# HANDBOOK OF RESEARCH ON SUSTAINABLE CONSUMPTION

# Handbook of Research on Sustainable Consumption

*Edited by*

Lucia A. Reisch

*Professor, Copenhagen Business School, Denmark*

John Thøgersen

*Professor, Aarhus University, Denmark*

Edward Elgar
PUBLISHING

Cheltenham, UK • Northampton, MA, USA

Published by
Edward Elgar Publishing Limited
The Lypiatts
15 Lansdown Road
Cheltenham
Glos GL50 2JA
UK

Edward Elgar Publishing, Inc.
William Pratt House
9 Dewey Court
Northampton
Massachusetts 01060
USA

A catalogue record for this book
is available from the British Library

Library of Congress Control Number: 2014952152

This book is available electronically in the Elgaronline
Social and Political Science subject collection
DOI 10.4337/9781783471270

MIX
Paper from responsible sources
FSC® C013056

ISBN 978 1 78347 126 3 (cased)
ISBN 978 1 78347 127 0 (eBook)

Typeset by Servis Filmsetting Ltd, Stockport, Cheshire
Printed and bound in Great Britain by T.J. International Ltd, Padstow

# Contents

# Contributors

**Gerrit Antonides** is a Professor of Economics of Consumers and Households at Wageningen University, the Netherlands. He has published in the areas of behavioural economics, economic psychology and consumer behaviour. He has been an editor of the *Journal of Economic Psychology* and has authored and co-authored several textbooks on consumer behaviour and economic psychology. The behavioural aspects of consumer decision making concerning issues of finance, household, environment and health are an important part of his current research activities.

**Christian Baatz** is Research Associate at the Department of Philosophy of Christian-Albrechts-Universität Kiel (Germany). His ongoing PhD thesis deals with compensating victims of climate change in developing countries. He is also part of the research project 'Arguing about Climate Engineering: Towards a Comprehensive Ethical Analysis of an Ongoing Debate' within the German Research Foundation's (DFG) priority programme on climate engineering. Besides climate ethics, his work centres on questions of global justice, human rights and environmental ethics. Originally, he received an education as environmental scientist at Leuphana University Lüneburg, Germany.

**Jan Willem Bolderdijk** received his PhD in Environmental Psychology in 2011 at the University of Groningen, the Netherlands. He is fascinated by people's tendency to make 'irrational' decisions, and frequently relies on field experiments to explore new research ideas in realistic consumer settings. He is currently employed as an Assistant Professor at the Department of Marketing, University of Groningen, where he studies ways to promote sustainable consumer behaviour. Besides being an academic, he is a cyclist and food enthusiast, and plays ukulele to his son Ties in his free time.

**Heather Chappells** is an Adjunct Professor in Geography at Saint Mary's University in Halifax, Nova Scotia, Canada. She is an interdisciplinary social scientist bringing perspectives from geography, sociology, and science and technology studies to address the sustainable management of materials and resources. Her research focuses specifically on the dynamics of infrastructure systems and their interface with practices of sustainable consumption, primarily in the energy, water and waste sectors. Publications include: *Infrastructures of Consumption: Environmental Innovation in the Utility Industries* (Earthscan, 2005), and *Sustainable Consumption: The Implications of Changing Infrastructures of Provision* (Edward Elgar, 2004).

**Mark A. Cohen** is the Justin Potter Professor of American Competitive Enterprise and Professor of Law at Vanderbilt University, USA. He also holds the title of University Fellow at Resources for the Future where he previously served as Vice President for Research. He previously served as staff economist at the US Environmental Protection Agency, the US Federal Trade Commission and the US Sentencing Commission. He received a BSFS in International Economics from Georgetown University, USA and an MA and PhD in Economics from Carnegie-Mellon University, USA. Professor Cohen has extensive experience analysing government enforcement policies as both an academic and as a government economist, with particular emphasis in the area of environmental and criminal justice issues. He has published over 100 articles and books on such diverse topics as: the effect of Community Right to Know laws on firm behaviour; why firms reduce toxic chemical emissions; and cost–benefit analysis of oil spill regulation and enforcement.

**Maurie J. Cohen** is Associate Professor and Director of the Program in Science, Technology, and Society at the New Jersey Institute of Technology, USA and Associate Fellow at the Tellus Institute, USA. He serves as the editor of *Sustainability: Science, Practice, and Policy* and is co-founder and an executive board member of the Sustainable Consumption Research and Action Initiative. His books include *Innovations in Sustainable Consumption: New Economics, Socio-technical Transitions, and Social Practices* (with Halina Szejnwald Brown and Philip Vergragt) and *Exploring Sustainable Consumption: Environmental Policy and the Social Sciences* (with Joseph Murphy).

**Hans Dagevos** is senior scientist at the Agricultural Economics Research Institute (LEI), and fellow at Economics of Consumers and Households, both at the Social Sciences Group of Wageningen University and Research Centre, the Netherlands. Hans Dagevos received his PhD from Utrecht University, the Netherlands in 1994 (*cum laude*). His research interests are in the field of the sociology of consumption with a special focus on food. He is co-editor of several books, and (co-)author of a variety of research reports and book chapters as well as articles in Dutch and international scientific journals.

**Wolfgang J. Fellner** is an economist by training and Assistant Professor in the Department of Socioeconomics at Vienna University of Economics and Business, Austria. His research approach is inspired by critical institutional economics and political economics. In his doctoral dissertation he developed an activity-based simulation model for consumer behaviour and demand. An activity-based approach assumes that people derive value from performing activities (that is, from the use of time) instead of from goods and services directly. Analysis of behaviour and motivation in the form of activities is still one of his major research areas. Besides that, his research deals with empirical measurement of activity preferences and economic strategies towards transformation to a socio-ecological economy.

**Connor J. Fitzmaurice** is a doctoral student in the Department of Sociology at Boston University (USA). He received a Bachelors of Arts degree from Boston College (USA) in 2010. As a researcher, his interests lie at the intersection of urban, cultural and economic sociology. Currently, his research focuses on consumer trends among 'foodies', ethical and ecological consumption, and alternative market arrangements and systems of valuation emerging in the 'sharing economy'.

**Margareta Friman**, who graduated from University of Gothenburg, Göteborg, Sweden, is Professor of Psychology and director of the Service and Market Oriented Transport Research Group (SAMOT) at Karlstad University (Sweden). SAMOT is a nationally funded excellence centre for research in public transport services. Her main research areas include consumer and transport psychology. She has conducted research on critical incidents, satisfaction and consumer-related emotions since the mid-1990s. She is author or co-author of about 50 internationally published journal articles and book chapters. She is a member of the editorial board of *Journal of Service Management* and an expert member of the European Cooperation in Science and Technology in the transport and urban development domain.

**Tommy Gärling** is Emeritus Professor of Psychology at the University of Gothenburg, Göteborg, Sweden. He graduated from Stockholm University, Sweden and after having held faculty positions at Umeå University, Sweden, he was appointed Professor of Psychology at University of Gothenburg. He is currently affiliated with an excellence centre in public transport research at Karlstad University. In collaboration with other centre members he has published extensively in international transportation journals. Recently he co-edited the *Handbook of Sustainable Travel* published by Springer in its Environmental Science series. He is a former president of the environmental psychology division of the International Association of Applied Psychology. Currently he is associate editor of the *Journal of Economic Psychology* and a member of the editorial boards of the *Journal of Environmental Psychology, Journal of Behavioral and Experimental Economics* (formerly *Journal of Socio-Economics*) and *Transportation*.

**Kirsten Gram-Hanssen** is professor at the Danish Building Research Institute, Aalborg University in Copenhagen, Denmark, where she studies household consumption, energy and everyday life. Her masters degree and PhD are from the Technical University of Denmark, within humanistic and science, technology and society (STS) approaches to technology. She uses qualitative and quantitative methods, analysed within different theoretical approaches including sociological theories of consumption, practice theory and technology studies. Kirsten Gram-Hanssen has been a project leader on national as well as international projects and has published numerous articles in international journals. She has also participated in organizing international conferences, presented keynote speeches and participated as an international expert in research councils.

**Wencke Gwozdz** is Associate Professor for Transformative Consumer Behaviour and Sustainability at Copenhagen Business School, Denmark. She holds a doctoral degree in economics and social sciences from the University of Hohenheim (Germany). As a consumer researcher, her main focus is on sustainable consumption, health behaviour and consumer policy. Her main topics are centred on obesity, well-being and fashion consumption. Among others, she is involved in European Union research projects on healthy eating and, in particular, on decision making in food choice (I. Family Study and Nudge-It). Moreover, she is the project leader for 'Sustainable Consumption and Consumer Behaviour' in the MISTRA Future Fashion project dealing with sustainability in the fashion industry.

**Dorothea Hauptstock** is a research fellow at the Wuppertal Institute for Climate, Environment and Energy, Germany. She is interested in policies and measures to support energy-efficient technologies, climate policy and sustainable consumer behaviour. She studied economics at the University of Heidelberg, Germany and at the Warsaw School of Economics, Poland with a focus on environmental economics and development policy. In her PhD thesis, she deals with energy efficiency-induced rebound effects at the household level in developing economies.

**Eva Heiskanen** has a PhD in Organization and Management from the Aalto University School of Economics, Finland and a master's degree from the University of Helsinki, Finland (major: consumer economics, minor: adult education). She works as a Research Professor at the Finish National Consumer Research Centre. Her research focuses on consumer and user acceptance, involvement and innovation in sustainable technologies and solutions, with an emphasis on energy-related technologies. She is also interested in science and technology studies and local sustainability experiments. She recently coordinated a European action research project bringing together researchers and practitioners working to change energy use patterns.

**Peter Hennicke** formerly served as President of the Wuppertal Institute, Germany. He worked as an energy policy expert for the Ministry of Environment and Energy of the Federal State of Hessen for two years and served as a member of three Inquiry Commissions of the German Parliament. From 2002 to 2006, Peter Hennicke was member of the Scientific and Technical Advisory Committee (STAP) of the Global Environment Facility (GEF). His work covers more than 230 articles, reports and various books mainly regarding national and international energy economy as well as energy and climate policy. Peter Hennicke ranks among the opinion leaders in the field of sustainability-oriented energy research in Germany. Today he works as a freelancer for the Wuppertal Institute. He received the prestigious 'German Environmental Award 2014' and is a member of various national and international advisory boards and committees (for example, a full member of the Club of Rome, a Management Board member of the European Environment Agency).

**Edgar G. Hertwich** is Professor of Energy and Process Engineering and director of the Industrial Ecology Programme at the Norwegian University of Science and Technology in Trondheim, Norway. He is a member of the International Resource Panel, where he leads the Working Group on the Environmental Impacts of Products and Materials. He served as a lead author of the energy chapter of the *IPCC 5th Assessment Report*. His most widely recognized research contributions are the first analysis of $CO_2$ emissions embodied in international trade and of the carbon footprint of nations. He seeks understanding of how activities in our society produce environmental pressures, the dynamics in our development that affect these driving forces and their resulting environmental pressures, and alternative courses of action that can reduce these pressures. What is the connection between human activities on the one hand, and emissions and resource use on the other hand?

**Sylvia Lorek** works as a researcher and policy consultant for sustainable consumption. She holds a PhD in consumer economics, and a diploma in household economics and nutrition (Oecotrophologie) and in economics. The combination of these different disciplines provides her with the tools – the individual microeconomic and the societal macroeconomic perspective – for a well-founded analysis of the contexts in which the scientific and societal discourses about sustainable consumption take place. Sylvia Lorek has been Project Coordinator at the Wuppertal Institute for Climate, Environment and Energy, Germany. Since 2000 she has been based at the Sustainable Europe Research Institute (SERI) and is head of SERI Germany e.V. Here she is working on studies and as a consultant for national and international organizations and institutes, among them the Organisation for Economic Co-operation and Development (OECD), the European

Union, the European Environment Agency and the United Nations Environment Programme (UNEP).

**Michael G. Luchs** is an Associate Professor at the College of William and Mary's Mason School of Business, USA. He earned his PhD from the University of Texas at Austin, USA. Dr. Luchs also earned an MBA from the University of Virginia's Darden Graduate School of Business, USA, as well as a BSE in Mechanical Engineering and a BA in Psychology from Tufts University, USA. His research interests include sustainable consumption, product innovation and sustainable design. Prior to earning his PhD, Dr Luchs worked for over a decade as a consultant and as a manager in industry specializing in new product development. His ongoing consulting work focuses on innovation and 'design thinking' methodology.

**Ellen Matthies** is Professor of Environmental Psychology at Otto von Guericke University Magdeburg, Germany. She holds a PhD in Psychology from Ruhr-University Bochum, Germany. Ellen Matthies has guided several research projects related to the fields of applied social psychology and environmental psychology (mainly funded by the German Research Foundation DFG but also by other institutions, like the European Union) on the role of personal and social norms in resource consumption, the role of habitualization for behavioural change, and on the development and evaluation of interventions to promote changes in sustainability related behaviours. She is a member of the German Advisory Council on Global Change (WBGU).

**Rebecca A. Miller** currently works in community and economic development, serving with the United States Peace Corps. She holds a bachelors degree in business administration from the College of William and Mary (USA). As an undergraduate, her main research focus was on sustainable consumption and consumer responsibility. Before joining the Peace Corps, she worked as a grant writer for a regional non-profit organization, raising funding to support small businesses through a non-profit loan fund. She also served as an AmeriCorps Volunteer in Service to America (VISTA), assisting with financial literacy for low-income populations.

**Oksana Mont** is Professor of Sustainable Consumption and Production and Director of PhD programme at the International Institute for Industrial Environmental Economics at Lund University, Sweden. She holds a PhD in Engineering, an MSc in Environmental Management and Policy, an MSc in Biology and Chemistry. Her main research area is sustainable consumption and production, in which she combines research on innovative business models with sustainable lifestyles and sustainable consumption policy. She leads projects on the role of policy and governance in shaping everyday choices of individuals, businesses and organizations and is engaged in high-level policy consulting.

**Sina Nitzko** is a research assistant at the Chair of Marketing of Agricultural Products and Food at the University of Goettingen, Germany. She obtained a diploma in psychology at the University of Magdeburg, Germany and a doctoral degree in psychology at the University of Mainz, Germany. Her main research interests focus on consumer behaviour, sustainable consumption, food marketing, market research, health psychology and nutritional psychology.

**Caroline L. Noblet** is an Assistant Professor in the School of Economics at the University of Maine, USA. She received her PhD in Economic Psychology from the University of Maine, and also holds a Master's in Resource Economics and Policy. Her work focuses on factors influencing sustainability behaviours and natural resource decision-making. She is interested in how one's own personal experiences, individual values, motivations and constraints influence understanding, processing and use of information in decision making. Her research extends current economic models to include interdisciplinary constructs, hypotheses and methods, with an eye towards future design of information policies.

**Konrad Ott** is Professor of Philosophy and Environmental Ethics at Christian-Albrechts-University of Kiel (Germany). He studied philosophy, history and literature in Frankfurt. In 1989, he did his PhD on the origins and epistemology of historical science. He was a post-doc at Tübingen University, Germany (1991–1995) and defended his habilitation thesis in 1995. From 1997 till 2012, Konrad Ott taught environmental ethics at Ernst-Moritz-Arndt-University Greifswald, Germany. His fields of research are discourse ethics, theories of justice, general environmental ethics, concepts of sustainability, nature conservation, water resources, and ethical aspects of climate change. He is a member of the Board for Sustainable Development of the Protestant Church of Germany and a member in the 'Deutscher Rat für Landespflege'. At Kiel University, he is founding director of the Gustav Radbruch Network which is devoted to the integration and ethical reflection of environmental disciplines.

**Ken Peattie** is Professor of Marketing and Strategy at Cardiff Business School, UK, which he joined in 1986 having previously worked in marketing and strategic management practice. His research interests focus on the impact of sustainability concerns on marketing and corporate strategy making; social marketing for sustainable lifestyles; and social enterprise and education for sustainability. He has published three books and numerous book chapters and journal papers on these topics. Between 2001 and 2012 he acted as Director to the Economic and Social Research Council funded interdisciplinary research centre for Business Relationships, Accountability, Sustainability and Society (BRASS). As BRASS Director he was involved in a range of projects delivering expert advice and research services to Welsh, UK and European policy organizations, funding bodies and businesses.

**Andreas Rasche** is Professor of Business in Society at the Centre for Corporate Social Responsibility (cbsCSR) at Copenhagen Business School, Denmark. He holds a PhD (Dr. rer. pol.) from the European Business School, Germany and a Habilitation (Dr. habil.) from Helmut-Schmidt-University, Hamburg, Germany. His research focuses on corporate responsibility standards (particularly the UN Global Compact), the political role of corporations in transnational governance, and the governance of global supply networks. He co-edited *The United Nations Global Compact: Achievements, Trends and Challenges* (Cambridge University Press) and recently published *Building the Responsible Enterprise* (Stanford University Press). Andreas Rasche collaborated with the UN Global Compact in the context of different projects and currently serves on the Global Compact LEAD Steering Committee. He is associate editor of *Business Ethics Quarterly*. He joined Copenhagen Business School from Warwick Business School, UK in August 2012.

**Lucia A. Reisch** is Professor of Intercultural Consumer Behaviour and Consumer Policy at Copenhagen Business School, Denmark. She holds a Doctorate in Economics and Social Sciences from the University of Hohenheim (Germany) and received an MBA education at the University of California, Los Angeles (USA). As a consumer researcher, her main research focus is on sustainable consumption, consumer and sustainability policy, behavioural economics and corporate sustainability. Besides running European Union research projects, she is engaged in high-level policy consulting. She is a member of the German Academy of Technical Sciences and editor-in-chief of the *Journal of Consumer Policy*.

**Deborah Roy** is a Research Associate at the University of Bath, UK where she has worked since 2010. She holds a Doctorate in Psychology from the University of Ulster, UK. Her research interests include the psychological determinants of environmental and socially responsible behaviour change, in particular ecological values, identity and temporal discounting. She is currently a member of the Sustainable Lifestyles Research Group and ad hoc reviewer for the *Journal of Environmental Psychology* and *Environment and Behavior*.

**Gerd Scholl** is an economist by training and received his PhD in Marketing from University of Oldenburg (Germany). He is a senior researcher at the Institute for Ecological Economy Research (IOEW) in Berlin, Germany and head of its department of Corporate Management and Consumption. His main research areas are sustainable consumption and production (SCP), sustainable marketing, sustainable product service systems, and consumers and new technologies. He has worked in leading roles in projects for the European Commission (DG Environment, DG Research), the United Nations Conference on Trade and Development (UNCTAD), and several German public authorities (for example, the Federal Environment Ministry, Federal Research Ministry). Gerd Scholl has been coordinator of CORPUS (Enhancing the Connectivity Between Research and Policy-Making in Sustainable Consumption) and main research partner in RESPONDER, both of which are major European Union projects dealing with sustainable consumption policies from a knowledge brokerage perspective.

**Juliet B. Schor** is Professor of Sociology at Boston College, USA and a member of the MacArthur Foundation Connected Learning Research Network. Her PhD is in economics, which she taught at Harvard University, USA from 1984 to 1995. Her current research topics include the sharing economy, sustainable lifestyles, and the relationship between time use and carbon emissions. Schor is the author of the national best-seller *The Overworked American: The Unexpected Decline of Leisure, The Overspent American: Why We Want What We Don't Need*, and most recently *True Wealth: How and Why Millions of Americans are Creating a Time-Rich, Ecologically Light, Small-Scale, High-Satisfaction Economy*.

**Sharon Shewmake** is an Assistant Professor in the Economics Department and a member faculty of the Institute for Energy Studies at Western Washington University in Bellingham, Washington (USA). She holds a Doctorate in Agricultural and Resource Economics from the University of California, Davis (USA). Her primary focus is on environmental economics including transportation, green labels and energy efficiency.

**Clive L. Spash** holds the Chair of Public Policy and Governance at WU, Vienna University of Economics and Business, Austria. His main interests are interdisciplinary research on human behaviour, environmental values and the transformation of the world political economy to a more socially and environmentally just system. This has also involved moving away from mainstream environmental and resource economics, looking at links with natural sciences, understanding applied ethics, exploring models of democracy and public participation in political science and linking with social psychology to develop models of human behaviour and motivation. For some time now, he has pursued this interdisciplinary work within the context of social ecological economics. He is editor-in-chief of *Environmental Values*, and has over 100 academic publications in journals and books.

**Achim Spiller** is a Professor of Food Marketing at the Department of Agricultural Economics and Rural Development at the University of Goettingen, Germany. His main research areas are food quality and safety, branding and labelling, management in agribusiness, consumer behaviour, organic food and animal welfare from a market research perspective. *Inter alia*, he is a member of the Agricultural Policies Scientific Council of the Federal Ministry of Food and Agriculture, member of the Board of Trustees of QS Qualität und Sicherheit GmbH, the major certification scheme for agriculture in Germany, and Chairman of the Scientific Council of the Animal Welfare Label of the Deutsche Tierschutzbund (the German Society for the Protection of Animals). Moreover Achim Spiller has been Dean of the Faculty of Agricultural Sciences of Georg-August-Universitaet Goettingen (since 2011) and member of the Academy of Sciences of the University of Goettingen (since 2013). He has published his research widely in scientific journals and books.

**Kjartan Steen-Olsen** is a PhD candidate in the Industrial Ecology Programme (IndEcol) at the Norwegian University of Science and Technology (NTNU) in Trondheim, Norway. He holds an MSc in Environmental and Energy Engineering, also from NTNU, with a thesis on the environmental impacts of European primary aluminium production. His PhD work is focused on the use of environmentally extended multiregional input–output models for assessments of environmental impacts embodied in trade and consumption.

**Linda Steg** is Professor of Environmental Psychology at the University of Groningen, the Netherlands. Her research focuses on factors and strategies promoting pro-environmental behaviour, and the effectiveness and acceptability of energy sources and environmental policies. Steg is member of the Scientific Board of the Groningen Energy and Sustainable Program (GESP) at the University of Groningen, and scientific director of the Kurt Lewin Institute, the Netherlands. Moreover, she was president of Division 4, Environmental Psychology, of the International Association of Applied Psychology (IAAP) from 2010 to 2014. Furthermore, she is an associated member of the Dutch Council for the Environment and Infrastructure, and was a member of the commission on Encouraging Sustainable Behaviour of this council.

**Paul C. Stern** is a senior scholar at the US National Research Council/National Academy of Sciences. His research interests include environmentally significant behaviour at the household level and processes for informing environmental decisions. He served on the

American Psychological Association's Task Force on the Interface between Psychology and Global Climate Change. He is co-author of the textbook *Environmental Problems and Human Behavior* (2nd edn, 2002) and co-editor of numerous National Research Council publications, including *Facilitating Climate Change Responses* (2010), *Environmentally Significant Consumption: Research Directions* (1997) and *Energy Use: The Human Dimension* (1984). Recent publications include 'Individual and household interactions with energy systems: toward integrated understanding' (*Energy Research and Social Science*, 2014) and 'Contributions of psychology to limiting climate change' (*American Psychologist*, 2011). He is a fellow of the American Association for the Advancement of Science and the American Psychological Association. He received his PhD in Psychology from Clark University, USA.

**Cass R. Sunstein** is the Robert Walmsley University Professor at Harvard University, USA. From 2009 to 2012, he was Administrator of the US White House Office of Information and Regulatory Affairs. He is the founder and director of the Program on Behavioral Economics and Public Policy at Harvard Law School. Cass Sunstein has testified before US congressional committees on many subjects, and he has been involved in constitution-making and law reform activities in a number of nations. Cass Sunstein is the author of many articles and books, including *Republic.com* (2001), *Risk and Reason* (2002), *Why Societies Need Dissent* (2003), *The Second Bill of Rights* (2004), *Laws of Fear: Beyond the Precautionary Principle* (2005), *Worst-Case Scenarios* (2001), *Nudge: Improving Decisions about Health, Wealth, and Happiness* (with Richard H. Thaler, 2008), *Simpler: The Future of Government* (2013) and most recently *Why Nudge?* (2014) and *Conspiracy Theories and Other Dangerous Ideas* (2014). He is now working on group decision making and various projects on behavioural economics and public policy.

**Mario F. Teisl** is a Professor in the School of Economics at the University of Maine, USA. He holds a PhD in Agricultural and Resource Economics from the University of Maryland, USA, and an MS in Agricultural and Resource Economics from the University of Maine. His research focuses on how the provision of environmental information affects demand behaviour. In this research he has focused on two themes. In one he focuses on ways to enhance the market conditions for environmentally certified and labelled products. In the other, he examines the effectiveness of eco-certification and labelling programmes. Dr Teisl's research has had specific policy and management ramifications for various industries (for example, food, fisheries, forestry, energy and transportation).

**John Thøgersen** is Professor of Economic Psychology at Aarhus University, School of Business and Social Sciences, Denmark. He heads the Marketing and Sustainability research group and the Virtual Community on Sustainability and Consumption. His research focus is on sustainable consumption in a broad sense, including sustainable lifestyles and 'spillover', social norms, values, intergenerational transfer, eco-labelling, energy consumption, travel mode choice and organic food. He has been a visiting scholar at many foreign universities, including Stanford University (USA), the Technical University of Berlin (Germany) and Sun Yat-sen University (Guangzhou, China). He is editor of the *Journal of Consumer Policy*, published by Springer.

**Frank Trentmann** is Professor of History at Birkbeck College, University of London, UK, and the principal investigator of the Arts and Humanities Research Council (AHRC) project on Material Cultures of Energy (2014–2017). He is also a member of the Engineering and Physical Sciences Research Council (EPSRC), the Economic and Social Research Council (ESRC) and research centre DEMAND (Dynamics of Energy, Mobility and Demand). He was the director of the Cultures of Consumption programme (2002–2007). His research has been in the history of consumption and politics broadly defined, with a particular focus on food, water and energy. Publications include *Free Trade Nation: Commerce, Consumption and Civil Society in Modern Britain* (OUP 2008) and *The Oxford Handbook of the History of Consumption* (OUP 2012).

**Arnold Tukker** is the Professor of Industrial Ecology and Director of the Institute of Environmental Sciences (CML) at Leiden University, the Netherlands. He further retains a position at the Netherlands Organisation for Applied Scientific Research (TNO) as senior researcher. Arnold Tukker has set up prominent European Union projects in the field of sustainable product design (SusProNet) and sustainable consumption and production (SCORE!). He was a core member of the 10 Million Euro Dutch Knowledge Network on Sustainable System Innovations. He currently co-ordinates €15 million worth of projects with 20 key European research institutes that build the world's most ambitious and detailed global energy, resource and economic input–output databases and models (EXIOBASE). He has authored six books, 47 refereed papers and seven special issues on sustainability research. He has been engaged with the work of the United Nations on the Green Economy Initiative, the Resources Panel, the Ten Year Framework of Programmes on Sustainable Consumption and Production and Sustainable Development Goals.

**Michael P. Vandenbergh** is David Daniels Allen Distinguished Chair of Law, Co-Director, Energy, Environment and Land Use Program, and Director, Climate Change Research Network, at Vanderbilt University Law School, USA. His work with Vanderbilt's Climate Change Research Network involves interdisciplinary teams that focus on energy use and carbon emissions from the household sector. His corporate work explores the social influences on firm behaviour and the emergence of private environmental governance. Before joining Vanderbilt's law faculty, Professor Vandenbergh was a partner at Latham & Watkins in Washington, DC. He served as Chief of Staff of the US Environmental Protection Agency from 1993 to 1995, and as a law clerk to Judge Edward R. Becker of the United States Court of Appeals for the Third Circuit in 1987–1988. A winner of the Hall-Hartman teaching award, he teaches courses in environmental law, energy and property.

**Muriel Verain** is a social scientist and obtained her Master's in Management, Economics and Consumer studies from Wageningen University, the Netherlands, with a specialization in consumer behaviour. She is currently pursuing a doctoral degree in the Economics of Consumers and Households group at Wageningen University. Her PhD research focuses on the identification of consumer lifestyle segments in the domain of healthy and sustainable food, and is conducted in cooperation with the Agricultural Economics Research Institute (LEI), part of Wageningen University and Research Centre. As a consumer researcher, her main research interests include healthy and sustainable food consumption, consumer segmentation, food attitudes and perceptions, and food-related lifestyles.

**Philip J. Vergragt**, is an academic and activist; a Fellow at Tellus Institute, Boston, USA; a Research Professor at Marsh Institute, Clark University, Worcester, MA, USA; he is a Professor Emeritus of Technology Assessment at Delft University of Technology, the Netherlands. He has co-authored more than 80 scientific publications and three books. His main research interests are sustainable technological and social innovations in transportation, energy, and housing; grass-roots innovations; socio-technical transitions; sustainable consumption and production; and technology assessment of emerging technologies. In the last five years, he has been the co-founder of SCORAI, the North American (and European) Sustainable Consumption and Action Initiative; of NARSPAC, the North American Roundtable on Sustainable Production and Consumption; of WoHEC, the Worcester Housing, Energy, and Community group, USA; and of GRF-SPaC, the Global Research Forum on Sustainable Production and Consumption, which held its inaugural meeting in Rio de Janeiro in June 2012. Dr. Vergragt obtained a PhD in Chemistry from the University of Leiden, the Netherlands, in 1976.

**Bas Verplanken** is a Professor of Social Psychology at the University of Bath, UK. He obtained his PhD at the Leiden University, the Netherlands, and held positions at the University of Nijmegen, the Netherlands and the University of Tromsø, Norway. His research is in social, health, consumer and environmental psychology, and includes topics such as attitude–behaviour relations, behaviour change, values, the self, environmental concern and impulsive buying. He has a particular interest in habitual behaviour and habitual thinking, and published a widely used scale to assess habit strength (the Self-Report Habit Index). He was an associate editor of the *British Journal of Social Psychology* and *Psychology and Health*. He is currently the Head of Department of Psychology at the University of Bath.

**Lieske Voget-Kleschin** studied landscape ecology and nature protection at Greifswald University, Germany in 1999–2005 and holds a Doctorate in Philosophy from Greifswald University. Her work focuses on environmental, food and agricultural ethics, sustainability and sustainable consumption and the capability approach. She has worked in research projects on ethical aspects of growing genetically modified plants, large-scale land acquisition in developing countries, and conscious meat consumption. She currently holds a postdoctural position at Kiel University, Germany.

**Hannah Wallis** is a psychologist and doctoral student of environmental psychology at the Otto-von-Guericke-University Magdeburg, Germany. Her PhD project focuses on characteristics of energy consumption in households with adolescents and aims at developing recommendations for targeted intervention programmes. The project is funded by the Helmholtz-Allianz ENERGY-TRANS and the state Saxony-Anhalt.

**Alan Warde** is Professor of Sociology in the School of Social Sciences, University of Manchester, UK; a Professorial Fellow of Manchester's Sustainable Consumption Institute (SCI); and Guest Professor, Department of Food and Nutrition, University of Uppsala, Sweden. His research interests are wide but recently have concerned the sociology of consumption and the sociology of food and eating in the context of issues of sustainability. Current projects are concerned with developing theories of practice, strategies for changing eating habits and changes in the organization of eating out in the UK.

**Daniel Welch** is a Research Associate at the Sustainable Consumption Institute, University of Manchester (UK) and was previously a researcher with the Sustainable Practices Research Group. He completed a PhD in Sociology at the University of Manchester in 2013. His thesis draws on theories of practice to examine the commercial field of sustainability communications and its significance for sustainable consumption and corporate sustainability. He is currently working on a practice theoretical account of the role of collectivity and collective actors in socio-technical change. His research interests include cultural intermediation, social ontology, socio-economic change, and sustainable consumption and production.

# Foreword

This handbook could not have come at a more appropriate time. Late in 2013 the European Union (EU) published its 7th Environmental Action Programme (7th EAP), which sets out a long-term vision promoting the goal of 'Living well, within the limits of our planet'. Concretely, the 7th EAP foresees a Europe in 2050 where: (1) low-carbon growth has been decoupled from resource use; (2) prosperity stems from an innovative, circular economy where nothing is wasted and resources are protected sustainably; and (3) biodiversity is protected, valued and restored in ways that enhance our society's resilience.

Such ambitions mean going far beyond existing policy targets, so the 7th EAP promotes new ways of thinking and innovation. Indeed, to meet these challenges we will have to fundamentally change the systems which underpin human well-being, including our food systems, energy systems, housing systems and mobility systems. Several decades of policy interventions have largely focused on improving the efficiency of these systems in order to reduce their environmental impacts. But it is becoming increasingly clear that incremental improvements are not enough. We need instead to completely rethink our systems and the business models that support them, and make a transition to new systems that continue to fulfil societal needs but do so in an essentially sustainable way.

Changing consumption behaviour is a crucial element in this journey. To properly target policy, we still need a great deal of information, including sound information on what drives consumption behaviour and how to influence different consumer segments. We will need better understanding of these things, and more, if we are to move towards truly sustainable consumption and production systems.

This handbook provides a much-needed overview of the latest research findings on sustainable consumption. This is a very relevant, even necessary publication, important for anyone trying to understand consumption behaviour and how to move it in a sustainable direction. Hence, I warmly welcome this book and I look forward to using it as a reference in my daily work at the European Environment Agency, and hope others do the same.

*Hans Bruyninckx*
*Executive Director of the European Environment Agency*
*Copenhagen, Denmark*
*June 2014*

# Research on sustainable consumption: introduction and overview

*Lucia A. Reisch and John Thøgersen*

Research on sustainable consumption (SC) sets out to understand (and promote) the types of consumption behaviours that are conducive for a sustainable development. While deeply embedded in the fields of consumer research, environmental and ecological economics as well as psychology, many more disciplines and research fields have profoundly contributed to the advancement of the field in recent years, among them: environmental sociology and its perspective of social embedment of individual behaviour in social settings and contexts; behavioural economics and its empirically based acknowledgment of consumer biases, heuristics and context dependencies; the political sciences and their view of the consumer as an active citizen consumer; applied philosophy and its theoretical insights regarding the ethical core of the concept; sustainability marketing and its expertise on how to convey the message to consumers and on how to make sustainable consumption attractive; innovation studies and their view on consumers as co-innovators and co-producers; systems analysis and its unescapable reference to the complexities and interconnectedness of the ecological, economic and social systems in which consumption takes place; and historical studies that remind us of the roots of sustainable consumption and its interdependencies with cultural and technological pathways. Last but not least, identifying and designing policy measures promoting sustainable consumption have been on the agenda for consumer policy studies since the mid-1990s. The *Journal of Consumer Policy* (which we co-edit) has been at the forefront of this discussion. Effective policy making requires an empirically robust evidence of actual consumer interest and needs, on behavioural tendencies and on probable impacts of policy tools as well as an understanding of the theoretical models that best predict behaviour.

Hence, research on sustainable consumption abounds in theories and methodological approaches that have been mostly developed and refined in neighbouring fields and applied to the field of SC. While having advanced tremendously in the two decades since its inception (which we think is the 1992 Rio Conference), it is still a young research field and ultimately still in its infancy. We think that this is a good moment to pause for a stocktaking exercise and to compile original contributions from leading experts in the different fields as sketched above. This is what this book aims to do: presenting a selection of highly relevant research that explores the key issues within sustainable consumption practice, policy and research from a multitude of disciplinary perspectives. In many cases, this is frontier work, and we appreciate the fact that what the authors deliver is first rate.

We have organized the chapters as follows: After this introduction, we start with the epistemology of the field and how it calls for interdisciplinary and transdisciplinary research (Part I). We then group chapters on major disciplinary approaches to SC

(Part II), followed by a part on diagnostic research, namely methods and measurements and their consequences for problem diagnosis (Part III). In Part IV, we compile concrete cases and issues of SC applied to the consumption domains of transport, housing and food as well as to public health. Part V features chapters on cross-cutting issues such as consumer habits, responsibility and socialization; while Part VI compiles contributions on different policies for SC. We finalize the book with a group of chapters suggesting and discussing key future directions for research on sustainable consumption (Part VII). In the following, we turn to a brief discussion about individual contributions to this book.

## I.1 OVERVIEW OF THE BOOK

### I.1.1 Part I

The opening chapter by Sylvia Lorek and Philipp J. Vergragt sets the stage by conceptualizing sustainable consumption as a systemic challenge that calls for inter- and transdisciplinary research and research questions. The aims of Chapter 1 are to document the unsustainability of present prevalent consumption patterns in what they call the 'overdeveloped' world, and to explore in more detail how a transition towards a more sustainable consumption system could be achieved. Consumption is viewed as part of a larger system of investments, production, trade, consumption and waste, and with comprising material, economic, cultural, institutional and power aspects. The chapter starts off by presenting empirical data that illustrate how unsustainable consumption actually is today and what problematic consequences so-called 'green consumerism' brings along. The authors present consumption as part of a complex, interacting system and argue that systemic change is needed that encompasses simultaneous changes in culture, production processes, consumption patterns, lifestyles, economics and politics. In closing, they elaborate which actions could contribute to such systemic change, and what the role of research could be to support such actions.

Similarly, Chapter 2 by Oksana Mont and Eva Heiskanen calls for a more systemic perspective, in their view based on industrial ecology and circular economy thinking. In 'Breaking the stalemate of sustainable consumption with industrial ecology and a circular economy' the authors share recent emerging ideas for alternative ways to organize our economy and society and explain why and how nature with its closed cycles is a source of inspiration for the evolving concepts of industrial ecology and circular economy. While the principles of industrial ecology and specifically the circularity idea have been mostly employed by the production side, implications for sustainable consumption and lifestyles have remained largely unexplored to date. This chapter focuses on the changes that need to take place in different stages of the production–consumption continuum in order to enable a shift from the currently linear economic system to a circular economy. In addition, it offers a discussion on the implications this shift might have for sustainable consumption and lifestyles and their institutional conditions. In particular, the chapter highlights the importance of emerging trends, such as collaborative consumption and the sharing economy, in changing the notion of social status and promoting less commoditized personal identity. It also reflects on the importance of the vintage economy and craft consumers in shaping values that may facilitate sufficiency and a circular economy.

Finally, the authors discuss the roles of various stakeholders in supporting the bricolage of emerging sustainable lifestyles from fragmented existing practices and initiatives to promote a circular economy.

### I.1.2 Part II

Part II of the book compiles explorations of different social sciences disciplines and research traditions in SC research. Widening the perspective from individual behaviour to the historical dynamics of practices can illuminate the changing resilience of human societies in the face of disruption and transition to new resources. Yet, the history of consumption in general – and the history of sustainable consumption in particular – have been understudied research fields for too long. Chapter 3 by Heather Chappells and Frank Trentmann is one of the few academic contributions to date to systematically explore sustainable consumption in history, with the subtitle: 'Ideas, resources and practices'. It places sustainability in a historical context and follows the career of the concept from the eighteenth century to the current paradigm of sustainable consumption and production. The increasingly integrated and global vision is examined alongside the local realities of sustainability challenges in three domains: water, energy and waste. Sustainability is presented as an evolving crisis concept, which has focused human efforts on conservation of resources and the revaluing of waste. Current approaches to conservation during energy crises and droughts are located in a longer history of tension between conservation, efficiency, and rising consumption and material flows. The chapter examines the emerging significance of consumers and their practices in recent responses to droughts in Britain and energy crises in California, to consider lessons for resilience and more sustainable demand management in rich societies. Those high levels of household waste, we learn, are persisting alongside greater recycling and reuse points to the limits of technological solutions or appeals to individual conscience. The chapter shows how deeply consumption is rooted in the social organization of daily life.

According to Linda Steg in Chapter 4, 'Environmental psychology and sustainable consumption', sustainable consumption is often associated with some behavioural costs and additional effort. Despite this, many consumers engage in sustainable consumption. She argues that consumers are more likely to engage in sustainable consumption when they strongly endorse biospheric and altruistic values, while strong egoistic and hedonic values are likely to inhibit sustainable consumption. Next, she discusses different processes through which values can affect sustainable consumption. Yet, we are reminded that strong endorsement of values may not be sufficient to promote sustainable consumption. Importantly, values need to be activated in order to be influential and steer decision making. The chapter discusses various situational factors that can activate and deactivate relevant values, thereby increasing the likelihood of sustainable consumption: value primes or value-related symbols, value-signalling behaviour of others that reflect the level of support for norms, cognitive demands in situations, and situational factors that affect the costliness of sustainable consumption. Her reasoning suggests that three strategies can be employed to promote sustainable consumption: strengthening biospheric or altruistic values, targeting situational cues that activate and support biospheric and altruistic values and/or deactivate egoistic and hedonic values, and targeting process variables through which values affect behaviour.

In the sociology of sustainable consumption, practice theoretical approaches provide an alternative to the cultural theory model of consumption dominant in sociology and related disciplines at the end of the last century. In Chapter 5 on theories of practice and sustainable consumption, Daniel Welch and Alan Warde take up the cudgels for practice theory and give an analytic account of the nature of the impact that theories of practice have had on approaches to sustainable consumption. The chapter briefly outlines the potential contribution of the practice theoretical approach to consumption in general. It then contrasts two major research programmes – exemplified by Spaargaren at the University of Wageningen and Shove at Lancaster University – which have applied theories of practice in different ways to research into sustainable consumption. According to the authors, the cultural theory model (which emphasises the conspicuous, communicative and symbolic aspects of consumption) offers only limited resources for the study of environmentally significant consumption. Practice theoretical approaches, by contrast, seem to afford distinctive understandings of the place of consumption in the accomplishment of everyday routine activities, that is, which activities have profound environmental impacts. The two exemplar programmes draw on differing theoretical resources and address different empirical foci, demonstrating the range of practice theoretical approaches applicable to the study of sustainable consumption. Finally, these points of departure between the two positions are used to suggest further avenues for sustainable consumption research informed by theories of practice: the relationship between consumption and production; the relationship between collective agency and everyday routines; and the relationship between the everyday performance of practice and the macro-institutional context.

In Chapter 6 on sustainability marketing, Ken Peattie focuses on the potential of a firm's marketing and commercial communication as a driver for more sustainable consumption; according to him, the most powerful and pervasive influence on consumer behaviour in relation to sustainability. Although frequently blamed for driving consumption to unsustainable levels, marketing surely has the potential to contribute to the development of more sustainable systems of consumption and production. The chapter considers how the relationship between marketing and sustainability has evolved, and how the next steps towards more sustainable marketing and consumption may be achieved. It reviews the ways in which marketers seek to understand consumers' willingness to adopt pro-sustainability behaviours, and the ways in which marketing variables can be manipulated to engage consumers with more sustainable market offerings. Finally, it reviews the future opportunities for research into sustainability marketing and how marketing scholarship and practice can contribute to the transformation of our societies to create substantively more sustainable ways of living, producing and consuming. Issues of ethics are also touched upon.

Sustainable development is at its core an ethical concept and applied philosophy has an important role to play in the research on sustainable consumption. In Chapter 7, 'Ethics and sustainable consumption', philosophers Lieske Voget-Kleschin, Christian Baatz and Konrad Ott provide a philosophical-ethical perspective on sustainable consumption. They start by outlining a concept of sustainable development based on an understanding of sustainable consumption as 'encompassing behaviour that reduces pressure on humanity's environmental and social base of livelihood, that respects other individuals' ability to live a decent human life and that does not overburden its addressees'. Subsequently, they introduce the distinction between weak and strong sustainable consumption and argue in favour of the latter. They then turn to (what in their view constitutes) the ethical core issue regarding sustainable consumption, namely: is it legitimate to claim that individuals need to consume more sustainably? The authors answer this question in the affirmative and distinguish three equally important, complementary individual duties: duties to comply, to promote and to contribute one's fair share. Finally, they turn back to the claim that such duties must not overburden individuals. The authors close by explaining why ethics cannot (exactly) delimit an individual's duties, while stressing that this does not yield individual duties the least bit less binding.

### I.1.3 Part III

Part III of the book consists of two chapters covering diagnostic research, that is, debates on methods and measurements of the relative (un)sustainability of consumption and production as well as on the options for and pitfalls of using these tools for evidence-based policy making and priority setting in sustainable consumption policy.

In Chapter 8, Kjartan Steen-Olsen and Edgar G. Hertwich evaluate life cycle assessment as a means to identify the most effective action for sustainable consumption. The chapter explains how everyday activities and purchases of private households adversely affect the environment through a highly complex web of interactions within and between the natural and man-made systems. In the effort to introduce behavioural change to reduce household environmental impacts, the authors argue, it is important for all to understand what types of activities and purchases affect the environment to a higher or lesser degree. Following Steen-Olsen and Hertwich, this understanding seems to be currently lacking. Instead, individuals tend to have black-and-white views of what activities are 'green', or not. Life cycle assessment (LCA) is proposed as an analytical tool well suited to compare product systems in terms of environmental impacts. By establishing a consistent framework to quantify the cumulative impacts of consumed products or services throughout their lifetime, including effects far upstream in the supply chain, LCA seems to offer fair evaluations of alternatives that without the life cycle perspective cannot be meaningfully compared, such as electrical versus petrol-powered cars. Previous research consistently highlights food, transport and housing as the most important consumption categories in this respect, issues and domains that are taken up in Part IV of this book. The authors address each in turn, summarizing some key findings of LCA research, and discuss the potential as well as the limitations of LCA as a guide for society towards a sustainable future.

Another diagnostic question is how priorities for sustainable consumption policies can best be determined. In Chapter 9, Arnold Tukker explains how environmental effects of economic activities are ultimately driven by consumption of households and governments. First, he explains, almost all consumption activities have direct environmental impacts. But second, consumption activities also have important indirect effects – such as the environmental impacts related to the production of food. Tucker sees essentially two ways of calculating such life cycle impacts of final consumption: via life cycle assessments, and via environmentally extended input–output analysis. The author shows that virtually all studies done for developed economies identify food consumption, the use of transport and activities in the home (housing, heating and leisure via electrical appliances) cause around three-quarters of the total life cycle impacts of consumption. Hence, he argues, these areas should be given priority by sustainability policies, either by cleaning production or greening products, or by more consumption-oriented measures like shared use of products and facilities, spending money on low-impact consumption activities, or even restructuring patterns of consumption and production in such a way that a higher quality of life can be realized at lower levels of economic expenditure.

### I.1.4 Part IV

In Part IV of this book, we compile contributions focusing on those most impacting consumption domains depicted above – namely travel, housing and food – as well as on the intersection of sustainable consumption and public health.

Fast, motorized transportation of people and cargo is essential in contemporary societies with their specialization of functions at different locations. Yet, the resulting unprecedented increase in motorized travel has both local short-term and global long-term detrimental effects on the environment, which must be mitigated. In Chapter 10, titled 'Unsustainable travel becoming (more) sustainable', Tommy Gärling and Margareta Friman review research assessing the effectiveness, public attitudes towards, and political feasibility of measures that limit local and global damage to the environment caused by automobile use. These measures include clean automobile technology, rebuilding the environment to increase accessibility by walking and bicycling, improving public transport, and reducing automobile use by implementing prohibition, pricing and information measures. The authors' conclusion is that no measure is sufficient alone but that several need to be combined. In particular, it is not even in the longer term likely that clean automobile technology, increasing accessibility by rebuilding the environment or improving alternative travel modes will suffice unless governments also implement measures that reduce automobile use. Since scientific evidence indicates that voluntary information and pricing measures may achieve 5–30 per cent reductions in urban areas, the often heard counter-argument from interest groups that automobile use cannot be reduced should not be taken seriously.

Next to travel (and interconnected), housing is essential from a sustainability perspective, both because this sector in itself stands for much of the resource consumption, and also because housing is central for the way consumption and production are organized in a society. In Chapter 11, Kirsten Gram-Hanssen puts housing in a sustainable consumption perspective. Policies related to sustainability in the housing sector have had a tendency to focus either on more efficient technologies or on changing user behaviour. In this chapter it is argued that technologies and the way people live in houses and use these technologies have to be dealt with in a much more integrated way than is done today, and that recent approaches of practices theory can help in the understanding of these relations. The author shares different approaches to sustainable housing development that have been promoted by both grass-roots initiatives and technological top-down approaches. The issue seems to be that policy initiatives have to understand the special meanings which people attach to housing: houses do not just provide shelter; they also form the basis for a home which represents security, familiarity and identity, and thus, according to the authors, any policy for a sustainable-consumption perspective on housing must also reflect this meaning of the home.

For the food domain, Achim Spiller and Sina Nitzko explore the role of meat in sustainable consumption in Chapter 12 titled 'Peak meat'. The chapter is based on the fact that global demand for meat and meat products is increasing, and with it the importance of the development of sustainable meat consumption. Besides social, economic, ecological and health-related criteria, ethical and animal welfare-related aspects play an additional role in the evaluation of sustainability of animal products. Following the 'less but better' approach discussed in this chapter, more sustainable meat consumption can be achieved by reducing the amount of meat consumed combined with enhancing the quality of the meat. In line with this, a typology of consumers that differ in their qualitative (ethical quality) and quantitative meat consumption is presented. Based on a consumer survey of a sample of the German population, the consumer types are validated and described. Furthermore, potential and existing policy measures to promote sustainable meat consumption in different target groups are suggested. The authors conclude by discussing challenges for the future development of more sustainable meat consumption.

Acknowledging that the consumption of meat accounts for a large proportion of the ecological footprint of contemporary Western diets, the following chapter also calls for a reduction in meat consumption to make a substantial contribution to a more sustainable food system. Muriel Verain, Hans Dagevos and Gerrit Antonides focus in Chapter 13 on 'flexitarianism' and the range of sustainable food styles it brings along. Flexitarianism displays itself in various ways of moderating meat consumption and appears to be acceptable for a large number of Dutch food consumers. What factors motivate flexitarianism, and what varieties of flexitarian food styles can be distinguished? The authors report on an empirical survey that has been conducted among 1312 Dutch consumers to identify clusters with different consumption styles with respect to meat. Differences across the clusters were found with respect to meat consumption, preferred societal actions to reduce meat consumption, and food neophobia. It is concluded that flexitarianism as a sustainable food style can take several forms. Several meat consumption reduction strategies to approach the different types of flexitarians are discussed.

Closely linked to modern Western food styles, obesity has increased tremendously worldwide, and the trend is still ongoing. In Chapter 14, Wencke Gwozdz discusses the nexus of obesity, sustainability and public health. The chapter acknowledges that the key drivers of obesity are not yet fully understood, yet consequences should have become obvious. Surely, the effects of obesity are not socially, economically or ecologically sustainable. Ecologically, current food production and consumption systems are responsible for a large share of greenhouse gas emissions. Economically, obesity is unsustainable with regard to health care systems and labour markets. And socially, obese consumers experience co-morbidities of obesity, an impairment in everyday life, discrimination and an overall reduced quality of life. The high prevalence of obesity and its unsustainable effects have led public health authorities worldwide to put obesity high on the policy agenda, and to make it an integral part of some nations' sustainability strategies. Promoting healthier lifestyles, including diets and physical activity of consumers, is one goal of public health, and if successful will have the power to reduce the unsustainable effects of obesity.

### I.1.5 Part V

In Part V of the book, we group chapters that cover a range of cross-cutting issues. Chapter 15 by Bas Verplanken and Deborah Roy focuses on consumer habits and sustainable consumption. It looks into what sustainable consumption means to consumers, why consumers make unsustainable decisions, and into potential avenues for promoting sustainable consumption. After reviewing some approaches to define sustainability, empirical evidence is presented showing how sustainable behaviours are cognitively clustered into sustainable technologies, sustainable energy use, sustainable food and shopping, sustainable environments and sustainable gardening. The authors continue to discuss the question why sustainability has such low priority in consumer decisions. Drawing on the decision making process literature, it is argued that unless sustainability is a top priority, linked to central values or prominently displayed it is unlikely to play a role at all due to the heuristic nature of most choices. The chapter then discusses the habitual nature of most consumer decisions and the consequences this has for making (un)sustainable choices. The authors focus in more detail on the habit discontinuity hypothesis, which states that behaviour change interventions are more effective when these capitalize on contexts where old habits are broken or suspended during life course changes, such as moving house or the transition to retirement. Finally, they address 'upstream' approaches to behaviour change, such as macro-level policy measures, transformations of the infrastructure or physical environments, or direct regulation of behaviour.

While academics and the press have paid significant and deserved attention to the issue of corporate social responsibility for a shift towards a more sustainable global economy, some have argued that there has been insufficient focus on the responsibility of the consumer. Michael G. Luchs and Rebecca A. Miller explore this issue in Chapter 16, titled 'Consumer responsibility for sustainable consumption'. In an effort to inform and promote future research on consumers' responsibility for sustainable consumption, they introduce a simple five-item scale of 'consumers' felt responsibility for sustainability' (CFRS) that builds on Schwartz's concept of activated personal norms as 'felt obligation'. The chapter aims at demonstrating the value of the CFRS scale in predicting sustainable consumption behaviours. They also explore consumers' conception of sustainability as well as their beliefs about the distribution of responsibility for sustainability amongst consumers, companies and governments. In addition, the authors describe preliminary results of research that explores the antecedents of CFRS using established constructs related to consumers' mind set, ideology and values, and demographics. The chapter concludes with a discussion about how a greater focus on consumer responsibility in general can advance research on sustainable consumption.

In the context of need for individual behavioural change, knowledge about family socialization and sustainable consumption is essential for developing effective policies. In Chapter 17, Ellen Matthies and Hannah Wallis develop two perspectives on sustainable consumer socialization, taking into consideration the level of impact and people's intentions to engage in sustainability. The first perspective focuses on how consumption behaviours that are particularly relevant in terms of environmental impact are transferred or have the potential to be transferred from parents to their children. The second perspective considers the transmission of pro-environmental values and norms within families. Earlier research has found relevant socialization influences from parents to children in a variety of domains, such as choice of travel mode and purchases of organic products and food. Adolescents appeared to be less influenced by their parents with regard to saving electricity. Thus, the transfer of specific consumption behaviours and the transmission of behaviour-specific norms seem to differ with respect to the domain of action. Studies indicate that communicating about the problems that are addressed by sustainable actions in families and children's observations of their parents' actions influence the socialization process. The authors close with suggestions on how to apply this knowledge to practical consumer socialization.

### I.1.6 Part VI

The following Part VI compiles chapters on promising policy instruments and tools that are applied to promote sustainable consumption. It spans from traditional instruments such as labelling and consumer information to more recent tools such as 'nudging'.

In Chapter 18, 'Carbon triage: a strategy for developing a viable carbon labelling system', Sharon Shewmake, Mark A. Cohen, Paul C. Stern and Michael P. Vandenbergh focus on carbon labelling as a way to fill gaps in governmental efforts to reduce the impact of human activity on global climate. Carbon labels can provide information that allows producers and consumers to develop and choose lower-impact products, but they have not become widespread, in part because of difficulties in developing valid and reliable labels for the universe of products. This chapter suggests a triage approach in which labelling begins with products that meet four criteria: magnitude of footprint, feasibility of assessment, and producer and consumer responsiveness. It presents an example of carbon labelling triage in the food industry and discusses three implementation issues: governance of the labelling system, geographic considerations and the content of carbon labels.

Caroline L. Noblet and Mario F. Teisl present a broader review of research on eco-labelling as sustainable consumption policy in Chapter 19. They start from the insight that the sustainability issues currently faced transcend region, place and generations; thus individuals must often rely on externally provided information to align their choices with their preferences. The wide-ranging use of eco-labels in the market suggests that they are perceived as an effective method of providing information to consumers, ultimately impacting upon consumer behaviour. The success of labelling programmes is contingent upon use of the labels in consumption decisions. Noblet and Teisl review factors influencing the decision to purchase eco-labelled products including characteristics of the individual, the programme and the product. Moreover, the potential for eco-labels to promote sustainability objectives is reviewed, including the benefits and limitations of eco-labels within the context of sustainable consumption.

Behavioural economics has been a late but crucial contributor to policy promoting sustainable consumption. In Chapter 20, 'Behavioural economics, consumption and environmental protection', one of the founding fathers of behavioural economics, Cass R. Sunstein, explains how behavioural economics, consumption and the environment can cooperate for the purpose of sustainable consumption. For a long time behavioural economists have shown that consumers may disregard the long term, display unrealistic optimism, ignore shrouded attributes, procrastinate, make mistaken judgements about probability, and suffer from 'internalities' that occur when people make decisions that hurt their future selves. Moreover, choice architecture, understood as the social or physical background, is always present and it can have major consequences for both consumption decisions and environmental outcomes. Small changes in the underlying architecture may have a large impact on consumer behaviour, potentially even larger than that of significant economic incentives. Such changes, he explains, may involve disclosure, warnings, default rules, increased salience, and use of social norms. We agree that in the domain of environmental protection, non-price interventions – preserving freedom of choice and avoiding people's reactance – have considerable potential.

Financial incentives are a highly popular tool to steer sustainable consumer behaviour, but they are not always effective, and can sometimes do more harm than good. Jan Willem Bolderdijk and Linda Steg offer insights into the conditions under which financial incentives are more or less effective. In Chapter 21, 'Promoting sustainable consumption: the risks of using financial incentives', their central point is that the persuasive power of incentives does not depend only on their instrumental value, but also on how these financial incentives affect people's underlying cognitions: money does something to people. Importantly, these cognitive responses may limit the persuasive power of incentives. Specifically, their instalment may lead consumers to adopt a business frame, disrupt the process of self-persuasion or taint the self-signal ensuing from the decision to act sustainably. This means that financial incentives can sometimes paradoxically discourage the very behaviour they are meant to encourage. Even when incentives are effective in promoting the target behaviour, they can still do more harm than good when they affect behaviour only temporarily, or simultaneously demotivate consumers to engage in other, more pertinent forms of sustainable actions that are not financially attractive. The chapter ends with discussing potential remedies against these risks, as well as directions for future research.

An instrument which impacts upon consumer behaviour indirectly is the corporate use of sustainability standards. In Chapter 22 on voluntary standards as enablers and impediments to sustainable consumption, Andreas Rasche discusses the role of voluntary standards for corporate sustainability and responsibility as enablers of and impediments to sustainable consumption. He starts by reflecting theoretically on the notion of standards, discussing different characteristics of this mode of regulation. Next he distinguishes different types of standards for corporate sustainability and responsibility. His subsequent analysis shows that standards enable sustainable consumption: firstly, by reducing information asymmetries, informing consumers about the social and environmental conditions under which products and services are created; secondly, by supporting the disclosure of firms' sustainability-related information (potentially leading to increased consumer loyalty); and thirdly, by further institutionalizing the discourse around sustainable consumption. The chapter also emphasizes that voluntary standards can impede sustainable consumption, the three reasons being: (1) the coexistence of a variety of competing initiatives in some sectors (for example, fair trade coffee) is likely to confuse consumers; (2) consumers may question the credibility of selected standards, since highly public scandals have revealed the limits of auditing and monitoring practices; and (3) while many standards are designed as multi-stakeholder initiatives, only few of them directly involve consumer representatives, leaving the impression that some standards define practices for consumers but not with them.

In parallel with policies for sustainable consumption gaining momentum, research into the barriers and drivers of more sustainable consumer behaviour has created a huge body of scientific evidence. However the impact of this knowledge on policy making has remained surprisingly small. In Chapter 23, 'Step across the border: knowledge brokerage for sustainable consumption', Gerd Scholl explores the reasons for the gap between science and policy on sustainable consumption and discusses ways to bridge it. After a brief overview of policies and research relevant to the field, different factors shaping the science–policy gap are presented. The concept of knowledge brokerage, which is essentially an approach to reduce the gap, is then introduced as a structured process of exchanging knowledge and creating links between different communities and of building capacities to perpetuate cross-community exchange. How this can look in practice is illustrated by the example of a European pilot project that experimented with and developed new integrative modalities of knowledge brokerage at the science–policy interface of sustainable consumption. The chapter concludes that conflicting time-frames and diverging agendas between science and policy still seem to be a major obstacle to more evidence-based policy making on sustainable consumption, and it suggests ways to overcome this mismatch by improving the availability of evidence (on demand) and by facilitating knowledge collaboration between the two communities. Recommendations for further research that can be derived from this conclusion cover topics such as cross-country analyses of different knowledge brokerage cultures, and explorations of the potential of social media for knowledge brokerage, amongst others.

### I.1.7 Part VII

The final part of the handbook looks into future directions for research on sustainable consumption. In Chapter 24, 'Decoupling resource consumption and economic growth: insights into an unsolved global challenge', Peter Hennicke and Dorothea Hauptstock argue that the decoupling of resource consumption from economic growth (that is, less used natural resources per unit of economic output) and impact decoupling (that is, reduced environmental impact of resource use and economic activities) are necessary conditions for sustainable development. The chapter demonstrates that a 'resource efficiency revolution' in combination with 'sufficiency policies' could be a promising step towards a solution. This might create much technological optimism. However we are reminded that there is much evidence that technological progress has to be accompanied by radical socio-economic transformation and new patterns of sustainable production and consumption to break the nexus between gross domestic product (GDP) growth and the use of nature. Thus, the authors call for more research on the social context of implementing 'greentec' and of the socio-economic drivers of 'lead markets' (for example, for energy and resource efficiency, sustainable mobility, recycling technologies or renewable energies). The authors conclude with a brief outlook on how the rapidly growing 'new consumer classes' (for example, in China and India) might change the overall picture dramatically.

Contemporary economic policy discourses are heavily oriented towards competition and efficiency, using modern conceptualization of the market as an institution for resource allocation and governance. Market-based policy approaches are considered necessary with sufficient instruments to achieve environmental goals while leaving individual freedom largely unaffected. In Chapter 25, 'The role of consumer sovereignty in sustaining the market economy', Wolfgang J. Fellner and Clive L. Spash challenge this neoliberal position in general and the underlying concept of consumer sovereignty specifically. According to the authors, this concept encapsulates the idea that individual consumption is the only source of value and consumers are able to enforce their interests on producers via their power in the market place. Despite the concept of consumer sovereignty having huge importance in contemporary economic theory and policy, its meaning remains opaque. The authors explore how consumer sovereignty has been employed for political instrumental, market ideal and economic instrumental reasons by classic liberals, neo-Austrian and neoclassical economists, respectively. They go on to show that the concept of consumer sovereignty depends upon a series of problematic assumptions and fails to bear much relationship to reality. The theoretical basis of consumer sovereignty on individual preferences proves problematic, not least due to its ethical presumptions. Environmentalists search for what makes a just and sustainable society, and neoliberalism is answering with the rhetoric of consumer sovereignty. This chapter shows why that answer needs to be rejected and why environmentalism actually means critically rethinking the role of markets in society.

New types of markets – and therewith new roles for market actors – are currently developing within the so-called 'sharing economy'. 'Collaborating and connecting: the emergence of the sharing economy' is the title of Chapter 26 by Juliet B. Schor and Connor J. Fitzmaurice. The authors show that while sharing is a long-standing form of exchange, new forms of sharing have emerged. What is innovative about today's sharing is that it is a market form in which strangers – rather than kin and communities – exchange goods and services. We learn that the contemporary sharing economy creates new ways of provisioning goods and services and opportunities for what the authors have called 'connected consumption', relying on peer-to-peer relationships rather than existing market actors to mediate exchanges. Schor and Fitzmaurice suggest that participation in the sharing economy is motivated by economic and ecological concerns, as well as a desire to increase social connections. However, they question how effective the sharing economy has been in meeting these goals. They emphasize the importance of digital technologies, facilitating the emergence of 'circuits of commerce', in overcoming the trust and reputational barriers that once restricted sharing to kin and community. Finally, Schor and Fitzmaurice suggest that the market orientation and organization of sharing economy platforms – as well as whether exchanges are monetized or non-monetized – are critical characteristics shaping these platforms and their potential to provide truly alternative economic arrangements.

In the final chapter in the book, American sociologist Maurie J. Cohen discusses the recent rise of numerous social innovations. Chapter 27, 'Toward a post-consumerist future? Social innovation in an era of fading economic growth', envisages such developments as incipient signals of a transition toward a heretofore inadequately theorized stage of social evolution, but contends that any such shift will invariably be a protracted and halting process. The author explains that while four decades have passed since social theorists first contemplated the waning of consumer society in the Anglo-European countries and Japan, this prospect was deferred in the early 1980s by new public policies favouring economic deregulation, trade liberalization and militarization. The political consensus that championed these strategies – and sustained lifestyles predicated on mass consumption – is said to have now broken down, and consumer-propelled economic growth is again becoming difficult to maintain. Cohen concludes that the reversal of once-favourable demographic, economic, social, cultural and environmental trends is undermining the pillars of consumerism today.

## I.2 SYNTHESIS AND LIMITATIONS

Together, the contributions to this book show that research on sustainable consumption is not only a young field, as we wrote earlier but is also a multifaceted, multidisciplinary, challenging and thriving field of research that has attracted brilliant scholars from all corners of the social and behavioural sciences. The research reported in this book spans from micro- to macro-level perspectives, from the past to the future, from what is to how to obtain what should be, from determining optimal individual choices to individuals' ethical responsibility for making these choices. More specifically, it spans from understanding the implications of the individual consumer's motives and constraints for the sustainability of choices and behaviour to attempting to grasp the complete system of production and consumption and its implications for sustainability. It spans from studies of the history of (un)sustainable consumption to systematic attempts to project the future of sustainable consumption. It spans from research attempting to build a better understanding of sustainable and unsustainable consumption (at the micro, various meso and the macro levels) to research on the most effective ways of changing lifestyles and creating more sustainable consumption patterns. It spans from research on measuring the sustainability of consumption options to research on the ethical responsibilities of individuals regarding the sustainability of their consumption choices.

However, despite its wide coverage, this book by necessity gives only a selective representation of current research. When deciding which specific topics to cover within the broad research field of sustainable consumption, we worked within the page constraints of a book in this series. In addition, even though we are thrilled by and grateful for the very positive responses we received to our invitations to contribute a chapter for this book, it is obvious that not everyone we invited was able to participate. These two limitations mean that there are important issues in sustainable consumption research that are not covered in this book. For example, we would have liked to have also included chapters that more systematically presented research on structural factors that limit consumer choices and thereby determine the sustainability of these choices, including research on the structural importance of prices (Ackerman and Gallagher 2000; Kågeson 1993; Pierce and Shoup 2013), including 'perverse subsidies' (Myers and Kent 2001; van Beers and van den Bergh 2001); research on how the law facilitates or impedes sustainable consumption (Garver 2013; Michalena and Frantzeskaki 2013; van Rijswick 2012), including mandatory standards (Boström and Klintman 2008); and research on the importance of the physical surroundings and infrastructure for sustainable consumption (Otnes 1988). One of us recently wrote an integrative review of how these and other factors contribute to unsustainable consumption (Thøgersen 2014).

As readers can confirm by checking the reference lists of the chapters of this book, research on sustainable consumption is published in core journals of the various disciplines, as well as in dedicated sustainability-oriented journals with a disciplinary or cross-disciplinary coverage, in policy-oriented journals and in books (like this one). These publication platforms have helped to establish and consolidate the research field, as well as to disseminate research results to other stakeholders within and outside research.

## I.3 FUTURE RESEARCH

As we write this in autumn 2014, three global work groups are in the process of publishing their contributions to IPCC's 5th assessment report on climate change. In the first two of three reports, Working Groups I and II (WGI and WGII) conclude that human activity is the main cause of global warming (with a certainty of more than 95 per cent) and that profound effects are already being felt around the world, but the effects are likely to get much worse (Field et al. 2014; Stocker et al. 2013). The report from Working Group III (WGIII), on mitigation of climate change, deals among other things with sustainable consumption and consumption growth (Edenhofer et al. 2014). This report concludes that, under conservative assumptions, interventions securing that we stay within atmospheric concentrations of carbon dioxide equivalent ($CO_2$eq) that are considered safe with regard to climate change entail an annualized reduction of consumption growth by 0.04 to 0.14 (median: 0.06) percentage points for the rest of this century, relative to annualized consumption growth in the baseline that is between 1.6 per cent and 3 per cent per year. This estimate does not include benefits of reduced climate change or co-benefits and adverse side-effects of mitigation. Consistent with research reported in the current book, WGIII judges that emissions can be substantially reduced through changes in consumption patterns, especially with regard to transport, energy use in buildings, and food (changing diets, reduced food wastes).

However it is symptomatic that the IPCC team assesses that the strength of the evidence this judgement is based on (only 'medium') and the level of agreement in the scientific community (also 'medium') is lower than for the key evidence presented in the reports from WGI and WGII. Behavioural science research has had, and still has, a relatively low priority among governments and other funders of sustainability research in general and climate research in particular. Until now, the focus has primarily been on creating sufficient certainty about the problem: that is, input for policy priorities and decisions about whether mitigation interventions are needed at all. There are good reasons for that, but it is now high time that research priorities and policy attention change and focus much more on mitigation, including how to make consumption more sustainable.

As written in an editorial in *Nature* when the WGI report was released, 'it is abundantly clear that the IPCC has done its job and is delivering what international policymakers need to do theirs . . . What is missing . . . is not science but political ambition' (Anonymous 2013). To advise them in 'doing their job' as effectively as possible, international policy makers need stronger, more unambiguous and more coordinated evidence from behavioural science research. Again, policy makers hold the most important key to this: sufficient research funds. However, behavioural scientists also carry their share of the responsibility by making their research more relevant and more accessible to international policy makers, including being better at coordinating our research and disseminating research evidence to policy makers and other key stakeholders. This volume is a small contribution towards this direction.

The development of research on understanding and promoting sustainable consumption, the research field covered in this book, has been facilitated by discipline-oriented scholarly associations creating subsections for this kind of research, and more recently by the creation of targeted cross-disciplinary communities such as the Sustainable Consumption Research and Action Initiative (SCORAI), the Virtual Community on Sustainability and Consumption, and the Global Research Forum on Sustainable Production and Consumption (GRF-SPaC).[1] Conferences, symposia and online dissemination activities organized by these communities are of tremendous importance for the coordination and dissemination of this research. These voluntary organizations of researchers also increase the vitality and dynamics of the research field, including exchange and testing of the newest results and ideas, and establishing collaborative research networks and projects. Hence, they are perhaps the best indication of the strong sense of responsibility that (also) behavioural researchers feel for contributing the needed evidence for deciding, designing and implementing effective mitigation action, regarding climate change as well as the other serious environmental threats that we are currently facing (Rockström et al. 2009).

In closing this introduction, we wish to express our deepest gratitude to the authors for giving their precious time and intellectual effort to our vision of this handbook. It was a real pleasure to edit it, not least due to the highly professional and always patient compliance with our many requests, suggestions for revisions, restrictions on (already carefully crafted) text length, and tight deadlines. We do owe a lot to our colleagues who have all contributed not just to this book but also to the advancement of research in SC in the past two decades. We hope that this handbook will prove valuable reference for policy makers and academicians interested in research on sustainable consumption.

## NOTE

1. See SCORAI.org, badm.au.dk/sustainabilityandconsumption, and grf-spc.weebly.com.

## REFERENCES


Ackerman, F. and K. Gallagher (2000), *Getting the Prices Wrong: The Limits of Market-Based Environmental Policy*, Medford, MA: Tufts University, Global Development and Environment Institute.

Anonymous (2013), 'Editorial: the final assessment', *Nature*, 501, p. 281.

Boström, M. and M. Klintman (2008), *Eco-Standards, Product Labelling and Green Consumerism*, Basingstoke: Palgrave Macmillan.

Edenhofer, O., R. Pichs-Madruga, Y. Sokona, S. Agrawala, I.A. Bashmakov, G. Blanco, J. Broome et al. (eds) (2014), *Climate Change 2014: Mitigation of Climate Change*, Working Group III contribution to the fifth assessment report of the Intergovernmental Panel on Climate Change, Cambridge, UK and New York, USA: Cambridge University Press.

Field, C.B., V.R. Barros, M.D. Mastrandrea, K.J. Mach, M.A.-K. Abdrabo, W.N. Adger, Y.A. Anokhin et al. (eds) (2014), *Climate Change 2014: Impacts, Adaptation, and Vulnerability. Volume I: Global and Sectoral Aspects*, Working Group II contribution to the fifth assessment report of the Intergovernmental Panel on Climate Change, Cambridge, UK and New York, USA: Cambridge University Press.

Garver, G. (2013), 'The rule of ecological law: the legal complement to degrowth economics', *Sustainability*, 5 (1), 316–337.
Kågeson, P. (1993), *Getting the Prices Right: A European Scheme for Making Transport Pay its True Costs*, Brussels: European Federation for Transport and Environment.
Michalena, E. and N. Frantzeskaki (2013), 'Moving forward or slowing-down? Exploring what impedes the Hellenic energy transition to a sustainable future', *Technological Forecasting and Social Change*, 80, 977–991.
Myers, N. and J. Kent (2001), *Perverse Subsidies: How Tax Dollars Can Undercut the Environment and the Economy*, Washington, DC: Island Press.
Otnes, P. (1988), 'Housing consumption: collective systems service', in P. Otnes (ed.), *The Sociology of Consumption*, Atlantic Highlands, NJ: Humanities Press, pp. 119–138.
Pierce, G. and D. Shoup (2013), 'Getting the prices right: an evaluation of pricing parking by demand in San Francisco', *Journal of the American Planning Association*, 79, 67–81.
Rockström, J., W. Steffen, K. Noone, Å. Persson, F.S. Chapin III, E. Lambin, T.M. Lenton et al. (2009), 'Planetary boundaries: exploring the safe operating space for humanity', *Ecology and Society*, 14 (2), 32.
Stocker, T.F., D. Qin, G.-K. Plattner, M. Tignor, S.K. Allen, J. Boschung, A. Nauels et al. (eds) (2013), *Climate Change 2013: The Physical Science Basis*. Contribution of Working Group I to the fifth assessment report of the Intergovernmental Panel on Climate Change. Cambridge, UK and New York, USA: Cambridge University Press.
Thøgersen, J. (2014), 'Unsustainable consumption: Basic causes and implications for policy', *European Psychologist*, 19, 84–95.
van Beers, C. and J.C.J.M. van den Bergh (2001), 'Perseverance of perverse subsidies and their impact on trade and environment', *Ecological Economics*, 36, 475–486.
van Rijswick, H.F. (2012), 'The road to sustainability: how environmental law can deal with complexity and flexibility', *Utrecht Law Review*, 8 (3), 1–6.

# PART I

# RESEARCH IN SUSTAINABLE CONSUMPTION AS AN INTERDISCIPLINARY AND TRANSDISCIPLINARY APPROACH

# 1. Sustainable consumption as a systemic challenge: inter- and transdisciplinary research and research questions

*Sylvia Lorek and Philip J. Vergragt*

## 1.1 THE CHALLENGE

Present consumption patterns in developed countries are unsustainable. We consume too many raw materials and use too much energy, create too much hazardous waste and even consume renewables at an unsustainable rate. In addition research has shown that more material consumption does not make us happier; it appears that above a certain level individual well-being is 'decoupled' from material throughput and energy use (Abdallah et al. 2009; Jackson 2009). Moreover there are strong indications that unsustainable consumption patterns contribute to greater inequity; and conversely, that inequities contribute to unsustainable consumption patterns (Vergragt 2013; Wilkinson and Picket 2009).

Developing countries are quickly following the same path of material over consumption and greater inequality. One-quarter of humanity – 1.7 billion people worldwide – now belongs to the 'global consumer class', having adopting the diets, transportation systems and lifestyles that were once mostly limited to the 'global North'. Today, the BRIC countries (Brazil, Russia, India and China) and other developing countries are home to growing numbers of these consumers.

Sustainable consumption is defined at the Oslo Roundtable (1994) as: 'the use of goods and services that respond to basic needs and bring a better quality of life, while minimizing the use of natural resources, toxic materials and emissions of waste and pollutants over the life cycle, so as not to jeopardize the needs of future generations'. It is thus a broad concept with a wide variety of meanings, for instance: consuming differently using less resource-intensive products; moving from material products to immaterial services; energy conservation; sharing the use of products; and using higher-quality products with longer life spans (Lebel and Lorek 2008). More generally it means a cultural shift away from the prevalent consumerist culture towards a culture which values sustainable lifestyles (Brown and Vergragt forthcoming). From an economic perspective, it means that the economy needs to move away from producing too many unsustainable consumer products, towards producing more sustainable services and infrastructures. However the present market economy is dominated by the economic growth paradigm which results in increasingly unsustainable production and consumption patterns (Jackson 2009).

Consumption is part of a larger system of investments, production, trade, consumption and waste; it has material, economic, cultural, institutional and power aspects. Changing consumption thus entails changing the entire system: it encompasses changing the economic system, the infrastructures, the dominant culture and lifestyles, and changing institutions and power relationships (Vergragt et al. 2014).

No full agreement exists among scholars about what constitutes the sustainable consumption research field. A first distinction can be made between research on existing (often unsustainable) consumption patterns and practices, and studies reflecting the aspiration of sustainable consumption. A second distinction is between individual consumption practices and the collective act of consumption, which is associated with the cultural notion of a consumer society and consumerist lifestyles. A third distinction can be made between material aspects, economic aspects and cultural notions. Material aspects are often expressed in life cycle assessments (LCAs) and materials flow analyses. Economic aspects are transactions between buyers and sellers as well as investments and trade. Cultural notions are researched at the individual level (norms and habits, identity) and the collective level (fashion, consumerist lifestyles).

Next to static analyses (such as the LCA of a product), dynamic analyses of change processes exist, such as the frameworks of socio-technical transitions, grassroots innovations and social movements. Change process can be analysed through the lens of power relationships between elements of the incumbent system and actors who want to change the system. Finally, scholars conceptualize production and consumption as a complex system and analyse the complexities of changing such systems. In Vergragt et al. (2014) an overview is presented of research fields comprising sustainable consumption research.

Consumerist culture is not a natural phenomenon. In the United States it was designed before the Second World War by powerful think-tanks, trade unions and government interventions serving big business interests (Botsman and Rogers 2010; Brown and Vergragt forthcoming; Cohen 2004; Ewens 1998; Garon 2012). The prevalent consumerist culture in consumer societies is closely related to the issues of (economic) power, which are so far insufficiently addressed in sustainable consumption research. It is beyond the scope of this chapter to discuss power issues in depth, but in general we can say that power plays a central role in creating structural barriers to sustainable consumption and in delimiting opportunities for intervention. The relationship between power and sustainable consumption also highlights fundamental questions of democracy: how can one assure equality in participation in today's democracies, which are characterized by large asymmetries in resources and access to institutions and decision makers? Power has structural and actor-specific elements as well as material and ideational sources (Fuchs 2013a, 2013b).

Consequently, modes and levels of consumption are hardly touched by politics. The prevalent market economy is ideologically based on 'free choice' and 'consumer sovereignty', and thus governments as well as civil society organizations are hesitant to interfere with individual lifestyle choices. Market-economy systems (as actually structured) need to constantly increase consumption in order to sustain the economy and, especially, full employment. Thus, in the name of sustainable consumption, their interventions are carefully calibrated to address environmental problems while not slowing down the economy. Consequently, the increased emphasis on efficiency and green consumerism has allowed governments to pay lip service to sustainable consumption while still allowing consumer sovereignty, and tacitly or explicitly encouraging continuous (over) consumption (Akenji 2014).

The aims of this chapter are to document the unsustainability of present prevalent consumption patterns in the overdeveloped world, and to explore in more detail how a transition towards a more sustainable consumption system could be achieved, based on research outcomes. In section 1.2 we present empirical data that illustrate unsustainable consumption and also the problems of 'green consumerism'. In section 1.3 we illustrate what we mean by 'systemic change'; we present consumption as part of a complex system; and argue that systemic change encompasses simultaneous changes in culture, production processes, consumption patterns, lifestyles, economics and politics. In section 1.4 we conclude by elaborating which actions could contribute to such systemic change, and what the role of research could be to support such actions.

## 1.2 EMPIRICAL EVIDENCE ON UNSUSTAINABLE CONSUMPTION

A huge variety of data illustrate that we are not at all approaching a sustainable level of consuming. The Global Footprint Network (2013), for example, annually calculates the day upon which the renewable resources which should last for a year are consumed already (Table 1.1). Since the mid-1980s the 'Earth Overshoot Day' appears earlier and earlier. In 2013 the resources were already used after two-thirds of the year. During the remaining months global population no longer consumes the fruits of nature but consumes from the stock, which is thus constantly shrinking.

Other sources offer more detailed facts, for example:

- Extraction of 'conventional' crude oil peaked in 2006; most major fields were discovered in the 1960s and production from them is declining at 4–6 per cent per year and 'new' oil cannot keep up (IEA 2010).
- Sixty-three of the 89 non-renewable resources that enable high-tech industrial society had become globally scarce by 2008 (Clugson 2012).
- Eighty-two per cent of monitored fish stocks were fully exploited or overexploited by 2008; 32 per cent are overexploited, up from 10 per cent in the 1970s (FAO 2010).
- Thirty per cent of the world's arable land has become unproductive; soil erosion and degradation continues at 10–40 times the rate of natural replenishment (Pimentel 2006).

Stopping and reversing these developments requires clear targets and timetables, as well as strategic approaches based on our knowledge of how systemic change could be influenced. Rockström et al. (2009) list nine processes for which it is necessary to define planetary boundaries. They illustrate that in three systems (rate of biodiversity

*Table 1.1 Development of Earth Overshoot Day*

| 1987 | 1990 | 1995 | 2000 | 2005 | 2007 | 2008 | 2009 | 2010 | 2011 | 2012 | 2013 |
|---|---|---|---|---|---|---|---|---|---|---|---|
| 19.12 | 07.12 | 21.11 | 01.11 | 20.10 | 26.10 | 23.09 | 25.09 | 21.08 | 27.09 | 22.08 | 20.08 |

*Note:* The discontinuity in 2009 is due to changes/improvements of the calculation methods.

*Source:* Global Footprint Network (2013).

loss, climate change and human interference with the nitrogen cycle) the safe operating boundaries have already been tremendously exceeded (Rockström et al. 2009).

Considering how to reduce the impacts on the environment, the IPAT formula (Ehrlich and Holden 1971; Thøgersen 2014) is still useful: the impact (I) on the environment is determined by population (P), affluence (A) and technology (T). We will briefly address each of the factors.

According to the *World Population Prospects* (UN DESA 2013) Europe's population (the 'P' factor) is projected to decline by 14 per cent until 2050. However, the current world population of 7.2 billion is projected to increase by almost 1 billion people within 12 years, reaching 8.1 billion in 2025, and 9.6 billion in 2050. Most of the population growth will occur in developing regions, which are projected to increase from 5.9 billion in 2013 to 8.2 billion in 2050. Growth is expected to be most rapid in the 49 least-developed countries, which are projected to double in size from around 900 million inhabitants in 2013 to 1.8 billion in 2050. Next to increasing fertility, life expectancy is also projected to increase and so contributes to the raising population number. The twentieth century witnessed the most rapid decline of mortality in human history. For the world as a whole, life expectancy at birth rose from 47 years in 1950–1955 to 69 years in 2005–2010. Over the next 40 years, life expectancy at birth is expected to continue on a similar path. At the global level, it is projected to reach 76 years in 2045–2050 and 82 years in 2095–2100. By the end of the century, people in developed countries could live on average around 89 years, compared to about 81 years in developing regions. As fertility declines and life expectancy rises, the proportion of the population above a certain age rises. This phenomenon, known as population ageing, is occurring throughout the world.

This is of concern because it reduces the 'fair Earth share' of resources per person. In its 2010 report *Transforming Cultures*, the World Watch Institute (2010) calculated a possible sustainable population in relation to Earth's biocapacity (see Table 1.2). This biocapacity would even allow 13.8 billion people 'if they would live on a biocapacity of one global hectare each'. As the World Watch Institute's figures indicate the income level of people – or in Ehrlich and Holden's terms, the affluence (A) factor – plays the even more important role. Both population and affluence have to be targeted to shrink our footprint to a size that fits the available biocapacity. So the challenging task of the developed nations is to shrink the affluence-related impacts, and for developing nations to increase affluence while not exceeding the fair Earth share.

*Table 1.2 Sustainable world population at different consumption levels*

| Consumption level | Per capita income (2005) (GNI, PPP, 2008 dollars) | Biocapacity/person (global hectares) | Sustainable population at this level (billion) |
|---|---|---|---|
| Low-income | 1.230 | 1.0 | 13.6 |
| Middle-income | 5.100 | 2.2 | 6.2 |
| High-income | 34.690 | 6.4 | 2.1 |
| United States | 45.580 | 9.4 | 1.4 |
| Global average | 9.460 | 2.7 | 5.0 |

*Source:* WorldWatch (2010).

As to the technology factor (T), the dominant paradigm still is that technology will be able to solve ecological problems through technological innovations, in combination with suitable policies. However it is becoming increasingly recognized that technology alone will not be able to solve these problems. Technological innovations have the potential to transform society, like the Internet; and also have the potential of reducing pollution and enhancing resource efficiency, for instance through dematerialization and through energy efficiency and renewable energy. However rebound effects (Herring and Sorrel 2008) on many levels are counteracting these efficiencies: on the individual level, if consumers spend their saved expenses on unsustainable activities; and on the economic level, when efficiencies spur innovations in more new products and services and economic growth (the Jevons paradox) (Alcott 2005).

For more than a decade scientific knowledge has been available on which product groups cause most environmental pollution; quite often due to fast technological development. The highest environmental impact per capita is caused by food, housing and mobility (Gatersleben et al. 2002; Lorek and Spangenberg 2001; Noorman et al. 1999). More recent and concrete data are provided by the European Environmental Agency (EEA 2013). Only a few product groups contribute significantly (between 30 and 50 per cent) to environmental pressures. These product groups are:

- construction works, that is, buildings and infrastructures;
- food products, beverages and alcohol;
- products of agriculture, forestry and fishing;
- electricity, gas, steam and hot water (the majority of which is electricity).

These four together contributed 42 per cent to greenhouse gas emissions, 52 per cent to acidifying emissions, 37 per cent to ground ozone precursors, and 55 per cent to the total material requirements (TMR) embodied in all consumed products in 2005. Interestingly they represent only 17 per cent of total consumption expenditure.

In addition the EEA claims that the production chains for additional seven products accumulate quite significant environmental pressures, though less than the first group of four. These are:

- wholesale and retail services;
- motor vehicles and other transport equipment;
- hotel and restaurant services;
- transport and auxiliary transport services;
- coke and refined petroleum;
- health and social work;
- public administration, defence and social security services.

All 11 key product groups together account for 75–85 per cent of the key environmental pressures caused by expenditure on goods and services.

So, recognizing, that all factors of the IPAT equation are increasing, including the impact on the environment, the question arises of whether the increase in A has at least some measurable benefits beyond just affluence. Research suggests that this is only the case to a very limited extent. There is a wealth of data showing that above a certain (low)

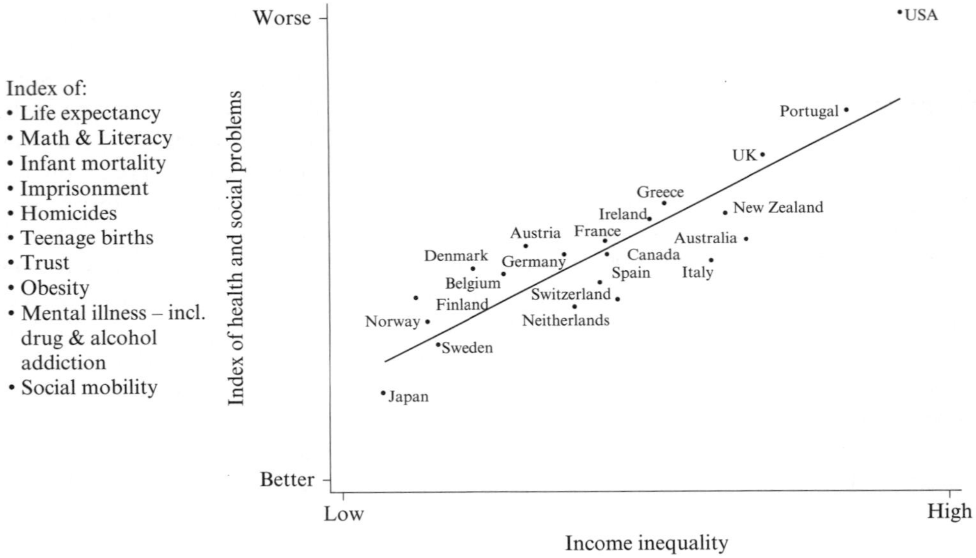


*Source:* Wilkinson and Picket (2009).

*Figure 1.1 Health and social problems in relation to income inequality*

income level, increased consumption of material goods does not increase happiness. For instance, in the US, a tripling of annual income since 1957 has made little or no effect on levels of happiness (Myers 1993). Across countries, above a certain level of income, subjective well-being hardly increased (Inglehart and Klingemann 2000).

In addition, since the 1980s inequality has increased in most countries. It has been amply documented that more equal societies perform better on a wide range of social indicators of well-being, including social trust and support for democratic institutions, political participation, educational outcomes, health status, crime and opportunities for social mobility (Wilkinson and Picket 2009) (Figure 1.1). A society with large income disparities provides the free market system with a perfect setting for exploiting the natural human tendency toward insatiability and positional consumption, and thus perpetuates and inflames the consumerist society. Less inequality will also mean lower material consumption and a smaller environmental burden, while providing greater life satisfaction and a higher standard of living for most people (Vergragt 2013).

## 1.3 TOWARDS SYSTEMIC CHANGE[1]

As a result of the argument above, some scholars insist that next to efficiency we need to consider sufficiency as a leading principle. Sufficiency explores the question: how much is enough? (Princen 2005). Sufficiency needs to be connected to two issues: one is individual and social well-being; and the other is ecological sustainability. Thus a sufficiency lifestyle should on the one hand remain within the ecological footprint that reflects a fair Earth share; and on the other hand enhance human and social well-being. There are many visions and scenarios for such sustainability lifestyles that reflect sufficiency, for instance the Tellus Institute's Great Transition Scenario (Great Transition Initiative 2013) and the SPREAD project (Sustaining Partnerships to enhance Rural Enterprise and Agribusiness Development) (Kuittinen et al. 2012; Mont et al. 2014). The challenge is not only to develop appealing visions of the future, but especially to develop strategies and policies about how to get there. So far, there is a deficiency in successful strategies and policies.

Based on scientific research, a number of strategies for systemic change have been developed over the last decade or so. The socio-technical transitions framework focuses mainly on technological innovations. The framework in essence stipulates that technological and social innovations are developed in niches, where social actors are able to experiment with the design and the implementation of new technologies, social arrangements and organizational structures (Geels and Schot 2007). Once experiments in niches have developed the innovation into a somewhat stable design, the niche may eventually challenge the mainstream, which is called a socio-technical regime (for example, the internal combustion motor regime). The destabilization of the socio-technical regime may be further enhanced when 'landscape' developments push in the same direction (for instance, the global challenges of climate change). The incumbent regime may eventually be replaced by a more sustainable regime.

A second framework of systemic change is the perspective of grass-roots innovations (Seyfang 2009; Seyfang and Smith 2007), which is also discussed under the heading of 'bounded socio-technical experiments' (BSTEs) (Brown and Vergragt 2008). BSTEs are in essence experiments in alternative technologies and social arrangements in niches; this framework focuses on the social learning processes that take place in those niches. The theory claims that learning occurs when actors with different world views (business, government, civil society and academia) collaborate in concrete projects, for instance on the design of a sustainable transportation system or a sustainable city concept. In such collaboration the actors, guided by their different world views, initially develop incompatible problem definitions (profit making, long-term social benefits, social change, knowledge creation). During the project, and especially in the design stage, actors mutually adjust their problem definitions (but not their world views, which are stable), and develop a joint problem definition that guides their collaboration. This development and stabilization of a common problem definition constitutes higher-order learning, and actors can transfer this learning to their subsequent projects.

Seyfang and Smith have studied 'grassroots innovations' existing in the 'social economy' of community activities and social enterprise, rather than in the market economy (Seyfang 2009, pp. 72–73; Seyfang and Smith 2007). Among their examples are: local currencies, local farmers' markets, non-traditional housing and others. The institutional forms of those initiatives are different from market institutions, including co-operatives, voluntary associations, informal community groups and other social enterprises. They are driven by two motivations – social and environmental needs, and ideology – and emphasize different social, ethical and cultural rules and values. Social and environmental needs could for instance consist of access to affordable and sustainable housing, fresh and sustainable food, sustainable transportation services and so on. Ideology refers to 'alternative ways of doing things, counter to the hegemony of the regime . . . Some grassroots innovations develop practices based on reordered priorities and alternative values. Examples are for instance the new economics, focusing on the quality of life rather than on economic growth per se' (Seyfang 2009, p. 74).

Another framework of systemic change has been developed under the heading of 'visioning and back casting' (Quist et al. 2011). Back casting can be defined as 'generating a desirable future, and then looking backwards from that future to the present in order to strategize and to plan how it could be achieved' (Vergragt and Quist 2011). It has gradually become more widely applied over the last decade. This is related to the rising popularity of the strongly normative concept of sustainability. Back casting also has a strongly normative nature, and therefore it is especially well equipped to be applied to sustainability issues. Backcasting works through envisioning and analysing sustainable futures and subsequently by developing agendas, strategies and pathways for how to get there. Visioning and back casting have been used for example in the SPREAD project (Corubolo et al. 2012; Kuittinen et al. 2012; Mont et al. 2014).

In the sociological literature the concept of 'new social movements' is relevant (Buechler 1990; Tarrow 2005; Tarrow et al. 2001). The most noticeable feature of new social movements is that they are primarily social and cultural and only secondarily, if at all, political. New social movements concentrate on bringing about social mobilization through cultural innovations, development of new lifestyles and transformation of identities. Some of them also emphasize post-material values in contemporary and post-industrial society, as opposed to conflicts over material resources. These contemporary social movements reject the materialistic orientation of consumerism and question the modern idea that links the pursuit of happiness and success closely to growth, progress and increased productivity, and promote alternative values and understandings in relation to the social world.

Akenji (2014) offers a useful conceptual model of change, the attitudes–facilitators–infrastructure (AFI) framework. It presents three conditions necessary to shift the system towards sustainability: the right attitudes by all stakeholders (shaped by values and knowledge); facilitators to translate attitudes into action (incentives and constraints); and sustainable infrastructure (including systems of provision and the physical infrastructure).

In addition to the above-mentioned approaches to systemic change, there are other useful approaches that are cross-cutting the field of sustainable consumption. One approach is the social practice theory (Halkier 2013; Shove and Walker 2010). Social practice scholarship views consumers of goods and services as practitioners immersed in the affairs of everyday life. Practices are the ways that people constitute the ordinary tasks of working, cooking, washing, preparing food, socializing and relaxing. Moreover most individuals typically regard themselves as practitioners engaged in the business of living, rather than as consumers of scarce commodities. This approach offers a useful new perspective on consumption practices; however it offers few insights into how to change established consumption practices.

Given that the individual is deeply embedded in societal, economic and political structures, governance for change will have to focus on structural changes, which in turn is where governments become important. This does not mean that individual, voluntary approaches should not be appreciated. However groups and movements such as the voluntary simplicity movement (Doherty and Etzioni 2003; Elgin 1993; Maniates 2002), which has recently gained attention in marketing concepts such as LOVOS (Lifestyle of Voluntary Simplicity) or voluntary downshifting (Hamilton 2010), tend to include small sectors of society only and thus are not sufficient to solve system-wide problems.

Several research approaches have started to explore governance opportunities for the kinds of substantial structural reforms that are needed; that is, that would go beyond the inclusion of external costs in prices or other market-related approaches. These approaches include system innovation research (Tukker 2008), evolutionary economics (Boulding 1991) and critical realism (Archer et al. 1998; Bhaskar 1978; Lorek 2010), for example.

A discussion that touches on sustainable consumption is the growth–degrowth debate, which is on the rise both within economics but also in the social movements around sustainable consumption (Demaria et al. 2013; Schneider et al. 2010; Sekulova et al. 2013). This debate is closely connected to the efficiency–sufficiency debate. Economic growth (measured in gross domestic product, GDP) has since the Second World War been the bedrock of economic theories and government policies. Economic growth is supposed to generate employment for most, as well as technological innovations, infrastructure development, and lifting the poor out of poverty. However, after the Great Recession it became clear that it did not deliver its promises (including a steep rise in inequality); and it had a strong negative impact on the environment (Harris 2013; Røpke 2013; Schneider et al. 2010, 2011).

In this context the notion of decoupling has emerged. Resource decoupling means reducing the rate of resource use per unit of economic activity measured in GDP. A distinction is often made between relative and absolute decoupling (Jackson 2009, Ch. 5). Relative decoupling is achieved when resource use grows less than GDP; it reflects a reduction of energy and materials use and emissions per unit of production. Unfortunately such a reduction is most often offset by further economic growth. Thus absolute decoupling is called for, meaning that resource use decreases in absolute terms in the sense of real dematerialization of societies, which is most often incompatible with economic growth in terms of GDP (O'Neill 2012).

In line with this, the degrowth movement argues that in (over)developed countries the economy should shrink in a planned and orderly way, not through recessions and economic calamities (Alperovitz 2011) or, as Victor (2008) phrased it: 'slower by design not disaster'. Some modelling has been performed on degrowth, which shows that public investments rather than private consumption, in combination with a shortening of the working week, could possibly achieve a degrowth scenario (Victor 2008, 2010).

Degrowth can be considered to be part of the 'new economy' movement, which conceptually has a macroeconomic component (Harris 2013; Røpke 2013) (degrowth of the economy, and different indicators than GDP for human and economic well-being); but also has a grass-roots innovation component, as it concentrates on socio-technical experiments, alternative currencies, experiments such as transition towns and different forms of company ownership such as co-operatives (Jackson and Victor 2013; Miller 2012).

Fuchs and Lorek (2005) make a useful distinction between weak and strong sustainable consumption, based on Neumayer's distinction of weak and strong sustainability (Neumeyer 2003). They suggest that the current 'green economy' or 'green growth' agenda is insufficient and potentially counterproductive to the long-term goal of sustainability because of its reliance on weak sustainability stimuli (Lorek and

Spangenberg 2014). Institutional change that promotes strong sustainable consumption is a necessary condition for sustainable development and calls for the greater involvement of government and powerful actors in encouraging public debate.

To better motivate a governance for change, a two-pronged strategy seems necessary: that is, a carrot and stick approach (Lorek 2010). The stick would be strong government regulations including capping unsustainable consumption levels, in combination with a communications strategy explaining why these are necessary (Thøgersen 2014).

The carrot for strong sustainable consumption is to raise the awareness of the fact that a slimming of the economy, that is, reducing its physical throughput, is accompanied by many positive side effects – if we are prepared for it. Well-being in developed countries has for some time already been decoupled from economic growth (Daly et al. 1990; Jackson 2009; Mulder et al. 2006). This needs to be communicated more effectively. Understanding and internalizing alternative measures of well-being (NEF 2009; Stiglitz et al. 2009) can help to overcome growth addiction (Van Griethuysen 2009), not by downplaying losses but by highlighting gains, for example, of time and self-realization (Grober 2012; Reisch 2001). It is important to sensitize people to the relevance of other elements of well-being beyond material consumption. Examples like the US initiative 'Take Back Your Time' for reducing working hours and extended holidays are a valid contribution to strong sustainable consumption without explicitly focusing on it (de Graaf 2003; Maniates 2010). Also, the public discourse on happiness can help in considering the limitations on increasing human well-being through material consumption (Hofstetter et al. 2006; Layard 2005).

Successful governance for strong sustainable consumption as well as successful degrowth governance will depend on governments taking responsibility and making tough choices (Lorek and Fuchs 2013). Capping and the protection of resources in the interest of societal sustainability are unavoidable (see also Princen 2010). It is governments' responsibility to phase out unsustainable consumption options (Church and Lorek 2007) or to carry out 'choice editing' as it is called more recently (Maniates 2009; Thaler and Sunstein 2008). As long as national governments understand their role in the governance of sustainable consumption as one of providing opportunities for the exchange of opinions and voluntary commitments that are not controlled, a significant drive will fail to materialize (Berg 2006). In consequence, pressuring governments to take responsibility is a crucial strategy to pursue.

To overcome socio-psychological lock-in – for consumers, policy makers and business decision makers – scenarios can help to imagine and compare the potential implications of choice options. For strong sustainable consumption they remain unrecognized, like the 'Great Transition' scenario mentioned earlier (Raskin et al. 2002). This makes the decision process abstract and hinders a broader perception of what the choice really encompasses. It can even result in the paradoxical effect that to some the ongoing degrowth debate strengthens rather than challenges the growth paradigm; for consumers as well as for political decision makers, as Berg and Hukkinen (2011) have shown in their narrative analysis of the Finnish sustainable consumption and production debate. Scenarios need to compare the suggested strong sustainable consumption option with the risks and costs of inaction, economic as well as social (Lorek and Spangenberg 2014; OECD 2008).

## 1.4 CONCLUSIONS

In this chapter we have argued that present 'Northern' lifestyles and consumption patterns have led to unsustainable environmental impacts, and also have led to deep inequalities which are equally unsustainable. Many publications and data sets have shown that these problems will increase due to population growth, urbanization and further increases of affluence due to the emerging of a new global middle class. Deep systemic changes are necessary in our current patterns of housing, transportation and food consumption. Green consumerism, setting the prices right and creating the right incentives for individual consumers are necessary, but will not be enough to address these problems. Such measures amount to what we have mostly called weak sustainable consumption.

Deep systemic changes need leadership and governance, learning from experiments, collaboration between stakeholders, new business models, and new framings and communications. Research can elucidate the conditions for success and failure, as well as help to more successfully communicate the urgency. Research also needs to generate clear and time-bound targets of what has to be reduced, by whom and when, if humanity aspires to stay within ecological limits. Such scenarios should highlight the social costs of inaction and the risks for social security from the local to the global level. Scientifically solid targets have to serve as orientation points for political and societal development.

Most research to date has either addressed the supply side and technological solutions, or has focused on behavioural change of individual consumers. To date, research has hardly begun to investigate a possible and necessary societal transition to new and sustainable production and consumption systems, which includes new economics, and a new post-consumerist culture. Research into these issues is complex and trans disciplinary. It needs to cover the various dimensions (material, technological, economic, cultural, psychological, historical and political) in an integrated way. It should cover domains such as food, housing, transportation and leisure. It should study successful examples and the conditions for success, and failures and causes of failure, and it should conduct comparative studies.

Research should ultimately contribute to developing a theory of social change that would contribute to systemic social change, including a transition to new and sustainable lifestyles and values. Technological change and individual consumption habits and patterns would be part of this research programme, but social change research would be an important and integral part of this endeavour.

## NOTE

1. Partially based on Vergragt et al. (2014).

## REFERENCES

Abdallah, S., S. Thompson, J. Michaelson, N. Marks and N. Steuer (2009), *The Happy Planet Index 2.0: Why Good Lives Don't Have to Cost the Earth*, London: NEF (New Economics Foundation).

Akenji, L. (2014), 'Consumer scapegoatism and limits to green consumerism', *Journal of Cleaner Production*, 63, 16–23.
Alcott, B. (2005), 'Jevons' paradox', *Ecological Economics*, 54 (1), 9–21.
Alperovitz, G. (2011), 'The New Economy movement', *Nation*, 13 June, available at http://www.thenation.com/article/160949/new-economy-movement# (accessed 24 February 2014).
Archer, M., R. Bhaskar, A. Collier, T. Lawson and A. Norrie (eds) (1998), *Critical Realism: Essential Readings*, Abingdon: Routledge.
Berg, A. (2006), 'Innovative governance or outsourcing politics? Discussing European forerunner cases of sustainable consumption and production', *Proceedings: The Ninth Biennial Conference of The International Society for Ecological Economics, Ecological Sustainability and Human Well-being*, New Delhi, India.
Berg, A. and J.I. Hukkinen (2011), 'The paradox of growth critique: narrative analysis of the Finnish sustainable consumption and production debate', *Ecological Economics*, 72, 151–160.
Bhaskar, R. (1978), *A Realist Theory of Science*, Brighton: Harvester Press.
Botsman, R. and R. Rogers (2010), *What's Mine is Yours: The Rise of Collaborative Consumption*, New York: Harper Collins.
Boulding, K.E. (1991), 'What is evolutionary economics?', *Journal of Evolutionary Economics*, 1, 9–17.
Brown, H.S. and P.J. Vergragt (2008), 'Bounded socio-technical experiments as agents of systemic change: the case of a zero-energy residential building', *Technological Forecasting and Social Change*, 75, 107–130.
Brown, H.S. and P.J. Vergragt (forthcoming), 'From consumerism to wellbeing: towards a cultural transition?', *Journal of Cleaner Production*.
Buechler, S.M. (1990), *Social Movements in Advanced Capitalism*, New York: Oxford University Press.
Church, C. and S. Lorek (2007), 'Linking policy and practice in sustainable production and consumption: an assessment of the role of NGOs', *International Journal of Innovation and Sustainable Development*, 2 (2), 230–240.
Clugson, C.O. (2012), *Scarcity: Humanity's Final Chapter?* Port Charlotte, FL: Booklocker.
Cohen, L. (2004), *Consumer Republic: The Politics of Mass Consumption in Postwar America*, New York: Vintage Books.
Corubolo, M., F. Jégou, A. Meroni, F. Piredda and Z. Zhang (2012), *Visual Material Presenting Emerging Best Practice and Emerging Visions on Sustainable Lifestyles*, Milan: Politecnico di Milano.
Daly, H.E., J.B. Cobb Jr and C.W. Cobb (1990), *For the Common Good: Redirecting the Economy Towards Community, the Environment and a Sustainable Future*, London: Green Print.
De Graaf, J. (ed.) (2003), *Take Back Your Time: Fighting Overwork and Time Poverty in America*, San Francisco, CA: Berrett-Koehler.
Demaria, F., F. Schneider, F. Sekulova and J. Martinez-Alier (2013), 'What is degrowth? From an activist slogan to a social movement', *Environmental Values*, 22, 191–215.
Doherty, D. and A. Etzioni (2003), *Voluntary Simplicity: Responding to Consumer Culture*, Lanham, MD: Rowman & Littlefield.
EEA (European Environmental Agency) (2013), 'Environmental pressures from European consumption and production', EEA Technical report 2/2013, Copenhagen: EEA.
Ehrlich, P. and J. Holden (1971), 'Impact of population growth', *Science*, 171, 1212–1217.
Elgin, D. (1993), *Voluntary Simplicity: Toward a Way of Life that is Outwardly Simple, Inwardly Rich*, rev. edn, New York: Harper Paperbacks.
Ewens, S. (1998), *PR: The Social History of Spin*, New York: Basic Books.
FAO (Food and Agriculture Organization) (2010), *The State of World Fishery and Aquaculture*, Rome: Food and Agriculture Organization.
Fuchs, D. (2013a), 'Sustainable consumption', in R. Falkner (ed.), *Handbook of Global Climate and Environmental Policy*, Hoboken, NJ: Wiley-Blackwell, pp. 215–230.
Fuchs, D. (2013b), 'Theorizing the power of global companies', in J. Mikler (ed.), *Handbook of Global Companies*, Hoboken, NJ: Wiley-Blackwell, pp. 77–95.
Fuchs, D. and S. Lorek (2005), 'Sustainable consumption governance – a history of promises and failures', *Journal of Consumer Policy*, 28, 261–288.
Garon, S. (2012), *Beyond Our Means: Why America Spends While the World Saves*, Princeton, NJ: Princeton University Press.
Gatersleben, B., L. Steg and C. Vlek (2002), 'Measurement and determinants of environmentally significant consumer behavior', *Environment and Behavior*, 34 (3), 335–362.
Geels, F. and J. Schot (2007), 'Typology of sociotechnical transition pathways', *Research Policy*, 36, 399–417.
Global Footprint Network (2013), 'Earth overshoot day', available at http://www.footprintnetwork.org/en/index.php/GFN/page/earth_overshoot_day/ (accessed 24 January 2014).
Great Transition Initiative (2013), available at http://gtinitiative.org (accessed 24 February 2014).
Grober, U. (2012), *Sustainability: A Cultural History*, Totnes: Green Books.
Halkier, B. (2013), 'Sustainable lifestyles in a new economy: a practice theoretical perspective on change

behavior campaigns and sustainability issues', in M. Cohen, H. Brown and P. Vergragt (eds), *Innovations in Sustainable Consumption: New Economics, Socio-Technical Transitions, and Social Practices*, Cheltenham, UK and Northampton, MA, USA: Edward Elgar, pp. 209–228.
Hamilton, C. (2010), 'Consumerism, self-creation and prospects for a new ecological consciousness', *Journal of Cleaner Production*, 18 (6), 571–575.
Harris, J. (2013), 'The macroeconomics of development without throughput growth', in M. Cohen, H. Brown and P. Vergragt (eds), *Innovations in Sustainable Consumption: New Economics, Socio-Technical Transitions, and Social Practices*, Cheltenham, UK and Northampton, MA, USA: Edward Elgar, pp. 31–47.
Herring, H. and S. Sorrell (eds) (2008), *Energy Efficiency and Sustainable Consumption: The Rebound Effect*, New York: Palgrave Macmillan.
Hofstetter, P., M. Madjar and T. Ozawa (2006), 'Happiness and sustainable consumption: psychological and physical rebound effects at work in a tool for sustainable design', *International Journal of Life Cycle Assessment*, 11 (1), 105–115.
IEA (International Energy Agency) (2010), *World Energy Outlook*, Paris: IEA.
Inglehart, R. and H.-D. Klingemann (2000), *Genes, Culture, and Happiness*, Boston, MA: MIT Press.
Jackson, T. (2009), *Prosperity without Growth: Economics for a Finite Planet*, London: Earthscan.
Jackson, T. and P. Victor (2013), 'Green economy at community scale', Toronto: Metcalf Foundation, available at http://metcalffoundation.com/wp-content/uploads/2013/10/GreenEconomy.pdf (accessed 8 January 2014).
Kuittinen, O., R. Mokka, A. Neuvonen, M. Orjasniemi, M. Ritola and M. Wikholm (2012), *I-Future Diversity of Sustainable Lifestyles*, Helsinki: Demos.
Layard, R. (2005), *Happiness: Lessons From a New Science*, New York: Penguin Press.
Lebel, L. and S. Lorek (2008), 'Enabling sustainable production–consumption systems', *Annual Review of Environment and Resources*, 33, 241–275.
Lorek, S. (2010), *Towards Strong Sustainable Consumption Governance*, Saarbrücken: LAP Publishing.
Lorek, S. and D. Fuchs (2013), 'Strong sustainable consumption governance – precondition for a degrowth path?', *Journal of Cleaner Production*, 38, 36–43.
Lorek, S. and J.H. Spangenberg (2001), 'Indicators for environmentally sustainable household consumption', *International Journal of Sustainable Development*, 4 (1), 101–120.
Lorek, S. and J.H. Spangenberg (2014), 'Sustainable consumption within a sustainable economy – beyond green growth and green economies', *Journal of Cleaner Production*, 63, 33–44.
Maniates, M. (2002), 'In search of consumptive resistance: the voluntary simplicity movement', in T. Princen, M. Maniates and K. Conca (eds), *Confronting Consumption*, Cambridge, MA: MIT Press, pp. 199–235.
Maniates, M. (2009), 'Editing out unsustainable behavior', in E. Assadourian, L. Starke and L. Mastny (eds), *State of the World 2010: Transforming Cultures, From Consumerism to Sustainability*, New York: W.W. Norton & Company, pp. 119–126.
Maniates, M. (2010), 'Cultivating consumer restraint in an ecologically full world: the case of "take back your time"', in L. Lebel, S. Lorek and R. Daniel (eds), *Sustainable Production and Consumption System*, Dordrecht: Springer, pp. 13–37.
Miller, E. (2012), 'Solidarity economy: key concepts and issues', in E. Kawano (ed.), *Solidarity Economy I: Building Alternatives for People and Planet; Papers and reports from the 2009 US Forum on the Solidarity Economy*, Amherst, MA: Center for Popular Economics, pp. 25–42.
Mont, O., E. Heiskanen, A. Neuvonen and S. Lähteenoja (2014), 'Sustainable lifestyles 2050: Stakeholder visions, emerging practices and future research', *Journal of Cleaner Production*, 63, 24–32.
Mulder, K., R. Costanza and R. Erickson (2006), 'The contribution of built, human, social and natural capital to quality of life in intentional and unintentional communities', *Ecological Economics*, 59 (1), 13–23.
Myers, D.G. (1993), *The Pursuit of Happiness: Who is Happy, and Why?*, New York: Harper Paperbacks.
NEF (New Economics Foundation) (2009), *National Accounts of Well-being: Bringing Real Wealth onto the Balance Sheet*, London: NEF.
Neumayer, E. (2003), *Weak Versus Strong Sustainability: Exploring the Limits of Two Opposing Paradigms*, 2nd edn, Cheltenham, UK and Northampton, MA, USA: Edward Elgar.
Noorman, K.J., W. Biesiot and H. Moll (1999), 'Changing lifestyles in transition routes towards sustainable household consumption patterns', *International Journal of Sustainable Development*, 2 (2), 231–244.
OECD (2008), *The Costs of Inaction on Key Environmental Challenges*, Paris: Organisation for Economic Co-operation and Development.
O'Neill, D.W. (2012), 'Measuring progress in the degrowth transition to a steady state economy', *Ecological Economics*, 84, 221–231.
Oslo Roundtable (1994), 'Part 1 – The imperative of sustainable production and consumption', available at http://www.iisd.ca/consume/oslo004.html (accessed 7 January 2014).
Pimentel, D. (2006), 'Soil erosion: a food and environmental threat', *Environment, Development and Sustainability*, 8, 119–137.

Princen, T. (2005), *The Logic of Sufficiency*, Cambridge, MA: MIT Press.
Princen, T. (2010), *Treading Softly – Paths to Ecological Order*, Cambridge, MA: MIT Press.
Quist, J., W. Thissen and P.J. Vergragt (2011), 'The impact and spin-off of participatory backcasting: from vision to niche', *Technological Forecasting and Social Change*, 78 (5), 883–897.
Raskin, P., T. Banuri, G. Gallopin, P. Gutman, A. Hammond, R. Kates and R. Stewart (2002), *Great Transition, the Promise and Lure of the Times Ahead*, Boston, MA: Stockholm Environment Institute and Tellus Institute.
Reisch, L.A. (2001), 'Time and wealth: the role of time and temporalities for sustainable patterns of consumption', *Time and Society*, 10 (2–3), 387–405.
Rockström, J., W. Steffen, K. Noone, Å. Persson, F.S. Chapin, E.F. Lambin, T.M. Lenton et al. (2009), 'A safe operating space for humanity', *Nature*, 461, 472–475.
Røpke, I. (2013), 'Ecological macroeconomics: Implications for the role of consumer-citizens', in M. Cohen, H. Brown and P. Vergragt (eds), *Innovations in Sustainable Consumption: New Economics, Socio-Technical Transitions, and Social Practices*, Cheltenham, UK and Northampton, MA, USA: Edward Elgar, pp. 48–64.
Schneider, F., G. Kallis and J. Martinez-Alier (2010), 'Crisis or opportunity? Economic degrowth for social equity and ecological sustainability', Introduction to Special Issue, *Journal of Cleaner Production*, 18 (6), 511–518.
Schneider, F., J. Martinez-Alier and G. Kallis (2011), 'Sustainable degrowth', *Journal of Industrial Ecology*, 15, 654–656.
Sekulova, F., G. Kallis, B. Rodríguez-Labajos and F. Schneider (2013), 'Degrowth: from theory to practice', *Journal of Cleaner Production*, 38, 1–6.
Seyfang, G. (2009), *The New Economics of Sustainable Consumption*, New York: Palgrave Macmillan.
Seyfang, G. and A. Smith (2007), 'Grassroots innovations for sustainable development: towards a new research and policy agenda', *Environmental Politics*, 16 (4), 584–603.
Shove, E. and G. Walker (2010), 'Governing transitions in the sustainability of everyday life', *Research Policy*, 39 (4), 471–476.
Stiglitz, J., A. Sen and J.P. Fitoussi (2009), *Report by the Commission on the Measurement of Economic Performance and Social Progress*, Paris: Commission on the Measurement of Economic Performance and Social Progress.
Tarrow, S. (2005), *The New Transnational Activism*, Cambridge: Cambridge University Press.
Tarrow, S., D. McAdam and C. Tilly (2001), *Dynamics of Contention*, Cambridge: Cambridge University Press.
Thaler, R.H. and C.R. Sunstein (2008), *Nudge, Improving Decisions about Health, Wealth, and Happiness*, New Haven, CT: Yale University Press.
Thøgersen, J. (2014), 'Unsustainable consumption: basic causes and implications for policy', *European Psychologist*, 19 (2), 84–95.
Tukker, A. (ed.) (2008), *System Innovation for Sustainability 1*, Sheffield: Greenleaf.
UN DESA (2013), *World Population Prospects: The 2012 Revision*, New York: United Nations, Department of Economic and Social Affairs, Population Division.
Van Griethuysen, P. (2009), 'Why are we growth-addicted? The hard way towards degrowth in the involutionary western development path', *Journal of Cleaner Production*, 18 (6), 590–595.
Vergragt, P.J. (2013), 'A possible way out of the combined economic-sustainability crisis', *Environmental Innovation and Societal Transitions*, 6, 123–125.
Vergragt, P., L. Akenji and P. Dewick (2014), 'Sustainable production, consumption, and livelihoods: global and regional research perspectives', *Journal of Cleaner Production*, 63, 1–12.
Vergragt, P.J. and J.N. Quist (2011), 'Backcasting for sustainability: introduction to a special issue', *Technological Forecasting and Social Change*, 78 (5), 747–755.
Victor, P.A. (2008), *Managing without Growth: Slower by Design, Not Disaster*, Cheltenham, UK and Northampton, MA, USA: Edward Elgar.
Victor, P.A. (2010), 'Questioning economic growth', *Nature*, 468, 370–371.
Wilkinson, R.G. and K. Picket (2009), *The Spirit Level: Why More Equal Societies Almost Always Do Better*, New York: Bloomsbury Press.
WorldWatch Institute (2010), *State of the World 2010: Transforming Cultures*, New York: WW Norton & Company.

# 2. Breaking the stalemate of sustainable consumption with industrial ecology and a circular economy

*Oksana Mont and Eva Heiskanen*

## 2.1 THE UNSUSTAINABILITY OF A LINEAR ECONOMY

We are living in times of great societal turmoil exacerbated by multiple environmental problems, ranging from climate change and the resource crunch to increasing levels of pollution. The assimilative capacity of our planet is reaching its limits (Rockström et al. 2009), and we are running out of some critical resources (UNEP 2012). We seem to be 'locked in' by the industrial system that emerged when natural resource limits were unknown and planetary sinks could still cope with the level of pollution and waste stemming from human activity (Beddoe et al. 2008).

As a result of technological progress improving the efficiency of industrial processes, labour productivity has increased by a factor 20 in the last 150 years (Lehner et al. 1999), whereas natural resource productivity has improved much less (Bleischwitz 2001). Although the environmental impacts per unit of product have decreased, growing consumption levels and the linear nature of the economic system have led to increased aggregate environmental problems. In the linear system, the fast replacement of goods is stimulated by advertising and marketing by businesses whose profits are directly linked to the volumes of sales of mostly material goods (Røpke 1999). Perhaps the most crucial problem with the prevailing market system is its failure to internalize the environmental and social costs associated with the production of products, which results in misleading market signals to both producers and consumers (Sanne 2002) and in the encouragement of throughput economy. Since the current economic system's reliance on unrestrained increase of resource-intensive economic activity is unsustainable on a finite planet, ideas for various alternative ways to organize production and consumption are emerging.

One such alternative is the concept of industrial ecology, which mimics the circular flows of resources in nature in the design of production processes and facilities. The circularity principle has been applied at the level of the entire economy (Fischer-Kowalski 1998), in large industrial constellations where many companies exchange resources and by-products (Ehrenfeld 1997) and at the level of circular business models with closed-loop resource cycles (Krikke et al. 2013). So, thus far, the principles of industrial ecology and specifically the circularity idea have been employed at the production side. However, the implications of the circularity principles for sustainable consumption and lifestyles remain largely unexplored.

This chapter aims to fill this gap by providing: (1) an overview of changes that need to take place in different life cycle stages to enable the shift from the currently linear economic system to a circular economy; and (2) reflections on the types of implications this shift might have for sustainable consumption and lifestyles.

Section 2.2 presents the concept of industrial ecology and its applications at local, regional and global levels. Section 2.3 outlines the idea of a circular economy and then reviews different life cycle stages – product design, production, retail, consumption and end-of-life – and discusses the type of changes needed in order to enable a circular economy. Section 2.4 discusses the implications of a circular economy for sustainable consumption and sustainable lifestyles. Section 2.5 discusses how a circular economy and sustainable lifestyles could be facilitated through policy development and institutional change.

## 2.2 INDUSTRIAL ECOLOGY: LEARNING FROM NATURE FOR THE BENEFIT OF THE SOCIETY

Industrial ecology is a field of study of the physical, chemical and biological interrelationships within and between industrial and ecological systems, and the development and implementation of strategies for emulating sustainable ecosystems in industrial systems (Frosch 1992). The aim of industrial ecology is to transform the current mostly linear industrial system into a circular one (Ehrenfeld 1997). The linear system extracts and processes raw materials to produce various goods, by-products and wastes. In a circular system, the input of raw materials is drastically reduced due to increased reuse and recycling of materials, by-products and waste in other products or processes. Fundamental to the field of industrial ecology is the study of flows of energy and materials, their transformation and dissipation in industrial, societal and natural systems. An important goal is to identify leakages into ecosystems by mapping and quantifying material flows and to develop strategies for reducing the impacts of these environmental burdens by improving the efficiency of material and energy use in industrial systems.

The principles of industrial ecology can be applied at the level of individual production processes (in-process recycling), or between different processes (for example, reuse and recycling), between different facilities in one company, between different co-located companies or among companies that are situated miles apart. The specific process of tracking material and energy flows in industrial systems is usually called industrial metabolism, while inter company relations and constellations that aim to optimize resource use by exchanging by-products, reusing waste products, producing energy from waste and sharing utility are called eco-industrial parks, industrial symbioses or industrial ecosystems.

However industrial ecology has rarely been seen as a means of advancing sustainable consumption, and in turn sustainable consumption policies have not explicitly included the principles of industrial ecology (Lehtoranta et al. 2011). Despite the lack of application in policies, the idea and principles of industrial ecology have been employed for tracing flows of resources and energy at global, regional or local levels, including cities or households. For example urban metabolism often analyses materials and energy flows in urban settings or sometimes also includes much broader technical and socio-economic processes that take place in cities (Agudelo-Vera et al. 2012; Broto et al. 2012; Lenzen and Peters 2009). The goal is to recreate the cycle between the city and the land around it, to secure resilience of both spaces and to improve inter dependability through the flow of resources and products. The concept of household metabolism refers both to direct flows of materials and energy that pass through households, and to indirect flows of materials associated with value chains of products and services that are used and consumed in households (Moll et al. 2008; Takase et al. 2008).

## 2.3 FROM LINEAR TO CIRCULAR ECONOMY

The current economy is based on linear systems where resources are extracted, transported, processed into goods, sold to consumers and disposed of after use, mostly to landfills or used to produce energy via incineration. Thus, on the one hand, the economy constantly demands input of resources from nature, and on the other hand, it continuously deposits large volumes of waste, emissions and pollution of different kinds – air, soil and water – to nature. To counteract the adverse environmental impacts, alternative economic models are being suggested, such as the recycling society based on principles of extended producer responsibility (Lindhqvist 1992), the service economy (Stahel 1994), and product–service systems (Mont 2004; Tukker and Tischner 2006). The key aim of these models is the reduction of aggregate throughput of resources by closing material loops and design for durability, reuse, upgrade and repair, based on the idea of a circular economy outlined by Kenneth E. Boulding (1966) and further developed by Walter Stahel and Genevieve Reday (1981).

In the circular economy three types of closed loops can be distinguished that relate to the consumption phase. In the first type, products are reused by the same or other consumers and for the same or a different purpose (for example, downgraded and reused). Products can also be repaired and their use can be extended with the same or an upgraded function (upcycling). In the second type, products are taken back, dismantled, and their parts are used as input in a remanufacturing/reverse logistics system (reuse of parts and modules). In the third type, neither products nor their parts can generate value in the economic system, but they instead enter the recycling system, where the value of materials is recovered. The cycles reduce the pressure on virgin natural resources by extending the use time of products, their parts and materials; decrease the amount of energy use and pollution from the production of new products; and cut production and post-consumer volumes of waste.

Although the idea of a circular economy has been on the policy agenda since the 1990s, the results have not been impressive. For example, globally only about 20 metals are being recycled with a recycling rate of 25 per cent or more (UNEP 2011). Twenty-one billion tonnes of materials enter production processes in Organisation for Economic Co-operation and Development (OECD) countries without being used in final products.[1] Losses in food supply chains amount to at least 30 per cent, and up to 60 per cent of the total waste generated in Europe is not reused, recycled or composted (Eurostat 2011).

Today, Japan is arguably the most advanced circular economy with its 98 per cent recycling of metals, 95 per cent reuse and recycling of household waste, and 75–90 per cent recovery of materials from appliances, feeding back to the same products from which they were reclaimed (Ministry of the Environment 2010). The circular economy was also identified as a priority area in China's 11th Five-Year Plan for 2006–2010 (Zhijun and Nailing 2007). Germany also has an official Raw Materials Resource Strategy (BMWI 2010). A recent report by the Ellen MacArthur Foundation estimated

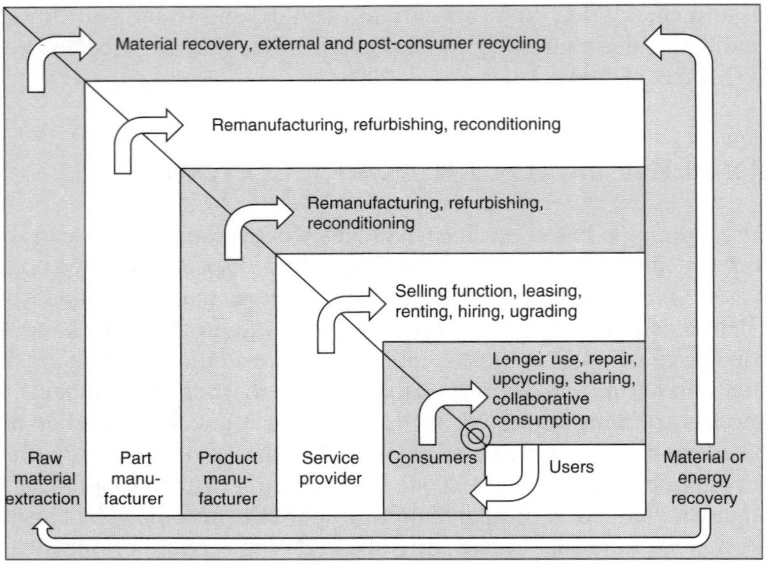


*Figure 2.1 Resource optimization strategies in various life cycle stages in a circular economy*

the global economic benefit of a circular economy to be about US$2 trillion (EMF 2012). The European Commission has also joined the efforts towards a circular economy, if only somewhat hesitantly and rhetorically, by stating that 'In a world with growing pressures on resources and the environment, the EU [European Union] has no choice but to go for the transition to a resource-efficient and ultimately regenerative circular economy' (European Commission 2012).

In order to better understand the practical and societal implications of a circular economy, in the following we analyse how it will affect the various stages of the production–consumption continuum. A quick overview of strategies used in different life cycle stages is shown in Figure 2.1.

### 2.3.1 Product Design: From Throwaway Junk to Multi-Life Goods

Product design determines the technical, economic and emotional durability of products (Chapman 2009) and up to 80 per cent of their environmental impact.[2] Design strategies to optimize the product lifespan by combating different types of obsolescence are as follows (Cooper 2010):

1. Obsolescence of technology can be addressed by design for reuse and upgrading, easy maintenance, replacement and remanufacturing.
2. Obsolescence of quality can be reduced by designing more robust products and by using more resilient and prone to impact materials.
3. Obsolescence of desire can be counteracted by timeless design, fashion durability and neutral aesthetics.

In a circular economy, products in which the greatest environmental impact occurs in the production stage should be built for durability (Cooper 2010) and reuse by multiple consumers (Lang 2011), while products in which the greatest environmental impact occurs in the use phase need to be upgraded or replaced more often. In both cases products need to be designed for easy repair and upgrade (Felton and Bird 2007), perhaps be produced in modules or with standardized parts that are easy to replace, or they need to be designed for quick dismantling and easy separation of different materials and parts (glued-welded versus screwed or put together with clips). For example, Google Nexus parts are screwed together, which makes it easy to both repair and reuse or recycle the product, whereas the iPad's parts are glued together.

Design for remanufacturing could for example reduce the cost of reconditioning and reusing mobile phones by 50 per cent compared to current costs (EMF 2012). Design for easier dismantling and materials recovery would lead to an increased proportion of recyclable materials in the post-consumer streams of products. For example, it is estimated that between 2012 and 2020 only 65 per cent of the potentially recyclable material in the UK will be returned back to the economy; and if the remaining 35 per cent of the material were captured, reused or recycled, it would generate £1.4 billion in revenues (ESA 2013). Some companies already design products that integrate a certain per cent of recycled material. For example, Levi's created two new lines of jeans and trucker jackets that contain at least 20 per cent of post-consumer recycled plastic, meaning eight 12–20 oz plastic bottles are used for each pair of jeans. With this effort, the company has already reused more than 3.6 million bottles and food trays for producing 300 000 'Waste<Less' jeans and jackets for its spring 2013 collection.

Obsolescence of desire leads to the premature replacement of products by consumers and is driven by ever-shorter fashion cycles. For example, in the 1980s, textile fashion was seasonal; nowadays collections are being changed every fortnight and American consumers buy a new clothing item every 5.4 days (Schor 2013). By choosing timeless or classic designs and high-quality materials, it is possible to prolong product life and perhaps increase profit margins per unit of product. Filippa K is an example of a company that builds on the notion of quality and timelessness in its design and marketing (Tikkanen 2012). Changing the mainstream fashion industry is however more difficult, and although design for emotional durability has been recognized as critical in promoting durable products (Packard 1963), practical tools for how this could be done are only just emerging (Chapman 2009).

### 2.3.2 Production: From Throughput to Cascaded Remanufacturing

In a linear economy, production processes are largely optimized for throughput of resources and rely on high levels of input energy. Recycling rates vary greatly among different sectors. For example the automotive industry reports high levels of recycling: 95 per cent is set as the EU target for 2015, while the majority of other sectors do not even achieve 25 per cent (EMF 2012). Yet, recycling might be problematic from a resource efficiency perspective, as large amounts of energy and labour embedded in products are lost when only the value of materials is recovered, as opposed to the value of the product design and functionality preserved during reuse or reconditioning. However, relatively few remanufacturing facilities exist in the linear economy.

In the circular economy goods are produced both from virgin raw materials and from remanufacturing old or used products in continuous cycles. To make such reverse manufacturing sustainable, several principles have been outlined (EMF 2012, p. 7):

- Minimized material use in the primary cycle when the product is designed and produced from virgin raw materials and used for as long as possible.
- Maximized number of consecutive cycles to enable product reuse and remanufacturing as many times as possible.
- Cascaded use when products are used and reused for their original purpose and then utilized for purposes that accept a lower quality of the products.
- Keeping pure material cycles to enable easy reuse and recycling of separated and clean material flows.

Following these principles, the circular economy could potentially reduce reliance on virgin materials and thereby exposure to fluctuations of resource prices. To enable this, new remanufacturing facilities need to be established or current production factories have to be upgraded; new technological solutions and new business models need to be found and new internal capacities, including skills and knowledge, have to be developed in companies to enable reconditioning, repair and reuse of products and recycling of materials. For example, Xerox redesigned its copy machines for remanufacturing, built remanufacturing facilities on all continents and developed a leasing-based business model to facilitate an organized return flow of products. Philips followed suit and built three remanufacturing facilities in North America and Europe for its high-end capital products such as medical equipment. The company collects its medical systems through a trade-in mechanism, after which the equipment is evaluated on quality criteria, such as performance, age and overall condition. The medical system is then disassembled and cleaned, refurbished and calibrated, upgraded with the latest software and, finally, undergoes quality testing. Philips offers a range of reconditioned medical systems through leasing contracts and provides customer care service packages and full warranties.

### 2.3.3 Retail: From Sales to Re-commerce

The role of distribution and retailers in a linear economy is to facilitate the throughput of products from producers to consumers. European large supermarkets are succeeding in this, offering about 45 000 products in their assortment in response to consumer demand for product variety, including environmentally and socially sound products. Consumers, on the other hand, are becoming increasingly confused by the choice of different products, offers, subscription, labels and advertising messages (Mitchell et al. 2005) and expect retailers to remove unsustainable products from the shelves. Retailers, in turn, struggle to manage environmental and social issues in complex global supply chains.

In the circular economy, products need to be collected from consumers, repaired and reused, and retail may play a role in such closed-loop business models. For example, baby prams are high-quality products with short first-consumer use time (typically one year) and relatively simple design that can be easily adjusted for reconditioning (Mont et al. 2006). Leasing prams instead of selling could ensure the return flow of products. At the end of the lease period, the products would come back to the retailer, who can refurbish them to an 'as new' state and lease them again to new users. To ensure the success of the system, retailers need to be educated in refurbishing and in marketing the leasing arrangements to consumers.

One can also imagine that, with time, retail outlets could become the centres for consumers to return their post-consumer goods for refurbishment and reuse. For example Marks & Spencer has started a project with Oxfam to help consumers donate 20 million items of clothing a year by 2015. There are also other examples of retailers who encourage and enable collection of textiles for reuse and repair, for example through the establishment of their own second-hand shops (Tojo et al. 2012) or by collaborating with second-hand outlets.

Even the food retail industry has a role to play in reducing the throughput of food produce in the economy (Mont 2013). For example, in order to reduce the amount of wasted food some shops cook and sell meals based on ingredients with close to 'the best before date', or from vegetables that deviate from the standard shape but are still fresh (Andersen et al. 2013). Other stores sort out their food waste and deliver it to biogas plants (Eriksson and Strid 2011).

### 2.3.4 Consumption: From Passive Transaction to Dynamic Interaction

Industrial ecology studies have identified four areas with the highest environmental impacts from households: housing (heating and electricity use), transport and food (Tukker and Jansen 2006), and manufactured products, especially electric and electronic appliances (Hertwich et al. 2010). Energy use in housing is not immediately influenced by a shift to a circular economy, but rather through the refurbishment of existing buildings, aiming to reduce energy consumption. However the principles of industrial ecology might be helpful when building houses that are self-sufficient in their energy use, such as zero- or plus-energy houses. In transport, a shift to shared use of modes of transport (for example, public transport, car sharing) can have a significant impact on both the specific energy use (due to more rapid upgrading of vehicles) and, especially, on the total energy use by consumers (due to more considered use of vehicles) (Heiskanen and Jalas 2003; Loose 2010). Food, as such, can only be used once, but a local circulation of nutrients reduces $CO_2$ emissions from fertilizer production and is essential for future food security (Cordell et al. 2009). However, the impacts of a circular economy are most visible in the category of manufactured products. According to Hertwich et al. (2010), manufactured products are the second or third most important contributor to the carbon footprint of rich countries, and their contribution to emissions rises with wealth. A substantial share of the pollution from such products occurs in developing countries, which have high emission intensities (Hertwich et al. 2010). A circular economy would relocalize the production of such products by closing cycles through reuse, remanufacturing and recycling, all of which suggest more local economic activity and reduced emissions at all stages of the product life cycle.

Consumers significantly influence how products are used, including the frequency and intensity of use; decisions about whether the product should be resold, shared or given away; when and whether to repair, refurbish or upcycle products; or at what stage the product could be discarded and in what way. Consumers need knowledge about the most efficient product use patterns and the care with which products should be used, including maintenance, cleaning and upgrading. To support product reuse, people need access to traditional channels, such as second-hand stores, or to formal or informal networks for the exchange of products and services. In order to promote recycling, consumers need access to recycling infrastructure, education on how to sort, collect and return materials to the appropriate collection points, and some kind of encouragement to participate in the system (McKenzie-Mohr 2011).

Perhaps even more importantly, a circular economy envisions a new role for consumers. This is especially visible in the recent trends of collaborative consumption and the sharing economy (Botsman and Rogers 2010). In addition to being consumers, individuals assume an active role in the co-production of utility (Ritzer et al. 2012). For example they become co-producers of electricity via smart grids or of food via urban gardens. Further consumers are rapidly (re)entering the 'maker movement' by fixing, repairing and upcycling products, from upgrading electric and electronic equipment, refurbishing houses to repairing and restoring cars. The fashion of making and fixing things is being spurred by open platforms and blogs for sharing knowledge and skills, open innovation and 'maker spaces' online (for example, the Instractables[3] or Fixperts[4]). Consumers also engage in co-creating alternative systems of consumption based on sharing and exchange (Botsman and Rogers 2010; Murray et al. 2010), which utilize the idling capacity of already produced but rarely used products or services (for example, Freecycle[5]), premises and facilities (for example, AirBnB[6]), or even spare time and skills (for example, Task Rabbit[7]). So consumers are no longer passive recipients of goods and services on the market, but are actively co-creating production–consumption systems with novel properties.

However, closing the loops might be insufficient to bring about a sustainable society due to the high volume and fast resource throughput stimulated by consumer demand. To ensure that the economy overall remains within the planetary limits in terms of assimilating pollution and using resources, the pace of the circular flows also needs to be adjusted (Reisch 2001).

### 2.3.5 End-of-Life: From Waste Management to 'Zero Waste' and Urban Mining

In a linear economy the waste management industry is the last stage in any product's life cycle. In most countries, apart from a few leading recyclers like Japan and Germany, the waste management industry currently provides the infrastructure and logistics to collect and dispose of some materials, while producing methane in landfills or energy in incinerators is a side activity. The circular economy envisions a new role for the waste industry as the resource industry that recovers and upcycles materials, that is, mines resources from society, rather than from nature.

In the circular economy, a larger portion of collected material will have to be returned as secondary resources to industries, in contrast to the current trend of wastefulness. For example, globally, 320 tonnes of gold and over 7500 tonnes of silver are used annually to produce electric and electronic equipment and only 15 per cent is being recovered. The combined value of the gold and silver is US$21 billion and thus, US$17.85 billion of value is lost in the waste bin (GeSi 2012). To enable the return of these and other materials to the economy, new technology and skills will need to be developed. The remaining materials that cannot be reused or recycled in any way should be used to produce biogas and energy to fuel public transport and provide heat and electricity to households, businesses and public facilities.

The notion of closing material loops is not without its weak points. Concerns have been raised about the potential increase of transportation if used products need to be returned to their original producers, which are often situated on the other side of the world. Technological solutions are lacking for the remanufacturing of some products or for recycling of some materials. Costs can be prohibitively high when the infrastructures for reverse logistics and remanufacturing are not yet established. Also problematic is the unpredictable flow of resources from the post-industrial or post-consumer use, both when it comes to the sheer volume of materials and products and to their composition, which are often comprised of composite materials or heterogeneous feed stocks. In addition, both the volume and composition of returned material changes over time, following consumption trends in the society.

These circumstances make it even more important for the waste industry to move from the traditional and somewhat passive role of taking care of end-of-life products towards redefining itself as a resource industry. The resource industry could work together with its 'suppliers' and set demands on the quality of materials it receives to ensure that products are designed and produced for recovery, reprocessing and recycling, as well as for durability and multiple uses. To ensure this, expertise and insights from different stages of the product life cycle have to come together in a process of multi-stakeholder co-innovation for circular economy.

## 2.4 IMPLICATIONS OF THE CIRCULAR ECONOMY FOR ADVANCING SUSTAINABLE LIFESTYLES

As demonstrated above, whatever changes to greening the production–consumption system could be made in different life cycle stages, the total throughput of resources needs to be reduced to sustainable levels. This cannot be done by efficiency measures alone; efficiency measures need to be accompanied by sufficiency strategies. In order to enable and create acceptance among the public to the latter, changes in mainstream lifestyles are needed. This has been understood by researchers (Spaargaren 1997), international organizations (TFSL 2010) and proactive representatives of the business community: 'efficiency gains and technological advances alone will not be sufficient to bring global consumption to a sustainable level; changes will also be required to consumer lifestyles' (WBCSD 2008).

So what are sustainable lifestyles? Following Giddens (1990), we understand lifestyles as social routines that help to create self-identity. They comprise not only material possessions, but also patterns of time use, such as household and gainful work, interests and leisure. Lifestyles encompass a narrative that gives meaning to routines and choices (Lorenzen 2012) and that serve as 'social conversations', in which people affiliate and differentiate themselves from other people. The notion of lifestyle also captures the interconnectedness of consumption practices. For example, petrol is purchased to be used in the car, whereas the car is necessary to get to work from the suburban house (Heiskanen and Pantzar 1997).

We define a sustainable lifestyle as a collection of social routines pertaining to everyday life, which: (1) has a much lower environmental impact than the present average; (2) is significantly more resource-efficient; and (3) (most importantly) progressively reduces dependence on a continuous flow of new commodities. Furthermore the concept of sustainable lifestyles broadens the focus from consumption activities to include a wider set of competencies and orientations that people employ in their lives. The notion of sustainable lifestyles acknowledges the interconnection (and even the blurring of boundaries) between gainful and household work, civic interests and leisure, and recognizes the importance of social norms and values that enable, support and normalize sustainable everyday practices and lifestyles.

Indeed, examples of collaborative consumption and the sharing economy (Botsman and Rogers 2010) suggest that the notion of social status based on the ownership of material possessions might be changing. Collaborative consumption takes the ideas of the circular economy further by offering innovative information and communication technology (ICT)-enabled ways of satisfying needs by unlocking the wealth of idle assets (a large pool of products, skills and services that people possess) and matching the 'haves' with the 'have-nots'. Needs are satisfied through non-virgin resources and through products that are upcycled. Collaborative consumption also offers the seeds of the decommoditization of consumption: a shift to 'doing, being or producing' rather than having and consuming (Dietz and O'Neill 2012).

To facilitate shared prosperity among people in the circular economy, different values from those propagated by the linear economic model need to be nurtured. Circularity builds on the idea of 'reuse and recycle', but the second-hand market grounded on this idea has traditionally benefited lower-income customer segments. However we are currently witnessing a renaissance of second-hand shopping and the rebirth and rebranding of charity shops, which now proudly profile themselves as part of the antique, luxury and vintage economy: 'Old is the new New'. More and more people find it socially acceptable and even cool to join the second-hand economy. Governmental campaigns can also help to promote the acceptance of swapping, hiring and sharing as demonstrated by the 'Use more, waste less' campaign in Denmark.[8] Through sharing, consumers can also authentically engage in an alternative mode of economic production. In this way, sustainable lifestyles in a circular economy can serve to 'challenge the powerlessness that people feel as individuated "consumers" by reconstituting a social, collective and non-commodified basis for personal identity' (Soron 2010, p. 180). Some authors highlight the rise of the 'craft consumer', referring to consumers who reappropriate mass-produced products into personalized ensembles via cooking, gardening or 'do-it-yourself' (DIY) work (Campbell 2005).

Other studies demonstrate how consumers engage in creative online activities, the results of which are freely shared with others; thus the driver is not personal gain as in the case of individuated consumers, but a desire to earn recognition in a community that shares one's passions (Himanen 2001).

Examples include the large communities of people developing Wikipedia and sharing instructional YouTube videos and other kinds of visual advice for a plethora of household and leisure activities (for example, cooking recipes, solar panel installations, DIY projects).

The aforementioned examples are fragmented and diverse. However, empirical analysis of people adopting 'green lifestyles' suggests that such lifestyles emerge out of a bricolage of existing routines, practices from family history and available cultural resources (Lorenzen 2012). Sustainable lifestyles are thus not always actively and purposively crafted, but emerge as people undertake new actions and at the same time reflect on them and their overall well-being. The notion of sustainable lifestyles is useful as it allows us to discuss such issues as the 'work–spend cycle' (Schor 1999), 'prosumerism' (Kotler 1986; Ritzer et al. 2012) and alternative measures of well-being in the context of a sustainable economy (Costanza et al. 2008; Dietz et al. 2009; O'Neill 2013).

While voluntary green lifestyles are still rare in our current society, perhaps a widening of potentially relevant sustainable practices (such as bartering and sharing) can serve to engage a wider group of people in a gradual process. However, this process is likely to require a stronger cultural narrative than the depoliticized notion of 'green consumerism' to support the transformative role of new consumer practices of non-market production. The circular economy and sustainable lifestyles are not likely to emerge without concerted multi-actor effort.

## 2.5 LIFTING OFF: REFLECTIONS ON POLICIES TO ENABLE CIRCULAR ECONOMY AND SUSTAINABLE LIFESTYLES

A range of changes in the policy context are needed to promote a circular economy and sustainable lifestyles. Policy makers need to support the circular economy by reducing the risks at different stages of the circle, by developing conditions for closing the resource loops, and by creating and supporting social norms and cultures conducive to the circular economy. One of the critical barriers is the short-termism that is currently practiced in policy making, in business and investment decisions. A move to long-term thinking and planning both in policy and in business is a fundamental prerequisite for a circular economy and sustainable lifestyles.

Long-term thinking in policy needs to be accompanied by the review of regulations that hinder reuse, repair and recycling, as well as sharing and bartering (for example, property rights legislation). Product policies, such as the EU Ecodesign Directive, need to include specifications for dismantling, recycling and the incorporation of recycled materials into products. Designing products for durability and recycling can become competitive only in the presence of markets for such products. Policy can support the creation of markets for recyclable and recycled materials, possibly by establishing third-party certification of recycled materials and by increasing demand for recycled content in products produced and consumed in Europe through green procurement policies. It is equally important to scale up, upgrade and optimize collection systems, for both households and businesses, and for different types of products, to maximize the materials recovery. And finally, to make sure that as many materials as possible are returned to the productive economy, targeted landfill bans on selected potentially recyclable materials could be introduced.

Perhaps the largest challenge for public policy is to support new kinds of businesses that will prosper in the circular economy. Such businesses are likely to be decentralized and agile, responding to the fast-changing localized contexts and various consumer segments, and relying on open-source and user-driven innovation to identify the most efficient ways for closing material loops. Since the circular economy suggests significant relocalization of activities, place-based enterprises (Shrivastava and Kennelly 2013) are more likely to benefit from the circular economy.

Local governments are critical in such efforts and they are uniquely positioned to create the conditions for the circular economy through the provision of infrastructure and public services and by encouraging new sustainable businesses. On the other hand, local governments can also benefit from increased resilience, a revival of community, improved life satisfaction of residents and a return of jobs, which suggests that they should have at least some incentive for advancing the circular economy.

Enhancing the circular economy requires the development of new knowledge in science, education and application. Funding agencies could help to create safe and innovative spaces for research and development (R&D), experimentation and testing for circularity and the sharing economy. Policy makers could help to boost investments in R&D to further the development of recycling technology and to promote design for circular business models. To enable innovative and competitive application of knowledge on circularity, the principles of circular systems need to be taught in universities, especially at faculties of economics, engineering, and environmental and social sciences.

Ideas of the circular economy and sustainable lifestyles need to be introduced and normalized at all levels of the society. One suggestion is to rejuvenate existing public services, such as libraries, to emphasize the idea of circularity and to add visibility to existing examples of more sustainable 'consumption' practices. Building on existing services that are well embedded in the society could help to legitimize the new ways of reusing and sharing other types of products. For example in Finland public libraries have also become hubs for sharing party costumes, paintings or metering devices.

Besides revamping existing public or private service systems, urban planning can also support sustainable lifestyles by offering open and common-use spaces to encourage and stimulate people to spend their lives on activities that boost creativity, promote serious leisure, and include collective and community projects to create a sense of ownership and responsibility for the common good.

Finally, the government could support research on developing alternative indicators of societal prosperity, which would judge the success of the economic system based on the well-being of the people the system is serving, not the other way around: how well the people – the nuts and bolts of the system – serve the system.

## NOTES

1. http://www.materialflows.net/home/.
2. Products that require input of resources during their use, for example energy, water, fuel and so on.
3. http://www.instructables.com/.
4. http://fixperts.org/.
5. http://www.freecycle.org/.
6. https://www.airbnb.com/.
7. https://www.taskrabbit.com/.
8. http://www.brugmerespildmindre.dk.

# REFERENCES


Agudelo-Vera, C.M., A. Mels, K. Keesman and H. Rijnaarts (2012), 'The urban harvest approach as an aid for sustainable urban resource planning', *Journal of Industrial Ecology*, 16 (6), 839–850.

Andersen, D., M. Brask, J.B. Eriksson, A. Hannukka, A. Harlén, J. Kjellin, N. Nebelius et al. (2013), *Från idé till förändring i din matbutik. En undersökning om hur ekoinnovationer uppstår inom detaljhandeln*, International Institute for Industrial Environmental Economics, Lund: Lund University.

Beddoe, R., R. Costanza, J. Farley, E. Garza, J. Kent, I. Kubiszewski, L. Martinez, et al. (2008), 'Overcoming systemic roadblocks to sustainability: the evolutionary redesign of worldviews, institutions and technologies', *Proceedings of the Academy of Sciences, PNAS*, 106 (8), 2483–2489.

Bleischwitz, R. (2001), 'Rethinking productivity: why has productivity focussed on labour instead of natural resources?', *Environmental and Resource Economics*, 19 (1), 23–36.

BMWI (Federal Ministry of Economics and Technology) (2010), *The German Government's Raw Materials Strategy. Safeguarding a Sustainable Supply of Non-Energy Mineral Resources for Germany*, Bonn: Federal Ministry of Economics and Technology.

Botsman, R. and R. Rogers (2010), *What's Mine Is Yours: The Rise of Collaborative Consumption*, New York: HarperBusiness.

Boulding, K.E. (1966), 'The economics of the coming spaceship earth', in H. Jarrett (ed.), *Environmental Quality in a Growing Economy*, Baltimore, MD, USA: Resources for the Future/Johns Hopkins University Press, pp. 3–14.

Broto, V.C., A. Allen and E. Rapoport (2012), 'Interdisciplinary perspectives on urban metabolism', *Journal of Industrial Ecology*, 16 (6), 851–861.

Campbell, C. (2005), 'The craft consumer: culture, craft and consumption in a postmodern society', *Journal of Consumer Culture*, 5 (1), 23–42.

Chapman, J. (2009), 'Design for (emotional) durability', *Design Issues*, 25 (4), 29–35.

Cooper, T. (ed.) (2010), *Longer Lasting Products. Alternatives to the Throwaway Society*, Farnham: Gower.

Cordell, D., J.-O. Drangert and S. White (2009), 'The story of phosphorus: global food security and food for thought', *Global Environmental Change*, 19, 292–305.

Costanza, R., B. Fisher, S. Ali, C. Beer, L. Bond, R. Boumans, J. Dickinson et al. (2008), 'An integrative approach to quality of life measurement, research, and policy', *Sapiens*, 1 (1), (online).

Dietz, R. and D. O'Neill (2012), *Enough Is Enough. Building a Sustainable Economy in a World of Finite Resources*, San Francisco, CA: Berrett-Koehler.

Dietz, T., E.A. Rosa and R. York (2009), 'Environmentally efficient well-being: rethinking sustainability as the relationship between human well-being and environmental impacts', *Human Ecology Review*, 16 (1), 114–123.

Ehrenfeld, J.R. (1997), 'Industrial ecology: a framework for product and process design', *Journal of Cleaner Production*, 5 (1–2), 87–95.

EMF (Ellen MacArthur Foundation) (2012), *Towards the Circular Economy Vol. 1: An Economic and Business Rationale for an Accelerated Transition*, Cowes: Ellen MacArthur Foundation.

Eriksson, M. and I. Strid (2011), *Livsmedelssvinn i butiksledet – en studie av butikssvinn i sex livsmedelsbutiker*, Uppsala: Lantbruksuniversitet.

ESA (Environmental Services Association) (2013), *Going for Growth. A Practical Route to a Circular Economy*, London: Environmental Services Association.

European Commission (2012), *Manifesto for a Resource-Efficient Europe*, Brussels: European Commission.

Eurostat (2011), *Waste Statistics*, Brussels: European Commission.

Felton, A.J. and E. Bird (2007), 'Design for recyclability: product function, failure, repairability, recyclability and disposability', in R.W. Sarsby and A.J. Felton (eds), *Geotechnical and Environmental Aspects of Waste Disposal Sites*, London: Taylor & Francis, pp. 311–318.

Fischer-Kowalski, M. (1998), 'Society's metabolism: the intellectual history of materials flow analysis, Part I, 1860–1970', *Journal of Industrial Ecology*, 2 (1), 61–78.

Frosch, R.A. (1992), 'Industrial ecology: a philosophical introduction', *Proceedings of Colloquium on Industrial Ecology, 20–21 May 1991*.

GeSi (Global e-Sustainability Initiative) (2012), 'Product design and development – urban mining worth billions', Global e-Sustainability Initiative, available at http://gesi.org/files/Articles/Product%20Design%20and%20Development%20-%20USA%20Urban%20Mining%20Worth%20Billions%20_%20.pdf (accessed 13 October 2013).

Giddens, A. (1990), *The Consequences of Modernity*, Cambridge: Polity Press.

Heiskanen, E. and M. Jalas (2003), 'Can services lead to radical eco-efficiency improvements? A review of the debate and evidence', *Corporate Social Responsibility and Environmental Management*, 10 (4), 186–198.

Heiskanen, E. and M. Pantzar (1997), 'Toward sustainable consumption: two new perspectives', *Journal of Consumer Policy*, 20 (4), 409–422.

Hertwich, E., E. van der Voet, S. Suh and A. Tukker (2010), *Assessing the Environmental Impacts of Consumption and Production: Priority Products and Materials*, Paris: UNEP.

Himanen, P. (2001), *The Hacker Ethic and the Spirit of the Information Age*, London: Vintage.

Kotler, P. (1986), 'The prosumer movement: a new challenge for marketers', *Advances in Consumer Research*, 13, 510–513.

Krikke, H., D. Hoffenk and Y. Wang (2013), 'Revealing an invisible giant: a comprehensive survey into return practices within original (closed-loop) supply chains', *Resources, Conservation and Recycling*, 73, 239–250.

Lang, P. (2011), 'Promoting the growth of high quality hoods and the phasing out of shoddy products', *International Journal of Green Economics*, 5 (2), 126–132.

Lehner, F., W. Bierter and T. Charles (1999), 'Factor 10: resource productivity, competitiveness, and employment in the advanced economies', Factor 10 Report, Chapter III, Carnoules: Factor 10 Institute.

Lehtoranta, S., A. Nissinen, T. Mattila and M. Melanen (2011), 'Industrial symbiosis and the policy instruments of sustainable consumption and production', *Journal of Cleaner Production*, 19 (16), 1865–1875.

Lenzen, M. and G.M. Peters (2009), 'How city dwellers affect their resource hinterland: a spatial impact study of Australian households', *Journal of Industrial Ecology*, 14 (1), 73–90.

Lindhqvist, T. (1992), 'Extended producer responsibility as a strategy to promote cleaner products', UNEP IE Cleaner Production invitational expert seminar, 4–5 May, Trolleholm Castle, Sweden, Department of Industrial Environmental Economics, Lund University.

Loose, W. (2010), *The State of European Car-Sharing*, Berlin: Bundesverband CarSharing.

Lorenzen, J.A. (2012), 'Going green: the process of lifestyle change', *Sociological Forum*, 27, 94–116.

McKenzie-Mohr, D. (2011), *Fostering Sustainable Behavior: An Introduction To Community-Based Social Marketing*, Gabriola Island, BC: New Society.

Ministry of the Environment (2010), *2010. Establishing a sound material-cycle society. Milestone toward a sound material-cycle society through changes in business and life styles*, Government of Japan.

Mitchell, V.-W., G. Walsh and M. Yamin (2005), 'Towards a conceptual model of consumer confusion', *Advances in Consumer Research*, 32, 143–150.

Moll, H.C., K.J. Noorman, R. Kok, R. Engström, H. Throne-Holst and C. Clark (2008), 'Pursuing more sustainable consumption by analyzing household metabolism in European countries and cities', *Journal of Industrial Ecology*, 9 (1), 259–275.

Mont, O. (2004), *Product-Service Systems: Panacea or Myth?*, IIIEE, Lund: Lund University.

Mont, O. (ed.) (2013), *Sustainability Landscape of Swedish Food Retailers in the European Context*, Lund: Lund University.

Mont, O., C. Dalhammar and N. Jacobsson (2006), 'A new business model for baby prams based on leasing and product remanufacturing', *Journal of Cleaner Production*, 14 (17), 1509–1518.

Murray, R., J. Caulier-Grice and G. Mulgan (2010), *The Open Book of Social Innovation*, London: Young Foundation.

O'Neill, D.W. (2013), 'How close are countries to a socially sustainable steady-state economy? Results from the Degrowth Accounts', 10th Biennal Conference of the European Society for Ecological Economics, Lille, France, 18–21 June.

Packard, V. (1963), *The Waste Makers*, London: Penguin.

Reisch, L.A. (2001), 'Time and wealth: the role of time and temporalities for sustainable patterns of consumption', *Time and Society*, 10 (2), 367–385.

Ritzer, G., P. Dean and N. Jurgenson (2012), 'The coming age of the prosumer', *American Behavioral Scientist*, 56, 379–398.

Rockström, J., W. Steffen, K. Noone, Å. Persson, F.S. Chapin, E.F. Lambin, T.M. Lenton, et al. (2009), 'A safe operating space for humanity', *Nature*, 461 (7263), 472–476.

Røpke I. (1999), 'The dynamics of willingness to consume', *Ecological Economics*, 28, 399–420.

Sanne, C. (2002), 'Willing consumers or locked-in?', *Ecological Economics*, 42 (1–2), 273–287.

Schor, J. (1999), *The Overspent American: Why We Want What We Don't Need*, New York: HarperPerennial.

Schor, J. (2013), 'From fast fashion to connected consumption: slowing down the spending treadmill', in N. Osbaldiston and J. Schor (eds), *The Culture of the Slow: Social Deceleration in an Accelerated World*, Basingstoke: Macmillan, pp. 34–51.

Shrivastava, P. and J.J. Kennelly (2013), 'Sustainability and place-based enterprise', *Organization and Environment*, 26, 83–101.

Soron, D. (2010), 'Sustainability, self-identity and the sociology of consumption', *Sustainable Development*, 18 (3), 172–181.

Spaargaren, G. (1997), 'Theorizing sustainable lifestyles and domestic consumption patterns in between deterministic and voluntaristic models of social change', Workshop 1: Consumption, Everyday Life and Sustainability, Lancaster, ESF-Term programme: Consumption, Everyday Life and Sustainability.

Stahel, W. (1994), 'The utilisation-focused service economy: resource efficiency and product-life extension', in B.R. Allenby and D.J. Richards (eds), *The Greening of Industrial Ecosystems*, Washington, DC: National Academy of Engineering, National Academy Press, pp. 178–190.

Stahel, W. and G. Reday (1981), *Jobs for Tomorrow, the Potential for Substituting Manpower for Energy*, New York: Vantage Press.

Takase, K., Y. Kondo and A. Washizu (2008), 'An analysis of sustainable consumption by the waste input–output model', *Journal of Industrial Ecology*, 9 (1–2), 201–219.

TFSL (Task Force for Sustainable Lifestyles) (2010), *Task Force for Sustainable Lifestyles*, Paris: UNEP.

Tikkanen, E. (2012), 'Fast fashion and slow fashion companies' constructions of authenticity. Two case studies of the category leaders' external communication from a discourse perspective', Department of Business Communication, Aarhus: Aarhus University.

Tojo, N., B. Kogg, N. Kiørboe, B. Kjær and K. Aalto (2012), 'Prevention of textile waste. Material flows of textiles in three Nordic countries and suggestions on policy instruments', Copenhagen: Nordic Council of Ministers.

Tukker, A. and B. Jansen (2006), 'Environmental impacts of products: a detailed review of studies', *Journal of Industrial Ecology*, 10 (3), 159–182.

Tukker, A. and U. Tischner (eds) (2006), *New Business for Old Europe. Product Services, Sustainability and Competitiveness*, Sheffield: Greenleaf.

UNEP (United Nations Environment Programme) (2011), *Recycling Rates of Metals – A Status Report*, Paris: International Resource Panel, United Nations Environment Programme.

UNEP (United Nations Environment Programme) (2012), *Responsible Resource Management for a Sustainable World: Findings from the International Resource Panel*, Paris: International Resource Panel, United Nations Environment Programme.

WBCSD (World Business Council for Sustainable Development) (2008), *Sustainable Consumption Facts and Trends. From a Business Perspective. The Business Role Focus Area*. Geneva: World Business Council for Sustainable Development.

Zhijun, F. and Y. Nailing (2007), 'Putting a circular economy into practice in China', *Sustainability Science*, 2, 95–101.

# PART II

# MAJOR APPROACHES TO THE STUDY OF SUSTAINABLE CONSUMPTION

# 3. Sustainable consumption in history: ideas, resources and practices

*Heather Chappells and Frank Trentmann*

A chapter on the history of sustainable consumption might be expected to be very short, if not impossible. After all, history has been a record of increasingly unsustainable forms of life. People started to clear land and extract resources in Southern China and the Near East 12 000 years ago. Irrigation and rice cultivation already started to raise methane levels some 5000 years ago. Whichever indicator we choose, the human pressure on the earth has grown exponentially, especially since the eighteenth century. The world's population grew more than sixfold between 1700 and 2000. The proportion of land devoted to cropland catapulted, from 2 per cent to 11 per cent; pasture grew even faster from 2 per cent to 24 per cent. The industrial revolution, which started in Britain in the late eighteenth century, intensified coal consumption and mineral extraction. In the twentieth century, synthetic nitrogen started to overtake the natural nitrogen cycle. Global water use increased fivefold. The extinction of species accelerated, as did the amount of carbon in the atmosphere, especially since the 1950s. Notwithstanding greater efficiency, material flows continue to rise per capita as well as in total; the only periods which saw a short-lived pause were the end of the Second World War and the collapse of the Soviet Union. Today, people carry a greater material rucksack on their back than at any other time in history (Klein Goldewijk 2010; Krausmann et al. 2009; Ruddiman 2005; Steffen et al. 2004).

Looking at these trends, it is tempting to see the present concern with 'sustainable development' as a healthy break with a catastrophic past. Instead of looking at past failures, where one generation after another ate into the future of the next, should we not look forward to a brighter future where the economy is once again in equilibrium with the environment and development is sustainable, meeting 'the needs of the present without compromising the ability of future generations to meet their own needs', in the famous words of the landmark report by the United Nations World Commission on Environment and Development, the Brundtland Commission, in 1987 (WCED 1987)?

To look forward without looking back, however, would be a mistake. This chapter highlights three ways in which history can add useful perspectives on sustainable consumption today and tomorrow. The first contribution of historical research is to uncover the evolution of the idea of sustainability itself. Experts who turned their focus on sustainable consumption in the 1980s and 1990s did not arrive out of nowhere. Visions of the future – such as plans for 2020 and 2050 – have a history, as do the methods and assumptions on which they are based. Where did these intellectual traditions come from? The second contribution is a greater appreciation of diversity, in terms of groups and regions. In today's discussions, a good deal of data is global and aggregated. This reflects the centrality of global warming. But even within the same society – indeed, even in the same city or district – people have led more or less sustainable lives. Attention to these different trajectories can shed light on the potential of pathways to sustainability today and the flexibility and stickiness of the practices that consume resources. Finally, history can tell us about the changing resilience of human communities in the face of shortages, disruption and transitions from one resource to another.

## 3.1 THE IDEA OF SUSTAINABILITY

Thinking about sustainability is not new. People have always had to consider how their activities might influence the future availability of forests, water, crops and other resources. For many agrarian communities managing the commons was a matter of everyday life. It also came to attract the attention of states and administrators. Venice, for example, passed conservation laws in the fifteenth century to prevent short-term deforestation and ensure sufficient timber for its fleet in the future. It was in 1713 that the term 'sustainable' made its first appearance, appropriately in the writings of the Saxon forestry and mining official Carl von Carlowitz (1645–1714). In his *Sylvicultura oeconomica* (1713) he offered a guide to sustainable forest management. At the time, Europe was gripped by fears of a 'wood famine', partly stoked by governments and landowners trying to limit the customary use of woodlands by the poor. Chopping down trees for short-term interests, von Carlowitz feared, put the future wealth and development of Saxony at risk: the local silver mines would run out of wood and charcoal. He recommended that wood be conserved and planted in such a way that it would enable a 'steady and sustainable [*nachhaltende*]' yield and use (von Carlowitz 1713, p. 105). The very survival of the country depended on it; future generations, he wrote, had a right to food and subsistence. A 'common interest' (*gemeines Wesen*) was at stake. He singled out three sets of measures: greater efficiency in consumption (such as energy-saving ovens); planned cultivation of saplings and trees; and a search for substitutes (such as peat).

Carlowitz's book became a set text for administrators in eighteenth-century Central Europe. Forests were measured, evaluated and taxed. As forest science advanced, the adjective evolved into a subject: 'sustainability' or *Nachhaltigkeit*. By the early nineteenth century, the French had '*production soutenu*', the Americans 'sustained yield forestry' (Grober 2002). In England, John Evelyn had already tackled the wood crisis in his *Sylva* in the 1660s, but here the urgency over wood receded as the country turned to coal.

The idea of sustainability gained clarity from a shift in knowledge about the soil. In the sixteenth century, soil, like the body, was understood via the theory of the humours. Health resulted from the right balance between different elements. This way of looking at the land meant problems could be rectified by short-term rebalancing, not long-term management. It was in the eighteenth century that attention shifted from balance to recycling nutrients via the injection of fresh manure into a field to restore fertility for a future harvest (Warde 2011).

Empire, war and population growth made the eighteenth century an early laboratory for exploring the limits to growth, especially in regions with marginal lands and limited resources and food supply. Botanists and agronomists saw their mission as extracting the treasures of the different climes that a providential God had created for the ingenuity of man to discover. Barren lands contained untapped value. The question was: how much value and by what means it could best be extracted? The late eighteenth century saw a major debate over the potential of the Scottish Highlands, where it was increasingly hard to sustain a growing population. On one side were liberal-minded reformers who blamed bad policy, not nature. Once evil laws like the salt and coal duties were lifted, backward Highland communities would develop into vibrant commercial societies, fishing and trading; 'excess' population, however, would still have to emigrate. On the other side were those who looked to the state, not the market, for development. Instead of spending on overseas colonies, where Highlanders could emigrate to, they argued that it would be much better to promote internal colonization. State-sponsored canals, peat extraction and model villages would support the population in their homeland. Tobacco and sugar beet could be grown in the Hebrides and the British army would be able to retain its Highlanders known for their war-like spirit. The Highlands (and Britain), in this view, needed hands-on state intervention not the 'invisible hand' of markets (Albritton Jonsson 2013).

The clash between market and state solutions mirrored contrasting views of nature. For liberal enlightenment thinkers like Adam Smith, nature and markets were broadly self-correcting: extremes balanced each other out. Natural historians were more pessimistic: nature was vulnerable, easily disturbed and needed careful management. From the 1790s, the mood was turning darker. Food crises gave 'limits' a new urgency. The big 'improvement' projects, like the Caledonian Canal, turned out to be expensive flops. Above all, fear of another shortage took hold: a coal famine. In 1789, John Williams revealed that he had been unable to find any coal reserves in Scotland. Even worse, he warned, Britain had managed to burn through half the coal ever mined in the country in the last 80 years alone. At that rate, coal would soon be exhausted and 'future inhabitants of this island must live, like its first inhabitants, by fishing and hunting' (Williams 1789, quoted in Albritton Jonsson 2013, p. 174). His answer was to stop coal exports and develop seams in Canada.

These episodes were milestones in the idea of sustainability. They shed light on several features. First, it is misleading to view modern history in terms of sequential phases, where unchecked industrialization gave way to an incipient new paradigm of sustainability. Rather, the concept of sustainability emerged in the heat of economic development and industrialization. Second, and related, it was the resource crises of development (the wood crisis, the coal famine) that focused contemporaries' minds on how to cultivate and conserve for the future. Sustainability is not some prelapsarian state: it is a crisis concept. And it is these crises that produced the science of measuring resource depletion, such as Williams's calculations of coal exhaustion. Third, limits to growth prompted ideological debate and different policy proposals. These operated with different geographic scales. Materials flows could be managed 'internally' by cultivating and conserving resources within a particular region or kingdom, or 'externally' by drawing on distant lands. In this sense, sustainability was not politically innocent, but tied to larger political battles over empire, markets and nation.

In these early developments, we can find ideas that parallel the current language of sustainable development: balancing economic life with nature and responsibility for the well-being of future generations. But we should not use history only to find ourselves in the past. History also reveals what is lost and different. Unlike today, all the authors mentioned above approached the question of limits from a regional perspective, not a shared global environment; Vernadsky introduced the 'biosphere' in the 1920s, but plural 'environments' only became a single global 'environment' after the Second World War (Robin et al. 2013). Williams's answer to the anticipated coal shortage was to mine coal in Nova Scotia, not to switch to renewable energies. Nor was sustainability an overarching goal. After all, Carlowitz wanted to conserve wood in order to extract and smelt more minerals. Finally, we need to note the significance of religious beliefs and emotional aesthetics in the call for sustainable use. As Carlowitz and generations of 'improvers' appreciated, human activity had consequences for future generations, but ultimately the world moved according to Divine time. Centuries were followed by eternity. Nature carried God's footprint, not just that of humans. It was always more than an economic unit: a store of divine beauty. For Carlowitz, trees were 'unspeakably beautiful'. In sum, the space of sustainability has widened to encompass the whole globe but narrowed in terms of its religious and cultural associations and temporal horizon (Mauch 2013, pp. 22–30, 48–56).

Material shortages and fears about future developments in the nineteenth and twentieth centuries – such as the efficiency movement of the years around 1900 and in the era of the two world wars – rang in new rounds in the battle between optimists and pessimists. Did the answer lie with greater efficiency or had natural limits been reached that required restraints on consumption and population growth? The debate reached a new height of alarm in the years of rapid growth after the Second World War. In 1955, the American conservationist Samuel Ordway warned that growth had become a dangerous religion and the world was approaching 'the limit of growth'. As resources were running short, costs would rise. He called for a new 'ethic for an age of conservation' (Ordway 1956). The establishment of the Club of Rome in 1968, with its mission to study the 'world problematique', strengthened the idea that the world faced an array of interconnected environmental and social problems. Its report on the *Limits to Growth* (Meadows et al. 1972) used computers to present future scenarios and model the interaction between accelerating industrialization, rapid world population growth, widespread malnutrition and poverty, dependence on non-renewable resources and their depletion, and a deteriorating environment. What made the Meadows report so influential was that it both defined and measured sustainable development in terms of achieving a balance between the economy, the need to maintain finite environmental resources and an improvement of social well-being.

The Brundtland Report in 1987 (WCED 1987) made sustainable development the organizing principle of transnational environmental policy. Concerns about resource allocation and material efficiency did not disappear but they were now recast in the economic language of natural capital stocks. The historian Emma Rothschild has stressed how Brundtland was widely interpreted as an injunction to 'maintain environmental capital intact' (Rothschild 2011, p. 194). At an institutional and policy level, this interpretation favoured the quantification of natural resources in national, regional and global environmental accounting systems. Human or social capital were also accounted for, but as Rothschild notes, this excluded many factors that added to well-being but did not have a measurable market value (Rothschild 2011). It was universalist and presentist, ignoring that cultures might value nature for different reasons, and that future generations might not share our yardsticks. It should be noted, though, that proponents of 'ecosystem services' continued to include the support of diverse cultures and aesthetic beauty and creativity among the list of nature's benefits upon which societies depended (Daily 1997).

The UN Conference on Environment and Development in Rio de Janeiro in 1992 operationalized the Brundtland approach and, by doing so, gave consumption greater visibility. Concrete initiatives and goals set out principles of economic, environmental and social sustainability for governance systems and consumer practice. The global, national and local sustainability action plan known as Agenda 21 dedicated a chapter to 'changing consumption patterns' (United Nations 1993). It emphasized the need to manage excessive demands and unsustainable lifestyles among richer societies. Excessive resource use in industrialized regions had to be redistributed to meet basic needs in poorer parts of the world. A more equitable rebalancing of resources at a global scale had thus been added to older concerns with regional sustainability.

Rio's Agenda 21 also gave greater attention to material flows. It called for an assessment of environmental impacts and resource requirements through the full life cycle of products and processes. This more fluid approach was reiterated at the Oslo Symposium on Sustainable Consumption two years later (Norwegian Ministry of the Environment 1994) and was formalized as a focus for national and global sustainability policy through the United Nations Environment Programme (UNEP) Sustainable Consumption and Production (SCP) Framework, to be implemented through the Marrakech Process (UNEP 2012). A fundamental objective of the increasingly influential SCP approach was to decouple economic growth from environmental degradation: nations could deliver more goods and services with less impact in terms of resource use, environmental degradation, waste and pollution (UNEP 2012). The vision of green growth marked a break with ideas that aligned sustainability with conservation and thrift.

SCP was founded on a resource-based, economistic approach which quantified the resource impacts of consumption and calculated the savings from more efficient technologies and processes. The objective was to reduce the material intensity of both production and consumer lifestyles by some measurable factor (Noorman and Uiterkamp 1998; von Weizsäcker et al. 1998). Agenda 21 and subsequent SCP policies looked to a multipronged strategy to manage demand via improved end-user and supply chain efficiencies, reducing wastage and limiting the use of finite resources in the production and consumption process. Market and voluntary instruments included eco-labelling, green tariffs, smart metering and environmental taxes. These would provide consumers and producers with signals about the environmental impact of their behaviours across the entire product chain. The Organisation for Economic Co-operation and Development (OECD)'s *Towards Sustainable Household Consumption?* saw the decisions of individual households as the main drivers of consumption and assumed that they would make the right pro-environmental choices given the right information and inducements (OECD 2002).

The career of the SCP paradigm was strangely at odds with the flourishing interest in consumption in the social sciences and humanities since the 1970s. While SCP policies approached consumption in individualistic terms of rational economic choice, sociologists, anthropologists and historians asked about status and distinction, meanings and communication, systems of provision, power and identity, and social practices (Bourdieu 1984; Brewer and Trentmann 2006; Miller 1998; Schama 1987; Shove 2003). In particular, SCP failed to take into account the structured and habitual nature of the many social practices that were responsible for the bulk of unsustainable forms of consumption, such as driving, bathing and showering, and cooling and heating (Shove 2003; Southerton et al. 2004; Warde and Gronow 2001; Welch and Warde, Chapter 5 in this book).

Today, it is widely acknowledged that the voluntary and market-based tools favoured by SCP have had little effect in reducing the intensity of material consumption and curbing unsustainable lifestyles or their global spread. In absolute terms, the global consumption of resources has continued to increase (OECD 2013). The limited achievements of global sustainable consumption policies have prompted a call to view consumption not only in economic terms but also through a social lens (UNEP 2012, p. 16). The gulf between the SCP approach and research in the social sciences has narrowed in recent years, although it certainly has not been bridged.

Looking at sustainable consumption through a social lens challenged the foundations of resource-based policy narratives. It highlighted the fact that people do not primarily consume resources, but the services they make possible. Shove's case studies showed how people did not value energy or water in themselves but for the services they provided: comfort, cleanliness and convenience (Shove 2003). This way of thinking also opened up a new perspective on the role of technologies in organizing consumption. In Agenda 21, technologies had been seen as tools for promoting eco-efficiency and curbing unsustainable behaviours. By contrast, historians of technology and socio-technical theorists used the concept of scripts, the idea that a vision of the world can be inscribed in the content of a technical object and shape how it is used (Akrich 1992), to explain how domestic appliances and devices structured unsustainable consumption. Infrastructure networks were also seen to embody the ideas of institutions about the efficient allocation and management of resources. Given the sunk costs of incumbent networks these notions could become locked in, making managers reluctant to explore sustainable alternatives (Arthur 1994). These studies challenged the more optimistic faith in consumer agency to make greener choices (Spaargaren and van Vliet 2000; van Vliet et al. 2005).

Contemporary sustainability policies acknowledge that solutions need to be tailored to local contexts, but they focus primarily on common environmental goals. Such a focus can ignore the diversity of cultural pathways to sustainability. The recent interest in alternative consumption in France, for example, has had little to do with the global project of promoting 'sustainable consumption'. The adoption of a 35-hour week and the revival of anti-consumerist movements were part of a social and political turn to 'discriminating consumerism', not driven by environmental directives (Sanches 2005).

## 3.2 RISING LEVELS OF CONSUMPTION

One way in which historians used to approach the growth of consumption was with the idea that eighteenth-century Britain gave birth to a 'consumer society' (McKendrick 1982). According to this idea, the eighteenth century amounted to a sharp break, after which the desire for and acquisition of goods took off. Hanoverian Britain appeared as a precursor of the 'take-off' model of economic development held out by W. Rostow and other champions of modernization during the Cold War. We now know that societies in Renaissance Italy (fifteenth century) and late Ming China (sixteenth–seventeenth centuries) had their own cultures of consumption and acquired a growing number of goods (Brook 1998; Clunas 1991; Welch 2005). So what changed? One change concerned a shift in orientation from public to private life. Renaissance town palaces did indeed fill up with more furniture and household objects, but, overall, consumption remained oriented towards public display and magnificence. Since then public consumption has not entirely disappeared, but in the course of modern history goods and services have increasingly assumed private meanings and functions. A second shift has been about flow and direction. A good deal of consumption in Renaissance Florence was circular: goods were borrowed, inherited, pawned and circled back and forth between families. Late Ming and early Qing China prized antiquity over novelty. Again, such circular flows have not entirely disappeared, but relatively they have been pushed aside by through-flow, that is, an accelerating injection of new stuff, a good deal of which is then discarded and disposed of.

From the seventeenth century onwards, with Holland and England in the lead, the movement has pretty much been in one direction: upward. English inventories document the rapid increase in mirrors, furniture, curtains, teapots, cutlery and much else in the years around 1700 (Weatherill 1996). Social, economic and cultural factors were at work: a cult of novelty (such as cotton textiles with vibrant colours and designs); an interest in exotic spices and drinks (cocoa, tea, coffee, sugar); the growing significance of 'comfort' and sociability which required and showcased consumer goods (the upholstered chair, curtains, tea parties); urbanization, which enhanced the significance of goods and fashions for communication and identity; and an appreciation of things for personal development, economic growth and national strength. While they never completely went away, earlier suspicions of luxury now faced serious defenders of 'modest' luxury in Enlightenment thinkers like David Hume and Adam Smith. The precocious embrace of things in Britain and Holland was favoured by comparatively open markets and competition that facilitated a transition from household self-provisioning to buying and selling goods in the market place. Elsewhere in Europe, by contrast, guilds and Church courts continued to discriminate against outside traders and punish their own womenfolk for buying fashionable clothes and trying to earn their own money (Ogilvie 2010).

The global advance of consumption was helped by empires, states and social movements; and this is important to stress, as many discussions of sustainability today focus on individual households as if they were the natural and only agents to consider. In the nineteenth century, European empires and missionary groups exported new lifestyles based on comfort and cleanliness. Western cities launched major infrastructure projects that delivered water, gas and electricity. In early twentieth-century Japan, housewives' associations worked together with state officials and architects to promote Western kitchens, fashions and lifestyles over traditional customs. At the same time and across the West, buyers' leagues were asserting the right and power of consumers as citizens. In liberal societies, growth, choice and a higher standard of living were attractive instruments to defuse class conflict. But fascism and Stalinism, too, promised their followers a future of material comfort. The acceleration in material flows and consumer goods since the 1950s needs to be located on this longer upward trajectory (Trentmann 2012).

In the following pages, we look at three domains that have particular bearing on sustainability to illustrate some of the historical dynamics of consumption: water, energy and waste.

### 3.2.1 Water Pressure

The history of changing water use illustrates how consumer practices came to be unsustainable and how they might be changed. The provision of clean, piped and constant water has been one of the central achievements of modern cities. This story has been mainly told from the perspective of engineering, infrastructures and supply. Yet, to understand the dynamics of demand, it is also necessary to look at the consumer's perspective. Water shows how what is considered 'normal' use is elastic. Whereas in the context of water sellers or communal wells, an inhabitant had once made do with 5 gallons a day, the arrival of piped supply suddenly led to the consumption of many more units. In Newark, USA, water consumption shot up from 20 gallons a day per person in 1870 to 113 gallons in 1898. In Atlanta, USA, it even reached a phenomenal 225 gallons or 885 litres per person per day in 1884. By contrast, people in European cities made do with 17 gallons (Berlin) and 44 gallons (London) in this period. In the 1880s, many American cities thus faced a serious sustainability challenge. The response was to impose meters. By 1888, Atlanta had managed to push consumption below the watermark of 100 gallons per capita per day. Metering also spread in European cities, with one significant exception: Britain. Here liberal political culture was opposed to a blanket intervention by the state in private life. Political ideas and institutions thus shaped the setting of consumer behaviour (Fuertes 1906; Grahn 1902; Royal Commission on Water Supply 1900).

One push in consumption's upward trajectory came from class-based ideals of 'civilized' practices, such as bathing. Victorian Britain is a good example. Once treated as an exceptional luxury and charged as such on a special rate by water companies, a bath became redefined as a 'need' from the middle of the nineteenth century. Instead of paying the water companies a higher special rate, middle-class citizens formed consumer defence leagues to fight for the new standard of a cheap, regular bath.

The shift from water pumped during certain hours to constant supply and ready availability 'on tap', day and night, further transformed habits, expectations and domestic technologies. When London introduced constant supply in the 1880s, landlords and public health reformers joined forces to eliminate 'dirty' cisterns in working-class districts. Such storage containers had been sources of resilience in the past. When London was hit by a series of harsh winters, which cracked pipes, and a European-wide drought in the 1890s, that resilience was gone. Consumers did not tolerate a return to limited hourly supply. Instead, they now left the taps on all day to make sure their tubs and containers would fill up while they were out. They also mobilized against the water companies, arguing that, far from a natural calamity, the drought was the man-made result of the profit hunger of private monopolies. The companies, in turn, accused consumers of criminal 'waste' and causing a water famine by taking advantage of constant supply not for 'normal' consumption but for watering gardens and even supplying ponds. Investigations revealed how much consumption was not the result of conscious individual choice, but caused by bad fittings and leaking taps. In the district of Shoreditch, water consumption was cut by half following the installation of regulated fittings. In 1903, London's water moved into public hands. The social democratic claim was that by giving all citizens a stake in water, inhabitants would behave responsibly, eliminating the risk of shortages in the future. Reality proved otherwise. While baths shrunk in size, per capita consumption continued to increase as new water-hungry practices spread (such as washing the car) and others intensified (more frequent baths and, later, showering) (Shove 2003; Taylor and Trentmann 2011; Taylor et al. 2009).

The global pattern of water use in the twentieth century was one of continuous climb overall, but some periods stand out for escalating demand. Global freshwater withdrawals grew most rapidly in the 1950s and 1960s. Culture, climate and shifting infrastructures and living arrangements help to explain why dependence on water intensified during this time. In Britain and Europe, it was during this period that internal baths and flushing toilets arrived in most people's homes. In Australia, most families by the 1960s were also able to turn a tap to obtain a copious supply of hot water, a convenience that came with more frequent and extravagant national bathing practices (Davison 2008). Yet how Australian families used water inside their homes paled beside their extravagant use outside. Melbourne water authorities calculated that the average consumption of water increased in the course of the 1970s by 15 per cent inside the house, but by 52 per cent outside. The main factors were rapid suburbanization and the transformation of the back garden, changes that were also visible elsewhere in the rich world. Once a utilitarian space for growing food, storing fuel and hanging up the laundry, the back garden became a place for leisure and socializing (Davison 2008). The metamorphosis involved extensive irrigation of lawns and flowerbeds, and the filling of swimming pools. It is these practices that became the focal point for discussions of excess use during subsequent water crises.

Over the last century, water management has broadly followed two distinct logics, each with its own understanding of network resilience and sustainability. From 1900 to the late 1970s, most consumers in the developed world paid a negligible price for water and received a steady supply via big public engineering projects (Duarte et al. 2011). Few efforts were devoted to conservation during this era of unlimited entitlement. From the mid-1970s, by contrast, water ceased to be considered cheap and abundant as infrastructures became ever costlier and environmental externalities received greater attention. A new paradigm emerged which looked to demand-side management and water saving. In reality, this paradigm shift was neither smooth, nor complete.

Twentieth-century droughts in advanced consumer societies such as Britain are instructive for how perspectives changed about what consumption is considered wasteful and what indispensable. Disruptions also illustrate the shifting balance between consumer and provider responsibilities for sustainable resource management. Experiences of drought in the post-1945 period challenged the idea that more supply and bigger infrastructures would solve rising demand (Taylor et al. 2009). During the 1959 drought, engineers and economists accused consumers of undervaluing water and treating it as infinite. Calls for water to be valued as an economic good became a recurrent theme in this and subsequent resource crises. Drought management methods have focused on regulating 'wasteful' consumption. Usually this has meant voluntary appeals urging citizens to curb non-essential water uses, primarily to stop watering their gardens and washing their cars. Occasionally it has meant restrictions. In the 1976 drought, national water authorities introduced water rationing and patrols to enforce hosepipe bans in some areas in order to protect supplies for big industrial consumers. Hosepipe bans for domestic consumers were again widespread in 1995 and 2006. Droughts also challenged what practices and purposes of water use should be treated as essential. In 2006 a swimming pool and hot tub could be filled with water, but it was not permitted to use a hosepipe to wash a private car or water a domestic garden. Droughts also showed the significance of people's hobbies, routines and values for how they adapted. Those who valued gardens for socialization or cultivation, for example, were more likely than others to use a watering can, even if this took considerable time and effort (Medd and Chappells 2008).

Rather than a clean shift from supply to demand management, however, British droughts point to an ongoing and evolving mix of provider and consumer responsibilities for sustainability. Thus in 1976 standpipes for consumers were complemented by measures to stretch the supply system to its limits by 'flogging the rivers and reservoirs' (Morren 1980). The 1990s looked for savings from greater efficiency, such as reducing the excessive 'demand' caused by leaking pipes. As in the 1890s, issues of provider responsibilities and of consumer rights continued to bubble up. In Yorkshire in 1995, some metered customers resisted water-saving measures in response to high water bills and distribution network leakage, which worsened the supply situation. Tankers were ultimately used to bring water into some villages. In 2006, greater environmental awareness supported a more integrated view of resilience where engaging consumers in demand management during the drought was seen as a way to pre-empt the need for supply-led adaptations, such as bulk transfers from other regions (Defra 2008). In turn, drought strategies today have started to concern themselves with long-term cultural adaptation as well as the short-term restrictions of the past (Environment Agency 2008). Instead of treating demand as the aggregate of a statistical average consumer, there is renewed interest in cultural change and in the diverse conditions, technologies and values that shape people's consumption (Medd and Chappells 2008).

The portion of the global population affected by chronic water shortages has expanded rapidly from around 9 per cent in 1960 to 35 per cent in 2005 (Kummu et al. 2010). As demand exceeds supply in more and more regions of the world, sustainability appears less and less achievable (Pacific Institute 2009). What adaptation approaches will drought-stricken regions come to embrace, and what visions of sustainable consumption will inform these? The case of California offers one illustration of how adaptations have been made in a region facing chronic shortage. California's historical struggles with drought exemplify the distributional challenges resulting from Americans' migration to hotter, drier regions in the twentieth century; the dream of California living drew 35 million new residents to the state in the course of the twentieth century (Brown 1999). The current drought (2013–2014) has prompted mandatory restrictions on lawn watering for some residents in addition to long-term approaches to supply-side resilience. Recycled municipal wastewater has become a significant source of water for golf course and landscape irrigation, and for drinking through groundwater replenishment. In such responses to chronic water shortage we see the re-emergence of a heroic engineering logic, but one that is now linked to conservation and reuse that are part of late twentieth-century principles. Water managers see the Carlsbad Desalination Project in San Diego County, the largest seawater desalination plant in the Western Hemisphere, as another solution to California's water woes. Ironically, this response to producing a resilient and stable water supply is not so sustainable in terms of energy consumption; desalination plants use about 30 per cent more energy than other current water supply options.

### 3.2.2 Energy

In Europe, total energy consumption increased sevenfold between 1870 and 2000. In per capita terms, three times as much energy was consumed at the end of the twentieth century as at the end of the nineteenth. The rise was most dramatic during the years of the post-war boom until the oil crises, from 1950 to 1973. Since then energy consumption has been uncoupled from economic growth, thanks to a major reduction in energy intensity. The aggregate trend is one of convergence; in 1870 per capita consumption in France and Spain was still only a quarter of that in Britain, today it is roughly the same. There has been a broad shift towards 'cleaner' fuels (such as gas) and cleaner electricity consumption. Britain, once the first industrial nation and the world's worst carbon emitter, has seen a decline in carbon emissions from energy since the 1970s, helped by deindustrialization. In general, the slight decrease in carbon emissions since the mid-1970s has come from a fall in energy intensity rather than decarbonization (Kander et al. 2013). There has been an overall rise in standards of heating and cooling comfort. In British homes, for example, insulation and central heating (mainly gas, and thus more sustainable than previous heating fuels) has facilitated a reduction in energy consumption even while average internal temperature in winter rose from 11 to 17 degrees Celsius between 1970 and 2010 (DECC 2013). American homes are now often cooler during the summer than in the winter, due to a reliance on air-conditioning. In 1955 fewer than 2 per cent of American households had air conditioning (Biddle 2008). In 2009, 87 per cent of US households were equipped with air conditioning (US EIA 2011). Such dramatic shifts resulted from a mix of factors: some about the ideal home as a place of security, comfort and family harmony, fostered by television and advertisers; others involving active policy support, such as when in 1957 the Federal Housing Administration began to include air conditioning as part of the mortgage cost (Cooper 1998).

Still, aggregate trends and averages can easily hide the significant diversity of energy consumption and the different habits, technologies, lifestyles and values that drive it. A few examples illustrate the persistence of diversity within affluent societies. In 1974 the German energy giant RWE surveyed use patterns in one neighbourhood. It found that 11 per cent of residents bathed several times a day, but 17 per cent only once a week. Half the residents cooked a warm lunch and dinner, 42 per cent cooked lunch only and ate cold cuts in the evening (RWE 1975). In Britain, at the time of writing in 2014, every tenth household lives in fuel poverty. Meanwhile, one in five households has a conservatory, most of which are heated. The richest 10 per cent of households consume more than four times as much gas as the bottom 20 per cent (DECC 2013, p. 60). Diversity extends to the shifting demands made by energy-hungry practices. British data shows that cooking draws half the energy today that it did in 1970. By contrast, electrical appliances have been using more and more: 5 per cent of household energy in 1970, 14 per cent in 2000 (DECC 2013). Alongside cookers and freezers (the big users of energy), homes have been invaded by hordes of new appliances and gadgets, a trend already discernible before the arrival of personal computing and electronic media. In the United States, there were 10 million aquariums in 1992. One in five homes had a waterbed. Some Americans used electric piano warmers. Transformers multiplied; in California in the early 2000s, 13 per cent of all residential energy went for standby or sleep mode (ACEEE 2000; Meier et al. 1992).

For interwar America it is sometimes said that the diffusion of appliances was prompted by the declining price of electricity (Kander et al. 2013, p. 317). But this has limited explanatory power for other periods. In Britain, in fact, the price of electricity has been rising since 1970 but appliances have proliferated nonetheless. To explain this we need to appreciate a basic point about the dynamics of consumption. Resources and fuels are a means for an end: they enable people to accomplish certain tasks and enjoy particular services, but these have their own logics and histories, relatively autonomous from the price of energy (about which most people know surprisingly little). The decline in home cooking, for example, has resulted from the rise of eating out in contemporary culture. At the same time, kitchens have evolved from badly lit sites of food preparation into bright and shiny places for socializing, with an unprecedented number of light fixtures. Compared to industry, households in Western countries have overall had a disappointing record when it comes to energy saving. To understand this we need to look at the changing meanings and functions of what people do, as well as at prices and regulation. The distinct trajectory of energy consumption in California holds some clues.

For the past 40 years, per capita residential electricity consumption has remained nearly constant in California while growing by 75 per cent in the rest of the United States. Geography and demography help to explain part of the divergence. California's mild climate means that heating and cooling demand has not increased as much as in other states, while the number of people per household has remained higher than elsewhere (Levinson 2013). Another reason, however, is California's progressive regulatory approach to energy efficiency. California's reaction to the 1973 oil crisis was distinctive. Growing population, environmental concerns and rapidly escalating costs for nuclear power plants made energy regulators turn towards consumers and demand-side management to cope with short supply. Energy saving was presented as a substitute power plant. Efficiency measures were conceived of in terms of 'negawatts' (Lovins 1989). Since the 1970s, a series of energy efficiency interventions, including building codes, have helped to slow the growth of Californian residential demand. Negawatts were cheaper in most periods than megawatts from finite fossil fuels or nuclear power plants. As the cost of natural gas fell during the 1990s, the focus on efficiency waned. But interest in demand-side management was rekindled by the electricity supply crisis of 2000–2001 and growing concern about long-term energy and environmental problems (Lutzenhiser 2010; Lutzenhiser et al. 2004). Californian households increasingly embraced voluntary conservation, continuing beyond the immediate crisis (Lutzenhiser et al. 2003).

Prior to 2000, California's demand-side programmes were mainly geared towards promoting efficiency, not conservation, with customers stimulated to reduce energy use while maintaining comparable levels of heating, cooling and lighting. This view started to change during the 2001 crisis as a call for conservation was met with collective altruism (Kunkle et al. 2004); for example, 6 per cent of households reported using no air conditioning at all and almost half took other conservation actions related to cooling or heating.

What will happen if consumers in China and India aspire to the same comfort standards as European or American societies? Energy consumption in residential buildings has increased markedly in China since 1990, helped by rapid growth and urbanization. Across Asia, air conditioning use has surged. By 1998, 70 per cent of urban households in Shanghai owned air conditioners. The demand for cooling energy is predicted to rise by up to 50 per cent by 2100 for Asia as a whole, driven by income growth, population increase, rapid urbanization, increases in house size and, paradoxically, climate change itself (Isaac and van Vuuren 2009). Initiatives to regulate cooling practices, however, may make a dent in this soaring demand. Some Chinese cities have adopted regulations that prohibit residents from setting thermostats below 26°C during the summertime. The oft-cited Cool Biz campaign in Japan combines similar thermostat rules and clothing policies to limit air conditioning demand in government offices.

The shift towards more energy-intensive ways of achieving comfort has been contributing to the intensity and experience of energy crises. Power cuts in Italy and France during the summer of 2003 were associated with a growing reliance on air conditioning (Trentmann 2009). In India, too, it has led to an increase in blackouts (Wilhite 2008). Across the world, many energy grids are at or close to their capacity at times of peak demand, creating significant problems for long-term resilience, health and security as well as for ecological sustainability.

Resilience in relation to managing future resource shortages will depend on an appreciation of diversity in consumer practice and in engaging consumers in keeping demand in balance with supply. The response to the California energy crisis of 2001 and to the drought in England in 2006 point to the possible role consumers might play in the future, with conservation and efficiency becoming a way of life.

### 3.2.3 Waste

Consumption puts pressure on sustainability as new goods and resources are acquired and put to use. But equally important is a later stage: when, where and how goods are disposed of. What happens to the value remaining in disposed goods is a major issue for sustainability, since the reuse of materials and their reintegration into the economy could reduce the pressure on untapped virgin resources. How has the expansion of consumption affected the dynamics and value of waste?

The last century and a half saw three revolutions in waste in the developed West. The first, in the late nineteenth century, introduced municipal waste management. From New York to Berlin, city authorities took over the collection of household waste and marginalized rag pickers. Solid waste was separated from human waste, which increasingly was flushed away into sewers rather than returned to the soil. This phase combined incineration and landfill with sorting at the household level and with the municipal separation of valuable material such as glass, metal and swill (for pigs) (Melosi 1981). A second phase, from the 1920s, made landfill ('controlled tipping') the preferred solution; by the 1960s, it handled 90 per cent of household waste in Britain and the United States, and 70 per cent in France and Germany. The 1970s ushered in a third phase: a turn away from landfill and a revival of recycling and of using waste for generating heat and energy. These were overlapping phases, not distinct waste regimes. It is worth recalling that as late as the early 1950s, New York City collected 600 tonnes of swill a day for pigs. Nor did all regions follow the same pattern. In the 1950s, Holland operated big sites that turned urban waste into compost. Shanghai mixed burning and burying waste with sending human excrement to neighbouring farms into the 1980s (Goldstein 2012). At the point of writing in 2014, rich societies continue to show considerable diversity, in terms of both how much waste they generate and how they treat it. In 2010, Germany and Belgium recycled 60 per cent of their municipal waste, while in Portugal and Greece it was a mere 20 per cent. Still, these phases give a sense of overall direction.

It is more problematic to draw a simple correlation between the growing amount of waste and a throwaway mentality. Earlier societies were not pure, austere communities where nothing of value was thrown out (Rathje and Murphy 1992). The Mayans and the Romans did it. Archaeologists have found barely chipped porcelain thrown out by colonial Americans in the eighteenth century. Reuse there was, but we should not romanticize it. Nor did materials flow only in locally integrated cycles. In the nineteenth century, textiles were pulped to produce paper, but such resources did not flow back to where they had been extracted. Clothing that had been made from Indian and Egyptian cotton ended up in newspapers and books in London and New York. Early municipal sorting machines in American cities found that households were throwing away a lot of bottles, metals and other valuable materials in 1900.

What changed in the twentieth century was not only the volume but also the composition of waste, its value and systems of regulation. Ash declined (as households shifted from heating with coal to gas and electricity), paper and (from the 1960s) plastics increased. Technological innovation disrupted processes of recycling in two main spheres. Thanks to the Haber–Bosch process, synthetic nitrogen eliminated the need for natural nitrogen from animal and human waste in farming. In paper-making, sulphites shifted processing from textile rags to wood pulp. Recycling campaigns continued in wartime drives for greater self-sufficiency as well as in years in peacetime when the price for material was rising. In Europe more so than in the more affluent United States, thrift, reuse and the experience of wartime salvage drives left a legacy after 1945; in Holland, for example, the women who pioneered recycling bins in the 1970s had been shaped by these earlier experiences (Oldenziel and Weber 2013). In many ways the problem was not that people during the affluent 1950s–1960s no longer cared about the destiny of their used glass and paper; there were many voluntary or Church-led collections in these years in Britain as well as on the Continent. Rather, prices for used materials were falling to such a low level that mountains of newspapers were piling up in church halls, unwanted by manufacturers. Still, even in those years, it is important to recognize that in some branches – such as steel or copper in the United States – industries had extensive recycling loops. Faced with chronic shortages, socialist countries developed impressive recycling networks and mobilized populations to show socialism's edge over wasteful capitalism. In reality, socialist waste management magnified the inefficiencies of the system, and in some areas (such as the collection of old car tyres in Hungary), developments went backwards in the course of the 1960s–1980s (Gille 2007).

In Western consumer societies, the 1970s–1980s ushered in a third phase, which looked to recycling. Environmental movements and the rising price of energy and materials initiated the shift but, arguably, it might have faded away in the long run as in earlier price cycles, if it had not been for national governments and, later, the European Community which introduced regulatory and price mechanisms that supported recycling and punished landfill; material recovery legislation and new waste laws were introduced by Japan (1970), Germany (1972) and Sweden (1975), and crowned by the European Landfill Directive in 1999. Demand for materials from China's rapidly growing economy and the liberalization of the European waste and recycling trade has helped, too. The integration of the European market in 1993 saw a major increase in the movement of waste and its reuse within Europe; the bulk of hazardous waste stays within Europe, although illegal shipments of e-waste to Africa continue to be a serious source of pollution and death (EEA 2013).

Recycling, however, has had paradoxical results. In Europe, bottle banks facilitated the triumph of the one-way bottle, although in Japan sake bottles are still reused 20 times. In Europe and the United States, household waste continued to expand from the 1970s to the early 2000s. In 2010, the average French person threw out four times as much as in 1970. In the EU-15, packaging waste alone increased by 10 million tonnes between 1997 and 2004. Food waste shows how these volumes are the result of social and technological factors: more fragmented meal times, the demands of conflicting schedules and social practices, refrigeration and over provisioning, and a fixation with expiry dates and 'freshness'. To blame a lack of individual morals is simplistic; in fact, most people feel bad when throwing wilted lettuce or other edible foods into the bin (Evans 2012).

In Europe, household waste has fallen slightly since 2008 but this may be the effect of the global recession rather than a long-term change in material use. The one exception to this trend has been Japan, which managed to reduce waste in the 1970s with the help of an integrated system of government regulation, neighbourhood civil activism and surveillance, education, fines and commercial recyclers (European Environment Agency 2013; Itoh 2004; OECD 2013). In general what recycling has done is make waste manageable. It has not led people to reduce their use of materials – the priority of the famed EU waste pyramid. Diversion from landfill has so far not translated into zero waste, that is, the recovery of enough materials from waste to make up for the wood, energy and water that would be used otherwise. Even the most progressive anti-waste city, San Francisco, only manages to recover half its waste; in Stockholm it is not even a quarter (Zaman and Lehmann 2013).

Throwing things away is not the only form of disposal, however. The centrality of other forms – from charitable and second-hand gifting to storage and collecting – urges us to be cautious when today's consumers are being reprimanded for having become wasteful, uncaring and indifferent to things. Anthropologists in Tucson (Arizona) found that when households replaced goods, only 6 per cent were actually thrown away; the majority was given or sold to family and friends, the rest handed to charity or stored at home (Gould and Schiffer 1981). In a major survey, the US Environmental Protection Agency (EPA) found that some 70 million computers and 104 million TV sets sit unused in lofts and garages (EPA 2011). Self-storage has mushroomed across the West in recent decades. Arguably, the problem is not that consumers are too profligate but that they are reluctant to let go of their stuff and allow rare metals and materials to find their way back into the cycle of production.

## 3.3 OUTLOOK

Sustainable consumption remains an emerging field in the study of history, notwithstanding the considerable advances in environmental history (McNeil 2001; Worster 1993). This chapter has highlighted the evolution of the concept and the interplay between practices, politics and networks that have shaped responses to shortages and crises in distinct historical contexts. There are two dimensions in particular which would benefit from more attention by future historians of consumption. The first is the interaction between households, firms and states. In the course of the twentieth century, the study of consumption became fixated with the private end-user. But a lot of resource use and consumption happens in firms and public places or, at least, is made possible by them, such as public leisure, hospitals, company canteens, housing and welfare benefits. In crises over water and energy, the demand of private consumers stands in tension with those of big industrial consumers. How these are negotiated and reconciled in different historical contexts, and with what consequences for sustainability, is a worthy field of inquiry. Secondly, our understanding of energy transitions and shifts in other resources has mainly proceeded from the contribution of technologies, networks and supply. We know surprisingly little about the role of households and how their habits and attitudes influenced the course of such transitions. Households are mainly treated as passive recipients of changes initiated elsewhere, a position that is at odds with the celebration of the active and creative consumer in the field of consumption more generally. We know, from the difficulties faced by champions of clean cooking stoves in the developing world, how important the culture of cooking and everyday life more generally is for the adoption of new technologies. How did households in the past respond to earlier transitions?

## ACKNOWLEDGEMENTS

We gratefully acknowledge support from the Arts and Humanities Research Council (AHRC), AH/K006088/1; the Dynamics of Energy, Mobility and Demand (DEMAND) centre (Engineering and Physical Sciences Research Council/ Economic and Social Research Council, EPSRC/ESRC); and (Frank Trentmann) the Leverhulme Trust for an International Fellowship.

## REFERENCES

ACEEE (American Council for an Energy-Efficient Economy) (2000), *Proceedings of the 2000 ACEEE Summer Study on Energy Efficiency in Buildings*, August, Washington, DC: American Council for an Energy-Efficient Economy.

Akrich, M. (1992), 'The de-scription of technical objects', in Wiebe Bijker and John Law (eds), *Shaping Technology / Building Society*, Cambridge, MA: MIT Press, pp. 205–224.

Albritton Jonsson, F. (2013), *Enlightenment's Frontier: The Scottish Highlands and the Origins of Environmentalism*, New Haven, CT: Yale University Press.

Arthur, W.B. (1994), *Increasing Returns and Path Dependence in the Economy*, Ann Arbor, MI: University of Michigan Press.

Biddle, J. (2008), 'Explaining the spread of residential air conditioning, 1955–1980', *Explorations in Economic History*, 45 (4), 402–423.

Bourdieu, P. (1984), *Distinction: A Social Critique of Judgment and Taste*, London: Routledge.

Brewer, J. and F. Trentmann (2006), *Consuming Cultures, Global Perspectives: Historical Trajectories, Transnational Exchanges*, London: Bloomsbury Academic.

Brook, T. (1998), *The Confusions of Pleasure: Commerce and Culture in Ming China*, Berkeley, CA: University of California Press.

Brown, T.C. (1999), 'Past and future freshwater use in the United States: a technical document supporting the 2000 USDA Forest Service RPA Assessment', General Technical Report RMRS-GTR-39, Fort Collins, CO: USDA.

von Carlowitz, H.C. (1713), *Sylvicultura oeconomica, oder haußwirthliche Nachricht und Naturmäßige Anweisung zur wilden Baum-Zucht*, Leipzig: Braun.

Clunas, C. (1991), *Superfluous Things: Material Culture and Social Status in Early Modern China*, Honolulu, HI: University of Hawaii Press.
Cooper, G. (1998), *Air Conditioning America: Engineers and the Controlled Environment, 1900–1960*, Baltimore, MD: Johns Hopkins University Press.
Daily, G.C. (ed.) (1997), *Nature's Services: Societal Dependence on Natural Ecosystems*, Washington, DC: Island Press.
Davison, G. (2008), 'Down the gurgler: historical influences on Australian domestic water consumption', in Patrick Troy (ed.), *Troubled Waters: Confronting the Water Crises in Australia's Cities*, Canberra: ANU Press, pp. 37–65.
DECC (Department of Energy and Climate Change) (2013), *United Kingdom Housing Energy Fact File: 2013*, London: Department of Energy and Climate Change.
Defra (Department for Environment, Food and Rural Affairs) (2008), 'Future water: the government's water strategy for England', London: Department for Environment, Food and Rural Affairs.
Duarte, R., V. Pinilla and A. Serrano (2011), 'Looking backward to look forward: water use and economic growth from a long-term perspective', No 1104, Documentos de Trabajo (DT-AEHE), Asociación Española de Historia Económica, available at http://econpapers.repec.org/paper/ahedtaehe/1104.htm (accessed 12 April 2014).
EEA (European Environment Agency) (2013), *Managing Municipal Solid Waste: A Review of Achievements in 32 European Countries*, Copenhagen: European Environment Agency.
Environment Agency (2008), 'International comparisons of domestic per capita consumption', Bristol: Environment Agency.
EPA (Environmental Protection Agency) (2011), 'Electronics waste management in the United States through 2009', Washington, DC: US Environmental Protection Agency.
Evans, D. (2012), 'Binning, gifting and recovery: the conduits of disposal in household food consumption', *Environment and Planning D: Society and Space*, 30 (6), 1123–1137.
Evelyn, J. (1664), *Sylva, or a Discourse of Forest-Trees*.
Fuertes, J.H. (1906), *Waste of Water in New York and its Reduction by Meters and Inspection*, New York: Merchant's Association of New York.
Gille, Z. (2007), *From the Cult of Waste to the Trash Heap of History: The Politics of Waste in Socialist and Postsocialist Hungary*, Bloomington, IN: Indiana University Press.
Goldstein, J. (2012), 'Waste', in Gould, R.A. and M.B. Schiffer (eds) (1981), *Modern Material Culture: The Archaeology of Us*, New York: Academic Press.
Gould, R.A. and M.B. Schiffer (eds) (1981), *Modern Material Culture: The Archaeology of Us*, New York: Academic Press.
Grahn, E. (ed.) (1902), *Die Städtische Wasserversorgung im Deutschen Reiche sowie in einigen Nachbarländern*, Munich and Leipzig: Oldenbourg.
Grober, Ulrich (2002), Tiefe Wurzeln: Eine kleine Begriffsgeschichte von 'sustainable development' – Nachhaltigkeit, *Natur und Kultur*, 3 (1), 116–128.
Isaac, M. and D.P. van Vuuren (2009), 'Modeling global residential sector energy demand for heating and air conditioning in the context of climate change', *Energy Policy*, 37, 507–521.
Itoh, H. (2004), *Waste Management in Japan*, Southampton: WIT Press.
Kander, A., P. Malanima and P. Warde (2013), *Power to the People: Energy in Europe over the Last Five Centuries*, Princeton, NJ: Princeton University Press.
Klein Goldewijk, K. (2010), 'Historical Database of the Environment (HYDE)', PBL Netherlands Environmental Assessment Agency, available at http://themasites.pbl.nl/tridion/en/themasites/hyde/index.html (accessed 14 April 2014).
Krausmann, F., S. Gingrich, N. Eisenmenger, K.H. Erb, H. Haberl and M. Fischer-Kowalski (2009), 'Growth in global materials use, GDP and population during the 20th century', *Ecological Economics*, 68 (10), 2696–2705.
Kummu, M., P.J. Ward, H. de Moel and O. Varis (2010), 'Is physical water scarcity a new phenomenon? Global assessment of water shortage over the last two millennia', *Environmental Research Letters*, 5 (3), available at http://iopscience.iop.org/1748-9326/5/3/034006 (accessed 12 April 2014).
Kunkle, R., L. Lutzenhiser, S. Sawyer and S. Bender (2004), 'New imagery and directions for residential sector energy policies', in *Proceedings of the 2004 ACEEE Summer Study on Energy Efficiency in Buildings*, Washington, DC: American Council for an Energy-Efficient Economy, pp. 171–182.
Levinson, A. (2013), 'California energy efficiency: lessons for the rest of the world, or not?', National Bureau of Economic Research (NBER) Working Paper No. 19123, June, Cambridge, MA: NBER.
Lovins, A. (1989), 'The Negawatt Revolution – solving the $CO_2$ problem', Keynote address at the Green Energy Conference, Montreal: Canadian Coalition for Nuclear Responsibility, available at http://www.ccnr.org/amory.html (accessed 12 April 2014).
Lutzenhiser, L. (2010), 'The evolution of energy efficiency policy', in D. Reeve, D.N. Dewees and B. Karney

(eds), *Current Affairs: Perspectives on Electricity Policy for Ontario*, Toronto: University of Toronto Press, pp. 158–193.
Lutzenhiser, L., R. Kunkle, J. Woods and S. Lutzenhiser (2003), 'Conservation behavior by residential consumers during and after the 2000–2001 California energy crisis', in California Energy Commission (ed.), *Public Interest Energy Strategies Report 100-03-012F*, Sacramento, CA: CEC, pp. 146–197.
Lutzenhiser, L., R. Kunkle, J. Woods, S. Lutzenhiser and S. Bender (2004), 'Lasting impressions: conservation and the 2001 California energy crisis', in *Proceedings of the 2004 ACEEE Summer Study on Energy Efficiency in Buildings*, Washington, DC: American Council for an Energy-Efficient Economy, pp. 229–240.
Mauch, C. (2013), *Mensch und Umwelt: Nachhaltigkeit aus historischer Perspektive*, Munich: Oekom.
McKendrick, N. (1982), 'The consumer revolution of eighteenth-century England', in N. McKendrick, J. Brewer and J.H. Plumb (eds), *The Birth of a Consumer Society: The Commercialization of Eighteenth Century England*, Bloomington, IN: Indiana University Press, pp. 9–33.
McNeil, J.R. (2001), *Something New Under the Sun: An Environmental History of the Twentieth-Century World*, New York: W.W. Norton & Company.
Meadows, D.H., D.L. Meadows, J. Randers and W.W. Behrens III (1972), *The Limits to Growth: A Report for the Club of Rome's Project on the Predicament of Mankind*, New York: Universe Books.
Medd, W. and H. Chappells (2008), 'Drought and demand in 2006: consumers, water companies and regulators', Final Report to UK Water Industry Research (UKWIR), April, Lancaster: Lancaster University.
Meier, A., L. Rainer and S. Greenberg (1992), 'Miscellaneous electrical energy use in homes', *Energy*, 17 (5), 509–518.
Melosi, M. (1981), *Garbage in Cities: Refuse, Reform and the Environment, 1880–1980*, Pittsburgh, PA: University of Pittsburgh Press.
Miller, D. (ed.) (1998), *Material Cultures: Why Some Things Matter*, London: UCL Press.
Morren, G. (1980), 'The rural ecology of the British drought of 1975–1976', *Human Ecology*, 8, 33–64.
Noorman, K.J. and T. Schoot Uiterkamp (eds) (1998), *Green Households? Domestic Consumers, Environment and Sustainability*, London: Earthscan.
Norwegian Ministry of the Environment (1994), *Report of the Symposium on Sustainable Consumption*, Oslo: Norwegian Ministry of the Environment.
OECD (Organisation for Economic Co-operation and Development) (2002), *Towards Sustainable Household Consumption? Trends and Policies in OECD Countries*, Paris: Organisation for Economic Co-operation and Development Publishing.
OECD (Organisation for Economic Co-operation and Development) (2013), *Environment at a Glance: OECD Indicators*, Paris: Organisation for Economic Co-operation and Development.
Ogilvie, S. (2010), 'Consumption, social capital, and the "industrious revolution" in early modern Germany', *Journal of Economic History*, 70 (2), 287–325.
Oldenziel, R. and H. Weber (2013), 'Introduction: reconsidering recycling', *Contemporary European History*, 22 (SI: 3), 347–370.
Ordway, S. (1956), 'Possible limits of raw material consumption', in W.L. Thomas (ed.), *Man's Role in Changing the Face of the Earth*, Chicago, IL: University of Chicago Press, pp. 987–1009.
Pacific Institute (2009), *Fact Sheet on Water Use in the United States*, Oakland, CA: Pacific Institute.
Rathje, W. and C. Murphy (1992), *Rubbish: The Archaeology of Garbage*, New York: Harper Collins.
Robin, L., S. Sörlin and P. Warde (2013), *The Future of Nature: Documents of Global Change*, New Haven, CT: Yale University Press.
Rothschild, E. (2011), 'Maintaining (environmental) capital intact', *Modern Intellectual History*, 8 (1), 193–212.
Royal Commission on Water Supply (UK) (1900), 'Final report', 38 (1), [Cd.25].
Ruddiman, W.F. (2005), *Plows, Plagues and Petroleum: How Humans Took Control of Climate*, Princeton, NJ: Princeton University Press.
RWE (1975), RWE Archive: Abt. Anwendungstechnik Marketing, June, Bericht ueber die Haushaltskundenbefragung 1974 im direkten RWE-Versorgungsgebiet.
Sanches, S. (2005), 'Sustainable consumption *à la française*? Conventional, innovative, and alternative approaches to sustainability and consumption in France', *Sustainability, Science, Practice and Policy*, 1 (1), 43–57.
Schama, S. (1987), *The Embarrassment of Riches: An Interpretation of Dutch Culture in the Golden Age*, New York: Alfred A. Knopf.
Shove, E. (2003), *Comfort, Cleanliness and Convenience: The Social Organization of Normality*, Oxford: Berg.
Southerton, D., H. Chappells and B. van Vliet (eds) (2004), *Sustainable Consumption: The Implications of Changing Infrastructures of Provision*, Cheltenham, UK and Northampton, MA, USA: Edward Elgar.
Spaargaren, G. and B. van Vliet (2000), 'Lifestyles, consumption and the environment: the ecological modernization of domestic consumption', *Environmental Politics*, 9 (1), 50–76.

Steffen, W., A. Sanderson, J. Jäger, P.D. Tyson, B. Moore III, P.A. Matson, K. Richardson et al. (2004), *Global Change and the Earth System: A Planet under Pressure*, Heidelberg: Springer.
Taylor, V., H. Chappells, W. Medd and F. Trentmann (2009), 'Drought is normal: the socio-technical evolution of drought and water demand in England and Wales, 1893–2006', *Journal of Historical Geography*, 35 (3), 568–591.
Taylor, V. and F. Trentmann (2011), 'Liquid politics: water and the politics of everyday life in the modern city', *Past and Present*, 211 (1), 199–241.
Trentmann, F. (2009), 'Disruption is normal: blackouts, breakdowns and the elasticity of everyday life', in E. Shove, F. Trentmann and R. Wilk (eds), *Time, Consumption and Everyday Life*, Oxford: Berg, pp. 67–84.
Trentmann, F. (2012), *Oxford Handbook of the History of Consumption*, Oxford: Oxford University Press.
United Nations (1993), *Agenda 21: Earth Summit – The United Nations Programme of Action from Rio*, New York: United Nations.
UNEP (United Nations Environment Programme) (2012), *Global Outlook on Sustainable Consumption and Production Policies: Taking Action Together*, Paris, United Nations Environment Programme.
US EIA (US Energy Information Association) (2011), 'Residential Energy Consumption Survey', Washington, DC: US Energy Information Association, available at http://www.eia.gov/consumption/residential/ (accessed 12 April 2014).
Van Vliet, B., H. Chappells and E. Shove (2005), *Infrastructures of consumption: Environmental Innovation in the Utility Industries*, London: Earthscan.
von Weizsäcker, E.U., A.B Lovins and L.H. Lovins (1998), *Factor Four: Doubling Wealth, Halving Resource Use – A Report to the Club of Rome*, London: Earthscan.
Warde, P. (2011), 'The invention of sustainability', *Modern Intellectual History*, 8 (1), 153–170.
Warde, A. and J. Gronow (2001), *Ordinary Consumption*, London: Routledge.
Weatherhill, L. (1996), *Consumer Behaviour and Material Culture in Britain, 1660–1760*, London: Routledge.
Welch, E.S. (2005), *Shopping in the Renaissance: Consumer Cultures in Italy, 1400–1600*, New Haven, CT: Yale University Press.
Wilhite, H.L. (2008), *Consumption and the Transformation of Everyday Life: A View From South India*, New York: Palgrave Macmillan.
WCED (World Commission on Environment and Development) (1987), *Our Common Future*, Oxford: Oxford University Press.
Worster, D. (1993), *The Wealth of Nature: Environmental History and the Ecological Imagination*, Oxford: Oxford University Press.
Zaman, A.U. and S. Lehmann (2013), 'The zero waste index: a performance measurement systems in a "zero waste city"', *Journal of Cleaner Production*, 50 (1), 123–132.

# 4. Environmental psychology and sustainable consumption

*Linda Steg*

Environmental psychology studies the transaction between human and the built and natural environment (Gifford 2007; Steg et al. 2012). On the one hand environmental psychologists examine how environmental conditions affect our thought, behaviour and well-being. This can provide important insights in whether and how different environmental (or: situational) factors affect environmental behaviour and sustainable consumption. Also it reveals which environmental conditions threaten or enhance well-being that could be changed by promoting sustainable consumption. On the other hand environmental psychologists study how to encourage pro-environmental behaviour and sustainable consumption. The latter involves understanding which factors affect sustainable consumption, and which strategies can be effectively employed to promote sustainable consumption. In doing so environmental psychologists tend to consider individual, social, cultural and situational factors influencing behaviour (change), as will be exemplified later in this chapter.

This chapter aims to explain how both strands of research can be employed to understand and promote sustainable consumption, focusing on the environmental impact of sustainable consumption. I first discuss some basic characteristics of sustainable consumption: sustainable consumption protects the environment but is often associated with behavioural costs and additional effort. Next I explain under which conditions consumers are likely to act sustainably, even though this is somewhat costly or effortful. I will argue that these conditions are not only defined by individual and social factors, but that situational factors, often overlooked in psychological research, play a key role in this respect as well. Finally I discuss which strategies can be employed to promote sustainable consumption, addressing key factors discussed in this chapter.

## 4.1 EXPLAINING SUSTAINABLE CONSUMPTION

### 4.1.1 Sustainable Consumption: Good but Costly

Sustainable consumption often involves a conflict between individual and collective interests (e.g. Lindenberg and Steg 2007; Vlek 1996). On the one hand sustainable consumption is aimed to benefit others (including future generations) and nature and the environment. Yet, on the other hand, in many cases acting sustainably is somewhat personally costly (Steg and Nordlund 2012). For example travelling by public transport instead of the car benefits others and the environment, but is generally perceived to be less comfortable, less convenient, more time-consuming and less pleasurable. Also, although being considered to be more sustainable, electric vehicles have less instrumental benefits than regular cars, and renewable energy sources are believed to be more costly and less convenient than fossil fuels (Noppers et al. 2014). Yet despite this, some consumers do purchase and use these sustainable products and services. What motivates them to do so? I propose that consumers are likely to engage in sustainable consumption when they strongly value nature and the environment, and when situational factors activate and support these values. In the next section I explain which values are most relevant to understand sustainable consumption, and via which processes values affect sustainable consumption. Next I will explain that although consumers may strongly value nature and the environment, they will not always act upon these values because situational factors can activate competing values that consumers endorse also.

### 4.1.2 Values

Values are 'desirable goals, varying in importance, that serve as guiding principles in people's lives' (Schwartz 1992, p. 21). Values reflect relatively stable and general goals that people strive for in life, which direct attention and influence how they evaluate different consequences of products, services and actions (Steg et al. 2014a; Stern and Dietz 1994). Values transcend situations, and thus may affect many different beliefs, preferences, attitudes, norms, intentions and behaviours (Feather 1995; Rokeach 1973). This makes it relevant to understand which values affect sustainable consumption, and how values affect sustainable consumption.

Literature reviews reveal that evaluations of and level of engagement in sustainable consumption particularly depends on the extent to which consumers prioritize self-enhancement values (in which case consumers particularly consider how behaviour affects themselves) versus self-transcendence values (in which case consumers particularly consider the consequences of their behaviours for others or the environment; Dietz et al. 2005; Steg and De Groot 2012). Two types of self-enhancement values appear to be most relevant for understanding sustainable consumption: hedonic values that make consumers focus on ways to improve their feelings and reduce effort; and egoistic values that make consumers focus on ways to secure or improve their resources (Steg et al. 2014b). In addition two types of self-transcendence values prove to be relevant for sustainable consumption: altruistic values that make consumers focus on how choices affect other people; and biospheric values that make consumers focus on the consequences of their behaviour for nature and the environment (De Groot and Steg 2007; Grønhøj and Thøgersen 2009; Nilsson et al. 2004; Steg et al. 2005; Steg 2008; Steg et al. 2014b). All four types of values are important to consumers to some extent, but they are likely to prioritize different values differently, which affects their evaluations of and engagement in sustainable consumption. Consumers who strongly endorse hedonic or egoistic values typically are less likely to evaluate sustainable consumption favourably and to act sustainably; while strong altruistic and biospheric values mostly promote favourable evaluations of and engagement in sustainable consumption (e.g. Nordlund and Garvill 2002; Schultz et al. 2005; Stern et al. 1995; Stern et al. 1998; Thøgersen and Ölander 2002), probably because sustainable consumption is often somewhat costly or effortful (see section 4.1.1). Importantly these four types of values appeared to be relevant for understanding preferences for and engagement in sustainable consumption in different countries and cultures across the world (see Steg and De Groot 2012, for a review).

Sustainable consumption preferences and behaviour seemed to be particularly related to biospheric values.

### 4.1.3 How Do Values Affect Sustainable Consumption?

Scholars generally assume that values mainly affect sustainable consumption indirectly, via behaviour-specific beliefs and norms. Below I discuss three different yet related processes through which values can affect sustainable consumption (Steg et al. 2014a).

First, as explained in section 4.1.2, values that are prioritized by a person steer attention and affect how consumers evaluate different consequences of actions, which in turn affect their preferences and sustainable consumption (Stern and Dietz 1994; Stern et al. 1995). This implies that values determine how important different consequences of choice alternatives are to people and how they evaluate these consequences, which will in turn affect the attractiveness of different alternatives and actual choices (Feather 1995). Values indeed appeared to affect the evaluation of the importance of different consequences of behaviour (Perlaviciute 2014; Steg et al. 2014a; Verplanken and Holland 2002). More specifically people with strong biospheric values are more likely to consider the environmental consequences of choice alternatives, while those with strong altruistic values particularly consider relevant altruistic consequences. Also consumers with strong hedonic values tend to focus on the hedonic consequences of choice alternatives, while those with strong egoistic values tend to evaluate egoistic consequences of choices as more important. In a similar vein, values determine whether people act upon information on (environmental) consequences of behaviour. For example an environmental campaign conveying the negative environmental consequences of a particular behaviour proved to increase environmental knowledge among the targeted population, but only promoted intentions to engage in pro-environmental behaviour among those who strongly endorse biospheric values, while intentions of people with weak biospheric values remained unchanged (Bolderdijk et al. 2013a). Apparently environmental information has little motivational force when consumers do not consider protecting the environment to be an important personal value.

Values not only affect which consequences consumers mostly consider when making choices, but also how they evaluate these consequences. Interestingly evaluations of choice alternatives seem to depend on how they will affect one's important values (De Groot et al. 2013; Perlaviciute 2014). For example consumers tend to evaluate behavioural options that have positive consequences for their central values favourably in many different respects, also with regard to aspects that are hardly linked to their central values. On the other hand behavioural alternatives that have negative consequences for one's central values tend to be evaluated negatively on many different aspects, again including aspects that are not very important on the basis of one's central values. This implies that consumers seem to stress any advantage and to downplay any disadvantage of behaviour alternatives that have positive consequences for their important values, and particularly stress disadvantages and downplay advantages of alternatives that have negative consequences for their important values. As a result, consumers tend to favour and choose alternatives that support the values they prioritize (De Groot et al. 2013; Perlaviciute 2014; Verplanken and Holland 2002).

Second, values can affect sustainable consumption via a process of norm activation

(Schwartz 1977; Stern 2000). In line with the reasoning in the previous paragraph, values affect the extent to which consumers are aware of the environmental problems caused by their behaviour (Nordlund and Garvill 2002; Steg et al. 2005; Stern et al. 1995). Consumers who strongly endorse biospheric values tend to be more aware of the negative environmental consequences of their behaviour than those with weak biospheric values, while the opposite is true for those who strongly endorse egoistic values. Higher problem awareness enhances one's feelings of responsibility for environmental problems and their solution, which in turn activates personal norms (that is, feelings of moral obligation) to engage in sustainable consumption that eventually promotes sustainable choices (Gärling et al. 2003; Steg and De Groot 2010; Steg et al. 2005).

Third, values can affect sustainable consumption via one's environmental self-identity, that is, the extent to which a person sees himself or herself as a pro-environmental person (Van der Werff et al. 2013b; Whitmarsh and O'Neill 2010). Consumers who strongly endorse biospheric values are more likely to see themselves as a pro-environmental person, which strengthens their personal norms to act accordingly, and in turn motivates them to engage in sustainable consumption (Van der Werff et al. 2013a). Values provide a stable basis for one's self-identity, as they affect one's environmental self-identity in the long term as well (Van der Werff et al. 2013b). Yet, the environmental self-identity can be changed to some extent by reminding consumers of their previous behaviour, especially when these behaviours clearly signal how pro-environmental they are (Cornelissen et al. 2008; Van der Werff et al. 2013a, 2014b). I come back to this issue in section 4.2.3.

### 4.1.4 Situational Factors Activate or Deactivate Values

In the previous section, I indicated that self-transcendence values, and particularly biospheric values, generally promote sustainable consumption. Interestingly, research has shown that consumers across the world strongly endorse biospheric values (e.g. De Groot and Steg 2007; Jakovcevic and Steg 2013; Jakovcevic et al. 2013; Nilsson et al. 2004; see Steg and De Groot 2012, for a review). If biospheric values are so widely endorsed, how can we explain that many consumers do not act accordingly and rather refrain from engaging in pro-environmental and sustainable consumption?

One important reason for the inconsistency between values and behaviour is that values need to be activated and supported by cues in a particular choice situation in order to be influential and to motivate people to act accordingly (Lindenberg and Steg 2013; Maio 2010; Steg et al. 2014a; Verplanken and Holland 2002). The extent to which consumers have the goal to act sustainably in a particular situation thus not only depends on one's values (that reflect their general goals in life), but also on situational cues that can activate or deactivate particular values (see Lindenberg 2012). Once values are activated, they are cognitively more easily accessible, and more likely to guide decision making in the particular situation. In contrast, consumers may fail to act upon their values when these values are not supported or activated by cues in the situation in which choices are made.

Various situational factors can serve as a cue that activates or deactivates specific values, thereby affecting the strength and influence of goals in a particular situation. On a general level, corporate capitalism that strongly emphasizes the pursuit of self-interest, competition and economic growth can make people focus on their hedonic and egoistic values (Kasser et al. 2007). Also feelings of insecurity increase the likelihood that people prioritize hedonic and egoistic values in that situation (Kasser and Sheldon 2000). In addition, values may be activated by specific cues in a given situation. For example bikini models or chocolate are likely to activate hedonic values; status symbols or signs of money or credit cards may activate egoistic values; while Bibles, churches, statues of Justitia or environmental symbols may activate altruistic and biospheric values (Lindenberg 2012; Lindenberg and Steg 2007; Perlaviciute 2014; Steg 2012; Verplanken and Holland 2002). Below I describe briefly three other ways in which situational factors can deactivate or activate values thereby influencing the likelihood of sustainable consumption: (signs of) behaviour of others that signal the level of support for norms; cognitive demands in a situation; and situational factors that affect the costliness of sustainable consumption.

First, signs of norm-violating behaviour signalling that others do not act in line with their biospheric or altruistic values may deactivate one's biospheric or altruistic values, thereby increasing the likelihood that the observer also engages in similar and other norm-violating behaviour (Keizer et al. 2008). For example people littered more in a littered environment (Cialdini 2003; Cialdini et al. 1990), but also when buildings in the specific environment were covered with graffiti, and when unreturned shopping carts were present, and they were even more likely to steal in a littered environment (Keizer et al. 2008). Such (cross-)norm inhibition effects were stronger when more people seemed to violate norms (Cialdini et al. 1990), or when norm violations were more salient (for example, an anti-litter sign in a littered environment makes people even more aware of the fact that many people violate this norm; Keizer et al. 2011). Also, (cross-)norm inhibition effects were stronger when those violating the norm were more similar to the observer (Gino et al. 2009). On the other hand situational cues can also signal that other people respect norms, which is likely to activate biospheric and altruistic values, thereby promoting sustainable actions. For example when people observed a person voluntarily removing other people's litter, they were less likely to litter themselves (Reno et al. 1993), and more likely to help a person in need (Keizer et al. 2013). These findings suggest that norm support cues can activate biospheric and altruistic values and promote sustainable actions (Keizer et al. 2013).

Second, consumers often have to manage and balance multiple goals in demanding situations. They may be less likely to act upon their biospheric and altruistic values when they face conflicting values in demanding situations. For example a driving simulator study revealed that drivers who adopted a fuel-saving goal saved less fuel when they were given an additional goal (that is, being on time) as compared to drivers who were not given this additional goal. Also, drivers indicated that they did not consider their fuel use when the traffic situation was highly demanding, suggesting that high task demands made them focus on the main goal (such as driving safely) and less on other goals (in this case reducing fuel use; Dogan et al. 2011). Related to this, as sustainable consumption is generally somewhat costly (in the sense of effort, money, comfort), consumers need to exercise self-control to act upon their biospheric and altruistic values and counter the impulse to opt for more attractive or profitable choices (Ruepert et al., in press). Consumers will be less likely to exercise sufficient self-control when their regulatory resources are depleted (Baumeister et al. 1998). For example after working on effortful or cognitive demanding tasks, the capability or willingness to engage in self-regulation will be reduced (Baumeister and Vohs 2007), which may inhibit consumers to act upon their biospheric or altruistic values.

Third, consumers may be less likely to act upon their biospheric or altruistic values when the relevant sustainable behaviour is very costly, as in this case sustainable consumption will seriously threaten the fulfilment of other values that are also important to them. Indeed, biospheric values and normative considerations appeared to be less predictive of sustainable consumption that is rather effortful, costly or uncomfortable (Abrahamse and Steg 2011; Bamberg and Schmidt 2003; Diekmann and Preisendörfer 2003; Harland et al. 1999). In such cases, it may be necessary to reduce the behavioural costs of sustainable consumption so as to facilitate consumers to act upon their biospheric and altruistic values.

In sum, biospheric values are more likely to predict behaviour when they are activated and supported by situational cues, making it more likely that these values actually guide behaviour in a particular situation. Yet consumers with rather strong biospheric or altruistic values may still engage in sustainable consumption even when situational cues do not fully support these values. That is, their biospheric or altruistic goals may still be strong and steer their behaviour in a given situation, even though situational cues may have weakened the strength of these goals somewhat.

## 4.2 PROMOTING SUSTAINABLE CONSUMPTION

Above, I argued that values as well as situational cues affect the strength of the goals that people strive for in specific situations that eventually determine which aspect people consider when making choices and the extent to which various behavioural-specific factors (including beliefs, evaluations, preferences, attitudes and norms) affect sustainable consumption. Please note that in many cases, sustainable consumption does not involve a conscious decision process: consumers may not be aware of how values, situational cues and goals affect their behaviour. So, what are the implications of this reasoning for developing effective strategies to promote sustainable consumption? How can we encourage consumers to act upon their biospheric or altruistic values, taking into account that sustainable consumption is often personally somewhat costly? Building upon the reasoning above, a key way to promote sustainable behaviour is by strengthening biospheric or altruistic values, and/or activating these values via situational cues. By doing so consumers are likely to adopt sustainable behaviour even when this is personally somewhat costly. Also, the process variables through which values affect behaviour can be targeted to promote sustainable consumption. I will elaborate on these three strategies below.

### 4.2.1 Strengthening Biospheric or Altruistic Values

An obvious strategy to encourage sustainable consumption is to strengthen consumers' biospheric or altruistic values, so that environmental consequences are more likely to be prioritized in a choice situation. Yet value theories suggest that this is more easily said than done. It is generally assumed that values develop in our lifetime and are relatively stable over time (Dietz et al. 2005; Feather 1995; Rokeach 1973; Schwartz 1997; Stern and Dietz 1994), which implies that they will not change easily. Yet, there is some initial evidence to suggest that the strength of values may change, for example when people encounter significant new experiences in their life (Brenchin and Kempton 1994; Hansen and Postmes forthcoming; Lönnqvist et al. 2011), probably particularly when these experiences take place over a longer period of time so that initial values are challenged over and over again (Bardi and Goodwin 2011). In addition value strength may change when one's significant others strongly endorse, or change their endorsement of, the relevant values (see Abrams et al. 1990). Also it has been argued that biospheric values may be strengthened when scientific evidence shows that unsustainable consumption seriously threatens our way of life, thereby providing arguments for the need to protect the environment (Lindenberg and Steg 2013). Although all plausible ways of how changes in value strength can be realized, as yet it is not clear whether these strategies will indeed be successful in strengthening biospheric and altruistic values. Future research is needed to systematically examine the conditions under which value priorities may change, and how biospheric and altruistic values can be strengthened.

### 4.2.2 Targeting Situational Cues that Activate or Deactivate Relevant Values

Another strategy to promote sustainable behaviour is to introduce situational cues that activate biospheric or altruistic values that generally promote sustainable consumption, or to remove situational cues that activate hedonic or egoistic values that mostly inhibit sustainable consumption. A wide variety of situational cues can activate biospheric or altruistic values, as I discussed earlier in this chapter, including moral (such as Bibles) or environmental symbols (Aquino et al. 2009; Perlaviciute 2014; Steg 2012; Verplanken and Holland 2002). Situational cues that activate hedonic or egoistic values (thereby deactivating biospheric and altruistic values) could be removed (such as symbols related to these values, for example bikini models, chocolate, business-related and material symbols; Kay et al. 2004; Steg 2012; Van den Bergh et al. 2008), and visceral cues such as an attractive ambient odour (Li et al. 2007). Please note that the addition or removal of situational cues will particularly affect the behaviour of those who relatively strongly endorse the relevant values; after all, values can only be activated or deactivated if these values are endorsed in the first place. Yet targeting situational cues can potentially be rather effective to promote sustainable consumption because, as indicated earlier, many people across the world do strongly endorse biospheric and altruistic values (see Steg and De Groot 2012, for a review). Future research should examine to what extent targeting various situational cues encourages consumers to act more consistently upon their biospheric or altruistic values.

Information can also be provided on the extent to which others engage in sustainable behaviour, which reflects whether they act in line with biospheric and altruistic values and respect pro-environmental norms. Research suggests that the provision of descriptive norm information (information on the behaviour of others) or socially comparative feedback (feedback about one's own performance compared with the performance of others) can be effective in promoting sustainable consumption, although the effect is not very strong (see Abrahamse and Steg 2013, for a meta-analysis). Such strategies should of course be particularly employed when most (significant) others do act sustainably; as discussed earlier, if consumers notice that the behaviour of most others is not that sustainable, and learn that most others disrespect pro-environmental norms, their biospheric and altruistic values are likely to be deactivated (see Schultz et al. 2007). Also information on value-signalling behaviour of others should be credible. For example it would be unwise to communicate that most others engage in sustainable consumption when it is obvious that this is not actually the case (see Terwel et al. 2009).

Moreover, the design of the environment can be altered so as to facilitate consumers to act upon their biospheric and altruistic values. As discussed earlier, consumers may be less likely to act upon their biospheric or altruistic values in cognitively demanding tasks that 'force' them to prioritize (other) values, or when their self-regulatory resources are depleted. A key solution here can be reducing the cognitive demands in a situation, so that consumers can allocate their scarce resources to act in line with their biospheric and altruistic values. Also, the need to exercise high levels of self-control to act upon one's biospheric or altruistic values can be reduced via environmental design. In this respect, ambient persuasive technology can be offered that promotes behaviour change without the need for the user's conscious attention, and hence with little cognitive effort (Midden and Ham 2012). For example processing interactive lighting feedback (such as: a light turns green when you conserve energy) is less cognitively demanding than processing factual feedback (such as statistics on your energy use). Ambient persuasive technologies can effectively change behaviour even when consumers lack the resources to consciously process all relevant information. More generally, when their self-regulatory resources are depleted, people are more likely to rely on heuristics when making choices (Janssen et al. 2008). Hence choice situations can be created that appeal to such heuristics, as to promote sustainable choices even when consumers have low levels of self-control. For example strategic placement of sustainable products in stores can promote their sales, and various social influence strategies can be employed to promote sustainable choices mostly outside consumers' conscious awareness (see Cialdini 2001).

Additionally, sustainable behaviour can (appear to) be made less costly so as to facilitate consumers to act upon their biospheric or altruistic values. Examples are subsidizing sustainable products, taxing unsustainable products and making sustainable behaviour fun (for example, thefuntheory.com) or convenient (for example, by increasing the availability of organic products). The actual costs and benefits of behavioural options can be changed (for example, via pricing policies, legal regulations or contextual changes; Bolderdijk et al. 2013b; Geller 2002; Steg and Vlek 2009), but in some cases it may be sufficient to change the perceptions of costs and benefits of options via information strategies as to correct misperceptions (Steg and Vlek 2009; Abrahamse and Matthies 2012). Changing the actual costs and benefits of behavioural options is particularly needed when sustainable choices are very unattractive, as high behavioural costs are likely to deactivate biospheric and altruistic values, making consumers prioritize their hedonic and egoistic values. Indeed, even those with very strong biospheric values are not likely to act upon these values when sustainable behaviour is very costly (see Steg et al. 2014a).

It is often believed that making sustainable choices relatively more attractive, or even the most attractive option, is a key strategy to promote sustainable behaviour. By employing this strategy, value conflicts can even be resolved, which implies that even consumers with strong hedonic or egoistic values would engage in sustainable behaviour, as this would also be the most pleasurable or profitable option. Yet there is a risk in solely targeting hedonic and egoistic values (for example, by making sustainable actions cheaper or more convenient), as this might activate people's egoistic and hedonic values (and deactivate their biospheric and altruistic values), thereby increasing the influence of these values on (subsequent) sustainable behaviour (Perlaviciute 2014; Steg et al. 2014a). As a consequence consumers may only engage in sustainable consumption when it is profitable or convenient to do so, and refrain from engaging in more costly or effortful sustainable behaviours (Thøgersen and Crompton 2009). Indeed people who focused on economic rather than environmental reasons for acting pro-environmentally appeared to be less inclined to engage in other sustainable behaviour on a following occasion (Evans et al. 2013). Interestingly, research suggests that durable sustainable behaviour is more likely when such behaviour is somewhat (but not too) costly or effortful (Van der Werff et al. 2014b). This counterintuitive finding can be explained by considering the effects of our previous behaviour on our environmental self-identity. As explained above, our environmental self-identity will be strengthened if we realize that we did engage in pro-environmental behaviour before (Cornelissen et al. 2008; Van der Werff et al. 2013a, 2014a), the more so when our previous actions clearly signal how pro-environmental we are (Van der Werff et al. 2014b). When sustainable behaviour is very easy, convenient or profitable, it is hard to claim that we engaged in the behaviour because we care for others and the environment. However, engaging in sustainable behaviour even though it is costly or effortful is more likely to signal care about others and the environment (see Gneezy et al. 2012).

In sum, it is sometimes necessary to change the costs and benefits of sustainable behaviour, but solely targeting hedonic and egoistic values may inhibit rather than promote durable sustainable choices. How can we solve this dilemma? One solution is targeting multiple values simultaneously (Steg et al. 2014a). For example when consumers purchase a subsidized sustainable product they can be praised for their sustainable choice (see also Bolderdijk and Steg, Chapter 21 in this book). More generally it could be clearly communicated that certain behaviours are facilitated and made more attractive because they are sustainable options, and people can be made aware of the fact that they chose a sustainable product or service. Future research is needed to test whether and under which conditions such approaches can be successful. Besides, sustainable behaviours sometimes support rather than threaten hedonic or egoistic values. For example, sustainable consumption can enhance consumers' status, as it signals to others that they have sufficient resources to make altruistic sacrifices (Griskevicius et al. 2010). In a similar vein the likelihood of adoption of sustainable innovations appears to be higher when consumers expect that such adoption would enhance their status and enable them to express their identity (Noppers et al. 2014). Moreover various studies suggest that people derive pleasure and satisfaction from engaging in sustainable consumption (Bolderdijk et al. 2012; Carrus et al. 2008; Pelletier et al. 1998). These findings suggest that it may be worthwhile to target different values simultaneously, by highlighting the hedonic and egoistic benefits of sustainable consumption in conjunction with its benefits for others and the environment.

### 4.2.3 Targeting Process Variables through which Values Affect Behaviour

The final strategy involves targeting the process variables through which values affect sustainable consumption. Below I discuss briefly key strategies that have proved to be effective in changing the process variables discussed earlier in this chapter (see section 4.1.2). To start with, information can be provided as to change consumers' beliefs about the pros and cons of sustainable consumption, and to increase their awareness of environmental and social problems caused by their consumption patterns. Yet, as indicated above, such information will be particularly effective when it resonates with consumers' central values (Bolderdijk et al. 2013a). This may be one of the reasons why general information campaigns appear to have limited effects on sustainable consumption (see Abrahamse et al. 2005; Schultz et al. 1995, for reviews). Information strategies have been more successful when they were tailored to the needs, wants and perceived barriers of the target population (Abrahamse et al. 2007; Thøgersen 2005).

Next, consumers could be made aware of the sustainable behaviour of others. This may not only activate their biospheric and altruistic values, as explained above, but also increase their feeling of outcome efficacy. That is, knowing that many others engaged in sustainable consumption may strengthen consumers' feeling that environmental problems can be reduced via sustainable consumption. Various social influence strategies can be employed in this respect, including block leader approaches, group feedback, socially comparative feedback, and social norm information and feedback; in particular, block leader approaches appear to be effective in promoting sustainable consumption (see Abrahamse and Steg 2013).

Besides commitment strategies (in which people make a promise to engage in sustainable behaviour), implementation intentions (in which people promise to engage in sustainable behaviour, and indicate how and when they will do so) appear to be effective in promoting sustainable consumption (see Abrahamse et al. 2005; Abrahamse and Steg 2013; Lokhorst et al. 2013, for reviews). Although little is known about the processes through which both strategies affect behaviour, one plausible explanation is that they strengthen personal norms; that is, once people commit themselves to engage in sustainable consumption, they are motivated to act in line with their promise as they want to (appear to) be consistent (Abrahamse and Steg 2013).

Finally, as explained earlier, the environmental self-identity can be strengthened by reminding people of their previous behaviours that signal how pro-environmental they are. Future research is needed to test how this insight can fruitfully be employed in campaigns and purchase situations.

## 4.3 SUMMARY AND CONCLUSION

Sustainable consumption is often associated with some behavioural costs and additional effort. Despite this, many consumers engage in sustainable consumption. In this chapter I discussed two key factors that motivate them to do so: values, and situational cues that affect the extent to which relevant values are activated in a given situation. I argued that consumers are more likely to act sustainably when they strongly endorse biospheric and altruistic values, while consumers with strong egoistic and hedonic values are less likely to act sustainably. I discussed three processes through which values affect sustainable consumption: values affect how consumers evaluate different consequences of behaviour, which influences their preferences and behaviour; values may affect sustainable consumption via a process of norm activation; and values affect sustainable consumption behaviour via the environmental self-identity, that is, the extent to which a person sees himself or herself as a pro-environmental person. Importantly, values need to be activated in order to be influential and steer decision-making. I discussed various situational factors that can activate and deactivate relevant values, thereby increasing the likelihood of sustainable consumption: value-activating cues, value-signalling behaviour of others that reflect the level of support for norms, cognitive demands in situations and situational factors that affect the costliness of sustainable consumption. Finally, I discussed three general strategies that can be employed to promote sustainable consumption: strengthening biospheric or altruistic values; targeting situational cues that activate biospheric and altruistic values and/or deactivate egoistic and hedonic values; and targeting process variables through which values affect behaviour.

## REFERENCES

Abrahamse, W. and E. Matthies (2012), 'Information strategies to promote pro-environmental behaviour: changing knowledge, awareness and attitudes', in L. Steg, A.E. van den Berg and J.I.M. de Groot (eds), *Environmental Psychology: An Introduction*, Oxford: John Wiley & Sons, pp. 223–232.

Abrahamse, W. and L. Steg (2011), 'Factors related to household energy use and intention to reduce it: the role of psychological and socio-demographic variables', *Human Ecology Review*, 18 (1), 30–40.

Abrahamse, W. and L. Steg (2013), 'Social influence approaches to encourage resource conservation: a meta-analysis', *Global Environmental Change*, 23, 1773–1785.

Abrahamse, W., L. Steg, C. Vlek and T. Rothengatter (2005), 'A review of intervention studies aimed at household energy conservation', *Journal of Environmental Psychology*, 25, 273–291.

Abrahamse, W., L. Steg, C. Vlek and T. Rothengatter (2007), 'The effect of tailored information, goal setting and tailored feedback on household energy use, energy-related behaviors and behavioral antecedents', *Journal of Environmental Psychology*, 27, 265–276.

Abrams, D., M. Wetherell, S. Cochrane, M.A. Hogg and J.C. Turner (1990), 'Knowing what to think by knowing who you are: self-categorization and the nature of norm formation, conformity, and group polarization', *British Journal of Social Psychology*, 29, 97–119.

Aquino, K., D. Freeman, A. Reed II, V.K.G. Lim and W. Felps (2009), 'Testing a social-cognitive model of moral behaviour: the interactive influence of situations and moral identity centrality', *Journal of Personality and Social Psychology*, 97, 123–141.

Bamberg, S. and S. Schmidt (2003), 'Incentives, morality or habit? Predicting students' car use for university routes with the models of Ajzen, Schwartz and Triandis', *Environment and Behavior*, 35 (2), 264–285.

Bardi, A. and R. Goodwin (2011), 'The dual route to value change: Individual processes and cultural moderators', *Journal of Cross-Cultural Psychology*, 42, 271–287.

Baumeister, R.F., E. Bratslavsky, M. Muraven and D.M. Tice (1998), 'Ego depletion: is the active self a limited resource?', *Journal of Personality and Social Psychology*, 74 (5), 1252–1265.

Baumeister, R.F. and K.D. Vohs (2007), 'Self-regulation, ego depletion, and motivation', *Social and Psychology Compass*, 1, 1–14.

Bolderdijk, J.W., M. Gorsira, K.E. Keizer and L. Steg (2013a), 'Values determine the (in)effectiveness of informational interventions in promoting pro-environmental behavior', *PLoS ONE*, 8 (12), e83911.

Bolderdijk, J.W., P.K. Lehman and E.S. Geller (2013b), 'Encouraging pro-environmental behaviour with rewards and penalties', in L. Steg, A.E. van den Berg and J.I.M. de Groot (eds), *Environmental Psychology: An Introduction*, Oxford: John Wiley & Sons, pp. 233–242.

Bolderdijk, J.W., L. Steg, E.S. Geller, P.K. Lehman and T. Postmes (2012), 'Comparing the effectiveness of monetary versus moral motives in environmental campaigning', *Nature Climate Change*, 3, 413–416.

Brenchin, S.R. and W. Kempton (1994), 'Global environmentalism: a challenge to the materialism thesis?', *Social Science Quarterly*, 75, 245–269.

Carrus, G., P. Passafaro and M. Bonnes (2008), 'Emotions, habits and rational choices in ecological behaviours: the case of recycling and use of public transportation', *Journal of Environmental Psychology*, 28, 51–62.

Cialdini, R.B. (2001), *Influence: Science and Practice*, 4th edn, Boston, MA: Allyn & Bacon.

Cialdini, R.B. (2003), 'Crafting normative messages to protect the environment', *Current Directions in Psychological Science*, 12 (4), 105–109.

Cialdini, R.B., R.R. Reno and C.A. Kallgren (1990), 'A focus theory of normative conduct: recycling the concept of norms to reduce littering in public places', *Journal of Personality and Social Psychology*, 58 (6), 1015–1026.

Cornelissen, G., M. Pandelaere, L. Warlop and S. Dewitte (2008), 'Positive cueing: promoting sustainable consumer behavior by cueing common environmental behaviors as environmental', *International Journal of Research in Marketing*, 25 (1), 46–55.

De Groot, J. and L. Steg (2007), 'Value orientations and environmental beliefs in five countries: validity of an instrument to measure egoistic, altruistic and biospheric value orientations', *Journal of Cross-Cultural Psychology*, 38 (3), 318–332.

De Groot, J.I.M., L. Steg and W. Poortinga (2013), 'Values, perceived risks and benefits, and acceptability of nuclear energy', *Risk Analysis*, 33 (2), 307–317.

Dogan, E.B., L. Steg and P. Delhomme (2011), 'The influence of multiple goals on driving behavior: the case of safety, time saving, and fuel saving', *Accident Analysis and Prevention*, 43, 1635–1643.

Diekmann, A. and P. Preisendörfer (2003), 'Green and greenback: the behavioural effects of environmental attitudes in low-cost and high-cost situations', *Rationality and Society*, 15 (4), 441–472.

Dietz, T., A. Fitzgerald and R. Shwom (2005), 'Environmental values', *Annual Review of Environmental Resources*, 30, 355–372.

Evans, L, G.R. Maio, A. Corner, C.J. Hodgetts, S. Ahmed and U. Hahn (2013), 'Self-interest and pro-environmental behaviour', *Nature Climate Change*, 3 (2), 122–125.

Feather, N.T. (1995), 'Values, valences, and choice: the influence of values on the perceived attractiveness and choice of alternatives', *Journal of Personality and Social Psychology*, 68, 1135–1151.

Gärling, T., S. Fujii, A. Gärling and C. Jakobsson (2003), 'Moderating effects of social value orientation on determinants of proenvironmental intention', *Journal of Environmental Psychology*, 23, 1–9.

Geller, E.S. (2002), 'The challenge of increasing proenvironmental behavior', in R.B. Bechtel and A. Churchman (eds), *Handbook of Environmental Psychology*, New York: Wiley, pp. 525–540.

Gifford, R. (2007), *Environmental Psychology: Principles and Practice*, Colville, WA: Optimal Books.

Gino, F., S. Ayal and D. Ariely (2009), 'Contagion and differentiation in unethical behavior: the effect of one bad apple on the barrel', *Psychological Science*, 20 (3), 393–398.

Gneezy, A., A. Imas, A. Brown, L.D. Nelson and M.I. Norton (2012), 'Paying to be nice: Consistency and costly prosocial behavior', *Management Science*, 58 (1), 179–187.

Griskevicius, V., J.M. Tybur and B. Van den Bergh (2010), 'Going green to be seen: status, reputation, and conspicuous conservation', *Journal of Personality and Social Psychology*, 98, 392–404.

Grønhøj, A. and J. Thøgersen (2009), 'Like father, like son? Intergenerational transmission of values, attitudes, and behaviours in the environmental domain', *Journal of Environmental Psychology*, 29, 414–421.

Hansen, N. and T. Postmes (forthcoming), How modernization instigates social change: laptop usage as a driver of gender equality and cultural value change in a developing country, *Journal of Cross-Cultural Psychology*.

Harland, P., H. Staats and H. Wilke (1999), 'Explaining proenvironmental behavior by personal norms and the theory of planned behavior', *Journal of Applied Social Psychology*, 29, 2505–2528.

Jakovcevic, A., J. Díaz-Marín, C. Moreno, S. Geiger and G. Tonello (2013), 'Valores y cuidado de la energía: implicancias para la educación ambiental en Argentina y Columbia', *Revista Latinoamericana de Psicología*, 45 (3), 387–398.

Jakovcevic, A. and L. Steg (2013), 'Sustainable transportation in Argentina: values, beliefs, norms and car use reduction', *Transportation Research-F*, 20, 70–79.

Janssen, L., B.M. Fennis, A.T.H. Pruyn and K.D. Vohs (2008), 'The path of least resistance: regulatory resource depletion and the effectiveness of social influence techniques', *Journal of Business Research*, 61, 1041–1045.

Kasser, T., S. Kohn, A.D. Kanner and R.M. Ryan (2007), 'Some costs of American corporate capitalism: a psychological exploration of value and goal conflicts', *Psychological Inquiry*, 18, 1–22.

Kasser, T. and K.M. Sheldon (2000), 'On wealth and death: materialism, mortality salience, and consumption behavior', *Psychological Science*, 11, 348–351.

Kay, A.C., S.C. Wheerler, J.A. Bargh and L. Ross (2004), 'Material priming: the influence of mundane physical objects on situational construal and competitive behaviour choice', *Organizational Behavior and Human Decision Processes*, 95, 83–96.

Keizer, K., S. Lindenberg and L. Steg (2008), 'The spreading of disorder', *Science*, 322, 1681–1685.

Keizer, K., S.M. Lindenberg and L. Steg (2011), 'The reversal effects of prohibition signs', *Group Processes and Intergroup Relations*, 14 (5), 681–688.

Keizer, K., S. Lindenberg and L. Steg (2013), 'The importance of demonstratively restoring order', *PLoS ONE*, 8 (6), e65137.

Li, W., I. Moallem, K.A. Paller and J.A. Gottfried (2007), 'Subliminal smells can guide social preferences', *Psychological Science*, 18, 1044–1049.

Lindenberg, S.M. (2012), 'How cues in the environment affect normative behavior', in L. Steg, A.E. Van den Berg and J.I.M. De Groot (eds), *Environmental Psychology: An Introduction*, New York: Wiley, pp. 119–128.
Lindenberg, S. and L. Steg (2007), 'Normative, gain and hedonic goal-frames guiding environmental behaviour', *Journal of Social Issues*, 63 (1), 117–137.
Lindenberg, S. and L. Steg (2013), 'Goal-framing theory and norm-guided environmental behavior', in H.C.M. van Trijp (ed.), *Encouraging Sustainable Behaviour*, New York: Psychology Press, pp. 37–54.
Lokhorst, A.M., C.M. Werner, H. Staats, E. van Dijk and J.L. Gale (2013), 'Commitment and behavior change: a meta-analysis and critical review of commitment making strategies in environmental research', *Environment and Behavior*, 45 (1), 3–34.
Lönnqvist, J.E., I. Jasinskaja-Lahti and M. Verkasalo (2011), 'Personal values before and after migration: a longitudinal case study on value change in Ingrian-Finnish migrants', *Social Psychology and Personality Science*, 2, 584–591.
Maio, G.R. (2010), 'Mental representations of social values', in M.P. Zanna (ed.), *Advances in Experimental Social Psychology*, San Diego, CA: Academic Press, pp. 1–43.
Midden, C. and J. Ham (2012), 'Persuasive technology to promote pro-environmental behaviour', in L. Steg, A.E. Van den Berg and J.I.M. De Groot (eds), *Environmental Psychology: An Introduction*, New York: Wiley, pp. 241–254.
Nilsson, A., C. Von Borgstede and A. Biel (2004), 'Willingness to accept climate change policy measures: the effect of values and norms', *Journal of Environmental Psychology*, 24, 267–277.
Noppers, E., K.E. Keizer, J.W. Bolderdijk and L. Steg (2014), 'The adoption of sustainable innovations: driven by symbolic and environmental motives', *Global Environmental Change*, 25, 52–62.
Nordlund, A.M. and J. Garvill (2002), 'Value structures behind pro-environmental behavior', *Environment and Behavior*, 34, 740–756.
Pelletier, L.G., K.M. Tuson, I. Green-Demers, K. Noëls and A.M. Beaton (1998), 'Why are you doing things for the environment? The motivation toward the environment scale', *Journal of Applied Social Psychology*, 28, 437–468.
Perlaviciute, G. (2014), 'Goal driven evaluations of sustainable products', PhD thesis, University of Groningen, Faculty of Behavioural and Social Sciences.
Reno, R.R., R.B. Cialdini and C.A. Kallgren (1993), 'The transsituational influence of social norms', *Journal of Personality and Social Psychology*, 64 (1), 104–112.
Rokeach, M. (1973), *The Nature of Human Values*, New York: Free Press.
Ruepert, A.M., L. Steg and K. Keizer (in press), 'Theoretical basis for organizational pro-environmental research', in J. Barling and J. Robertson (eds), *The Psychology of Green Organisations*, Oxford: Oxford University Press.
Schultz, P.W., V.V. Gouveia, L.D. Cameron, G. Tankha, P. Schmuck and M. Franěk (2005), 'Values and their relationship to environmental concern and conservation behavior', *Journal of Cross-Cultural Psychology*, 36, 457–475.
Schultz, P.W., J.M. Nolan, R.B. Cialdini, N.J. Goldstein and V. Griskevicius (2007), 'The constructive, destructive, and reconstructive power of social norms', *Psychological Science*, 18, 429–434.
Schultz, P.W., S. Oskamp and T. Mainieri (1995), 'Who recycles and when? A review of personal and situational factors', *Journal of Environmental Psychology*, 15, 105–121.
Schwartz, S.H. (1977), 'Normative influences on altruism', in L. Berkowitz (ed.), *Advances in Experimental Social Psychology*, New York: Academic Press, pp. 221–279.
Schwartz, S.H. (1992), 'Universals in the content and structure of values: theoretical advances and empirical tests in 20 countries', in M. Zanna (ed.), *Advances in Experimental Social Psychology*, Orlando, FL: Academic Press, pp. 1–65.
Schwartz, S.H. (1997), 'Values and culture', in D. Munro, S. Carr and J. Schumaker (eds), *Motivation and Culture*, New York: Routledge, pp. 69–84.
Steg, L. (2008), 'Promoting household energy conservation', *Energy Policy*, 36, 4449–4453.
Steg, L. (2012), 'Niets duurt voort behalve verandering: De mens als sleutel tot duurzaamheid', inaugural talk, Groningen: University of Groningen, Faculty of Behavioural and Social Sciences.
Steg, L., J.W. Bolderdijk, K.E. Keizer and G. Perlaviciute (2014a), 'An integrated framework for encouraging pro-environmental behaviour: The role of values, situational factors and goals', *Journal of Environmental Psychology*, 38, 104–115.
Steg, L. and J.I.M. De Groot (2010), 'Explaining prosocial intentions: testing causal relationships in the norm activation model', *British Journal of Social Psychology*, 49 (4), 725–743.
Steg, L. and J.I.M. De Groot (2012), 'Environmental values', in S. Clayton (ed.), *The Oxford Handbook of Environmental and Conservation* Psychology, New York: Oxford University Press, pp. 81–92.
Steg, L., L. Dreijerink and W. Abrahamse (2005), 'Factors influencing the acceptability of energy policies: testing VBN theory', *Journal of Environmental Psychology*, 25 (4), 415–425.
Steg, L. and A. Nordlund (2012), 'Models to explain environmental behaviour', in L. Steg, A.E. van den

Berg and J.I.M. de Groot (eds), *Environmental Psychology: An Introduction*, Oxford: John Wiley & Sons, pp. 1–11.
Steg, L., G. Perlaviciute, E. Van der Werff and J. Lurvink (2014b), 'The significance of hedonic values for environmentally-relevant attitudes, preferences and actions', *Environment and Behavior*, 46 (2), 163–192.
Steg, L., A.E. Van den Berg and J.I.M. De Groot (eds) (2012), *Environmental Psychology: An Introduction*, Oxford: John Wiley & Sons.
Steg, L. and C. Vlek (2009), 'Encouraging pro-environmental behaviour: an integrative review and research agenda', *Journal of Environmental Psychology*, 29, 309–317.
Stern, P.C. (2000), 'Toward a coherent theory of environmentally significant behavior', *Journal of Social Issues*, 56 (3), 407–424.
Stern, P.C. and T. Dietz (1994), 'The value basis of environmental concern', *Journal of Social Issues*, 50, 65–84.
Stern, P.C., T. Dietz and G.A. Guagnano (1998), 'A brief inventory of values', *Educational and Psychological Measurement*, 58 (6), 984–1001.
Stern, P.C., T. Dietz, L. Kalof and G.A. Guagnano (1995), 'Values, beliefs, and pro-environmental action: attitude formation toward emergent attitude objects', *Journal of Applied Social Psychology*, 25, 1611–1636.
Terwel, B.W., F. Harinck, N. Ellemers and D.D.L. Daamen (2009), 'How organizational motives and communications affect public trust in organizations: the case of carbon dioxide capture and storage', *Journal of Environmental Psychology*, 29, 290–299.
Thøgersen, J. (2005), 'How may consumer policy empower consumers for sustainable lifestyles', *Journal of Consumer Policy*, 28, 143–178.
Thøgersen, J. and T. Crompton (2009), 'Simple and painless? The limitations of spillover in environmental campaigning', *Journal of Consumer Policy*, 32, 141–163.
Thøgersen, J. and F. Ölander (2002), 'Human values and the emergence of a sustainable consumption pattern: a panel study', *Journal of Economic Psychology*, 23, 605–630.
Van den Bergh, B., S. Dewitte and L. Warlop (2008), 'Bikinis instigate generalized impatience in intertemporal choice', *Journal of Consumer Research*, 35, 85–97.
Van der Werff, E., L. Steg and K.E. Keizer (2013a), 'It is a moral issue: The relationship between environmental self-identity, obligation-based intrinsic motivation and pro-environmental behaviour', *Global Environmental Change*, 23, 1258–1265.
Van der Werff, E., L. Steg and K.E. Keizer (2013b), 'The value of environmental self-identity: the relationship between biospheric values, environmental self-identity and environmental preferences, intentions and behavior', *Journal of Environmental Psychology*, 34, 55–63.
Van der Werff, E., L. Steg and K.E. Keizer (2014a), 'I am what I am, by looking past the present: the influence of biospheric values and past behaviour on environmental self-identity', *Environment and Behavior*, 46 (5), 626–657.
Van der Werff, E., L. Steg and K.E. Keizer (2014b), 'Follow the signal: when past pro-environmental actions signal who you are', *Journal of Environmental Psychology*, 40, 273–282.
Verplanken, B. and R.W. Holland (2002), 'Motivated decision making: effects of activation and self-centrality of values on choices and behaviour', *Journal of Personality and Social Psychology*, 82, 434–447.
Vlek, C. (1996), 'Collective risk generation and risk management: the unexploited potential of the social dilemmas paradigm', in W.B.G. Liebrand and D.M. Messick (eds), *Frontiers in Social Dilemmas Research*, Berlin: Springer, pp. 11–38.
Whitmarsh, L. and S. O'Neill (2010), 'Green identity, green living? The role of pro-environmental self-identity in determining consistency across diverse pro-environmental behaviours', *Journal of Environmental Psychology*, 30, 305–314.

# 5. Theories of practice and sustainable consumption

*Daniel Welch and Alan Warde*

The year 2001 saw the publication of a book entitled *The Practice Turn in Contemporary Theory* (Schatzki et al. 2001). More a declaration of intent than a monument to a newly established orthodoxy, it marks a point of theoretical confluence which has had significant impact on the study of sustainable consumption. Theories of practice – in the plural, for there is no single accepted version of such a theory – are applicable in principle to any domain of activity, and have been adopted for use within many social scientific disciplines, but they seem to have produced particularly promising applications in the understanding of sustainable consumption. Theories of practice make several moves in the explanation of personal conduct and social organization which are unorthodox. For example when giving an account of human activity the roles of conscious intention, of individual autonomy and of decision making are played down, and explanation focuses on the organization of practices rather than on individuals.

Such recalibrations of perspective throw a different light on activities such as consumption and, *a fortiori*, on sustainable consumption. Protecting Planet Earth from the consequences of human-induced climate change and environmental degradation will be a formidable, collective, political endeavour which entails a radical transformation in the patterns, forms and levels of consumption in wealthier societies. Research conducted under the auspices of theories of practice has picked up on the near impossibility of current responses successfully resolving the problem. This chapter is therefore designed against the background of a highly intractable set of political difficulties upon which a new theoretical perspective offers fresh insight about the nature of the problem and its solution.

In this chapter we present a brief history of the construction of basic elements of the theories of practice as formulated in the later twentieth century. There are many disputes within the camp of practice theorists and the general movement is very much a project still in the making. Exposition of internal differences in approach is therefore essential, even at the expense of exposition being sometimes rather detailed. We present the development of practice theoretical approaches to sustainable consumption by way of a (somewhat stylized) contrast between two research programmes: one emerging from ecological modernization theory, the other more entrenched in or heavily dependent upon current 'strong' revisions of theories of practice. We detect some degree of convergence between the two at the beginning of the second decade of the twenty-first century. Nevertheless the contrast serves to reveal points of tension within practice-theoretical-inspired research strategies and to identify contrasting proposals for political intervention in the name of sustainability. Consequently we reveal some of the internal problems of theories of practice, some of which have been (sometimes tortuously) resolved. We conclude by identifying three analytic problems whose clarification and resolution would enhance the power of practice theories: the first concerns the relationship between production and consumption; the second concerns the relationship between collective agency and quotidian routine; and the third concerns the relationship between the minutiae of everyday performances of practices and the macro-institutional context.

## 5.1 THE DEVELOPMENT OF THEORIES OF PRACTICE

Theories of practice are currently widely employed across the disciplines of the humanities and social sciences and have become increasingly prominent in discussions of sustainable consumption. We refer to theories in the plural because there are several different, though of course related, versions. Concepts of practice and praxis have a long history in the social sciences (see Nicolini 2012). However the forms in which they are currently manifested derive from attempts in the 1970s to resolve some fundamental puzzles in social theory, ones of particular interest to sociologists and anthropologists (Ortner 1984; Rouse 2006). Probably the most important of these was the issue of the relationship between structure and agency, but controversy over the relative merits of holism and methodological individualism was also significant.

Recently Nicolini (2012) has surveyed in magisterial fashion the full and wide range of practice theories now in circulation. He distinguishes between: the praxeological theories of Giddens (1984) and Bourdieu (1977); practice as tradition and community (Wenger 1998; MacIntyre 1981); practice as activity (Vygotsky and cultural and historical activity theory); practice as accomplishment, in the manner of ethnomethodology; practice as the locus of the social (as in Schatzki's 1996, 2002 reworking of Heidegger and Wittgenstein); and practice as discourse, which he elaborates via conversation analysis and a review of Foucault. It is difficult to specify what these theories have in common. Nicolini (2012) concurs with Schatzki (2001) that there is no unified practice approach. Nevertheless he notes 'a number of family resemblances' among theories from which he isolates some suggestions for how to undertake empirical studies (Schatzki 2001, p. 11). Reckwitz (2002) helpfully observes that while all cultural theories oppose both the utilitarian or rational-choice models of social action and order, and the classical sociological norm-orientated model of social action and order (that is, Durkheim and Parsons), what unites the heterogeneity of practice theories is the contention that social order and action is a feature of, and established through, the field of human practices. Practice theories' central claim is to move beyond problematic dualisms like structure and agency, methodological individualism and holism, determinism and voluntarism, and subject and object. Moreover, as Schatzki (2001, p. 14) suggests, 'these accounts all undermine the traditional individual–nonindividual divide by availing themselves of features of both sides'. Social practices, then, rather than individuals (and their attitudes and preferences), norms, cultural codes, discourses, macro-level trends or social structures become the central unit of analysis; and in policy-oriented accounts of sustainable consumption, they become the central unit of intervention (Shove 2010; Shove and Walker 2010; Spurling et al. 2013).

Whilst there is considerable variation in the definition of what constitutes a social practice,[1] a minimal definition might be an organized, and recognizable, socially shared bundle of activities that involves the integration of a complex array of components: material, embodied, ideational and affective. Practices are sets of 'doings and sayings'; they involve both 'practical activity and its representations' (Warde 2005, p. 134).

A useful analytical distinction can be made between practices as performances and practices as entities (Schatzki 1996; Shove et al. 2012; Warde 2005). Practices as entities have a history and a trajectory, or path of development, but at the same time only exist through their performance. Performance and entity are therefore recursively related rather as agency and structure in Giddens's theory of structuration.

Theories of practice began to be applied explicitly to the analysis of consumption at the beginning of the twenty-first century. Warde's (2005) paper, 'Consumption and theories of practice', is widely regarded as the first programmatic application of practice theory to the field of consumption (e.g. Halkier et al. 2011; Røpke 2009). Perhaps the central contribution of the paper is to reconceptualize consumption as 'not itself a practice but . . . rather, a moment in almost every practice' (Warde 2005, p. 137). Thus for Warde, whilst there are practices in which people may understand their behaviour as 'consuming', such as shopping, these are by far the exception amongst practices in which consumption is a moment. The figure of 'the consumer' is decentred from accounts of consumption as 'wants are fulfilled only in practice, their satisfaction attributable to effective practical performances' (Warde 2005, p. 142):

> The analytic focus shifts from the insatiable wants of the human animal to the instituted conventions of collective culture, from personal expression to social competence, from mildly constrained choice to disciplined participation. From this angle the concept of 'the consumer' . . . evaporates. Instead the key focal points become the organization of the practice and the moments of consumption enjoined. (Warde 2005 p. 146)

Warde defines the generic components of practice as: understandings (know-how and practical interpretation), procedures (rules, principles, instructions) and engagements (affective and normative orientations). The identification of the components of practice, their coordination, histories and dynamics, thus becomes a core task for the analysis of practices in the field of sustainable consumption (e.g. Halkier 2010).

Advocacy of practice theories emanated in part from dissatisfaction with aspects of the analysis of consumption when viewed through the lens of cultural theory. The context was one of reaction to 'the cultural turn' in the human and social sciences, which was hegemonic during the final quarter of the twentieth century. The cultural turn emphasized the symbolic and the conspicuous aspects of consumption, their role in communication and their support for 'expressive individualism'. Indeed when the editors of the first social science collection addressing sustainable consumption (Cohen and Murphy 2001, p. xi) brought together environmental social scientists with scholars of consumption, the subject area of the latter was described as 'attention on the role of consumption in identity formation and communication'. An even more prevalent, and complementary, tendency was to offer individualistic explanations in terms of the figure of 'the consumer'. Thus analysis of consumption was founded upon models of an empowered individual, exercising freedom of choice through voluntary decisions.

In studying consumption, theories of practice promise new perspectives: first, by providing an alternative to models of individual choice, whether based upon the sovereign or the expressive individual; and second, by uncovering and exploring phenomena normally concealed in cultural analysis. It was a reaction both to the overbearing tendency to offer explanations of action in terms of the individual actor and to the exaggeration of the importance of the symbolic in the steering of consumption. Against the model of the sovereign consumer, practice theory emphasizes routine over actions, flow and sequence over discrete acts, dispositions over decisions, and practical consciousness over deliberation. In reaction to the cultural turn, emphasis is placed upon doing over thinking, the material over the symbolic, and embodied practical competence over expressive virtuosity in the fashioned presentation of self.

When Ortner (1984) spotted a tendency for practice theory to be (re-)emergent in the social sciences during the 1970s, she discussed at length three figures who turned out to dominate subsequent debates in sociological theory in Europe: Bourdieu, Giddens and Foucault. Subsequent work by Schatzki (1996, 2002) also played a very important role in reorienting discussion. We suggest that much of the variation in, and potential use of, theories of practice can be attributed to the different positions of these four authors. Of the first three, Giddens had the major impact in the early development of sociological approaches to sustainable consumption. Initially Giddens's theory of structuration seemed to offer an attractive general solution to the structure–agency problem. His insistence upon the need to develop an appropriate concept of agency (Giddens 1984), which was in reaction to the earlier dominance of structuralist and functionalist theories, seemed especially attractive and was enthusiastically adopted by leading scholars as a foundation for practice-theoretical approaches to environmentally relevant consumption – by Spaargaren and Shove especially. Despite his seminal influence on the sociology of consumption Bourdieu's work has made little impact in the field of sustainable consumption, though there are currently signs of recuperation. Foucault has been a persistent background influence, as well as providing resources for a small body of work addressing sustainable consumption as 'green governmentality' implicated in the neoliberal project of 'responsibilization of the consumer' (e.g. Rumpala 2011; see Barnett et al. 2011 for a critique of this position).

## 5.2 THE SOCIOLOGY OF SUSTAINABLE CONSUMPTION

Theories of practice have been deployed in a growing corpus of empirical studies of consumption in research areas including eating, recreational enthusiasms and listening to music. However, probably the most important domain of application has been sustainable consumption.

Sustainable consumption was initially conceived as the necessary 'downstream' complement to the 'ecological modernization' of production required in order to achieve a transition towards environmental sustainability (Spaargaren and Martens 2005). Sustainable consumption policy focused attention on the huge impact of specifically domestic consumption and deployed behaviour change strategies drawing primarily on psychology and behavioural economics, which deploy individualistic models. Whilst some influential works of environmental sociology had stressed the role of consumption in the ecological crisis (e.g. Redclift 1996) they failed to provide an adequate account of the determinants of behaviour relevant to environmental impacts. Equally Shove and Warde (2002) noted that the extant sociology of consumption offered limited tools in this area, and that understanding sustainable consumption would require the sociology of consumption to move beyond a focus on the individual consumer to the social organization of consumption. The burgeoning policy area of sustainable consumption offered the sociology of consumption a new research agenda, and theories of practice the theoretical and methodological resources to implement it.

Theories of practice have an affinity with the analysis of sustainable consumption for several reasons. Firstly, one is that the inconspicuous consumption of energy and resources in the use of goods and services in the accomplishment of everyday routine tasks (for example, doing the laundry, showering or commuting) as opposed to simply their acquisition, has profound environmental impacts. Furthermore such use is not amenable to explanations based on models of consumer choice, and approaches to consumption based in cultural theory have little purchase, due to their concern with symbolic display, communication and the presentation of self (Shove and Warde 2002). Secondly, goods and services are primarily put to use for the accomplishment of social practices (for example, sharing a meal, playing sport or gardening), rather than for their consumption per se, drawing attention to the dynamics of social practices for explanatory resources for the escalating environmental impact of consumption (Warde 2005). Thirdly, theories of practice offer the sociology of sustainable consumption an understanding of social action that promised a way out of the cul-de-sac of the 'value–action' or 'attitude–behaviour' gap: the phenomenon of the discrepancy between reported pro-environmental values and obdurately unsustainable behaviour.

The purported gap between attitudes and actions, which has become the centrepiece of so much policy intervention and analysis, arises from widely shared conceptual premises that social action is driven by anterior conditions, variously: norms (in classical sociology), attitudes (in social psychology) and preferences or interests (in economics). It derives from a common model of the human subject, which Hindess (1990) calls 'the portfolio model', wherein the subject possesses a more or less stable portfolio of beliefs and desires and selects from them to decide on the course of action. This ontology is shared, despite all their apparent opposition, by both theoretical traditions of structuralism and methodological individualism. Thus for the structuralist the 'content of the portfolio is a function of the actor's social location' (Hindess 1990, p. 88). The rational-choice model of the sovereign consumer makes a further refinement of the model, adding the assumption that the actor's portfolio of desires has a utilitarian structure (ibid.).

From the perspective of theories of practice this model of action structurally overestimates the role of deliberation in routine purposive tasks, and fundamentally underestimates the extent to which individuals' autonomous action is constrained by infrastructures and socio-technical systems and by the collective and normative derivation of most consumption, routinely conducted within the context of resource constraints: social, cultural and economic (Southerton et al. 2004).

This said, the topic of agency remains one of considerable controversy. Indeed we suggest that the understanding of agency marks a key contrast between two, relatively distinct, major programmes in the field of sustainable consumption.

## 5.3 TWO PRACTICE-THEORETICAL PROGRAMMES FOR SUSTAINABLE CONSUMPTION

The two programmes can each be exemplified by a key theorist in the sociology of sustainable consumption: Gert Spaargaren and Elisabeth Shove. While there are multiple points of contact between the two, each draws on different intellectual resources, addresses distinct empirical areas of enquiry, and envisages differing political and policy implications.

Spaargaren drew on Giddens's structuration theory to explore the behaviour, roles and capacities of 'citizen-consumers' in promoting the 'ecological modernisation' of consumption, in the context of globalized environmental governance (Spaargaren and Van Vliet 2000). This first programme therefore focuses on purposive projects and social and cultural activities explicitly oriented by sustainable consumption: sustainability policy initiatives and behaviour change programmes; 'citizen-consumer' engagements and 'sustainable lifestyles' (e.g. Spaargaren 2003; Spaargaren and Martens 2005; Spaargaren and Oosterveer 2010).

Shove, on the other hand, is centrally concerned with understanding the dynamics of everyday practices, how practices emerge, persist and disappear, and how expectations and conventions become naturalized. This programme seeks to understand the complex causalities that lead to more (or less) resource-intensive practices (e.g. Shove 2003, 2004), and the implications of such for policy (e.g. Shove 2010; Shove and Walker 2010; Shove et al. 2012; Spurling et al. 2013). Shove suggested a fundamental rethinking of the research agenda for the sociology of sustainable consumption, arguing that:

> [I]nvestigations into the beliefs and actions of self-confessed environmentalists represent something of a distraction. What counts is the big, and in some cases, global swing of ordinary, routinized and taken-for-granted practice . . . Only by setting 'the environment' aside as the main focus of attention will it be possible to follow and analyse processes underpinning the normalization of consumption and the escalation of demand. (Shove 2003, p. 9)

Spaargaren's understanding of the 'transformative capacity' of individual and collective agency mediated by social structures, whilst acknowledging the constraining force of those structures, posited human agency 'as something that could explain the dynamics of systems of provision' (Spaargaren and Van Vliet 2000, p. 63). Shove (2003, pp. 12–13), on the other hand, drawing intellectual inspiration from science and technology studies (e.g. Akrich 1992) and innovation studies (e.g. Rip and Kemp 1998), emphasized how ways of life 'are situated and inscribed in tools, devices and material objects', the 'mutual constitution of technologies and their . . . users', and the 'potentially constitutive role of things and sociotechnical systems'. Spaargaren professed optimism in citizen-consumers' conscious efforts to alter the organization of practices, in reflexive subjects' capacity to establish new, more sustainable routines, and in the dynamics of capitalism to shift in a sustainable direction. Shove, by contrast, professed scepticism that environmentally inspired consumers' commitments could redefine conventions of everyday life, questioned whether explicit contestation was a prerequisite for enduring change, and emphasized processes of path-dependency (Shove 2003, 2004; Chappells et al. 2011). Before turning to what appears to be a convergence of the two programmes let us outline the different methodological resources that, at their most distinctive, each offers.

### 5.3.1 Citizen-Consumers at the Consumption Junction

Within Giddens's structuration theory individual behaviour subsists within social practices, the rules and resources of which both enable and constrain actors, and constitute the structures that are involved in the reproduction of social practices. In this recursive relationship structures are both the media and the outcomes of human action (Spaargaren and Van Vliet 2000). This 'duality of structure' is examined methodologically by, on the one hand, 'institutional analysis' of social practices, where agency is bracketed out, and on the other 'the analysis of strategic conduct' in which the rules and resources of practices are taken as given in order to focus on actors' use of structures.

For the purposes of Spaargaren's programme, the relative power of citizen consumers to achieve a reduction in the environmental impacts of different domains of consumption (housing, food, travel and so on) can be assessed through analysis of the rules and resources of the consumption practices afforded them by the different domains' systems of provision (or systemic interactions between consumption and production). The task of policy becomes to enable that power, conceived not simply as capacity for consumer choice of 'green options' but as the enhancing of 'the authority of consumers . . . to exert democratic control over the actors involved' (Spaargaren 2003, p. 691). Spaargaren and Oosterveer (2010, p. 1893) offer a conceptualization of environmental power as 'the capacity of social actors to reduce the environmental impacts of consumption and production where these impacts are directly connected to sets of practices predominantly under the control of other actors'.

Spaargaren's programme thus explicitly seeks to further the 'new consumer-oriented environmental politics' that arises in the context of the increasing importance of the hybrid role of citizen-consumer for companies, policy makers and social movements under conditions of globalization and reflexive modernity (Spaargaren 2003, 2006). Core areas that it seeks to address include: the changing role of citizen-consumers in globalizing environmental politics; the changing social relations between producers and citizen-consumers in globalizing systems of provision; the appropriation of socio-technical innovations within social practices; social change as socio-technical innovation rooted in systems of provision, lifestyles or both; the assessment of levels of ecological modernization and the relative capacities of different actor groups to enable transitions towards sustainability in different consumption domains; and the role of companies in incorporating sustainability-enabling ideas, information and products into consumption routines of citizen-consumers.

Two central concepts deserve attention: 'lifestyle' and 'consumption junction'. The place of the citizen-consumer within this programme foregrounds Giddens's descriptive concept of lifestyle: a specific form of integration of practices enacted by actors, in which consumption often plays a key role, to form a reasonably coherent unity. Lifestyles are equally the discursive accounts by which actors connect practices, 'clusters of habits and story lines' and 'narratives of self identity' (Spaargaren 2006, p. 24). If Spaargaren's programme foregrounds the cultural politics of sustainable consumption, lifestyle is an organizing principle of that politics, and 'consumption junctions' the sites in which this politics is often fought. Consumption junctions are where demand and provision, or the social practices of consumption and production, meet and where actors may enact social change through incorporating socio-technical innovations into everyday life (Spaargaren 2006; Spaargaren and Van Vliet 2000).

Spaargaren and Oosterveer's (2010) exploration of citizen-consumers' role in effecting change and Spaargaren and van Koppen's (2009) instrumental suggestions for the role of companies in enabling more sustainable consumption routines delineate the programme's empirical approach to practice theory.

### 5.3.2 Conventions, Competence and Kit

Shove aimed to reframe the problem of sustainable consumption from one of the promotion of more efficient, sustainable technologies, to one of the promotion of more sustainable practices; which practices co-evolve with technological innovation and infrastructures of provision. Such an approach animates diverse questions relevant to sustainable consumption, such as: why has daily showering widely replaced weekly bathing? (Hand et al. 2005); what are the dynamics of escalating energy demand from digital technologies? (Røpke and Christiansen 2013); and what accounts for the rapid global diffusion of air conditioning? (Shove et al. 2013). The material and functional properties of things, neglected in cultural analysis, are made central to accounts of consumption.

This reframing recognizes that promoting more efficient technologies alone may not ameliorate their environmental impact: improved refrigeration technology, for example, may simply lead to the use of increased refrigerated space at the same cost. Moreover increased efficiency may have the unintended consequence of inadvertently naturalizing ultimately less sustainable conventions and expectations, that become embedded in routine practices of everyday life and escalate aggregate consumption's environmental impact: 'what matters is the relation between (more or less efficient) technologies, systems and appliances, and co-evolution of routines, habits and practices' (Shove 2004, p. 1054).

In *Comfort, Cleanliness and Convenience* (2003, p. 61) Shove unpacks dimensions of social and technical co-evolution, and the ensuing dynamics of escalating demand, through these social conventions or 'composite services'. Comfort – in the form of lighting and indoor temperature control – is examined to demonstrate global processes of standardization and convergence, and their local translation. This 'vertical' structuring of normal practice is contrasted with the very different mechanisms of 'horizontal' ordering presented by evolving conventions and practices of cleanliness. Here the circulation of elements of practice – images, meanings, technologies – is again implicated in escalating demand (in, for example, the rapid diffusion of the practice of frequent showering); and an account that cannot be accommodated in standard models of socio-technical co-evolution. 'Convenience' introduces the temporal dimension, which forms an intersection between the two axes, and is itself an engine of change (2003, p. 192). Shove does not present an all-encompassing account of the social organization of normality, or a universal schema for social change, but rather identifies multiple intersecting dynamics. The approach does however identify some abstract mechanisms of change, such as a ratcheting of demand through unidirectional path-dependency and temporary configurations able to stabilize in more or less resource intensive forms.

This interdependence of technical systems and practices suggests two key insights. First, levels of demand and patterns of consumption are the outcome of both (Shove

2004, p. 1055). Second, there are multiple possible points of intervention and innovation for steering practices towards more sustainable forms. If much of the environmental impact of consumption arises through the routine reproduction of normal life, interventions may be targeted at disrupting or challenging cultural conventions and meanings (Shove 2003).

However Shove's programme also challenges a dominant assumption within sustainable consumption research (e.g. Spaargaren and Van Vliet 2000), that changing embedded habits and practices requires de- and re-routinization through deliberative engagement and reflexive renegotiation: 'An alternative practice-based perspective suggests that enduring change emerges through the amplification of existing social orientations and does not necessarily depend upon explicit contestation and debate' (Chappells et al. 2011, p. 701).

This approach, then, focuses on the dynamics of practice and their relation to escalating impacts of consumption, analysing the intersection of conventions, understandings and competences on the one hand, and institutions, infrastructures and technologies on the other.

## 5.4 AGENCY, CHANGE AND CONVERGENCE

Central to the further development of theories of practice for sustainable consumption has been the work of Schatzki (especially 1996, 2002). Schatzki has rigorously elaborated a social ontology of practice, in critical dialogue with the practice theories of Bourdieu, Foucault and Giddens, by way of the philosophies of Wittgenstein and Heidegger. This ontology establishes a 'strong' version of practice theory in which both social order and individuality result from practices. It asserts that there is no macro level beyond the realm of social practices, which are 'not merely "sites" of interaction but are, instead, ordering and orchestrating entities in their own right' (Shove and Walker 2010, p. 471).

The programme we have associated with Shove has attempted to develop the implications of this stance (e.g. Shove and Spurling 2013). This strong practice theory approach advances an abstract description of dynamics between and within practices (e.g. Shove et al. 2012), but without seeking to produce a unified model of change that can be applied across whole categories of practices. Rather it enables the identification of critical, context-specific (often recursive) processes and complex causal interactions that result in resource-intensive patterns of everyday consumption. Key dimensions of such processes are materiality and temporality. Novel material components of practice may either transform or fail to transform existing practices, with important implications for sustainable consumption. Røpke and Christensen (2013) analyse this first process in the context of how the generic functionalities of information and communication technologies (ICTs) become embedded in a huge range of existing everyday practices and projects, transforming many in the process; including those with no self-evident relation to ICTs, such as sports, hobbies and do-it-yourself (DIY). Such embedding of digital technologies in everyday life has profound consequences for energy demand and resource use. The second process is explored by Yli-Kauhaluoma et al. (2013) with respect to the obdurate materiality of paper, which resists the promise of the 'paperless office' offered by those self-same digital technologies.

Crucially, these dynamics operate both across space and in time. The temporal ordering of practices, 'embedded conventions of duration, sequence and timing' (Shove 2009, p. 25), and the synchronization of personal and collective schedules, have significant implications for the consumption of energy and the development of infrastructure: in, for example, transport infrastructure designed to cope with rush hours, or energy systems designed to cope with peak loads. The temporal coordination of practices, their sequencing and synchronization within collective life, not only has profound importance for the environmental impact of everyday life but equally presents novel opportunities for achieving substantial shifts in behaviours (Southerton et al. 2011; Spurling et al. 2013).

Any brief summary of the field would be incomplete without acknowledging the important recent book by Shove, Pantzar and Watson, *The Dynamics of Social Practice* (Shove et al. 2012), which is both an important general contribution to the application of practice theory and explicitly orientated to promoting transitions in practice. It presents an avowedly 'radically simplified' account of practice theory, the better to elucidate complex dynamics. Central to this project is to model practices as composed as three generic elements: meaning, competence and material. It stresses the relative independence of the trajectories of these elements of practices from practices themselves. Practices come into being and are transformed through the circulation and recombination of elements. Shove et al. (2012) elaborate Giddens's (1984) notion of the 'reproduction circuit' or feedback between the self-monitoring of actors and social structure. 'Circuits of reproduction' include: the reproduction of practice through the integration of elements; cross-practice configurations of elements that affect the former; and inter-practice circuits (Shove et al. 2012, p. 114).

In the UK, the Sustainable Practices Research Group, SPRG (2010–2013), has explicitly conducted empirical research engaging with the stronger programme and its concerns with the emergence, diffusion, normalization, persistence, change, variation across social space and disappearance of practices. The SPRG applied variations of practice theory to several empirical areas, including: the diffusion of air conditioning (Shove et al. 2013); how eating habits change (Darmon 2013); understanding domestic water consumption through variations in domestic practices (Browne et al. 2013); and comparative international configurations of drinking water (Harvey 2012).

More recently Spaargaren and collaborators have also drawn upon these intellectual resources to address the criticisms that their emphasis on citizen-consumers and lifestyles amounts to a regression to methodological individualism and an exaggeration of individuals' transformative capacities, with a concomitant neglect of materiality and structural constraints (Spaargaren and Oosterveer 2010, p. 1897–1898). As such there has been, to a certain extent, a theoretical convergence of this programme with that of Shove.

However, there remain differences in position regarding in particular the nature of change. Indeed some of the aficionados of the stronger programme also have reservations about the manner in which change is analysed. One nuanced but important difference from Spaargaren can be found in a useful distinction. Spaargaren (2013, p. 233) notes that '[i]t is practices that "produce" and co-constitute individuals . . . not the other way round'; nevertheless 'human subjectivity is at the heart of process of structuration'. The 'strong' practice theory understanding of practices as entities with causal powers is overshadowed by the model of agency implicit in the optimistic understanding of citizen-consumers as 'change agents'. Social practices become a device for analysing citizen-consumers' roles as bearers of ecological citizenship, political consumption and lifestyle politics (Spaargaren and Oosterveer 2010), rather than practices themselves taking centre stage in the analysis of social change. Political actors overshadow other dynamics, such as the circulation of practice elements, whether concepts or technologies (Shove and Walker 2010), and of endogamous change (Chappells et al. 2011). Conversely the strategic move of Shove away from the 'distraction' of environmentalists' motivations has led to a neglect of the cultural dimensions of sustainable consumption (Spaargaren 2013). Perhaps this programme focuses overzealously on analysing the dynamics of everyday practice as a route to better understanding transitions toward sustainable practices at the expense of collective mobilization and macro-level institutional processes. Thus there appears to be a need to construct a plausible set of connections between the habits and routines of everyday life and lay normativity and collective mobilization.

Recently, a number of researchers drawing upon Schatzki and the resources of the 'stronger' version of practice theory have addressed activities organized and represented explicitly in the name of sustainable consumption, which have come to increasing prominence since the early 2000s. Thus, for example: Barnett et al. (2011) have explored practices of 'ethical consumption'; Gram-Hanssen (2011) has analysed an intervention aimed at reducing consumers' standby consumption; Hargreaves (2011) has applied practice theory to an organizational environmental behaviour change programme; Crivits and Paredis (2013) have analysed sustainable food practices; Middlemiss (2011) has addressed initiatives of community-based organizations for sustainable lifestyles; and Wheeler (2012) has examined practices of 'Fairtrade support'. In these cases, participants consider themselves to be acting to make consumption more sustainable.

Similarly Halkier (2010) foregrounds the reflexive effects of the mediatized discourse of sustainable consumption. This is a refreshing contrast to the focus on the routinized, habitual character of 'inconspicuous consumption' that drew attention away from the role of cultural intermediaries, the public sphere and media in the wider dynamics of sustainable consumption. Halkier (2010) put to work the practice component categories of understandings, procedures and engagements (Warde 2005) to explore the performance of everyday food practices in the context of their problematization through media discourses of environmental sustainability, risk and health. Halkier notes that the very problematization of consumption (in which sustainable consumption plays such a significant part) draws attention to consumption routines *qua* consumption. Indeed the intention of media discourses and the many purposive interventions of non-governmental organizations, public bodies and companies that ascribe societal responsibility to 'consumers' is often to nominate everyday activities explicitly as consumption practices in order to open them up for revision (Halkier 2010; Barnett et al. 2011). This presents a caveat to Warde's (2005, p. 137) contention that consumption is a 'moment in almost every practice' rather than itself being a practice. Halkier argues that an engaged form of environmentally friendly food consumption can indeed be viewed as a practice in its own right, through the integration of a specific set of understandings, routinized procedures and engagement with a normative project of sustainability:

> In identifying with environmentally friendly food consumption, practitioners express understandings in their sayings oriented towards specific tasks (such as using organic food), and practitioners express engagements in their doings that amount to practice projects . . . This can be seen as performing political consumption practices. (Halkier 2010, p. 74)

In stressing the everyday normative negotiations attendant upon sustainable food consumption, Halkier points to areas which recent theoretical approaches have avoided: discursivity, lay normativity, social interaction[2] and the creation of norms which produce shared understandings and common procedures. Her empirical research indicates that interaction within social networks and practical procedures is often more important than individual normative commitments in driving the 'normativized performing' characterizing sustainable food consumption (ibid.). This has significant implications for policy interventions, communication strategies and behaviour change initiatives.

Sustainable consumption is a notion born of policy initiatives and much of the practice-theoretical research is ultimately oriented to informing policy. The two programmes offer contrasting approaches to policy, which undoubtedly partly reflects the very different national political contexts of the key protagonists in the Netherlands and the UK. Spaargaren's programme seeks to operationalize social science for direct application in policy initiatives – assessing levels of green provisioning, developing 'environmental heuristics' and so forth (e.g. Spaargaren 2003, 2006) – thus working with the grain of conventional politics. Shove (2010), on the other hand, rejects the individualized, voluntaristic model of consumption which dominates policy approaches, those which she calls the attitude–behaviour–choice (ABC) model, which in turn reflect the 'portfolio model' of the actor. Her critique challenges the policy focus on information provision and social marketing in behaviour change programmes, reflecting theoretical scepticism towards the role of deliberative action in changing social practice as well as emphasizing processes of co-evolution (Evans et al. 2012; Spurling et al. 2013). Furthermore such framings of policy lead to the 'more powerful drivers of consumption practices and social dynamics that continue to perpetuate undesirable patterns of resource use [being] largely ignored' (Chappells et al. 2011, p. 712).

## 5.5 PROSPECTS

Theories of practice have made an important contribution to the study of sustainable consumption. Overcoming traditional theoretical antinomies through positing the generative interdependence of structure and agency enables pertinent accounts of complex causality. Their sensitivity to the constitutive role of material elements (tools, infrastructures) in socio-technical change and the active appropriation of technologies and commodities in local contexts is specifically suited to the analytical needs of sustainable consumption: identifying systematic links of social, cultural, economic and technological processes of innovation, normalization and disruption. The integration of socio-cultural and material elements is of particular relevance to the multidisciplinary research programmes that have been commonplace in sustainable consumption research and to strategies for political intervention.

There are at least three important outstanding analytic problems whose clarification and resolution would enhance the power of practice theories. The first concerns the relationship between production and consumption. While Shove (2003) set out to develop a framework encompassing innovation in consumption and production and the dynamic process between the two, most practice-theoretical empirical research has engaged in micro-sociological studies of everyday life to the neglect of the sphere of economic production. Shove's programme was at least in part directed against producer-oriented accounts of socio-technical change in innovation studies and the multi-level perspective (MLP) of the 'socio-technical transitions' literature (Geels 2002) (e.g. Shove 2003; Shove and Walker 2010; Shove et al. 2013). However, the 'horizontal' dynamics of end-use consumption and everyday life might now be enhanced by taking greater account of other phases of systems of provision.

MLP, for example, offers a heuristic framework which distinguishes between levels of niche (or relatively unstabilized practice), regime (or relatively stabilized incumbent configurations) and landscape (or broad cultural and historical context). The ontological compatibility of practice theory and MLP is contentious (see Geels 2010; and Schatzki 2011 for a critique). The recent stress of MLP proponents that their model primarily distinguishes degrees of institutionalization, defined as the stability and consistency of interactions and power relations over time and space, goes some way to address these concerns (Geels 2011; Grin 2012; Spaargaren et al. 2012).

Recent pragmatic moves towards a synthesis of practice theory and the socio-technical transition approaches is therefore a welcome development (Cohen et al. 2013; Crivits and Paredis 2013; Geels 2010, 2011; McMeekin and Southerton 2012; Spaargaren et al. 2012; Watson 2012). McMeekin and Southerton (2012) propose, echoing Spaargaren's earlier emphasis on 'consumption junctions', that better conceptualization of the dynamics between production and consumption in sustainability transitions would result from a fuller account of the institutional space, the 'mediation junction', in which these processes take place and address the ability of intermediaries 'in terms of their ability to shape elements within the nexus of practices that occupy [that] space' (2012, p. 356).

A second issue concerns the relationship between collective agency and everyday routines which perpetuate and reproduce patterns of consumption. Theories of practice have tended to neglect the role of collective social and political projects, ideologies and cultural discourses. This is ironic given that sustainable consumption was initiated as a purposive project, promoted by powerful collective actors and expressed via a cultural, reflexive discourse. Grin (2012) for example, through a study of the modernization of food consumption and production in the Netherlands, takes practice approaches to task for not acknowledging the extent to which 'regime actors' directly govern and shape practices. Similarly Harvey (2004), in critique of Shove (2003), points to social struggles over standardization as quality-of-life issues; he cites the examples of clean air regulation and improved cleanliness in the workplace.

Barnett et al. (2011) make an important contribution by counteracting a lack of theorization of collective social action and actors.[3] Challenging the assumption that 'the consumer' is the primary agent of change in efforts to politicize consumption practices, Barnett et al. (2011) draw on practice-theoretical resources to stress how the politicization and problematization of consumption 'is an outcome of organized efforts by a variety of collective actors to practically re-articulate the ordinary ethical dispositions of everyday consumption': '"the consumer" is not so much a locus of sovereignty and agency as it is a rhetorical figure and point of identification only contingently related to the politics of consumption' (Barnett et al. 2011, p. 19). Sustainable consumption is from this perspective understood 'as an organised field of strategic interventions' (ibid.,

p. 13) in which, following a Foucauldian route, consumption is taken up as the object of problematizing discourse.

A final concern is the relationship between the minutiae of everyday performances of practices and the macro-institutional context. This is a perpetual theoretical dilemma for sociology as a whole, but appears in stark relief with respect to the stronger programme's account of practice bundles.

Arguably, the 'horizontal' circulation of ideas and representations may provide an account of change within discrete practices but says less about the supra-practice configurations that these elements may subtend. How the analytical categories of generic components of practice are conceptualized may have a bearing. Schatzki's (2002) later schema explicitly adds the category 'general understandings'. General understandings are common to many practices and condition the manner in which practices are carried out, as well as being expressed in their performance. They constitute external understandings of the overall project in which the practice is engaged (Nicolini 2012, p. 167). Schatzki gives the example of the Shaker view of labour as a sanctification of the earthly sphere, which conditioned the manner in which many of their labouring practices were carried out, as well as being explicitly formulated in doings and sayings (Schatzki 2002, p. 86).

Schemas (e.g., Shove et al. 2012) which lack analytical differentiation between very general cultural understandings and practice-specific orders of meaning run the risk of obscuring the structuring effects upon practices of widespread, adjacent or overarching cultural discourses. Such discourses may animate purposive programmes, such as those of 'modernization', 'neoliberalism' or indeed 'sustainable consumption', or be found in diffuse but powerful cultural trends such as 'Americanization', or even very general cultural notions such as 'authenticity'. Conceptualizing such general understandings simply as common ideational elements shared by discrete practices potentially misses important processes of change. Shove et al. (2012, p. 110) have recourse to 'meso-level discourses and categories that have orchestrating and co-ordinating effects in their own right', such as obesity, 'simultaneously reproduced in "micro" and "macro" form', from bathroom scales to public health initiatives. However, it is moot whether such a move is compatible with the 'high order ontological sameness' of Schatzki's (2011) flat ontology, which itself offers disappointing analytical or explanatory resources. The ends to which practices are put, the kind of objects that they seek to act upon, the nature of problems they admit to, and the form of interventions thus enjoined, suggest patterning and configuration on a supra-practice level. Practice theories at present lack persuasive theoretical or conceptual answers. It is in this context that the conceptual instruments of Bourdieu and Foucault, both of whom managed to reconcile practice-theoretical foundations with macro-level structural and historical explanation, might yet be useful. In their absence there still seems no reason why empirical investigation, and indeed strategic intervention, cannot proceed in a profitable manner.

## NOTES

1. Widely cited definitions include Reckwitz (2002, p. 249), Schatzki (1996, p. 89; 2002, p. 77), Shove et al. (2012, p. 23) and Warde (2005, p. 134).
2. Halkier points out that social interaction tends to be left implicit in practice theory '"dressed" conceptually

as recognition or coordination' and demands more explicit conceptual and analytical elaboration, not least specifically in the area of sustainable consumption where communication processes play such a key role (2010, p. 172).

3. Kaidesoja (2013, p. 311) notes that the distributed approach to human cognition that practice theory tends to support supports a notion of collective agents with emergent causal powers.

## REFERENCES


Akrich, M. (1992), 'The de-scription of technical objects', in W. Bijker and J. Law (eds), *Shaping Technology/ Building Society*, Cambridge, MA: MIT Press, pp. 205–244.

Barnett, C., N. Clarke, P. Cloke and A. Malpass (2011), *Globalizing Responsibility: The Political Rationalities of Ethical Consumption*, Chichester: Wiley-Blackwell.

Bourdieu, P. (1977), *Outline of a Theory of Practice*, Cambridge: Cambridge University Press.

Browne, A.L., M. Pullinger, W. Medd and B. Anderson (2013), 'Patterns of practice', *International Journal of Social Research Methodology*, 17 (1), 27–43.

Chappells, H., W. Medd and E. Shove (2011), 'Disruption and change: drought and the inconspicuous dynamics of garden lives', *Social and Cultural Geography*, 12 (7), 701–715.

Cohen, M.J., H.S. Brown and P.J. Vergragt (eds) (2013), *Innovations in Sustainable Consumption: New Economics, Socio-technical Transitions and Social Practices*, Cheltenham, UK and Northampton, MA, USA: Edward Elgar.

Cohen, M.J. and J. Murphy (eds) (2001), *Exploring Sustainable Consumption: Environmental Policy and the Social Sciences*, London: Pergamon.

Crivits, M. and E. Paredis (2013), 'Designing an explanatory practice framework', *Journal of Consumer Culture*, 13 (3), 306–336.

Darmon, I. (2013), 'Change in eating habits: the contribution of new local food infrastructures', SPRG Discussion Paper 3. www.sprg.ac.uk.

Evans, D., A. McMeekin and D. Southerton (2012), 'Sustainable consumption, behaviour change policies and theories of practice', in A. Warde and D. Southerton (eds), *The Habits of Consumption, COLLeGIUM* 12, 1–25, Helsinki Collegium for Advanced Studies.

Geels, F.W. (2002), 'Technological transitions as evolutionary reconfiguration processes: a multi-level perspective and a case study', *Research Policy*, 31, 1257–1274.

Geels, F.W. (2010), 'Ontologies, socio-technical transitions (to sustainability), and the multi-level perspective', *Research Policy*, 39 (4), 495–510.

Geels F.W. (2011), 'The multi-level perspective on sustainability transitions: responses to eight criticisms', *Environmental Innovation and Societal Transitions*, 1, 24–40.

Giddens, A. (1984), *The Constitution of Society*, Cambridge: Polity Press.

Gram-Hanssen, K. (2011), 'Understanding change and continuity in residential energy consumption', *Journal of Consumer Culture*, 11, 61–78.

Grin, J. (2012), 'Changing governments, kitchens, supermarkets, firms and farms', in G. Spaargaren, P. Oosterveer and A. Loeber (eds), *Food Practices in Transition*, London: Routledge, pp. 35–58.

Halkier, B. (2010), *Consumption Challenged*, Farnham: Ashgate.

Halkier, B., T. Katz-Gerro and L. Martens (2011), 'Applying practice theory to the study of consumption: theoretical and methodological considerations', *Journal of Consumer Culture*, 11 (1), 3–13.

Hand, M., D. Southerton and E. Shove (2005), 'Explaining showering: a discussion of the material, conventional, and temporal dimensions of practice', *Sociological Research Online*, 10 (2), http://www.socresonline.org.uk/10/2/hand.html.

Hargreaves, T. (2011), 'Practice-ing behaviour change: applying social practice theory to pro-environmental behaviour change', *Journal of Consumer Culture*, 11(1), 79–99.

Harvey, M. (2004), 'Book review: *Comfort, Cleanliness and Convenience*', *Journal of Consumer Culture*, 4, 419–421.

Harvey, M. (2012), 'Drinking-water and drinking water: trajectories of provision and consumption in the UK, Taiwan and Delhi', CRESI Working Paper 2012-02, University of Essex.

Hindess, B. (1990), 'Analyzing actors' choices', *International Political Science Review*, 11 (1), 87–97.

Kaidesoja, T. (2013), 'Overcoming the biases of microfoundationalism', *Philosophy of the Social Sciences*, 43 (3), 301–322.

MacIntyre, A.C. (1981), *After Virtue*, London: Duckworth.

McMeekin, A. and Southerton, D. (2012), 'Sustainability transitions and final consumption: practices and socio-technical systems' *Technology Analysis and Strategic Management*, 24 (4), 345–361.

Middlemiss, L. (2011), 'The power of community', *Society and Natural Resources*, 24 (11), 1157–1173.
Nicolini, D. (2012), *Practice Theory, Work and Organization*, Oxford: Oxford University Press.
Ortner, S. (1984), 'Theory in anthropology since the sixties', *Comparative Study of Society and History*, 16, 126–166.
Reckwitz, A. (2002), 'Towards a theory of social practices', *European Journal of Social Theory*, 5 (2), 243–263.
Redclift, M. (1996), *Wasted*, London: Earthscan.
Rip, A. and R. Kemp (1998), 'Technological change', in S. Rayner and E. Malone (eds), *Human Choices and Climate Change*, Columbus, OH: Battelle, pp. 327–400.
Røpke, I. (2009), 'Theories of practice', *Ecological Economics*, 68 (10), 2490–2497.
Røpke, I. and T.H. Christensen (2013), 'Transitions in the wrong direction?', in E. Shove and N. Spurling (eds), *Sustainable Practices: Social Theory and Climate Change*, London: Routledge, pp. 49–68.
Rouse, J. (2006), 'Practice theories', in D.M. Gabbay, P. Thagard and J. Woods (eds), *Handbook of Philosophy and Social Science*, Vol. 15, Cambridge, MA: Elsevier, pp. 500–540.
Rumpala, Y. (2011), '"Sustainable consumption" as a new phase in a governmentalization of consumption', *Theory and Society*, 40, 669–699.
Schatzki, T. (1996), *Social Practices: A Wittgensteinian Approach to Human Activity and the Social*, New York: Cambridge University Press.
Schatzki, T. (2001), 'Introduction: practice theory', in T.R. Schatzki, K. Knorr Cetina and E. Savigny (eds), *The Practice Turn in Contemporary Theory*, London: Routledge, pp. 10–23.
Schatzki, T. (2002), *The Site of the Social*, University Park, PA: Pennsylvania State University Press.
Schatzki, T. (2011), 'Where the action is (on large social phenomena such as sociotechnical regimes)', SPRG Working Paper 1, www.sprg.ac.uk.
Schatzki, T.R., K. Knorr Cetina and E. Savigny (eds) (2001), *The Practice Turn in Contemporary Theory*, London: Routledge.
Shove, E. (2003), *Comfort, Cleanliness and Convenience: The Social Organization of Normality*, Oxford: Berg.
Shove, E. (2004), 'Efficiency and consumption: technology and practice', *Energy and Environment*, 15 (6), 1053–1065.
Shove, E. (2009), 'Everyday practice and the production and consumption of time', in E. Shove, F. Trentmann and R. Wilk (eds), *Time, Consumption and Everyday Life*, New York: Berg, pp. 17–34.
Shove, E. (2010), 'Beyond ABC: climate change policy and theories of social change', *Environment and Planning A*, 42, 1273–1285.
Shove, E., M. Pantzar and M. Watson (2012), *The Dynamics of Social Practice*, London: Sage.
Shove, E. and N. Spurling (eds) (2013), *Sustainable Practices: social theory and climate change*, London: Routledge.
Shove, E. and G. Walker (2010), 'Governing transitions in the sustainability of everyday life', *Research Policy*, 39, 471–476.
Shove, E., G. Walker and S. Brown (2013), 'Transnational transitions: the diffusion and integration of mechanical cooling', *Urban Studies*, 50 (14), 1–14.
Shove, E. and A. Warde (2002), 'Inconspicuous consumption', in R.E Dunlap, F.H. Buttel, P. Dickens and A. Gijswijt (eds), *Sociological Theory and the Environment*, London: Rowman & Littlefield, pp. 230–241.
Southerton, D., C. Diaz-Mendez and A. Warde (2011), 'Behavioural change and the temporal ordering of eating practices: a UK–Spain comparison', *International Journal of Sociology of Agriculture and Food*, 19 (1), 19–36.
Southerton, D., A. Warde and M. Hand (2004), 'The limited autonomy of the consumer: implications for sustainable consumption', in D. Southerton, H. Chappells and B. Van Vliet (eds), *Sustainable Consumption: The Implications of Changing Infrastructures of Provision*, Cheltenham, UK and Northampton, MA, USA: Edward Elgar, pp. 32–48.
Spaargaren, G. (2003), 'Sustainable consumption: a theoretical and environmental policy perspective', *Society and Natural Resources: An International Journal*, 16 (8), 687–701.
Spaargaren, G. (2006), 'The ecological modernization of social practices at the consumption junction', Discussion paper for the ISA-RC-24 conference Sustainable Consumption and Society, Madison, WI, June.
Spaargaren, G. (2013), 'The cultural dimension of sustainable consumption practices', in M.J. Cohen, H.S. Brown and P.J. Vergragt (eds), *Innovations in Sustainable Consumption*, Cheltenham, UK and Northampton, MA, USA: Edward Elgar, pp. 229–251.
Spaargaren, G. and S. Martens (2005), 'Globalization and the role of citizen-consumers in environmental politics', in F. Wijen, K. Zoeteman and J. Pieters (eds), *A Handbook of Globalisation and Environmental Policy*, Cheltenham, UK and Northampton, MA, USA: Edward Elgar, pp. 211–245.
Spaargaren, G. and P. Oosterveer (2010), 'Citizen-consumers as agents of change in globalizing modernity: the case of sustainable consumption', *Sustainability*, 2010 (2), 1887–1908.
Spaargaren, G., P. Oosterveer and A. Loeber (2012), 'Sustainability transitions in food consumption, retail and

production', in G. Spaargaren, P. Oosterveer and A. Loeber (eds), *Food Practices in Transitions*, London: Routledge, pp. 1–33.

Spaargaren, G. and C.S.A. van Koppen (2009), 'Provider strategies and the greening of consumption practices', in H. Lange and L. Meier (eds), *The New Middle Classes*, Dordrecht and Heidelberg, Germany; London, UK; New York, USA: Springer, pp. 81–100.

Spaargaren, G. and B. Van Vliet (2000), 'Lifestyles, consumption and the environment', *Environmental Politics*, 9 (1), 50–76.

Spurling, N., A. McMeekin, E. Shove, D. Southerton and D. Welch (2013), 'Interventions in practice', SPRG Report, www.sprg.ac.uk.

Warde, A. (2005), 'Consumption and theories of practice', *Journal of Consumer Culture*, 5 (2), pp. 131–153.

Watson, M. (2012), 'How theories of practice can inform transition to a decarbonised transport system', *Journal of Transport Geography*, 24 (September), 488–496.

Wenger, E. (1998), *Communities of Practice*, Cambridge: Cambridge University Press.

Wheeler, K. (2012), 'The practice of fairtrade support', *Sociology*, 46 (1), 126–141.

Yli-Kauhaluoma, S., M. Pantzar and S. Toyoki (2013), 'Mundane materials at work', in E. Shove and N. Spurling (eds), *Sustainable Practices*, London: Routledge, pp. 69–85.

# 6. Sustainability marketing

*Ken Peattie*

Within any consumer society, most of what we consume will have been marketed to us. Not just the goods and services that we associate with the notion of 'consumption', but also the public services we use, the charities we patronize, the politicians we vote for, the places we visit and even the institutions and ideas that we think of as part of our society. There will be exceptions to this, such as when people grow their own food, make their own furniture or entertainment, or generate their own energy. In poorer countries, consumption on a self-sufficiency and barter basis outside the formal economy may be the norm for many citizens. Within consumer economies however our consumption is facilitated and influenced by marketing thinking, processes and practices, and for that reason marketing sometimes takes the blame for the unsustainable nature of our consumption (Kjellberg 2008). Despite this, marketing can play a pivotal role in developing more sustainable systems of production and consumption within our societies in future (Belz and Peattie 2012).

The term 'marketing' can refer to an academic discipline, a business process, an organizational function or division or a management philosophy. The focus of all of these is the customer. In business-to-business or organizational marketing, customers will be companies or public sector organizations. Such marketing is still relevant to the sustainability of consumer lifestyles, since marketing practices within industry supply chains will strongly influence the sustainability of consumer goods (see Sharma et al. 2010). However, the form of marketing most visible, both in scholarship and in daily life, and which forms the focus of this chapter, is consumer marketing.

A growing phenomenon within marketing practice over the last three decades has been the intersection between societal concerns about sustainability, consumer behaviour and the marketing of products and services across a range of key markets (many of which are discussed in Part IV of this book). This in turn has been reflected in a growing body of research into the influence of marketing processes and practices on elements of consumption such as product choice, price sensitivity, consumer satisfaction and post-purchase consumption behaviours.

## 6.1 MARKETING AND SUSTAINABILITY: AN EVOLVING RELATIONSHIP

Marketing has continually evolved throughout history, from the informal marketing practices of pre-industrial artisans through to the sophisticated social media and relationship-based marketing of the twenty-first century. During the first half of the twentieth century, marketing scholarship evolved from the study of how to efficiently sell and distribute products to consumers, to increasingly sophisticated efforts to research and understand consumers, and to develop products and services to meet their needs.

During the 1960s and 1970s what is often referred to as 'modern mainstream marketing' emerged based on a marketing philosophy centring companies' efforts around the needs and wants of the customer as the means to deliver profits and growth (Bartels 1988). It also emphasized research on understanding the customer and the marketing environment, which then allowed for the effective targeting of a customized mix of marketing variables at specific market segments.

By the late twentieth century, this conventional mainstream was being challenged on several fronts including its failure to address marketing's socio-environmental impacts. Another critical school of thought focused on the discipline's preoccupation with marketing as an economic transaction and on the tangible products provided to consumers. Such critics argued that the field needed to evolve to reflect a service provision mindset, partly due to the increasing dominance of services markets within developed economies. They called for marketing to be reconsidered as a process of building and managing relationships with customers with an emphasis on the intangible dimensions of those relationships and the companies behind them (Vargo and Lusch 2004).

### 6.1.1 The Marketing–Sustainability Relationship

The relationship between marketing and socio-environmental sustainability can be categorized into three 'ages' (Peattie 2001a). It began with 'ecological marketing' in the 1970s that focused on pressing environmental problems, such as air pollution, depleting oil reserves and the environmental impact of pesticides (e.g. Henion and Kinnear 1976). It impacted upon a narrow range of industries and largely focused on technical solutions to resource use, pollution or waste concerns (for example, the addition of catalytic converters to cars). The 1980s era of 'environmental marketing' focused on developing products with superior socio-environmental performance with the aim of marketing them to the 'green consumer' in search of competitive advantage. This was more opportunity-focused and involved a far wider range of industries. It reflected growing consumer interest in sustainability issues, and higher levels of information available through the development of sustainability-oriented guides and labels. The third age, of 'sustainable marketing', involves the transformation of markets and marketing to achieve substantive progress towards the internalization of socio-environmental costs previously treated as externalities. Since 'sustainable marketing' implies it having reached a sustainable end state (which ultimately is both impossible to judge and dependent on the sustainability of the society within which it takes place), it is more helpful to talk about 'sustainability marketing'. This is marketing that seeks to integrate the ecological and ethical concerns of the green marketing era, along with a relationship marketing focus, to create a form of marketing that develops long-term, sustainability-oriented value relationships with customers (Belz and Peattie 2012).

Most sustainability marketing activity and research has focused on the ecological sustainability of products and production systems rather than on their contribution to greater social justice (with some particular exceptions such as FairTrade marketing which is primarily social). However, in practice, social and environmental issues are so intertwined within the sustainability agenda that it is unhelpful to draw a clear distinction between them. This chapter will use terms such as 'green', 'sustainable', 'ethical', 'environmental' and 'ecological' in ways that reflect the source research material. It is more helpful to consider all of these terms as referring to either social and ethical or ecological issues, or both, reflecting Hopwood et al.'s (2005) conception of business sustainability initiatives as plotted on a two-dimensional space with degree of improved social justice and ecological protection representing the two axes.

### 6.1.2 Marketing Sub-types

Marketing's evolution has involved the emergence of marketing subdisciplines. Several are important for sustainability due to their socio-environmental impacts and/or the extent to which consumers are sensitive to sustainability issues. These include travel and tourism marketing and particularly eco-tourism (Middleton and Hawkins 1998); arts and culture marketing and its role in promoting and protecting cultural resources (Boorsma 2006); charitable and not-for-profit marketing that supports pro-sustainability causes (Kotler and Andreasen 1996); and financial marketing of ethical investment and banking products (Getzner and Grabner-Krauter 2004). A particularly important subtype is social marketing (Kotler and Lee 2007), which involves non-commercial organizations using commercial marketing techniques to change peoples' behaviours to contribute to social goals linked to health, environmental protection and social equity.

**Services marketing**

The largest marketing subdiscipline is services marketing, which recognizes the distinctive characteristics of marketing intangible services compared to tangible products. Although sustainability issues are reflected in research for specific services (such as ecotourism or ethical banking), in the generic services literature there is a comparative lack of consideration of sustainability (van der Zwan and Bhamra 2003). This is surprising given that service provision has a key role in the potential transformation to a more sustainable economy through the substitution of resource-intensive product elements of companies' offerings with services (van der Zwan and Bhamra 2003). This is most obvious in 'use' services where instead of owning a product, customers access the benefits of use through rental or leasing arrangements (for example car-sharing services versus car ownership and use). A core strategy for the dematerialization and improved sustainability of many markets is through 'product–service systems' that integrate elements of tangible products and service provision through innovative business models (Tukker 2004). However, van der Zwan and Bhamra (2003) note that the success of such business models depends on understanding how consumers perceive behaviours such as renting and leasing as a different form of consumption to purchase and ownership, and on designing strategies to address consumer concerns about issues such as the continuity of service provision.

**Macro-marketing**

Like economics, marketing scholarship has a dual focus. Micro-marketing considers the efforts of particular companies to develop attractive and profitable offerings, including more sustainable offerings, for their customers. Macro-marketing seeks to systematically consider the interrelationship between marketing as a field and society as a whole, with an emphasis on the (often unintended) socio-environmental impacts (Hunt 1981). This 'big picture' view of marketing remains a field of academic interest for a specialist few, whilst the mainstream field has increasingly focused on the technical minutiae of micro-marketing (Wilkie and Moore 2003). In relation to environmental concern, in a review of marketing research between 1971 and 1997, Kilbourne and Beckman (1998) noted that up until 1995 it was dominated by micro-marketing, managerialist studies, after which more macro-marketing and critical studies emerged (but remained a minority). This chapter will focus on micro-marketing perspectives and the ways in which marketing scholars and practitioners seek to understand and influence consumers and their behaviour.

## 6.2 UNDERSTANDING CONSUMERS

Effective marketing depends upon gathering research data on consumers and the influences on their behaviour, and applying analytical approaches to interpret the data in search of insight. It is worth noting that marketing-oriented research into sustainable consumption is heavily biased towards purchasing aspects of consumer behaviour. This is unsurprising, since from the marketer's perspective purchases ultimately remain the yardstick of success or failure. Another aspect of consumer behaviour that features relatively prominently is recycling as a post-purchase behaviour. Other elements of consumption including non-consumption decisions (particularly through product boycotts), product repair and maintenance, product resale and the sharing of products all feature in the research literature but comparatively rarely. Recent research has seen attempts to develop more multi-dimensional notions of pro-sustainability consumption behaviours (PSCBs) such as Webb et al.'s (2008) 'Socially Responsible Purchase and Disposal Scale' encompassing pro-sustainability purchasing choices, recycling and avoidance or reduced use of products due to their environmental impact.

### 6.2.1 Marketing Research

Researching and analysing consumers to understand how to promote PSCBs is an endeavour that marketing scholars and practitioners have engaged in over the past decades. However, this research has focused on a narrow range of markets, particularly packaged goods and other relatively low-involvement purchases (Prothero et al. 2011). It has also tended to focus on consuming differently in terms of substitutions between product types, rather than on consuming less (Mont and Pleyps 2008). There has been some exploration of lifestyles of voluntary simplicity (Bekin et al. 2005) or anti-consumption (Cherrier et al. 2011), but the majority of research focuses on individual purchases rather than a broader understanding of consumption as a process, consumer lifestyles and alternatives to purchasing (including consumption reduction).

It is also worth noting that much of the scholarly research into sustainable consumer behaviour comes not from marketing academics but from environmental psychologists, environmental economists, social geographers and sociologists.

### 6.2.2 Consumer Behaviour Modelling

A key focus of sustainability consumer research has involved models of behaviour that have the potential to inform marketing strategies. There are a range of different types of model developed which are usefully reviewed by Jackson (2005). One of the most common approaches are extensions of the 'theory of planned behaviour' (Ajzen 1991), although other approaches apply attitude–behaviour–context (ABC) theory (Stern 2000), the motivation–ability–opportunity model (Ölander and Thøgersen 1995), 'norm activation theory' (Schwartz 1992), and value–belief–norm theory (Stern 2000; Stern et al. 1999). These modelling approaches are split between those that apply conventional models of consumer behaviour (such as the theory of planned behaviour) to sustainability contexts, and those such as ABC theory that have been specifically developed to explain sustainable consumer behaviours. Although each of these modelling approaches has produced results that suggest some explanatory power, they all tend to focus on a relatively small set of key variables linked to complex behaviours and situations (Jackson 2005), and as such their application in, and usefulness to, marketing practice is limited. Further consideration of the use of such behavioural models to understand sustainable consumer behaviour is provided in Steg, Chapter 4 of this book.

### 6.2.3 Segmenting Consumer Markets

A key marketing task is the grouping of consumers into distinctive market segments. Segmentation aims to identify groups of consumers who share particular traits that make them meaningfully similar in their consumption behaviour, and different to people in other segments. Segmentation has been enthusiastically applied to markets for more sustainable goods and services in an attempt to identify, and market to, 'green' or 'ethical' consumers by using a range of segmentation bases. Many of the early attempts focused on demographic factors such as age, gender or educational attainment. Later studies attempted to segment markets using psychographic bases such as personality variables (particularly, perceived locus of control and alienation), values and identity (both social and self-identity). Behavioural and attitudinal factors have also been used, particularly environmental knowledge, ecological concern and consciousness, perceived social norms and 'environmental affect' (the emotional response of consumers to sustainability issues). Segmentation is discussed further in Vérain et al., Chapter 13 in this book (and for a broader review of segmentation bases see do Paco and Raposo 2009; Straughan and Roberts 1999).

One type of consumer that may be particularly important to understand is the so-called 'early adopter'. More sustainable consumption behaviours may be achieved through engaging consumers with innovative products and services, encouraging consumers to adopt new types of behaviour, or engaging consumers in new types of business model to deliver benefits to them. Marketing innovative products such as electric vehicles requires early adopters to take a lead that more conservative consumers can later follow, in order for markets to grow beyond small niches (Gärling and Thøgersen 2001). Bhate and Lawler (1997) found that willingness to choose more sustainable product offerings was associated with innovativeness as a personality trait.

### 6.2.4 Consistency in Sustainable Consumer Behaviour

The focus of behavioural modelling and segmentation studies has been to identify those consumers most likely to respond positively to pro-sustainability marketing offerings, and therefore those consumers who are relatively consistent in their PSCB. Unfortunately perhaps the most common observations about research in the field concern: (1) the contradictory results and the lack of consistency about the significance of many of the key bases on which consumers have been segmented (do Paco and Raposo 2009; Kilbourne and Beckmann 1998; Straughan and Roberts 1999); and (2) that the behaviour of particular consumers will vary considerably in different contexts. For example Dolnicar and Grun (2009) found that consumers rarely maintained their 'at home' PSCBs when on holiday.

The notion that there is a particular group of 'green' consumers goes against the proposition of Kardash (1976) that all consumers (barring a contrary few) are potentially environmentally responsible consumers in that, given the choice between two products that are identical in all respects other than their socio-environmental performance, they will choose the more sustainable option. Therefore variations in consumers' willingness to purchase greener products can partly be understood by their perception of any other differences between sustainable and conventional goods and services. Perceived differences of price, value, convenience, reliability or technical performance will vary across different purchase contexts. Peattie (2001b) proposed two explanatory factors for the success of sustainable market offerings:

1. The degree of compromise involved, which could be a price premium, the need to travel further to make a purchase or to accept some reduction in technical performance. Although consumer acceptance of premium prices is one of the most widely researched topics via willingness-to-pay studies (see section 6.3.2; and Bolderdijk and Steg, Chapter 21 in this book), Bhate and Lawler (1997) found that consumers were more willing to accept price increases than an increase in the effort required to access more sustainable products.
2. The degree of confidence consumers have in the significance of the relevant socio-environmental issue, the sustainability benefits of the offering and the contribution that a purchase will make, which equates to the notion of perceived consumer effectiveness (PCE) which has been shown to be a significant influence on their PSCB (Straughan and Roberts 1999).

McDonald and Oates (2006) provided an empirical test of a simplified version of these factors by asking consumers to score 40 PSCBs according to the consumer effort required and the perceived difference or contribution they make towards sustainability. This revealed that perceived effort and difference are influential in consumers' propensity to engage in PSCB, that individuals tended to exhibit relatively consistent patterns in their attribution of effort or worth to a range of PSCBs, and whilst some PSCBs were perceived relatively consistently by consumers (for example, switching off lights or engaging in kerbside recycling perceived as high worth, low effort), others such as purchasing organic produce, composting or ethical banking were perceived very inconsistently across consumers in terms of effort and worth.

The subject of consistency across PSCBs was also explored by McDonald et al. (2012) as they attempted to understand how consumers reconcile sustainability concerns with their lifestyles. A key group identified in their study were 'exceptors', consumers who generally followed through on their sustainability-oriented values within their lifestyle, but would treat certain categories of consumption (such as use of a private car or foreign holidays) as distinct from their other everyday consumption activities and an exception.

**Attitude–behaviour gaps**

An important stream of research concerns the apparent gap between consumers' pro-sustainability attitudes, values and expressed intentions and their actual behaviours and actions (Pickett-Baker and Ozaki 2008; Prothero et al. 2011). Several explanations are offered for such attitude–behaviour (or value–action) gaps. One is simply that consumers over-report socio-environmental concerns as a form of social acceptability bias. Biel and Dahlstrand (2005) suggest that the barrier to action is the comparatively large amount of cognitive effort required to translate sustainability-oriented values into purchases. White et al. (2012) showed that marketing activities could reduce this gap, for example by making clearer to consumers the improvement in social justice that FairTrade purchases could deliver (see also: Steg, Chapter 4 and Verplanken and Roy, Chapter 15 in this book).

**Scepticism, uncertainty and trust**

Whether or not consumers believe marketers' claims about products and companies is crucial to the success of any form of marketing. It is arguably more crucial in an arena such as sustainability where cynicism about companies' motives and behaviour is evident and problematic for marketers (Carlson et al. 1993; Mohr et al. 1998). Osterhus (1997) found that consumer trust was a highly significant moderator of consumer willingness to respond to marketers' attempts to market products on a sustainability basis. Even when consumers are not overtly sceptical of marketing claims, the complexities and ambiguities involved in many sustainability issues can generate uncertainties that undermine consumers' willingness to engage in PSCBs (Van Dijk et al. 2004). Given the importance of trust, it is perhaps surprising that there has not been more exploration of its link to the attitude–behaviour gap.

### 6.2.5 Perceived Consumer Social Responsibility

One emerging sustainability marketing issue is the notion of perceived consumer social responsibility as a corollary to corporate social responsibility (CSR) (Wells et al. 2011). This is a radical proposition for marketers, since the marketing discipline is founded on the principle of consumer sovereignty and consumer rights rather than responsibilities. Perhaps for this reason, despite being a potentially worthwhile approach to understanding and influencing consumers, it has been under-researched (Wells et al. 2011). Empirical evidence is emerging that consumers feel a sense of partial responsibility towards both causing and tackling issues such as climate change, and that this can influence their behaviour (Wells et al. 2011). A further exploration of notions of consumer responsibility is provided in Luchs and Miller, Chapter 16 in this book.

What stands out most from the research about consumers, and how they relate to companies and products in relation to sustainability issues, is the sheer complexity of potential influences on behaviour. As Jackson (2005) noted, a difficulty facing consumer behaviour modelling is that any model comprehensive enough to be realistic is rendered untestable by its complexity (see, e.g., Bagozzi et al. 2002), and any model that is testable will be unrealistically simplistic. Consumer behaviour reflects a wide range of consumers' demographic, psychographic, attitudinal and behavioural traits; and also the context in which consumer decision making and behaviour takes place in terms of time, place, social linkages and other situational factors. Finally, consumer behaviour will reflect what it is that the consumer is being offered and how they perceive both that offer and the company behind it. Research evidence suggests that consumers will respond positively to CSR initiatives amongst companies that go beyond improvements to individual products and their production systems (Brown and Dacin 1997). Success partly depends on promoting issues that consumers perceive as consistent with the nature of the product and business, since they can respond negatively if they perceive companies to be inappropriately or insincerely appropriating socio-environmental issues for marketing purposes (Sen and Bhattacharya 2001).

## 6.3 INFLUENCING CONSUMERS: THE MARKETING MIX

Once marketers have targeted a market, their strategy is implemented through a 'marketing mix' of variables. The standard mix model is the '4Ps'developed by McCarthy (1960) of product, price, place (referring to distribution) and promotion. Despite decades of criticism, its memorability and simplicity have allowed it to endure. However it has been criticized from a sustainability perspective for overemphasizing product and production issues at the expense of consumers and consumption (Belz and Peattie 2012).

### 6.3.1 Offerings to Consumers

A company's offering to its consumers can usefully be thought of as a bundle of benefits, or as a solution to a particular want or need. The move towards providing 'solutions' rather than products is more typical of business-to-business marketing, but it also resonates with both the shift towards a service-based logic in marketing (Vargo and Lusch 2004), and a move towards product–service systems as a means to create more sustainable consumer markets (Tukker 2004).

Improved socio-environmental performance of an offering can come via specific features (such as low-energy appliances or low-emission vehicles), through production or service delivery characteristics (such as recycled paper, organic food or ethical banking), or from additional services or attributes (such as provision for recycling end-of-life products). Many environmental product attributes such as recyclability or recycled content, low-energy or low-emission performance, or a reduction in ecologically sensitive ingredients requires their specification through a design-for-environment process (Chen 2001). Some sectors are using processes of 'co-design' to work collaboratively with consumers in search of environmental improvements and innovation (Lebel and Lorek 2008). Heiskanen and Lovio (2010), in a study of the low-energy housing market in Finland, found that close cooperation between builders and prospective purchasers led to both design innovations and improvement in householders' use of energy-saving features.

Whether or not perceived sustainability performance impacts upon consumer perceptions of technical quality is a subject of some controversy. Research from Landor

Associates (2007, quoted in Connelly et al. 2011) shows that consumers associate improved socio-environmental performance with an increase in technical product quality, whilst other research suggests that consumers may draw negative inferences about the technical performance of more sustainable products (Luchs et al. 2010).

### 6.3.2 Cost–Price Issues

Whether or not consumers are willing to pay a premium for more sustainable products has been a core research topic, particularly through 'willingness-to-pay' studies in markets such as green energy and organic food (see, e.g., Laroche et al. 2001). Since the influence of pricing on sustainable consumption behaviour is central to Bolderdijk and Steg (Chapter 15 in this book), this field of research will not be explored further here. However two points are worth making. The first is that such studies perpetuate a view of sustainable products as luxuries that command a premium price, and of their conventional competitors as 'normally' priced. In many cases more sustainable product prices reflect the internalization of socio-environmental costs that conventional competitors treat as externalities and leave unmet. Unfortunately research is rarely phrased in terms of whether or not consumers view as acceptable conventional products with unrealistically low prices because they are subsidized by environmental destruction and human suffering (Belz and Peattie 2012).

The second point worth noting is that the transformation of markets towards more sustainable systems of consumption and production may make conventional notions of price less applicable as we move away from business models based on the sale of products towards more product–service systems. In such cases price becomes less meaningful than the transaction costs (including all financial and psychological costs) associated with accessing and using products and services (including product disposal costs). A transaction costs approach is advanced as a way to explore the viability of sustainability marketing strategies when applied both to the internal processes of developing sustainability solutions and to understanding the consumer's response (Connelly et al. 2011) and presents research opportunities across a range of markets.

### 6.3.3 Distribution

The notion of the 'place' marketing mix variable has conventionally related to the management of distribution channels for tangible products or places of service encounter. For tangible consumer goods, much of their environmental impact is linked to energy and resource consumption within distribution channels and also in consumer travel to and from retail locations (Pretty et al. 2005). Developing eco-efficient distribution channels is a significant subject for research in marketing scholarship and practice, and although consumers have a vested interest in it through the impact on the distribution component of costs and prices, it is not generally an issue that concerns them directly. There has been an exception to this in the food market through consumer concern about food miles and a growing interest in more 'local' food consumption.

The other significant field for research linked to product distribution is in the role played by retailers in building relationships with consumers and influencing their behaviour through their sustainability marketing strategies (Jones et al. 2011).

### 6.3.4 Communications Media

Although all aspects of marketing activity tend to communicate with consumers and other stakeholders, there are a range of specific media that companies use (often in integrated ways) to build stakeholder relationships and influence consumers.

**Advertising**

Advertising is the most visible form of marketing communications encompassing print, broadcast, outdoor and online media. The popularity of sustainability-oriented advertising has varied over time (Leonidou et al. 2011) with a particular spike in its use in the period 1990 to 1992, perhaps explaining the flurry of marketing scholarship looking at its use and effects in the mid-1990s. Some of this research sought to classify ads according to various criteria linked to the style of appeal and 'depth' of green-ness presented. Other research has sought to understand such advertising's influence on consumers, but has tended to produce contradictory results (Leonidou et al. 2011). There is also direct mail advertising, although its associations with generating waste, as indicated by the term 'junk mail', make it a challenging medium to use for sustainable consumption-based messages (Belz and Peattie 2012).

**Sales promotion**

Sales promotion covers a range of techniques that seek to elicit a response from consumers (usually a sale, but also possibly a product trial or the gathering of information) through the offer of additional benefits as a 'special offer'. Vouchers, coupons, contests, free gifts, samples, multi-buy offers, cash-back offers, loyalty schemes and consumer clubs are just some of the promotions used by companies. Their role in stimulating sales, and in the case of 'buy-one-get-one-free' type offers, potentially encouraging overconsumption, has led to criticism of promotions as marketing tools. Despite the prevalence of sales promotion offers in the retailing of packaged foods in particular, there is surprisingly little research exploring their role and effectiveness in influencing consumer behaviour in relation to sustainability. In one study Thøgersen (2009) found that the use of a promotional one-month travel card did significantly increase consumers' willingness to commute by public transport. Behavioural change was even to an extent evident several months after the promotional offer ended, which is in line with broader findings about the ability of short-term promotions to break habits and change longer-term behaviours.

**Selling**

Personal selling is more usually associated with industrial than consumer marketing. However there are consumer markets including cosmetics, cars, new homes and high-technology goods in which selling plays a key role, and these include some of the most significant contributors to consumers' ecological impacts (Belz and Peattie 2012). Despite the important role that sales staff could play in the sustainability marketing communications process, the research literature relating to this is very limited and skewed towards industrial markets.

**Public relations, sponsorship and events**

Products may be promoted through a range of activities under the umbrella terms of public relations including press releases, product launch events, celebrity endorsements, sponsorship activities and 'experiential' marketing. The most comprehensively researched amongst these media is public relations, where there is a significant overlap with corporate brand communications and CSR strategies (Gregory 2007). Research in relation to these media tends to focus on individual cases and rarely with a direct link to their influence on consumer behaviour.

**Point-of-sale**

In-store communication provides opportunities for retailers and manufacturers to engage with consumers on sustainability issues during the shopping and purchasing process, and at a moment that many purchase decisions are made. In a comparison of in-store communications practices amongst leading UK grocers, Jones et al. (2011) found that most such communication was about promoting, rather than restraining, consumption. Sustainability communications tended to be insignificant compared to communications about value and special offers. With the exception of Marks and Spencer's 'Plan A' communications materials that were thematically linked, most in-store communication addressed sustainability issues in a piecemeal way, including topics such as FairTrade, local sourcing, use of reusable shopping bags, sustainably sourced fish and recycled packaging.

### 6.3.5 Interactive Marketing

Online and mobile phone-based communication has been a key growth area in marketing communications in recent years. Leonidou et al. (2011) noted that a common means to connect companies' print advertisements to their environmental agenda was through a reference to online environmental resources (either a specific environmental website or an environmental section of the conventional site). The benefits of communicating online with consumers about sustainability are considerable. Online resources can provide as much depth and detail on product ingredients, production methods and supply chain impacts as the consumer wants. The interactive nature of online communication allows companies to create a dialogue about sustainability improvements, allowing any expressed consumer concerns or scepticism to be tackled directly. Online media also allow consumers to self-select the sustainability issues that most concern them, allowing companies to develop more customized communication than conventional mass-media campaigns providing blanket messages (Minton et al. 2012).

### 6.3.6 Communications Messages

Research into marketing communication messages has largely concerned advertising campaigns and the style of appeal they employ (White et al. 2012). One key stream of research has focused on the nature of environmental claims, which Carlson et al. (1993) classify as product-oriented, process-oriented, image-oriented and environmental fact-based. Leonidou et al. (2011) note that over a 20-year period there has been a gradual shift away from process-oriented, image-oriented or environmental fact-based advertising campaigns towards focusing more on specific product-oriented claims that are easier to observe and for consumers to understand, and more closely related to practical environmental improvements.

### 6.3.7 Packaging and Labelling

Product packaging provides a range of consumer benefits by protecting products, portioning them for convenience and helping to attract consumer attention and communicate information to them at the points of both sale and use. Packaging is also responsible for a considerable portion of products' environmental impact through resource use and the generation of waste. This has led to packaging becoming the focus of consumers' environmental concerns (Bech-Larsen 1996) and company strategies to develop more sustainable offerings (Underwood and Ozanne 1998). Research findings suggest that consumers express concern about the environmental consequences of packaging, but a lack of certainty on the part of consumers about the relative environmental merits of different types of packaging limits its influence on consumer behaviours, particularly in food purchasing where behaviour is strongly driven by habit (Bech-Larsen 1996).

Labelling is a core research area in sustainable marketing, particularly in markets such as organic foods and low-energy appliances, and is considered in detail in Noblet and Teisl (Chapter 19 in this book). From a marketer's perspective sustainability labels have been shown to positively influence consumer behaviour (Grankvist et al. 2007; Thøgersen et al. 2010). It is however challenging to communicate accurately on complex sustainability issues using labels that must also accommodate a growing list of mandatory requirements about ingredients (and in the case of foodstuffs, nutrition and allergy information), and address increasingly international markets using multiple languages. The space available for labelling information is also often shrinking, with attempts to reduce the amount of packaging required by products (Prothero et al. 1997). The persuasive power of labels is particularly strengthened by the use of independent certification of product claims that reflect a full life cycle analysis of the product's socio-environmental performance.

### 6.3.8 Greenwashing

Another stream of research concerns 'greenwashing' and the ways in which environmentally oriented product claims and other marketing communications vary between those that are factually accurate and acceptable, and those that are flawed due to omissions, ambiguity or claims that are untrue or misleading (Kangun et al. 1991). Research into greenwashing has generally focused on understanding it as a marketing practice rather than on its impact on consumer perceptions and behaviour. However studies like that of Chen and Chang (2013) have shown that greenwashing reduces consumers' trust and increases their uncertainty and perception of risks.

## 6.4 SOCIAL MARKETING

Social marketing reflects the use of commercial marketing techniques by governments and public sector bodies to promote behavioural change in the pursuit of social goals.

Although the majority of applications and research studies concern health behaviours, since being established as a field in the early 1970s, social marketing has been applied to an increasingly wide range of behaviours linked also to injury and accident prevention, community involvement and environmental protection (Kotler and Lee 2007). Although social marketing campaigns typically target people with behavioural change interventions in their role as citizens, there can be a significant overlap with their role as consumers. Health campaigns promoting dietary improvement, promoting cycling and walking behaviours over driving, or promoting responsible alcohol consumption all focus on important aspects of consumption. Environmental social marketing campaigns tend to focus on energy, water and waste reduction, and the promotion of PSCBs such as recycling, car sharing, safe pesticide use, and the consumption of local and seasonal produce (Peattie and Peattie 2011).

'Community-based social marketing' addresses the behaviour of citizens at a collective community level (McKenzie-Mohr 2000), recognizing that many elements of consumption (such as energy, transport, recycling and food purchasing) are largely dependent on the provisioning systems within a community and the choices they offer to consumers. Individually, consumers may face very restricted choices in terms of being able to accept or reject what is offered. At its simplest level, consumers cannot car share on their own. Collectively, communities can make sustainable consumption behaviours more feasible, more impactful, and can widen the choices available to consumers through the development of community food, energy, transport or waste schemes (Carrigan et al. 2011). A combination of community-based social marketing campaigns to motivate consumers, and sustainable community enterprises aiming to develop and market sustainable goods and services on a community basis, may represent one of the most promising pathways towards substantively more sustainable consumption. It will however take marketing practice and research away from the familiar territory of international scale systems of production and consumption and supply chains that have come to dominate the research agenda in recent decades.

## 6.5 FUTURE RESEARCH AGENDA

Chabowski et al. (2011), conducted a bibliometric evaluation of the structure of scholarship in marketing and sustainability, taking in 1320 sustainability-focused articles in 36 academic marketing and business journals over a 51-year period. On exploring their results, perhaps the most remarkable finding goes unremarked in the paper itself: that for a discipline that prides itself on its customer orientation, consumers and their behaviour are conspicuous only by their relative absence. The majority of studies focus on marketing strategies, organizational cultures, processes and activities, resources, performance measures and profitability, the ethics and conduct of marketers, advertisers, sales staff and other employees, and the relationship between marketing, CSR and corporate citizenship. Of 35 'clusters' of marketing and sustainability literature identified in the study, only one explicitly mentions 'consumers', and that is in relation to their response to CSR strategies rather than specific marketing efforts. Marketing as a field appears fascinated by the impact that sustainability concerns are having upon itself, whilst leaving the consumer's response comparatively under-researched. Given that progress towards more sustainable systems of consumption and production will depend upon consumer responses to the sustainability agenda and to the innovations in products, services and business models that companies introduce, this is both baffling and worrying.

Prothero et al. (2011) and Chabowski et al. (2011) both review the existing literature on marketing and sustainability and seek to identify future research opportunities. Many of their recommendations for future research focus more on the management of marketing assets, strategy development, macro-marketing issues and broader stakeholder management than understanding the marketing–consumer relationship in a sustainability context. Prothero et al. (2011), argue for the need to broaden the scope of consumer research in marketing beyond the existing emphasis on purchasing, and to understand purchases in the context of consumer lifestyles. In this way the aggregate impacts of consumption behaviours can be understood and reflected in marketing strategies. Prothero et al. (2011) also highlight the research opportunities provided by the blurring of the traditional roles of citizen and consumer, emerging notions of consumer responsibility, and the rise of sustainable consumption practices such as sharing, collaborative consumption and co-creation.

An important contribution that marketing can make to sustainable consumption is through de-marketing activities taken to reduce demand and consumption (Peattie and Peattie 2009). Although usually associated with social marketing and the reduction of consumption of harmful products such as cigarettes, de-marketing has been applied in commercial markets such as tourism to limit access in order to protect the quality of a destination or to restrict demand in the search for exclusivity and increased prices. More de-marketing-focused research would help to shift the agenda beyond the integration of sustainable consumption behaviours and practices into conventional models of consumption and marketing. Instead it would begin to use an understanding of sustainable consumption behaviours and practices to challenge those conventional models of consumption and marketing to move the field from one that seeks to perpetuate our existing consumption–production systems, to one that seeks to challenge and transform them in a search for substantive progress towards a sustainable society (Varey 2010).

## REFERENCES

Ajzen, I. (1991), 'The theory of planned behavior', *Organizational Behavior and Human Decision Processes*, 50 (2), 179–211.

Bagozzi, R., Z. Gürnao-Canli and J. Priester (2002), *The Social Psychology of Consumer Behaviour*, Buckingham: Open University Press.

Bartels, R. (1988), *The History of Marketing Thought*, 3rd edn, Homewood, IL: Richard D. Irwin.

Bech-Larsen, T. (1996), 'Danish consumers' attitudes to the functional and environmental characteristics of food packaging', *Journal of Consumer Policy*, 19 (3), 339–363.

Bekin, C., M. Carrigan, and I. Szmigin (2005), 'Defying marketing sovereignty: voluntary simplicity at new consumption communities', *Qualitative Marketing Research*, 8 (4), 413–429.

Belz, F.M. and K. Peattie (2012), *Sustainability Marketing: A Global Perspective*, 2nd edn, Chichester: Wiley.

Bhate, S. and K. Lawler (1997), 'Environmentally friendly products: factors that influence their adoption', *Technovation*, 17 (8), 457–465.

Biel, A. and U. Dahlstrand (2005), 'Values and habits: a dual-process model', in S. Krarup and C.S. Russell (eds), *Environment, Information and Consumer Behaviour*, Cheltenham, UK and Northampton, MA, USA: Edward Elgar, pp. 33–50.

Boorsma, M. (2006), 'A strategic logic for arts marketing: Integrating customer value and artistic objectives', *International Journal of Culture Policy*, 12 (1), 73–92.

Brown, T.J. and P.A. Dacin (1997), 'The company and the product: corporate associations and consumer product responses', *Journal of Marketing*, 61 (1), 68–84.
Carlson, L., S.J. Grove and N. Kangun (1993), 'A content analysis of environmental advertising claims: a matrix method approach', *Journal of Advertising*, 22 (3), 27–39.
Carrigan, M., C. Moraes and S. Leek (2011), 'Fostering responsible communities: a community social marketing approach to sustainable living', *Journal of Business Ethics*, 100 (3), 515–534.
Chabowski, B.R., J.A. Mena and T.L. Gonzalez-Padron (2011), 'The structure of sustainability research in marketing 1958–2008: a basis for future research opportunities', *Journal of the Academy of Marketing Science*, 39 (1), 55–70.
Chen, C. (2001), 'Design for the environment: a quality-based model for green product development', *Management Science*, 47 (2), 250–263.
Chen, Y.-S., and C.-H. Chang (2013), 'Greenwash and green trust: the mediation effects of green consumer confusion and green perceived risk', *Journal of Business Ethics*, 114 (3), 489–500.
Cherrier, H., I.R. Black and M. Lee (2011), 'Intentional non-consumption for sustainability: consumer resistance and/or anti-consumption?', *European Journal of Marketing*, 45 (11–12), 1757–1767.
Connelly, B.L., D.J. Ketchen and S.F. Slater (2011), 'Towards a "theoretical toolbox" for sustainability research in marketing', *Journal of the Academy of Marketing Science*, 39 (1), 86–100.
do Paco, A. and M. Raposo (2009), '"Green" segmentation: an application to the Portuguese consumer market', *Marketing Intelligence and Planning*, 27 (3), 364–379.
Dolnicar, S. and B. Grun (2009), 'Environmentally friendly behavior: can heterogeneity among individuals and contexts/environments be harvested for improved sustainable management?', *Environment and Behavior*, 41 (5), 693–714.
Gärling, A. and J. Thøgersen (2001), 'Marketing of electric vehicles', *Business Strategy and the Environment*, 10 (1), 53–65.
Getzner, M. and S. Grabner-Kräuter (2004), 'Consumer preferences and marketing strategies for "green shares": specifics of the Austrian market', *International Journal of Bank Marketing*, 22 (4), 260–278.
Grankvist, G., U. Dahlstrand and A. Biel (2007), 'The impact of environmental labeling on consumer preference: negative vs. positive labels', *Journal of Consumer Policy*, 27 (2), 213–230.
Gregory, A. (2007), 'Involving stakeholders in developing corporate brands: the communication dimension', *Journal of Marketing Management*, 23 (1–2), 59–73.
Heiskanen, E. and R. Lovio (2010), 'User–producer interaction in housing energy innovations: energy innovation as a communication challenge', *Journal of Industrial Ecology*, 14 (1), 91–102.
Henion, K.E. and T.C. Kinnear (1976), *Ecological Marketing*, Chicago, IL: American Marketing Association.
Hopwood, B., M. Mellor and G. O'Brien (2005), 'Sustainable development: mapping different approaches', *Sustainable Development*, 13 (1), 38–52.
Hunt, S.D. (1981), 'Macromarketing as a multidimensional concept', *Journal of Macromarketing*, 1 (1), 7–8.
Jackson, T. (2005), *Motivating Sustainable Consumption: A Review of Evidence on Consumer Behaviour and Behavioural Change*, London: Policy Studies Institute.
Jones, P., D. Hiller and D. Comfort (2011), 'Shopping for tomorrow: promoting sustainable consumption within food stores', *British Food Journal*, 113 (7), 935–948.
Kangun, N., L. Carlson and S.J. Grove (1991), 'Environmental advertising claims: a preliminary investigation', *Journal of Public Policy and Marketing*, 10 (2), 47–58.
Kardash, W.J. (1976), 'Corporate responsibility and the quality of life: developing the ecologically concerned consumer', in K.E. Henion and T.C. Kinnear (eds), *Ecological Marketing*, Chicago, IL: American Marketing Association.
Kilbourne, W.E. and S. Beckmann (1998), 'Review and critical assessment of research on marketing and the environment', *Journal of Marketing Management*, 14 (6), 513–532.
Kjellberg, H. (2008), 'Market practices and over-consumption', *Consumption, Markets and Culture*, 11 (2), 151–167.
Kotler, P. and A.R. Andreasen (1996), *Strategic Marketing for Nonprofit Organizations*, 5th edn, Upper Saddle River, NJ: Prentice Hall.
Kotler, P. and N.R. Lee (eds) (2007), *Social Marketing: Influencing Behaviors for Good*, Thousand Oaks, CA: Sage.
Laroche, M., J. Bergeron and G. Barbaro-Forleo (2001), 'Targeting consumers who are willing to pay more for environmentally friendly products', *Journal of Consumer Marketing*, 18 (6), 503–521.
Lebel, L. and S. Lorek (2008), 'Enabling sustainable production–consumption systems', *Annual Review of Environment and Resources*, 33, 241–275.
Leonidou, L.C., C.N. Leonidou, D. Palihawadana and M. Hultman (2011), 'Evaluating the green advertising practices of international firms: a trend analysis', *International Marketing Review*, 28 (1), 6–33.
Luchs, M.G., R. Walker-Naylor, J.R. Irwin and R. Raghunathan (2010), 'The sustainability liability: potential negative effects of ethicality on product preference', *Journal of Marketing*, 74 (5), 18–31.

McCarthy, E.J. (1960), *Basic Marketing, A Managerial Approach*, Homewood, IL: Richard D. Irwin.
McDonald, S. and C. Oates (2006), 'Sustainability: consumer perceptions and marketing strategies', *Business Strategy and the Environment*, 15 (3), 157–170.
McDonald, S., C. Oates, P.J. Alevizou, C.W. Young and K. Hwang (2012), 'Individual strategies for sustainable consumption', *Journal of Marketing Management*, 28 (3–4), 445–468.
McKenzie-Mohr, D. (2000), 'Promoting sustainable behavior: an introduction to community-based social marketing', *Journal of Social Issues*, 56 (3), 543–554.
Middleton, V.T.C. and R. Hawkins (1998), *Sustainable Tourism: A Marketing Perspective*, Oxford: Butterworth-Heineman.
Minton, E., C. Lee, U. Orth, C. Kim and L. Kahle (2012), 'Sustainable marketing and social media: a cross-country analysis of motives for sustainable behaviors', *Journal of Advertising*, 41 (4), 69–84.
Mohr, L.A., D. Eroglu and P.S. Ellen (1998), 'The development and testing of a measure of skepticism toward environmental claims in marketers' communications', *Journal of Consumer Affairs*, 32 (1), 30–55.
Mont, O. and A. Plepys (2008), 'Sustainable consumption progress: should we be proud or alarmed?', *Journal of Cleaner Production*, 16 (4), 531–537.
Ölander, F. and J. Thøgersen (1995), 'Understanding consumer behaviour as a prerequisite for environmental protection', *Journal of Consumer Policy*, 18 (4), 345–385.
Osterhus, T. (1997), 'Pro-social consumer influence strategies: when and how do they work?', *Journal of Marketing*, 61 (4), 16–30.
Peattie, K. (2001a), 'Towards sustainability: the third age of green marketing', *Marketing Review*, 2 (2), 129–146.
Peattie, K. (2001b), 'Golden goose or wild goose? The hunt for the green consumer', *Business Strategy and the Environment*, 10 (4), 187–99.
Peattie, K. and S. Peattie (2009), 'Social marketing: a pathway to consumption reduction?', *Journal of Business Research*, 62 (2), 260–268.
Peattie, S. and K. Peattie (2011), 'Social marketing for a sustainable environment', in G. Hastings, C. Bryant and K. Angus (eds), *The SAGE Handbook of Social Marketing*, London: Sage, pp. 343–358.
Pickett-Baker, J. and R. Ozaki (2008), 'Pro-environmental products: marketing influence on consumer purchase decision', *Journal of Consumer Marketing*, 25 (5), 281–93.
Pretty, J.N., A.S. Ball, T. Lang and J.I.L. Morison (2005), 'Farm costs and food miles: an assessment of the full cost of the UK weekly food basket', *Food Policy*, 30 (1), 1–20.
Prothero, A., S. Dobscha, J. Freund, W.E. Kilbourne, M.G. Luchs, L.K. Ozanne and J. Thøgersen (2011), 'Sustainable consumption: opportunities for consumer research and public policy', *Journal of Public Policy and Marketing*, 30 (1), 31–38.
Prothero, A., K. Peattie and P. McDonagh (1997), 'Communicating greener strategies: a study of on-pack communication', *Business Strategy and the Environment*, 6 (2), 74–82.
Schwartz, S. (1992), 'Universals in the content and structure of human values: theoretical advances and empirical tests in 20 countries', in M. Zanna (ed.), *Advances in Experimental Social Psychology*, Vol. 25, San Diego, CA: Academic Press, pp. 1–65.
Sen, S. and C.B. Bhattacharya (2001), 'Does doing good always lead to doing better? Consumer reactions to corporate social responsibility', *Journal of Marketing Research*, 38 (2), 225–243.
Sharma, A., G.R. Iyer, A. Mehrota and R. Krishnan (2010), 'Sustainability and business-to-business marketing: a framework and implications', *Industrial Marketing Management*, 39 (2), 330–341.
Stern, P. (2000), 'Toward a coherent theory of environmentally significant behavior', *Journal of Social Issues*, 56 (3), 407–424.
Stern, P., T. Dietz, T. Abel, G. Guagnano and L. Kalof (1999), 'A value–belief norm theory of support for social movements: the case of environmental concern', *Human Ecology Review*, 6 (2), 81–97.
Straughan, R.D. and J.A. Roberts (1999), 'Environmental segmentation alternatives: a look at green consumer behaviour in the new millennium', *Journal of Consumer Marketing*, 16 (6), 558–75.
Thøgersen, J. (2009), 'Promoting public transport as a subscription service: effects of a free month travel card', *Transport Policy*, 16, 335–343.
Thøgersen, J., P. Haugaard and A. Olesen (2010), 'Understanding consumer responses to ecolabels', *European Journal of Marketing*, 44 (11/12), 1787–1810.
Tukker, A. (2004), 'Eight types of product–service system: eight ways to sustainability? Experiences from SusProNet', *Business Strategy and the Environment*, 13 (4), 246–260.
Underwood, R. and L. Ozanne (1998), 'Is your packaging an effective communicator? A normative framework for increasing the communicative competences of packaging', *Journal of Marketing Communications*, 4 (4), 207–220.
van der Zwan, F. and T. Bhamra (2003), 'Services marketing: taking up the sustainable development challenge', *Journal of Services Marketing*, 17 (4), 341–356.
Van Dijk, E., A. Wit, H. Wilke and D.V. Budescu (2004), 'What we know (and do not know) about the effects

of uncertainty on behavior in social dilemmas', in R. Suleiman, D.V. Budescu, I. Fischer and D.M. Messick (eds), *Contemporary Psychological Research on Social Dilemmas*, Cambridge: Cambridge University Press, pp. 315–331.
Varey, R. (2010), 'Marketing means and ends for a sustainable society: a welfare agenda for transformative change', *Journal of Macromarketing*, 30 (2), 112–126.
Vargo, S.L. and R.F. Lusch (2004), 'Evolving to a new dominant logic for marketing', *Journal of Marketing*, 68 (1), 1–17.
Webb, D., L.A. Mohr and K.E. Harris (2008), 'A re-examination of socially responsible consumption and its measurement', *Journal of Business Research*, 61 (3), 91–98.
Wells, V., C. Ponting and K. Peattie (2011), 'Behaviour and climate change: consumer perceptions of responsibility', *Journal of Marketing Management*, 27 (7–8), 803–833.
White, K., R. MacDonnell and J.H. Elland (2012), 'Belief in a just world: consumer intentions and behaviours towards ethical products', *Journal of Marketing*, 76 (1), 103–118.
Wilkie, W.L. and S.E. Moore (2003), 'Scholarly research in marketing: exploring the "4 eras" of thought development', *Journal of Public Policy and Marketing*, 22 (2), 116–46.

# 7. Ethics and sustainable consumption

*Lieske Voget-Kleschin, Christian Baatz and Konrad Ott*

Ethics constitutes the subdiscipline of philosophy dedicated to the academic study of human practices, customs and conventions (Düwell et al. 2002). One way to describe philosophy is that it is concerned with reflections upon basic concerns within human life. Consuming things essentially belongs to human life. A philosophical-ethical perspective on sustainable consumption aims to make transparent the implicit and sometimes unquestioned assumptions behind arguments. This renders such assumptions accessible and subject to critique (see Ott et al. 2011).

Sustainable development (SD) constitutes a leading model for contemporary societal development. Despite or probably because of this, the complex idea of SD has often been used as a catchphrase without specific meaning. Different parties interpret the concept according to their particular interests. Insofar as this is the case, the concept is no longer suited for guiding societal development. Therefore, to approach sustainable consumption from a philosophical-ethical perspective first of all necessitates delineating what we mean when we speak about SD (section 7.1). This then allows briefly specifying our notion of sustainable consumption (section 7.2).

Normative ethics focuses on what humans owe to each other as moral persons (Scanlon 2000). Thus, a normative-ethical approach towards sustainable consumption asks if we as a society as well as everyone of us as a single individual are obliged to take up sustainable consumption (section 7.3). A general principle in ethics is 'ought implies can'. A moral imperative that cannot be met is not valid. The ability to meet moral demands is not limited to cognitive and physical ability but also needs to take into account the psychological 'costs' of complying with obligations. Ensuring that claims for sustainable consumption do not overburden individuals is a constitutive and important part of a normative-ethical approach towards sustainable consumption (section 7.4). Section 7.5 concludes.

## 7.1 A NORMATIVE CONCEPT OF SUSTAINABLE DEVELOPMENT

Though there exist a multitude of definitions and conceptions of sustainability, they all take responsibility of contemporary humans for posterity as a starting point (Becker 2012; Burger and Christen 2011; Christen and Schmidt 2012; Norton 2005). Acknowledging responsibilities for future humans, it would be inconsistent not to recognize responsibilities towards contemporary humans. Thus there is a strong link between sustainability questions and questions of intra- and intergenerational justice (Schultz et al. 2008; Schultz et al. 2013). We therefore understand SD as claiming that all contemporary and future human beings should be able to live a decent human life (WCED 1987).

Furthermore it is constitutive of SD to acknowledge that the ability to live a decent human life necessarily presupposes certain environmental and social conditions. Accordingly we understand the concept of SD to encompass two kinds of claims (Voget-Kleschin 2013):[1]

1. Direct claims for justice ask us to behave in a way that our interaction with other people avoids violating their ability to live a decent human life.
2. Indirect claims for justice encompass claims for a handling of our social and natural environment that qualifies as not undermining contemporary and future humans' ability to live such a decent human life.

Finally, we understand direct and indirect claims for justice as equally important and mutually constraining each other. Direct claims for justice entail claims in regard to our consumption behaviour insofar as this involves interactions with other people. By way of example, this holds for our interaction with sales personnel at the point of sale, meaning that such interactions must not violate their ability to live a decent human life. Furthermore in buying certain products we arguably interact with individuals in the commodity chain. Thus in buying fair trade rather than conventional coffee we contribute to fostering certain production conditions. Direct claims for justice entail that in any such interactions we need to respect other people's claims to a decent human life. In addition focusing on direct claims for justice allows for a further insight: for an individual (or group or society), changing behaviour towards more sustainable consumption is often costly in terms of money, time and effort.[2] Thus, claims for more sustainable consumption burden individuals. Acknowledging that SD is about direct claims for justice does imply that to qualify as more sustainable consumption, a measure or act must not violate the claim to a decent human life of those individuals or societies which we expect to consume sustainably. To put it simply, claims for sustainable consumption must not overburden their addressees. We will come back to this issue in section 7.4.

Indirect claims for justice imply that an act or measure only qualifies as (more[3]) sustainable consumption if it results in less pressure on humanity's environmental and social base of livelihood than conventional consumption. Whether, and by how far, a certain act or measure complies with such claims depends on its consequences. It is therefore closely linked to empirical questions (see Part III of this book). Yet the question of what qualifies as pressure and sufficient reduction of such pressures, respectively, involves not only empirical information but also value judgements.

The paradigmatic example regards the debate about weak versus strong sustainability. Proponents of weak sustainability argue that natural capital (that is, the natural base of human livelihood) can be substituted for by human and real capital. Therefore, according to weak sustainability, what we need to preserve for future generations is the aggregate capital stock, that is, the sum total of natural, human and real capital: 'Loosely speaking, according to WS [weak sustainability] it does not matter whether the current generation uses up non-renewable resources or pollutes the environment as long as enough machineries, roads and ports as well as schools and universities are built in compensation' (Neumayer 2010, p. 1). By contrast, strong sustainability negates such substitutability. It therefore claims that we need to maintain at least part if not all of natural capital (ibid.). Elsewhere we have argued in favour of strong sustainability (e.g. Ott et al. 2011). Among the arguments discussed we have named a critique of the general economic framework on which the concept of weak sustainability relies, adherence to the precautionary principle and a better compatibility with the argumentative framework of environmental ethics (ibid.). It should be obvious that these arguments – as well as any potential refutation – cannot rely on empirical information alone but necessarily draw on value judgements.

## 7.2 SPECIFYING MORE SUSTAINABLE CONSUMPTION

The distinction between weak and strong sustainability is closely connected to distinguishing between weak and strong sustainable consumption.[4] Weak, or mainstream (Seyfang 2011), sustainable consumption primarily focuses on improving consumption efficiency; that is, the amount of environmental burden per product unit consumed. It maintains the notion of consumption as a proxy for utility. Thus it can be dubbed 'green' or 'ethical' consumerism. The problem with such a notion of sustainable consumption lies in that it retains 'consumerism'. However as soon as the rate of increase in consumption exceeds the rate of increase of consumption efficiency, this results in an absolute increase rather than decrease of consumption.[5]

By contrast, strong, or 'new economics' (Seyfang 2011), sustainable consumption aims at reducing absolute consumption levels. It therefore avoids rebounds. Strong sustainable consumption recognizes that consumption of goods and services is not necessarily linearly correlated to well-being and investigates alternative, non-consumptive or less consumptive ways of achieving well-being. Furthermore it acknowledges individuals' embeddedness in infrastructures of provision as well as social institutions (ibid.). This allows diagnosing, first, how certain infrastructures and institutions inhibit more sustainable consumption; and second, how changing infrastructures and institutions contributes to facilitating more sustainable consumption. Thus strong sustainable consumption constitutes a broad notion encompassing individual lifestyle changes that are not directly related to consuming goods or services as well as institutional and infrastructural changes aiming at governing individuals towards such more sustainable lifestyles. Table 7.1 juxtaposes characteristic features of mainstream and new economics models of sustainable consumption.

In the remainder of this chapter we adhere to a position of strong sustainable consumption. The first reason for doing so is that we adhere to strong sustainability (see Ott et al. 2011; Voget-Kleschin 2013, 2014). Strong sustainability *inter alia* encompasses a critique of the general economic framework of neoclassical mainstream economics (Neumayer 2010; Ott et al. 2011). As demonstrated in Table 7.1, weak or mainstream sustainable consumption is very much grounded in these same neoclassical assumptions. Accordingly, we hold that from a position of strong sustainability, strong sustainable consumption is much more convincing than weak sustainable consumption. More specifically, we hold that weak sustainable consumption will run into rebound effects (see above, especially note 5) and therefore fails to relieve the pressure on natural capital. Because of this, it is not universalizable. In our view, weak sustainable consumption constitutes an improvement in comparison to today's consumptive patterns in rich societies but does not offer a role model for a globally emerging middle class. This is so because we do not conceive of weak sustainable consumption as a first step that might or will

*Table 7.1 Comparing mainstream and new economics models of sustainable consumption*

| | Mainstream sustainable consumption | New economic sustainable consumption |
|---|---|---|
| Objective | Incremental improvements in resource efficiency; continual economic growth through 'consuming differently' | System-wide changes in infrastructures of provision to reduce absolute consumption levels by 'consuming less' |
| Mechanism | Sustainable consumers send market signals for sustainably-produced goods and services, which drives innovation and improvement | Collective action reshapes socio-technical infrastructures of provision, creating new systems and non-market alternatives where necessary |
| Consumers | Individual green consumers | Ecological citizens within communities of place, practice and interest |
| Progress measured by | Traditional measures of economic growth; consumption as a proxy for utility (happiness) | New measures of sustainable well-being; consumption not necessarily related to wellbeing |
| Theories of consumption | Utilitarian<br>Social/psychological | Social/ psychological<br>Infrastructures of provision |
| Examples | Green and ethical consumerism; corporate greening of global capitalism; social marketing | Local provisioning e.g. farmers' markets; mutual aid e.g. LETS; self-reliance e.g. low-impact development |

*Source:* Seyfang (2011, p.21).

eventually lead into strong(er) sustainable consumption. Rather, in our view, insofar as weak and strong sustainable consumption are grounded in different objectives and theories of consumption they constitute two different trajectories.

As Table 7.1 shows, strong sustainable consumption asks for more radical lifestyle changes. Therefore ethical questions related to sustainable consumption are more pronounced in regard to strong sustainable consumption. This constitutes the second reason for our focusing on strong sustainable consumption in the remainder of this chapter. However the ethical questions we discuss subsequently also occur in regard to weak sustainable consumption, though are probably less pronounced. Accordingly even those readers not convinced by our (necessarily brief) justification of strong sustainable consumption might gain from the subsequent discussion of related ethical issues.

## 7.3 IS IT LEGITIMATE TO ASK INDIVIDUALS TO CONSUME IN A (MORE) SUSTAINABLE MANNER?[6]

In the philosophical literature on individual obligations regarding what are called 'environmental duties', several authors have denied that there is such a thing as duty to change one's individual behaviour such as one's consumption behaviour (e.g. Cripps 2013; Johnson 2003; Neuteleers 2010; Sandberg 2011; Sinnot-Armstrong 2010). These authors generally argue that obligations regarding SD primarily apply to governments. Governments are assigned the duty to implement political institutions that ensure SD. Obviously this is not without implications regarding individual behaviour. First, the aim of political institutions is to govern individual behaviour. Therefore, for institutions to be effective requires individuals to comply with these institutions. Second, although political institutions result from collective action broadly conceived, such collective action is not detached but rather emerges from individual behaviour. Therefore, in a situation where political institutions are lacking, a claim for collective action aiming at implementing such institutions yields a corresponding individual obligation to engage in collective action to promote such political institutions. Thus the above-mentioned authors reason that individuals' obligations encompass duties to comply and duties to promote.

### 7.3.1 Duties to Comply

Formal political institutions constrain individual behaviour.[7] It seems plausible that individuals promote such formal political institutions only if they are prepared to accept the corresponding constraints. Democratic political changes necessitate that a majority of individuals promotes institutional changes. However political institutions do not only bind those individuals who show their acceptance by politically promoting them or at least accepting them for internal reasons (rather than because they are linked to external sanctions). On the contrary, institutions bind everybody falling under their scope.

Institutions aiming at more sustainable consumption typically result in constraints on so far (rather) unconstrained behavioural possibilities, namely such that are widely conceived of as private, for example, mobility behaviour, behaviour related to one's place of living or food consumption. Therefore an important line of argument against such institutions points to the liberal principle according to which the state should not interfere with individuals' ideas about how to live (principle of neutrality).[8] However as Rawls (1988) points out, some of the connotations the term 'neutrality' evokes are highly misleading. To put it simply, as social practice theory demonstrates, any kind of individual behaviour is always influenced by social constraints, norms of social interaction, infrastructures and material organization of spaces, timescapes and routines (see Southerton et al. 2004; Welch and Warde, Chapter 5 in this book). Although political institutions cannot determine any of these, they deliberately aim to, and in fact do influence all of them. However if any institutional frame affects individual choices as well as the impact these choices have on individuals' quality of life, it is inadequate to assume that a situation prior to the implementation of an institution aiming at eliciting more sustainable consumption generally involves fewer constraints in comparison to a situation post such implementation. Take the example of introducing a tax on aviation fuel. Assume that the aim of such a tax was to govern individuals to increase train and coach rides at the expense of air travel. Our argument than reads as pointing out that it is more adequate to perceive the situation prior to the implementation of this tax as involving different constraints (for example, no tax on aviation fuel, tax on railway and coach travel) as compared to a situation post such implementation (for example, tax on aviation fuel, tax on railway and coach travel). While the situation with a tax on aviation fuel arguably entails disincentives regarding air travel, so does the situation without such a tax entail disincentives regarding other forms of travel.

Thus the state cannot avoid setting some institutional frame. Therefore it cannot avoid influencing people's choices, ranging from narrow market choices to more seminal choices such as where to live or which job to take. This means that neutrality of influence is chimerical (Rawls 1988). Rather than asking if constraints resulting from institutions aiming at overcoming global environmental problems are legitimate we need to focus on how and to what degree individuals' choices can be legitimately constrained (see Voget-Kleschin 2014).[9] We will come back to this issue in section 7.4.

### 7.3.2 Duties to Promote

Duties to promote initially refer to any kind of action that primarily aims at promoting yet non-existent formal institutions as well as infrastructure, for example, public transport systems. Examples for duties to promote include classical political actions such as voting and participating in demonstrations but also action such as supporting an environmental organization, participating in a consumer boycott or trying to convince friends of an opinion (Neuteleers 2010). However possibilities for promoting are not limited to such political behaviour. Rather, individual behaviour not primarily aimed at promoting formal institutions may nevertheless contribute towards promotion. First, it can act as a political signal to policy makers. By way of example, if I, as well as a sufficient amount of other people, each decide to commute via public transport rather than by private car, this can motivate the authority in charge to increase frequency of public transport. Thus my behaviour can promote formal institutions (ibid.). Furthermore my behaviour may also feature communicative value towards fellow citizens. Accordingly my behaviour might, first, directly motivate other people to adopt certain consumption choices. Thus a friend of mine might like my tasty vegetarian cooking and try out some vegetarian recipes herself (direct diffusion; see Neuteleers 2010). Second, if many people change their lifestyles in a certain way, this might influence customs, habits, norms and status; that is, informal institutions (indirect diffusion; ibid.). Finally, the communicative value of individual behaviour is not limited to positive signals towards more sustainable consumption. Rather, it can also work in the opposite direction. By way of example, Sinnot-Armstrong (2010) thinks it legitimate to adhere to a certain behaviour such as driving a fuel-guzzling sports utility vehicle (SUV) for fun while concurrently engaging politically to constrain just such behaviour. He reasons this claim by the allegedly higher effectiveness of political behaviour as opposed to individual behavioural change. However he overlooks the communicative disvalue of his act: his Sunday joy ride might well undermine his political efforts by rendering them hypocritical. Thus individual behaviour that runs counter to one's political efforts towards more sustainable consumption antagonizes the success of such efforts by undermining an individual's credibility.[10]

### 7.3.3 A Third Kind of Individual Duties

The contentious issue that the above-mentioned authors negate relates to the question of whether there exists a third type of duty, namely a duty to change one's lifestyle[11] even if this does not have any kind of communicative value. A typical example refers to reducing time in the shower, or showering with cold water, so as to save energy and water (see Neuteleers 2010). Given that most people might not be inclined to discuss their showering habits with others, this action does not feature communicative value. Rather, the intuitive argument behind such a duty is that each individual should contribute their bit towards collective sustainable development. It can thus be designated as a duty to contribute one's fair share (see Baatz 2014). It is important to note that the question is not whether we have a duty to comply and promote *or* a duty to contribute our individual fair share. Rather, the question at stake is whether, *in addition* to our duties to comply and promote, we *also* have a duty to contribute our individual fair share. A common argument against such a duty points out that individual behavioural changes feature negligible effects only (Sandberg 2011). However, first, the empirics of this claim can be contested (Hiller 2011; Nolt 2011, 2013). Furthermore, insofar as this claim does hold, one could argue that it applies to duties to promote as well. That is, political institutions usually emerge by individuals lobbying for such actions. However, imagine I engage in a Greenpeace campaign to cut GHG emissions or lobby for a green party. Given that I might be a very poor campaigner or a bad team player, not only might the effect of my joining the collective effort be negligible, but it might even constrain rather than support the political endeavour.

A second important argument against duties to contribute one's fair share points out that such duties overburden individuals. That is, taking up more sustainable consumption necessitates individual resources such as knowledge, competence, being prepared to turn away from beloved routines and habits, not to mention time and (sometimes) money. The argument goes that asking individuals to invest these resources into more sustainable consumption is asking for too much. However, once again this argument does not specifically cover duties to contribute one's fair share. Rather, it applies to duties to promote as well. This is because, obviously, complying with duties to promote might be as demanding in terms of the individual resources listed above as complying with a duty to contribute one's fair share.

Meanwhile we hold the argument to be very important that claims for individual contributions (in terms of promoting institutions and in terms of contributing one's fair share) can overburden individuals. This is so because according to the understanding of SD as laid down in this chapter (see section 7.1), demands that overburden individuals do not qualify as contributing towards SD at all. Nevertheless we hold that pointing to such possibilities of overburdening does not undermine the task of reasoning claims for individual contributions towards SD. Rather, it highlights that such claims need to be specified in a way that avoids such overburdening. We will address this issue in section 7.4. Figure 7.1 summarizes the spectrum of individual duties.

## 7.4 SPECIFYING OBLIGATIONS: INDIVIDUAL DUTIES AS IMPERFECT DUTIES

Lifestyle changes may be linked to quite substantial economic, social and/or psychological costs. These costs will vary, depending on the circumstances individuals are in.[12] By way of example, it will presumably be easier for an urban single person to give up her car than it will be for a rural family to abandon even their second car. The obligation to

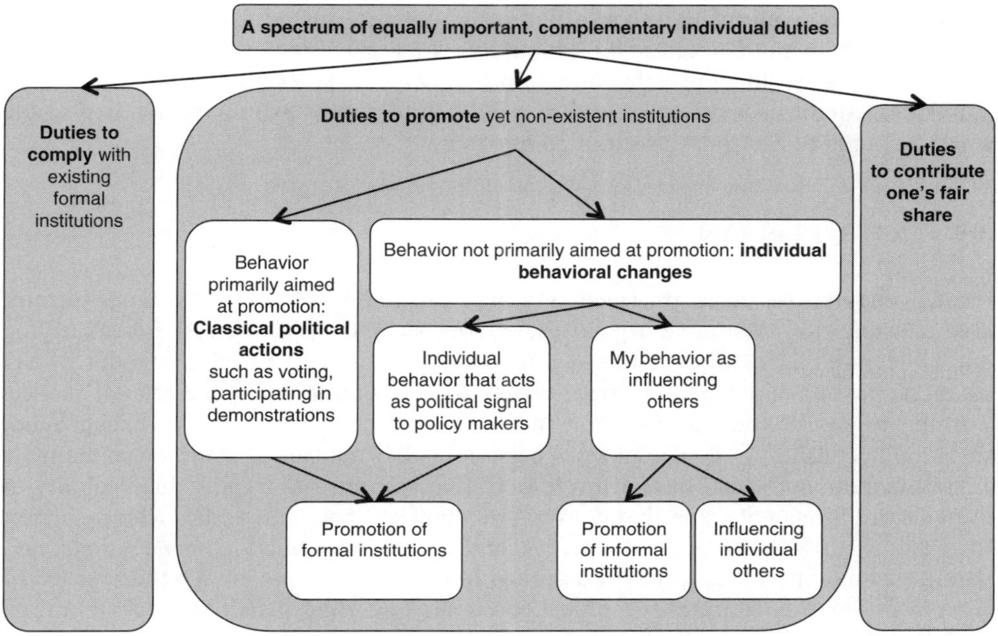


*Source:* Based on Neuteleers (2010, p. 510).

*Figure 7.1 A spectrum of equally important, complementary individual duties*

change one's lifestyle only holds if doing so can be reasonably demanded. On a general level of analysis, it is not possible to specify this claim, because to determine whether or not certain obligations overburden individuals, we need information regarding the circumstances an individual is in. If we knew the exact circumstances a person is in, we would be able to determine whether or not certain obligations overburden her. However we cannot know, because of structural reasons. That is to say, we cannot determine from the outside (from the perspective of a fellow citizen) how big the costs involved in certain actions are for specific individuals. Returning to the shower example, how big the burden of taking a cold shower really is cannot be determined from the outside but can only be judged by the individual herself. Therefore individual lifestyle changes are imperfect duties in the Kantian sense (Johnson 2011).[13] According to Kant (1996, p. 156), perfect duties are determinate, whereas imperfect duties are wide duties in that 'the duty has in it a latitude for doing more or less, and no specific limits can be assigned to what should be done'. Insofar as ethics thus cannot (exactly) delimit an individual's duties, imperfect duties mark limits of ethics as ethics.

However this does not mean that what should be done is left to an individual's convenience. Imperfect duties remain duties. First, insofar as they have information regarding the situation individuals are in, common deliberation among moral persons can determine a range within which the fulfilment of imperfect obligations should fall. For example we might judge that it is less problematic to nudge or even oblige an urban single to give up her car than to apply the same measures to a rural family. Second, that duties are imperfect only means that their extent cannot be determined from the outside. This does not make them the slightest bit less binding. In terms of our example, the individual herself must assess how great the burden of taking a cold shower is for her. That is, an individual cannot do as she pleases but must (try to) assess as impartially as possible what she ought to do from the moral point of view.

## 7.5 CONCLUSION

In this chapter we have provided a philosophical-ethical perspective on sustainable consumption. We have argued that doing so first of all necessitates clarifying our understanding of SD. In this regard we have briefly outlined a concept of SD as encompassing direct and indirect claims for intra- and intergenerational justice. Turning to sustainable consumption, we have argued that against this background, sustainable consumption encompasses behaviour that reduces pressure on humanity's environmental and social base of livelihood, that respects other individuals' ability to live a decent human life, and that does not overburden those individuals who we expect to consume sustainably. Subsequently we introduced the distinction between weak and strong sustainable consumption and argued in favour of the latter. We then turned to what in our view constitutes the ethical core issue regarding sustainable consumption: namely, whether it is legitimate to claim that individuals need to consume more sustainably. We answered this question in the affirmative and distinguished three equally important, complementary individual duties: duties to comply, to promote and to contribute one's fair share. Finally we turn back to the claim that such duties must not overburden individuals. We explain why ethics cannot (exactly) delimit an individual's duties, but stress that this does not result in individual duties being the least bit less binding.

## NOTES

1. It is important to note, first, that such a concept of SD is embedded in higher-ranking normative positions regarding normative ethics. In our case this takes the form of a commitment to discourse ethics. Second, depicting SD as encompassing direct and indirect claims for justice as such does not suffice for reasoning action-guiding claims. Rather, action guidance necessitates further specifications, most notably in regard to the scope, pattern and currency of justice (see Voget-Kleschin 2014).
2. It is questionable whether such a behavioural change is necessarily costly. On the one hand there are win–win possibilities, especially in regard to monetary costs. Thus, reducing travel, living space or meat consumption goes along with reducing expenses in these areas. On the other hand, the relation is less clear in regard to time and effort. Insofar as most if not all everyday behaviour is based upon routines and habits, any change will initially produce costs in terms of time and effort. As new routines and habits develop, these initial costs will cease. In regard to the general question of whether more sustainable practices are more or less costly regarding time and effort, we tentatively propose an inverse relation regarding time and effort: some more sustainable practices, such as travelling less, will indeed free up time. However we propose that many individuals will experience such drastic changes as being rather costly in terms of reducing their quality of life. Other, less radical changes such as substituting a private car by public transport will be less costly in terms of effort but will prove more time-consuming.
3. We do not hold it to be possible to define a (group of) lifestyle(s) as sustainable. What we do hold is that it is possible to ordinally rank different lifestyles according to their sustainability. Again, we do not hold that it is possible to give a complete ordering. The less demanding thesis we presuppose here is

that it is (sometimes) possible to identify different choices as well as different lifestyles as more and less sustainable.

4. However it is important to note that though they are closely connected, the two distinctions do not necessarily coincide.
5. This phenomenon is generally designated as the rebound effect. Historically, this effect was first described by William Stanley Jevons (see Jevons 1866 [2009]). Since increase in consumption as a result of increase in efficiency runs counter to popular intuition, the effect was historically called 'Jevons' paradox'.
6. The arguments in this section draw on Voget-Kleschin and Baatz (2013).
7. As discussed in the introduction to section 7.3, duties to comply and to promote are grounded in an argument according to which governments are assigned the duty to implement political institutions that ensure SD. Accordingly, in duties to comply with institutions the term 'institutions' refers to a narrow understanding of formal institutions. This is not to say that we generally equalize the term 'institutions' with formal institutions. Rather, in adopting a strong sustainable consumption perspective we explicitly acknowledge the existence and importance of informal institutions. Furthermore, in regard to duties to promote we discuss the promotion of both formal and informal institutions (see section 3.2).
8. See Grunwald (2010). Corresponding arguments are often implied in popular protest against regulations of so far unregulated issues, such as public smoking. A recent and rather vigorous example consist in the protest against a proposal of a mandatory vegetarian day in all public canteens, issued by the German Greens in the course of their election campaign (see Hawley 2013).
9. Note that thus constraining choices is not paternalistic if citizens themselves democratically opt for laws, regulations and incentives that constrain their behaviour.
10. Note that the credibility of persons who promote (strong) sustainable consumption will always be challenged by opponents who try to find remaining 'weak points'. Those who will not change at all always like to accuse forerunners as hypocrites.
11. In the following, whenever we speak of duties to change one's lifestyle, we presuppose that the current lifestyle is unsustainable.
12. Among others, these circumstances also encompass whether others do their fair share. The question of whether and how non-compliance by other individuals affects the duty of complying agents is a major question within so-called non-ideal theory (see Murphy 2003).
13. Johnson discusses duties to lower one's GHG emissions but his argument equally applies to individual lifestyle changes more generally.

# REFERENCES

Baatz, C. (2014), 'Climate change and individual responsibility to reduce GHG-emissions', *Ethics, Policy and Environment*, 17 (1), 1–19.

Becker, C.U. (2012), *Sustainability Ethics and Sustainability Research*, Dordrecht, New York: Springer.

Burger, P. and M. Christen (2011), 'Towards a capability approach of sustainability', *Journal of Cleaner Production*, 19 (8), 787–795.

Christen, M. and S. Schmidt (2012), 'A formal framework for conceptions of sustainability: a theoretical contribution to the discourse in sustainable development', *Sustainable Development*, 20 (6), 400–410.

Cripps, E. (2013), *Climate Change and the Moral Agent: Individual Duties in an Interdependent World*, Oxford: Oxford University Press.

Düwell, M., C. Hübenthal and M. Werner (2002), 'Einleitung. Ethik: Begriff – Geschichte – Theorie – Applikation', in M. Düwell (ed.), *Handbuch Ethik*, Stuttgart: Metzler, pp. 1–23.

Grunwald, A. (2010), 'Wider die Privatisierung der Nachhaltigkeit. Warum ökologisch korrekter Konsum die Umwelt nicht retten kann', *Gaia*, 19 (3), 178–182.

Hawley, C. (2013), 'Hands off my sausage', *Spiegel Online International*, 6 August, available at http://www.spiegel.de/international/germany/spat-over-meat-consumption-livens-german-campaign-a-915064.html (accessed 30 January 2014).

Hiller, A. (2011), 'Climate change and individual responsibility', *Monist*, 94 (3), 349–368.

Jevons, W.S. (1866 [2009]), *The Coal Question*, La Vergne, TN: General Books.

Johnson, B. (2003), 'Ethical obligations in a tragedy of the commons', *Environmental Values*, 12 (3), 271–287.

Johnson, B. (2011), 'The possibility of a joint communique: my response to Hourdequin', *Environmental Values*, 20 (2), 147–156.

Kant, I. (1996), *Kant: The Metaphysics of Morals*, Cambridge: Cambridge University Press.

Murphy, L.B. (2003), *Moral Demands in Nonideal Theory*, Oxford: Oxford University Press.

Neumayer, E. (2010), *Weak Versus Strong Sustainability: Exploring the Limits of Two Opposing Paradigms*, 3rd edn, Cheltenham, UK and Northampton, MA, USA: Edward Elgar.
Neuteleers, S. (2010), 'Institutions versus lifestyle: do citizens have environmental duties in their private sphere?', *Environmental Politics*, 19 (4), 501–517.
Nolt, J. (2011), 'How harmful are the average American's greenhouse gas emissions?', *Ethics, Policy and Environment*, 14 (1), 3–10.
Nolt, J. (2013), 'Replies to critics of "How harmful are the average American's greenhouse gas emissions?"', *Ethics, Policy and Environment*, 16 (1), 111–119.
Norton, B.G. (2005), *Sustainability. A Philosophy of Adaptive Ecosystem Management*, Chicago, IL: University of Chicago Press.
Ott, K., B. Muraca and C. Baatz (2011), 'Strong sustainability as a frame for sustainability communication', in J. Godemann and G. Michelsen (eds), *Sustainability Communication. Interdisciplinary Perspectives and Theoretical Foundations*, Dordrecht, New York: Springer, pp. 13–26.
Rawls, J. (1988), 'The priority of right and ideas of the good', *Philosophy and Public Affairs*, 17 (4), 251–276.
Sandberg, J. (2011), 'My emissions make no difference', *Environmental Ethics*, 33 (3), 229–248.
Scanlon, T. (2000), *What We Owe to Each Other*, Cambridge, MA: Belknap Press of Harvard University Press.
Schultz, E., M. Christen, L. Voget-Kleschin and P. Burger (2013), 'A sustainability-fitting interpretation of the capability approach: integrating the natural dimension by employing feedback loops', *Journal of Human Development and Capabilities*, 14 (1), 115–133.
Schultz, J., F. Brand, J. Kopfmüller, K. Ott (2008), 'Building a "theory of sustainable development": two salient conceptions within the German discourse', *International Journal of Environment and Sustainable Development*, 7 (4), 465–482.
Seyfang, G. (2011), *The New Economics of Sustainable Consumption: Seeds of Change*, Basingstoke: Palgrave Macmillan.
Sinnot-Armstrong, W. (2010), 'Its not my fault: global warming and individual moral obligations', in S.M. Gardiner (ed.), *Climate Ethics: Essential Readings*, Oxford, UK and New York, USA: Oxford University Press, pp. 332–346.
Southerton, D., A. Warde and M. Hand (2004), 'The limited autonomy of the consumer: implications for sustainable consumption', in D. Southerton, H. Chappells and B. van Vliet (eds), *Sustainable Consumption: The Implications of Changing Infrastructures of Provision*, Cheltenham, UK and Northampton, MA, USA: Edward Elgar, pp. 32–48.
Voget-Kleschin, L. (2013), 'Large-scale land acquisition: evaluating its environmental aspects against the background of strong sustainability', *Journal of Agricultural and Environmental Ethics*, 26 (6), 1105–1126.
Voget-Kleschin, L. (2014), 'Employing a normative conception of sustainability to reason and specify sustainable food consumption', *Journal of Agricultural and Environmental Ethics*, DOI: 10.1007/s10806-014-9503-1.
Voget-Kleschin, L. and C. Baatz (2013), 'Individual responsibility for global environmental problems. Climate change, sustainability, and an ethics of an open future', in Societas Ethica (24 August 2013), 50th Societas Ethica Annual Conference, Soesterberg.
WCED (World Commission on Environment and Development) (1987), *Our Common Future*, New York, USA and Oxford, UK: WCED.

# PART III

# DIAGNOSTIC RESEARCH: METHODS AND MEASUREMENTS

# 8. Life cycle assessment as a means to identify the most effective action for sustainable consumption

*Kjartan Steen-Olsen and Edgar G. Hertwich*

What kind of responses would you get if you took a poll to the streets asking people what actions they should take to reduce the environmental burden of their lifestyle? It is likely that common replies would involve installing energy-efficient light bulbs and water-efficient shower heads, switching to reusable shopping bags, driving electric cars and so on. But how much, if at all, do these individual actions actually contribute? The sustainable society, though hardly controversial as a vision for the global community, is as challenging as it is ambitious, and it does not help that sustainability is intrinsically hard to measure.

One challenge for consumers is the plethora of information they are exposed to from media, official agencies, commercial actors, friends and family. Even for those who are motivated to do so, changing behaviour on environmental grounds takes cognitive effort, which consumers economize (Stern et al. 2010). As such, it is in the interest of all parties that those behaviour changes that are successfully introduced to the public carry as much weight for the environment as possible.

In research on environmental psychology and sustainable consumption, the term 'environmentally significant behaviour' has emerged to highlight the need for studies to take into account both the size of the environmental impact and the possibility of changing that impact through behaviour change (behavioural plasticity; see for example Stern 2000). Not all types of environmental behaviour matter equally; for instance, major infrequent decisions such as what kind of car to buy, or whether to buy a car at all, typically have larger environmental impacts than whether or not people reuse their shopping bags (Stern 2000).

Clearly a consumer-oriented environmental policy measure that is successful in changing consumer behaviour will not be effective if the net impact per person who changes their behaviour is low. Gatersleben et al. (2002) report highly variable correlations between the perceived and actual environmental impact of different types of household consumption. The overall environmental impact of a certain purchase or activity is usually not intuitively obvious, but will be a combination of several effects that can be different in a number of ways:

- Temporally: in addition to the direct effects incurred during its use, a purchased product might have caused environmental harm in the past, or it is committed to do so in the future. A nuclear power plant may deliver virtually emission-free electricity in the present, but will have to deal with the handling of radioactive waste in the future. A fine whisky purchased today contributed to emissions two decades ago.
- Spatially: in contrast to pre-industrial times, when trees logged for ship building and firewood would come from (and visibly diminish) local forests, the globalized

economy of today has increasingly separated consumers from producers, and retail goods currently available to consumers in the Western world can contain parts designed, manufactured and assembled in dozens of countries.

- Chemically: the production, use and disposal of consumer goods frequently involve emissions of thousands of chemical compounds, each affecting the environment in different, often unknown ways.
- Mechanistically: there might be several causal pathways between emitted substances and ultimate adverse effects. For instance inhalation of mercury vapour has been known for centuries to be hazardous, but today we know that mercury also accumulates in the food chain and represents an additional health risk to humans and large predators through ingestion.
- Categorically: the release of pollutants and wastes to the environment, and the intake of resources from it, during the lifetime of a product may affect the environment in many different ways. One such harmful impact category is adverse climate change from anthropogenic greenhouse gas emissions; other examples include increased cancer incidence or species extinction.

Life cycle assessment (LCA) is a well-established method to quantify the overall environmental impacts of consumption activities, put forward by the United Nations as a central tool to achieve sustainable consumption (UNO 2002). LCA describes the impacts associated with consumption of services provided by a product system, where the product system includes the production, distribution, operation, maintenance and disposal of the product. LCA can hence facilitate a consumption-based approach to understanding environmental problems. The life of a product in this respect starts with the extraction of natural resources, such as iron ore from the ground, and ends with their return to nature as landfill or as emissions.

The consideration of indirect (upstream) emissions is highly important when addressing sustainable consumption. Roughly half of the energy use of households is indirect, and the share increases with increased affluence (Hertwich 2011; Moll et al. 2005). For other impact categories, such as terrestrial and marine eco-toxicity, the share will be much higher because emissions occur in the producing and extracting industries, far away from the consumer.

The published assessments of the overall environmental impacts of households generally agree on which household consumption activities contribute more or less towards the total, when consumption is broken down in broad categories. Specifically, researchers single out food, shelter and mobility as being most important, overall (Hertwich 2011; Hertwich and Peters 2009; Tukker et al. 2008; Tukker et al. 2010). In the remainder of this chapter, following a section devoted to an introduction to the general structure of a life cycle assessment, these three household consumption categories will be dealt with in turn, in an attempt to summarize some general insights in each of them from the LCA literature over the last decade or so. The chapter is concluded with a general discussion of the potential contributions of LCA to the international debate on sustainable consumption, along with a word of caution as to its limitations.

## 8.1 THE STRUCTURE OF AN LCA

Life cycle assessments are standardized under ISO 14040, which outlines four key assessment phases to be conducted in an LCA (International Organization for Standardization 2006): (1) goal and scope definition; (2) inventory analysis; (3) impact assessment; and (4) interpretation. In this section, these four elements will be introduced briefly.

Any LCA should start with defining the goal and scope of the analysis. To ensure that LCA studies are not taken as evidence to support practices or products without sufficient grounds, and to avoid comparison of LCA studies that are in fact not comparable, it is of utmost importance that the researchers set out by clearly and unambiguously defining the goal and scope of the study. A central part of this is the definition of a 'functional unit' as the fundamental unit under study. It specifies the service or product to be delivered to the customer, and for which the total embodied environmental impacts is to be quantified. Since LCAs are frequently used to compare the environmental performance of two or more alternative ways of delivering a service, it is important that the functional unit is described precisely, and that the focus is on the service required rather than on a specific type of product. For instance, rather than defining the functional unit simply as a desk lamp, it may be defined as the provision of adequate working light for one office worker during the course of one standard working year; or rather than a can of soda, the functional unit might be specified as a certain volume of packaged carbonated beverage (see e.g. Amienyo et al. 2013).

Also important in the goal and scope phase is specifying the system boundaries, that is, which processes are included in the analysis and which are not. The supply chain of a functional unit can in principle be modelled with extreme complexity, because every industrial process is indirectly dependent on a wide range of inputs in addition to the direct inputs of production. The assembly of a desk lamp directly requires the lamp components, but the manufacturing also requires a factory, labour inputs, energy to heat and illuminate the factory, roads and other infrastructure to service the factory, and so on. All these upstream processes may in turn have equally complex supply chains of their own. Since the supply chain of any product hence is in principle infinitely long, any LCA requires a system boundary, outside of which potentially relevant processes are excluded – whether this boundary is explicitly defined or not.

Inventory analysis is the compilation of an inventory of primary flows, that is, material, energy and other exchanges with nature, along the life cycle of the product system. Exchanges with nature include uses of natural resources as well as emission and waste flows back to nature. This stage, which is usually the most time-consuming, involves the organization of a system of industrial processes and the quantification of their material and energy exchanges with nature as well as with other industrial processes. In an LCA the industrial system that ultimately delivers the functional unit is modelled as a network of processes that take material and energy inputs from each other and nature in order to deliver their output product. For the analysis, the process diagram is reformulated in matrix form following the Leontief model.

In practice, analysts will typically model a foreground system consisting of the most relevant processes for the system under study, and link this to a background system in the form of a commercial LCI database of generic products and services. For instance an analyst assessing a solar cell panel would probably focus on modelling the individual components of the panel, but would rely on a background database to provide life cycle results for the steel in its frame.

Impact assessment is the process of translating the result of the inventory analysis into environmental consequences. The life cycle inventory gives a quantitative account of all the environmental interventions (sometimes enumerating emissions of thousands of chemicals) resulting from the functional unit over its life cycle. This includes total resource use and emissions incurred directly and indirectly in the supply chain, as well as in the production, use and disposal of the product under study. As such the LCI could be viewed as a complete analysis result; however for most purposes this is not very useful as an environmental assessment. In the impact assessment phase, knowledge of the various environmental mechanisms is applied to calculate the contributions of individual primary flows to a set of environmental impact categories, each category quantified in units of some reference compound or damage indicator. For instance emissions of carbon dioxide ($CO_2$) and methane ($CH_4$) are both counted towards global warming potential (GWP) impact; however since $CH_4$ is a more potent greenhouse gas (GHG), it is assigned a weight to allow the two emissions to be added and expressed in the single unit of kilograms of $CO_2$ equivalents ($CO_2$e).

Finally ISO 14040 defines interpretation as a separate phase to be conducted concurrently throughout the study, to provide guidance to an iterative process between the first three stages. The interpretation part of an LCA should serve to inform readers about the relevance, validity and conclusions of the study, and should discuss the sensitivity analysis of the results, if any has been performed (International Organization for Standardization 2006).

## 8.2 LCA INSIGHTS ON SOME IMPORTANT CONSUMPTION CATEGORIES

### 8.2.1 Food

Studies of the environmental impacts of household consumption consistently highlight food consumption as one of the most important categories contributing towards total impacts of consumption (Tukker et al. 2008). Food is one of the areas where LCA has contributed significantly to the understanding of the environmental impacts, on different scales. A range of assessments have been published; see for example Roy et al. (2009) or de Vries and de Boer (2010) for reviews of recent life cycle assessments of food products.

Within the food category, meat and dairy products are singled out as the most significant products in terms of environmental impacts (Carlsson-Kanyama and González 2009; Hertwich et al. 2010; Tukker and Jansen 2006). Meat carries a lot of embodied resources and energy due to the rather inefficient transfer of energy from feed to meat; the differences in conversion efficiencies also explain why beef generally has higher environmental impacts than pork or chicken (Carlsson-Kanyama et al. 2003; de Vries and de Boer 2010; Weber and Matthews 2008). Adding to the effect of lower conversion efficiency, a lower reproduction rate for cattle compared to chickens or pigs also drive up the life cycle land and energy requirements (de Vries and de Boer 2010). In terms of global warming potential (GWP), meat is different from most other products in that

$CH_4$ and nitrous oxide ($N_2O$) emissions contribute more towards the total than does $CO_2$ (de Vries and de Boer 2010). $CH_4$ emissions are particularly important for meat from ruminants, due to emissions from enteric fermentation in the rumen; whereas $N_2O$ emissions are primarily due to fertilizer use (this applies to all agriculture, not only meat production).

In the dairy category, milk and cheese are important products. In an LCA of industrial milk production, Eide (2002) compared dairies of various sizes and found the agricultural stage to be the overall most important in terms of environmental impacts; however, milk produced from the smallest dairies carried very high life cycle energy requirements due to electricity consumption at the dairy itself. This efficiency difference led to total life cycle energy requirements of 6.3 MJ/litre for milk from the smallest dairy versus only 3.6 MJ/litre for the largest. Though milk is consumed in greater quantities than cheese (103 kg per capita and 18 kg per capita, respectively, in Norway in 2010; Johansson 2011), LCA results reported by Carlsson-Kanyama and González (2009) for Sweden show 11 times higher life cycle GWP per kilogram of cheese compared to milk when both are domestically produced; in fact cheese is more GHG-intensive per kilogram than pork and chicken meat.

The promotion of organically farmed food as a more sustainable option has spurred some public debate, due to doubts of the net effect of organic products when factors such as production efficiency are taken into account. This is the kind of research question which LCA is ideally suited to answer, and there have been some attempts to do so. Williams et al. (2006) compared organic to conventional meat production, and found that in UK conditions, organic beef had a higher carbon footprint; however for mutton the result was the opposite. Pork had a similar carbon footprint whether organically or conventionally grown. Wood et al. (2006) compared organic to conventional farming in Australia and conclude that though the organic farms had higher on-farm energy use, the conventional farms carried much higher embodied energy use upstream, leading to higher life cycle energy requirements. Overall, LCA research seems to confirm the notion that the benefits of reduced use of pesticides and mineral fertilizer comes at the price of somewhat reduced efficiency, particularly in terms of land area requirements (Cederberg and Mattsson 2000; Haas et al. 2001). Organically produced milk exhibits a similar trade-off pattern as meat (Cederberg and Mattsson 2000; Williams et al. 2006).

Related to the debate of organic versus conventional food products, there have been campaigns promoting locally produced food to reduce the environmental impacts of food transport. However, an influential study on the climate impact of food in the United States concluded that in general, the transport stage is of minor importance compared to the production stage, contributing only 11 per cent of the total food-related carbon footprint for the average household (Weber and Matthews 2008). Milà i Canals et al. (2007) studied apples consumed in Europe, and found lower primary energy requirements for domestically grown apples when the apples were in season, but variable results out of season; other studies support this notion of favouring local produce only when it is in season (Carlsson-Kanyama et al. 2003). Among imported products, the distance and mode of transport can significantly influence life cycle results: in particular, air-transported food carries high embodied impacts (Jungbluth et al. 2000).

In order to limit global warming to 2°C above pre-industrial levels, emissions related to food and diet will have to be addressed, as one of the major sources of GHG

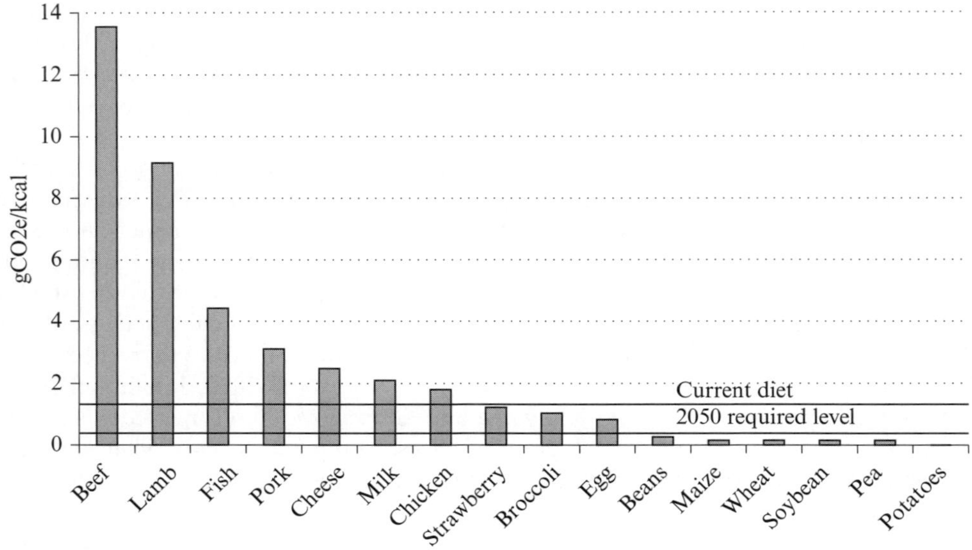


*Notes:*
Current global average and 2050 target levels shown for reference, based on Girod et al. (2013).
$gCO_2e$ = grams of $CO_2$ equivalents.

*Source:* Based on González et al. (2011).

*Figure 8.1 Life cycle GHG emissions per kcal of some food items*

emissions. The energy and greenhouse gas intensity of meat and meat products seems to suggest vegetarian diets are preferable from a sustainability perspective. In a comprehensive review of life cycle inventories of 84 food items, González et al. (2011) concluded that plant-based food was overall much more efficient than animal-based foods in terms of protein delivery per unit energy use or GHG emitted. Girod et al. (2013) estimate that life cycle GHG emissions per calorie will have to be reduced from a global average of 1.3 to 0.37 $gCO_2e$/kcal from 2000 to 2050, which will put strict limitations on the share of animal-based products in our diets (see Figure 8.1).

When comparing environmental impacts of different types of food using LCA, the selection of functional unit is not obvious. For instance on a mass basis, milk has lower land use requirements than meat, because of the high water content of milk (de Vries and de Boer 2010). Since the primary function of food is to provide nutrition for the body, comparisons based on fixed amounts of protein or energy might be better suited than mass-based comparisons; see Schau and Fet (2008) for an overview of some food LCAs and the various functional units chosen in them. Roy et al. (2009) found chicken to be the most environmentally efficient meat if protein was chosen as the functional unit, whereas pork performed better per calorie delivered. Due to this possible ambiguity, Carlsson-Kanyama (1998) recommends comparisons to be made on complete meals or diets with comparable nutritional qualities, rather than on single products.

### 8.2.2 Shelter

The 'shelter' category in analyses of household environmental impacts concerns dwellings, including the construction, maintenance and ultimate demolition stages; and the energy required for space and water heating (or cooling). When assessing the environmental impacts of household consumption over a year, the shelter category entails some additional considerations in contrast to analyses of food consumption.

What are the environmental impacts of the occupancy of a house over a year? Aside from the energy used for space and water heating, cooking, cleaning, and so on, the lifetime energy requirements of the building itself are significant. However most of this energy use is generally required in the construction phase with only smaller additional requirements for structural maintenance and upgrades over the years. Obviously these high initial energy requirements must be distributed over the years the dwelling will be used and the assumed lifetime of buildings will significantly affect the annualized embodied energy requirements.

Increased focus on energy consumption in buildings has led to significant advances in the energy efficiency of buildings in recent years, ranging from small-scale improvements of furnishings and appliances such as energy-efficient light bulbs and hot water taps, to larger structural changes such as improved thermal insulation in walls and ceiling, and triple-glazed windows. Buildings with especially low energy requirements are referred to as low-energy buildings or 'passive houses', while self-sufficient or zero-energy houses are even better insulated and also generate their own electric or thermal energy so that they are not dependent on an external energy supply.

Due to the structural complexity of low- and zero-energy buildings compared to conventional houses, however, there have been concerns about their overall life cycle impacts. Following this, several LCAs have been published, attempting to quantify life cycle energy requirements and emissions by including also the emissions incurred in the construction, maintenance and demolition stages. Though there are considerable differences in structural characteristics and climatic conditions among them, the numerous case studies published (see Hertwich 2011; Ramesh et al. 2010; Sartori and Hestnes 2007; Ürge-Vorsatz et al. 2012 for overviews of some relevant studies) seem to allow at least two general conclusions to be drawn. Firstly, even after accounting for embodied energy use, the operation stage dominates the life cycle energy use of residential buildings, and the bulk of this energy use is associated with space conditioning (heating and cooling) and hot water provision. Most of the remainder consists of the embodied (construction-phase) energy, with maintenance and demolition contributing only to a smaller degree to the overall requirements (Fay et al. 2000). As houses become more energy-efficient, the contribution of heating and other direct energy use will decrease. The LCA of a low-energy house compared to a standard house by Blengini and Di Carlo (2010) suggests that after the heating requirements have been reduced, life cycle energy requirements are no longer dominated by any single factor, which means further improvements will be more challenging and require a more systematic approach.

Secondly, although low-energy houses have indeed been found to carry higher embodied energy, this (slight) energy cost is several times outweighed by the lifetime energy savings gained in the operations stage through lower heating requirements (Blengini and Di Carlo 2010; Dahlstrøm et al. 2012; Dodoo et al. 2010; Thiers and Peuportier 2008).

However, the marginal net life cycle savings diminish as increasing steps are taken to lower the operational energy requirements of the buildings; in fact, the annualized total energy requirements of the most efficient low-energy houses may be lower than those of completely self-sufficient houses (Sartori and Hestnes 2007). Hernandez and Kenny (2010) highlight the same trade-off effect for insulation levels in low-energy buildings, and find that the energy ratio, defined as the ratio of the decrease in annual energy use to the increase in annualized embodied energy, diminishes steadily with increased insulation thickness and after a few increments drops below 1, implying negative lifetime energy savings on the margin.

The choice of materials obviously impacts upon the energy use and environmental impacts embodied in buildings. The production of concrete entails significant energy use and $CO_2$ emissions; in a comparative LCA of embodied emissions Börjesson and Gustavsson (2000) find concrete buildings to have 60–80 per cent more embodied primary energy than a wooden equivalent. Wood also offers a potential for in-stock carbon storage, as well as energy recovery after demolition (Ürge-Vorsatz et al. 2012).

In the environmental assessment of most goods and products, a pertinent question as new and more energy and environmentally efficient technologies and standards of some products evolve is whether or when to replace the product in order to minimize the environmental impacts. Kim et al. (2006) apply a life cycle optimization model to determine optimal lifetimes of household refrigerators in the US to minimize energy, GWP and costs, and conclude from model runs from 2004 to 2020 that 'current owners should replace refrigerators that consume more than 1000 kWh/year of electricity (typical mid-sized 1994 models and older) as an efficient strategy from both cost and energy perspectives'.

Along the same lines, life cycle type assessments have been used to determine whether existing buildings should be retrofitted to comply with current standards or whether it would be preferable to demolish and rebuild entirely. Itard and Klunder (2007) perform a comparative life cycle assessment of four cases of increasing levels of interventions, from maintenance through consolidation and transformation, through redevelopment, and find transformation to be environmentally preferable to demolition and rebuilding. Dodoo et al. (2010) assess several retrofitting measures on an existing wooden house, and find significant potential for life cycle energy savings; however the net gains depend largely on the heating technology of the house, with the greatest savings for electrical resistance heating and lower savings for houses using heat pumps or district heating. Figure 8.2 compares life cycle impacts of conventional and passive houses using electric resistance or heat pump space heating.

### 8.2.3 Mobility

Household energy requirements in the developed world have increased greatly over the past century, and mobility, particularly private car use, has been one of the major contributors to this development (Fuglestvedt et al. 2008). Across the world, though the onset came at different times throughout the twentieth century, as soon as private cars have become publically available and affordable the per capita stocks soon soared; in the United States the ownership rate is approaching 0.8 cars per capita (Pauliuk et al. 2011). To consumers, car use is perhaps the most intuitively obvious private con-

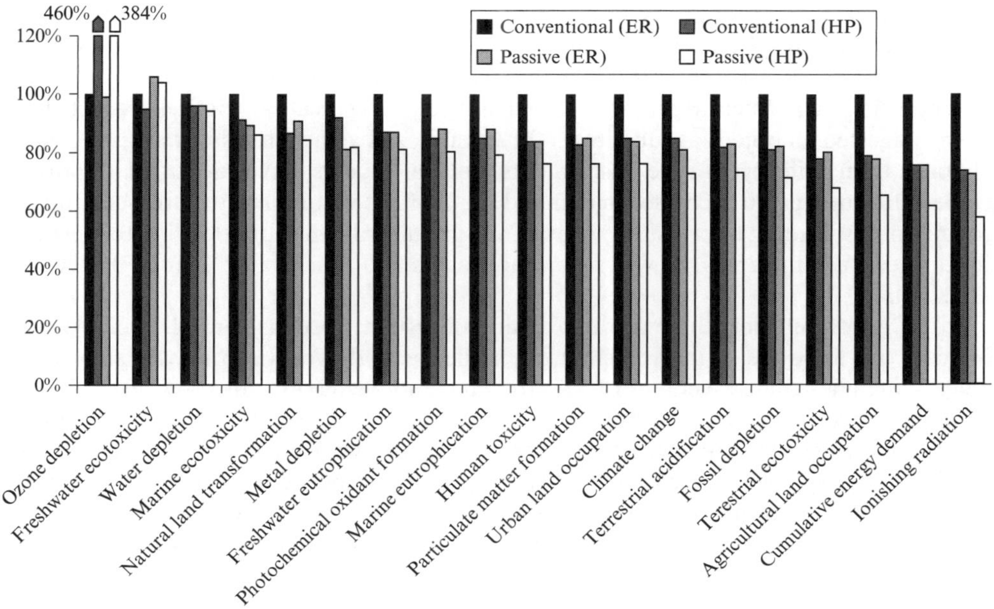


*Note:* Impacts are shown relative to conventional houses (with ER heating). For four of the impact types, the contribution of embodied (construction, materials and demolition) impacts are indicated as shaded areas. The high ozone depletion potential of the HP cases is due to refrigerant leakages from the heat pumps.

*Source:* Based on Dahlstrøm et al. (2012).

*Figure 8.2 Various life cycle impacts of conventional versus passive houses using either electric resistance (ER) or heat pump (HP) for space heating*

sumption activity that contributes to household environmental impacts. Combustion of petrol simultaneously entails resource use, energy use and emissions of $CO_2$ plus a range of other pollutants. As such, the mobility category offers significant potential for consumption-oriented strategies and policies for sustainability. In this section, we have chosen to focus on private car use, which is the most important of the various transport modes included in the mobility category.

When evaluating strategies to reduce the environmental impacts of private car use, LCA can serve to avoid the pitfall of environmental problem shifting. Problem shifting refers to situations where an effort to reduce environmental impacts of one process leads to other adverse impacts instead. Problem shifting can occur as simple relocations of fundamentally equivalent emissions, either geographically (by importing rather than producing emission-intensive components) or within the production chain. Electric vehicles are sometimes marketed as emission-free because there are no tailpipe emissions; however the generation of the electricity with which their batteries are charged will require emissions at the power plant instead, thus the vehicle emissions are effectively relocated further up the supply chain.

Other than relocations of a specific type of emission, problem shifts can also manifest themselves in terms of other types of environmental impacts. In the impact assessment stage of LCA, the system's impacts in terms of several different types of environmental impacts are usually assessed, thus allowing a simultaneous assessment of widely different potential impacts. Such a problem shift has been identified for biofuels, which have been suggested as potential substitutes for fossil-based vehicle fuels to mitigate climate change. Using life cycle type assessments, several studies have identified important trade-offs: anticipated increases in demand for biofuels would imply increased land use requirements, leading to pressures on existing agricultural land (thus leading to increased food prices in some areas) as well as on rainforests and other natural land (Bringezu et al. 2012).

In LCAs of vehicles, there are two main subsystems to consider. The vehicle cycle includes the life cycle of the vehicle itself, while the fuel cycle (also known as 'well-to-wheel') includes the conversion of fuel to vehicle movement ('tank-to-wheel') and the complete upstream process of delivering fuel to the vehicle ('well-to-tank'). As was the case for housing, the LCA literature unsurprisingly shows that for conventional internal combustion engine (ICE) vehicles fuelled by petrol or diesel, the operating stage is the most important in terms of energy requirements and GWP (MacLean and Lave 2003a). However for the various low-carbon alternatives available, indirect impacts become more important in relative terms, and probably also in absolute terms (Schäfer et al. 2006).

Several LCAs evaluate different vehicle fuel options. MacLean and Lave (2003b) review a dozen studies on alternative fuels and propulsion technologies for cars and light trucks, and conclude that no one technology can be singled out as preferable, because they have different advantages and disadvantages. Ultimately, the question is how we should weight the different impact types and environmental problems against each other.

Bioethanol has been used in fuel blends in Brazil for decades, and has been put forward as a low-hanging fruit for decarbonization of car fuels, because existing conventional cars can run on petrol blends with up to 10 per cent ethanol (E10) without any modifications (MacLean and Lave 2003a). Niven (2005) assesses the sustainability of ethanol–petrol blends in Australia based on a review of available literature, and concludes that for such E10 blends, from a life cycle perspective the GHG reductions are small and come at a significant price in terms of other environmental impacts, notably soil and groundwater contamination, air pollution and land use. In another review article, von Blottnitz and Curran (2007) evaluate 47 published LCAs of bioethanol compared to conventional fuel, and find large variations depending on the well-to-tank side of the bioethanol. Using tropical sugar crops as feedstock appears preferable; however the authors point to potential land use conflicts. In terms of energy use and GWP, bioethanol performs well throughout, while for other impact categories the authors find divergent or unclear results across studies.

The case of electrical versus conventional passenger cars was recently assessed by Hawkins et al. (2013), who perform a comparative LCA of the environmental impacts of 1 kilometre driven with a typical European small car powered with either a conventional internal combustion engine or a battery-electric powertrain (see Figure 8.3). Assuming a common vehicle glider (that is, the car except powertrain) and vehicle and battery lifetimes of 150 000 km, the authors quantify life cycle impacts per kilometre driven within ten different impact categories. They assess different fuels for the conventional vehicles,

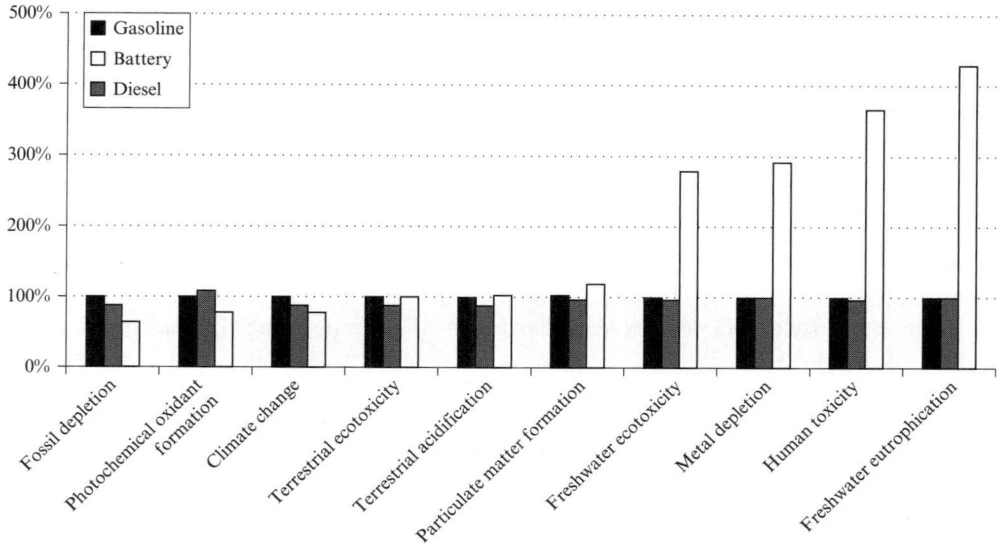


*Note:* BEV results are averages across two types of Li-ion batteries with similar results, assuming a European average electricity mix.

*Source:* Based on Hawkins et al. (2013).

*Figure 8.3 Various life cycle impacts of a battery-electric vehicle (BEV) versus a comparable conventional vehicle (petrol or diesel fuelled) shown as relative to petrol vehicle results*

and different battery types as well as different electricity sources for the electric vehicles, and find overall a 10 per cent to 24 per cent decrease in GWP when assuming the present European electricity mix. However the electric vehicles perform worse in terms of several other impact categories, such as human toxicity potential, freshwater ecotoxicity and eutrophication potentials, and metal depletion potentials, chiefly originating from battery production. It should be emphasized that vehicle batteries are still an emerging technology and that changes in production methods are likely to affect environmental impacts of future battery production.

## 8.3 DISCUSSION: THE ROLE OF LCA IN SOCIETAL SUSTAINABILITY ASSESSMENTS

The global growth in overall material and energy use per capita as well as in absolute numbers; the increased material and technological complexity of products and services and their international supply chains; the progressing scientific understanding of the interconnectedness of natural systems and the various types of environmental challenges associated with them; all these factors point to the need for a holistic, life cycle type approach to sustainability. Though a powerful and versatile analytical tool, life cycle assessments alone cannot uncover the path towards a sustainable future. An important limitation of LCAs in this respect lies on the consumer side. For instance the overall impacts of LCA findings on the sustainability of different types of travel modes, car types and fuel types may be diminished by the fact that consumers may ultimately prefer big, powerful trucks with loud engines (MacLean and Lave 2003a). Furthermore, there is good reason why the ISO standard names interpretation as one of the four main steps of any LCA. Two examples highlight the importance of interpreting LCA results, especially when attempting to draw conclusions on the bigger picture. Firstly, significant advances in technology and management have led life cycle GHG emissions of air travel to be comparable to those of cars per passenger-kilometre. However in the detail of this functional unit (which is perfectly standard to use) lies a devil: aeroplanes travel many times faster than cars, allowing consumers to travel vast distances on a regular basis. Long-weekend intercontinental trips are becoming popular among an increasing group of well-off people, something that would be unthinkable with any other mode of transport. In other words, on a per time basis, air travel is much more emissions-intensive than cars, allowing much higher overall per capita carbon footprints. Secondly, in an interesting article Cullen and Allwood (2009) illustrate the 'washing machine effect', whereby a synthesis of individual subsystem analyses may lead to a distorted picture of the overall system. The name of the effect was drawn from an example of washing laundry, where individual energy-use LCAs of separate stages, including the machine itself, the detergent, the process of washing clothes, all conclude that the operations stage – that is, the energy used in the washing cycle – is clearly the most important stage, while a combination of the three into one larger system revealed the materials and production stages to be equally important.

As illustrated in this chapter, life cycle assessment is a powerful tool for analysing complex process chains and the way industrial processes interact with each other and nature. Using LCA, analysts can simultaneously assess a system's impacts across a range of different impact types and identify benefits and trade-offs between similar products. The points made in the previous paragraph, however, illustrate that the results of life cycle assessments must be carefully interpreted before they are used to create environmental policies. For design of efficient policies and strategies for sustainability, LCA results should also be evaluated in light of the growing body of literature from the fields of consumer and behavioural research, since, as pointed out by Stern (2011), the overall effect of an attempted shift in consumer patterns to lessen environmental impacts is ultimately the product of the technical potential for reduction and the share of the population able and willing to make the change.

## REFERENCES

Amienyo, D., H. Gujba, H. Stichnothe and A. Azapagic (2013), 'Life cycle environmental impacts of carbonated soft drinks', *International Journal of Life Cycle Assessment*, 18 (1), 77–92.

Blengini, G. and T. Di Carlo (2010), 'Energy-saving policies and low-energy residential buildings: an LCA case study to support decision makers in Piedmont (Italy)', *International Journal of Life Cycle Assessment*, 15 (7), 652–665.

Börjesson, P. and L. Gustavsson (2000), 'Greenhouse gas balances in building construction: wood versus concrete from life-cycle and forest land-use perspectives', *Energy Policy*, 28 (9), 575–588.

Bringezu, S., M. O'Brien and H. Schütz (2012), 'Beyond biofuels: assessing global land use for domestic consumption of biomass: a conceptual and empirical contribution to sustainable management of global resources', *Land Use Policy*, 29 (1), 224–232.
Carlsson-Kanyama, A. (1998), 'Climate change and dietary choices – how can emissions of greenhouse gases from food consumption be reduced?', *Food Policy*, 23 (3–4), 277–293.
Carlsson-Kanyama, A., M.P. Ekström and H. Shanahan (2003), 'Food and life cycle energy inputs: consequences of diet and ways to increase efficiency', *Ecological Economics*, 44 (2–3), 293–307.
Carlsson-Kanyama, A. and A.D. González (2009), 'Potential contributions of food consumption patterns to climate change', *American Journal of Clinical Nutrition*, 89 (5), 1704S–1709S.
Cederberg, C. and B. Mattsson (2000), 'Life cycle assessment of milk production – a comparison of conventional and organic farming', *Journal of Cleaner Production*, 8 (1), 49–60.
Cullen, J.M. and J.M. Allwood (2009), 'The role of washing machines in life cycle assessment studies', *Journal of Industrial Ecology*, 13 (1), 27–37.
Dahlstrøm, O., K. Sørnes, S.T. Eriksen and E.G. Hertwich (2012), 'Life cycle assessment of a single-family residence built to either conventional or passive house standard', *Energy and Buildings*, 54, 470–479.
de Vries, M. and I.J.M. de Boer (2010), 'Comparing environmental impacts for livestock products: a review of life cycle assessments', *Livestock Science*, 128 (1–3), 1–11.
Dodoo, A., L. Gustavsson and R. Sathre (2010), 'Life cycle primary energy implication of retrofitting a wood-framed apartment building to passive house standard', *Resources, Conservation and Recycling*, 54 (12), 1152–1160.
Eide, M. (2002), 'Life cycle assessment (LCA) of industrial milk production', *International Journal of Life Cycle Assessment*, 7 (2), 115–126.
Fay, R., G. Treloar and U. Iyer-Raniga (2000), 'Life-cycle energy analysis of buildings: a case study', *Building Research and Information*, 28 (1), 31–41.
Fuglestvedt, J., T. Berntsen, G. Myhre, K. Rypdal and R.B. Skeie (2008), 'Climate forcing from the transport sectors', *Proceedings of the National Academy of Sciences*, 105 (2), 454–458.
Gatersleben, B., L. Steg and C. Vlek (2002), 'Measurement and determinants of environmentally significant consumer behavior', *Environment and Behavior*, 34 (3), 335–362.
Girod, B., D.P. van Vuuren and E.G. Hertwich (2013), 'Global climate targets and future consumption level: an evaluation of the required GHG intensity', *Environmental Research Letters*, 8 (2), 14–16.
González, A.D., B. Frostell and A. Carlsson-Kanyama (2011), 'Protein efficiency per unit energy and per unit greenhouse gas emissions: potential contribution of diet choices to climate change mitigation', *Food Policy*, 36 (5), 562–570.
Haas, G., F. Wetterich and U. Köpke (2001), 'Comparing intensive, extensified and organic grassland farming in southern Germany by process life cycle assessment', *Agriculture, Ecosystems and Environment*, 83 (1–2), 43–53.
Hawkins, T.R., B. Singh, G. Majeau-Bettez, and A.H. Strømman (2013), 'Comparative environmental life cycle assessment of conventional and electric vehicles', *Journal of Industrial Ecology*, 17 (1), 53–64.
Hernandez, P. and P. Kenny (2010), 'From net energy to zero energy buildings: defining life cycle zero energy buildings (LC-ZEB)', *Energy and Buildings*, 42 (6), 815–821.
Hertwich, E.G. (2011), 'The life cycle environmental impacts of consumption', *Economic Systems Research*, 23 (1), 27–47.
Hertwich, E.G. and G.P. Peters (2009), 'Carbon footprint of nations: a global, trade-linked analysis', *Environmental Science and Technology*, 43 (16), 6414–6420.
Hertwich, E.G., E. van der Voet, S. Suh, A. Tukker, M. Huijbregts, P. Kazmierczyk, M. Lenzen et al. (2010), 'Assessing the environmental impacts of consumption and production: priority products and materials', A Report of the Working Group on the Environmental Impacts of Products and Materials to the International Panel for Sustainable Resource Management, United Nations Environment Programme.
International Organization for Standardization (2006), *Environmental Management – Life Cycle Assessment – Principles and Framework*, Geneva: ISO.
Itard, L. and G. Klunder (2007), 'Comparing environmental impacts of renovated housing stock with new construction', *Building Research and Information*, 35 (3), 252–267.
Johansson, L. (2011), Utviklingen i norsk kosthold 2011, Oslo: Norwegian Directorate of Health.
Jungbluth, N., O. Tietje and R. Scholz (2000), 'Food purchases: Impacts from the consumers' point of view investigated with a modular LCA', *International Journal of Life Cycle Assessment*, 5 (3), 134–142.
Kim, H.C., G.A. Keoleian and Y.A. Horie (2006), 'Optimal household refrigerator replacement policy for life cycle energy, greenhouse gas emissions, and cost', *Energy Policy*, 34 (15), 2310–2323.
MacLean, H.L. and L.B. Lave (2003a), 'Life cycle assessment of automobile/fuel options', *Environmental Science and Technology*, 37 (23), 5445–5452.
MacLean, H.L. and L.B. Lave (2003b), 'Evaluating automobile fuel/propulsion system technologies', *Progress in Energy and Combustion Science*, 29 (1), 1–69.

Milà i Canals, L., S. Cowell, S. Sim and L. Basson (2007), 'Comparing domestic versus imported apples: a focus on energy use', *Environmental Science and Pollution Research – International*, 14 (5), 338–344.

Moll, H.C., K.J. Noorman, R. Kok, R. Engström, H. Throne-Holst and C. Clark (2005), 'Pursuing more sustainable consumption by analyzing household metabolism in European countries and cities', *Journal of Industrial Ecology*, 9 (1–2), 259–275.

Niven, R.K. (2005), 'Ethanol in gasoline: environmental impacts and sustainability review article', *Renewable and Sustainable Energy Reviews*, 9 (6), 535–555.

Pauliuk, S., N.M.A. Dhaniati and D.B. Müller (2011), 'Reconciling sectoral abatement strategies with global climate targets: the case of the Chinese passenger vehicle fleet', *Environmental Science and Technology*, 46 (1), 140–147.

Ramesh, T., R. Prakash and K.K. Shukla (2010), 'Life cycle energy analysis of buildings: an overview', *Energy and Buildings*, 42 (10), 1592–1600.

Roy, P., D. Nei, T. Orikasa, Q. Xu, H. Okadome, N. Nakamura and T. Shiina (2009), 'A review of life cycle assessment (LCA) on some food products', *Journal of Food Engineering*, 90 (1), 1–10.

Sartori, I. and A.G. Hestnes (2007), 'Energy use in the life cycle of conventional and low-energy buildings: a review article', *Energy and Buildings*, 39 (3), 249–257.

Schäfer, A., J.B. Heywood and M.A. Weiss (2006), 'Future fuel cell and internal combustion engine automobile technologies: a 25-year life cycle and fleet impact assessment', *Energy*, 31 (12), 2064–2087.

Schau, E.M. and A.M. Fet (2008), 'LCA studies of food products as background for environmental product declarations', *International Journal of Life Cycle Assessment*, 13 (3), 255–264.

Stern, P.C. (2000), 'New environmental theories: toward a coherent theory of environmentally significant behavior', *Journal of Social Issues*, 56 (3), 407–424.

Stern, P.C. (2011), 'Contributions of psychology to limiting climate change', *American Psychologist*, 66 (4), 303–314.

Stern, P.C., G.T. Gardner, M.P. Vandenbergh, T. Dietz and J.M. Gilligan (2010), 'Design principles for carbon emissions reduction programs', *Environmental Science & Technology*, 44 (13), 4847–4848.

Thiers, S. and B. Peuportier (2008), 'Thermal and environmental assessment of a passive building equipped with an earth-to-air heat exchanger in France', *Solar Energy*, 82 (9), 820–831.

Tukker, A., M.J. Cohen, K. Hubacek and O. Mont (2010), 'The impacts of household consumption and options for change', *Journal of Industrial Ecology*, 14 (1), 13–30.

Tukker, A., S. Emmert, M. Charter, C. Vezzoli, E. Sto, M. Munch Andersen, T. Geerken et al. (2008), 'Fostering change to sustainable consumption and production: an evidence based view', *Journal of Cleaner Production*, 16 (11), 1218–1225.

Tukker, A. and B. Jansen (2006), 'Environment impacts of products: a detailed review of studies', *Journal of Industrial Ecology*, 10 (3), 159–182.

UNO (2002), *Plan of Implementation of the World Summit on Sustainable Development*, A/CONF.199/20, New York: United Nations Organizations.

Ürge-Vorsatz, D., N. Eyre, P. Graham, D. Harvey, E. Hertwich, Y. Jiang, C. Kornevall et al. (2012), 'Energy end-use: buildings', in T.B. Johansson, A. Patwardhan, N. Nakicenovic and L. Gomez-Echeverri (eds), *Global Energy Assessment. Toward a Sustainable Future*, Cambridge, UK and New York, USA: Cambridge University Press, and the International Institute for Applied Systems Analysis, pp. 649–760.

von Blottnitz, H. and M.A. Curran (2007), 'A review of assessments conducted on bio-ethanol as a transportation fuel from a net energy, greenhouse gas, and environmental life cycle perspective', *Journal of Cleaner Production*, 15 (7), 607–619.

Weber, C.L. and H.S. Matthews (2008), 'Food-miles and the relative climate impacts of food choices in the United States', *Environmental Science and Technology*, 42 (10), 3508–3513.

Williams, A.G., E. Audsley and D.L. Sandars (2006), *Determining the Environmental Burdens and Resource Use in the Production of Agricultural and Horticultural Commodities*, Bedford: Cranfield University and Defra.

Wood, R., M. Lenzen, C. Dey and S. Lundie (2006), 'A comparative study of some environmental impacts of conventional and organic farming in Australia', *Agricultural Systems*, 89 (2–3), 324–348.

# 9. Priorities for sustainable consumption policies

*Arnold Tukker*

Environmental effects of economic activities are ultimately driven by consumption by households and governments. First, almost all consumption activities have direct environmental impacts. Obvious examples are the emissions from the use of fossil fuels to heat our homes and drive our cars. But, second, consumption activities also have important indirect effects. Cooking food may cause direct emissions if a gas stove is used, but in addition this food obviously is part of a product life cycle that ranges from agricultural production, the production of auxiliary inputs such as fertilizers for agriculture, usually processing and packaging of the food in the food industry, and storage and transportation until it reaches the final consumer. For food, the emissions and resources used in this supply chain are much more important than the emissions and impacts caused during the use phase. There are obviously such impacts in the supply chain for all products for final consumption. And next to this, after their useful life, waste products are subject to transport, storage and treatment, again causing impacts. In the box labelled 'Society's economic system', Figure 9.1 gives a simplified representation of this production–consumption chain.

Historically, environmental policies have attempted to reduce environmental impacts by end-of-pipe or cleaner production measures in the production stage. Later more emphasis was put on stimulating the development and production of 'greener' products. Currently, analysing how more sustainable patterns of consumption can be stimulated forms the basis of an innovative next generation of environmental policy (e.g. Simons et al. 2001). Consumption-oriented environmental policies require clear knowledge about the final consumption expenditures and related purchases of products and services causing the greatest environmental impacts, as well as insight into where impact reductions can be most easily realized. This chapter discusses methods and gives examples on the former point and outlines via which strategies impacts of consumption can be reduced. The latter point is discussed in other chapters of this book (mainly in Shewmake et al., Chapter 18 in this book).

## 9.1 THE SUSTAINABILITY PROBLEM

Since the industrial revolution, the global economy has grown at a rate unprecedented in human history. This growth was obviously made possible by technical progress. But the size of the economic system built around these novel technologies means that humanity now uses unprecedented amounts of finite, non-renewable resources, has transformed a large part of the available ecosystems into cultivated land, and uses nature as a sink for waste and emissions at a troubling scale. Since the economic system by definition is embedded in the Earth's natural system, it is a manifest question for how long this economic growth can continue (see Figure 9.1).

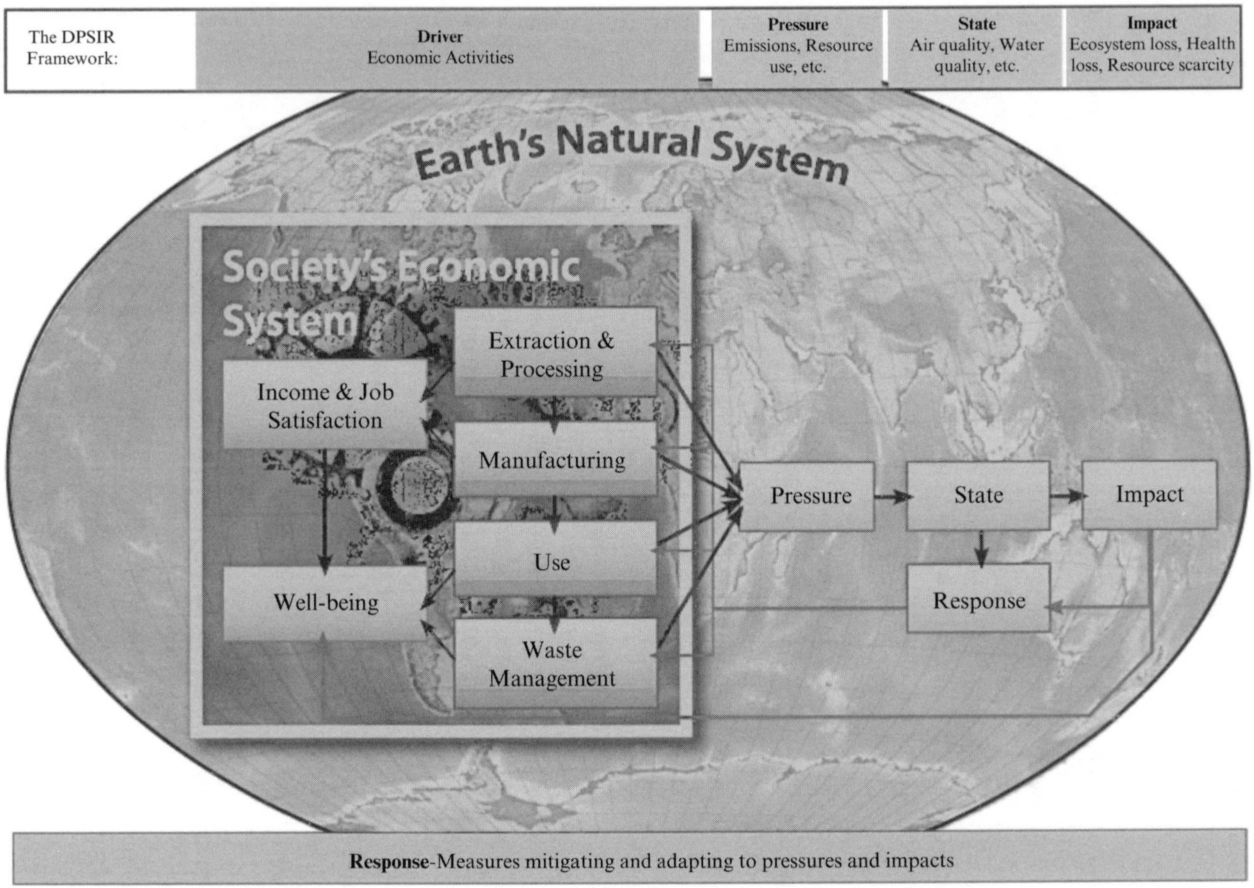


*Source:* UNEP (2010).

*Figure 9.1 The Earth's natural system enveloping the global economic system, and the source and sink function of nature*

The problem of continued economic growth can be further illustrated as follows. The world has currently just over 7 billion people, of which 1 billion live in high-income Organisation for Economic Co-operation and Development (OECD) countries; 1–2 billion live in rapidly developing, 'emerging' economies; and 4–5 billion people have to get by on just a few dollars a day. The new and rapidly expanding middle class in emerging economies such as China and India is quickly closing the wealth gap with the West (Myers and Kent 2004). With the projected population growth, by 2050 we will have 9 billion people. Of these, 2–3 billion will have an income similar to the current rich: some $40 000–$50 000 per capita/year. Some 6–7 billion people will be less rich, but in order to fulfil the Rio+20 promise of poverty eradication they need an income of some $10 000–$15 000/ per capita/year. A myriad of studies show that a level below this means a higher child mortality, shorter life expectancy, lower literacy rate or, in short, clearly negative impacts on happiness indices and the Human Development Index. However a scenario that would not affect the income of the current rich, that would fulfil the aspirations and expectations of the new middle class and that would eradicate the poverty of the remaining people would imply the need for a US$200 trillion global economy by 2050 (Tukker 2013). This is four times as big as the current US$50 trillion economy. And this should happen in a world where already the economy seems to 'crash against the Earth' (Speth 2008).

At the same time, in order to keep global warming below 2°C above pre-industrial levels, by 2050 the use of fossil fuels and related carbon emissions need to be reduced by around 80 per cent compared to levels of around 2000 (IPCC 2013; Meinshausen et al. 2009). By 2030, at a global level the difference between freshwater needs and the amount that can be extracted from sustainable sources – the 'water gap' – is predicted to reach 40 per cent (locally, the mismatch can be much higher, cf. Water Resources Group 2009). The human appropriation of net primary production of biomass (simply said: the amount of biomass the Earth produces annually and that is somehow used for human purposes) is already around 35 per cent, and cannot grow much higher (Vitousek et al. 1986).

It is pretty clear that in these areas – global warming, water use and appropriation of biomass – our economy operates close to or over the limits of the 'safe operating space' of the Earth's natural capacity (Rockström et al. 2009). The need to quadruple the global economy by 2050 in order to provide decent lives for all, in combination with the aforementioned constraints, imply a need, for instance, to reduce the carbon emissions per dollar gross domestic product (GDP) by a factor of more than ten, and the water use and biomass extraction per dollar GDP by at least a factor of two, by 2050.

## 9.2 PRIORITIES FROM A CONSUMPTION-ORIENTED PERSPECTIVE: METHODS

To decide the focus of consumption-oriented sustainability policies, one obviously needs to know which consumption activities drive the use of natural resources and create most impacts. In principle, two different approaches can be followed to assess the life cycle environmental impacts of final consumption of a country, for example. Some studies select a number of products as being representative for an expenditure category.

They then use life cycle assessment (LCA) data for these products, followed by scaling up the volume to the total expenditure in a country, to estimate the impacts related to this expenditure category. This is called the 'bottom-up' approach. Other studies use input–output (IO) tables with environmental extensions to calculate the impacts that should be allocated to different final expenditure categories. This is called the 'top-down' approach. I discuss both approaches in more detail below, but since LCA is treated in more depth in another chapter of this book (Steen-Olsen and Hertwich, Chapter 8), this chapter will focus more on the IO approach.

### 9.2.1 Bottom-Up Approach

The bottom-up approach follows the classic ISO 14040 approach to LCA (e.g. Guinée 2002): (1) define the goal and the scope of the study; (2) create an inventory of impacts; and (3) impact assessment.

**Goal and scope definition**
This phase involves defining the purpose of the study, its scope and a method of quality assurance for the results. A functional unit of a product is defined in order to be able to compare products on the basis of the functions they fulfil rather than their quantitative amount. In case one wants to analyse the impacts of final consumption in a country, one has to define a number of products that are deemed representative for final consumption categories such as food, housing and related appliances, mobility, and so on. For instance for food, one may define a typical food basket of beef, pig meat, chicken meat, dairy, bread and vegetables. However, one can never cover all the hundreds of thousands of products for final consumption; this would make doing the LCAs an impossible task. Instead, one may have to limit oneself to a few dozen, up to 100, products deemed representative for the full basket.

**Inventory**
For the products defined in step (1) a system is developed that includes all relevant process chains for the manufacture, use and waste management of the product function in question. For each process in this chain, the relevant environmental interventions (emissions to air and water and extraction of primary resources) are inventoried in relation to the process's contribution to the central product function. Since doing primary data collection would be a massive task, usually databases such as the ILCD, Eco-invent or others in combination with LCA software such as SIMAPRO or Gabi will be used here. Interventions caused by each process that is part of the considered system are added by intervention type. The final result is a list of all environmental interventions associated with the product's function. The list is known as the life cycle inventory (LCI) table. A typical inventory table may list 100 or more interventions, such as the total emissions of lead, sulphur dioxide ($SO_2$) and other substances to air and to water.

If we want to know the inventory related to the full final consumption of a country, rather than a simple functional unit (for example, 1 kg of beef with a specific nutritional value), the LCI for the product must be scaled up to the total volume of that product used in a country. For a consumption category such as Classification of Individual Consumption According to Purpose (COICOP) categories 01 and 02 (food and drink) this may be done as follows. For the food and drink items most relevant in terms of volume, environmental impacts and expenditure LCIs are made and scaled up to actual volumes consumed in the country in question. These volumes can be retrieved from, for example, food balance sheets or other statistical sources. Hopefully, the top 20–25 products for which an LCI is made cover the main part of the monetary value of purchased food products. One then could assume that the remainder fraction of food products has the same average impact as for the food basket for which LCIs have been made.

**Impact assessment (classification, characterization and valuation)**

The purpose of the impact assessment step is to aggregate the information obtained in the inventory. First, a classification of impact categories is chosen, usually reflecting a common mechanism of environmental threat (for example, global warming, acidification and ozone depletion). In the characterization step, the environmental interventions listed in the inventory table are translated to scores on each impact category. This step is based as far as possible on natural science and generally according to the following formula:

$$S_i = {}_{1-j}S\ (e_{ij} * E_j)$$

where:

$S_i$ = score on impact category (theme) $i$

$E_j$ = magnitude of environmental intervention $j$

$e_{ij}$ = equivalency factor; a factor that indicates the contribution of one unit of intervention $j$ to impact category $i$.

The result of this operation is called the impact profile of a functional unit of a product. In principle, the impact categories can be aggregated, by means of weighting, to give a single score for the environmental impact of a product.

### 9.2.2 Top-Down Approach

The top-down approach in essence follows the same steps. The goal and scope step as well as the impact assessment steps hardly differ. The goal and scope again is to assess the environmental impacts of final consumption in a country. The impact assessment, in essence aggregating a life cycle inventory to more aggregated indicators, is done via the same method as depicted above. The main difference is in the inventory step where the top-down approach uses so-called 'environmentally extended input–output tables' to calculate the life cycle inventory related to final consumption.

'Supply and use tables' (SUTs) and input–output tables (IOTs) are a component of the System of National Accounts (SNA; UN et al. 1993), which is the standard used by national statistical offices to report data about national economies. In short, SUTs and IOTs split up the economy of a country into a number of sectors and/or products and show all the financial relations between these sectors and/or products in the economy. As I will explain in more detail below, for each element of final consumption this makes it possible to 'trace back' which industry sector has made which contribution to that particular final consumption activity. The SUTs and IOTs published by the statistical office of the European Union, Eurostat, discern 59 products and industries.

For each of the 59 industries, supply tables as published by Eurostat (2011) show the monetary volume of goods and services they produce, discerning 59 product categories. Usually one industry produces one main product, but often also secondary products. The use table shows the use of products (goods and services) for each of the 59 industries, but also the use of products for final consumption by consumers and government. Usually, the number of products used by a specific industry is much higher than the number of products in the supply table or output. For instance the agricultural sector will use fuel, automotive equipment (tractors), chemicals (fertilizers) and so on, but will only have agricultural products as output. Next to domestically produced products, the supply table also contains the imports for each product, and next to (intermediate and final) domestic consumption the use table also contains the exports of each product (Eurostat 2008).

The supply and use tables are two distinct tables, but they have to obey some obvious identities. The most important one is that the supply of products always equals the use of products.[1] Another is that for each industry the supply (or sales) of products always equals the use (purchase) of products, plus added value (that is, wages for employees, depreciation of assets, net taxes and subsidies, and profit or loss).[2]

For practical purposes, it is easier that the supply and use tables are combined into so-called 'input–output tables' (IOTs). The IOT is constructed by merging the supply table and the use table into one single table. A so-called 'industry-by-industry' IOT now describes how much input each industry uses from another industry; and conversely, shows for the output of this industry in which other industries and final consumption activities (consumers, government, exports) this output is used.[3]

An interesting feature is that for each industry the SUTs and IOT can be 'extended'. For instance, such extensions can show the direct emissions, primary resource extraction or land use by industry. Using the same sector classification as in its SUTs and IOT, Eurostat now has air emission data available for about eight substances, mainly greenhouse gases (GHGs) (Eurostat, 2005, 2009). The same applies for materials extraction, whereas from other sources such as FAOSTAT, data on land use and water use per industry sector can easily be made available. This relatively simple accounting structure forms a very powerful tool to understand the economic relations in a country, with all relevant environmental impacts made visible in the same structure. 'Environmentally extended' (EE) SUTs and IOTs (EE SUTs and EE IOTs) allow for a direct calculation of the emissions intensity or resource intensity per euro production of each industry sector.

However a country or European Union (EU) EE SUT/IOT (SUIOT) gives no information on how imported (intermediate and final) products were produced and what emissions this has caused. Accounting for such pollution embodied in imports is highly relevant. For various countries it has been shown that an apparent decoupling of carbon dioxide ($CO_2$) emissions or primary material use from gross domestic product (GDP) growth is the result of the relocation of materials- and energy-intensive production abroad (Druckman and Jackson 2009; Giljum et al. 2008; Wiedmann et al. 2010). Also a significant part of land use and water use embodied in final consumption can take place abroad. For that reason, ideally the country SUTs and IOTs are linked via trade: that is, in a table making visible which part of the products used in country A is imported from

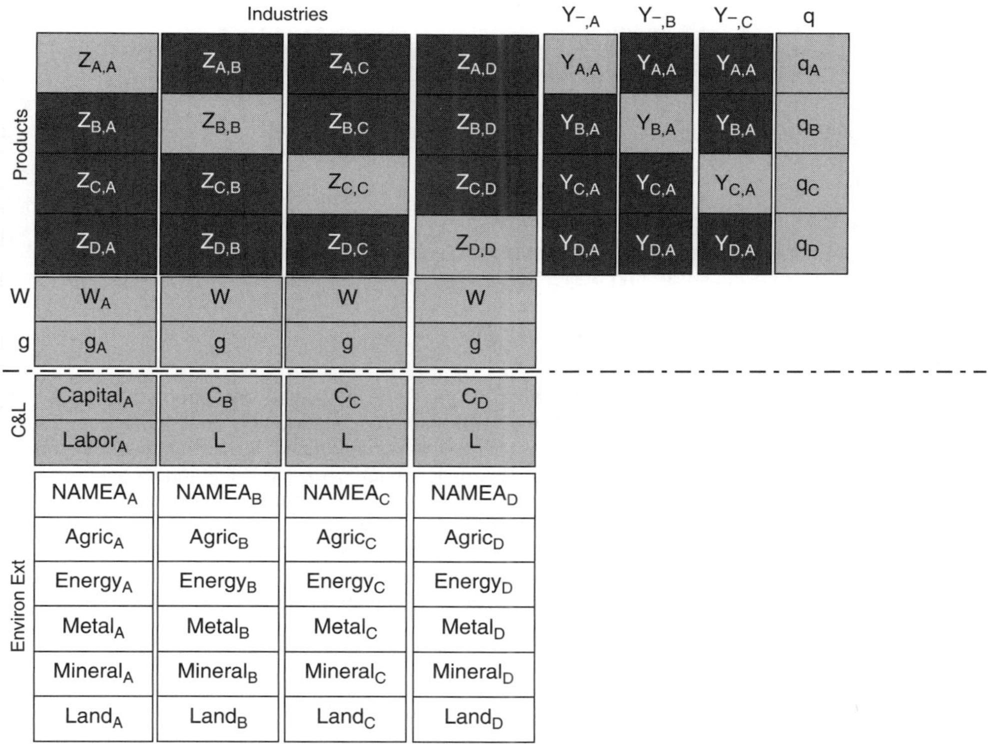


*Note:* grey: country tables including intermediate consumption, final consumption and added-value; dark grey: trade; white: extensions such as emissions and resource extraction.

*Figure 9.2 Schematic example of a multi-regional environmentally extended SUIOT for four countries*

country B, C, and so on. This then leads to so-called 'multi-regional' (MR) EE SUTs or IOTs, combining the SUTs and IOTs of a number of countries. Figure 9.2 gives a schematic example of such an MR EE SUIOT for four countries.

Such (MR) EE SUTs and IOTs have become a popular tool to estimate the life cycle environmental impacts of final consumption expenditure in a country or region. First, since the SUT or IOT contains all transactions in an economy, one can calculate for a specific final consumption category which industry sectors contributed which part of the final impact. But, second, the SUT or IOT also gives emissions by industry (and hence emissions by unit turnover). This allows calculating for each final demand or product category in the SUIOT how much emissions take place over its product life cycle (see Box 9.1; for details refer to, for example, Miller and Blair 2009). In this way, using the data in the EE SUT or IOT, the life cycle inventory for each of the 59 broad product groups discerned in the Eurostat tables can be calculated.

While the calculation as such is quick and easy, an obvious drawback is that SUTs and IOTs provide limited product detail (for example, Eurostat's SUIOTs have one

### BOX 9.1 CALCULATING ENVIRONMENTAL PRESSURES OF FINAL CONSUMPTION WITH EE IO TABLES

An input–output model describes how supply x follows demand with the following identity:

$$\mathbf{X} = \mathbf{AX} + \mathbf{f}$$

In this x is total output, A the matrix of direct input coefficients and f the vector of final demand. Solving the model for output gives (Miller and Blair 2009):

$$\mathbf{X} = (\mathbf{I}-\mathbf{A})^{-1}\,\mathbf{f} = \mathbf{Lf}$$

The matrix $(\mathbf{I} - \mathbf{A})^{-1}$ is commonly referred to as the Leontief-inverse and denoted by **L**, the multiplier matrix of direct and indirect industry output requirements per unit of final demand. In the Leontief quantity model, from which the backward multipliers are derived, the assumption is made that prices are fixed in the near term. Another assumption in IO modelling is that input coefficients do not change regardless of output, final demand, or other relevant changes. The structure of the economy is taken to be constant, at least in the near term.

The environmental extensions are given as a matrix of direct impact coefficients $\mathbf{D} = d_{kj}$ of which each element represents the amount (in physical units per euro worth of output) of the environmental factor k used in the production of sector j. These environmental extensions can be emissions, pollution, raw material, land use, water use, etc. The total requirement of environmental factors $x^E$ can be calculated as:

$$\mathbf{X}^{E} = \mathbf{Dx} = \mathbf{D}(\mathbf{I}-\mathbf{A})^{-1}\,\mathbf{f}$$

For an international input–output table the same equation holds, where x is now a vector of all individual country sub vectors $x_R$, for all countries R.

The total requirement of environmental factors $x^E$ (both resources and emissions/sinks) signifies the dependency of a sector on environmental resource inputs. Resource use and emissions may take place domestically, but especially for the countries that are not well endowed with material resources, these requirements will be imported.

agricultural production sector, making it impossible to distinguish between beef and vegetable production and consumption, despite their differences in impacts per kilogram or euro) and limited availability of official extensions (emissions, resource uses and so on). Further, while it is essential to have MR EE SUTs and IOTs available to take into account pollution embodied in imports, statistical offices usually only publish data for their own country, since that is within their mandate. There are no MR EE SUTs and IOTs published by official statistical offices or supra-national organizations (Tukker and Dietzenbacher 2013).

To overcome these problems, practitioners have built detailed so-called global 'multi-regional' EE SUIOTs that link country SUIOTs via trade, with a high number of extensions. Examples of such detailed MR EE SUIOT databases are EXIOBASE (Tukker et al. 2013) and EORA (Lenzen et al. 2012). For instance, EXIOBASE covers 43 countries and the 'rest of world', has 170 sectors and products per country, and includes 40 emissions, and 80 types of resources, land and water per sector.

### 9.2.3 Reflection: The Two Approaches Compared

The bottom-up and top-down approaches both have strengths and weaknesses. An advantage of the bottom-up LCA approach is that in principle a very high level of detail is possible with regard to product categories. Further, due to the use of comprehensive LCI databases, a much larger number of emissions types is covered than in most EE IO tables. Particularly for issues such as water and land embodied in trade, primarily related to agricultural products, it is an advantage that the full detail of the available trade data can be used, in combination with information about land use and water use per kilogram of crop in the country of origin (for example, from FAOSTAT or similar databases).

However the LCA approach also has obvious disadvantages. It is a laborious approach and in practice it is limited to around 100 product groups. There is a need for scaling up data from the product groups covered by LCIs to the full basket of products consumed in a country, which inevitably gives errors. Scaled-up LCIs rarely match the top-down reported emissions of, for example, greenhouse gases at country or world level. Further, most LCI databases are available for Europe, Japan and the USA. Hence, these give an incorrect picture of the life cycle impacts of production for production steps taking place in other countries. More generally, LCIs do not adequately take into account the fact that value chains for most products are complex and that parts of such products are made in different, sometimes myriad, countries. And finally one needs to use different LCI databases to cover a sufficient range of product groups, which may imply using LCI data that are not fully consistent.

A clear advantage of the top-down approach is that an MR EE SUT or IOT forms an inherently complete and consistent accounting system. All emissions and resource extractions for which country or global totals are available are allocated to the sectors that extract these resources and emit these emissions. In this way, all these emissions and resource extractions are also allocated to final consumption categories. There is no danger of double counts or unallocated impacts. Value chains across countries and country-specific emissions and resource extraction profiles are taken into account. And finally, once a global MR EE SUIOT is available, the calculation and analyses can be done with minimal effort.

But the top-down approach also has disadvantages. An MR EE SUT or IOT usually has less detail in product categories and covers less emissions than an LCI. An MR EE SUT or IOT usually also has less detail in trade flows than, for instance, water and land footprint methods. Since these footprints are mainly related to agricultural products, whose primary production takes place in one country, the advantage of having a better value chain perspective does not count here. And finally an MR EE SUT or IOT by definition uses an economic allocation of inventory items. This may not always be the most adequate.

## 9.3 SOME PRACTICAL ANALYSES

In this section I review some practical analyses using the bottom-up and top-down approaches. The examples and explanations are taken from earlier publications on the Environmental Impact of Products (EIPRO) project (Tukker 2006; Tukker et al. 2006) and the Externality Data and Input–Output Tools for Policy Analysis (EXIOPOL) project (Tukker et al. 2013).

Table 9.1 shows the results of the EIPRO report: a comparison across various studies of the results for the indicators related to energy use and carbon emissions, and which hence allow for a comparison across studies. Two remarks are made on the allocation of original product categories in the different studies to COICOP categories. First, Collins et al. (2006) considered government expenditure as a separate category. The (relative) percentages in this study were therefore calculated for private consumption only. Second, Palm et al. (2006) included energy-related household emissions as a single, separate sector in their IO table. In order to be comparable with the other studies, this sector should be further divided and distributed to housing and transport, which was not possible to do due to lack of data.

The table shows a clear pattern. Food, housing and transport dominate in virtually all studies, with a total contribution to energy-related impacts of typically 70 per cent, while being responsible for only 55 per cent of the total expenditure in the EU25. Results that seemingly defy this overall pattern are usually due to idiosyncrasies and hence of limited relevance. Notably, food was not included in Nemry et al. (2002) and was under-addressed in Labouze et al. (2003).[4] Some studies use energy and $CO_2$ as indicators and miss, for example, methane ($CH_4$) emissions from agriculture, which is a significant contribution to global warming potential (GWP). The somewhat lower relative contributions in these studies hence do not mean a lower priority. Housing scored high in the bottom-up studies, probably because these studies cover direct energy use (which is mainly in the home and for transport) quite well, but may miss some of the indirect energy use in the other COICOP categories due to cut-offs in the underlying LCAs used. The score of Palm et al. (2006) on transport would rise considerably if part of the energy purchases they reported separately were allocated here. The relatively high score on transport of Peters and Hertwich (2006) is probably due to the relatively low overall $CO_2$ emissions in Norway, where hydropower is the source for most other types of energy use. Recreation is relatively important in the work of Nijdam and Wilting (2003) since they include (package) holidays, probably including transport. In other studies transport is not so integrated and included under category 07, transport. Finally, some studies simply did not classify their expenditures in a way that allowed us to 'fill' all COICOP categories, implying that the scores for some COICOP categories had to be left blank.

The EIPRO study (Tukker et al. 2006) made qualitative comparisons on other indicators as far as they were included in the different studies. Space does not allow for a full reproduction of the analysis so I limit myself to the main conclusions for some important (groups of) indicators. The impact on resource use has been covered in two different ways: via the life cycle impact assessment (LCIA)-based indicator of 'resource depletion potential' and different types of total material requirement. Despite the enormous variety of scope and methods, the studies covering this impact category give priority to housing (buildings), transport and in some cases food. The studies considering land use as an impact category, despite applying rather different methodologies, consistently give food and housing as priorities. For water use, a comparison is not possible, since the two studies covering this impact category did so in completely different ways. Nemry et al. (2002) only considered tap water (with, as a logical priority, sanitary use) whereas Nijdam and Wilting (2003) considered total water use (leading to dominance of food

*Table 9.1 Contribution per COICOP category to energy-related impact indicators in different studies*

| | | | 1 | 2 | 3 | 5 | 6 | 7 | 8 | 9 | 10 |
|---|---|---|---|---|---|---|---|---|---|---|---|
| COICOP | Study | % of total expenditure in EU25 (Tukker et al. 2006) | Collins et al.(2006) (%) | Dall et al. (2002) (%) | Labouze et al. (2003) (%) | Moll et al. (2004) (%) | Jansen and Thollier (2006) (%) | Nijdam and Wilting (2003) (%) | Palm et al. (2006)* (%) | Peters and Hertwich (2006) (%) | Huppes et al. (2006) (%) |
| | Geographical focus | EU25 | Cardiff | Denmark | EU15 | Germany | Belgium | Netherlands | Sweden | Norway | EU25 |
| | Indicator | | Footprint | Energy | GWP | Energy | GWP | GWP | $CO_2$ | $CO_2$ | GWP |
| | Main approach | | Top-down/ hybrid | Bottom-up | Bottom-up | Top-down | Bottom-up | Top-down | Top-down | Top-down | Top-down |
| CP01i–02 | Food | 19.3 | 21.0 | 26.2 | 7.0** | 13.0 | 3.6** | 22.1 | 7.7 | 12.2 | 31.0 |
| CP03 | Clothing | 3.1 | 0.8 | 1.3 | 3.3 | 2.2 | 1.3 | 6.5 | 0.7 | 10.3 | 2.4 |
| CP04–05 | Housing | 25.1 | 30.8 | 40.8 | 58.8 | 54.3 | 53.5 | 33.4 | 32.3 | 24.9 | 23.6 |
| CP06 | Health | 3.9 | 0.3 | n/a | n/a | 1.8 | 0.3 | 0.3 | 1.0 | 1.1 | 1.6 |
| CP07 | Transport | 14.1 | 22.4 | 19.5 | 29.6 | 18.3 | 32.9 | 17.3 | 12.3 | 34.5 | 18.5 |
| CP08 | Communication | 4.0 | 0.5 | | 0.0 | | 2.9 | 0.0 | 1.7 | 2.1 | 2.1 |
| CP09 | Recreation | 9.1 | 8.3 | 7.2 | 0.0 | 8.1 | n/a | 15.1 | 0.5 | 0.5 | 6.0 |
| CP10 | Education | 1.4 | 0.3 | n/a | n/a | 1.8 | n/a | 0.7 | 0.3 | 0.1 | 0.5 |
| CP11 | Restaurants | 9.6 | 11.0 | n/a | n/a | n/a | n/a | 2.8 | 1.8 | 1.3 | 9.1 |
| CP12 | Miscellaneous | 10.3 | 4.5 | 5.1 | 1.3 | 0.4 | 5.4 | 1.8 | 6.6 | 13.1 | 5.2 |
| Other | Refined petroleum products / Direct household energy* | | | | | | | | 35.0 | | |
| | TOTAL | 100 | 100 | 100 | 100 | 100 | 100 | 100 | 100 | 100 | 100 |

*Notes:*
* Palm et al. (2006) reported energy use by households as a separate category. To be distributed over housing and transport.
** Jansen and Thollier (2006) and Labouze et al. (2003) under-addressed food for a variety of reasons in their work.
n/a Not visible as a specific category in the study at stake.

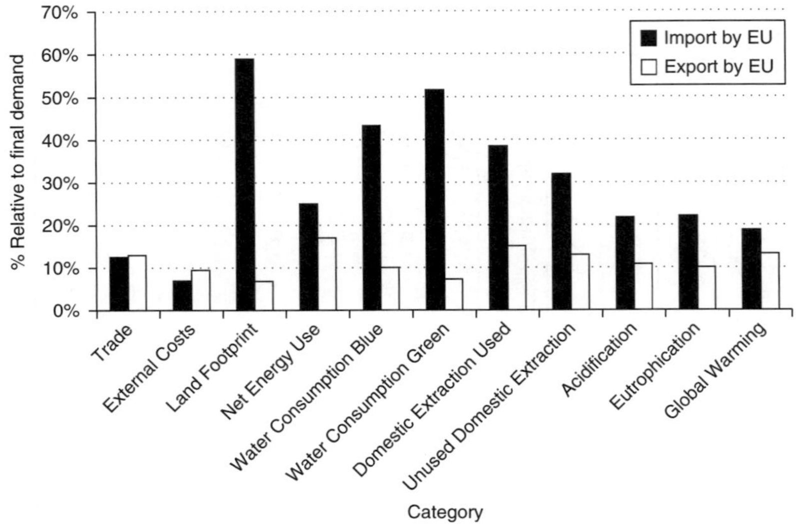


*Notes:*
Trade taken relative to Europe's GDP.
The global warming excludes emissions from land use change.
Green water is rainwater. Blue water is water sourced from rivers or aquifers.
See Tukker et al. (2013) for a more extensive account of the external costs related to the emissions embodied in imports.

*Figure 9.3 Impacts embodied in Europe's imports and exports, relative to impacts caused by EU final demand in 2000*

and, at a distance, clothes). The studies covering acidification agree that transport and cars, building structures and heating, and food are priorities.

With regard to eutrophication, studies covering this impact category agree that food dominates all other product and expenditure categories. For photochemical smog formation, transport and cars, building structures and food consistently show up as priorities. Finally, results for waste volume differ strongly among studies, mainly because they define waste in different ways.

The EXIOPOL study additionally gives information on how relevant is the pollution embodied in imports to Europe. Figure 9.3 provides the results for pollution embodied in imports and exports as a percentage of the impacts of final consumption in Europe (Tukker et al. 2013). The figure makes clear that for land use, green and blue water use, and material extraction, Europe depends largely on other countries. This is an interesting finding since at this stage policy is mainly concerned about GWP or $CO_2$ emissions embodied in trade. Figure 9.3 makes clear that the imbalance in water, land and materials embodied in trade is much more pronounced.

Europe is a rather densely populated continent, and it is hence logical that it does not concentrate on land-intensive products (mainly agricultural and forestry products, which are also responsible for most green and blue water use). Each continent will concentrate on producing goods fitting best with its natural resources and skills base so the fact that trade imbalances exist is as such not a priori a concern. However, it shows that Europe may have a significant responsibility with regard to land use and water use abroad, and that it should allow the countries from which it imports to avoid negative impacts on, for example, biodiversity related to this land and water use.

## 9.4 REFLECTION, IMPLICATIONS AND CONCLUSIONS

The conclusion of the comparison in Table 9.1 is straightforward. On the most common indicators used, food, transport and housing (the building and energy use) always show up as the highest contributors. Given the very different approaches followed in the studies represented in Table 9.1, this result must be regarded as extremely robust. With the possible exception of food, the results were to be expected: these categories include all expenditures on car fuel, gas, oil and electricity use. The results have later been validated by other authoritative reports, such as a United Nations Environment Programme (UNEP) Resource Panel study on the environmental impacts of products and resources (UNEP 2010). Apart from identifying these priorities for sustainable consumption and sustainable product categories, the EXIOPOL study further makes clear that particularly when it comes to impacts such as water use, land use and resource extraction, Europe relies heavily on production abroad.

Given the need to reduce impacts considerably, action is essential. As indicated in the first sections of this chapter, significant reductions in impact intensities are needed: for greenhouse gases around a factor of ten, and for water, land use and biodiversity impacts at least a factor of two. In principle, there are five main strategies to reduce the impacts of consumption:

- cleaning production;
- greening products;
- intensifying use of products ('product services');
- shifting expenditure to immaterial consumption;
- improving quality of life without changing monetary consumption.

Table 9.2 shows, on the basis of earlier analyses (Tukker 2014), the ballpark reduction that each of these strategies can provide. Where each decoupling strategy on its own has difficulties in realizing a 'factor 10' or more decoupling, all strategies in combination may deliver such reductions. Where this seems promising news, the existing realities in sustainability policy should lead to a more prudent conclusion. It seems safe to say that most existing sustainability policies focus on cleaning production and greening products, often via rather marginal adaptations, and hardly touch consumption. From such policies one cannot expect radical 'factor X' decoupling. It is essential that the potential of the other decoupling strategies is used. Policies should also focus on shifting expenditure to less material consumption; that is, buying product categories with lower impacts. Also, lowering economic consumption while maintaining quality of life is essential, which in essence leads to policy agendas that pursue quality of life first, rather than a high GDP. This, in turn, may entail all kinds of other goals, such as limiting income inequality, allowing a good work–life balance, enhancing social cohesion and so on. It

*Table 9.2 Ballpark data on the potential contribution of various intervention mechanisms to decoupling of impact and quality of life*

| Intervention mechanism | Potential reductions of impact per unit Quality of Life (excluding rebounds) |
|---|---|
| Enhancing impact efficiency of production | Small mass flows: several factors by end of pipe or cleaner technology<br>Large mass flows: limited |
| Enhancing product function efficiency output of production | Limited to intermediate, in case of incremental improvements and redesign<br>Factor X in case of system innovation |
| Enhancing the intensity of use of product functions | Factor 2 or more, depending on the sharing, pooling or function combination system |
| Reducing the product composition of expenditure | Factor 2 (if limited to changes within existing product and service categories) |
| Enhancing the ratio of Quality of Life to consumer expenditure | Several factors? |

is hence essential that radical shifts in policy take place, focusing more on policies that influence consumption and life style patterns.

To conclude, whatever their (dis)advantages for specific applications, the bottom-up and top-down methods point at the same priorities for an environmental consumption and product policy. Such policies should in particular focus on housing, mobility and food (meat and dairy, followed by the rest). Particularly the latter category is very important with regard to impacts of Europe abroad (water and land use). How to embark on effective policies to achieve the needed radical changes is the subject of other chapters in this book.

## ACKNOWLEDGEMENTS

Various parts of this chapter benefited from the contributions of the EIPRO and EXIOPOL project teams, projects on which this chapter relies heavily. See the full references to the EIPRO (Tukker et al. 2006) and EXIOPOL projects (Tukker et al. 2013).

## NOTES

1. The use table also provides a column for changes in inventories: when production is higher than consumption, the surplus is stored and administered as a change in inventory.
2. For a company, income (= sales) is by definition equal to expenses (purchases, wages, depreciation, taxes) plus profit or loss.
3. A product-by-product IOT describes which products in which quantities are used to produce another product, and for what other products this product output is used.
4. Labouze et al. (2003) used the bottom-up approach, but did not have a good representation of meat and dairy consumption in their LCI basket, whereas it is now known that these count for around 50 per cent of the impact of food consumption.

# REFERENCES


Collins, A., A. Flynn, T. Wiedmann and J. Barrett (2006), 'The environmental impacts of consumption at a sub-national level: the ecological footprint of Cardiff', *Journal of Industrial Ecology*, 10 (3), 9–24.

Dall, O., J. Toft and T.T. Andersen (2002), 'Danske husholdningers miljøbelastning, København: Miljøstyrelsen', Arbejdsrappport 13, available at http://www.mst.dk/udgiv/ Publikationer/2002/87-7972-094-3/pdf/87-7972-095-1.PDF.

Druckman, A. and T. Jackson (2009), 'The carbon footprint of UK households 1990–2004: a socio-economically disaggregated, quasi-multi-regional input–output model', *Ecological Economics*, 68 (7), 2066–2077.

Eurostat (2005), 'NAMEA for air emissions. Compilation guide', Joint Eurostat EFTA group, meeting 11–13 May, Doc EA1/016/10.1/ (2005), DG Eurostat, Unit E-5, Environment, Luxemburg, available at http://forum.europa.eu.int/Public/irc/dsis/envirmeet/library?l=/11-130505_environmental/namea_air/namea_workshop&vm=detailed&sb=Title.

Eurostat (2008), *Eurostat Manual of Supply, Use and Input–Output Tables*, Luxembourg: Office for Official Publications of the European Communities.

Eurostat (2009), *Manual for Air Emissions Accounts*, Luxembourg: Office for Official Publications of the European Communities.

Eurostat (2011), *Creating Consolidated and Aggregated EU27 Input–Output Tables, Adding Environmental Extensions (Air Emissions), and Conducting Leontief-Type Modelling to Approximate Carbon and other 'Footprints' Of EU27 Consumption for 2000 to 2006*, Luxembourg: Office for Official Publications of the European Communities.

Giljum, S., A. Behrens, F. Hinterberger, C. Lutz and B. Meyer (2008), 'Modelling scenarios towards a sustainable use of natural resources in Europe', *Environmental Science and Policy*, 112 (3), 204–216.

Guinée, J.B. (ed.) (2002), *Handbook on Life Cycle Assessment: Operational Guide to the ISO Standards*, Eco-Efficiency in Industry and Science, Vol. 7, Dordrecht: Springer.

Huppes, G., A. de Koning, S. Suh, R. Heijungs, L. van Oers, P. Nielsen and J.B. Guinée (2006), 'Environmental impacts of consumption in the European Union using detailed input–output analysis', *Journal of Industrial Ecology*, 10 (3), 129–146.

IPPC (International Panel on Climate Change) (2013), *Climate Change 2013: The Physical Science Base*, Geneva: International Panel on Climate Change.

Jansen, B. and K. Thollier (2006), 'Bottom-up LCA methodology for the evaluation of environmental impacts of product consumption in Belgium', *Journal of Industrial Ecology*, 10 (3), 41–55.

Labouze, E., V. Monier, Y. Le Guern and J.-B. Puyou (2003), *Study on External Environmental Effects Related to the Lifecycle of Products and Services – Final Report Version 2*, Paris: European Commission, Directorate General Environment, Directorate A – Sustainable Development and Policy Support.

Lenzen, M., K. Kanemoto, D. Moran and A. Geschke (2012), 'Mapping the structure of the world economy', *Environmental Science and Technology*, 46 (15), 8374–8381.

Meinshausen, M., N. Meinshausen, W. Hare, S.C.B. Raper, K. Frieler, R. Knutti, D.J. Frame et al. (2009), 'Greenhouse-gas emission targets for limiting global warming to 2° C', *Nature*, 458, 1158–1162.

Miller, R.E. and P.D. Blair (2009), *Input–Output Analysis: Foundations and Extensions*, Cambridge: Cambridge University Press.

Moll, S., J. Acosta and A. Villanueva (2004), *Environmental Implications of Resource Use – Insights from Input–Output Analyses*, prepared by The European Topic Centre on Waste and Material Flows (ETC WMF), Copenhagen: European Environment Agency.

Myers, N. and J. Kent (2004), *The New Consumers: The Influence of Affluence on the Environment*, Washington, DC: Island Press.

Nemry, F., K. Thollier, B. Jansen and J. Theunis (2002), 'Identifying key products for the federal product and environment policy – final report, for Federal Services of Environment Department on Product Policy', Namur/Mol: Institut Wallon de Développement Économique et Social et d'Aménagement du Territoire ASBL/Vlaamse Instelling voor Technologisch Onderzoek.

Nijdam, D.S. and H. Wilting (2003), 'Milieudruk consumptie in beeld' [A view on environmental pressure on consumption], RIVM rapport 7714040004, Bilthoven: RIVM.

Palm, V., A. Wadeskog and G. Finnveden (2006), 'Swedish experiences of using environmental accounts data for integrated product policy (IPP) issues', *Journal of Industrial Ecology*, 10 (3), 57–72.

Peters, G.P. and E.G. Hertwich (2006), 'The importance of imports for household environmental impacts', *Journal of Industrial Ecology*, 10 (3), 89–109.

Rockström, J., W. Steffen, K. Noone, Å. Persson, F. Stuart Chapin, III, E.F. Lambin, T.M. Lenton et al. (2009), 'A safe operating space for humanity', *Nature*, 461, 472–475.

Simons, L.P., A. Slob, H. Holswilder and A. Tukker (2001), 'The fourth generation: new strategies call for new eco-indicators', *Environmental Quality Management*, 11 (2), 51–61.
Speth, J.G. (2008), *The Bridge at the Edge of the World*, Yale, CT, USA and London, UK: Yale University Press.
Tukker, A. (ed.) (2006), *Special Issue on Priorities for Environmental Product Policy*, *Journal of Industrial Ecology*, 10 (3).
Tukker, A. (2013), 'Knowledge collaboration and learning by aligning global sustainability programs: reflections in the context of Rio+20', *Journal of Cleaner Production*, 48, 272–279.
Tukker, A. (2014), 'Strategies for enhancing resource efficiency', in M. Angrick, A. Burger and H. Lehmann (eds), *Factor X – Policies, Strategies and Instruments for Sustainable Resource Use*, Heidelberg and Berlin, Germany; Dordrecht, the Netherlands: Springer.
Tukker, A., A. de Koning, R. Wood, T. Hawkins, S. Lutter, J. Acosta, J.M. Rueda Cantuche et al. (2013), 'EXIOPOL – Development and illustrative analyses of a detailed global MR EE SUT/IOT', *Economic Systems Research*, 25 (1), 50–70.
Tukker, A. and E. Dietzenbacher (2013), 'Global multiregional input–output frameworks: an introduction and outlook', *Economic Systems Research*, 25, 1–19.
Tukker, A., G. Huppes, S. Suh, T. Geerken, B. Jansen and P Nielsen (2006), *Environmental Impacts of Products. Literature Review and Input-Output Analyses on 500 Product groupings for the EU's Integrated Product Policy*, Seville: European Science and Technology Observatory (ESTO) and Institute for Prospective Technological Studies (IPTS).
UN (United Nations), World Bank, OECD (Organisation for Economic Co-operation and Development), EC (European Commission) and IMF (International Monetary Fund) (1993), *System of National Accounts 1993*, Brussels, Belgium; Luxembourg; New York and Washington, DC, USA; Paris, France: United Nations, World Bank, Organisation for Economic Co-operation and Development, Commission of the European Communities and International Monetary Fund.
UNEP (United Nations Environment Programme) (2010), *Assessing the Environmental Impacts of Consumption and Production: Priority Products and Materials*, A Report of the Working Group on the Environmental Impacts of Products and Materials to the International Panel for Sustainable Resource Management, Paris: United Nations Environment Programme.
Vitusek, P., P. Ehrlich, A. Ehrlich and P. Matson (1986), 'Human appropriation of the products of photosynthesis', *BioScience*, 36 (6), 368–373.
Water Resources Group (2009), 'Charting our water future. economic frameworks to inform decision-making', available at http://www.2030wrg.org/wp-content/uploads/2014/07/Charting-Our-Water-Future-Final.pdf.
Wiedmann, T., R. Wood, J.C. Minx, M. Lenzen, D. Guan and R. Harris (2010), 'Carbon footprint time series of the UK – results from a multi-region input–output model', *Economic Systems Research*, 22 (1), 43–63.

# PART IV

# TRANSPORT, HOUSING, FOOD AND PUBLIC HEALTH

# 10. Unsustainable travel becoming (more) sustainable

*Tommy Gärling and Margareta Friman*

Fast motorized transportation of people and cargo is essential in contemporary societies with their specialization of functions at different locations. Cargo needs to be transported between different units in the manufacturing process as well as from manufacturers to retailers. People need to travel to and from work, shops and other locations. It is not likely that telecommunication in the future will substantially reduce the need for physical travel (Moktharian et al. 2006). Neither is it likely that electronic commerce will (Rotem-Mindali and Weltenwreden 2013).

For the benefits of the individual as well as society, time for travel could be spent in better ways. In urban areas of developed countries, travel still contributes to well-being by increasing opportunities for residents to purchase the most attractive goods at the lowest prices, patronize the best restaurants, visit recreational places, attend entertaining and cultural events, and meet with relatives and friends (Leyden et al. 2011; Reardon and Abdallah 2013). In sparsely populated rural areas travel is essential for sustenance. Some travel is also enjoyed for its own sake (Moktharian and Salomon 2001). Examples include driving a new car or enjoying a recreational sailing trip in the sunshine. Today for busy people in the workforce, travel furthermore provides the privacy and time for recovery from stress (Hartig 2007). If not for recreation, travel allows work at a distance, including reading memos, preparing for meetings and using available telecommunication devices (Ettema and Verschuren 2007).

The present chapter focuses on environmental sustainability of daily personal travel in urban areas. Long-distance holiday travel, business travel and freight transportation are beyond its scope. For these topics the reader is referred to chapters in Gärling et al. (2014). Neither does the chapter cover research examining the role played by motorized travel for sedentary life styles in Western societies. A review is found in Handy (2014).

## 10.1 THE UNSUSTAINABILITY OF TRANSPORTATION

Passenger and freight transportation have both local short-term and global long-term detrimental effects on the environment. The unprecedented increase in motorized travel is primarily responsible for this (van Wee 2014). Locally, urban environments are made less liveable due to accident risks, particle emissions, noise and road infrastructure infringement on land that crowds out other uses as well as destroys historical and cultural values. The global long-term effects include primarily the contribution to the global warming from emissions of greenhouse gases (GHGs) caused by motorized traffic. These emissions are substantial and increasing. The use of land that otherwise could produce food for an increasing world population is another global long-term effect. Still another effect is shortage of materials and fossil energy due to the production and use of motorized petrol-powered vehicles.

Constructing road infrastructure, controlling noise (for example, replacing old road surfaces with new quiet ones; building protective walls along the roads), preventing and mitigating damage from accidents, medical treatment of accident victims and loss of work hours due to injuries are societal costs accrued to taxpayers, insurance companies and, directly and indirectly, road users. Congestion is also considered a societal cost.

## 10.2 WHY PERSONAL TRAVEL BECAME UNSUSTAINABLE: THE RISE OF THE AUTOMOBILE

The automobile has drastically altered the development of the world like few other human inventions. In the developed countries, and now in developing countries, its versatility strongly contributes to why it is preferred for urban, suburban and rural travel (Jakobsson 2007). Instrumental motives still do not alone explain its choice. The automobile is also attractive because it is attractive to drive and ride, provides privacy and security, and signals social status (Gatersleben 2014).

Even though cars were available at the beginning of the twentieth century, it was only in the years after the Second World War with the subsequent spread of affluence and the acceleration of automobile mass production that ownership was brought within the reach of a majority of households in the industrialized world. Car ownership is related to household socio-economic characteristics (for example, income, household composition, employment status), the characteristics of the transport system (for example, car purchase costs, available road infrastructure, non-access to public transport) and attributes of the built environment (for example, population density, access to services and amenities) (Giuliano and Dargay 2006).

Bonsall (2000) shows that car ownership in the UK rose from 30 per cent of households in 1960 to 70 per cent in 1995. Pucher (1999) provides evidence of a similar large increase for the US: per capita car ownership increased from 0.31 in 1960 to 0.65 in 1996. Considering only licensed drivers, Southworth (2001) calculates that an average of more than one vehicle per licensed driver has already been reached. Such a growth in car ownership is not limited to these Anglo-Saxon countries, to which Australia and Canada can be added with increases in cars per capita for the period 1970 to 1992 from 0.31 to 0.45, and from 0.31 to 0.49, respectively (Dargay and Gately 1999). Similar trends have been observed for other industrialized countries, including several in the European Union. As an example Vilhelmson (2005) estimates that in Sweden almost all growth in daily travel since the 1950s is attributable to the increase in car use. Eurostat (2011) estimates that the automobile accounts for more than 80 per cent of the total daily distance of passenger travel; the corresponding figure for the USA is similar (Pucher 1999). When car use is indexed as the number of trips as opposed to distance travelled, the car accounts for 45 per cent of urban trips in European countries but a staggering 90 per cent in the USA. Perhaps reflecting a similar development in Europe, Mackett (2001) notes an increase in the number of short car trips in the UK.

To some extent these alarming figures may be offset by recent evidence of a discontinued increase of private automobile travel (Millard-Ball and Schipper 2011). Thus referred to as ‘peak car use’, stagnation or even a decrease has been observed in eight developed countries (Australia, Canada, France, Germany, Japan, Sweden, the UK and the USA).

Different explanations have been offered. Millard-Ball and Schipper (2011) propose that increasing fuel prices accounts for the peak car use. Litman (2012) highlights a number of additional determinants: automobile saturation, wealth effects, ageing populations, increased urbanization, improved alternative travel options and incentives, changing consumer preferences, and increased concerns for health and the environment. Goodwin (2012) argues that peak car use should be considered a turning point followed by decline. As long as an explanation of peak use car is not conclusively supported empirically, this remains speculation however. Also, current levels of automobile use in developed countries are still not sustainable.

Suggesting instead that the future is even darker, sharply increasing automobile ownership and use are observed in countries only beginning the industrialization process (for example, China, India) or which are to some extent industrialized such that citizens are beginning to experience income growth and the spread of affluence (for example, South Korea, Taiwan) (Kitamura and Mohamad 2009). Indeed according to Sperling and Claussen (2004), the fastest growth has been observed in Latin America and Asia, with vehicle sales in China, for example, having increased by more than 50 per cent per year in recent years (from 700000 in 2001, to 1.1 million in 2002, and about 1.7 million in 2003).

## 10.3 HOW TRAVEL CAN BECOME (MORE) SUSTAINABLE: THE FALL OF THE AUTOMOBILE

A conclusion about which most agree is that personal travel needs to be (more) sustainable in the future and that this requires changes in current private automobile use. Yet opinions differ about how this can be accomplished (van Wee 2012). Some believe automobile travel already needs to be substantially reduced today. Others have faith in waiting for the long-term development of sustainable vehicles and fuels. Still others with a similar long-term horizon argue that the environment needs to be planned differently. This section examines future prospects of implementing clean automobile technology; changing infrastructure that increases accessibility without travel or with travel by more sustainable modes; and reducing automobile use by implementing prohibition, pricing and information measures.

### 10.3.1 Clean Automobile Technology

Developing and implementing clean automobile technology appears to be a win-all solution that globally reduces energy use and GHG emissions and locally particle pollution without requiring changes in current automobile use. Will automobiles running on clean fuels (electricity, hydrogen, biofuels, natural gas) soon penetrate markets such that these become dominant in the fleet? A few years ago more than 99 per cent of all on-road vehicles consisted of internal combustion engine vehicles (ICEVs) and 94 per cent of transportation fuels came from petroleum (International Energy Agency 2009). Alternative fuels including electricity (for rail) represented about 4 per cent and biofuels about 2 per cent. This gives a sense of the challenge.

Which are the technical options and how can these be implemented? Consensus appears to be that there is no single vehicle or fuel of the future but that a diverse mix is likely (Ogden 2012). The long time horizon and the high degree of uncertainty furthermore favour a portfolio approach. This is in stark contrast to the short-lived enthusiasm for one technology after another characterizing mass media coverage, public opinions and policy proposals.

The portfolio approach includes in the short term increasing the fuel efficiency of ICEVs by diminishing vehicle weights, aerodynamic streamlining and improving engines, transmissions and drive trains. Even if there is still considerable scope for improvement, considering also the recent developments of hybridized drive trains, these technological changes will not alone suffice. Low- or zero-emissions electric vehicles (EVs) are still in a phase of development with several recognized previous failures of market penetration (Gärling and Thøgersen 2001). Costs and performance of batteries remain unresolved issues. Zero-emissions hydrogen and fuel cell vehicles appear more promising in the near future (National Research Council 2008). Biofuels blended with the petrol or diesel that currently power automobiles are estimated to contribute about a quarter of fuel supply in the longer term (Parker et al. 2011). Here the crucial issue is whether biofuels sufficiently increase the sustainability of transportation. Natural gas supply has been growing (Massachusetts Institute of Technology 2011). It is a low-carbon fuel but may still not make a sufficient contribution.

Governments, in order to succeed, would need to fund research to speed up the development of low-carbon or zero-emissions vehicles as well as to initially subsidize their production. For their market penetration substantial infrastructure investments are also required. Another important issue is whether current automobile owners are willing to purchase clean automobiles and how these should be marketed to sell. Whether powered by battery or fuel cells from hydrogen, EVs differ importantly from current automobiles in having a limited driving range, longer refuelling times, limited space for cargo, and at least currently high purchase prices. On the basis of a UK survey of potential EV adopters, these were found to be reasons for why automobile owners are reluctant to replace their petrol-powered automobile (Schuitema et al. 2013). Yet it was also demonstrated that low pleasure of driving and identity derived from owning an EV are even more important obstacles.

Gärling and Thøgersen (2001) outlined a two-phase strategy to market EVs based on the theoretical framework proposed by Rogers (1962) positing that early adopters of innovations augment investments in product development and marketing, that in turn increases the likelihood of a wide market penetration. Governments may subsidize or reduce taxes for early adopters among fleet operators such as utility, postal service, public transport, taxi and car rental companies. Launching demonstration projects may be effective both in the development of the product and to make it visible. Other potential early adopters include companies marketing themselves as environmentally friendly as well as multi-car households to whom an EV as a second car may be less disadvantageous. Segments of automobile users with pro-environmental attitudes may also become early adopters. This was found by Jansson et al. (2009) in studies of early adopters of alternative-fuel vehicles.

The process of adopting a new product has been studied by means of agent-based models simulating macro-level consequences of micro-level product characteristics driving adoption (Meade and Islam 2006). Recently Delre et al. (2010) developed a modified agent-based model by adapting percolation models in statistical physics of how information spread in networks. The model is designed to make realistic predictions of how in a network of consumers preferences are influenced by word of mouth as well as by high-status persons. Applying this model may demonstrate that spreading of pro-environmental attitudes is essential for a wide EV adoption.

### 10.3.2 Increasing Accessibility

Accessibility is generally either defined as individuals' access to destinations (origin-based accessibility) or access to destinations by individuals belonging to different subpopulations (destination-based accessibility) (Curl et al. 2011). Origin-based accessibility in urban areas entails policies to change future land use to decrease distances to destinations, and policies to change the transportation system to increase access to more destinations including infrastructure improvements (for example, new walking and cycle paths).

Origin-based accessibility that reduces travel may be reached by integrating transport and land use planning policies. If services and other facilities are located closer to homes, people can walk or cycle. Yet, on the basis of a review of several studies, Handy and Van Wee (2014) conclude that in the short term land-use policies are likely to only result in minor reductions of unsustainable travel and that persistence in implementation, as well as governmental and municipality funding, will determine the likely reductions in the long term. Four extensive case studies in Europe still demonstrate that it is possible to reduce car travel through a modal shift away from the car or through reduced travel distances by car (Marshall and Banister 2000).

Strategies to increase destination-based accessibility depart from descriptions of individual needs (for example, shaped by age, income and educational level), abilities (for example, physical fitness) and opportunities (for example, travel budget). Limanond and Niemeier (2003) analyse how the distribution of these individual characteristics in subpopulations influences aggregated access to destinations. Both neighbourhood accessibility and regional accessibility are found to influence travel mode and destination choice for shopping journeys.

### 10.3.3 Alternative Travel Modes

A study by Kenworthy (2011) of transport, urban form, energy use and GHG emissions in 84 cities in Africa, Asia, Australia, Canada, China, Europe, Latin America, the Middle East and the USA showed that energy use in automobile-dependent cities (mainly in the USA) is very high. In comparisons between private and public transport, it was found that regardless of level of service and frequency of use, public transport energy use per capita and carbon dioxide emissions are only a fraction of that of private automobile use, with rail being the least damaging to the environment. Walking and cycling have the lowest environmental impacts, whereas that of public transport varies with type of vehicle, fuel, trip route and loading. Even though different combinations of these factors would change the impacts on sustainability, public transport is by far more sustainable than private automobile use, partly due to its comparatively low share of trips and partly due to its larger efficiency in moving people.

Rates of walking and cycling are very low in the USA compared to many European countries (Handy 2014). This is partly understandable since a recent review by Heinen et al. (2010) indicates that choices to cycle to and from work increase with the availability of attractive and safe cycle paths. Providing this has traditionally been limited in the USA. A short distance (travel time, physical exertion) is the most important among other factors promoting cycling (Martens 2004). A climate with moderate temperatures and little rain also increases the share of cycling. All these factors promoting cycling, as well as attractive neighbourhoods (Brown et al. 2013), likewise promote walking. In order to motivate people to start walking or cycling, persuasion leading to attitude changes and social pressure are effective (Bird et al. 2013). Self-monitoring feedback techniques (for example, pedometers or smartphone apps) are effective for interventions.

Women and older persons are generally less likely to walk or cycle (Dickinson et al. 2003). Other personal factors favouring walking and cycling include the desire to be physically active to increase fitness (Oja et al. 1998), previous habits to walk or cycle (Lemieux and Godin 2009), and positive attitudes towards protection of the environment (Bopp et al. 2011). Not everyone is able to or should cycle, however. People with health problems (older people; people with sight, hearing or cognitive impairments) are not able to cycle and sometimes not even to walk at an acceptable speed (Frye 2013).

Many people are thus excluded from walking and cycling, either because they live too far from work places, shops and other facilities, or because of age or health problems. Public transport is the only sustainable travel mode remaining. Redman et al. (2013) identify the most likely attributes of public transport quality to attract automobile users. In Table 10.1 these attributes are roughly categorized as physical or perceived. Assumptions are made about how physical attributes impact on users, since their measurements do not involve users. In contrast, measurements of perceived attributes require that users are observed directly or indirectly.

*Table 10.1 Definitions of public transport service quality attributes*

| | Attribute | Definition |
|---|---|---|
| Physical | Reliability | Match to actual timetable |
| | Frequency | Frequency of operation during different hours |
| | Travel time | Time spent travelling from origin to destination |
| | Accessibility | Accessibility of public transport to number of destinations and people |
| | Price | Monetary cost of travel |
| | Information | Information about departure/arrival times, routes and interchanges |
| | Ease of transfer | Simplicity of connections including wait times |
| Perceived | Vehicle condition | Physical and mechanical condition of vehicles including frequency of breakdowns |
| | Comfort | Vehicle comfort including seat access, noise level, driver handling and indoor climate |
| | Safety | Safety from traffic accidents and personal security |
| | Convenience | Simplicity of use and contribution to ease of mobility |
| | Aesthetics | Appeal of vehicles, stations and waiting areas |

*Source:* Adapted from Redman et al. (2013).

Reliability and frequency of service have been found to be key attributes in determining attractiveness of and satisfaction with public transport. Reduced travel time has however primarily been targeted in interventions to promote public transport. Successful strategies to improve travel time include bus rapid-transit systems, light rail replacing buses, and integrated public transport, also referred to as 'seamless transportation', that brings travellers from door to door. Other targeted quality attributes are reliability, frequency of service, fares, vehicle comfort, convenience and access. Redman et al. (2013) conclude that a basic service quality is needed to match the quality of private automobile use. They also suggest that context-specific, perceived quality attributes should be improved to appeal to automobile users. Furthermore the benefits of these quality attributes must be communicated and demonstrated to ensure that the quality is perceived as such.

A problem with public transport is routing that precludes easy access for everyone. In cities with high-quality public transport services, walking, cycling or feeder bus services are common access modes (Mees 2000). Car access to public transport has however often been obstructed by failures of park-and-ride schemes due to lack of parking space and high implementation costs (Meek et al. 2008; Parkhurst 2000).

### 10.3.4 Automobile Use Reduction Measures

None of the measures discussed so far is likely to succeed if automobile users do not drive less. This requires the implementation of prohibition, pricing or information measures.

**Prohibition**

Prohibition is by definition effective. Automobile use cannot however be prohibited everywhere at all times. The effectiveness of prohibition therefore depends on what exemptions are made for certain types of traffic (for example, delivery and emergency vehicles) and its spatial and temporal scale. A GIS-based feasibility study in a Swedish municipality using national travel diary data (Loukopoulos et al. 2005a) demonstrated that prohibiting car traffic in the central business district substantially reduced automobile travel even when restricted to different hours during weekdays. It is still possible that some of the suppressed automobile trips would be substituted by trips to more distant (for example, shopping) destinations. This may possibly be counteracted if prohibition is combined with increased accessibility by public transport. Positive effects would still be observed of reduced local emissions of particles and noise, and more liveable streets that are attractive and safe for walking.

Public attitudes towards prohibition have been found to be more positive than towards information and pricing measures (as described below) (Jones 2003; Loukopoulos et al. 2005b). This seemingly paradoxical finding is explained in that prohibition is perceived to be effective. It is also perceived to be fair in that it strikes everyone equally. At the same time restricting freedom of choice reduces the positive attitude (Eriksson et al. 2006; Jakobsson et al. 2000).

**Pricing**

Imposing additional taxes and charges on automobile users is attractive to policy makers but less so to the automobile users themselves. Examples include vehicle purchase and fuel taxes, kilometre charges, road and cordon tolls, and parking charges. Purposes include to finance maintenance of old infrastructure and investments in new infrastructure for alternative sustainable travel modes (for example, light rail, high-speed trains), to reduce traffic congestion in urban areas, and to abate adverse environmental effects caused by automobile use.

Pricing measures are theoretically grounded in neoclassical economics: consumption is regulated by supply and demand such that if the price of the product (transportation) increases, its demand will decrease, and vice versa (Emmerink et al. 1995; Rothengatter 2003). Such market-based measures have become increasingly popular in recent years, particularly among neoliberal politicians trusting free-market solutions. Although there are reasons to regulate transport to maintain quality, reliability and safety, it is believed that if unnecessary regulations are reduced, other objectives are reached through competition, innovation and diversity (Klein et al. 1997).

The increasing popularity among politicians is however mismatched by scepticism among researchers. For pricing to be viewed as a first-best instrument for decreasing car use it needs to be assumed that: (1) full information on all costs is available to the automobile users; and (2) the automobile users maximize utility (Emmerink et al. 1995). Yet the habitual nature of car use with its consequences of limiting pre-decisional information search (Gärling et al. 2001) renders the first assumption dubious. The second assumption of rational (expected) utility maximization has frequently been empirically violated (Gigerenzer and Gaissmaier 2011; Shafir and LeBoeuff 2002). Lack of competitive alternatives is another impediment.

Independent lines of empirical research show that at least in the short term, vehicle purchases and fuel taxes are associated with low price elasticities (Goodwin et al. 2004). Jakobsson (2004) summarizes the mainly negative outcomes of a limited number of field experiments evaluating the effectiveness of kilometre charges. It is believed that differentiated charges are more effective by influencing when and where automobile users drive. A reason for a generally less-than-expected effectiveness is that they are implemented without knowledge of how motivation and cognitive capacity influence automobile users' processing of the price information (Bonsall et al. 2007). In order to have an impact, differentiated charges may also need to be supplemented by customized information about travel alternatives (Jakobsson et al. 2002) (see the next subsection).

In recent years several European cities have implemented cordon tolls following the early example of Singapore. In London, cordon tolls were introduced in 2003. An unexpectedly high 30 per cent reduction of congestion was initially registered, attributed to both switches to public transport and drivers avoiding crossing the cordon (Transport for London 2008). Another example is Stockholm, for which the effects have been broadly assessed (Eliasson et al. 2009). The cordon tolls started as a seven-month field trial in the beginning of 2006 followed by a referendum, resulting in the municipality politicians permanently implementing the tolls 12 months later. An average 20 per cent reduction of crossings of the cordon was observed and appeared to be sustained after five years (Börjesson et al. 2012). Initially a 14 per cent reduction of carbon dioxide emissions was observed within the cordon area, corresponding to a 2–3 per cent reduction in the metropolitan area at large. Other positive effects within the cordon area include reduction of particle emissions, increased accessibility by walking and cycling, increased liveability, and reduction of traffic accidents. Reduced private automobile travel to the inner city due to improvements of public transport services before the implementation probably played a role in the satisfactory outcomes (Kottenhoff and Brundell Freij 2009).

Possibly because of the strong beliefs in the effectiveness of pricing measures, empirical research has focused on understanding the generally negative public attitudes towards such measures, perceived to be an obstacle to their (desired) implementation. While in previous research this has been referred to as assessments of 'acceptability' (before the implementation of the pricing measure) or 'acceptance' (after the implementation), 'attitude', referring to relatively stable evaluations (Eagly and Chaiken 1993), seems appropriate to cover both. According to dominant theories (Fishbein and Ajzen 2010) attitudes towards pricing measures may be assumed to be formed based on the likelihood and evaluation of salient consequences associated with these measures. Emotional responses (for example, fear or wishes) may sometimes override a consequence-based attitude formation. Another important factor is whether the consequences associated with the pricing measures are experienced directly, in which case (positive or negative) impacts may increase.

Although early studies (Jones 2003) found that the public had negative attitudes toward pricing measures, awareness of the problem (for example, emissions, congestion) made the attitudes less negative. In a Swedish sample of car owners Jakobsson et al. (2000) measured attitudes towards and intention to vote for or against kilometre charges. The results demonstrated influences of both personal consequences (perceived threats to freedom of choice to drive) and collective or societal consequences (fairness). Similar Swedish results were reported by Eriksson et al. (2006). An additional strong influence of perceived effectiveness was demonstrated by Bamberg and Rölle (2003) for a German sample. Concern for fairness has been investigated further by Schuitema et al. (2011), demonstrating that societal consequences such as protecting the environment in the interest of future generations, and affecting all equally, render attitudes more positive towards pricing measures than selfishly comparing oneself to others. Still another influential factor is the degree to which the pricing measure is favoured by others (Bamberg and Rölle 2003; Jakobsson et al. 2000). Not surprisingly the charge level negatively affects the attitude (Steg and Schuitema 2007). A difficult trade-off is implied in that automobile users' attitudes to a pricing measure appear to be more positive if the revenues are allocated to benefit automobile use (for example, investment in road infrastructure), while at the same time the measure may then have less effect (Steg and Schuitema 2007).

While the reviewed research illuminates the influences of policy factors including charge level, time–space differentiation (through fairness concerns) and revenue allocation, measurements have been made in advance of a proposed implementation. An opportunity to measure attitudes towards the cordon tolls before and after their actual implementation arose during the Stockholm seven-month field trial described above. In a study of a panel surveyed before and after the implementation, Schuitema et al. (2010) found that attitudes towards the cordon tolls were more positive after than before the implementation, due to participants' experiences of more positive and less negative consequences than expected.

Pricing measures are not politically feasible to implement if the public attitudes are negative (Gärling and Schuitema 2007; Jones 2003). Empirical support includes politicians demanding that a majority voted for the permanent implementation of the cordon tolls in Stockholm (Eliasson et al. 2009). Another impediment is political goal conflicts. Based on surveys of the local politicians in a Swedish municipality, Johansson et al. (2003) found that for the leading Social Democrat, Conservative, Liberal and Christian Democrat Parties, the national sustainability goal of reduced GHG emissions was in conflict with fairness and fiscal goals. Only the Left and Green Parties prioritized the national goal. Implementing a pricing measure to reduce congestion was a political compromise expected to lead to more efficient use of existing road infrastructure that reduces or even eliminates costly new investments, to reduce negative local effects, and to provide a non-negligible financial surplus to the municipality. It was still not sufficient to contribute to achieving the national sustainability goal.

**Information**

People are information processing systems. They acquire information from different sources about what to think, how to judge and evaluate, and how to act. The information is acquired in advance (referred to as feed-forward), after having acted (feedback or knowledge of results), or both. In order to change automobile use authorities should provide appropriate information. One example from the European Union is 'Do The Right Mix' (www.youtube.com/watch?v=55yhNqMtdxA).

It is essential to accurately conceptualize personal travel in order to know what information to disseminate. A majority of all personal travel is motivated by needs, desires and obligations to participate in out-of-home activities (e.g., Axhausen and Gärling 1992). Therefore as has been argued (Gärling et al. 2002), car-use reduction should be viewed broadly as an adaptation by car users that potentially has consequences for their engagement in different activities and the satisfaction they experience from them (Jakobsson Bergstad et al. 2012).

Information measures aim at increasing automobile users' awareness of more sustainable alternatives than their current car use, and empowering them to switch to these alternatives (Ampt 2004). Although the main evaluation criterion is reduced negative consequences of current car use, the potential changes that car users may make to attain this are several: suppressing car trips (possibly using telecommunication instead), choosing more sustainable travel modes (for example, walking or cycling instead of driving short distances), driving to closer destinations (for example, stores in the neighbourhood instead of distant shopping malls), combining more errands on the same car trips, and sharing car trips with other household members or acquaintances. In particular in the USA, eco-driving is still another alternative which may result in a 10 per cent reduction in fuel consumption (Barkenbus 2010).

In Australia, Germany, Japan and the UK automobile users have participated in large-scale projects targeting car-use reduction (Brög et al. 2009; Cairns et al. 2008; Fujii and Taniguichi 2006; Taylor 2007). Participants are recruited in residential areas, at workplaces or in schools. They obtain customized (feed-forward) information about sustainable alternatives to car use. Meta-analyses show that while a maximum of 30–40 per cent of automobile users participate in the projects, for the total number in a targeted area relatively stable 5–15 per cent car-use reductions are attained (Fujii et al. 2009; Möser and Bamberg 2008). Cost-effectiveness is claimed to be high (Brög et al. 2009).

Since information measures are voluntary, they meet with little opposition. At the

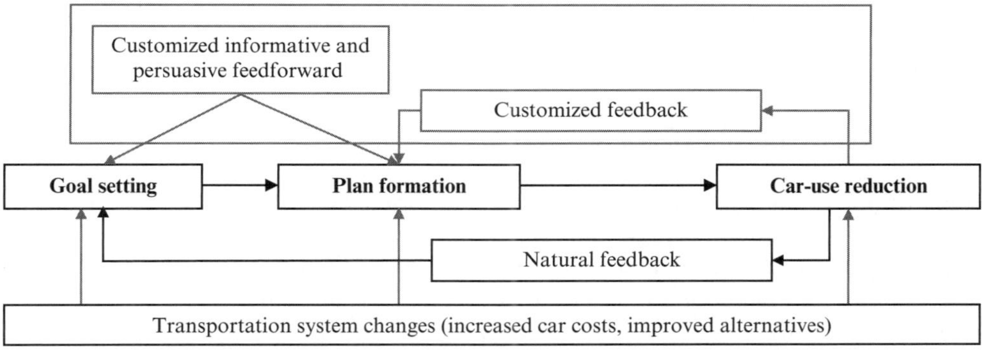


*Figure 10.1 A model of the effects of information measures on car-use reduction when the transportation system is changed*

same time only a minority of automobile users participate. In order to render information measures effective, they may therefore need to be combined with prohibition and pricing measures (sometimes referred to as 'hard' measures in contrast to the 'soft' information measures) (Fujii and Taniguchi 2014). They may also need to use persuasion techniques (Bamberg et al. 2011). Figure 10.1 illustrates a model[1] of how information measures influence car-use reduction when automobile users face changes in the transportation system. The process starts with the automobile user setting a car-use reduction goal, prompted by the changes in the transportation system (for example, increased car-use costs due to the implementation of pricing measures), strengthened by persuasive and customized informative feed-forward information. Such information is also provided by public transport companies, the Internet (for example, Google Maps) or word of mouth. Setting a high and specific reduction goal followed by a request to form a plan for how to achieve the goal has been found to be particularly effective (Fujii et al. 2009). Knowledge of the change outcome (for example, feedback about travel times, costs, carbon dioxide emissions) is customized such that participants are able to improve on their change plan.

## 10.4 SUMMARY AND CONCLUSIONS

Few dispute that current private automobile use is unsustainable, although motorized freight transportation, and long-distance holiday and business travel by air also contribute importantly to the unsustainability of transportation. This chapter has reviewed research assessing the effectiveness of, public attitudes towards and political feasibility of measures that limit local and global damage to the environment caused by daily automobile use in urban areas. A conclusion is that no measure is sufficient alone, but that several need to be combined. It is not likely that clean automobile technology, increasing accessibility by rebuilding the environment or improving alternative travel modes will suffice unless prohibition, pricing and information measures are implemented to reduce automobile use. Since research evidence indicates that voluntary measures may achieve reductions of 5–15 per cent and pricing measures even more, the often heard counter-argument from interest groups that automobile use cannot be reduced should not be taken seriously.

## ACKNOWLEDGEMENTS

Preparation of this chapter was financially supported by grant (2004–0297) from the Swedish Governmental Agency for Innovation Systems (VINNOVA) to the SAMOT research group at Karlstad University. We thank Cecilia Jakobsson Bergstad, Johan Jansson, Maria Johansson, Jonas Eliasson, Anita Gärling and Karl Kottenhoff for valuable comments.

## NOTE

1. More elaborate similar models have been proposed by Bamberg (2013) and Jones and Sloman (2006).

## REFERENCES

Ampt, E.S. (2004), 'Understanding voluntary travel behaviour change', *Transport Engineering in Australia*, 9, 53–66.

Axhausen, K.W. and T. Gärling (1992), 'Activity-based approaches to travel analysis: conceptual frameworks, models, and research problems', *Transport Reviews*, 12, 323–341.

Bamberg, S. (2013), 'Changing environmentally harmful behaviors: a stage model of self-regulated behavioral change', *Journal of Environmental Psychology*, 34, 151–159.

Bamberg, S., S. Fujii, M. Friman and T. Gärling (2011), 'Behaviour theory and soft transport policy measures', *Transport Policy*, 18, 228–235.

Bamberg, S. and D. Rölle (2003), 'Determinants of people's acceptability of pricing measures: replication and extension of a causal model', in J. Schade and B. Schlag (eds), *Acceptability of Transport Pricing Strategies*, Amsterdam: Elsevier, pp. 238–248.

Barkenbus, J.N. (2010), 'Eco-driving: an overlooked climate change alternative', *Energy Policy*, 18, 762–769.

Bird, E.L., G. Baker, N. Mutrie, D. Ogilvie, S. Sahlqvist and J. Powell (2013), 'Behavior change techniques used to promote walking and cycling: a systematic review', *Health Psychology*, 32, 829–838.

Bonsall, P.W. (2000), 'Legislating for modal shift: background to the UK's new Transport Act', *Transport Policy*, 7, 179–184.

Bonsall, P.W., J.D. Shires, B. Matthews, J. Maule and J. Beale (2007), 'Responses to complex pricing signals: theories, evidence and implications for road pricing', *Transportation Research Part A*, 41, 672–683.

Bopp, M., A.T. Kaczynski and P. Wittman (2011), 'The relationship of eco-friendly attitudes with walking and biking to work', *Journal of Public Health Management and Practice*, 17, 9–17.

Börjesson, M., J. Eliasson, M.B. Hugosson and K. Brundell-Freij (2012), 'The Stockholm congestion charges – 5 years on: effects, acceptability and lessons learnt', *Transport Policy*, 20, 1–12.

Brög, W., E. Erl, I. Ker, J. Ryle and R. Wall (2009), 'Evaluation of voluntary travel behaviour change: experiences from three continents', *Transport Policy*, 16, 281–292.

Brown, B.B., K.R. Smith, H. Hanson, J.X. Fan, L. Kowaleski-Jones and C. Zick (2013), 'Neighborhood design for walking and biking: physical activity and body mass index', *American Journal of Preventive Medicine*, 44 (3), 231–238.

Cairns, S., L. Sloman, C. Newson, J. Anable, A. Kirkbride and P. Goodwin (2008), 'Smarter choices: Assessing the potential to achieve traffic reduction using "soft measures"', *Transport Reviews*, 28, 593–618.

Curl, A., J.D. Nelson and J. Anable (2011), 'Does accessibility planning address what matters? A review of current practice and practitioner perspectives', *Research in Transportation Business and Management*, 2, 3–11.

Dargay, J. and D. Gately (1999), 'Income's effect on car and vehicle ownership, worldwide: 1960–2015', *Transportation Research Part A*, 33, 101–138.

Delre, S.A., W. Jager, T.H.A. Bijmolt and M.A. Janssen (2010), 'Will it spread or not? The effects of social influences and network topology on innovation diffusion', *Journal of Product Innovation Management*, 27, 267–282.
Dickinson, J.E., S. Kingham, S. Copsey and D.J.P. Hougie (2003), 'Employer travel plans, cycling and gender: will travel plan measures improve the outlook for cycling to work in the UK?', *Transportation Research Part D*, 8, 53–67.
Eagly, A.H. and S. Chaiken (1993), *The Psychology of Attitudes*, Fort Worth, FL: Harcourt Brace Jovanovich.
Eliasson, J., L. Hultkrantz, L. Nerhagen and L. Smidfelt Rosqvist (2009), The Stockholm congestion charging trial 2006: overview of effects, *Transportation Research Part A*, 43, 240–250.
Emmerink, R.H.M., P. Nijkamp and P. Rietveld (1995), 'Is congestion pricing a first-best strategy in transport policy? A critical review of arguments', *Environment and Planning B*, 22, 581–602.
Eriksson, L., J. Garvill and A. Nordlund (2006), 'Acceptability of travel demand management measures: the importance of problem awareness, personal norm, freedom, and fairness', *Journal of Environmental Psychology*, 26, 15–26.
Ettema, D. and L. Verschuren (2007), 'The effect of multi-tasking on the value of travel time savings', *Transportation Research Record: Journal of the Transportation Research Board*, 2010, 19–25.
Eurostat (2011), 'Themes/transport', available at http://epp.eurostat.cec.eu.int. (accessed 15 October 2013).
Fishbein, M. and I. Ajzen (2010), *Predicting and Changing Behavior*, New York: Psychology Press.
Frye, A. (2013), 'Disabled and older persons and sustainable urban mobility', thematic study prepared for Global Report on Human Settlements 2013, available at http://www.unhabitat.org/grhs/2013.
Fujii, S., S. Bamberg, M. Friman and T. Gärling (2009), 'Are effects of travel feedback programs correctly assessed?', *Transportmetrika*, 5, 43–57.
Fujii, S. and A. Taniguchi (2006), 'Determinants of the effectiveness of travel feedback programs – a review of communicative mobility management measures for changing travel behaviour in Japan', *Transport Policy*, 13, 339–348.
Fujii, S. and A. Taniguchi (2014), 'Theoretical understanding of practical strategies of changing travel behavior', in T. Gärling, D. Ettema and M. Friman (eds), *Handbook of Sustainable Travel*, Dordrecht: Springer, pp. 151–162.
Gärling, A. and J. Thøgersen (2001), 'Marketing of electric vehicles', *Business Strategy and the Environment*, 10, 53–65.
Gärling, T., D. Eek, P. Loukopoulos, S. Fujii, O. Johansson-Stenman, R. Kitamura, R. Pendyala and B. Vilhelmson (2002), 'A conceptual analysis of the impact of travel demand management on private car use', *Transport Policy*, 9, 59–70.
Gärling, T., D. Ettema and M. Friman (eds) (2014), *Handbook of Sustainable Travel*, Dordrecht: Springer.
Gärling, T., S. Fujii and O. Boe (2001), 'Empirical tests of a model of determinants of script-based driving choice', *Transportation Research Part F*, 4, 89–102.
Gärling, T. and G. Schuitema (2007), 'Travel demand management targeting reduced private car use: effectiveness, public acceptability, and political feasibility', *Journal of Social Issues*, 63 (1), 139–153.
Gatersleben, B. (2014), 'Psychological motives for car use', in T. Gärling, D. Ettema and M. Friman (eds), *Handbook of Sustainable Travel*, Dordrecht: Springer, pp. 85–94.
Gigerenzer, G. and W. Gaissmeier (2011), 'Heuristic decision making', *Annual Review of Psychology*, 62, 4511–482.
Giuliano, G. and J. Dargay (2006), 'Car ownership, travel and land use: a comparison of the US and Great Britain', *Transportation Research Part A*, 40, 106–124.
Goodwin, P. (2012), 'Three views on peak car', *World Transport Policy and Practice*, 17, 8–18.
Goodwin, P.B., J. Dargay and M. Hanly (2004). 'Elasticities of road traffic and fuel consumption with respect to price and income: a review', *Transport Reviews*, 24, 275–292.
Handy, S. (2014), 'Health and travel', in T. Gärling, D. Ettema and M. Friman (eds), *Handbook of Sustainable Travel*, Dordrecht: Springer, pp. 199–214.
Handy, S. and B. van Wee (2014), 'Do future land-use policies increase sustainable travel?', in T. Gärling, D. Ettema and M. Friman (eds), *Handbook of Sustainable Travel*, Dordrecht: Springer, pp. 231–242.
Hartig, T. (2007), 'Congruence and conflict between car transportation and psychological restoration', in T. Gärling and L. Steg (eds), *Threats from Car Traffic to the Quality of Urban Life: Problems, Causes, and Solutions*, Oxford: Elsevier, pp. 103–122.
Heinen, E., B. van Wee and K. Maat (2010), 'Commuting by bicycle: an overview of the literature', *Transport Reviews: A Transnational Transdisciplinary Journal*, 30, 59–96.
International Energy Agency (2009), 'Transport, energy, and $CO_2$: moving toward sustainability', Paris: International Energy Agency IEA/OECD, available at www.iea.org.
Jakobsson, C. (2004), 'Motivational and volitional control of private automobile use: the effectiveness of transport policies', Doctoral dissertation, Göteborg: Göteborg University, Department of Psychology.
Jakobsson, C. (2007), 'Instrumental motives for private car use', in T. Gärling and L. Steg (eds), *Threats*

*from Car Traffic to the Quality of Urban Life: Problems, Causes, and Solutions*, Oxford: Elsevier, pp. 205–217.

Jakobsson, C., S. Fujii and T. Gärling (2000), 'Determinants of private car users' acceptance of road pricing', *Transport Policy*, 7, 153–158.

Jakobsson, C., S. Fujii and T. Gärling (2002), 'Effects of economic disincentives on private car use', *Transportation*, 29, 349–370.

Jakobsson Bergstad, C.J., A. Gamble, O. Hagman, M. Polk, T. Gärling, D. Ettema, M. Friman and L.E. Olsson (2012), 'Influences of affect associated with routine out-of-home activities on subjective well-being', *Applied Research in Quality of Life*, 7, 49–62.

Jansson, J., A. Marell and A. Nordlund (2009), 'Elucidating green consumers: a cluster analytic approach to proenvironmental purchases and curtailment behaviors', *Journal of Euromarketing*, 18, 245–267.

Johansson, L.-O., M. Gustafsson, G. Falkemark, T. Gärlingand O. Johansson-Stenman (2003), 'Goal conflicts in political decision making: a survey of municipality politicians' views of road pricing', *Environment and Planning C: Government and Policy*, 21, 615–624.

Jones, P. (2003), 'Acceptability of road user charging: meeting the challenge', in J. Schade and B. Schlag (eds), *Acceptability of Transport Pricing Strategies*, Amsterdam: Elsevier, pp. 27–62.

Jones, P. and L. Sloman (2006), 'Encouraging behavioral change through marketing and management: what can be achieved?', in K.W. Axhausen (ed.), *Moving Through Nets: The Physical and Social Dimensions of Travel*, Oxford: Elsevier, pp. 189–218.

Kenworthy, J.R. (2011), 'Transport energy use and greenhouse emissions in urban passenger transport systems: a study of 84 global cities', in P. Droege (ed.), *Urban Energy Transition: From Fossil Fuels to Renewable Power*, Amsterdam: Elsevier, pp. 211–239.

Kitamura, R. and J. Mohamad (2009), 'Rapid motorization in Asian cities: urban transport infrastructure, spatial development and travel behavior', *Transportation*, 36, 269–274.

Klein, D., A. Moore and B. Reja (1997), *Curb Rights: A Foundation for Free Enterprise in Urban Transit*, Washington, DC: Brookings Institution Press.

Kottenhoff, K. and K. Brundell Freij (2009), 'The role of public transport for feasibility and acceptability of congestion charging: the case of Stockholm', *Transportation Research Part A*, 43, 297–305.

Lemieux, M. and G. Godin (2009), 'How well do cognitive and environment variables predict active commuting?', *International Journal of Behavioral Nutrition and Physical Activity*, 6, 1–9.

Leyden, K.M., A. Goldberg and P. Michelbach (2011), 'Understanding the pursuit of happiness in ten major cities', *Urban Affairs Review*, 47, 861–888.

Limanond T. and D.A. Niemeier (2003), 'Accessibility and mode–destination choice decisions: exploring travel in three neighborhoods in Puget Sound, WA', *Environment and Planning B: Planning and Design*, 30, 219–238.

Litman, T. (2012), 'Current mobility trends: Implications for sustainability', in B. van Wee (ed.), *Keep Moving, Towards Sustainable Mobility*, The Hague: Eleven International Publishing, pp. 23–44.

Loukopoulos, P., T. Gärling and B. Vilhelmson (2005a), 'Mapping the potential consequences of car-use reduction in urban areas', *Journal of Transport Geography*, 13, 135–150.

Loukopoulos, P., C. Jakobsson, T. Gärling, C.M. Schneider and S. Fujii (2005b), 'Public attitudes towards policy measures for reducing private car use', *Environmental Science and Policy*, 8, 57–66.

Mackett, R.L. (2001), 'Policies to attract car drivers out of their cars for short trips', *Transport Policy*, 8, 295–306.

Marshall, S. and D. Banister (2000), 'Travel reduction strategies: Intentions and outcomes', *Transportation Research Part A: Policy and Practice*, 34, 321–338.

Martens, K. (2004), 'The bicycle as a feedering mode: experiences from three European countries', *Transportation Research Part D*, 9, 281–294.

Massachusetts Institute of Technology (2011), 'The future of natural gas: an interdisciplinary MIT study', available at www.mit.edu/mitel/research/studies/naturalgas.

Meade, N. and T. Islam (2006), 'Modelling and forecasting the diffusion of innovation: a 25-year review', *International Journal of Forecasting*, 22, 519–545.

Meek, S., S. Ison and M. Enoch (2008), 'Role of bus-based park and ride in the UK: a temporal and evaluative review', *Transport Reviews: A Transnational Transdisciplinary Journal*, 28, 781–803.

Mees, P. (2000), *A Very Public Solution: Public Transport in the Dispersed City*, CarltonVictoria: Melbourne University Press.

Millard-Ball, A. and L. Schipper (2011), 'Are we reaching peak travel? Trends in passenger transport in eight industrialized countries', *Transport Reviews: A Transnational Transdisciplinary Journal*, 31, 357–378.

Moktharian, P.L. and I. Salomon (2001), 'How derived is the demand for travel? Some conceptual and measurement considerations', *Transportation Research Part A*, 31, 35–50.

Moktharian, P.L., I. Salomon and S. Handy (2006), 'The impact of ICT on leisure activities and travel: a conceptual exploration', *Transportation*, 33, 263–289.

Möser, G. and S. Bamberg (2008), 'The effectiveness of soft transport policy measures: a critical assessment and meta-analysis of empirical evidence', *Journal of Environmental Psychology*, 28, 10–26.
National Research Council (2008), *Transitions to Alternative Transportation Technologies: A Focus on Hydrogen*, Washington, DC: National Research Council, National Aacademies of Engineering.
Ogden, J.M. (2012), 'Modalities and technical advancement', in B. van Wee (ed.), *Keep Moving, Towards Sustainable Mobility*, The Hague: Eleven International Publishing, pp. 45–84.
Oja, P., I. Vuori and O. Paronen (1998), 'Daily walking and cycling to work: their utility as health enhancing physical activity', *Patient Education and Counselling*, 33, 87–94.
Parker, N., B. Jenkins, P. Dempster, B. Higgins and J. Ogden (2011), 'The biofuels pathway', in J.M. Ogden and L. Anderson (eds), *Sustainable Transportation Energy Pathways: A Research Summary for Decision Makers*, Davies, CA: Regents of the University of California, pp. 15–37.
Parkhurst, G. (2000), 'Influence of bus-based park and ride facilities on users' car traffic', *Transport Policy*, 7, 159–172.
Pucher, J. (1999), 'Transportation trends, problems, and policies: an international perspective', *Transportation Research Part A*, 33, 493–503.
Reardon, L. and S. Abdallah (2013), 'Well-being and transport: taking stock and looking forward', *Transport Reviews*, 33 (6), 634–657.
Redman, L., M. Friman, T. Gärling and T. Hartig (2013), 'Quality attributes of public transport that attract car users', *Transport Policy*, 25, 119–127.
Rogers, E.M. (1962), *Diffusion of Innovations*, New York: Free Press.
Rotem-Mindali, O. and J.W.J. Weltevreden (2013), 'Transport effects of e-commerce: what can be learned after years of research?', *Transportation*, 40, 867–885.
Rothengatter, W. (2003), 'How good is first best? Marginal cost and other pricing principles for user charging in transport', *Transport Policy*, 10, 121–130.
Schuitema, G., J. Anable, S. Skippon and N. Kinnear (2013), 'The role of instrumental, hedonic and symbolic attributes in the intention to adopt electric vehicles', *Transportation Research Part A*, 48, 39–49.
Schuitema, G., L. Steg and S. Forward (2010), 'Explaining differences in acceptability before and acceptability after the implementation of a congestion charge in Stockholm', *Transportation Research Part A*, 44, 99–109.
Schuitema, G., L. Steg and M. van Kruining, M. (2011), 'When are transport pricing policies fair and acceptable?', *Social Justice Research*, 24, 66–84.
Shafir, E. and R. LeBoeuff (2002), 'Rationality', *Annual Review of Psychology*, 53, 491–517.
Southworth, F. (2001), 'On the potential impacts of land use change policies on automobile vehicle miles of travel', *Energy Policy*, 29, 1271–1283.
Sperling, D. and E. Claussen (2004), 'Motorizing the developing world', *Access*, 24 (Spring), 10–15.
Steg, L. and G. Schuitema (2007), 'Behavioural responses to transport pricing: a theoretical analysis', in T. Gärling and L. Steg (eds), *Threats from Car Traffic to the Quality of Urban Life: Problems, Causes, and Solutions*, Oxford: Elsevier, pp. 103–122.
Taylor, M. (2007), 'Voluntary travel behavior change programs in Australia: the carrot rather than the stick in travel demand management', *International Journal of Sustainable Transportation*, 1, 173–192.
Transport for London (2008), 'Central London congestion charging. Impacts monitoring. Sixth Annual Report', available at http://www.tfl.gov.uk/assets/downloads/sixth-annual-impacts-monitoring-report-2008-07.pdf.
van Wee, B. (ed.) (2012), *Keep Moving, Towards Sustainable Mobility*, The Hague: Eleven International Publishing.
van Wee, B. (2014), 'The unsustainability of car use', in T. Gärling, D. Ettema and M. Friman (eds), *Handbook of Sustainable Travel*, Dordrecht: Springer, pp. 69–83.
Vilhelmson, B. (2005), 'Urbanisation and everyday mobility: long-term changes of travel in urban areas of Sweden', *Cybergeo*, 302, 1–13.

# 11. Housing in a sustainable consumption perspective

*Kirsten Gram-Hanssen*

In a global perspective, sustainability includes a social, an economic and an environmental perspective (United Nations 1987). In this chapter I focus on the environmental perspective from a North-Western point of view, and in this context sustainable consumption is mainly about reducing the use of non-renewable resources as well as avoiding environmental pollution and waste. Resource consumption, emissions and waste related to housing can be assessed either from 'above' or from 'below'. When counting from below, from the point of the individual consumer, three main consumption areas are usually deemed most (and about equally) important: travelling, food and housing (Tukker et al. 2010). Based on different ways of counting resource use, it can be shown that housing, roughly speaking, takes up one-quarter of an average Western consumer's ecological footprint, and transportation and food consumption about the same (for Denmark, see Dall and Toft 2002). Another approach is to look at consumption from above, for example from a national perspective, and see how resource consumption and emissions are distributed between sectors. For example the housing sector in Denmark takes up roughly one-third of all energy consumed (Danish Energy Authority 2010). Thus irrespective of whether one approaches the topic from above or from below, housing is important when dealing with sustainable consumption.

Quantifications of ecological footprint sometimes combine calculations of the carrying capacity of the Earth with democratic arguments of sharing between all humans. Typically, such calculations result in demands for reductions of carbon dioxide ($CO_2$) emissions in the wealthy part of the world by a factor of between four and ten (Schmidt-Bleek 2008). Following this line of thought, it can be argued that sustainable consumption requires completely different ways of living, transporting, producing and consuming, rather than debating how to reduce consumption within different sectors (see for example Fuchs and Lorek 2005, for a discussion of this in relation to weak and strong sustainability). However, also within a more radical approach to sustainability, housing seems to be a core issue, as the way housing is provided in a society is intimately linked with different ways of relating production and consumption as well as with the need for transportation.

Thus sustainable housing can relate to some quite specific targets to reduce, for example, energy and water consumption in the housing sector. It might also relate more broadly to the organization of everyday life and the way production, consumption and transportation are combined in and around the home. In this chapter, I take up questions relating to sustainable housing in both approaches, relating them to a theoretical understanding of consumption and to policy discussions about how to change consumption.

In the public debate, as well as in mainstream policy approaches to sustainable housing, such as saving energy at home, focus is often either on the more technical aspect of improving energy efficiency of houses and appliances, or it is on how to make people change their daily habits in less consuming directions, such as turning off the light when leaving a room or turning off a running tap to avoid wasting resources (Gram-Hanssen 2013; Wilhite et al. 2000). Both of these approaches have been debated and criticized by research. Specifically, the technical approach has been criticized for failing to see that new and more efficient technologies often do not result in less consumption (e.g. Gram-Hanssen et al. 2012; Shove 2003); whereas the individual behaviour approach has been criticized for being too focused on the individuals, failing to see the more structural aspects of how human resource consumption is constituted in our societies (Shove 2010).

Basically, however, housing is not about consuming energy or any other materials. Housing is about being at home and having a physical shelter that provides an environment for the everyday activities of caring for oneself and others (Després 1991; Gullestad 1991; Mallett 2004). On the other hand, housing is also a physical structure that builds on and reflects long historical roots, as well as representing huge economic investments; both these aspects represent a considerable degree of inertia for change. Demolishing all existing buildings and the infrastructures connecting them is not desirable, neither from an environmental nor from a cultural perspective (Thomsen and van der Flier 2009). So how, then, can we manage a sustainable transition of housing? This is the core question taken up in this chapter.

In the following I first review some studies on the importance of, and the relation between, the technical and the consumer aspect of energy consumption in homes and a social-science perspective is used to explain why the technical and the human perspectives cannot be separated from each other. Theories of practice are then used as the framework for discussing how daily habits are linked with technological developments. Then follows a section on housing as both a technical and a meaning-giving structure, and the chapter concludes with a discussion of the policy aspects of combining these insights.

## 10.1 TECHNOLOGIES AND HUMANS IN (NON-) SUSTAINABLE HOUSING

In policy and technological research dealing with energy efficiency and lowering energy consumption in housing, there is a growing interest in the importance of the habit aspects for understanding actual energy consumption (for example, see Special Issue 1, 2014, of *Architectural Engineering and Design Management* on 'The impact of the building occupant on energy consumption'). From a consumer perspective, the question could be whether it is more relevant to buy more efficient technologies and energy upgrades at home or to change daily habits. A recent study dealt with this question using two different approaches: (1) a comparative study of similar buildings with varying consumption; and (2) a historical approach using national statistics (Gram-Hanssen 2013).

The comparative approach included looking at housing areas with identical buildings and then analysing how energy consumption varies with the different households living in them. A Danish study found that the households using the least for heat consumption use less than a third of those using the most (Gram-Hanssen 2013). Likewise older studies from the USA and Sweden found similar results (Palmborg 1986; Sonderegger 1977/78), and newer studies focusing on variation in identical low-energy housing showed variation by a factor of two in Sweden (Karlsson and Moshfegh 2007) and by a factor of three in the UK (Gill et al. 2010). Thus it seems that variation in consumption in similar buildings is as large in new efficient buildings as in older, less energy-efficient buildings.

To answer the question whether daily habits or efficient technology is the more important, these studies should be compared with variations in consumption between energy-efficient buildings and 'ordinary' buildings. In the above-mentioned UK study, the average consumption in the low-energy houses is 92.9 kWh/m2 and the corresponding average for the local area is 172 kWh/m2 (Gill et al. 2010). There is thus a factor of two between average heat consumption for 'normal housing' and for low-energy housing in the UK. Based on nine Danish low-energy houses, it is concluded that on average the low-energy houses use 53 per cent of a 'normal' house's energy consumption for heating (Kristensen et al., 2010). Thus there is a factor of two between the average energy consumption for heating low-energy houses and 'normal' houses in Denmark too. Together these studies suggest that the daily habits count for a factor of two to three, and the technological factor counts for a factor of two, when comparing energy consumption for heating in buildings. The habitual aspect is thus equally or more important compared to the technology efficiency when understanding heat consumption.

The question of whether efficiency or use of technology is the more important for sustainability can also be approached from a historical perspective. Data on the development of the energy efficiency of appliances sold in Denmark over the last 20 years, and the corresponding development in the number of appliances in Danish households during the same period, are presented in Figure 11.1. In the top part of this figure, it is seen that the average electricity consumption per appliance sold in Denmark decreased substantially over these 20 years (except for TV sets). In the part of the figure to the right, it is seen that the stock of the same types of appliances rose during the same years. By combining the left and the bottom part of this figure, we learn that the energy saving due to the growing energy efficiency of appliances gained over the last 20 years is counterbalanced by the growing number of appliances in use.

Figure 11.2 describes a corresponding development within the housing sector in Denmark. It is seen that the average energy efficiency increased in residential buildings, so that in 2010 a specific area could be heated by using only 85 per cent of the energy used for heating it in 1990. However in the same period the heated area grew by 20 per cent, resulting in a final energy consumption that has been more or less stable during the last 20 years. It is important to note that the growing heated area represents a growing amount of living space per person, as the Danish population increased by only 9 per cent during this period (statistikbanken.dk).

These data on the last 20 years' development in efficiency, number and size of appliances and buildings suggest that the increasing efficiency in technology is balanced by a growing demand for appliances and living space. A relevant question is whether there is a connection between the development in efficiency and the corresponding growth in consumption. This question is discussed in the literature about the rebound effect, which concerns the extent to which the efficiency gained through technical improvements of buildings and appliances is reflected in increased consumption; for instance, greater comfort (Greening et al. 2000; Sanne 2000; Shipper and Grubb 2000). In a review of studies of the rebound effect within the household sector, it was concluded that the rebound effect for heating is approximately 20 per cent (Sorrel et al. 2009). This means

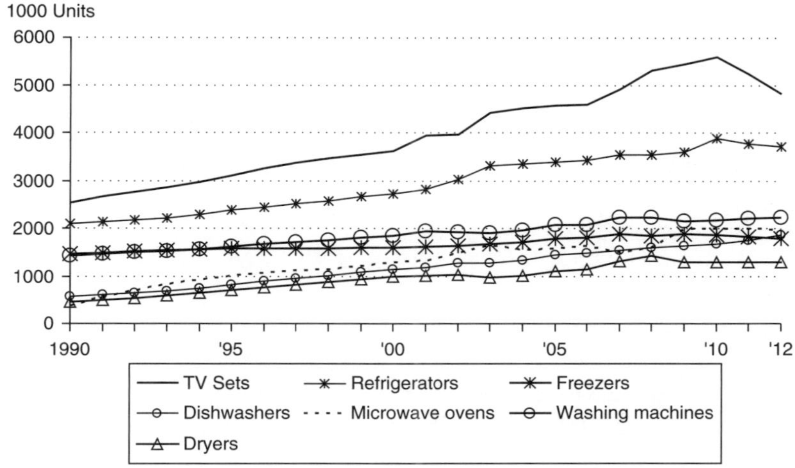


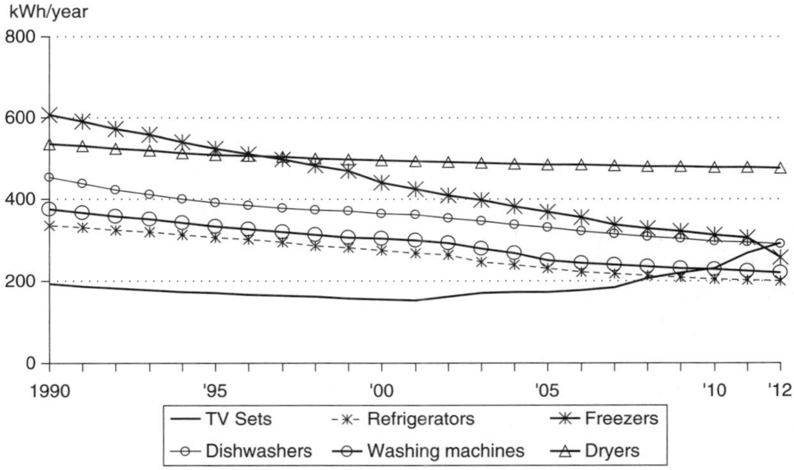


*Source:* Danish Energy Authority (2010).

*Figure 11.1 Number of appliances in Danish households 1990–2010, top ('000 units) and energy efficiency of Danish household appliances 1990–2010, bottom (KWh/year)*

that about 20 per cent of the efficiency gained through technical improvements of buildings and appliances is turned into greater comfort, such as maintaining higher temperatures. This understanding of the rebound effect primarily builds on the assumption that people consume more because they can afford it, due to the reduced costs resulting from energy efficiency. A recent Danish study on substitution of direct electric heating with air-to-air heat pumps showed similar results (Gram-Hanssen et al. 2012). However this study points at more sociological and psychological reasons for the increase in consumption. If people feel that they have done something to save energy, such as buying

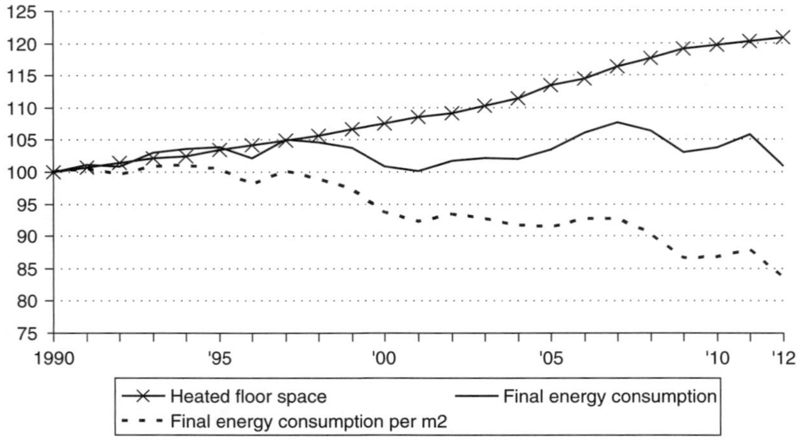


*Note:* Index 1990= 100; data are climate adjusted.

*Source:* Danish Energy Authority (2010).

*Figure 11.2 Energy consumption for space and water heating in Danish households*

an energy-efficient heat pump, then they might feel that they do not have to think so much about how they use it. Within environmental psychology this is analysed as part of a negative spillover effect (Thøgersen and Crompton 2009). In this way, a direct link might exist between efficient technology, changing habits and growing consumption. Thus consumer policy to spread energy-efficient technologies in households should also take account of this link.

However, of course not all types of growing consumption relate to energy efficiency. The growing number of appliances and inhabited floor area are also a consequence of other societal processes, which have been described as drivers behind consumption, including changing social norms and expectations resulting from new technical possibilities (Røpke 1999).

Thus efficiency is normally followed by some increase in consumption; but growing consumption also relates to other societal processes. In both cases, the historical approach to efficiency shows that growing consumption has to be taken into account when designing energy-saving interventions towards sustainable consumption. Efficiency alone will not do it. The next section deals with the social processes behind both daily habits and growing consumption.

## 10.2 UNDERSTANDING TECHNOLOGY, HABITS AND CONSUMPTION

In the last decade, a growing number of researchers have used practice theories as the framework for understanding consumer practices in a sustainability perspective. This research and tradition is thoroughly introduced elsewhere in this book (Welch and

Warde, Chapter 5), so a brief outline of the framework will suffice here. Practise theories emphasize the collectiveness of practices and see the individual as a carrier of practices. Practices are 'doings' and 'sayings' which are held together by different elements. The naming and number of elements vary slightly between different authors, the most important difference being that Schatzki (1996) explicitly states that technologies are not a part of the elements holding practices together; rather, they are a result of practices. In contrast, Shove sees technologies or products as an important element that holds practices together (e.g. Shove and Walker 2010; Shove et al. 2012). In line with Schatzki (1996) and Warde (2005), but adding technology, I distinguish between four elements holding practices together: habits, knowledge, meanings and technologies (Gram-Hanssen 2010, 2011). Compared to Shove et al., I distinguish between implicit non-verbal habits and more conscious explicit knowledge elements, which she combines in one element, called competences.

Practice theories can be used for understanding the variations between households living in identical houses, where some households use three times as much energy for heating as others (Gram-Hanssen 2010). According to this understanding, different households (or the members in the household) are all carriers of a common practice – the practice of keeping a comfortable indoor climate – though they perform it in slightly different ways. These differences can then be related to differences in either of the elements holding the practice together, including differences in knowledge, in meanings or in habits relating to different experiences from previous housing or from their workplace. The reason to be interested in understanding these differences in practices is, on one hand, that these differences in practices, as described, have substantial influence on the actual energy consumption. However another reason to be interested in variations in practices is that these variations might be involved in broader societal changes in practices over time. Although it was raised by Warde (2005), this last point, about how individuals performing practices in different ways may take part in changing the common structure of this practice over time, has up to now been under-researched within practice theories.

Practice theories are also useful for understanding the general development and growth of consumption (Røpke and Christensen 2013; Shove 2003). For example a practice-theory approach has been used in a study of historical developments regarding the use of electric lighting, appliances and information and communication technology (ICT) (Gram-Hanssen 2008). The study shows how social, cultural and technological structures together structure everyday life and the different energy-consuming practices, while emphasizing the collective nature of practices. It also makes visible how commercial and governmental interests influence these structures; so far primarily in a more resource-consuming direction. For example authorities in Denmark have played a key role in developing Denmark into a front-runner in the use of ICT (Müller et al. 2013). Public infrastructure decisions and investments, tax incentives, education and, most recently, the decision to only use digital communication between the authorities and the public have now in reality forced all households to have a computer and Internet connection. From a practice-theory perspective, it could be said that the authorities have worked effectively to change and form knowledge, technology and meaning elements, which now take part in holding different ICT-based practices together. In this way policy has had a strong influence on the practice of communication and the use of computers, although visions of sustainable consumption have not been part of this. The result is that electricity consumption for ICT in households in Denmark has more than doubled in the last decade (Jensen et al. 2009).

## 10.3 HOUSING AS CONSUMPTION, MATERIAL STRUCTURE AND MEANING

Housing as a consumer object differs from most other types of consumption, such as food that is bought daily and which can be consumed in the sense of used up; or clothes, where consumers typically buy new items regularly, use them over time and then throw them out. Most people only acquire new housing a few times in their life, and the house is not used up or thrown away afterwards; it is sold or rented out to other people. The housing market is also different from most other consumer markets in that it contains both rented and owner-occupied markets, with different possibilities and limitations for different consumers. The owner-occupied housing is mainly regulated through the income and capital of consumers, but as prices of housing vary with the overall economic situation, different cohorts or generations might have different possibilities on this market. The economy of the housing market also implies that housing can be an investment, contrary to most other types of consumption. Other parts of the housing market are rented accommodation, either with a private landlord or as social housing. The regulation of these markets varies between countries, but often, personal network and familiarity with the systems facilitates entry to the market. These social structures of the housing market have to be included when considering policy for sustainable housing consumption.

The housing market thus contains elements like a high degree of reuse and the possibility of renting rather than owning, which for other types of consumer goods might be viewed as more sustainable. However the negative side of these elements from a sustainable point of view is that old, inefficient housing is only very slowly being replaced by more energy-efficient new housing, and that those living in these old houses cannot always decide themselves to make sustainable improvements to the building.

The high degree of reuse in housing follows from the fact that most housing in the Western world can last for more than 100 years. This means that the majority of the housing that we have now was built more than half a century ago, and that the majority of the housing in 2050 has already been built (Power 2008). There are huge economic and physical resources invested in buildings and in the infrastructures around the buildings, as well as cultural heritage in the architecture, and therefore these are some of the most slowly changing material structures in society. Buildings might be reinterpreted and renovated for changed use, but the material layouts still structure the new possibilities. In those cases where housing is actually demolished, this often has more to do with the location of the residence rather than with the physical condition of the building. Currently buildings in marginalized districts of the countryside are often left empty, with no potential buyers, and new buildings are more often seen in new urban districts in order to meet the demand from the migration from the countryside to metropolitan areas (Andersen et al. 2011).

However housing is neither primarily a consumer object nor a material structure; it is primarily a home for households. The home is the centre of people's everyday life, it is the setting for caring for oneself and for others, and more generally speaking it is the centre for reproduction (Després 1991; Mallett 2004). As such the home is the centre for many other types of consumption, and it is also the centre for most of our everyday practices; the home is where we depart from and return to (Gullestad 1991). The home is a place for security and identity formation, and understanding housing in a (sustainable) consumption perspective must also reflect this understanding of the home.

Ideas of sustainable housing have been formulated by different groups and organizations for the last 30 years. In the bottom-up approach, people redefine, rebuild and change the practices and organization of their everyday life and housing in order to live and consume in more sustainable ways. Initiatives and experiments in this approach have been more or less radical. In Denmark some of these have taken the form of eco-villages, where people live in communities producing and consuming more sustainably, locally and collectively than people in the rest of the society (Marckmann 2009). Other experiments have taken place in urban districts, where local residents work together to change buildings, infrastructures and practices in more sustainable directions. The top-down approaches include flagship renovation projects in urban renewal processes in many Danish cities during the 1990s, where different types of green technologies for energy production, water savings, wastewater treatment and so on were included in the renovation of old apartment blocks. Also, the development of different types of certification schemes for sustainable buildings and districts can be viewed as part of the top-down approach (for an overview of both top-down and bottom-up experiments in Denmark, see Gram-Hanssen and Jensen 2005; Jensen and Gram-Hanssen 2008). So far these sustainable housing agenda initiatives have not to any substantial degree influenced the mainstream housing development, whereas what can be called the low-energy building regime has had a huge influence, especially on new buildings (Jensen et al. 2014).

The low-energy building regime is closely linked to the building regulations at national level, and to the Energy Performance of Buildings Directive (EPBD) at European Union (EU) level. Since 1979, building regulation in Denmark has, as in many other countries, included provisions on the energy efficiency of all new buildings, and the regulations have since then regularly been tightened; on the one hand to influence the building components industry to continue developing more efficient products, and on the other hand to regulate all new buildings to include the most efficient products on the market. Today all new buildings are thus low-energy buildings and the main challenge is found within the existing buildings. Policy to influence the energy upgrading of existing buildings is also widespread, though not yet as successful (Gram-Hanssen 2014). It includes mandatory energy labels and certificates on all buildings sold in the EU, regulations stating that if a building is renovated it has to be updated on energy efficiency as well, and different forms of communication strategies and financial schemes in different countries.

Where the low-energy building regime focuses on the individual building, the urban planning approach focuses on the layout and location of buildings. Within a sustainability approach, the main discussions and initiatives have been on the location of new buildings near public transportation, as well as regulation to protect the natural environment and green spaces. Another main discourse has focused on the strength of dense cities in contrast to urban sprawl in order to minimize transportation (Næss et al. 1996; Newman and Kensworthy 1989) and land use, to gain energy efficiency from high-rise buildings rather than detached buildings, as well as other benefits (Gordon and Richardson 1997; Thinh et al. 2002; van der Waals 2000). A strong relation between urban form and sustainability is not easy to document, however (van der Waals 2000). The possibilities of local production also speak against larger and denser cities. However due to development based on economic mechanisms, metropolitan areas all over the world are expanding, regardless of the ideas of the sustainable city.

Rather than focusing on the buildings and urban planning, other initiatives have dealt with what people are doing in buildings and cities. During the energy crisis of the 1970s, campaigns often focused simply on saving energy by insulating the buildings or closing windows and doors. As a result of the Brundtland report, many campaigns during the 1990s were locally situated and supported grass-roots ideas. Later more specific campaigns have promoted different efficient products like CFL (compact fluorescent lamp) lightbulbs or the replacement of old oil boilers. In 2011 the most expensive Danish campaign within energy savings to that date focused on persuading homeowners to energy upgrade their buildings. In general, it seems that the majority of recent Danish campaigns have focused on promoting energy-efficient technologies rather than on changing habits. Notably one of the key public organizations responsible for energy savings in Denmark, the now terminated Elsparefonden, based its activities on the premise that public authorities neither could nor should interfere in the everyday life of citizens (personal communication, Elsparefonden's chief executive officer, CEO). Research also questions whether public mass communication campaigns really have any substantial influence on people's daily habits (Staats et al. 1996).

All of these different top-down approaches to sustainable buildings and cities have, to different degrees, contributed positively to more sustainable housing. However when it comes to the questions of changing habits, and especially reducing overall growing consumption in relation to housing, they do not contribute substantial input. Regarding the bottom-up approaches, the picture is more varied. Habits in particular can be seen to be regulated through the social interaction of a community that shares norms about sustainability and that can support each other in performing more sustainable practices, as shown in a study on lighting practices (Jensen 2013). On the other hand, not all conventional norms are necessarily open for discussion in these types of eco-communities. In Marckmann's (2009) study on establishing a new group in an existing eco-village, it was apparent that the size of the home was not open for discussion, and the general norm of building more spacious homes was not to be challenged from a sustainability perspective, which rather included discussion of what energy type should be used for heating, and so on.

Yet another issue related to (non-)sustainable housing, which is not challenged within any of these approaches, is the way households are formed, including the size of them. In Western societies ever more people are living alone, and today more than 40 per cent of Danish households consist of only one person (Statistikbanken.dk n.d.), partly explaining the growing number of heated square metres, as well as the growing number of appliances. It has been argued that the trend towards an increasing share of one-person households is unsustainable (Williams 2007). Explanations for the growing number of one-person households can be found in various tendencies in society such as demographic transitions (Hall et al. 1997), economic growth, divorce rates and individualization. However, so far, none of this has been challenged or in any way dealt with, within a sustainable housing consumption perspective.

## 10.4 POLICY FOR A SUSTAINABLE HOUSING CONSUMPTION

This chapter started by stating that substantial reductions in emissions and resource consumption within housing are needed, and continued by showing that efficient technologies alone will not do the job. The unconscious habits of everyday life, and not least the expectations and norms of growing consumption, have to be taken into account when developing solutions. Policy has so far had a quite strong influence on the energy efficiency of new buildings in particular. However, habits and, especially, norms of consumption have not been successfully addressed. I have argued that practice theory is useful for understanding both habits and norms of consumption, and in this section I will discuss how practice theory might inspire policy initiatives to work on all aspects of sustainable housing consumption, and to take into account the special consumer object that housing is.

Housing as such is not a practice; it is rather the site of many different practices, such as doing laundry or cooking. However making and maintaining a home can be considered a practice, which is carried out by a household and which includes acquiring a home, maintaining and decorating it, tidying up and cleaning it, as well as controlling the indoor climate to keep it comfortable as regards air quality and temperature. In the following I discuss how policy might contribute to making this practice more sustainable.

The practice of making and maintaining a home is held together by different elements, including habits, knowledge, technologies and meanings. As described previously, the meanings of homemaking practices focus on different variations of caring for oneself and other household members, privacy, security and identity, and economic investment or social status (Després 1991; Mallett 2004). The meaning of homemaking thus cannot be to be sustainable; however, sustainability might influence or be part of what we relate to caring, identity, investment or status. This, however, relates to common structures of meanings related to home. If general norms of caring for your children mean providing them with large private rooms, it might feel like deprivation if more children share the same room. If there is social status in living in big detached villas, living in a small apartment might similarly feel like deprivation. Understanding how these kinds of commonly shared norms are established is essential for understanding how norms of the opposite might fall into place. For instance can identity and status be attached to small sustainable homes, where people live close to each other and share rooms and equipment, appliances and so on with other households? Understanding how norms are established is the domain of sociology in a broader sense. Bourdieu described how, for example, social status is distributed to different consumer objects through mechanisms and distribution of economic and cultural capital (Bourdieu 1984). However, the question is whether it is possible or desirable from a policy perspective to work actively on these kinds of meaning or whether this would be considered a kind of propaganda that does not belong in democracies. Arguably, too often the opposite is seen: that campaigns to promote low-carbon technologies in different ways reinforce unsustainable norms. For example a 2006 advertisement in the customer magazine from a local energy company promoting heat pumps had the title: 'Save cash on your heating bill – and enjoy a nice warm summerhouse all the year round' (Christensen et al. 2011). In this way, the advert promoting the energy-efficient heat pump was also promoting a change in norms to heat a summerhouse all year round (which is a quite unsustainable practice as compared to the widespread norm of not using and heating the summerhouse in the wintertime).

Another element in what holds practices together is knowledge. It is often stated in sociology that information alone is not enough (Shove 2010). This is also true when it comes to sustainable housing. However, it is important to acknowledge that knowledge and information are always part of practices, although they cannot stand alone. People rarely change practices just because they get new knowledge. However, in an advanced Western society, where the home and everyday life are filled with technologies, knowledge of how these technologies work is part of being able to use them. Being a homeowner includes having knowledge of how to maintain your house and, for example, regulate the heat; or at least it includes knowledge of how to contact people who possess this knowledge. From a sustainability perspective, it is relevant whether this knowledge also includes knowledge of what is more or less sustainable, and that different types of knowledge do not conflict, for example as regards what is healthy and what is saving energy.

A way of working with the knowledge element of sustainable housing that has received much attention in recent years is through giving feedback to consumers on their energy consumption (Darby 2010; Fischer 2008). As energy is consumed indirectly, depending on habits related to various practices, people are often not aware of how much energy they are consuming and what the consumption relates to. Policy makers often have high confidence in the effect of giving targeted feedback to consumers on their consumption (Darby 2010). However, research finds that feedback information, alone or combined with elements of competition or other elements relating to consumption of other households, may show reductions of from 0 up to 15 per cent (Darby 2010). No matter whether feedback actually gives a major contribution to the sustainability of housing, it will surely continue as part of the future. Smart metering is statutory in many places, and digital meters that can provide different types of feedback are already widespread, together with ideas of smart energy futures (Strengers 2013).

Technologies, including the buildings themselves, are obviously an important element in the practice of making and maintaining a home. Focus has long been on the efficiency of technologies and buildings when it comes to energy and water savings. However, as shown in this chapter, efficiency alone is not enough. Technology development needs to include a focus on how buildings and technologies take part in shaping practices, and how they can be designed so that they are not only efficient, but also support a sustainable low-consumption practice (Vlasova and Gram-Hanssen 2014). The rebound effect must also be taken into account when forming policy for sustainable housing. This includes questions of how efficient technologies are introduced to the market. Efficient technologies for heating, such as heat pumps, are often sold with promises to deliver both greater comfort and energy savings. Hence it is not surprising that consumers use the more efficient technologies for also turning up their demands.

Daily habits are a fourth and final element of holding together the practice of making and maintaining a home. Habits are in general difficult to change (Verplanken and Roy,

Chapter 15 in this book). However, sometimes changes of habits happen very fast, for example in line with the introduction of new technologies such as information and communication technologies (smartphones, tablets and so on). Unfortunately the changes of habits, together with the introduction of new information and communication technologies, often move in an unsustainable direction (Røpke and Christensen 2013). Sometimes habits are also changed based on conscious decisions and knowledge, not as a simple straightforward process (Ilmonen 2001) but as an ongoing dialogue, as there is no sharp line between the conscious and the unconscious habits (Halkier 2001).

As shown in this chapter, sustainable housing is not just about more efficient technologies or about campaigns for changing behaviour. However, awareness and efficient technologies are also part of forming more sustainable housing. Hence when designing policy for sustainable housing, all four elements of what holds together the practice of making and maintaining a home must be included and integrated, as they are mutually dependent and equally important for the development of new and more sustainable ways of living.

## REFERENCES

Andersen, H.T., L. Møller-Jensen and S. Engelstoft (2011), 'The end of urbanization? Towards a new urban concept or rethinking urbanization', *European Planning Studies*, 19 (4), 595–561.

Bourdieu, P. (1984), *Distinction. A Social Critique of The Judgment of Taste*, Cambridge: Polity Press.

Christensen, T.H., K. Gram-Hanssen, P.E. Petersen, T.F. Larsen, E. Gudbjerg, L. Stryhn and P. Munter (2011), 'Air-to-air heat pumps: A wolf in sheep's clothing?', in *ECEEE 2011 Summer Study. Energy Efficiency First: The Foundation of a Low-Carbon Society*, Stockholm: European Council for an Energy Efficient Economy, ECEEE.

Dall, O. and J. Toft (2002), *Danske Husholdningers miljøbelastning*, Copenhagen: Miljøstyrelsen, Miljø- og Energi Ministeriet.

Danish Energy Authority (2010), 'Energistatistikken 2010', Copenhagen: Energistyrelsen.

Darby, S. (2010), 'Smart metering: What potential for householder engagement?', *Building Research and Information*, 38 (5), 442–457.

Després, C. (1991), 'The meaning of home: literature review and directions for future research and theoretical development', *Journal of Architectural and Planning Research*, 8, 96–115.

Fischer, C. (2008), 'Feedback on household electricity consumption: a tool for saving energy?', *Energy Efficiency*, 1 (1), 79–104.

Fuchs, D.A., and S. Lorek (2005), 'Sustainable consumption governance: a history of promises and failures', *Journal of Consumer Policy*, 28, 261–288.

Gill, Z.M., M.J. Tierney, I.M. Pegg and N. Allan (2010), 'Measured energy and water performance of an aspiring low energy/carbon affordable housing site in the UK', *Energy and Buildings*, 43, 117–125.

Gordon, P. and H.W. Richardson (1997), 'Are compact cities a desirable planning goal?', *Journal of the American Planning Association*, 63 (1), 95–106.

Gram-Hanssen, K. (2008), 'Consuming technologies – developing routines', *Journal of Cleaner Production*, 16 (11), 1181–1189.

Gram-Hanssen, K. (2010), 'Residential heat comfort practices: understanding users', *Building Research and Information*, 38 (2), 175–186.

Gram-Hanssen, K. (2011), 'Understanding change and continuity in residential energy consumption', *Journal of Consumer Culture*, 11 (1), 61–78.

Gram-Hanssen, K. (2013), 'Efficient technologies or user behaviour, which is the more important when reducing households' energy consumption?', *Energy Efficiency*, 6 (3), 447–457.

Gram-Hanssen, K. (2014), 'Existing buildings – users, renovations and energy policy', *Renewable Energy*, 61 (1), 136–140.

Gram-Hanssen, K. T.H. Christensen and P.E. Petersen (2012), 'Air-to-air heat pumps in real-life use: are potential savings achieved or are they transformed into increased comfort?', *Energy and Buildings*, 53 (12), 64–73.

Gram-Hanssen, K. and J.O. Jensen (2005), 'Green buildings in Denmark: from radical ecology to consumer oriented market approaches', in S. Guy and S. Moore (eds), *Sustainable Architecture*, London: Marcel Dekker Inc., pp. 165–185.

Greening, L.A., D.L. Greene and C. Difglio (2000), 'Energy efficiency and consumption: the rebound effect – a survey', *Energy Policy*, 28, 389–401.

Gullestad, M. (1991), 'The transformation of the Norwegian notion of everyday life', *American Ethnologist*, 18 (3), 480–499.

Halkier, B. (2001), 'Routinisation or reflexivity? Consumers and normative claims for environmental considerations', in J. Gronow and A. Warde (eds), *Ordinary Consumption*, London: Routledge, pp. 25–44.

Hall, R., P.E. Ogden and C. Hill (1997), 'The pattern and structure of one-person households in England and Wales and France', *International Journal of Population Geography*, 3, 61–181.

Ilmonen, K. (2001), 'Sociology, consumption and routine', in J. Gronow and A. Warde (eds), *Ordinary Consumption*, London: Routledge, pp. 9–24.

Jensen, C.J. (2013), 'Sharing conventions for energy efficient lighting?', in T. Laitinen Lindström (ed.), *Conference Proceedings: Proceedings of ECEEE 2013 Summer Study*, European Council for an Energy Efficient Economy.

Jensen, J.O. and K. Gram-Hanssen (2008), 'Ecological modernization of sustainable buildings: a Danish perspective', *Building Research and Information*, 36 (2), 146–158.

Jensen, J.O., K. Gram-Hanssen, I. Røpke and T.H. Christensen (2009), 'Household's use of information and communication technologies: a future challenge for energy savings?', *Conference Proceedings: ECEEE Summer Studies 2009*, Ile Saint-Denis: ECEEE.

Jensen, J.O., O.M. Jensen, K. Gram-Hanssen (2014), 'Omstilling til bæredygtigt byggeri', in J. Holm, B. Søndergård, I. Stauning and J.O. Jensen (eds), *Bæredygtig omstilling af bolig og byggeri*, Frederiksberg: Frydenlund, pp. 73−106.

Karlsson, J.F. and B. Moshfegh (2007), 'A comprehensive investigation of a low-energy building in Sweden', *Renewable Energy*, 32, 1830–1841.

Kristensen, L., O.M. Jensen, H.N. Knudsen, T.V. Rasmussen, N.C. Bergsøe, J. Kragh, H. Arvedsen and T. Olsen (2010), 'Erfaringsopfølgning på lavenergibyggeri klasse 1 og 2: med "Fremtidens Parcelhuse" som eksempel', Det Grønne Hus.

Mallett, S. (2004), 'Understanding home: a critical review of the literature', *Sociological Review*, 52, 62–89.

Marckmann, B. (2009), 'Hverdagslivets Kritik: Økosamfund i Danmark', PhD dissertation, Copenhagen: Copenhagen University.

Müller, L., O. Mont and K. Gram-Hanssen (2013), 'Vem bestämmer över konsumtionen?', in M. Jiborn and A. Kander (eds), *Generationsmålet: Kontroverser kring klimat och konsumtion*, Stockholm: Dialogos Förlag, pp. 64−99.

Næss, P., S.L. Sandberg and P.G. Røe (1996), 'Energy use for transportation in 22 Nordic towns', *Scandinavian Housing and Planning Research*, 13, 79–97.

Newman, P.W.G. and J.R. Kensworthy (1989), *Cities and Automobile Dependence*, Aldershot: Gower Publications.

Palmborg, C. (1986), 'Social habits and energy consumer behavior in single family homes', *Energy*, 11 (7), 643–650.

Power, A. (2008), 'Does demolition or refurbishment of old and inefficient homes help to increase our environmental, social and economic viability?', *Energy Policy*, 36, 4487–4501.

Røpke, I. (1999), 'The dynamics of willingness to consume', *Ecological Economics*, 28, 399–420.

Røpke, I. and T.H. Christensen (2013), 'Transitions in the wrong direction? Digital technologies and daily life', in E. Shove and N. Spurling (eds), *Sustainable Practices*, London: Routledge, pp. 49–68.

Sanne, C. (2000), 'Dealing with environmental savings in a dynamic economy – how to stop chasing your tail in the pursuit of sustainability', *Energy Policy*, 28, 487–495.

Schatzki, T.R. (1996), *Social Practices: A Wittgensteinian Approach to Human Activity and the Social*, Cambridge: Cambridge University Press.

Schmidt-Bleek, F. (2008), 'Factor 10: the future of stuff', *Sustainability: Science, Practice, and Policy*, 4 (1), 1–4.

Shipper, L. and M. Grubb (2000), 'On the rebound? Feedback between energy intensities and energy uses in IEA countries', *Energy Policy*, 28, 367–388.

Shove, E. (2003), *Comfort, Cleanliness and Convenience: The Social Organization of Normality*, Oxford, UK and New York, USA: Berg.

Shove, E. (2010), 'Beyond the ABC: climate change policy and theories of social change', *Environment and Planning A*, 42 (6), 1273–1285.

Shove, E., M. Pantzar and M. Watson (2012), *The Dynamics of Social Practice. Everyday Life and How It Changes*, London: Sage.

Shove, E. and G. Walker (2010), 'Governing transitions in the sustainability of everyday life', *Research Policy*, 39 (4), 471–476.

Sonderegger, R.C. (1977/78), 'Movers and stayers: the resident's contribution to variation across houses in energy consumption for space heating', *Energy and Buildings*, 1, 313–324.
Sorrel, S., J. Dimitropoulos, M. Sommerville (2009), 'Empirical estimates of the direct rebound effect: a review', *Energy Policy*, 37, 1356–1371.
Staats, H.J., A.P. Wit and C.Y.H. Midden (1996), 'Communicating the greenhouse effect to the public: evaluation of a mass media campaign from a social dilemma perspective', *Journal of Environmental Management*, 46 (2), 189–203.
Statistikbanken.dk (n.d.), 'Danmarks Statistik', available at http://www.statistikbanken.dk/statbank5a/default.asp?w=1600.
Strengers, Y. (2013), *Smart Energy Technologies in Everyday Life. Smart Utopia?* Basingstoke: Palgrave Macmillan.
Thinh, N.X., G. Arlt, B. Heber, J. Hennersdorf and I. Lehmann (2002), 'Evaluation of urban land-use structures with a view to sustainable development', *Environmental Impact Assessment Review*, 22, 475–492.
Thøgersen, J. and T. Crompton (2009), 'Simple and painless? The limitations of spillover in environmental campaigning', *Journal of Consumer Policy*, 32, 141–163.
Thomsen, A. and K. van der Flier (2009), 'Replacement or renovation of dwellings: the relevance of a more sustainable approach', *Building Research and Information*, 37, 5–6.
Tukker, A., M. Cohen, K. Hubacek and O. Mont (2010), 'The impacts of household consumption and options for change', *Journal of Industrial Ecology*, 14, 13–30.
United Nations (1987), *Our Common Future*, Report of the World Commission on Environment and Development (The Brundtland Report), Oxford: Oxford University Press.
van der Waals, J. (2000), 'The compact city and the environment: a review', *Tijdschrift voor Economische en Sociale Geografie*, 91 (2), 111–121.
Vlasova, L. and K. Gram-Hanssen (2014), 'Incorporating inhabitants' everyday practices into domestic retrofits', *Building Research and Information*, 42 (4), 512–524.
Warde, A. (2005), 'Consumption and theories of practice', *Journal of Consumer Culture*, 5 (2), 131–153.
Wilhite, H., E. Shove, L. Lutzenhiser and W. Kempton (2000), 'Twenty years of energy demand management: we know more about individual behavior but how much do we really know about demand?', *Proceedings ACEEE Summer Study on Energy Efficiency in Buildings*, 8, 8.435–8.453.
Williams, J. (2007), 'Innovative solutions for averting a potential resource crisis – the case of one-person households in England and Wales', *Environment, Development and Sustainability*, 9, 325–354.

# 12. Peak meat: the role of meat in sustainable consumption

*Achim Spiller and Sina Nitzko*

The issue of sustainable meat consumption is inextricably linked with aspects of animal welfare and ethical treatment. In the context of a growing worldwide demand for animal products, sustainable meat consumption may take several forms. We take a theoretical approach to segmenting consumers into four types that differ in their qualitative and quantitative meat consumption. Based on a consumer survey of a sample of the German population, we then validate and describe these consumer types. We then give an overview of existing and potential policy measures to promote sustainable meat consumption within these different target groups, including methods of libertarian (soft) and hard paternalism, before summarizing the future challenges of sustainable meat consumption.

## 12.1 MEAT AND SUSTAINABLE CONSUMPTION

A sustainable diet is a key part of responsible consumption. Generally, sustainability includes economic, ecological and social attributes. Additionally for food, the health values of the products as well as animal welfare aspects of animal products are also important factors in sustainability (Reisch et al. 2013). Through their link to animals, the consumption of meat and other animal products (such as eggs, milk or dairy products) raise certain ethical questions that are almost unique to these categories. Livestock farming and the consumption of meat are, therefore, classical topics in the debate surrounding responsible consumption.

The treatment of animals, from birth to slaughter, is an important characteristic of a civilization and requires ethical justification. Thus, there have been, and will continue to be, philosophical approaches examining human–animal relationships, animal welfare and attitudes towards meat consumption (Foer 2009; Singer 1975).

The sustainable consumption of animal products is also a relevant topic in the context of global food security. The production of animal-based food products requires considerably more resources than that of plant-based products. For example about 31 $m^2$ of land is needed to produce 1000 kcal of beef, whilst cereals require only 1.1 $m^2$ (Peters et al. 2007). As the global population grows, the available amount of agricultural land per person is reducing. According to estimates, in the year 2025 there will be less than 2000 $m^2$ of agricultural land per person available to produce the food and renewable resources needed (Flachowsky 2003). As the global pressure on resources from meat production is expected to continue to rise, responsible meat consumption in Organisation for Economic Co-operation and Development (OECD) countries, which currently consume the majority of global meat production, is becoming a critical issue (FAO 2009).

The present chapter discusses the (sustainable) farming of animals from the consumer research perspective, specifically considering consumers in developed countries. We do not include fish, because the characteristics and problems of sustainable farming and consumption of fish differ in important aspects (production structure, intensity and so on) from that of the farm animals considered here, namely pigs, poultry and cattle. After presenting the associations between meat consumption and sustainability, we describe worldwide developments concerning the consumption of animal products. After that, the different aspects of sustainable meat consumption, for example, ethical and health aspects, are described in detail. The presentation of the quantity–quality dilemma leads to the introduction of a typology of meat consumers. Using empirical data, we investigate to what extent this theoretical typology of meat consumption patterns can be confirmed. The chapter closes with an overview of policy measures for promoting sustainable meat consumption and an outlook on future developments.

## 12.2 THE CONSUMPTION OF ANIMAL PRODUCTS

The demand for animal products has been considerably increased over recent decades. However this growth in consumption has been greater in some parts of the globe than in others, leading to a high discrepancy in the per capita demand between industrialized (82.3 kg of meat per year) and developing economies (31.2 kg) (FAO 2008). By 2050, a simple continuation of this trend predicts a further rise to 103 kg/per person in industrial economies and 44 kg in developing economies (FAO 2009), which would mean a growth in global meat consumption of 85 per cent compared to 2005–2007 (Bruinsma 2009). The key driver of global meat consumption is now the relatively high income elasticity of demand for meat in emerging and developing economies (for example, in China, income elasticity for meat is 1.34; Liao and Chern 2007).

Alongside the general growth in demand, in recent decades there have also been shifts within the meat categories. Whilst the global demand for beef rose by 1.1 per cent per year during the period between 1981 and 2001, the demand for pork and poultry rose by 2.9 and 5.1 per cent, respectively. The feed conversion rate (that is, the amount of body weight gained for every kilogram of consumed feed) of poultry is comparatively high, which makes the production relatively cost-efficient.

Considering the relationship between meat consumption and socio-demographic characteristics, it appears that men generally consume more meat than women (Prättälä et al. 2006). In addition, meat consumption decreases with age (Gossard and York 2003), and there are differences based on social class and educational level. Gossard and York (2003) showed that in developed countries, highly educated people, the self-employed and people in the service sector eat less meat than people with a lower educational level and manual workers. Apart from socio-demographic differences, there are also regional differences concerning meat consumption between different countries. Whilst the average annual meat consumption in the USA is 122.8 kg per person per year, in Asia comparatively little meat is consumed, especially in countries such as India (3.3 kg per person per year) (Nordgren 2012). Big discrepancies can also be found within individual countries. In Germany in 2013, around 3.8 per cent of the population followed a vegetarian or vegan diet, whilst 4.9 per cent of men consumed three times the national average of meat (Cordts et al. 2013b). These differences underline the importance of lifestyle-related factors concerning meat consumption (Grunert 2006).

Motivations for a vegetarian diet are manifold. Ruby (2012) suggests that ethical considerations concerning the rearing and slaughter of farm animals are the most frequent drivers. Worries about health are the second most frequently mentioned. Further reasons for vegetarianism are the environmental effects of meat consumption, spiritual purity and rejection of the sensory qualities of meat. When comparing vegans with vegetarians, it becomes clear that vegans have stronger political, as well as animal welfare and environmental motivations for their choice in diet (Haverstock and Forgays 2012).

In addition to quantity, the question of product quality is also highly important for sustainable consumption decisions. Whilst these debates have in many countries so far been focused on food safety, questions about animal welfare and global food security are gaining increasing attention (Godfray et al. 2010).

## 12.3 CHARACTERISTICS OF SUSTAINABLE MEAT CONSUMPTION

### 12.3.1 Aspects of Animal Ethics

Discussions of animal ethics centre on moral questions of the status of animals, and the responsibilities of humans in their treatment of them. There is a long tradition of philosophical reflections on animals from a moral perspective, dating back to early human history (Wibbecke 2013). From an animal ethics perspective, animals are considered as creatures capable of experiencing pain and suffering that have the right to physical integrity and a life under species-appropriate conditions (Baumgartl-Simons 2013). Veterinary medical and neurobiological research is also producing increasing evidence for the cognitive and emotional abilities of animals (Kornum and Knudsen 2011; Sneddon 2009), leading to a growing awareness of their needs. In addition, people in high-income countries do not differentiate so strongly between domestic pets and farm animals, which is presumably a result of the increasing alienation between farming and consumers in industrialized countries (von Alvensleben and Mahlau 1998). In this respect, there are cross-cultural and species-specific differences, for example concerning the consumption of horse meat. While eating this kind of meat is unthinkable in the UK, it is sold as a delicacy in Switzerland or Italy.

Due to strong competitive pressure, the common forms of intensive livestock farming today represent a compromise between the dominant economic and animal welfare demands (Lusk and Norwood 2011). This type of husbandry has little in common with traditional forms of farming, leading to increased discussion of livestock rights (Baumgartl-Simons 2013). A basic framework for the analysis and evaluation of animal welfare is provided by the ‘five freedoms’, which were established in the Brambell Report of 1965, and apply to farm animals that are kept or used by humans. They consider both physical and mental suffering, and include: (1) freedom from thirst, hunger and malnutrition; (2) freedom from discomfort; (3) freedom from pain, injury and disease; (4) freedom to express normal behaviour; and (5) freedom from fear and distress (Webster 2001). Whilst the five freedoms aim to protect animals from unnecessary suffering, recent approaches have focused on opportunities for animals to express species-specific behaviour (Miele et al. 2011) and thereby experience positive emotions (Boissy et al. 2007).

### 12.3.2 Ecological Aspects

Recent decades have seen a change from extensive (that is, grassland-based) to industrialized production systems for livestock (Naylor et al. 2005) that are independent of local feed production or land availability. Livestock in industrialized systems are no longer fed on grass and low-value by-products but on cereals and high-value feed such as soy, maize and potatoes (FAO 2009).

An increasing proportion of the global agricultural area used for feed production and grazing is subjected to excessive fertilization, overuse and/or land degradation due to the constantly growing demand for meat (Sutton et al. 2013). The use of pesticides to increase yields may affect not only the plant, but also the groundwater and the food products (for example, through residues) (Steinfeld et al. 2006). New agricultural areas are created by clearance, in many regions of the world by fire, which is accompanied by destruction of the natural vegetation and a decrease in biodiversity. In emerging and developing economies in particular, negative social consequences have been seen due to the expansion of agriculture, such as the dispossession or displacement of local communities (Lambin and Meyfroidt 2011).

The production of animal feed products is also characterized by a high use of primary energy, as it is energy-inefficient to use the energy stored in plants via plant-eating animals. Between 65 per cent and 90 per cent of the energy from plant-based food is lost in the conversion to animal-based food (Strahm 1995).

From an environmental perspective, the climate-related consequences of food production and consumption are similarly problematic (EEA 2013). Around 80 per cent of the emissions related to food production are caused by animal-based food (McMichael et al. 2007), demonstrating that human diets play a large role in the release of greenhouse gases.

### 12.3.3 Social Aspects

The majority of feed imports, which play a large role in the economic viability of intensive livestock production in industrialized countries, come from developing countries. However, farming for export is frequently associated with competition for land and with the production of food for the local or national population. Particularly in developing economies, the production of crops for export is partly linked to the destruction of natural habitats (see section 12.3.2) and rural depopulation (von Koerber and Kretschmer 2000).

The availability of food worldwide is very unequal. Theoretically, world hunger could be eliminated if meat consumption was reduced (Strahm 1995; see section 12.3.2). However, this ignores the fact that the main cause of hunger is poverty. Whilst a reduction in meat consumption in industrialized countries could improve the global availability of biomass (Stehfest et al. 2009), its effect on food security would be limited unless the purchasing power and access to food for malnourished populations is improved (Grethe et al. 2011).

### 12.3.4 Health Aspects

Meat is generally considered as a nutritionally valuable foodstuff due, above all, to its protein, vitamins as well as iron, zinc and selenium content (Honikel 1995). Therefore the consumption of meat in limited quantities is positive, especially for developing countries. Current recommendations from health and nutritional organizations vary regarding consumption quantity. The German Nutrition Society (2005), for example, recommends the consumption of a maximum of 300 to 600 g of meat and processed meat products per week. The World Cancer Research Fund/American Institute for Cancer Research (2007) specify a maximum of 300 g of red meat per week. In the industrialized nations, the average per capita consumption clearly exceeds these recommendations (e.g., German Nutrition Society 2012). Various empirical studies have shown that sustained increased consumption of meat, and in particular red and processed meats, is associated with negative health impacts (Micha et al. 2010). This includes an increased risk of developing coronary heart disease (Hu et al. 2000), type 2 diabetes (mellitus) (Song et al. 2004) and various types of cancer (Chao et al. 2005). Furthermore higher meat consumption is frequently associated with a generally unhealthy lifestyle (Vergnaud et al. 2011), which in turn promotes excessive weight and obesity. Within the context of the prevention and curing of diseases related to high-meat diets, reducing meat intake is an essential element of a sustainable diet and lifestyle (see Gwozdz, Chapter 14 in this book).

### 12.3.5 Trade-Offs and Rebound Effects

Livestock rearing involves a number of trade-offs between the objectives of sustainable development, specifically between animal welfare and resource management (Sutton and Dibb 2013). Through efforts to optimize feed conversion by reducing animal movement with restrictive housing, improving fattening rates through calculated feeding regimes and continuous advances in genetics, modern livestock rearing has achieved a reduction in the amount of feed needed to produce a certain amount of meat. Today, feed conversion rates for broiler chickens are only about 1:1.6 in modern industrialized farming systems (de Beer et al. 2011). With the improvement of feed conversion and the housing of animals in barns, ecological goals such as reducing the carbon footprint or the energy and water use can also be considerably improved. Processing losses are thereby minimized, and the environmental drawbacks of a diet including animal products compared to a strictly plant-based diet are reduced. At the same time, the price of meat has decreased so that it has become more accessible to low-income groups of consumers (Beran and Dyckhoff 2011). Production costs for 1 pound of live chicken dropped from US$2.32 in 1934 to US$1.08 in 1960, and further to US$0.45 in 2004 (in today's money; USDA 2006). On the other hand the above-mentioned factors such as breeding to target feed conversion efficiency, minimizing energy loss through restriction of movement, animals being kept 100 per cent indoors, and so on, are important causes of animal welfare problems (FAO 2005). One-sided livestock rearing leads, for example in the poultry industry, to a greater risk of microfractures in the animals' bones, considerably restricts their movement and can prevent basic behaviour such as simple walking (Tuyttens et al. 2008). The preventative use of antibiotics in livestock leads to the development of resistant bacteria, and they may remain in the meat after slaughter and enter the food chain (Witte 2000).

Besides such trade-offs, which make the evaluation of overall sustainability difficult, sustainable consumer behaviour is hindered through rebound effects. A decline in the demand for meat in industrialized countries would indirectly, via the mechanism of a decrease in world market prices, contribute to an increase in meat consumption, especially in affluent consumer groups in emerging and developing countries. This would be associated with an attenuation of the decline in global animal production (Cordts et al. 2013a).

## 12.4 MEAT CONSUMPTION AND SUSTAINABLE LIFESTYLES

### 12.4.1 Less but Better: The Two Sides of Sustainable Meat Consumption

The predominant meat consumption patterns in industrialized countries are currently characterized by high per capita consumption of meat, produced with emphasis on low costs. Making this more sustainable requires on the one hand a reduction in the quantity of meat consumed ('less meat approach'), and on the other the enhancement of the quality attributes of meat ('better meat approach'; Dagevos and Voordouw 2013).

Through a reduction in quantity, individuals in OECD countries would still be provided with the necessary nutrients, whilst simultaneously reducing the risk of developing diseases linked to the excessive consumption of meat. Furthermore, on a national and international scale, lower meat consumption would contribute to environmental protection goals.

Better meat quality means the preference for healthy meat, for example with low saturated fat, products from high-welfare systems, environmentally friendly meat from ruminants grazing marginal land (Ridoutt et al. 2012), eating broiler chicken with a lower carbon footprint (de Beer et al. 2011), and so on (Sutton and Dibb 2013).

'Less but better' as the combination of a sufficiency with a quality approach takes both parts of consumption behaviour into account. While meat is quite expensive compared to vegetarian alternatives, a reduction of meat consumption would mean that individuals could spend the money saved on better quality. This strategy is not useful for poor people in poor countries, but for developed countries and the growing middle class in emerging countries it supports individual health objectives and social responsibility.

Nevertheless, meat consumption is deeply rooted in food culture and individual habits. To change this behaviour, autonomous lifestyle changes (for example, adopting the principle of sufficiency and perceiving it as an improvement of quality of life) as well as policy interventions are needed.

### 12.4.2 Changing Attitudes Towards Meat Consumption

In earlier periods of human history, meat was seen as a very valuable good. Its consumption demonstrated the high social status of the eater and was a symbol of power, strength and manliness. For a long time meat was, therefore, a luxury product and served to differentiate between the social classes (Fiddes 2011).

Nowadays, there is a tendency towards the opposite relationship, at least for some countries in North-Western Europe. Consuming a larger quantity of meat in industrialized countries is increasingly a characteristic of socially disadvantaged classes (Perrin et al. 2002). With the transition into the post-industrial society, so-called 'peak meat' could have been reached; that is, a maximum per capita meat consumption, followed by a decrease in consumption quantities in some developed countries (Hirschfelder and Lahoda 2012). This is due to the reduction in meat consumption in certain groups that are characterized by greater sustainability orientation and accompanying responsible meat consumption (de Boer et al. 2007).

The motivations for not consuming meat are complex. For example high health awareness and ethical motivations seem to be drivers of the reduction in meat consumption or its exclusion from a consumer's diet (Hoek et al. 2004; Tobler et al. 2011). Socio-demographic aspects, such as gender also play a role, in that women generally consume less meat than men (Prättälä et al. 2006).

The values and attitudes leading to lower consumption of meat are, therefore, very similar to the ones promoting better meat quality. This may lead to an apparent dilemma: people who do not consume a product cannot drive the market. For the industry, the preferences of the intensive buyer are key.

## 12.5 THE QUANTITY–QUALITY DILEMMA

### 12.5.1 A Typology of Meat Consumers

Following the principle of 'less but better', two dimensions of meat consumption are important in the context of sustainability: quantity and the (ethical) quality of animal products. Both dimensions are crucial, but there are essential trade-offs between the strategies, which may hinder developments towards sustainable meat consumption. This can be explained with the example of vegetarians, who often have strong beliefs about animal husbandry without having any influence on the meat market as consumers. The possible relationships between the quantity of meat consumed and the quality requirements can be developed into a simple theoretical model (see Figure 12.1). Depending on the strength of the characteristics in the different consumer groups, there are different sustainability-related implications and different effects on the meat market. Figure 12.1 only considers meat consumers; vegans are not included, as they follow an ethical code but by definition have no influence on the meat market. Vegetarians are also not included as they have a much lower influence (through milk and egg consumption) on livestock farming. In the following, the four meat consumer groups and their consumption patterns are described in more detail:

- Low meat consumer (I): these consumers are characterized by low meat consumption together with a lack of interest in the ethical quality of the product. This group is generally a passive market participant, whose influence on the meat market is low, but their behaviour is fairly sustainable due to their low consumption level.
- Benign carnivore (II): McMahan (2008) defines benign carnivores as meat consumers that consider meat eating justified if (and only if) the short life of the

| | | | |
|---|---|---|---|
| Importance of the ethical quality of animal products | high | II (Benign carnivore) | IV (Shifter) |
| | low | I (Low meat consumer) | III (Bad influence) |
| | | low | high |
| | | Level of meat consumption | |

*Figure 12.1* *A simple model of the links between the level of meat consumption and the importance of the ethical quality of the animal product*

animal was as comfortable as possible. Accordingly consumers in this group eat little meat but attribute great importance to the ethical quality of the meat that they do eat. Their influence on the meat market is, however, small due to their low consumption volume.

- Bad influence (III): consumers in this group are characterized by high meat consumption. The ethical quality of the products is not considered very important. Suppliers clearly orientate themselves according to the needs of this group (that is, large quantities of meat at the cheapest price). However, regarding sustainability (social and individual), the influence of this group is generally negative.
- Shifter (IV): people with this consumption pattern are characterized by high levels of meat consumption but with serious consideration of the quality of the meat. Ethically motivated consumption of large quantities of meat has a positive effect on the quality level in the market. For the industry, this target group is perfect; they consume large quantities of meat of high ethical quality that is probably characterized by higher prices. Nevertheless, the large volume consumed has negative consequences for the environment and climate, as well as the health of the individual consumers in this group.

In the following, we summarize the results of a consumer survey investigating to what extent this theoretical typology of meat consumption patterns can be confirmed (see Verain et al., Chapter 13 in this book).

### 12.5.2 Empirical Results

In an online survey, 1175 German consumers were recruited in January 2013 via a professional online panel provider, using a standardized questionnaire. The sample is approximately representative regarding age, sex, geographical region and income of the German population. Considering meat consumption, 85.6 per cent of participants are meat eaters, 11.7 per cent are flexitarians (that is, only occasional consumption of meat products), 3.5 per cent vegetarians and 0.3 per cent vegans (Cordts et al. 2013c).

Within the online survey, participants answered questions on meat consumption and

*Table 12.1 Results of the confirmatory factor analysis*

| Factor: Ethically motivated meat consumption (KMO = 0.734; $R^2$ = 53.28%; Cronbach's Alpha = 0.702) | |
|---|---|
| Item | Factor loading |
| If I knew which meat came from happy animals, I would only buy this. | 0.781 |
| I am willing to pay twice the amount for high-quality meat. | 0.738 |
| When buying food, I place great value on animal welfare. | 0.726 |
| I value quality above quantity in meat. | 0.659 |

attitudes related to meat quality and animal welfare, and willingness to pay. To judge the level of meat consumption, we asked how many days per week meat or processed meat products were eaten for breakfast, lunch or the evening meal (on a scale of 0–7 meals with meat per week). The importance of the ethical quality of consumed meat products was captured using four statements that were scored on a five-point Likert scale and combined into a single index (verified by a confirmatory factor analysis; see Table 12.1).

The factor 'ethically motivated meat consumption' and the 21-scale variable for the level of meat consumption were both included as cluster-forming variables in the hierarchical cluster analysis. Applying the Ward method showed that a five-cluster solution was appropriate (see Table 12.2).

The resulting consumer typology contains the following five clusters (see Figure 12.2):

- Cluster 1: 15.1 per cent of consumers are assigned to this cluster, which is characterized by a relatively large proportion of males. These consumers have a fairly average level of meat consumption and the lowest ethical orientation and willingness to pay for high-quality meat. Due to its strong price orientation, this consumer group is generally difficult for the meat market as well as for sustainability goals ('bad influence').
- Cluster 2: The second cluster contains 22.3 per cent of consumers. This group has the second-lowest meat consumption, the second-lowest ethical motivation, and the second-lowest willingness to pay for high-quality meat. This group therefore consumes relatively little meat, but the price is more important than ethical attributes. Through their low consumption of meat, the consumers in this group have a very small influence on the meat market and, therefore, a generally passive role ('low meat consumer').
- Cluster 3: This cluster contains 27.7 per cent of consumers, the largest group, characterized by a large proportion of males eating the highest amount of meat. Compared to the other clusters, the educational level is the lowest and their age is the highest. The ethical motivation for meat consumption is moderate, as is the willingness to pay for high-quality meat. For the development of the meat market, this relatively large group could play an important role. These consumers are characterized by high consumption levels and a slightly above-average sustainability orientation ('indifferent heavy meat consumer').
- Cluster 4: This is the smallest cluster, with 9.9 per cent of survey respondents, but

*Table 12.2 Results of the cluster analysis (consumer typology)*

| | Cluster 1 (N = 177) | Cluster 2 (N = 250) | Cluster 3 (N = 326) | Cluster 4 (N = 116) | Cluster 5 (N = 262) |
|---|---|---|---|---|---|
| | M (SD) | M (SD) | M (SD) | M (SD) | M (SD) |
| Cluster forming variables: mean (standard deviation) | | | | | |
| Level of meat consumption[1] *** | 11.62 (2.80) | 5.23 (2.22) | 15.22 (3.57) | 2.41 (1.60) | 8.39 (2.40) |
| Ethically motivated meat consumption[2] *** | 2.54 (0.50) | 3.03 (0.42) | 3.56 (0.52) | 4.32 (0.43) | 4.16 (0.46) |
| Cluster describing variables: mean (standard deviation) or percentage | | | | | |
| Age (in years) | 45.54 (13.11) | 46.05 (12.75) | 47.88 (13.93) | 47.26 (14.01) | 46.57 (13.44) |
| Males / Females (in %) *** | 62.7/37.3 | 44.8/55.2 | 62.6/37.4 | 28.4/71.6 | 45.4/54.6 |
| (Vocational) university entrance qualification (in %) | 42.9% | 47.4% | 41.2% | 52.2% | 46.6% |
| I am willing to pay twice the amount for high quality meat. (M [SD])[2] *** | 1.88 (0.82) | 2.29 (0.93) | 2.71 (1.03) | 3.77 (0.96) | 3.60 (0.97) |

*Notes:*
[1] The number of meals containing meat per week; the frequencies for breakfast/lunch/evening meal (each scored between 0 and 7) were summed into 'frequency of meat consumption' on a scale of 0 to 21 meals containing meat per week.
[2] Scale: 1 = not at all; to 5 = completely.
* $p \leq 0.05$; ** $p \leq 0.01$; *** $p \leq 0.001$ (based on Chi squared tests or one-way ANOVAs).

the largest proportion of women. Compared to other clusters, this group has the lowest meat consumption, and can be considered as 'benign carnivores' because of their very positive attitudes towards animal welfare and meat quality.

- Cluster 5: The second-largest cluster (22.3 per cent) contains slightly more women than men and is characterized by a high household income. These consumers have the third-highest meat consumption and the second-highest ethical orientation and willingness to pay for high-quality meat. This relatively large group could, as 'shifters', influence the market as well as sustainability goals. Both their ethical orientation and their willingness to pay are above average.

In general the results empirically reveal at least a partial trade-off between the level of meat consumption and sustainability orientation. A significant proportion of the consumers that are particularly sustainability-oriented consume relatively little meat and can, therefore, have only a limited influence on the market through their buying behaviour. These flexitarians as well as the vegetarians are not suited to drive issues such as animal welfare or social standards in the market. For businesses, this

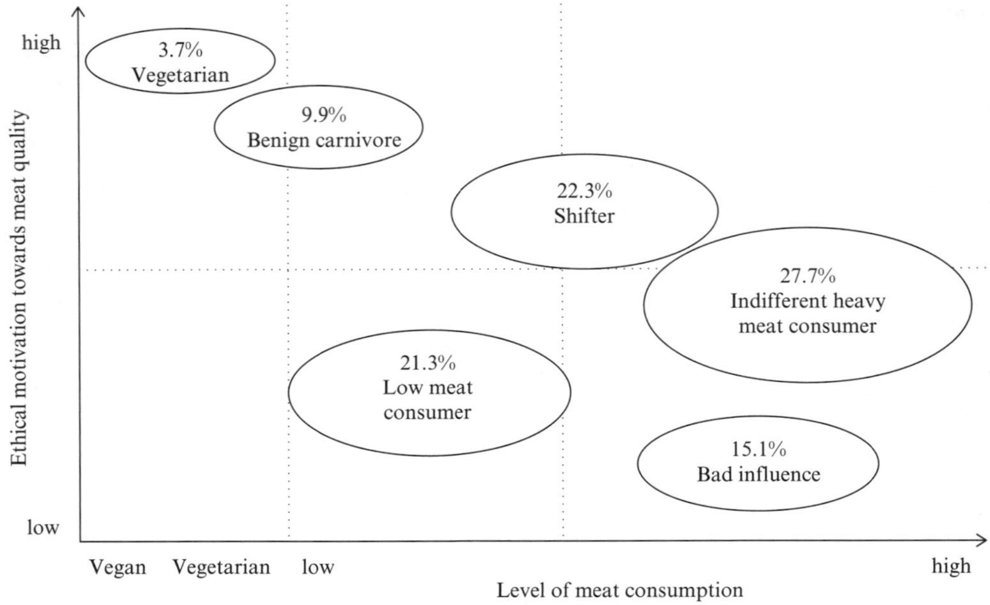


*Figure 12.2 Sustainable meat consumption in Germany 2013*

means that they need to take into account the sometimes very significant differences between consumer and citizen preferences. About 15 per cent of German consumers have no or only minor influence on the meat market but probably a huge effect as citizens through their strong ethical orientation (citizen–consumer gap; Schröder and McEachern 2004).

For economic reasons, the supply side is focused on the values and attitudes of the cluster of 'indifferent heavy meat consumers'. Their preferences drive production decisions due to the demand power of this group, accounting for roughly half of the meat consumption of the whole population. If this group consumes less but better meat, the sustainability of the market will improve quickly. Because two-thirds of this group are men, sustainable meat consumption heavily relies on gender aspects. Males seem to change their eating habits especially for health reasons (Kiefer et al. 2005) which calls for target-group-specific policy tools.

## 12.6 POLICY MEASURES FOR SUSTAINABLE MEAT CONSUMPTION

The quantity–quality dilemma is an important concept to explain differences between citizen and consumer preferences, and is therefore central to the development of policy interventions. In the case of meat consumption, this means measures to reduce consumption as well as to promote quality. Table 12.3 gives an overview of different regulatory options.

*Table 12.3 Overview of consumer-oriented policy measures and examples*

| Consumer information/ education/ nudging | | Financial incentives (economic instruments) | Regulatory requirements | |
|---|---|---|---|---|
| Libertarian (soft) paternalism | | | Hard paternalism | |
| Information provision/ product labelling | Nudging | Taxes or subsidies | Obligations | Prohibitions |
| • 'Less but Better' campaign (United Kingdom) (Sutton and Dibb 2013)<br>• Animal welfare label (de Jonge and van Trijp 2013)<br>• Meadow-grazed milk label (FrieslandCampina 2013) | • In-store product placement of vegetarian articles<br>• Increased promotion for healthy labelled meals (Thunström and Nordström 2013) | • Fat tax (Denmark) (Villanueva 2011)<br>• Junk food tax (Mexico, Hungary) (Holt 2011) | • Vegetarian day in public canteens (Lombardini and Lankoski 2013; Wahlen et al. 2012) | • Maximum size of meat portions in meals |

### 12.6.1 Interventions to Reduce Meat Consumption

Measures to influence consumer decisions can be divided into three general categories: consumer education, financial incentives and regulatory mechanisms (see Table 12.3; Tänzler et al. 2005). The first two measures, which allow consumers free choice, are referred to in the modern literature as libertarian (soft) paternalism (Thaler and Sunstein 2003). Information-based instruments included in this category serve to increase awareness of, develop understanding of and establish commitment to meat reduction (for example, information campaigns to increase the consumption of plant-based foods) (Dagevos and Voordouw 2013). An example of this is the World Wide Fund for Nature (WWF) non-governmental organization (NGO) campaign for less but better meat (Sutton and Dibb 2013). Choice architecture is another method of libertarian paternalism, in which the consumer is 'nudged' towards the desired decision; for example, a more visible product placement of meat substitutes in communal catering. Consumer behaviour in this context is seen as habitual or routine, which can be moulded by influencing the contextual conditions in which the consumers make their choice (Thaler and Sunstein 2008; see Sunstein, Chapter 20 in this book).

Financial incentives involve raising the cost of the harmful consumption option, for example through a tax on unhealthy food products (Thunström and Nordström 2013) such as the fat tax in Denmark (Villanueva 2011) or the junk food taxes in Mexico and Hungary (Holt 2011).

In hard paternalism (command and control), certain options are excluded through obligations and prohibitions. In recent years, some European countries have controversially discussed an obligatory vegetarian day in public cafeterias (Lombardini and Lankoski 2013; Wahlen et al. 2012).

In general there have only been a few first attempts promoting meat reduction, which so far have not been very successful (for example, the failed vegetarian day campaign in Germany, and the abolition of the fat tax in Denmark; see Snowdon 2013), demonstrating that meat consumption is a highly complex phenomenon.

Austgulen (2014) identified the lack of consensus on the environmental problems associated with meat consumption in the public debate as a barrier for consumers to consume meat more sustainably. Both negative and positive aspects of red meat consumption and production for environment are emphasized by different interest groups, making the discourse confusing for consumers.

### 12.6.2 Interventions to Improve Quality

Compared to meat quantity reduction ('less'), it seems easier to influence the quality standards in the meat market ('better'). However, characteristics of more sustainable or higher-quality meat are, from an information economic perspective, credence attributes (Jahn et al. 2005). These are process properties that cannot be observed in the end product. In order to guarantee these hidden attributes and make them transparent for the consumer, certification systems and meat labels that cover the whole supply chain and ensure scrutiny of each stage of the production process are necessary. Food labels can be private, facultative or mandatory (WBVE/WBA 2011).

Whilst private global certification systems have developed very quickly in the field of food safety in recent years (for example, GlobalGap), the use of animal welfare labels is still low. Exceptions are the UK (Freedom Food), Switzerland (private labels from retailers), Germany (Animal Welfare Label of the German Animal Welfare Federation) and the Netherlands (Better Leven) (Ministerie van Economische Zaken 2013). Most other countries do not have animal welfare labels, or the existing ones cover only very small niches (de Jonge and van Trijp 2013).

This great difference between attitudes of citizens and the low relevance of special meat qualities in the market is referred to as a welfare preference paradox (Sullivan 2013). Possible causes are manifold: for example, ambivalence towards meat eating, a low degree of product differentiation, high price differences between market niche programmes (organic meat with small market shares) and the dominating mainstream markets (de Jonge and van Trijp 2013). The presented survey additionally reveals the quantity–quality dilemma; that is, the limited buying power of most sustainability-oriented groups.

## 12.7 VEGETARIANS, BENIGN CARNIVORES AND SUSTAINABLE SHIFTERS

A fundamental part of sustainable meat consumption is sufficiency and moderation (Notter et al. 2013). Nevertheless, through their buying behaviour, consumers with low meat consumption and vegetarians have little influence on the quality of meat production. Their influence does not depend on loyalty, but on raising their voice in society and politics (Hirschman 1970), hence acting as 'citizen consumers'.

Meat suppliers are more oriented towards the preferences of consumers with higher levels of meat consumption. This quantity–quality dilemma is a rarely discussed but is an important characteristic of sustainable consumption. As a result, market shares of sustainable products often remain small due to the low market influence of consumers with high ethical preferences but low buying intensity.

In general, strong sustainable consumption (that is, sufficiency) provides the greatest benefits for sustainable development. Nevertheless, it may simultaneously hinder weak sustainability approaches (that is, efficiency and quality) due to the reduced consumer power of groups with ethically motivated behaviour. In this case, policy interventions are justified to close the 'citizen versus consumer gap' (Prothero et al. 2011).

## REFERENCES


Austgulen, M.H. (2014), 'Environmentally sustainable meat consumption: An analysis of the Norwegian public debate', *Journal of Consumer Policy*, 37 (1), 45–66.

Baumgartl-Simons, C. (2013), 'Über den Tierschutz zu den Tierrechten. Gedanken zur Werteentwicklung in unserer Gesellschaft', *TIERethik*, 5 (6), 9–11.

Beran, L. and H. Dyckhoff (2011), 'Biomasse als industrieller Faktor einer nachhaltigen Weltwirtschaft?', in H. Corsten and S. Roth (eds), *Nachhaltigkeit. Unternehmerisches Handeln in globaler Verantwortung*, Wiesbaden: Springer Gabler, pp. 171–190.

Boissy, A., G. Manteuffel, M.B. Jensen, R.O. Moe, B. Pruijt, L.J. Keeling, C. Winckler et al. (2007), 'Assessment of positive emotions in animals to improve their welfare', *Physiology and Behavior*, 92 (3), 375–397.

Bruinsma, J. (2009), 'The resource outlook to 2050: by how much do land, water and crop yields need increase by 2050', available at ftp://ftp.fao.org/docrep/fao/012/ak971e/ak971e00.pdf (accessed 25 October 2013).

Chao, A., M.J. Thun, C.J. Connell, M.L. McCullough, E.J. Jacobs, W.D. Flanders, C. Rodriguez et al. (2005), 'Meat consumption and risk for colorectal cancer', *Journal of the American Medical Association*, 293 (2), 172–182.

Cordts, A., N. Duman, H. Grethe, S. Nitzko and A. Spiller (2013a), 'Auswirkungen eines verminderten Konsums von tierischen Produkten in Industrieländern auf globale Marktbilanzen und Preise für Nahrungsmittel', in Edmund Rehwinkel-Stiftung der Landwirtschaftlichen Rentenbank (ed.), *Sicherung der Welternährung bei knappen Ressourcen*, Schriftenreihe der Rentenbank Band 29, pp. 103–135, available at http://orgprints.org/22744/2/Schriftenreihe_ Band29_final.pdf (accessed 12 November 2013).

Cordts, A., A. Spiller, S. Nitzko, H. Grethe and N. Duman (2013c), 'Imageprobleme beeinflussen den Konsum', *Fleischwirtschaft*, 7, 59–63.

Cordts, A., F. Wittig, B. Schulze, M. Eisinger-Watzl, T. Heuer, A. Spiller and I. Hoffmann (2013b), 'A typology comparing male organic purchasers: nutrition, health and buying behaviours', *Ernährungs Umschau International*, 60 (3), 36–42.

Dagevos, H. and J. Voordouw (2013), 'Sustainability and meat consumption: Is reduction realistic?', *Sustainability: Science, Practice, and Policy*, 9 (2), 60–69.

de Beer, M., D. Elfick and D.A. Emmerson (2011), 'Is a feed conversion ratio of 1:1 a realistic and appropriate goal for broiler chickens in the next 10 years?', *Recent Advances in Animal Nutrition – Australia*, 18, 9–16.

de Boer, J., C.T. Hoogland and J.J. Boersema (2007), 'Towards more sustainable food choices: value priorities and motivational orientations', *Food Quality and Preference*, 18 (7), 985–996.

de Jonge, J. and H.C.M. van Trijp (2013), 'Meeting heterogeneity in consumer demand for animal welfare: a reflection on existing knowledge and implications for the meat sector', *Journal of Agricultural and Environmental Ethics*, 26 (3), 629–661.

EEA (European Environment Agency) (2013), 'European Union $CO_2$ emissions: different accounting perspectives', EEA Technical report No 20/2013, available at http://www.eea.europa.eu/publications/european-union-co2-emissions-accounting/at_download/file (accessed 17 February 2014).

FAO (Food and Agriculture Organization) (2005), *Animal Welfare and the Intensification of Animal Production: An Alternative Interpretation*, Rome: Food and Agriculture Organization.

FAO (Food and Agriculture Organization) (2008), 'Food outlook: global market analysis', available at ftp://ftp.fao.org/docrep/fao/011/ai474e/ai474e00.pdf (accessed 25 October 2013).

FAO (Food and Agriculture Organization) (2009), 'How to feed the world in 2050', available at http://www.fao.org/fileadmin/templates/wsfs/docs/expert_paper/How_to_Feed_the_World_in_2050.pdf (accessed 25 October 2013).

Fiddes, N. (2011), *Meat: A Natural Symbol*, New York: Routledge.

Flachowsky, G. (2003), 'Tierernährung: Gras, Getreide, Wasser – und was noch in der Tierernährung im Jahre 2025?', *Landbauforschung Voelkenrode*, 262, 81–92.
Foer, J.S. (2009), *Eating Animals*, Boston, MA, USA: Little, Brown & Company.
FrieslandCampina (2013), 'Outdoor grazing', available at http://www.frieslandcampina.com/english/responsibility/outdoor-grazing.aspx (accessed 20 December 2013).
German Nutrition Society (DGE) (2005), '10 guidelines of the German Nutrition Society (DGE) for a wholesome diet', available at http://www.dge.de/modules.php?name=Content&pa=showpage&pid=15 (accessed 25 October 2013).
German Nutrition Society (DGE) (ed.) (2012), *12. Ernährungsbericht*, Bonn: DGE.
Godfray, H.C., J.R. Beddington, I.R. Crute, L. Haddad, D. Lawrence, J.F. Muir, J. Pretty et al. (2010), 'Food security: the challenge of feeding 9 billion people', *Science*, 327 (5967), 811–818.
Gossard, M.H. and R. York (2003), 'Social structural influences on meat consumption', *Human Ecology Review*, 10 (1), 1–9.
Grethe, H., A. Dembele, and N. Duman (eds) (2011), *How to Feed the World's Growing Billions: Understanding FAO World Food Projections and their Implications*, Berlin: WWF Germany.
Grunert, K.G. (2006), 'Future trends and consumer lifestyles with regard to meat consumption', *Meat Science*, 74, 149–160.
Haverstock, K. and D.K. Forgays (2012), 'To eat or not to eat: a comparison of current and former animal product limiters', *Appetite*, 58 (3), 1030–1036.
Hirschfelder, G. and K. Lahoda (2012), 'Wenn Menschen Tiere essen. Bemerkungen zu Geschichte, Struktur und Kultur der Mensch-Tier-Beziehungen und des Fleischkonsums', in J. Buchner-Fuhs and L. Rose (eds), *Tierische Sozialarbeit – Ein Lesebuch für die Profession zum Leben und Arbeiten mit Tieren*, Wiesbaden: VS Verlag für Sozialwissenschaften, pp. 147–166.
Hirschman, A.O. (1970), *Exit, Voice, and Loyalty: Responses to Decline in Firms, Organizations, and States*, Cambridge, MA: Harvard University Press.
Hoek, A.C., P.A. Luning, A. Stafleu and C. de Graaf (2004), 'Food-related lifestyle and health attitudes of Dutch vegetarians, non-vegetarian consumers of meat substitutes, and meat consumers', *Appetite*, 42 (3), 265–272.
Holt, E. (2011), 'Hungary to introduce broad range of taxes', *Lancet*, 378 (9793), 755.
Honikel, K.-O. (1995), 'Inhaltsstoffe von Fleisch und Fleischwaren', in Bundesanstalt für Fleischforschung (ed.), *Fleisch: Gesundheit – Tierschutz – Umwelt*, Kulmbach: Bundesanstalt für Fleischforschung, pp. 59–87.
Hu, F.B., E.B. Rimm, M.J. Stampfer, A. Ascherio, D. Spiegelman and W.C. Willett (2000), 'Prospective study of major dietary patterns and risk for coronary heart disease in men', *American Journal of Clinical Nutrition*, 72 (4), 912–921.
Jahn, G., M. Schramm and A. Spiller (2005), 'The reliability of certification: quality labels as a consumer policy tool', *Journal of Consumer Policy*, 28 (1), 53–73.
Kiefer, I., T. Rathmanner and M. Kunze (2005), 'Eating and dieting differences in men and women', *Journal of Men's Health and Gender*, 2 (2), 194–201.
Kornum, B.R. and G.M. Knudsen (2011), 'Cognitive testing of pigs (Sus scrofa) in translational biobehavioral research', *Neuroscience and Biobehavioral Reviews*, 35 (3), 437–451.
Lambin, E.F. and P. Meyfroidt (2011), 'Global land use change, economic globalization, and the looming land scarcity', *Proceedings of the National Academy of the United States of America*, 108 (9), 3465–3472.
Liao, H. and W.S. Chern (2007), 'A dynamic analysis of food demand patterns in urban China', available at http://ageconsearch.umn.edu/bitstream/9770/1/sp07li09.pdf (accessed 12 November 2013).
Lombardini, C. and L. Lankoski (2013), 'Forced choice restriction in promoting sustainable food consumption: intended and unintended effects of the Mandatory Vegetarian Day in Helsinki schools', *Journal of Consumer Policy*, 36 (2), 159–178.
Lusk, J.L. and F.B. Norwood (2011), 'Animal welfare economics', *Applied Economic Perspectives and Policy*, 33 (4), 463–483.
McMahan, J. (2008), 'Eating animals the nice way', *Daedalus*, 137 (1), 66–76.
McMichael, A.J., J.W. Powles, C.D. Butler and R. Uauy (2007), 'Food, livestock production, energy, climate change, and health', *Lancet*, 370 (9594), 1253–1263.
Micha, R., S.K. Wallace and D. Mozaffarian (2010), 'Red and processed meat consumption and risk of incident coronary heart disease, stroke, and diabetes mellitus: a systematic review and meta-analysis', *Circulation*, 121 (21), 2271–2283.
Miele, M., I. Veissier, A. Evans and R. Botreau (2011), 'Animal welfare: establishing a dialogue between science and society', *Animal Welfare*, 20, 103–117.
Ministerie van Economische Zaken (2013), 'Monitor Duurzaam Voedsel 2012', available at http://www.rijksoverheid.nl/documenten-en-publicaties/rapporten/2013/06/11/monitor-duurzaam-voedsel-2012.html (accessed 30 October 2013).

Naylor, R., H. Steinfeld, W. Falcon, J. Galloway, V. Smil, E. Bradford, J. Alder and H. Mooney (2005), 'Losing the links between livestock and land', *Science*, 310 (1621), 1621–1622.
Nordgren, A. (2012), 'Ethical issues in mitigation of climate change: the option of reduced meat production and consumption', *Journal of Agricultural Environmental Ethics*, 25, 563–584.
Notter, D.A., R. Meyer and H.-J. Althaus (2013), 'The western lifestyle and the long way to sustainability', *Environmental Science and Technology*, 47 (9), 4014–4021.
Perrin, A.E., C. Simon, G. Hedelin, D. Arveiler, P. Schaffer and J.L. Schlienger (2002), 'Ten-year trends of dietary intake in a middle-aged French population: relationship with educational level', *European Journal of Clinical Nutrition*, 56 (5), 393–401.
Peters, C.J., J.L. Wilkins and G.W. Fick (2007), 'Testing a complete-diet model for estimating the land resource requirements of food consumption and agricultural carrying capacity – the New York State example', *Renewable Agriculture and Food Systems*, 22 (2), 145–153.
Prättälä, R., L. Paalanen, D. Grinberga, V. Helasoja, A. Kasmel and J. Petkeviciene (2006), 'Gender differences in the consumption of meat, fruit and vegetables are similar in Finland and the Baltic countries', *European Journal of Public Health*, 17 (5), 520–525.
Prothero, A., S. Dobscha, J. Freund, W.E. Kilbourne, M.G. Luchs, L.K. Ozanne and J. Thøgersen (2011), 'Sustainable consumption: opportunities for consumer research and public policy', *Journal of Public Policy and Marketing*, 30 (1), 31–38.
Reisch, L.A., U. Eberle and S. Lorek (2013), 'Sustainable food consumption: an overview of contemporary issues and policies', *Sustainability: Science, Practice and Policy*, 9 (2), 7–25.
Ridoutt, B.G., P. Sanguansri, M. Nolan and N. Marks (2012), 'Meat consumption and water scarcity: beware of generalizations', *Journal of Cleaner Production*, 28, 127–133.
Ruby, M.B. (2012), 'Vegetarism: a blossoming field of study', *Appetite*, 58 (1), 141–150.
Schröder, M.J.A. and G. McEachern (2004), 'Consumer value conflicts surrounding ethical food purchase decisions: a focus on animal welfare', *International Journal of Consumer Studies*, 28 (2), 168–177.
Singer, P. (1975), *Animal Liberation – A New Ethics for our Treatment of Animals*, London: Jonathan Cape.
Sneddon, L.U. (2009), 'Pain perception in fish: indicators and endpoints', *ILAR Journal*, 40 (4), 338–342.
Snowdon, C. (2013), 'The proof of the pudding: Denmark's fat tax fiasco', Institute of Economic Affairs, available at http://www.iea.org.uk/sites/default/files/publications/files/The%20Proof%20of%20the%20Pudding.pdf (accessed 14 February 2014).
Song, Y., J.E. Manson, J.E. Buring and S. Liu (2004), 'A prospective study of red meat consumption and Type 2 Diabetes in middle-aged and elderly woman', *Diabetes Care*, 27 (9), 2108–2115.
Steinfeld, H., P. Gerber, T. Wassenaar, V. Castel, M. Rosalesm and C. de Haan (2006), 'Livestock's long shadow: environmental issues and options', Rome: Food and Agriculture Organization of the United Nations, available at http://www.fao.org/docrep/010/a0701e/a0701e00.HTM (accessed 10 February 2013).
Stehfest, E., L. Bouwman, D.P. Van Vuuren, M.G.J. Den Elzen, B. Eickhout and P. Kabat (2009), 'Climate benefits of changing diet', *Climatic Change*, 95 (1–2), 83–102.
Strahm, R.H. (1995), *Warum wir so arm sind – Arbeitsbuch zur Entwicklung der Unterentwicklung in der Dritten Welt*, Wuppertal: Hammer.
Sullivan, S.P. (2013), 'Empowering market regulation of agricultural animal welfare through product labeling', *Animal Law Review*, 19 (2), 391–422.
Sutton, C. and S. Dibb (2013), 'Prime cut: valuing the meat we eat', Discussion Paper for WWF-UK and the Food Ethics Council.
Sutton, M.A., A. Bleeker, C.M. Howard, M. Bekunda, B. Grizzetti et al. (2013), 'Our nutrient world: the challenge to produce more food and energy with less pollution. Global overview of nutrient management', Centre for Ecology and Hydrology, Edinburgh on behalf of the Global Partnership on Nutrient Management and the International Nitrogen Initiative, available at http://initrogen.org/uploads/rte/ONW.pdf (accessed 1 January 2014).
Tänzler, D., A. Schulz and A. Carisus (2005), 'Nachhaltigkeit und Verbraucherpolitik: Ansätze und Maßnahmen in anderen Ländern', available at http://download.ble.de/04hs049.pdf (accessed 10 February 2013).
Thaler, R.H. and C.R. Sunstein (2003). 'Libertarian paternalism', *American Economic Review*, 93 (2), 175–179.
Thaler, R.H. and C.R. Sunstein (2008), *Nudge: Improving Decisions about Health, Wealth, and Happiness*, New Haven, CT: Yale University Press.
Thunström, L. and J. Nordström (2013), 'The impact of meal attributes and nudging on healthy meal consumption', *Modern Economy*, 4 (10a), 1–8.
Tobler, C., V.H.M. Visschers and M. Siegrist (2011), 'Eating green: consumers' willingness to adopt ecological food consumption behaviors', *Appetite*, 57 (3), 674–682.
Tuyttens, F., M. Heyndrickx, M. de Boeck, A. Mareels, A. van Nuffel, E. van Poucke, E. van Coillie et al. (2008), 'Broiler chicken health, welfare and fluctuating asymmetry in organic versus conventional production systems', *Livestock Sciences*, 113 (2–3), 123–132.

USDA (United States Department of Agriculture) (2006), 'Poultry yearbook', available at http://usda.mannlib.cornell.edu/MannUsda/viewDocumentInfo.do?documentID=1367 (accessed 5 September 2013).
Vergnaud, A.-C., T. Norat, D. Romaguera, T. Mouw, A.M. May, N. Travier, J. Luan et al. (2011), 'Meat consumption and prospective weight change in participants of the EPIC-PANACEA study', *American Journal of Clinical Nutrition*, 92 (2), 664–664.
Villanueva, T. (2011), 'European Nations launch tax attack on unhealthy foods', *Canadian Medical Association Journal*, 183 (17), E1229–E1230.
von Alvensleben, R. and G. Mahlau (1998), 'The decline of the meat image and consequences for the meat marketing in Germany', available at http://orgprints.org/1652/1/imagec.pdf (accessed 30 October 2013).
von Koerber, K. and J. Kretschmer (2000), 'Sustainable nutrition – health, environmental, economic and social compatibility in the food sector', *Zeitschrift für Ernährungsoekologie*, 1 (1), 39–46.
WBVE/WBA (2011), 'Politikstrategie Food Labelling', available at http://www.bmelv.de/SharedDocs/Downloads/Ministerium/Beiraete/Verbraucherpolitik/2011_10_PolitikstrategieFoodLabelling.pdf?__blob=publicationFile (accessed 6 January 2014).
Wahlen, S., E. Heiskanen and K. Aslto (2012), 'Endorsing sustainable food consumption: prospects from public catering', *Journal of Consumer Policy*, 35 (1), 7–21.
Webster, A.J.F. (2001), 'Farm animal welfare: the five freedoms and the free market', *Veterinary Journal*, 161 (3), 229–237.
Wibbecke, A.-L. (2013), *Tier-Mensch-Pädagogik: Analyse einer Integration von Tierrechten in die Pädagogik*, Wiesbaden: Springer.
Witte, W. (2000), 'Selective pressure by antibiotic use in livestock', *International Journal of Antimicrobial Agents*, 16 (Supplement 1), S19–S24.
World Cancer Research Fund and American Institute for Cancer Research (2007), 'Second expert report, food, nutrition, physical activity, and the prevention of cancer: a global perspective', available at http://www.dietandcancerreport.org/cancer_resource_center/downloads/chapters/chapter_12.pdf (accessed 30 October 2013).

# 13. Flexitarianism: a range of sustainable food styles

*Muriel Verain, Hans Dagevos and Gerrit Antonides*

People who don't abstain from meat as a matter of principle may still eat less of it.
(Steven Pinker, *The Better Angels of our Nature*, 2011, p. 472)

A shift in Western meat consumption patterns could significantly reduce the ecological effects of the food system. The consumption of meat accounts for a large proportion of the ecological footprint of consumers. Therefore reduction of meat consumption is important in making more sustainable food choices. Although the average consumer may not consider meat consumption as a highly relevant sustainability issue, in scholarly thinking the ecological effects and energy-intensiveness of meat consumption and production have been acknowledged for more than 20 years. As a result of the worldwide rising levels of meat consumption and production, experts increasingly express urgent reasons to adjust meat consumption to more sustainable levels. Although discussions on more sustainable food consumption patterns are mainly focused on meat reduction, from a sustainability perspective a transition is needed towards a diet that is less dependent on all types of animal proteins, including dairy, eggs and fish (see Reisch et al. 2013; Tukker et al. 2011; Westhoek et al. 2011). A switch towards less animal-based and more plant-based diets would not only benefit the sustainability of our diets, but also positively affect consumer health (see Van Dooren et al. 2014).

Sustainability in the food system is a matter of both production and consumption (McMeekin and Southerton 2012), hence it is doubtful that technological innovations to reduce unsustainable aspects of animal production and livestock systems will be sufficient to overcome environmental problems. Therefore we stress the importance of taking into account consumers as possible change agents. Consumers have the ability and inclination to adopt more environmentally friendly food styles by making more sustainable food choices, and developing more sustainable food consumption patterns. But it would be naive to think that adopting a more sustainable food style would be easily realized, even for those consumers who are highly motivated. In addition to consumers' willingness to change their diets, structural constraints that influence the change possibilities are important to study. Such constraints include the material conditions of choice (availability, affordability, and so on) as well as opportunities and obstacles in the form of intangible 'codes of conduct' (cultural values, social norms, institutional support, advertising, and so on) (see Dolan 2002; Vinnari and Vinnari 2014). It is important to keep this contextualization of consumption in mind with respect to sustainable consumption in general (see also Jackson 2005) as well as, more specifically, with respect to meat production and consumption, given their central position to the food system and the central place of meat on our plates.

Our objective in this research is to improve understanding of meat consumption reducers (flexitarians) by identifying and describing clusters of (food) consumers who differ in the type of flexitarianism. Empirical results will be presented about consumer opinions concerning meat consumption and meat reduction. This study focuses on symbolic ethical variables beyond an 'economic' view implying rational choice, utility value and functionality of consumer goods. We believe that food consumption cannot be understood completely by rational behavioural determinants. Particularly with respect to sustainable food consumption, moral beliefs or ethical concerns cannot be omitted. Strikingly enough, suggestions to modify the well-known 'theory of planned behaviour' and the Food Choice Questionnaire have focused on the incorporation of so-called consumer concerns (for example, animal welfare, fair trade, environmental protection) in order to improve our understanding of (sustainable) food consumption (see Dowd and Burke 2013; Fotopoulos et al. 2009; Lindeman and Väänänen 2000; Raats et al. 1995).

Although consumer concerns could be seen as altruistic, other-oriented or pro-social, at the other end of the spectrum more hedonistic and egoistic or pro-self considerations could also motivate sustainable consumption. Self-interest motives should not be excluded from discussions about sustainable behaviour and behavioural change. The idea of 'green to be seen' offers (controversial) avenues for consumers to move in more sustainable directions (Griskevicius et al. 2010). We can only pay limited attention to these discussions about 'conspicuous sustainable consumption' by including status in our analytic framework as a perceived symbolic value of meat.

In section 13.1, we present definitions and describe several types of flexitarianism, summarize various motives behind flexitarianism, and describe several pathways aimed at achieving a flexitarian food style. Section 13.2 presents our empirical study and the results. Section 13.3 provides conclusions and a discussion.

## 13.1 FLEXITARIANISM AS A SUSTAINABLE FOOD STYLE

### 13.1.1 Flexitarianism and Food Styles

After the emergence of the word 'flexitarianism' at the beginning of this century, the term evolved from a definition of a vegetarian consumption pattern, occasionally including meat products, to a broader interpretation of reduced meat consumption without avoiding meat altogether. Seen from this perspective, 'flexitarianism' is a new term that can be found in the literature under different synonyms. For example Fox and Ward (2008) talk about 'partial vegetarians'. Janda and Trocchia (2001) study 'pseudo-vegetarians', defined as people who abstain from meat-based products, but occasionally eat some meat. Beardsworth and Keil (1991, 1992) identified 'type I vegetarians', who consider themselves vegetarian, but occasionally consume red meat or poultry, for example when vegetarian food options are unavailable or in cases where they want to avoid embarrassment in social settings where meat is being served. Rothgerber (2014) studies consumers who identify themselves as vegetarians but who report eating animal flesh occasionally, to varying degrees, and labels these consumers 'semi-vegetarians'. Baker et al. (2002) study meat reducers, reporting that they consciously endeavour to reduce the amount of meat they eat. And finally Povey et al. (2001) distinguish a group of meat avoiders who abstain from eating meat but who do eat fish.

The above-mentioned varieties of meat reducers show that the differences between flexitarian and vegetarian categories are gradual. However, it is clear that to many contemporary consumers the total elimination of meat from the diet (vegetarianism) is less acceptable than meat reduction (flexitarianism), implying either the substitution of meat with other protein-rich types of food or no substitution at all. Every food consumer who abstains from eating meat at least one day a week may be called a flexitarian, regardless of the reason for abstention.

### 13.1.2 Motives for Meat Eating, Meat Reduction and Meat Avoidance

Flexitarianism is not necessarily a stepping stone towards vegetarianism (Baker et al. 2002) and can be regarded as a 'food style', a certain style or culture of eating, including a broad range of attitudes and activities related to food (see Askegaard and Madsen 1998; Korthals 2012). Food styles are not mutually exclusive and overlap to some degree. Two consumers who consume the same kind of foods may have completely different motivations. For example a vegetarian food style may be motivated by health benefits, by environmental concerns and/or by concerns for animal welfare. In order to gain a better understanding of flexitarian behaviour, it is important to obtain insights into underlying motives for meat curtailment. As research on flexitarianism is very limited, it can be helpful to place flexitarianism on a spectrum with vegetarianism at one end and a meat-centred diet at the other, and investigate both poles. The main motives for vegetarianism are moral and ethical beliefs and concerns about animal welfare and the killing of animals, followed by health reasons. Other motives are environmental concern, disgust with eating meat, religion and aspirations to belong to a reference group (Fox and Ward 2008; Hoek et al. 2004; Janda and Trocchia 2001; Lea and Worsley 2001; Povey et al. 2001; Rozin et al. 1997; Ruby 2012). The main motives for eating meat are perceived healthiness, taste appreciation and eating enjoyment, as well as the unwillingness to change eating habits, value for money or the appeal of such product characteristics as lean, easy to prepare or safe to eat (see Lea and Worsley 2003; Povey et al. 2001; Verbeke and Viaene 1999). In addition, meat is perceived as a symbol of power, status and masculinity (Rothgerber 2012; Rozin et al. 2012; Ruby and Heine 2011).

With respect to environmental concern, flexitarians are much more similar to meat eaters than to vegetarians (Janda and Trocchia 2001). Rothgerber (2014) has found that semi-vegetarians, who eat meat occasionally, express more liking for meat, are less disgusted by meat and have less emotional resistance to meat consumption compared to vegetarians, but they experience more feelings of guilt compared to meat eaters. Motivations for this flexitarian behaviour are evenly divided between health, ethics and a combination of both these aspects.

### 13.1.3 Meat Reduction Studies

Given the growing awareness and concern in the past few decades about meat products as energy-intensive and ecologically burdensome foods, it is notable that only few scholars have addressed the moderation of meat consumption as a topic of research. Notable early exceptions are Richardson et al. (1994a, 1994b) and Baker et al. (2002) in the UK, and more recently, a few Northern European studies (Latvala et al. 2012; Nordgren 2012; Vinnari et al. 2010). Also in the Netherlands flexitarians have been newly studied

(Dagevos 2014; Dagevos and Voordouw 2013; De Bakker and Dagevos 2012; Schösler et al. 2012).

Three studies on meat reduction are worth mentioning, as they relate to our empirical work. Latvala et al. (2012) investigated meat consumption patterns in Finland. Six consumer segments, categorized into three cluster blocks, were identified: the first cluster block (48 per cent) has no intention to change their established meat consumption pattern; the second cluster block (13 per cent) has made a shift toward less meat and more vegetable consumption in the past year; the third cluster block (39 per cent) consists of consumers who are in the middle of a change towards a reduction in the use of meat and an increase in the use of vegetables. The most important overall reason for change was healthiness. Environmental concern and animal welfare are important reasons for change in some clusters, particularly in the cluster with the intention to decrease their meat consumption in all meat categories and increase their vegetable consumption.

Hoek et al. (2004) categorized their respondents as vegetarians, consumers of meat substitutes (non-vegetarians) or meat consumers. They found that the group of meat substitute consumers had a socio-demographic profile comparable to vegetarians, but their food-related lifestyle and health attitudes mainly were in-between those of vegetarians and meat eaters.

Vanhonacker et al. (2013) identified five distinct consumer clusters or segments which can be differentiated on the basis of their meat consumption frequency. The so-called 'conscious' and 'unwilling' segments (41 per cent of the sample) have the highest meat consumption frequency and the 'active' segment (19 per cent of the sample) reports the lowest meat consumption frequency and the highest incidence of consuming less meat per meal. This Flemish sample confirms that meat eating prevails and meat reduction is still in its infancy.

### 13.1.4 Pathways Towards a Flexitarian Food Style

In the literature, several behavioural strategies towards more sustainable food consumption are discussed. Insights into these distinct pathways can be helpful in identifying, understanding and stimulating several types of flexitarianism. The two main pathways that are often distinguished are minor adjustments to habitual consumption patterns (weak sustainable consumption) and undertaking radical transformations (strong sustainable consumption). Flexitarians following the first pathway choose products that are less burdening for the environment (for example, hybrid meat products), whereas the latter make fundamental changes in consumption patterns (for example, substantial reduction of consumption levels of meat) (Fuchs and Lorek 2005; Lorek and Fuchs 2013; Scholl et al. 2010; see also De Bakker and Dagevos 2012). These two pathways differ in both quality – consuming differently and efficiently; and quantity – consuming less. Alternatively the distinction may be reformulated by contrasting an (eco-)efficiency approach and a sufficiency approach (Boulanger 2010), in which the first puts emphasis on meat reduction strategies through consumers opting for sustainably produced meat products or low-meat products, while the second stresses behavioural dietary change by consumers. Alternatively, the first approach may be called product-related consumption, the second act-related consumption (Verain et al. 2012).

Two studies identified pathways to reduce meat consumption more specifically. Schösler et al. (2012) identify four pathways towards meat substitution. The first and most difficult path entails challenging existing meal formats and food hierarchies. It is about food choices that deviate from the cultural norm and require breaking with conventional diets, such as the use of tofu or lentils instead of meat. Eating in a 'different', more sustainable way can become important to one's identity. The second pathway entails an incremental change towards more health-conscious vegetarian meals by replacing meat with other 'regular' products such as fish, eggs and cheese. As these meat alternatives are still animal-based, this route is not very promising in terms of sustainability, but can be a first step in a shift towards a more plant-based diet. The third pathway contains meat substitution in convenience food. Meat is already less visible in most convenience products compared to traditional meals and therefore can be substituted easily. The last pathway entails reducing meat portion size. This pathway should be seen as an addition to substitution-oriented pathways.

De Bakker and Dagevos (2012) identify three broader routes to moderating meat consumption. The first one is labelled 'sustainability by stealth' and entails the acceptance of rather unnoticeable sustainable food innovations. An example is the incorporation of plant products in meat products to form more sustainable hybrid products. This rather technological route is particularly suitable for uninvolved or passive consumers. This route is most similar to the third pathway discussed by Schösler et al. (2012), the convenience-oriented path. The second route involves social debate and small practical steps towards more sustainable food consumption such as meat reduction through moderating meat portion size and/or incorporation of meatless days. This route requires at least moderately involved consumers and is similar to the fourth pathway identified by Schösler et al. (2012). The third route, involving cultural change, is an extension of the second route. This route includes lifestyle alternatives that are structurally different from current consumption practices. Cultural values need to be changed. This route requires high food involvement and ethical motives and is related most to the first pathway identified by Schösler et al. (2012).

Next, the results of an empirical survey will be presented. Section 13.2.2 provides detailed analysis of meat consumption clusters based on their motives and opinions about meat consumption.

## 13.2 EMPIRICAL SURVEY

### 13.2.1 Method

The survey was conducted in October 2011 in a sample of 1312 individuals, randomly drawn from a panel of a Dutch marketing research agency (see also Dagevos 2014; Dagevos and Voordouw 2013). The panel is representative for the Netherlands with respect to gender, age and education level. Since vegetarians and vegans do not consume meat at all, and therefore do not fall within the definition of flexitarians, they were removed from the data set, resulting in 1253 individuals eligible for analysis. Fifty per cent of the sample were male, about 50 per cent were older than 45 years of age, 33 per cent had obtained higher education, 23 per cent lived in a one-person household,

39 per cent lived in a two-person household, and 38 per cent lived in households with three or more persons.

The participants completed an online questionnaire including questions concerning current meat consumption (number of days per week), meat consumption increase in the past year and intended meat consumption increase in the next year (both measured on a seven-point scale running from 1 'Much less meat' to 7 'Much more meat', and 4 indicating no change). Further questions related to norms, perceptions and opinions concerning meat consumption and meat substitution. All answers were given on a seven-point Likert scale (1 = 'Totally disagree' to 7 = 'Totally agree').

Personal norms concerning meat consumption reduction (Cronbach's Alpha = 0.86), were operationalized through two items: 'Because of my own values and norms, I feel morally obliged to eat less meat' and 'It is important that people in general eat less meat'.

Perceived positive health effects of reduced meat consumption (Cronbach's Alpha = 0.89), were operationalized through four items: 'Eating meat is unhealthy', 'Meat causes heart diseases', 'Meat causes cancer' and 'Meat fattens'.

Perceived status of meat consumption (Cronbach's Alpha = 0.70), was operationalized through four items: 'Eating meat is "cool"', 'By eating meat, I feel I am on top of the food chain', 'Eating meat gives one status' and 'By eating less meat I feel myself as being unworthy'.

Appreciation of meatless meals (Cronbach's Alpha = 0.70), was operationalized through three items: 'The day after a barbeque with meat, I eat less meat', 'I like a meal without meat' and 'It is easy to prepare a tasty meal without meat'.

Need for meat consumption (Cronbach's Alpha = 0.72), was operationalized through two items: 'After a day without meat I feel extra need for meat' and 'If I do not eat meat for a whole day, I feel weaker'.

Importance of environment and animal-friendliness (Cronbach's Alpha = 0.82), was operationalized through three items: 'If I buy meat I want to know it has been produced in an animal-friendly way', 'If I buy meat I want to know it has been produced in an environmentally friendly way' and 'Animal well-being is important to me'.

Dislike of animals as a source of meat (Cronbach's Alpha = 0.60), was operationalized through two items: 'The idea that meat comes from animals gives me an unhappy feeling' and 'I can accept that meat comes from animals' (reverse scored).

Two single items dealt with spending money on meat: 'Meat is not expensive' and 'Meat is worth its money'.

To reduce the influence of answering tendencies, the scales were centred before the cluster analysis, by subtracting the average scale score of each respondent from that individual's raw scale scores. In addition to the above-stated questions, several questions concerning the strategy on how to reduce meat and food neophobia were asked. Finally several questions concerning responsibility for societal action on meat reduction (for example, own responsibility, government, supermarkets, societal organizations), and the type of actions that should be taken (for example, taxes, campaigns, increase availability of meat alternatives), were included.

### 13.2.2 Results

In order to cluster the sample based on norms, perceptions and opinions concerning meat consumption, cluster analysis was conducted based on the constructs mentioned above, except for information about meat consumption, the type of meat substitution, the opinions about who should take responsibility in bringing about changes in meat consumption and food neophobia, which were used to profile the clusters. This approach was chosen because consumption is assumed to result from associations with meat. If the clusters are to be used in sustainable policy making aimed at reducing meat consumption, the variables to be influenced should be norms, perceptions and opinions. The clusters were then profiled on current meat consumption, intention to reduce meat consumption and socio-demographic variables.

Hierarchical agglomerative cluster analysis was conducted using Ward's method, minimizing the squared deviations from the cluster means of all input variables. Inspection of the dendrogram – a figure indicating the relative distance of the clusters – and judging the feasibility of the cluster solution for interpretation led to five clusters. With more than five clusters, the clusters became much less distinctive; with less than five clusters, important information distinguishing the clusters seemed to be lost. The resulting clusters were profiled with univariate analyses of variance (ANOVAs) (with post hoc Tukey comparisons of mean scores) and cross-tabulations (with Pearson $\chi^2$) to test for significant differences between the identified segments on the segmentation and profiling variables.

Although the cluster analysis was based on the centred scale values, Table 13.1 reports the uncentred average values of the scales to facilitate the interpretation of the results. We observe that meat consumption is the lowest in cluster 3 which scores the most favourable on norms, perceptions and opinions regarding meat reduction and has the highest percentage of females. Cluster 4 scores the highest on meat consumption, followed by cluster 1, but these clusters differ in personal norms, status, appreciation of meatless meals, need for meat consumption, importance attached to the environment and animal friendliness, and dislike of animals as source of meat. Clusters 2 and 5 score in-between on meat consumption but differ on status, appreciation of meatless meals, the need for meat, dislike of animals as a source of meat, and on the money values, as indicated by superscripts in Table 13.1. Gender and age differed significantly across the clusters. Education level, income and family size were not significantly different and are not reported in Table 13.1. Next, the clusters will be described in more detail.

**Cluster 1, meat lovers (22.2 per cent)**

This cluster considers meat as relatively inexpensive and worth the money. The 'light' flexitarians in this cluster do not appreciate meatless meals much and do not dislike animals as a source of meat. They have relatively high current meat consumption (about five days a week), which has remained the same in the past and will remain the same in the future. The percentage of males is relatively high, the 46–65 years age class is relatively large and the youngest age group is relatively small. On the other variables, this cluster does not differ very much from the other clusters. However, cluster 1 differs from cluster 4, the other high meat consumption cluster, in that they appreciate meatless meals a bit more, and do not express a high need for meat consumption.

*Table 13.1 Cluster variable means, reported meat consumption, gender and age by cluster*

| | Clusters | | | | | |
|---|---|---|---|---|---|---|
| Segmentation variables (scales) | 1 | 2 | 3 | 4 | 5 | Total |
| Personal norm to consume less meat | 2.01[a] | 3.44[b] | 5.19[c] | 1.61[d] | 3.52[b] | 3.30 |
| Perceived positive health effects of less meat | 2.25[a] | 3.17[b] | 3.78[c] | 2.02[a] | 2.61[d] | 2.92 |
| Status of meat consumption | 2.00[a] | 2.87[b] | 1.65[c] | 2.94[b] | 1.66[c] | 2.33 |
| Appreciation of meatless meal | 3.33[a] | 3.88[b] | 5.59[c] | 2.27[d] | 5.49[c] | 4.10 |
| Need for meat consumption | 2.45[a] | 3.36[b] | 1.58[c] | 4.98[d] | 1.38[c] | 2.77 |
| Importance of environment/animal friendliness | 4.21[a] | 4.08[a,b] | 5.36[c] | 3.79[b] | 4.42[a] | 4.36 |
| Dislike of animals as source of meat | 1.92[a] | 3.07[b] | 3.36[b] | 1.55[c] | 1.74[a,c] | 2.60 |
| Meat is not expensive | 3.94[a] | 3.33[b] | 2.57[c] | 3.82[a] | 4.52[d] | 3.48 |
| Meat is worth its money | 5.63[a] | 4.13[b] | 3.78[c] | 5.94[a] | 5.18[d] | 4.67 |
| Reported meat consumption and intentions | | | | | | |
| Days of meat consumption per week | 5.17[a] | 4.58[b] | 3.54[c] | 5.87[d] | 4.35[b] | 4.61 |
| Increase of meat consumption last year | 3.92[a] | 3.57[b] | 2.92[c] | 4.09[a] | 3.39[b] | 3.55 |
| Intention of meat consumption increase next year | 3.94[a] | 3.64[b] | 3.00[c] | 4.17[a] | 3.50[b] | 3.62 |
| Socio-demographic variables | | | | | | |
| Male (%) | 57.2[a,b] | 52.5[b] | 31.7[c] | 68.9[a] | 38.0[c] | 49.6 |
| Age 18–29 years (%) | 14.7[a] | 25.5[b] | 15.9[a] | 18.9[a,b] | 19.0[a,b] | 20.0 |
| Age 30–45 years (%) | 28.8[a] | 33.1[a] | 28.9[a] | 32.0[a] | 27.3[a] | 30.6 |
| Age 46–65 years (%) | 46.4[a] | 31.5[b] | 44.3[a] | 41.8[a,b] | 42.1[a,b] | 39.3 |
| Age 65+ years (%) | 10.1[a] | 9.9[a] | 11.0[a] | 7.4[a] | 11.6[a] | 10.1 |
| Cluster size (%) | 22.2 | 38.8 | 19.6 | 9.7 | 9.7 | 100 |

*Notes:* a – d. In each row, different superscripts indicate significantly different cluster means or column proportions, respectively ($p < 0.05$).

**Cluster 2, unconscious flexitarians (38.8 per cent)**

This cluster scores relatively high on dislike of animals as a source of meat, and together with cluster 4 scores the highest on status derived from meat consumption. Its level of meat consumption is average. The 46–65 years age group is slightly under-represented in this cluster of 'medium' flexitarians. They differ from cluster 5, the other cluster of 'medium' flexitarians, in that they derive more status from meat consumption, appreciate meatless meals less, need meat less, dislike animals as a source of meat more, find meat more expensive and less worth its money. Cluster 2 is the largest cluster, and it seems they are willing to consider alternatives for meat, most likely the cheaper ones.

**Cluster 3, conscious flexitarians (19.6 per cent)**

This cluster's answers to the questionnaire indicate relatively positive attitudes towards reduced meat consumption. It has the lowest frequency of weekly meat consumption, on average 3.5 days per week. Many food consumers in this cluster of 'heavy' flexitarians have reduced meat consumption in the past and will reduce it further in the future. Sixty-eight per cent are women; the youngest age group is under-represented, whereas the 46–65 years age group is slightly over-represented.

**Cluster 4, compulsive meat consumers (9.7 per cent)**
This cluster's answers to the questionnaire indicate negative attitudes towards reduced meat consumption. In contrast with cluster 1, the other 'light' flexitarian cluster, they do not appreciate meatless meals, and express a higher need for meat. Sixty-nine per cent are males. This cluster has the highest meat consumption on average, about six times per week, which is stable over time. This cluster reports a high need for meat and does not seem to be willing to consider meat alternatives at all. In other words, the level of flexitarianism in this cluster is very 'light' and more a matter of coincidence than commitment.

**Cluster 5, potential flexitarians (9.7 per cent)**
This cluster hardly derives status from meat consumption, seems to appreciate meatless meals and has a low need for meat. It has an average level of meat consumption. These factors differ positively with respect to reduced meat consumption from those in cluster 2, the other cluster of 'medium' flexitarians. However they less often dislike animals as a source of meat, and find meat less expensive and more worth its money than cluster 2. Sixty-two per cent are female. This cluster might consider meat alternatives, especially because of environmental and animal welfare reasons.

**Analysis**
With regard to the consumption of meat alternatives, it appears that fish, eggs, cheese, 'no alternative', mushrooms, pulses, vegetarian burgers, nuts and tofu are used as meat substitutes in decreasing order (see Table 13.2). This order is more or less similar across the clusters, and calls to mind the hierarchy of foods (Twigg 1983; see also Dagevos and Voordouw 2013). It is notable that meat reduction without substitution for an alternative is even more likely than substitution by mushrooms, pulses, vegetarian burgers, nuts and tofu.

Regarding preferences for meat alternatives, differences across the clusters exist, except for fish, which is the most preferred alternative to meat in all clusters. Eggs and cheese are preferred almost equally by the potential flexitarians (cluster 5) and the conscious flexitarians (cluster 3). Eggs seem to be somehow acceptable in the other clusters, even to the compulsive meat consumers (cluster 4). Cheese, mushrooms and pulses seem to be acceptable alternatives in both the conscious flexitarian (cluster 3) and the potential flexitarian cluster (cluster 5).

With regard to the way of reducing meat, there is a striking difference between conscious flexitarians in cluster 3 and potential flexitarians in cluster 5, and the other clusters. Conscious flexitarians and potential flexitarians indicate much more often that they use meat substitutes and that they leave meat out of the meal entirely. These clusters are also most open to consuming smaller meat portions, although this way to reduce meat consumption is also used by unconscious flexitarians. Interestingly, among conscious flexitarians leaving meat out of the meal entirely is used more than lowering portion size, whereas for potential flexitarians and unconscious flexitarians, the difference in these two

*Table 13.2 Meat alternatives and meat reduction behaviour*

| | Clusters | | | | | |
|---|---|---|---|---|---|---|
| Meat alternatives (%) | 1 | 2 | 3 | 4 | 5 | Total |
| Fish | $68.3^{a}$ | $64.9^{a}$ | $70.1^{a}$ | $72.1^{a}$ | $73.0^{a}$ | 68.2 |
| Egg | $44.1^{a}$ | $53.0^{a,b}$ | $57.7^{b}$ | $50.0^{a,b}$ | $58.6^{a,b}$ | 52.7 |
| Cheese | $29.2^{a}$ | $27.0^{a}$ | $35.5^{a}$ | $19.1^{a}$ | $34.2^{a}$ | 29.7 |
| No alternative | $23.3^{a,b}$ | $19.9^{b}$ | $31.2^{a}$ | $20.6^{a,b}$ | $31.5^{a,b}$ | 24.5 |
| Mushroom | $14.9^{a,b}$ | $15.4^{b}$ | $31.6^{c}$ | $10.3^{a,b}$ | $27.0^{a,c}$ | 20.0 |
| Pulses | $11.4^{a}$ | $15.7^{a}$ | $26.9^{b}$ | $13.2^{a,b}$ | $21.6^{a,b}$ | 17.9 |
| Vegetarian burger | $7.9^{a,b}$ | $15.7^{b}$ | $29.5^{c}$ | $2.9^{a}$ | $16.2^{a,b,c}$ | 16.5 |
| Nuts | $5.4^{a}$ | $6.3^{a}$ | $15.4^{b}$ | $4.4^{a,b}$ | $8.1^{a,b}$ | 8.3 |
| Tofu | $3.0^{a}$ | $7.3^{a,b}$ | $14.1^{b}$ | $4.4^{a,b}$ | $7.2^{a,b}$ | 7.8 |
| Other | $4.0^{a}$ | $4.8^{a}$ | $3.8^{a}$ | $11.8^{a}$ | $4.5^{a}$ | 4.8 |
| Evaluation of meat alternative | | | | | | |
| Fish | $5.78^{a,b}$ | $5.28^{a}$ | $6.02^{b}$ | $5.33^{a}$ | $6.13^{b}$ | 5.62 |
| Egg | $4.38^{a}$ | $4.38^{a}$ | $5.28^{b}$ | $4.06^{a}$ | $5.31^{b}$ | 4.61 |
| Cheese | $3.88^{a}$ | $3.84^{a,b}$ | $4.70^{c}$ | $3.35^{b}$ | $4.50^{c}$ | 4.04 |
| Pulses | $3.14^{a}$ | $3.48^{a}$ | $4.63^{b}$ | $2.55^{c}$ | $4.40^{b}$ | 3.63 |
| Mushrooms | $3.16^{a,b}$ | $3.36^{a}$ | $4.64^{c}$ | $2.70^{b}$ | $4.41^{c}$ | 3.60 |
| Vegetarian burger | $2.66^{a}$ | $3.30^{b}$ | $4.52^{c}$ | $1.99^{d}$ | $3.79^{b}$ | 3.32 |
| Nuts | $2.70^{a,b}$ | $3.01^{a}$ | $4.17^{c}$ | $2.36^{b}$ | $3.66^{d}$ | 3.17 |
| Tofu | $2.27^{a}$ | $2.89^{b}$ | $4.05^{c}$ | $1.83^{a}$ | $3.55^{c}$ | 2.94 |
| How to reduce meat? (%) | | | | | | |
| Use meat substitute | $23.0^{a}$ | $30.7^{a}$ | $63.0^{b}$ | $8.2^{c}$ | $50.4^{b}$ | 35.0 |
| Leave meat out of meal | $16.9^{a}$ | $21.6^{a}$ | $45.5^{b}$ | $5.7^{c}$ | $33.9^{b}$ | 24.9 |
| Eat smaller portions | $11.2^{a}$ | $26.5^{b}$ | $32.5^{b}$ | $5.7^{a}$ | $31.4^{b}$ | 22.7 |
| Don't eat particular type of meat | $7.9^{a,b}$ | $15.6^{c}$ | $28.5^{d}$ | $4.9^{b}$ | $16.5^{a,c,d}$ | 15.5 |
| Other | $1.1^{a,b}$ | $1.0^{b}$ | $4.5^{a}$ | $3.3^{a,b}$ | $0.8^{a,b}$ | 1.9 |

*Notes:* a – e. In each row, different superscripts indicate significantly different cluster means or column proportions, respectively ($p < 0.05$).

ways to reduce meat consumption is much smaller and even reversed among unconscious flexitarians. In addition, conscious flexitarians distinguish themselves by being the most critical regarding eating particular types of meat, as opposed to meat lovers (cluster 1) and compulsive meat eaters (cluster 4), who seem to consume every type of meat.

With respect to taking responsibility for reducing meat consumption, differences across clusters also exist (see Table 13.3). Conscious flexitarians (cluster 3) agree the most with statements indicating that consumers in general and the respondents themselves should reduce meat consumption, in contrast with meat lovers (cluster 1) and compulsive meat eaters (cluster 4). These 'heavy' flexitarians also most strongly believe that the government should take action in reducing meat consumption, increase taxes or run campaigns. Meat lovers (cluster 1) and compulsive meat eaters (cluster 4) do not agree with such opinions, and the two remaining 'medium' clusters partly agree with such statements. Corresponding differences in reactions across clusters are expressed when it

*Table 13.3 Preferred actions of societal institutions and neophobia*

| | Clusters | | | | | |
|---|---|---|---|---|---|---|
| **Who should reduce meat consumption?** | **1** | **2** | **3** | **4** | **5** | **Total** |
| Other parties | 2.24$^{a}$ | 3.17$^{b,c}$ | 3.62$^{b}$ | 1.73$^{d}$ | 3.07$^{c}$ | 2.90 |
| Consumers themselves | 3.50$^{a}$ | 4.15$^{b}$ | 5.86$^{c}$ | 2.77$^{d}$ | 4.69$^{e}$ | 4.26 |
| I myself | 2.43$^{a}$ | 3.74$^{b}$ | 4.70$^{c}$ | 1.89$^{d}$ | 3.81$^{b}$ | 3.47 |
| **What should government do?** | | | | | | |
| Reduce meat consumption | 2.33$^{a}$ | 3.30$^{b}$ | 4.42$^{c}$ | 1.69$^{d}$ | 3.23$^{b}$ | 3.14 |
| Increase meat tax | 1.51$^{a}$ | 2.58$^{b,c}$ | 2.95$^{c}$ | 1.31$^{a}$ | 2.26$^{b}$ | 2.26 |
| Campaigns | 2.72$^{a}$ | 3.66$^{b}$ | 5.02$^{c}$ | 2.30$^{a}$ | 3.98$^{b}$ | 3.62 |
| **What should supermarkets do?** | | | | | | |
| Reduce meat consumption | 1.97$^{a}$ | 3.09$^{b}$ | 3.99$^{c}$ | 1.59$^{a}$ | 2.78$^{b}$ | 2.84 |
| Increase meat alternatives | 2.15$^{a}$ | 3.10$^{b}$ | 4.49$^{c}$ | 1.60$^{d}$ | 3.07$^{b}$ | 3.01 |
| Promote meat | 4.73$^{a}$ | 4.27$^{a}$ | 3.48$^{b}$ | 5.50$^{c}$ | 4.21$^{a}$ | 4.33 |
| **What should organizations do?** | | | | | | |
| Reduce meat consumption | 2.31$^{a}$ | 3.32$^{b}$ | 4.43$^{c}$ | 1.78$^{d}$ | 3.52$^{b}$ | 3.18 |
| Protest against cheap meat | 2.64$^{a}$ | 3.50$^{b}$ | 4.80$^{c}$ | 2.08$^{d}$ | 3.88$^{b}$ | 3.47 |
| Guide consumers | 2.98$^{a}$ | 3.71$^{b}$ | 5.19$^{c}$ | 2.44$^{d}$ | 4.27$^{e}$ | 3.77 |
| **Neophobia** | | | | | | |
| Try new food | 4.29$^{a,b}$ | 4.10$^{a}$ | 4.73$^{b,c}$ | 4.14$^{a}$ | 4.80$^{c}$ | 4.34 |
| Don't trust new food | 2.73$^{a}$ | 3.37$^{b}$ | 2.97$^{a,b}$ | 2.98$^{a,b}$ | 2.71$^{a}$ | 3.05 |
| Don't try if ingredients unknown | 3.05$^{a}$ | 3.58$^{b}$ | 3.88$^{b}$ | 3.00$^{a}$ | 3.45$^{a,b}$ | 3.45 |
| Like ethnic food | 5.53$^{a}$ | 4.84$^{b}$ | 5.70$^{a}$ | 5.48$^{a}$ | 5.73$^{a}$ | 5.31 |
| Ethnic food looks weird | 2.79$^{a,b}$ | 3.41$^{c}$ | 2.56$^{a,d}$ | 3.16$^{b,c}$ | 2.34$^{d}$ | 2.98 |
| Try food at a dinner | 4.21$^{a}$ | 4.06$^{a}$ | 4.47$^{a,b}$ | 4.02$^{a}$ | 4.71$^{b}$ | 4.23 |
| Don't try unknown food | 2.73$^{a}$ | 3.32$^{b}$ | 2.72$^{a}$ | 2.75$^{a}$ | 2.47$^{a}$ | 2.93 |
| Being precise about food | 3.51$^{a}$ | 3.73$^{a}$ | 4.54$^{b}$ | 3.55$^{a}$ | 3.95$^{a}$ | 3.85 |
| I eat everything | 5.07$^{a}$ | 4.48$^{b}$ | 4.84$^{a,b}$ | 5.11$^{a}$ | 5.12$^{a}$ | 4.80 |
| Like to try new food in new restaurant | 4.26$^{a,b}$ | 4.05$^{a}$ | 4.55$^{b,c}$ | 4.26$^{a,b}$ | 4.76$^{c}$ | 4.28 |

*Notes:* a – e. In each row, different superscripts indicate significantly different cluster means ($p < 0.05$).

comes to actions and responsibilities of supermarkets and other societal organizations with respect to addressing the reduction of meat consumption.

With regard to neophobia, it appears that the (potential) flexitarians of clusters 3 and 5 are the most willing to try new or unknown foods, whereas they also are fastidious about the type of food they eat. The other clusters are less open to try new foods.

## 13.3 CONCLUSIONS AND DISCUSSION

To a considerable number of Dutch consumers eating meat is not always self-evident. Flexitarianism does exist. From the perspective of sustainability, flexitarianism may be qualified as a first and insufficient step towards more sustainable food consumption choices and patterns, particularly when meat is substituted by other animal-based products (for example, fish, eggs, cheese) rather than plant-based substitutes. However, from the perspective of the dominancy of meat-eating habits in the current food culture the emerging trend of flexitarianism signifies a cautious break with carnivorous traditions and therefore contains a significant step towards a future of sustainable food consumption.

The identified clusters show that consumers contribute differently to sustainable food consumption habits or diets containing less meat. The meat consumption frequency of meat lovers and compulsive meat eaters is higher and in that sense more unsustainable compared to conscious flexitarians, for example. Although we did not study within-consumer conflicts, different clusters seemed to favour different motives. The two clusters of 'medium' flexitarians (unconscious flexitarians and potential flexitarians) differ with respect to status derived from meat consumption, need for meat, and value for money. This result suggests different routes of sustainable policy making aimed at different clusters. For unconscious flexitarians, attractive and high-status meat alternatives may be offered to reduce meat consumption. Such offerings might be accompanied by information suggesting that consumers themselves are responsible for meat reduction in their diets. Since the cluster of unconscious flexitarians is relatively large, such a policy may be efficient. For potential flexitarians, price measures may be relatively effective. However this cluster is relatively small, which renders such a policy less efficient.

We have attempted to improve our insight into different types of flexitarians by conducting a cluster analysis based on the segmentation variables measuring symbolic and ethical associations with meat outlined above. Meat consumption was only analysed in the cluster profiling. Mainly because meat consumption was excluded from the cluster variables, the clusters presented here differ partly from those reported in Dagevos and Voordouw (2013). There seems to be no specific rule for applying cluster analysis on behavioural variables or on background variables. Vanhonacker et al. (2013) use meat consumption in the cluster profiling, whereas Latvala et al. (2012) use meat consumption as input to the clustering procedure. This state of affairs makes it difficult to compare results across studies. For policy purposes it would be useful to study which measures affect meat consumption most effectively in different clusters.

The different strategies towards meat reduction discussed so far can be categorized into five broad strategies: (1) reducing meat portion size; (2) replacing part of the meat in meat-based products by plant-based alternatives (so-called hybrid meats); (3) consumption of meat substitutes (for example, vegetarian burgers); (4) replacing meat by other (animal-based or plant-based) protein-rich products; and (5) leaving out meat from the dish without replacement. In addition to these five strategies, a sixth strategy deserves attention. If meat needs to be reduced because of environmental and animal welfare concerns, meat could be replaced by other more environmentally friendly and animal-friendly meat products (for example, organic or free-range meat) (see Vanhonacker et al. 2013). This 'weak', product-related sustainable consumption strategy could be applied in approaching consumer segments that highly value their meat consumption and are not willing to reduce it. In this way gains in terms of environmental impact and animal welfare issues can still be achieved to some degree (see De Jonge and van Trijp 2013).

The five identified clusters need different approaches towards changing their meat consumption. The meat lovers do like meat a lot, but they do not express a high need for meat consumption. This offers opportunities towards meat reduction. Consuming smaller portions of meat, replacing meat in convenience food or consumption of hybrid meat products could be effective strategies. In addition, 'light flexitarians' in cluster 1 could be willing to buy more environmentally friendly and animal-friendly meat products, as this cluster expresses relatively high importance to environmental and animal welfare issues. This cluster also indicates that meat is worth its money and therefore might be willing to pay somewhat more for these more sustainable meat products. Health motivation appeared to be less strong in this cluster and therefore an approach through health messages does not seem very effective.

The unconscious flexitarians of cluster 2 perceive positive health effects of less meat, dislike animals as a source of meat, believe meat is rather expensive and indicate relatively little need for meat. However they also indicate that meat consumption gives status, and they do not appreciate meatless meals. Therefore this cluster might benefit from information and skills on preparing meatless meals. Fancy, tasty, low-meat meals could be attractive to them and may be perceived as relatively healthy. In contrast to the meat lovers, this cluster may be approached via 'strong' curtailment strategies rather than the consumption of more sustainable meat products.

Cluster 3 of 'heavy' conscious flexitarians has the most positive attitudes towards meat reduction and is most open for all possible meat-reduction strategies. This cluster should mainly be stimulated to enforce their current behaviour (curtailment), for example by providing the right context for making the flexitarian choice the easy choice, and by focusing on health and the environment.

The compulsive meat eaters of cluster 4 are probably the most difficult to change, as this cluster indicates a high need for meat, does not appreciate meatless meals and is not open to any of the meat reduction strategies. The only way to lower their meat consumption seems to be to improve 'sustainability by stealth' through the implementation of rather unnoticeable innovations such as in hybrid meats, a product-related strategy (De Bakker and Dagevos 2012; Verain et al. 2012).

Finally, cluster 5 of potential flexitarians is characterized by a low need for meat, a relatively high appreciation of meatless meals and a high level of concern about environmental issues and animal friendliness. This cluster is also the least neophobic, indicating that these flexitarians are open-minded to changes in their diet. Possibly their current level of meat consumption is very much the result of dietary habits. Making these 'medium' flexitarians more aware of ill-health effects and environmental consequences of low or moderate meat consumption, and informing them about meat alternatives and more sustainable dietary patterns, might be sufficient to amplify and consolidate their meat reduction behaviour. Concluding, it appears that flexitarianism is a promising trend toward more sustainable food consumption. Different approaches and measures should be applied to help different food consumers to adjust their meat consumption to more sustainable levels.

## REFERENCES

Askegaard, S. and T.K. Madsen (1998), 'The local and the global: exploring traits of homogeneity and heterogeneity in European food cultures', *International Business Review*, 7 (6), 549–568.

Baker, S., K.E. Thompson and D. Palmer-Barnes (2002), 'Crisis in the meat industry: a values-based approach to communications strategy', *Journal of Marketing Communications*, 8 (1), 19–30.

Beardsworth, A.D. and T. Keil (1991), 'Vegetarianism, veganism and meat avoidance: recent trends and findings', *British Food Journal*, 93 (4), 19–24.

Beardsworth, A. and T. Keil (1992), 'The vegetarian option: varieties, conversions, motives and careers', *Sociological Review*, 40 (2), 253–293.

Boulanger, P.M. (2010), 'Three strategies for sustainable consumption', *Sapiens*, 3 (2), 1–10.

Dagevos, H. (2014), 'Flexibility in the frequency of meat consumption: empirical evidence from The Netherlands', *EuroChoices*, 13 (2), 40–45.

Dagevos, H. and J. Voordouw (2013), 'Sustainability and meat consumption: is reduction realistic?', *Sustainability: Science, Practice, and Policy*, 9 (2), 60–69.

De Bakker, E. and H. Dagevos (2012), 'Reducing meat consumption in today's consumer society: questioning the citizen–consumer gap', *Journal of Agricultural and Environmental Ethics*, 25 (6), 877–894.

De Jonge, J. and H.C.M. van Trijp (2013), 'Meeting heterogeneity in consumer demand for animal welfare: a reflection on existing knowledge and implications for the meat sector', *Journal of Agricultural and Environmental Ethics*, 26, 629–661.

Dolan, P. (2002), 'The sustainability of "sustainable consumption"', *Journal of Macromarketing*, 22 (2), 170–181.

Dowd, K. and K.J. Burke (2013), 'The influence of ethical values and food choice motivations on intentions to purchase sustainably sourced foods', *Appetite*, 69, 137–144.

Fox, N. and K. Ward (2008), 'Health, ethics and environment: a qualitative study of vegetarian motivations', *Appetite*, 50 (2–3), 422–429.

Fotopoulos, C., A. Krystallis, M. Vassallo and A. Pagiaslis (2009), 'Food choice questionnaire: suggestions for the development of an enhanced general food motivation model', *Appetite*, 52, 199–208.

Fuchs, D.A. and S. Lorek (2005), 'Sustainable consumption governance: a history of promises and failures', *Journal of Consumer Policy*, 28 (3), 261–288.

Griskevicius, V., J.M. Tyler and B. Van den Bergh (2010), 'Going green to be seen: status, reputation, and conspicuous conservation', *Journal of Personality and Social Psychology*, 98 (3), 392–404.

Hoek, A.C., P.A. Luning, A. Stafleu and C. De Graaf (2004), 'Food-related lifestyle and health attitudes of Dutch vegetarians, non-vegetarian consumers of meat substitutes, and meat consumers', *Appetite*, 42 (3), 265–272.

Jackson, T. (2005), '*Motivation Sustainable Consumption: A Review of Evidence on Consumer Behaviour and Behavioural Change*', Guildford: University of Surrey.

Janda, S. and P.J. Trocchia (2001), 'Vegetarianism: toward a greater understanding', *Psychology and Marketing*, 18 (12), 1205–1240.

Korthals, M. (2012), 'Two evils in food country: hunger and lack of representation', in D.M. Kaplan (ed.), *The Philosophy of Food*, Berkeley, CA: University of California Press, pp. 103–122.

Latvala, T., M. Niva, J. Mäkelä, E. Pouta, J. Heikkilä, J. Kotro and S. Forsman-Hugg (2012), 'Diversifying meat consumption patterns: consumers' self-reported past behaviour and intentions for change', *Meat Science*, 92 (1), 71–77.

Lea, E. and A. Worsley (2001), 'Influences on meat consumption in Australia', *Appetite*, 36 (2), 127–136.

Lea, E. and A. Worsley (2003), 'Benefits and barriers to the consumption of a vegetarian diet in Australia', *Public Health Nutrition*, 6 (5), 505–511.

Lindeman, M and M. Väänänen (2000), 'Measurement of ethical food choice motives', *Appetite*, 34, 55–59.

Lorek, S. and D. Fuchs (2013), 'Strong sustainable consumption governance – precondition for a degrowth path?', *Journal of Cleaner Production*, 38, 36–43.

McMeekin, A. and D. Southerton (2012), 'Sustainability transitions and final consumption: practices and socio-technical systems', *Technology Analysis and Strategic Management*, 24 (4), 345–361.

Nordgren, A. (2012), 'Ethical issues in mitigation of climate change: the option of reduced meat production and consumption', *Journal of Agricultural and Environmental Ethics*, 25 (4), 563–584.

Pinker, S. (2011), *The Better Angels of our Nature: The Decline of Violence in History and its Causes*, London: Allen Lane.

Povey, R., B. Wellens and M. Conner (2001), 'Attitudes towards following meat, vegetarian and vegan diets: an examination of the role of ambivalence', *Appetite*, 37 (1), 15–26.

Raats, M.M., R. Shepherd and P. Sparks (1995), 'Including moral dimensions of choice within the structure of the theory of planned behaviour', *Journal of Applied Social Psychology*, 25 (6), 484–494.

Reisch, L., U. Eberle and S. Lorek (2013), 'Sustainable food consumption: an overview of contemporary issues and policies', *Sustainability: Science, Practice, and Policy*, 9 (2), 1–19.

Richardson, N., H. MacFie and R. Shepherd (1994a), 'Consumer attitudes to meat eating', *Meat Science*, 36 (1–2), 7–65.

Richardson, N., R. Shepherd and N. Elliman (1994b), 'Meat consumption, definition of meat and trust in

information sources in the UK population and members of the vegetarian society', *Ecology of Food and Nutrition*, 33 (1–2), 1–13.
Rothgerber, H. (2012), 'Real men don't eat (vegetable) quiche: masculinity and the justification of meat consumption', *Psychology of Men and Masculinity*, 14 (4), 363–375.
Rothgerber, H. (2014), 'A comparison of attitudes toward meat and animals among strict and semi-vegetarians', *Appetite*, 72, 98–105.
Rozin, P., J.M. Hormes, M.S. Faith and B. Wansink (2012), 'Is meat male? A quantitative multimethod framework to establish metaphoric relationships', *Journal of Consumer Research*, 39 (3), 629–643.
Rozin, P., M. Markwith and C. Stoess (1997), 'Moralization and becoming a vegetarian: the transformation of preferences into values and the recruitment of disgust', *Psychological Science*, 8 (2), 67–73.
Ruby, M.B. (2012), 'Vegetarianism: a blossoming field of study', *Appetite*, 58 (1), 141–150.
Ruby, M.B. and S.J. Heine (2011), 'Meat, morals, and masculinity', *Appetite*, 56 (2), 447–450.
Scholl, G., F. Rubik, H. Kalimo, K. Biedenkopf and O. Söebech (2010), 'Policies to promote sustainable consumption: Innovative approaches in Europe', *Natural Resources Forum*, 34 (1), 39–50.
Schösler, H., J.D. Boer and J.J. Boersema (2012), 'Can we cut out the meat of the dish? Constructing consumer-oriented pathways towards meat substitution', *Appetite*, 58 (1), 39–47.
Tukker, A., R.A. Goldbohm, A. de Koning, M. Verheijden, R. Kleijn, O. Wolf, I. Pérez-Domínguez et al. (2011), 'Environmental impacts of changes to healthier diets in Europe', *Ecological Economics*, 70 (10), 1776–1788.
Twigg, J. (1983), 'Vegetarianism and the meanings of meat', in A. Murcott (ed.), *The Sociology of Food and Eating*, Farnborough: Gower, pp. 18–30.
Van Dooren, C., M. Marinussen, H. Blonk, H. Aiking and P. Vellinga (2014), 'Exploring dietary guidelines based on ecological and nutritional values: a comparison of six dietary patterns', *Food Policy*, 44, 36–46.
Vanhonacker, F., E.J. Van Loo, X. Gellynck and W. Verbeke (2013), 'Flemish consumer attitudes towards more sustainable food choices', *Appetite*, 62, 7–16.
Verain, M.C.D., J. Bartels, H. Dagevos, S.J. Sijtsema, M.C. Onwezen and G. Antonides (2012), 'Segments of sustainable food consumers: a literature review', *International Journal of Consumer Studies*, 36 (2), 123–132.
Verbeke, W. and J. Viaene (1999), 'Beliefs, attitude and behaviour towards fresh meat consumption in Belgium: empirical evidence from a consumer survey', *Food Quality and Preference*, 10, 437–445.
Vinnari, M., P. Mustonen, and P. Räsänen (2010), 'Tracking down trends in non-meat consumption in Finnish households, 1966–2006', *British Food Journal*, 112, 836–852.
Vinnari, M. and E. Vinnari (2014), 'A framework for sustainable transition: the case of plant-based diets', *Journal of Agricultural and Environmental Ethics*, 27, 369–396.
Westhoek, H., T. Rood, M. van den Berg, J. Janse, D. Nijdam, M. Reudink and E. Stehfest (2011), *The Protein Puzzle: The Consumption and Production of Meat, Dairy, and Fish in the European Union*, The Hague: Netherlands Environmental Assessment Agency.

# 14. Obesity, sustainability and public health

*Wencke Gwozdz*

## 14.1 A POTENTIAL NEXUS BETWEEN OBESITY, SUSTAINABILITY AND PUBLIC HEALTH

In the individual, obesity is a risk factor for numerous health problems, including hypertension, high cholesterol, diabetes, cardiovascular disease, respiratory problems (asthma), musculoskeletal disease (arthritis), infertility and certain forms of cancer, including leukaemia, breast and colon cancer (OECD 2012). The tremendous increase in overweight and obesity worldwide, however, shifts the challenge from being simply a matter of individual risk factors to a major public health concern across the globe. In fact, since 2010, the World Health Organization (WHO) has classified obesity as a disease whose consequences have a lasting impact on communities, nations and individuals not only today but across future generations. Obesity therefore is anything but sustainable.

Before elaborating on the possible nexus between obesity and sustainable consumption, however, it is pertinent to discuss its prevalence and development worldwide (section 14.2), as well as its key drivers (section 14.3); some identified, others unknown. The interplay between these drivers, in particular, is as yet little understood, which makes it difficult to fight obesity and its consequences effectively. What is clear is that if obesity harms not only the individual but society at large, its consequences and related consumption patterns are unsustainable in all aspects: social, economic and ecological (section 14.4). This unsustainability can, however be alleviated by decreasing obesity – a primary goal of public health (section 14.5). Yet to curb obesity effectively, public health must rely on an understanding of its drivers, a goal that motivates this chapter on the potential nexus between obesity, sustainability and public health. Section 14.6 concludes with a discussion.

## 14.2 OBESITY: AN INDIVIDUAL OR SOCIETAL CHALLENGE?

Since 1980, obesity rates have nearly doubled worldwide, an increase of epidemic proportions that cannot be attributed to individual responsibility alone. In 2008, more than 34.5 per cent (1.46 billion) adults were overweight while around 9.8 per cent (205 million) of men and 13.8 per cent (297 million) of women were obese, compared to 4.8 per cent and 7.9 per cent, respectively, in 1980 (Finucane et al. 2011). The highest prevalence is in the USA, with 69 per cent of the population being either overweight or obese and more than a third being obese in 2009–2010 (Flegal et al. 2012). This rate was topped only by Middle Eastern and Southern African women, with obesity rates of 44–48 per cent and 36.4 per cent, respectively (Finucane et al. 2011). In Europe, the average for overweight and obesity is more than 52 per cent of the adult population, with 17 per cent

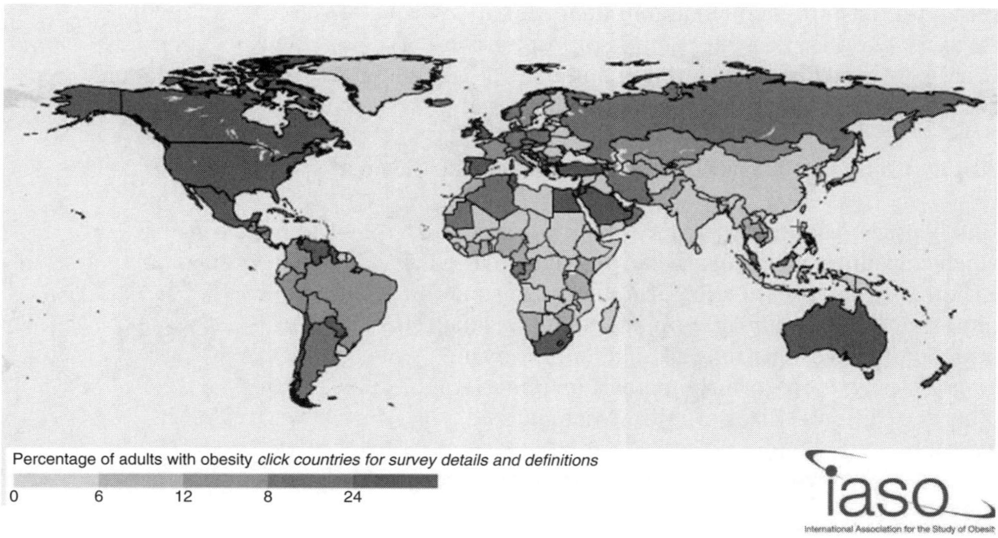


*Source:* IASO (2013) http://www.iaso.org/resources/world-map-obesity/ (with permission from IASO).

*Figure 14.1 Adult obesity prevalence worldwide, 2000–2013*

being obese. Nevertheless obesity rates vary greatly between European countries, with Romania and Switzerland at the lower bound with 8 per cent, and Hungary and the UK at the upper bound with 25 per cent (OECD 2012). In Africa, South America and the Asia-Pacific, data must be interpreted carefully because of their scarcity; nevertheless obesity rates are also increasing in these regions. Figure 14.1 illustrates the prevalence of overweight and obesity worldwide.

The estimates for children, graphed in Figure 14.2, paint a similar picture: overweight and obesity rates doubled over the last 20 years, resulting in about 150 million overweight children and approximately 50 million obese children, with an average 13 per cent being overweight or obese at age 15 (OECD 2012). It is the harmful effects of such obesity on children's emotional and physical health that underlies the WHO's concern, especially the high likelihood of obesity transmission into adulthood, and the elevated risk of cardiovascular diseases or diabetes even when excess weight is lost in adulthood by formerly obese children (WHO Europe 2009).

The different levels of obesity across the world clearly show specific, predictable patterns in subpopulations. In low-income countries, for example, a higher prevalence of obesity occurs among middle-aged adults living in wealthy urban areas, with women affected more than men. In high-income countries, in contrast, obesity is not dependent on age or sex, but prevalence is higher in those with low socio-economic status (SES) (Swinburn et al. 2011). The common trend observed over the last two decades, however, is that with few exceptions, overweight and obesity rates are increasing across the globe. The only stable or decreasing rates are observed for women in a handful of Central and Eastern European countries, and for men in parts of Central Africa and South

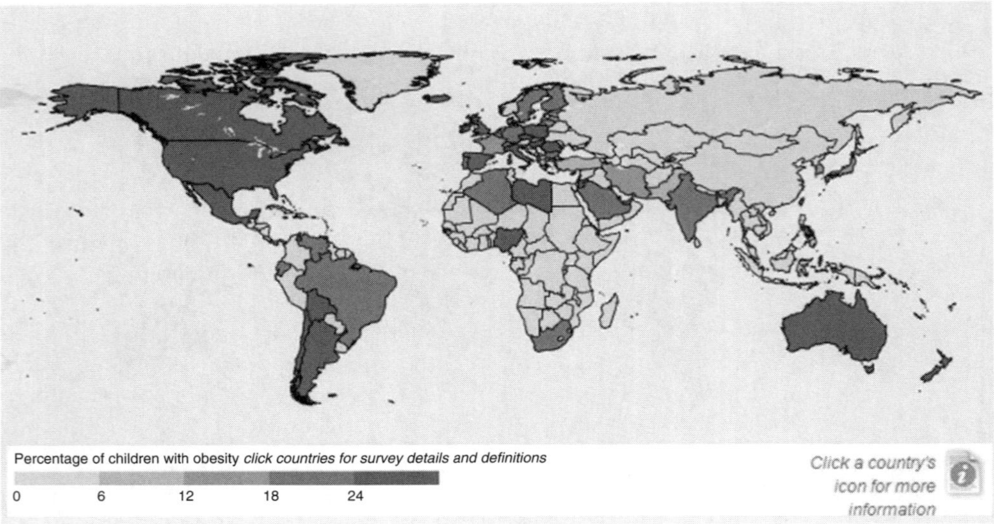


*Source:* IASO (2013) http://www.iaso.org/resources/world-map-obesity/ (with permission from IASO).

*Figure 14.2 Child obesity prevalence worldwide, 2000–2013*

Asia (Finucane et al. 2011). For children, a levelling off since 1999 has been identified in some countries, including Australia, Denmark, Greece, Sweden, the UK and the US; however in the past, such stable periods have usually been followed by an increase in obesity prevalence in all of these countries except Sweden (Rokholm et al. 2010). Moreover although the causes of these observed trends are not yet well understood, forecasts for the US predict a 33 per cent increase in obesity rates over the next two decades (Finkelstein et al. 2012), and it seems reasonable to assume this upward trend will continue worldwide.

## 14.3 KEY DRIVERS OF OBESITY

To understand and slow this rise in obesity, it is necessary to understand its key drivers. What is recognized is that they are both interdependent and complex, a complexity that can be reduced somewhat through classification. One such classification offered by the human ecological approach (e.g., Story et al. 2008) consists of four levels that influence health behaviour: the individual, social, environmental and societal. It should be noted, however, that the human ecological model, like all such classifications of obesity drivers, remains imperfect because the distinctions between its four levels are arbitrary and not mutually exclusive. Nevertheless such a framework is useful for structuring the drivers of the dietary behaviour and physical activity that ultimately are at the core of obesity.

### 14.3.1 Individual Drivers

The individual level incorporates biological (for example, genetics, metabolic factors), psychological (for example, beliefs or attitudes) and lifestyle factors (for example, meal and activity patterns). Yet despite the high priority given to research on genetics and obesity, only a few genes have been directly related to obesity (Darnton 2009). Independent of genetic predisposition, decision-making on diet choices and physical activity is the responsibility of the individual. Yet behavioural economics suggests that such decisions are actually made in the automatic system (Cohen 2008; Johnson and Hasher 1987), meaning that they are based on neuropsychological responses to environmental, physiological and interpersonal cues and thus beyond individual awareness. More specifically, consumers' decisions are influenced through the use of heuristics or rules of thumb or the framing of information, as well as by inconsistent, non-stable preferences such as those constructed at the point of sale (Thaler and Sunstein 2008). These constructive preferences – sometimes boosted by limited self-control – can contradict long-term preferences such as a healthy life (Scharff 2009). Another contributory factor is hyperbolic discounting (see e.g. Thaler 1981): the fact that consumers discount the costs and benefits of the long-term health consequences of current lifestyle choices. Consumer decision making is also influenced by framing, the way that information is presented to them (e.g. Tversky and Kahnemann 1981), as well as habitual behaviour, which makes everyday life easier by routinizing and automating decision making so that it requires little cognitive effort (e.g. Posner and Snyder 1975). Because habits are often reinforced by short-run rewards that can outweigh the long-term benefits of behavioural change, such behaviour is difficult to change.

### 14.3.2 Social Drivers

Because consumers are social animals, their behaviour is subject to social influences from family, peers and social networks. Within the family, two influences are particularly relevant: common genetic drivers and exposure to a shared environment and lifestyles (Silventoinen et al. 2010). Both genetics and parental food and health behaviours, values, awareness and knowledge conveyed to children contribute to the strong correlation between parental and child body mass index (BMI). Such a correlation is also observed (albeit more weakly) in partners, perhaps because of partner selection and behavioural influences (Sassi 2010). In general, depending on the child's stage of socialization, parents act more or less as role models and gatekeepers. Individual BMI, however, is also related to peers' BMI (Cunningham et al. 2012; Trogdon et al. 2008) through peer ability to change two factors: norms of acceptable weight and weight-related behaviour. Thus individual lifestyle choices have an influence on others and vice versa, a dynamic often termed the 'social multiplier effect', which has important implications for policies and interventions to fight obesity (Trogdon et al. 2008).

### 14.3.3 Environmental Drivers

Social drivers are difficult to isolate from environmental drivers because they are often shared by different social agents (family members, peers). Such a shared environment can be more or less 'obesogenic'; that is, likely to provide more or fewer stimuli to becoming overweight or obese (Lobstein et al. 2004): Obesogenic environments favour a sedentary lifestyle and the easy availability, accessibility and affordability of high-energy-dense foods (Reisch and Gwozdz 2011). The development of such environments can be traced back to the 1960s, when massive changes occurred in the food retailing sector (Elinder and Jansson 2008). Specifically, smaller shops were replaced by large out-of-town supermarkets, often resulting in urban food deserts in which healthy food was more expensive and less available than unhealthy food (especially in poorer areas). At the same time, locations for eating outside the home, particularly fast food restaurants, began serving cheap, energy-dense foods, leading to accusations that they were contributing to the rise in obesity. The workplace and schools have also been targets for intervention because of the way they influence and shape consumers' dietary patterns and behaviours.

Built environments can also be obesogenic, increasing obesity by decreasing levels of physical activity (Darnton 2009). Availability, affordability and accessibility are important with regard to active transportation such as bicycles – versus passive transportation such as cars – and recreational opportunities. The features that determine their obesogenicity include population density; the presence and quality of pavements; perceptions of safety; and access to parks, green spaces and leisure facilities (Lake and Townshend 2006). Not only is the number of leisure facilities in a neighbourhood correlated with physical activity, but walkability and bikeability (the perceived ease of walking and biking in a neighbourhood) are associated with higher levels of physical activity and lower body weight (Darnton 2009). Because of their influence on diet and physical activity, such environmental drivers hold great potential for preventative measures and interventions to create less obesogenic environments by nudging individuals towards healthier dietary choices, less sedentary behaviour and increased levels of physical activity.

### 14.3.4 Societal Drivers

The sum of societal drivers influencing obesity has been referred to as the 'obesogenic society' (Ogilvie and Hamlet 2005) and comprises policy, economy, technology enabling or promoting consumption, food supply, marketing environments and media influences. An obesogenic society naturally shapes (non-) obesogenic environments, individual and social factors, and ultimately individual behaviour, even though in a more distal and indirect way. One oft-mentioned driver on the societal level is the provision of easily available, accessible and affordable energy-dense food, whose increasing presence in the US readily explains the rise in obesity since the 1970s (Swinburn et al. 2009). Major contributors to this increased food supply are technological innovations and agricultural policies that lead to decreased food prices and more convenient food consumption. As a result, food is highly processed and energy dense and served in larger packages and portion sizes, blocking consumer awareness of the hidden energy (ibid.). This modernized and increased food supply, which shapes consumers' decision-making through the influence of the immediate context (for example, in-store marketing, product offers, easy access to food) (Reisch and Gwozdz 2011), has induced major changes in food cultures. In Europe, diets are more homogeneous than a few decades ago, favouring traditional continental European diets characterized by more animal fat and a lower intake of vegetables and fruits over the more healthy Mediterranean diet (Elinder and Jansson 2008). Also contributing to this trend are the more sophisticated marketing and persuasion techniques used by marketers to increase consumption of their products. These include creating positive images of the foods they produce, building on existing behavioural patterns to channel social norms, and convincing consumer of the foods' benefits (Grier et al. 2007).

Obesity is also driven by government policies such as agricultural subsidies and other fiscal measures that affect commodity prices, transport (public and private) and urban planning (recreational areas or opportunities for physical activity) (Sassi 2010). Yet agricultural subsidy patterns that boost the marketing of unhealthy foods are in fact economically unsustainable, as amply demonstrated by the case of the Scottish sugar industry, boosted by high subsidies in the 1800s that made sugar one of today's most popular and easily accessible foods (Renton 2006). Since then, the Scots have been suffering the negative consequences: dental decay rates comparable to those in developing countries and much higher overweight and obesity rates than in other parts of the UK, all resulting in severe health costs (ibid.).

Despite the major contributions of the factors outlined above, the global rise in obesity over the past four decades cannot be fully explained by individual, social and environmental drivers. Individual lifestyle choices, for example, as well as the consequences of obesity, are likely to be triggered by such societal drivers as increased food supply, which as yet are not fully understood. What is widely recognized, however, is that individuals alone do not pay the full price for their conditions; it is society at large that pays for the obesity-related social, economic and environmental costs that cannot be sustained by either present or future generations.

## 14.4 OBESITY AND ITS UNSUSTAINABLE CONSEQUENCES

In 1987, the Brundtland Commission defined sustainable development as 'development that meets the needs of the present without compromising the ability of future generations to meet their own needs' (Brundtland and the World Commission on Environment and Development 1987). Since then, the United Nations (UN 2005), adopting the overarching objectives of eradicating poverty, unsustainable consumption and production patterns and managing natural resources responsibly, has identified three interdependent and mutually reinforcing components of sustainability: social development, economic development and environmental protection. Unfortunately the obesity epidemic is unsustainable with regard to all three of these pillars of sustainable development.

### 14.4.1 Obesity and Social Sustainability

The consequences of obesity are socially unsustainable because they threaten social cohesion, equity and fairness (Reisch and Gwozdz 2011); that is, obesity is closely linked to deteriorating health, reduced mobility, stigma, lower SES (only in developed countries), income inequality and premature mortality resulting in an overall poorer quality of life (Foresight 2007). Above all, obese individuals experience deteriorating health, such as a seven (men) or 12 (women) times higher risk of diabetes than normal-weight individuals (Guh et al. 2009). Obesity is also associated with cardiovascular diseases, including coronary heart disease (32 per cent increased risk over normal-weight individuals), stroke (64 per cent increased risk) and cardiovascular death (53 per cent increased risk) (Strazzullo et al. 2010). Overweight and obesity are also linked to respiratory diseases such as asthma, with a 50 per cent higher risk for the obese (Beuther and Sutherland 2007). Although the link between obesity and cancer remains unclear, there is evidence for increased risk for some kinds of cancer. Obesity is linked to lower fertility, being possibly responsible for about 25 per cent of the infertility in the US (Rich-Edwards et al. 2002). Obesity is also co-morbid with mobility-reducing conditions like osteoarthritis, lower back pain and chronic generalized pain (Taylor et al. 2013), and results in reduced functional mobility that impairs general mobility and participation in everyday life activities (Forhan and Gill 2013).

Because of these increased health risks and impairments, obesity is also related to premature mortality. In fact, obesity and its co-morbidities are currently the second most frequent cause of death (after tobacco consumption) in the UK (HM Government 2008), where obesity has decreased the average life expectancy for men by two years. Moreover if forecasted trends hold true, this two-year decrease will rise to five years by 2050 (Haslam and James 2005). Such an association between BMI and cause-specific mortality was the subject of an analysis by the Prospective Studies Collaboration (2009), which observed the lowest mortality for a BMI between 22.5 and 25.0 $kg/m^2$. At a BMI of 30–35 $kg/m^2$, life expectancy is already reduced by 2–5 years, while a BMI of 40–45 $kg/m^2$ shortens the expected age by as much as 6–10 years. This latter is comparable to the expected mortality of smokers.

Social sustainability is further jeopardized by 'weight-related stigma', defined as negative attitudes and discriminatory behaviours directed towards obese individuals (Puhl and Heuer 2009). In the US, the prevalence of weight-related discrimination is believed to be equal to that of race-related discrimination (Puhl et al. 2008). These discriminatory behaviours, which stereotypically attribute to obese people such characteristics as laziness, lack of self-control or motivation, incompetence and/or non-compliance (ibid.), include insulting comments, social exclusion, discrimination in the workplace and health care settings, and depreciatory representation in the media. They thus make obese individuals vulnerable to social injustice, unfair treatment and impaired quality of life. Job discrimination, for example, is induced through disadvantages in hiring, wages, promotions and job termination (Puhl and Heuer 2009). Likewise, obese individuals receive around 10 per cent lower wages than their non-obese counterparts even given equal occupation, education and job experience (Sassi 2010). According to McCormick and Stone (2007), the lower employment rates of obese individuals result from an assumption that their productivity will be lower because they will need more sick days or will die prematurely. In fact research does indeed show a correlation between obesity and sick leave days, as well as decreased productivity. According to Sassi (2010), however, such a link should be seen not as a justification for discrimination but rather as an alert for public health actors.

Poorer employment opportunities are also associated with lower SES. Yet there is ample empirical evidence that, in developed countries, members of a low SES group are more likely to be obese than any other social group (McLaren 2007). Even in developing countries, such as those in Central and Southern America, where the opposite used to be true, a shift has been observed (Monteiro et al. 2007). One explanation for this higher prevalence of obesity in lower SES groups is the poor access to and the higher prices for healthy food, as well as fewer opportunities for physical activity (Robertson et al. 2007). Nevertheless the relation between obesity and SES is bidirectional: belonging to a lower SES group increases the probability of becoming obese, while being obese decreases the opportunities to improve SES. In developed countries, obesity is also related to income inequality; that is, the higher the income inequality, the higher the prevalence of obesity (Pickett et al. 2005).

All of the above factors – deteriorating health, reduced mobility, premature mortality, stigmatization, poorer employment opportunities and lower SES – affect overall quality of life. When all these factors are linked to obesity, it is no surprise that research has found a negative, bidirectional relation between obesity and quality of life (e.g. Taylor et al. 2013), including poorer self-image and social ostracism for individuals, and routine difficulties (like finding suitable seating) in daily life (Witkowski 2007).

### 14.4.2 Obesity and Economic Sustainability

Economic sustainability means maintaining or increasing current standards of living without decreasing the living standards of others, especially those of future generations. The economic consequences of obesity, however, are severe with regard to both health care systems and labour markets. As regards the first, national health systems are burdened by obesity's many co-morbidities, which make public spending on health care and long-term care a challenge for Western policy makers. In Europe, since 2010, health spending has experienced severe cuts following a trend of steady increases, with health expenditures remaining stable or declining an average 9 per cent of gross domestic product (GDP) (OECD 2012). Yet on average, less than 3 per cent of health expenditures are used for preventative measures such as vaccinations or campaigns against alcohol abuse, smoking and obesity (ibid.).

In particular, health care costs have increased because of obesity-related chronic diseases. According to Finkelstein et al. (2009), obesity is responsible for approximately 1–3 per cent of total health expenditures in most countries, except in the US where it was responsible for 9 per cent of total health expenditures (~US$86 billion) in 2006. Cawley and Meyerhoefer (2012), on the other hand, using the same data but a different empirical approach, estimate the costs of obesity in the US at more than 21 per cent of national health expenditures or around US$190 billion. On the individual level, health care expenditures for an obese person are on average at least 25 per cent higher than those for a normal-weight person (Withrow and Alter 2010). Hence projections for the US and UK, assuming a continued rise in obesity, foresee costs of US$48–66 billion per year in the US and £1.9–2 billion per year in the UK in 2030 (Wang et al. 2011).

In addition to the health expenditures, resources forgone because of health conditions also generate indirect costs, most notably perhaps, the losses in productivity. These indirect costs, however, are harder to trace and nowhere coherently defined, although the National Obesity Observatory (2010) suggests that they include labour market-related lost earnings from attributable sickness and premature mortality. Depending on the calculation method, these indirect costs are estimated to be up to twice the direct costs. In the US for example in 2008, the estimated obesity-related lost working days and costs of absenteeism amounted to a loss of 1.7–3.0 productive person-years in the working population, with a corresponding cost of US$390–580 billion (Wang et al. 2011). Nevertheless these indirect costs are very much dependent on the actual labour market situation and on the structure of the welfare system.

The long-term costs of obesity over a lifetime have been little researched, and the few studies that do exist offer no consistent findings. Whereas some suggest that health care costs for obese individuals are actually lower than for normal-weight individuals because of premature mortality, others claim that the costs of obesity outweigh the health care expenditures of the longer life expectancy of non-obese individuals (see Sassi 2010). The more important observation might be that the costs of obesity for a health care system arise in a certain period of time, so during that period, an obese population costs more than a lean population (Wang et al. 2011). Nevertheless although such an economic modulation could be policy makers' strongest argument for prevention and intervention, basing intervention decisions on calculated costs over a lifetime of normal-weight versus obese individuals raises serious ethical questions.

### 14.4.3 Obesity and Ecological Sustainability

Finally, obesity is closely connected to ecological unsustainability because current food production and consumption are characterized by an excessive use of energy and water (Reisch et al. 2013). Globally, food production accounts for about one-fifth of greenhouse gas (GHG) emissions, while food-related transport accounts for an additional 14 per cent (Haines et al. 2009). In the European Union (EU), food and non-alcoholic beverages account for 21 per cent of the GHG emissions of private consumption, with meat, meat products and dairy being the largest contributors (EEA 2013). In fact, with the earlier-mentioned changes in food production and supply (Reisch et al. 2013), local farmers have become more likely to feed their products into the large industrial food system instead of trading them locally, thereby increasing transportation or food miles. This tendency in turn increases transport distances between farmers, industry and consumers.

Food production also requires masses of fresh water, accounting for about 75 per cent of total water use in Germany, 40 per cent directly consumed within the country and 60 per cent consumed indirectly through production elsewhere (virtual water consumption) (WWF 2009). Another important aspect is food waste, primarily during food manufacturing and consumption. Around 90 megatonnes of food are wasted in the European Union every year, 39 per cent generated from food manufacturing and 42 per cent from consumption, which latter accounts for 170 megatonnes of GHG equivalent emissions (about 3 per cent of the EU's total GHG emissions), 45 per cent directly from consumers (BioIS 2010). The overall effect on GHG emissions of rising obesity is estimated by Edwards and Roberts (2009). They show that compared to a normal population with about 3.5 per cent obese and a mean BMI of 24.5 (equivalent to the UK in the 1970s), a population with 40 per cent obese and a mean BMI of 29.0 (equivalent to the UK in the 2010s) requires 16 per cent more food energy. In a population of 1 billion people, such an increase would result in a 0.4–1.0 gigatonne rise in carbon dioxide equivalents per year in GHG emissions from food production and transportation. Hence, reducing the BMI should have equally beneficial effects for the environment.

In fact, changes in current diets could substantially reduce environmental impacts, as clearly shown by studies on the effects of diet changes on GHG emissions (Stehfest et al. 2009) and water use (Vanham and Bidoglio 2013). The point of departure for such investigation is diets high in meat and low in vegetable consumption, versus healthier diets in which consumers adhere to current food-based dietary guidelines or move towards vegetarian diets that have greater potential to reduce not only obesity but also GHG emissions and water use. Changes in purchasing behaviour – that is, better planning – could also reduce food waste by about 13 per cent (Faber et al. 2012). Hence, shifting consumer behaviour towards healthier diets (decreased animal product consumption, increased vegetable and fruit consumption) could have a substantial impact on both obesity reduction and environmental sustainability.

## 14.5 OBESITY, SUSTAINABILITY AND PUBLIC HEALTH

As already emphasized, obesity is a major challenge for both sustainable development and public health. The enormity of the economic costs, the decreased quality of life and the other social and environmental impacts have heightened global political attention to obesity and made it a target in national sustainable consumption and production (SCP) strategies and plans. As clearly illustrated in earlier sections, the effects of obesity are unsustainable either socially, economically or environmentally, making curtailment of the obesity epidemic a primary and necessary goal for public health systems. In fact, from a public health perspective, obesity harms nearly every aspect of physical wellbeing, from premature mortality to elevated risks of chronic diseases. Thus, halting or even reversing obesity will fulfil public health goals and lead to more sustainability, both of which achievements provide strong justification for intervention.

Public health interventions can be targeted either at the societal level through regulation or law-based policy intervention or at a more micro level through health promotion programmes (Swinburn et al. 2011). Policy interventions, however, although their effect on obesity reduction is supposedly greater because they affect larger population shares and produce systemic modifications that induce further environmental, social and individual changes (ibid.), are also more difficult to implement. Health promotion, in contrast, may have smaller effects but such programmes are easier to implement and more target-group-specific. Both types of intervention are explained in more detail below.

### 14.5.1 Policy Interventions

Policy interventions include such regulation as food taxation and subsidies, food labelling and health claims, product reformulation and banning of unhealthy food marketing to children; measures often anchored in sustainability strategies and national action plans. Obesity is included, for instance, in the EU Sustainable Development Strategy to promote equality in public health and improve protection against health threats (EC 2006). Many countries worldwide (for example, most European countries, Australia, Canada and the USA) have also developed and implemented national action plans on obesity, diet and physical activity, leading the WHO to compile its comprehensive database on Nutrition, Obesity and Physical Activity (NOPA). This database encompasses a wide range of policy documents from general action plans to legally binding policies whose main purpose is to monitor progress on obesity, diet and physical activity interventions (WHO Europe 2013). Both supranational and national public health strategies provide the background for such intervention programmes and set the general frame in terms of not only the major approaches and methods applied but also the focus areas, targets, relevant actors and their respective responsibilities.

One relevant actor is the food industry, which on the one hand lobbies powerfully against regulation (Corporate Europe Observatory 2010) and follows short-term goals to satisfy its shareholders, but on the other hand, like retailers, is no longer blamed for the obesity epidemic and has since the early 2000s become part of the solution. In 2005, for example, the EU Directorate General for Health and Consumers launched a round table on 'Diet, Physical Activity and Health', bringing together all relevant stakeholders with the aim of encouraging voluntary actions across Europe (EC 2008). In particular, the combined pressure felt from consumers, governments and non-governmental organizations (NGOs) has created an opportunity for the industry to take advantage of the growing markets for health-promoting products (EC JRC 2014). As a result, some policy interventions – for example (self-)regulation of marketing to children, food labelling and product reformulation – are co-driven by the food industry.

One of the most important of these changes, product reformulation to decrease energy intake in diets, involves the reduction of salt, fat or sugar in food, as well as the reduction of packaging and portion sizes. Product reformulation can also mean the fortification of products with desirable nutrients such as vitamins or minerals – so-called 'functional food' – aimed at improving foods' nutritional value. In the EU, several such initiatives have been implemented over the last few years, driven by both industry and government (EC JRC 2014). Nevertheless important problems remain to be solved, including the emerging costs of reformulations, technical issues related to sensory properties and food safety, and the regulatory framework surrounding standards and dietary recommendations.

As far back as the early 1990s, Canada, Sweden and Norway banned all advertising targeted at children from children's public television programming (WHO 2004). However the evidence on the Swedish regulation's success was controversial, leading policy makers, including the European Commission, to promote and support more flexible, voluntary initiatives within the advertising sector (EIM 2008). These initiatives were followed by the provision of a common framework for national voluntary agreements on responsible food and beverage communication by the Confederation of the Food and Drink Industry of the EU (CIAA). This framework stipulated that advertising activities should not mislead children, not promote excessive consumption and not impede parents' role as gatekeepers (Harris et al. 2009). The Union of European Beverages Associations (UNESDA-CISDA) likewise developed its own guidelines, including the prohibition of soft drinks advertising in printed media or on the Internet or children's television (WHO 2007). As of today, most European countries have implemented codes of conduct on marketing to children, although the evaluation of industry self-regulation that was supposed to take place in 2010 never materialized. Hence the European Parliament recently requested that the existing national codes be evaluated to assess whether further regulatory steps are necessary (EC JRC 2014).

Food consumption that is sensitive to price can be partly controlled through fiscal measures (e.g. Andreyeva et al. 2010), so in recent years, taxation on foods considered unhealthy has either been introduced or come under debate. For instance Finland and Denmark have implemented a sugar tax, France a soda tax and Hungary a junk food tax; while Ireland plans a sugar tax, Romania a fast food tax (EPHA 2012) and Mexico the 2014 introduction of a tax on sugar-sweetened beverages and junk food. That such taxes have risks, however, is clearly illustrated by the case of the Danish fat tax, implemented in October 2011 and abandoned after only 14 months. Aimed at products containing more than 2.3 per cent saturated fat, this tax was levied on food manufacturers and food importers, who then passed the price increase on to consumers. In 2013, the tax was abandoned because of implementation issues, such as unclear definition of the products affected and the cumbersomeness of having food manufacturers calculate the levy themselves. According to media reports, it also resulted in increased cross-border shopping and lower profits for Danish food manufacturers while having only a dubious effect on consumer behaviour. That is, although Jensen and Smed (2013) estimate a 10–15 per cent drop in fat consumption in Denmark during its implementation, the tax existed for too short a time for its long-term effects to become clear.

Another obesity-fighting instrument is evidence-based, food-based dietary guidelines that serve to inform consumers about a healthy diet. Such guidelines, by standardizing and simplifying existing food labelling schemes, can reduce consumer confusion about the 'healthiness' of any given food (Thøgersen 2002). Examples include the general daily allowances (GDAs), the 'traffic light' system or the Nordic 'green keyhole', one of the few positive labels signifying a relatively healthier choice within one food group. In fact research has shown that consumers do indeed use such information when it is prominently displayed and easy to understand (Grunert and Wills 2007). The advantages and disadvantages of the different labelling schemes, however remain the subject of intense discussion among policy makers, the food industry, NGOs and researchers, with no conclusion as yet reached on the European level other than the UK's adoption of the traffic light system (EC JRC 2014). Nevertheless there does exist more consensus on and regulation of health claims within the EU in the sense that all must be verified by the European Food safety Authority (EFSA) and approved by the European Commission before usage (ibid.). In general, all such claims must be clear, accurate and evidence-based in order to avoid misleading consumers.

### 14.5.2 Health Promotion

Health promotion's main goal is to eliminate or at least decrease obesity drivers (that is, barriers to healthier lifestyles), while enhancing drivers of healthier lifestyles so as to reduce and prevent obesity. The major challenges in health promotion are affordability and sustainability; that is, the long-lasting effects. In this case, the targeted drivers and barriers stem primarily from the individual, social or environmental level, and most initiatives, such as public campaigns and educational programmes, are information-based. Such initiatives assume that consumers lack information about health consequences, meaning that once awareness and knowledge are raised, consumers will react accordingly (Swinburn et al. 2011).

Such raising of knowledge and awareness about healthy eating and physical activity is especially important whenever imperfect or asymmetric information exists between suppliers and consumers. Hence, information-based public campaigns targeting any type of population employ social marketing tools, often through media communication. These campaigns usually target a specific issue, such as reducing salt intake while increasing the intake of fish or fruit and vegetables (Capacci et al. 2012). The evaluation of these campaigns, however, is mostly restricted to awareness and knowledge – and in some instances self-reported behaviour – that allow no conclusions about actual changes in behaviour. In fact, studies on the effectiveness of informational campaigns suggest that the resulting changes are small (ibid.). Educational programmes, on the other hand, are mainly targeted at children in the hope of shaping taste preferences or habits at an early age that will then assumedly transfer into adulthood. These programmes vary greatly in terms of geography, intensity and content, which makes them difficult to compare and evaluate. In general both information-based campaigns and educational programmes increase consumer awareness and knowledge on health issues but fail to induce behavioural change. They do have the advantage of comparatively low costs, but even these vary with the complexity of the information delivered, the accessibility of the target group and the choice of communication channel.

Lately, therefore, these rather general approaches have been losing ground to what is referred to as 'nudging'; that is, behaviourally informed social regulation that leverages the biases influencing individual decision making, often by changing the context (Sunstein 2011). Such behaviourally informed instruments regulate through disclosure requirements, default rules, simplification or social norms, and are thus seen as less intrusive than imposed regulation (Thaler and Sunstein 2008). These newer approaches to health promotion draw on insights from behavioural economics and are also generally linked with low costs.

Successful forms of nudging often employ choice architecture, for example the highly effective strategy of displaying healthier foods more prominently than unhealthier choices in workplace or school canteens (Just and Wansink 2009). Also common in schools are fruit and milk schemes designed to establish healthy nutritional habits among children and adolescents. In Sweden, for example, school lunches, which are free, are subject to nutritional guidelines, which makes the healthy choice available to all. Vending machines selling unhealthier choices, on the other hand, are often banned on school campuses. Other forms of nudging are more informational: for instance, in some US states, nutritional information (for example, calories) has been a requirement on menus since 2010 (Capacci et al. 2012).

Nudging is also visible in major efforts to promote physical activity; for example, urban planning may systematically integrate opportunities and stimuli for physical activities in the regional infrastructure. Many countries, for instance, are striving to improve the physical and legal infrastructure for bicycle use by building attractive and safe cycle lanes and by enacting regulation that increases the road safety for cyclists and translates the idea of 'bikes first!' into practice. Another example is the provision of public bicycles for temporary use in urban areas (Sassi 2010). These interventions, rather than limiting choice, modify the available choice options in a manner that still seems cost-effective.

## 14.6 DISCUSSION

Despite many efforts to combat obesity worldwide, the trends are mostly heading one way: upwards. Yet the obesity epidemic is not simply an individual problem; it is also a societal challenge. That is, the current development of obesity is not merely a result of individual irrationality but rather is shaped by obesogenic environments and obesogenic societies. Unfortunately its consequences are unsustainable: it is costly in economic, social and environmental terms. As a result, (supra-)national sustainability strategies and public health strategies are acting in concert to fight obesity, all striving to find cost-effective interventions today rather than tomorrow.

Obesity arises from current dietary and physical activity patterns, especially in the West where diets and transportation patterns are ecologically unsustainable. Hence, changes in diet (for example, from meat-based to vegetarian-based) and related consumer behaviour (for example, food waste) have huge potential for obesity reduction. Such reduction would in turn alleviate the economically and socially unsustainable effects of obesity; for example by decreasing costs for health care systems and labour markets. Moreover besides decreasing the health deterioration and premature mortality caused by obesity, it may lower the incidence of social injustice and discrimination against the overweight and obese, thereby increasing overall quality of life.

Given the issues outlined above, decreasing obesity is one of public health's main targets, one traditionally approached by focusing on changing consumers' diets and physical activity behaviour; that is, decreasing energy intake while increasing energy expenditure. Nevertheless because the success of past public health interventions varies – whether societal policy measures or micro-level health promotions – a growing number of studies and reviews are carefully examining the evidence on intervention effectiveness. Such investigation has determined that policy interventions such as labelling, making health claims and marketing to children do affect consumer behaviour (Capacci et al. 2012), while alternatives such as product reformulation, although not yet widely evaluated, are potentially effective. Research also points to the effectiveness of health promotion initiatives such as educational and promotional programming, while behavioural economics suggests that exposure to specific contextual factors is at least as relevant for health and dietary choices as attitude, preference and intention. In fact interventions that combine health education and promotion, regulation and nudging have the greatest potential to curb the obesity epidemic (OECD 2012).

Because policies for healthier lifestyles are not simply a matter of state politics but are driven by civil society, consumers, industry, health organizations, the educational sector and the media, public health policies must be developed and implemented with the support and involvement of a range of actors, both public and private, at national, regional and community levels. Above all, such policies must be based in sound scientific evidence. As highlighted earlier in this chapter, the key drivers of obesity and their independencies are not yet fully understood, but are essential to promote healthier lifestyles of consumers.

# REFERENCES


Andreyeva, T., M.W. Long and K.D. Brownell (2010), 'The impact of food prices on consumption: a systematic review of research on the price elasticity of demand for food', *American Journal of Public Health*, 100 (2), 216–222.

Beuther, D.A. and E.R. Sutherland (2007), 'Overweight, obesity, and incident asthma: a meta-analysis of prospective epidemiologic studies', *American Journal of Respiratory and Critical Care Medicine*, 175 (7), 661–666.

BioIS (Bio Intelligence Service) (2010), 'Preparatory study on food waste across EU-27', Final Report for DG Environment, Contract Number: 07.0307/2009/540024/SER/G4, London: Policy Studies Institute.

Brundtland, G.H. and the World Commission on Environment and Development (1987), *Our Common Future*, Oxford: Oxford University Press.

Capacci, S., M. Mazzocchi, B. Shankar, J. Brambila Macias, W. Verbeke, F.J.A. Pérez-Cueto, A. Kozioł-Kozakowska et al. (2012), 'Policies to promote healthy eating in Europe: a structured review of policies and their effectiveness', *Nutrition Reviews*, 70 (3), 188–200.

Cawley, J. and C. Meyerhoefer (2012), 'The medical care costs of obesity: an instrumental variables approach', *Journal of Health Economics*, 31 (1), 219–230.

Cohen, D.A. (2008), 'Neurophysiological pathways to obesity: below awareness and beyond individual control', *Diabetes*, 57 (7), 1768–73.

Corporate Europe Observatory (2010), 'A red light for consumer information: the food industry's €1-billion campaign to block health warnings on food', Brussels: Corporate Europe Observatory.

Cunningham, S.A., E. Vaquera, C.C. Maturo and K.M. Venkat Narayan (2012), 'Is there evidence that friends influence body weight? A systematic review of empirical research', *Social Science and Medicine*, 75 (7), 1175–1183.

Darnton, A. (2009), 'The determinants of obesity', unpublished manuscript, London: British Department of Health.

EC (European Commission) (2006), 'Review of the EU Sustainable Development Strategy (EU SDS): renewed strategy', available at http://register.consilium.europa.eu/pdf/en/06/st10/st10917.en06.pdf (accessed 31 October 2013).

EC (European Commission) (2008), 'EU platform on diet, physical activity and health: 2008 annual report', Brussels: DG SANCO.

EC JRC (European Commission, Joint Research Centre) (2014), 'Tomorrow's healthy society: research priorities for foods and diets', background document, Brussels: European Commission, Joint Research Centre, Foresight Studies.

Edwards, P. and I. Roberts (2009), 'Population adiposity and climate change', *International Journal of Epidemiology*, 38 (4), 1137–1140.

EEA (European Environmental Agency) (2013), 'Environmental pressures from European consumption and production', EEA Technical Report No 2/2013, Copenhagen.

EIM (2008), 'Self-regulation practices in SANCO policy areas: final report', Brussels: EIM Business & Policy Research.

Elinder, L.S. and M. Jansson (2008), 'Obesogenic environments? Aspects on measurement and indicators', *Public Health Nutrition*, 12 (3), 307–315.

EPHA (European Public Health Alliance) (2012), 'Food taxation in Europe: evolution of the legislation', European Public Health Alliance, October update, available at http://www.epha.org/a/4814 (accessed 31 October 2013).

Faber, J., A. Schroten, M. Bles, M. Sevenster, A. Markowska, M. Smit, C. Rohde et al. (2012), 'Behavioural climate change mitigation options and their appropriate inclusion in quantitative longer term policy scenarios', Main Report for DG Climate Change, contract number 070307/2010/576075/SER/A4, CE Delft.

Finkelstein, E.A., O.A. Khavjou, H. Thompson, J.G. Trogdon, L. Pan, B. Sherry and W. Dietz (2012), 'Obesity and severe obesity forecasts through 2030', *American Journal of Preventive Medicine*, 42 (6), 563–570.

Finkelstein, E.A., J.G. Trogdon, J.W. Cohen and W. Dietz (2009), 'Annual medical spending attributable to obesity: payer- and service-specific estimates', *Health Affairs*, 28 (5), w822–w831.

Finucane, M.M., G.A. Stevens, M.J. Cowan, G.Danaei, J.K. Lin, C.J. Paciorek, G.M. Singh et al. (2011), 'National, regional, and global trends in body-mass index since 1980: systematic analysis of health examination surveys and epidemiological studies with 960 country-years and 9.1 million participants', *Lancet*, 377 (9765), 557–567.

Flegal, K.M., M.D. Carroll, B.K. Kit and C.L. Ogden (2012), 'Prevalence of obesity and trends in the distribution of body mass index among US adults 1999–2010', *Journal of the American Medical Association*, 307 (5), 491–497.

Foresight (2007), 'Foresight tackling obesities: Future Choices Project', London: Department for Innovation, Universities and Skills, Government Office for Science.

Forhan, M. and S.V. Gill (2013), 'Obesity, functional mobility and quality of life', *Best Practice and Research Clinical Endocrinology and Metabolism*, 27 (2), 129–137.

Grier, S.A., J. Mensinger, S.H. Huang, S.K. Kumanyika and N. Stettler (2007), 'Fast-food marketing and children's fast-food consumption: exploring parents' influences in an ethnically diverse sample', *Journal of Public Policy and Marketing*, 26 (2), 221–235.

Grunert, K. and J. Wills (2007), 'A review of European research on consumer response to nutrition information on food labels', *Journal of Public Health*, 15 (5), 385–399.

Guh, D.P., W. Zhang, N. Bansback, Z. Amarsi, C.L. Birmingham and A.H. Anis (2009), 'The incidence of co-morbidities related to obesity and overweight: A systematic review and meta-analysis', *BMC Public Health*, 9, 88.

Haines, A., A.J. McMichael, K.R. Smith, I. Roberts, J. Woodcock, A. Markandya, B.G. Armstrong et al. (2009), 'Public health benefits of strategies to reduce greenhouse-gas emissions: overview and implications for policy makers', *Lancet*, 374 (9707), 2104–2114.

Harris, L.H., J.L. Pomeranz, T. Lobstein and K.D. Brownell (2009), 'A crisis in the marketplace: how food marketing contributes to childhood obesity and what can be done', *Annual Review of Public Health*, 30 (1), 211–225.

Haslam, D.W. and W.P.T. James (2005), 'Obesity', *Lancet*, 366 (9492), 1197–1209.

HM Government (2008), 'Healthy weight, healthy lives: a cross-government strategy for England', Cross-Government Obesity Unit, London: Department of Health and Department of Children, Schools and Families.

Jensen, J.D. and S. Smed (2013), 'The Danish tax on saturated fat: short run effects on consumption, substitution patterns and consumer prices of fats', *Food Policy*, 42 (0), 18–31.

Johnson, M. and L. Hasher (1987), 'Human learning and memory', *Annual Review of Psychology*, 38, 631–668.

Just, D.R. and B. Wansink (2009), 'Smarter lunchrooms: Using behavioural economics to improve meal selection', *Choices*, 24 (3), 1–7.

Lake, A. and T. Townshend (2006), 'Obesogenic environments: exploring the built and food environments', *Journal of the Royal Society for the Promotion of Health*, 126 (6), 262–267.

Lobstein, T., L. Baur and R. Uauy (2004), 'Obesity in children and young people: a crisis in public health', *Obesity Reviews*, 5 (S1), 4–85.

McCormick, B. and I. Stone (2007), 'Economic costs of obesity and the case for government intervention', *Obesity Reviews*, 8 (S1), 161–164.

McLaren, L. (2007), 'Socioeconomic status and obesity', *Epidemiologic Reviews*, 29 (1), 29–48.

Monteiro, C.A., W.L. Conde and B.M. Popkin (2007), 'Income-specific trends in obesity in Brazil: 1975–2003', *American Journal of Public Health*, 97 (10), 1808–1812.

National Obesity Observatory (2010), 'The economic burden of obesity', available at http://www.noo.org.uk/uploads/doc/vid_8575_Burdenofobesity151110MG.pdf (accessed 28 October 2013).

OECD (Organisation for Economic Co-operation and Development) (2012), 'Health at a glance: Europe 2012', OECD Publishing, available at http://dx.doi.org/10.1787/9789264183896-en (accessed 19 September 2013).

Ogilvie, D. and N. Hamlet (2005), 'Obesity: the elephant in the corner', *British Medical Journal*, 331, 1545–1548.

Pickett, K.E., S. Kelly, T. Lobstein, E. Brunner and R.G. Wilkinson (2005), 'Wider income gaps, wider waistbands? An ecological study of income inequality and obesity', *Journal of Epidemiology and Community Health*, 59 (8), 670–674.

Posner, M. and C. Snyder (1975), 'Facilitation and inhibition in the processing of signals', in P. Rabbit and S. Dornic (eds), *Attention and Performance V*, London: Academic Press, pp. 450–469.

Prospective Studies Collaborations (2009), 'Body-mass index and cause-specific mortality in 900,000 adults: collaborative analyses of 57 prospective studies', *Lancet*, 373 (9669), 1083–1096.

Puhl, R.M., T. Andreyeva and K.D. Brownell (2008), 'Perceptions of weight discrimination: prevalence and comparison to race and gender discrimination in America', *International Journal of Obesity*, 32, 992–1000.

Puhl, R.M. and C.A. Heuer (2009), 'The stigma of obesity: a review and update', *Obesity*, 17 (5), 941–964.

Reisch, L.A., U. Eberle and S. Lorek (2013), 'Sustainable food consumption: an overview of contemporary issues and policies', *Sustainability: Science, Practice, and Policy*, 9 (2), 7–25.

Reisch, L.A. and W. Gwozdz (2011), 'Chubby cheeks and climate change: childhood obesity as a sustainable development issue', *International Journal of Consumer Studies*, 35 (1), 3–9.

Renton, A. (2006), 'The rot starts here', *Observer Food Monthly*, 28 May, available at http://www.guardian.co.uk/lifeandstyle/2006/may/28/foodanddrink.features2 (accessed 28 October 2013).

Rich-Edwards, J.W., D. Spiegelman, M. Garland, E. Hertzmark, D.J. Hunter, G.A. Colditz, W.C. Wilett et al. (2002), 'Physical activity, body mass index, and ovulatory disorder infertility', *Epidemiology*, 13 (2), 184–190.

Robertson, A., T. Lobstein and C. Knai (2007), 'Obesity and socio-economic groups in Europe: evidence review and implications for action', Brussels: European Commission, DG SANCO.

Rokholm, B., J.L. Baker and T.I.A. Sørensen (2010), 'The levelling off of the obesity epidemic since the year 1999: a review of evidence and perspectives', *Obesity Reviews*, 11 (12), 835–46.
Sassi, F. (2010), *Obesity and the Economics of Prevention: Fit not Fat*, Paris: OECD Publishing.
Scharff, R.L. (2009), 'Obesity and hyperbolic discounting: evidence and implications', *Journal of Consumer Policy*, 32 (1), 3–21.
Silventoinen, K., B. Rokholm, J. Kaprio and T.I.A. Sorensen (2010), 'The genetic and environmental influences on childhood obesity: a systematic review of twin and adoption studies', *International Journal of Obesity*, 34 (1), 29–40.
Stehfest, E., L. Bouwman, D.P. van Vuuren, M.G.J. den Elzen, B. Eickhout and P. Kabat (2009), 'Climate benefits of changing diet', *Climatic Change*, 95 (1–2), 83–102.
Story, M., K.M. Kaphingst, R. Robinson-O'Brien and K. Glanz (2008), 'Creating healthy food and eating environments: policy and environmental approaches', *Annual Review of Public Health*, 29, 253–272.
Strazzullo, P., L. D'Elia, G. Cairella, F. Garbagnati, F.P. Cappuccio and L. Scalfi (2010), 'Excess body weight and incidence of stroke: meta-analysis of prospective studies with 2 million participants', *Stroke*, 41, e418–e426.
Sunstein, C. (2011), 'Empirically informed regulation', *University of Chicago Law Review*, 78 (4), 1349–1429.
Swinburn, B.A., G. Sacks, K.D. Hall, K. McPherson, D.T. Finegood, M.L. Moodie and S.L. Gortmaker (2011), 'The global obesity pandemic: shaped by global drivers and local environments', *Lancet*, 378 (9793), 804–814.
Swinburn, B., G. Sacks and E. Ravussin (2009), 'Increased food energy supply is more than sufficient to explain the US epidemic of obesity', *American Journal of Clinical Nutrition*, 90 (6), 1453–56.
Taylor, V.H., M. Forhan, S.N. Vigod, R.S. McIntyre and K.M. Morrison (2013), 'The impact of obesity on quality of life', *Best Practice and Research Clinical Endocrinology and Metabolism*, 27 (2), 139–146.
Thaler, R.H. (1981), 'Some empirical evidence on dynamic inconsistency', *Economics Letters*, 8, 201–207.
Thaler, R.H. and C.R. Sunstein (2008), *Nudge: Improving Decisions about Health, Wealth, and Happiness*, New Haven, CT: Yale University Press.
Thøgersen, J. (2002), 'Promoting green consumer behavior with eco-labels', in T. Dietz and P. Stern (eds), *New Tools for Environmental Protection: Education, Information, and Voluntary Measures*, Washington, DC: National Academy Press, pp. 83–104.
Trogdon, J.G., J. Nonnemaker and P. Jais (2008), 'Peer effects in adolescent overweight', *Journal of Health Economics*, 27 (5), 1388–1399.
Tversky, A. and D. Kahnemann (1981), 'The framing of decisions and the psychology of choice', *Science*, 211, 453–458.
UN (2005), '2005 world summit outcome', available at http://www.who.int/hiv/universalaccess2010/worldsummit.pdf (accessed 25 October 2013).
Vanham, D. and G. Bidoglio (2013), 'A review on the indicator water footprint for the EU28', *Ecological Indicators*, 26 (0), 61–75.
Wang, Y.C., K. McPherson, T. Marsh and S.L. Gortmaker (2011), 'Health and economic burden of the projected obesity trends in the USA and the UK', *Lancet*, 378 (9793), 815–825.
WHO (World Health Organization) (2004), 'Marketing food to children: the global regulatory environment', Geneva: World Health Organization.
WHO (World Health Organization) (2007), 'Marketing food to children: changes in the global regulatory environment 2004–2006', Geneva: World Health Organization.
WHO (World Health Organization) (2010), 'International statistical classification of disease and related health problems', available at http://apps.who.int/classifications/icd10/browse/2010/en#/E65-E68 (accessed 19 September 2013).
WHO (World Health Organization) Europe (2009), 'Prevalence of overweight and obesity in children and adolescents', Fact Sheet No. 2.3, European Environment and Health Information Systems, Geneva: World Health Organization.
WHO (World Health Organization) Europe (2013), 'Database on nutrition, obesity and physical activity', available at http://data.euro.who.int/nopa/ (accessed 1 November 2013).
Withrow, D. and D.A. Alter (2010), 'The economic burden of obesity worldwide: a systematic review of the direct costs of obesity', *Obesity Reviews*, 12 (2), 131–41.
Witkowski, T.H. (2007), 'Food marketing and obesity in developing countries: analysis, ethics, and public policy', *Journal of Macromarketing*, 27 (2), 126–137.
WWF [World Wildlife Fund] (2009), *Der Wasser Fußabdruck Deutschlands: Woher stammt das Wasser, das in unseren Lebensmitteln steckt?* Berlin: WWF Germany.

# PART V

# CROSS-CUTTING ISSUES

# 15. Consumer habits and sustainable consumption

*Bas Verplanken and Deborah Roy*

When you ask people if sustainable consumption is a good thing, you can expect an overwhelmingly positive response. Yet, as this *Handbook of Research on Sustainable Consumption* makes clear, there is still a long way to go. And this may even be the optimistic view: most people show little interest in making truly sustainable choices, but rather follow their natural tendency to focus on short-term benefits and tangible outcomes, which more often than not do not contribute to a sustainable lifestyle. The content of the present volume is a testimony to the complexity and difficulty of sustainable consumption. While realizing that our focus only represents a thin slice of a much richer reality, this chapter focuses on individual consumers, and in particular on consumer habits and sustainability. We first address the question: what is meant by sustainable consumption? We then discuss the process of making sustainable choices, and define and position the concept of habit. Finally we turn to the important question of behaviour change and prospects for interventions to promote more sustainable lifestyles.

## 15.1 WHAT IS SUSTAINABLE CONSUMPTION?

Sustainable consumption is a loosely defined concept, which encompasses a large variety of behaviours and domains. A plethora of labels can be found that seem to be considered as more or less synonymous with sustainable behaviour, such as pro-environmental, ecological, green or ethical behaviour. In defining sustainable consumption, we may adopt various approaches. A 'high-level' approach is the notion that sustainable consumption contributes to, or at least does not jeopardize, the survival of future generations. This was implied in the definition of sustainable consumption as stated in the seminal Brundtland Report released by the World Commission on Environment and Development (WCED 1987): 'Sustainable development is development that meets the needs of the present without compromising the ability of future generations to meet their own needs' (p. 43).

Obviously, the WCED definition does not answer the question of which behaviours should or should not be considered as sustainable consumption. A more pragmatic approach is to define specific behaviours or behavioural domains as sustainable. For instance the Department for Environment, Food, and Rural Affairs (Defra) in the United Kingdom defined specific sustainable behaviours, organized in broader categories, such as using energy and water wisely (for example, line-drying laundry), travelling sustainably (for example, combining trips) and being part of improving the environment (for example, volunteering) (Defra 2008). The benefits of such lists are that citizens and policy makers are provided with concrete examples of behaviours, which might be improved. The downside is that such lists might be incomplete, become outdated, or are influenced by other policy agendas than promoting sustainability.

Finally, sustainability might be defined by what 'ordinary people' are telling us. For example, we posed this question in interviews with UK citizens (Roy and Verplanken 2014). What came to our interviewees' mind most rapidly was recycling, with an emphasis on minimization of waste. Another immediate association was preserving resources for future generations. Sustainability also represented addressing the negative impact humanity is having on the natural world and the depletion of natural resources. However any impact was seen as rather abstract, far away and set in the future. One interviewee expressed this as follows:

> As we know, some of the rain forests, which have a big effect on weather patterns and wildlife, are disappearing, and we may not see the full impact that this has during our lifetime, but things are changing at the moment but certainly for the next generation to come if things aren't looked at and sorted out, if you like, now, then it will have an effect on later generations.

This illustrates the fact that phenomena such as climate change may be subject to temporal and spatial discounting; due to the large perceived psychological distance, risks are perceived to be less urgent and there is less involvement of motivating emotions (e.g. Gifford 2011; Spence et al. 2012).

In a survey among students in the USA and the UK, we asked which worries they had about the natural environment (Verplanken and Roy 2013). The top five worries mentioned were global warming and climate change; pollution and environmental damage; extinction of species and biodiversity; resource depletion and lack of renewables; and deforestation. This study also demonstrated that habitual worrying about the environment was constructive, rather than pathological, as it was associated with pro-environmental attitudes and behaviours and with a personality structure characterized by imagination and an appreciation for new ideas.

An indication of how people think about sustainable living might also be obtained from how they mentally organize sustainable behaviours. We asked a sample of citizens how often they performed a set of 25 sustainable behaviours. When presenting the questions, the behaviours were grouped into five domains: energy saving, waste reduction, water conservation, transport and miscellaneous behaviours. However, a cluster analysis of participants' responses revealed a different organization than the way the behaviours were presented, namely into sustainable technologies, sustainable energy use, sustainable food and shopping, sustainable environments and sustainable gardening (Figure 15.1).

It is important to note some caveats. Firstly, behaviours vary widely in their actual contribution to sustainability (Whitmarsh 2009). It is extremely difficult for the ordinary citizen to have accurate views on sustainability, for instance comparing the impact of switching off lights with buying locally produced food or a flight to Spain. Also, whereas some choices may be carefully considered, most behaviours are performed relatively mindlessly, and considerations about sustainability may then not easily appear in one's consciousness. We will elaborate on this in the next section.

## 15.2 TO THINK OR NOT TO THINK ABOUT SUSTAINABILITY? THAT IS THE QUESTION

In order to change behaviour into a more sustainable direction, an important question is whether or when people consider sustainability as an attribute of their choice alterna-

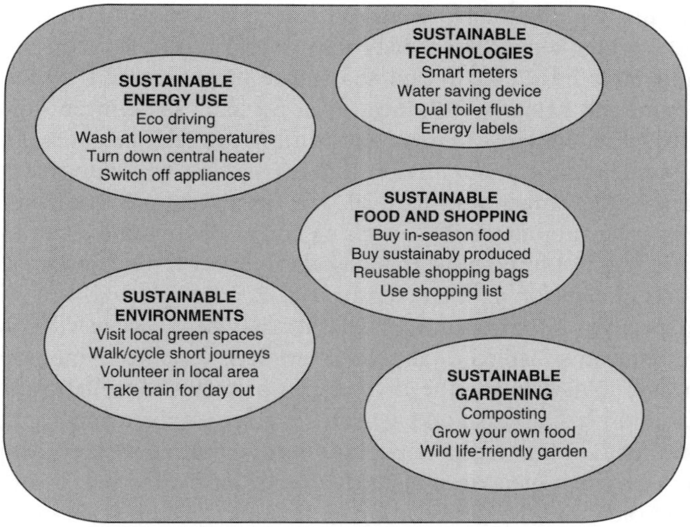


*Figure 15.1 Mental clustering of sustainable behaviours*

tives. We have known for a long time that people do not follow normative 'rational' decision rules, but often ignore information, take short cuts and use their intuition in arriving at choices (e.g. Slovic et al. 2002). For instance, given a choice between products which vary in a number of attributes, a rational decision rule would be to weigh each attribute by its importance or impact, consider the values of each choice alternative on all attributes, combine these values with the weights of the attributes, and choose the alternative which has the highest weighted value. If sustainability is one of the attributes, this decision rule would take sustainability into account, no matter whether its weight was large or small. However, we seldom or never follow this rule, but rather use less elaborate and thus less effortful decision strategies. A large number of such 'short cuts' have been described in the decision making literature (e.g. Payne et al. 1993). For instance the elimination-by-aspect rule drops alternatives that do not meet a set criterion on the most important attribute, and then continues this process with the second most important attribute, and so on, until one alternative remains. Following the lexicographic decision rule the decision maker first establishes the most important attribute, and then chooses the alternative that scores best on that attribute. The satisficing rule is even simpler, and considers alternatives one at a time in the order they occur, and settles for the first alternative that meets a certain need, that is, 'is doing the job'.

What these cognitively 'easier' decision rules have in common is that if sustainability or sustainability-related attributes are not considered as top priority (for example, compared to price, comfort or quality), such attributes may not feature *at all* in consumers' decision making. This is more likely in busy or otherwise pressing choice environments. For instance, while energy labels may have some effect on making more sustainable choices (e.g. Grankvist and Biel 2006), such effects may quickly vanish when choices are made under time pressure, due to the use of the more heuristic-based decision rules (Verplanken and Weenig 1993). Only if sustainability is considered as an important attribute (e.g. Honkanen et al. 2006), or is linked with important values (e.g. Honkanen and Verplanken 2004), it may play a role in the decision making process. Verplanken and Holland (2002) found that more environment-friendly choices were made if environmental values were central to a person's self-concept and these values were cognitively activated. However, such conditions are relatively rare, and can only be found among segments of the population that are genuinely committed to the sustainability agenda (cf. Verplanken and Roy 2013; Verplanken and Svenson 1997). On the other hand, under certain conditions, such as when sustainability features are prominently presented, it is not impossible that sustainability will play a more significant role in heuristic forms of decision making (Bradu et al. 2014).

Another perspective on the question of whether (if, when) people will consider sustainability can be found in so-called dual-process models, which became popular in social and consumer psychology during the 1990s (e.g. Fazio 1990; Ouellette and Wood 1998; Petty and Cacioppo 1986; Strack and Deutsch 2004; see Chaiken and Trope 1999). These models describe behaviour in terms of two different operating systems, which may guide behaviour. In one system behaviour is a function of motivated processing or intention, which is thus characterized by deliberation, conscious decision making; in other words, willpower. These processes are relatively elaborate and cognitively effortful, and are typically portrayed in socio-cognitive models of behaviour (e.g. Ajzen 1991). Alternatively, behaviour may unfold in cognitively less demanding and more spontaneous ways. A variety of such spontaneous processes have been proposed, for instance automatic elicitation of strong attitudes (Fazio 1990), salient context cues (Petty and Cacioppo 1986), schema-based impulses (Strack and Deutsch 2004) or habit (Ouellette and Wood 1998), to which we will turn in the next section. The key to the question of which process will prevail (conscious deliberation or a spontaneous reaction) is whether there is sufficient motivation and cognitive capacity to deliberate or process information. In general, high motivation combined with sufficient cognitive capacity lead to more elaborate, deliberate and effortful processes. A lack in motivation and/or capacity leads to the cognitively less demanding spontaneous responses. Following our previous reasoning with respect to decision rules, as sustainability is very often a secondary attribute of products and services, it will be most likely only be considered under conditions of high elaboration, that is, high motivation and sufficient cognitive capacity. And again, such conditions are less prevalent compared to the default condition where either motivation or capacity, or both, are lacking.

A logical conclusion that may follow from a dual-process analysis is that interventions may be developed that 'kick' people from spontaneous to deliberate modes of processing. In fact, some of the successful interventions in the sustainability domains can be interpreted along these lines (e.g. Bamberg 2006; Eriksson et al. 2008; Fujii and Kitamura 2003).

## 15.3 THE CASE OF HABIT

Many of the behaviours which individuals or households are engaged in and are relevant to the sustainability agenda are executed repetitively and routinely. During the last decade the insight has gained ground that this has consequences for behaviour change (e.g. Verplanken and Wood 2006). Based on a meta-analysis on the relationship between past and future behaviour, Ouellette and Wood (1998) proposed a dual-process model in which past behaviour may guide future choices via the deliberate route through intentions or, when behaviour has been repetitively conducted, via a spontaneous route through habituation (e.g. Verplanken 2006).

Habits comprise a form of automaticity in responding which develops as people repeat actions in stable circumstances (e.g. Verplanken and Wood 2006). Habit can be characterized by three important 'pillars' (e.g. Verplanken 2010). The first, obviously, is repetition, which has always been the key feature to define habit. Repetition is not only a key feature of habit, it is also what makes a habit significant with respect to its impact: the cumulative effect of repetitive behaviours performed by large numbers of people is what creates problematic levels of unsustainability. There is no harm whatsoever for the environment in making the occasional leisure trip by car, but there is an impact on the environment when large populations habitually commute by car instead of using alternative modes of transport.

The second pillar is automaticity. This may be broken down into a number of features, that is, lack of awareness and conscious intent, mental efficiency and limited feelings of control (e.g. Verplanken and Orbell 2003). The automaticity pillar represents how habits make up our everyday experience of behaviour as being fluent and not consisting of discrete 'choices', which in fact we are constantly making. We may experience this when we are not able to perform our usual habits, for instance when we are shopping in a different supermarket than we are used to, and realize we have to 'work' on finding the products we usually grab in a more or less mindless fashion. Habituation frees up mental resources, and makes it possible to do or think about other things, while executing the habitual act. Another aspect of automaticity is that strong habits may lead to 'tunnel vision': individuals are less likely to attend to new information, even if this might lead to more optimal choices, such as when an efficient bus line is introduced (Klöckner and Verplanken 2013; Verplanken et al. 1997). Habits may also lead to perceptual biases, such as overestimating disadvantages of non-habitual alternatives (Fujii et al. 2001).

The third pillar is not so much a feature of habit itself, but one of the context in which habits are executed: while habits form by repetitive associations between the behaviour and features of the performance context, once habits are formed these features may automatically trigger the habit, that is, without the need to deliberate or make a conscious decision (e.g. Orbell and Verplanken 2010; Wood and Neal 2007). Another way of looking at this is from the perspective of locus of control over behaviour. When behaviour is guided by attitudes and intentions, control is largely located within the person; it is the person's motivation or willpower which make things happen. When behaviour is triggered by context cues, as in the case of habits, control has somewhat shifted from the person to the environment; it is no longer a person's willpower which makes things happen, but the cues that have been empowered to trigger the habit.

In line with Ouellette and Wood's (1998) analysis of the relationship between intention, past behaviour and future behaviour, intentions and habits are often found to be in competition: when habits are strong, intentions are not an active force, and vice versa (e.g. Danner et al. 2008; Ji and Wood 2007; Triandis 1977; Verplanken et al. 1998). For instance Verplanken et al. (1998) assessed intentions and habit strength of car use, and assessed actual car use from travel diaries which were kept by participants during the course of a week. They thus demonstrated that intentions predicted car use well when car use habit was weak, but that intentions were uncorrelated with behaviour when car use habit was strong. In the previous section we concluded that if sustainability is to feature in people's choices, this is more likely to happen through a more effortful and deliberate choice process than through a heuristic choice process. The presence of strong habits thus does not bode well for sustainable choices.

In addition, there is another issue related to habits, which particularly may form a barrier to sustainability. Many habits are goal-directed, and the activation of a goal (for example, going to work) may automatically trigger a habit (for example, taking the car; Aarts and Dijksterhuis 2000). The problem with many behaviours that are relevant for the sustainability agenda, such as those related to transportation, energy use, shopping or waste, is that unless an individual entertains sustainability as a core value central to their self-concept, the goals that are associated with these habits are not to create a more sustainable world, but rather to accomplish other ends, such as efficiency, reducing costs or increasing comfort (e.g. Hansla et al. 2013). And because these habits are performed without much deliberation, the chances are high that the sustainability argument will not feature in individuals' decision making.

## 15.4 CHANGING BEHAVIOUR: THE HABIT DISCONTINUITY HYPOTHESIS

The classical approach of general information campaigns aimed at raising awareness and changing attitudes and values in an undefined population, in the hope that behaviours follow suit, has not been convincingly effective in producing significantly higher levels of sustainable consumption (e.g. Weenig and Midden 1997). Although the quality of the 'package' delivered in an intervention (for example, information, specific directives, activities) is of the utmost importance, interventions may prove more effective if these are tailored to the targeted audience or the dynamics of the context in which change is projected (e.g. Hawe et al. 2009). A variety of such approaches are available in the sustainability domain, such as those using segmentation and phase models to identify sections of the population, which might be more receptive to interventions (e.g. Bamberg 2013; Dahlstrand and Biel 1997), or social networks as vehicle for change (e.g. Weenig and Midden 1991).

The present analysis of (un)sustainable behaviours as habits may lead to another approach, one that capitalizes on the timing at which interventions are delivered, and in particular on circumstances where habits are temporarily broken or suspended, which was denoted as the 'habit discontinuity hypothesis' (Verplanken et al. 2008; Verplanken and Wood 2006). Such discontinuities occur in many forms and varieties during the course of an individual's life, such as leaving school for further education or work, starting a family, moving house, changing job or retirement. These transitions come with relatively sudden changes in the way people organize their lives. Habits are part of this shake-up. Old habits may not be applicable in the new situation, or not in the form in which they have always been executed. New behaviours may have to be negotiated and established. Such discontinuities may provide unique opportunities for interventions; there may be brief windows in time during which people have to reorientate themselves, and find new solutions or ways of doing things. Interventions might be more effective when aimed at such discontinuities (Bamberg 2006; Jones and Ogilvie 2012; Thøgersen 2012; Verplanken and Roy 2014; Verplanken and Wood 2006; Verplanken et al. 2008; Walker et al. 2014; Wood et al. 2005).

In a survey among commuters, Verplanken et al. (2008) provided circumstantial evidence for a habit discontinuity effect in a cross-sectional study. These authors assessed the strength of participants' pro-environmental values, whether they commuted by car or alternative transportation, and how long ago they had moved house. Not surprisingly, participants with strong pro-environmental values were less likely to commute by car. However this relationship was only found among those who had moved house in the previous year. These results were at least compatible with the hypothesis that context change may make people think and, in this case, consider their pro-environmental values in assessing their options (cf. Verplanken and Holland 2002).

In terms of actual interventions, some research has focused on interventions that were delivered in the aftermath of 'naturally' occurring discontinuities. For instance Bamberg (2006) provided a free transportation ticket and personal schedule information of public transportation to people who recently had relocated. Compared to a no-intervention control group, the intervention resulted in a strong increase in the use of public transport from pre-relocation to post-relocation. While this study did not include a comparison with residents who had not relocated, the results are in line with the habit discontinuity hypothesis. Walker et al. (2014) followed commuters who had switched away from car use to more sustainable travel modes after an office relocation. They demonstrated how the new habit strengthened, while the old habit decayed in strength, over a four-week period after the relocation.

Thøgersen (2009) demonstrated that significant proportions of car drivers who had expressed an intention to use public transport in the future, and were given a free one-month travel card on public transport, indeed switched to this mode of transportation compared to a no-intervention control group. A secondary analysis of these data took into account whether or not participants had recently changed either residence or workplace (Thøgersen 2012). This analysis revealed that, in line with the habit discontinuity hypothesis, the intervention effect could only be detected among those who had recently undergone such a transition.

A rigorous test of the habit discontinuity hypothesis was provided in a field experiment conducted in Peterborough, UK (Verplanken and Roy 2014). In that study, 400 households were given an intervention promoting sustainable behaviours. The intervention consisted of a household visit and interview, free sustainable items, tailored advice and general information. Another 400 households served as a no-intervention control condition. In both groups half of the households had moved house in the previous six months, while the other half had not. Movers and non-movers were matched on key features, while a clustered randomization procedure was used to designate the intervention and control households. Self-reported frequencies of 25 behaviours were assessed at baseline and eight weeks later. At baseline a host of traditional determinants of behaviour were measured as well, such as intentions, perceived control, habit strength, personal norms and environmental values.

There were two key results in this study. One was that after controlling for all baselines assessments, there was support for the habit discontinuity hypothesis in the form of a small but statistically significant interaction effect between having received an intervention and recently having moved house; the intervention was more effective among those who had recently moved house. The second key finding was revealed when we analysed in more detail when exactly people had moved house; the discontinuity effect appeared to be confined to those who had moved house in the previous three months. No effects were found for participants who had relocated six months earlier or longer ago. This study thus provided proof of concept for the idea that interventions provide more value for money when delivered to people who have recently moved house.

If habit discontinuity effects prove to be robust in future research, an important question will be how long exactly a window of opportunity exists. While Verplanken and Roy's (2014) study suggested that this window existed during the first three months after moving house, which also happened to be the time frame in Thøgersen's (2012) analysis, this is by no means set in stone, and may be different in other contexts. It is also not unthinkable that a window of opportunity opens before the actual discontinuity takes place, for instance when commuting options are considered in order to decide on a location. Jones and Ogilvie (2012) found evidence to suggest that a window only opened some time after participants had moved; commuters in their study started to review their commuting options after moving house or workplace, and only made changes months later. The bottom line for sustainability interventions which capitalize on habit discontinuities is that it is imperative to investigate when and for how long the period exists during which people are most likely to consider more sustainable alternatives.

## 15.5 UPSTREAM INTERVENTIONS

An alternative for interventions that target individuals' behaviours are so-called 'upstream' approaches (e.g., Maio et al. 2007; McKinlay 1993; Verplanken 2011; Verplanken and Wood 2006). These involve large-scale macro-level policy changes, such as tax and other economic incentives (for example, road pricing, congestion tax), transformations of the infrastructure or physical environments (for example, closing city centres to private automobiles, building energy-efficient homes), restricting the availability of options (for example, abolishing traditional light bulbs or the use of certain chemicals in food production systems), or directly regulating behaviour (for example, enforcing speed reductions). Such interventions obviously take time and require political willpower. The latter is particularly difficult when a politician's survival depends on local support.

Some large-scale upstream interventions, such as mandatory seatbelt use, smoking bans and abolishing traditional light bulbs, have been extremely successful not only in terms of behaviour change, but also by receiving wide public acceptance (e.g. Poortinga et al. 2013; cf. Eriksson et al. 2010). Upstream interventions may have implications that go further than mere behaviour change. One is that such interventions may influence social practices, such as the way we commute or do our shopping, in which habits are embedded (e.g., Kurz et al. 2014; Shove et al. 2012). Also, while the traditional thinking about behaviour change has often been to target attitudes and values in order to change behaviour, this process may well be reversed. When upstream interventions successfully change behaviour, we may capitalize on that by designing interventions that bring people's attitudes and values in line with the (already changed) behaviours. Behaviour change may thus be consolidated. This may even lead to spillover effects to other behaviours which were not targeted in the first place, although this is still a somewhat elusive phenomenon (e.g. Poortinga et al. 2013; Thøgersen and Ölander 2003).

## 15.6 FINAL REMARKS

The notions that our habitat is vulnerable and resources are finite have been widely accepted in our societies. Compared to where we were 40 or 50 years ago, much progress has been made in raising this awareness and in taking measures to mitigate these risks. There has also been tremendous progress in technological developments, which have contributed to more sustainable ways of living, producing and consumption. However the world population has also grown massively, perhaps partly because of the technological advancements, and thus continues to put enormous pressure on our ecosystems. Although many people believe that action is needed to achieve a more sustainable balance, it is also clear that sustainability has never gained a key position in the decisions of the majority of consumers or, for that matter, businesses and governments. Consumers are driven by tangible personal benefits that are more certain, rather than invisible long-term risks; businesses are driven by profit; and policy makers by the next election. However there are individual citizens, green movements, ethical businesses and a handful of responsible politicians who are genuinely concerned, and who do prioritize sustainability (Nilsson et al. 2004; Verplanken and Roy 2013). These are the forces that have to carry the sustainability agenda forward. It is hoped that when our great-grandchildren look back at the beginning of this century, they will feel proud that these people never lost hope.

## REFERENCES


Aarts, H. and A. Dijksterhuis (2000), 'Habits as knowledge structures: automaticity in goal-directed behavior', *Journal of Personality and Social Psychology*, 78, 53–63.

Ajzen, I. (1991), 'The theory of planned behavior', *Organizational Behavior and Human Decision Processes*, 50, 179–211.

Bamberg, S. (2006), 'Is a residential relocation a good opportunity to change people's travel behavior? Results from a theory-driven intervention study', *Environment and Behavior*, 38, 820–840.

Bamberg, S. (2013), 'Applying the stage model of self-regulated behavioral change in a car use reduction intervention', *Journal of Environmental Psychology*, 33, 68–75.

Bradu, C., J.L. Orquin and J. Thøgersen (2013), 'The mediated influence of a traceability label on consumer's willingness to buy the labelled product', *Journal of Business Ethics*, 124 (2), 283–295.

Chaiken, S. and Y. Trope (1999), *Dual-Process Theories in Social Psychology*, New York: Guilford.

Dahlstrand, U. and A. Biel (1997), 'Pro-environmental habits: Propensity levels in behavioral change', *Journal of Applied Social Psychology*, 27, 588–601.

Danner, U., H. Aarts and N.K. de Vries (2008), 'Habit vs. intention in the prediction of future behaviour: the role of frequency, context stability and mental accessibility of past behaviour', *British Journal of Social Psychology*, 47, 245–265.

Defra (Department for Environment, Food and Rural Affairs) (2008), *Framework for Pro-Environmental Behaviour*, London: Department for Environment, Food, and Rural Affairs.

Eriksson, L., J. Garvill and A.M. Nordlund (2008), 'Interrupting habitual car use: the importance of car habit strength and moral motivation for personal car use reduction', *Transportation Research Part F*, 11, 10–23.

Eriksson, L., A.M. Nordlund and J. Garvill (2010), 'Expected car use reduction in response to structural travel

demand management measures', *Transportation Research Part F: Traffic Psychology and Behaviour*, 13, 329–342.
Fazio, R.H. (1990), 'Multiple processes by which attitudes guide behavior: the MODE model as an integrative framework', *Advances in Experimental Social Psychology*, 23, 75–109.
Fujii, S., T. Gärling, and R. Kitamura (2001), 'Changes in drivers' perceptions and use of public transport during a freeway closure: effects of temporary structural change on cooperation in a real-life social dilemma', *Environment and Behavior*, 33, 796–808.
Fujii, S. and R. Kitamura (2003), 'What does a one-month free bus ticket do to habitual drivers?', *Transportation*, 30, 81–95.
Gifford, R. (2011), 'The dragons of inaction: psychological barriers that limit climate change mitigation and adaptation', *American Psychologist*, 66, 290–302.
Grankvist, G. and A. Biel (2006), 'The impact of environmental information of professional purchasers' choice of products', *Business Strategy and the Environment*, 16, 421–429.
Hanlsa, A., T. Gärling and A. Biel (2013), 'Attitude toward environmental policy measures related to value orientation', *Journal of Applied Social Psychology*, 43, 582–590.
Hawe, P., A. Shiell and T. Riley (2009), 'Theorising interventions as events in systems', *American Journal of Community Psychology*, 43, 267–276.
Honkanen, P. and B. Verplanken (2004), 'Understanding attitudes towards genetically modified food: the role of values and value strength', *Journal of Consumer Policy*, 27, 401–420.
Honkanen, P., B. Verplanken and S.O. Olsen (2006), 'Ethical values and motives driving organic food choice', *Journal of Consumer Behaviour*, 5, 420–430.
Ji, M.F. and W. Wood (2007), 'Purchase and consumption habits: not necessarily what you intend', *Journal of Consumer Psychology*, 17, 261–276.
Jones, C.H.D. and D. Ogilvie (2012), 'Motivations for active commuting: a qualitative investigation of the period of home or work relocation', *International Journal of Behavioural Nutrition and Physical Activity*, 9, 109.
Klöckner, C.A. and B. Verplanken (2013), 'Yesterday's habits preventing change for tomorrow? About the influence of automaticity on environmental behaviour', in L. Steg, A.E. van den Berg and J.I.M. de Groot (eds), *Environmental Psychology: An Introduction*, Chichester: Wiley-Blackwell, pp. 197–209.
Kurz, T., B. Gardner, B. Verplanken and C. Abraham (2014), 'Habitual behaviours or patterns of practice? Explaining and changing repetitive climate-relevant actions', *WIREs Climate Change*, DOI: 10.1002/wcc.327.
Maio, G.R., B. Verplanken, A.S.R. Manstead, W. Stroebe, C.S. Abraham, P. Sheeran and M. Conner (2007), 'Social psychological factors in lifestyle change and their relevance to policy', *Social Issues and Policy Review*, 1, 99–137.
McKinlay, J.B. (1993), 'The promotion of health through planned sociopolitical change: challenges for research and policy', *Social Science and Medicine*, 36, 109–117.
Nilsson, A., C. von Borgstede and A. Biel (2004), 'Willingness to accept climate change strategies: the effect of values and norms', *Journal of Environmental Psychology*, 24, 267–277.
Orbell, S. and B. Verplanken (2010), 'The automatic component in health behavior: habit as cue-contingent automaticity', *Health Psychology*, 29, 374–383.
Ouellette, J.A. and W. Wood (1998), 'Habit and intention in everyday life: the multiple processes by which past behavior predicts future behavior', *Psychological Bulletin*, 124, 54–74.
Payne, J.W., J.R. Bettman and E.J. Johnson (1993), *The Adaptive Decision Maker*, New York: Cambridge University Press.
Petty, R.E. and J.T. Cacioppo (1986), *Communication and Persuasion: Central and Peripheral Routes to Attitude Change*, New York: Springer.
Poortinga, W., L. Whitmarsh and C. Suffolk (2013), 'The introduction of a single-use carrier bag charge in Wales: attitude change and behavioural spillover effects', *Journal of Environmental Psychology*, 36, 240–247.
Roy, D. and B. Verplanken (2014), 'Sustainable living and how younger and older generations are making sense of it', manuscript.
Shove, E., M. Pantzar and M. Watson (2012), *The Dynamics of Social Practice: Everyday Life and How it Changes*, London: Sage.
Slovic, P., M. Finucane, E. Peters, and D.G. MacGregor (2002), 'The affect heuristic', in T. Gilovich, D. Griffin and D. Kahneman (eds), *Heuristics and Biases: The Psychology of Intuitive Judgment*, Cambridge: Cambridge University Press, pp. 397–420.
Spence, A., W. Poortinga and N. Pidgeon (2012), 'The psychological distance of climate change', *Risk Analysis*, 32, 957–972.
Strack, F. and R. Deutsch (2004), 'Reflective and impulsive determinants of social behavior', *Personality and Social Psychology Review*, 8, 220–247.

Thøgersen, J. (2009), 'Promoting public transport as a subscription service: effects of a free month travel card', *Transport Policy*, 16, 335–343.
Thøgersen, J. (2012), 'The importance of timing for breaking commuters' car driving habits', in A. Warde and D. Southerton (eds), *The Habits of Consumption*, Helsinki: Helsinki Collegium for Advances Studies, pp. 130–140.
Thøgersen, J. and F. Ölander (2003), 'Spillover of environmental-friendly behaviour', *Journal of Environmental Psychology*, 23, 225–236.
Triandis, H.C. (1977), *Interpersonal Behaviour*, Monterey, CA: Brooks/Cole.
Verplanken, B. (2006), 'Beyond frequency: habit as mental construct', *British Journal of Social Psychology*, 45, 639–656.
Verplanken, B. (2010), 'Habit: from overt action to mental events', in C.R. Agnew, D.E. Carlston, W.G. Graziano and J.R. Kelly (eds), *Then a Miracle Occurs: Focusing on Behavior in Social Psychological Theory and Research*, Oxford: Oxford University Press, pp. 68–88.
Verplanken, B. (2011), 'Old habits and new routes to sustainable behaviour', in L. Whitmarsh, S. O'Neill and I. Lorenzoni (eds), *Engaging the Public with Climate Change*, London: Earthscan, pp. 17–30.
Verplanken, B., H. Aarts and A. van Knippenberg (1997), 'Habit, information acquisition, and the process of making travel mode choices', *European Journal of Social Psychology*, 27, 539–560.
Verplanken, B., H. Aarts, A. Knippenberg and A. Moonen (1998), 'Habit versus planned behaviour: a field experiment', *British Journal of Social Psychology*, 37, 111–128.
Verplanken, B. and R. Holland (2002), 'Motivated decision-making: effects of activation and self-centrality of values on choices and behavior', *Journal of Personality and Social Psychology*, 82, 434–447.
Verplanken, B. and S. Orbell (2003), 'Reflections on past behavior: a self-report index of habit strength', *Journal of Applied Social Psychology*, 33, 1313–1330.
Verplanken, B. and D. Roy (2013), '"My worries are rational, climate change is not": habitual ecological worrying is an adaptive response', *PLoS ONE*, e74708.
Verplanken, B. and D. Roy (2014), 'Empowering interventions to promote sustainable lifestyles: testing the habit discontinuity hypothesis in a field experiment', manuscript.
Verplanken, B. and O. Svenson (1997), 'Personal involvement in human decision-making: on conceptualizations and effects on decision processes', in R. Ranyard, W.R. Crozier and O. Svenson (eds), *Decision Making: Cognitive Models and Explanations*, London: Routledge, pp. 40–57.
Verplanken, B., I. Walker, A. Davis and M. Jurasek (2008), 'Context change and travel mode choice: combing the habit discontinuity and self-activation hypotheses', *Journal of Environmental Psychology*, 28, 121–127.
Verplanken, B. and M.W.H. Weenig (1993), 'Graphical energy labels and consumers' decisions on home appliances: a process tracing approach', *Journal of Economic Psychology*, 14, 739–752.
Verplanken, B. and W. Wood (2006), 'Interventions to break and create consumer habits', *Journal of Public Policy and Marketing*, 25, 90–103.
Walker, I., G.O. Thomas and B. Verplanken (2014), 'Old habits die hard: travel habit formation and decay during an office relocation', *Environment and Behavior*, DOI: 10.1177/0013916514549619.
Weenig, M.W. and C.J. Midden (1991), 'Communication network influences on information diffusion and persuasion', *Journal of Personality and Social Psychology*, 61, 734–742.
Weenig, M.W.H. and C.J.H. Midden (1997), 'Mass-media information campaigns and knowledge-gap effects', *Journal of Applied Social Psychology*, 27, 945–958.
Whitmarsh, L. (2009), 'Behavioural responses to climate change: asymmetry of intentions and impacts', *Journal of Environmental Psychology*, 29, 13–23.
Wood, W. and D.T. Neal (2007), 'A new look at habits and the habit–goal interface', *Psychological Review*, 114, 843–863.
Wood, W., L. Tam and M. Guerrero Witt (2005), 'Changing circumstances, disrupting habits', *Journal of Personality and Social Psychology*, 88, 918–933.
WCED (World Commission on Environment and Development) (1987), *Our Common Future*, Oxford: Oxford University Press.

# 16. Consumer responsibility for sustainable consumption

*Michael G. Luchs and Rebecca A. Miller*

For many of us, the mention of the word 'responsibility' in relation to sustainability evokes images of companies that market environmentally responsible products and/or that promote various social causes. One might instead imagine companies that manufacture products with questionable social value and/or who exploit the human and physical resources within their supply chains and beyond. This focus on the corporation seems appropriate given the significant presence and influence of brands and branded products in modern society.

Similarly, many academics interested in researching sustainability have also paid significant attention to the responsibility of the corporation. For example, academics within the fields of management and marketing have studied the effect of corporate social responsibility (CSR) on firm performance (Luo and Bhattacharya 2009; Sen and Bhattacharya 2001) and consumer responses to corporate ethics and CSR activities (Becker-Olsen et al. 2006; Brown and Dacin 1997; Folkes and Kamins 1999; Jackson 2005).

While significant and deserved attention has been paid to corporate responsibility, some have argued that there has been relatively less focus on the concurrent responsibility of another critical actor: the consumer (Devinney et al. 2006; Wells et al. 2011; Williams 2005). While it is plausible that business academics and consumer behaviour researchers have not focused sufficiently on consumer responsibility, a substantial amount of research has been published in related fields such as social psychology, environmental psychology, and consumer policy. Much of this research has been inspired by academics who have addressed the need for a greater focus on consumer responsibility within the context of an economic evolution, shifting from a model based on consumer sovereignty to a new model of sustainable consumption that emphasizes consumers' responsible use of their 'demand power' (Hansen and Schrader 1997, p. 458). However while the underlying social, environmental and economic issues have become even more clear and pressing over time, researchers still bemoan the gap between consumers' sustainability related attitudes and behaviours (Phipps et al. 2013; Prothero et al. 2011) and, therefore, continue to promote the need for more research on consumers' 'mindful consumption' (Sheth et al. 2011).

Our belief is that while the motivation for more research on consumer responsibility has existed for some time, research has been somewhat impeded by the lack of a simple, easy-to-deploy scale of consumers' felt responsibility for sustainability. One objective of this chapter is to introduce such a scale. To do so, we revisit a highly relevant theory of pro-social behaviour, the norm activation model (Schwartz 1973, 1977), and then discuss the concept of consumers' felt responsibility for sustainability as a specific type of personal norm. We then proceed with the introduction of a scale for 'consumers' felt responsibility for sustainability' (CFRS) and we review preliminary results from recent research that employs this scale. Another objective of this chapter is to consider how a greater focus on consumer responsibility in general can advance research on sustainable consumption.

## 16.1 THEORETICAL BACKGROUND AND A PROPOSED DEFINITION OF CONSUMERS' FELT RESPONSIBILITY FOR SUSTAINABILITY (CFRS)

### 16.1.1 Consumer Social Responsibility

Devinney et al. (2006) define consumer social responsibility as 'the conscious and deliberate choice to make certain consumption choices based on personal or moral beliefs'. Note that they use 'social' in this context in a broad sense to include environmental issues as well. Indeed, the use of the term 'social' is likely intended to parallel the oft-used term 'corporate social responsibility', itself a bit of a misnomer since responsible production is also often motivated by environmental concerns. Devinney et al. (2006) propose that consumer social responsibility manifests in three ways:

1. Expressed activity with respect to causes, such as donations and boycotts.
2. Purchasing or non-purchasing behaviour.
3. Expressed opinions in market research.

Note that when consumer responsibility is measured by (1) and (3), a positive picture emerges; consumers appear to be very responsible, at least when the personal cost to act responsibly is low. However when considering (2), that is, actual behaviours at the heart of consumption, a different picture emerges: consumers mostly do not tend to consume the products and services that reflect their pro-social or moral beliefs, at least not in proportion to what one might expect given their expressed opinions and attitudes. To better understand behaviour in this context, we proceed with a discussion of one of the most influential models of pro-social behaviour: the norm activation model.

### 16.1.2 Norm Activation, Personal Norms and Consumers' Felt Responsibility for Sustainability

While business academics characterize research on consumer responsibility as rare and scarce (Peattie 2010; Wells et al. 2011), there has been a significant amount of research on the broader concept of personal norms (e.g. Harland et al. 2007; Stern 2000; Thøgersen 2006) building on Schwartz's norm activation model (Schwartz 1977). Schwartz (1977) described personal norms (PN) as 'self-expectations . . . experienced as feelings of moral obligation generated when perception of another's need activates the internalized structure of values and norms' (p. 223). Schwartz's (1973) study of altruism in the context of bone marrow donation was highly influential because it showed that it was these personal norms, once activated, that most influenced behaviour and not behavioural intentions nor attitudes towards specific behaviours, such as transplant donations. Schwartz (1973) also showed that the effect of personal norms on behaviour was moderated by a measure of 'ascription of responsibility'. Schwartz (1973, p. 354) described ascription of responsibility, or AR, as an 'individual difference in the tendency to deny personal responsibility for one's actions and their negative consequences once the sense of responsibility has been aroused'. For example, one of the measures of AR used by Schwartz (1968) was as follows: 'Being very upset or preoccupied does not excuse a person for doing anything he would ordinarily avoid.' Therefore, AR is a measure of one's tendency to rationalize the acceptance, or denial, of responsibility; in Schwartz's words, 'AR measures the tendency to use a mode of defense' (Schwartz 1973, p. 361). To fully appreciate his thinking, however, it is important to understand that for Schwartz the process of norm activation is an iterative one. According to Schwartz, the situation activates personal norms, the cost of acting on these activated norms is considered, and then the situation is reassessed and redefined, potentially leading to a heightened or, more typically, a dampened sense of felt obligation to act responsibly. With respect to behaviour, what ultimately matters according to Schwartz are activated personal norms, that is, the pre-behavioural outcome of this iterative norm activation process. The ascription of responsibility was simply one variable that influenced the strength of personal norms or the degree to which initially activated personal norms remained activated. Thus, within the context of sustainable consumption we will focus on this sense of felt responsibility, akin to Schwartz's activated personal norms.

The mere use of the word 'responsibility' in AR, and its non-use in PN, could easily be inferred to mean that responsibility is more closely related to AR than to PN; for reasons just discussed, a sense of responsibility – as felt obligation – is instead more akin to activated PN. Further, as discussed by De Groot and Steg (2009), there are somewhat equivocal results in the literature about the relationship between PN, AR and behaviour. Some studies show evidence of a mediation model, in which PN mediates the effect of AR on behaviour; other studies support a moderation model, whereby the effect of PN on behaviour is moderated by AR, consistent with Schwartz (1973). As De Groot and Steg (2009) note, however AR has historically been operationalized in a variety of ways, which could help to explain these equivocal results. Whereas some have operationalized AR as reflecting whether individuals feel responsible for creating these problems, that is, looking backward in time, others treat AR as the extent to which individuals feel they are responsible for helping to solve these problems, that is, looking forward (De Groot and Steg 2009). These nuances illustrate the challenge of conducting research on consumer responsibility and the consequent opportunity for a clear definition that is specific to the context of sustainable consumption, as well as a scale to measure it. Hence, we propose the following definition: consumers' felt responsibility for sustainability (CFRS) refers to the consumer's sense of responsibility, or felt obligation, to consume in ways that simultaneously promote their self-oriented values, and their pro-social and/or pro-environmental values. Next, we proceed with the introduction of a new scale for measuring CFRS, followed by a discussion of preliminary results from a study using this scale.

## 16.2 A SCALE OF CFRS

In order to better understand the role of consumer responsibility in the context of studying sustainable consumption behaviours, we wanted to develop a measure consistent with Schwartz's conception of personal norms as 'felt obligation' and consistent with recent calls for research on consumers' 'sense of personal responsibility' (Peattie 2010). However we also wanted to use a measure that would be specific to the context of sustainable consumption. Some prior research on personal norms has been criticized for the use of single-item measures (Manstead 2000). While Stern et al. (1999) use a nine-item scale to assess 'personal normative beliefs' within the context of environmental issues, their scale includes items that address the responsibility of multiple actors, for example the government and industry, in addition to the consumer. Further, Stern et al.'s scale focuses on specific environmental issues such as climate change, and does not address sustainability more broadly, which increasingly has been described as addressing social and economic issues as well (Luchs et al. 2010; Prothero et al. 2011; Simpson and Radford 2012).

Therefore, we instead adapted a scale developed in the field of management, focused on felt responsibility in the context of the work environment, for use within the current context. While Hackman and Oldham (1976) initially proposed the concept of felt responsibility in the workplace, Morrison and Phelps (1999) developed the first published scale as a five-item measure of employees' felt responsibility for promoting constructive change (FRCC) in the workplace. Fuller et al. (2006, p. 1092) describe FRCC as a 'future oriented construct . . . that reflects an assumed obligation or willingness to be held accountable for future behaviour'. Given the successful use of this measure in conceptually related research and its consistency with Schwartz's description and operationalization of activated personal norms, we adapted the Morrison and Phelps (1999) scale by modifying the object of interest in each question – from promoting change in the workplace to promoting sustainability in the context of consumption. For example, the item 'I feel a personal sense of responsibility to bring about change at work' was modified to 'I feel a personal sense of responsibility to be more sustainable in my product choices'. We refer to this scale as the scale of 'consumers' felt responsibility for sustainability', or CFRS (see Appendix A for the five items).

## 16.3 PREDICTING BEHAVIOUR WITH CFRS

In an initial study to test the reliability and usefulness of the CFRS scale, 66 undergraduate students were presented with a choice between two kitchen blenders. While one blender had relatively superior 'product performance', the other was superior with respect to 'sustainability'.

Participants were shown two product scorecards with information about these blenders and were instructed to indicate which blender they would be most likely to purchase and then how much they would be willing to pay (WTP) for each blender. Following the focal choice and WTP questions, participants responded to the set of five CFRS scale questions. Upon analysis, the scale demonstrated strong reliability, with a Cronbach alpha score of 0.78.

Overall, participants chose the product with superior performance over the more sustainable product (45:21). Choice was, as expected, predicted by CFRS, such that as CFRS increased, so did the choice likelihood of the more sustainable product. To illustrate, we used a median split on CFRS to define low and high CFRS groups. Within the low CFRS group, choice was strongly biased in favour of the higher-performing (and less sustainable) option (31:4). However, in the high CFRS group both were equally likely to be chosen (14:17).

Similarly, while participants were overall willing to pay an average of $4.40 more for the higher-performing product than for the more sustainable product, this difference in the WTP for each product was predicted by CFRS, such that the more responsible the consumer felt for sustainability, the less of a premium they were willing to pay for high performance (versus sustainability). Thus, the results from this study provide preliminary evidence suggesting that our proposed scale of consumers' felt responsibility for sustainability (CFRS) could be a useful predictor of sustainable consumption behaviours.

While the simplicity of this five-item scale can be a virtue, enabling inclusion in future research studies, it also begs the question of how exactly consumers construe sustainability itself. In other words, when a consumer responds to scale questions about their felt responsibility for sustainability, what do they think sustainability means? We return to this question subsequently.

## 16.4 SHARED RESPONSIBILITY

This chapter began with a discussion of responsibility in the context of sustainable consumption and the observation that relatively little research has been conducted on consumers' responsibility. While more research is needed on consumers' responsibility in this context, it is important to consider that responsibility for future behaviours is likely viewed by the various stakeholders as a shared responsibility (Heiskanen and Pantzar 1997; Kalamas et al. 2014; Lenzen et al. 2007). Indeed, this sharing of responsibility is one of the challenges we face, given known effects of shared responsibility on behaviour in general (Darley and Latané 1968; Hardin 1968). A starting point in the current context is to at least understand how the various stakeholders view their responsibility with respect to other actors. Toward that end, we provide some preliminary evidence suggesting that consumers' distribution of responsibility depends, in part, on the perspective or frame through which they view the issue.

### 16.4.1 Consumers' Conception of Sustainability

We first investigated how consumers construe sustainability by means of an open-ended pilot study, followed by a closed-response survey to validate the findings from the pilot study. For the pilot study, our sample included 84 participants who were simply asked to respond to the following open-ended question: 'How would you define sustainability? In other words, when you think about sustainability, what attributes come to mind (list as many as you can think of)?' After coding the responses, it became clear that in addition to defining sustainability with respect to the traditional 'triple bottom line' perspective of environmental, social and economic issues, many comments identified behaviours that aligned with a life cycle perspective, that is, addressing behaviours and decisions related to the production of products, product purchase and usage, and product disposal. Therefore, following several rounds of coding, we converged on a conceptual model that included both of these dimensions, as shown in Figure 16.1.

Next, we recruited a new sample of 171 participants, drawn from 23 US states, to participate in an online survey. Participants were randomly presented with each of the nine descriptions of the elements of sustainability depicted within the conceptual model (Figure 16.1). They rated the degree to which they agreed that each statement reflected their own definition of sustainability on a scale from 1 (strongly disagree) to 7 (strongly agree). Our analysis suggested that participants overall believed that all nine elements of the conceptual model were relevant to their own definition of sustainability. Specifically, the mean ratings of all of the elements were all statistically significantly higher than the midpoint of 4. Note from Figure 16.2, however, that participants were especially likely to agree that sustainability relates to: (1) environmental issues; and (2) the disposal stage of the life cycle. Thus, although not limited to environmental issues and disposal, consumers' conception of sustainability – at least in the US – appears to reflect an historical emphasis on environmentalism, and may also be a reflection of the disposal behaviours that public policy has attempted to most influence in the past (for example, recycling). These consumer perceptions are important to keep in mind when interpreting results from studies on sustainable consumption (including those reported here) and when determining the relevance of prior research in contexts related to, but different from, sustainable consumption (for example, willingness to donate blood).

### 16.4.2 Consumers' Distribution of Responsibility

In the same online survey described in the prior section, participants reviewed each of the six statements given in Appendix B and indicated how responsible various groups were for each of these dimensions of sustainability. This was accomplished by allocating a percentage, from 0 to 100 per cent, to each of three groups – consumers, governments and companies – for each of the six dimensions. Note that this task used six statements, each aligned with one of the three outcome dimensions (environmental, social, economic) or the three behavioural dimensions (production, purchase and usage, disposal).

As seen in Figure 16.3, the distribution of responsibility was relatively consistent across the three outcome dimensions. On average, participants believed that consumers are 31 per cent responsible, while governments are 33 per cent responsible and companies are 36 per cent responsible. On the other hand, substantial variance emerged across the three behavioural dimensions. Participants on average indicated that consumers are 19 per cent responsible when considering production, 52 per cent responsible when considering purchase and usage, and 42 per cent responsible when considering disposal. This variance suggests that a behavioural framing of sustainability forces a focus on discrete choices and behaviours, which can be more clearly attributed to different groups as opposed to a perspective focused on outcomes, where perceived responsibility is more diffuse.

These results are limited given the sampling frame, and therefore the details need to be viewed with caution. However they do highlight the importance of considering how perceptions of relative responsibility can depend significantly on how the issues are

| | Production | Purchase & usage | Disposal |
|---|---|---|---|
| **Environmental** | Minimizing harm to the environment by reducing the use of energy and raw materials, and reducing pollution during the development and production of products and services. | Minimizing harm to the environment by consuming fewer goods, purchasing "green" products, using less energy, buying organic products, and reducing pollution from personal use of vehicles and consumer goods. | Minimizing harm to the environment by re-using and repairing existing products, recycling materials used in the production of goods, recycling packaging and used products, and disposing of waste in the appropriate way. |
| **Social** | Engaging in socially responsible business practices during the development and production of products and services by treating workers fairly, e.g. fair wages and safe working conditions, and avoiding testing of products on animals. | Improving the welfare of society by encouraging business involvement in the community, buying products to promote social causes and buying safe and healthy products. | Disposing of waste in a fair and equitable way (e.g., not shipping it to other countries) and finding socially beneficial uses for used items, e.g., donating used items to charities. |
| **Economic** | Increasing value in the production of goods by developing and maintaining efficient manufacturing and office processes and efficiently using financial and human resources to ensure long term financial viability. | Gaining the most value from investments by engaging in balanced consumption, balanced saving of personal funds, and enabling businesses to gain a competitive edge so that both consumers and businesses are financially sound. | Gaining the most value from money already spent by reusing products, reusing production materials and other resources to improve long-term financial viability. |

*Note:* The text within each cell is a representative composite of the open-ended responses provided by participants.

*Figure 16.1 Conceptual model of sustainability within the context of consumption*

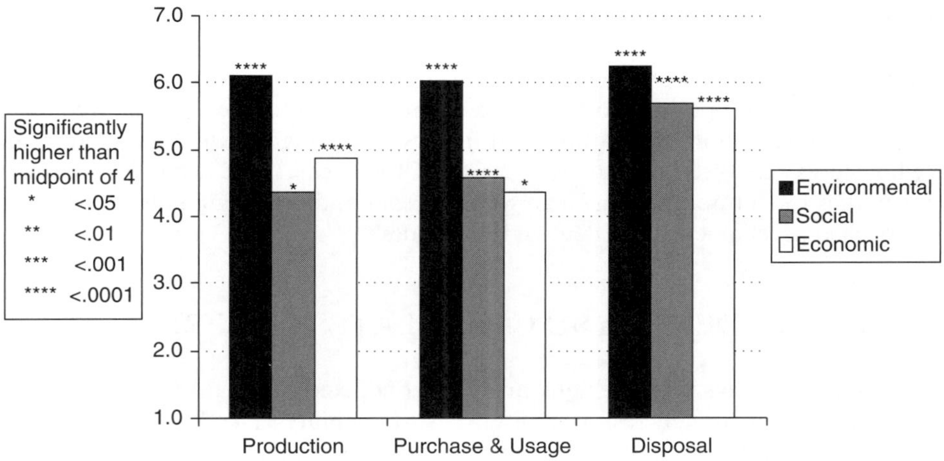


*Figure 16.2* *Ratings of the relevance of each element of conceptual model to the definition of sustainability*

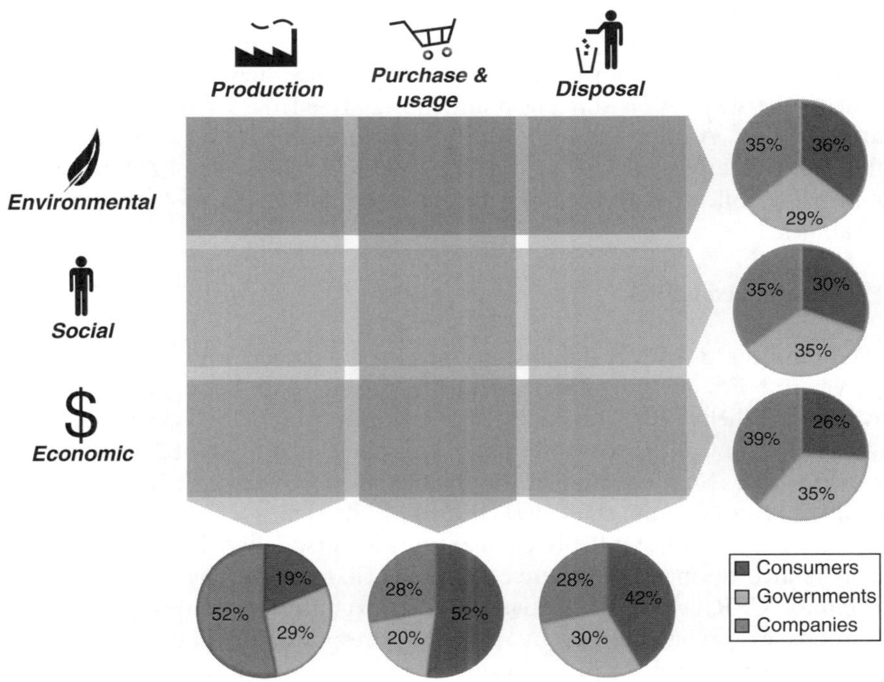


*Figure 16.3* *Distribution of shared responsibility for sustainability*

described and framed. Consumers' perceptions of their responsibility may, for example, be higher when specific behaviours and decisions are identified, such as purchase and usage decisions, as opposed to general outcomes such as environmental damage.

Thus far, we have provided some evidence that CFRS could be a useful predictor of sustainable consumption behaviour. What factors, then, might be useful in understanding who scores relatively high, or low, on the CFRS scale? And what insights – and opportunities for future research – can we gain from understanding how CFRS relates to established psychometric and demographic scales?

## 16.5 ANTECEDENTS AND CORRELATES OF CFRS

Following are findings from various analyses conducted using the CFRS scale as a measure of consumers' felt responsibility for sustainability. The focus will be on the findings and not on the details of methods, procedures and analyses. Therefore, these findings should be viewed as preliminary and are intended to inspire future research, not to circumvent it.

The data were compiled across five separate surveys that included CFRS together with various other measures. The sample size for each analysis ranged from 464 participants to 1048 participants drawn from a variety of sources including national online panels in the United States as well as two college campuses in the United States. All findings identified as statistically significant had $p$ values of 0.01 or lower, unless mentioned otherwise. As a starting point, we analysed the CFRS scale itself across the entire data set. All five measures were significantly correlated as expected, with an overall Cronbach alpha of 0.81, suggesting good reliability. We organize the findings below into the following three major categories: mindset, values and ideology, and demographics.

### 16.5.1 Mindset and CFRS

First we found that CFRS is significantly positively related to the 'need for cognition' (NFC), where NFC measures the tendency to engage in and enjoy effortful cognitive endeavours. In other words, individuals with a relatively high (low) CFRS score also had a relatively high (low) NFC score. We used Cacioppo et al.'s (1984) 18-item short version of the NFC scale. Next we studied the relationship between CFRS and the 'big five personality inventory' (John et al. 1991) using Gosling et al.'s (2003) simple ten-item personality inventory (TIPI). Of the five dimensions of personality, CFRS was most clearly positively related to openness, where openness is characterized by originality, curiosity and ingenuity. CFRS was also positively related to conscientiousness ($p = 0.02$), where conscientiousness is characterized by orderliness, responsibility and dependability. The latter is consistent with prior research showing that a sense of responsibility in general is related to conscientiousness (John and Srivastava 1999). CFRS was also somewhat related to agreeableness ($p < 0.05$), where agreeableness is characterized by good-naturedness, cooperativeness and trust. We found no relationship between CFRS and either extraversion or neuroticism.

We also found that CFRS is related to regulatory focus (a 'promotion focus' versus a 'prevention focus', Higgins 1997). We used the 20-item modified 'general regulatory focus measure' (GRFM) as per Summerville and Roese (2008) in which a promotion orientation is characterized by an emphasis on pursuing desirable outcomes whereas a prevention orientation is characterized by an emphasis on avoiding bad outcomes. Our analysis suggests that CFRS is positively associated with a promotion orientation; we found a negative but weak relationship between CFRS and a prevention orientation ($p = 0.05$). This suggests that an increase in consumers' sense of responsibility in the context of sustainability may be motivated more by the possibilities of improved sustainability rather than by the negative consequences of the unsustainable status quo. This finding, if supported by future research, could be important from a public policy perspective since it seems somewhat counter to the dominant tone of public discourse around sustainability, which currently focuses more on the avoidance of bad outcomes rather than the achievement of good outcomes. Finally, we also found that CFRS is positively related to Joireman et al.'s (2012) 14-item scale of the consideration of future consequences (CFC) which is a measure of the tendency to emphasize long-term consequences over short-term consequences.

### 16.5.2 Values, Ideology, and CFRS

Not surprisingly, we found that CFRS is positively related to the 'new environmental paradigm' (NEP) revised scale as per Dunlap et al. (2000) which emphasizes the interconnectedness between humans and the environment. In a separate analysis, we also found that CFRS is positively (negatively) related to liberal (conservative) political ideology, using a single-item measure (Farwell and Weiner 2000).

A logical question to consider at this point is whether CFRS is materially different than consumers' attitudes towards CSR. In order to address this question, we created a measure of consumers' attitudes towards CSR by averaging responses for the following three items (Cronbach alpha = 0.89):

- The issue of environmental corporate responsibility is important to me (for example, energy use, resource usage, pollution).
- The issue of social corporate responsibility is important to me (for example, factory safety, labour practices, community service).
- It is important to me that companies maintain high ethical standards in general.

We found that while CFRS is correlated with consumers' attitudes towards CSR (Pearson $r^2 = 0.34$), they are somewhat independent. This suggests that a consumer's attitude towards corporate social and environmental responsibility does not necessarily translate into or depend upon a greater sense of felt personal responsibility for sustainability-related behaviours.

### 16.5.3 Demographics and CFRS

Our data suggest that CFRS is positively related to level of education, but is unrelated to income. In addition, we found that CFRS is positively related to age and is also higher amongst women than men. These latter findings are consistent with prior research on the relationship between age, gender and attitudes towards ethical issues and corporate social responsibility (e.g. Albaum and Peterson 2006).

## 16.6 LOOKING AHEAD

The overall purpose of this chapter was to increase the focus on consumers' responsibility for sustainable consumption as a discrete, important and under-researched topic – and to promote future research. To that end, we have provided a definition for 'consumers' felt responsibility for sustainability', based on the concept of activated personal norms (Schwartz 1973, 1977), as well as a simple scale to enable future research. In addition, we have provided some evidence to demonstrate the value of this scale and to explore its relationship to other established constructs. These results are preliminary, however, and need to be developed and built upon. Regardless of whether this specific scale is ultimately adopted in its current form by others, we believe that a renewed focus on defining and measuring consumer responsibility – as perceived by the consumer – is warranted for both theoretical and practical reasons.

A variety of well-documented models of pro-social behaviour have been used to study sustainable consumption (see Jackson 2005 for a review), yet there is still more to learn. Researchers continue, for example, to try to further explain the gap between consumers' attitudes and behaviours in the context of sustainable consumption (Phipps et al. 2013; Prothero et al. 2011). Consumers' felt responsibility for sustainability might help to explain why this gap persists. Might the effect of positive attitudes towards sustainable consumption on behaviour be mediated by felt responsibility? Or, instead, might a moderation model be more appropriate; that is, the effect of positive attitudes on sustainable behaviours depends on whether consumers do, or do not, also feel a sense of responsibility?

Similarly, using a measure of felt responsibility conceived as an activated personal norm and specific to the context of sustainable consumption might help to clarify results from prior research. For example, research on the relationships between variables within the norm activation model (NAM) has yielded somewhat mixed results. De Groot and Steg (2009) advance our understanding by providing evidence supporting a mediation model for the variables within NAM as opposed to a moderation model, as indicated by some prior research. However, in an effort to generalize their findings, they apply somewhat different interpretations of variables within their studies, yielding results open to different interpretations. Further research exploring consumers' felt responsibility – conceived as an activated personal norm – might help to further clarify its role within NAM and other models of pro-social behaviour applied to the context of sustainable consumption.

In addition, a specific measure of consumer responsibility could support the vision set forth by others who have offered conceptual perspectives on the role of consumers within a sustainable economy. For example, Hansen and Schrader (1997) discuss consumers' responsible use of their 'demand power' as a way to promote ecological and social progress. Their conception of consumer responsibility is predicated on consumers' active reflection on their needs which, they argue, can manifest at different levels from non-consumption for certain needs, to the intentional consumption of ecologically and/or socially superior goods when consumption is justified. Similarly, Sheth et al. (2011) explore the concept of 'mindful consumption', which 'is premised on consciousness in thought and behaviour about consequences of consumption' (p. 27). A scale of consumer responsibility would make it easier to identify and study consumers in order to understand what specific activities – such as deliberate reflection prior to, or after, a purchase – underlie the development and practices of the responsible consumer.

Finally, from a practical perspective, a clear and simple way to measure consumer responsibility could benefit both public policy initiatives and company practices. For example consumer policy often emphasizes consumer education about underlying issues and desired behaviours. Likewise, companies often promote the sustainable attributes of their products. It is plausible that a greater focus on both understanding and even influencing consumers' perceptions of their own responsibility for sustainable consumption might significantly contribute to the shift towards a more sustainable economy, one that ultimately depends on a consensus of mutual responsibility.

## REFERENCES

Albaum, G. and R.A. Peterson (2006), 'Ethical attitudes of future business leaders: do they vary by gender and religiosity?', *Business and Society*, 45 (3), 300–321.

Becker-Olsen, K.L., A.B. Cudmore and R.P. Hill (2006), 'The impact of perceived corporate social responsibility on consumer behavior', *Journal of Business Research*, 59 (1), 46–53.

Brown, T.J. and P.A. Dacin (1997), 'The company and the product: corporate associations and consumer product responses', *Journal of Marketing*, 61 (1), 68–84.

Cacioppo, J.T., R.E. Petty and C.F. Kao (1984), 'The efficient assessment of need for cognition', *Journal of Personality Assessment*, 48 (3), 306–307.

Darley, J.M. and B. Latané (1968), 'Bystander intervention in emergencies: diffusion of responsibility', *Journal of Personality and Social Psychology*, 8 (4, 1), 377–383.

De Groot, J.I.M. and L. Steg (2009), 'Morality and prosocial behavior: the role of awareness, responsibility, and norms in the norm activation model', *Journal of Social Psychology*, 149 (4), 425–449.

Devinney, T.M., G.M. Eckhardt, P. Auger and T. Birtchnell (2006), 'The other CSR: consumer social responsibility', *Stanford Social Innovation Review*, 4 (3), 30–37.

Dunlap, R.E., K.D. Van Liere, A.G. Mertig and R.E. Jones (2000), 'Measuring endorsement of the New Ecological Paradigm: a revised NEP scale', *Journal of Social Issues*, 56 (3), 425–442.

Farwell, L. and B. Weiner (2000), 'Bleeding hearts and the heartless: popular perceptions of liberal and conservative ideologies', *Personality and Social Psychology Bulletin*, 26 (7), 845–852.

Folkes, V.S. and M.A. Kamins (1999), 'Effects of information about firms' ethical and unethical actions on consumers' attitudes', *Journal of Consumer Psychology*, 8 (3), 243–259.

Fuller, J.B., L.E. Marler and K. Hester (2006), 'Promoting felt responsibility for constructive change and proactive behavior: exploring aspects of an elaborated model of work design', *Journal of Organizational Behavior*, 27 (8), 1089–1120.

Gosling, S.D., P.J. Rentfrow and W.B. Swann Jr. (2003), 'A very brief measure of the big five personality domains', *Journal of Research in Personality*, 37 (6), 504–528.

Hackman, R.J. and G.R. Oldham (1976), 'Motivation through the design of work: test of a theory', *Organizational Behavior and Human Performance*, 16 (2), 250–279.

Hansen, U. and U. Schrader (1997), 'A modern model of consumption for a sustainable society', *Journal of Consumer Policy*, 20 (4), 443–468.

Hardin, G. (1968), 'The tragedy of the commons', *Science*, 162, 1243–1248.

Harland, P., H. Staats and H.A.M. Wilke (2007), 'Situational and personality factors as direct or personal norm mediated predictors of pro-environmental behavior: questions derived from norm-activation theory', *Basic and Applied Social Psychology*, 29 (4), 323–334.

Heiskanen, E. and M. Pantzar (1997), 'Toward sustainable consumption: two new perspectives', *Journal of Consumer Policy*, 20 (4), 409–442.

Higgins, E.T. (1997), 'Beyond pleasure and pain', *American Psychologist*, 52 (12), 1280–1300.
Jackson, T. (2005), 'Motivating sustainable consumption: a review of evidence on consumer behavior and behavioral change', University of Surrey, Centre for Environmental Strategy.
John, O.P., E.M. Donahue and R.L. Kentle (1991), 'The big five inventory – Versions 4a and 54', Berkeley, CA: University of California, Berkeley, Institute of Personality and Social Research.
John, O.P. and S. Srivastava (1999), 'The big five trait taxonomy: history, measurement, and theoretical perspectives', in L.A. Pervin and O.P. John (eds), *Handbook of Personality: Theory and Research 2*, New York: Guilford Press, pp. 102–138.
Joireman, J., M.J. Shaffer, D. Balliet and A. Strathman (2012), 'Promotion orientation explains why future-oriented people exercise and eat healthy: evidence from the two-factor consideration of future consequences scale', *Personality and Social Psychology Bulletin*, 38 (10), 1272–1287.
Kalamas, M., M. Cleveland and M. Laroche (2014), 'Pro-environmental behaviors for thee but not for me: green giants, green gods, and environmental locus of control', *Journal of Business Research*, 67 (2), 12–22.
Lenzen, M., J. Murray, F. Sack and T. Wiedmann (2007), 'Shared producer and consumer responsibility – theory and practice', *Ecological Economics*, 61 (1), 27–42.
Luchs, M.G., R.W. Naylor, J.R. Irwin and R. Raghunathan (2010), 'The sustainability liability: potential negative effects of ethicality on product preference', *Journal of Marketing*, 74 (5), 18–31.
Luo, X. and C.B. Bhattacharya (2009), 'The debate over doing good: corporate social performance, strategic marketing levers, and firm-idiosyncratic risk', *Journal of Marketing*, 73 (6), 198–213.
Manstead, A.S.R. (2000), 'The role of moral norm in the attitude–behavior relation', in D.J. Terry and M.A. Hogg (eds), *Attitudes, Behavior, and Social Context: The Role of Norms and Group Membership*, Mahwah, NJ: Lawrence Erlbaum, pp. 11–30.
Morrison, E.W. and C.C. Phelps (1999), 'Taking charge at work: extrarole efforts to initiate workplace change', *Academy of Management Journal*, 42 (4), 403–419.
Peattie, K. (2010), 'Green consumption: behavior and norms', *Annual Review of Environmental Resources*, 35 (1), 195–228.
Phipps, M., L.K. Ozanne, M.G. Luchs, S. Subrahmanyan and S. Kapitan (2013), 'Understanding the inherent complexity of sustainable consumption: a social cognitive framework', *Journal of Business Research*, 66 (8), 1227–1234.
Prothero, A., S. Dobscha, J. Freund, W.E. Kilbourne, M.G. Luchs, L.K. Ozanne and J. Thøgersen (2011), 'Sustainable consumption: opportunities for consumer research and public policy', *Journal of Public Policy and Marketing*, 30 (1), 31–38.
Schwartz, S.H. (1968), 'Words, deeds, and the perception of consequences and responsibility in action situations', *Journal of Personality and Social Psychology*, 10 (3), 232–242.
Schwartz, S.H. (1973), 'Normative explanations of helping behavior: a critique, proposal, and empirical test', *Journal of Experimental Social Psychology*, 9 (4), 349–364.
Schwartz, S.H. (1977), 'Normative influences on altruism', in L. Berkowitz (ed.), *Advances in Experimental Social Psychology*, New York: Academic Press, pp. 222–275.
Sen, S. and C.B. Bhattacharya (2001), 'Does doing good always lead to doing better? Consumer reactions to corporate social responsibility', *Journal of Marketing Research*, 38 (2), 225–243.
Sheth, J.N., N.K. Sethia and S. Srinivas (2011), 'Mindful consumption: a customer-centric approach to sustainability', *Journal of the Academy of Marketing Science*, 39 (1), 21–39.
Simpson, B.J.K. and S.K. Radford (2012), 'Consumer perceptions of sustainability: a free elicitation study', *Journal of Nonprofit & Public Sector Marketing*, 24 (4), 272–291.
Stern, P.C. (2000), 'Toward a coherent theory of environmentally significant behavior', *Journal of Social Issues*, 56 (3), 407–424.
Stern, P.C., T. Dietz, T. Abel, G.A. Guagnano and L. Kalof (1999), 'A value–belief–norm theory of support for social movements: the case of environmentalism', *Human Ecology Review*, 6 (2), 81–97.
Summerville, A. and N.J. Roese (2008), 'Self-report measures of individual differences in regulatory focus: a cautionary note', *Journal of Research in Personality*, 42 (1), 247–254.
Thøgersen, J. (2006), 'Norms for environmentally responsible behaviour: an extended taxonomy', *Journal of Environmental Psychology*, 26 (4), 247–261.
Wells, V.K., C.A. Ponting and K. Peattie (2011), 'Behaviour and climate change: consumer perceptions of responsibility', *Journal of Marketing Management*, 27 (7–8), 808–833.
Williams, A. (2005), 'Consumer social responsibility', *Consumer Policy Review*, 15 (2), 34–35.

# APPENDICES

## Appendix A: Scale Questions for Consumers' Felt Responsibility for Sustainability (CFRS)

### BOX 16A.1 CONSUMERS' FELT RESPONSIBILITY FOR SUSTAINABILITY (CFRS)

I feel obligated to try to implement sustainable practices where appropriate.
It's up to me to bring about improvements in sustainability.
I feel little obligation to challenge or change the way sustainability related practices have been conducted. (R)
I feel a personal sense of responsibility to be more sustainable in my product choices.
Correcting sustainability related problems is not really my responsibility. (R)

*Source:* Adapted from Morrison and Phelps (1999), 'scale of felt responsibility for constructive change' (FRCC).

## Appendix B: Dimensions of Sustainability

'Please allocate a percentage to each of the following categories, indicating whose beliefs, values and behaviours have contributed the most to current sustainability related problems as they relate to . . .'

Outcome dimensions:

- **the environment**, where environmental sustainability is engaging in environmentally friendly practices and behaviours, and taking part in activities that do not harm the environment and avoiding activities that hurt the environment.
- **social justice**, where social sustainability involves showing concern for the social aspects of production, consumption, and disposal of goods.
- **the economy**, where economic sustainability means preserving economic success on a personal, corporate, and national level.

Behavioural dimensions:

- **the production of goods and services**, where sustainability during production refers to the behaviours and activities during the extraction of raw materials, the production of goods, and rendering of services that ensure sustainability.
- **the consumption and use of goods and services**, where sustainability during consumption refers to the choices made during the purchase and use of products and services by both individual consumers and companies.
- **disposal and recycling**, where sustainability during disposal refers to the chosen methods of disposal of goods and materials, that is, any behaviour or action that occurs post-use.

# 17. Family socialization and sustainable consumption

*Ellen Matthies and Hannah Wallis*

## 17.1 THE SIGNIFICANCE OF FAMILY SOCIALIZATION IN THE CONTEXT OF SUSTAINABILITY-RELEVANT CONSUMPTION ACTS

Consumption behaviour at an individual household level has been identified as an important domain in which to determine how sustainable consumption can be achieved (EEA 2012; Rijnhout and Lorek 2012). But how do we develop specific behavioural routines that will result in sustainable consumption? Families are units in which close social interactions take place and especially in which parents function as the primary socialization agents for their children. These day-to-day conditions of family life may lead to some degree of synchronization in values, concerns and behaviours between generations (e.g. John 1999; Grusec and Davidov 2008; Grønhøj and Thøgersen 2009). Consequently knowledge about the socialization of sustainable consumption acts within the family is essential for developing effective policies.

In the context of climate change and ambitious national aims to limit carbon dioxide ($CO_2$) emissions, direct and indirect energy consumption is particularly relevant (EEA 2012). In this context, housing, transportation and food are recognized as the main priorities for reducing household $CO_2$ emissions (EEA 2012). The suggested domains in which actions are likely to have the greatest impact are the type and use of heating system and of (electrical) energy-consuming devices (Dietz et al. 2009); the choice of transportation (Dietz et al. 2009); food consumption, the consumption of meat in particular (Tukker et al. 2011), and the general tendency toward a higher level of food consumption per person (Edwards and Roberts 2009). For an overview of relevant consumption acts, also see Chapter 4 in this book.

All of the relevant areas of consumption that were reported above involve all members living in a household and affect their everyday lives. It therefore makes sense to take a closer look at the relevance of family interactions and socialization for sustainable consumption. Referring to a definition of family established in family psychology, families are units that are related socially, biologically or by law, containing two generations or more. Moreover family members follow specific shared purposes, such as producing common goods (for example, the education of children) (Schneewind 2010). Children learn everyday practices within the household and become citizens who will influence the extent to which society follows the goal toward a more sustainable consumption and use of resources (Grønhøj and Thøgersen 2009). Routines can be viewed as a strong barrier to behavioural change toward a sustainable lifestyle (Jackson 2005a). This alone makes it necessary to look at the contexts in which lifestyles may be developed.

### 17.1.1 Sustainable Consumption

According to Fischer et al. (2011, p. 72), 'a primary goal of sustainable development is to ensure that both now and in the future, all people should be given the opportunity to satisfy their objective needs in order to be able to develop universally valid human characteristics and capabilities'. As a consequence, a main point by which to identify a consumption act as sustainable should be the extent to which the consumption practices of the individual contribute to this development. Fischer et al. (2011, p. 74) also offer a doubly focused definition of individual consumption as sustainable consumption: 'Ideally, individual acts of consumption are sustainable if they are oriented towards the objectives of sustainable development (intention-oriented), and actually contribute to their accomplishment (impact-oriented).' We agree that these two foundations of the sustainability of individual consumption are necessary and complementary aspects.

Since there is more empirical research in this than in other areas of sustainable consumption, the current chapter will mainly focus on the socialization of consumption acts that are relevant for reducing $CO_2$ emissions. Reducing $CO_2$ emissions is highly relevant for sustainability, as it will have a strong influence on the capacity of human beings to achieve sustainable development in the future.

### 17.1.2 Consumer Socialization

How do individuals, and children in particular, learn specific consumption acts? According to Moschis and Churchill (1978, p. 599), 'Consumer socialization is the process by which young people develop consumer-related skills, knowledge, and attitudes' (see also Ward 1974). On the basis of more recent psychological research, we suggest that the acquisition of habits and norms also be taken into consideration (e.g. Matthies and Klöckner forthcoming). Some common ways in which children learn are by observing and imitating behaviours (for example, parental behaviours, behavioural representations in films or books, and so on) and through reinforcement (Bandura 1977). Moreover we can expect that individuals will be more likely to transfer knowledge from one situation to another when they detect familiar elements in the new situation (Thorndike 1913). Knowledge about the learning process – and more specifically the socialization of specific consumption acts that have strong environmental impacts – is a prerequisite for the development of intervention programmes targeted toward producing sustainable consumption.

Several agents, such as the family, peers, the media and school, are influential in the process of consumer socialization (Easterling et al. 1995; John 1999; Moschis 1985; Moschis and Churchill 1978). This chapter focuses on the family as the primary socialization agent but also takes into account that other agents tend to increase in importance as the child grows older (e.g. Hurrelmann 2007).

In the following, we will first focus on the socialization processes of high-impact behaviours, such as the use of cars, warm water and electricity (17.2). Other consumption acts with an environmental impact (for example, food consumption and purchases of environmentally friendly products) will be briefly discussed as well. In section 17.3 we will consider more generally how norms and values with regard to sustainable consumption may be developed within the family. In the last section we will step back and discuss some implications for policy making.

## 17.2 FROM SUSTAINABLE CONSUMER SOCIALIZATION IN GENERAL TO SOCIALIZATION PROCESSES OF SPECIFIC CONSUMPTION ACTS

In line with Fischer et al.'s (2011) twofold definition of sustainable consumption, we will present two perspectives on sustainable consumer socialization (Figure 17.1). The first perspective views sustainable consumption as behaviours and decisions that are relevant because of their impact. Accordingly we will look at how these everyday practices are (or could be) transferred from parents to children and adolescents. The second perspective focuses on the intention behind sustainable consumption patterns and considers the question of how values or norms are related to sustainable consumption and transferred within the family.

We assume that socialization processes may differ between specific consumption acts: for example it seems likely that learning how to purchase organic products is different from learning how to save electricity. Also, in a recent study, Matthies et al. (2012) found that the influence parents have on children's consumption acts differs depending on where the act is conducted (for example, within the household versus in a school context).

In the following, we will review research – mainly in environmental psychology and consumer research – on family socialization with regard to direct energy consumption behaviours (for example, choice of travel mode, warm water and electricity use) as well as behaviours with indirect implications for energy consumption (for example, recycling and food consumption). We also discuss the new practices of giving, sharing and reusing, related to the recent discussion of sufficiency as a behavioural strategy (e.g., Fischer et al. 2013; Rijnhout and Lorek 2012), and develop suggestions for how to promote these practices via socialization within the family.

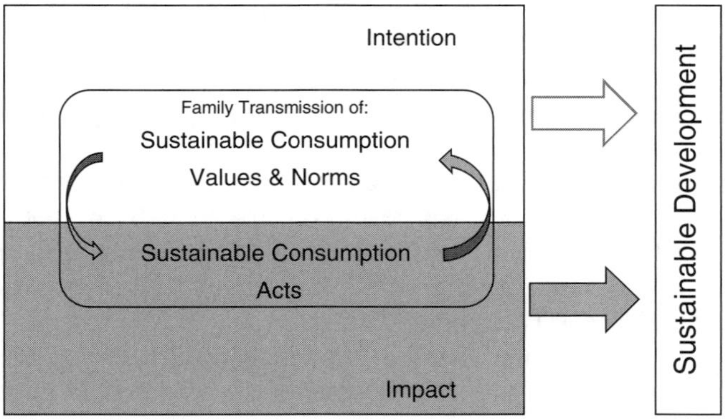


*Figure 17.1 A dual view on the family transmission of sustainable values, norms and consumption acts with regard to sustainable development*

### 17.2.1 Energy-Consumption-Relevant Behaviours

When addressing energy-relevant behaviours, Gardner and Stern (2002) proposed a distinction between curtailment actions and actions aimed at increasing energy efficiency. The first type of action achieves a reduction in energy consumption because the consumer directly consumes less (for example, decreasing the length of showers, turning down the thermostat or switching off lights when leaving the room). Efficiency behaviours achieve a reduction in energy consumption indirectly because the consumer purchases new and more efficient devices (for example, a new refrigerator or a new energy-efficient car). Two main arguments support this separation of energy-saving consumption behaviours.

First, energy efficiency behaviours have a higher potential to save energy than curtailment behaviours (Gardner and Stern 2002; Gardner and Stern 2008). In their 'Short List of Effective Actions' Gardner and Stern (2008) reported the 17 most impact-relevant behaviours for saving energy, and six of the top ten are efficiency behaviours.

Second, actions that foster increased efficiency are influenced by different factors than the ones that influence curtailment actions (see Black et al. 1985). Most curtailment behaviours are daily behaviours that are practiced frequently and are therefore, to a large extent, habitual (Jackson 2005a; Quellette and Wood 1998; Verplanken and Roy, Chapter 15 in this book). On the other hand, buying a more energy-efficient washing machine or installing a new heating system requires a certain amount of financial capital and information. Among others, decisions about whom to consult for this consumption decision may be made (Gardner and Stern 2002).

Most energy efficiency behaviours are mostly up to adults (for example, investing in new energy-efficient technology), and this can complicate investigations of socialization influences on energy efficiency behaviours. Long-term studies would be required to examine the parent-to-child influence on these behaviours. Due to lack of research, the socialization processes of energy efficiency-producing behaviour is under-represented in this chapter. However it can be assumed that the development of specific consumption norms in childhood may influence the decision making process of practicing consumption behaviours as an adult.

Research on the socialization of direct energy consumption acts can be found in two domains: choice of travel mode and use of warm water and electricity at home.

**Choice of travel mode**

The socialization of travel mode choice – and in particular, the preference for the private car – has been a topic in environmental psychology and sociology for years (for a recent overview, see Matthies and Klöckner, forthcoming). As car use in most societies is restricted to adolescents and adults, it is more the preference for the use of the private car that has been the focus of attention. Authors generally assume various socialization agents for travel mode preferences: mainly parents, peer groups and the media. However, empirical studies have usually focused on parents as socialization agents. In particular, it is car ownership and car use in the family that have been found to be relevant here.

Baslington (2008) found that in car-free households, a higher percentage of children could imagine living without a car in adulthood compared with children from households that own a car. The relationship between parents' car ownership and children's attitudes toward different modes of transportation has been confirmed in other studies as well (e.g. Cahill et al. 1996; Sandqvist 2002).

The socialization of travel mode preferences can also be understood as a side effect of environmental conditions. Engelbert (1986) investigated the type of residential area and travel behaviour of children. She found that children growing up in areas with high traffic density had less autonomous travel experiences (going by foot, bike or bus) for their regular commute to nursery school or school. For a sample of Swedish families, Johansson (2006) reported that parents' chauffeuring behaviour for the leisure travel of their children was related to environmental factors (traffic environment and quality of foot and bicycle paths) as well as to the car ownership of the respective households. Thus, they found that travel mode socialization was not only an effect of the deliberate socialization actions of parents but was also a by-product of certain environmental conditions (for example, accessibility of cars, traffic environment).

When focusing on the mode preferences and actual travel mode choices of adults, it does not seem sufficient to investigate only preferences at early stages of childhood; rather, it also makes sense to consider socialization processes in adolescence. Mode experiences undergo relevant changes in this phase of development (for example, older children and adolescents travel more often and across longer distances), and it was assumed (see Flade 1994) that the travel experiences themselves become increasingly relevant for adolescents' attitudes and preferences. From the perspective of socialization, it is particularly interesting that adolescents in general experience car driving as a privilege and as the achievement of a higher status (Flade 1994). In a German study, Flade (1994) reported that adolescents recognize and complain about the long waiting times for pedestrians compared with the waiting times for cars at intersections.

Empirical research on travel mode socialization from an adult's perspective is rare. Klöckner and Matthies (2009) found that habits mediate the influence of three aspects of travel mode socialization on current car use in Germany: the frequency of parents' former use of public transportation, experiencing the acquisition of a driver's licence as an initiation rite to adulthood, and the former multi-mobility of the peer group. In an online survey, Haustein et al. (2009) retrospectively measured three different aspects of socialization: communication with parents about the environmental impact of travel mode choice; the symbolic-affective importance of the acquisition of a driver's licence at age 18 and multi-mobility in the peer group. Analyses revealed a significant impact of all three socialization constructs mediated via norms to reduce car use or car use habit.

Taken together, the results of empirical travel mode socialization research propose that later mode choices are influenced by socialization agents, mainly parents, and by the environment (car ownership, rural versus urban environment). Based on retrospective studies, it can be concluded that habit is a central mediating variable, but norms to reduce car use are also influenced by socialization and seem relevant for later mode preferences.

**Warm water use and electricity**

Only a few studies have been concerned with the socialization of the consumption of warm water and electricity within families. Recent research on energy use in households has suggested that, among others, age is a relevant socio-economic factor for predicting electricity consumption (McLoughlin et al. 2012) and energy-saving behaviour

(Martinsson et al. 2011). Martinsson et al. (2011) found more energy-saving behaviour (especially hot water saving) in older than in younger people. However their study sample was between 20 and 85 years old and, hence, no conclusions could be drawn for children or adolescents. Thøgersen and Grønhøj (2010) and Gram-Hanssen (2004) reported that the number of teenagers in a household, in particular, increases electricity consumption. Hence, it seems worth looking at socialization processes in the domain of water and energy for adolescents.

In a study of family communication about 'green' consumer practices based on interviews with 30 parents, Grønhøj (2006) found that water and energy are domains that inspire frequent discussions between parents and teenagers, in particular about showering habits. Grønhøj (2006) interpreted parents' responses to their children as an attempt to save energy in the household and to teach responsible behaviours to their children. Other empirical evidence also suggests that adolescents and parents act in quite different ways with regard to saving electricity in households (Grønhøj and Thøgersen 2009). Grønhøj and Thøgersen (2009) investigated the intergenerational transmission of values, attitudes and behaviours in the environmental domain. Six hundred and one dyads consisting of parents and their adolescent children completed an online survey on values, attitudes and behaviours with regard to purchasing environmentally friendly products, saving electricity and separating waste. Results showed that children and parents' electricity-saving behaviours were correlated, but only weakly so. This finding stands in contrast to the purchasing of environmentally friendly products and recycling, for which adolescents' and parents' behaviours were much more similar. Across all three domains, adolescents performed the behaviours less frequently than their parents. For the saving of electricity, this gap was particularly wide. Hence, it seems that family socialization is less influential for saving electricity than in other domains. Grønhøj and Thøgersen (2009) suggested different reasons for this.

First, adolescents may be more sensitive to behavioural costs than parents. For example, buying organic and environmentally friendly products may be less associated with behavioural costs for adolescents, because parents commonly pay for household purchases, whereas saving electricity is associated with behavioural costs for both generations. Moreover, saving electricity potentially saves money for parents. In a recent focus group study, adolescents indicated that it is a barrier preventing the conservation of energy in households that only the parents save money from such actions (Toth et al. 2013, p. 36).

Life-stage barriers are a second possible reason for the lower commitment of younger generations to environmentally sustainable consumption (Grønhøj and Thøgersen 2009). Adolescents begin to rebel against the consumption norms of their parents in order to achieve some degree of independence (Hurrelmann 2007); thus, some differences in behaviour may be only temporary. Third, the authors suggested that an action's visibility might moderate parent-to-child influences. They argued that separating waste is highly visible whereas saving electricity is not (Grønhøj and Thøgersen 2012). Countering this, one could argue that turning off the TV after watching it or turning off lights can easily be observed by children. As the discussed results were based on a more general questioning of adolescents (whether they save electricity and whether their parents save electricity), the question of the extent to which electricity-saving behaviours are visible to children remains open.

Children will be able to observe at least some of their parents' electricity-saving behaviours, but do they also understand the reasons behind the observed actions? In a study of recycling and reuse of paper in 206 parent–child dyads, Matthies et al. (2012) found that not only is observing parental behaviour important for socialization, but so is communication about motives or the problem that the behaviour is supposed to address. Perhaps these results can be transferred to the use of electricity.

Studies of teenagers' (ranging in age from ten to 19) stories and diaries revealed that older teenagers (16–19 years) concentrated on personal electricity use in homes when thinking about energy, whereas younger teenagers (10–15 years) reported a wide range of energy types, including personal physical energy (Toth et al. 2013). This indicates that younger teenagers have a special understanding of energy use, without viewing personal electricity use as a really important consumption domain. Even if they observe how their parents turn off the lights after leaving the room, the motive behind the action is not automatically delivered with the action. For example, turning off the TV when not in use can have several meanings that range from saving money, to reducing media influence, to saving energy. If an explanation of the problem behind the action is missing, this may lead to lower parent-to-child influences compared with other actions for which the motivations are more obvious. For instance, children can directly observe their parents purchasing organic products in supermarkets instead of conventional products. The use of organic products because they are pro-health and pro-environment is a subject of commercial, family and public discussions and is easily accessible to children. Therefore, parents' motives for purchasing organic products seem to be more obvious. Grønhøj and Thøgersen's (2012) results support this argument. For the purchase of green products, children's behaviours were correlated with parents' attitudes. By contrast, no influence of parents' attitudes on their children's behaviours was found for saving electricity.

Collectively, adolescents' energy consumption behaviours differ from their parents. Adolescents seem to use more electricity and also admit that they save energy less frequently than adults. In line with such findings, socialization influences for saving electricity in the family seem to be less strong than for other specific consumption behaviours. The reported studies have primarily investigated adolescents, and thus it is possible that socialization influences might not be found due to this age group's specific developmental characteristics, which may include protests against the consumption norms of the family. It is also possible that adolescents are more sensitive to behavioural costs than other age groups.

### 17.2.2 Purchasing Environmentally Friendly Products

The purchasing of environmentally friendly products includes the consumption of organic food, organic clothes and local produce. Without distinguishing between products, further analyses of habits and of the financial costs of these kinds of behaviours become more difficult. Organic coffee, for example, may be purchased on a daily or weekly basis, whereas environmentally friendly clothes are purchased less frequently. Furthermore, it is important to notice that children and adolescents usually do not pay for family purchases, and this may influence their behaviour in this domain. Therefore, the possibility that children and adolescents are less concerned than their parents about the higher costs of environmentally friendly products has to be considered (Grønhøj and Thøgersen 2009).

Nevertheless in an investigation of the importance of several socialization agents for purchasing environmentally friendly products, participants reported that the family was the first and most important factor that determined their purchases (Yan and Xu 2010). Similarly a study of 340 secondary school students' self-reported purchases of organic products found that these were influenced by their perceptions of others' expectations, especially the expectations of their parents (Gotschi et al. 2007). Grønhøj and Thøgersen (2009) found that adolescents and parents showed more congruence in purchasing environmentally friendly products than for other behaviours.

Taken together, research on the purchasing of environmentally friendly products indicates significant socialization influences from parents to their children. The moderating influence of the frequency and costs of purchases on the strength of socialization influences are interesting issues for further investigation.

### 17.2.3 Sustainable Food Consumption

Research on socialization with regard to food consumption has a long history in clinical psychology and public health research, most often embedded in the context of the psychological or physical risks of childhood obesity (e.g. Jahnke and Warschburger 2008; Warschburger and Kröller 2012). Reisch and Gwozdz (2011a) looked at the issue of obesity from the perspective of sustainable consumption by outlining the effects on the social and economic sustainability of societies (see Gwozdz, Chapter 14 in this book, for further information). They supported the assumption of a direct connection between obesity and greenhouse gas emissions based on the finding that a population with a higher body mass index (BMI) has higher energy use due to a higher demand for transportation and food production (Edwards and Roberts 2009). Considering the relevance of the consumption of beef and dairy products for our carbon footprint (see Tukker et al. 2011), it is important to study how eating habits are formed (see also Vérain et al., Chapter 13 in this book).

Reisch and Gwozdz (2011a) reported that parents act as gatekeepers who have a major influence on their children's risk for obesity. In addition to parents, there seem to be further influential factors that shape children's food consumption practices (Reisch and Gwozdz 2011a). Reisch et al. (2011) identified potential key factors that influence children's obesity such as advertisements, the media and the food industry. It is further assumed that specific environments can promote overconsumption and subsequently add to obesity (Reisch and Gwozdz 2011b). Results have indicated that the children of parents with healthy food practices and a critical attitude toward advertisements have good knowledge of healthy food. This shows that parents influence children in the domain of food choice. However children's food knowledge is not related to their food preferences (Reisch and Gwozdz 2011b).

Possible consumer resocialization (Easterling et al. 1995), which means that children may influence the purchasing decisions of their parents, should be considered in this context as well. For instance, a study on communication about 'green' consumer practices found that, in some cases, parents chose not to buy organic products due to the influences of their children (Grønhøj 2006). Today, children influence a large proportion of their parents' purchases in direct and indirect ways (McNeal 1999). Larsson et al. (2010) argue that the influence of children on domestic consumption has increased because the policies of today encourage children to participate. A review study (McDermott et al. 2006) outlined that food advertising fosters children's requests of certain food from their parents. More importantly children mainly request food that is rich in sugar, salt or fat, and such requests seem to influence parents to make less healthy decisions about their food purchases.

Moreover it is known in developmental psychology that independent purchases are a main area in which adolescents begin to rebel against their parents' rules (Hurrelmann 2007). In addition, Pettersson et al. (2004) found that teenagers were more involved in and influential of the family's food purchases than younger children.

### 17.2.4 Consuming Less

Sustainable consumption does not only imply changes in consumption patterns but also often implies 'consuming less' in order to follow a more sustainable lifestyle (Jackson 2005b, p. 19). Taking fewer hot showers, using the car less frequently and wasting less food or consuming less meat involve a reduction or a sacrifice. In the context of socialization, it is interesting how the idea of sufficiency is generally involved in consumer socialization. Research targeting this issue seems to be lacking, but there is research on the socialization of materialism within families. This research suggests that a certain communication style in families promotes a tendency for children to embrace materialism (e.g. Moschis and Moore 1979). Parents often reward children with money or other material goods for their accomplishments (for example, good grades in school; McNeal 1999). A major concern is that our entire culture (not just the family) socializes children to believe that one achieves personal happiness by consuming material goods (John 1999). When families support a material orientation, it is likely to influence children's consumption styles (e.g. Flouri 1999). However ideas such as sustainable gift-giving seem to be gaining in popularity. For instance, a German company (erlebnisgeschenke.de) recently promoted a guidebook for sustainable gift-giving, recommending that parents give second-hand toys as gifts instead of new ones, or organize time for joint ventures with their children (Steinhoff et al. 2013).

Hence, it appears that parents influence the material orientation of their children. In order to investigate the kinds of socialization that influence children to consume less, future research could examine recent ideas such as sustainable gift-giving with respect to socialization influences.

### 17.2.5 Conclusion: Family Experiences and their Relevance for Later Consumption Behaviours

Research in a variety of domains has found that the sustainability-relevant behaviours of adolescents and later of adults are influenced by actual or former family practices and norms. This is true, for example, for travel mode choice and buying organic products. Parents influence children's food consumption as well, but research on how food preferences are transferred to children is still inconclusive.

The impact of socialization differs between environmentally relevant behaviours. In the domain of electricity use, adolescents seem to be less influenced by their parents than in other domains; they seem to consume more energy and to be less willing to accept the behavioural costs of a sustainable lifestyle.

## 17.3 VALUES, NORMS AND THE INTENTION TO CONSUME IN A LESS PROBLEMATIC WAY: LESSONS FROM ENVIRONMENTAL PSYCHOLOGY

Complementing our discussion of how specific sustainability relevant consumption behaviours are developed and transferred within the family, we now turn to how norms and values may be developed and transferred with regard to sustainable consumption. Again, we will primarily focus on the environmental aspects of sustainability.

In line with the tradition of Piaget's theory of intellectual development (Ginsburg and Opper 1988), John (1999) argues that the process of 'green' consumer socialization is strongly connected to cognitive and social developments (see also Easterling et al. 1995). As an example, the consumption motives of younger children may be driven primarily by highly valuing the act of possession, such as having more of something (Baker and Gentry 1996). However older children (11–16 years), may reach a more reflective stage, including developing an emerging understanding of the social meaning and value of their consumption (John 1999).

There is a growing body of empirical evidence – although weak in some domains – suggesting that norms and values are important determinants of pro-environmental behaviour (e.g. Matthies et al. 2012; Thøgersen and Ölander 2002). Two psychological theories have formed the background of most studies investigating the relations of values and norms with pro-environmental behaviours: The 'norm activation model' (NAM; Schwartz 1977) and the value–belief–norm theory (VBN; Stern et al. 1999). (This book provides detailed information about environmental psychology in Steg, Chapter 4.)

In the context of family socialization, values and attitudes open the door to pro-environmental actions and are transmitted from parents to children (Grønhøj and Thøgersen 2009). Research on the strength of these transmissions is still in its infancy. However, some research has indicated that family communication about environmental problems and about the consequences of behaviours activates an awareness of needs and consequences for children. On the basis of this emerging understanding of environmental consequences, children may develop a personal norm to embrace pro-environmental behaviours (Matthies et al. 2012). In addition, children seem to develop attitudes toward specific consumption behaviours by observing their parents' actions. For actions such as separating waste and purchasing organic products, family norms reflected in parental behaviours appear to be as important to adolescents as their own attitudes (Grønhøj and Thøgersen 2012). Likewise for recycling, children seem to be influenced mostly by observing their parents' behaviour directly (e.g. Matthies et al. 2012). Across different behavioural conditions, communication about problems and observations of parental behaviours seems to have diverse influences. For example children's reuse of paper is mainly influenced by communication about paper use within the family rather than by observing behaviours (Matthies et al. 2012). Similar conditions are assumed for the saving of electricity. As the understanding of household electricity is just emerging in later adolescents (Toth et al. 2013), communication about the concept of electricity seems to be necessary to evoke an understanding of the problem of wasting electricity in children's perceptions. Without an awareness of the needs and consequences connected to a problem to support parental actions, it will be unlikely that children will feel obliged to save energy as well.

Although people may have the motivation to change their behaviour, they often do not succeed; a problem that has been discussed under the heading of an 'attitude–behaviour gap' (e.g. Bamberg and Möser 2007). Explanations for this include habits that block behavioural change (Verplanken and Wood 2006) as well as behaviour change requiring going through a series of stages (Bamberg 2013). This strengthens the point that the socialization of more sustainable consumption should embrace the transfer of both norms and habits.

## 17.4 CONCLUSIONS

Considering the two aspects of sustainable consumption (impact and intention), there seem to be two strategies that may improve sustainable consumption via family socialization: (1) directly building up sustainable consumption habits; and (2) supporting the development of a more general understanding and motivation. Across several fields of consumption acts, it seems evident that the family influences the development of consumption habits via infrastructure, environment and the modelling of parents' behaviour (for example, transportation preferences, consumption of organic and fair trade products). Against this background special attention should be given to approaches that aim to change problematic structural conditions in families (for example, offering family-friendly dwelling facilities in a green environment with good infrastructure). Compensatory approaches (for example, offering public transportation as the primary way to get to school, and so on) also seem advisable. Alternative strategies should be considered for adolescents' electricity use, as family socialization seems less effective here. Adolescence is a time in which young people are yearning for independence, which can involve protests against their parents' value system. Therefore, programmes underlining the benefits for the environment and society as well as addressing personal interests instead of focusing on the family might be useful.

To conclude, observing parental behaviours seems to be a key element in the family socialization of sustainable consumption acts. However, teaching behaviours alone is not enough, especially for consumption acts that are hard for children to observe or understand. Regarding the increasing progress in new technological and social innovations, it seems crucial also to provide background information and to help children to understand the norms and values behind the concept of sustainable development. Sufficiency behaviours in particular, such as consuming less or sharing instead of owning, require citizens who are motivated by the normative idea of sustainable development.

## ACKNOWLEDGEMENTS

We would like to thank all those who scientifically or practically supported us during the preparation of this chapter. Special thanks go to our colleagues from the Helmholtz Alliance ENERGY-TRANS who gave us valuable input during the preparation of this chapter.

## REFERENCES

Baker, S.M. and J.W. Gentry (1996), 'Kids as collectors: a phenomenological study of first and fifth graders', *Advances in Consumer Research*, 23, 132–137.

Bamberg, S. (2013), 'Changing environmentally harmful behaviors: a stage model of self-regulated behavioral change', *Journal of Environmental Psychology*, 34, 151–159.

Bamberg, S. and G. Möser (2007), 'Twenty years after Hines, Hungerford, and Tomera: a new meta-analysis of psycho-social determinants of pro-environmental behaviour', *Journal of Applied Social Psychology*, 27 (8), 14–25.

Bandura, A. (1977), *Social Learning Theory*, Englewood Cliffs, NJ: Prentice-Hall.

Baslington, H. (2008), 'Travel socialization: a social theory of travel mode behavior', *International Journal of Sustainable Transportation*, 2 (2), 91–114.

Black, S., P. Stern and J. Elworth (1985), 'Personal and contextual influences on household energy adaptations', *Journal of Applied Psychology*, 70 (1), 3–21.

Cahill, M., T. Ruben and S. Winn (1996), 'Children and transport: travel patterns, attitudes and leisure activities of children in the Brighton area', *Health and Social Policy Research Centre, Report*, 96/4, Brighton: University of Brighton, Health and Social Policy Research Centre.

Dietz, T., G.T. Gardner, J. Gilligan, P.C. Stern and M.P. Vandenbergh (2009), 'Household actions can provide a behavioral wedge to rapidly reduce US carbon emissions', *Proceedings of the National Academy of Sciences*, 106 (44), 18452–18456.

Easterling, D., S. Miller and N. Weinberger (1995), 'Environmental consumerism – a process of children's socialization and families' resocialization', *Psychology and Marketing*, 12 (6), 531–550.

Edwards, P. and I. Roberts (2009), 'Population adiposity and climate change', *International Journal of Epidemiology*, 38 (4), 1137–1140.

EEA (European Environment Agency) (2012), 'Consumption and the environment: 2012 update – the European environment state and outlook 2010', Copenhagen: European Environment Agency.

Engelbert, A. (1986), *Kinderalltag und Familienumwelt: Eine Studie über die Lebenssituation von Vorschulkindern*, Frankfurt/M.: Campus.

Fischer, C., R. Grießhammer, R. Barth, B. Brohmann, C. Brunn, D.A. Heyen, F. Keimeyer and F. Wolf (2013), 'Mehr als nur weniger, Suffizienz: Begriff, Begründung und Potentiale', Working Paper 2, Freiburg: Öko-Institut e.V., available at http://www.oeko.de/oekodoc/1836/2013-505-de.pdf (accessed 20 January 2014).

Fischer, D., G. Michelsen, B. Blättel-Mink and A. Di Guilio (2011), 'Sustainable consumption: how to evaluate sustainability in consumption acts', in R. Defila, A. Di Giulio and R. Kaufmann-Hayoz (eds), *The Nature of Sustainable Consumption and How to Achieve It*, Munich: Oekom, pp. 67–80.

Flade, A. (1994), 'Effekte des Straßenverkehrs auf das Wohnen', in A. Flade (ed.), *Mobilitätsverhalten*, Weinheim: Psychologie Verlags Union, pp. 155–169.

Flouri, E. (1999), 'An integrated model of consumer materialism: can economic socialization and maternal values predict materialistic attitudes in adolescents?', *Journal of Socio-Economics*, 28 (6), 707–724.

Gardner, G.T. and P.C. Stern (2002), 'Choosing the behaviors to change and the points to intervention', in G.T. Gardner and P.C. Stern (eds), *Environmental Problems and Human Behavior*, Boston, MA: Pearson Custom, pp. 253–276.

Gardner, G.T. and P.C. Stern (2008), 'The short list: The most effective actions US households can take to curb climate change', *Environment: Science and Policy for Sustainable Development*, 50 (5), 12–25.

Ginsburg, H.P. and S. Opper (1988), *Piaget's Theory of Intellectual Development*, 3rd edn, Englewood Cliffs, NJ: Prentice-Hall.

Gotschi, E., S. Vogel and T. Lindenthal (2007), 'High school students' attitudes and behaviour towards organic products: survey results from Vienna', Institute for Sustainable Economic Development, DoE aSS, University of Natural Resources and Applied Life Sciences, Vienna.

Gram-Hanssen, K. (2004), 'Domestic electricity consumption – consumers and appliances', in I. Røpke and L.A. Reisch (eds), *The Ecological Economics of Consumption*, Cheltenham, UK and Northampton, MA, USA: Edward Elgar, pp. 132–150.
Grønhøj, A. (2006), 'Communication about consumption: a family process perspective on "green" consumer practices', *Journal of Consumer Behaviour*, 5 (6), 491–503.
Grønhøj, A. and J. Thøgersen (2009), 'Like father, like son? Intergenerational transmission of values, attitudes, and behaviours in the environmental domain', *Journal of Environmental Psychology*, 29 (4), 414–421.
Grønhøj, A. and J. Thøgersen (2012), 'Action speaks louder than words: the effect of personal attitudes and family norms on adolescents' pro-environmental behaviour', *Journal of Economic Psychology*, 33 (1), 292–302.
Grusec, J.E. and M. Davidov (2008), 'Socialization in the family: the roles of parents', in J.E. Grusec and P.D. Hastings (eds), *Handbook of Socialization: Theory and research*, New York: Guilford Press, pp. 284–308.
Haustein, S., C. Klöckner and A. Blöbaum (2009), 'Car use of young adults: the role of travel socialization', *Transportation Research Part F: Traffic Psychology and Behaviour*, 12, 168–178.
Hurrelmann, K. (2007), *Lebensphase Jugend: Eine Einführung in die sozialwissenschaftliche Jugendforschung*, 9th edn, Weinheim: Beltz Juventa.
Jackson, T. (2005a), *Motivating Sustainable Consumption: A Review of Evidence on Consumer Behavior and Behavioral Change*, London: Policy Studies Institute.
Jackson, T. (2005b), 'Live better by consuming less? Is there a "double dividend" in sustainable consumption?', *Journal of Industrial Ecology*, 9, 19–36.
Jahnke, D.L. and P.A. Warschburger (2008), 'Familial transmission of eating behaviors in preschool-aged children', *Obesity*, 16, 1821–1825.
Johansson, M. (2006), 'Environment and parental factors as determinants of mode for children's leisure travel', *Journal of Environmental Psychology*, 26 (2), 156–169.
John, D.R. (1999), 'Consumer socialization of children: a retrospective look at twenty-five years of research', *Journal of Consumer Research*, 26 (3), 183–213.
Klöckner, C.A. and E. Matthies (2009), 'Structural modeling of car use on the way to the university in different settings: interplay of norms, habits, situational restraints, and perceived behavioral control', *Journal of Applied Social Psychology*, 39 (8), 1807–1834.
Larsson, B., M. Andersson and C. Osbeck (2010), 'Bringing environmentalism home, children's influence on family consumption in the Nordic countries and beyond', *Childhood*, 17 (1), 129–147.
Martinsson, J., L.J. Lundqvist and A. Sundström (2011), 'Energy saving in Swedish households: the (relative) importance of environmental attitudes', *Energy Policy*, 39 (9), 5182–5191.
Matthies, E. and C.A. Klöckner (forthcoming), 'Car fixation, socialization and opportunities for change', in R. Hickman, M. Givoni, D. Bonilla, and D. Banister (eds), *International Handbook on Transport and Development*, Cheltenham, UK and Northampton, MA, USA: Edward Elgar.
Matthies, E., S. Selge and C.A. Klöckner (2012), 'The role of parental behaviour for the development of behaviour specific environmental norms – the example of recycling and re-use behaviour', *Journal of Environmental Psychology*, 32 (3), 277–284.
McDermott, L., M. Stead, G. Hastings and T. O'Sullivan (2006), 'International food advertising, pester power and its effects', *International Journal of Advertising*, 25 (4), 513–539.
McLoughlin, F., A. Duffy and M. Conlon (2012), 'Characterising domestic electricity consumption patterns by dwelling and occupant socio-economic variables: an Irish case study', *Energy and Buildings*, 48, 240–248.
McNeal, J.U. (1999), *The Kids Market: Myths and Realities*, Ithaca, NY: Paramount Market.
Moschis, G.P. (1985), 'The role of family communication in consumer socialization of children and adolescents', *Journal of Consumer Research*, 11 (4), 898–913.
Moschis, G.P. and G.A. Churchill Jr. (1978), 'Consumer socialization: a theoretical and empirical analysis', *Journal of Marketing Research*, 15 (4), 599–609.
Moschis, G.P. and R.L. Moore (1979), 'Family communication and consumer socialization', *Advances in Consumer Research*, 6 (1), 359–363.
Pettersson, A., U. Olsson and C. Fjellström (2004), 'Family life in grocery stores – a study of interaction between adults and children', *International Journal of Consumer Studies*, 28 (4), 317–328.
Quellette, J.A. and W. Wood (1998), 'Habit and intention in everyday life: the multiple processes by which past behaviour predicts future behaviour', *Psychological Bulletin*, 124 (1), 54–74.
Reisch, L.A. and W. Gwozdz (2011a), 'Chubby cheeks and climate change: childhood obesity as a sustainable development issue', *International Journal of Consumer Studies*, 35 (1), 3–9.
Reisch, L.A. and W. Gwozdz (2011b), 'Childhood obesity, sustainable development, and behavioral economics', SCORAI, Socio-technical Transitions, Social Practices, and the New Economics: Meeting the Challenge of a Constrained World, available at http://research.cbs.dk/portal/en/publications/childhood-obesity-sustainable-development-and-behavioral-economics(a718ea6d-e4a6-4946-bd82-4b5911e31747).html.
Reisch, L.A., W. Gwozdz and S.C. Beckmann (2011), 'Consumer behavior in childhood obesity research and

policy', in L.A. Moreno, I. Pigeot and W. Ahrens (eds), *Epidemiology of Obesity in Children and Adolescents – Prevalence and Aetiology*, Heidelberg: Springer, pp. 431–454.
Rijnhout, L. and S. Lorek (2012), 'EU Sustainable Lifestyles Roadmap and Action Plan 2050 "Pathways for enabling social innovation and behavior change"', available at http://www.sustainable-lifestyles.eu/fileadmin/images/content/Roadmap.pdf (accessed 15 November 2013).
Sandqvist, K. (2002), 'How does a family car matter? Leisure, travel and attitudes of adolescents in inner city Stockholm', *World Transport Policy and Practice*, 8 (1), 11–18.
Schneewind, Klaus A. (2010), *Familienpsychologie*, 3rd edn, Stuttgart: Kohlhammer.
Schwartz, S.H. (1977), 'Normative influence on altruism', in L. Berkowitz (ed.), *Advances in Experimental Social Psychology*, New York: Academic Press, pp. 221–279.
Steinhoff, T., S. Morvay, B. Wilde and V. Hamel (2013), 'Nachhaltig schenken', München: erlebnisgeschenke.de, available at http://www.erlebnisgeschenke.de/nachhaltig-schenken/ (accessed 21 November 2013).
Stern, P.C., T. Dietz, T. Abel, G.A. Guagnano and L. Kalof (1999), 'A value-belief-norm theory of support for social movements: the case of environmentalism', *Human Ecology Review*, 6 (2), 81–97.
Thøgersen, J. and A. Grønhøj (2010), 'Electricity saving in households – a social cognitive approach', *Energy Policy*, 38 (12), 7732–7777.
Thøgersen, J. and F. Ölander (2002), 'Human values and the emergence of a sustainable consumption pattern: a panel study', *Journal of Economic Psychology*, 23, 605–630.
Thorndike, E.L. (1913), '*Educational Psychology: Vol. 1. The Psychology of Learning*', New York: Teachers College Press.
Toth, N., L. Little, J.C. Read, D. Fitton and M. Horton (2013), 'Understanding teen attitudes towards energy consumption', *Journal of Environmental Psychology*, 34, 36–44.
Tukker, A., R.A. Goldbohm, A. De Koning, M. Verheijden, R. Kleijn, O. Wolf, I. Pérez-Domínguez and J.M. Rueda-Cantuche (2011), 'Environmental impacts of changes to healthier diets in Europe', *Ecological Economics*, 70 (10), 1776–1788.
Verplanken, B. and W. Wood (2006), 'Interventions to break and create consumer habits', *Journal of Public Policy and Marketing*, 25 (1), 90–103.
Ward, S. (1974), 'Consumer socialization', *Journal of Consumer Research*, 1 (2), 1–14.
Warschburger, P. and K. Kröller (2012), 'Childhood overweight and obesity: maternal perceptions of the associated health risks and the need for action', *BMC Public Health*, 12 (1), 1–8.
Yan, R. and H. Xu (2010), 'Understanding green purchase behavior: college students and socialization agents', *Journal of Family and Consumer Sciences*, 102 (2), 27–32.

# PART VI

# POLICIES FOR SUSTAINABLE CONSUMPTION

# 18. Carbon triage: a strategy for developing a viable carbon labelling system

*Sharon Shewmake, Mark A. Cohen, Paul C. Stern and Michael P. Vandenbergh*

The Intergovernmental Panel on Climate Change has expressed increasing scientific certainty about the anthropogenic influence on climate change, concluding in 2013 that the influence is 'extremely likely' (IPCC 2013). Despite these developments, the policy response remains quite uncertain. The prospects for international agreement on a comprehensive climate treaty under the United Nations Framework Convention on Climate Change process are dim, and the prospects for comprehensive national climate legislation in the United States and many other major emitting countries look no more promising. In this environment, scholars and policy makers over the past several years have become increasingly interested in other governance options, including regime complexes (Keohane and Victor 2011) and climate 'clubs' (Victor 2011) at the international level, as well as subnational strategies such as polycentric governance (Ostrom 2012), bottom-up approaches (Stewart et al. 2013) and private governance (Vandenbergh 2013).

One such option is carbon labelling, which involves representing on a product label (or otherwise at the point of sale) the product's contribution across its life cycle to net emissions of gases that contribute to global warming. The calculations are often made in carbon dioxide equivalents ($CO_2$eq) to aggregate across types of emissions, hence the term 'carbon labelling'. Carbon labelling initiatives can in principle bypass the current government gridlock, influence corporate and individual behaviour across international boundaries, and yield near-term, cost-effective emissions reductions (Cohen and Vandenbergh 2012; Cohen and Viscusi 2012; Vandenbergh et al. 2011).

Although public or private carbon labelling programmes could fill current gaps in government mitigation efforts and play a complementary role after governments have adopted more comprehensive laws and policies, recent attempts to provide carbon labels that are meaningful to consumers and firms and effective in reducing the carbon footprints of products have had mixed results. The most widely known private carbon labelling programme was initiated by Tesco, a UK supermarket chain that vowed in 2007 to begin labelling all 70000 of its products. Five years later, Tesco abandoned its plans, due to the high cost of labelling each of its products and the lack of other retailers following its lead (Vaughan 2012). In the meantime, government-sponsored programmes in Japan, Korea, Thailand, Australia, the UK, France, Germany, Switzerland, Sweden and elsewhere have been established with guidelines for measuring and labelling (Langley et al. 2012; Vandenbergh et al. 2011). In addition several eco-labels include carbon considerations among the issues included in their screening criteria.[1] Some of these efforts are government-sponsored; others have been developed by non-profit organizations and individual companies. Many have been undertaken on a limited scale and have been independent from each other. No convergence has occurred on a labelling protocol of demonstrated validity that could be applied globally. Considering the globalization of many product life cycles, there are clear advantages to developing a carbon labelling system with global applicability.

Set against the recent history and the difficulties of achieving valid and widely applicable carbon labels are two compelling reasons to continue working to develop carbon labelling systems. One is the lack of progress with national and international legislative approaches to reducing the carbon footprints of product streams. The other is evidence of the promise of labelling approaches. Experience around the world with energy-saving labels on appliances, motor vehicles and other consumer goods, experiments in grocery stores and florists shops (Michaud et al. 2013; Vanclay et al. 2011), and survey evidence (Onozaka et al. 2012) all suggest that carbon labels could influence consumption patterns and reduce greenhouse gas emissions. One reason for Tesco's failure is that it was trying to do too much at once. In this chapter we propose a system for prioritizing which products to label and a strategy for making the system feasible.

Critics of carbon labelling claim that labels are unlikely to result in substantial changes in purchase or use decisions, and will have little effect on aggregate emissions (e.g. Hailes 2010). They also note that some product categories have only minor carbon emission differences among competing products, or complex and variable supply chains that make life cycle emission assessments costly and unreliable. These are legitimate concerns. However our research suggests that if properly conceived, a carbon-labelling programme can provide valid information, support meaningful carbon reductions, and be cost-effective (Cohen and Vandenbergh 2012). If applied to a basket of 50 or 100 of the most promising goods, this approach has the potential to generate substantial carbon emissions reductions and to serve a proof-of-concept function. What is missing is a screening methodology to identify the most promising initial candidates for carbon labelling.

This chapter outlines strategies for a carbon labelling system that has the potential for prompt adoption and relatively significant carbon emissions reductions. In light of the failures of recent efforts to label all products, we first discuss how to prioritize the products to carbon label. To identify the most promising products to label, our research suggests a triage approach that targets products in categories that have large aggregate carbon footprints, products where the carbon assessment may be reliable and feasible, and products that are likely to have the largest producer and consumer responses to a labelling system. We illustrate these results with an example from the dairy industry and discuss implementation issues. We begin in the next section by listing the four criteria for determining which goods are best suited for carbon labels. Based on these criteria, we provide an example of how these principles can help prioritize product categories in the case of dairy products. Finally, we explore several important implementation issues, including questions about the geography of product life cycles, whether the labelling programme should be mandatory or voluntary, and how the label may effectively communicate a product's carbon content.

## 18.1 CRITERIA FOR CHOOSING PRODUCTS TO LABEL

This section details four criteria that can be used to prioritize products for carbon labelling. In general, to be a good candidate for labelling: (1) the product category must produce a significant amount of carbon emissions; (2) there must be adequate data on life cycle emissions; (3) firms must be able to adjust their production, acquisition, distribution and/or disposal mechanisms in ways that significantly reduce the life cycle carbon emissions of individual products; and (4) the ultimate consumers of the product (which may be individuals or organizations concerned with their carbon footprints) must respond to the labelling programme in ways that ultimately result in significant carbon reductions through switching their purchases to lower carbon products. These principles are detailed below.

### 18.1.1 Magnitude of Footprint

Consumer products represent a significant source of carbon emissions through both their embedded carbon content and the energy they consume during the use phase.[2] However, not every product has enough potential to reduce carbon emissions to justify the costs of testing and labelling. We propose focusing on products in categories that have relatively large life cycle carbon intensity or a large sales volume, recognizing that the product of these two factors represents the aggregate carbon footprint of the good. This analysis can be conducted with available information in many cases, and does not require in-depth data collection at the screening stage. For many product categories, this information has already been collected. For example, CleanMetrics and ecoinvent maintain databases with the tools to estimate process-based carbon, energy and water footprints for agriculture, packaging materials, building construction and operating, metals and metal processing, bedding and furniture, clothing and apparel, electronics, transportation, product distribution and logistics, and waste treatments (CleanMetrics 2011; ecoinvent 2013). Furthermore, input–output models can provide more aggregated estimates of carbon footprints. These tools could be used to provide such an initial screen. Priorities may depend on the geographic reach of the label because of very different sales volumes in different countries. Consider the example of a food labelling system for the United States. Lamb has a high carbon footprint per kilogram, but the amount of lamb consumed in the United States is less than 0.5 kg per person per year. Cheese has a lower carbon footprint than lamb by weight but the average American consumes approximately 14 kg of cheese per year. Thus, in the USA, cheese has a much bigger total impact on the carbon footprint of the country's food.

The situation could be quite different for a food label aiming for a more global reach. Cheese consumption is highly concentrated in Europe and North America. Greece's consumption of cheese is 32.6 kg per person per year (Wisconsin Milk Marketing Board n.d.) while world cheese consumption is projected to reach only 3 kg per person per year by 2015 (Global Industry Analysts 2010). Meanwhile lamb consumption is higher in Asia and the Middle East and worldwide lamb consumption is approximately 1.8 kg per person annually (Brester 2012). Since carbon content is 13.5 kg of $CO_2$eq per kg of cheese compared to 39.2 kg of $CO_2$eq per kg of lamb, if the sole criterion were aggregate global carbon emissions, lamb would have a higher priority for a globally targeted label.[3]

### 18.1.2 Feasibility of Assessment

A second criterion for prioritizing products for labelling is that the cost of obtaining relatively accurate information is low. The availability of accurate life cycle data including production, transport, storage and sales, consumption and disposal varies by product category. Goods with more complex or shifting supply chains may not be promising initial candidates for carbon labelling. Many products are frequently redesigned and researchers may face proprietary data constraints. For example mobile phones are redesigned as often as every nine months. Carbon footprints of other consumer electronics such as laptops and desktop computers have been found to be inconsistent and lacking transparency (Andrae and Anderson 2010; Teehan and Kandlikar 2012).

Varying consumer usage patterns also affect the carbon footprint of products. De Koning et al. (2010) provide an example of the uncertainties associated with comparing the carbon footprint of ultra-liquid to compact powder laundry detergent. Although they find that standardizing several key parameters (such as washing machine efficiency, electricity sources and water temperature) results in ultra-liquid detergent always having a lower carbon footprint compared to compact powder detergent, if all parameters are allowed to vary, the compact powder detergent sometimes has lower emissions. This example does not mean that carbon labelling is infeasible, only that the firm or standard-setting body engaged in labelling needs to determine the feasibility of producing reliable and valid carbon footprint labels for the major products within a product category that are meaningful in terms of consumer choices, considering the parameters involved in estimating the carbon footprint for each product.

Several organizations have recently developed life cycle protocols using similar principles and a multi-stakeholder approach. These protocols are the British Standards Institute's (2011) Publicly Available Specification 2050 and the Greenhouse Gas Protocol's (2011) Product Life Cycle Accounting and Reporting Standard. The International Organization for Standardization (ISO) also issued a technical specification for life cycle analysis of carbon footprints in 2013, ISO/TS 14067.[4] While these organizations do not themselves provide estimates of carbon footprints, they move the world closer to standardized protocols so that consumers of carbon labels will be able to obtain comparable and meaningful carbon footprint information.

It may not be necessary to conduct a detailed analysis of all aspects of the life cycle of a good to set priorities for labelling. Methods such as economic input–output life cycle analysis (EIO-LCA) can readily provide approximate carbon footprint estimates that are good enough to identify high-footprint products without detailed process analyses that often take months (Hendrickson et al. 2006). The EIO-LCA approach does this by calculating the average carbon intensity of each sector using an emissions database and then linking that sector's contribution to the production of final goods using national input–output accounts.[5] The EIO-LCA model takes into account transportation and can be modified to account for usage and end-of-life phases. EIO-LCA models have been developed for the United States, Canada, Japan and various European countries. Even if more detailed and reliable estimates are ultimately desired for establishing carbon footprints, the EIO-LCA approach can aid in the initial screening and prioritization process.

A carbon label could proceed with information using the EIO-LCA methodology as an approximation. Such a label could be sufficiently reliable and valid to offer useful information for producers and consumers. Footprint information using this approach could also be presented during a trial period during which actors in the product's supply chain could have the opportunity to contest the proposed label data.

### 18.1.3 Producer Responsiveness, or Supply-Side Plasticity

Another important criterion for prioritizing carbon labelling is the extent to which firms are likely to change their product content, mix of product offerings, acquisition of materials, manufacturing processes or locations, transportation methods, power sources or disposal practices to reduce the product's life cycle carbon footprint. We call this responsiveness 'plasticity' (Dietz et al. 2009). The impact (*I*) that a label can have can be analysed as the product of the potential reduction in carbon emissions that could be achieved by technical changes in the product's life cycle (*t*), the number of products affected by the label (*n*), and the degree to which the technically possible improvements are made, or plasticity (*p*); thus, $I = tpn$ (Stern 2011). Plasticity can be achieved both through the actions of firms across the product life cycle and through changes in consumer behaviour. Since firms with high plasticity or responsiveness are more likely to participate in voluntary carbon labelling systems, their product categories are good candidates for prioritization.

Firm responsiveness depends on four key factors: available technology for reducing carbon footprints, brand visibility, industry competitiveness and consumer demand, which is further discussed in the next subsection. Firms might be more receptive to altering their products' carbon footprints if there are cheap lower-carbon production alternatives such as new production technologies, low-cost renewable energy sources, or options to reduce overall transportation footprints by choosing alternative suppliers or changing processing locations. Without cost savings, firms are less likely to respond even with a demand-side pull.

Prior experience with voluntary product labels suggests that firms at the downstream end of the supply chain with fast-moving consumer goods and visible brands are more responsive to demand-side pressures (for example, boycotts or firm reputation campaigns) and hence more likely to change behaviour (Steering Committee 2012). Firms may respond to these general reputational concerns by reformulating products offered to consumers, even if consumers do not change behaviour in response to the new product information (Cohen and Vandenbergh 2012). This process may explain the behaviour of firms such as McDonald's, which purchased certified seafood long before it announced that fact to its consumers (Gunther 2013). These types of responses may occur because of a rational perception about the importance of reputational concerns or because of an overestimation of consumer awareness of the information, a phenomenon that has been called the 'tell-tale heart effect' (Loewenstein et al. 2013). Finally, the market structure of an industry may be important if some firms see a tactical opportunity in differentiating themselves. For example, industries that sell primarily to governments with environmental procurement standards may see an advantage in proactively reducing the carbon footprints of their goods. Similarly, firms that are selling to environmentally sensitive consumers might be more receptive to reducing carbon emissions. Although the evidence is sparse, one study of investor-owned electric utilities (Delmas et al. 2010) found that those who sell more of their electricity to households (as opposed to firms) were more responsive in changing their fuel mix when confronted with mandatory disclosures. Another possible example of responsiveness to possible consumer sensitivity is Microsoft, which made a commitment in 2012 to achieve carbon neutrality beginning in 2013 (UN n.d.). The firm appears to be on track to meet this goal (Bernard 2013).

### 18.1.4 Consumer Responsiveness, or Demand-side Plasticity

Finally, the selection of high-priority products for labelling should consider the extent to which consumer behaviour is likely to change upon receiving new information about the carbon content of competing products. Consumer motivation and opportunity are both important. Goods may differ in the extent to which consumers are likely to attend to eco-labels and in the substitutes available. For example some studies report that household consumers respond to carbon labels on apples, tomatoes, roses and pet food, but not to labels for different sizes of milk (Michaud et al. 2013; Onozaka et al. 2012; Vanclay et al. 2011).

One way to predict consumer responsiveness is to use own- and cross-price elasticities. Elasticities measure the responsiveness of demand for a good to the change in the price of that good (own-price elasticity) or to another good (cross-price elasticity). Insulin is an example of a good with an own-price elasticity close to zero, that is, a very inelastic demand. A change in the price of insulin is not likely to induce large changes in the quantity of insulin consumed. Insulin would also be a poor choice for a carbon label since diabetics who need insulin are not likely to be persuaded from using it as a result of its carbon footprint. On the other hand, labels on elastic products, such as roses, are more likely to be successful.

In addition to the own-price elasticity, it may be useful to know which products consumers consider to be substitutes. Cross-price elasticities convey this information by quantifying the relationship between a change in the price of one product and the change in the quantity demanded of a different product. For instance, if the cross-price elasticity of pork with respect to beef is 0.48, then a 1 per cent increase in the price of beef will increase pork consumption by 0.48 per cent. An elasticity close to zero implies that an increase in the price of one good has no influence on the demand for the other good and hence those two products are not substitutes. High-carbon goods that have low-carbon substitutes, as measured by cross-price elasticities, are better candidates for a carbon label than high-carbon goods with only other high-carbon substitutes.

To quantify these relationships and predict consumer demand shifts in response to a carbon label, Shewmake et al. (2013) developed a model that integrated elasticities, willingness to pay for personal carbon footprint reductions, and estimates of carbon footprints. A carbon label is assumed to change the perception of a good's carbon footprint, which can then be related to a change in price through the willingness to pay for personal carbon footprint reductions. This approach is in contrast to the many studies that estimate potential carbon footprint reductions from consumers using ad hoc judgements about which products are substitutes. Instead of simply assuming that chicken is a substitute for beef, the model quantifies the shift from beef to chicken that results from informing the consumer as to beef and chicken's actual carbon footprints. Although beef and chicken are obvious substitutes, many other products are not. Vanclay et al. (2011) were surprised to find that consumers were not willing to switch from a pint of milk to a gallon of milk despite the pint having a higher carbon footprint per unit. The cross-price elasticity of milk with regard to container size is close to zero largely due to milk being perishable (Stockton and Capps 2005). If Vanclay et al. had examined cross-price elasticities, they would have been able to predict the unwillingness to switch milk container sizes and might have focused on bottled waters or carbonated beverages. Consumers are willing to switch between different sizes of bottled water and carbonated drinks according to their cross-price elasticities.

The demand side of the market for carbon-emitting products is not limited to individuals and households. Many products are purchased and consumed by firms as intermediate products in a production process or by public or private sector organizations as ultimate consumers. Some firms and sectors have demonstrated far greater willingness to pressure suppliers to reduce carbon emissions than others. Several examples suggest the potential importance of such activity: Wal-Mart announced in 2010 that it planned to assist its suppliers in reducing their carbon footprints by 20 million metric tons by 2015 (Rosenbloom 2010). In connection with the WWF's (World Wildlife Fund) Climate Savers programme, Hewlett-Packard recently announced a goal for a 20 per cent decrease from 2010 in its first-tier manufacturing and product transportation-related greenhouse gas (GHG) emissions intensity by 2020 (Hewlett-Packard 2013), and Coca-Cola developed system-wide supply chain goals to reduce 'the drink in your hand' carbon emissions by 25 per cent (Coca-Cola 2013). Wal-Mart and many other large retailers recently participated in a programme that imposes restrictions on beef suppliers to reduce Brazilian deforestation, a leading contributor to global carbon emissions (Downie 2009).

## 18.2 IMPLICATIONS OF THE PRODUCT LIFE CYCLE FOR CARBON LABELLING

In the previous section, we identified four principles for determining the most promising candidates for carbon labelling. However, these factors must not be viewed in isolation. The total carbon footprint of a good can be decomposed into its footprints in the four phases of its life cycle: production, transportation, usage and disposal. It matters for labelling that some products differ greatly in terms of how these phases contribute to the life cycle carbon footprint. For example, long-lived household technologies that consume energy in use, such as motor vehicles and many home appliances, have carbon footprints dominated by the usage phase; whereas other products, such as fresh fruits, have almost no carbon footprints in usage, but may have footprints dominated by other phases, such as production and transportation. Thus, suppose a product category has a very large total carbon footprint due to the usage stage but not the production stage, and that producers are responsive but consumers are not. This product category might not be a good candidate for carbon labelling because little of the potential for carbon reduction is likely to be affected. On the other hand, if consumers are responsive but producers are not, this product category might be a perfect candidate.

In addition, for products with usage-dominated footprints, it may be sufficient to use existing labels available for the usage phase, such as energy consumption labels (Energy Star in the USA, for example), if these labels are already guiding consumers to lower-footprint products. Although this might be the case, we caution that some energy labels might not convey adequate information about related consumer product usage. For example, while a washing machine might be labelled Energy Star or contain a label comparing its energy efficiency to the average competing product, this type of information does not inform consumers of the dramatic difference in energy consumption when using cold versus warm versus hot water – a factor that dominates the $CO_2$ emissions associated with choice of laundry detergent. In this example, either an energy label on the washing machine that compared energy use by water temperature or a carbon label on the detergent that compared average energy use by water temperature would serve similar purposes.

## 18.3 AN EXAMPLE OF CARBON LABELLING TRIAGE IN THE FOOD INDUSTRY

We focus our example on the food sector. Organic, local and sustainable designations have been popular with food products, but these do not give information on the carbon footprint. The livestock sector is responsible for 18 per cent of worldwide anthropogenic greenhouse gas emissions (FAO 2006; Pelletier and Tyedmers 2010) and thus meets the first criterion for carbon labelling: a sufficient magnitude of the carbon footprint. Furthermore, livestock production is expected to increase as populations and incomes rise. Pelletier and Tyedmers (2010) estimate that the livestock sector alone could produce enough greenhouse gas emissions to account for between 52 and 294 per cent of what is thought to be a safe level of emissions by 2050.

The feasibility of assessment criterion is also satisfied: the cattle and dairy sectors are relatively well studied as a source of greenhouse gas emissions, with many estimates available across geographies and methods of production (see, e.g., Capper 2011, 2012; de Vries and de Boer 2010; Doreau et al. 2011; ecoinvent 2013; Environmental Working Group 2011; Nguyen et al. 2010; Pelletier et al. 2010). Beef and dairy products often come with origin designations, which facilitate calculations of the transportation element of the carbon footprint.

Producers of cattle and dairy have multiple opportunities to reduce the carbon footprints of their products. Carbon footprints can be lowered by improvements in animal genetics and diet, by increased efficiency in feed production including the incorporation of by-products from other sectors such as distillers' grains and citrus pulp, by changes to the cow–calf breeding system as well as finishing and feedlot systems, by increases in land use intensity, by using electricity from lower-carbon sources such as wind and natural gas, by using more energy-efficient transport modes, by better managing manure and by changes in processing and packing processes. Indeed, many changes have already occurred in response to the profit motive. The carbon footprint of a glass of milk in 2007 was 37 per cent of what it was in 1944 (Capper et al. 2009) and the carbon footprint of a kilogram of beef was reduced by 16.3 per cent from 1977 to 2007 (Capper 2011). Technological advances in the developed world and higher rates of adoption of energy-saving technologies in developing countries may be able to lower the carbon footprints of meat and dairy with minimal impacts on producer profits.

Producer responsiveness may be high due to the wide variety of market niches and the substantial retail consumer exposure of beef and dairy products. Although cheese and beef producers may be reluctant to label their high-carbon goods, some grocery stores or health food stores may choose to label beef and dairy products as a way to find niches as low-carbon suppliers. Many stores already label on the basis of how food animals are raised, to respond to consumer interest in animal welfare.

Finally there is reason for optimism about consumer responsiveness. A preliminary study estimated that if consumers were to learn the carbon impact of beef, they would decrease their beef consumption by approximately 3–4 per cent (Shewmake et al. 2013). This is not taking into account their ability to switch between types of beef and is thus an underestimate. Even though consumers would increase their consumption of substitutes such as pork, poultry, fish, eggs and other foods, the net impact of a label would be to reduce emissions by approximately 450 000 tonnes of $CO_2$eq per year in the United States. Examining other products and accounting for the magnitude of their carbon footprints, feasibility of assessment, firm responsiveness and consumer responsiveness should lead researchers to find additional products that could be feasibly and effectively labelled. This would allow labelling efforts to proceed without having to solve the daunting problem of labelling all goods.

## 18.4 IMPLEMENTATION ISSUES

This chapter sketches out a framework and criteria to prioritize products for carbon labelling; but selecting promising products is only the first step. To implement a successful carbon label scheme, it will be important to address several implementation challenges. We briefly discuss three of these: the governance of the labelling scheme, geographic considerations, and the content and format of carbon labels. We also discuss some potential solutions to these implementation issues.

### 18.4.1 Governance

We anticipate that, for the foreseeable future, any carbon labelling programme will be voluntary; that is, product suppliers will not be required by law to participate. Voluntary labelling programmes could be established by private, public or public–private partnership entities (such as the European Eco-label; www.ecolabel.eu). They could also be adopted as stand-alone carbon labelling programmes or added to existing eco-label programmes. In any case, they will need to meet the four key challenges facing all voluntary environmental programmes: sponsorship (finding actors who will invest resources to get the programme operating), recruitment of suppliers as members, prevention of shirking (typically through monitoring, enforcement and providing incentives to ensure that member firms keep to their commitments), and marketing the programme to stakeholders (Potoski and Prakash 2013). Programmes will also benefit from implementing principles that apply generally to efforts to provide environmental public goods, such as engaging the interested and affected parties in the needed scientific analysis and monitoring (National Research Council 1996; Stern 2013).

Available evidence indicates that successful voluntary environmental programmes are those that fit well into their institutional contexts (Potoski and Prakash 2013; Prakash and Potoski 2006). In the case of carbon labelling, two key challenges appear to be:

obtaining support for the research needed to develop and validate labels; and identifying an entity or entities that can conduct the research, update labels as needed, monitor their use, and identify and report cases of misuse. If these challenges can be met for labelling one class of products, the lessons learned and institutional mechanisms created may be adaptable to other product types. Food products may be a good candidate for initial efforts because recruitment of suppliers and marketing of labels have both proven easier with products for which end-users already want environmental information (Potoski and Prakash 2013). Moreover, existing non-governmental organizations (NGOs) could represent the concerns of environmentally oriented food consumers and could help to build consumer demand for carbon labels, participate in designing them and, if adequate monitoring is in place, sanction suppliers who violate the labelling regime with reputational costs. Funding for developing the label data and format and for supporting an organization to do monitoring and sanctioning remains a challenge, but might come from a private foundation that supports environmental causes or from an interested government.

### 18.4.2 Geographic Considerations

One of the most basic implementation concerns about carbon labelling is that the carbon emissions associated with the life cycle of a product vary with the places where it is produced and used. Products that require electricity or other sources of energy at various points in their life cycles will have different carbon footprints depending upon the sources of energy used at each of these points. For example, life cycle analyses of carbon emissions from electric vehicles vary depending upon whether local electricity is powered by coal, natural gas, nuclear or renewables,[6] as well as on the sources and amounts of energy used to produce the vehicles and move them to market (Zivin et al. 2012). For products like these, for which electricity in use has a major carbon footprint, labels may need to provide alternative carbon footprint indicators depending upon the sources of local electricity in target markets.

Similarly, for products sold in widely different geographic locations and for which transportation to market has a large carbon footprint, labels may need to provide different information in different places. Transportation footprints vary depending on whether or not a good is produced locally or is shipped from a long distance to the consumer. A French wine may have a lower carbon footprint than a California wine when consumed in New York, but not in San Francisco. If such differences are small, there might be no need to customize the carbon footprint by location. However, if they are large, it might require individualized labels depending upon the point of sale. Over time, it may be possible to take advantage of 'intelligent packaging' in which embedded nanostrips convey information that can be read at the point of sale, allowing for specific in-store labelling. For some products, where there is great variation in carbon footprint due to differences in production, transportation and usage, the labelling task may be so complex that the product fails to meet the 'feasibility' criterion for valid labelling. Countering the above difficulties related to geography is the point that many of the costs of a label – designing the label, calculating the footprints, testing and educating consumers – are fixed costs. Developing a label in one nation or region may make using the label in other regions more likely. This was seen in the Energy Star programme that was started by the United

States Environmental Protection Agency in 1992 but became a de facto international standard as the Energy Star symbol gained international recognition (Meier 2003). Manufacturers of Energy Star products used the Energy Star logo to differentiate their products and preferred an international standard. A related issue that is often raised in the context of product labelling is whether a labelling programme might be construed as a trade barrier under international agreements. This is a complicated and sometimes contentious issue that has been discussed in the international law literature in the context of eco-labels. Cohen and Vandenbergh (2012) summarize these legal arguments and note that the World Trade Organization (WTO) tries to balance the right of members to advance legitimate goals such as environmental protection against the international goal of free trade. In particular, a carbon labelling programme should avoid applying arbitrary standards that are not aligned with greenhouse gas emissions and it should not serve as disguised protectionism. Thus, a well-designed carbon labelling system may be able to withstand WTO challenges. Furthermore, Cohen and Vandenbergh (2012) conclude that private (as opposed to government mandated) carbon labelling is even less vulnerable to serious WTO challenges.

### 18.4.3 Content of Carbon Labels

Much has been written elsewhere about the design of labelling schemes and labels themselves (see generally Magat and Viscusi 1992; Cohen and Viscusi 2012 in the context of carbon labelling). An important implementation issue is the level of precision a carbon label should provide. It is useful to distinguish three levels of precision. One is binary, as in a seal of approval. Examples include the Energy Star label, the organic label on foods, and many other labels that distinguish only two categories of products: those that do or do not meet some preset standard. A higher level of precision is ordinal. Ordinal scales are sometimes presented as ratings such as letter grades of A–F or ratings using one to five stars. Such scales allow finer comparisons than a seal of approval but do not tell users how much better one level is than the adjacent one, and do not even imply that the distances between adjacent levels are all equal. Still greater precision is offered by a numerical estimate of carbon footprint, such as a measure of carbon dioxide equivalent emissions in grams across an item's life cycle. Such measures, commonly called ratio scales because they allow for valid calculation of ratios, provide sufficiently precise information for users to calculate, for instance, benefit–cost ratios that estimate the amount of emission reductions that would be achieved by spending a given amount on a more climate-friendly model of a product.

Climate scientists and others might prefer the highest possible level of precision in a carbon label, but there are several reasons why it may not be best to provide labelling information to consumers using ratio scales. One is that reliable and valid information may not be available at the required level of precision, because key parameters cannot be measured accurately or because they vary greatly according to where the product is made, how it is transported, or other factors. A second reason is that high precision may not be necessary to inform consumers as they make product choices. A third reason is that less-precise labels may be more user-friendly, easier to understand and therefore more effective in changing behaviour among household consumers.

Whether seals of approval or ordinal evaluative categories provide useful information to consumers depends in part upon the current product mix. For example, if virtually all products in a category now meet the Energy Star threshold, there is little value to manufacturers of exceeding that standard. At that point, there is little incentive for manufacturers to improve and little consumer responsiveness to the label unless the standard is ratcheted up for receiving the seal.

Research derived from surveys and choice experiments has shown that household consumers are more responsive to seal-of-approval labels than to raw numbers (Teisl et al. 2008), and that they pay more attention to quality information when it is presented in ordinal evaluative categories (such as one to five stars) rather than as percentages (Hibbard and Peters 2003). Framing effects can also influence the effectiveness of a label (Heinzle and Wüstenhagen 2012). A general principle from the consumer behaviour perspective is that labels should convey information that is accurate at the level of precision they offer, that consumers can understand as intended, and that they can act upon. At a minimum, a carbon label should allow a consumer to compare alternative products available for purchase in terms of their carbon footprints, and thus inform choices that may involve trading off carbon footprint against other product attributes. Pre-testing, through relatively inexpensive choice experiments and surveys, should be performed before the label is introduced to ensure consumers respond to and understand the labels.

It is worth re-emphasizing that carbon labels provide information not only for the individuals and households who are the most typical consumers, but also for producers, intermediate consumers and organizational consumers, all of whom may be able to make good use of information at a higher level of precision than is 'user-friendly' to typical household consumers.

## 18.5 CONCLUSION

With the slow development of international and national efforts to adopt a carbon tax or cap and trade programme, attention has turned to other measures such as public or private carbon labelling programmes. A voluntary carbon labelling system has the potential to be adopted and implemented in the near term and to complement an international or national carbon price when one is adopted. A key stumbling block is the tendency to seek a comprehensive system that labels all products or includes all relevant information. If time matters, as it does with climate change mitigation (Gilligan and Vandenbergh 2014; Nordhaus 2013), then a triage strategy may be desirable. This chapter outlines ways to think about carbon labelling that could lead to prompt development of an effective system.

## NOTES

1. For example a certification programme in Australia called Global Green Tag rates products based on greenhouse gas emissions along with human health and toxicity, biodiversity and other corporate social responsibility activities. See www.ecolabelindex.com.
2. One analysis suggests that consumer goods account for roughly a quarter of the carbon emissions from the average American, with food accounting for another 14 per cent (Union of Concerned Scientists et al.

2012). Labelling also could affect emissions from home energy use, which account for 32 per cent; and transportation, which accounts for 28 per cent of the average American's carbon emissions.
3. Carbon footprint numbers per kilograms are for the US and are taken from Environmental Working Group (2011).
4. The Greenhouse Gas Protocol is a co-operative initiative of the World Resources Institute and the World Business Council for Sustainable Development. According to the Greenhouse Gas Protocol, the two existing standards are very similar and unlikely to result in significant differences in their measurement outcomes. Both provide principles on how to develop transparent life cycle measures for products. However they are not detailed enough to provide aggregation rules or sector-specific assumptions. The ISO/TS 14067 technical specifications are guidelines that were developed in collaboration with both organizations. See 'Quantifying the greenhouse gas emissions of products: PAS 2050 & the GHG protocol product standard', http://www.ghgprotocol.org/standards/product-standard.
5. For example if the manufacture of $1 million worth of milk requires $16000 worth of services from the banking sector, we would multiply $16000 by the average carbon intensity of the banking sector and add it to all the other sectors that are used in the production of milk.
6. This point has been made in the case of China's recent push to adopt electric vehicles. In many parts of the country, there might be little or no carbon benefit from an electric vehicle under present electricity generation technologies (Earley et al. 2011).

# REFERENCES


Andrae, A.S.G. and O. Anderson (2010), 'Life cycle assessments of consumer electronics – are they consistent?', *International Journal of Life Cycle Assessment*, 15, 827–836.

Bernard, R. (2013), 'Earth Day 2013 – reflecting on our commitment to sustainability', available at http://blogs.msdn.com/b/microsoft-green/archive/2013/04/22/earth-day-2013-reflecting-on-our-commitment-to-sustainability.aspx (accessed 22 April 2013).

Brester, G. (2012), 'International lamb profile', available at http://www.agmrc.org/commodities__products/livestock/lamb/international-lamb-profile/ (accessed 22 October 2013).

British Standards Institution (2011), 'PAS 2050: 2011 – specification for the assessment of the life cycle greenhouse gas emissions of goods and services', available at http://shop.bsigroup.com/en/forms/PASs/PAS-2050/ (accessed 29 October 2013).

Capper, J.L. (2011), 'The environmental impact of dairy production: 1977 compared with 2007', *Journal of Animal Science*, 89, 4249–4261.

Capper, J.L. (2012), 'Is the grass always greener? Comparing the environmental impact of conventional, natural and grass-fed beef production systems', *Animals*, 2, 127–143.

Capper, J.L., R.A. Cady and D.E. Bauman (2009), 'The environmental impact of dairy production: 1944 compared with 2007', *Journal of Animal Science*, 87, 2160–2167.

CleanMetrics (2011), 'Product LCA and carbon footprint analysis', available at http://www.cleanmetrics.com/html/carbon_footprints.htm (accessed 29 October 2013).

Coca-Cola (2013), 'The Coca-Cola Company and World Wildlife Fund expand global partnership, announce new environmental goals', Press release, 9 July, available at http://www.coca-colacompany.com/press-center/press-releases/the-coca-cola-company-and-world-wildlife-fund-expand-global-partnership-announce-new-environmental-goals (accessed 29 October 2013).

Cohen, M.A. and M.P. Vandenbergh (2012), 'The potential role of carbon labeling in a green economy', *Energy Economics*, 34, S53–S63.

Cohen, M.A. and W.K. Viscusi (2012), 'The role of information disclosure in climate mitigation policy', *Climate Change Economics*, 3 (4), 1250020:1–1250020:21.

de Koning, A., D. Schowanek, J. Dewaele, A. Weisbrod and J. Guinée (2010), 'Uncertainties in a carbon footprint model for detergents; quantifying the confidence in a comparative result', *International Journal of Life Cycle Assessment*, 15, 79–89.

Delmas, M., M.J. Montes-Sancho and J.P. Shimshack (2010), 'Information disclosure policies: evidence from the electricity industry', *Economic Inquiry*, 48, 483–498.

de Vries, A., and I.J.M. de Boer (2010), 'Comparing environmental impacts for livestock products: a review of life cycle assessments', *Livestock Science*, 128, 1–11.

Dietz, T., G.T. Gardner, J. Gilligan, P.C. Stern and M.P. Vandenbergh (2009), 'Household action can provide a behavioral wedge to rapidly reduce US carbon emissions', *Proceedings of the National Academy of Sciences*, 106 (44), 18452–18456.

Doreau, M., H.M.G. van der Werf, D. Micol, H. Dubroeucq, J. Agabriel, Y. Rochette and C. Martin (2011),

'Enteric methane production and greenhouse gases balance of diets differing in concentrate in the fattening phase of a beef production system', *Journal of Animal Science*, 89, 2518–2528.
Downie, A. (2009), 'Can Nike and Wal-Mart save the Amazon?', *Christian Science Monitor*, available at http://www.csmonitor.com/World/Americas/2009/0922/p06s07-woam.html (accessed 31 October 2013).
Earley, R., L. Kang, F. An and L. Green-Weiskel (2011), 'Electric vehicles in the context of sustainable development in China', Commission on Sustainable Development, Background Paper No. 9. CSD19/2011/BP9, New York: United Nations Department of Economic and Social Affairs, available at http://www.un.org/esa/dsd/resources/res_pdfs/csd-19/Background-Paper-9-China.pdf (accessed 28 October 2013).
ecoinvent (2013), 'The ecoinvent database', available at http://www.ecoinvent.org/database/ (accessed 29 October 2013).
Environmental Working Group (2011), 'Meat eater's guide to climate and health', available at http://www.ewg.org/meateatersguide/ (accessed 23 September 2013).
FAO (Food and Agricultural Organization) of the United Nations (2006), 'Livestock's long shadow', available at http://www.fao.org/docrep/010/a0701e/a0701e00.HTM (accessed 29 October 2013).
Gilligan, J.M. and M.P. Vandenberg (2014), 'Accounting for political opportunity costs in climate instrument choice', *Virginia Environmental Law Journal*, 32 (1), 1–6.
Global Industry Analysts (2010), 'Cheese: a global strategic business report', available at http://www.prweb.com/releases/cheese_cheddar/organic_artisan/prweb3489924.htm (accessed 22 October 2013).
Greenhouse Gas Protocol (2011), 'Product life cycle accounting and reporting standard', World Resources Institute and World Business Council for Sustainable Development, Washington, DC, available at http://www.ghgprotocol.org/standards/product-standard (accessed 29 October 2013).
Gunther, M. (2013), 'Coffee and the consumer: can McDonald's mainstream sustainability?', *Guardian*, 24 September, available at http://www.theguardian.com/sustainable-business/mcdonalds-coffee-sustainability (accessed 28 October 2013).
Hailes, J. (2010), 'Carbon footprint and carbon labelling', briefing paper.
Heinzle, S.L. and R. Wüstenhagen (2012), 'Dynamic adjustment of eco-labeling schemes and consumer choice – the revision of the EU energy label as a missed opportunity?', *Business Strategy and the Environment*, 21 (1), 60–70.
Hendrickson, C., L. Lave and H.S. Matthews (2006), *Environmental Life Cycle Assessment of Goods and Services: An Input–Output Approach*, Washington, DC: Resources for the Future Press.
Hewlett-Packard (2013), 'HP announces supply chain greenhouse gas (GHG) emissions reduction goal', press release, 23 September, available at http://www8.hp.com/us/en/hp-news/press release.html?id=1489007#.UmL8RhAvs_g (accessed 29 October 2013).
Hibbard, J.H. and E. Peters (2003), 'Supporting informed consumer health care decisions: data presentation approaches that facilitate the use of information in choice', *Annual Review of Public Health*, 24, 413–433.
IPCC (Intergovernmental Panel on Climate Change) Working Group I (2013), 'Climate change 2013: the physical science basis', available at http://www.climatechange2013.org/report/ (accessed 28 October 2013).
Keohane, R.O. and D.G. Victor (2011), 'The regime complex for climate change', *Perspectives on Politics*, 9 (1), 7–23.
Langley, E., A. Dickman, M. Jenner, C. Duke, J. Suter, M. Sinn, S. Boulos et al. (2012), *Research on EU Product Label Options: Final Report to EU*, available at http://ec.europa.eu/energy/efficiency/studies/doc/2012-12-research-eu-product-label-options.pdf (accessed 22 October 2013).
Loewenstein, G., C.R. Sunstein and R. Golman (2013), 'Disclosure: psychology changes everything', Working Paper, available at http://ssrn.com/abstract=2312708 (accessed 29 October 2013).
Magat, W.A. and W.K. Viscusi (1992), *Informational Approaches to Regulation*, Cambridge, MA: MIT Press.
Meier, A. (2003), 'The future of Energy Star and other voluntary energy efficiency programs', *ECEEE 2003 Summer Study Proceedings*, Panel 4, pp. 675–680.
Michaud, C., D. Llerena and I. Joly (2013), 'Willingness to pay for environmental attributes of non-food agricultural products: a real choice experiment', *European Review of Agricultural Economics*, 40 (2), 313–29.
National Research Council (1996), *Understanding Risk: Informing Decisions in a Democratic Society*, Committee on Risk Characterization, Commission on Behavioral and Social Sciences and Education, P.C. Stern and H.V. Fineberg (eds), Washington, DC: National Academy Press.
Nguyen, T.L.T., J.E. Hermansen and L. Mogensen (2010), 'Environmental consequences of different beef production systems in the EU', *Journal of Cleaner Production*, 18, 756–766.
Nordhaus, W. D. (2013), *The Climate Casino: Risk, Uncertainty, and Economics for a Warming World*, New Haven, CT: Yale University Press.
Onozaka, Y., W. Hu and D. T. McFadden (2012), 'Market based innovations to alter environmental outcomes: can eco-labeling affect the overall carbon emissions?', working paper.
Ostrom, E. (2012), 'Nested externalities and polycentric institutions: must we wait for global solutions to climate change before taking actions at other scales?', *Economic Theory*, 49 (2), 353–69.

Pelletier, N., R. Pirog and R. Rasmussen (2010), 'Comparative life cycle environmental impacts of three beef production strategies in the Upper Midwestern United States', *Agricultural Systems*, 103, 380–389.
Pelletier, N. and P. Tyedmers (2010), 'Forecasting potential global environmental costs of lifestock production 2000–2050', *Proceedings of the National Academy of Sciences*, 107 (43), 18371–18374.
Potoski, M. and A. Prakash (2013), 'Green clubs: collective action and voluntary environmental programs', *Annual Review of Political Science*, 16, 399–419.
Prakash, A. and M. Potoski (2006), *The Voluntary Environmentalists: Green Clubs, ISO 14001, and Voluntary Environmental Regulations*, Cambridge: Cambridge University Press.
Rosenbloom, S. (2010), 'Wal-Mart unveils plan to make supply chain greener', *New York Times*, 25 February, B3.
Shewmake, S., A. Okrent, L. Thabrew and M.P. Vandenbergh (2013), 'Carbon labeling for consumer food groups', Vanderbilt Law School Working Paper.
Steering Committee of the State-of-Knowledge Assessment of Standards and Certification (2012), *Toward Sustainability: The Roles and Limitations of Certification*, Washington, DC: RESOLVE, Inc.
Stern, P.C. (2011), 'Contributions of psychology to limiting climate change', *American Psychologist*, 66 (4) 303–314.
Stern, P.C. (2013), 'Design principles for governing risks from emerging technologies', in T. Dietz and A. Jorgenson (eds), *Structural Human Ecology: Essays in Risk, Energy and Sustainability*, Pullman, WA: Washington State University Press, pp. 91–118.
Stewart, R., M. Oppenheimer and B. Rudyk (2013), 'Building a more effective global climate regime through a bottom-up approach', *Theoretical Inquiries in Law*, 14 (1), 273–306.
Stockton, M. and O. Capps Jr. (2005), 'A micro level demand analysis of selected non-alcoholic beverages with emphasis on container size', Working Paper, Texas A&M University, available at http://ageconsearch.umn.edu/bitstream/19137/1/sp05st02.pdf (accessed 23 October 2013).
Teehan, P. and M. Kandlikar (2012), 'Sources of variation in life cycle assessments of desktop computers', *Journal of Industrial Ecology*, 16 (s1), S182–S194.
Teisl, M.F., J. Rubin and C.L. Noblet (2008), 'Non-dirty dancing? Interactions between eco-labels and consumers', *Journal of Economic Psychology*, 29, 140–159.
UN Department of Economic and Social Development (n.d.), 'Carbon neutrality', UN Sustainable Development Knowledge Platform, available at http://sustainabledevelopment.un.org/index.php?page=view&type=1006&menu=1348&nr=807 (accessed 7 August 2013).
Union of Concerned Scientists, S. Shulman, J. Deyette, B. Ekwurzel, D. Friedman, M. Mellon, J. Rogers and S. Shaw (2012), *Cooler Smarter: Practical Steps for Low-Carbon Living*, Washington, DC: Island Press.
Vanclay, J.K., J. Shortiss, S. Auselbrook, A.M. Gillespie, B.C. Howell, R. Johanni, M.J. Maher et al. (2011), 'Customer response to carbon labeling of groceries', *Journal of Consumer Policy*, 34, 153–160.
Vandenbergh, M.P. (2013), 'Private environmental governance', *Cornell Law Review*, 99 (1), 129–200.
Vandenbergh, M.P., T. Dietz and P.C. Stern (2011), 'Time to try carbon labeling', *Nature Climate Change*, 1, 4–6.
Vaughan, A. (2012), 'Tesco drops carbon-label pledge', *Guardian*, 30 January, available at http://www.guardian.co.uk/environment/2012/jan/30/tesco-drops-carbon-labelling (accessed 22 October 2013).
Victor, D.G. (2011), *Global Warming Gridlock: Creating More Effective Strategies for Protecting the Planet*, Cambridge: Cambridge University Press.
Wisconsin Milk Marketing Board (n.d.), 'Cheese statistics', available at http://media.eatwisconsincheese.com/dairyimpact/statistics/cheeseStatistics.aspx (accessed 22 October 2013).
Zivin, J.S.G., M. Kotchen, and E.T. Mansur (2012), 'Spatial and temporal heterogeneity of marginal emissions: Implications for electric cars and other electricity-shifting policies', NBER Working Paper No. 18462.

# 19. Eco-labelling as sustainable consumption policy

*Caroline L. Noblet and Mario F. Teisl*

Changing people's purchase behaviours is important in mitigating negative environmental impacts because their consumption habits contribute directly and indirectly to environmental degradation (Schrader and Thøgersen 2011). However, consumers who want to purchase environmentally friendly goods cannot normally identify them because the environmental profile of a product (for example, the environmental impact of pesticides sprayed in an apple orchard) is a credence attribute; that is, consumers cannot assess them even after purchase (Darby and Karni 1973; Teisl and Roe 1998). Even though this information is known to producers, they may find it difficult to market these environmentally better products as it is difficult to build consumer trust with credence attributes (Bonroy and Constantatos 2013) because, without a robust eco-labelling and certification programme, some firms will have an incentive to 'greenwash' (for example, see Greenpeace's Greenwash campaign) or misrepresent the environmental attributes of their product (Cason and Gangadharan 2002; Hussain 2000). Many sellers are therefore willing to pay for eco-certification, and to be supportive of eco-label monitoring to ensure environmental claims are trusted and 'greenwashers' are unable to take advantage of unearned price premiums (Cason and Gangadharan 2002; Kirchhoff 1998).

A key component of market efficiency is that consumers have information sufficient to make decisions align with their preferences. When information costs are high,[1] sellers and buyers have different levels of product information; this 'asymmetric' information (Akerlof 1970) leads to a market that is inefficient and prevented from reaching equilibrium (Teisl and Roe 1998). The above information-based market failures have increased interest in eco-labelling programmes as potentially corrective policy (Teisl and Roe 1998), as they can present product information to consumers (Darby and Karni 1973; Hanss and Böhm 2012) while minimizing search costs (Payne et al. 1988) and easing the decision process (Thøgersen et al. 2010; Thøgersen et al. 2012). Eco-labels also help producers by allowing them to build a reputation based on consumer perceptions of the credence attributes (Bonroy and Constantatos 2013). Finally, purchasing eco-labelled products send signals to industry and government about consumer preferences for natural resource and societal investments (Kaufmann et al. 2012; Stern and Dietz 1999).

Eco-labels can be defined by how they provide information. A Type I (ISO 14024) label or 'eco-seal' indicates whether a product meets a threshold level and offers no further comparison among product qualities (Allison and Carter 2000; Bonroy and Constantatos 2013). The threshold criteria are set by a third party based on the product's life cycle impacts.[2] Examples include the Nordic Swan and German Blue Angel. There are limitations to this system, including the following. First, the threshold conditions are not typically included on the actual label (yet another information asymmetry), thus such programmes operate under an assumed level of consumer familiarity with the underlying standards or by faith or trust with the certifying organization. Second, these types of programmes reduce incentives for firms to exceed the quality level required by the label, incentives which may exist under more detailed labelling schemes (Bonroy and Constantatos 2013; Dröge 2001). Third, if these labels create 'excessive' product differentiation, then consumers who are willing to pay modest amounts for environmental improvement may be made worse off due to a choice between quality standards set too high or too low (Bonroy and Constantatos 2013). Therefore trust in a label's source is of particular importance and yields confidence in the presented information (Koos 2011). Finally, under specific conditions, these Type I labels can reduce trade and the benefits of market integration (Roe and Sheldon 2007).

A Type II (ISO 14021) label is a set of self-declarations by producers on a single attribute (Allison and Carter 2000). In contrast, a Type III (ISO/TR 14025) label provides detailed information about the life cycle attributes of a product. Type III labels indicate all the components of a product have been verified, monitored or certified by a third party (Cobut et al. 2012). These labels may be government-sponsored or privately provided (Cason and Gangadharan 2002). Since consumer constraints (time, cognitive abilities) and values (Bradu et al. 2013; Grankvist et al. 2007; Verplanken and Holland 2002) vary, consumers will vary in how much detailed information they will process (Kahneman 2011); we address these differences further in section 19.2.

This chapter considers eco-labels as supporting sustainable consumption. The metric of success for an eco-label is ultimately reduction of the environmental impacts of the production and/or consumption of a product (Osbaldiston and Schott 2011), but few studies have examined these links (Rotherham 2005), and those that have, indicate weak to no positive impact (Auld et al. 2008; Blackman and Rivera 2010). However, eco-labels are successfully achieving related goals, such as increasing eco-labelled purchases across a range of products (e.g. see Bjørner et al. 2004; Brouhle and Khanna 2012; Siriwardena et al. 2012; Teisl et al. 2002). Eco-labels are increasingly important to policy makers[3] (Cashore et al. 2003) who want to combine 'hard policy' structural or incentive interventions with 'soft policy' psychological interventions aimed at motivating voluntary changes. Additionally, policies linking environmental deterioration with values and outcomes understandable to consumers (for example, weather changes resulting from global climate change) can increase the utility of consuming eco-labelled products (Lin and Huang 2012). While early eco-labels may have been implemented by government decision makers (for example, Blue Angel from Germany in 1977) there is an emergence of non-state labels which often combine environmental, social and economic performance and increase the standards for producers to earn a label (Gulbrandsen 2005). The objective of this chapter is to review the potential benefits and limitations of eco-labels within the context of sustainable consumption.

## 19.1 FACTORS INFLUENCING THE DECISION TO PURCHASE ECO-LABELLED PRODUCTS

Consumers do not buy goods for the sole purpose of protecting the environment, but also to increase their utility (Thøgersen 2000). However, consumers may take on a green identity to impact upon supplier decisions (Cox 2010) and to diminish their consumption impact by choosing environmentally better goods. This internal motivation is a unique factor in environmental consumption, where other consumption may be motivated by extrinsic (for example, price) concerns[4] (Welsch and Kühling 2010). Individuals may underestimate the happiness achieved from an intrinsically motivated purchase (such as buying green) and overestimate happiness gained from overall consumption (Welsch and Kühling 2010). Individuals can attain higher utility levels (for example, feel a 'warm glow' by contributing to others' welfare; Andreoni 1990; Brécard et al. 2009) by reducing overall consumption and the associated environmental impacts; thus eco-labels may create a market for environmental protection where consumer preferences will be revealed in the prices consumers pay and the quantity consumed (Bruce and Laroiya 2007). Empirical evidence of consumer willingness to pay for eco-labelled products supports this attainment of higher utility; for example, paper products with a Nordic Swan label had a price premium of 13–18 per cent (Bjørner et al. 2004).

Thøgersen (2000) indicates that buying eco-labelled products becomes a tougher sell when consumers perceive a large compromise. One can imagine perceived inferiority may monopolize a consumer's attention and thus decrease the likelihood of buying green. This perceived inferiority may stretch into the potential for consumers to re-evaluate mainstream products, and the retailer and supply chain which provide them, even if there is no comparable eco-labelled product. Consumers may assume that the lower-priced mainstream product lacks sustainability and therefore feel guilt and perceived inferiority for purchasing the product (Binnekamp and Ingenbleek 2008; Brécard et al. 2009; Teisl 2003). Additionally, associating a product with sustainability may negatively influence the evaluation of strength characteristics of the product, the so-called 'sustainability liability' (Luchs et al. 2010). Consumers are aware that budget-constrained firms must make trade-offs, thus increased sustainability may indicate a (perceived) decrease in another desirable attribute.

The effectiveness of eco-labels rests on consumers' ability to simultaneously meet their consumption needs and act in a manner consistent with their chosen identity, including a desire to lessen impact on the environment and behave pro-socially (Bamberg and Möser 2007). Only by understanding what drives individuals to (or away from) environmentally responsible behaviour can effective policy instruments be designed (Ek and Söderholm 2008). Here we review the factors that successfully encourage consumers to select eco-labelled products. Influences on individual eco-label purchase decision range from the characteristics of the person (for example, socio-economic, norms), the programme (for example, Type I versus Type III label) and the product (for example, prices) (Brécard et al. 2009; Teisl et al. 2008).

### 19.1.1 Characteristics of the Person

For personal characteristics to influence behaviours, researchers suggest these characteristics must be salient or activated by a situation (Tietenberg 1998; Verplanken and Holland 2002). For example eco-labels can trigger latent environmental beliefs by providing contextual signals to act in accordance with these beliefs (Tietenberg 1998; Thøgersen et al. 2012; Torjusen et al. 2001). Here we review personal characteristics believed to impact upon eco-label purchase behaviour.

**Concern**

Eco-labels are supported by relatively well-informed and environmentally concerned individuals (Coad et al. 2009; Thøgersen et al. 2010), as labels provide an opportunity for them to express their preferences. Evidence suggests that consumers with higher levels of environmental concern respond more favourably to labels (Bamberg 2003), link green products with higher levels of other values (functional, social, emotional, conditional and epistemic) (Lin and Huang 2012) and are more likely to choose green products. Grankvist et al. (2004) also find that individuals with stronger environmental concern are more influenced by environmental information. Although, if other characteristics of a good monopolize a consumer's attention, the role of environmental concern in the decision will be lessened (Thøgersen 2000). Related to concern, an individual's awareness of the consequences should an environmental problem go unaddressed (Schwartz 1977; Stern 2000) increases the likelihood of buying eco-labelled goods; for example awareness of marine resource issues yields an increased desire for eco-labelled products (Brécard et al. 2009).

**Perceived consumer effectiveness**

Eco-labels provide an opportunity for environmentally concerned consumers to feel that their own actions can improve the problem, a metric often known as perceived consumer effectiveness[5] (Ellen et al. 1991). Some consumers need to perceive that enough other consumers are buying the green option (that is, not free-riding), because the consumer needs to be assured that their purchases provide a significant environmental pay-off (Bougherara et al. 2005). While the potential for free-riders may exist, the empirical evidence of willingness to pay for eco-labelled products and the current prevalence of eco-labels indicates that the potential for free-riders does not override consumer's willingness to purchase eco-labelled products (Bruce and Laroiya 2007). In addition, while people may feel responsibility (and utility) as consumers, they may feel limited in their own ability to act as a correcting force, and instead expect other consumers, the government and institutions to be involved (Fraj and Martinez 2007).

**Norms**

Normative expectations of others influences an individual's behaviour (Ajzen and Fishbein 1980; Bamberg and Möser 2007). Gould and Golob (1998) found that the behaviours of others influences people's driving behaviour; drivers often felt no personal responsibility for vehicle air pollution when they noted worse offenders. Eco-labels can activate a consumer's personal and perceived social environmental norms by highlighting consequences or benefits to self and others (Ajzen and Fishbein 1980; Bamberg and Möser 2007; Stern 2000). Further, the belief that other consumers will also make the environmentally preferred choice will nudge a consumer to purchase an eco-labelled product (Berger and Corbin 1992; Koos 2011). Noblet et al. (2006) found that consumers will consider the emission profile of a vehicle during purchase if information is provided; however the impact of the label differs based on personal perceptions and norms. Further, the value an individual places on their relationships with others influences their willingness to purchase eco-labels: Grankvist et al. (2007) find that individuals who value 'warm relationship' have a more positive attitude toward eco-labels in comparison to consumers who value personal or financial security.

**Socio-economic**
Socio-demographic characteristics (for example, income, age, gender and education) have also been found to influence environmental behaviour (Thøgersen 2005). Studies have found an inverse U-shaped age effect where younger consumers and older consumers are less willing to purchase eco-labelled products, but middle-aged consumers are more likely (Koos 2011); others have found declining eco-label purchase with age (Brécard et al. 2009). Being female, more educated or of higher socio-economic status increases the likelihood of purchasing eco-labelled products (Brécard et al. 2009; Koos 2011).

### 19.1.2 Characteristics of the Programme and Product

The strength of context in decision making can also depend on label characteristics, such as familiarity, clarity through standardization, and how the information is framed.

**Familiarity**
Consumer adoption of a new eco-label is found to increase with the number of other eco-labels known and used by the consumer (Thøgersen et al. 2010), and the presence of eco-labels draw attention to sustainability issues (Barham 2002; Gulbrandsen 2005). Eco-labels are important in supporting sustainable consumption due to their worldwide prevalence. The US Environmental Protection Agency's Energy Star programme alone certifies 63000 different household machines (Schuetze 2013), and current estimates indicate that there are 437 eco-labels in 197 countries across 25 industry sectors (www.ecolabelindex.com).

In order for eco-labels to be successfully used as a tool by consumers in decision-making, awareness of and familiarity with the label is required.[6] Zajonc (1968) reveals that familiarity breeds acceptability, and mere exposure enhances one's attitude towards a good. Further, trustworthiness and reliability may also be associated with frequent exposure where familiar labels, such as the Nordic Swan, may be perceived as indicative of enhanced sustainability over unfamiliar products (Hanss and Böhm 2012); thus, revising existing eco-labels may weaken the efficacy of well-established labels (Heinzle and Wüstenhagen 2012). Adoption by larger segments of the population requires recognition and understanding of the label as well as trust in the certifying entity (Thøgersen et al. 2010). Importantly, increasing the availability of eco-labelled products can increase the investment of both consumers and producers in eco-labels (Koos 2011).

**Standardization**
The disconnect between stated willingness to pay for eco-labelled products and actual purchase behaviour may in part be explained by consumer inability to determine environmentally preferred products even with an eco-label scheme (Brécard et al. 2009). Competing eco-labels may confuse consumers and reduce trust in established labels (Gulbrandsen 2005); studies suggest that standardized[7] displays provide the largest benefit to consumers (Kleinmutz and Schkade 1993; Schkade and Kleinmutz 1994) because they increase the number of products or attributes considered during choice, allowing for more accurate choice decisions (Coupey 1994; Winneg et al. 1998).

Further, when labelling is voluntary, the effects of label standardization can be dependent on the degree of information detail. Teisl (2003) finds that when respondents view multiple products bearing a standard environmental seal and different prices, they assume that the environmental characteristics of the products are similar and are not willing to pay a price differential between the two certified products. However, when respondents view a similar situation with different environmental seals they assume that the environmental characteristics of the higher-priced product are better, and at least some of these individuals are willing to pay the price differential between the two certified products. When similar comparisons are made with more detailed labels, Teisl does not find a similar result.

**Framing and habit**

Many eco-labels (for example, Nordic Swan, German Blue Angel) present information in a positive manner (for example, when a product meets a specification; Grankvist et al. 2004), especially when the eco-labels are voluntary, as producers are not likely to negatively label their own product. However, consumers' aversion to losses and their increased attention to negative information suggest that negative information may be a more powerful force in decision-making (Fiske 1980; Kahneman and Tversky 1984). For example Grankvist et al. (2004) suggest that some consumers are 'avoiding environmentally bad things' rather than looking for 'environmentally good' ones; they find that individuals with lower environmental concern avoid purchasing negatively labelled products, but these consumers did not necessarily purchase positively labelled products but rather they purchased neutral items. Importantly, Grankvist et al. (2004) indicate that negative information is more successful in breaking existing habits and getting the attention of consumers who may not currently be focused on eco-labels. Given that consumers make initial 'green' choices by using environmental information, but continue to make these purchases out of habit (Thøgersen et al. 2010, 2012), it is increasingly important to understand this aspect of purchase behaviour. This work suggests that eco-label programmes should mandate positive, neutral and negative labels for maximum effectiveness.

**Trust in labelling**

An additional component to examine in the disconnect between stated willingness to pay for eco-labelled products and actual purchase behaviour is lack of trust in certifying agencies (Teisl et al. 2008). Two key elements may increase consumers' trust of labels: involvement of the government and increased number of other known labels (Koos 2011; Thøgersen et al. 2010). Teisl and Roe (2005) find a significant effect of state-sponsored labels in the likelihood of purchasing eco-labelled products; however this effect vanishes when trust and supply-side characteristics are controlled for. However, government labelling systems may be insufficient if labels do not convey the information required or desired by the consumer for purchase. Consumers may prefer if the government monitors 'certification' of firm claims rather than mandating the content of the claim (Bruce and Laroiya 2007). This preference for government certification of claims may result from a perception that private certifying agencies have an incentive to deceive consumers and certify products not meeting the standards (Bonroy and Constantatos 2013). As noted by Bonroy and Constantatos (2013), third-party certification not only faces the challenge of credibility, but also certifying specific levels of an attribute is costly and may produce data too difficult for consumers to absorb.

Consumers may face different challenges in selecting eco-labels and receive very different rewards from an eco-label purchase dependent upon their personal factors and those of the programme[8] or product. The consideration of demand-side factors, which influence eco-label purchases, has shed light on the ability of consumers to be a driving force behind eco-labelled sustainable consumption. While this research has often focused on individual reasons to engage in eco-labels, we must also consider the influences of organization and structural factors on decision-making (Koos 2011).

## 19.2 CAN LABELS HELP SUSTAINABILITY?

The above review of factors that promote the effectiveness of labels leads to further crucial questions regarding eco-label effectiveness, and sustainable impact. First, are eco-labels promoting sustainability improvements and yielding reduced environmental impacts – the ultimate metric? Second, are there remaining barriers to the use and promotion of eco-labels?

### 19.2.1 Certification Standards

Challenges to the effectiveness of eco-labels may also exist in the production side of the market. Labels can cause firms to seek increased market power by unduly influencing certifying entities responsible for labelling (Bonroy and Constantatos 2013; Bougherara et al. 2005). Eco-labels may also lead to imperfection in product markets and yield barriers to trade[9] (Bruce and Laroiya 2007; Kirchhoff 1998). The structure (for example, standard-setting) and operation (for example, monitoring and enforcement) of certification programmes that underlie most eco-labelling affect the cost of participation and thus influence the effectiveness of the eco-labels in enhancing sustainability. For example, to the extent that certification and labelling costs are borne by firms (consumers), setting environmental quality standards too high can lead to decreased profits (increased prices) and more firms producing (consumers buying) products with lower environmental quality (Bonroy and Constantatos 2013). Other characteristics that can affect labelling costs include: the frequency with which standards are revised (Amacher et al. 2004); the setting of tolerance, chain-of-custody or segregation requirements (Teisl and Caswell 2002); the number of environmental impacts included (Bruce and Laroiya 2007); and the size of the firms (Bruce and Laroiya 2007). Here we review two internationally known single-issue labels to glean insight into the factors that yield success or portend failure in contributing to sustainability.

### 19.2.2 Wood Certification

The Forest Stewardship Council (FSC) is an international certification, with region-based levels of standards for wood products (Cashore et al. 2003). The label addresses the issues of private ownership of forests through a chain of custody and the adherence to criteria for well-managed forests (Gulbrandsen 2005). This label provides key lessons for future labelling efforts. First, organizers of the label utilized market forces when government policy gains appeared limited. Proponents of the FSC indicate that the label revealed latent demand for certified forest products and led some large-scale retailers to supply only FSC-certified products; however these firms have experienced difficulty in providing such products due to supply limitations (Gulbrandsen 2005).

Second, labels promoted by non-profit organizations may differ from industry-supported labels. The Sustainable Forestry Initiative (SFI) is a North American competing label to FSC developed by the forest industry. Similar to other industry-dominated labels, the SFI label relies on an environmental management system which directs the producers to meet goals and improve performance through a focus on processes. In contrast, labels chartered by environmental organizations focus more on outcomes or performance. This is a surprising result for environmental economists who typically note that industry prefers outcome-based environmental policy because it allows firms to pursue the outcome using least-cost process methods, which may differ firm by firm. It is hoped that the FSC and SFI labels increase international scrutiny of forest-product production practices which may lead to a 'reversal of the "downward" effect of globalization' (Cashore et al. 2003, p. 226). However, certification seems to have mostly moved certified forest operations to more-developed countries where the costs of meeting the certification standards are relatively low (because more-developed countries already have existing regulations that are relatively close to the certification standards) (Auld et al. 2008).

### 19.2.3 Marine Resources

The Marine Stewardship Council (MSC) labels 'sustainable' seafood in an effort to undertake market-based consumer awareness of marine resource depletion issues. A third-party certifier determines whether fisheries meet the set criteria; as of 2012, if fisheries currently under review attain certification, 10 per cent of global catch will be labelled (Christian et al. 2013). The label is designed to complement, not replace, international regulations (Gulbrandsen 2005). Of interest, there are no private benefits of labelled seafood, such as associated human health benefits (Christian et al. 2013). Similar to FSC-labelled products above, when large retailers (here, Wal-Mart in 2006) agreed to supply only MSC-certified sustainable fish there was an enormous pressure on supply of the resource.

This label provides interesting insight into the strong role of incentives in eco-label programmes. First, the fishery applying for certification may select its own third-party certifier, leading to the selection of entities most likely to produce positive outcomes. Further, if the fishery is certified, the same certifier will be asked to complete 'annual monitoring' and reassessments. Second, the access to markets given to MSC products, and the accompanying price premiums, draw many fisheries to seek certification, which has led to some stress within the industry. Approximately 12 per cent of MSC fisheries which are currently certified received objections to their certifications; in tonnage this represents 35 per cent of MSC-certified seafood. Statistics are also available regarding MSC certified stocks which show evidence of overfishing or depletion (Froese and Proelss 2013).

Future labelling efforts may benefit from careful a review of lessons learned during development of the MSC label. All MSC-certified fisheries use the logo and the phrase 'certified sustainable seafood', with no indication of the controversy over the certification of specific fisheries, nor the general standards for certification. Ultimately we must consider whether certification improves the resource it was intended to protect. Nine per cent of fisheries which were certified have since declined to below certification standards during their yearly audit, while 9 per cent below the standard rose to above it in an effort to become certified (Christian et al. 2013). This appears to indicate that the greatest opportunity for environmental impacts may be in the pre-assessment stage of certification when suppliers are trying to meet standards. The lessons learned from forestry and marine resource labelling reinforce the importance of understanding whether eco-labels are able to change patterns of consumption, and ultimately influence methods of production.

## 19.3 FUTURE DIRECTIONS

Eco-labels, like all policy tools, pose questions necessitating further investigation. Perhaps the most challenging aspect of eco-label research is the notable time lag between introduction of the label and influence on consumer behaviour (Teisl and Roe 1998). Any eco-label policy implemented will require time for consumers to adjust to the label before an evaluation of the policy can take place. Labels may also be viewed as political by bringing to the market 'processes of norm formation that we often expect to occur in other social arenas' (Barham 2002, p. 354). However, the institutionalization of norms may be considered part of societal change. Further, the impact of negative attribution may be strong: consumers blame companies for non-preferred practices rather than reward the firms which produce eco-labelled products (Binnekamp and Ingenbleek 2008). Additionally some proponents of eco-labels may in fact be 'cheap talkers' who indicate a support for information policy because it is 'relatively harmless policy that will not cost them anything' (Coad et al. 2009, p. 2082). Moreover products may be considered environmentally preferred on three grounds: during consumption by reduced emissions or consumption externalities; product-related production such as reduction of toxins in the actual product; or non-product-related production methods including reduction of production externalities (Dröge 2001). However, government social planners must seek to maximize total welfare for both producers and consumers where production externalities (typically the focus of eco-labels) are but one component of this social welfare (Bonroy and Constantatos 2013).

The gravest concern facing eco-labelling programmes is the tenuous link between changed consumer awareness due to eco-labels and actual change in purchase behaviour (Teisl et al. 2002) or upstream environmental impacts (Bonroy and Constantatos 2013; Gulbrandsen 2005). Eco-labels provide fact and value learning (Dietz 2003) which may alter attitudes and motivation during, and after, purchase (Coad et al. 2009). Sustainable consumption is generally considered a conscious and deliberate decision for sustainable goods and services; however current research work is based upon definitions of sustainability that may not encompass the broad range of impacts desired (Hanss and Böhm 2012). Consumer support for eco-labels lies in peril of being influenced by social desirability effects, where one purports to engage in environmentally preferred behaviour for social approval (Fletcher and Downing 2011). Understanding the initial and maintenance forces behind sustainable behaviour is far from an idle issue, particularly when assumptions are made about consumer behaviour after the purchase of eco-labelled products. There is emerging evidence of spillover effects, where engaging in one sustainable behaviour increases the likelihood of engaging in future, perhaps more impactful actions (Thøgersen and Noblet 2012). However, evidence suggests that this spillover may be less likely to occur when people make a decision for externally motivated or self-interested reasons such as social approval (Tabernero and Hernandez 2012). Additionally, studies have hypothesized, or found evidence of, licensing in sustainability behaviours, where preliminary sustainable choices yield a belief that a 'fair contribution' has already been made and no further action is required (Mazar and Zhong 2010). In contrast, external intervention into sustainable consumption markets through eco-labels may cause some individual consumers to reduce their own sustainable consumption either because it is believed policy may relieve the issue, or because consumers' own intrinsic motivation is 'crowded out' by the policy (Frey 1999). These complex linkages between policy and consumption yield an increased need for consideration of policy combinations to encourage sustainable consumption with both financial and information policies. Financial incentives may target mainstream consumers who lack internal motivation to engage in a sustainable manner. Green consumers may also be heartened by implementation of these joint policies which may ensure a critical mass in eco-label purchasing; internally motivated consumers may realize the differences between consumption patterns and lose their faith in others (Coad et al. 2009). Further, understanding what motivates a consumer to perform green behaviour, and the link that eco-labelled consumption has to environmental impacts, are necessary next steps in understanding the long-term success and ramifications of sustainable consumption.

## NOTES

1. Consumers with limited money (Capon and Lutz 1983; Kirchhoff 2000), time or cognitive abilities (Hoyer 1984; Payne et al. 1988; Simon 1955, 1959; Thøgersen et al. 2012) are unable to search for additional information.
2. A variant of Type I (eco-seal) labels is the single-issue label that does not use a life cycle approach, but focuses on a subset of environmental metrics; examples include: dolphin-safe, energy-efficiency, Forest Stewardship Council and Marine Stewardship Council labels (Allison and Carter 2000).
3. Policy makers may prefer eco-labelling to government regulation as labels are viewed as more 'democratic' (Coad et al. 2009), and are more easily supported by those holding a free-market ideology.
4. Financial incentives can motivate consumers who are extrinsically motivated, but may alienate intrinsically motivated consumers; while information programmes are likely to 'kindle intrinsic motivation' (Coad et al. 2009, p. 2081).
5. Implying 'ascription of responsibility to self' according to Stern (2000).
6. Without familiarity the role of innovators and diffusion of innovation becomes important, where early adoption depends not only on an individual's knowledge of the issue and of eco-labels (Rogers 2003; Thøgersen et al. 2010).
7. Standardization is the degree to which regulations require the information be provided in a standardized fashion across products.
8. Challenges may include increased display of information during the time of purchase or directing consumers to non-package information (Bruce and Laroiya 2007).
9. Eco-labels may be perceived as a non-tariff trade barrier. World Trade Organization (WTO) intervention is not possible when a label is voluntary or certified by a private organization (Dröge 2001).

# REFERENCES


Ajzen, I. and M. Fishbein (1980), *Understanding Attitudes and Predicting Social Behaviour*, Englewood Cliffs, NJ, USA: Prentice Hall.

Akerlof, G.A. (1970), 'The market for "lemons": quality uncertainty and the market mechanism', *Quarterly Journal of Economics*, 84 (3), 488–500.

Allison, C. and A. Carter (2000), 'Study on different types of environmental labelling (ISO Type II and III Labels) – proposal for an environmental labelling strategy', Report prepared by ERM Consultants for DG Environment, Brussels, Belgium.

Amacher, G.S., E. Koskela and M. Ollikainen (2004), 'Environmental quality competition and eco-labeling', *Journal of Environmental Economics and Management*, 47 (2), 284–306.

Andreoni, J. (1990), 'Impure altruism and donations to public goods: a theory of warm-glow giving', *Economic Journal*, 100 (401), 464–477.

Auld, G., L.H. Gulbrandsen and C.L. McDermott (2008), 'Certification schemes and the impacts on forests and forestry', *Annual Review of Environment and Resources*, 33 (1), 187–211.

Bamberg, S. (2003), 'How does environmental concern influence specific environmentally related behaviors? A new answer to an old question', *Journal of Environmental Psychology*, 23 (1), 21–32.

Bamberg, S. and G. Möser (2007), 'Twenty years after Hines, Hungerford, and Tomera: a new meta-analysis of psycho-social determinants of pro-environmental behaviour', *Journal of Environmental Psychology*, 27 (1), 14–25.

Barham, E. (2002), 'Towards a theory of values-based labeling', *Agriculture and Human Values*, 19 (4), 349–360.

Berger, I.E. and R.M. Corbin (1992), 'Perceived consumer effectiveness and faith in others as moderators of environmentally responsible behaviors', *Journal of Public Policy and Marketing*, 2 (2), 79–89.

Binnekamp, M. and P. Ingenbleek (2008), 'Do "good" food products make others look "bad"? Spin-off effects of labels for sustainable food production in the consumer perception', *British Food Journal*, 110 (9), 843–864.

Bjørner, T.B., L.G. Hansen and C.S. Russell (2004), 'Environmental labeling and consumers' choice – an empirical analysis of the effect of the Nordic Swan', *Journal of Environmental Economics and Management*, 47 (3), 411–434.

Blackman, A. and J. Rivera (2010), 'The evidence base for environmental and socioeconomic impacts of "sustainable" certification', Resources for the Future Discussion Paper RFF DP 10-17, Washington, DC, available at SSRN 1579083.

Bonroy, O. and C. Constantatos (2013), 'On the economics of labels: a review of the theoretical literature', Working Paper 2013–01, Grenoble Applied Economics Laboratory (GAEL).

Bradu, C., J.L. Orquin and J. Thøgersen (2013), 'The mediated influence of a traceability label on consumer's willingness to buy the labelled product', *Journal of Business Ethics*, DOI 10.1007/s10551-013-1872-2.

Brécard, D., B. Hlaimi, S. Lucas, Y. Perraudeau and F. Salladarré (2009), 'Determinants of demand for green products: an application to eco-label demand for fish in Europe', *Ecological Economics*, 69 (1), 115–125.

Bougherara, D., G. Grolleau and L. Thiébaut (2005), 'Can labelling policies do more harm than good? An analysis applied to environmental labelling schemes', *European Journal of Law and Economics*, 19 (1), 5–16.

Brouhle, K. and M. Khanna (2012), 'Determinants of participation versus consumption in the Nordic Swan eco-labeled market', *Ecological Economics*, 73, 142–151.

Bruce, C. and A. Laroiya (2007), 'The production of eco-labels', *Environmental and Resource Economics*, 36 (3), 275–293.

Capon, N. and R.J. Lutz (1983), 'The marketing of consumer information', *Journal of Marketing*, 47 (3), 108–113.

Cashore, B., G. Auld and D. Newsom (2003), 'Forest certification (eco-labeling) programs and their policy-making authority: explaining divergence among North American and European case studies', *Forest Policy and Economics*, 5 (3), 225–247.

Cason, T.N. and L. Gangadharan (2002), 'Environmental labeling and incomplete consumer information in laboratory markets', *Journal of Environmental Economics and Management*, 43 (1), 113–134.

Christian, C., D. Ainley, M. Bailey, P. Dayton, J. Hocevar, M. LeVine and J. Jacquet (2013), 'A review of formal objections to Marine Stewardship Council fisheries certifications', *Biological Conservation*, 161, 10–17.

Coad, A., P. de Haan and J.S. Woersdorfer (2009), 'Consumer support for environmental policies: an application to purchases of green cars', *Ecological Economics*, 68 (7), 2078–2086.

Cobut, A., R. Beauregard and P. Blanchet (2012), 'Using life cycle thinking to analyze environmental labeling: the case of appearance wood products', *International Journal of Life Cycle Assessment*, 18 (3), 722–742.

Coupey, E. (1994), 'Restructuring: constructive processing of information displays in consumer choice', *Journal of Consumer Research*, 21 (1), 83–99.

Cox, R. (2010), *Environmental Communication and the Public Sphere*, 2nd edn, Thousand Oaks, CA: Sage.

Darby, M.R. and E. Karni (1973), 'Free competition and the optimal amount of fraud', *Journal of Law and Economics*, 16 (1), 67–88.
Dietz, T. (2003), 'What is a good decision? Criteria for environmental decision making', *Human Ecology Review*, 10 (1), 33–39.
Dröge, S. (2001), 'Ecological labelling and the World Trade Organization', DIW-Diskussionspapiere, No. 242.
Ek, K. and P. Söderholm (2008), 'Norms and economic motivation in the Swedish green electricity market', *Ecological Economics*, 68 (1–2), 169–182.
Ellen, P.S., J.L. Wiener and C. Cobb-Walgren (1991), 'The role of perceived consumer effectiveness in motivating environmentally conscious behaviors', *Journal of Public Policy and Marketing*, 10 (2), 102–117.
Fiske, S.T. (1980), 'Attention and weight in person perception: The impact of negative and extreme behavior', *Journal of Personality and Social Psychology*, 38 (6), 889–906.
Fletcher, J. and P. Downing (2011), 'Consumer understanding of green terms: a supplementary report on consumer responses to environmental labels', a research report completed for the Department for Environment, Food and Rural Affairs by Brook Lyndhurst and Icaro Consulting, February.
Fraj, E. and E. Martinez (2007), 'Ecological consumer behaviour: an empirical analysis', *International Journal of Consumer Studies*, 31 (1), 26–33.
Frey, B. (1999), 'Morality and rationality in environmental policy', *Journal of Consumer Policy*, 22 (4), 395–417.
Froese, R. and A. Proelss (2013), 'Is a stock overfished if it is depleted by overfishing? A response to the rebuttal of Agnew et al. to Froese and Proelss "Evaluation and legal assessment of certified seafood"', *Marine Policy*, 38, 548–550.
Gould, J. and T.F. Golob (1998), 'Clean air forever? A longitudinal analysis of opinions about air pollution and electric vehicles', *Transportation Research Part D: Transport and Environment*, 3 (3), 157–169.
Grankvist, G., U. Dahlstrand and A. Biel (2004), 'The impact of environmental labelling on consumer preference: negative vs. positive labels', *Journal of Consumer Policy*, 27 (2), 213–230.
Grankvist, G., H. Lekedal and M. Marmendal (2007), 'Values and eco- and fair-trade labelled products', *British Food Journal*, 109, 169–181.
Gulbrandsen, L.H. (2005), 'Mark of sustainability? Challenges for fishery and forestry eco-labeling', *Environment: Science and Policy for Sustainable Development*, 47 (5), 8–23.
Hanss, D. and G. Böhm (2012), 'Sustainability seen from the perspective of consumers', *International Journal of Consumer Studies*, 36 (6), 678–687.
Heinzle, S.L. and R. Wüstenhagen (2012), 'Dynamic adjustment of eco-labeling schemes and consumer choice – the revision of the EU energy label as a missed opportunity?', *Business Strategy and the Environment*, 21 (1), 60–70.
Hoyer, W. (1984), 'An examination of consumer decision making for a common repeat purchase product', *Journal of Consumer Research*, 11 (3), 822–829.
Hussain, S. (2000), 'Green consumerism and ecolabelling: a strategic behavioural model', *Journal of Agricultural Economics*, 51 (1), 77–89.
Kahneman, D. (2011), *Thinking, Fast and Slow*, London: Macmillan.
Kahneman, D. and A. Tversky (1984), 'Choices, values, and frames', *American Psychologist*, 39 (4), 341–350.
Kaufmann, H.R., M.F.A.K. Panni and Y. Orphanidou (2012), 'Factors affecting consumers' green purchasing behavior: an integrated conceptual framework', *Amfiteatru Economic*, 14 (31), 50–69.
Kirchhoff, S. (1998), 'Overcompliance, labeling, and lobbying: the case of credence goods', unpublished PhD dissertation, Department of Resource Economics, University of Maryland.
Kirchhoff, S. (2000), 'Green business and blue angels', *Environmental and Resource Economics*, 15 (4), 403–420.
Kleinmuntz, D.N. and D.A. Schkade (1993), 'Information displays and decision processes', *Psychological Science*, 4 (4), 221–227.
Koos, S. (2011), 'Varieties of environmental labelling, market structures, and sustainable consumption across Europe: a comparative analysis of organizational and market supply determinants of environmental-labelled goods', *Journal of Consumer Policy*, 34, 127–151.
Lin, P.C. and Y.H. Huang (2012), 'The influence factors on choice behavior regarding green products based on the theory of consumption values', *Journal of Cleaner Production*, 22 (1), 11–18.
Luchs, M.G., R.W. Naylor and J.R. Irwin (2010), 'The sustainability liability: potential negative effects of ethicality on product preferences', *Journal of Marketing*, 74 (5), 18–31.
Mazar, N. and C.B. Zhong (2010), 'Do green products make us better people?', *Psychological Science*, 21, 494–498.
Noblet, C.L., M.F. Teisl and J. Rubin (2006), 'Factors affecting consumer assessment of eco-labeled vehicles', *Transportation Research Part D: Transport and Environment*, 11 (6), 422–431.
Osbaldiston, R. and J.P. Schott (2011), 'Environmental sustainability and behavioral science: meta-analysis of proenvironmental behavior experiments', *Environment and Behavior*, 44 (2), 257–299.
Payne, J.W., J.R. Bettman and E.J. Johnson (1988), 'Adaptive strategy selection in decision making', *Journal of Experimental Psychology: Learning, Memory, and Cognition*, 14 (3), 534–552.

Roe, B. and I. Sheldon (2007), 'Credence good labeling: the efficiency and distributional implications of several policy approaches', *American Journal of Agricultural Economics*, 89 (4), 1020–1033.
Rogers, E.M. (2003), *Diffusion of Innovations*, 5th edn, New York: Free Press.
Rotherham, T. (2005), 'The trade and environmental effects of ecolabels: assessment and response', United Nations Environment Programme.
Schkade, D.A. and D.N. Kleinmuntz (1994), 'Information displays and choice processes: differential effects of organization, form, and sequence', *Organizational Behavior and Human Decision Processes*, 57 (3), 319–337.
Schrader, U. and J. Thøgersen (2011), 'Putting sustainable consumption into practice', *Journal of Consumer Policy*, 34 (1), 3–8.
Schuetze, C.F. (2013), 'What's in a label? Not necessarily sustainability', *New York Times*, 17 September.
Schwartz, S.H. (1977), 'Normative influences on altruism', in L. Berkowitz (ed.), *Advances in Experimental Social Psychology, Volume 10*, New York: Academic Press, pp. 221–279.
Simon, H.A. (1955), 'A behavioral model of rational choice', *Quarterly Journal of Economics*, 69 (1), 99–118.
Simon, H.A. (1959), 'Theories of decision-making in economics and behavioral science', *American Economics Review*, 49 (3), 253–283.
Siriwardena, S., G. Hunt, M.F. Teisl and C.L. Noblet (2012), 'Effective environmental marketing of green cars: a nested-logit approach', *Transportation Research Part D: Transport and Environment*, 17 (3), 237–242.
Stern, P.C. (2000), 'New environmental theories: Toward a coherent theory of environmentally significant behavior', *Journal of Social Issues*, 56 (3), 407–424.
Stern, P. and T. Dietz (1999), 'A value–belief–norm theory of support for social movements: the case of environmentalism', *Human Ecology Review*, 6 (2), 81–97.
Tabernero, C. and B. Hernandez (2012), 'A motivational model for environmentally responsible behavior', *Spanish Journal of Psychology*, 15 (2), 648–658.
Teisl, M.F. (2003), 'What we may have is a failure to communicate: labeling environmentally certified forest products', *Forest Science*, 49 (5), 668–680.
Teisl, M.F. and J.A. Caswell (2002), 'Information policy and genetically modified food: weighing the benefits and costs', paper presented at the 2nd World Congress of Environmental and Resource Economists, Monterey, CA.
Teisl, M.F. and B. Roe (1998), 'The economics of labeling: an overview of issues for health and environmental disclosure', *Agricultural and Resource Economics Review*, 27, 140–150.
Teisl, M.F. and B. Roe (2005), 'Evaluating the factors that impact the effectiveness of eco-labelling programmes', in S. Krarup and C.S. Russel (eds), *Environment, Information and Consumer Behaviour*, Cheltenham, UK and Northampton, MA, USA: Edward Elgar, pp. 65–90.
Teisl, M.F., B. Roe and R. Hicks (2002), 'Can eco-labels tune a market? Evidence from dolphin-safe labeling', *Journal of Environmental Economics and Management*, 43, 339–359.
Teisl, M.F., J. Rubin and C.L. Noblet (2008), 'Non-dirty dancing? Interactions between eco-labels and consumers', *Journal of Economic Psychology*, 29 (2), 140–159.
Thøgersen, J. (2000), 'Psychological determinants of paying attention to eco-labels in purchase decisions: model development and multinational validation', *Journal of Consumer Policy*, 23 (3), 285–313.
Thøgersen, J. (2005), 'How may consumer policy empower consumers for sustainable lifestyles?', *Journal of Consumer Policy*, 28 (2), 143–177.
Thøgersen, J., P. Haugaard and A. Olesen (2010), 'Consumer responses to ecolabels', *European Journal of Marketing*, 44 (11–12), 1787–1810.
Thøgersen, J., A.-K. Jørgensen and S. Sandager (2012), 'Consumer decision making regarding a "green" everyday product', *Psychology and Marketing*, 29 (4), 187–197.
Thøgersen, J. and C.L. Noblet (2012), 'Does green consumerism increase the acceptance of windpower?', *Energy Policy*, 51, 854–862.
Tietenberg, T. (1998), 'Disclosure strategies for pollution control', *Environmental and Resource Economics*, 11, 587–602.
Torjusen, H., G. Lieblein, M. Wandel and C. Francis (2001), 'Food system orientation and quality perception among consumers and producers of organic food in Hedmark County, Norway', *Food Quality and Preference*, 12 (3), 207–216.
Verplanken, B. and R.W. Holland (2002), 'Motivated decision making: effects of activation and self-centrality of values on choices and behavior', *Journal of Personality and Social Psychology*, 82 (3), 434–447.
Winneg, K., M.J. Herrmann, A.S. Levy and B. Roe (1998), 'Label testing: results of mall-intercept study', Consumer Information Disclosure Series, Regulatory Assistance Project, Gardiner, ME.
Welsch, H. and J. Kühling (2010), 'Pro-environmental behavior and rational consumer choice: evidence from surveys of life satisfaction', *Journal of Economic Psychology*, 31 (3), 405–420.
Zajonc, R. (1968), 'Attitudinal effects of mere exposure', *Journal of Personality and Social Psychology*, 9 (2), 1–27.

# 20. Behavioural economics, consumption and environmental protection

*Cass R. Sunstein*

Why do consumers choose as they do? Economists and social scientists have long answered by assuming that consumers are 'rational', in the sense that they maximize their utility. If consumers purchase energy-efficient appliances, it is because those are the appliances they prefer, and if not, it is because the benefits of energy-efficient appliances fail to justify the costs. In either case, the choices of consumers maximize their utility. On this view, the role of government is straightforward. Public officials should correct market failures by ensuring that consumers are adequately informed and by adopting policies to reduce transaction costs that prevent mutually advantageous deals or to correct for externalities (as when the environmental consequences of consumer choices are not internalized by consumers themselves).

This simple framework has a great deal of power, but in recent decades it has been placed under serious strain (LeBoeuf and Shafir 2012). Sometimes consumers display bounded rationality, in the sense that they depart from the standard account in predictable ways. Because of those departures, consumers can make serious errors by their own lights, even in the absence of externalities (Allcott et al. 2012; Luth 2010). They may, for example, decline to purchase energy-efficient appliances even when it would be in their economic interest to do so (Allcott and Greenstone 2012). Consumers may suffer from 'internalities', the now standard term within behavioural economics that is meant to capture the losses that people incur when they make decisions that hurt their future selves (Allcott et al. 2012). If we understand human beings as a series of selves extending over time, internalities can be seen to create a kind of intrapersonal collective action problem, whose solution could provide significant benefits.

These points about bounded rationality should not be taken to suggest that consumers are 'irrational', but they do suggest both challenges and opportunities for policy makers. For example consumers can be greatly affected by apparently modest and inconsequential aspects of the social environment. Small changes in that environment may have a large impact on consumer behaviour, potentially even larger than that of economic incentives (Banerjee and Duflo 2011; Chetty et al. 2012; Thaler and Sunstein 2008).

Behavioural economists have also explored two concepts that have implications for consumer behaviour and environmental protection. The first is choice architecture, understood as the background (social and natural) against which consumer decisions are made (Thaler and Sunstein 2008). Consumers do not decide in a vacuum; choice architecture is always present, and it has major consequences for both decisions and outcomes. If one nation has a far more serious pollution problem than another, it may well be because of differences in the relevant choice architecture, not because of any fundamental differences between the preferences or values of the citizens of the two nations

(Jones et al. 2013). An understanding of choice architecture may well help to identify a series of potential reforms.

The second concept is libertarian paternalism, understood to include approaches that preserve freedom of choice but nonetheless incline or steer people in a particular direction. The hope of libertarian paternalism is that inexpensive and seemingly modest policy initiatives can have large and highly beneficial effects on consumer behaviour. These initiatives take the form of 'nudges' – low-cost, choice-preserving, behaviourally informed approaches to regulatory problems, including disclosure requirements, default rules, simplification, and use of salience and social norms (Allcott 2011b; Luth 2010; Newell and Siikamäki 2013; Sunstein 2013a; Thaler and Sunstein 2008).

In the United States regulatory efforts have been directly informed by behavioural findings, and behavioural economics has played an unmistakable role in numerous domains involving consumer behaviour (Sunstein 2013a). The relevant initiatives can be found in multiple areas, including fuel economy, energy efficiency, environmental protection, health care, financial products and obesity (Sunstein 2011). In the United Kingdom, Prime Minister Cameron has created a Behavioural Insights Team with the specific goal of incorporating an understanding of human behaviour into policy initiatives (Jones et al. 2013). The official website states that its 'work draws on insights from the growing body of academic research in the fields of behavioural economics and psychology which show how often subtle changes to the way in which decisions are framed can have big impacts on how people respond to them' (Cabinet Office n.d.; see also Jones et al. 2013). The Team has used these insights to promote initiatives in numerous areas, including consumer behaviour and environmental protection (Jones et al. 2013). In 2013 the United States created a Behavioral Insights Unit of its own.

Behavioural economics has drawn attention in Europe more broadly. The Organisation for Economic Co-operation and Development (OECD) has published a Consumer Policy Toolkit that recommends a number of initiatives rooted in behavioural findings (OECD 2010). In the European Union, the Directorate-General for Health and Consumers has also shown the influence of behavioural economics (DG SANCO 2010). A report from the European Commission, called 'Green behaviour', enlists behavioural economics to outline policy initiatives to promote environmental protection (European Commission 2012). Behavioural findings have attracted attention in other nations as well (Low 2012). In addition private organizations are using behavioural insights to promote a variety of environmental, health-related and other goals (see iNudgeYou.com n.d.; greeNudge.no n.d.).

The central purpose of this chapter is to outline the relevant behavioural findings and to use those findings to explore how public officials might provide environmental benefits in a matter that is compatible with job creation and economic growth; goals of special importance, above all in an economically challenging time. Many actual and potential initiatives, involving choice architecture, promise to produce large environmental gains without compromising economic goals, and perhaps even while promoting them. A key task is the development of non-price interventions that nonetheless influence consumer behaviour. Such interventions have the important advantage of promoting environmental goals without requiring the expenditure of either public or private funds.

Of course it is also true that further progress will require the use of more standard tools, including economic incentives and regulation (Sunstein 2013a). No one contends that nudges are sufficient in this domain. The more modest suggestion is that an understanding of choice architecture and libertarian paternalism significantly expands the policy toolbox (Johnson et al. 2012; Jones et al. 2013; Thaler and Sunstein 2008). The idea of a 'psychological state' (Jones et al. 2013), attuned to human psychology and behaviour, may seem a bit alarming, but the straightforward goal is to identify effective, low-cost instruments for achieving valuable social goals.

## 20.1 WHAT WE KNOW ABOUT CONSUMER BEHAVIOUR

### 20.1.1 Findings

For purposes of understanding consumer behaviour, the central findings of behavioural research fall into four categories.

**Inertia and procrastination**

Default rules often have a large effect on social outcomes. Both private and public institutions often establish 'default rules': rules that determine the result if people make no affirmative choice at all. In part because of the power of inertia, default rules can be extremely important. The most well-studied area, with implications for many environmental issues, involves retirement savings, where the default rule has significant consequences (Thaler and Sunstein 2008). When people are asked whether they want to opt in to a retirement plan, the level of participation is far lower than if they are asked whether they want to opt out (Thaler and Sunstein 2008). Automatic enrolment significantly increases participation. With respect to energy and the environment, the same proposition holds (Sunstein and Reisch 2013a, 2013b): consumers are greatly affected by the default rule (Pichert and Katsikopoulos 2008).

More generally, people may decline to change from the status quo even if the costs of change are low and the benefits substantial. In the context of energy and the environment, for example, it is reasonable to predict that consumers would neglect to switch to fuel-efficient alternatives even when it is in their interest to do so (see Allcott 2011a). In such cases, 'internalities' may turn out to be high (Allcott et al. 2012), and the intrapersonal collective action problem may not be solved. It follows that complexity can have serious adverse effects, by increasing the power of inertia, and that ease and simplification (including reduction of paperwork burdens) can produce significant benefits.

Procrastination can have significant adverse effects. According to standard economic theory, consumers will consider both the short term and the long term. They will appropriately discount the future. In practice, however, some people procrastinate or neglect to take steps that impose small short-term costs but that would produce large long-term gains; an especially important phenomenon in the environmental area (Zandstra et al. 2012). Consumers may, for example, delay insulating their homes, enrolling in a retirement plan, starting to exercise, ceasing to smoke or using some valuable, energy-efficient, cost-saving technology (Devoto et al. 2012). When procrastination is creating significant problems, automatic enrolment in relevant programmes might be helpful; simplification is also important (Devoto et al. 2012).

When people are informed of the benefits or risks of engaging in certain actions, they are far more likely to act in accordance with that information if they are simultaneously provided with clear, explicit information about how to do so (Leventhal et al. 1965; Nickerson and Rogers 2010). The classic experiment, outside of the environmental area, shows that those who are informed of the benefits of a vaccine are more likely to become vaccinated if they are also given specific plans and maps describing where to go (Leventhal et al. 1965). Similarly, consumer behaviour is significantly affected if people are informed, not abstractly of the value of 'healthy eating', but specifically of the advantages of buying 1 per cent fat milk (as opposed to whole milk) (Heath and Heath 2010). With respect to energy efficiency and environmental protection, the identification of a specific, clear, unambiguous path or plan has an important effect on social outcomes; complexity or vagueness can ensure inaction, even when people are informed about risks and potential improvements.

**Framing and presentation**

Consumers are influenced by how information is presented or 'framed' (Levin et al. 1998; Redelmeier et al. 1993). Human beings display loss aversion (Tversky and Kahneman 1991). If consumers are informed that they will gain a certain amount of money by using energy-efficient products, they may be less likely to change their behaviour than if they are told that they will lose the same amount of money by not using such products (Gonzales et al. 1988). It follows that a product that is labelled '90 per cent fat-free' may well be more appealing than one that is labelled '10 per cent fat'. Behaviourally informed efforts to frame environmental outcomes can increase the likelihood that consumers will attend to delayed rewards (Zandstra et al. 2012).

Information that is vivid and salient can have a larger impact on consumer behaviour than information that is statistical and abstract. With respect to the environment and public health, vivid displays can be more effective than abstract presentations of statistical risks (Nisbett and Ross 1980). This point bears on the design of effective warnings. Attention is a scarce resource, and vivid, salient and novel presentations may trigger attention in ways that abstract or familiar ones cannot.

A related but more general point is that many costs (or benefits) are less salient than purchase prices; they are 'shrouded attributes' to which some consumers do not pay much attention (Gabaix and Laibson, 2006). Such 'add-on' costs may matter a great deal but receive little consideration, because they are not salient. Delayed rewards fall in the same category (Zandstra et al. 2012).

**Social influences**

In multiple domains, consumer behaviour is greatly influenced by the perceived behaviour of other people (Hirshleifer 1995). With respect to littering, recycling, obesity, consumption, smoking, becoming vaccinated and much more, the perceived decisions of others have a significant influence on individual behaviour and choice. The behaviour of peers has been found to have a significant effect on risky behaviour among adolescents, including tobacco smoking, marijuana use and truancy (Bisin et al. 2011; Card and Guiliano, 2011). Similarly, energy use is greatly affected by the perceived behaviour of others (Allcott and Rogers 2012; Schultz et al. 2007; Thaler and Sunstein 2008). In multiple domains, consumer decisions may well depend on what consumers believe that their neighbours are doing. One reason involves information: in deciding what to choose, a consumer learns from the behaviour of others. Another reason involves reputation: in deciding what to choose, a consumer might want to receive approval or to avoid disapproval.

**Probability assessment and attitude to risk**

In some domains, people show unrealistic optimism (Jolls 1998; Sharot 2011; Shepherd et al. 2013). Many consumers have unrealistically optimistic views about the objective risks that they face and also about how the risks they face compare to those of similarly situated others (Shepherd et al. 2013). The 'above average' effect is common (Shepherd et al. 2013; Weinstein 1987): many consumers believe that they are less likely than others to suffer from various misfortunes, including automobile accidents and adverse health outcomes. One study found that while smokers do not underestimate statistical risks faced by the population of smokers, they nonetheless believe that their personal risk is less than that of the average smoker (Slovic 1998). These points have evident implications for environmental risks in general.

Consumers often use heuristics, or mental shortcuts, when assessing risks (Kahneman and Frederick 2002). For example judgements about probability are often affected by whether a recent event readily comes to mind (Tversky and Kahneman 1973). If an event is cognitively 'available', people may well overestimate its probability, and if an event remains unavailable, they might well underestimate its likelihood (availability bias). Optimistic bias does of course produce an unduly low estimate of probability; availability bias can serve to overcome unrealistic optimism (Shepherd et al. 2013).

**Beyond incentives**

With respect to consumer behaviour, none of these findings is inconsistent with the conventional economic emphasis on the importance of material incentives; actual and perceived costs and benefits certainly matter. But apart from strictly material incentives of this kind, evidence suggests the independent importance of choice architecture and prevailing social norms. If, for example, healthy foods are prominent and easily accessible, consumers are more likely to choose them; one study finds an 8–16 per cent decrease in intake simply by making food more difficult to reach (as, for example, by varying its proximity by 10 inches or altering the serving utensil) (Rozin et al. 2011). The problem of childhood obesity is, at least in part, a result of the easy availability of unhealthy foods. The same point bears on smoking and alcohol abuse. In some areas, including those that involve the environment, automatic enrolment might have larger effects than even significant economic incentives (Chetty et al. 2012; Sunstein and Reisch 2013b).

On all of these issues, a great deal remains to be learned; future work is indispensable (on whether consumers ignore the long-term, see Allcott and Greenstone 2012). But with respect to consumer behaviour, existing research suggests that four approaches have particular promise: (1) behaviourally informed disclosure; (2) appropriate default rules; (3) increasing the salience of certain factors or variables; and (4) enlisting social norms through private–public partnerships and other approaches that operate in the service of desirable public goals.

## 20.2 BEHAVIOURALLY INFORMED DISCLOSURE: INFORMING CHOICE

### 20.2.1 Examples

In many nations, public officials have often recognized that information disclosure can be a useful regulatory tool, replacing or complementing other approaches. Central examples include efforts to require disclosure of potential consumer savings from energy efficiency (Newell and Siikamäki 2013), of the risks associated with smoking, of credit card payments and debt (Soll et al. 2013), and of information that bears on health (Fung et al. 2008).

In the area of energy efficiency, information disclosure can have a significant impact, at least if the relevant information is clear, simple and meaningful (Newell and Siikamäki 2013). Monetary information, making it clear what consumers have to gain in economic terms, can operate as a significant 'nudge', resulting in substantial savings (Kallbekken and Saelen 2013; Newell and Siikamäki 2013). Interpretive labels, of the sort in use in the European Union, add to this effect (Newell and Siikamäki, 2013). With respect to costs and benefits over time, consumers' discount rates of course play a significant role. In this domain, many consumers tend to show a high discount rate, which will affect any judgement about the appropriate policy. If a high discount rate reflects some kind of error, giving rise to the 'energy paradox' (by which consumers fail to purchase energy-efficient goods from which they would save money), then there is special reason for policy makers to respond. The evidence remains inconclusive (Allcott and Greenstone 2012).

It is also true that information disclosure, showing what consumers have to gain, will not work unless the gain is non-trivial. If consumers learn that they can save $20 a year on their electricity bill by paying close attention all the time, they might conclude that the gain is not worth the effort. In such cases emphasizing the monetary gain might be counterproductive. In other cases a small incentive will have no effect at all. There is also a risk that an emphasis on economic benefits may 'crowd out' intrinsic motivation (Frey 1998).

In the domain of nutrition, a number of disclosure requirements are in place. To take just one example, a final rule has been issued by the US Department of Agriculture (USDA), requiring provision of nutritional information to consumers with respect to meat and poultry products. Nutrition facts panels must be provided on the labels of such products. Under the rule, the panels must contain information with respect to calories and both total and saturated fats (9 CFR § 317.309).

The rule clearly recognizes the potential importance of framing. If a product lists a percentage statement such as '80 per cent lean', it must also list its fat percentage. This requirement should avoid the confusion that can result from selective framing; a statement that a product is 80 per cent lean, standing by itself, makes leanness salient, and may therefore be misleading.

### 20.2.2 How, Not Only Whether

As behavioural economists have shown, policy makers should devote care and attention to how, not only whether, disclosure occurs. Accurate disclosure of information may be ineffective if the information is too abstract, vague, detailed, complex, poorly framed or overwhelming to be useful. Disclosure requirements should be designed for Homo sapiens, not Homo oeconomicus.

A good rule of thumb is that disclosure should be concrete, straightforward, simple, meaningful, timely and salient. If the goal is to inform people about how to avoid risks or to obtain benefits, disclosure should avoid abstract statements (such as, for example, of 'healthy eating') and instead clearly identify the steps that might be taken to obtain the relevant goal (by specifying, for example, what specific actions parents might take to reduce the risk of childhood obesity).

### 20.2.3 Avoiding Confusion

If not carefully designed, disclosure requirements can produce ineffective, confusing and potentially misleading messages. Behaviourally informed approaches are alert to this risk and suggest possible improvements (Soll et al. 2013).

In the United States, for example, the Department of Agriculture has abandoned the 'Food Pyramid', used for decades as the central icon to promote healthy eating. The Pyramid has long been criticized as insufficiently informative; it does not offer people with any kind of clear 'path' with respect to healthy diet and does not connect to people's actual experience with food (Heath and Heath 2010). In response, the USDA replaced the Pyramid with a new, simpler icon, consisting of a plate with clear markings for fruit, vegetable, grains and protein. The plate is accompanied by straightforward guidance, including 'make half your plate fruits and vegetables', 'drink water instead of sugary drinks' and 'switch to fat-free or low-fat (1 per cent) milk'. This approach has the key advantage of informing people what to do, if they seek to have a healthier diet.

To be sure, mandatory disclosure can impose costs and burdens on both private and public institutions, and those costs and burdens should be considered in deciding how to proceed. Empirical evidence on the actual effects of disclosure policies is indispensable (Greenstone 2009; Loewenstein et al. 2013; Soll et al. 2013).

## 20.3 DEFAULT RULES

Behavioural research provides strong evidence that starting points, or default rules, greatly affect social outcomes (Chetty et al. 2012; Johnson et al. 1993). In some contexts, it is possible to promote social goals with sensible default rules that preserve freedom of choice and that might help to avoid the rigidity, cost and unintended adverse consequences of mandates and bans.

### 20.3.1 Automatic Enrolment and Default Rules: Two Examples

**Savings**

In the United States, employers have long asked workers whether they want to enrol in 401(k) pension plans; under a common approach, the default rule is non-enrolment. Even when enrolment is easy, the number of employees who enrol, or opt in, has sometimes been relatively low (Gale et al. 2009; Madrian and Shea 2001). A number of employers have responded by changing the default to automatic enrolment, by which employees are enrolled unless they opt out. The results are clear: significantly more employees end up enrolled with an opt-out design than with opt-in (Chetty et al. 2012; Gale et al. 2009). This is so even when opting out is easy.

**Energy**

In Germany, many people say that they would use green energy if presented with a choice, but the number of people who opt for green is limited (Pichert and Katsikopoulos 2008): in almost all communities, the green usage rate was for a long period under 1 per cent (though it has significantly increased in recent years; see Sunstein and Reisch 2013b). Even when the green usage rate was very low, two communities showed far higher rates, and the reason is simple: they used green defaults.

The first such community is Schönau in the Black Forest, consisting of about 2500 people and (notably) dominated by conservatives, with a weak Green Party (receiving only about 5 per cent of recent ballots). In the aftermath of the Chernobyl disaster in the 1980s, a citizen referendum established an environmentally friendly energy supply, in which the Schönau Power Company became the incumbent utility, and many of the Schönau citizens became owners of the co-operative. That company promotes solar energy and places a great deal of reliance on renewables. Customers are allowed to opt out and to use other energy sources, but they have to find relevant information in order to identify alternatives. Almost no one opts out: in recent years, the opt-out rate has been only slightly above 0 per cent.

The second natural experiment involves Energiedienst GmbH, which supplies energy to an area in southern Germany (Pichert and Katsikopoulos 2008). In 1999, the company established three separate tariffs. The default was green, and it turned out to be 8 per cent cheaper than the previous tariff. The second option was less green but cheaper (by an additional 8 per cent) and the third was greener but more expensive (by an additional 23 per cent). If customers did not respond, they would remain with the default. About 94 per cent of customers so remained, with 4.3 per cent switching to the cheaper tariff, and the rest switching either to the greener alternative or to a different supplier (Pichert and Katsikopoulos 2008).

These results testify to the power of defaults. Recall that elsewhere in Germany, the use of green energy was at the time of the study less than 1 per cent, even though consumers said that they would be willing to pay a premium for it. But outside of the two areas just described, people must affirmatively elect green energy, and they overwhelmingly do not. It is fair to speculate that, at least within a large range, the default rule is the determinant of social outcomes.

Similar results have been found in the United States. The Department of Energy has found that significantly more customers enrol in time-based rate programmes (designed to promote smarter energy use) with opt-out offers than with opt-in offers (US Department of Energy 2013). The average participation rate was merely 11 per cent under opt-in, by which customers were informed of the study and asked to join. The participation rate jumped to 85 per cent under an opt-out approach, by which customers were automatically enrolled. In a related finding, a reduction in the size of plates was found to reduce the amount of food waste in hotel restaurants by about 20 per cent

(Kallbekken and Saelen 2012); the finding is related because plate size creates something akin to default rules for food consumption.

### 20.3.2 Automatic Enrolment and Consumer Behaviour: Mechanisms and Complexities

A great deal of research has attempted to explore exactly why default rules have such a large effect on outcomes (Carroll et al. 2009; Dinner et al. 2009; Gale et al. 2009; Johnson and Goldstein 2013; Sunstein 2013b). There appear to be three contributing factors. The first involves inertia and procrastination. To alter the effect of the default rule, consumers must make an active choice to reject the default. In view of the power of inertia and the tendency to procrastinate, people may simply continue with the status quo.

The second factor involves what might be taken to be an implicit endorsement of the default rule. Many people appear to conclude that the default was chosen for a reason; they believe that they should not depart from it unless they have particular information to justify a change.

The third factor involves the reference point for consumer decisions; the established reference point has significant effects because people dislike losses from that reference point. If, for example, the default rule favours energy-efficient light bulbs, then the loss in terms of reduced efficiency may loom large, and there will be a tendency to continue with energy-efficient light bulbs. But if the default rule favours less efficient (and initially less expensive) light bulbs, then the loss in terms of up-front costs may loom large, and there will be a tendency to favour less efficient light bulbs (Johnson and Goldstein 2013; Sunstein and Reisch 2013b).

In the environmental domain, it might be possible to achieve social goals, and to do so while maintaining freedom of choice and at low cost, by selecting good default rules and by avoiding harmful ones. One approach is to select the default rule that reflects what most people would choose if they were adequately informed. Suppose, for example, that a particular default rule would place a strong majority of the relevant population in the situation that they would favour if they made an informed choice. If so, there is a legitimate reason to adopt that default rule (with the understanding that for those who differ from the majority, it remains possible to opt out).

Some default rules apply to all of the relevant population, subject to the ability to opt out. Other default rules are personalized, in the sense that they draw on available information about which approach best suits individuals in the relevant population (Jones and Goldstein 2013). A personalized default might be based on geographical or demographic variables; for example, income and age might be used in determining appropriate default rules for retirement plans. Alternatively, a personalized default might be based on people's own past choices to the extent that they are available (unless those choices are based on an absence of information, manipulation, or some kind of bias).

An advantage of personalized default rules is that they may well be more accurate than 'mass' default rules (Sunstein 2013b). As technology evolves, it should be increasingly possible to produce personalized defaults, based on people's own choices and situations, and likely to be far more accurate than more general ones. There will be excellent opportunities to use default rules to promote consumer welfare. To be sure, any such rules must respect the applicable laws, policies and regulations involving personal privacy and should avoid unduly crude proxies.

It is important to note that default rules may not 'stick' when the relevant population has strong contrary preferences. For example, a study in the United Kingdom found that most people rejected a savings plan with an unusually high default contribution rate (12 per cent of before-tax income) (Beshears et al. 2010). Only about 25 per cent of employees remained at that rate after a year, whereas about 60 per cent of employees remained at a lower default contribution rate. One implication is that 'extreme' defaults are less likely to stick; another implication, based on the lower incomes of those who stayed with the default, is that default rules may be more influential for low-income workers than for their higher-earning counterparts (Beshears et al. 2010). These points must be considered in designing default rules that involve energy and the environment (Sunstein and Reisch 2013b).

### 20.3.3 Active Consumer Choices

An alternative approach, sometimes worth serious consideration, is to avoid any default rule and to require active choices (Carroll et al. 2009; Sunstein 2013b). Under this approach, people are required to make an actual choice among the various options; they are not defaulted into any particular alternative. With respect to energy, for example, an employer might reject both opt-out and opt-in and simply require employees to indicate their preferences. Evidence suggests that active choices result in far higher levels of savings than a default rules that requires people explicitly to opt in (Carroll et al. 2009).

If inertia and procrastination are playing a significant role, then active choosing may be better than opt-in, in which people end up with outcomes that they would not prefer if they were to make a choice. In such circumstances, active choosing increases the likelihood that people will end up with their preferred outcomes.

Active choosing might also be preferred when public officials lack relevant information, so that the chosen default rule might be harmful. This is an especially important point. If officials are inadequately informed, and if the default rule is no better than a guess, that rule might lead consumers in the wrong direction. The same point argues against a default rule when self-interested private groups have managed to call for it, even though it is not in the interest of those on whom it is imposed. Active choosing is much less risky on these counts.

As compared with either opt-in or opt-out, active choosing can have significant advantages when the relevant group has a great deal of diversity, so that a single approach is unlikely to fit variable circumstances. In some contexts that involve energy and the environment, a unitary default rule may also be harmful, because the power of inertia, or the force of suggestion, may mean that many consumers will end up in a situation that is not in their interest. For this reason active choosing may be better, because it can handle heterogeneity.

On the other hand, active choosing can have significant disadvantages. One disadvantage is that in situations of unfamiliarity or great complexity, in which consumers lack information or experience, active choosing may impose unjustified or excessive burdens. These burdens include the resources required to enforce the requirement to choose and the time required for people to obtain relevant information and to make the choice. As compared with a default rule, active choosing increases the costs of decisions, possibly significantly; it also might increase errors, possibly significantly, if the area is unfamiliar and confusing. In such situations, opt-in or opt-out might produce better outcomes for consumers. Whether this is so in the environmental area depends on the nature of the problem involved. And when the relevant activity imposes costs on third parties (as is frequently the case for environmental issues), active choosing might well be inferior to opt-out, simply because the latter provides safeguards against those costs; although in such cases, regulatory requirements, without opt-out, might be desirable instead (Sunstein and Reisch 2013b).

## 20.4 SALIENCE

It is often possible to promote environmental goals by making certain features of a product or a situation more salient to consumers. As a simple example of salience effects, consider alcohol taxes. There is evidence that when such taxes are specifically identified in the posted price, increases in such taxes have a larger negative effect on alcohol consumption than when they are applied at the register (Chetty et al. 2009; Finkelstein 2009). Incentives matter, but in order to matter, they must be salient. Sensible regulatory policies, especially those that involve disclosure, are attentive to the importance of salience. And if we are attentive to salience, we will be alert to the possibility that what was salient at one time might become background noise at another. Information disclosure and warnings should be attentive to this risk.

People's attention is limited, and regulatory goals are not always served merely by altering policy or disclosing information. The relevant policy or information must also be salient. In the context of fiscal policy, consider the question whether to provide payments in the form of a one-off cheque or instead in the form of reduced withholding. Would one or another approach lead to increased spending?

In the abstract, it may be predicted that there would be no difference as a result of delivery method. But evidence suggests that a one-off stimulus payment has significantly greater effects in increasing spending than does an economically equivalent reduction in withholding (Sahm et al. 2011). A potential explanation, with support in the evidence, involves the importance of salience or visibility. Indeed, a majority of households did not notice the withholding changes in the relevant study, and households who found 'a small but repeated boost to their pay cheques' appear to be less likely to use the money for significant purchases.

With respect to environmental protection, there are many potential applications. Well-designed energy efficiency labels make relevant factors salient to those who will see them (Newell and Siikamäki 2013). The significant consequences of easy accessibility and convenience (returning to the issue of obesity) can be seen as a close cousin of salience effects.

Energy-efficient products can save money, but for many consumers the potential savings may not be salient at the time of purchase, even if those savings are significant. The 'energy paradox' refers to the fact that some consumers do not purchase energy-efficient products even when it is clearly in their economic interest to do so. As suggested, the evidence remains unclear on the magnitude and seriousness of the problem (Allcott and Greenstone 2012; Allcott et al. 2012). But empirical work does suggest that non-price interventions, making the effects of energy use more salient, can change consumers' decisions and significantly reduce electricity use (Mullainathan and Allcott 2010). Such interventions can lead to private as well as public savings (Howarth et al. 2000). For energy conservation, non-price interventions have been found to be both effective and cost-effective, and to compare favourably to use of more standard regulatory tools (Mullainathan and Allcott 2010). In addition, the effect of an economic incentive may well depend on the kind of information that is used to promote it (Stern 1999).

## 20.5 SOCIAL NORMS AND CONSUMER BEHAVIOUR

Social scientists have emphasized the immense importance of social practices and norms, which have a significant influence on individual decisions. If people learn that they are using more energy than similarly situated others, their energy use may decline, saving money while also reducing pollution (Allcott and Rogers 2012). Studies of a well-established programme, designed to inform people about how their energy use compares with that of their neighbours, demonstrates that display of comparative information can have a significant effect on consumer behaviour (Allcott 2011b). Indeed the effect is about the same as that of a short-run electricity price increase of 11 per cent to 20 per cent. Repeated reminders can be important to ensure long-term effects (Allcott and Rogers 2012).

The behaviour of relevant others can provide a valuable signal about sensible or appropriate courses of action. Informational cascades are a possible consequence (Hirshleifer 1995), as people rely on, and thus amplify, the informational signals produced by the actions of their predecessors, potentially producing significant and unanticipated changes in consumer behaviour (Hirshleifer 1995; Salganik et al. 2006). Similarly, those actions can provide information about what others will approve and disapprove.

These points have strong implications for consumer behaviour and public policy in general (Salganik et al. 2006), and in the environmental area in particular. For example smoking and seat belt regulations appear to have worked hand in hand with emerging social norms, helping to reduce deaths and injuries. In the context of seat belt usage, there has been a dramatic change in behaviour in the United States, with an increase in a few decades from usage rates under 15 per cent to usage rates over 70 per cent, in significant part a product of social norms that operated in concert with educational campaigns, warnings and regulatory changes (see Sunstein 2011).

In other areas, such norms have helped consumers to save money while also protecting the environment (Allcott and Rogers 2012; Costa and Kahn 2013). If people are informed that others are engaged in environmentally harmful behaviour, they are more likely to engage in such behaviour themselves (Schultz et al. 2007). At the same time, environmentally beneficial behaviour can be contagious, especially if relevant norms can be activated (Schultz et al. 2007). Multiple equilibria are possible, and in principle, changes by some consumers can produce changes by many (Watts 2011). Public–private partnerships can be especially important in this domain, as those in the private sector enlist existing or emerging norms that can improve consumer choices.

## 20.6 A CONCLUDING NOTE

As I have suggested, it is implausible to suggest that uses of choice architecture, or nudges, exhaust the policy toolkit in the environmental domain. Standard policy instruments, including regulation, are indispensable. But for those who are sceptical of the potential effects of choice architecture, it is worthwhile to consider three findings. First, in the context of savings, automatic enrolment has had a larger effect than quite significant economic incentives (Chetty et al. 2012). Second, efforts to enlist social norms, by providing comparative information about energy use, have had an effect comparable to that of significant increases in the cost of energy (Allcott 2011b; see also Mullainathan and Allcott 2010). Third, in the context of college attendance, simplification of existing application forms has the same effect as several thousand dollars in additional subsidies (Bettinger et al. 2012). These findings reveal that even if initiatives of the kind discussed here do not impose significant costs, they can have large consequences for behaviour; consequences that are comparable to, and perhaps even larger than, those of more conventional economic instruments.

## REFERENCES

Allcott, H. (2011a), 'Consumers' perceptions and misperceptions of energy costs', *American Economic Review*, 101 (3), 98–104.

Allcott, H. (2011b), 'Social norms and energy conservation', *Journal of Public Economics*, 95 (9–10), 1082–1095.

Allcott, H. and M. Greenstone (2012), 'Is there an energy efficiency gap?', *Journal of Economic Perspectives*, 26 (1), 3–28.

Allcott, H., S. Mullainathan and D. Taubinsky (2012), 'Energy policy with externalities and internalities', NBER Working Paper No. 17977, available at https://files.nyu.edu/ha32/public/research/AMT%20NBER%20WP%20-%20Energy%20Policy%20with%20Externalities%20and%20Internalities.pdf.

Allcott, H. and T. Rogers (2012), 'The short-run and long-run effects of behavioral interventions: experimental evidence from energy conservation', NBER Working Paper No. 18492, available at http://www.nber.org/papers/w18492.

Banerjee, A. and E. Duflo (2011), *Poor Economics*, New York: Public Affairs.

Beshears, J., J. Choi, D. Laibson and B. Madrian (2010), 'The limitations of defaults', unpublished manuscript, available at http://www.nber.org/programs/ag/rrc/NB10-02%20Beshears,%20Choi%20et%20al%20SUMMARY.pdf.

Bettinger, E.P., B.T. Long, P. Oreopoulos and L. Sanbonmatsu (2012), 'The role of application assistance and information in college decisions: results from the H&R Block FAFSA experiment', *Quarterly Journal of Economics*, 127 (3), 1205–1242.

Bisin, A., A. Moro and G. Topa (2011), 'The empirical content of models with multiple equilibria in economies with social interactions', NBER Working Paper No. 17196, available at http://www.nber.org/papers/w17196.

Cabinet Office (n.d.), 'The behavioural insights team', available at http://www.cabinetoffice.gov.uk/behavioural-insights-team.

Card, D. and L. Giuliano (2011), 'Peer effects and multiple equilibria in the risky behavior of friends', NBER Working Paper No. 17088, available at http://www.nber.org/papers/w17088.

Carroll, G.D., J.J. Choi, D. Laibson, B.C. Madrian and A. Metrick (2009), 'Optimal defaults and active decisions', *Quarterly Journal of Economics*, 124 (4), 1639–1674.

Chetty, R., J. Friedman, S. Leth-Petersen, T. Nielsen and T. Olsen (2012), 'Active vs. passive decisions and crowdout in retirement savings accounts: evidence from Denmark', NBER Working Paper No. 18565, available at http://www.nber.org/papers/w18565.

Chetty, R., A. Looney and K. Kroft (2009), 'Salience and taxation: theory and evidence', *American Economic Review*, 99 (4), 1145–1177.

Costa, D.L. and M.E. Kahn (2013), 'Energy conservation "nudges" and environmentalist ideology: evidence

from a randomized residential electricity field experiment', *Journal of the European Economic Association*, 11 (3), 680–702.
Devoto, F., E. Duflo, P. Dupas, W. Pariente and V. Pons (2012), 'Happiness on tap: piped water adoption in urban Morocco', *American Economic Journal: Economic Policy*, 4 (4), 68–99.
DG SANCO (2010), 'Consumer affairs', available at http://ec.europa.eu/consumers/docs/1dg-sanco-brochure-consumer-behaviour-final.pdf.
Dinner, I.M., E.J. Johnson, D.G. Goldstein and K. Liu (2009), 'Partitioning default effects: why people choose not to choose', unpublished manuscript, available at http://ssrn.com/abstract=1352488.
European Commission (2012), 'Green behaviour', Future Brief, Science for Environment Policy, available at http://ec.europa.eu/environment/integration/research/newsalert/pdf/FB4.pdf.
Finkelstein, A. (2009), 'E-ZTAX: tax salience and tax rates', *Quarterly Journal of Economics*, 124 (3), 969–1010.
Frey, B. (1998), *Not Just For the Money: An Economic Theory of Personal Motivation*, Cheltenham, UK and Lyme, NH, USA: Edward Elgar Publishing.
Fung, A., M. Graham and D. Weil (2008), *Full Disclosure: The Promise and Perils of Transparency*, New York: Cambridge University Press.
Gabaix, X. and D. Laibson (2006), 'Shrouded attributes, consumer myopia, and information suppression in competitive markets', *Quarterly Journal of Economics*, 121 (2), 505–32.
Gale, W., J. Iwry and S. Walters (2009), 'Retirement savings for middle- and lower-income households: the Pension Protection Act of 2006 and the unfinished agenda', in W.G. Gale, et al. (eds), *Automatic*, Harrisburg, VA: R.R. Donnelley, pp. 11–27.
Gonzales, M.H., E. Aronson and M.A. Costanzo (1988), 'Using social cognition and persuasion to promote energy conservation: a quasi-experiment', *Journal of Applied Social Psychology*, 18 (12), 1049–1066.
Greenstone, M. (2009), 'Toward a culture of persistent regulatory experimentation and evaluation', in D. Moss and J. Cisternino (eds), *New Perspectives on Regulation*, Cambridge, MA: Tobin Project, pp. 111–125.
greeNudge.no (n.d.), 'GreeNudge', available at: http://www.greenudge.no.
Heath, C. and D. Heath (2010), *Switch: How to Change Things when Change is Hard*, New York: Crown Business.
Hirshleifer, D. (1995), 'The blind leading the blind: social influence, fads, and informational cascades', in M. Tommasi and K. Ierulli (eds), *The New Economics of Human Behaviour*, Cambridge: Cambridge University Press, pp. 188–215.
Howarth, R.B., B.M. Haddad and B. Paton (2000), 'The economics of energy efficiency: insights from voluntary participation programs', *Energy Policy*, 28 (6–7), 477–486.
iNudgeYou.com (n.d.), 'Resources', available at http://www.inudgeyou.com/resources.
Johnson, E. and D. Goldstein (2013), 'Decisions by default', in E. Shafir (ed.), *Behavioral Foundations of Public Policy*, Princeton, NJ: Princeton University Press, pp. 417–428.
Johnson, E.J., J. Hershey, J. Meszaros and H. Kunreuther (1993), 'Framing, probability distortions, and insurance decisions', *Journal of Risk and Uncertainty*, 7 (1), 35–51.
Johnson, E., S. Shu, B. Dellaert, C. Fox, D. Goldstein, G. Haubl, R. Larrick, J. Payne, E. Peters, D. Schkade, B. Wansink and E. Weber (2012), 'Beyond nudges: tools of a choice architecture', *Marketing Letters*, 23 (2), 487–504.
Jolls, C. (1998), 'Behavioral economics analysis of redistributive legal rules', *Vanderbilt Law Review*, 51 (6), 1653–1677.
Jones, R., J. Pykett and M. Whitehead (2013), *Changing Behaviours: On the Rise of the Psychological State*, Cheltenham, UK and Northampton, MA, USA: Edward Elgar Publishing.
Kahneman, D., and S. Frederick (2002), 'Representativeness revisited: attribute substitution in intuitive judgment', in T. Gilovich, D. Griffin and D. Kahneman (eds), *Heuristics and Biases: The Psychology of Intuitive Judgment*, Cambridge: Cambridge University Press, pp. 49–81.
Kallbekken, S. and H. Saelen (2013), '"Nudging" hotel guests to reduce food waste as a win–win environmental measure', Economics Letters, 119 (3), 325–327.
LeBoeuf, R. and E. Shafir (2012), 'Decision making', in K. Holyoak and R. Morrison (eds), *The Oxford Handbook of Thinking and Reasoning*, Oxford: Oxford University Press, pp. 301–21.
Leventhal, H., R. Singer and S. Jones (1965), 'Effects of fear and specificity of recommendation upon attitudes and behavior', *Journal of Personality and Social Psychology*, 2 (1), 20–29.
Levin, I.P., S.L. Schneider and G.J. Gaeth (1998), 'All frames are not created equal: a typology and critical analysis of framing effects', *Organizational Behavior and Human Decision Processes*, 76 (2), 149–188.
Loewenstein, G., C.R. Sunstein and R. Golman (2013), 'Disclosure: psychology changes everything', unpublished manuscript, available at https://papers.ssrn.com/sol3/papers.cfm?abstract_id=2312708.
Low, D. (2012), *Behavioural Economics and Policy Design: Examples from Singapore*, Singapore: World Scientific.

Luth, H. (2010), *Behavioural Economics in Consumer Policy: The Economic Analysis of Standard Terms in Consumer Contracts Revisited*, Antwerp: Intersentia.
Madrian, B.C. and D.F. Shea (2001), 'The power of suggestion: Inertia in 401(k) participation and savings behavior', *Quarterly Journal of Economics*, 116 (4), 1149–1187.
Mullainathan S. and H. Allcott (2010), 'Behavior and energy policy', *Science*, 327 (5970), 1204–1205.
Newell, R. and J. Siikamäki (2013), 'Nudging energy efficiency behavior: the role of information labels', NBER Working Paper No. 19224, available at http://www.nber.org/papers/w19224.
Nickerson, D.W. and T. Rogers (2010), 'Do you have a voting plan? Implementation intentions, voter turnout, and organic plan making', *Psychological Science*, 21 (2), 194–199.
Nisbett, R.E. and L. Ross (1980), *Human Inference: Strategies and Shortcomings of Social Judgment*, Englewood Cliffs, NJ: Prentice-Hall.
OECD (Organisation for Economic Co-operation and Development) (2010), 'Consumer policy toolkit', available at http://www.oecd.org/sti/consumerpolicy/consumerpolicytoolkit.htm.
Pichert, D. and K.V. Katsikopoulos (2008), 'Green defaults: information presentation and pro-environmental behaviour', *Journal of Environmental Psychology*, 28 (1), 63–73.
Redelmeier, D.A., P. Rozin and D. Kahneman (1993), 'Understanding patients' decisions', *JAMA: The Journal of the American Medical Association*, 270 (1), 72–76.
Rozin, P., S. Scott, M. Dingley, J.K. Urbanek, H. Jiang and M. Kaltenbach (2011), 'Nudge to Nobesity I: minor changes in accessibility decrease food intake', *Judgment and Decision Making*, 6 (4), 323–332.
Sahm, C.R., M.D. Shapiro and J. Slemrod (2011), 'Check in the mail or more in the paycheck: does the effectiveness of fiscal stimulus depend on how it is delivered?', available at http://www.federalreserve.gov/pubs/feds/2010/201040/201040pap.pdf.
Salganik, M.J., P. Sheridan Dodds and D.J. Watts (2006), 'Experimental study of inequality and unpredictability in an artificial cultural market', *Science*, 311 (5762), 854–856.
Schultz, P.W., J. Nolan, R. Cialdini, N. Goldstein and V. Griskevicius (2007), 'The constructive, destructive, and reconstructive power of social norms', *Psychological Science*, 18 (5), 429–434.
Sharot, T. (2011), The Optimism Bias: A Tour of the Irrationally Positive Brain, New York: Knopf Publishing.
Shepherd, J., W. Klein, E. Waters and N. Weinstein (2013), 'Taking stock of unrealistic optimism', *Perspectives on Psychological Science*, 8 (4), 395–411.
Slovic, P. (1998), 'Do adolescent smokers know the risks?', *Duke Law Journal*, 47 (6), 1133–1141.
Soll, J., R.L. Keeney, R.P. Larrick (2013), 'Consumer misunderstanding of credit card use, payments, and debt: causes and solutions', *Journal of Public Policy and Marketing*, 32 (1), 66–81.
Stern, P.C. (1999) 'Information, incentives, and proenvironmental consumer behavior', *Journal of Consumer Policy*, 22 (4), 461–478.
Sunstein, C.R. (2011), 'Empirically informed regulation', *University of Chicago Law Review*, 78 (4), 1349–1429.
Sunstein, C.R. (2013a), *Simpler*, New York: Simon & Schuster.
Sunstein, C.R. (2013b), 'Deciding by default', *University of Pennsylvania Law Review*, 162, 1–56.
Sunstein, C.R. and L.A. Reisch (2013a), 'Green by default', *Kyklos*, 66 (3), 398–402.
Sunstein, C.R. and L.A. Reisch (2013b), 'Automatically green: behavioral economics and environmental protection', *Harvard Environmental Law Review*, 38, 128–158.
Thaler, R.H. and C.R. Sunstein (2008), *Nudge: Improving Decisions about Health, Wealth and Happiness*, New Haven, CT: Yale University Press.
Tversky, A. and D. Kahneman (1973), 'Availability: a heuristic for judging frequency and probability', *Cognitive Psychology*, 5 (2), 207–232.
Tversky, A. and D. Kahneman (1991), 'Loss aversion in riskless choice: a reference-dependent model', *Quarterly Journal of Economics*, 106 (4), 1039–1061.
US Department of Energy (2013), 'Analysis of customer enrollment patterns in time-based rate programs', available at http://energy.gov/sites/prod/files/2013/07/f2/CustomerEnrollmentPatterns.pdf.
Watts, D. (2011), *Everything Is Obvious: How Common Sense Fails Us*, New York: Crown Business.
Weinstein, N. (1987), 'Unrealistic optimism about susceptibility to health problems: conclusions from a community-wide sample', *Journal of Behavioral Medicine*, 10 (5), 481–500.
Zandstra, E., K. Miyapuram and P. Tobler (2012), 'Understanding consumer decisions using behavioral economics', in V.S. Chandrasekhar Pammi and N. Srinivasan (eds), Decision Making: Neural and Behavioural Approaches, Amsterdam: Elsevier, pp. 197–211.

# 21. Promoting sustainable consumption: the risks of using financial incentives

*Jan Willem Bolderdijk and Linda Steg*

Scientists agree that many of today's most pressing environmental issues (for example, resource depletion, water pollution, climate change) can ultimately be attributed to specific behaviour of consumers. Whether we decide to live in poor or well-insulated houses, travel by plane or train, put beef or locally grown vegetables on our plate, on an aggregate level, substantially influences the amount of energy, water and land that is involved in housing, moving and feeding humanity (Hammond 2006; Hoekstra 2013). Consequently, a key component to mitigating environmental problems lies with changing the behaviour of individual consumers (Dietz et al. 2009). But how should consumers be motivated to act pro-environmentally?

Sustainable consumption often involves some degree of physical or financial discomfort on behalf of the consumer. For example locally grown vegetables are typically less readily available than mass-produced, greenhouse-grown alternatives which are typically offered in supermarket settings. Sustainable consumption is sometimes also financially expensive; adding more insulation to one's home for instance requires a steep initial financial investment. Thus, many sustainable consumption patterns are not inherently rewarding. Consequently it is argued that some kind of external incentive is needed to make sustainable consumption attractive from an individual consumer perspective.

A widespread notion is that consumers are primarily motivated by (economic) self-interest (Miller 1999), and are not motivated to act pro-environmentally unless some personal benefit is implicated (Penn 2003). Hence, it is not surprising that policy aimed at 'greening' consumer behaviour – for example, environmental taxes, subsidies for energy-efficient vehicles – often appeals to consumers' economic sense. Indeed, money is one of the most powerful and universal sources of motivation, and can trigger behaviours (people are likely to try behaviours they believe are financially rewarding) and reinforce them (people tend to repeat actions that have resulted in financial gain; Lea and Webley 2006). Consequently it is assumed that people would be motivated to engage more often in sustainable consumption by positioning such behaviour as financially attractive (for example, rebates, subsidies, tax credits) and positioning unsustainable behaviour as costly (for example, levies, taxes, tolls). Simply change the price structure, and consumers will change accordingly.

Financial incentives (we use the term 'incentive'[1] in this chapter to denote any situation in which specific consumer behaviour is purposefully linked to a financial consequence in an attempt to increase motivation, including monetary feedback) have often been used in promoting sustainable consumer behaviour. However, the effects were mixed. Although financial incentives have been effective in improving some targeted behaviours, such as recycling (Levitt and Leventhal 1986), composting (Thøgersen 2003) and fuel-efficient driving (Bolderdijk et al. 2011), research also documented instances in which the introduction of financial incentives did not improve (for example, in the case of a tax on air travel) or even reduced desired behaviour (for example, in the case of financial reimbursement for residents living close to a nuclear waste depository; Frey and Oberholzer-Gee 1997).

Nevertheless, incentives remain a highly popular tool to steer consumer behaviour. Importantly, however, financial incentives constitute just one of several policy options. Consequently – just like a carpenter who relies on more than just his hammer to get the job done – incentives should not be the only tool to steer consumer behaviour. Unfortunately, incentives are often applied under the implicit assumption that they would be effective in any circumstance, without taking the specific situation (such as type of target behaviour, motivation present with the consumer) into regard, with null or potentially counterproductive effects as a consequence.

In this chapter, we aim to offer insights into the conditions under which financial incentives are a more or less suitable tool to promote sustainable consumer behaviour. We do so by reviewing the literature for potential limitations and risks of financial incentives. Moreover we identify literature gaps that may spur future research. As such, this chapter may aid social marketers, policy makers and scholars in their attempts to shape more sustainable consumer behaviours.

## 21.1 WHAT MONEY DOES FOR PEOPLE VERSUS WHAT MONEY DOES TO PEOPLE

In order to better understand when financial incentives may be more or less suitable to promoting sustainable consumption, we first address the question of how incentives affect behaviour. We review two perspectives on the effects of financial incentives: what money does *for* people (the instrumental value of money) versus what money does *to* people (the cognitive impact of money).

Money, according to the traditional perspectives that one may find in economics textbooks and in the public domain, has several functions. First, it is a unit of account: money can be used to express the market value of goods or services. Second, it is a store of value: money is a means to save, store and retrieve value. Third, and most importantly, it is a medium of exchange: money facilitates the trading of goods and services. According to this reasoning, money itself has no intrinsic value, and people only desire to obtain money for the sake of what it allows them to purchase. Thus, money derives its persuasive power from its instrumental value (Lea and Webley 2006) – money does something for people.

This instrumental analysis of money offers some straightforward predictions about the effects of money as a tool for behaviour change. Financial incentives (for example, discounts, deposits, rebates, subsidies) make desired consumer behaviour (for example, the purchase of organic food, recycling cans) financially attractive. They are considered to be persuasive insofar as they allow consumers to save money, which can be used to purchase more of the goods and services they desire. Similarly financial disincentives (for example, surcharges, fines, fees, taxes) make undesired consumer behaviour (for example, buying excessive packaging) financially unattractive because they limit the amount of desirable goods and services people can purchase.

In sum, because incentives impact the amount of money available to spend on other products and services, larger incentives should result in more behaviour change. This prediction is in line with some formal predictions and assumptions that are prevalent in the economic literature. Within the neoclassical economic framework, people are modelled as rational agents, who make optimal decisions and are mainly focused on pursuing self-interest and personal wealth ('*Homo economicus*'; Thaler 2000). Accordingly they are presumed to react 'rationally' to money as a tool of persuasion. Incentives (for example, subsidies, energy taxes) make specific behaviours financially more or less attractive, and should consequently increase or reduce demand for those behaviours. Thus, this basic economic framework predicts a monotonic relation between anticipated financial consequences and behaviour (Gneezy and Rustichini 2000): the larger the monetary incentive, the more likely it is that consumers will change their behaviour.

A host of studies indeed suggest that the implementation of financial incentives – both small and large ones – can be effective in promoting specific types of sustainable behaviours (e.g. Levitt and Leventhal 1986; Poortinga et al. 2013). This however does not mean that making sustainable consumption financially attractive is always required or even conducive to promoting certain kinds of behaviour. The sales of the Toyota Prius in the US, for instance, did not plummet after the tax credit for hybrid cars ended in 2006. On the contrary, sales increased by 68.9 per cent, suggesting that tax credits no longer seemed crucial once a sufficiently large critical mass was reached (Griskevicius et al. 2010). In fact, there are cases in which financial incentives could do more harm than good. Recent studies for instance suggest that reminding consumers of the financial benefits associated with energy-saving actions may in fact demotivate them from taking appropriate actions (Bolderdijk et al. 2013; Handgraaf et al. 2013). Additionally, both basic (Ariely et al. 2009b) and applied studies (Heberlein and Warriner 1983) suggest that larger incentives do not necessarily translate into stronger changes in behaviour. Evidently, the effects of money on behaviour cannot be fully captured by referring to money's instrumental function (see also Thøgersen 2003). Perhaps there is more to money as a tool for persuasion than initially meets the eye.

The instrumental perspective of money implies that people desire to obtain money for the sake of what it allows them to buy. However, money appears to be more than a neutral medium of exchange. In fact, psychological and sociological studies suggest that money has consistent and predictable cognitive effects: 'Money is found to have value and an emotional charge that is not predicted by its economic use' (Lea and Webley 2006). The mere activation of the concept of money, for instance, may already affect people's decisions; screenshot pictures of a dollar bill were found to elicit a self-sufficient orientation among observers, making them less susceptible to the needs of others (Vohs et al. 2006). This example illustrates that, as we will argue throughout this chapter, money's persuasive power does not depend only on its instrumental value, but also on how money affects people's underlying cognitions: money does something to people. Importantly, these cognitive responses may limit the persuasive power of incentives. It is therefore important to bear such cognitive responses in mind when trying to understand and predict the effectiveness of financial incentives. In the remainder of this chapter, we explain this point in more detail.

## 21.2 THE PSYCHOLOGICAL IMPACT OF INCENTIVES

Incentives can have a host of cognitive effects: they can affect the amount of trust in others (Mulder et al. 2006; Tenbrunsel and Messick 1999), make people more self-sufficient (Vohs et al. 2006), and narrow people's attention (Ariely et al. 2009b). Here we review the most pertinent effects to persuasion. We start by discussing how incentives affect the decision frame of consumers (section 21.2.1). Next we discuss how incentives affect and interact with people's self-concept, which has implications for self-persuasion (21.2.2), as well as the type of signal that ensues from acting sustainably (21.2.3). In doing so, we identify some important risks associated with the application of incentives as a tool for persuasion.

### 21.2.1 Incentives Change the Decision Frame

Many consumers engage in environmentally sustainable actions when there is no explicit financial gain in doing so (Pelletier et al. 1998; Thøgersen 2006). Consider for instance consumers who buy organic products or recycle batteries and glass. Such actions are often spurred by normative considerations: not engaging in such sustainable actions would be considered inappropriate (not in line one's standards) and may result in internal sanctions (for example, experiencing guilt). For these consumers, the decision whether or not to act sustainably is not a matter of cost–benefit analysis, but one regarding morality and ethics (Lindenberg and Steg 2007).

Different studies have suggested that financial incentives may interact with such normative considerations (Gneezy et al. 2011). Consider for instance a field experiment conducted at an Israeli daycare centre (Gneezy and Rustichini 2000). In an attempt to stimulate parents to collect their children before closing time, daycare employees installed a financial fine for latecomers. The goal of the penalty was to reinforce the punctuality norm: parents are expected to be on time to prevent daycare centre employees from working overtime. But rather than supporting this norm, the penalty seemed to stimulate norm violations: parents were late more often after the penalty was installed; by paying the penalty, parents no longer had to face the personal and social repercussions that are associated with violating a norm; they had purchased the 'right' to be late (Gneezy and Rustichini 2000).

In other words, incentives can undermine the influence of normative considerations. This risk also seems relevant when incentives are used to promote sustainable consumption, given that many of such behaviours are spurred by normative considerations. For instance, financial rewards actually reduced employees' discretionary energy conservation practices (for example, turning off their computer screens during the lunchtime break; Handgraaf et al. 2013). A related study established direct empirical support for the underlying role of normative considerations (Schwartz et al. 2013). Households were exposed to three different advertisements for energy-saving programmes, emphasizing either financial benefits ('reduce your electricity bill'), environmental benefits ('reduce your environmental impact') or both ('reduce your electricity bill and your environmental impact'). Afterwards respondents from the three groups indicated their willingness to enrol for the said energy-saving programme. Emphasizing the monetary benefits, either as the single argument used, or as an addition to environmental arguments, turned out to reduce respondents' willingness to enrol relative to the advertisement where only environmental benefits were stressed. Follow-up mediation analyses confirmed the crucial role of normative considerations in this process: by highlighting monetary benefits, the financial and combined advertisements shifted respondents' attention away from the environmental benefits of enrolling for the energy-saving programme, which seemed to be the central argument for respondents to enrol in the first place. In sum, incentives can shift people's attention away from the normative reasons for behaviour, and paradoxically discourage the very behaviour they were meant to stimulate.

Arguably, the incentive discussed above all included relatively small monetary stakes, which may explain their ineffectiveness. One could argue that such a shift in underlying motivations is not relevant as long as a sufficiently large incentive is used that is effective in changing the target behaviour. There are however some problems with this reasoning. First, given that the instalment of incentives is often a consequence of political debate and economic tides, their presence cannot be guaranteed over time. Second, and more importantly, the shift away from normative considerations may not only affect the onset of the target behaviour, but may also reduce the likelihood that consumers spontaneously engage in other, related types of sustainable consumption. When respondents for instance read about the financial benefits (less fuel costs) instead of the environmental benefits (less emissions) that were associated with carpooling, they were less likely to engage in an ostensibly unrelated sustainable behaviour: disposing of their waste paper in the recycling bin (Evans et al. 2012). Hence, by appealing to selfish motives, incentives could inhibit positive spillover effects; although they may be effective in promoting specific kinds of sustainable consumption practices, they are unlikely to simultaneously lead to increases in other types of sustainable consumption. The explanation here is that by drawing people's attention to people's self-enhancing (selfish) reasons for sustainable consumption, financial appeals fail to elicit a more general self-transcendent (pro-environmental) orientation, which is required for positive spillover to occur (Thøgersen 2013). More generally, by exclusively appealing to self-interest, financial incentives may reinforce the undesirable societal norm that acting sustainably should only be considered worthwhile or appropriate when there is sufficient financial gain in doing so (Thøgersen and Crompton 2009).

We have explained how financial incentives, by undermining shifting people's attention, may demotivate sustainable behaviours that result from normative motivations. More broadly, by changing the type of information people attend to and base their decision on, incentives may turn an otherwise ethical decision ('Is it appropriate for me to do so?') into business decision ('What's in it for me?'). In other words, incentives can change the decision frame (Tenbrunsel and Messick 1999). This process has two, closely related, implications. First, as explained above, incentives may undermine or crowd-out normative considerations. There is however a second, closely related effect that warrants mention: the instalment of incentives can direct people's attention to trade-off between the size of compensation and the effort or inconvenience required (Heyman and Ariely 2004). In other words, incentives stimulate people to engage in explicit cost–benefit analysis before engaging in sustainable actions. As a consequence, consumers will only consider changing their behaviour when the introduced incentive is considered worthwhile (Dogan et al. 2014). This effect is not problematic as long as a sufficiently large incentive can be offered in return, for instance in the case of a substantive tax break on the purchase of energy-efficient vehicles. But what happens when only a relatively small incentive can be offered in return for a rather effortful type of behaviour?

Given that most people prefer some money to no money at all, one could reason that offering a small incentive, at best, would improve motivation, or, at worst, fail to affect behaviour. As illustrated earlier, however, small incentives can in fact demotivate people. The underlying process was illustrated in a classic experiment (Heyman and Ariely 2004). Respondents were paid either 10 cents ('small incentive') or $4 ('medium incentive') or no payment (control) for participating in a highly tedious task: using the computer mouse to drag a grey circle across the computer screen as often as possible in three minutes. Not surprisingly, performance was much lower in the small- compared to the medium-incentive condition. The researchers also included a control condition in which no payment was offered at all. Interestingly, unpaid participants performed significantly better than respondents who received the small incentive. Apparently the small incentive of 10 cents was not enough to justify the effort that was associated with the mind-numbing task of dragging balls across a computer screen. Relative to offering no payment, offering a small financial incentive thus seemed to demotivate respondents.

In sum, offering financial compensation that is perceived as too small in relation to the costs may potentially do more harm than good. Given that many sustainable consumer behaviours involve seemingly small financial gains (for example, using public transport instead of one's own car, cutting the amount of showers per week, switching to vegetarian meals), but may require substantial effort and inconvenience, it is questionable whether appealing to monetary concern is the most effective strategy (Schultz 2010). This point seems especially relevant for feedback devices that reveal the exact financial consequences associated with specific energy-saving actions, such as setting the thermostat lower, or flicking off specific devices (Jain et al. 2013). Although in general, instant feedback about the consequences of one's actions may enhance learning (Kluger and DeNisi 1996), a potential risk of financial feedback specifically is that previously ignorant consumers become aware of how little financial benefit is actually to be gained by engaging in specific sustainable actions. As a consequence, financial feedback can demotivate, rather than motivate, sustainable behaviours, particularly when these behaviours are perceived as rather effortful (Dogan et al. 2014).

Thus far, we have discussed how incentives can change the decision frame of consumers. However, incentives affect not only the type of decision (business versus ethical) that consumers are making, but also the implications that consumers derive from choosing to act sustainably: they affect and interact with consumers' self-concept. The relevance of this point will become evident in the next two subsections.

### 21.2.2 Incentives Disrupt the Process of Self-Persuasion

Incentives are meant to provide consumers with an external reason to change. This is the core assumption underlying many applications of incentives; the inherent consequences of behaviour are not enough to motivate change, so external consequences need to be added (Lehman and Geller 2004). Large incentives give people a justification to adopt behaviours they otherwise would not consider. However, precisely because of this reason, large incentives may also fail to simultaneously change people's underlying attitudes, and therefore fail to change behaviour in the long run, as will become apparent below.

Let us explain this process by describing another classic experiment (Festinger and Carlsmith 1959). Students were asked to engage in a highly boring chore, which took about an hour. Afterwards they were asked to tell the next respondent (a confederate who was waiting outside) that the boring task was 'fun' and 'interesting' – an obvious lie. One group of respondents received a small incentive ($1) for telling this lie, while others received a large incentive ($20). Next, respondents indicated how enjoyable they found the task, and whether they were willing to participate in a similar task again should the opportunity arise. The group who received a large incentive was honest: they did not claim to enjoy the boring task, and would not engage in a similar task if asked to do so. In contrast, the small-incentive group claimed they found the task enjoyable, and indicated they were willing to engage in a similar task.

So what explains this group difference? According to cognitive dissonance theory, people strive for consistency between their attitudes and actions, and experience discomfort when they engage in behaviours that are not in line with their attitudes. Dissonance is stronger when behaviours are the result of one's own choice, and not caused by external influences, such as incentives. In the example above, students who were paid $20 for lying about how much fun the task was had a clear external justification: they were generously paid for doing so. Consequently, they experienced less dissonance and felt no need to change their opinion on the subject; they just indicated that the task was not enjoyable. Students who received the small incentive, however, did not have a convincing justification for lying to others about how much fun the task would be. When later asked how much fun the task really was, they dealt with the ensuing dissonance by changing their attitudes: they convinced themselves the task actually was fun.

So what is the relevance for sustainable consumption? Incentives, by offering an external justification for specific behaviour, may be effective in promoting specific types of behaviour, but at the same time prevent consumers from ascribing compliance to their own free will – they prevent consumers from engaging in self-persuasion (Aronson 1999). Consequently, incentives for sustainable consumption (for example, subsidies for solar panels, air travel taxes, 'bottle bills' or container deposit laws) run the risk of only being effective as long as they are in place. Since the underlying attitudes have not changed, behaviour may relapse to its old levels when the incentive is removed.

This effect has been documented in many instances. Consider a field experiment that tested effects of incentives on speeding (Bolderdijk et al. 2011). Changing speeding behaviour requires nothing more than simply being a bit less zealous when pushing the accelerator pedal; in other words, it involves a relatively straightforward type of behaviour, and there are no barriers that prevent motivations from translating to change. Consequently, the circumstances are met where incentives can be expected to enhance performance (Stern 1999; Ariely et al. 2009b). Results showed that a relatively large financial incentive (€50 per month) was successful in motivating sustainable consumption: drivers significantly reduced their driving speeds during the months in which they were incentivized. Specifically, drivers in the incentive group tended to decrease their speeds after the incentive was installed, while respondents in the control group did not exhibit a similar drop in speeding levels. Importantly, drivers in the incentive group pushed the accelerator pedal again after the financial incentive was removed. Apparently drivers discovered no additional benefit in reduced driving speeds during the incentivized period; the only reason keeping them from speeding was the financial reward. They did not develop different attitudes towards speeding during the four-month period, so when the initial justification for driving slower was removed, drivers relapsed to their old levels of speeding.

We have explained how incentives may only lead to short-term change, as they do not foster self-persuasion and thus not facilitate changes in underlying attitudes. However a lack of self-persuasion not only prevents long-term change, but is also another impediment preventing spillover to other domains, as we explain next.

Self-perception theory (Bem 1972) suggests that people derive their self-concept from their actions: people use their past actions as a way to construct their self-concept. Given that the self-concept determines the likelihood that people will engage in specific actions (Benabou and Tirole 2006), any change in self-concept could also affect a range of related behaviours. Indeed, when people realize that they have acted pro-environmentally in the past, they are more likely to reconstrue themselves as a person who acts pro-environmentally (as reflected in a strong environmental self-identity), which in turn promotes subsequent pro-environmental actions (Van der Werff et al. 2014b).

Research suggests that incentives may interact with this process. In an attempt to pinpoint the exact mechanism driving the 'foot-in-the-door' effect, an experiment was conducted that also illustrates one of the risks associated with incentives (Burger and Caldwell 2003). While waiting in the lab for the experimenter, respondents received an initial request by a confederate to sign a petition to battle homelessness (most respondents did). Some respondents received a financial incentive for signing, while others received no reward. Two days later, the same respondents were asked whether they were willing to spend a few weekend hours to help out at a local homelessness shelter. Respondents who were not paid for signing the petition were more likely to comply with the request to help at the homeless shelter in the weekend.

Here again the results can be explained by self-persuasion: respondents who were not paid for signing the petition underwent a change in self-perception; they were not forced to sign, and consequently saw themselves as being more altruistic. Importantly, the financial incentive for signing the petition disrupted the process of self-persuasion: respondents who were paid for signing did not see themselves as being altruistic, and were consequently less likely to comply with the request to help the homeless shelter during their weekend break.

This study also offers important insights for sustainable consumption. When consumers are exclusively motivated by financial rewards, they are less likely to attribute any ensuing behaviour to themselves. Consequently they are less likely to develop a general 'green' self-concept and to take environmental considerations into account in other situations. A recent study for instance found that when people's attention was directed to the environmental benefits of their prior pro-environmental actions, their environmental self-identity was strengthened, making it more likely that they engaged in subsequent pro-environmental actions. Yet, when attention was directed to the financial benefits of their previous pro-environmental actions, no changes in the environmental self-identity were observed, and no positive spillover took place (Van der Werff and Steg forthcoming). Hence a lack of self-persuasion may be another process explaining why incentives may fail to bring about the aforementioned positive spillover effects that are considered crucial to the success of environmental campaigning (Thøgersen and Crompton 2009).

In sum, by reviewing how incentives affect consumers' self-concept, we identified another cognitive side effect that is associated with the introduction of financial incentives: incentives may disrupt the process of self-persuasion. So while perhaps being effective in temporarily affecting the target behaviour, incentivized action does not simultaneously change consumers' underlying attitudes and self-concepts. As such, incentives only affect behaviour as long as the incentive is in place, and may prevent the spontaneous onset of other sustainable consumption behaviours.

### 21.2.3 Incentives Taint the Signal Ensuing from Sustainable Actions

As argued before, there are many reasons why consumers may want to act sustainably, reasons that go beyond the motive of simply wanting to save money. Incentives may shift people's attention away from these motives. Incentives may also directly negate the influence of such non-economic motives. Specifically, some consumers may be motivated to act or purchase sustainably out of image concerns (Ariely et al. 2009a). These consumers want to appear 'green' in the eyes of others or to themselves (Griskevicius et al. 2010; Dunning 2007).

Consumers may thus act sustainably in order to signal their green intentions to themselves or others. However, one's actions will be particularly diagnostic of true pro-environmental intentions when they come at some expense, for example effort or financial costs (Van der Werff et al. 2014a). After all, if there is no personal cost involved, the same behaviour may as well be perceived to be spurred by selfish concerns. One can for instance hardly claim to be a true environmentalist if a government programme paid for the solar panels on one's roof. So while incentives may boost demand for sustainable products by making certain sustainable products cheaper, they may simultaneously demotivate consumers who are interested in demonstrating their green intentions to themselves and others. As a consequence, lowering prices for green products (a common and potentially effective way to stimulate demand) may paradoxically demotivate a subset of consumers who are motivated to purchase green products out of reputational concerns (Griskevicius et al. 2010).

There is another, related risk in the reliance on self-interest as a motive to spur green consumption. As exemplified by the labels 'miser', 'cheapskate' and 'scrooge', being exclusively preoccupied with obtaining money can be considered socially inappropriate. In fact, the relentless pursuit of money can also signal a disregard for others' needs, and thereby carry the risk of social exclusion. People who demanded monetary compensation for pro-social behaviour (donating blood, for instance) were perceived as being morally unworthy (Kretzmann 1992). Thus, although people desire to obtain money for themselves, they may also want to avoid acting in a way that makes them look asocial, as callous and uncaring for others (Dunn et al. 2010). These image concerns can have important implications for consumption decisions. The fear of appearing 'cheap' may for instance explain why people sometimes shy away from publicly engaging in actions that lead to very small financial gains, such as redeeming coupons (Ashworth et al. 2005). The same fear of appearing greedy may lead consumers to forego desirable products that can be obtained at very low prices (Gneezy et al. 2012). Taken to the extreme, positioning sustainable consumption as purely an economical choice carries the risk of shunning consumers who fear being seen as exclusively occupied with monetary gain.

The relevance of image concerns for pro-environmental persuasion was examined in a recent study (Bolderdijk et al. 2012). The researchers designed and posted three different sandwich board signs at a local US petrol station, each advocating tyre pressure checks by either referring to the economic (reduced fuel costs), environmental (reduced emissions) or safety (better grip) benefits of proper tyre pressure. Additionally, a control appeal was included, which merely reminded people to get a tyre check without offering a specific rationale. Compliance was measured by counting the amount of free tyre check coupons that were taken per type of appeal.

A pilot study showed that the economic message was deemed most persuasive by respondents. However, economic pleas may not be very motivating to consumers who are driven by image motives: consumers who are motivated to see themselves as green, or those worried about appearing cheap. Indeed results revealed that the economic tyre-check message was the least effective of all: while the other three signs (including the control sign) elicited some level of compliance, not a single coupon was taken while the economic sandwich board was posted. Additional studies suggest that respondents preferred the environmental over the economic appeal, as the former made them feel better about themselves. Importantly, this preference was more pronounced when respondents' self-concept was activated, thus alluding to the role of image concerns in consumers' responses to persuasive appeals: their self-concept defines the range of behaviours that people can afford (Mazar et al. 2008).

In sum, incentives can affect the self-signal that is associated with the decision to act sustainably. A decision that otherwise would have been diagnostic for a pro-environmental orientation may be perceived as a self-interested choice if compliance is explicitly linked to some specific financial benefit. Moreover, by making products cheaper, incentives could unwittingly also undermine another source of motivation for some consumers: image concerns. Additionally there is the risk that financial incentives can demotivate those consumers who are motivated to appear green, as well as consumers who are worried about appearing cheap in the eyes of others.

## 21.3 RISKS OF EMPLOYING FINANCIAL INCENTIVES AND POTENTIAL REMEDIES

By reviewing some of the cognitive effects that may ensue from the implementation of incentives, we have identified several risks that are associated with financial incentives as: incentives may sometimes be ineffective or even counterproductive, only have a temporary effect, or fail to foster related types of sustainable consumption. So how can each specific risk be remedied? In the remainder of this chapter, we offer some guidelines that may help policy makers in mitigating the specific risks that are lurking when applying financial incentives to promote sustainable consumption. While doing so, we identify avenues for further research.

### 21.3.1 Adding Incentives May Not Improve Target Behaviour

We previously discussed the risk of small incentives: incentives may create a business mindset in consumers, in which a cost–benefit analysis precedes compliance. Consequently, small incentives may be ineffective or even counterproductive when used to stimulate behaviours that require some effort. Additionally, consumers who fear coming across as 'cheap' may not want to be associated with very small monetary gains. But how do we reconcile this pattern with the fact that small incentives are sometimes effective in promoting sustainable consumption practices? A minor charge for single-use carrier bags has, for instance, recently been found to reduce demand (Poortinga et al. 2013).

One obvious possibility is that some types of behaviour (for example, bringing one's own shopping bag to the shops rather than using plastic bags) require very little effort, and thus even a small incentive may perceived to outweigh the cost. Indeed research on mindless decision making suggest that any type of motivation may be sufficient to spur behaviours that involve no or very little inconvenience (Langer et al. 1978). The idea here is that as long as the stakes are very low, people tend to economize on conscious thinking and rely on automatic processes instead. Consequently any kind of argument, no matter how trivial, can be sufficient to automatically trigger behaviour change. Indeed, when sustainable behaviour is relatively convenient and requires little effort (for example, turning an idling car engine off while waiting), even very small amounts of money may boost behaviour change (Dogan et al. 2014).

One implication of this reasoning therefore is that incentives, particularly when they are relatively small, should be introduced in concert with other measures that reduce the costs of compliance. This conclusion resonates with earlier studies in which researchers concluded that offering an incentive for energy efficiency by itself is not sufficient to motivate people. Rather, financial incentives are particularly effective when they are combined with marketing efforts (to draw attention to the presence of the incentive) and facilitation efforts (to help people translate their intentions to save energy to relevant actions; Stern 1999). So while incentives (provided that they are large enough to justify the effort required) may trigger motivation, motivation in itself is not always enough to trigger change. Rather, in this situation it is important to consider other factors, such as barriers that may prevent people's motivation translating to behaviour (Geller 2002).

So even small incentives may be effective if the costs of the promoted behaviour are low enough. This explanation can however not account for the fact that small incentives can also spur more difficult types of behaviour, such as the relatively burdensome behaviour of recycling. Recycling may require collecting and returning empty plastic bottles to the supermarket, rather than the much more convenient option of throwing them in the bin (Levitt and Leventhal 1986). A business frame would thus lead consumers to conclude that the benefit does not reciprocate the effort. Still, many consumers do recycle bottles. Why? One option (see Thøgersen 2003, for a discussion of additional accounts) is that these consumers are acutely aware of, and personally subscribe to, the underlying goal of the incentive: reducing waste. It seems that many consumers are personally convinced that plastic waste should be minimized. For these consumers, the introduction of an incentive may not induce a business frame; the decision about whether or not to recycle remains an ethical decision. If true, one could wonder, what is the added benefit of adding an incentive in the first place? Would these consumers not recycle anyway? Although speculative, one could reason that such incentives operate as a reminder for consumers to act on their pre-existing attitudes. Future research is needed, however, to study whether, and under which conditions, this process can be empirically validated.

### 21.3.2 Incentives May Only Affect Behaviour Temporarily

The possibility that consumers may adopt a business frame, and fail to engage in self-persuasion, may prevent them from maintaining their changed behaviour after the incentive is removed. So does this mean that the benign effects of incentives always cease after they are removed? Not necessarily so. First, while some behaviours require repeated action (for example, reducing showering time; also known as 'curtailment' behaviours), other behaviours require only a single action (for example, insulating one's home; 'efficiency' behaviours; Gardner and Stern 2002). So if a financial incentive can bring consumers to adopt one single action with lasting impact (for example, purchasing a more fuel-efficient vehicle), the incentive will have had a lasting sustainable effect (whenever the car is used, lower fuel emissions result). Second, incentives may have an impact after they have been removed if they succeeded in changing underlying attitudes, for example if the relevant behaviour turns out to have benefits that were not recognized beforehand. Car drivers, for instance, kept on using public transport after being forced to use it temporarily due to road works (Fujii and Gärling 2005) or after being lured to try public transport during a free trial period (Thøgersen 2009); consumers discovered that travelling by bus was more pleasant than they had anticipated in advance (their attitudes shifted), and they kept on doing so after the initial reason for this had disappeared.

### 21.3.3 Incentives May Not Affect Broader Types of Sustainable Consumption

Incentives can be effective in promoting some specific sustainable action, but may not result in positive spillovers if consumers are not personally convinced that acting sustainably is the right thing to do. We discussed the relevant study by Burger and Caldwell (2003) earlier: when respondents were paid for signing the petition, they were unlikely to ascribe their support to themselves (they did not engage in self-persuasion), and were therefore unlikely to agree to a related, bigger request: helping at the homelessness centre during the weekend break.

So incentives may disrupt the process of self-persuasion. This is not however the only relevant insight from this study. In an attempt to undermine the disrupting effect of incentives, some paid respondents in the study received praise after signing the petition (they were informed that they were 'helpful'), while others did not receive such praise. Despite having being offered a financial incentive, respondents receiving praise underwent a change in their self-concept (they saw themselves as being more altruistic), and consequently did exhibit a positive spillover effect: these respondents were more likely to say yes to the request to help at the homeless shelter over the weekend.

This insight seems relevant for sustainable consumption as well. We know that incentives may disrupt positive spillover in the environmental domain (Evans et al. 2012), but apparently this need not always be the case; it likely depends on how the initial action is perceived by the consumer. Indeed, some studies suggest that relabeling the same neutral action as 'green' can affect consumers' environmentally conscious self-concept, and encourage related pro-environmental actions on subsequent occasions (Cornelissen et al. 2008). Future research should therefore examine the possibility that incentives can sometimes lead to positive spillover, provided that initial compliance is relabelled as a 'green' action.

## 21.4 CONCLUSION

According to the instrumental perspective on money, incentives are effective in motivating consumers insofar as they allow consumers to purchase more of the services and products they desire. Consequently, incentives (particularly large ones) can be an effective and required tool to promote sustainable consumer behaviour. However they should not be considered as the only tool, given the fact that they have some important limitations. Specifically, incentives do something to people: they have some important cognitive side effects that are not always known or considered by policy makers. Specifically, their instalment may lead consumers to adopt a business frame, disrupt the process of self-persuasion, or taint the self-signal ensuing from the decision to act sustainably. This means that incentives can sometimes paradoxically discourage the very behaviour they are meant to encourage. Even when incentives are effective in promoting the target behaviour, they can still do more harm than good when they only affect behaviour temporarily, or simultaneously demotivate consumers to engage in other, more pertinent forms of sustainable actions that are not financially attractive.

By alerting policy makers to the risks associated with financial incentives, as well directing them to potential remedies (for example, considering the size of the incentive, introducing incentives in concert with supporting policies, explicitly linking advertised actions to environmental benefits), we hope that this chapter leads to a more efficient deployment of incentives. We also hope that this chapter triggers policy makers to more quickly consider alternatives where incentives are less appropriate; in situations where the potential risks associated with the implementation of incentives outweigh their intended benefits.

## NOTE

1. We use this definition for for the sake of simplicity. Note that the word 'incentive' may signify different concepts depending on context or discipline; see for example Bolderdijk et al. (2012).

## REFERENCES

Ariely, D., A. Bracha and S. Meier (2009a), 'Doing good or doing well? Image motivation and monetary incentives in behaving prosocially', *American Economic Review*, 99 (1), 544–555.

Ariely, D., U. Gneezy, G. Loewenstein and N. Mazar (2009b), 'Large stakes and big mistakes', *Review of Economic Studies*, 76 (2), 451–469.

Aronson, E. (1999), 'The power of self-persuasion', *American Psychologist*, 54 (11), 875–884.

Ashworth, L., P.R. Darke, and M. Schaller (2005), 'No one wants to look cheap: trade-offs between social

disincentives and the economic and psychological incentives to redeem coupons', *Journal of Consumer Psychology*, 15 (4), 295–306.
Bem, D.J. (1972), 'Self-perception theory', in L. Berkowitz (ed.), *Advances in Experimental Social Psychology*, New York: Academic Press, pp. 1–62.
Benabou, R. and J. Tirole (2006), 'Incentives and prosocial behavior', *American Economic Review*, 96 (5), 1652–1678.
Bolderdijk, J.W., J. Knockaert, E.M. Steg and E.T. Verhoef (2011), 'Effects of pay-as-you-drive vehicle insurance on young drivers' speed choice: results of a Dutch field experiment', *Accident Analysis and Prevention*, 43 (3), 1181–1186.
Bolderdijk, J.W., P.K. Lehman and E.S. Geller (2012), 'Encouraging pro-environmental behaviour with rewards and penalties', in L. Steg, A.E. van den Berg and J.I.M. de Groot (eds), *Environmental Psychology. An Introduction*, Oxford: John Wiley & Sons, pp. 233–242.
Bolderdijk, J.W., L. Steg, E.S. Geller, P.K. Lehman and T. Postmes (2013), 'Comparing the effectiveness of monetary versus moral motives in environmental campaigning', *Nature Climate Change*, 3, 413–416.
Burger, J.M. and D.F. Caldwell (2003), 'The effects of monetary incentives and labeling on the foot-in-the-door effect: evidence for a self-perception process', *Basic and Applied Social Psychology*, 25 (3), 235–241.
Cornelissen, G., M. Pandelaere, L. Warlop and S. Dewitte (2008), 'Positive cueing: promoting sustainable consumer behavior by cueing common environmental behaviors as environmental', *International Journal of Research in Marketing*, 25 (1), 46–55.
Dietz, T., G.T. Gardner, J. Gilligan, P.C. Stern and M.P. Vandenbergh (2009), 'Household actions can provide a behavioral wedge to rapidly reduce US carbon emissions', *PNAS Proceedings of the National Academy of Sciences of the United States of America*, 106 (44), 18452–18456.
Dogan, E.B., J.W. Bolderdijk and L. Steg (2014), 'Making small numbers count: financial and environmental feedback in eco-driving', *Journal of Consumer Policy*, 37, 413–422.
Dunn, E.W., C.E. Ashton-James, M.D. Hanson and L.B. Aknin (2010), 'On the costs of self-interested economic behavior: how does stinginess get under the skin?', *Journal of Health Psychology*, 15 (4), 627–633.
Dunning, D. (2007), 'Self-image motives and consumer behavior: how sacrosanct self-beliefs sway preferences in the market place', *Journal of Consumer Psychology*, 17 (4), 237–249.
Evans, L., G.R. Maio, A. Corner, C.J. Hodgetts, S. Ahmed and U. Hahn (2012), 'Self-interest and pro-environmental behaviour', *Nature Climate Change*, 3, 122–125.
Festinger, L. and J.M. Carlsmith (1959), 'Cognitive consequences of forced compliance', *Journal of Abnormal and Social Psychology*, 58 (2), 203–210.
Frey, B.S. and F. Oberholzer-Gee (1997), 'The cost of price incentives: an empirical analysis of motivation crowding-out', *American Economic Review*, 87 (4), 746–755.
Fujii, S. and T. Gärling (2005), 'Temporary structural change: a strategy to break car-use habit and promote public transport', in G. Underwood (ed.), *Traffic and Transport Psychology*, Amsterdam, the Netherlands and London, UK: Elsevier, pp. 585–592.
Gardner, G. and P. Stern (2002), *Environmental Problems and Human Behavior*, Boston, MA: Pearson Custom Publishing.
Geller, E.S. (2002), 'The challenge of increasing proenvironmental behavior', in A. Churchman (ed.), *Handbook of Environmental Psychology*, New York: John Wiley & Sons, pp. 541–553.
Gneezy, A., U. Gneezy, G. Riener and L.D. Nelson (2012), 'Pay-what-you-want, identity, and self-signaling in markets', *Proceedings of the National Academy of Sciences*, 109 (19), 7236–7240.
Gneezy, U., S. Meier and P. Rey-Biel (2011), 'When and why incentives (don't) work to modify behavior', *Journal of Economic Perspectives*, 25 (4), 191–210.
Gneezy, U. and A. Rustichini (2000), 'A fine is a price', *Journal of Legal Studies*, 29 (1), 1–18.
Griskevicius, V., J.M. Tybur and B. Van den Bergh (2010), 'Going green to be seen: status, reputation, and conspicuous conservation', *Journal of Personality and Social Psychology*, 98 (3), 392–404.
Hammond, G.P. (2006), 'People, planet and prosperity: the determinants of humanity's environmental footprint', *Natural Resources Forum*, 30 (1), 27–36.
Handgraaf, M.J.J., M.A. Van Lidth de Jeude and K.C. Appelt (2013), 'Public praise vs. private pay: effects of rewards on energy conservation in the workplace', *Ecological Economics*, 86, 86–92.
Heberlein, T. and G.K. Warriner (1983), 'The influence of price and attitude on shifting residential electricity consumption from on- to off-peak periods', *Journal of Economic Psychology*, 4 (1), 107–130.
Heyman, J. and D. Ariely (2004), 'Effort for payment: a tale of two markets', *Psychological Science*, 15 (11), 787–793.
Hoekstra, A.Y. (2013), *The Water Footprint of Modern Consumer Society*, London: Routledge.
Jain, R.K., J.E. Taylor and P.J. Culligan (2013), 'Investigating the impact eco-feedback information representation has on building occupant energy consumption behavior and savings', *Energy and Buildings*, 64, 408–414.

Kluger, A.N. and A. DeNisi (1996), 'Effects of feedback intervention on performance: a historical review, a meta-analysis, and a preliminary feedback intervention theory', *Psychological Bulletin*, 119 (2), 254–284.
Kretzmann, M.J. (1992), 'Bad blood: The moral stigmatization of paid plasma donors', *Journal of Contemporary Ethnography*, 20 (4), 416–441.
Langer, E.J., A. Blank and B. Chanowitz (1978), 'The mindlessness of ostensibly thoughtful action: the role of "placebic" information in interpersonal interaction', *Journal of Personality and Social Psychology*, 36 (6), 635–642.
Lea, S.E.G. and P. Webley (2006), 'Money as tool, money as drug: the biological psychology of a strong incentive', *Behavioral and Brain Sciences*, 29 (2), 161–209.
Lehman, P.K. and E.S. Geller (2004), 'Behavior analysis and environmental protection: accomplishments and potential for more', *Behavior and Social Issues*, 13 (1), 13–32.
Levitt, L. and G. Leventhal (1986), 'Litter reduction: how effective is the New York state bottle bill?', *Environment and Behavior*, 18 (4), 467–479.
Lindenberg, S. and L. Steg (2007), 'Normative, gain and hedonic goal frames guiding environmental behavior', *Journal of Social Issues*, 63 (1), 117–137.
Mazar, N., O. Amir and D. Ariely (2008), 'The dishonesty of honest people: a theory of self-concept maintenance', *Journal of Marketing Research (JMR)*, 45 (6), 633–644.
Miller, D.T. (1999), 'The norm of self-interest', *American Psychologist*, 54 (12), 1053–1060.
Mulder, L.B., E. van Dijk, D. De Cremer and H.A.M. Wilke (2006), 'Undermining trust and cooperation: the paradox of sanctioning systems in social dilemmas', *Journal of Experimental Social Psychology*, 42 (2), 147–162.
Pelletier, L.G., K.M. Tuson, I. Green-Demers, K. Noels and A.M. Beaton (1998), 'Why are you doing things for the environment? The motivation toward the environment scale (MTES)', *Journal of Applied Social Psychology*, 28 (5), 437–468.
Penn, D.J. (2003), 'The evolutionary roots of our environmental problems: towards a Darwinian ecology', *Quarterly Review of Biology*, 78 (3), 275–301.
Poortinga, W., L. Whitmarsh and C. Suffolk (2013), 'The introduction of a single-use carrier bag charge in Wales: attitude change and behavioural spillover effects', *Journal of Environmental Psychology*, 36, 240–247.
Schultz, P.W. (2010), 'Making energy conservation the norm', in K. Ehrhart-Martinez and J. Laitner (eds), *People-Centered Initiatives for Increasing Energy Savings*, Washington, DC: American Council for an Energy-Efficient Economy, pp. 251–262.
Schwartz, D., W. Bruine de Bruin, B. Fischhoff and L. Lave (2013), 'Advertising energy saving programs: the potential environmental cost of emphasizing monetary savings', paper presented at the Preconference EACR 'Moral Dynamics and Socially Responsible Consumer Behavior', Barcelona, 3 July.
Stern, P.C. (1999), 'Information, incentives, and proenvironmental consumer behavior', *Journal of Consumer Policy*, 22, 461–478.
Tenbrunsel, A. and D. Messick (1999), 'Sanctioning systems, decision frames, and cooperation', *Administrative Science Quarterly*, 44 (4), 684–707.
Thaler, R.H. (2000), 'From homo economicus to homo sapiens', *Journal of Economic Perspectives*, 14 (1), 133–141.
Thøgersen, J. (2003), 'Monetary incentives and recycling: behavioral and psychological reactions to a performance-dependent garbage fee', *Journal of Consumer Policy*, 26, 197–228.
Thøgersen, J. (2006), 'Norms for environmentally responsible behaviour: an extended taxonomy', *Journal of Environmental Psychology*, 26 (4), 247–261.
Thøgersen, J. (2009), 'Promoting public transport as a subscription service: effects of a free month travel card', *Transport Policy*, 16, 335–343.
Thøgersen, J. (2013), 'Psychology: inducing green behavior', *Nature Climate Change*, 3, 100–101.
Thøgersen, J. and T. Crompton (2009), 'Simple and painless? The limitations of spillover in environmental campaigning', *Journal of Consumer Policy*, 32, 141–163.
Van der Werff, E. and L. Steg (forthcoming), 'Pro-environmental behaviour should not pay off'.
Van der Werff, E., L. Steg and K. Keizer (2014a), 'Follow the signal: when past pro-environmental actions signal who you are', *Journal of Environmental Psychology*, 40, 273–282.
Van der Werff, E., L. Steg and K. Keizer (2014b), 'I am who I am, by looking past the present: the influence of biospheric values and past behavior on environmental self-identity', *Environment and Behavior*, 46, 626–657.
Vohs, K.D., N.L. Mead and M.R. Goode (2006), 'The psychological consequences of money', *Science*, 314 (5802), 1154–1156.

# 22. Voluntary standards as enablers and impediments to sustainable consumption

*Andreas Rasche*

Voluntary standards for corporate sustainability and responsibility have proliferated over the last two decades. Examples of such standards include ISO 14001, the United Nations Global Compact, the Global Reporting Initiative and the Forest Stewardship Council. Although these standards differ significantly in terms of how they function and what they aim to achieve – ranging from broad principles to stipulate organizational learning around responsible business (Rasche 2012) to initiatives which certify and label organizations, products and services (Berliner and Prakash 2013) – they jointly reflect what Waddock (2008) calls a 'new institutional infrastructure' for corporate sustainability and responsibility. Such standards have been subject of intense scholarly debate. Research has explored how selected initiatives are produced (Tamm Hallström 2008), in what ways standards can achieve legitimacy (Bernstein and Cashore 2007), what impact standard adoption has on social and environmental problems (Bartley 2007; Potoski and Prakash 2005), what factors determine standard diffusion (Delmas 2002) and whether adopters walk their talk when signing up to initiatives (Behnam and Maclean 2011).

This chapter examines in what ways standards enable and impede sustainable consumption. Standards enable sustainable consumption in at least three different ways. First, standards can inform consumers about the social and environmental conditions under which products and services are created, because some initiatives form the basis of labelling schemes (for example, seafood eco-labels as such as the Marine Stewardship Council). Second, several standards support the disclosure of relevant information through sustainability reports (for example, the Global Reporting Initiative). Although it is unlikely that individual consumers look at these reports, the disclosed information influences whether a firm is perceived as a responsible actor in society. Research shows that consumers become more loyal if firms are broadly perceived to have a distinguishable profile in terms of their social and environmental performance (Bhattacharya and Sen 2004). Hence reporting standards can facilitate positive word-of-mouth recommendations and enhance consumers' overall identification with an organization. Third, standards can help to further institutionalize the discourse around sustainable consumption. Some initiatives, such as ISO 26000, aim at creating a common understanding of key terms and organizational practices related to sustainable consumption. Such standardization can help to ensure a broader uptake of practices (for example, the use of labelling schemes), also showing the relevance and potential impact of these practices to other actors (for example, consumer protection agencies).

However, standards can also impede sustainable consumption. First, the coexistence of a variety of competing standards in some sectors (for example, fair trade coffee) is likely to confuse consumers, who are unable to distinguish the specific characteristics of different initiatives. Second, consumers may question the credibility of standards and their associated labels, since highly public scandals have revealed the limits of auditing and monitoring practices (for example, in the context of the Bangladesh factory collapse in 2013). Finally, while many standards are designed as multi-stakeholder initiatives, only a few of them directly involve consumer representatives. This lack of inclusiveness can impede the further institutionalization and acceptance of sustainable consumption, as some practices may be defined for consumers, but not with them.

The discussion in this chapter is focused on voluntary standards that cannot be directly enforced through legal action. While my analysis distinguishes between voluntary standards and mandatory legal instruments, it is clear that many rules that impact upon sustainable consumption are also fixed through laws (Thøgersen 2005). For instance emission levels for cars and insulation standards for houses are legally set rules that are often understood as standards. Limiting my analysis to voluntary initiatives does not imply that I neglect their potential effects on legislation. Regulators can endorse certain standards (for example, through recommendations) and also integrate them into binding legal frameworks. Standards are just one policy solution within the broader regulatory spectrum that underlies sustainable consumption.

This chapter is structured as follows. The analysis starts by theoretically reflecting on the notion of standards, discussing different characteristics of this mode of regulation. Section 22.2 introduces different types of standards for corporate sustainability and responsibility, showing that while much of the debate is focused on certification schemes, relevant standards have also emerged in other contexts. The next section (22.3) discusses how different types of standards act as enablers of sustainable consumption, emphasizing that there is a need to distinguish between standards' direct impacts on purchasing behaviour (for example, via labels) and more indirect impacts (for example, on how consumers identify with a company). Section 22.4 complements this analysis by discussing how standards can potentially impede sustainable consumption. The concluding section contains a summary of the key arguments.

## 22.1 STANDARDS: WHAT'S IN A NAME?

The term 'standard' has been used in numerous ways (Timmermans and Epstein 2010), mostly because standards occur in different social contexts, ranging from technical interface standards to standards for corporate sustainability and responsibility. I here adopt the definition by Brunsson et al. (2012, p.616) and define a standard as 'a rule for common and voluntary use, decided by one or several people or organizations'. This definition highlights several important characteristics. First, standards are voluntary consensus instruments to regulate behaviour. They do not rest on the hierarchical authority of a state, although states can recommend and encourage the adoption of standards. The regulative authority of standards is mostly based on their perceived legitimacy and coercive pressure by third parties (for example, when certain buyers only cooperate with certified suppliers; Guler et al. 2002). This makes standards different from laws. Even though the content of a standard can move into law, they are not the same. While laws are binding for all actors and are enforced through legal sanctions, standards are voluntarily adopted and rest on non-legal sanctions (for example, revoking a certification).

Second, standards rest on specific type of rules: that is, rules that are explicitly available and are deliberately decided by certain people or organizations. This makes standards different from social norms, which have a more implicit character and are the result of socialization processes (Brunsson and Jacobsson 2000). We learn to accept social norms over time through our interactions with others, while we deliberately decide upon the content of standards. Emphasizing the deliberate nature of standard production implies that so-called de facto standards are excluded from this theoretical treatment. De facto standards emerge if a large number of actors adopt the same solution which subsequently serves as a commonly agreed-upon model (for example, the QWERTY layout for typewriters; David 1985). Since it is hard to deviate from these solutions, they are perceived as de facto standards.

Finally, the above-mentioned definition highlights that the rules of standards are designed for common use. Standards define rules that are supposed to be relevant for not just one but many social actors. Timmermans and Epstein (2010, p. 71) observe in this context that standardization is a 'process of constructing uniformities across time and space, through the generation of agreed upon rules. The standards thereby created tend to span more than one community of practice or activity site'. This makes standards an attractive mode of regulation under conditions of globalization. Since states often fail to agree on binding rules to govern transnational economic activities, regulation increasingly relies upon standards. These standards have a substantial reach, both in terms of geographic scope but also in terms of the number of potential adopters, as their underlying rules can be applied in separate and diverse local contexts (Scherer and Palazzo 2011).

The literature distinguishes four types of standards (Timmermans and Epstein 2010). First, design standards specify certain features of products, services or tools. Most technical standards fall into this category, as they define components of technical systems and specify how these components are supposed to interact (Garud and Kumaraswamy 1993). For instance a widely used technical standard is the HyperText Markup Language (HTML) which influences how content is displayed on websites. Second, terminological standards are concerned 'with terms, usually accompanied by definitions, and sometimes explanatory notes, illustrations, examples, etc.' (ISO and IEC 1996). The main task of such standards is to ensure that there is a certain stability of meaning to essential terms across different contexts. For instance, the International Classification of Diseases (ICD) is used by health care organizations to support the use of common terms within medical billing.

Third, performance standards define outcome specifications that adopters have to fulfil (for example, maximum pollution levels). One precondition of using such standards is that outcomes can be clearly identified and measured (Werner and Katz 1976). For instance the International Finance Corporation (IFC) has defined a variety of performance standards related to environmental and social risks that clients have to follow (for example, with regard to labour and working conditions). Finally, process standards delineate the characteristics of processes (for example, quality management) without specifying any particular outcomes. For instance, the quality management standard ISO 9001 focuses on the processes that are necessary for creating products and services that meet consumer expectations. The impact of process standards remains contested in some areas, because the mere existence of certain processes does not necessarily bring about the desired results (Christmann and Taylor 2006). These four categories provide useful analytical distinctions, although many standards combine elements of these four categories.

It is necessary to distinguish standards from labels. Labelling refers to 'any words, particulars, trade marks, brand names, pictorial matter or symbols on any packaging, document, notice, label, board or collar accompanying or referring to a product' (European Council 1991, p. 6). While all labels refer to a certain set of standardized rules, which provide the grounds upon which the label is awarded, not all standards reflect labels. Labels are only used if a standardizer wants to communicate to a broader audience that adopters are in compliance with the rules of the standard. In most cases, certification mechanisms (for example, third-party audits) are used to verify whether a certain product can carry a label. Labels have a signalling function, providing consumers with information about certain product features or distinguishable characteristics of production methods. Some labels refer to production methods that leave an identifiable trace in the product (for example, cotton grown without pesticides), while other labels refer to methods that do not leave such traces (for example, toys produced by using clean energy; see Fliess et al. 2007).

## 22.2 STANDARDS FOR CORPORATE SUSTAINABILITY AND RESPONSIBILITY

### 22.2.1 Types of Standards

We can define standards for corporate sustainability and responsibility as 'voluntary predefined rules, procedures and methods to systematically assess, measure, audit and/or communicate the social and environmental behaviour and/or performance of firms' (Gilbert et al. 2011, p. 24). Often these standards are characterized as soft law, emphasizing the nonlegal nature of the underlying regulations as well as the involvement of non-state actors in the creation and enforcement of rules (Abbott et al. 2000). Four categories of standards for corporate sustainability and responsibility can be distinguished (Rasche 2010).

First, some standards reflect broadly defined principles; for example the Principles for Responsible Investment, the Equator Principles, the Organisation for Economic Co-operation and Development (OECD) Guidelines for Multinational Corporations, the Caux Round Table Principles and the United Nations (UN) Global Compact. The principles that underlie these initiatives serve as a starting point for dialogue, learning and the exchange of best practices. Principle-based standards define (often vague) outcome expectations and in some cases also give guidance on implementation processes. Such initiatives usually reflect a combination of performance and process standards. The UN Global Compact, for instance, rests on ten universal principles (for example, that firms should work against corruption) and defines best practices outlining how businesses should realize these outcomes (Rasche 2009). Principle-based standards do not reflect compliance mechanisms that can be used to assess firms' behaviour, although in some cases soft compliance mechanisms exist (for example, the delisting of participants; Knudsen 2011). Critics have pointed to the potential misuse of such standards by arguing that corporations can exploit them for public relations purposes (Baccaro and Mele 2011).

Second, certification standards aim at monitoring production facilities against predefined criteria. Examples of such standards include: the Forest Stewardship Council (FSC), Fairtrade, UTZ Certified, the Marine Stewardship Council (MSC), Social Accountability (SA) 8000 and the Fair Labor Association (FLA). There are considerable differences between these initiatives. Some certification standards are used as product labels for the end consumer (for example, FSC-certified paper), while other initiatives cannot be used in this way (for example, SA 8000 certifies supply factories but is not a label for end consumers). Certification standards also differ with regard to what is being certified. Some standards certify processes and management systems (for example, ISO 14001), while other standards put more emphasis on outcome-based compliance benchmarks (for example, WindMade), and yet other standards base certifications on a combination of process and outcome measures (for example, the FLA Workplace Code of Conduct covers outcome-based compliance benchmarks and process-based criteria for management systems). Certification standards have emerged in a variety of sectors (for example, coffee, apparel, forestry, palm oil, cut flowers, footwear), creating a market for sustainable goods in some cases (Reinecke et al. 2012).

Third, reporting standards have emerged to harmonize non-financial reporting practices among corporations. In the 1990s, more and more corporations started to disclose information on their social and environmental performance, resulting in a wide variety of reports. Firms' reports differed substantially in terms of: (1) the covered issues (and the metrics that were used to disclose information on these issues); and (2) the underlying reporting principles (for example, in terms of defining the scope of reporting). Standards such as the Global Reporting Initiative (GRI) or the Carbon Disclosure Project were developed to harmonize non-financial reporting across regions and sectors (Fortanier et al. 2011). Although such standards define common metrics to measure a firm's sustainability performance, they do not pass judgement on this performance. For instance, the GRI guidelines define a variety of standard disclosures in different areas, but the standard does not benchmark performance vis-à-vis these disclosures. Competition among different reporting standards is limited, as the GRI is widely recognized as the de facto global standard for disclosing non-financial information (Etzion and Ferraro 2010) and also acts as a reference point for other reporting frameworks. For instance, the German Sustainability Code is based on key performance indictors defined by the GRI (Rat für Nachhaltige Entwicklung 2012).

Finally, process standards define how certain management processes and practices, which are related to corporate sustainability and responsibility, should look (for example, processes for stakeholder engagement). Unlike some certification standards with a focus on processes, these standards do not certify compliance. Process standards help adopters to create an organizational framework around corporate sustainability and responsibility by outlining best practices in selected areas and by providing general guidance and definitions (Göbbels and Jonker 2003). For instance the AccountAbility 1000 Stakeholder Engagement Standard (AA1000SES) outlines processes related to the design, implementation, assessment and communication of stakeholder engagement (for example, how to map stakeholders and integrate them into governance). ISO 26000 also supports the standardization of intra-organizational processes (for example, how to communicate on relevant topics), although the standard is not positioned as a certifiable management systems standard. ISO 26000 provides broader guidance on social responsibility (for example, by defining core subject areas; see Helms et al. 2012), including, but not limited to, promoting a common understanding of how to design organizational practices.

The four categories overlap and it is often difficult to find standards that exclusively fit into one category. For instance, most certification standards also contain elements of process standards (for example, SA 8000's focus on management systems; see Gilbert and Rasche 2007), while some principle-based initiatives have adopted separate reporting guidelines (for example, the UN Global Compact's Communication on Progress policy; see Rasche 2009).

### 22.2.2 Actors Driving Standardization

Standards for corporate sustainability and responsibility are often defined by actor collectives and thus differ from firm-level codes of conduct (for example, when a buyer defines a code to be used by its suppliers). Standards in the four categories are different in terms of how the respective actor collectives are composed, making it necessary to distinguish between standards designed by a single group of stakeholders and multi-stakeholder initiatives.

Some standards are exclusively driven by businesses (for example, the chemical industry's Responsible Care initiative), while other standards are driven entirely by actors from civil society; for example, the non-governmental organization (NGO) corporate social responsibility (CSR) Frame of Reference. Governments have also been the exclusive drivers of some initiatives (for example, the OECD Guidelines for Multinational Enterprises). Standards produced by governments are voluntary and hence reflect recommendations and exemplary models for business practice rather than legally binding rules. However certain elements of standards may be consistent with laws (for example, as emphasized in the OECD Guidelines for Multinational Enterprises; OECD 2011, p. 9), and governments can also encourage businesses to adopt the standards developed by non-state actors (for example, the Act amending the Danish Financial Statements Act in 2008 encourages firms to use the GRI standard for reporting).

Standards that are drawn up by a single stakeholder group often lack legitimacy, as the inclusion of those affected by an issue into standard production is seen as a precondition for creating legitimate rules (Mena and Palazzo 2012). Multi-stakeholder initiatives emerged as a response to this lack of legitimacy. Such initiatives usually involve a mix of business representatives and civil society actors, and in some cases also include governments, academic institutions, consumer groups and trade unions (Rasche 2012; Rasche and Esser 2006). Even though multi-stakeholder initiatives are supposed to balance the interest of all involved parties (for example, by allowing for equal voting rights), research has emphasized that some initiatives remain limited in terms of their inclusiveness and the distribution of power among participants (Boström 2006).

Since standard production is an unregulated activity, we have witnessed a proliferation of initiatives with very similar objectives. For instance, there are numerous certification standards in the global coffee industry (Reinecke et al. 2012). Competing standards exist because actor groups with an interest in a particular area of regulation have different problem definitions, potential solutions and organizational agendas (Fransen 2011). For example the emergence of the Forest Stewardship Council, a multi-stakeholder standard for sustainable forestry, was 'countered' by the creation of an industry-backed scheme, the so-called Sustainable Forestry Initiative (Gulbrandsen 2012). Standard multiplicity is also caused by the fragmented nature of the NGO community. Since NGOs position themselves differently vis-à-vis businesses, they support those initiatives that are most aligned with their own beliefs. While it can be argued that competing standards converge over time due to stakeholder pressure (for example, consumers who may be confused by too many unconnected certification schemes), competing initiatives may also continue to coexist because each standard setter perceives its own niche as being too important to give up (Fransen 2011).

## 22.3 STANDARDS AS ENABLERS OF SUSTAINABLE CONSUMPTION

How do standards for corporate sustainability and responsibility affect sustainable consumption? Although it is hard to find a conclusive answer to this question, as the influence of standards is often indirect and hard to observe, we suggest that standards enable sustainable consumption in at least three different ways.

### 22.3.1 Standards as Providers of Product-Specific Market Signals

Standards are one way to organize markets, since they are able to reduce information asymmetries (Akerlof 1970). The market for sustainable goods faces such asymmetries, as the underlying qualities of products are hard to observe for consumers, making it hard or even impossible to ascertain the utility of the good. There are many reasons why consumers are faced with incomplete information. The sustainability features of some products are hard to understand for a layperson, because the underlying issues are complex and dynamic (for example, the debate around biofuels). Moreover, the production of sustainable goods relates to internal businesses processes (or processes of supply partners), which are unobservable for individual consumers (Terlaak 2007). Interested consumers are also facing a certain level of confusion, as corporate talk around sustainability is 'cheap' (that is, largely unregulated), leading to an oversupply of supposedly sustainable goods (Cason and Gangadharan 2002; Delmas and Burbano 2011).

Certification standards reflect one way to cope with such information asymmetries. Certifications transform unobservable credence attributes (that is, attributes that must be taken on faith) into observable search attributes (that is, attributes that can be assessed prior to purchase; see Caswell and Padberg 1992). In other words, standards emit signals which contribute to the availability and accuracy of the information used by consumers to make purchasing decisions. Signals that are relevant for consumers are based on product labels. Labels signal that a product conforms to the codified requirements of a particular certification standard (see above). For instance, labels signal certain product features (for example, paper with a specific amount of recycled content) or communicate to consumers that products were produced under specific conditions (for example, textiles produced under just working conditions). Labels allow for a swifter comparison of sustainable and unsustainable products, leading to improved choice and lowered search costs (Horne 2009).

One precondition for the creation of a market for sustainable goods is that consumers react to labels' signals. The question of whether or not consumers prefer labelled over non-labelled products has been the subject of considerable scholarly debate. At the heart of this debate rests a tension. On the one hand, studies show that a large number of consumers demand more sustainable goods and that they are also willing to pay price premiums. Bjørner et al. (2004) found that the Nordic Swan label had a significant effect on consumers' brand choices for toilet paper, and that consumers were willing to pay between 13 and 18 per cent as a price premium for labelled products. Teisl et al. (2002b) showed that the dolphin-safe label increased the market share of canned tuna in the United States, while Loureiro and Lotade (2005) found that consumers were willing to pay a premium for fair trade labelled coffee. Labels make the sustainability attributes of a particular product or service salient, which often has a positive effect on perceived quality (Larceneux et al. 2012).

On the other hand, research demonstrates that there is a gap between consumers' intention to buy sustainable products and their actual purchasing behaviour. Sedjo and Swallow's (2002) study, for instance, cautioned that a mere willingness of consumers to pay price premiums does not ensure that higher prices are realized in practice. Other research showed that while some consumers are willing to pay price premiums for sustainable goods, most are not willing to sacrifice functional attributes of the product (for example, quality). In other words, consumers are only willing to pay higher prices for labelled products when the functional attributes of such products are fulfilling their needs (Bhattacharya and Sen 2004; Devinney et al. 2006).

Methodological challenges to scholarly work in this area explain why studies paint no consistent picture. First, as many studies of purchase intentions are based on experimental settings, they tend to induce an artificial awareness for sustainability (Öberseder et al. 2011). Consumers, however, only have a limited awareness of social and environmental problems and challenges (Pomering and Dolcinar 2009). Second, studies often suffer from a social desirability bias; that is, consumers publicly declare that they prefer labelled products (as they believe that this answer is socially accepted), while they act differently when faced with an actual purchasing decision (Auger and Devinney 2007). This is not to say that labels lack influence on purchasing decisions. Rather, consumer reactions to labels are heterogeneous and highly contingent upon the characteristics of the consumer, the labelled product, the label itself, the geographic context of consumption and the underlying social or environmental problem (Smith 2008). For instance, research has emphasized that consumers' willingness to pay premiums for labelled goods differs across product categories (Ozanne and Vlosky 1997) and also depends on whether consumers believe that their purchasing decision makes a difference (for example, when seeing a connection between high usage of a product and environmental impact). Teisl et al. (2002a) also found that the credibility of the standard-setting organization influenced purchasing behaviour (for example, consumers were suspicious of labels that were endorsed by industry groups).

### 22.3.2 Standards as Facilitating the Disclosure of Company-Level Information

Reporting standards facilitate the disclosure of company-level information on corporate sustainability and responsibility. The emergence of the GRI has enabled the institutionalization of non-financial reporting in different regions and has harmonized reporting metrics and principles (Etzion and Ferraro 2010). Of the 250 largest corporations in the world, 95 per cent disclose information on their social and environmental performance, while small and medium-sized enterprises are catching up (KPMG 2011). Regulators increasingly mandate sustainability reporting. A recent study of 180 policies on different aspects of non-financial reporting in 45 countries found that 72 per cent of these policies were mandatory (KPMG et al. 2013), although legislation is often based on a 'report or explain' approach (that is, firms have the choice to report or explain why it is not done). Voluntary reporting standards play a critical role in this context, as regulators often encourage their adoption so that firms disclose information against commonly accepted frameworks. Even stock exchanges have started to look into non-financial reporting. Some of them make reporting a listing requirement, while others follow a voluntary approach (for example, the Singapore Stock Exchange encourages listed firms to use the GRI guidelines; see Singapore Stock Exchange 2012).

Apart from a handful of 'CSR mavens' (Bhattacharya and Sen 2004, p. 14), consumers rarely look directly into firms' non-financial reports. Although consumers are interested in learning more about firms' social and environmental practices (Dawkins 2004), only a few actively use information from sustainability reports when making purchasing decisions. There may be at least two reasons for this. First, consumers do not put a lot of trust in self-reported information. A recent survey showed that only 15 per cent of consumers worldwide trust information coming from sustainability reports (BBMG et al. 2013). Although standards like the GRI have helped to increase the quality of disclosure and moved reporting beyond public relations, the general public still puts more trust in claims originating from sources beyond a firm's control (Edelman 2012). Second, interested consumers usually look for product-related information that can be compared and benchmarked, while sustainability reports contain company-level information. Often, this information contains a myriad of technical details and hence remains inaccessible to a non-expert audience.

While only a few action-oriented consumers may read sustainability reports, the disclosure of relevant information can still support sustainable consumption in more indirect ways. First, standards like the GRI create higher levels of transparency, because they allow other actors to benchmark a firm's sustainability performance vis-à-vis its industry peers and vis-à-vis its past promises. NGOs often use this information to expose inconsistencies between companies' public claims and their actions. For instance, numerous cases show that there is a non-alignment between firms' corporate political activities and their reported corporate responsibility activities (den Hond et al. 2014). NGOs regularly draw upon such inconsistencies when mobilizing consumers via boycotts. Boycotts help consumers to express their identity, as they feel part of a larger movement, and hence provide a platform for creating sustainable consumption patterns (Yates 2011).

Second, third parties can endorse a firm's reported sustainability information. Such endorsements can make the information more accessible to consumers. Numerous rankings, awards and indices base their assessment on non-financial reports. These endorsements translate the myriad of (often technical) metrics into recognizable labels that are easy to understand and communicate (for example, 'The World's Most Sustainable Corporation'; see www.global100.org). Firms use such endorsements in their communication with relevant stakeholders (for example, to differentiate themselves). Although third-party endorsements of reported information may not directly impact upon sales, they can still generate indirect effects that have economic consequences. Research shows that firms' distinguishable profiles in terms of their social and environmental performance create effects on increased customer loyalty, positive word of mouth, and a greater preparedness to overlook or even forgive a lapse in behaviour (Bhattacharya and Sen 2004; Smith 2008). Third-party endorsements would hardly be possible without reporting standards. Meaningful comparisons require shared metrics, which translate qualitative information into quantitative measures (Espeland and Sauder 2007). Reporting standards provide such metrics and hence simplify the construction of rankings, awards and indices.

### 22.3.3 Standards as Influencing the Discourse on Sustainable Consumption

Standards can also influence the discourse around sustainable consumption. This discourse enables sustainable consumption, because it shapes the agenda in ways favourable to the protection of consumer rights (for example, by setting priorities and defining key terms). One way in which standards affect this discourse is by including consumer groups into standard-setting processes. For instance, consumer groups played a significant role in producing ISO 26000. In 2001, the ISO Council requested that the Consumer Policy Committee (COPOLCO) of the International Organization for Standardization (ISO) should consider the possibility and viability of setting up a standard in the area of corporate responsibility. The COPOLCO Working Group on 'Consumer Protection in the Global Market' concluded that 'from a consumer perspective, ISO CR MSSs [Corporate Responsibility Management Systems Standards] are both desirable and feasible' (ISO COPOLCO 2002, p. v). Although the Working Group also considered the perspectives of other stakeholders, the initial report was 'written from a decidedly consumer perspective' (ISO COPOLCO 2002, p. iii). Once the official development phase of the standard began in 2005, the ISO included consumers as one of six core stakeholder groups (Tamm Hallström 2010). Overall, more than 80 consumer experts from different regions participated in the development of the standard (Martens 2010).

The involvement of consumer representatives into standard production helps to diffuse and legitimize an agenda for sustainable consumption. Due to the participation of consumer groups in the development of ISO 26000, the standard contains an entire section on 'Consumer Issues'. This section defines key terms and principles which are supposed to guide firms' socially responsible practices towards consumers, including, but not limited to: sustainable consumption, fair marketing, consumer protection, consumer service and support, and data protection. ISO 26000 defines sustainable consumption as the 'consumption of products and resources at rates consistent with sustainable development' (ISO 2010, p. 55). The standard also lays out how organizations can contribute to sustainable consumption; for example, by providing consumers with relevant and traceable information about products and by making use of labelling schemes.

Although most large companies and policy makers are aware of what sustainable consumption is and how it can be enabled, the availability of definitions creates a common frame of reference for all actors and thus helps to further institutionalize relevant practices. Two points concerning the relationship between standardization and institutionalization are important in this context. First, standards produce 'texts' which allow thoughts and actions to transcend diverse local settings (Phillips et al. 2004), making exemplary practices available to new actors (for example, small and medium-sized enterprises) and encouraging them to adopt these practices. For example, consumer protection agencies could use the language defined by standards like ISO 26000 to evaluate and benchmark companies' activities in the field of sustainable consumption. Second, since renowned actors are often involved in standard development (for example, the International Labour Organization in the case of ISO 26000), the resulting standard often legitimizes key definitions and practices. This increases the perceived relevance of standard content and supports its diffusion.

## 22.4 STANDARDS AS IMPEDIMENTS TO SUSTAINABLE CONSUMPTION

Standards can under certain conditions impede sustainable consumption. Three topics are particularly noteworthy. First, the coexistence of a range of competing standards with overlapping objectives may impede the signalling function of associated labels. Standards have in some cases created new markets for certified goods (for example, the market for grass-fed beef; Weber et al. 2008). As these markets evolve and mature, they become attractive to standardizers with different agendas, such as NGOs and industry groups. The resulting multiplicity of standards creates a situation in which it is increasingly difficult to oversee what initiatives exist and what purpose they serve. For instance, the Ecolabel Index is currently tracking 440 labels in 197 countries and 25 sectors (see www.ecolabelindex.com). While one could see such numbers as evidence that labelling has gone mainstream, it is clear that the coexistence of many competing labels also impedes sustainable consumption (SustainAbility 2011). It gives standard adopters flexibility to strategically choose initiatives with low entrance barriers, thereby building up a legitimacy façade which consumers can hardly uncover (Mueller et al. 2009). The coexistence of competing labels for single product categories can also confuse consumers who are facing a plethora of undifferentiated information, especially when keeping in mind that only some consumers actively compare labels. Suppliers often face similar problems, as they need to obtain multiple certifications in order to maintain relationships with different brand name companies (Mutersbaugh 2005). Overall, the coexistence of multiple standards lowers the recognition for single labels. This questions whether product labels can support a broader uptake of sustainable consumption.

Second, research has emphasized that the monitoring and auditing mechanisms, which provide the basis upon which certifications are granted, are sometimes incomplete, unreliable and inconsistent (Fransen and Kolk 2007; O'Rourke 2006). Much of this discussion relates to certification practices in global supply chains. Often, a narrow 'going by the book' approach limits the quality of audits. O'Rourke (2002), for instance, found that auditors simply worked their way through long checklists without reflecting on the context of the audit (for example, with regard to local customs), making it hard to uncover non-obvious problems such as discrimination. Other documented problems include: (1) forcing suppliers to adopt standards without much dialogue, thereby decreasing their motivation to fully implement them (Mamic 2005); and (2) a lack of credible and transparent information about audit results for interested consumers (Fung

2003). Can labels credibly signal sustainable product attributes, if the certifications that underlie labels are perceived to be weak? Although only a few consumers may be familiar with these problems at the moment, the ongoing media coverage around highly publicized scandals can raise greater awareness (for example, in the context of the collapse of a factory in Bangladesh in 2013; see Bhasin 2013). In the end, there is a risk that consumers may distrust selected labels and that reported problems in the context of some labels may spill over to other initiatives.

Finally, even though standards such as ISO 26000 have given a voice to consumers, their overall influence on the institutionalization of sustainable consumption remains limited to date. While many standards see consumers as 'game changers' to mainstream sustainable business practices, only a few initiatives involve consumer groups directly in standard development and governance. Many initiatives are based on deliberations between businesses, governments and NGOs, while consumer representatives are only involved in a few cases (for example, EcoMark: Japan and Naturemade). The missing inclusiveness of standard-setting processes can lead to a neglect of consumer concerns. While this may be less of a problem in the context of certification standards, as these initiatives are usually directly related to sustainable consumption, it is certainly a problem when looking at other types of standards for corporate sustainability and responsibility. For instance, the UN Global Compact, which by now is the world's largest network of business and non-business actors in support of sustainability (with over 10000 participants, as of October 2013), has not yet initiated discussions around sustainable consumption.

## 22.5 CONCLUSION

Those who define and enforce standards exercise influence. This is true in different areas of life, ranging from the design of technical interfaces to the definition of rules for corporate behaviour. Standards for corporate sustainability and responsibility have swiftly emerged as a form of regulating business conduct, mostly because other types of regulation (for example, laws) cannot sufficiently cope with the political and economic complexities of globalized markets. This chapter has highlighted that such standards enable sustainable consumption in three different ways. Certification standards can signal product-related attributes through labels and thus impact upon purchasing behaviour directly, although only a limited number of consumers currently respond to such labels. Reporting standards act as carriers of company-level information on social and environmental performance. This information can help firms to build a distinguishable profile in terms of their sustainability performance, creating effects on some consumers (for example, in terms of their loyalty towards the company). Finally, standards can influence the broader discourse around sustainable consumption, helping to define and institutionalize definitions of key terms and practices. The discussion also emphasized that standards can potentially impede the evolution of sustainable consumption, since consumers may be confused by the coexistence of competing labels in certain product categories. Consumers may also distrust labels because the public is increasingly aware of the limits of auditing and monitoring practices associated with certifications.

To conclude, the analysis shows that the influence of a standard on sustainable consumption is contingent upon the nature of the standard. Certification standards enable sustainable consumption in other ways than reporting, process or principle-based initiatives. So far, much of the scholarly debate has been limited to studying the link between labels and consumer behaviour. Giving more consideration to the existence of different types of standards can broaden the scholarly debate, because it shows the need to differentiate between direct effects on purchasing behaviour and more indirect effects on consumer loyalty and resilience. Future scholarly work will have to investigate more closely how different types of standards influence whether and how consumers identify with a company. For instance, we know too little about how broader principle-based initiatives such as the UN Global Compact may impact upon consumers' perceptions of a firm. Does a firm's affiliation with a trusted entity like the UN create positive identification effects?

Future research also needs to explore how business-to-business certifications (for example, SA 8000) enable sustainable consumption practices. Although such certifications cannot be used as product labels for end consumers, they are an important driver of sustainable production in global supply networks and thus provide the basis for sustainable consumption. One key question in this context is whether increased transparency in business-to-business operations can help consumers to better understand the impact of a product. Recent innovations such as phone apps that allow consumers to scan barcodes to directly access supply chain-related information (see www.goodguide.com) show that enhanced transparency can directly impact upon consumer behaviour.

## REFERENCES


Abbott, K.W., R.O. Keohane, A. Moravcsik, A.-M. Slaughter and D. Snidal (2000), 'The concept of legalization', *International Organization*, 54 (3), 401–419.

Akerlof, G.A. (1970), 'The market for "lemons": quality uncertainty and the market mechanism', *Quarterly Journal of Economics*, 84 (3), 488–500.

Auger, P. and T.M. Devinney (2007), 'Do what consumers say matter? The misalignment of preferences with unconstrained ethical intentions', *Journal of Business Ethics*, 76 (4), 361–383.

Baccaro, L. and V. Mele (2011), 'For lack of anything better? International organizations and global corporate codes', *Public Administration*, 89 (2), 451–470.

Bartley, T. (2007), 'Institutional emergence in an era of globalization: the rise of transnational private regulation of labor and environmental conditions', *American Journal of Sociology*, 113 (2), 297–351.

BBMG, GlobeScan and SustainAbility (2013), *RE:Thinking Consumption: Consumers and the Future of Sustainability*, New York: BBMG.

Behnam, M. and T.L. MacLean (2011), 'Where is the accountability in international accountability standards? A decoupling perspective', *Business Ethics Quarterly*, 21 (1), 45–72.

Berliner, D. and A. Prakash (2013), 'Signaling environmental stewardship in the shadow of weak governance: the global diffusion of ISO 14001', *Law and Society Review*, 47 (2), 345–373.

Bernstein, S. and B. Cashore (2007), 'Can non-state global governance be legitimate? An analytical framework', *Regulation and Governance*, 1 (4), 347–371.

Bhasin, K. (2013), 'In Bangladesh factory disasters – auditing process fails workers', available at: http://www.huffingtonpost.com/2013/04/26/bangladesh-factory-disaster_n_3164040.html (accessed 2 October 2013).

Bhattacharya, C.B. and S. Sen (2004), 'Doing better at doing good: when, why, and how consumers respond to corporate social initiatives', *California Management Review*, 47 (1), 9–24.

Bjørner, T.B., L.G. Hansen and C.S. Russell (2004), 'Environmental labeling and consumers' choice – an empirical analysis of the effect of the Nordic Swan', *Journal of Environmental Economics and Management*, 47 (3), 411–434.

Boström, M. (2006), 'Regulatory credibility and authority through inclusiveness: standardization organizations in cases of eco-labeling', *Organization*, 13 (3), 345–367.

Brunsson, N. and B. Jacobsson (2000), 'The contemporary expansion of standardization', in N. Brunsson and B. Jacobsson (eds), *A World of Standards*, Oxford, UK and New York, USA: Oxford University Press, pp. 1–17.
Brunsson, N., A. Rasche and D. Seidl (2012), 'The dynamics of standardization: three perspectives on standards in organization studies', *Organization Studies*, 33 (5–6), 613–632.
Cason, T.N. and L. Gangadharan (2002), 'Environmental labeling and incomplete consumer information in laboratory markets', *Journal of Environmental Economics and Management*, 43 (1), 113–134.
Caswell, J.A. and D.I. Padberg (1992), 'Toward a more comprehensive theory of food labels', *American Journal of Agricultural Economics*, 74 (2), 460–468.
Christmann, P. and G. Taylor (2006), 'Firm self-regulation through international certifiable standards: determinants of symbolic versus substantive implementation', *Journal of International Business Studies*, 37 (6), 863–878.
David, P.A. (1985), 'Clio and the economics of QWERTY', *American Economic Review*, 75 (2), 332–337.
Dawkins, J. (2004), *The Public's View of Corporate Responsibility*, MORI White Paper Series, London: MORI.
Delmas, M.A. (2002), 'The diffusion of environmental management standards in Europe and in the United States: an institutional perspective', *Policy Sciences*, 35 (1), 91–119.
Delmas, M.A. and V.C. Burbano (2011), 'The drivers of greenwashing', *California Management Review*, 54 (1), 64–87.
Den Hond, F., K.A. Rehbein, F.G.A. de Bakker and H.K. van Lankveld (2014), 'Playing on two chessboards: reputation effects between Corporate Social Responsibility (CSR) and Corporate Political Activity (CPA)', *Journal of Management Studies*, 51 (5), 790–813.
Devinney, T.M., P. Auger, G. Eckhardt and T. Birtchnell (2006), 'The other CSR', *Stanford Social Innovation Review*, 4 (3), 30–37.
Edelman (2012), 'Edelman 2012 trust barometer findings', available at: http://www.scribd.com/doc/79026497/2012-Edelman-Trust-Barometer-Executive-Summary (accessed 30 September 2013).
Espeland, W.N. and M. Sauder (2007), 'Rankings and reactivity: how public measures recreate social worlds', *American Journal of Sociology*, 113 (1), 1–40.
Etzion, D. and F. Ferraro (2010), 'The role of analogy in the institutionalization of sustainability reporting', *Organization Science*, 21 (5), 1092–1107.
European Council (1991), 'Council regulation (EEC) on organic production of agricultural products and indicators referring thereto on agricultural products and foodstuffs', No. 2092/91, 24 June, Brussels: European Council.
Fliess, B., H.-J. Lee, O.L. Dubreuil and O. Agatiello (2007), 'CSR and trade: informing consumers about social and environmnetasl conditions of globalized production', OECD Trade Policy Working Paper No. 47 – PART I, Paris: OECD Publications.
Fortanier, F., A. Kolk and J. Pinkse (2011), 'Harmonization in CSR reporting', *Management International Review*, 51 (5), 665–696.
Fransen, L. (2011), 'Why do private governance organizations not converge? A political-institutional analysis of transnational labor standards regulation', *Governance*, 24 (2), 359–387.
Fransen, L.W. and A. Kolk (2007), 'Global rule-setting for business: a critical analysis of multi-stakeholder standards', *Organization*, 14 (5), 667–684.
Fung, A. (2003), 'Deliberative democracy and international labor standards', *Governance*, 16 (1), 51–71.
Garud, R. and A. Kumaraswamy (1993), 'Changing competitive dynamics in network industries: an exploration of sun microsystems' open systems strategy', *Strategic Management Journal*, 14 (5), 351–369.
Gilbert, D.U. and A. Rasche (2007), 'Discourse ethics and social accountability: the ethics of SA8000', *Business Ethics Quarterly*, 17 (2), 187–216.
Gilbert, D.U., A. Rasche and S. Waddock (2011), 'Accountability in a global economy: the emergence of international accountability standards', *Business Ethics Quarterly*, 21 (1), 23–44.
Göbbels, M. and J. Jonker (2003), 'AA1000 and SA8000 compared: a systematic comparison of contemporary accountability standards', *Managerial Auditing Journal*, 18, 54–58.
Gulbrandsen, L.H. (2012), *Transnational Environmental Governance: The Emergence and Effects of the Certification of Forests and Fisheries*, Cheltenham, UK and Northampton, MA, USA: Edward Elgar.
Guler, I., M.F. Guillen and J.M. Macpherson (2002), 'Global competition, institutions, and the diffusion of organizational practices: the international spread of ISO 9000 quality certificates', *Administrative Science Quarterly*, 47 (2), 207–232.
Helms, W.S., C. Oliver and K. Webb (2012), 'Antecedents of settlement on a new institutional practice: negotiation of the ISO 26000 standard on social responsibility', *Academy of Management Journal*, 55 (5), 1120–1145.
Horne, R.E. (2009), 'Limits to labels: the role of eco-labels in the assessment of product sustainability and routes to sustainable consumption', *International Journal of Consumer Studies*, 33 (2), 175–182.

ISO (International Organization for Standardization) (2010), *International Standard ISO/DIS 26000: Guidance on Social Responsibility*, Geneva: ISO.

ISO (International Organization for Standardization) and IEC (International Electrotechnical Commission) (1996), *Standardization and Related Activities: General Vocabulary*, Geneva: ISO.

ISO COPOLCO (International Organization for Standardization Consumer Policy Committee) (2002), *The Desirability and Feasibility of ISO Corporate Social Responsibility Standards*, Geneva: ISO.

Knudsen, J. (2011), 'Company delistings from the UN Global Compact: limited business demand or domestic governance failure?', *Journal of Business Ethics*, 103 (3), 331–349.

KPMG (2011), *KPMG International Survey of Corporate Responsibility Reporting 2011*, Amsterdam: KPMG.

KPMG, Center for Corporate Governance in Africa, Global Reporting Initiative and United Nations Environment Programme (2013), *Carrots and Sticks: Sustainability Reporting Policies Worldwide – Today's Best Practice, Tomorrow's Trends*, Amsterdam: KPMG.

Larceneux, F., F. Benoit-Moreau and V. Renaudin (2012), 'Why might labels fail to influence consumer choices? Marginal labelling and brand equality effects', *Journal of Consumer Policy*, 35 (1), 85–104.

Loureiro, M.L. and J. Lotade (2005), 'Do fair trade and eco-labels in coffee wake up the consumer conscience?', *Ecological Economics*, 53 (1), 129–138.

Mamic, I. (2005), 'Managing global supply chain: the sports footwear, apparel and retail sectors', *Journal of Business Ethics*, 59 (1–2), 81–100.

Martens, J. (2010), 'Consumers international (interview with Joost Martens)', *ISO Focus+*, 1 (9), 3–6.

Mena, S. and G. Palazzo (2012), 'Input and output legitimacy of multi-stakeholder initiatives', *Business Ethics Quarterly*, 22 (3), 527–556.

Mueller, M., V.G. dos Santos and S. Seuring (2009), 'The contribution of environmental and social standards towards ensuring legitimacy in supply chain governance', *Journal of Business Ethics*, 89 (4), 509–523.

Mutersbaugh, T. (2005), 'Fighting standards with standards: harmonization, rents, and social accountability in certified agrofood networks', *Environment and Planning A*, 37 (11), 2033–2051.

O'Rourke, D. (2002), 'Monitoring the monitors: a critique of corporate third-party labor monitoring', in R. Jenkins, R. Pearson and G. Seyfang (eds), *Corporate Responsible Ethical Trade: Codes of Conduct in the Global Economy*, London: Earthscan, pp. 196–208.

O'Rourke, D. (2006), 'Multi-stakeholder regulation: privatizing or socializing global labor standards?', *World Development*, 34 (5), 899–918.

Organisation for Economic Co-operation and Development (OECD) (2011), *OECD Guidelines for Multinational Enterprises*, Paris: OCED Publishing.

Ozanne, L.K. and R.P. Vlosky (1997), 'Willingness to pay for environmentally certified wood products: a consumer perspective', *Forest Products Journal*, 47 (6), 39–48.

Öberseder, M., B.B. Schlegelmilch and V. Gruber (2011), '"Why don't consumers care about csr?": a qualitative study exploring the role of CSR in consumption decisions', *Journal of Business Ethics*, 104 (4), 449–460.

Phillips, N., T.B. Lawrence and C. Hardy (2004), 'Discourse and institutions', *Academy of Management Review*, 29 (4), 635–652.

Pomering, A. and S. Dolnicar (2009), 'Assessing the prerequisite of successful CSR implementation: are consumers aware of CSR initiatives?', *Journal of Business Ethics*, 85 (S2), 285–301.

Potoski, M. and A. Prakash (2005), 'Green clubs and voluntary governance: ISO 14001 and firms' regulatory compliance', *American Journal of Political Science*, 49 (2), 235–248.

Rasche, A. (2009), '"A necessary supplement": what the United Nations Global Compact is and is not', *Business and Society*, 48 (4), 511–537.

Rasche, A. (2010), 'Collaborative governance 2.0', *Corporate Governance*, 10 (4), 500–511.

Rasche, A. (2012), 'Global policies and local practice: loose and tight couplings in multi-stakeholder initiatives', *Business Ethics Quarterly*, 22 (4), 679–708.

Rasche, A. and D.E. Esser (2006), 'From stakeholder management to stakeholder accountability: applying Habermasian discourse ethics to accountability research', *Journal of Business Ethics*, 65 (3), 251–267.

Rat für Nachhaltige Entwicklung (2012), 'The German Sustainability Code', available at: http://www.nachhaltigkeitsrat.de/uploads/media/RNE_The_German_Sustainability_Code_GSC_text_No_41_January_2012_01.pdf (accessed 22 January 2014).

Reinecke, J., S. Manning and O. von Hagen (2012), 'The emergence of a standards market: multiplicity of sustainability standards in the global coffee industry', *Organization Studies*, 33 (5–6), 791–814.

Scherer, A.G. and G. Palazzo (2011), 'The new political role of business in a globalized world: a review of a new perspective on csr and its implications for the firm, governance, and democracy', *Journal of Management Studies*, 48 (4), 899–931.

Sedjo, R.A. and S.K. Swallow (2002), 'Voluntary eco-labeling and the price premium', *Land Economics*, 78 (2), 272–284.

Singapore Stock Exchange (2012), 'Guide to sustainability reporting for listed companies', available at http://

rulebook.sgx.com/net_file_store/new_rulebooks/s/g/SGX_Sustainability_Reporting_ Guide_and_Policy_Statement_2011.pdf (accessed 30 September 2013).
Smith, N.C. (2008), 'Consumers as drivers of CSR', in A. Crane, D. Matten, A. McWilliams, J. Moon and D. Siegel (eds), *The Oxford Handbook of Corporate Social Responsibility*, Oxford: Oxford University Press, pp. 281–302.
SustainAbility (2011), *Signed, Sealed . . . Delivered? Behind Certifications and Beyond Labels*, London: SustainAbility.
Tamm Hallström, K. (2008), 'ISO expands its business into social responsibility', in M. Boström and C. Garsten (eds), *Organizing Transnational Accountability*, Cheltenham, UK and Northampton, MA, USA: Edward Elgar, pp. 46–60.
Tamm Hallström, K. (2010), 'The use of democratic values in the ISO 26000 process on social responsibility', in G. Sundström, L. Soneryd and S. Furusten (eds), *Organizing Democracy. The Construction of Agency in Practice*, Cheltenham, UK and Northampton, MA, USA: Edward Elgar, pp. 48–64.
Teisl, M.E., S. Peavey, F. Newman, J. Buono and M. Hermann (2002a), 'Consumer reactions to environmental labels for forest products: a preliminary look', *Forest Products Journal*, 52 (1), 44–50.
Teisl, M.F., B. Roe and R.L. Hicks (2002b), 'Can eco-labels tune a market? Evidence from dolphin-safe labeling', *Journal of Environmental Economics and Management*, 43 (3), 339–359.
Terlaak, A. (2007), 'Order without law? The role of certified management standards in shaping socially desired firm behaviors', *Academy of Management Review*, 32 (3), 968–985.
Timmermans, S. and S. Epstein (2010), 'A world of standards but not a standard world: toward a sociology of standards and standardization', *Annual Review of Sociology*, 36 (1), 69–89.
Thøgersen, J. (2005), 'How may consumer policy empower consumers for sustainable lifestyles?', *Journal of Consumer Policy*, 28, 143–178.
Waddock, S. (2008), 'Building a new institutional infrastructure for corporate responsibility', *Academy of Management Perspectives*, 22 (3), 87–108.
Weber, K., K.L. Heinze and M. DeSoucey (2008), 'Forage for thought: mobilizing codes in the movement for grass-fed meat and dairy products', *Administrative Science Quarterly*, 53 (3), 529–567.
Werner, R.O. and B.J. Katz (1976), 'regulation of product characteristics', *Journal of Marketing*, 40 (3), 95–97.
Yates, L.S. (2011), 'Critical consumption', *European Societies*, 13 (2), 191–217.

# 23. Step across the border: knowledge brokerage for sustainable consumption

*Gerd Scholl*

This chapter explores the question of how one can enhance the impact of research on policy making for sustainable consumption. Policies aiming to foster more sustainable consumer behaviours have lately become more prominent, at international, European and national level. At the same time, researchers from a variety of disciplines have undertaken major efforts to analyse the factors that both prevent and drive the proliferation of sustainable consumption patterns. However, there is reason to believe that the existing body of scientific evidence goes largely underutilized in the design, implementation and assessment of sustainable consumption policies. Therefore recent calls for more evidence-based policy making (e.g. Campbell et al. 2007; European Commission 2010) are valid for this policy domain as well.

In order to better understand the science–policy gap in sustainable consumption this chapter starts off with an overview of relevant policies and research endeavours. It then discusses the factors that shape this gap and concludes that distinct efforts are needed to bridge it. The set of efforts required is then introduced under the notion of 'knowledge brokerage', representing a structured process of exchanging knowledge and creating links between different communities and of building capacities to perpetuate cross-community exchange. In the subsequent section the case of a European knowledge brokerage project is described to illustrate different ways in which knowledge brokerage can be put into practice. This three-year pilot project experimented with and developed new integrative modalities of knowledge brokerage at the science–policy interface of sustainable consumption. The chapter closes with some considerations on future issues for research on knowledge brokerage for sustainable consumption.

## 23.1 POLICIES AND RESEARCH ON SUSTAINABLE CONSUMPTION

Sustainable consumption has only recently emerged as a policy domain. At international level the United Nations (UN) Conference on Environment and Development held in Rio de Janeiro in 1992 and its follow-up conference, the Johannesburg Summit from 2002, paved the way to a global commitment to more sustainable consumption patterns. The subsequent Marrakech Process informed the elaboration of a ten-year framework of programmes, which was adopted at the Rio+20 Conference in 2012. The framework aims to develop, multiply and scale up initiatives in the area of sustainable consumption and production (SCP). At European level the action plan on Sustainable Consumption and Production and Sustainable Industrial Policy (European Commission 2008a), the flagship initiative 'A Resource-Efficient Europe', which calls for consumers to be empowered to move to resource-efficient consumption (European Commission 2011), and the recent communication 'Building the single market for green products' (European Commission 2013) have largely framed policy development. In addition many countries have introduced their own initiatives to further accelerate the transition towards sustainable consumption (e.g. Szlezak et al. 2008; UNEP 2012).

Alongside the formation of policies at global, European and national level, a toolbox has been created for implementing existing policies. The instruments include regulatory approaches, such as bans and standards; economic instruments, such as fees and taxes; informational tools, such as labels and campaigns; and investments in infrastructure or green procurement by public authorities (e.g. European Commission 2012a; Scholl et al. 2013). With respect to consumption domains the housing sector, including buildings as well as household goods, the mobility sector and the food sector are at the centre of policy making for sustainable consumption, the main reason being their high environmental impact (e.g. Tukker et al. 2006).

Sustainable consumption policies cover a wide range of issues. They encompass greener market transformation through the promotion of eco-efficient products (e.g. Carter et al. 2012); the encouragement of environmentally and socially sound consumer behaviours, for example through tax incentives or conducive choice architectures ('nudging', e.g. Oullier and Sauneron 2011; Thaler and Sunstein 2009); and, more recently, questions of equity, fairness, the good life and individual well-being (e.g. SDC 2011). Hence the scope of (notably) European policy making has gradually expanded from focusing on the product alone towards encompassing consumer behaviour beyond the purchasing decision, for instance the way people use goods and treat goods after use, in order to influence people's lifestyles and the values that underlie the way they live their lives.

Except for anecdotal evidence, little is known about the effectiveness of sustainable consumption policies (e.g. Wolff and Schönherr 2011). An explanation for this might be that the so-called rebound effect makes the calculation of policy impacts difficult. The rebound effect occurs when efficiency gains are compensated by a rise in demand caused by income saved through efficiency improvements (Hertwich 2008). In addition to this effect, a general rise in ownership of for example household equipment has offset large parts of the advances in product efficiency (EEA 2012), which again may counteract the positive impacts of policies. These phenomena challenge policies that merely focus on single, incremental improvements and neglect the 'bigger picture' of multifaceted consumption systems. As a consequence, more strategic approaches to sustainable consumption policies (Berg 2011) and a societal transition perspective on the desired change in consumption patterns (Tukker et al. 2008b) have been advocated in literature. Apart from conceptual limitations in policy design, Mont et al. (2013) identified numerous myths about sustainable consumption, such as the myth that more consumer information will lead to more sustainable consumption, which strongly determine current thinking by decision makers and prevent them from implementing more effective policies.

In summary, there is a variety of policies promoting sustainable consumption patterns. They cover a broad array of consumption domains, leading to comprehensive and complex policy agendas. However, very few policies follow a strategic approach and design policies from a more systemic perspective. One such policy might be Sweden's abandoned SCP programme 'Think Twice!' (Ministry of Agriculture, Food and Consumer Affairs 2005). Overall, this should imply a huge demand for knowledge not only about the sustainability impacts of products and services, but also essentially about the drivers of current consumer behaviours and the barriers to more sustainable ones.

These issues have been put centre stage in sustainable consumption research[1] for a few decades now. Besides a substantial amount of research addressing the life cycle impacts of products and services (e.g. Tukker et al. 2006; Tukker et al. 2009), which is primarily informed by natural and engineering sciences, a huge body of knowledge has been created in social sciences and humanities as well (e.g. Cohen and Murphy 2001; European Commission 2012b; Jackson 2006; Jackson and Michaelis 2003; Tukker et al. 2008a). The foci of this strand of research are as diverse as the topics covered. One focus is on policy instruments employed to foster the emergence and proliferation of sustainable consumer behaviours (e.g. European Commission 2012a; OECD 2011; Rubik et al. 2009; Scholl et al. 2010). Within this area of research some special attention has been paid to product labelling (e.g. Rubik and Frankl 2005; Rubik and Scholl 2002; Thøgersen et al. 2010) and more generally to communication and marketing strategies for sustainable consumption (e.g. Belz and Peattie 2009; Godemann and Michelsen 2011; Sachs and Finkelpearl 2010). Moreover, the sustainability of consumer behaviour has been addressed from different disciplinary angles, such as (behavioural) economics (e.g. Dolan et al. 2010; Reisch and Røpke 2004), sociology (e.g. McMeekin and Southerton 2012; Shove 2003; Shove et al. 2012; and Welch and Warde, Chapter 5 in this book) and psychology (e.g. Kaiser and Gutscher 2003; Manning 2009; and Steg, Chapter 4 in this book). Some of that research explores the role of habits, routines and life events in the observed lack of transition towards more sustainable consumer behaviour (e.g. Defra 2011a, 2011b; and Verplanken and Roy, Chapter 15 in this book), and furthermore provides evidence on consumer and lifestyle segmentation (e.g. Backhaus et al. 2012; Defra 2008; Schultz and Stieß 2008; and Vérain et al., Chapter 13 in this book). This vast amount of scientific evidence multiplies when sustainable consumer behaviour is approached from the point of view of consumption domains. There is a plethora of knowledge available on sustainable food consumption (e.g. Reisch et al. 2013), sustainable mobility (e.g. Geerken et al. 2009; Holden 2007; and Gärling, Chapter 10 in this book), sustainable housing (e.g. Lahlou 2011; and Gram-Hanssen, Chapter 11 in this book) and sustainable clothing (e.g. Niinimäki 2010; Niinimäki and Hassi 2011).

Hence the existing body of scientific knowledge on sustainable consumption (policies) is huge. It is informed by a variety of disciplines and covers a vast array of topics in different consumption domains. The evidence is scattered across various publication channels such as scientific journals, monographs, edited books, grey literature and others. The sheer amount and the confusingly broad dissemination of knowledge limit its accessibility, in particular for stakeholders outside the research system, such as policy makers.

## 23.2 THE SCIENCE–POLICY GAP IN SUSTAINABLE CONSUMPTION

As briefly sketched above, sustainable consumption policies are fairly new and deal with a wide range of issues. On the other hand there is a huge body of research addressing the promoting and inhibiting factors of sustainable consumption. These scientific endeavours, however, have not yet achieved a significant impact on policy making. The following example illustrates the gap between science and policy in sustainable consumption.

In the case of food, consuming more sustainably also means considering the environmental impacts of transporting produce and foodstuffs. Policy making can provide guidance for consumers, for example through labels or guidelines, on the basis of proper assessments of the different options. Life cycle assessment (LCA), for instance, is a valuable tool in this respect as it discloses the environmental impacts along the entire supply chain (e.g. Andersson 2000). LCAs have been applied to a variety of food products, sometimes yielding surprising results. For example while apples produced locally in Germany are more climate-friendly – despite the indispensable cold storage – than apples imported to Germany from New Zealand, lettuce imported to Germany from Spain during the winter months is more environmentally friendly than locally produced lettuce grown in heated greenhouses (Reinhardt et al. 2009). Against this background, the popular concept of minimizing food miles turns out to be an inadequate basis for policy making.

Given this example, the following question arises: what factors hamper a more resolute uptake of research findings in policy-making for sustainable consumption? Answers to this question can be drawn from generic studies dealing with the science–policy interface, such as Nutley et al. (2002) and Oldham and McLean (1997). Additional insight is provided by work exploring ways to enhance the impact of science on health policies (e.g. Choi et al. 2005). More recently, similar questions have been dealt with in the context of environmental and sustainability policies (e.g. Holmes and Clark 2008; Magnuszewski et al. 2010; Michaels 2009). Sustainable consumption has not been at the forefront of these analyses but many factors elaborated on in these studies are also important for explaining the gap between science and policy in sustainable consumption. Figure 23.1 provides an overview of the different factors that will be introduced below.

One factor shaping this gap is related to the nature of environmental problems that are often associated with high levels of uncertainty (Magnuszewski et al. 2010, p. 41); even more so when not only the environment but also the interaction between the environment and society is targeted. On the one hand this framing of consumption-oriented policies at the interface of the natural environment and societal conduct admittedly increases the proximity of policy making to real-world challenges. On the other hand it adds to the problem of the unpredictability of policy interventions which are geared towards human behaviour in daily life.

Another set of factors relates to the internal rationale of the academic system. Usually scientists have little incentive to actively communicate their findings to policy makers (e.g. Holmes and Clark 2008) as academic performance is traditionally measured by the number of publications in peer-reviewed journals rather than by the number of policy briefs being produced. Also scientists often show poor communication skills when it comes to conveying at least the policy-relevant parts of their research (e.g. European Commission 2008b; Michaels 2009). The quest for excellence, which often prevents research contributing to the solution of societal problems (e.g. Holmes and Lock 2010; Sterk et al. 2009) and, related to this, the narrow definition of disciplinary boundaries in science (e.g. Shanley and López 2009) further exacerbate the use of scientific evidence in policy making. Last but not least, science has no strong need to increase its engagement

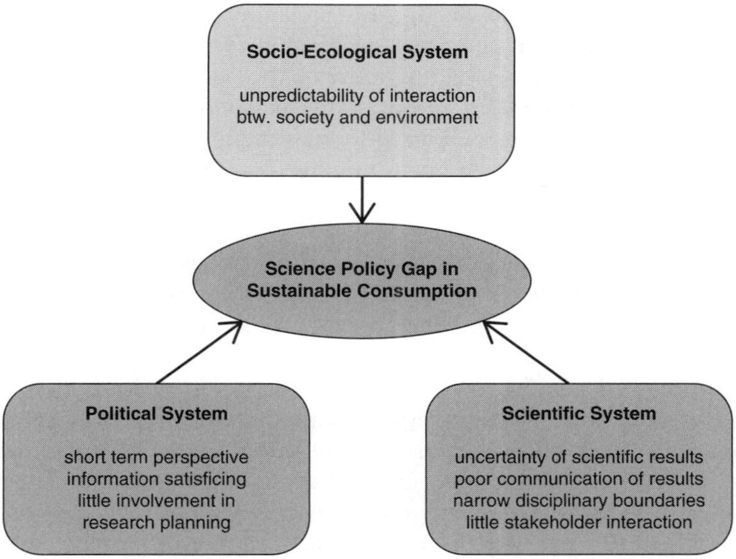


*Figure 23.1 Factors shaping the science–policy gap*

with public stakeholders (e.g. European Commission 2008a, 2008b; Shanley and López 2009), which may again impair its relevance for policy making.

All these factors hold true for the gap between science and policy in sustainable consumption; most of them, however, in an attenuated fashion. Poor and inadequate dissemination of results is still a problem in sustainable consumption research but efforts have been made in recent times to widen its outreach. The European Union (EU)-funded network project SCORE,[2] for instance, served as the EU's central support structure for the United Nations 10-Year Framework of Programmes. The conference series European Roundtable on Sustainable Consumption and Production (ERSCP), which has just evolved into a scientific society (European Society for the ERSCP), is a non-profit forum providing a platform for academics as well as practitioners to stimulate, develop and disseminate new initiatives aimed at fostering the implementation of sustainable consumption and production. A third example, the network initiative SCORAI (Sustainable Consumption Research and Action Initiative), founded in North America and recently expanded to Europe, aims to establish a community that drives forward-thinking, innovative research in the area of sustainable consumption, while also bridging academic research with mainstream thinking and policy making.

In parallel to these improved dissemination and networking initiatives, transdisciplinary modes of research have increasingly found their way into the science of sustainable consumption. Transdisciplinarity has three main features: it stands for a focus on socially relevant problems, for mutual learning between researchers from different scientific disciplines as well as between academic and societal actors, and for the creation of solution-oriented knowledge. Accordingly, practical solutions to real-life problems are pursued through collaborative problem framing and collaborative research designs integrating a range of disciplines and stakeholders (Lang et al. 2012). A research programme on sustainable consumption following this research approach was completed recently in Germany (Defila et al. 2013). It comprises projects on various topics including the question of how life events such as relocation, retirement or childbirth can provide windows of opportunity for a transition to more sustainable behaviours (Schäfer et al. 2012) or by what means homeowners can be mobilized to take energy-saving measures (Weiß et al. 2012). This highly applied research on sustainable consumption might well contribute to overcoming the barriers stemming from the very nature of the traditional academic system.

Some factors hindering the uptake of research in policy making are rooted in the internal rationale of the political system. One such factor is conflicting timelines (e.g. Choi et al. 2005; Hukkinen 2009). While policy makers usually take a short-term perspective, which is justified by the need to find quick fixes for real-life problems, scientists undertake research – depending on the scope of the grant – with a mid- to long-term perspective. Research projects dealing with sustainable consumption typically run from one to three or five years, plus a preparation phase that often lasts more than one year. Within such time frames policy issues can undergo several changes, thus reinforcing the mismatch between knowledge demand and knowledge supply. This mismatch is further increased by the fact that many of the issues in sustainable consumption, such as market transformations and lifestyle changes, are long-term per se and hence go beyond the duration of current policy cycles.

Moreover, policy makers can be considered information satisficers rather than information optimizers (Michaels 2009) due to a lack of time, skills, understanding and so on (Magnuszewski et al. 2010). As information satisficers they tend to apply the first information that works for them. Doing this naturally limits the uptake of scientific evidence as the usefulness of any additional piece of information is rapidly offset by the costs associated with its acquisition. The observation made by Heiskanen et al. (2013), that Nordic policy makers regard research on consumer behaviour as too complex and wide-ranging to process, supports this hypothesis.

Another factor that is stressed in the literature refers to the lack of participation by policy makers in future research planning (e.g. Holmes and Clark 2008; Holmes and Lock 2010). Whether this is an impediment at the science–policy interface in sustainable consumption strongly depends, however, on the source of research funding. In the case of research commissioned by government departments, the involvement of policy makers in research planning will usually be high, as opposed to research funded by national research councils, for example. One can assume that both commissioned and funded research is found in sustainable consumption, which puts this hindering factor into perspective.

The gap between science and policy can be widened further when policy makers use the uncertainty of scientific results[3] as an argument against taking action (Surridge and Harris 2007). It is difficult to tell whether and to what extent this holds true for sustainable consumption. Nevertheless the moderate ambitions of current consumption policies suggest that – at least in some cases – ambiguities and uncertainties regarding scientific results might be part of the reason for, or employed to justify, the observed lack of action.

In sum, there are a multitude of factors shaping the gap between science and policy, some of which are related to the very nature of consumption as a social-ecological entity and others resulting from the essential features of both the scientific and political systems. Many of the factors addressed in literature can be transferred to sustainable consumption, implying that efforts to bridge the gap – by means of knowledge brokerage – are certainly required.

## 23.3 BRIDGING THE SCIENCE–POLICY GAP THROUGH KNOWLEDGE BROKERAGE

This section deals with the question of how the gap between research and policy making in sustainable consumption can be bridged. It draws on relevant literature on knowledge brokerage and, by doing so, prepares the discussion of a specific brokerage case that is presented in the next section.

To start with there is little consensus on appropriate tools and methods to bridge the gap between science and policy (e.g. Michaels 2009) and, moreover, little is known about the effectiveness of these (e.g. Magnuszewski et al. 2010; Nutley et al. 2007). At least there is some consensus that bridging requires a significant effort and its own approach, which is commonly referred to as knowledge brokerage. Michaels (2009) describes knowledge brokerage as a 'two way facilitative process between researchers and policy makers' (p. 996), the aim of which is 'to encourage policy makers to be open to making use of research findings and to encourage researchers to undertake policy relevant research and to communicate with policy-makers such that policy-makers value the findings' (van Kammen et al. 2006, cited in Michaels 2009, p. 996). This characterization acknowledges that pushing research evidence to potential users is not enough. The knowledge push rather needs to be supplemented by the creation of a pull for evidence by those who may benefit from it (Nutley et al. 2002).

Understanding knowledge brokerage as a bidirectional process is at the very core of the literature (e.g. Magnuszewski et al. 2010; Meyer 2010). An often-quoted source, Oldham and McLean (1997), distinguishes between three dimensions of knowledge brokerage covering this essential feature as well. The first dimension, knowledge system framework, deals with the procedural elements of knowledge, such as its creation, acquisition, assimilation, use and dissemination. Knowledge brokerage in this sense is basically about knowledge transfer from one domain to another. In the transactional framework of knowledge brokerage, the stakeholders involved in the process of mutual knowledge transfer are taken into account as well. In this regard knowledge brokerage mainly deals with building linkages and fostering mutual exchange between different communities and actors. The third dimension, social change framework, highlights the building of capacities within society, for example by providing training to knowledge users, in order to enhance overall access to knowledge, thereby achieving positive social results. In light of these three dimensions, knowledge brokers may act as knowledge managers, linkage agents and capacity builders (Ward et al. 2009).

Depending on the role they take on, knowledge brokers can follow different brokerage strategies. While Creech and Willard (2001) present a broad distinction of three strategies – information provision, nurturing relationships and joint action – which define different levels of an engagement pyramid, Michaels (2009) offers a more differentiated view of how brokerage can operate in practice. When adopting the strategy of informing, brokers help to disseminate content, for example by adequately packaging information. In the case of consulting, brokers identify experts who can advise on a problem articulated by someone seeking counsel, and also facilitate the appropriate form of communication between the two parties. In matchmaking, brokers find out what expertise is required to address a specific problem and who could provide it, and they connect knowledge providers and knowledge users who would otherwise not connect. Engaging as another strategy of knowledge brokerage means implementing a process, which is framed by the party addressing the problem and which actively involves a number of experts during the course of the related decision-making process. In contrast, in the collaborating strategy the problem and the interactive process aiming to address it are framed by both parties. This also holds for the brokerage strategy of building capacity, which however aims at establishing proper structures for knowledge exchange in the mid- to long term. Hence this latter strategy is less temporary and transient than the other strategies and more profoundly committed to ensuring longevity in the effort to bridge the science–policy gap.

Besides different roles and strategies that one may encounter in knowledge brokerage, the quality of information which is processed in a knowledge brokerage endeavour influences the outcome of the process. Cash et al. (2003) report that information is most effective when it is perceived by the relevant stakeholders not only as credible (that is, scientifically adequate) but also as salient (that is, meeting the needs of the decision maker) and legitimate (that is, respecting divergent values and beliefs as well as opposing views and interests). These three properties can be simultaneously enhanced by knowledge brokerage systems that facilitate active, iterative and inclusive communication between researchers and policy makers, that achieve mutual understanding between experts and decision makers through proper translation, and that create a legitimate, transparent and open process by means of suitable mediation.

## 23.4 CORPUS: A CASE STUDY IN KNOWLEDGE BROKERAGE FOR SUSTAINABLE CONSUMPTION

Knowledge brokerage can be put into practice in different ways. It can be implemented by single actors, such as an individual or an organization, or by a set of processes, strategies, techniques and tools (e.g. Magnuszewski et al. 2010; Michaels 2009; Sheate and Partidário 2009). The EU-funded project CORPUS (Enhancing the Connectivity Between Research and Policy-Making in Sustainable Consumption) is an example of the latter. It dealt with knowledge brokerage between science and policy on sustainable consumption and can be regarded an orchestrated set of processes and tools designed to enhance the connectivity between the two communities. CORPUS was a three-year pilot project aiming to experiment with and develop new integrative modalities of knowledge brokerage at the science–policy interface. The project consortium consisted of nine research organizations and two ministries. The knowledge brokerage system implemented in CORPUS comprised a web platform as a central information gateway and online interaction forum and a series of offline interaction exercises with researchers and policy makers in priority areas of sustainable consumption (food, mobility and housing) (see Figure 23.2).

The interaction exercises, which were promoted as 'Policy Meets Research' workshops, explored novel modalities of knowledge brokerage through different forms of

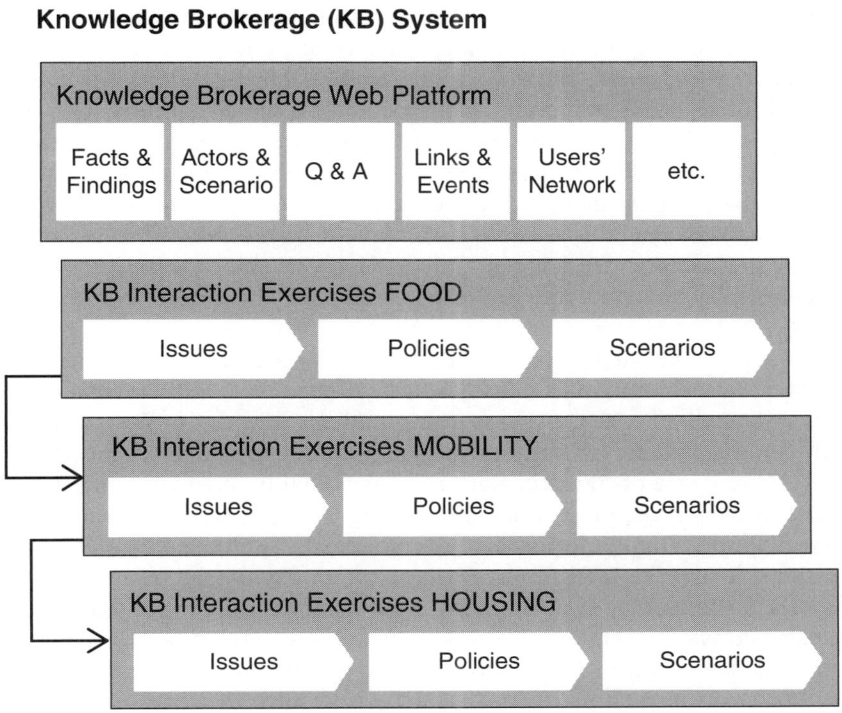


*Source:* CORPUS.

*Figure 23.2 The knowledge brokerage system implemented in CORPUS*

face-to-face dialogues. A series of three workshops was conducted in each policy domain within a period of approximately seven months. Throughout the events the organizers experimented with various techniques for knowledge translation and community building, such as poster sessions, cognitive mapping exercises, participatory scenario building, backcasting, building a joint research agenda, and so on (Scholl et al. 2013).

The web platform was a reference point for high-quality information and networking among European professionals working in sustainable consumption. In each of the three consumption areas the site offered all users a large collection of the latest research and policy documents, a chronological database of events, a selection of useful links to further information as well as information on the CORPUS interaction exercises. Registered users could interactively upload information, such as their own publications, events, and policy documents, and were able to communicate with one another. There was also a question and answer (Q&A) function to facilitate dialogue among users (Scholl et al. forthcoming).

Hence the knowledge brokerage system implemented in CORPUS was mainly geared towards the management of knowledge and the creation of linkages and exchange between the two targeted communities. Through its online knowledge database it also made some contribution to capacity building.

Strategy-wise, CORPUS went through all levels of the engagement pyramid: it comprised the provision of information through online and offline tools, such as news tickers, background papers, poster sessions, and so on, as well as the nurturing of relationships through the facilitation of online and offline encounters. The latter were particularly successful, not only in terms of the number of professionals participating in the events and the substantial share of policy makers among them, but also given that many of the attendees participated repeatedly. Last but not least, CORPUS enabled joint action through the collaborative development of future visions and backcasting strategies in the scenario workshops and through the co-development of a domain-specific research agenda involving researchers and policy makers over the course of two workshops.

With respect to the quality of the information processed by the knowledge brokerage system implemented in CORPUS, a high level of credibility was achieved by engaging renowned researchers from inside and outside the project team as either presenters in workshops or authors of background papers and knowledge units. Moreover, the salience of the information was ensured by involving policy makers, in particular those from the project team, in setting the agendas and selecting the topics for the workshops. Finally, legitimacy was practically addressed by facilitating open conversations during the workshops, for example in a mapping session or during discussions of a poster, or by systematically combining keynote input with the views of critical discussants.

The main contribution of CORPUS to capacity building was the development and implementation of the web platform. The experience of using the online tool revealed that providing up-to-date evidence for experts is the foundation of successful knowledge brokerage. For the sake of high usability, good organization and intuitive navigation is key, as is an effective method for searching through the information. Turning a knowledge repository into a social web with high interaction among users is challenging, though. In the case of CORPUS this involved expanding the platform to additional media outlets such as a LinkedIn group and a Facebook page. Although these social media have become more commonly used in professional contexts in recent years, they do not yet seem to fully accommodate the knowledge acquisition routines of the majority of policy makers (Scholl et al. 2013).

## 23.5 FUTURE RESEARCH ON KNOWLEDGE BROKERAGE FOR SUSTAINABLE CONSUMPTION

In the preceding sections the gap between research and policy making on sustainable consumption, the factors that shape this gap and possible ways to bridge it – illustrated with the example of a European pilot project – have been described. One can conclude from the information presented that conflicting time-frames and diverging agendas still seem to be major obstacles to more evidence-based policy making on sustainable consumption. This has two major implications for knowledge brokerage in sustainable consumption policies and underpins the need to establish a proper knowledge system framework as well as a transactional framework (Scholl et al. forthcoming):

- Providing evidence on demand: policy makers need the right knowledge at the right time. Hence relevant scientific evidence should feed into a reservoir and be easily available for the time when policy practitioners can make most use of it.
- Facilitating knowledge collaboration: in the area of sustainable consumption, policy makers and researchers are connected and yet separate. They are accustomed to knowledge exchange but still operate in different professional environments. Thus, creating room for collaboration around specific problems in which they have a shared interest can help to strengthen the flow of knowledge between the two communities.

These insights raise a number of important issues and questions with regard to future research dealing with the science–policy interface in sustainable consumption. The CORPUS project revealed that the nature and scope of knowledge brokerage between science and policy for sustainable development is country-specific. Some countries are characterized by more structured and active knowledge collaboration than others.[4] Investigation into national decision making and related knowledge brokerage cultures could thus provide further insights into how more evidence-based policy making can be achieved.

It is somewhat obvious that knowledge collaboration or, more precisely, co-production of knowledge between science and policy for sustainable consumption could enhance the impact of research on policy making. But how should this look in practice, given the restrictions both communities still face within their professional environments? How would policy makers and researchers need to interact in research planning and implementation in order to produce results that have greater impact on policy making? The answers to these questions would include finding ways to better exploit the potential of social media for creating more connectivity between research and policy making on sustainable consumption. Social media have certainly become more widely used in professional contexts but apparently not so much in policy making. Therefore the preconditions and proper means for further activating the use of social media in strengthening cross-community collaboration deserve further investigation.

Finally, the type of knowledge with the most potential for policy impact would require research attention too. Information on good policy practice, for instance, was highly appreciated by policy makers in the CORPUS project. However, this kind of information is usually anecdotal and not scientifically 'proven'. Hence, another question would be how one can increase the transferability of experiential evidence without creating a prohibitively high amount of scientific assessment.

The issues raised here – carrying out cross-country analyses of knowledge brokerage cultures, exploring practical ways to co-produce knowledge, bringing out the potential of social media for brokerage and strengthening the transferability of experiential evidence – cannot be claimed to be anything close to an exhaustive list. The complexities related to research and policy making on sustainable consumption and to knowledge brokerage as a method to bridge the gap between the two communities lead one to conclude that there are more questions about the effectiveness and efficiency of knowledge brokerage for sustainable consumption than are sketched here. However, with the latest experience gained in projects such as CORPUS, a good start has been made in discovering the promising terrain of knowledge brokerage.

## ACKNOWLEDGEMENTS

The research leading to these results has received funding from the European Community's Seventh Framework Programme (FP7/2007–2013) under grant agreement no. 244103 (CORPUS, www.scp-knowledge.eu). The author would like to thank all consortium partners who contributed to the CORPUS project, notably Gerald Berger, Elisabeth Freytag, Márton Herczeg, Francois Jégou, Harri Kalimo, Tamas Kallay, Lucia Reisch, Sauli Rouhinen, Frieder Rubik, Benoît Simon and Pål Strandbakken. Moreover I am very grateful to all professionals who took part in the workshop series and engaged with the web platform.


## NOTES

1. Research is regarded as 'any investigation towards increasing the sum of knowledge based on planned and systematic enquiry' (Nutley et al. 2007, p. 20). From this perspective, evidence and knowledge respectively result from the interpretation of research findings and, hence, include not only technical and objective assessments but also subjective and contextualized ones (ibid., pp. 23ff).
2. SCORE is the acronym for Sustainable Consumption Research Exchange (2005–2008), the results of which have been published, amongst others, in a series of edited books (e.g. Tukker et al. 2008a; Geerken et al. 2009; Lahlou 2011).
3. The result of (social sciences) research is 'often contentious, may be reliant on controversial theories, draws on multiple and sometimes disputed methods, and may lead to contestable and at times ambiguous findings' (Nutley et al. 2007, p. 21).
4. This observation is in line with what has been found by the European Commission (2008b, p. 14): 'Some countries have a greater tradition of encouraging communication between both fields and in providing appropriate forums and channels to facilitate communication. This is particularly true of Scandinavia and the United Kingdom, and countries with more decentralized models of decision-making.'

## REFERENCES


Andersson, K. (2000), 'LCA of food products and production systems', *International Journal of Life Cycle Assessment*, 5 (4), 239–248.

Backhaus, J., S. Breukers, O. Mont, M. Paukovic and R. Mourik (2012), *Sustainable Lifestyles: Today's Facts and Tomorrow's Trends – D1.1 Sustainable Lifestyles Baseline Report*, Amsterdam: Energy Research Centre of the Netherlands.

Belz, F.-M. and K. Peattie (2009), *Sustainability Marketing: A Global Perspective*, Chichester: John Wiley & Sons.

Berg, A. (2011), 'Not roadmaps but toolboxes: analysing pioneering national programmes for sustainable consumption and production', *Journal of Consumer Policy*, 34, 9–23.

Campbell, S., S. Benita, E. Coates, P. Davies and G. Penn (2007), *Analysis for Policy: Evidence-Based Policy in Practice*, London: Government Social Research Unit.

Carter, R., J. Fawcett, J. Hindson and P. Owen (2012), *Evaluation of the Market Transformation Programme*, Birmingham: Databuild.

Cash, D.W., W.C. Clark, F. Alcock, N. Dickson, N. Eckley, D.H. Guston, J. Jäger et al. (2003), 'Knowledge systems for sustainable development', *Proceedings of the National Academy of Sciences of the United States of America*, 100, 8086–8091.

Choi, B.C.K., T. Pang, V. Lin, P. Puska, G. Sherman, M. Goddard, M.J. Ackland et al. (2005), 'Can scientists and policy makers work together?', *Journal of Epidemiology and Community Health*, 59 (8), 632–637.

Cohen, M.J. and J. Murphy (eds) (2001), *Exploring Sustainable Consumption: Environmental Policy and the Social Sciences*, New York, USA and Amsterdam, the Netherlands: Pergamon.

Creech, H. and T. Willard (2001), *Strategic Intentions: Managing Knowledge Networks for Sustainable Development*, Winnipeg: International Institute for Sustainable Development.

Defila, R., A. Di Giulio and R. Kaufmann-Hayoz (eds) (2013), *The Nature of Sustainable Consumption and How to Achieve It*, Munich: oekom.
Defra (Department for Environment, Food and Rural Affairs) (2008), *A Framework for Pro-Environmental Behaviours*, London: Department for Environment, Food and Rural Affairs.
Defra (Department for Environment, Food and Rural Affairs) (2011a), *Habits, Routines and Sustainable Lifestyles*, London: Department for Environment, Food and Rural Affairs.
Defra (Department for Environment, Food and Rural Affairs) (2011b), *'Moments of Change' as Opportunities for Influencing Behavior*, London: Department for Environment, Food and Rural Affairs.
Dolan, P., M. Hallsworth, D. Halpern, D. King and I. Vlaev (2010), *Mindspace: Influencing Behavior through Public Policy*, London: Institute for Government.
EEA (European Environment Agency) (2012), *Consumption and the Environment – 2012 Update*, Copenhagen: European Environment Agency.
European Commission (2008a), *Action Plan on Sustainable Consumption and Production and Sustainable Industrial Policy (No. 397/3)*, Brussels: European Commission.
European Commission (2008b), *Scientific Evidence for Policy-Making*, Brussels: European Commission.
European Commission (2010), *Communicating Research for Evidence-Based Policymaking. A Practical Guide for Researchers in Socio-Economic Sciences and Humanities*, Brussels: European Commission.
European Commission (2011), *Resource-Efficient Europe – Flagship Initiative under the Europe 2020 Strategy*, Brussels: European Commission.
European Commission (2012a), *Policies to Encourage Sustainable Consumption*, Brussels: European Commission.
European Commission (2012b), *Future Brief: Green Behaviour*, Brussels: European Commission.
European Commission (2013), 'Building the single market for green products: facilitating better information on the environmental performance of products and organisations', Communication from the Commission to the European Parliament and Council, Brussels: European Commission.
Geerken, T., M. Borup and A. Vercalsteren (eds) (2009), *System Innovation for Sustainability 2. Case Studies in Sustainable Consumption and Production – Mobility*, Sheffield: Greenleaf Publishing.
Godemann, J. and G. Michelsen (eds) (2011), *Sustainability Communication. Interdisciplinary Perspectives and Theoretical Foundation*, Dordrecht: Springer.
Heiskanen, E., O. Mont and K. Power (2013), 'A map is not a territory – making research more helpful for sustainable consumption policy', *Journal of Consumer Policy*, 37 (1), 1–18.
Hertwich, E. (2008), 'Consumption and the rebound effect: an industrial ecology perspective', *Journal of Industrial Ecology*, 9 (1–2), 85–98.
Holden, E. (2007), *Achieving Sustainable Mobility: Everyday and Leisure Time Travel in the EU*, Aldershot: Ashgate.
Holmes, J. and R. Clark (2008), 'Enhancing the use of science in environmental policy-making and regulation', *Environmental Science and Policy*, 11, 702–711.
Holmes, J. and J. Lock (2010), 'Generating the evidence for marine fisheries policy and management', *Marine Policy*, 34, 29–35.
Hukkinen, J.I. (2009), 'Science–policy brokerage: enhancing connectivity between research and policy-making in sustainable development', Report to European Commission's Directorate-General Research, Directorate I – Environment, Brussels: European Commission.
Jackson, T. (ed.) (2006), *The Earthscan Reader in Sustainable Consumption*, London: Earthscan.
Jackson, T. and L. Michaelis (2003), *Policies for Sustainable Consumption*, London: Sustainable Development Commission.
Kaiser, F.G. and H. Gutscher (2003), 'The proposition of a general version of the theory of planned behavior: predicting ecological behavior', *Journal of Applied Social Psychology*, 33 (3), 586–603.
Lahlou, S. (ed.) (2011), *System Innovation for Sustainability 4. Case Studies in Sustainable Consumption and Production – Energy Use and the Built Environment*, Sheffield: Greenleaf Publishing.
Lang, D.J., A. Wiek, M. Bergmann, M. Stauffacher, P. Martens, P. Moll, M. Swilling and C.J. Thomas (2012), 'Transdisciplinary research in sustainability science: practice, principles, and challenges', *Sustainability Science*, 7 (1), 25–43.
Magnuszewski, P., K. Sodomkova, A. Slob, M. Muro, J. Sendzimir and C. Pahl-Wostl (2010), 'Report on conceptual framework for science-policy barriers and bridges. Final version 22.12.2010 of deliverable No. 1.1 of the EC FP7 project PSI-connect. EC contract No. 226915. July 2010', Delft.
Manning, C. (2009), 'The psychology of sustainable behavior. Tips for empowering people to take environmentally positive action', St. Paul, MN: Minnesota Pollution Control Agency.
McMeekin, A. and D. Southerton (2012), 'Sustainability transitions and final consumption: practices and socio-technical systems', *Technology Analysis and Strategic Management*, 24 (4), 345–361.
Meyer, M. (2010), 'The rise of the knowledge broker', *Science Communication*, 32 (1), 118–127.
Michaels, S. (2009), 'Matching knowledge brokering strategies to environmental policy problems and settings', *Environmental Science and Policy*, 12, 994–1011.

Ministry of Agriculture, Food and Consumer Affairs (2005), 'Think twice! An action plan for sustainable household consumption. Government Communication 2005/06:107', Ministry of Agriculture, Food and Consumer Affairs.

Mont, O., E. Heiskanen, K. Power and H. Kuusi (2013), *Nordic Policy Brief: Improving Nordic Policymaking by Dispelling Myths on Sustainable Consumption*, Copenhagen: Nordic Council of Ministers.

Niinimäki, K. (2010), 'Eco-clothing, consumer identity and ideology', *Sustainable Development*, 18 (3), 150–162.

Niinimäki, K. and L. Hassi (2011), 'Emerging design strategies in sustainable production and consumption of textiles and clothing', *Journal of Cleaner Production*, 19 (16), 1876–1883.

Nutley, S., H. Davies and I. Walter (2002), 'Evidence based policy and practice: cross sector lessons from the UK', Working Paper 9, St Andrews: ESRC UK Centre for Evidence Based Policy and Practice.

Nutley, S., I. Walter and H.T.O. Davies (2007), *Using Evidence: How Research can Inform Public Services*, Bristol: Policy Press.

OECD (Organisation of Economic Co-operation and Development) (2011), *Greening Household Behaviour: The Role of Public Policy*, Paris: Organisation for Economic Co-operation and Development Publishing.

Oldham, G. and R. McLean (1997), *Approaches to Knowledge-Brokering*, Winnipeg: IISD Publications Centre.

Oullier, O. and S. Sauneron (2011), *"Green Nudges": New Incentives for Ecological Behaviour*, Paris: Centre d'analyse stratégique.

Reinhardt, G., S. Gärtner, J. Münch and S. Häfele (2009),*Ökologische Optimierung regional erzeugter Lebensmittel: Energie- und Klimagasbilanzen*, Heidelberg: IFEU – Institut für Energie- und Umweltforschung.

Reisch, L., U. Eberle and S. Lorek (2013), 'Sustainable food consumption: an overview of contemporary issues and policies', *Sustainability: Science, Practice, and Policy*, 9 (2), 7–25.

Reisch, L. and I. Røpke (2004), *The Ecological Economics of Consumption*, Cheltenham, UK and Northampton, MA, USA: Edward Elgar.

Rubik, F. and P. Frankl (eds) (2005), *The Future of Ecolabelling: Making Environmental Product Information Systems Effective*, Sheffield: Greenleaf.

Rubik, F. and G. Scholl (2002), 'Eco-labelling practices in Europe: an overview of environmental product information schemes', *Schriftenreihe des IÖW (Institut für ökologische Wirtschaftsforschung) 162/02*, Berlin: Institut für ökologische Wirtschaftsforschung.

Rubik, F., G. Scholl, K. Biedenkopf, H. Kalimo, F. Mohaupt, Ó. Söebech, E. Stø et al. (2009), 'Innovative approaches in European sustainable consumption policies', *Schriftenreihe des IÖW (Institut für ökologische Wirtschaftsforschung) 192/09*, Berlin: Institut für ökologische Wirtschaftsforschung.

Sachs, J. and S. Finkelpearl (2010), 'From selling soap to selling sustainability: social marketing', in E. Assadourian (ed.), *State of the World 2010 Transforming Cultures: From Consumerism to Sustainability*, Washington, DC: Worldwatch Institute, pp. 151–225.

Schäfer, M., M. Jaeger-Erben and S. Bamberg (2012), 'Life events as windows of opportunity for changing towards sustainable consumption patterns? Results from an intervention study', *Journal of Consumer Policy*, 35, 65–84.

Scholl, G., G. Berger, E. Freytag, M. Herczeg, F. Jégou, H. Kalimo, T. Kallay et al. (forthcoming), 'Knowledge brokerage for sustainable consumption – enhancing the connectivity between research and policy-making', in A. Martinuzzi and M. Sedlacko (eds), *Knowledge Brokerage for a Sustainable Europe: Innovative tools for Increasing the Impacts of Research and Promoting Evidence Based Policy Making*, Sheffield: Greenleaf.

Scholl, G., K. Power, G. Berger, F. Rubik, E. Freytag, M. Herczeg, F. Jégou et al. (2013), 'Enabling sustainable consumption: making better use of research evidence in policy-making', CORPUS Policy Brief, February, Berlin: Institut für ökologische Wirtschaftsforschung.

Scholl, G., F. Rubik, H. Kalimo, K. Biedenkopf and Ó, Söebech (2010), 'Policies to promote sustainable consumption: innovative approaches in Europe', *Natural Resources Forum*, 34, 39–50.

Schultz, I. and I. Stieß (2008), 'Linking sustainable consumption to everyday life: a social-ecological approach to consumption research', in A. Tukker, M. Charter and C. Vezzoli (eds), *Perspectives on radical Changes to Sustainable Consumption and Production. System Innovation for Sustainability 1*, Sheffield: Greenleaf, pp. 288–300.

Shanley P. and C. López (2009), 'Out of the Loop: 'Why research rarely reaches policy makers and the public and what can be done', *Biotropica*, 41 (5), 535–544.

Sheate, W.R. and M.R. Partidário (2009), 'Strategic approaches and assessment techniques – potential for knowledge brokerage towards sustainability', *Environmental Impact Assessment Review*, 30, 278–288.

Shove, E. (2003), *Comfort, Cleanliness and Convenience: The Social Organization of Normality*, Oxford: Berg.

Shove, E., M. Pantzar and M. Watson (2012), *The Dynamics of Social Practice: Everyday Life and how it Changes*, London: Sage.

Sterk, B., P. Carberry, C. Leeuwis, M.K. van Ittersum, M. Howden, H. Meinke, H. van Keulen et al. (2009), 'The interface between land use systems research and policy: multiple arrangements and leverages', *Land Use Policy*, 26, 434–442.

Surridge, B. and B. Harris (2007), 'Science-driven integrated river basin management: a mirage?', *Interdisciplinary Science Reviews*, 32 (3), 298–312.

SDC (Sustainable Development Commission) (2011), *Making Sustainable Lives Easier. A Priority for Governments, Business and Society*, London: Sustainable Development Commission.

Szlezak, J., A. Reichel and H. Reisinger (2008), 'National sustainable consumption and production (SCP) strategies in the EU – a comparative review of selected cases', *Environmental Research, Engineering and Management*, 45, 54–60.

Thaler, R.H. and C.R. Sunstein (2009), *Nudge: Improving Decisions about Health, Wealth and Happiness*, London: Penguin Books.

Thøgersen, J., P. Haugaard and A. Olesen (2010), 'Consumer responses to ecolabels', *European Journal of Marketing*, 44 (11–12), 1787–1810.

Tukker, A., S. Bausch-Goldbohm, M. Verheijden, A. de Koning, R. Kleijn, O. Wolf and I. Pérez Domínguez (2009), *Environmental Impacts of Diet Changes in the EU*, Seville: Joint Research Centre.

Tukker, A., M. Charter, C. Vezzoli, E. Stø and M.M. Andersen (eds) (2008a), *System Innovation for Sustainability 1: Perspectives on Radical Changes to Sustainable Consumption and Production*, Sheffield: Greenleaf.

Tukker, A., S. Emmert, M. Charter, C. Vezzoli, E. Sto, M. Munch Andersen, T. Geerken, U. Tischner and S. Lahlou (2008b), 'Fostering change to sustainable consumption and production: an evidence based view', *Journal of Cleaner Production*, 16 (11), 1218–1225.

Tukker, A., G. Huppes, J. Guinée, R. Heijungs, A. Koning, L. Oers, S. Suh et al. (2006), 'Environmental impact of products (EIPRO)', draft report of the Institute for Prospective Technological Studies (IPTS) and the European Science and Technology Observatory (ESTO) EIPRO, European Commission Joint Research Centre and Institute for Prospective Technological Studies.

UNEP (United Nations Environment Programme) (2012), *Global Outlook on Sustainable Consumption and Production Policies: Taking Action Together*, Paris: United Nations Environment Programme.

Van Kammen, J., D. de Savigny and N. Sewankambo (2006), 'Using knowledge brokering to promote evidence-based policy-making: the need for support structures', *Bulletin of the World Health Organization*, 84, 608–612.

Ward, V., A. House and S. Hamer (2009), 'Knowledge brokering: the missing link in the evidence to action chain?', *Evidence & Policy: A Journal of Research, Debate and Practice*, 5, 267–279.

Weiß, J., T. Vogelpohl and E. Dunkelberg (2012), 'Improving policy instruments to better tap into homeowner refurbishment potential: lessons learned from a case study in Germany', *Energy Policy*, 44, 406–415.

Wolff, F. and N. Schönherr (2011), 'The impact evaluation of sustainable consumption policy instruments', *Journal of Consumer Policy*, 34, 43–66.

# PART VII

# FUTURE DIRECTIONS

# 24. Decoupling resource consumption and economic growth: insights into an unsolved global challenge

*Peter Hennicke and Dorothea Hauptstock*

In the face of climate change, global demographic developments and growing resource use, natural capital in the form of not only resources but also sinks (for example the atmosphere as a dump for greenhouse gas emissions) is becoming increasingly scarce. Therefore, the decoupling of resource consumption from economic growth (that is, less used natural resources per unit of economic output) and impact decoupling (that is, reduced environmental impact of resource use and economic activities) are necessary condition for sustainable development (UNEP 2011). To this day, there exists no agreed solution for this challenge, despite the increasing risks of irreversible changes of the global earth system ('tipping points'[1]). To minimize these risks, politics, business and civil society have to take considerably more action than they have done until today. Although unsustainable trends have driven the world economy 'beyond the limits' (Meadows et al. 1992) and an overshoot of 'planetary boundaries' (Rockström et al. 2009) is threatening mankind, a resource efficiency revolution in combination with sufficiency policies could be a promising step towards a solution. Scenarios for the global energy sector (e.g. WWF et al. 2011) and for specific countries such as Germany (see Hennicke et al. 2011 for a comparison of scenarios) have clearly demonstrated the technical feasibility for absolute decoupling of gross domestic product (GDP) from primary energy consumption up to 2050. Thus, theoretically, we know enough about technological options to solve the climate problem 'simply by scaling up'[2] (Pacala and Sokolow 2004). This could create much technological optimism. However, based on past experience of only relative decoupling, there is much evidence that technological progress has to be accompanied by radical socio-economic transformation in order to break the nexus between GDP growth and the use of nature. Thus more research on the social context of implementing 'green-tech' and of the socio-economic drivers of 'lead markets' (for example for energy and resource efficiency, sustainable mobility, recycling technologies or renewable energies) is needed. 'Scaling up' is not simple at all. It might even be the core of the problem.

There is no realistic alternative strategy to ambitious improvements in resource efficiency on a global scale, because of manifold reasons: the increasing scarcity of resources (for example biodiversity loss, scarcity of critical metals, overfishing and acidification of oceans, stress on water, scarcity of arable land) and the associated resource conflicts could trigger worldwide crises on a similar scale as climate change. And the frightening perspective is that all these components of a global ecological, economical and societal crisis are getting more and more interlinked (Hennicke and Schneidewind 2012).

The inconvenient truth is: transferring the pattern of consumption and production of the global North to a worldwide population of projected 9.6 billion people by 2050 (UN 2013) is impossible on account of the associated economic, environmental and social problems. Hence there is an imperative to foster decoupling by the increase of resource productivity. Moreover, not taking the opportunity of improved resource efficiency now means huge lost opportunities and economic loses in the future. Increasing scarcity of natural capital and global competition can drive countries into a race to be the most resource efficient global player. Green technology can lead to falling material costs and therewith an improved competitive position; it can lower the dependence on imports and prices and improve raw material security. But we are running out of time: because of existing market failures and manifold barriers, politics must take the lead to establish supporting frame conditions to foster a 'Great Transfomation' (Distelkamp et al. 2010a; WBGU 2011).

With this in mind, this chapter implicitly links the concept of sustainable consumption with the systemic aspects of sustainable production as well as resource and sufficiency policies. This understanding of sustainable consumption goes beyond individual behaviour changes. In case of an urgent necessity for absolute decoupling in the future, two questions have to be answered: (1) On the condition that absolute decoupling is possible, how far can democracies go to change consumption patterns by policy interventions? and (2) How much should policy interventions be focused on sustainable production to enable shifts of sustainable consumption? It seems that there are many as yet unexplored fields of interdisciplinary research that could help us to answer these questions. To frame this research, the chapter is organized along the following lines. First, indicators and key areas for decoupling are presented. Second, the analysis is differentiated for the global North (industrialized countries) and the global South (developing and emerging countries). Third, a concept of absolute decoupling for the case of Germany is described. Fourth, a short outlook is given on how the rapidly growing 'new consumer classes' (for example in China and India) might change the overall picture dramatically.

## 24.1 HOW TO MEASURE DECOUPLING AND WHAT KEY AREAS SHOULD BE ADDRESSED

Global economic and social development over the last two centuries has been largely achieved through intensive, inefficient and unsustainable use of the Earth's finite resources. Over the course of the twentieth century, global resource extraction and consumption increased by around a factor of eight (UNEP 2011). Global population grew around half as fast, while GDP grew at a significantly higher rate (by a factor of 23). The resource category with the highest growth rate was construction minerals (which grew by a factor of 34), followed by industrial ores and minerals (factor of 27) and fossil fuels (factor of 12). The use of biomass increased by a factor of 3.6, reflecting a shift from non-renewable mineral resources to renewable biotic ones. However the scarcity of land and food security constrains a further increase of biotic raw materials for industry or energy production (UNEP 2011; Hennicke and Khosla 2014).

Hence improvements of material productivity happen, but these are mainly driven by autonomous market and price trends and rarely supported by strategic policies. The potential for global technological 'leap-frogging' and possible impacts of international technical cooperation policies (for example transfer of globally best available technologies, BATs) is indicated by the fact that the increase of material productivity in some

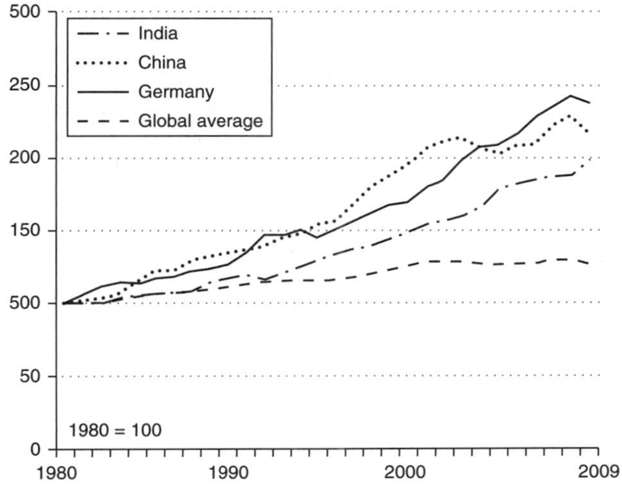


*Note:* GDP in purchasing power parity, const. 2005.

*Source:* Based on IFEU et al. (2013, p. 28).

*Figure 24.1 Material efficiency in India, China, Germany and globally (resource productivity in GDP / DMC)*

countries, such as Germany, is much higher than the global average. However, China and India are catching up (see Figure 24.1). 'South–South' technical cooperation and options for leap-frogging from the global South to less developed countries could increase in the future.

The problem is that absolute material consumption per capita still remains on a high level, especially in industrialized countries: 8.5 tonnes domestic material consumption (DMC) per capita and year were consumed globally in 2008 (Dittrich et al. 2012). In that year, India's consumption was around 4 tonnes per capita, whereas on average, Germany consumed around 14.8 tonnes per capita. According to the Global Footprint Network (2012), if current economic and production trends persist, we will need the equivalent of two Earths to support us by 2030. The World Business Council for Sustainable Development estimates that significant improvements in resource efficiency will be needed by 2020 and they will need to increase by four to ten times until 2050 (WBCSD 2010). The global economy thus needs to reduce dependence on primary resource extraction, while still enabling satisfactory, fulfilling lives for an increasing world population. These scenarios offer clear indications that current levels of resource consumption exceed what is considered sustainable; at least three of nine identified 'planetary boundaries' have already been exceeded and others are dangerously close to scientifically 'safe' thresholds (Rockström et al. 2009, p. 472). Moreover 60 per cent of the world's major ecosystems that ensure the reproduction of renewable resources have already been degraded or are being used unsustainably (MEA 2005).

### 24.1.1 Indicators for Resource Consumption

The results of decoupling analysis depend on the choice of indicators. A comparison of different indicators currently being used shows that the strategic objectives for resource use in environmental policy up to now tend to be general in nature, with the exception of greenhouse gas (GHG) emissions and renewable energy (EEA 2012). The debate on the 'right set' of indicators continues, but should hopefully soon be settled by developing pragmatic, measurable, reliable and easy-to-understand indicator sets for politics, business and civil society. Another challenge is the question of how quantitative indicators should be used for target setting and what they mean in the context of global regimes aimed at reducing resource consumption. In light of the painful negotiations on a global climate regime, up to now there is little political consensus among national governments for setting quantitative targets both nationally and globally. This is not only because of a general political reluctance to make commitments even on indicative, less binding quantitative targets, but also due to a lack of definite measurement methodologies.

The simplest input and consumption indicators used for international comparisons are direct material input (DMI) and domestic material consumption (DMC), which only take direct flows into account. A second set of indicators, raw material input (RMI) and raw material consumption (RMC), try to take indirect flows also into account. Total material requirement (TMR) and total material consumption (TMC) are the most comprehensive indicators, incorporating both indirect flows and unused extraction (e.g. Bringezu and Schütz 2010; Dittrich et al. 2012).

It should be noticed that all these macro indicators are only based on quantities of resources, neglecting impacts because of methodological and data problems. Nevertheless impact decoupling is of the utmost importance. Impact decoupling means maintaining or even raising economic output while reducing negative environmental impacts along the value chain of extraction, production, produce use and waste management. These impacts can be estimated by life cycle analysis (LCA) in combination with various input–output techniques. In general it is very demanding to measure impact decoupling, especially as at the aggregated system level such as a national economy or an economic sector (see Hirschnitz-Grabers et al. 2012) many environmental impacts need to be considered, their trends may be quite different or not even monitored over time, and system boundaries as well as weighting procedures are often contested. Additionally it should be recognized that even a dramatic specific increase of the resource productivity of buildings, processes, vehicles and products etc. could be eaten up by rebound effects, growth, increased comfort and lifestyle changes (see section 24.2).

Last but not least, we have to look at GDP, the numerator of resource productivity. There is now a growing consensus that GDP is only a very rough indicator of welfare, and might be even misleading if it comes to the measurement of happiness and life satisfaction (Clark et al. 2008; Costanza et al. 2014; Frey 2008; see also section 24.4). Thus a necessary and more sufficient condition and indicator for sustainable development implies simultaneous structural change and innovation processes which can be called a triple decoupling: first, life satisfaction from GDP; second, GDP from resource consumption; and third, resource consumption from impacts. Figure 24.2 illustrates this process of triple decoupling, when the impact decoupling is subsumed under the heading of 'less natural resource use' (Hennicke and Welfens 2012).

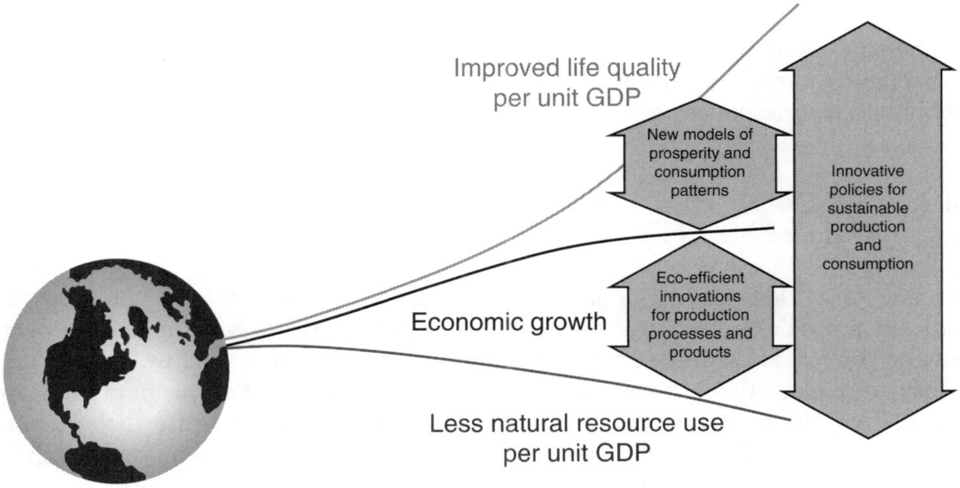


*Source:* Based on Hennicke and Welfens (2012, p. 213).

*Figure 24.2 Conditions for sustainability: the decoupling of quality of life, economic growth and resource use*

### 24.1.2 Key Areas of Action

The potential to use resources more efficiently is vast. But the question is, how can the hot spots and priority areas for change be identified? At the sector level, input–output analysis can pinpoint sectors and product groups that are especially resource-intensive. Recent research has revealed that five product groups are responsible for the majority of resource use at the final consumption end of Europe's economy (ETC/SCP 2011):[3]

- construction;
- food, beverages and tobacco;
- agriculture, forestry and fishing;
- electricity, gas and water;
- coal, refined petroleum products and nuclear fuels.

Strategies to foster resource productivity in these sectors are driven by economics, for example global competition, as well as favourable frame conditions and politically induced incentives to reduce resource costs. McKinsey (2011) identified 15 groups of opportunities to foster resource productivity on a global scale and calculated their total resource benefit as well as their cost–benefit ratios. Taking a societal perspective, it turns out that about 75 per cent of the total resource savings potential in 2030 could be implemented with an attractive cost-efficiency ratio. Fourteen out of 15 groups have a cost–benefit ratio below 1. According to estimates by McKinsey (2011), on a global scale the economic opportunities from raising resource productivity amounts to up to $2.9 trillion in 2030 (for example, energy efficiency alone creating nearly $700 billion in resource benefits), of which 70 per cent have an internal rate of return of more than 10 per cent at current prices. Due to data deficits these figures should be taken only as a rough and preliminary calculation. But based on more detailed national data and scenarios these global figures might be confirmed as being robust if existing barriers can be overcome by ambitious resource policies (see Distelkamp et al. 2010a).

## 24.2 COMMON BUT DIFFERENTIATED RESPONSIBILITIES AND BENEFITS

Sustainable worldwide development is only possible if industrialized countries dramatically reduce their resource consumption per capita. At the same time, the growing demand for resources in developing countries needs to be supported by modern technology to reduce growth rates and to keep the absolute resource consumption as low as possible. The aim should be that industrialized countries decrease their resource consumption per capita faster than developing countries increase resource consumption per capita. With smart resource management this could theoretically create a 'tunnel' for an acceptable standard of living within the given resource boundaries. The described concept is called contraction and convergence (e.g. Jochem 2004). Figure 24.3 illustrates the very ambitious long-run reduction path (up to a factor of ten).

To ensure a global sustainable level all countries have to reach, according to Bringezu (2009), a yearly resource consumption of approx. 6 tonnes (TMC abiotic) per capita in the long run. Countries with higher resource consumption per capita have to approach this level by means of an adequate policy package. Countries below this level have to raise their consumption, so that an acceptable quality of life with a decent level of

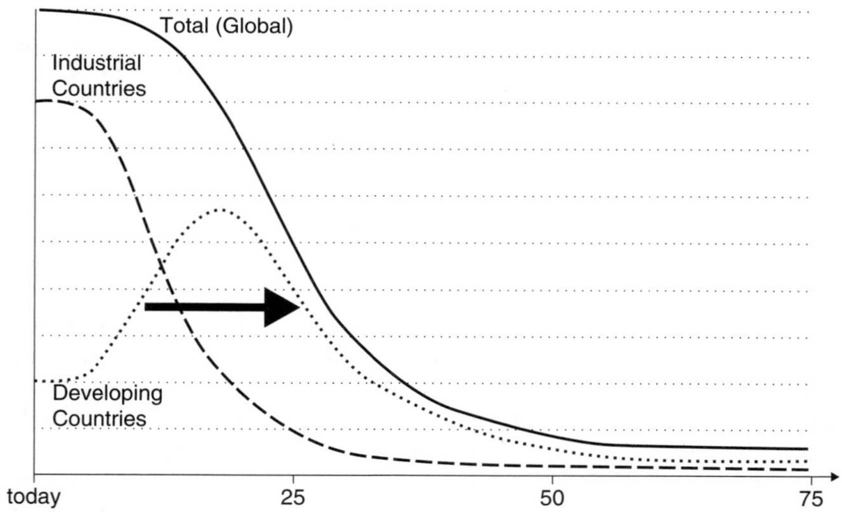


*Source:* Based on Khosla (2011).

*Figure 24.3 Contraction and convergence: in industrial countries, developing countries and globally*

education, health and income of the citizens is ensured, respecting criteria of fair access to resources. Following the concept of contraction and convergence, industrialized and developed countries have to achieve an absolute decoupling, meaning that aggregated resource consumption has to decline irrespectively of the economic growth rate. Developing countries should pursue relative decoupling, meaning that the growth rate of resource consumption is lower than the economic growth rate (that is, an increase in resource productivity). This means that the resource consumption might increase in absolute terms, but its growth rate slows down. If a decent standard of living is reached in a developing country, the adoption of measures to achieve an absolute decoupling should be undertaken.

### 24.2.1 Formal Illustration of Decoupling Challenges

Common but differentiated opportunities and challenges of decoupling in developed and developing countries can be made clearer by referring to the following formula (Ekins 2000, based on Ehrlich and Holdren 1971 and Commoner 1971):

$$I = P \text{ x } A \text{ x } T$$

where $I$ = environmental impact; $P$ = population; $A$ = affluence per capita; $T$ = technology.

To make an international comparison easier and to reduce data problems, resource use ($R$) can be taken as a proxy and indicator for $I$, $Y/P$ (per capita income) as the indicator for 'affluence' and $T$ as the indicator for resource intensity (reciprocal of resource productivity). Then the formula can be rewritten as follows (Hennicke and Sewerin 2008):

$$R = P \text{ x } Y/P \text{ x } R/Y.$$

Formulated in terms of growth rates, the formula becomes:

$$w_R = w_P + w_{Y/P} + w_{R/Y},$$

from which we can derive a simple conclusion: with a positive growth rate of population ($w_P$) and per capita affluence ($w_{Y/P}$), just to keep the global environmental impact constant ($w_R = 0$) requires that the resource intensity decreases by the added growth rates of population and per capita affluence, that is, $(w_P) + (w_{Y/P})$.

The strategic message on a global scale is quite clear: the resource shortages and environmental impacts of resource use will become constraints on human progress unless: (1) the growth of population ($P$) is reduced, (2) lower standards of living ($Y$) are accepted and/or (3) resource productivity is significantly raised.

### 24.2.2 Growth, Resource Protection, Jobs: A 'Knife-Edge' Problem of Absolute Decoupling

In most countries of the North the acceptance of a strategy on absolute decoupling of GDP from the use of nature will be low if it is not connected with at least stabilizing or, better, increasing employment. This can be taken as a necessary condition of sustainable development. It can be demonstrated by a formal comparison of growth rates that this condition can be perceived as a societal 'knife-edge' problem under *ceteris paribus* conditions (all other factors being constant).

Using the following definitions:

*Labour productivity (LP) = Gross domestic product (GDP) / Jobs (J)*
*Resource productivity (RP) = Gross domestic product (GDP) / Total material requirement (TMR)*
*Energy productivity (EP) = Gross domestic product (GDP) / Energy (E)*

a necessary condition for sustainable development – more jobs, less use of nature – can be demonstrated by the following:

$$\textit{Only if } w_{GDP} > w_{LP} \rightarrow \textit{Employment increases}$$

On the other hand:

$$\textit{Only if growth rate of } w_{GDP} < w_{RP\ (or\ EP)} \rightarrow \textit{Resource use (or energy) decreases}$$

Thus to meet the necessary condition of sustainable development the following formal inequality must hold:

$$w_{LP} < w_{GDP} < w_{RP} \text{ (example for annual rates: } 1.5\% < 2\% < 2.5\%)$$

Thus focusing economic policies only on maximizing economic growth without fostering resource productivity will not lead to absolute decoupling. On the other hand, the growth rate of GDP must be high enough for additional jobs to be created considering the growth of labour productivity (*ceteris paribus*). To alleviate this 'knife-edge' problem other strategic options such as the reduction of average labour time, structural changes to a service and recycling economy, new models of wealth, lifestyle changes and sufficiency policies have to be taken into account.

### 24.2.3 The Decoupling Triangle

One basic challenge of fostering global decoupling by increasing resource productivity is supporting micro-level activities that are compatible with long-term goals and conditions. This requires a systemic perspective and a way to link the micro level of where change happens to the macro level of where impacts are measured, policies are made and targets are set.

It also requires knowledge on how to cushion rebound effects (Madlener and Alcott 2011) and other counterproductive effects[4] over time. For example even though the technical feasibility of an absolute decoupling and a tremendous increase of resource productivity were demonstrated by scenarios and might be the aim of national resource policies, counteracting social and economic reactions (direct and indirect rebound effects; growth, structural and quantity effects) can 'eat up' even massive increases in product, process or sector specific resource productivities. Therefore, resource policies based on technology-driven scenario analysis and respective policy mixes to overcome barriers and to disseminate advanced technologies should always be aware of these counterproductive side effects. It is the triangle of efficiency ('more with less'), sufficiency ('less can be more') and consistency ('better than more') upon which policies and measures for decoupling should be based (see BUND and Misereor 1996; BUND et al. 2008). At the end of the day, what counts from an ecological and ethical perspective is to sustain ecosystem services for all peoples and generations to come.[5]

## 24.3 GERMANY: A CASE STUDY

### 24.3.1 Framing Resource Policies[6]

In Germany, as well as in other European countries, there is an influential new debate in the research community and civil society on the topic of the 'limits of growth' or the 'post-growth society' (Seidl and Zahrnt 2010). The debate started in the 1970s with the Meadows report to the Club of Rome (Meadows et al. 1972), but its revival is currently much more differentiated and policy-oriented. Based on historical evidence of only relative decoupling in even the most resource-efficient countries (ETC/SCP 2011), some 'anti-growth' advocates argue that also in the future an absolute decoupling will not be probable or might even be impossible (e.g. Jackson 2009; Seidl and Zahrnt 2010). Their claim, in short, is that climate and resource protection strategies will not work as long as efficiency gains are eaten up by growth. This thesis is mainly based on the assumption that macroeconomic rebound effects cannot be avoided even with the strongest efforts to raise energy, material and resource productivity in specific products and production processes, if economic growth is not reduced and stopped later on.

The counterproductive impact on public opinion of this simplified thesis can be that it is used as an argument against any ambitious efficiency strategies, be they focused only on raising energy efficiency or – at a broader scale – on resource productivity. Thus it is necessary to critically analyse the 'no decoupling possible' thesis for specific countries, and using appropriate modelling tools (for example dynamic input–output models). For example, the Wuppertal Institute for Climate, Environment and Energy in cooperation with 30 partners from research and business conducted a comprehensive study of decoupling in Germany on behalf of the Ministry of Environment, on Material Efficiency and Resource Consumption (MaRess).[7] This project also contributed to pave the way to establish a governmental strategy, the German Resource Efficiency Programme (ProgRess, see below).

The MaRess project started with the basic question of whether resource policies in Germany could be based on new opportunities to shape technical and social progress ('nature saving, labour augmenting') in a manner which helps to conserve nature, creates jobs and is economically attractive at the same time. Under conditions of global competition, one could even ask: is there any alternative to forcing increased resource efficiency? Because not taking advantage of the economic opportunities of resource efficiency and structural change to a greener economy may mean becoming a loser in global competition (Kristof and Hennicke 2010a).

From a business perspective, in Germany, material costs account for over 45 per cent of total costs (including approximately 2 per cent energy costs) in the manufacturing industries,[8] whereas total labour costs account for approximately 20 per cent (Kristof and Hennicke 2010a). There is evidence that in other developed and emerging economies the average share of material costs of processing industries is also very high (see e.g. IFEU et al. 2013). Thus advanced nature-conserving technology, so called 'green-tech', contributes on the one hand to reduce national material costs, and on the other hand creates opportunities on the export lead markets (Kristof and Hennicke 2010b).

The German consultancy company Roland Berger (2009) identified, on behalf of the German Ministry of Environment, six global 'lead markets':

- energy efficiency (39 per cent);
- sustainable water management (26 per cent);
- sustainable mobility (14 per cent);
- environmental friendly power (11 per cent);
- material efficiency (7 per cent); and
- waste management (3 per cent).

The percentages (in brackets) are based on a total global potential of €1400 billion (2007) of the six 'lead markets' with a probable rise to €3100 billion in 2020 (Roland Berger 2009; UBA 2011).

From a technological perspective these green 'lead markets' are technological options to substitute 'brown' technologies (for example, fossil fuels), to reduce material and resource use, and at the same time to mitigate climate change and foster sustainable development. Thus one important political focus of the MaRess project was to identify and recommend integrated resource and climate protection strategies for the German government.

Apparently there is a large amount of overlap between a climate protection strategy and a forced resource conservation strategy. This applies both to the shared portfolio of applied technologies and to the synergies of the implementation strategies. This increases the demands on an integrated and goal-oriented economic, environmental and research policy. A large incentive to implement this sort of integrated policy would be if a dedicated climate protection policy were amplified through the integration of resource conservation to create additional benefits for the economy.

MaRess modelling results on the combination of resource and climate protection policies show that for Germany even a limited use of resource policy tools already leads to positive acceleration of economic and environmental effects, if combined with an ambitious climate mitigation strategy. The MaRess simulation assumed a selected portfolio of resource policies, including for example the introduction of a primary buildings material tax, certain quota obligations to encourage the use of recycled materials, information (audits) and incentives to identify and implement cost-effective material reduction potentials, especially in small and medium-sized enterprises (SMEs). Based on these policy strategies the simulation with the Panta Rhei model[9] for the year 2030 resulted in the following effects; relative to a reference approach with active climate protection, which has been estimated to ensure a reduction in greenhouse gases of 54 per cent by 2030 (Distelkamp et al. 2010b):

- a reduction in the absolute material consumption of around 20 per cent;
- an increase of the gross domestic product by around 14 per cent;
- an increase in employment levels of around 1.9 per cent (under consideration of demographic factors and productivity-oriented wage developments); and
- a reduction of €251 billion in the federal budget by the year 2030.

Overall, the MaRess simulation came to the conclusion that a consistent resource efficiency policy strengthens Germany's international competitive position if industrial policy drives green innovation. Though further empirical research is still needed, the dynamic input–output analysis demonstrated for the first time for a high-technology country that 'combining a committed climate protection policy with a policy to increase material efficiency can achieve an absolute decoupling of economic growth from resource consumption' (Kristof and Hennicke 2010a, p. 18; based on Distelkamp et al. 2010a). This simulation result is also interesting because it provides a new understanding of the balancing of the structural effects of green growth industries and shrinking risk industries in the national economy. In addition, the development of more sustainable consumption and production patterns, and the limiting of macroeconomic 'rebound' and comfort effects, can be quantified and examined in more detail with modelling tools. This is a new and promising field of international research on socio-economic transformation processes. On the one hand, it could encourage an in-depth analysis of the potentials and hot spots of absolute decoupling. On the other hand, it strongly supports the integration of policies for climate, resource protection and sustainable development.

### 24.3.2 Selected Policies and Measures

The numerous obstacles to efficient utilization of resources, such as a lack of information, external costs or path-dependencies, demand a targeted framework as well as stimuli and incentives which promote increased resource efficiency. Therefore a sort of toolbox was developed in MaRess for the government framework conditions, for the business sector and for consumers. Some policies and measures are selected below.[10]

**Framework conditions**

Regulatory, fiscal and contract-based tools can be used to trigger search processes as well as innovations, diffusion and green investments in resource efficiency technology.

*Regulatory approaches* Reporting requirements for manufacturers and importers. A lack of information on the use of materials is a key problem when it comes to resource policy. This problem is in particular a result of globalized supply chains and product life cycles. Manufacturers should be obligated to provide information on the material groups and materials used in their products. This tool provides the knowledge base for further incentive tools (for example production input regulations, labelling).

Product input regulations can be used in order to influence the design and composition of products. Up to now, approaches in the area of resource conservation were primarily targeting the waste streams. Input regulations, however, apply to the product design phase. Requirements can also be tied to market access regulations.

The EU Ecodesign Directive is suitable as the basis for regulatory approaches. It should be expanded to additional product groups and indicators which go beyond energy consumption.

*Fiscal tools* Taxation of primary building materials. The suggested amount is €2 per tonne, with the goal of increasing resource efficiency and reducing consumption. Differentiated value-added tax (VAT) approaches can be used to reduce the tax burden on resource-efficient products at the expense of inefficient products. One could also consider a tax advantage for secondary building materials or devices, which contain a large percentage of recycled material.

*International covenant* An agreement based on private law between public agencies and stakeholders along the product life cycle can serve to close metal material cycles which cross international boundaries (for example, vehicles). In this case, one would define concrete goals to increase resource efficiency, for example by ensuring that recycling is performed in other countries.

**Business level**

*Financing-based incentives* The goal is to establish resource efficiency as a key factor for the power to compete in the financial sector: as a cost reduction approach and for the dynamic growth of green technology:

- Performance: resource-based key performance indicators (R-KPI) allow the financial sector to apply resource efficiency criteria in everyday business, for financial supervision and in company reporting.
- Dialogue: establishing an inquiry commission, 'Resource Efficiency and Sustainability in the Financial Sector', in order to support the debate on the role of the financial sector in the protection of resources; development of a political strategy with all stakeholders.
- Research: implementation of a federal research programme worth €10 million could relate the financial sector perspectives with the well-founded results of environment and sustainability research, so that the results can be used functionally by politics and the financial sector.

*Public efficiency awareness and performance*

- Increasing the willingness to change behaviours and beneficial external offers and framework conditions.
- Supporting small and medium-sized enterprises (SMEs) locally: expansion of the consultant pool and regional structures in order to improve understanding of the topic of resource efficiency and to communicate it locally.

The MaRess-Project was one cornerstone in developing the German Resource Efficiency Programme (ProgRess). Figure 24.4 summarizes the complex structure of the planned ProgRess.

For the first time in Europe, a comprehensive programme to foster resource efficiency was formulated. Mainly due to political priorities on implementing the ambitious

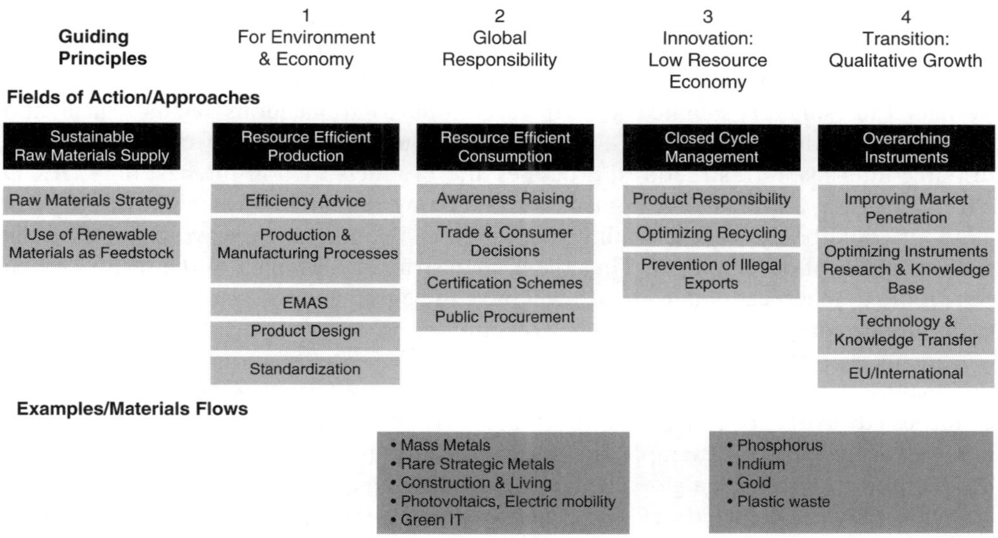


*Source:* Based on BMU (2012).

*Figure 24.4 Structure of the German Resource Efficiency Programme, ProgRess*

German roadmap to a nuclear and (almost) fossil-fuel-free energy system up to 2050 ('Energiewende') the implementation of this programme has been postponed. It can be argued that integration of the Energiewende (focused on renewables and energy efficiency) with resource and material efficiency policies would create additional macroeconomic benefits. Thus there might be an opportunity to develop an integrated energy and material efficiency programme to support the Energiewende.

## 24.4 OUTLOOK

There is much evidence in Organisation for Economic Co-operation and Development (OECD) countries that after a certain threshold rising GDP is decoupled from life satisfaction. For example instead of growing in parallel with GDP, the genuine progress indicator (GPI), showing the level of life satisfaction, has remained at a constant level since the 1970s globally (Costanza et al. 2014 based on Kubiszewski et al. 2013). The indicator reveals that for 17 countries the (about half of the world population) GDP per capita and GPI per capita developed similarly from 1950 until 1970, but then decoupled dramatically.

Thus it is necessary to focus the decoupling agenda much more than in the past on how much quality of life (life satisfaction) or happiness can be derived from GDP growth. This is not only a debate on the right metrics or on indicators, but also a fundamental societal and political challenge, especially for developed countries, but also for the growing urban middle class of developing and emerging countries.

Research on the environmental Kuznets curve suggests that the environmental impact of production and consumption increases with increasing prosperity in a first development phase, but beyond a certain point of prosperity it then decreases (e.g. Dasgupta et al. 2002). Development patterns according to the Kuznets curve will dramatically overrun the planetary boundaries. However, due to tremendous technological and societal innovations, developing and emerging countries can leap-frog to much less resource-intensive infrastructures, processes and products than in the past (e.g. OECD 2011). Thus the Kuznets development phase 'getting rich and dirty' might not happen at all, or could be shortened, if failures of developed countries were avoided during the take-off phase of development. Thus the needed structural changes of the sectors which contribute to macroeconomic growth will have to be tremendous, and decoupling needs to be supported by a resource efficiency revolution.

It seems especially useful to identify joint technical, societal and structural leap-frog options for sustainable production and consumption between developed and developing countries, to avoid lock-in effects (cf. GEA 2012) and path-dependencies from technologies of the past (for example, inefficient building stock or highly centralized energy production). It would be a global tragedy if developing countries try to copy past technological patterns, which developed countries are currently changing in favour of more environmentally, economically and socially benign decentralized and energy-efficient options.

It has been predicted that India and China's share of global middle class consumption[11] will grow rapidly between 2025 and 2050 (EEA 2010). According to these projections, in 2050 India's share could rise to 31 per cent and China's to 22 per cent, leaving the European Union (EU), USA and Japan (together approximately 13 per cent) far behind. The challenge for emerging economies such as India or China is to find a way to circumvent the highly capital-intensive, unsustainable infrastructure as an indicator of development. Not only are such installations (for example in energy and water supply) locking up more and more capital; but they are also impeding research and development (R&D) or the adaptation of smaller-scale, ecosystem-based services options and, especially, circular economy approaches. New 'green-tech' and 'green-soc' innovations such as energy co-operatives, prosumers (increased rate of energy autarky), smart grids, integrated city mobility, urban gardening or social enterprises, guilds and other artisan groups, might be applicable in Germany as well as in emerging economies.

## ACKNOWLEDGEMENTS

This chapter is partly based on a background paper prepared for the Indo-German Expert Group on Green and Inclusive Economy; see Hennicke and Khosla (2014). We thank Ann-Cathrin Klappert for finalizing the text.

## NOTES

1. 'The term "tipping point" commonly refers to a critical threshold at which a tiny perturbation can qualitatively alter the state or development of a system' (Lenton et al. 2008). Tipping points can be fundamental changes in the global climate system (for example, instability of pole ice sheets, monsoon transformation) due to overshooting the global 2° C target.

2. 'Humanity can solve the carbon and climate problem in the first half of the century simply by scaling up what we already know to do' (Pacala and Socolow 2004, p. 968).
3. Calculations refer to nine European Union (EU) countries for 2005: Austria, the Czech Republic, Germany, Denmark, France, Italy, the Netherlands, Portugal and Sweden.
4. In this chapter the term 'rebound effect' is used in a general way to include direct and indirect rebound effects as well as growth, structural and quantity effects. To answer the questions whether and by how much resource effects are caused by efficiency increase, a much more sophisticated analysis is needed.
5. This simplified definition summarizes the often-cited Brundtland definition of sustainable development; the strength and impact of substitution between 'nature' and 'capital' (strong versus weak concepts of sustainability) cannot be debated in this context.
6. Text based on Hennicke and Khosla (2014) and Hennicke and Sewerin (2008).
7. See the project website at http://ressourcen.wupperinst.org/en/home/index.html.
8. According to official statistics, material costs are defined as: 'Raw materials and other preliminary products obtained from third parties, auxiliary and operating materials including third-party components, energy, water, fuels, office and advertising material, and non-activated low-value commodities' (DESTATIS, FS 4, line 4.3., cost structures in producing trades). Therefore the material costs also include the advance services of upstream production stages. The stated cost fraction of 45 per cent is based on the average production value of the processing industry.
9. For an explanation of the model see Meyer (2005).
10. See also the policy part of the MaRess project (http://ressourcen.wupperinst.org/en/project/policies/index.html) as well as the summary in Hennicke and Schneidewind (2012).
11. In this study 'middle class' is defined as households with per capita daily spending between US$10 and US$100 (purchasing power parity).

# REFERENCES


BMU (Federal Ministry for the Environment, Nature Conservation, Building and Nuclear Safety) (2012), *The German Programme Resource Efficiency*, Berlin: BMU.

Bringezu, S. (2009), 'Visions of a sustainable resource use', in S. Bringezu and R. Bleischwitz (eds), *Sustainable Resource Management. Global Trends, Visions and Policies*, Sheffield, UK: Greenleaf, pp. 155–215.

Bringezu, S. and H. Schütz (2010), 'Material use indicators for measuring resource productivity and environmental impacts', workshop, Berlin, 25–26 February, Final report, Paper within the framework of the 'Material Efficiency and Resource Conservation' (MaRess) Project, Wuppertal: Wuppertal Institute for Climate, Environment and Energy.

BUND (Bund Umwelt und Naturschutz Deutschland) and Misereor (1996), *Zukunftsfähiges Deutschland. Ein Beitrag zu einer global nachhaltigen Entwicklung*, Eine Studie des Wuppertal Instituts für Klima, Umwelt, Energie, Basel: Birkhäuser.

BUND (Bund Umwelt und Naturschutz Deutschland), Brot für die Welt and eed (Evangelischer Entwicklungsdienst) (2008), *Zukunftsfähiges Deutschland in einer globalisierten Welt. Ein Anstoß zur gesellschaftlichen Debatte*, Eine Studie des Wuppertal Instituts für Klima, Umwelt, Energie, Frankfurt/Main: Fischer.

Clark, A., P. Frijters and M.A. Shields (2008), 'Relative income, happiness, and utility: an explanation for the Easterlin Paradox and other puzzles', *Journal of Economic Literature*, 46 (1), 95–144.

Commoner, B. (1971), *The Closing Circle: Confronting the Environmental Crisis*, London: Jonathan Cape.

Costanza, R., I. Kubiszewski, E. Giovannini, H. Lovins, J. McGlade, K.E. Pickett, K.V. Ragnarsdóttir, et al. (2014), 'Development: time to leave GDP behind', *Nature*, 505, 283–285.

Dasgupta, S., B. Laplante, H. Wang and D. Wheeler (2002), 'Confronting the environmental Kuznets curve', *Journal of Economic Perspectives*, 16 (1), 147–168.

Dittrich, M., S. Giljum, S. Lutter and C. Polzin (2012), 'Green economies around the world? Implications of resource use for development and the environment', Study supported by UNIDO, UBA, Factor 10 Institute, FOE, Heinrich Böll Stiftung, GIZ and Swiss Confederation, Vienna.

Distelkamp, M., B. Meyer and M. Meyer (2010a), 'Quantitative und qualitative Analyse der ökonomischen Effekte einer forcierten Ressourceneffizienzstrategie', Kurzfassung der Ergebnisse des Arbeitspakets 5 des Projekts 'Materialeffizienz und Ressourcenschonung' (MaRess), Ressourceneffizienz Paper 5.2, Wuppertal: Wuppertal Institute for Climate, Environment and Energy.

Distelkamp, M., B. Meyer and M. Meyer (2010b), 'Quantitative and qualitative effects of a forced resource efficiency strategy', Summary report of Task 5, in *Final Report on the Material Efficiency and Resource Conservation (MaRess) Project*, Wuppertal: Wuppertal Institute for Climate, Environment and Energy.

Ehrlich, P.R. and J.P. Holdren (1971), 'Impact of population growth', *Science*, 171, 1212–1217.
Ekins, P. (2000), *Economic Growth and Environmental Sustainability*, New York: Routledge.
EEA (European Environment Agency) (2010), *The European Environment. State and Outlook 2010, Material Resources and Waste*, Copenhagen: European Environment Agency.
EEA (European Environment Agency) (2012), *Environmental Indicator Report 2012 – Ecosystem Resilience and Resource Efficiency in a Green Economy in Europe*, Copenhagen: European Environment Agency.
ETC/SCP (European Topic Centre on Sustainable Consumption and Production) (2011), 'Key messages on material resource use and efficiency in Europe. Insights from environmentally extended input–output analysis and material flow accounts', ETC/SCP Working Paper 3/2011, Copenhagen: European Topic Centre of Sustainable Consumption and Production, EEA.
Frey, B. (2008), *Happiness: A Revolution in Economics*, Cambridge, MA: MIT Press.
GEA (Global Energy Assessment) (2012), *Toward a Sustainable Future*, Cambridge: Cambridge University Press.
Global Footprint Network (2012), 'Glossary', available at http://www.footprintnetwork.org/en/index.php/GFN/page/glossary/ (accessed 4 February 2014).
Hennicke, P. and Khosla, A. (2014), 'Decoupling Economic Growth From Resources Consumption. A Transformation Strategy with Manifold Socio-Economic Benefits For India and Germany', Deutsche Gesellschaft für Internationale Zusammenarbeit (GIZ). Berlin.
Hennicke, P. and U. Schneidewind (2012), 'Material efficiency and resource conservation – selected results from the large-scale project MaRess', in econsense – Forum for Sustainable Development of German Business (ed.), *Resource Efficiency Challenge. Opinions, Examples, and Management Tools*, Berlin: econsense, pp. 27–32, available at http://www.econsense.de/sites/all/files/Ressource%20Efficiency%20Challenge.pdf (accessed 4 February 2014).
Hennicke, P. and S. Sewerin (2008), 'Developing strategies and policy instruments to foster material efficiency and resource conservation in Germany', *Nikkei Ecology*, 8, 165, available at http://wupperinst.org/uploads/tx_wupperinst/Decoupling-GDP.pdf (accessed 4 February 2014).
Hennicke, P. and P.J.J. Welfens (2012), *Energiewende nach Fukushima: Deutscher Sonderweg oder weltweites Vorbild?*, München: oekom.
Hennicke, P., S. Samadi and T. Schleicher (2011), Ambitionierte Ziele – untaugliche Mittel: Deutsche Energiepolitik am Scheideweg. Hintergrundpapier der Vereinigung Deutscher Wissenschaftler (VDW) zur Energie- und Klimapolitik in Deutschland, Berlin: VDW-Materialien, available at http://www.vdw-ev.de/images/stories/vdwdokumente/aktuelles/vdw%20materialien%201%202011.pdf (accessed 4 February 2014).
Hirschnitz-Garbers, M., T. Srebotnjak, L. Porsch, M. Grünig, P. Hand and K. Timeus Crezo (2012), 'Integrating resource efficiency, greening of industrial production and green industries – scoping of and recommendations for effective indicators', Berlin: Ecologic Institute.
IFEU (Institute for Energy and Environmental Research), TERI (The Energy and Resources Institute), SERI (Sustainable Europe Research Institute), Wuppertal Institute for Climate, Environment and Energy, GIZ (Deutsche Gesellschaft für Internationale Zusammenarbeit) and M. Dittrich (2013), *India's Future Needs for Resources. Dimensions, Challenges and Possible Solutions*, Heidelberg, Germany and New Delhi, India: GIZ.
Jackson, T. (2009), *Prosperity Without Growth. Economics for a Finite Planet*, London: Earthscan.
Jochem, E. (ed.) (2004), *Steps towards a Sustainable Development. A White Book for R&D of Energy-efficient Technologies*, Zurich: Novatlantis.
Khosla, A. (2011), 'Sustainable Energy and Resource Management – Some Basic Systems Principles for International Negotiations', presentation at Club of Rome meeting in Basel October 2011, available at http://www.clubofrome.org/cms/wp-content/uploads/2011/10/Ashok-Khosla-Sustainable-Energy-and-Resource-Management1.pdf (accessed 4 February 2014).
Kristof, K. and P. Hennicke (2010a), 'Argumentationslinie für Ressourceneffizienzpolitik: Policy Paper zu Arbeitspaket 7 des Projekts "Materialeffizienz und Ressourcenschonung" (MaRess)', Wuppertal: Wuppertal Institute for Climate, Environment and Energy.
Kristof, K. and P. Hennicke (2010b), 'Final Report on the Material Efficiency and Resource Conservation (MaRess) Project', Wuppertal: Wuppertal Institute for Climate, Environment and Energy.
Kubiszewski, I., R. Costanza, C. Franco, P. Lawn, J. Talberth, T. Jackson and C. Aylmer (2013), 'Beyond GDP: measuring and achieving global genuine progress', *Ecological Economics*, 93, 57–56.
Lenton, T., H. Held, E. Kriegler, J.W. Hall, W. Lucht, S. Rahmstorf and H.J. Schellnhuber (2008), 'Tipping elements in the Earth's climate system', *Proceedings of the National Academy of Sciences*, 105 (6), 1786–1793.
McKinsey Global Institute and McKinsey Sustainability and Resource Productivity Practice (2011), 'Resource revolution: meeting the world's energy, materials, food, and water needs', McKinsey & Company.
Madlener, R. and B. Alcott (2011), 'Herausforderungen für eine technische-ökonomische Entkoppelung von Naturverbrauch und Wirtschaftswachstum: unter besonderer Berücksichtigung der Systematisierung von

Rebound-Effekten und Problemverschiebungen', Enquete Commission 'Growth, Well-being and Quality of Life' of the German Parliament.
Meadows, D., D. Meadows and J. Randers (1992), *Beyond the Limits*, White River Junction, VT: Chelsea Green.
Meadows, D.H., D.L. Meadows, J. Randers and W.W. Behrens III (1972), *The Limits to Growth*, New York: New American Library.
MEA (Millennium Ecosystem Assessment) (2005), *Ecosystems and Human Well-Being: Synthesis*, Washington, DC: Island Press.
Meyer, B. (2005), 'The economic–environmental model PANTA RHEI and its application', GWS Discussion Paper, Osnabrück: GWS, available at http://www.gws-os.de/downloads/gws-paper05-3.pdf (accessed 4 February 2014).
OECD (Organisation for Economic Co-operation and Development) (2011), *Towards Green Growth*, Paris: OECD Publishing.
Pacala, S. and R. Sokolow (2004), 'Stabilization wedges: solving the climate problem for the next 50 years with current technologies', *Science*, 305, 968–972.
Rockström, J., W. Steffen, K. Noone, Å. Persson, F. Stuart Chapin III, E.F. Lambin, T.M. Lenton, et al. (2009), 'A safe operating space for humanity', *Nature*, 461, 472–475.
Roland Berger (2009), *GreenTech Made in Germany 2.0*, Federal Ministry for the Environment, Nature Conservation, Building and Nuclear Safety (BMU) (ed.), Munich: Franz Vahlen.
Seidl, I. and A. Zahrnt (eds.) (2010), *Postwachstumsgesellschaft: Konzepte für die Zukunft*, Marburg: Metropolis.
UBA (Federal Environment Agency) (2011), 'Report on the environmental economy 2011 – facts & figures for Germany', Berlin: BMU/UBA.
UN (2013), 'World population prospects. The 2012 revision. Volume II: Demographic profiles', available at http://esa.un.org/wpp/Documentation/pdf/WPP2012_Volume-II-Demographic-Profiles.pdf (accessed 4 February 2014).
UNEP (United Nations Environment Programme) (2011), 'Decoupling natural resource use and environmental impacts from economic growth', A Report of the Working Group on Decoupling to the International Resource Panel, M. Fischer-Kowalski, M. Swilling, E.U. von Weizsäcker, Y. Ren, Y. Moriguchi, W. Crane, F. Krausmann, N. Eisenmenger, S. Giljum, P. Hennicke, P. Romero Lankao, A. SiribanManalang and S. Sewerin, available at http://www.unep.org/resourcepanel/decoupling/files/pdf/decoupling_report_english.pdf (accessed 4 February 2014).
WBCSD (World Business Council for Sustainable Development) (2010), 'Vision 2050. The new agenda for business', Geneva: World Business Council for Sustainable Development.
WBGU (German Advisory Council on Global Change) (2011), *World in Transition – A Social Contract for Sustainability*, Berlin: Wissenschaftlicher Beirat der Bundesregierung Globale Umweltveränderungen.
WWF (World Wide Fund For Nature), Ecofys and OMA (Office for Metropolitan Architecture) (eds) (2011), 'The energy report: 100% renewable energy by 2050', Gland: WWF, available at http://awsassets.panda.org/downloads/the_energy_report_lowres_111110_2.pdf (accessed 4 February 2014).

# 25. The role of consumer sovereignty in sustaining the market economy

*Wolfgang J. Fellner and Clive L. Spash*

In today's market economy the politics of neoliberalism dominate. A central weapon in the formidable armoury of economists sympathetic to the neoliberal agenda is that of the sovereign consumer. This encapsulates in one simple analogy the idea that individuals can command the organizations composing an exchange market to do what they want, as a monarch might command their troops in the field of battle. On the simple expression of demand by the consumer, the mechanism of the market will respond, resources will be reallocated and goods and services will be supplied.

In this consumer-driven world of mainstream economists there are only two actors, firms and consumers, who operate in a market which is idealized as being free of government (by state or any other authority). The political economy of the real world is a little more complex than that. Markets themselves are constructed in many different ways involving various institutional arrangements (conventions, norms and rules). Markets are constituted of formally sanctioned rules that are enforced and maintained by government. The rules are manipulated and changed by national vested interest groups and authorities (for example, unions, employers' federations, city councils, health and safety, advertising and trading standards) and international organizations (for example, the World Bank, World Trade Organization, multinational corporations) in accord with their own interests and their power to enforce those interests. The economy is inseparable from this world of power, so there is only a political economy.

Behind the power game lies the supportive discourse of academic economists providing the rhetoric, concepts and formal arguments that power players use to assure others that free-market institutions are the best means of operating human society. Government, as a major potential player, then needs to be made subservient to the interests of the market players, primarily corporations. This is the new industrial state of Galbraith (2007 [1967]) that today has been realized in a new form. For now we have both his technostructure empowered and the neoliberal coup of a hollowed-out state (Rhodes 1996).

In order to explore the role of consumer sovereignty in this complex we take a critical and analytical history of thought approach to tracing the development of the concept. This allows us to gain a better understanding of how the initial analogy has been reinterpreted over time and used for different purposes to support alternative ideological positions. More specifically we trace out three arguments (political instrumental, market ideal and economic instrumental) that have been used to support the importance of maintaining that consumers are sovereigns in the market economy. These arguments are associated with three forms of political economy, namely those of classical liberalism, Austrian and neoclassical economics. The development of consumer sovereignty in a classical liberal political tradition has facilitated a close association with Austrian economics encouraging some merging of positions. Neoclassical economists hold a somewhat distinct role for consumer sovereignty as a desirable instrumental means for achieving economic efficiency backed by rational choice theory.[1] This allows for government intervention in the neoclassical economics tradition, that is, as guarantor of consumer rights and the smooth operation of the price mechanism, often contra corporate power. However, despite some fundamental differences, all three arguments can be seen as combining to support neoliberalism and the current economic faith in a corporate capitalist market system. Internal contradictions merely obscure meaning and provide a shield rather than a weakness. Neoliberalism then creates a mist of self-belief through which criticism cannot easily penetrate. This position is maintained in spite of, and in fact has been bolstered by, the recent financial crisis (Mirowski 2013).

In the following section we start by sketching out the historical context of economic thought from which consumer sovereignty arose. Next we explore the three positions mentioned above. These are explained as involving three distinct roles for consumer sovereignty: as a political instrument, a market ideal and an instrument of economic efficiency. Neoliberalism is noted as having combined aspects of all three positions, gaining allegiance from members of all three camps. Next we investigate arguments as to why consumers are not sovereign in a capitalist market economy. This raises the need to distinguish between choices and preferences, the place of consumers in the structure of real modern economies, and the power that others (for example, producers, the state) have over consumer preferences. We conclude by drawing out some lessons for the needed transformation of society away from the capitalist market exchange model of political economy and towards a socially just, environmentally harmonious political economy.

## 25.1 THE DEVELOPMENT OF MODERN POLITICAL ECONOMY

Classical economists recognized that the production of goods and services was not an end in itself, although producers might seek to profit at the consumer's expense (for example, via protectionism under a mercantilist system). Thus Adam Smith (1976 [1776], p. 877) wrote:

> Consumption is the sole end and purpose of all production; and the interest of the producer ought to be attended to only so far as it may be necessary for promoting that of the consumer. The maxim is so perfectly self evident that it would be absurd to attempt to prove it. But in the mercantile system the interest of the consumer is almost constantly sacrificed to that of the producer; and it seems to consider production, and not consumption, as the ultimate end and object of all industry and commerce.

However, Smith's theoretical exploration did not revolve around the fulfilment of the unlimited interests of consumers, utilitarianism or maximizing hedonic pleasures. For him, the legitimacy of a liberal market economy was based on providing superior results under conditions where people's behaviour is fundamentally subject to moral constraints (Smith 1982 [1759]). Economic policy analysis could then be seen as a search for a system that could provide the material basis for a moral society. In contrast, modern economics moved to supporting the unquestioned individual preference-based desire to consume ever more. That later position appeals to the hedonism of David Hume which became encapsulated in the utilitarianism of Bentham that then was adopted and adapted by neoclassical economists.

Nevertheless the predominant focus of classical economics was to expand production. In the real world capital accumulation and the spread of the market was causing major transformations (Polanyi 1944). The second half of the nineteenth century was characterized by serious social and political struggles. Class conflict became a direct battle between capitalist factory owners and workers' unions (Screpanti and Zamagni 2001). Political economy in general and the labour theory of value in particular were under heavy attack by liberal economists who could point to the writings of Marx (1867), and Romantic socialist thinkers such as Morris (1993 [1890]) and Ruskin (1907 [1862]), as providing the fuel for political discontent and social tensions.

In this context, one group of economists wanted to free the profession from politics and ethics and instead make it into a scientific objective theory. As a result, during the marginalist revolution of the 1870s, the way in which power was conceived within economics became substantially altered. Utility theory replaced the labour theory of value and made consumerism a core concept of neoclassical economics. The new neoclassical economists formulated their models as direct analogies of classical mechanics (Mirowski 1989), and converted economics from an ethical to an engineering profession (Sen 1987). They employed Rene Descartes's philosophy of science, his deductive epistemology and belief in universal mechanistic laws. Firms were conceived as isolated mechanical profit maximizing devices. Consumers were now the atomistic utility maximizing elements to which all else could be reduced and of which all else was merely an aggregate.

Neoclassical economists wanted to claim for their subject the status of physics as an objective truth-revealing science. Mirowski (1989) documents how this was carried out in a crude fashion by substituting economic variables directly into mechanical equations. Perhaps this is not surprising given that a key founder, William Stanley Jevons, was an engineer. Such an approach clearly paid little attention to any distinguishing features of economic or social reality which became analogous to a man-made machine. Marginal utility theory and *Homo oeconomicus* averted attention from unpleasant social problems. The new economics appeared as factual rather than a set of contentious and ideologically loaded metaphysical presuppositions and inappropriate metaphors. This allowed the deletion of concepts such as social class, labour power, exploitation and surplus in the interests of proprietors (Screpanti and Zamagni 2001). Economics was now on the road to becoming a value-free science.

While Smith's political economy was deeply rooted in the moral philosophy of the Stoics (Raphael and Macfie 1982, pp. 5–10), the marginalist revolution soon led to the divorce of economics from politics and power and also any affiliation with moral or ethical questions. Here the British empiricists' approach to science was adopted with its belief in a naive objectivism denying the need for conceptual interpretation and ontology. This was facilitated by adopting David Hume's fact–value dichotomy now encapsulated in the split between positive and normative economics. The success of this transition is then linked to the asserted ability of consumers to enforce their interests on producers via the price mechanism.

## 25.2 THE ROLE OF CONSUMER SOVEREIGNTY IN ECONOMIC THOUGHT

In the economic literature, the analogy of the consumer as sovereign has been developed by those favouring capitalism and market exchange, as the primary means of social organization. Those economists sympathetic to the concept of consumer sovereignty have attributed to it three different interpretations. These we identify as being associated with distinct uses made of the concept, namely: a political instrumental use by classical liberals, a market idealist role in Austrian economics and an economic instrumental function in neoclassical economics. Each interpretation has its own implications for the characterization of the political economy of the modern market system. Key aspects of that characterization are the legitimacy attributed to the role of government in economic policy, the need for intervention in the market system and the extent to which society is reduced to a sum of individual actors.

### 25.2.1 The Political Instrumental Argument

The origins of the term 'consumer sovereignty' are usually traced to William H. Hutt (1899–1988), an English-born economist who classified himself as a classical liberal. He is also often closely identified with Austrian economics. In *Economists and the Public: A Study of Competition and Opinion* he explores the features of consumer sovereignty. This is defined as follows (Hutt 1936, p. 257): 'The consumer is sovereign when, in his role of citizen, he has not delegated to political institutions for authoritarian use the power which he can exercise socially through his power to demand (or refrain from demanding).'

This implies that individuals have two options for the exercise of power in society. First, they may delegate their authority and transfer power to political institutions, in accord with the traditional classical liberal arguments of Hobbes and Locke. Second, they might exercise their power directly as consumers via their purchasing decisions over goods and services.

Exploring the way in which consumers determine production, Hutt argues that there is a direct parallel between choices in the marketplace and at the ballot box. This voting analogy fits nicely with the desire to claim that market economies are naturally democratic and so supportive of a liberal democratic ideal. However the analogy proves far from obviously appropriate. For example, unlike consumer preferences, political preferences in a democracy are weighted equally because one person gets one vote. In the marketplace the richest get millions, or even billions, of votes compared to the poorest. Neither do consumers require the majority of others to agree with their preferences to get what they want. Indeed, Hutt realizes there are problems with claiming that the voting analogy could exist in reality. Consequently he argues in favour of changing reality to match his model: that is, the need to create equality of opportunity in the marketplace so that consumers could get an equal vote. He advocates public education, progressive income taxes and heavy inheritance taxes as necessary preconditions for consumer sovereignty to operate as he desires. This places state government in the role of guarantor of a fair and level playing field for citizens in their active participation as consumers.

For Hutt consumer sovereignty is not then an end in itself. The crucial argument for consumer sovereignty is that people will appreciate living in a society which allows them the fullest possible expression of liberty, and the society to achieve this is a capitalist exchange economy. Consumer sovereignty is therefore regarded as instrumental to social stability. Thus, Persky (1993, p. 188) claims that: 'The reason behind liberty and tolerance and hence consumer sovereignty lies in the useful role they play in allowing people to live constructively together. It is this productive social peace that Hutt really advances as the ultimate good.'

Division of labour in a specialized industrial economy implies that production and consumption become separated spheres in everyday life. The majority of people are regarded as having the ability to exercise power in their role as consumers and this is deemed sufficient to assuage any doubt about the system. That individuals then suppress any questions concerning social or class relations, or the conduct of the system, is regarded as successfully creating social stability. Put quite simply, people are consumers who accept the need to adhere to market institutions to get what they want. Similarly, producers accept the need to comply with consumers' wishes in this Panglossian world.[2]

Hutt treats as separate issues questioning what consumers actually do and whether they act in their own best interest. Persky (1993, p. 190) notes that: 'Hutt's defense of consumer sovereignty, appealing as it does to a broad commitment to a tolerant society, requires no assumptions concerning the self-knowledge and rationality of consumers.' Hutt had grave doubts about the ability of consumers to know their best interests. Like many other economists of his time, he was convinced that tastes and desires are acquired and imposed on people, whose behaviour is largely based on habits (Hutt 1936, p. 283). As nobody can legitimately pretend to know about people's preferences, nobody can claim that increases in efficiency provide a rationale for interventionist measures. Hutt explicitly deals with questions about the formation and evolution of preferences and is interested in exploring the limitations of the concept of consumer sovereignty and obstacles to achieving it. This approach to consumer sovereignty claims validity for it as an analogy but also involves promoting it as politically desirable and requiring empirical investigation to help make it fully operational.

Hutt's argument in favour of an extensive government framework to guarantee equitable participation of people in the economy raised doubts in the liberal camp. For example Jacob Viner has been cited as fearing that Hutt's book would provide the enemies of consumer sovereignty with too much ammunition (Persky 1993, p. 186). This criticism points towards the desire for a more dogmatic formulation of consumer sovereignty, as developed by Austrian economists.

### 25.2.2 The Market Ideal Argument

Based on Ludwig von Mises' book *Human Action*, the Austrian economist Gunning (2009 p. 3) proposes the following definition of consumer sovereignty: 'Under the conditions of the pure market economy, the entrepreneur role always and exclusively acts in the interests of individuals in the role of the consumer.' This definition does not make any direct reference to power. Instead it refers to the pure market economy as an idealized unrestricted set of exchange relations between consumers and 'entrepreneurs'. This notion of consumer sovereignty provides the underpinning of major theorems in Austrian economics.

Claiming that there is such an object in the world as a pure market economy is then employed to substantiate an objective value-free role for the economic analyst. The facts about the purity of the market being contaminated are all that is necessary for analysis. Thus Gunning (2009, p. 1) believes economists can make 'value-free evaluations of arguments in favour of or against government intervention in otherwise free markets'.

Such Austrian economists use this as a prescriptive means of defining who is a legitimate economist, in their opinion. Gunning argues that the general acceptance and tradition of the criteria of value-free analysis (or positivism) in economics renders economists who reject it non-economists. Furthermore, he appeals to Mises' claim that this would also be a rejection of 'science' (Gunning 2009, p. 3). Austrian economists in this vein advocate science as a value-free domain of research in which they include economics. This naive objectivism assumes that the world is a collection of facts that require no interpretation or conceptualization but can merely be observed and noted by the scientific investigator (for more on the fallacy of such a position, see Sayer 1992).

In Austrian economics market power does not pose a threat to consumer sovereignty. Instead of describing the behaviour of firms, Mises deals with behaviour of individuals in three distinct roles: as consumers, factor owners (rentiers) and entrepreneurs. Monopoly gains result from the fact that people in their role as owners of a factor of production are able to charge a monopoly price. Entrepreneurs are regarded as separate actors whose profits have nothing to do with power. They depend on the entrepreneur's ability to understand consumers' desires and meet them through the products they supply. Consequently, there are no conflicts of interest between buyers and sellers (Mises 1949). 'Individuals acting in the entrepreneur role always act in the rightly understood interests of individuals acting in the role of consumer-saver' (Gunning 2009, p. 14f).

Austrian economics does not consider market power a reason for interventionist measures to establish consumer sovereignty. The dogma of consumer sovereignty provides no space at all for any intervention in a pure market economy. All challenges associated with production and the allocation of resources can be assigned to markets. The only remaining question is whether all necessary preconditions for markets are met to enable a pure market economy to exist.[3] The only remaining legitimate purpose for state action and the exercise of political power is to establish a pure market economy. Markets become ends in themselves.

Consumer sovereignty in Austrian economics implies an *ex ante* equal distribution of opportunities that renders an *ex post* comparison of individuals unnecessary and misleading (that is, what people start with is just, and what they end up with is irrelevant). Individuals are assumed to be rewarded according to their marginal productivity, or that of factors they own if rentiers. As rewards determine ability to pay for goods and services there is no need for questioning income distribution. The hypothesis that a specific allocation of resources can exclusively be explained in terms of consumers' expressed interests is meant to be empirically testable. In practice this is impossible, not least because of the inability to know individual preferences *ex ante*.

Consumer sovereignty then becomes a dogma requiring that people behave in specific ways. Any behaviour implying that outcomes are not entirely determined by the interests of consumers has to be ruled out as non-economic. Thus Mises' approach to human action is entirely devoted to that objective. His praxiology is about discrediting any kind of behaviour failing to conform with the principle of consumer sovereignty. For example, he distinguishes between ascetic and non-ascetic world views. If an actor is a hermit or an ascetic they are not considered part of a market economy (Gunning 2009, p. 12).

The endeavour of the classical liberal argument for exploring the conditions that allow consumers to exercise power in the economy is replaced in Austrian economics by the imperative statement that 'consumers are the only ones who can legitimately exercise power in the economy'. This notion of consumer sovereignty as a doctrine of economic dogma is fundamental to understanding Austrian economics. It is a necessary precondition for their concepts and axioms.

### 25.2.3 The Instrumental Efficiency Argument

The primary focus of neoclassical economics is on allocation. It aims to derive from first principles a logical argument for the existence of a market exchange economy and how it can best operate. Evaluating whether an economy is acting successfully in the allocation of resources requires a criterion of assessment. Neoclassical economists employ a concept of efficiency defined by the Pareto criterion. That is, resources are efficiently allocated when there is no longer any ability to make at least one person better off and none worse off by a reallocation. This criterion is entirely defined in terms of the preferences of consumers.

As no comprehensive empirical mapping of consumers' preferences is possible, the assessment of efficiency is exclusively based on behavioural assumptions. Those assumptions are necessary for a general market equilibrium to exist, and supposed to imply consumer sovereignty (Thomasberger 2002). Neoclassical analysis and the resulting theorems relying on those assumptions are consequently restricted to circumstances where all economic agents behave in accordance with rational choice theory that is, the conceptualization of humans as *Homo oeconomicus*. On this basis, Torre (1998, pp. 23–24) describes the neoclassical conceptualization of consumer sovereignty in terms of four attributes: (1) pursuit of self-interest; (2) individualism; (3) consumers' wants as determinants of the quantity and quality of products; and (4) consumers' power largely determining market prices. These are essential features of rational choice theory or derived from it. In dogmatic vein, Becker has argued that rational choice theory is the only reasonable way of describing and understanding human behaviour (Becker 1976).

The branch of neoclassical economics which deals with assessments of allocations is (new) welfare economics. This is the only branch of mainstream economics that explicitly admits the need for and legitimacy of value judgements. It is therefore segregated off as being 'normative economics', as opposed to the rest of economics which is meant to be 'positive', that is, value-free. Comparing allocations at the social level requires a social welfare function. The first theorem of welfare economics states that irrespective of the initial distribution of endowments, competitive market exchange will lead to an efficient allocation of resources. Market power decreases efficiency and poses a threat to consumer sovereignty. Therefore, market power provides a rationale for state intervention to establish competitive markets. This highlights the notion of consumer sovereignty in neoclassical economics as an ethical imperative: 'consumers should be able to impose their interests on producers'.[4] Consumer sovereignty is then the means by which the goal of efficiency is to be achieved. For the neoclassical economist, the main obstacle that might prevent the consumer from exercising their sovereignty power is the countervailing force posed by uncompetitive firms (that is, monopoly, oligopoly). They therefore favour strong state government to intervene on behalf of the consumer.

### 25.2.4 The Neoliberal Synthesis

'Neoliberalism' often appears a vague, imprecise and contested term. However, as a social movement backed by various economists it is currently a real political force in society. The historical rise of this social movement, and its increasing influence over the world political economy, has been explored in detail by several authors in the edited volume of Mirowski and Plehwe (2009). The hegemony of neoliberalism since the financial crisis is documented by Mirowski (2013). What these works explain is the broad alliance of liberal, Austrian economic and neoclassical economic thought in support of a neoliberal political economy that empowers banking, finance and corporate interests at the national and multinational levels. This alliance of economists exists despite the internal contradictions and incoherence of a united position. The link between neoclassical economics and the neoliberal is sometimes denied, not least because of apparent differences over the role of government. However, this relationship has actually become stronger since the recent financial crisis. In a book-length thesis, Mirowski (2013) makes an extensive, well-documented argument to substantiate his observation that: 'Neoclassical economics was not intrinsically neoliberal over its entire one-and-a-half-century history; but it sure looks like they are working in tandem now' (Mirowski 2013, p. 13).

Neoliberalism, in its present form, can be traced back to an elitist social movement of the 1940s and the foundation of the Mont Pelerin Society. Although clear definitions of a common position have largely been avoided, there was an attempt in 1947 which produced a draft unifying statement. Point 2 of the ten positions then drafted runs as follows:

> The freedom of the consumer in choosing what he shall buy, the freedom of the producer in choosing what he shall make, and the freedom of the worker in choosing his occupation and his place of employment, are essential not merely for the sake of freedom itself, but for efficiency in production. Such a system of freedom is essential if we are to maximize output in terms of individual satisfactions. Departure from these individual liberties leads to the production not only of fewer goods and services but of the wrong goods and services. We cannot enrich ourselves merely by consenting to be slaves. (Plehwe 2009, p. 23)

As Plehwe (2009) makes clear, the Mont Pelerin Society has acted as a unifying organization bringing together key neoliberal thinkers and thought. Amongst its presidents have been both Austrian economists, including von Hayek who helped to produce the above draft statement, and a range of neoclassical economists, including both Stigler and Becker. These three are high-profile economists representing a core set of ideals supporting a market capitalist political economy and a specific conceptualization of freedom based upon the individual. All three have been awarded the Sveriges Riksbank Prize in Economic Sciences in Memory of Alfred Nobel.

## 25.3 CONSUMERS ARE NOT SOVEREIGNS

The notion of consumer sovereignty has been criticized for various reasons. In this section we explain three objections. First, consumer sovereignty relies upon a specific conceptualization of individual rationality and an associated interpretation of what choice means. This theory is then open to criticism as an unrealistic, inadequate and inappropriate explanation of both human behaviour and choice. Second, the structure of the modern industrial state is such that the role of the consumer in determining resource allocation is highly circumscribed. Third, the real power in an affluent society resides with the producer who exercises it over the consumer, as opposed to vice versa.

### 25.3.1 Individual Choice and Preferences

The mainstream economic approach describes the consumer as having stable and given preferences, being able to compare and choose between any two given bundles of goods, and possessing all the required information about those bundles, their constituents and the choices involved. Rationality in this model is the ability to make such choices and trade off more of one thing for less of another. The approach is strictly consequentialist and individuals are assumed to look after their own best interests which can be summarized as maximizing their own preference-based utility.

Behaviour in accordance with this rationalization of choice is a crucial precondition for consumer sovereignty because it guarantees an exact correspondence between consumer choices expressed in the marketplace and individual preferences. Without this correspondence market prices would be deemed to convey misleading information. They would fail to depict the 'true' desires of individuals, and this would affect how scarce resources were allocated and so prices as a measure of relative scarcity. There is then a foundational presupposition that consumers have 'true' preferences, which are preformed or a priori, and these drive the whole economic system. Preferences have come to form a core metaphysical concept in mainstream economics, and one which goes unexplained and unquestioned. Choices in the marketplace are observed; preferences can only be inferred.

The direct link between individual preferences and choice in markets can be questioned on several grounds. Problems include issues of preference formation and the role of knowledge (Spash 2002), lexicographic preferences and the resulting refusals to make trade-offs (Spash 1998, 2000; Spash and Hanley 1995), incommensurability (Aldred 2006; Chang 1997; O'Neill 1997) and the difference between choosing as opposed to preferring something (Holland 2002; Spash 2008). A range of questions confronts the economic logic, such as: Do people have well formed preferences? Do preferences reflect an individual's own best interests? Do people choose in accordance with their preferences?

Once the idea of perfect information is dropped, the provision of information becomes a crucial precondition for consumer sovereignty. Information here is regarded as some neutral conveyance of factual knowledge. This allows the maintenance of a model where preferences are informed rather than formed by new information. In reality the same piece of new information will inform some and be crucial to forming the preferences of others (Spash 2002). Yet the belief remains prevalent that neutral factual information can be provided to make markets function according to the model.[5]

The idea in mainstream microeconomics that there is a state of 'imperfect information' leads to a major justification for policy intervention. For example, the concept of asymmetric information is used to describe one party to a transaction (buyer or seller) having an information advantage over the other, and so power over a transaction to be completed which would otherwise not occur. Mainstream economists discuss problems of moral hazard and adverse selection. Information here hides other factors which mainstream economists have tried to remove from their subject, such as ethics and power. The dominant belief is that consumers remain sovereign and government can act to correct market failures but leave the individual in control.

Economists supporting the idea that consumers can be informed to make choices then regard government as merely acting to perfect flows of factual information to achieve optimal consumer choices. Yet the reality is somewhat different. As Rothenberg (1968) states:

> In fact, most public intervention arose not out of theoretical analyses of subtle consumer sub-optimization but as a response on concrete national traumas – dramatic scandals concerning damage from specific foods and drugs, scandals concerning massive fraud and irregularity in financial markets, etc. Thus, laissez-faire was cast aside not on theoretical grounds but on the evidence of acute malfunctioning of markets.

Yet, accepting that there is no such thing as a fully informed human being with perfect information means undermining the very foundations for believing consumers can be sovereign. Government intervention may then be recommended to, say, maintain quality standards of traded goods and services not because consumers are unable to acquire information but because they cannot assimilate it or judge for themselves what is best. The decisions here involve judgement as to what is toxic, harmful, polluting, exploitative in production, and damaging socially and environmentally. Markets may then be regarded as the wrong institutions for addressing these problems, and the appeal to preferences and self-interested individuals as totally misguided.

In addition, the whole premise of price distortion due to 'externalities' is that they will mislead consumers in their optimal choice behaviour. That is, where prices are absent too much undesired activity occurs (for example, pollution) and not enough desired activity (for example, wildlife provision). Things that are regarded by mainstream economists as external to the market pricing mechanism do not, according to them, get taken into account.[6] The Coase theorem is then used to justify allocation of private property rights and consumer sovereignty is used to justify the outcome. For example, common property should be privatized along with wildlife, the atmosphere and water in order that they can be optimally allocated to consumers on the basis of their preferences. That consumers may not have any preferences for essential aspects of ecosystem function and structure (even after being 'informed' about them) merely means they have no value and are dispensable. Nature is not valued in itself but only instrumentally and then only via individuals' preferences. There is no room for judgement or thoughtful reflection, only selection on the basis of what is preferred (or not) for whatever reason (Spash 2008). Choosing to preserve ecosystems' function and structure, stop the loss of endangered species or take action to control human-induced climate change, is just the same for the mainstream economist or neoliberal as choosing a flavour of ice cream.

### 25.3.2 The Structure of the Economy

The earlier sections have outlined how modern mainstream economics has attempted to divorce economics from politics. This diverts attention away from the influence of various vested interest groups in society, who do not passively respond to or reflect consumers' interests. Galbraith famously described the threat to American democracy posed by the professional corporate managers whom he termed the 'technostructure' (Galbraith 2007 [1967]). The technostructure is able to capture those elements of government which are meant to regulate its activities or, rather, regulate the activities of the organizations in which the technostructure resides. This creates a power bloc which serves the corporate interest.

That the power structure of modern economies brings into question the idea of resource allocation on the basis of consumer preferences can quickly be exemplified. Consider military expenditure in the USA. A permanent peacetime arms industry arose after the Second World War for the first time and was soon dominating the economy. In 1960, this led President Eisenhower to state, in his last address to the nation, that: 'In the councils of government, we must guard against the acquisition of unwarranted influence, whether sought or unsought, by the military–industrial complex. The potential for the disastrous rise of misplaced power exists and will persist.'

His term 'military–industrial complex' referred to a major power bloc connected to corporate interests (such as aerospace and arms manufacture). This potential threat to democracy has nothing to do with consumer sovereignty, but is responsible for ongoing innovation and product placement, for example satellites, jet aircraft, the Internet, nuclear power. This produces spin-off products and services for civil society; products that have been heavily supported by government in their development and promotion. Basic military expenditure in the USA in recent years has been running at around a quarter to a third of tax revenues,[7] and according to the Fiscal Year 2013 Budget accounts for a fifth of Federal Budget spend. So a major aspect of production and consumption in the political economy is just ignored by mainstream economic theory and analysis.

Interestingly Eisenhower pointed in the same speech to the dangers arising from science and technology. He noted that public policy could itself become the captive of a scientific-technological elite. What we observe today is not just public policy domination but also domination of the consumer by the latest gadgets, digital machinery, telecommunications devices, computer technology, home entertainment systems, cars, heating systems, cooling systems, 3D (three-dimensional) cinema, domestic electric convenience devices, drugs, beautifying chemicals and so on. New things to do old jobs do not necessarily improve life, but they certainly change it. Old products are therefore removed regardless of consumer preferences, and soon become unsupported and unavailable. This is clearest in the information technology modern world where both hardware (computers, phones, printers, scanners, entertainment devices) and software (computer programs) are regularly 'updated'.

The structure of the economy is heavily interwoven with the need for capital accumulation and economic growth. The promotion of mass consumption is not something that can be left for individuals to reject. They must consume and consume more all the time, because that is the imperative of the material and energy throughput economy.

Once again we can borrow from Eisenhower's speech where he notes that we: 'must avoid the impulse to live only for today, plundering, for our own ease and convenience, the precious resources of tomorrow'. In fact humanity is doing the exact opposite and, according to mainstream economists and neoliberals, this is simply the right result based on consumer preferences being expressed in a free society.

### 25.3.3 Power over Preferences

The previous section has already raised some aspects of the need for the capitalist market economy to promote material and energy throughput. Whilst neoclassical economics deals with power over prices (that is, market power) it ignores power over preferences (that is, pervasive persuasion). Galbraith (2001) points out that rather than consumers being sovereign they are subject to manipulation.[8] He notes that, rather than consumer choice, producer manipulation of consumer response is the determining factor in production. As he states: 'Salesmanship, design and innovation are all utilized to attract and capture the consumer' (Galbraith 2001, p. 31). Similarly, Kapp (1978b) details practices such as the use of sales promotion, planned obsolescence and cut-throat competition in his book on the social costs of business enterprise.

For Galbraith, the ability of producers to influence consumers (that is, producer sovereignty) is crucial to understanding the dynamics of industrial economies (Galbraith, 1969 [1958]). The requirement to persuade consumers and manage demand arises at different levels: individual firms, industries and on the macroeconomic level. At the firm level, demand management is in many cases a precondition for investment and technical progress. It aims at avoiding sunk costs and putting established industrial organizations into jeopardy. The risk associated with investments in sophisticated technology, large commitments of capital, long time horizons in product development and production, has to be mitigated (Galbraith 1970). To achieve those targets sometimes firms have to cooperate at the industry level to bring the state to support their efforts in creating and managing consumer preferences. For example the automobile companies get the roads that are essential for a consumer preference for automobile transportation. Airline and aircraft manufacturing companies can win public financing for the development of new types of aircraft, in the past under a military guise (Galbraith 1970). At the macroeconomic level persuasion of consumers to buy more of anything and everything is a necessary precondition for 'sustained' economic growth.

The collective effort of producers and the state imposes cultural developments that perpetuate scarcity of resources and market products, unrecognized by mainstream economics:

> The concept of consumer sovereignty acts with marked force to inhibit questions concerning the cultural achievements of the system. It will surely be agreed that whatever the effects of advertising its ultimate effect is an extremely powerful and sustained propaganda on the importance of goods. No similar case is made on behalf of artistic, educational, or other humane achievement. The notion of consumer sovereignty suppresses the response. (Galbraith 1970, p. 476)

Galbraith regarded the interrelatedness of consumer wants and production as a problem for the affluent society. This he saw as worsening with the acceleration of economic growth. Greater affluence leads to more superfluous consumption and more manipulation of demand (for example, fashion, throwaway products):

> The fact that wants can be synthesized by advertising, catalyzed by salesmanship, and shaped by discreet manipulations of the persuaders shows that they are not very urgent. A man who is hungry need never be told of his need for food . . . Increases in consumption, the counterpart of increases in production, act by suggestion or emulation to create wants. Or producers may proceed actively to create preferences through advertising and salesmanship. Wants thus come to depend on output. (Galbraith 1969 [1958], p. 158)

He termed this the 'dependence effect'. A qualification to Galbraith's argument is perhaps necessary because even at very low incomes specific products may be heavily marketed, for example cheap fast food lacking nutrition, drinks such as Coca-Cola heavily consumed in less developed countries, cigarettes and alcohol. However the key point from Galbraith is that higher levels of production require higher levels of want creation. The satisfaction of these wants has nothing to do with addressing preformed consumer preferences or improving human well-being; they are necessary for the growth economy to continue.

The policy implications of power over preferences go far beyond a mere regulation of advertising and sales promotion. Economic policy needs a new foundation upon which to analyse the allocation of resources and must reopen a fundamental question: 'What is the purpose of economic activity?' The concept of consumer sovereignty denies the legitimacy of questioning industrial practice and cultural criticism of consumption practices in general (Schor 2007). Once consumers' sovereignty is rejected, the social and cultural aims of production and consumption are subject to scrutiny and can clearly be found wanting socially, environmentally and economically.

## 25.4 CONCLUSIONS

The claim that consumers are sovereign, reigning over what is produced in a capitalist market economy, remains an item of faith in economic doctrine. This belief is upheld by classical liberals, Austrian and neoclassical economists. Their arguments combine to support an ideological position that claims individual freedom is the highest ideal, that freedom is only achievable via a market economy and such an economy must have as its primary goal the efficient allocation of resources. From this viewpoint a generally accepted provision for a successful market economy is minimal government. Every state action beyond establishing a pure market economy has to be understood as an illegitimate intervention causing a deterioration of people's ability to meet their interests. This is the basic foundation of the neoliberal political economy that dominates today.

One implication of claiming consumers are sovereign is to lay the blame for the state of the world at their feet. After all, they command what is produced and where resources should be allocated. This position requires that consumers are fully informed about their choices. As we have been at pains to explain, the fully informed individual is a concept divorced from reality, akin to being fully enlightened. However, let us assume that the concept of 'being informed' makes sense and that consumers might be able to be pretty well informed in today's society. Further assume that there exists a country where everyone is literate and has access to readily available meaningful information at little or no cost, so that they can actually achieve 'being informed'. The argument still places the preferences of such (potentially) well-informed individuals above all else, and those preferences are to remain unquestioned. In addition, society is to be run by the expression of those preferences on the basis of disposable income.

If consumers do not buy 'green' products then they are not wanted. If they demand plastic trees instead of real ones they should be provided. If they dislike certain species, and are not prepared to pay for their survival, then they should become extinct. The sovereign consumer lives in the best of all possible worlds and pollution or environmental disruption is optimal. There is no judgement here as to what is right or wrong on any grounds beyond the fulfilment of hedonic pleasures, whether they be egoistic, sadistic, masochistic, sociopathic, psychopathic or whatever. The world is an instrument provided for maximizing personal utility on the basis of what is preferred by the individual regardless of why.

This raises questions over the role and meaning of individual choice. Choice over which flavour of ice cream to consume may be considered a matter of preference. Choice over luxury items in a modern consumer market of an affluent society might also be deemed a matter of the rich consumer's preference. However, generalizing this approach to taking decisions about everything in the world reduces everything down to being as trivial as selecting flavours of ice cream or unnecessary luxuries. Life goes on without such things and as trivia they may add little or nothing to the meaningfulness of a person's life. Indeed the consumer framing removes much that is important for being human and humane, or living a good or meaningful life in the Aristotelian sense.

There is indeed too much that is important that is missing from this world view. For example, consider what most humans in developed market economies spend much of their lives doing: that is, working for a wage. Work itself has no meaning except as a means to obtain goods and services. Work is a necessary ill rather than a potentially meaningful role. Choice over consumer goods is emphasized, while that over work life is ignored. Yet the lack of choice an individual has over their work life and its conditions has major impacts on health and well-being. The value of a person is as a worker (that is, labour) and that value is their productive output that can be sold in the marketplace. Those who do not work in the marketplace cannot command consumption goods and have no value, for example housewives, the unemployed, students. Regarding the primary goal of humanity as consumption excludes other more important roles that individuals play in society.

That consumers are not in fact in command of the economy or their role in it, although they may be complicit in its operation, is something consumer sovereignty denies or sees as correctible through appropriate policy measures. What it also denies is that perceived wants are socially and culturally constructed, and can easily be changed through legislation, given the political will to do so. Who 'wanted' let alone demanded the car, air flights, the computer, a mobile phone? A considerable political will lay behind the provision of all these things and a massive infrastructure investment has supported them all and still does. The same is true of genetically modified crops, nanotechnology, fracking or any number of developments trying to maintain the 'growth society'.

That this is true also means that a different society is possible. However, such an alternative will not be achieved by waiting for the mythical sovereign consumer to be nudged into doing the right thing by a new behavioural economics, or forced to buy the right products by old-fashioned price incentives. The problems go much deeper than that and concern the very foundations of what is the purpose of human society. Indeed, why would anyone want to sustain the modern consumer society? Modernity has conceptualized development as technological change and economics has become a corporate capitalist market system trapped in the need for ever more energy and material consumption. The sovereign consumer is a myth employed to divert attention away from reality and the need for personal and social development in harmony with the biophysical world.

## NOTES

1. Rational choice theory basically reduces all decisions down to the individual, regarded as a consequential calculating machine that judges the best action on the sole basis of personal interest, that is, *Homo oeconomicus*.
2. The problem with power as described in this context is that consumers are expected to have power over producers. However, simultaneously, economists argue that exchange is entered into by individuals of their own free will and entails a conceptualization of freedom to act. Buyers and sellers are free agents entering into a contract without coercion. If this is so then producers would be under no compulsion to meet consumers' demands. So there is a logical contradiction here.
3. Gunning (2009, p. 13) specifies the conditions for this existence as being: the division of labour, a complete private property system, completely free enterprise, neutral money, absence of fraud and deception, and an absence of coercion (except for that employed by the government to enforce private property rights and laws against fraud).
4. New welfare economics provides a vague argument for state intervention beyond potential Pareto improvements on the basis of interpersonal comparisons. Despite being unable to construct a social welfare function, it theoretically legitimizes interventions that redistribute income to improve social welfare. This qualifies the role of consumer sovereignty as leading to the best welfare outcome.
5. Austrian economics tries to avoid the problem by claiming that the entrepreneur aims to fulfil the desires of the consumer and is rewarded with profits for doing so. However any information flow from producer to consumer will impact upon consumers' preferences. The only way it cannot is to maintain the fiction that all information is neutral, factual and objective.
6. Kapp (1978a) describes the actions behind the creation of social and environmental harms as relating to 'cost shifting' rather than being something external to the market or its actors. As such they are deliberate acts consciously undertaken to avoid costs. They are an integral part of the market system with its utility and profit maximizing agents purposefully creating 'externalities' for their own advantage. They are not external to such market systems, or matters of the wrong prices misleading well-intentioned agents.
7. Such figures may underestimate the full costs by excluding various categories of expenditure, such as 'homeland security'; and when a war is on there will typically be some overseas forces, and their budgets are separated out (for example, Iran, Iraq, Afghanistan).
8. Galbraith (2001, p. 31) actually thought that, due to his attacks on the concept, the role of consumer sovereignty had declined in economics. As he states: 'In the end, however, circumstance, fact, had their effect: the established belief was undermined; perhaps it could even be said that consumer sovereignty was set aside as a dominant factor in the economic system. From my reading of the literature, including the textbooks, it no longer enjoys its old role as the center of truth in shaping the economy.' However, he seems totally incorrect on this count, and died before the full-scale dominance of neoliberalism of recent times had occurred, along with the resurgence of the powerful myth.

## REFERENCES

Aldred, J. (2006), 'Incommensurability and monetary valuation', *Land Economics*, 82, 141–161.
Becker, G.S. (1976), *The Economic Approach to Human Behavior*, Chicago, IL: University of Chicago Press.
Chang, R. (1997), *Incommensurability, Incomparability and Practical Reason*, Cambridge, MA: Harvard University Press.
Galbraith, J.K. (1969 [1958]), *The Affluent Society*, Boston, MA: Houghton Mifflin.
Galbraith, J.K. (1970), 'Economics as a system of belief', *American Economic Review*, 60, 469–478.

Galbraith, J.K. (2001), 'The myth of consumer sovereignty', in J.K. Galbraith (ed.), *The Essential Galbraith*, Boston, MA: Houghton Mifflin, pp. 31–39.

Galbraith, J.K. (2007 [1967]), *The New Industrial State*, Princeton, NJ: Princeton University Press.

Gunning, J.P. (2009), *Consumer Sovereignty: The Key to Mises's Economics*, Smithfield, RI: Bryant University.

Holland, A. (2002), 'Are choices tradeoffs?', in D.W. Bromley and J. Paavola (eds), *Economics, Ethics, and Environmental Policy: Contested Choices*, Oxford, UK and Malden, MA, USA: Blackwell, pp. 17–34.

Hutt, W.H. (1936), *Economists and the Public: A Study of Competition and Opinion*, London: Jonathan Cape.

Kapp, K.W. (1978a), *The Social Costs of Business Enterprise*, 3rd edn, Nottingham: Spokesman.

Kapp, K.W. (1978b), 'The social costs of cutthroat competition, planned obsolesence and sales promotion', in K.W. Kapp (ed.), *The Social Costs of Business Enterprise*, 3rd edn, Nottingham: Spokesman, pp. 224–247.

Marx, K. (1867), *Das Kapital. Kritik der Politischen Ökonomie. Buch I: Der Produktionsprozess des Kapitals*, Hamburg: Otto Meissner.

Mirowski, P. (1989), *More Heat than Light: Economics as Social Physics, Physics as Nature's Economics*, Cambridge: Cambridge University Press.

Mirowski, P. (2013), *Never Let a Serious Crisis go to Waste: How Neoliberalism Survived the Financial Meltdown*, London: Verso.

Mirowski, P. and D. Plehwe (eds) (2009), *The Road to Mont Pèlerin: Making of the Neoliberal Thought Collective*, Cambridge, MA: Harvard University Press.

Mises, L. v. (1949), *Human Action: A Treatise on Economics*, New Haven, CT: Yale University Press.

Morris, W. (1993 [1890]), 'News from nowhere', in C. Wilmer (ed.), *Penguin Classics*, London: Penguin, pp. 41–228.

O'Neill, J.F. (1997), 'Value, pluralism, incommensurability and institutions', in J. Foster (ed.), *Valuing Nature? Economics, Ethics and Environment*, London: Routledge, pp. 75–88.

Persky, J. (1993), 'Retrospectives: consumer sovereignty', *Journal of Economic Perspectives*, 7 (1), 183–191.

Plehwe, D. (2009), 'Introduction', in P. Mirowski and D. Plehwe (eds), *The Road to Mont Pèlerin: Making of the Neoliberal Thought Collective*, Cambridge, MA: Harvard University Press, pp. 1–42.

Polanyi, K. (1944), *The Great Transformation*, New York, USA and Toronto, Canada: Rinehart & Company.

Raphael, D.D. and A.L. Macfie (1982), 'Introduction', in D.D. Raphael and A.L. Macfie (eds), *Adam Smith: The Theory of Moral Sentiments*, Indianapolis, IN, USA: Liberty Fund.

Rhodes, R.A.W. (1996), 'The new governance: governing without government', *Political Studies*, 44, 652–667.

Rothenberg, J. (1968), 'Consumer sovereignty', in D.L. Sills and R.K. Merton (eds), *International Encyclopedia of the Social Sciences*, New York: Macmillan and Free Press, pp. 326–335.

Ruskin, J. (1907 [1862]), *'Unto This Last': Four Essays on the First Principles of Political Economy*, London: Routledge.

Sayer, A. (1992), 'Theory, observation and practical adequacy', in A. Sayer (ed.), *Method in Social Science: A Realist Approach*, London: Routledge, pp. 45–84.

Schor, J.B. (2007), 'In defense of consumer critique: revisiting the consumption debates of the twentieth century', *Annals of the American Academy of Political and Social Science*, 611, 16–30.

Screpanti, E. and S. Zamagni (2001), *An Outline of the History of Economic Thought*, New York: Oxford University Press.

Sen, A.K. (1987), *On Ethics and Economics*, Oxford: Blackwell.

Smith, A., (1976 [1776]), *An Inquiry into the Nature and Causes of the Wealth of Nations*, Chicago, IL: Chicago University Press.

Smith, A. (1982 [1759]), *The Theory of Moral Sentiments*, Indianapolis, IN: Liberty Fund.

Spash, C.L. (1998), 'Investigating individual motives for environmental action: lexicographic preferences, beliefs and attitudes', in J. Lemons, L. Westra and R. Goodland (eds), *Ecological Sustainability and Integrity: Concepts and Approaches*, Dordrecht: Kluwer, pp. 46–62.

Spash, C.L. (2000), 'Ecosystems, contingent valuation and ethics: the case of wetlands re-creation', *Ecological Economics*, 34, 195–215.

Spash, C.L. (2002), 'Informing and forming preferences in environmental valuation: coral reef biodiversity', *Journal of Economic Psychology*, 23, 665–687.

Spash, C.L. (2008), 'How much is that ecosystem in the window? The one with the bio-diverse trail', *Environmental Values*, 17, 259–284.

Spash, C.L. and N. Hanley (1995), 'Preferences, information and biodiversity preservation', *Ecological Economics*, 12, 191–208.

Thomasberger, C. (2002), 'Menschliches Handeln und marktwirtschaftliche Strukturen. Traditionelle Neoklassik, ökonomischer Ansatz und sozioökonomische Gegenbewegungen', in W. Ötsch and S. Panther (eds), *Ökonomik und Sozialwissenschaft. Ansichten eines in Bewegung geratenen Verhältnisses*, Marburg: Metropolis, pp. 81–118.

Torre, D. (1998), 'Consumer Sovereignty', in R. Arena and C. Longhi (eds), *Markets and Organization*, Berlin and Heidelberg: Springer, pp. 23–41.

# 26. Collaborating and connecting: the emergence of the sharing economy

*Juliet B. Schor and Connor J. Fitzmaurice*

Sharing, or practices by which individuals use, occupy, or enjoy something with others, is long-standing. Anthropologists analyse the ways that sharing produces and reproduces social relations (Belk 2009; Gell 1986). In the United States, scholars have studied early examples of sharing in the close-knit farming towns of the colonial Northeast (Merrill 1977). In the mid-twentieth century, Carol Stack described sharing as a survival mechanism for African-Americans living in a community beset by poverty and discrimination (Stack 1974).

New forms of sharing have emerged in recent years, in part as a result of the Internet. What is innovative about today's sharing is that it is a market form in which strangers – rather than kin and communities – exchange goods and services. This contemporary sharing economy creates new ways of provisioning goods and services, and opportunities for what we have called 'connected consumption', and what others have termed 'collaborative consumption'. Connected consumption is predicated on peer-to-peer relationships rather than existing market actors to mediate exchange. As such, it represents an innovation that is capable of reallocating wealth across the 'value chain', specifically away from middlemen and towards small producers and consumers. In 2011, *Time* magazine identified collaborative consumption as one of its ten ideas that will change the world. While the phenomenon is still in its early stages in many product or service categories, its combination of economic rationality, technological infrastructure and cultural appeal will likely lead it to grow significantly over the next decade (Gansky 2011; Schor 2010). If it does, it has the potential to enhance sustainability and reduce ecological and carbon footprints in a number of key areas.

In this chapter, we will begin by offering a broad definition of the sharing economy and the categories of practices it includes. Next we discuss salient motivations for participation and describe the size and growth of these types of exchanges and the complexities of definition. We will then review the existing academic literature on the sharing economy, and suggest key themes and areas of investigation. We conclude by addressing the challenges faced by participants engaging in these emergent practices. Throughout, our discussion is based on four years of qualitative case study research, which includes roughly 150 interviews and hundreds of hours of observation with sharing economy participants, mainly those aged 18–35.[1]

## 26.1 THE SHARING ECONOMY EMERGES

In the last 15 years, a growing number of young adults, as both business innovators and users of these services, have attempted to transform the sphere of consumption. (We focus on young adults because they are disproportionately active in these innovations.) They advocate shared ownership and use, reuse and resale of goods, and optimizing use of assets by renting or loaning out durable goods and spaces. The movement they represented was originally dubbed the 'sharing economy', and later also came to be known as 'collaborative consumption', as the result of a popular book and website of that name (Botsman and Rogers 2010). We call it 'connected consumption' to emphasize its social and digital dimensions. All three terms, which we will use interchangeably, refer to a wide and varied range of old, revamped and new practices whose central characteristics are the ability to save or make money, provide a novel consumer experience, reduce ecological and carbon footprints, and strengthen social ties. Not all the practices have all of these characteristics; however, most attempt to. Of course, there is considerable room for debate about the boundaries of the phenomenon. What is common across the 'space', as it is colloquially referred to, is that participants are transforming consumption practices as well as markets for consumer goods and services.

As they pertain to consumption, the new sharing practices fall into four major categories: recirculation of goods, exchange of services, optimizing use of assets and building social connections. In our reading of the history, the first innovation was sites devoted to the recirculation of goods, in particular eBay and Craigslist. Both were founded in 1995 as online marketplaces for individuals to exchange used products. Both eventually moved beyond their beginnings to encompass a much wider range of offerings, and moved out of the niche of the sharing economy into the consumer mainstream. The intensification of purchasing that occurred in the late 1990s and 2000s was key to their success because it led to a ready supply of items for resale. What we have elsewhere called the 'fast-fashion' model, that is, the speed-up of consumer acquisition and discard (Schor 2010), was crucial to the emergence of connected consumption: increased consumer purchases and the subsequent social superfluity of goods led to the development of secondary markets (that is, markets where goods are exchanged a second time). In addition, digital technology and sophisticated online software reduced what had traditionally been high transaction costs in secondary markets. Thus, a combination of technological and socio-economic changes facilitated the growth of connected consumption. eBay and Craigslist are now enormous entities, and their example has been followed by many similar ventures. There are now scores, if not hundreds, of Internet sites that facilitate the exchange of used goods. They range from sites that handle many products to specialized sites. Modes of exchange include two-way trades, gifting, sale and multiple-party exchanges.

Apparel has been an especially fertile area for secondary outlets, on account of extensive growth in apparel purchasing in the US and Europe as a result of the globalization of production and the decline in prices (Schor 2013). Swapstyle.com is a clothing exchange site that has been operating for ten years and boasts more than 55000 participants and more than 4 million completed trades. Registrants browse a worldwide inventory of fashion items and negotiate swaps with others. If suitable swaps are not forthcoming, items may be purchased with cash. Threadflip is oriented to the resale of high-end designer item and does not include a swapping dimension. Other examples are Dig n' Swap, 99 Dresses, I-Ella, Rehashclothes, ThredUp and Rent the Runway, in addition to a growing number of local, face-to-face clothing exchange organizations and events.

Outside of apparel, the range of goods now being exchanged includes nearly the full portfolio of consumers' possessions, from items such as books, DVDs and toys, where there are 'thick' or densely populated markets, to the thinner markets of sporting equipment, furniture and other home goods. Goods can be swapped, 'gifted' or purchased online using a variety of exchange formulae at sites such as Swap, Netcycler and Bartercard. Freecycle emphasizes the creation of a community and operates with a gift model in which people join a local group and all exchange is free. The expectation is that members both give and receive, and over time develop social bonds (Nelson et al. 2007). At Yerdle, if the consumer is unable to find what he or she is looking for, the site provides a link to a retail store where it can be purchased. Another variant of the exchange model is the sale of new, but home- or hand-made items. Etsy, a craft marketplace, is the largest and best known of these sites.

Another early innovator was Zipcar, a business-to-peer company founded by Robin Chase, a visionary entrepreneur with a strong sustainability motive. Zipcar was a membership organization that placed vehicles in convenient locations in urban areas and rented them out for short periods of time. A central goal was to reduce urban car ownership. Over time, car sharing became very popular, particularly among young people, whose car ownership is lower than that of previous generations. The concept of car sharing entered the mainstream and Zipcar expanded dramatically. Eventually, the company was acquired by Avis and car sharing in one form or another began to be adopted by large transportation corporations, including car manufacturers such as BMW.

The rationale behind Zipcar represents the second major type of connected consumption: schemes for optimizing the use of durable goods or other economically productive assets. In a wealthy economy, individuals and households can afford to purchase durable goods that are used only intermittently, or to own assets that are not operated to capacity. Examples include spare bedrooms, unused garage or other storage space, unproductive lawns and square footage in office environments.

After the 2009 recession, deploying unused assets for economic gain took on added appeal and schemes for offering idle capacity emerged. Quite a few were focused on durable goods, such as lawn mowers, tools or expensive equipment for specialized uses. Some of these initiatives had histories that long antedated Zipcar. For example tool libraries had developed decades earlier in low-income communities. However earlier efforts tended to be small and local, in order to facilitate the transfer and use of heavy items as well as to solve the problems of trust and credibility which arise with lending schemes. A number of neighbourhood sites attempted to replicate that functionality online, but with a local focus, by including durable goods sharing as one dimension of their efforts. Examples include Share Some Sugar, the Front Porch, Neigh*goods, Hey, Neighbor, and Neighborgoods.

In 1999, Couchsurfing built a platform that matched people who had empty sofas (or beds) and were willing to lend them, to people looking for a cheap way to travel. Originally a non-profit, Couchsurfing is now a benefit corporation operating on a large scale and around the world. It reports having 6 million members hosting in more than 100 000 cities (https://www.couchsurfing.org/n/about, accessed 14 February 2014). It aims to create 'a better world', through fostering new social experiences and connections. Couchsurfing led to AirBnB, which is a for-profit bed-and-breakfast in which people host travellers in their spare rooms, which we discuss in more detail below. Other sites include Roomarama and Tourboarder. Practices such as ratings, comments and feedback have helped to address the problems of trust that are present in a context where people are opening their homes or lending expensive possessions to strangers.

The idea of renting excess space was extended to empty garages, attics and parking spaces. Other variants include land sharing, which matches unused land with would-be gardeners who lack acreage, and co-working, in which unrelated individuals share office space. A related concept is to mobilize idle capacity in publically owned assets. One example is Neighborhood Fruit, which identifies and publicizes publically owned fruit trees and also helps to transfer excess fruit from tree owners to consumers. In their peer-to-peer versions, these innovations provide people with low-cost access to goods and capacity and allow owners to earn modest amounts of money to supplement regular income streams.

The third major type of connected consumption involves the exchange of services, rather than goods. Here the originator is time banking, a practice whose origins as a formal institution date to the 1980s (Cahn and Rowe 1992; Collom et al. 2012; Seyfang 2004). Time banks are typically community-based non-profits whose members trade services on an egalitarian basis in which each member's time is equivalent in value to every other member's. Time banking participants offer services such as babysitting, painting or massage, and earn 'time dollars' when they provide services to others. This currency can then be used to receive services. Time banks explicitly aim to circumvent monetized market exchange and create more egalitarian relations. There are now an estimated 276 time banks officially operating in the United States and time banks exist in 26 countries (http://en.wikipedia.org/wiki/Time_banking, accessed 9 February 2014).

The impetus to innovate in the connected consumption space has led to variants of time banking which use money or, in some cases, a convertible 'social currency'. Zaarly and Task Rabbit are sites in which some users request services and others bid (in dollars) for the opportunity to do them. Hub Culture is a social networking site for management professionals offering advice, skills acquisition and other services. Delivery is partly face-to-face, and the currency earned is called Ven, which has dollar convertibility. The other major service-sharing category is in transportation, where a number of ride-sharing sites operate.

A variant between goods and service provision involves the exchange of home-produced goods, such as food, crafts and the like. The largest of these sites is etsy, which has more than one million sellers. Other sites include Mama Bake, Soup Sharing and EatWithMe, which are oriented toward creating more social connection and social experience. This is a goal shared by many of the connected consumption platforms, but it is the key motivator for a number of the neighbourhood sites, such as those mentioned above. Facilitating peer-to-peer connection and avoiding financial institutions is also at the root of social lending sites such as Prosper, Zopa and the Lending Club, which allow people to go online, learn about initiatives that require financial investment, and transfer money or invest in them. Finally there are sites whose purpose is to help people build their own skills and capacities, such as Skillshare.com, which offers peer-to-peer workshops to democratize access to skill and knowledge and to supplant traditional educational institutions.

## 26.2 MOTIVATIONS FOR NEW FORMS OF SHARING

In our research, we have found multiple motivations for participation in the sharing economy. The first is economic. Because these sites are peer-to-peer they are able to redistribute value across the supply chain, to producers and consumers, and away from middlemen. They both deliver more value to consumers and create new income-earning opportunities for producers. Sharing sites boast that people are able to earn significant sums by renting out their spare rooms or cars, or doing tasks for money. One consequence is that these sites can be highly disruptive of established or 'legacy' businesses and interests in these sectors. Hotel demand can fall when AirBnB activity rises. Taxi and limousine drivers have organized against Uber and Lyft, which sell rides online (Chen 2012). While proponents of collaborative consumption extol its virtues, they rarely discuss its negative economic impact on old economy businesses and employees.

The second motivation is to reduce ecological impact, including carbon and eco-footprints. Most sites advertise their green credentials and impacts, and many of the users care about eco-impact. In some cases, the effect seems obvious. Recirculation of goods, rather than buying new, involves a lower footprint. Staying in existing homes reduces the demand for new hotels. Sharing space is less resource-intensive than letting it sit empty. In general, however, we have found that ecological impacts have been largely assumed and there are relatively few studies of how these new practices affect resource intensity and greenhouse gas emissions. One careful study of car sharing (Martin and Shaheen 2010) found that the practice had a significant negative impact on greenhouse gas emissions. However this was due to the fact that only a few households used car sharing to reduce their emissions by a substantial amount. For the majority of households, the practice increased emissions. The authors conclude that because the impacts of car sharing vary so greatly across households, broad generalizations about climate impacts cannot be inferred. This is likely true for a number of sharing economy platforms. One reason is that by creating new markets for used goods, they expand the volume of commerce and inject additional purchasing power into the economy, which in turn creates impact. First round effects which seem 'obvious' may be misleading.

The third motivation is to increase social connection and build social networks. Many sites advertise this feature of their business, and we have found in our case studies that this motivation is common among users. However, we have also discovered that a number of these platforms fail to deliver durable social ties. In our time bank case, we found many participants were disappointed in the extent of social connection they developed (Dubois et al. 2014). In her study of car sharing, Fenton found that the two parties to the transaction often never met, on account of remote access technology (Fenton 2013).

We have also found that technophilia accounts for people's interest in connected consumption. They like using the Internet to do things efficiently and easily. They enjoy the sophisticated interfaces offered by many of the sites. Many users have been 'digitally primed' by years of online sharing of files, music and other cultural products. Also, a significant number of our respondents are themselves in the world of digital technology as programmers or website designers.

A final motivation is that many participants are ideologically committed to the concepts of sharing and collaborating, and many have critiques of market provision, especially in services. In our time bank research (Dubois et al. 2014), half our respondents are ideologically motivated to engage in non-market, personal types of service exchange. In the food swap case, all of the founders and many of the participants are motivated by ideas surrounding organic and local food, membership in community supported agriculture (CSA) programmes, and other aspects of the alternative food movement (Fitzmaurice and Schor 2014). Indeed, the founding of the food swap itself was due to issues associated with alternative food practices. More generally, for many participants, especially early adopters, joining sharing or swapping initiatives is an intentional political act with the purpose of helping to construct an alternative to normative market provision. In this way, we find that our respondents do believe in what Viviana Zelizer (2007) has termed the 'hostile worlds' view of the relation between the market and intimate life. But they are not so concerned about how the market is undermining private life, as in the classic cases Zelizer discusses. Rather, they are trying to construct new kinds of markets that produce personalized exchange relations. We find this in research on time banking, food swapping, lodging exchange and service provisioning.

## 26.3 QUANTIFYING AND DEFINING THE SHARING ECONOMY

To our knowledge, there is not yet a serious quantification of the size and extent of the phenomenon. However there is considerable anecdotal evidence of its growing reach. In 2013, Rachel Botsman reported that the peer-to-peer (or P2P) rental market had reached $26 billion (Botsman 2013). Jeremiah Oywang, a marketing consultant, estimated that in 2013 there were 200 companies with more than $2 billion in venture funding, although this includes only for-profit sites and those that have advanced to the venture capital stage (http://www.web-strategist.com/blog/2013/06/14/infographic-collaborative-economy-startups-proliferating/). We have gathered data from some of the largest sites in a few of the major categories, which are shown in Table 26.1. These platforms range considerably in size: AirBnB, which is the largest, logged a cumulative total of 10 million overnight stays by 2012; Freecycle has more than 6 million members. Among the transportation sites, the trend is towards availability in a growing number of cities; this is also the case with bike sharing programmes, which are expanding rapidly.

Defining the limits of the sharing economy is difficult. What specific characteristics make these forms of exchange part of the sharing economy, rather than novel market forms? An even more complex issue is what distinguishes these phenomena from older practices of sharing. We have identified three characteristics that can help to define which practices warrant inclusion in this emergent economy.

First, the new sharing economy is distinguished from previous forms of sharing by its ability to facilitate sharing between strangers, rather than among kin or within communities. In contrast to monetized commodity exchange, sharing necessitates at least a modicum of social connection. As Russell Belk has argued, in standard market exchanges, one-off trades are possible and participants are not required to encounter each other again. 'Commodity exchange is about the reproduction of rights to objects, not the reproduction of relationships between people' (Belk 2009, p. 718). As a result, sharing has historically been associated with exchanges within the home or community. Previous forms of sharing have not been characterized by the participation of strangers.

*Table 26.1 Websites*

| Site | Statistics | Source |
|---|---|---|
| AirBnB | Total guests: 9 million+<br>Total guest nights booked: 10 million+ as of June 2012<br>Cities: 34 000+<br>Countries: 192 | https://www.airbnb.com/about/about-us |
| Couchsurfing | Members: 7 million+<br>Cities: 100 000 | https://www.couchsurfing.org/n/about |
| Uber | Countries: 20<br>Cities: 72 | https://www.uber.com/cities |
| Lyft | Cities: 20 | http://help.lyft.com/ |
| Zipcar | Cities: 181 | http://www.zipcar.com/?redirect_p=0 |
| Capital Bikeshare | Trips per month on average: 218 000+<br>Annual members: 41 000+<br>24-hour passes per month: 380 000+ | http://cabidashboard.ddot.dc.gov/CaBiDashboard/ |
| CitiBikes | Annual membership: 85 000+<br>Total miles travelled: 8 million+<br>Trips taken: 3.5 million+ | http://cf.datawrapper.de/DJ3mf/2/ |
| Freecycle | Groups: 5120<br>Membership: 6 912 829 | http://www.freecycle.org/ |

*Note:* Websites accessed on 11 February 2014.

The historical restriction of sharing practices to familiar 'others' is largely due to two limitations of sharing in comparison to market exchanges. The first has been described as the problem of the 'leaky self' and involves fears of contagion, be it biological or social (Belk 2009). The act of sharing inevitably blurs social boundaries, in relation to both the commodities and the social actors involved. 'When this happens we symbolically become one so that, at least for a moment, the former me and you, as well as mine and yours, become us and ours' (Belk 2009, p. 728). The social obligations of sharing imply that exchange partners do not come together as prototypical self-interested, autonomous actors. As a result, the usual markers of social distinction such as race, class, gender and cultural capital (Bourdieu 1984 [1979]) can become salient. With familiar individuals such information is easily known, and exchange partners are likely similar. Among strangers, exchange partners are forced to ask with whom are they willing to share, and whether or not they are willing to become associated with such 'others'.

A related characteristic of sharing that historically limited such practices to kin and communities is the problem of establishing trust. Trust can be conceptualized as 'a disposition to engage in social exchanges that involve uncertainty and vulnerability, but that are also potentially rewarding' (Bicchieri et al. 2004, p. 286). However, among strangers, exchange partners often lack the necessary information or previous experience necessary to establish trust. As a result, individuals must rely upon impersonal trust, presenting exchange partners with a one-sided social dilemma (Bicchieri et al. 2004). 'The standard solution to "social dilemmas" is to introduce some form of formal or informal social control', which can range from institutional monitoring to 'repetition itself, with its possibilities for signalling, retaliation and reputation formation' (Bicchieri et al. 2004, p. 287). Sharing among kin and community ensures that exchange partners have a basis for trust based on pre-existing social relationships. But it also ensures the types of informal social controls needed to generate impersonal trust. Among strangers, the market has typically provided solutions to the problem of trust by minimizing risk. In our view, the ability to facilitate sharing between strangers is a defining feature of institutions and practices that are part of the emergent sharing economy.

Second, practices comprising the sharing economy can be distinguished from previous forms of sharing by their strong reliance on digital technologies. Digital technologies provide mechanisms for crowd-sourcing information to create accountability, ratings and reputation indicators. This solves some of the barriers to generating impersonal trust among strangers. However, digital platforms also help to coordinate sharing among strangers by facilitating connections between goods and services and their potential users and consumers. Sharing within households and communities requires little complex coordination because needs are either known or readily discerned. However, among strangers coordination costs arise; a problem that impersonal market exchanges have heretofore resolved. The Internet dramatically reduces the costs of coordination in terms of time and money (Schifferes 2014).

Finally, the contemporary sharing economy can be distinguished from other systems of sharing by the participation of high cultural capital consumers. Increasingly, such consumers are electing to share, rather than sharing out of necessity. While anthropological studies have certainly documented the social roles of sharing beyond providing for necessities (Belk 2009), in wealthy countries sharing has been best documented sociologically as a survival mechanism among the most disadvantaged (Stack 1974). Moreover, Robert Putnam has noted that along with declining levels of community and civic engagement there has been a decline in generalized reciprocity and trust in the United States, and a related reticence to engage in the types of sharing that once characterized neighbourhoods, such as raking up another's leaves (Putnam 2000). The sharing economy is a reversal of this trend, as sharing practices are being adopted by high cultural capital consumers as a distinctive consumption preference (Carfagna et al. 2014). Our argument is not that the sharing economy is limited to elite consumers. Rather, a distinctive feature of sharing economy platforms and practices is their ability to involve such consumers in practices that they previously refrained from.

These characteristics distinguish the sharing economy from other forms of sharing. Additionally, many platforms within the sharing economy establish what Viviana Zelizer has termed 'circuits of commerce' (Zelizer 2010), which distinguishes them from traditional conceptions of sharing as sporadic and often bilateral. Zelizer has identified five criteria that must be met for a pattern of interactions to constitute a circuit of commerce rather than a market or a social network. These are: social ties among a group of individuals, economic exchanges stemming from those relationships, a common system of evaluation and accounting, shared meaning attached to the exchanges and a boundary defining membership in the circuit (Zelizer 2010). Sharing economy platforms often serve to bring together bounded groups of people into circuits to facilitate such exchanges. This is another way in which these platforms address the problems of trust associated with sharing among strangers.

## 26.4 TRUST AND REPUTATION STUDIES

The ability to overcome barriers of trust is not only a defining characteristic of sharing economy platforms: trust and reputation has become the central question in the social science literature on the sharing economy. In the previous section we noted that crowd-sourcing of information from participants is the key mechanism for creating trust and reputation. Additional research has shown that online reputation systems shift revenue in markets as consumers gain access to more information. Yelp reviews, for example, have been shown to shift consumer spending away from chains (about which, historically, greater reputational information was available) to independent establishments (Luca 2011).

However, much of the academic literature explores the limitations of the reputational mechanisms that sharing platforms provide. For example, Lauterbach et al. (2009) have examined reputation and trust among Couchsurfers and find that the number of exchanges facilitated by the Couchsurfing platform is the result of its reputation system, which allows users to vouch for each other through references and descriptions of their experiences. They also find significant problems with the reliability of the information that is offered. A quarter of members had vouched for each other, which is a sign that vouching is too freely given by members who only know each other through the site and may be inflating members' reputations. Moreover, due to the public nature of the platform's reputational system, vouching can be induced by social pressures rather than genuine affirmations of a member's trustworthiness (Lauterbach et al. 2009).

Also using Couchsurfing as an exemplary case, Overgoor et al. (2012) note a similarity to other peer-to-peer (hereafter P2P) public reputation systems: anonymity can lead to misinformation. The public nature of these systems produces positive biases as users seek to avoid retribution for less positive reviews. Similar problems have been found across online, peer-rated, public trust systems. Wang and Nakao (2010) suggest that P2P reputation systems – which aggregate a community's evaluation of a user's trustworthiness – are vulnerable to attack by what they term 'front peers'. These are individuals who cooperate and collude with peers to inflate their own reputations. Ott et al. (2012) find that for P2P reputation systems which have low posting costs and allow any user to post reviews without safeguards to ensure reviewers actually used the service, the prevalence of dishonest 'deceptive opinion spam' has increased. The popular site Yelp.com fits this model.

The remainder of the literature on the sharing economy has focused on the consumer side. An influential theoretical paper by Takahashi (2000) addresses the problem of how norms of generalized exchange, critical for many sharing platforms, can arise when people are assumed to be rational actors. Takahashi shows that altruism is unnecessary for exchanges to take place and demonstrates that norms of generalized exchange can emerge as long as individuals have a personal sense of fairness.

Other research has investigated the ability of the sharing economy to foster community. Ozanne and Ballantine (2010) found that a toy-sharing library provided a space for collective mobilization of anti-consumption values. Albinsson and Perera (2012) suggest that individuals involved in the sharing economy through the creation of alternative markets built community on the local level as 'citizen-consumers' seeking more sustainable futures. Finally, Setiffi's (2011) analysis suggests the need to consider how the sharing or recirculation of goods conveys social meaning and suggests a theorization of the 'culture of the used'.

In contrast, as we noted above, our research and that of others has revealed less evidence of social connection within the sharing economy than proponents suggest. In their study of Zipcar, Bardhi and Eckhardt (2012) found that users resisted the creation of brand communities. They argue that the altruism typically associated with sharing might be limited by the market mediation of sharing exchanges and by platforms that allow participants to remain anonymous to each other. Similarly, our research on time banking has pointed to limitations in the ability of the sharing economy to build social capital and community (Dubois et al. 2014). Participants often engaged in one-off trades, or were reluctant to provide services in their areas of expertise, both because they could be better compensated for those skills in the market and because they desired opportunities to try out skills they would not be rewarded for in the labour market due to inexperience. Fenton's study of RelayRides users challenged the potential of such platforms to truly build community and users described their interactions as 'anonymous' and 'sterile' (Fenton 2013).

Some studies have provided evidence for the reproduction of inequality within the sharing economy. In our study of food swaps we have observed the ways in which cultural capital – as reflected in the products, packaging and even the appearance of participants – limited the trades members are willing to make, and who feels comfortable at the events. Only participants who possess the 'right' taste will be traded with and, in many cases, will feel comfortable returning (Fitzmaurice and Schor 2014). In the time bank we found that the skills individuals are willing to trade for reproduces inequality on the basis of participants' cultural capital (Dubois et al. 2014). Finally, Edelman and Luca (2014) have identified racial bases of discrimination among AirBnB users. They found that white users were able to charge 12 per cent more for rentals than non-white users for comparable properties, controlling for all other information available on listings.

## 26.5 CLASSIFYING THE SHARING ECONOMY: A TYPOLOGY OF PLATFORMS AND PRACTICES

Having suggested the characteristics distinguishing the platforms and practices of the sharing economy from other forms of sharing, and reviewed the primary concerns of the academic literature on sharing, we suggest that certain features are particularly useful when classifying these emergent platforms and practices. These characteristics are the predominant influences giving shape to the platforms, provide organizing logics, and also determine how disruptive to mainstream market models a platform may be and the ability of platforms to expand. To that end, in Table 26.2 we suggest a typology for categorizing sharing economy platforms.

*Table 26.2 A sharing economy platforms typology*

| | | Organization | |
|---|---|---|---|
| | | Peer-to-peer (P2P) | Business-to-peer (B2P) |
| Market orientation | Non-profit | P2P Non-profit sharing e.g. food swaps, time banks | B2P Non-profit sharing |
| | For-profit | P2P For-profit sharing e.g. Relay Rides, AirBnB | B2P For-profit sharing e.g. Zipcar |

The first characteristic that influences the nature of sharing economy platforms and practices is the organization's orientation towards profits and value creation. While all sharing economy platforms effectively create 'markets in sharing' by facilitating sharing amongst strangers, the imperative for a platform to generate a profit influences how sharing ultimately takes place. For-profit sharing platforms such as Zipcar and AirBnB have become market leaders. However many of the for-profit entities in the sharing economy – such as RelayRides and AirBnB – earn money by taking a commission on the peer-to-peer exchanges they facilitate. As a consequence, revenue growth depends on increasing the number of peer-to-peer exchanges occurring on the platform. This is a significant departure from business models that seek to maximize revenue per transaction, an approach that is more common on business-to-peer platforms.

This difference points to a second characteristic of consequence: whether a sharing platform operates peer-to-peer (P2P) or business-to-peer (B2P) exchanges. Peer-to-peer exchanges are more like the traditional idea of sharing, except that exchange partners often begin as strangers. Individual participants can set the terms of exchange, and loan and exchange their own goods and services. Business-to-peer exchanges have the tendency to assume the form of more conventional rental arrangements. Consider the differences between Zipcar (B2P) and RelayRides (P2P). RelayRides allows vehicle owners to share their own cars and earn income from their vehicles. It allows members to choose rentals based on their needs, owner-determined rates, and availability. Zipcar functions in a manner much more akin to a short-term car rental company: members pay a specific membership fee and hourly charges for access to company-owned vehicles.

## 26.6 WHAT DOES THE SHARING ECONOMY LOOK LIKE IN PRACTICE?

Having outlined the main characteristics that shape the practices and organization of exchange platforms within the sharing economy, we turn our attention to examples of what the sharing economy looks like in practice. Below, we offer four short descriptions of different platforms and practices. Data is drawn from our own research. These examples span the various spectrums we have outlined, yet all provide opportunities for novel forms of exchange.

Food swaps are an example of a peer-to-peer, non-profit sharing platform for barter exchange (Fitzmaurice and Schor 2014). Although there are online resources to connect interested individuals to local swaps, swaps are autonomously organized and can range from small groups of interested individuals to as many as 50 participants. At food swap events, individuals bring products they have made, foraged, or grown themselves. Most often, these are foods such as granola, jam, baked goods and spice blends. Swaps operate using a silent auction format. After a period of sampling, individuals bid on goods with the aim of enacting bilateral exchanges. Transactions are finalized when two individuals express mutual interest in each other's products. At the food swap we have studied, participants tend to be white women ranging in age from their mid-20s to middle age.

RelayRides is a peer-to-peer, for-profit car-sharing platform in which owners list their vehicles for rent (https://relayrides.com/how-it-works). In exchange for connecting vehicle owners to renters, RelayRides receives a commission from the rental cost. We have found that car owners often decided to rent on RelayRides as a result of working from home, traveling often, or simply using their car infrequently. Owners reported being able to cover their loan payments or maintenance costs, and occasionally making a profit. Unlike other car sharing programmes, owners set the terms of rental as well as the hourly or daily rental fee. Renters include those who do not own cars or need a particular car for a unique task. Unlike with food swapping, the digital component is critical in facilitating this sort of sharing. The platform connects renters to cars by allowing them to search for cars that are available near them and provides a solution to trust barriers through reputational rating systems for both owners and renters. Additionally, unlike the food swap model – which allows participants to more efficiently produce new products – RelayRides facilitates a form of sharing that creates opportunities for individuals to earn money by tapping into the existing idle capacity of their unused vehicles.

AirBnB is a similar platform to RelayRides, making use of the idle capacity of a room, apartment or home. The accommodation platform was founded in 2008 and now operates in over 33000 cities located in 192 countries worldwide (https://www.airbnb.com/about/about-us). Like RelayRides, it is an online, peer-to-peer, for-profit sharing platform that generates revenue via service fees on bookings. In our research, we found that AirBnB hosts seek to supplement their incomes, as well as to meet travellers and introduce them to their communities. Guests were found to use this service as an affordable alternative to traditional hotels that is less commercialized and perceived as offering a more 'authentic' experience of place.

In both RelayRides and AirBnB the online platform is critical for facilitating sharing. An online profile for each listing provides information about the accommodations, rates and guidelines for renters. Users are able to review ratings for both hosts and prospective renters. The platform provides a system for overcoming the barriers of trust involved in sharing among strangers by providing a consistent system for evaluating user reputations.

Our final example, Task Rabbit, is an online, for-profit, peer-to-peer marketplace that connects local individuals to complete specific tasks for others (https://www.taskrabbit.com/about). As such, it functions as a shared labour market, in which Task Posters create listings for tasks they are seeking to have completed, and Task Rabbits (recently renamed 'Taskers') bid for the chance to carry out these tasks for their desired level of compensation. Task Rabbit monetizes the traditional sharing relationships of neighbours, and expands such sharing practices from the spheres of kin and community to strangers.

Task Posters create listings describing the tasks, including information on the location and the deadline for when a task must be completed. Posters originally designated prices for tasks, or accepted bids from Rabbits, although the site has recently introduced fixed prices. Posters can consult the reviews that are located on Task Rabbits' profiles. Unlike the previously described forms of sharing, Task Rabbit mediates exchanges between individuals with particular skills and surplus time with those needing various services. Moreover it provides an efficient online platform for evaluating reputations and competencies of participants, as well as a basis for monetizing such sharing exchanges.

## 26.7 CONCLUDING THOUGHTS: TRANSFORMATIVE POTENTIALS AND CHALLENGES

To what extent can the sharing economy lead to a sustainable and more humane regime of consumption and production, a goal shared by many of its participants? In 2013, this question attracted considerable attention in the popular media, as the ambitious claims of proponents were scrutinized by analysts with a more critical view, particularly of the for-profit platforms. (Golumbia 2013; Slee 2013). Critics raised the question of whether these sites can create a more progressive and socially just economy, a frequently articulated goal of advocates. Agyeman et al. (2013) argued that the key to keeping sharing economies socially just is to emphasize shared urban space, and collective, public forms of sharing as well as an explicit politics of sharing, a view we endorse.

The ongoing debate about the potential for social transformation associated with these initiatives is due to the fact that their long-term impacts are currently unknown (Schor 2014). Some of these efforts, if they can scale up, do have the possibility of creating new economic relations that are more equal, sustainable and socially cohesive. On the other hand, others reproduce existing inequalities, foster high-impact consumer demand, or are likely to converge to business-as-usual if they are successful. The likelihood of going one way or another, is determined by a range of factors, such as the business model, whether they are non-profit or for-profit, and the nature of the service they provide.

While most of the for-profits identify social goals as part of their mission, in some cases as they grow and mature, they come to behave very similarly to existing profit-centric businesses. Zipcar seems to be an example of this. Carbon footprint reduction was central to its original purpose, however its partnership with Ford Motor Company involved offering sport utility vehicles. Furthermore, its goal of putting cars on college campuses, where cars were rare, may end up increasing car use, rather than reducing car usage. In contrast, some of the for-profit sites may be able to maintain their footprint reducing, or socially progressive goals as they grow, particularly in cases where their service or product is itself low-impact, eg., clothing swaps or Etsy. And yet, eBay started by selling used items, but eventually included a large range of new products. Similarly, sites such as Craigslist, which began as a non-profit, can convert to for-profit status, as it did.

A second issue is whether the site uses money as a medium of exchange (versus goods, time or an invented currency such as Ven). Those that create a new currency or trade in used goods have a much greater likelihood of fostering new economic relations. Time banks use an internal currency, measured as time dollars or hours. They therefore facilitate a new 'economy' in which participants can deploy a relatively more equally distributed asset (time). This counteracts the highly unequal market distribution of financial assets and skills and creates opportunities for people whose labour market options are constrained. We have also found that this can be a limiting feature of time banks, particularly in good economic times. If highly-skilled professionals can sell their time on the market, they are unlikely to participate in trades with others whose market wage is low. (Trading plumbing services for babysitting is not appealing for plumbers.) But trades among more equal partners can be attractive in a labour market where professionals are unable to work to their desired capacities. Ourgoods.com, a site for artists, is an example of this type of platform. Coding Cupboard and Concept Cupboard are others. Other sites, such as Zaarly and TaskRabbit, operate within the dollar economy, and give people with excess time and inadequate cash a chance to sell their services to others with the reverse situation. We find that TaskRabbit seems to differ little from an inexpensive errand service, and is likely to evolve into a conventional business if it is successful, but one in which employees lack secure hours, income streams and protections.

Given that connected consumption is so new, it is impossible to say how this sector will evolve. What we do believe is that it is likely to grow, including in its more transformative forms. The demand for sharing comes in part from its capacity to foster economic activity among people with constrained earning power in the formal economy. In our research, we also find that people want to share because they crave connection with others, are concerned about climate change and because they fervently believe in the need to humanize what has become a dysfunctional and anti-social market.

## ACKNOWLEDGEMENTS

The authors would like to thank the MacArthur Foundation for generous funding, and all the members of the Connected Consumption Research Team whose work contributed to this chapter: Luka Carfagna, Will Attwood-Charles, Emilie Dubois, Alison Wawrzynek, Lea Oriol and Nathan Schwan.

## NOTE

1. Information about our project, which is called Connected Consumption and is funded as part of the MacArthur Connected Learning Research Network, can be found at: http://clrn.dmlhub.net/projects/connected-consumption.

## REFERENCES

Agyeman, J., D. McLaren and A. Schaefer-Borrego (2013), 'Sharing cities', Friends of the Earth Briefing Paper.

Albinsson, P.A. and Y. Perera (2012), 'Alternative market places in the 21st century: building community through sharing events', *Journal of Consumer Behavior*, 11, 303–315.

Bardhi, F. and G.M. Eckhardt (2012), 'Access-based consumption: the case of car sharing', *Journal of Consumer Research*, 39 (4), 881–898.

Belk, R. (2009), 'Sharing', *Journal of Consumer Research*, 36, 715–734.

Bicchieri, C., J. Duffy and G. Tolle (2004). 'Trust among strangers', *Philosophy of Science*, 71 (3), 286–319.

Bourdieu, P. (1984 [1979]), *Distinction: A Social Critique of the Judgment of Taste*, London: Routledge & Kegan Paul.

Botsman, R. (2013), 'The rise of the sharing economy', *The Economist*, 9 March, available at http://www.economist.com/news/leaders/21573104-internet-everything-hire-rise-sharing-economy (accessed 9 February 2014).

Botsman, R. and R. Rogers (2010), *What's Mine is Yours: The Rise of Collaborative Consumption*, New York: HarperCollins.

Cahn, E. and J. Rowe (1992), *Time Dollars*, Emmaus, PA: Rodale Press.

Carfagna, L.B., E. Dubois, C. Fitzmaurice, T. Laidley, M. Ouilmette, J. Schor and M. Willis (2014), 'An emerging eco-habitus: the reconfiguration of high cultural capital practices among ethical consumers', *Journal of Consumer Culture*, 14 (2), 158–178.

Chen, B.X. (2012), 'A feisty start-up is met with regulatory snarl', *New York Times*, 3 December, B1, available at http://www.nytimes.com/2012/12/03/technology/app-maker-uber-hits-regulatory-snarl.html?pagewanted=all (accessed 9 February 2014).

Collom, E., J.N. Lasker, and C. Kyriacou (2012), *Equal Time, Equal Value: Community Currencies and Time Banking in the US*, Aldershot: Ashgate.

Dubois, E., J. Schor and L. Carfagna (2014), 'New cultures of connection in a Boston time bank', in J.B. Schor and C.J. Thompson (eds), *Practicing Plenitude*, New Haven, CT: Yale University Press, pp. 95–124.

Edelman, B.G. and M. Luca (2014), 'Digital discrimination: the case of Airbnb', Harvard Business School Working Papers.

Fenton, A. (2013), 'Making markets personal: exploring market construction at the micro level in the car-sharing and time bank markets', unpublished manuscript, Harvard University.

Fitzmaurice, C. and J. Schor (2014), 'Handmade matters: (re)imagining "homemade" food at the boundaries of food swap circuits', paper presented at Consumers and Consumption session, American Sociological Association Annual Meeting, San Francisco, August 2014..

Gansky, L. (2011), 'Do more, own less: a grand theory of the sharing economy', available at http://www.theatlantic.com/business/archive/2011/08/do-more-own-less-a-grand-theory-of-the-sharing-economy/244141/ (accessed 2 September 2011).

Gell, A. (1986), 'Newcomers to the world of goods: consumption among the Muria Gonds', in A. Appadurai (ed.), *The Social Life of Things: Commodities in Cultural Perspective*, Cambridge: Cambridge University Press, pp. 110–138.

Golumbia, D. (2013), 'Cyberlibertarians' digital delection of the left', *Jacobin Magazine*, https://www.jacobinmag.com/2013/12/cyberlibertarians-digital-deletion-of-the-left/ (accessed 14 February 2014).

Lauterbach, D., H. Tmong, T. Shah and L. Adamic (2009), 'Surfing a web of trust: reputation and reciprocity on Couchsurfing.com.' *Proceedings of the IEEE Social Computing 2009*, Vancouver, British Columbia, Canada.

Luca, M. (2011), 'Reviews, reputation, and revenue: the case of Yelp.com', Harvard Business School, Working Paper.

Martin, E.W. and S.A. Shaheen (2010), 'Greenhouse gas impacts of car sharing in North America', Mineta Transportation Institute Report 09–11, San Jose, CA: Mineta Transportation Institute.

Merrill, M. (1977), 'Cash is good to eat: self-sufficiency and exchange in the rural economy of the United States', *Radical History Review*, 13, 42–71.

Nelson, M.R., M.A. Rademacher and H.-J. Paek (2007), 'Downshifting consumer = upshifting citizen? An examination of a local freecycle community', *Annals of the American Academy of Political and Social Science*, 611, 141–156.

Ott, M., C. Cardie and J. Hancock (2012), 'Estimating the prevalence of deception in online review communities', *Proceedings of the 21st International Conference on the World Wide Web*, pp. 201–210.

Overgoor, J., E. Wulczyn and C. Potts (2012), 'Trust propagation with mixed-effects models', International AAAI Conference on Weblogs and Social Media.

Ozanne, L.K. and P.W. Ballantine (2010), 'Sharing as a form of anti-consumption? An examination of toy library users', *Journal of Consumer Behaviour*, 9 (6), 485–498.

Putnam, R. (2000), *Bowling Alone: The Collapse and Revival of American Community*, New York: Simon & Schuster.

Schifferes, J. (2014), 'There's more to shops than shopping', *RSA*, 14 January, available at http://www.rsablogs.org.uk/2014/social-economy/shops-shopping/ (accessed 9 February 2014).

Schor, J.B. (2010), *Plenitude: The New Economics of True Wealth*, London: Penguin Press.

Schor, J.B. (2013), 'The paradox of materiality: fashion, marketing, and the planetary ecology', in M. McAllister and E. West (eds), *Routledge Companion to Advertising and Promotional Culture*, London: Routledge, pp. 435–448.

Schor, J.B. (2014), 'Debating the sharing economy', essay published by the Great Transition Initiative, Tellus Institute, available at http://www.greattransition.org/, October 2014.

Setiffi, F. (2011), 'Reflections on the cultures of the new and the second hand in Italy', *Italian Sociological Review*, 3, 12–20.

Seyfang, G. (2004), 'Time banks: rewarding community self-help in the inner city?', *Community Development Journal*, 39 (1), 62–71.

Slee, T. (2013), 'Sharing and caring', *Jacobin Magazine*, available at https://www.jacobinmag.com/2014/01/sharing-and-caring/ (accessed 14 February 2014).

Stack, C.B. (1974), *All our Kin: Strategies for Survival in a Black Community*, New York: Harper & Row.

Takahashi, N. (2000), 'The emergence of generalized exchange', *American Journal of Sociology*, 105 (4), 1105–1134.

Wang, Y.F. and A. Nakao (2010), 'On cooperative and efficient overlay network evolutions based on group selection pattern', *IEEE Transcripts on Systems, Man, and Cybernetics Part 1*, 40 (3), 493–504.

Zelizer, V.A. (2007), *The Purchase of Intimacy*, Princeton, NJ: Princeton University Press.

Zelizer, V.A. (2010), *Economic Lives: How Culture Shapes the Economy*, Princeton, NJ: Princeton University Press.

# 27. Toward a post-consumerist future? Social innovation in an era of fading economic growth[1]

*Maurie J. Cohen*

While there is a tendency to attribute the advent of contemporary consumer society in the United States and other affluent nations to a combination of heroic entrepreneurship and historic inevitability, more prudent analysis points to the critical role of state intervention at key moments during the twentieth century (Cohen 2003; de Grazia 2006; Garon 2013; Prasad 2012; Seiji 1999). Starting in most countries with the provision of guaranteed pensions, which reduced the need to accumulate personal retirement savings and increased propensities to spend, governments enacted an expanding array of policies and programmes to bolster consumerist lifestyles. These interventions combined and co-evolved with several auspicious social and economic factors during the post-1945 period: a relatively youthful population, a sustained pattern of rising per capita income, a growing middle class, and a quest for affordable housing and mobility (see in particular Field 2012). Demonstrable evidence of a weakening in the capacity of mass consumption to drive economic growth began to appear during the 1970s and these conditions were exacerbated by high inflation, rising and unusually volatile energy prices, and expanding public attentiveness to the environmental consequences of industrial production. In response, a grand political bargain was struck in the United States favouring deregulation of key economic sectors (particularly finance), liberalization of international trade, and reassertion of military power abroad that reinvigorated household consumption, prompting a new wave of acquisitive social striving and competitive spending (Collins 2002; Yarrow 2010). It has subsequently been necessary to refresh these measures from time to time so as to ensure sufficient flow of raw materials and to keep retail prices aligned with household budgets.

Mass consumption as the foundation of social organization is now variously showing new signs of fatigue in nations where it has taken deepest root (Acemoglu and Robinson 2012; Benett and O'Reilly 2010; Etzioni 2011; Ferguson 2012; Frank 2009). Since 2008, much of the global North has been caught up in another period of slackening economic growth, and the accompanying turbulence is encouraging incipient expressions of 'post-consumerism' (Cohen 2013; Etzioni 2004, 2009; Frank 2009; Gilding 2011; Ivanova 2011). Stalwart commitment to a perverse kind of anti-Keynesianism has stifled consumer demand and exacerbated near-recessionary conditions in many G-20 countries.

A similar process has been under way in Japan for more than two decades and this head start has arguably given the nation frontrunner status in this putative transition (Cohen 2011; Hama 2012; Horioka 2006; Kato 2010, 2013). Rather than a speculative projection, 'degrowth' (or a condition closely approximating it) is now a candid and legitimate description of economic reality in a growing number of ostensibly wealthy countries (Heinberg 2011; Jackson 2009; Klitgaard and Krall 2012; Latouche 2010; Lloyd 2009; Victor 2009). Moreover prevailing conditions are showing signs of becoming systemic. A 'long malaise' is how the economist Joseph Stiglitz (2013) has recently described the state of affairs in the United States. 'The American dream,' he writes, 'a good life in exchange for hard work – is slowly dying.'

This sort of sober appraisal shifts the valence of debate beyond normative claims about the efficacy of consumer society to salient questions about the continued feasibility of an economic model founded on continual expansion of energy and material throughput (Coyle 2011; Speth 2009). Keeping the wheels of consumerism turning in the future will require considerable renewal of the current economic system, but political interest in undertaking the necessary difficult work is inadequate to the task. At the same time, a wave of social innovation predicated on shared use, self and collective provisioning, and a variety of novel business models seems to be building as prevailing conditions both inspire and compel lifestyle reinventions.[2] There are indications that in some locales these experimental activities are starting to swell up and radiate outward because conventional arrangements are becoming strained and people are reaching for – or fashioning for themselves – more workable options. Over time these novel practices may achieve sufficient scale to confront, and perhaps even to supplant, incumbent arrangements.

The aim of this chapter is to identify hints of the early emergence of post-consumerism in the United States and to suggest that these developments may presage the initial breakdown of consumer society in Anglo-European countries (and Japan) more generally. Section 27.1 highlights the changing circumstances for economic growth in the global North and describes why we are unlikely to see a return to prior conditions. Section 27.2 then explores the first tentative social innovations that may herald a post-consumerist transition, and the concluding section outlines the reasons why this societal transformation is likely to be slow and spatially uneven.

## 27.1 THE WINDING DOWN OF ECONOMIC GROWTH

All economic systems rest upon supportive pillars that require periodic reinforcement to maintain their viability. For instance, when supplies of critical raw materials run short, substitutes must be identified or technological changes introduced. Failure to do so in a timely manner runs the risk of gradual attrition or, in certain more dramatic cases, precipitous decline (Diamond 2004; Tainter 1990). Current developments at the heart of contemporary consumer society suggest that a difficult and unsettling period may loom in the near future in the absence of significant revitalization (Packer 2013; Wuthnow 2006).

For the last several decades mass consumption in the United States has been enabled by three dependable mainstays: favourable demographics, rising and relatively equal household income, and malleable consumer sensibilities. Spanning these props have been reliable joists, most notably facilitative government policies that have resolutely privileged consumer-driven economic expansion and guaranteed access to ample natural resources (Collins 2002; Prasad 2012). Under these circumstances, few people questioned the efficacy or indomitability of consumer society; it was simply taken to be a normal condition of everyday life.

Several cross-cutting currents are now weakening the scaffold of American consumer society. First, the demographic profile of the United States is getting older, with notable implications for consumption practices. Second, the implications of income stagnation were buffered for several decades by rising home prices and lax credit policies, but these strategies have lost much of their effectiveness. Third, new consumer sensibilities favouring access over ownership are starting to permeate American society, a process that is most readily discernible among members of the so-called 'millennial generation'. Fourth, the federal government in the United States is locked into a state of political paralysis and the venerable consensus on how best to advance economic growth has dissolved. Finally, new sources of resource scarcity are becoming manifest and price variability is now an ever-present characteristic of the global economy. The following subsections look at each of these factors in greater detail.

### 27.1.1 Demographics

The median age of the American population reached its post-Second World War nadir in 1970 at 27.7 years. It has since risen to 36.8 years today and is expected to level out at 39.0 by 2050. Driving this process has been the ageing of the 'baby boomers', born between 1946 and 1964.The birth of this generation reversed the prior trend, injected an unprecedented youthfulness into the country's demographic profile, launched the first truly mass wave of suburbanization during the 1950s, impelled demand for unprecedented throughputs of material goods and, in due course, animated consumerist lifestyles (Roszak 2009). The great burst of economic growth associated with this activity and its subsequent reverberations – houses (and their furnishings), shopping centres, business parks and roads – is a push that, as economist Robert Gordon (2012) has recently observed, can only play out once.

These developments are consequential because the boomers comprise one of the two largest demographic cohorts in the country (Doherty and Leinberger 2010). (The other outsized cohort is the children of boomers – the so-called 'echo boomers' – discussed separately below.) As boomers reach retirement age, their consumption preferences are shifting dramatically: toward smaller homes, fewer goods and more health care services. Accordingly, we are now seeing a contraction in demand for the customary array of consumer products and a downscaling in the appurtenances of consumerist lifestyles.

This retrenchment is evident in a changing merchandising landscape in the United States. Retail sales (annually now approximately $4 trillion) have been flattening over the last few years and even normally ebullient industry advocates are ambivalent about opportunities for future improvement. In particular, establishments that feature products targeted predominantly to a middle-class clientele are experiencing financial strain and announcement of the downsizing or liquidation of familiar firms is becoming a regular and relatively unremarkable event (Harris 2014; Schwartz 2014). Explanations attributing the downturn to lingering effects of the post-2008 financial crisis are starting to wear thin as awareness that more penetrating – and demographically driven – adjustments are taking hold.[3]

### 27.1.2 Household Income

During the years following the Second World War, robust industrial employment and relatively progressive tax policies combined in the United States to broadly lift wages and to markedly reduce income inequality (Crowie 2012; Stein 2011). Median household income for the population as a whole attained a high of just under $55 000 in 1999 (measured in 2011 dollars) but a decade later was down to approximately $50 000. Disaggregating the data by income quintiles provides, however, a more variegated view with sizeable increases at the uppermost strata and stagnation and decline at the lower levels. Income inequality, as measured by the Gini coefficient (a standard statistical measure of income distribution) fell to a historic low in the late 1960s and then reversed course (US Census Bureau 2012). While easy access to credit cushioned some of the impacts of these developments, it also contributed to rising levels of indebtedness, bankruptcy and foreclosure, especially for the poor (Blinder 2013; Hacker 2008; Michaelson 2009; Noah 2012; Sullivan et al 2001).

These trends call into question an important premise of a well-functioning consumer society first instituted in 1914 by Henry Ford. The pioneering car manufacturer understood that worker-consumers must earn an income beyond subsistence to be able to afford the products of their labour (Brinkley 2003; Snow 2013).[4] For this strategy to be effective, however, a collective action problem must first be overcome. Capitalist-producers have an incentive to keep the salaries of their own employees low and to rely on other firms to raise wages, yet if all act on this logic, consumer demand will be insufficient to absorb available production (Ubert and Bell 2013).

Recent developments thus raise a critical question: Can a consumer society persist in the face of a shrinking middle class? It seems unlikely, because increasing income inequality deepens the divide between affluent cognoscenti of positional goods and cash-strapped shoppers of quotidian commodities (Faux 2012; Freeland 2012). Predominant consumption practices predicated on the compensation policies of Walmart are strikingly different from the routines sparked a century ago by the revolutionary Fordist $5 per day. Reversal of this trend is a political task, but there seems to be little motivation to marshal the necessary will to do so. In the meantime, new business strategies grounded in the concept of an 'hourglass society' are gaining ground as firms realign their products away from the mass market and toward the upper and lower ends of an increasingly bifurcated income distribution (Byron 2011; Lansley 2013).[5]

### 27.1.3 New Consumer Sensibilities

Market research suggests that the current youth generation, comprising people born during the 1980s and 1990s and often referred to as the 'millennial generation' (or 'Generation Y') is expressing decidedly different consumption preferences than its predecessors (Benett and O'Reilly 2010; Fairnington 2010). In particular, this cohort evinces diminished interest in material possessions, subscribes to less regularized employment practices (in part due to prevailing labour-market conditions), and relies heavily on social media to manage relationships and daily activities (see e.g. Burstein 2013; Winograd and Hais 2011).[6] Novel social routines pioneered by Generation Y-ers are beginning to induce broader changes in consumer society, and an especially salient example pertains to the hitherto most celebrated good: the personal automobile. In the United States (and a number of other affluent countries), a growing proportion of the current youth generation is not even bothering to acquire a driver's licence, let alone purchase a vehicle (Cohen 2012; see also Delbosc and Currie 2013). Not surprisingly, car manufacturers are becoming more and more disconcerted by their inability to cultivate among members of this age group the kind of passionate enthusiasm for cars that has long been an undisputed tenet of American youth culture and consumerism more generally.

It is not difficult to intuit the reasons for this new cast of mind.[7] After all, for a typical teenager a car is, first and foremost, a means of maintaining connectivity with a social network, and motorized transportation is less essential in an era of ubiquitous mobile communications. The commodity fetishism that was previously associated with cars has been transferred to hand-held electronic devices. In addition, Generation Y-ers in the United States and beyond favour urban lifestyles, making it possible to dispense with the cost and inconvenience of a personal automobile or at least to reassign a less commanding role to it (Metz 2013; Thompson and Weissmann 2012).

As the conventional position of cars in American society is reshaped, its consumptive companion, the suburban home, is also coming in for re-examination. This housing alternative would never have become dominant in the absence of widespread financial supports ranging from the tax deductibility of mortgage interest to generous public subsidies for land development. The political commitment to these entitlements may now be faltering, with ongoing consideration being devoted to the recommendations issued in 2010 by the National Commission on Fiscal Responsibility and Reform (known more generally as the Simpson–Bowles Commission) (Ehrenhalt 2013; Gallagher 2013; Pozen 2011).[8]

Meanwhile, the primary facilitator of home purchases – a low-interest mortgage with a 30-year term – has become more elusive in the wake of the financial crisis and the collapse (and slow recovery) of the housing market. The national homeownership rate in the United States, after climbing steeply between 1995 and 2005, is now at its lowest level in a decade and this trend is unlikely to change direction without injection of massive – and improbable – federal assistance. More important, though, may be the shift that the real-estate debacle has prompted in terms of the sacrifice that borrowers are prepared to make to retain a home in the face of financial adversity (Lowenstein 2010; Vigeland 2011). Strategic default now carries less social stigma and without the ability to rely on moral suasion to ensure repayment, long-term home financing at fixed rates loses its viability. Additionally a sizeable fraction of the country's distressed suburban housing stock is now being acquired by hedge funds and private equity firms and offered to occupants on a rental basis (Corkery 2014; Dayen 2013). While resale at some point in the future is an option, the vast size of these investment portfolios may make it difficult to do so at scale without depressing the market. In some parts of the country, neighbourhoods that were once comprised exclusively of owner-occupied homes are now inhabited by an increasing number of renters (Dewan 2013). This development suggests the possibility of an enduring structural shift in how housing in the country will be provided in the future. There are also likely to be implications of growing home rental on public policy activities ranging from the provision of municipal services to the design of household energy-efficiency programmes.

### 27.1.4 Political Paralysis

The post-Second World War era in the United States has been marked by resolute political concordance on the desirability – and indeed the non-negotiable necessity – of economic growth (Friedman 2006; Lowry 2012, 2013). There has been in the country, regardless of party affiliation, a resolute commitment to expansionary policies and to reliance, during periods of slack demand, on deficit spending by government. Concurrently, economic growth, by increasing public revenues, has ameliorated numerous governance problems, particularly conflicts surrounding equitable distribution. In short, 'growthism' has served as a kind of grease to the wheels of political decision making.

During the immediate aftermath of the 2008 financial crisis there were indications in the United States (and elsewhere) of a turn toward neo-'New Deal' economic policies (sometimes even cast as a 'Green New Deal'). However the prospect for such action quickly faded in the face of implacable political divisions. Plentiful rhetoric, to be sure, continues to be devoted to the inviolability of economic growth, but there is little common ground between adherents of 'free-market' neoliberalism and proponents of a return to Keynesian fiscal policy. The present stalemate in the United States, in all likelihood, will continue for some time at the federal level (Bartels 2008; Edsall 2012; see also Smaghi 2013). Many state and local governments, caught in their own austerity traps, have implemented policies that perversely sap the potential for meaningful rejuvenation (Blyth 2013; Kuttner 2013; Stuckler and Basu 2013).

Dissolution of the political consensus on economic growth is taking a toll on several fronts relevant to maintaining American consumer society. Education is just one area where the ramifications are particularly evident. Current political dysfunction is closely bound up with faltering commitment to quality public education and this situation raises concerns about the country's ability to compete in a globalized economy in coming decades. Despite a seemingly endless stream of reports from august commissions over the last couple of decades, there has been little systemic effort to stem the erosion, let alone move the country onto a different trajectory.[9] The United States seems to be reaching a critical tipping point where a positive and debilitating feedback loop is being triggered with further adverse consequences for economic growth. A cycle of decline is becoming manifest where falling levels of educational achievement reinforce a parochial understanding of social problems, diminish public capacity to appreciate complexity, stimulate a tendency to embrace superficial interventions, and narrow world views.

### 27.1.5 Resource Scarcity

The global system faces several types of resource scarcity, ranging from shortages of precious metals to insufficient freshwater in densely populated regions (Heinberg 2010; Klare 2012). However it is the remaining supply of oil that has captured most attention because of the pivotal role that relatively inexpensive petroleum has played for the past century fuelling industrial production and existing forms of transportation. Cheap energy has also been indispensable in propelling economic growth during this period and it is extremely challenging to imagine how we might maintain even modest expansion in the face of steadily increasing prices and dwindling supplies (Nel and Cooper 2009; Nel and van Zyl 2010; Rubin 2012).

Most recent attention on the future of energy has centred on the notion of 'peak oil', the point at which global production reaches its zenith and then begins to inexorably decline. We may now be nearing this historic juncture (Murphy and Hall 2011). First, the rate of discovery has slackened considerably in recent decades and we are presently consuming four barrels of oil for every newly identified one (Campbell 2013).[10] Second, despite appreciable increases in both market price and global demand over the past decade, producers have made little effort to expand conventional supplies and this development suggests, in the minds of many observers, that the severity of impending circumstances is becoming more widely acknowledged (Heinberg 2010). Finally, the growth of deepwater drilling and the advent of tar-sands development suggest that the era of readily exploitable supplies has come to an end and in the future it will be necessary to pursue evermore inaccessible – as well as expensive and environmentally problematic – sources.

It is, though, unnecessary for purposes of the current discussion to scrupulously parse the ensuing debates on each of these points. Instead, we need only focus on the extreme price volatility that exists in oil markets today due to burgeoning demand in China, India and elsewhere (Moyo 2012). One would need to search for quite some time to find a reputable analyst who envisions that this situation will lead to decreasing oil prices rather than the all but inevitable obverse. This pattern of upward trending prices will pose pronounced difficulties for the United States because the country has not done an especially effective job of preparing for such an eventuality. Despite improvements in recent decades, the United States has the third-highest energy intensity (amount of energy required to produce $1000 of gross domestic product) among nations that comprise the Organisation for Economic Co-operation and Development (OECD).[11] Furthermore, the country has been slow to reduce the oil dependency of its surface transportation fleet or to encourage large-scale uptake of alternative fuel vehicles.[12] The point then is that over the course of the past two centuries the United States has benefited enormously from low-cost sources of energy and this favourable situation has facilitated the development of an entrenched and fuel-inefficient consumer society. Any significant change in the price of oil or its availability will have profound effects on the country's prospects for economic growth and ability to maintain current volumes of material throughput (Lipson 2011; Steiner 2009).

## 27.2 SOCIAL INNOVATIONS FOR A POST-CONSUMERIST FUTURE

The winding down of consumer society can evoke an unsettling image of indolent livelihoods, diminished and without much dynamism. This is the disquieting vision that many observers of the current scene hold for the United States, with the country sliding down much the same slippery slope that Japan has travelled over its past two 'lost' decades (Bullard 2010; Chen and Frieden 2011). However, such an inauspicious future is not inevitable, and probably not even likely. By adopting a longer-term perspective, we can envisage a stepwise developmental trajectory from agrarianism (pre–1800) to industrialism (1800–1945) to consumerism (1945–present) (Frankel 1987; Giddens 1991; Kumar 1995).

One of the most prevalent – and arguably most influential – expressions of this mode of thinking over the past half century has been Rostow's (1964) 'stages of growth' model that conceives a series of phases moving from traditional society, to take-off, and then to maturation. The process culminates with high mass consumption. From this standpoint, the United States and other similarly situated countries now seem to be reaching the limits of this model and it is a useful opportunity to consider what happens after the putative climax stage of high mass consumption.

Aside from the work of future-oriented social scientists such as Daniel Bell (1973) and Alvin Toffler (1980), the challenge of envisioning post-consumerist scenarios has to date attracted little attention. As consumer society begins to give way, the auguries of the next, but heretofore largely unanticipated, phase of Rostow's model are starting to come into view. We are seeing today a notable upsurge in social innovation organized around local living economies, 'prosuming', collaborative consumption, peer-to-peer provisioning, self- and communal cultivation and fabrication, community-based energy and food programmes, social lending and 'unconsumption', that in aggregate portend the arrival of post-consumerist arrangements (e.g. Benett and O'Reilly 2010; Botsman and Rogers 2010; Gansky 2012; Gerzema and D'Antonio 2011) (see the Appendix).[13] These alternative systems are frequently premised on new business models organized around distributed networks, novel allocation of surplus capacity, and shared use and rental or leasing schemes that unbundle the use of goods from actual title to them (Chase 2011; Geron 2013; Porter and Kramer 2011; Sheth et al 2011). This array of approaches aims to facilitate 'value co-creation' and, under certain conditions, to nurture what some marketing analysts refer to as 'mindful consumption'.

While little more than experiments at this stage, these initiatives are challenging familiar systems for delivering household goods and services and demonstrating the potential for scaling up (Schor 2010; Walljasper 2010). For instance the trading of second-hand goods has become valorized, swap meets are popular social activities, and craft reskilling is now a trendy pastime (Crawford 2010; Shirky 2011; see also Sennett 2009). It might be tempting to surmise that these developments are confined to 'hipster' subcultures but such a conclusion would fail to capture the fact that mainstream commerce is becoming actively engaged. This largely uncoordinated activity to create alternatives to current modes of mass consumption is the beginning of what will be a prolonged process. In coming years, numerous – and conceivably disparate – social innovations will need to fit together, and how they will ultimately converge in ways that enable effective competition with dominant practices remains to be seen. However, our inability to foresee carefully worked-out solutions should not detract us from considering how the underlying conditions of contemporary consumer society are changing. It would, after all, have been preposterous in the middle of the eighteenth century to call for a blueprint of how the industrial age would ultimately unfold. On the basis of historical experience, a societal transformation beyond consumerism will proceed in fits and starts, with variance across regions. Some people will benefit and others will come up short, perhaps severely so. Nonetheless, earlier transitions, such as from medieval European agrarianism to industrialism and then to globalized consumerism, hold instructive lessons (Braudel 1992; Ferguson 2011; Landes 1969). In brief, these prior shifts required extensive micro- and macro-scale adjustment over time, sparking significant disruptions in political power, economic affairs and rhythms of everyday life.

A counter-argument to the claim presented here, of course, might be that consumer society has encountered and overcome various obstacles in the past and, in due course, will successfully do so again. Accordingly, declarations of demise are unjustified, and it is premature, if not dangerous, to talk about an impending transition. Some champions of mass consumption even suggest that this system of social organization is so essential to human flourishing that we would be foolish to let it slip away (Livingston 2011; Stephens 2013). The faltering of consumer-propelled economic growth and the fraying of contemporary consumerist lifestyles, though, make such assertions seem brash and quixotic.

## 27.3 CONCLUSION

If a historic change in the underpinnings of consumer society is in the air, it is reasonable to ask where one might go to most readily glimpse it in fledgling form. After all, someone in the late eighteenth century interested in the then nascent industrial age would have been wise to head to Lancashire and the city of Manchester. Los Angeles and its environs would have been a good place to observe the flowering of post-Second World War lifestyles premised on mass consumption. Today, the Brooklyn neighbourhood of Williamsburg, because of its social diversity, cultural creativity, adaptable infrastructure and proximity to Manhattan (see below) may hold vanguard status in the transition to post-consumerism (see e.g. Lipinski 2010; Robbins 2011; Schiller 2011; see also Ehrenhalt 2013; Florida 2009). Other possible contenders in the United States could be Berkeley (California) and Cambridge (Massachusetts).

On one hand, it is pertinent to note that these communities have become what sociologists Jason Kaufman and Matthew Kaliner (2011) call destinations for 'idio-cultural migration'. In short, the prevalence of alternative lifestyle practices in these places is now sufficient to induce the relocation of like-minded people, and this movement continues to expand in numbers and effects. On the other hand, such circumstances suggest the paradox that social innovation flourishes in propinquity to city-regions that are archetypes of the incumbent economic system. It is probably not an accident that the three aforementioned crucibles of lifestyle reinvention in the United States are in proximate distance of, respectively, Manhattan, San Francisco and Silicon Valley, and Boston. It is not unusual for the ostensible vanguard of post-consumerism to leverage the financial and social capital of the conventional economy and to redirect small measures of it to jump-starting alternative modes of consumption (and production). An evocative example might be a household where one member is a partner in a Wall Street investment bank while her companion devotes himself to urban gardening, clothing swaps and micro-scale furniture production in the couple's Brooklyn neighbourhood. Such circumstances suggest a close entwining – possibly even an inextricable linkage and unavoidable dependency – between the old and the new.[14]

This reflection provides instructive insight into how a transition to post-consumerism might plausibly reveal itself. Novel practices cannot spring into existence in whole form. Incipient routines will inevitably emerge out of prevailing ways of doing in a halting and partial manner, and will not quickly or thoroughly displace the customary institutions that support and facilitate still prevalent lifestyles. It merits recognizing that industrialism only gradually supplanted agrarianism, developing a co-dependent relationship with it (industrial workers had to eat and farmers increasingly needed tractors). Moreover, there is currently no indication that global society, and certainly not many of the world's most affluent countries, could get along without mass consumption any more than it might manage without agriculture or manufacturing. Rather than leaving consumerism completely behind, ongoing changes with respect to demography, politics, economics and so forth are likely to progressively destabilize the dominant system as it continues to lose its ability to deliver satisfactory livelihoods. To be sure, many outstanding questions remain about how a putative move to post-consumerism might unfold and the shape that it could take in the end. Regardless of the eventual outcome, these changes demonstrate that consumer society will not be the final chapter of human experience.

## NOTES

1. This chapter is a revised version of a keynote address delivered at the conference on Modernization and Global Change sponsored by the China Center for Modernization Research, Chinese Academy of Sciences, Beijing, 8–9 August 2013.
2. The implied contention here is that innovation is not, as is conventionally thought to be the case, the exclusive domain of business firms and engineers, but occurs as well with respect to daily practices as individuals invent and seek out new alternatives with which to organize and conduct their lives. For work on social innovation and lifestyles see, for example, Huber (1979), Green and Vergragt (2002), Walker (2011), Lundström and Zhou (2011), Scott et al. (2011), Edwards-Schachter et al. (2012), van den Hove (2012) and Chalmers (2013).
3. With 14.2 billion square feet of retail space (46.6 square feet per person), retail capacity in the United States exceeds by large margins the amount of space devoted to this purpose in all comparable countries. Even after considerable contraction over the past few years, the retail sector remains heavily overbuilt. The shift to online shopping is also contributing to retrenchment of customary retail establishments and over time this process will free up land to construct new post-consumerist landscapes (Phelps et al. 2010).
4. It must be noted that Ford was not necessarily motivated – at least initially – by a desire to sell automobiles to his factory workers, but rather by a need to improve productivity through reduction in the rate of employee turnover. Nonetheless, the indirect effect of his wage policy was to put more money in the pockets of his (and other) labourers and to thus contribute to the promotion of automobile-based mass consumption.
5. Recent developments in commercial air travel offer an especially evocative example. First-class and business-class accommodation has become increasingly sumptuous, while space for passengers seated in the economy-class cabin has become ever more compressed and uncomfortable. See Mouawad (2013) and Mouawad and White (2013).
6. Determination of the extent to which the social practices of Generation Y-ers are cause or consequence of the more unstable and uncertain employment conditions in which they have come of age is difficult to discern. There is presumably a pattern of circular dependency at work.
7. A common expression to describe this phenomenon in Japan is '*kuruma banare*', which translates roughly as 'walking away from the car'.
8. A number of countries have eliminated or substantially reduced allowable limits for the tax deductibility of mortgage interest in recent years. For example, Finland instituted a major overall of this entitlement in 1993 and the UK did away with it in 2000. A lively debate on the issue has been taking place in the Netherlands for the past several years. See Bartlett (2013).
9. The issue becomes particularly salient when the examination results of the Programme for International Student Assessment (PISA) are released by the Organisation for Economic Co-operation and Development (OECD).
10. Global oil discovery peaked in 1965 when approximately two new barrels were being found for each barrel consumed.
11. Among OECD countries, the United States ranks ahead of only Luxembourg and Canada on this measure. It also bears noting that the improvement in energy intensity in OECD countries is to a large extent attributable to the relocation of industrial production to developing countries, and the importation of goods that were previously domestically produced.
12. The advent of hydraulic fracturing (or 'fracking') to extract natural gas and the exploitation of domestic oil sources has played a significant role in reducing oil imports to the United States in recent years, but these developments have had little influence on reducing end-user demand for energy.
13. Each of these categories of post-consumerist practices has given rise to its own body of scholarly literature which is too extensive to detail here. For useful examples, see Exner and Lauk (2012), Seyfang and

Haxeltine (2012), Albinsson and Yasanthi Perera (2012) and Ritzer et al. (2012). The emergent field of 'new economics' strives to capture several of these developments. See, for example, Boyle and Simms (2009), Schor (2010), Marglin (2012) and Speth (2013) as well as various reports issued by the New Economics Foundation.

14. Current expressions of urban social innovation raise interesting questions about the trade-offs between geographic proximity and Internet-based interactivity. See, for example, websites such as Shareable, Amplifying Creative Communities and Yoxi.

## REFERENCES


Acemoglu, D. and J. Robinson (2012), *Why Nations Fail: The Origins of Power, Prosperity, and Poverty*, New York: Crown.

Albinsson, P. and B. Yasanthi Perera (2012), 'Alternative marketplaces in the 21st century: Building community through sharing events', *Journal of Consumer Behavior*, 11 (4), 303–315.

Bartels, L. (2008), *Unequal Democracy: The Political Economy of the New Gilded Age*, New York: Princeton University Press.

Bartlett, B. (2013), 'The sacrosanct mortgage interest deduction', *New York Times*, 6 August.

Bell, D. (1973), *The Coming of Post-Industrial Society: A Venture in Social Forecasting*, New York: Basic Books.

Benett, A. and A. O'Reilly (2010), *Consumed: Rethinking Business in the Era of Mindful Spending*, New York: Palgrave Macmillan.

Blinder, A. (2013), *After the Music Stopped: The Financial Crisis, the Response, and the Work Ahead*, New York: Penguin.

Blyth, M. (2013), *Austerity: The History of a Dangerous Idea*, New York: Oxford University Press.

Botsman, R. and R. Rogers (2010), *What's Mine Is Yours: The Rise of Collaborative Consumption*, New York: Harper Business.

Boyle, D. and A. Simms, (2009), *The New Economics: A Bigger Picture*, London: Earthscan.

Braudel, F. (1992), *Civilization and Capitalism, 15th–18th Century*, Berkeley, CA: University of California Press.

Brinkley, D. (2003), *Wheels for the World: Henry Ford, His Company, and a Century of Progress, 1903–2003*, New York: Viking.

Bullard, J. (2010), 'Seven faces of "the peril"', *Federal Reserve Bank of St Louis Review*, 92 (5), 339–352.

Burstein, D. (2013), *Fast Future: How the Millennial Generation is Shaping Our World*, Boston, MA: Beacon Press.

Byron, E. (2011), 'As middle class shrinks, P&G aims high and low', *Wall Street Journal*, 12 September.

Campbell, C. (2013), *Campbell's Atlas of Oil and Gas Depletion*, 2nd edn, Dordrecht: Springer.

Chalmers, D. (2013), 'Social innovation: an exploration of the barriers faced by innovating organizations in the social economy', *Local Economy*, 28 (1), 17–34.

Chase, R. (2011), 'Remixing excess capacity', *Journal of Urban Regeneration and Renewal*, 4 (4), 354–357.

Chen, M. and J. Frieden (2011), *Lost Decades: The Making of America's Debt Crisis and the Long Recovery*, New York: W. W. Norton.

Cohen, L. (2003), *A Consumers' Republic: The Politics of Mass Consumption in Postwar America*, New York: Vintage.

Cohen, M. (2011), 'Turning Japanese', *Sustainability: Science, Practice, and Policy*, 7 (2), 1–3.

Cohen, M. (2012), 'The future of automobile society: a socio-technical transitions perspective', *Technology Analysis and Strategic Management*, 24 (4), 377–390.

Cohen, M. (2013), 'Collective dissonance and the transition to post-consumerism', *Futures*, 52, 42–51.

Collins, R. (2002), *More: The Politics of Economic Growth in Postwar America*, New York: Oxford University Press.

Corkery, M. (2014), 'Wall Street's new housing bonanza', *Wall Street Journal*, 29 February.

Coyle, D. (2011), *The Economics of Enough: How to Run the Economy as if the Future Matters*, Princeton, NJ: Princeton University Press.

Crawford, M. (2010), *Shop Class as Soulcraft: An Inquiry into the Value of Work*, New York: Penguin.

Crowie. J. (2012), *Stayin' Alive: The 1970s and the Last Days of the Working Class*, New York: New Press.

Dayen, D. (2013), 'Your new landlord works on Wall Street', *New Republic*, 12 February, available at http://www.newrepublic.com/article/112395/wall-street-hedge-funds-buy-rental-properties.

de Grazia, V. (2006), *Irresistible Empire: America's Advance through Twentieth Century Europe*, Cambridge, MA: Harvard University Press.

Delbosc, A. and G. Currie (2013), 'Causes of youth licensing decline: a synthesis of evidence', *Transport Reviews*, 33 (3), 271–290.
Dewan, D. (2013), 'As renters move in, some homeowners fret', *New York Times*, 28 August.
Diamond, J. (2004), *Collapse: How Societies Choose to Fail or Succeed*, New York: Viking.
Doherty, P. and C. Leinberger (2010), 'The next real estate boom', *Washington Monthly*, November–December.
Edsall, T. (2012), *The Age of Austerity: How Scarcity Will Remake American Politics*, New York: Doubleday.
Edwards-Schachter, M., C. Mati and E. Alcántara (2012), 'Fostering quality of life through social innovation: a living lab methodology study case', *Review of Policy Research*, 29 (6), 672–692.
Ehrenhalt, A. (2013), *The Great Inversion and the Future of the American City*, New York: Vintage.
Etzioni, A. (2004), 'The post-affluent society', *Review of Social Economy*, 62 (3), 407–420.
Etzioni, A. (2009), 'Spent: American after consumerism', *New Republic*, 17 June, available at http://www.tnr.com/article/spent#.
Etzioni, A. (2011), 'The new normal', *Sociological Forum*, 26 (4), 779–798.
Exner, A. and C. Lauk (2012), 'Social innovations for economic degrowth', *Solutions*, 3 (4), available at http://www.thesolutionsjournal.com/node/1143.
Fairnington, A. (2010), *The Age of Selfish Altruism: Why New Values are Killing Consumerism*, Hoboken, NJ: Wiley.
Faux, J. (2012), *The Servant Economy: Where America's Elite is Sending the Middle Class*, Hoboken, NJ: Wiley.
Ferguson, N. (2011), *Civilization: The West and the Rest*, New York: Penguin.
Ferguson, N. (2012), *The Great Degeneration: How Institutions Decay and Economies Die*, London: Allen Lane.
Field, A. (2012), *A Great Leap Forward: 1930s Depression and US Economic Growth*, New Haven, CT: Yale University Press.
Florida, R. (2009), *Who's Your City? How the Creative Economy is Making Where to Live the Most Important Decision of Your Life*, New York: Basic Books.
Frank, R. (2009), 'Post-consumer prosperity: finding new opportunities amid the economic wreckage', *American Prospect*, 29 (3), 12–15.
Frankel, B. (1987), *The Post-Industrial Utopians*, Malden, MA: Polity Press.
Freeland, C. (2012), *Plutocrats: The Rise of the New Global Super Rich and the Fall of Everyone Else*, New York: Penguin.
Friedman, B. (2006), *The Moral Consequences of Economic Growth*, New York: Vintage.
Gallagher, L. (2013), *The End of the Suburbs: Where the American Dream is Moving*, New York: Portfolio.
Gansky, L. (2012), *The Mesh: What's the Future of Business is Sharing*, New York: Portfolio.
Garon, S. (2013), *Beyond Our Means: Why America Spends While the World Saves*, Princeton, NJ: Princeton University Press.
Geron, T. (2013), 'Airbnb and the unstoppable rise of the share economy', *Forbes*, 23 January, available at http://www.forbes.com/sites/tomiogeron/2013/01/23/airbnb-and-the-unstoppable-rise-of-the-share-economy.
Gerzema, J. and M. D'Antonio (2011), *Spend Shift: How the Post-Crisis Values Revolution is Changing the Way We Buy, Sell, and Live*, San Francisco, CA: Jossey-Bass.
Giddens, A. (1991), *The Consequences of Modernity*, Palo Alto, CA: Stanford University Press.
Gilding, P. (2011), *The Great Disruption: Why the Climate Crisis Will Bring on the End of Shopping and the Birth of a New World*, New York: Bloomsbury.
Gordon, R. (2012), 'Is US economic growth over? Faltering innovation confronts the six headwinds', NBER Working Paper No. 18315, Boston, MA: National Bureau of Economic Research.
Green, K. and P. Vergragt (2002), 'Towards sustainable households: a methodology for developing sustainable technological and social innovations', *Futures*, 34 (5), 381–400.
Hacker, J. (2008), *The Great Risk Shift: The New Economic Insecurity and the Decline of the American Dream*, New York: Oxford University Press.
Hama, N. (2012), 'Japanization needn't be an economic curse word', *Japan Times*, 28 November.
Harris, E. (2014), 'Retailers ask: Where did teenagers go?', *New York Times*, 1 February.
Heinberg, R. (2010), *Peak Everything: Waking Up to the Century of Declines*, Gabriola Island: New Society Publishers.
Heinberg, R. (2011), *The End of Growth: Adapting to Our New Economic Reality*, Gabriola Island: New Society Publishers.
Horioka, C. (2006), 'The case of Japan's "lost decade": the role of household consumption', *Japan and the World Economy*, 18 (4), 378–400.
Huber, J. (1979), 'Limiting the system and reshaping lifestyles: solving unemployment by social and technical innovations', *Technological Forecasting and Social Change*, 15 (1), 37–54.
Ivanova, M. (2011), 'Consumerism and the crisis: wither "the American dream"?', *Critical Sociology*, 37 (3), 329–350.
Jackson, T. (2009), *Prosperity Without Growth: Economics for a Finite Planet*, London: Earthscan.
Kato, N. (2010), 'Japan and the ancient art of shrugging', *New York Times*, 21 August.

Kato, N. (2013), 'Japan in a post-growth age', *New York Times*, 2 December.

Kaufman, K. and M. Kaliner (2011), 'The re-accomplishment of place in twentieth century Vermont and New Hampshire: history repeats itself, until it doesn't', *Theory and Society*, 40 (2), 119–154.

Klare, M. (2012), *The Race for What's Left: The Global Scramble for the World's Last Resources*, New York: Metropolitan Books.

Klitgaard, K. and L. Krall (2012), 'Ecological economics, degrowth, and institutional change', *Ecological Economics*, 84, 247–253.

Kumar, K. (1995), *From Post-Industrial to Post Modern Society*, New York: Blackwell.

Kuttner, R. (2013), *Debtors Prison: The Politics of Austerity Versus Possibility*, New York: Knopf.

Landes, D. (1969), *The Unbound Prometheus: Technological Change and Industrial Development in Western Europe*, New York: Cambridge University Press.

Lansley, S. (2013), 'The hourglass society', *Los Angeles Review of Books*, 28 May.

Latouche, S. (2010), *Farewell to Growth*, Malden, MA: Polity Press.

Lipinski, J. (2010), 'A commune grows in Brooklyn', *New York Times*, 17 September.

Lipson, D. (2011), 'Is the great recession only the beginning? Economic contraction in an age of fossil fuel depletion and ecological limits to growth', *New Political Science*, 33 (4), 555–575.

Livingston, J. (2011), *Against Thrift: Why Consumer Culture is Good for the Economy, the Environment, and Your Soul*, New York: Basic Books.

Lloyd, B. (2009), 'The growth delusion', *Sustainability*, 1 (3), 516–536.

Lowenstein, R. (2010), 'Walk away from your mortgage!' *New York Times*, 10 January.

Lowry, A. (2012), 'Income inequality may take toll on growth', *New York Times*, 16 October.

Lowry, A. (2013), 'The low politics of low growth', *New York Times*, 12 January.

Lundström, A. and C. Zhou (2011), 'Promoting innovation based on social sciences and technologies: the prospect of a social innovation park', *Innovation: The European Journal of Social Science Research*, 24 (1–2), 133–149.

Marglin, S. (2012), *Premises for a New Economy*, Boston, MA: Tellus Institute, available at http://www.gtinitiative.org/documents/issueperspectives/gti-perspectives-premises_for_a_new_economy.pdf.

Metz, D. (2013), 'Peak car and beyond: the fourth era of travel', *Transport Reviews*, 33 (3), 255–270.

Michaelson, A. (2009), *The Foreclosure of America: The Inside Story of the Rise and Fall of Countrywide Home Loans, the Mortgage Crisis, and the Default of the American Dream*, New York: Berkeley Books.

Mouawad, J. (2013), 'The race to build a better business class', *New York Times*, 3 August.

Mouawad, J. and M. White (2013), 'On jammed jets, sardines turn on one another', *New York Times*, 22 December.

Moyo, D. (2012), *Winner Take All: China's Race for Resources and What It Means for the World*, New York: Basic Books.

Murphy, D. and C. Hall (2011), 'Energy return on investment, peak oil, and the end of economic growth', *Annals of the New York Academy of Sciences*, 1219 (1), 52–72.

Nel, W. and C. Cooper (2009), 'Implications of fossil fuel constraints on economic growth and global warming', *Energy Policy*, 37 (1), 166–180.

Nel, W. and G. van Zyl (2010), 'Defining limits: energy constrained economic growth', *Applied Energy*, 87 (1), 168–177.

Noah, T. (2012), *The Great Divergence: America's Growing Inequality Crisis and What We Can Do About It*, New York: Bloomsbury.

Packer, G. (2013), *The Unwinding: An Inner History of the New America*, New York: Farrar, Straus & Giroux.

Phelps, N., A. Wood and D. Valler (2010), 'A postsuburban world? An outline of a research agenda', *Environment and Planning A*, 42, 366–383.

Porter, M. and M. Kramer (2011), 'Creating shared value', *Harvard Business Review*, 89 (1–2), 62–87.

Pozen, R. (2011), 'Heretic reality: mortgage interest deduction needs to be slashed', *Forbes*, 25 March.

Prasad, M. (2012), *The Land of Too Much; American Abundance and the Paradox of Poverty*, Cambridge, MA: Harvard University Press.

Ritzer, G., P. Dean and N. Jurgenson (2012), 'The coming age of the prosumer', *American Behavioral Scientist*, 56 (4), 379–398.

Robbins, L. (2011), 'Back to the simple life, with needle and thread', *New York Times*, 5 August.

Rostow, W. (1964), *The Stages of Economic Growth: A Non-Communist Manifesto*, New York: Cambridge University Press.

Roszak, T. (2009), *The Making of an Elder Culture: Reflections on the Future of America's Most Audacious Generation*, Gabriola Island: New Society.

Rubin, J. (2012), *The Big Flatline: Oil and the No-Growth Economy*, New York: Palgrave Macmillan.

Schiller, B. (2011), 'Brooklyn as a lab to amplify urban ideas', FastCo.EXIST, 10 November, available at http://www.fastcoexist.com/1678795/brooklyn-as-a-lab-to-amplify-urban-ideas.

Schor, J. (2010), *Plenitude: The New Economics of True Wealth*, New York: Penguin.

Schwartz, N. (2014), 'The middle class is steadily eroding. Just ask the business world', *New York Times*, 2 February.
Scott, K., C. Bakker and J. Quist (2011), 'Designing change by living change', *Design Studies*, 33 (3), 279–297.
Seiji, T. (1999), *Japan's Consumer Society: A Critical Introduction*, New York: ARC Publishing.
Sennett, R. (2009), *The Craftsman*, New Haven, CT: Yale University Press.
Seyfang, G. and A. Haxeltine (2012), 'Growing grassroots innovations: exploring the role of community-based initiatives in governing sustainable energy transitions', *Environment and Planning*, 30 (3), 381–400.
Sheth, J., N. Sethia and S. Srinivas (2011), 'Mindful consumption: a customer-centric approach to sustainability', *Journal of the Academy of Marketing Science*, 39 (1), 21–39.
Shirky, C. (2011), *Cognitive Surplus: How Technology Makes Consumers into Collaborators*, New York: Penguin.
Smaghi, L. (2013), *Austerity: European Democracies against the Wall*, Brussels: Centre for European Policy Studies.
Snow, R. (2013), *I Invented the Modern Age: The Rise of Henry Ford*, New York: Scribner's.
Speth, J. (2009), *The Bridge at the Edge of the World: Capitalism, the Environment, and Crossing from Crisis to Sustainability*, New Haven, CT: Yale University Press.
Speth, J. (2013), *America the Possible: Manifesto for a New Economy*, New Haven, CT: Yale University Press.
Stein, J. (2011), *Pivotal Decade: How the United States Traded Factories for Finance in the Seventies*, New Haven, CT: Yale University Press.
Steiner, S. (2009), *$20 Per Gallon: How the Inevitable Rise in the Price of Gasoline Will Change Our Lives for the Better*, New York: Grand Central.
Stephens, D. (2013), *The Retail Revival: Reimagining Business for the New Age of Consumerism*, Hoboken, NJ: Wiley.
Stiglitz, J. (2013), 'Inequality is holding back the recovery', *New York Times*, 9 January.
Stuckler, D. and S. Basu (2013), *The Body Economic: Why Austerity Kills*, New York: Basic Books.
Sullivan, T., E. Warren and J. Westbrook (2001), *The Fragile Middle Class: Americans in Debt*, New Haven, CT: Yale University Press.
Tainter, J. (1990), *The Collapse of Complex Societies*, New York: Cambridge University Press.
Thompson, D. and J. Weissmann (2012), 'The cheapest generation: why Millennials aren't buying cars or houses, and what that means for the economy', *Atlantic*, September.
Toffler, A. (1980), *The Third Wave*, New York: Bantam Books.
Ubert, E. and M. Bell (2013), 'Welcome to the consumption line: sustainability, social organization, and the wage-price gap', in M. Cohen, H. Brown and P. Vergragt (eds), *Innovations in Sustainable Consumption: New Economics, Socio-technical Transitions, and Social Practices*, Cheltenham, UK and Northampton, MA, USA: Edward Elgar, pp. 87–112.
US Census Bureau (2012), *Income, Poverty, and Health Insurance Coverage in the US: 2011*, Washington, DC: US Census Bureau.
van den Hove, S., J. McGlade, P. Mottet, and M. Depledge (2012), 'The innovation union: a perfect means to confused ends', *Environmental Science and Policy*, 16, 73–80.
Victor, P. (2009), *Managing Without Growth: Slower By Design, Not Disaster*, Cheltenham, UK and Northampton, MA, USA: Edward Elgar.
Vigeland, T. (2011), 'They walked away, and they're glad they did', *New York Times*, 8 November
Walker, G. (2011), 'The role for community in carbon governance', *Wiley Interdisciplinary Reviews: Climate Change*, 2 (5), 777–782.
Walljasper, J. (2010), *All That We Share: How to Save the Economy, the Environment, the Internet, Democracy, Our Communities and Everything Else that Belongs to Us*, New York: New Press.
Winograd, M. and M. Hais (2011), *Millennial Momentum: How a New Generation is Remaking America*, New Brunswick, NJ: Rutgers University Press.
Wuthnow, R. (2006), *American Mythos: Why Our Best Efforts to Be a Better Nation Fall Short*, Princeton, NJ: Princeton University Press.
Yarrow, A. (2010), *Measuring America; How Economic Growth Came to Define American Greatness in the Late Twentieth Century*, Amherst, MA: University of Massachusetts Press.

# APPENDIX: POST-CONSUMERIST SOCIAL INNOVATIONS

## Collaborative Consumption, or the Sharing Economy

Collaborative consumption involves using durable goods more efficiently, often through collective use and rental arrangements. These modes of exchange are facilitated by the Internet, which reduces search costs and readily connects buyers and sellers, owners and users, for short-term exchanges of cars, household space, tools and much more.

## Community Energy and Food Production

Rather than procure energy and food from distant and anonymous producers, the notion of community energy and food production stresses the importance of relocalization and frequently features the establishment of collective ownership as a means of ensuring local control of supplies.

## Local Living Economy

Developed in large part in the USA by the Business Alliance for Local Living Economies (BALLE), this approach facilitates the development of community-based systems of production and consumption, the strengthening of localized economic relationships, and the promotion of fair exchange.

## Mindful Consumption

Proponents of mindful consumption strive to make a business case for reducing the purchase and use of consumer products and enabling consumers to achieve lifestyle satisfaction in ways that do not involve material goods.

## Peer-to-Peer (P2P) Provisioning

P2P provisioning is an extension of Internet-based collaborative networks that allow participants to engage directly in transactional activities without the need for a retail intermediary. Vehicle sharing and social lending are two particularly prominent examples of this mode of activity.

## Prosumption

Prosumption refers to co-creation of economic value through the combined efforts of producers and consumers. The term was coined in 1980 by futurist Alvin Toffler and captures activities ranging from operation of an automatic teller machine to community-supported agriculture.

**Self and Communal Cultivation and Fabrication**

This mode denotes production and consumption activities that are carried out on an individual or collective basis. Notable examples include home-based and communal vegetable gardening as well as the personal manufacture of furniture and other artefacts. The advent of 3D (three-dimensional) printing technology is sometimes envisaged as an important enabler of this type of provisioning.

**Unconsumption**

Unconsumption refers to post-acquisition activities pertaining to the recycling, creative reuse and repurposing of goods, as well as to efforts to maximize satisfaction from the use of purchased products.

# Index

# 42 WAYS

## MAKING HUMAN INTELLIGENCE WORK IN THE AGE OF AI

Azim Shaik Gregory P. Steffine

Sanderson
Pittsburgh

**42 WAYS: Making Human Intelligence Work in the Age of AI**


**First Edition**
ISBN: 978-1-7320108-4-0 (Paperback)
ISBN: 978-1-7320108-5-7 (Hardcover)
ISBN: 978-1-7320108-6-4 (eBook)

**BISAC**
BUSINESS & ECONOMICS/Decision-Making & Problem-Solving
COMPUTERS / Artificial Intelligence / General
BUSINESS & ECONOMICS / Business Ethics

Cover design by *the*BookDesigners
Interior design by Leo & Tedy

Sanderson

**Sanderson Press, LLC**
Pittsburgh, PA
USA

# Dedication

To our families, friends, and colleagues.

Without your encouragement, this book would not exist.

# Dedication

To our families, friends, and colleagues.

Without your encouragement, this book would not exist.

## Companion Website

42waysthebook.com

This book features a dedicated companion website of supplemental material. It includes exercises, lecture slides, errata, and other valuable resources tailored for business professionals, educators, and students.

# The Authors

## Azim Shaik, MS, MBA

Azim Shaik is a Lead Enterprise Architect with over a decade of experience spear-heading AI-driven innovation and cloud transformation in the financial services sector. Azim serves as a Board Member at Kent State University and remains deeply engaged with academia as an alumnus of the institution. In addition to his corporate leadership, he is a veteran hackathon participant with more than 100 events to his name. He frequently shares his knowledge as a podcaster and YouTuber, offering insights into the rapidly evolving worlds of technology, AI, and entrepreneurship. Azim holds an MS in Computer Science from Kent State University and an MBA from the University of Illinois Urbana-Champaign (UIUC).

## Gregory P. Steffine

Gregory Steffine is a consultant, business intelligence strategist and analytics leader with more than 30 years of experience helping organizations translate data into competitive advantage. Known for equipping leaders to think sharper and act faster, his work has consistently bridged the gap between insight and execution. He is an award-winning author of two books on data-driven performance and most recently served as Head of Analytics Enablement for one of the nation's largest bank-based financial services firms. Today, he continues to write about the evolving field of analytics and other topics.

# The Contributor

## Foreword by Kathleen L.D. Maley

Kathleen Maley is a seasoned analytics leader with deep expertise in predictive modeling, data-informed product innovation, and advanced decisioning strategies. As Senior Vice President of Analytics & Commercialization at Experian, she leads the development and deployment of AI-powered models and analytical frameworks that help businesses transform data into actionable insights for smarter, faster decisions across the lending lifecycle. Kathleen is a Research Fellow at the International Institute for Analytics and an adjunct faculty member at the University of California San Diego.

# Table of Contents

The future of analytics and AI will be defined by how well we integrate algorithms into the fabric of how we think, decide, and act.

*Kathleen L.D. Maley*

# Foreword

## "The answer is 42."

So says Deep Thought, the supercomputer in Douglas Adams' classic *The Hitchhiker's Guide to the Galaxy,* offering what is supposed to be "the answer to the ultimate question of life, the universe, and everything." But by the time the answer arrives, the humans who asked the question are long gone, so no one knows exactly what the question was. They have little more context than you did when you read my first sentence.

The computer's answer is a joke, of course—but also a real reminder: answers without context, interpretation, or human insight are meaningless. That's something to keep in mind as humanity barrels toward a future where artificial intelligence is an ever-present frenemy—helping us find answers and move faster, but also sometimes feeding us false or even harmful information.

For those who use AI search engines and casually follow discussions about AI on social media and elsewhere, one question tends to linger: "How do we use AI to take humankind to a better place without unleashing an army of killer robots that destroy us?"

*42 Ways* doesn't answer that question directly. And who could really trust a confident, dogmatic answer this early in the journey anyway?

Instead, it offers something more credible and more useful: a set of perspectives, patterns, and practices to help us navigate a world where data is abundant, technology is accelerating, and human decisions matter more than ever. What authors Azim Shaik and Gregory Steffine understand—and what this book articulates with uncommon clarity—is that success in the age of AI is not about replacing human intelligence but deliberately designing for it.

For much of my career, I've worked at the intersection of analytics, decision-making, and product innovation.

I've watched organizations wrestle with both the promise and the peril of increasingly sophisticated technology. The pattern is remarkably consistent: leaders invest heavily in platforms, tools, and models, yet struggle to turn those investments into sustained value. AI initiatives stall.

Trust erodes. Talented people disengage. And ethics are often treated as an afterthought—until a crisis makes them unavoidable.

This failure is rarely technical. It is almost always human—and it requires thoughtful human interaction to fix.

That's why Azim and Greg are such effective and indispensable guides on the road to AI success.

I met Greg in 2017.

At the time, I was leading enterprise analytics within a shared services organization. Greg was leading an enterprise analytics center of excellence within the technology group. We had a similar mandate: to make data and analytics more accessible and help business leaders make better, data-informed decisions. We were both working to solve the same problem—but in very different ways.

One day he invited me to a workshop he was running. I showed up skeptical—and maybe a bit grumpy. I fully expected to be told that what I was doing was wrong, and that there was a better, more "correct" way to do it. Instead, when I told him I disagreed with his approach, he paused and said, "Interesting. Tell me more about that."

It was a small moment, but it changed everything. In that instant, the conversation shifted from positioning to understanding. I knew he was actually listening. More importantly, I knew he was willing to challenge his own assumptions—not just mine. We didn't suddenly agree on everything. We still don't. But we found a way to debate with respect, to push each other's thinking, and, over time, to build a shared language.

This is a book that will change how you think about your work—not by giving you a single answer, but by helping you see the system more clearly. You'll start to notice where decisions break down, where assumptions go unchallenged, and where opportunities exist so you can connect the dots more effectively.

As you move into the chapters that follow, I encourage you to approach them the same way Greg approached our early conversation—with curiosity, openness, and a willingness to reconsider your assumptions.

Success in the age of AI will not be defined by who has the most advanced models. It will belong to organizations that build a strong data sense: the ability to think clearly, decide wisely, and act with intention in an environment overwhelmed by noise, constant change, and opportunity.

But recognize that what worked even two years ago is unlikely to be sufficient today. This book reflects that reality and underscores the importance of continuous learning, experimentation, and adaptation.

In *The Hitchhiker's Guide,* the answer "42" was unsatisfying because no one understood the question. In analytics and AI, we face a similar risk. We can generate answers faster than ever before, but if we are not asking the right questions, those answers won't matter.

*42 Ways* helps you ask better questions. It challenges you to think differently about how your organization operates. It provides a roadmap—not a rigid prescription—for building capabilities that are resilient, scalable, and human-centered. And it does so in a way that is accessible to both technical and non-technical audiences.

Whether you are an executive shaping strategy, a leader trying to drive change, or a practitioner building models, you will find something in these pages that resonates.

In the end, the future of analytics and AI will not be defined by algorithms alone. It will be defined by how well we integrate those algorithms into the fabric of how we think, decide, and act.

How best to do that is, in many ways, the real answer we are all searching for.

This book is an excellent place to begin.

Humans still decide which
questions are worth asking.
The rest is execution.

*Azim Shaik*

# Introduction

We're at a moment when human intelligence and artificial intelligence are coming together to reshape how we work, create, and solve problems.[1] **Artificial intelligence**, commonly known as AI, is "technology that enables computers and machines to simulate human learning, comprehension, problem solving, decision making, creativity and autonomy."[2] While AI can automate routine tasks, surface new insights, and speed up evidence-based decisions, it's still the human side—our creativity, empathy, judgment, and values—that ultimately drives meaningful progress.[3] The future will favor leaders who treat machine capability and human wisdom as collaborators, not rivals.

Building this kind of enterprise takes more than buying advanced tools. It requires clear choices about how to best organize people, redesign processes, select technology, and manage data. That work plays out across four tightly connected areas: people, process, technology, and data:

- **People remain the heart of every organization.** Cultivating a data-driven culture, forming multidisciplinary teams, and empowering employees to work alongside intelligent systems are essential for success.[4] As roles evolve, ongoing investment in skills, leadership, cross-generational collaboration, and ethics builds a workforce that can thrive in constant change.
- **Process is the connective tissue that aligns human and machine capabilities.** Agile workflows that support rapid iteration, governance that balances innovation with accountability, and inclusive decision-making methods help organizations respond quickly to new challenges.[5] When ethical principles are built into day-to-day processes and reinforced by continual improvement, organizations earn trust and stay adaptable.
- **Technology, the great enabler, accelerates productivity and opens new possibilities.** Its real value shows up when interoperable systems are integrated in ways that support collaboration and broaden access to insight.[6] When you choose platforms carefully and design for scalability, security, and transparency, technology serves people rather than the other way around.

- **Data forms the foundation for innovation and insight in a digital enterprise.** High data quality, fewer silos, strong stewardship, and a culture of trust in analytics are vital to unlocking value.[7] Comprehensive governance and compliance frameworks support responsible use, while strategies that tap both structured and unstructured data deepen understanding and amplify business impact.

The 42 Ways in this book offer concrete guidance for building a future-ready enterprise—one that can take advantage of the expected growth in AI-related jobs in the years ahead.[8] Together, these themes draw on expert perspectives and lived experience to help leaders and change agents put human intelligence to work in a world increasingly shaped by AI.

## Setting the Stage for Enterprise Analytics Excellence

In the digital age, data runs through every part of the enterprise, creating big opportunities and real challenges. Organizations in every industry are trying to use analytics and AI to innovate, simplify operations, and stay competitive. But technology alone is not enough; sustained success depends on an integrated approach that brings together people, process, technology, and data around clear business goals.

This book starts from the premise that enterprise analytics, powered by AI, is no longer optional—it is a core strategic capability. It distills deep industry experience, modern approaches, and working practices into a guide that helps business and technology leaders build and scale analytics functions that deliver measurable value.

## Why This Book Matters

Many organizations still face fragmented analytics efforts, weak data governance, misaligned technology investments, and cultural resistance. Even with heavy spending on tools, failure rates remain high, often because leaders overlook the human and process side of analytics. The challenge only grows as teams try to make real use of new AI capabilities.

This book is designed to help close those gaps. It offers actionable guidance, evidence-informed methods, and concrete examples to help you avoid common pitfalls and accelerate analytics and AI maturity. Whether you are launching your first initiative or scaling to an enterprise program, the approaches outlined here are meant to serve as a working playbook, not just theory.

## How This Book Is Structured

To reflect the complexity of analytics and AI, this book organizes the 42 Ways into four core sections: people, process, technology, and data. Each chapter follows a consistent structure so you can quickly find and apply what you need:

- Abstract
- Objectives
- Terms to know
- Key topic narratives
- Case studies or thought experiments
- Success metrics
- Practical advice for leaders
- Conclusion
- Parenthetical notes

For quick reference, you will also find a tables and charts index, a consolidated terms-to-know index, and a full bibliography.

## Who Should Read This Book

This book is written for business executives, analytics leaders, data scientists, IT professionals, and consultants who want to build strategic, durable analytics programs. It also supports students who are building a foundation in analytics that uses AI. You do not need technical expertise to understand the content, but you will get the most value if you are actively involved in shaping or running an analytics initiative.

## How to Use This Book

Treat this book as both a primer and a reference for 42 high-impact themes in analytics that rely on AI. The content is designed to support real-world execution and to spark the strategic conversations your team needs to have for long-lasting success. Each chapter goes deep enough that you can put its ideas to work in your organization right away. Because analytics that uses AI is a fast-moving and complex field, any one chapter could easily grow into its own book; use the citations and bibliography as starting points for further study.

## Acknowledgments

We owe special thanks to the many pioneers, scholars, and practitioners whose ideas and experiences shaped this work. Their willingness to ask hard questions, challenge assumptions, and share what they have learned made it possible to trace the themes and perspectives collected here. Whatever value this book offers rests on the foundations they laid, and we are deeply grateful to everyone whose contributions informed and inspired these pages.

## AI Disclosure Statement

In developing this book, the authors used Perplexity AI and Grok AI as research assistants to help identify, summarize, and cite potential source material. The authors then selected, organized, and adapted content for each of the 42 Ways, and designed and edited the book's final manuscript themselves.

## Notes

[1] Workhuman Editorial Team. "Human-AI Collaboration: Shaping the Future of Intelligent Partnerships." *Workhuman,* 13 Feb. 2025, workhuman.com/blog/human-ai-collaboration/.

[2] "What Is Artificial Intelligence (AI)?," *IBM,* accessed May 12, 2026, ibm.com/think/topics/artificial-intelligence.

[3] Forbes. "Human-AI Collaboration Is Redefining the Modern Workplace." *Forbes,* 13 June 2025, forbes.com/councils/forbestechcouncil/2025/06/13/the-new-era-of-work-human-ai-collaboration-is-redefining-the-modern-workplace/.

[4] World Economic Forum. "Here's How Human-Centric AI Can Shape the Future of Work." *WEF,* 15 Sept. 2025, weforum.org/stories/2025/09/human-centric-ai-shape-the-future-of-work/.

[5] McKinsey & Company. "AI in the Workplace: A Report for 2025." *McKinsey,* 27 Jan. 2025, mckinsey.com/ai-in-the-workplace-report-2025.

[6] Salesforce. "Human-AI Collaboration: The Future of Work." *Salesforce,* 3 Apr. 2025, salesforce.com/agentforce/human-ai-collaboration/.

[7] Collibra. "Top 6 Best Practices of Data Governance." *Collibra,* 10 Apr. 2022, collibra.com/blog/data-governance-best-practices.

[8] Rathindran, Randeep. "Forget Layoffs: AI Is Coming for Inefficiency, Not People." *Gartner,* 9 Dec. 2025, gartner.com/en/articles/ai-is-coming-for-inefficiency.

# Part One: People

In the age of AI, people remain the heart of every organization. Human strengths in culture, ethics, and continuous learning ultimately determine whether human-machine collaboration succeeds.

## Key topics explored in this chapter:

- Why Culture Is the Bedrock
- Recognizing and Overcoming Cultural Resistance
- The Curiosity Dividend
- Making Data Accessible
- Storytelling with Data
- Celebrating Data Champions
- Blending Evidence with Judgment
- Aligning Data with Organizational Values

# WAY 1

# Cultivate a Data-Driven Culture


## Abstract[1]

A data-driven culture is the foundation of effective enterprise analytics and a prerequisite for using AI responsibly. This chapter shows how people at every level can treat data and intelligent systems as everyday tools for making better decisions. You will see how to reduce cultural resistance, spark curiosity, and encourage a mindset that values evidence and human judgment side by side. Along the way, we highlight practical steps such as storytelling with data, elevating data champions, and aligning data and AI work with your organization's values. By the end, you will see cultural change not as a side project, but as the first real and important step toward trustworthy AI.


## Objective

After completing this chapter, you will be able to:

- Define a data-driven culture and explain why it is the foundation of AI readiness.
- Spot and address common sources of cultural resistance to analytics and intelligent systems.
- Use curiosity, storytelling, and better access to data to build AI literacy and adoption.
- Balance algorithmic insight with human expertise when decisions matter.
- Lead in ways that connect data and AI initiatives to your organization's values and mission.

# Terms to Know

**AI Literacy**[2] - The basic understanding of what AI systems can and cannot do, so employees can read outputs, question them, and use them appropriately.

**AI Readiness**[3] - How prepared your organization is to adopt AI, based on culture, data access, skills, and leadership commitment.

**Analytics Adoption**[4] - The degree to which people use data and analytics in real workflows, not just in reports and slide decks.

**Behavior Change**[5] - The shift from relying mostly on gut feel to routinely using data and AI to inform decisions.

**Communication Strategy**[6] - How leaders use storytelling, transparency, and recognition to make data and AI feel relevant and safe.

**Data-Driven Culture**[7] - A shared mindset in which teams expect to use data and AI in everyday decisions, while still honoring experience and context.

**Data Literacy**[2] - The ability to read, interpret, and question data and AI-generated insights, including recognizing limits and bias.

**Leadership**[3] - The way executives and managers model data-driven behavior, reward curiosity, and keep AI initiatives aligned with values.

**Organizational Change**[8] - The longer transition from siloed, intuition-heavy habits to a more collaborative way of working with analytics and AI.

# Introduction

Shifting an organization from gut instinct to data-driven action is not a paper exercise. It is a multi-year, whole-team transformation. At the heart of every analytics success story is a culture where curiosity is normal, data informs day-to-day decisions, and people at every level feel both empowered and responsible to act on evidence.

This chapter starts with a simple premise: culture makes or breaks analytics and AI. You can have the right strategy, platforms, algorithms, and talent, but if people do not trust the data or see how it helps them, very little will change. This chapter makes culture concrete. We will look at how resistance shows up, what it means to "democratize data," and how storytelling, recognition, and values come together.

By the end, you will have a clearer picture of what a data-driven culture looks like in real meetings and decision-making, and a set of steps you can start using right away to make that culture stick.

## Why Culture Is the Bedrock[9]

Data strategy, new platforms, and advanced algorithms all matter. But they only create value when the broader organization sees data as part of everyday decision-making. In a genuine data-driven culture, information is no longer the private domain of analysts. It becomes everyone's business.

AI raises the stakes. It amplifies the culture you already have. If your culture is siloed or biased, AI will scale those flaws. If your culture values learning, transparency, and shared responsibility, AI will help you move faster in the right direction. Getting culture right turns analytics and AI from side projects into core muscles for how the organization works.

## Recognizing and Overcoming Cultural Resistance[10]

Any meaningful change generates resistance, and culture change is no exception. For some people, "data-driven" triggers anxiety. Long-tenured staff may see it as a threat to experience and intuition. Managers may worry that new reports will expose blind spots. Teams may fear more work or, more acutely, that AI exists to replace them.

Strong leaders name these fears openly. They explain why data matters, what it will change, and what it will not. They show that AI is meant to act as a co-pilot, not a replacement. They also treat healthy skepticism as an asset rather than a problem. Tough questions improve models and sharpen insights. Finally, they tackle the "black box" problem directly. People are much more willing to use AI-supported insights when they can see how results were produced and when they know human judgment still has the final say.

## The Curiosity Dividend[11]

Organizations that excel with data have one trait in common: they reward curiosity. This is not about questioning for its own sake. It is about normalizing questions like "Why do we think that?" and "How do we know?" as part of good work. In a world where AI can generate answers quickly, the ability to ask better questions becomes a real advantage.

Curious teams do not just accept metrics or model outputs at face value. They dig into the assumptions, look for patterns that do not fit, and ask what the data might be missing. Leaders can turn routine meetings into learning sessions by modeling this behavior—asking for the thinking behind results, inviting dissent, and pausing on surprising trends long enough to understand them.

## Making Data Accessible[12]

A data-driven culture depends on broad, practical access to information. Traditional organizations treat data as something to be handed out on a "need-to-know" basis. High-performing organizations do the opposite. They work hard to remove silos and make relevant data easy to find and use. This often means investing in simple dashboards, self-service analytics, conversational interfaces, and clear data dictionaries so non-specialists can explore on their own. But access is only half the story. People also need the skills to interpret what they see and to understand the limits of AI-generated probabilities. Ongoing education, hands-on demonstrations, and regular learning sessions help ensure that access turns into action.

## Storytelling with Data[6]

Data on its own rarely changes behavior. The leaders who make analytics land are the ones who turn numbers into stories. AI can surface patterns, but humans connect those patterns to customers, operations, and strategy. Effective storytelling puts data in context. It might compare "before and after" results, highlight a single customer story behind a metric, or pair a simple visual with a clear narrative about what needs to change. When done well, stories make insights memorable and they give people a reason to act.

## Celebrating Data Champions[13]

One of the fastest ways to shift culture is to celebrate the people who already behave the way you want the organization to behave. Most companies have early adopters—managers who reorganize their teams around evidence, analysts who make insights easy to act on, and citizen developers who experiment with new AI tools to solve old problems. When leaders highlight these examples through recognition, shout-outs, or internal spotlights, they send a clear signal about what matters. Over time, skeptics see that data-driven behavior is not a passing fad but a path to impact and career growth.

### Blending Evidence with Judgment[14]

No healthy culture relies only on data. Experience, context, and judgment still matter. You don't want to replace intuition but to refine it. The most effective leaders show teams how to put evidence and judgment in conversation. When data and instinct line up, decisions are easier to make and easier to defend. When they diverge, that is a cue to pause and investigate rather than to pick sides. Framing data as a respected partner to human insight prevents a "tyranny of numbers" while still raising the overall quality of decisions.

### Aligning Data with Organizational Values[8]

A real data-driven culture reflects the values you say you care about. If transparency is a stated value, that should show up in how you share metrics, explain models, and report AI-supported decisions. If innovation is core, data should be central to how you test ideas and learn from experiments. Leaders can reinforce this connection by talking about analytics and AI in the language of the organization's mission. When teams see dashboards, models, and reports as expressions of what the company stands for—not just tools for control—they are more likely to engage deeply and use them well.

## Case Studies

### Case Study #1: MTN Ghana's Proactive Service Shift[15]

MTN Ghana reshaped customer service by opening up real-time network data to both engineers and frontline reps. Instead of waiting for complaints, cross-functional huddles used shared dashboards to spot congestion early and fix issues before customers felt the impact. Churn dropped to historic lows.

The lesson is straightforward. When more people can see and question the same data, analytics stops being a specialist function and starts to shape everyday decisions. MTN Ghana built AI readiness not by buying new tools first, but by using shared data to fuel curiosity and joint problem-solving.

## Gut Instinct vs. Data-Driven Decisions[16]

The contrast is clear when you put gut-driven and data-driven decision-making side by side. Gut decisions are fast but depend heavily on personal experience and can easily miss patterns. Data-driven and AI-supported decisions are still fast, but they benefit from broader evidence and can scale across products, regions, and teams. In MTN Ghana's case, shared analytics turned "I think we have a problem" into "The data shows a problem here—let's fix it now."

| Aspect | Gut Instinct | Data-Driven + AI |
|---|---|---|
| **Decision Speed** | Fast but error-prone | Accelerated by self-service tools |
| **Bias Risk** | High (experience silos) | Reduced via diverse data probing |
| **Scalability** | Limited to individuals | Enterprise-wide via dashboards/AI |
| **Outcome Example** | Missed patterns (e.g., stockouts) | 20-40% efficiency gains (MTN, XpressGas) |
| **Human Role** | Dominant, unrefined | "Informed intuition" co-pilot |

## Case Study #2: Standard Bank's Frontline Upskilling[17]

Standard Bank South Africa took a different path to the same goal. They invested in analytics training for tellers and officers and tied executive incentives to data-literacy goals. Over time, frontline staff began to use dashboards to spot suspicious activity, including potential loan fraud, and were recognized for doing so.

As more people saw peers succeed with data, participation grew. Clients also noticed the shift. Conversations were anchored in facts, not just impressions, which strengthened trust. Standard Bank's experience shows how upskilling and recognition can turn "analytics" from a back-office function into a frontline habit.

# Success Metrics[18]

Culture change can feel fuzzy if you do not measure it. To keep progress visible, many organizations track a small set of leading indicators. These might include how often decisions reference data, how many employees complete AI and analytics training, how frequently data champions are recognized, and how many people actively use AI-enabled tools.

The aim is not to hit perfect numbers overnight, but to see steady movement in the right direction. When leaders review these metrics regularly—and talk about them in the same breath as financial or customer KPIs—it signals that culture is not a side conversation. It is part of how the business runs.

### Culture Change KPIs

| KPI | Description | Target/Metric |
|---|---|---|
| **Data Usage Rate** | % of decisions referencing analytics | ≥ 70% |
| **Literacy Penetration** | Employees completing AI training | 100% |
| **Champion Nominations** | Internal recognitions awarded quarterly | Quarterly recognitions retrospectives |
| **AI Adoption** | Active users of AI tools (e.g., natural language queries) | Ongoing growth in active users |

## Practical Advice for Leaders[19]

- **Model data-driven habits.** When you make decisions, explain which data you relied on and where judgment came in.
- **Make access easy.** Clear away bottlenecks so people can get to relevant, timely, and reliable data without jumping through hoops.
- **Invest in dual literacy.** Help teams learn both how to read analytics and how to work with AI systems in their domain.
- **Tell stories with numbers.** Use data-backed stories to make the case for change, not just charts on slides.
- **Reward curiosity.** Call out and recognize people who ask better questions, challenge assumptions, and follow the evidence.
- **Recognize diverse champions.** Make sure recognition reaches voices from different levels, functions, and backgrounds so your data culture reflects your whole organization.
- **Balance numbers with insight.** Invite experienced colleagues to interpret what the data is saying, rather than treating analytics as the final word.
- **Tie analytics to outcomes.** Keep reminding teams how better use of data and AI moves the organization closer to its mission and goals.

# Conclusion[20]

A real data-driven culture amplifies everything else you invest in—strategy, technology, and talent. It helps teams make sharper decisions, respond faster to change, and hold themselves accountable in a fairer, more transparent way. Over time, it turns analytics and AI from isolated projects into part of how the organization thinks.

The shift won't happen in a single quarter. Culture change is a series of small, visible steps repeated over time: leaders asking for data, teams sharing what they learn, and champions being recognized. Every time you reinforce those behaviors, you move a little closer to a culture where data and AI feel natural, not forced. When that happens, your organization is not just coping with a data-rich, AI-shaped world—it is using that world to its advantage.

# Notes

[1] Data-driven culture, AI readiness, leadership strategies, and the role of curiosity, access, and values—all informing the Abstract, learning outcomes, and closing summary—are examined across Emmanuel Boadi's "Data-Driven Culture - Key Strategies and Case Studies"; AZTech Training's "How to Build a Data-Driven Culture with AI?"; IBM's "Foster a Culture of Data Literacy"; Pointury's "A Data and AI Driven Culture"; DOOR Training & Consulting's "Cultural Levers Driving Digital Transformation in Banking"; and KPMG's "A Data-Driven Culture Will Differentiate the Winners from the Losers."

[2] AI literacy and data literacy, as used in this chapter, are defined in Visium's "The Role of Data Literacy in Building a Data-Driven Culture."

[3] AZTech Training's "How to Build a Data-Driven Culture with AI?" addresses AI readiness and the "co-pilot" framing of AI.

[4] Analytics adoption and decision practices are described in Siddharth Tumkur's "Data-Driven Decision-Making: How to Foster a Culture of Analytics."

[5] Behavior change and the culture metrics used here are drawn from *CDO Magazine*'s "Data-Driven Culture Measurement Framework: Foundation of Data Literacy."

[6] Communication strategy and the role of storytelling with data in culture change are explored in Newmath's "Cultivating a Data-Driven Culture: Leadership Strategies for Success."

[7] A data-driven culture and its link to competitive differentiation are set out in KPMG's "A Data-Driven Culture Will Differentiate the Winners from the Losers."

[8] Organizational change, values alignment, transparency, and innovation in data and AI initiatives are addressed in DOOR Training & Consulting's "Cultural Levers Driving Digital Transformation in Banking."

[9] *MIT Sloan Management Review*'s "Building a Data-Driven Culture: Four Key Elements" makes the case that culture is foundational to data-driven decision-making and AI success.

[10] Leadership behaviors that address resistance, promote skepticism as a positive force, and model evidence-based decision-making are drawn from Tumkur's "Data-Driven Decision-Making: How to Foster a Culture of Analytics."

[11] IBM's "Foster a Culture of Data Literacy" emphasizes curiosity, questioning, and data literacy as core enablers of a data-driven culture.

[12] Democratized access, dashboards, and self-service analytics as supports for a data-driven culture are described in Boadi's "Data-Driven Culture - Key Strategies and Case Studies."

[13] AZTech Training's "How to Build a Data-Driven Culture with AI?" provides examples of recognizing data champions and early adopters who use AI and analytics to drive impact.

[14] "Informed intuition" and the idea that AI amplifies existing culture and bias are developed in Pointury's "A Data and AI Driven Culture."

[15] The MTN Ghana case study illustrating proactive service and shared data access appears in Boadi's "Data-Driven Culture - Key Strategies and Case Studies."

[16] Gut instinct vs. data-driven decision-making—covering bias reduction, scalability, and outcome gains—is compared across Boadi, KPMG, and Visium.

[17] Visium's "The Role of Data Literacy in Building a Data-Driven Culture" provides the Standard Bank frontline upskilling example and its focus on data literacy and fraud detection.

[18] Culture success metrics—data usage rate, literacy penetration, recognition of champions, and AI adoption—are drawn from *CDO Magazine*'s "Data-Driven Culture Measurement Framework: Foundation of Data Literacy"; IBM's "Foster a Culture of Data Literacy"; and AZTech Training's "How to Build a Data-Driven Culture with AI?"

[19] Practical leadership guidance on modeling data-driven habits, investing in access, balancing analytics with insight, and tying analytics to an organization's mission is collected from *CDO Magazine*'s "Data-Driven Culture Measurement Framework: Foundation of Data Literacy"; IBM's "Foster a Culture of Data Literacy"; *MIT Sloan Management Review*'s "Building a Data-Driven Culture: Four Key Elements"; DOOR's "Cultural Levers Driving Digital Transformation in Banking"; and Pointury's "A Data and AI Driven Culture."

[20] Claims in the conclusion about performance acceleration, collaboration, and the ongoing journey of AI-enabled decision-making are supported by AZTech Training's "How to Build a Data-Driven Culture with AI?"; and KPMG's "A Data-Driven Culture Will Differentiate the Winners from the Losers."

## Key topics explored in this chapter:

- The Power of Diversity in Analytics
- Structuring the Analytics Organization
- Role Clarity: The Antidote to Confusion
- Enabling Synergy Across Roles
- Cross-Training: Broadening the Toolkit
- Leveraging Strengths: From Talent to Impact
- Resolving Collaboration Challenges
- Leaders as Catalysts for Multidisciplinary Success
- Build Demographic Diversity for Ethical AI
- Team Maturity Evolution: From Formation to Optimization

# WAY 2

# Build Multidisciplinary Teams


## Abstract[1]

Strong analytics and AI work depends on teams that bring together different kinds of expertise. This chapter shows how to build teams that combine technical depth, business understanding, and ethical judgment so AI-supported insights are trustworthy and useful. It explains how to structure those teams, clarify roles, and remove common barriers to collaboration. It also highlights cross-training, role alignment, and intentional use of individual strengths so teams can produce better insights and better outcomes. When those pieces come together, human and machine capabilities reinforce each other in practical, measurable ways.


## Objective

After completing this chapter, you will be able to:

- Compare centralized, decentralized, and hybrid models for structuring AI and analytics organizations.
- Define roles that balance technical depth, business knowledge, and ethical oversight in human-AI teams.
- Use cross-training and collaboration rituals to reduce friction across disciplines.
- Design talent-mapping approaches that put individual strengths to work for the team.
- Measure team effectiveness with AI-specific metrics and support steady team development over time.

# Terms to Know

**AI Roles**[2] - Specialized positions such as prompt engineers, model auditors, and ethics reviewers that help integrate AI into human workflows.

**Analytics Talent**[3] - The mix of technical skill, business understanding, and interpersonal ability needed to build and scale analytics and AI work.

**Cross-Functional Collaboration**[4] - Structured work across disciplines so teams can combine technical, business, and operational perspectives in one solution.

**Human-AI Teaming**[5] - A working model in which people and intelligent systems complement each other, with humans providing judgment, oversight, and context.

**Leadership**[3] - The role leaders play in setting direction, removing barriers, and creating conditions for healthy collaboration.

**Multidisciplinary Teams**[6] - Teams made up of people with different specialties who work together on shared goals rather than in isolated handoffs.

**Organizational Design**[3] - How reporting lines, decision rights, and team structures are arranged to support effective work.

**Talent Development**[6] - The deliberate building of skills, experience, and adaptability so teams can grow with changing business and technology demands.

**Team Structure**[3] - The way people, roles, and responsibilities are organized to deliver analytics and AI outcomes.

# Introduction

Transformative AI and analytics are team sports. No single function can carry the full load. Technical specialists may know how to build models and pipelines, but they still need business context, operational insight, and ethical judgment to make those outputs useful. The strongest teams bring those perspectives together early, not at the end. That is why multidisciplinary teams matter so much. They help organizations move from isolated technical work to shared problem-solving.

This chapter looks at how to structure those teams, define roles clearly, broaden collaboration, and build maturity over time. But it's not just about assembling a group of specialists. It's about helping them work as one team.

## The Power of Diversity in Analytics[7]

Good analytics depends on more than technical excellence. It depends on the range of perspectives brought to the problem. Diverse teams are better at spotting assumptions, surfacing risks, and asking questions a more uniform group might miss. That matters even more in AI work, where models can easily scale blind spots if teams do not catch them early.

Diversity here includes more than demographics, though demographics matter. It also includes differences in discipline, operating experience, problem-solving style, and proximity to customers or frontline decisions. The more varied the perspective at the table, the better the odds that the team will build solutions people can trust and use.

## Structuring the Analytics Organization[8]

There is no one perfect team model for every organization. Some companies benefit from centralized structures that create consistency, shared standards, and deeper technical communities. Others gain speed from decentralized models that place analytics talent closer to business units. Many organizations do best with a hybrid approach that combines shared governance with local responsiveness.

The right structure depends on your size, regulatory environment, talent pool, and business complexity. What matters most is clarity. People need to know where accountability sits, how decisions get made, and when work should be shared across the enterprise rather than duplicated in silos.

## The Analytics Organization Model

| Model | Strengths | Weaknesses | Best For |
|---|---|---|---|
| **Centralized** | Standardization, best practices, economies of scale | Slower business alignment, less context awareness | Early-stage AI maturity, enterprise standards |
| **Decentralized** | Business relevance, agility, ownership | Duplication, inconsistent quality | Mature organizations with strong governance |
| **Hybrid (Federated)** | Balances control + customization | Requires sophisticated coordination | Most enterprises scaling AI broadly |

Multidisciplinary teams work best when each person knows what they own and how their role connects to the rest of the group. Without that clarity, teams waste time in overlap, duplication, and avoidable conflict. One person assumes someone else owns the business framing. Another assumes validation is handled elsewhere. Important work slips between the cracks. Role clarity is the antidote to confusion.

## Role Clarity: The Antidote to Confusion[9]

| Role | Core Responsibilities | AI-Specific Focus |
|---|---|---|
| **Data Engineer** | Pipeline construction | Scalable data lakes for ML training |
| **Data Scientist** | Modeling, validation | Hyperparameter tuning, bias detection |
| **Prompt Engineer** | LLM optimization | Chain-of-thought prompting, RAG systems |
| **Ethics Auditor** | Fairness assessment | Demographic parity, counterfactual testing |
| **Business Translator** | Stakeholder alignment | ROI modeling, change management |

Clear roles do not make teams rigid. They make collaboration easier. When responsibilities are understood, people can move faster, ask for help sooner, and coordinate work with less friction. In AI and analytics environments, that clarity is especially important because technical, business, and governance responsibilities often intersect.

## Enabling Synergy Across Roles[10]

A multidisciplinary team should feel like a system, not a lineup. The aim is not simply to gather specialists in the same meeting, but to help them solve problems together. That means creating routines that encourage open exchange across roles: shared planning, joint review sessions, regular demos, and working sessions where technical and business teams shape the solution together.

When this happens consistently, synergy stops being an abstract idea. Teams begin to combine strengths in real time. Analysts frame insights in language leaders can use. Domain experts improve model relevance. And risk and governance partners flag issues before they become expensive, harmful mistakes.

## Cross-Training: Broadening the Toolkit[11]

Cross-training isn't about turning everyone into a generalist. Its purpose is to help people understand enough about adjacent disciplines so they can collaborate intelligently. A data scientist doesn't need to become a compliance officer but should understand the practical constraints compliance introduces. A business stakeholder doesn't have to engineer pipelines but should know enough to ask better questions about data quality and feasibility.

This kind of fluency makes teams more resilient. It reduces miscommunication, speeds handoffs, and creates more empathy across roles. Over time, it also helps organizations build adaptable talent that can grow as analytics and AI capabilities evolve.

## Leveraging Strengths: From Talent to Impact[12]

Strong teams do not treat people as interchangeable. They look closely at what each person does best and aligns work accordingly. One person may excel at technical depth. Another may be gifted at translation across business and technical groups. Another may see process risks early or bring unusual creativity to experimentation.

The point of multidisciplinary teaming is not to blur all distinctions. It is to use complementary strengths on purpose. When leaders do that well, talent turns into impact more quickly because people are not just busy—they are contributing where they add the most value.

## Resolving Collaboration Challenges[13]

Even strong teams run into friction. Different functions bring different priorities, assumptions, and even vocabularies. Technical teams may push for rigor and precision. Business partners may push for speed. Governance teams may focus on control and risk. None of those instincts are wrong, but they can clash if the team lacks a shared way of working.

The answer is not to eliminate tension. It's to make tension productive. Teams need clear decision rules, agreed escalation paths, and a culture that treats disagreement as part of better problem-solving rather than as a personal threat. When handled well, collaboration challenges become a source of stronger solutions, not stalled progress.

## Common Pitfalls and Mitigations[14]

| Pitfall | Symptom | Mitigation |
|---|---|---|
| **Role Ambiguity** | Project delays, finger-pointing | RACI matrix + quarterly refreshers |
| **Trust Gaps** | SME resistance to AI outputs | Explainability training + joint retrospectives |
| **Silo Thinking** | "Ivory tower" analytics | Mandatory role rotations + AI demo days |
| **Skill Gaps** | Failed model scaling | Skills inventories + cross-training mandates |
| **Lack of Diversity** | Bias amplification in AI | Blind hiring + diverse interview panels |

## Leaders as Catalysts for Multidisciplinary Success[15]

Leaders shape whether multidisciplinary teams struggle or thrive. They decide whether teams get clear priorities, enough time for joint planning, and the psychological safety to question assumptions. They also set the tone for whether collaboration is treated as real work or as an extra burden on top of "the real job."

Strong leaders do more than sponsor teams from a distance. They remove bottlenecks, reinforce shared accountability, and reward the behaviors that make collaboration work. Over time, these signals shape the culture around analytics and AI just as much as org charts do.

## Build Demographic Diversity for Ethical AI[16]

Demographic diversity is not a side issue in AI work. It affects how teams identify harm, interpret outcomes, and question whether a model is fair or useful across different groups. Teams with broader representation are more likely to spot where data, design choices, or deployment assumptions could create unequal outcomes.

That does not mean demographic diversity alone solves bias. But it is an important part of building teams that are more likely to ask the right ethical questions and less likely to normalize a narrow set of assumptions. In AI, that is both a performance issue and a responsibility issue.

# Case Studies

## Case Study #1: Google's PAIR Initiative[17]

Google's People + AI Research initiative showed what can happen when technical experts, designers, and user-centered thinkers work together from the start. Instead of treating AI as a purely engineering problem, the work connected system capability with usability, transparency, and human judgment.

The larger lesson is that multidisciplinary collaboration improves not only model performance, but also how well people can understand and use AI-supported systems. Teams build better tools when they design for both technical quality and human experience.

## Case Study #2: Mayo Clinic's AI Diagnostics Team[18]

Mayo Clinic's work in combining clinicians, researchers, and technical specialists illustrates why AI needs strong domain partnership. Medical AI cannot succeed if it is built in isolation from the people who understand patient care, workflow realities, and practical decision stakes.

The broader lesson applies outside healthcare as well. AI becomes more useful when domain experts help define the problem, interpret the output, and shape how results fit into real decisions.

## Case Study #3: Reliance Jio (India)[19]

Reliance Jio's experience highlights the challenge of coordinating large, multidisciplinary efforts across a fast-moving environment. At scale, team effectiveness depends not just on who is on the team, but on how clearly teams are connected, governed, and supported.

This reinforces a simple point: as analytics and AI work spreads, structure matters more, not less. Growth without coordination creates duplication, confusion, and uneven quality.

# Success Metrics[20]

Multidisciplinary teamwork improves when leaders measure it directly instead of assuming it is happening because the org chart says it should. Useful indicators can include delivery speed, stakeholder satisfaction, model adoption, and bias detection:

## AI Team Effectiveness Metrics

| Metric | Target | Measurement Method |
|---|---|---|
| **Model Adoption Rate** | 75% business units | Quarterly stakeholder surveys |
| **Cross-Training Completion** | 90% team members | Learning management system tracking |
| **Project Delivery Velocity** | 20% faster than baseline | Sprint retrospectives and throughput metrics |
| **Bias Detection Rate** | 95% flagged issues caught | Ethics audit scores and model review logs |
| **Stakeholder Satisfaction** | 4.2/5.0 | Post-project NPS-style surveys |

No single metric tells the full story. What matters is whether the team is becoming more coordinated, more trusted, and more capable of turning technical work into business value. Good metrics make that progress visible to stakeholders.

## Team Maturity Evolution: From Formation to Optimization[21]

Multidisciplinary teams don't achieve high performance overnight. They usually move through stages. Early on, the main work is role definition, trust-building, and basic coordination. Later, teams can focus more on speed, refinement, and continuous improvement because they already know how to work well together.

Recognizing this progression helps leaders stay realistic. A newly assembled team should not be judged by the same standard as a mature one. What matters is whether the team is learning, improving, and building the habits that make collaboration stronger over time.

## AI Team Maturity Roadmap[22]

| Stage | Timeline | Key Focus | Milestones | Success Indicators |
|---|---|---|---|---|
| **Formation** | 0-6 months | Structure: Role clarity + basic collaboration | RACI matrices deployed; daily standups established | 80% role understanding (survey); zero project stalls from ambiguity |
| **Synergy** | 6-18 months | Building habits: Cross-training + rituals | "AI teach-ins" complete; first demo day held | 75% cross-training completion; Model Adoption Rate >50% |
| **Optimization** | 18+ months | Innovation: Metrics-driven evolution | Bias detection at 95%; quarterly rotations | Project Velocity 20%+ faster; Stakeholder NPS 4.2+ |

The AI Team Maturity Roadmap gives you a straightforward way to gauge where your team is today and what to focus on next. Use it in retrospectives to mark your current stage: Formation teams focus on structure, Synergy teams on building durable habits, and Optimization teams on continuous innovation. The roadmap also helps you avoid common "maturity traps," where early wins stall out before the team has a chance to fully evolve.

# Practical Advice for Leaders[23]

- **Clarify roles early.** Make sure every team member understands what they own, how decisions are made, and where responsibilities might overlap.
- **Hire and organize around complementary skills.** Build teams with a mix of technical depth, business insight, and ethical awareness rather than overloading one profile.
- **Create shared working rituals.** Use planning sessions, reviews, and demos to keep collaboration active rather than occasional.
- **Invest in cross-training.** Help people understand adjacent disciplines well enough to communicate and coordinate better.

- **Use strengths intentionally.** Assign work based not only on title, but also on where each person contributes most effectively.
- **Treat conflict as signal.** Use friction to surface assumptions and improve decisions instead of forcing artificial consensus.
- **Reward team behavior.** Recognize collaboration, translation, and shared accountability-not just individual technical output.
- **Build diversity on purpose.** Broader representation improves both team judgment and AI quality.

# Conclusion[24]

Multidisciplinary teams are not a nice-to-have in analytics and AI; they are one of the strongest indicators that technical capability will translate into real business value. When organizations bring together diverse expertise with clear roles, regular collaboration, and grounded leadership, they make better decisions and build more trustworthy systems.

Just remember: these teams don't come together by accident. They have to be intentionally designed, supported, and refined over time. When that happens, the payoff is substantial: sharper insights, stronger execution, and AI efforts that are more practical, ethical, and built to last.

# Notes

[1] Multidisciplinary AI teams, role diversity, and objectives in the Abstract—including organizational models, conflict resolution tactics, and human-AI teaming—are examined in *The Art of Service Academy*'s "AI-Driven Business Transformation: Strategies and Frameworks"; Google PAIR's People + AI Guidebook and related resources (including research overviews at pair.withgoogle.com and the "People + AI Research (PAIR)" initiative); *DeepMind Blog*'s "Human-Centered Mechanism Design with Democratic AI"; *Science*'s "AI can help humans find common ground in democratic deliberation"; and Mayo Clinic News Network's "Using AI in Radiology Clinical Practice."

[2] AI roles and responsibilities—prompt engineers, ethics reviewers, and model auditors—are defined in *Google Research Blog*'s "Responsible AI at *Google Research*: PAIR"; and *Science*'s "AI can help humans find common ground in democratic deliberation."

[3] *The Art of Service Academy*'s "AI-Driven Business Transformation: Strategies and Frameworks" develops the concepts of analytics talent, leadership in AI teams, organizational design choices, and team structures.

[4] Cross-functional collaboration as a means of validating AI outputs against real-world contexts is central to *DeepMind Blog*'s "Human-Centered Mechanism Design with Democratic AI."

[5] Human-AI teaming—the combination of human judgment and creativity with AI's pattern-recognition and scale—is elaborated in *Science*'s "AI can help humans find common ground in democratic deliberation."

[6] Multidisciplinary teams, talent development, and cross-training practices are addressed in *Google Design*'s "People + AI Research" and *The Art of Service Academy*'s "AI-Driven Business Transformation: Strategies and Frameworks."

[7] Cross-functional diversity—its capacity to challenge silos, improve robustness, and prevent naive techno-optimism, with examples including churn, triage, and misinformation—is explored in *Google Research*'s "People + AI Research (PAIR)"; *Science*'s "AI can help humans find common ground in democratic deliberation"; and *DeepMind Blog*'s "Human-Centered Mechanism Design with Democratic AI."

[8] Centralized, decentralized, and hybrid analytics structures—and guidance on evolving from a central "tiger team" to embedded specialists—are compared in *The Art of Service Academy*'s "AI-Driven Business Transformation: Strategies and Frameworks"; and *Google Design*'s "People + AI Research (PAIR)."

[9] Role definitions—data engineer, data scientist, prompt engineer, ethics auditor, business translator—along with RACI matrices and lifecycle examples such as next-best-action recommenders, are drawn from *Google Research Blog*'s "Responsible AI at *Google Research*: PAIR"; and Mayo Clinic News Network's "Using AI in Radiology Clinical Practice."

[10] *DeepMind Blog*'s "Human-Centered Mechanism Design with Democratic AI" supplies the practices that build synergy—daily standups, rotating leads, and AI teach-ins—as well as norms of respectful dissent.

[11] Cross-training techniques and baseline literacy in prompt engineering and interpretability are set out in *Google Design*'s "People + AI Research (PAIR)."

[12] Skills inventories as a tool for aligning technical, strategic, and ethical strengths with AI project roles are detailed in *The Art of Service Academy*'s "AI-Driven Business Transformation: Strategies and Frameworks."

[13] Mayo Clinic News Network's "Using AI in Radiology Clinical Practice" offers strategies for addressing trust gaps—explainability tools, joint retrospectives, and clinical examples where AI triage and human intuition diverge.

[14] Common pitfalls—role ambiguity, trust gaps, silo thinking, skill gaps, lack of diversity—and their mitigations are catalogued in *The Art of Service Academy*'s "AI-Driven Business Transformation: Strategies and Frameworks"; Mayo Clinic News Network's "Using AI in Radiology Clinical Practice"; and *DeepMind Blog*'s "Human-Centered Mechanism Design with Democratic AI."

[15] Leadership behaviors—attending AI demo days, praising cross-functional work, and tying incentives to team-level metrics—are examined in *Google Design*'s "People + AI Research (PAIR)"; and *DeepMind Blog*'s "Human-Centered Mechanism Design with Democratic AI."

[16] Demographic diversity—gender, ethnicity, neurodiversity—inclusive hiring practices, and the impact of diverse teams on AI fairness are addressed in *Patterns*' "Bringing AI Participation Down to Scale"; and *Science*'s "AI can help humans find common ground in democratic deliberation."

[17] *Google Research*'s "People + AI Research (PAIR)"; *Google PAIR*'s "People + AI Guidebook"; and *Science*'s "AI can help humans find common ground in democratic deliberation" document the Google PAIR initiative—its multidisciplinary composition, the People + AI Guidebook, and human-AI feedback loops in election forecasting.

[18] The Mayo Clinic diagnostics example—radiologists, data scientists, engineers, ethicists, AI as a "second set of eyes," and reduced false positives—draws on Mayo Clinic News Network's "Using AI in Radiology Clinical Practice"; and *The New York Times*' "Your A.I. Radiologist Will Not Be With You Soon."

[19] The Reliance Jio case study—hybrid teams combining engineers, rural domain experts, and ethicists to optimize telecom networks—is drawn from *DeepMind Blog*'s "Human-Centered Mechanism Design with Democratic AI"; and *The Art of Service Academy*'s "AI-Driven Business Transformation: Strategies and Frameworks."

[20] Success metrics—model adoption rate, cross-training completion, project velocity, bias detection rate, and stakeholder satisfaction—are drawn from *The Art of Service Academy*'s "AI-Driven Business Transformation: Strategies and Frameworks"; *CDO Magazine*'s "Data-Driven Culture Measurement Framework: Foundation of Data Literacy"; IBM's "Foster a Culture of Data Literacy"; and Mayo Clinic News Network's "Using AI in Radiology Clinical Practice."

[21] Team maturity stages and the importance of roles, rituals, and metrics in evolving multidisciplinary AI teams are set out in *Google Design*'s "People + AI Research (PAIR)"; and *The Art of Service Academy*'s "AI-Driven Business Transformation: Strategies and Frameworks."

[22] The AI Team Maturity Roadmap—Formation, Synergy, Optimization—and its milestones are developed in *The Art of Service Academy*'s "AI-Driven Business Transformation: Strategies and Frameworks."

[23] Practical leadership advice is drawn from *The Art of Service Academy*'s "AI-Driven Business Transformation: Strategies and Frameworks"; *Google Design*'s "People + AI Research (PAIR)"; *DeepMind Blog*'s "Human-Centered Mechanism Design with Democratic AI"; *Google Research Blog*'s "Responsible AI at *Google Research*: PAIR"; and Mayo Clinic News Network's "Using AI in Radiology Clinical Practice."

[24] The claim that multidisciplinary teams turn AI into a durable competitive advantage by combining technical, ethical, and domain strengths is grounded in *Google Research*'s "People + AI Research (PAIR)"; and *Science*'s "AI can help humans find common ground in democratic deliberation."

Cohesive team dynamics in multidisciplinary settings enhance collaboration, knowledge sharing, and overall organizational performance when implementing AI.

*International Journal of Information Management*

"AI-Driven Performance in Organizations"

Ullah et al.

March 2026

## Key topics explored in this chapter:

- Rethinking Leadership in the Age of AI
- Building Trust in AI Systems Without Blind Reliance
- Defining Clear Roles and Responsibilities
- Cultivating a Culture of Augmentation Over Replacement
- Enhancing Decision-Making Through Joint Problem-Solving
- Anticipating and Managing Risks

# WAY 3

# Lead AI-Human Collaboration


## Abstract[1]

The AI-human collaboration works best when organizations are clear about what machines do well, what people must still own, and how the two work together in practice. This chapter explains how to build that partnership so AI strengthens judgment rather than weakening it. It focuses on trust, role design, shared problem-solving, and risk management so teams can use AI confidently without surrendering accountability. The larger goal is not automation for its own sake, but a working model in which human expertise and machine capability reinforce one another.


## Objective

After completing this chapter, you will be able to:

- Explain the distinctive strengths and limitations of AI systems versus human decision-makers, and why collaboration outperforms either alone.
- Design Human-in-the-Loop (HITL) frameworks that specify when, where, and how humans oversee, challenge, and correct AI outputs.
- Build and sustain trust in AI by emphasizing transparency, explainability, and continuous bias monitoring while avoiding automation bias and overreliance.
- Cultivate a culture of augmentation over replacement, where AI is positioned as a capability multiplier and employees are actively upskilled to work with intelligent systems.

- Define and track success metrics—such as override rates, adoption rates, and bias reduction—that indicate whether AI-human collaboration is healthy and improving over time.
- Anticipate and manage key risks, including skill erosion, ethical drift, and inappropriate task assignment between humans and AI, through structured governance and leadership behaviors.

# Terms to Know

**AI-Human Collaboration**[2] - A working relationship in which AI systems and people contribute different strengths to tasks or decisions.

**Augmented Intelligence**[3] - An approach that highlights how AI enhances human abilities rather than replacing them, aiming for stronger combined performance instead of making people obsolete.

**Automation Bias**[4] - The tendency to trust machine output too quickly, even when human review is still needed.

**Ethical AI**[4] - The practice of designing, deploying, and monitoring AI systems in ways that uphold fairness, transparency, accountability, and respect for human rights.

**Human-in-the-Loop (HITL)**[5] - A design pattern in which humans are explicitly required to review, approve, or correct AI outputs, and their feedback is used to retrain or improve models.

**Leadership**[6] - The capacity of executives and managers to shape AI strategy, model healthy use, communicate its limits clearly, and build a culture where AI is probed and refined rather than blindly followed.

**Organizational Change**[7] - The planned evolution of structures, processes, and culture needed to integrate AI-human collaboration into everyday work.

**Workforce Development**[3] - Ongoing investment in employee skills, mindsets, and career paths so that workers can effectively partner with AI and remain employable as technology evolves.

# Introduction

The fusion of artificial intelligence with human expertise reshapes how organizations diagnose problems, generate options, and act. AI often discerns patterns and processes data at a scale no human team can match. Yet, it still struggles with ambiguity, conflicting values, and tacit knowledge—the kind rooted in lived experience and empathy. The central leadership challenge isn't choosing between AI or humans; it's designing the conditions where the two genuinely complement each other.

Without intentional leadership, organizations often swing between extremes: either fearing AI as a threat to identify and jobs or romanticizing it as an infallible oracle. This chapter advocates a third path: a deliberate AI-human collaboration. Here, leaders define clear roles, establish trust through guardrails, and continuously measure the effectiveness of this new and unique partnership.

## Rethinking Leadership in the Age of AI[8]

Traditionally, leadership centered on directing human tasks and optimizing workflows. Today, in the AI era, it's all about orchestrating a hybrid system of people and machines. Effective leaders understand that AI is strong in speed, scale, and pattern detection, but weak in human experience, ethical reasoning, and contextual nuance. Rather than treating AI as a black box, they act as translators and integrators. They interpret, question, and explain AI outputs in ways that connect to organizational priorities and values. They encourage teams to treat AI recommendations as strong hypotheses, not final answers. They also normalize questions such as, "What might this system be missing?" Leaders who do this well consistently model three behaviors:

- **Curiosity toward AI:** Investigating how it works and where it may fail.
- **Humility about AI:** Acknowledging its limits and trade-offs.
- **Courage with AI:** Being willing to deploy, monitor, and revise systems in the open.

These behaviors set the tone for healthy skepticism and ongoing learning.

## Building Trust in AI Systems Without Blind Reliance[9]

AI adoption depends on trust. If employees see AI as opaque, biased, or arbitrary, they'll either ignore it or work around it. But blind trust can produce serious errors and reputational damage. The objective is "calibrated trust:" a level of confidence that aligns with the system's actual reliability and known limits. Leaders build calibration by reinforcing three pillars: explainability, bias monitoring, and expectations.

## Three Pillars of Trust

| Trust Element | Leadership Action | Example Impact |
|---|---|---|
| **Explainability** | Require models to surface reasons, features, or examples that justify outputs | Clinicians or analysts can challenge AI recommendations using domain knowledge |
| **Bias Monitoring** | Establish regular audits comparing outcomes across groups and scenarios | Early detection of skewed decisions before they become systemic |
| **Setting Expectations** | Communicate clearly where AI is strong and weak; publish "AI capability labels" | Users avoid overextending AI into use cases where it was not trained |

When trust breaks down, adoption falls and shadow processes emerge as teams return to manual workarounds. Leaders should invite feedback on where AI feels untrustworthy and respond with system improvements or explicit constraints instead of defensiveness.

## Defining Clear Roles and Responsibilities[10]

Unclear boundaries around what AI should do and what humans must retain can quickly undermine collaboration, especially in high-stakes settings. Confusion can lead either to over-delegation to AI or to wasteful double work where both people and AI repeat the same analysis. A useful starting point is to distinguish between four broad types of tasks:

- **Routine processing:** Repetitive, well-defined tasks that follow clear rules.
- **Pattern detection:** Finding trends, regularities, or anomalies in large data sets.
- **Ethical judgment:** Choosing what ought to be done in situations with moral or social consequences.
- **Creative synthesis:** Combining ideas, data, or styles into novel concepts, stories, or designs.

## Who Does What?

| Task Type | Primary Actor | Human Role | AI Role |
|---|---|---|---|
| **Routine Processing** | AI | Exception handling and escalation | Automate repetitive calculations and checks |
| **Pattern Detection** | AI | Validate and interpret in context | Surface anomalies, clusters, and correlations |
| **Ethical Judgment** | Human | Final decision-making and accountability | Provide structured information and scenario analysis |
| **Creative Synthesis** | Human | Generate options, narratives, and strategies | Suggest options based on patterns and prior examples |

Leaders should clearly separate prediction, where AI is often strongest, from judgment, where humans should remain central; this is especially relevant with ethically sensitive or mission-critical decisions. Clear HITL protocols define when people must approve, comment on, or override AI recommendations so responsibilities are not left to improvisation.

## Cultivating a Culture of Augmentation Over Replacement[11]

Without strong messaging and visible action, employees often assume AI will eventually replace them, especially in sectors shaped by earlier waves of automation. Leaders who want healthy AI-human collaboration have to frame AI as augmentation rather than substitution.

In practice, that means emphasizing AI's role in removing drudgery, highlighting risk, and surfacing opportunity so people can focus on relationship-building, creativity, and complex judgment. Leaders can highlight teams that have reshaped roles alongside AI and publicly commit to upskilling and redeploying people affected by automation rather than quietly reducing headcount. Stories of augmentation should be as concrete as technical demos. For example, customer-service agents can use AI-generated summaries to personalize conversations rather than simply increase ticket volume.

## Enhancing Decision-Making Through Joint Problem-Solving[12]

The strongest AI-human relationships work as an ongoing dialogue rather than a one-time handoff. AI systems surface patterns, anomalies, and forecasts. Humans question the logic, add experiential knowledge and ethical considerations, and ask AI to explore sharper follow-up questions. This creates a continuous improvement cycle: a simple **four-step joint problem-solving loop** that looks like this:

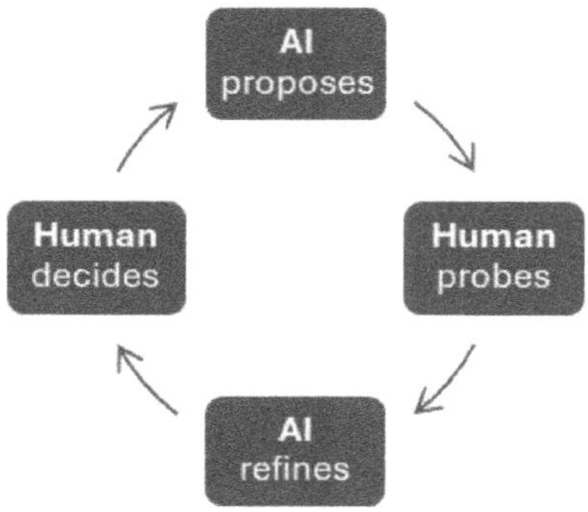


1. **AI proposes:** The system generates predictions, clusters, or recommended actions.
2. **Human probes:** Decision-makers test outputs against experience, exploring edge cases and potential harms.
3. **AI refines:** Feedback is incorporated for retraining, recalibration, or rule adjustments.
4. **Human decides:** A person or committee makes the final call, documenting rationale and any deviations from AI recommendations.

Leaders reinforce this loop by praising teams that improve AI through constructive challenge, not only teams that maximize usage metrics. That keeps collaboration, rather than automation volume, at the center of the success story.

# Case Studies

## Case Study #1: AI-Assisted Clinical Decision Support[13]

A large hospital network introduced an AI-powered clinical decision support tool to flag high-risk patients for readmission, reflecting broader trends in machine learning for medicine. Initially, clinicians distrusted the system, feeling it "saw numbers but not people," and override rates were high as staff relied on their own judgment.

Leadership responded by forming cross-functional rounds where physicians, data scientists, and nurses jointly reviewed flagged cases and documented reasons for accepting or overriding AI suggestions. Over several months, the model was retrained to better account for social determinants of health and contextual variables. Clinicians reported that the AI helped them notice subtle risk patterns previously overlooked, contributing to improved readmission metrics without displacing clinical input and judgment.

## Case Study #2: Human-AI Collaboration in Recruitment[14]

A global consumer-goods company deployed AI screening tools to analyze large applicant pools for early-career roles, echoing well-known challenges around biased recruiting algorithms. Instead of allowing the AI to fully rank and filter candidates, HR leaders established a HITL pipeline in which AI scored candidates on specific job-relevant attributes while human reviewers focused on qualitative signals and cultural fit.

They also implemented periodic audits to check for demographic bias, and one early review revealed that the model was down-ranking resumes from certain underrepresented universities, prompting adjustments to training data and feature weighting. Human reviewers were encouraged to override AI scores with documented rationale. Eventually, time-to-hire decreased while workforce diversity improved, demonstrating the value of AI-human co-design over AI-only automation.

# Success Metrics[15]

To know whether AI-human collaboration is working, leaders need explicit metrics that capture both performance and risk. The portfolio that follows offers a strong starting point:

### Collaboration Effectiveness Metrics

| Metric | Target Range | What It Indicates |
|---|---|---|
| **AI Adoption Rate** | ~70% of eligible users | Level of trust and integration into daily work |
| **Override Frequency** | 10-20% of AI recommendations | Balance between healthy skepticism and over trust |
| **Bias Reduction** | ≥ 20-30% reduction in identified bias incidents year-over-year | Effectiveness of ethical governance |
| **Productivity Gain** | 15-30% improvement in key process KPIs | Value generated by AI augmentation |
| **Literacy Penetration** | ≥ 80-90% of target workforce trained | Readiness of staff to collaborate with AI |

Override frequency is especially important. Near-zero overrides may suggest rubber-stamping and weak critical thinking, while very high override rates may point to poor calibration or low trust. Leaders should track this metric over time, investigate deviations from the target range, and adjust training, communication, or model design as needed.

## Practical Advice for Leaders[16]

- **Mandate explainable AI** in production systems by requiring teams to deploy only models that can provide interpretable reasons, feature importances, or examples for their outputs.
- **Institutionalize HITL reviews** by asking every people manager to run a set number of documented AI-output reviews each quarter, examining both decision quality and user experience.
- **Tie incentives to collaborative outcomes** by linking a portion of bonuses or performance evaluations to hybrid metrics such as productivity gains plus bias reduction, rather than raw AI utilization.
- **Encourage diverse human validators** by involving people from different backgrounds, disciplines, and communities in validation and audit processes to surface algorithmic blind spots.
- **Run regular "AI and Ethics" retrospectives** where teams review recent AI-influenced decisions, celebrate good catches, and identify areas where oversight needs tightening.

- **Prevent skill erosion** by rotating staff between AI-augmented roles and more traditional analytical or customer-facing work to keep core human capabilities sharp.
- **Create safe experimentation zones** through "AI office hours" or sandboxes where employees can test tools on non-critical tasks, building familiarity and surfacing failure modes before high-stakes deployment takes place.

These practices reinforce the message that leadership cares not only about using AI, but about using it wisely and humanely.

## Anticipating and Managing Risks[17]

Making common risks explicit helps leaders monitor for early warning signs instead of waiting for major incidents.

### Risk Management Matrix

| Risk | Symptom | Mitigation Strategy |
|---|---|---|
| **Automation Bias** | Users rarely challenge AI outputs | Require periodic overrides with documented rationale; training on critical evaluation |
| **Skill Erosion** | Declining human expertise over time | Role rotations and continuing education programs |
| **Ethical Drift** | Gradual normalization of harmful patterns | Regular ethics reviews, external audits, and escalation channels |
| **Misplaced Tasks** | AI used where ambiguity is high | Task-mapping workshops and governance approvals for AI use cases |

By naming these risks and linking them to observable symptoms, organizations can embed monitoring into governance processes and respond before trust or performance is severely damaged.

# Conclusion[18]

AI-human collaboration isn't a passing trend. It is becoming the defining operating model for AI-enabled organizations. Leaders who succeed in this environment recognize that their role is not simply to assign tasks, but to coordinate a complex relationship among data, algorithms, and people while balancing efficiency, ethics, and human meaning.

Building calibrated trust in AI, protecting distinctly human domains of ethics and interpretation, and measuring collaboration outcomes alongside financial results is how organizations produce new levels of agility, resilience, and creativity. The chapters that follow build on that foundation by extending these collaborative principles deeper into workflows, products, and customer experiences.

# Notes

[1] AI-human collaboration, joint problem-solving, and the benefits of pairing machine analysis with human judgment and values—as synthesized in the Abstract and learning outcomes—are examined in *Science*'s "AI can help humans find common ground in democratic deliberation"; *DeepMind Blog*'s "Human-Centred Mechanism Design with Democratic AI"; Mayo Clinic News Network's "Using AI in Radiology Clinical Practice"; and *The New York Times*' "Your A.I. Radiologist Will Not Be With You Soon."

[2] HITL design patterns and AI-human collaboration definitions are grounded in *Science*'s "AI can help humans find common ground in democratic deliberation"; and Mayo Clinic News Network's "Using AI in Radiology Clinical Practice."

[3] On augmented intelligence and workforce development in AI-rich environments, see *The New York Times*' "Your A.I. Radiologist Will Not Be With You Soon."

[4] Automation bias and ethical AI, including overreliance on AI and fairness concerns, are analyzed in *Patterns*' "Bringing AI Participation Down to Scale."

[5] For practical HITL frameworks and clinical oversight patterns, see Mayo Clinic News Network's "Using AI in Radiology Clinical Practice."

[6] Leadership roles in AI governance, calibrated trust, and democratic oversight of AI systems are explored in *DeepMind Blog*'s "Human-Centred Mechanism Design with Democratic AI."

[7] On organizational change considerations when integrating AI-human collaboration, see *The Art of Service Academy*'s "AI-Driven Business Transformation: Strategies and Frameworks."

[8] Reconceptualizing leadership as orchestrating human-AI systems—and the associated behaviors of curiosity, humility, and courage around AI—draws on *Science*'s "AI can help humans find common ground in democratic deliberation"; *DeepMind Blog*'s "Human-Centred Mechanism Design with Democratic AI"; and Mayo Clinic News Network's "Using AI in Radiology Clinical Practice."

[9] Calibrated trust, explainability requirements, bias monitoring, and AI capability labels are grounded in Mayo Clinic News Network's "Using AI in Radiology Clinical Practice"; *DeepMind Blog*'s "Human-Centred Mechanism Design with Democratic AI"; and *Science*'s "AI can help humans find common ground in democratic deliberation."

[10] *Science*'s "AI can help humans find common ground in democratic deliberation" sets out the task taxonomy separating routine processing, pattern detection, ethical judgment, and creative synthesis between AI and humans.

[11] Cultural framing of augmentation versus replacement, fear of automation, and narrative strategies for AI in the workplace are examined in *Patterns*' "Bringing AI Participation Down to Scale."

[12] The iterative human-AI problem-solving loop—including AI proposals refined by human probing and feedback—is developed in *Science*'s "AI can help humans find common ground in democratic deliberation."

[13] Mayo Clinic News Network's "Using AI in Radiology Clinical Practice" and *The New York Times*' "Your A.I. Radiologist Will Not Be With You Soon" supply the AI-assisted clinical decision support example, including override patterns, retraining on contextual variables, and preserved clinical judgment.

[14] Recruitment case study patterns of AI scoring plus human review, demographic bias audits, and diversity improvements appear in *Patterns*' "Bringing AI Participation Down to Scale"; and Jeffrey Dastin's "Amazon Scraps Secret AI Recruiting Tool That Showed Bias against Women" in *Reuters.*

[15] Collaboration success metrics—adoption, override frequency, bias reduction, productivity gains, literacy penetration, and their target ranges—are compiled from internal "AI and Data Analytics KPIs" documentation.

[16] Practical leadership actions—mandating explainable AI, institutionalizing HITL reviews, collaborative incentives, diverse validators, ethics retrospectives, role rotations, and safe experimentation zones—are drawn from *DeepMind Blog*'s "Human-Centred Mechanism Design with Democratic AI"; Mayo Clinic News Network's "Using AI in Radiology Clinical Practice"; *Patterns*' "Bringing AI Participation Down to Scale"; and internal "AI and Data Analytics KPIs" documentation.

[17] Key risks including automation bias, skill erosion, ethical drift, and misplaced tasks—along with their symptoms and mitigation strategies—are addressed in *DeepMind Blog*'s "Human-Centred Mechanism Design with Democratic AI"; and *Patterns*' "Bringing AI Participation Down to Scale."

[18] *Science*'s "AI Can Help Humans Find Common Ground in Democratic Deliberation" and *The New York Times*' "Your A.I. Radiologist Will Not Be With You Soon" support the conclusion's claims that AI-human collaboration is a defining operating model and a source of agility, resilience, and creativity.

## Key topics explored in this chapter:

- The AI Resistance Multiplier Effect
- Understanding Resistance
- Transparent Communication
- Early Wins Framework
- Resistance Heatmap
- Maturity Progression Roadmap: From Mobilization to Sustainability

# WAY 4

# Overcome Resistance to Change


## Abstract[1]

AI and analytics transformations inevitably trigger resistance, often rooted in deep-seated fears of job displacement, skill obsolescence, and the unsettling opacity of "black box" systems. This chapter provides you with proven methods to identify the root causes of resistance, foster empathetic communication, secure early stakeholder commitment, and transform skeptics into advocates through tangible results and psychological safety. It also illustrates how rigorous diagnostics, strategic stakeholder engagement, structured pilots, and longitudinal metrics can transition change management from a defensive activity into a core driver of successful AI adoption, while maintaining human dignity and sustaining organizational morale.


## Objective

After completing this chapter, you will be able to:

- Diagnose specific resistance archetypes (fear of the unknown, status quo bias, AI distrust, and skill-gap anxiety) using structured assessment methods.
- Design stakeholder-specific communication plans that address existential automation anxieties and clearly articulate the purpose and benefits of AI.
- Execute pilot programs that generate early AI wins, building credibility and momentum while minimizing perceived risk.
- Create psychological safety protocols that enable candid feedback on AI limitations and failures without fear of punishment.

- Monitor transformation health through adoption metrics, sentiment indicators, and resistance hotspots, and adjust strategies accordingly.
- Embed continuous improvement mindsets that ensure sustained AI readiness and adaptability beyond the initial rollout.

Ultimately, this chapter establishes resistance management as the fourth essential pillar of enterprise AI maturity—the point where skilled leadership transforms skepticism into collaborative momentum.

## Terms to Know

**AI Anxiety**[2] - An existential fear that intelligent automation threatens job security, professional identity, and human agency.

**Change Advisory Groups**[3] - Cross-functional teams that provide early feedback, represent stakeholder perspectives, and co-design AI implementations to reduce resistance and improve fit.

**Psychological Safety**[4] - An organizational climate in which employees can ask questions, express doubts, and report AI issues without fear of ridicule or reprisal.

**Resistance Archetypes**[5] - Common patterns of pushback, such as status quo bias, distrust of algorithms, and fear of skill gaps, that call for targeted responses rather than generic messaging.

**Stakeholder Engagement**[3] - The proactive, ongoing involvement of affected groups in shaping AI rollout decisions, communication, and training.

**Transformation Momentum**[6] - A self-reinforcing cycle in which early wins and positive experiences with AI build trust, increase adoption, and generate demand for further innovation.

## Introduction

When organizations undertake analytics and AI transformations, resistance is not the exception. It's the norm. Change disrupts familiar habits, pushes people outside their comfort zones, and in the age of AI can feel like a direct challenge to professional identity: Will the machine make my judgment irrelevant? The first task for any serious leader is to recognize resistance as a normal, predictable human response.

What separates organizations that stall from those that move ahead is not whether resistance appears, but how leadership anticipates it, interprets it, and redirects it into useful momentum. This chapter looks at resistance in the specific context of AI and advanced analytics, where the stakes often feel higher than in a typical IT rollout because these technologies are seen as carrying a form of autonomous intelligence.

## The AI Resistance Multiplier Effect[7]

Resistance to AI looks different from ordinary technology pushback because intelligent systems appear to think. When a traditional reporting system fails, employees usually blame the tool or the data. But when an AI model hallucinates or makes obviously poor recommendations, people are more likely to conclude that AI itself cannot be trusted. One visible failure can taint perceptions of the broader AI portfolio, causing category-level rejection instead of concern about a single tool. That is the AI resistance multiplier: one chatbot mistake or bad prediction can trigger rejection of multiple tools carrying the AI label if leaders fail to effectively intervene and do it in a timely manner.

**The psychological cascade** often looks like this:

Leaders need to treat early errors as learning moments, not embarrassing setbacks to hide. Clear communication about what went wrong, what was learned, and how the system was improved is essential for preserving trust.

## Understanding Resistance[5]

AI resistance rarely shows up as open revolt. More often, it appears as delayed adoption, quiet workarounds, or half-hearted participation in training. To respond well, leaders need a diagnostic lens that identifies the root causes instead of treating resistance as one vague, undifferentiated problem.

The Resistance Diagnostic Framework links each archetype to psychological triggers, observable symptoms, AI-specific expressions, and diagnostic questions.

## Resistance Diagnostic Framework

| Archetype | Psychological Trigger | Observable Symptoms | AI-Specific Manifestations | Diagnostic Question |
|---|---|---|---|---|
| **Fear of Unknown** | Existential threat to identity | Passive avoidance, absenteeism from training | "AI will automate my job entirely." | Do employees ask about severance or redeployment plans? |
| **Status Quo Bias** | Loss of familiar control | Workflow workaround, "shadow processes" | "Our spreadsheets work fine; why change?" | Are people exporting dashboards to Excel to "double check"? |
| **Distrust (Black Box)** | Algorithmic opacity + past failures | Rejection after a single visible AI error | "AI hallucinated once = useless forever." | Does one model mistake cause rejection of all AI tools? |
| **Skill Gap Anxiety** | Perceived incompetence | Training no-shows, helpdesk overload | "I don't understand model confidence scores." | Are basic interactions with AI tools failing or avoided? |

Leaders can use short, anonymous pulse surveys that include these diagnostic questions. The survey results can then be paired with manager interviews and helpdesk data to build a resistance map by business unit or role. Quarterly reassessment matters because these archetypes shift over time: fear often dominates early, distrust can spike after a visible AI error, and skill-gap anxiety tends to grow as tools become more complex.

## Transparent Communication[1]

Communication about AI-driven change often fails because it is generic and one-directional. Leaders may send a single email announcing a new platform with a slide deck on "the power of AI" and assume the job is done, while each stakeholder group actually brings distinct anxieties, expectations, and information needs.

The matrix that follows helps tailor messages to these differences, turning communication into a strategic tool for reducing resistance.

## Stakeholder Communication Matrix

| Stakeholder Group | Core Anxiety | Primary Message | Channel | Cadence | Success Metric |
|---|---|---|---|---|---|
| **C-Suite** | ROI and risk | "AI can deliver X% margin or risk reduction." | Executive briefings | Quarterly | Budget approval, sponsor-ship strength |
| **Middle Managers** | Team disruption | "AI frees 15 hours/week for strategic work." | Manager workshop s and playbooks | Monthly | Adoption compliance in their teams |
| **Frontline Users** | Job security | "AI removes drudgery; you focus on relation-ships." | Town halls, videos, and FAQs | Weekly | Training attendance, qualitative sentiment |
| **Power Users, Champions** | Influence and mastery | "Help us co-design the next AI features." | Slack, Teams, design sessions | Weekly, Daily | No. of feature suggestions and pilot participants |

Using a "What's In It For Me?" lens keeps messages concrete and relevant; for example, explaining to call center agents that AI will summarize interaction history so they can spend more time solving problems, not hunting for information. Testing draft messages with small focus groups from each audience helps validate emotional resonance and identify potential unintended triggers before wide release.

## Early Wins Framework[6]

Choosing the wrong "early AI" projects can seriously damage trust and progress. High-risk, high-complexity pilots that touch sensitive decisions—like key-customer pricing or employee performance scoring—can backfire if anything goes wrong, reinforcing every resistance archetype at once.

It's best to identify opportunities where value is visible but risk is both acceptable and manageable.

## Early Wins Selection Matrix

| Category | Example | Risk Level | Expected Impact | Timeline | AI Role |
|---|---|---|---|---|---|
| **Reporting Automation** | Monthly sales dash-boards | Low | 80% time savings | ~4 weeks | Data aggregation, visualization |
| **Predictive Alerts** | Inventory stockout prediction | Medium | 30% error/ rework reduction | ~8 weeks | Anomaly detection, forecasting |
| **Customer Personaliza-tion** | Next-best-offer suggestions | Low | 10-15% conversion uplift | ~6 weeks | Pattern matching, segmenta-tion |
| **Avoid Early: Complex Judgment** | Dynamic pricing, performance rankings | High | Uncertain, politically sensitive | 6+ months | Defer until trust and literacy established |

Leaders should select two or three early use cases across functions and deliberately choose teams with a mix of openness and constructive skepticism. Communicating expected outcomes upfront and sharing simple before-and-after stories helps build credibility and momentum.

## Resistance Heatmap[5]

Not all AI initiatives face the same level of resistance, so sequencing projects intelligently avoids overloading the organization's capacity for change. A conceptual "resistance heatmap" distinguishes zones of likely pushback from workers.

- **High-resistance zone:** AI that appears to replace complex human judgment (e.g., promotion decisions, compensation, disciplinary actions) and AI that touches identity-rich work (e.g., creative outputs without clear human credit).
- **Medium-resistance zone:** AI that changes daily workflows but clearly reduces repetitive tasks (e.g., automated case triage, scheduling assistants).
- **Low-resistance zone:** AI that invisibly improves existing processes (e.g., background anomaly detection, internal search relevance).

Mapping each proposed initiative onto this heatmap guides sequencing and engagement intensity, reserving high-resistance projects for later phases when foundational trust and Change Advisory Groups are in place.

# Case Studies

## Case Study #1: GE's Predix Platform Turnaround[7]

GE's initial rollout of the Predix IoT analytics platform in its industrial businesses encountered strong resistance from factory engineers, who felt the system had been imposed without understanding real maintenance workflows. Engineers perceived AI alerts as noisy, irrelevant, or politically motivated, leading to stalled adoption and reversion to older tools.

Leadership responded by forming "Engineer Councils" at key sites—groups of respected frontline engineers empowered to co-design dashboards, alert thresholds, and workflow integrations. These councils refined AI signals to focus on real failure patterns and on-the-ground context, and within six months adoption reached roughly two-thirds of the target audience, a milestone originally projected to take much longer. Former critics became vocal advocates once they saw their input visibly incorporated into the system design.

## Case Study #2: DBS Bank's AI Teller Transformation[8]

DBS Bank in Singapore introduced AI assistants to support branch tellers with routine transactions, customer lookups, and next-best-action prompts as part of a broader AI strategy. Initially, many tellers feared that the assistants would make their roles redundant or reduce them to blindly following machine recommendations.

To address these concerns, DBS designed pilots in which AI explicitly augmented rather than replaced teller work, with AI handling low-value tasks and tellers retaining responsibility for complex issues and relationship-building. The bank also invested heavily in staff retraining and repositioned teller roles toward advisory and relationship work. Over time, tellers reported higher job satisfaction as repetitive work declined and they spent more time on meaningful customer interactions.

## Case Study #3: Nubank's AI Customer Service Transformation (Brazil)[9]

Nubank, Latin America's largest digital bank, deployed AI-powered "agent copilot" tools and assistants to help handle surging customer inquiries across multiple markets. Customer service agents initially viewed AI as a direct competitor, worried that automation would make their roles increasingly obsolete.

Nubank created co-design forums where frontline agents collaborated with data scientists to design conversation flows, tone guidelines, and escalation rules. AI tools began drafting responses, but humans remained firmly in the loop to accept, edit, or reject suggestions. Within a few months, AI handled a large share of routine queries while complex or emotionally sensitive cases escalated to human agents, and satisfaction scores rose as response times fell and human interactions became more focused and empathetic.

# Success Metrics

Leaders need more than anecdotes to judge whether resistance is decreasing and adoption is healthy. This dashboard tracks key indicators across three phases of transformation.

## AI Transformation Health Dashboard[10]

| Phase | Key Metric | Target | Data Source | Intervention Trigger |
|---|---|---|---|---|
| **Mobilize Months 1-3** | Training completion | ≥ 80% of target audience | LMS/training records | Mandatory sessions if < 70% completion |
| **Accelerate Months 4-9** | Active usage | ≥ 70% within 90 days | Tool telemetry | Retrain or re-engage if < 50% usage |
| **Sustain Months 10-18** | Net Promoter Score (NPS) | ≥ +40 | Post-interaction surveys | Culture audit if NPS declines |
| **Ongoing** | Resistance tickets | < 5% of workforce | Help desk categorization | Targeted interventions for hotspots |

A 70% active usage target within 90 days is often a sign of healthy adoption: people are using tools but still exercising judgment about when they are appropriate. Near-100% usage can signal compliance without genuine buy-in, while strong NPS scores in later phases suggest that tools have shifted from “forced change” to perceived value.

## Maturity Progression Roadmap: From Mobilization to Sustainability[11]

Transformation does not happen all at once; organizations evolve through distinct phases that demand different leadership behaviors. Analysis of digital and AI transformations indicates that progress hinges on matching actions to phase-specific needs rather than generic "change programs."

## AI Transformation Maturity Roadmap

| Phase | Timeline | Leadership Focus | Diagnostic Milestone | Success Signal |
|---|---|---|---|---|
| **Mobilize** | 0-3 months (Q1) | Diagnose resistance and craft messaging | ≥ 80% of resistance patterns identified via surveys and interviews | Diagnostic survey completion > 90%; Change Advisory Groups formed |
| **Accelerate** | 4-9 months (Q2-Q3) | Execute pilots and share early wins | ≥ 70% adoption across at least 3 pilot initiatives | "Before/after" stories circulating; peer evangelists identified |
| **Sustain** | 10+ months (Q4+) | Embed culture and continuous improvement | NPS ≥ +40; resistance tickets < 5% of employees | Employees propose AI use cases and improvements unprompted |

Quarterly assessment helps leaders determine which phase they are truly in; if core diagnostics are not complete at Month 6, the organization is likely still in Mobilize even if tools are live. Each phase demands a leadership pivot: empathy and listening in Mobilize, disciplined execution and storytelling in Accelerate, and coaching and governance in Sustain. Red flags such as lagging adoption or declining NPS signal misaligned actions or unresolved friction.

# Practical Advice for Leaders[12]

- **Launch three-month pilot sprints** aimed at clearly defined benefits, such as 20 percent time savings in reporting, so the organization can see quick, credible wins.

- **Form cross-level Change Advisory Groups** that include skeptics, frontline staff, and supporters, and have them meet regularly to surface resistance hotspots and co-design improvements.
- **Mandate AI error reporting** as a positive behavior and treat good catches as contributions worth recognizing, reinforcing psychological safety.
- **Elevate diverse resistors into champion roles** by inviting them onto pilot teams, so any later support they offer carries more weight than a generic endorsement.
- **Run weekly "AI Office Hours"** where employees can bring their questions, frustrations, and ideas to a live support and coaching session.
- **Tie a portion of relevant bonuses** to a mix of adoption and satisfaction metrics, ensuring leaders care about both usage and user experience, not just deployment.

## Conclusion[13]

When workers resist AI, it isn't proof that something has gone wrong. It is evidence that people are paying attention to changes that matter. Leaders who dismiss resistance as obstruction miss the chance to learn from it. Leaders who diagnose patterns, tailor communication, sequence early wins, engage skeptics, and track progress with clear metrics can turn resistance from a barrier into a catalyst. In that kind of organization, intelligent systems do not weaken human judgment or trust. They strengthen both.

## Notes

[1] AI and analytics transformations face distinctive cultural and psychological resistance—and the emphasis on communication, early wins, and change management that runs through the Abstract and learning outcomes—is documented across Fountaine et al., "Building the AI-Powered Organization," *Harvard Business Review*; "AI Implementation Is a Classical Change Management," *Data Invision*; *McKinsey*'s "Bias Busters: The Cognitive Brakes on the Gen AI Accelerator"; and *Rewired: The McKinsey Guide to Outcompeting in the Age of Digital and AI.*

[2] AI Anxiety—the fear of job loss and diminished agency, grounded in prior automation experiences—is examined in "AI Implementation Is a Classical Change Management," *Data Invision*; and Attupurathu's "Organizational Resistance to AI: A Strategic Approach," LinkedIn.

[3] On Change Advisory Groups and stakeholder engagement in AI transformations, see Fountaine et al., "Building the AI-Powered Organization"; and "Innovative Human Capital: Applied Agentic AI for Organizational Transformation." Innovative Human Capital.

[4] Psychological safety in AI error reporting and learning is examined in *McKinsey & Company*'s "Bias Busters: The Cognitive Brakes on the Gen AI Accelerator"; and *Rewired: The McKinsey Guide to Outcompeting in the Age of Digital and AI.*

[5] Resistance archetypes—status quo bias, distrust of algorithms, skill-gap anxiety—and diagnostic approaches are mapped in Attupurathu's "Organizational Resistance to AI: A Strategic Approach"; and "Consequence of Resistance to Change on AI Readiness: Mediating ...." *SAGE Open.*

[6] Early low-risk, high-impact AI pilots, their selection criteria, and the resulting transformation momentum are emphasized in Fountaine et al., "Building the AI-Powered Organization"; and *Rewired: The McKinsey Guide to Outcompeting in the Age of Digital and AI.*

[7] The GE Predix example—initial resistance, creation of engineer councils, and subsequent adoption gains—appears in "Building the AI-Powered Organization" (case materials and licensing PDFs associated with HBR article R1904C); and "Building the AI-Powered Organization," The Case Centre.

[8] DBS Bank's AI teller and staff retraining initiatives—including the shift from transactional work to advisory roles—are documented in DBS Bank, *Digital Transformation Annual Report* 2022; "Singapore's Biggest Bank DBS to Cut 4,000 Roles as It Embraces AI," *BBC News*; and "Singapore's DBS Girds for AI as Tellers Morph Into Bankers." *Bloomberg.*

[9] Nubank's AI customer support "agent copilot" tools, co-design forums, and impact on satisfaction and response times are covered in "Empowering Customer Support Agents with Generative AI," Building Nubank; "Brazil's Nubank Is Leveraging OpenAI to Transform Customer Support," Weekly Fintech Pulse; and "Nubank Elevates Customer Experiences with OpenAI," OpenAI.

[10] AI Transformation Health Dashboard metrics—training completion, active usage, NPS, resistance tickets—and their target thresholds are examples drawn from internal company documents and "What It Really Takes to Scale Artificial Intelligence," *McKinsey Digital.*

[11] The Mobilize-Accelerate-Sustain maturity roadmap and its associated leadership focuses are laid out in *Rewired: The McKinsey Guide to Outcompeting in the Age of Digital and AI*; and Welch's "Overcoming Leadership Barriers in AI Adoption: A Socio-Technical Perspective."

[12] Practical leadership interventions—pilot sprints, Change Advisory Groups, AI Office Hours, incentive design, and "Resistance Radar" dashboards—are treated in Fountaine et al., "Building the AI-Powered Organization"; "AI Implementation Is a Classical Change Management"; and "Innovative Human Capital: Applied Agentic AI for Organizational Transformation."

[13] Fountaine et al., "Building the AI-Powered Organization"; and "Consequence of Resistance to Change on AI Readiness." *SAGE Open* support the concluding view that resistance, when surfaced and addressed, becomes a catalyst for stronger AI-enabled organizations.

## Key topics explored in this chapter:

- Why Skills Matter More Than Ever
- Mapping Current Skills and Defining Future Needs
- Prioritizing Gaps for Business Impact
- Designing Tailored Training Programs
- Embedding Continuous Learning and Knowledge Sharing
- Applying Technology to Scale Training
- Measuring Impact and Continuous Improvement

# WAY 5

# Close Skill Gaps Through Training


## Abstract[1]

As analytics and AI tools evolve, they reshape how data is gathered, how insights are produced, and how decisions are made, often faster than organizations can keep up. In that environment, both technical and human skill gaps widen quickly, making structured and repeatable upskilling a strategic requirement rather than a nice extra. This chapter offers a practical roadmap for identifying and closing workforce skill gaps through continuous, role-specific development. It introduces ways to assess current capabilities, anticipate emerging skill demands, and turn those insights into targeted learning initiatives that improve performance, confidence, and innovation in measurable ways.


## Objective

After completing this chapter, you will be able to:

- Map current AI and analytics skills and forecast emerging capability needs, using skills taxonomies and skills-graph technologies common in modern HR platforms.
- Prioritize learning investments by strategic value and risk exposure, acknowledging that skill gaps are now seen by a majority of employers as the top barrier to transformation.
- Design adaptive training programs matched to role, proficiency, and learning style, reflecting best practices from large-scale corporate learning initiatives.
- Embed continuous learning into day-to-day culture and work so that reskilling keeps pace with AI's rapid half-life of skills.

- Use AI-powered platforms to scale and personalize workforce development programs.
- Measure impact with clear metrics connecting learning to business outcomes, including productivity, innovation, and employee retention.

# Terms to Know

**AI Fluency**[2] **-** The ability of non-specialists to understand and work effectively with AI systems, including interpreting outputs and incorporating machine insights into decisions.

**Analytics Talent**[3] **-** Professionals who can turn raw data into usable insights across domains such as data science, engineering, statistics, and communication, including "citizen analysts" who combine domain knowledge with foundational analytics or AI skills.

**Continuous Learning**[4] **-** A practice where learning becomes routine and embedded in work, emphasizing ongoing adaptation and curiosity rather than one-time training events.

**Data Literacy**[5] **-** The ability to read, interpret, question, and communicate data responsibly and effectively.

**Prompt Engineering**[6] **-** The practice of crafting precise, context-aware prompts to elicit accurate and relevant responses from AI systems, with prompt quality increasingly tied to productivity and error reduction.

**Skills Development**[4] **-** Structured efforts to strengthen knowledge, technical capability, and professional judgment through education, mentoring, and practice, often combining coursework, coaching, and project-based learning.

**Training Programs**[4] **-** Designed learning interventions—courses, labs, bootcamps, or academies—that build specific competencies aligned with organizational strategy, often delivered through blended and microlearning formats.

**Upskilling**[5] **-** Expanding or strengthening capabilities so people can stay effective and employable as technology and business demands change, now a core response to AI-driven job transformation.

**Workforce Development**[7] **-** Long-term strategic investment in people's capabilities to ensure adaptability and sustained employability as technology and markets evolve.

# Introduction

The pace of AI advancement has outstripped organizations' capacity to reskill their workforce. Leading labor market analyses[1] project nearly two-fifths of core worker skills will transform by 2030, and most employees will need substantial training to remain effective. Tools rooted in machine learning and automation have certainly transformed how data is collected, analyzed, and communicated—yet many organizations still struggle to apply them effectively.

An organization's future resilience depends not just on owning advanced technology, but on nurturing a workforce that can reason about data, understand model boundaries, and balance automation with ethics. Surveys of global employers reveal skill gaps as the primary barrier to business transformation, ahead of factors like regulation or capital. Closing skill gaps through structured training isn't optional; it's the bedrock of sustainable digital transformation.

## Why Skills Matter More Than Ever[8]

Technical mastery and human judgment form a dual-competence model of readiness. AI can automate routine analysis, but it cannot replicate context, empathy, or cross-domain reasoning—the very strengths humans bring to complex decision-making. It is the skilled employee who decodes model outputs, spots ethical dilemmas, and translates numbers into narratives stakeholders can act on.

Without these abilities, organizations often underutilize or misapply even the most basic AI tools. Global employer surveys and industry research consistently identify a lack of AI skills and data literacy as a primary barrier to effective AI implementation. Moreover, as demand for AI and big-data skills continues to outpace supply, it's the balancing of technical and human competencies that emerges as the central design constraint for any AI strategy.

## Mapping Current Skills and Defining Future Needs[9]

The first leadership priority is visibility into what skills exist today and what will be needed tomorrow. Many organizations lack a coherent skills inventory; capabilities are inferred from job titles, résumés, or outdated training records rather than from direct evidence of performance, obscuring hidden strengths and emerging gaps.

Modern platforms increasingly support AI-enabled skills mapping by aggregating HR data, credentials, project histories, and work artifacts into living "skills graphs." These tools reveal clusters of strength, and they identify "deserts" where new capabilities like prompt engineering or AI risk management are missing. Effective mapping combines three lenses—current state, desired state, and gap distance—often visualized via heatmaps or radar charts. Skills-based approaches recommended in HR and strategy research encourage defining work by discrete capabilities rather than static roles, enabling precise training investments instead of generic courses.

## Prioritizing Gaps for Business Impact[10]

Once the skills map is built, leaders must determine which gaps matter most for performance and risk. Some skills are foundational, some differentiating, and others aspirational; so, not every gap warrants immediate investment. Here's one model you can use for evaluation:

## Skills Prioritization Model

| Priority Tier | Description | Business Link | Example Skills |
|---|---|---|---|
| **Critical** | Capabilities whose absence directly threatens current operations, safety, or compliance | Avoids regulatory fines, safety incidents, and quality failures | AI transparency, data privacy, secure analytics workflows |
| **Emergent** | Skills enabling innovation, new business models, or next-generation products | Opens new revenue streams and differentiation | Generative AI for coding, agentic workflow design, synthetic data methods |
| **Supportive** | Broader literacy and collaboration enablers that raise the baseline | Improves cross-functional collaboration and adoption | Data storytelling, stakeholder communication, basic AI literacy |

Aligning the training portfolio with strategy means prioritizing essential skills to stabilize risk, investing in emergent capabilities to drive future growth, and reinforcing supportive skills so technical expertise translates into trusted, widely adopted solutions. This portfolio logic mirrors how leading firms manage innovation investments, and it positions learning as a value-managed asset rather than a generic expense.

## Designing Tailored Training Programs[11]

With priorities in hand, attention turns to training design. One-size-fits-all learning rarely changes behavior; employees disengage if content feels too basic or too abstract, so effective programs are tailored by role, skill tier, and learning modality.

These role-specific pathways distinguish between executives (who need AI strategy, risk, and ethics), managers and analysts (who need to translate business questions into data questions), technical specialists (who need deep labs on ML and MLOps), and frontline staff (who need accessible AI and data literacy modules focused on safe use and simple prompts). Often training can be structured across foundational, applied, and advanced levels. Not everyone needs to become a machine learning expert, but everyone should develop practical AI fluency relevant to their roles and reinforced through blended, hands-on learning that's tied to real business challenges.

## Embedding Continuous Learning and Knowledge Sharing[12]

Training as a "series of events" is fragile; training as a "culture" is resilient. Learning and development research shows that organizations now prioritize continuous learning models because skills degrade quickly in AI-related domains, making it essential to embed learning into daily work rather than confining it to the HR calendar. Communities of practice create ongoing forums for data professionals and domain experts to share techniques and lessons learned, while coaching and mentoring accelerate skill development and spread tacit knowledge. Internal certifications and badging provide visible signals of capability tied to transparent skill methods, strengthening engagement and internal mobility. Knowledge repositories—such as wikis, code libraries, and pattern books—preserve institutional memory and support self-directed learning.

## Applying Technology to Scale Training[13]

AI is not just the subject of training; it's part of the training solution. Learning technologies, like those presented in the following table, increasingly use AI to personalize recommendations and assess learning at scale. These tools make it feasible to offer personalized development and align with evidence that employees engage more deeply when learning pathways reflect their roles, aspirations, and current proficiency.

## Training Benefit Matrix

| Technology | Core Capability | Organizational Benefit |
|---|---|---|
| **Learning Management System (LMS)** | Centralizes content delivery, tracking, and reporting | Provides visibility into participation and compliance |
| **Adaptive Learning Engine** | Adjusts content difficulty and pacing based on learner behavior and assessments | Increases engagement and reduces drop-off |
| **Virtual Labs and Sandboxes** | Provide safe experimental environments for analytics tools and datasets | Build confidence and skills before production use |
| **Microlearning Platforms** | Deliver short, just-in-time lessons via mobile or desktop | Support learning "in the flow of work" |
| **Skills Analytics Dashboards** | Correlate learning activities with performance and career outcomes | Enable evidence-based talent decisions and demonstrate ROI |

## Measuring Impact and Continuous Improvement[14]

Executives are more likely to support training when its impact is visible and quantifiable. Measurement should combine learning metrics (what people know) with performance metrics (what people do differently and how that affects results)

Consider the following training effectiveness metrics and the insight they provide.

### Training Effectiveness Matrix

| Metric | Target Range | Leadership Insight |
|---|---|---|
| **Skill Competency Gain** | ≥ 25% avg. improvement on post-training assessments | Indicates knowledge acquisition and basic mastery |
| **AI and Analytics Adoption Rate** | ~70% of eligible users regularly using key tools | Reflects confidence, usability, and trust |
| **Training Participation and Completion** | ≥ 80% of targeted staff completing assigned learning | Signals cultural engagement and access |
| **Productivity or Quality Lift** | 10-30% improvement in key process KPIs linked to trained teams | Connects learning directly to business outcomes |
| **Retention and Mobility** | Higher retention and internal movement for trained employees | Suggests learning is valued and career-relevant |

These metrics should feed continuous improvement loops such as curriculum reviews, content refresh cycles, and updated role-specific learning paths, creating a virtuous cycle where data about learning informs better design and, in turn, better performance.

## Case Studies

### Case Study #1: Financial Firm Boosts Analytics Speed[15]

A multinational bank discovered through AI-assisted skills mapping that many employees outside its analytics group already had intermediate coding and statistical skills but lacked formal recognition or guidance. Rather than hire exclusively from outside, the bank launched a "Citizen Analyst Academy" combining foundational AI literacy, data ethics modules, and hands-on labs focused on automating repetitive reporting tasks. Within eight months, analytics project backlog times dropped nearly 30% while internal promotion rates into analytics-adjacent roles rose.

### Case Study #2: Healthcare Network Builds Trust Through Literacy[16]

A regional healthcare system sought to implement predictive AI tools for readmission risk but faced clinician skepticism about "black-box" algorithms. Leaders responded with layered literacy programs in which clinicians learned how models were trained, how to interpret risk scores, and how to document overrides, co-taught by data scientists using anonymized real cases. Over time, readmissions declined while clinicians reported higher trust and more nuanced use of AI recommendations.

### Case Study #3: Tech Enterprise Drives Innovation via Peer Learning[17]

A mid-size technology firm created peer-led "Data Guilds" where volunteers from product, operations, and HR met weekly to share AI use cases and teach one another new techniques. The company supplied a basic curriculum and sandboxes but let guilds self-organize, and within a year a majority of new internal automation ideas and several prototype features originated from guild members.

## Success Metrics[18]

Beyond course-level measures, organizations increasingly track broader indicators of skills health. The metrics in the following table provide an important view of how well the organization is keeping pace with technological change.

### Skill Development Metrics

| Metric | Definition | Target Range | What Success Looks Like |
|---|---|---|---|
| **Skill Penetration Rate** | % of workforce with baseline AI/data literacy | 80-90% | Majority can interpret dashboards and recognize AI limits |
| **Innovation Origination Rate** | New ideas/prototypes from trained employees | 20%+ innovations | Training cohorts generate measurable business ideas |
| **Learning Agility Index** | Days from skill gap ID to training launch | <60 days | Rapid response to emerging needs such as new AI tools |
| **Cross-Functional Diffusion** | % of practices adopted outside origin team | 40%+ adoption | Practices spread |
| **Skills Obsolescence Rate** | % of skills needing refresh annually | <15% retraining | Proactive curriculum keeps workforce current |

Global benchmarks indicate that organizations with higher reskilling rates experience fewer disruptions during technological transitions.

## Practical Advice for Leaders[19]

- **Signal learning as a strategic priority** by publicly connecting upskilling goals to transformation milestones and performance expectations, in line with evidence that employers intend to prioritize reskilling in coming years.
- **Allocate protected time** by dedicating a defined percentage of working hours to learning activities so employees do not have to choose between training and "real work."
- **Invest** in both depth and breadth by funding deep training for key technical roles alongside broad literacy programs for the wider workforce.
- **Pair training with real projects** so major cohorts deliver scoped improvements or prototypes linked to new skills, reinforcing applied learning and business value.
- **Reward contributions to learning** by recognizing and rewarding mentors, course creators, and internal community leaders, and continuously refresh the curriculum (perhaps annually) to match technology trends and skills half-life in tech domains.

## Conclusion[20]

Closing skill gaps is the human counterpart to AI transformation. Technology investments alone won't deliver impact; real value emerges when people have the confidence and competence to use intelligent tools responsibly and creatively—giving organizations the resilience to adapt to new capabilities, regulations, and market shifts without the strain of constant disruption.

Organizations that neglect skills development risk creating "technology graveyards"—costly systems that are poorly understood, underused, or resisted by the very people they're meant to serve. By contrast, treating skills as strategic assets transforms training from a cost center into a compounding source of competitive advantage, innovation, and important employee engagement.

# Appendix

## AI Skills Quick-Start Checklist[21]

### 4-Week Launch | $150-250K First Year (Scalable)*

| Week | Phase | Actions |
|---|---|---|
| 1 | **DIAGNOSE** | ☐ AI skills audit (LinkedIn Skills/Degreed)<br>☐ Map top 3 critical gaps (use Step 2 Skill Prioritization Model)<br>☐ Benchmark vs WEF Future of Jobs 2025 |
| 2 | **PLAN** | ☐ Budget: 60% Critical / 30% Emergent / 10% Supportive<br>☐ Platforms: Coursera Business + LMS<br>☐ Design role paths (Step 3) |
| 3 | **PILOT** | ☐ Launch 50-person cohort (10 each role type)<br>☐ Assign 1:5 mentors + weekly CoPs<br>☐ Build 3 core metric dashboards (Step 6) |
| 4 | **SCALE** | ☐ Post-training assessments (target 25% gain)<br>☐ Calculate ROI (productivity vs cost)<br>☐ Expand to 200+ employees |

### Zero-Code Tool Stack (<$10K Setup)*

| Tool | Purpose | Cost* |
|---|---|---|
| **LinkedIn Learning** | Skills mapping | $399/user/year |
| **Coursera Business** | Content delivery | $400/user/year |
| **MS Viva Insights** | Progress tracking | Included w/ M365 |
| **Slack #AI-Guild** | Learning community | Existing licenses |

* Costs are for illustrative purposes only

# Notes

1 AI skill gaps as a strategic necessity—including the projection that a large share of workers will need training by 2030—is laid out in SHIFT eLearning's "The Urgent Case for Reskilling: Key Insights and Practical Tips to Get Started"; and *New Economy Skills: Unlocking the Human Advantage,* World Economic Forum.

2 AI fluency, role expectations, and the need for AI literacy are defined in *McKinsey*'s "Redefine AI Upskilling as a Change Imperative."

[3] "How Growth-Focused Organizations Can Meet the Needs of a Shifting Workforce," *Harvard Business Review* describes analytics talent categories, including citizen analysts.

[4] Continuous learning, skills development, and modern training program design are examined in Allied OneSource's "From Training to Transformation: How Continuous Learning Cultivates a Future-Ready Workforce."

[5] Data literacy and analytical thinking as priorities in the skills outlook, alongside the rise of upskilling for future jobs, are documented in *The Future of Jobs Report* 2025, World Economic Forum, and related skills-outlook coverage.

[6] Prompt engineering, generative AI, productivity gains, and error reduction are linked in Paylocity's "Upskilling for AI: Workforce Training Strategies."

[7] Workforce development as strategic capability building is developed in *New Economy Skills: Unlocking the Human Advantage*, World Economic Forum.

[8] The dual-competence model of technical and human skills, growth of AI skills demand, and skills as a constraint are set out in *New Economy Skills: Unlocking the Human Advantage*, World Economic Forum; and "Skills, 2025," *TD Magazine.*

[9] Skills mapping practices, skills graphs, and three-lens diagnostics (current, desired, gap) are covered in "How Growth-Focused Organizations Can Meet the Needs of a Shifting Workforce," *Harvard Business Review*; and World Economic Forum coverage on employers prioritizing reskilling.

[10] The Critical/Emergent/Supportive prioritization logic and employer views of skill gaps as top transformation barriers draw on *The Future of Jobs Report* 2025, World Economic Forum; and WEF commentary on employers prioritizing reskilling.

[11] Role-specific pathways, tiered skill levels, and blended learning tied to real business problems are addressed in Allied OneSource; McKinsey & Company's AI upskilling guidance; Paylocity's AI upskilling article; and World Economic Forum's jobs-of-the-future skills pieces.

[12] Continuous learning cultures, Communities of Practice, and internal certifications and badging are treated in SHIFT eLearning; Paylocity; and *New Economy Skills: Unlocking the Human Advantage*, World Economic Forum.

[13] AI-powered learning technology—adaptive engines, virtual labs, microlearning, and skills analytics dashboards—is surveyed in McKinsey & Company's AI upskilling blog; Allied OneSource; SHRM coverage on real-time upskilling; and *New Economy Skills: Unlocking the Human Advantage.*

[14] Measurement frameworks connecting learning metrics to business outcomes and adoption appear in Allied OneSource; Paylocity's AI upskilling strategies; and World Economic Forum reports on skills and growth.

[15] Internal academies and citizen-analyst programs that reduce backlogs and increase internal promotions are illustrated in Davenport and Bean's "Why Companies That Wait to Upskill Their Workforce Will Struggle," *Harvard Business Review.*

[16] Literacy programs in clinical AI adoption, model interpretation, and override documentation are examined in Rajkomar et al., "Machine Learning in Medicine," New England Journal of Medicine.

[17] Peer-led data guilds and cross-functional innovation via communities are explored in Allied OneSource and related organizational learning case examples.

[18] Portfolio-level skills metrics—penetration, learning agility, diffusion, and obsolescence—are drawn from SHIFT eLearning; SHRM real-time upskilling articles; Paylocity; and World Economic Forum skill-focused reports.

[19] Practical leadership advice on signaling priority, modeling learning, allocating time, pairing training with projects, and curriculum refresh is drawn from World Economic Forum's reskilling guidance; McKinsey & Company's AI upskilling perspective; SHRM's coverage of learning time allocation; Paylocity's AI workforce strategies; and "Skills, 2025," *TD Magazine.*

[20] The conclusion's claims about "technology graveyards," skills as strategic assets, and links between reskilling and reduced disruption rest on *The Future of Jobs Report* 2025, World Economic Forum; and *New Economy Skills: Unlocking the Human Advantage.*

[21] Short-horizon launch plans, zero-code tool stacks, and upskilling urgency are addressed in Davenport and Bean's "Why Companies That Wait to Upskill Their Workforce Will Struggle," *Harvard Business Review.*

Diverse development teams are better at identifying biases, improving transparency, and enhancing the trustworthiness of AI systems.

*Empirical Software Engineering*

"The Role of Team Diversity in AI Systems Development"

Santos et al.

March 2026

## Key topics explored in this chapter:

- The Cost of Role Ambiguity in Analytics and AI
- Four Principles for Defining Roles Well
- Mapping the Analytics and AI Organization
- Using RACI to Clarify Project Responsibilities
- Role Evolution in an AI-Enabled Workforce
- Special Consideration: Cross-Border and Multi-Region Teams

# WAY 6

# Define Roles and Responsibilities


## Abstract[1]

Clear roles and responsibilities are essential to trustworthy analytics and AI work. This chapter explains how organizations can reduce friction, speed delivery, and improve accountability by defining who owns which decisions, tasks, interfaces, and outcomes. It also shows how role charters, RACI matrices, and planned role evolution can help organizations move from informal analytics work to a more disciplined operating model. The central idea is simple: when people know what they own and how their work connects, analytics and AI become more reliable, scalable, and useful.


## Objective

After completing this chapter, you will be able to:

- Describe the core roles that make up a healthy analytics and AI function and how they fit together.
- Use RACI matrices to remove confusion about who is responsible, accountable, consulted, and informed for key tasks.
- Create role charters that give people clear scope, deliverables, and decision rights.
- Design role evolution paths so jobs keep up with AI automation and growing organizational maturity.
- Put in place governance and communication practices that keep roles aligned as the business changes.
- Track role clarity with simple, meaningful metrics that link directly to delivery, collaboration, and innovation.

## Terms to Know

**Accountability**[2] - Clear ownership of outcomes for a given area or decision, including the authority to make trade-offs and escalate issues.

**AI Ethicist**[2] - A role focused on identifying, assessing, and mitigating fairness, transparency, and societal risks in AI systems.

**AI Governance**[2] - The structures, policies, and practices that ensure AI is developed and used in a way that is ethical, compliant, and aligned with organizational values.

**Analytics Governance**[3] - The oversight of analytics practices, including standards, data policies, and processes that uphold quality and trust.

**Data Stewardship**[3] - The day-to-day responsibility for maintaining data quality, lineage, and compliant use across the organization.

**Organizational Alignment**[2] - The degree to which individual and team roles support and reinforce broader business strategy.

**RACI Matrix**[4] - A Responsibility Assignment tool that defines who is Responsible, Accountable, Consulted, and Informed for specific tasks or decisions.

**Role Charter**[4] - A one-page document that spells out a role's purpose, scope, key outputs, interfaces, and success measures.

**Role Evolution**[4] - The planned progression of a role over time as technology, skills, and organizational strategy change.

## Introduction[5]

Many analytics and AI failures are not technical failures at all. The models run, the dashboards refresh, and the proofs of concept look promising. The breakdown often happens between people: no one owns an important handoff, several teams assume someone else will validate the output, or everyone claims success while problems are quietly blamed on "the data."

As organizations introduce AI-assisted workflows, those risks become more serious:

- If a system recommends an action, who is accountable for acting on it?
- If AI-generated output contains subtle bias or poor reasoning, who is responsible for detecting and addressing it?

Without clear answers, organizations accumulate risk while teams work in avoidable friction. Role clarity transforms that friction into flow. The objective is to create a dependable and trustworthy operating rhythm.

## The Cost of Role Ambiguity in Analytics and AI[6]

Role ambiguity shows up in analytics and AI work in familiar and expensive ways. In fact, leaders often recognize the symptoms before they can diagnose the cause:

- **Duplicated work:** Different teams clean the same dataset or build similar models in parallel because ownership was never agreed upon.
- **Accountability gaps:** No one feels responsible for verifying an AI model's behavior in production, so issues emerge only when a customer or regulator complains.
- **Bottlenecks and rework:** Reports bounce between teams because it's unclear who can sign off on assumptions or definitions.

In AI-heavy environments, this ambiguity carries an important twist. Automated systems can now draft code, generate reports, and propose actions. If the "human in the loop" is not clearly defined—by role, not just by hope—organizations risk either over trusting the system or ignoring it entirely. In both cases, investments can underperform.

Leaders who treat role clarity as a one-time HR exercise miss the point. It is a strategic lever that shapes how quickly analytics moves from data to decision, how safely AI scales, and how confidently employees engage with intelligent tools.

## Four Principles for Defining Roles Well[7]

Effective role design rests on four simple yet demanding principles.

- **Principle #1 - Scope:** Scope answers, "What should this role actually do?" It defines the core responsibilities, typical deliverables, and decisions that sit with a person in that role. When scope is fuzzy, people either overreach into others' territory or underperform because they fear stepping on toes.
- **Principle #2 - Accountability:** Accountability clarifies who owns outcomes, not just activities. Two people can contribute to a dashboard, but only one person should be accountable for its overall correctness and usefulness. Without this clarity, blame shifts and decisions stall when trade-offs are needed.

- **Principle #3 - Interfaces:** This principle describes how roles connect—where they hand work off, where they need feedback, and where they must coordinate. In analytics and AI, interfaces between technical roles (engineers, scientists) and business roles (analysts, product leaders) are particularly important. Tight interfaces reduce rework and shorten cycle times.
- **Principle #4 - Evolution:** Evolution acknowledges that roles are not static. As AI automates manual tasks and the organization matures, roles must shift upward toward more judgment, design, and oversight. Designing these shifts in advance helps avoid talent gaps and morale issues when job content changes.

Many organizations find it useful to embed these four principles into their role charter templates, so every role description forces a conversation about scope, accountability, interfaces, and how the role will evolve over the next 12-18 months.

### Role Charter Template

A practical role charter can answer five questions:

- **Purpose:** Why does this role exist?
- **Scope:** What key work and decisions belong here?
- **Outputs:** What deliverables or outcomes is the role expected to produce?
- **Interfaces:** Which roles must this person work with closely?
- **Success Measures:** How will effectiveness be judged?

Organizations that embed these questions and their answers into role charters usually create better alignment than organizations relying on job titles alone.

## Mapping the Analytics and AI Organization[8]

A mature analytics and AI function is not built around a single "data team." It is an ecosystem of roles that together move from raw data to sustained business impact. The following table outlines common role clusters and how they fit together in practice.

## Ecosystem of Roles

| Role Cluster | Primary Function | Key Contributions | Typical "Customer" |
|---|---|---|---|
| **Executive Sponsor** | Set strategic direction and priorities | Approves portfolio, secures budget, removes roadblocks | Board, C-suite, business units |
| **Chief Data/AI Officer** | Lead data and AI capabilities | Sets standards, builds teams, oversees governance | Executive sponsor, IT, business |
| **Data Engineer** | Build and maintain data infrastructure | Pipelines, warehousing, data reliability | Data scientists, analysts |
| **Data Scientist** | Develop models and advanced analytics | Predictive models, experiments, optimization | Analysts, product teams |
| **Data Analyst** | Translate data into business insights | Dashboards, KPI tracking, exploratory analysis | Business leaders, frontline teams |
| **Business Analyst** | Capture requirements and define use cases | Problem framing, user stories, acceptance criteria | Product owners, business sponsors |
| **Data Steward** | Govern data quality and compliance | Data standards, lineage, access control | CDO, legal, risk & compliance |
| **AI Ethicist / Risk Lead** | Oversee ethical and responsible AI use | Bias reviews, impact assessments, escalation pathways | CDO, legal, executive sponsor |

This mapping does two things. First, it helps leaders see where they have coverage and where there are gaps; for example, organizations with strong engineers and scientists but no clear steward or ethicist role. Second, it makes it easier to define interfaces: the analyst relies on the scientist for model outputs, and the scientist relies on the engineer for stable pipelines.

A simple exercise is to print this table and ask each team to mark where they see themselves today. Many organizations discover that multiple people are informally playing the same role under different titles, or that nobody is playing one of the roles at all.

## Using RACI to Clarify Project Responsibilities[9]

Even with roles defined at a high level, confusion often resurfaces at the project level. This is where a RACI matrix is helpful. Instead of assuming everyone knows what they own, the project team explicitly assigns who is **R**esponsible, **A**ccountable, **C**onsulted, and **I**nformed for each key task.

The example below is a RACI from a customer churn prediction initiative. The exact roles may vary, but the pattern is widely applicable.

## Example RACI Matrix

| Task | Data Engineer | Data Scientist | Business Analyst | Analytics Leader | Executive Sponsor |
|---|---|---|---|---|---|
| **Define Business Problem** | I | C | R/A | C | C |
| **Prepare and Validate Data** | R/A | C | C | I | I |
| **Build and Test Model** | C | R/A | C | I | I |
| **Review Ethical and Bias Risk** | I | C | I | A | C |
| **Design Dashboards and Reports** | I | C | R/A | C | I |
| **Deploy to Production** | R/A | C | I | C | I |
| **Review Results and Iterate** | C | R | R | A | I |

Two things matter most when using this tool. First, every row should have exactly one "A"—the person ultimately accountable for that step. Second, the team should revisit the matrix when scope changes. When AI agents are introduced for code generation or report drafting, they can be listed as "R" for certain tasks, but a human role must always hold the "A."

Embedding the habit of building a RACI at the start of each major project dramatically reduces finger-pointing later. It also gives executives a clear line of sight into who to support and who to hold accountable for project outcomes.

## Role Evolution in an AI-Enabled Workforce[11]

AI tools are quietly changing what "junior" and "mid-level" work looks like. Tasks that once filled early-career job descriptions—such as basic data cleaning, simple SQL queries, or routine slide production—are now partially or fully automated. If leaders do not proactively redesign roles, they risk leaving people stuck in work that no longer adds much value or feeling threatened by tools rather than empowered by them.

A more strategic response is to shift roles upward along the value chain. For example:

- Junior data analysts move from manually creating reports to validating AI-generated outputs, refining prompts, and learning how to interpret subtle model behavior.
- Mid-level analysts take on more responsibility for experiment design, storytelling, and change management around the firm's analytics initiatives.
- Senior leaders focus increasingly on orchestration: setting direction, designing portfolios of use cases, and overseeing important AI risk.

A simple career path for data analysts in this context might look like something this:

- **Level 1 - Analyst (AI-assisted):** Builds dashboards, validates AI-generated analyses, learns to ask better questions.
- **Level 2 - Senior Analyst:** Designs use cases, shapes experiments, partners closely with business stakeholders.
- **Level 3 - Analytics Lead:** Guides teams, resolves trade-offs, steers portfolio-level priorities, works with executives on analytics strategy.

Making these paths explicit and tying them to learning opportunities helps people see AI as a way to grow their impact rather than as a threat to their relevance.

# Case Studies

## Case Study #1: Multinational Manufacturer Cuts Delays by 40%[12]

A global manufacturing firm invested heavily in analytics platforms but kept missing critical delivery deadlines. Root cause analysis revealed that data engineers and data analysts were constantly disputing who owned data preparation versus business logic. Engineers claimed analysts were "sneaking transformations into dashboards," while analysts complained that engineers "never finished the pipelines on time."

The chief data officer convened a cross-functional workshop and mapped out RACIs for the firm's twelve highest-impact analytics projects. Role charters were created for engineers, analysts, and project leads, with clear accountability lines. Weekly 30-minute standups focused on interfaces and handoffs rather than rehashing blame.

Within nine months, on-time delivery of analytics projects improved by roughly 40%. Business stakeholders reported far fewer surprises, and the analytics team regained credibility as a reliable partner rather than a bottleneck. Role clarity, not new technology, delivered the breakthrough.

## Case Study #2: Healthcare Balances Centralized Governance and Local Insight[13]

A regional healthcare system had created a centralized data team to standardize metrics and improve quality. While the data was now more consistent, clinicians in different departments felt that analytics lacked nuance. They complained that "headquarters doesn't understand what happens on the ward" and often worked around the central dashboards with their own spreadsheets.

To address this, the organization created a hybrid model. Core roles—data stewards, engineers, and a small group of data scientists—remained centralized under the chief data officer. At the same time, each clinical service line received an embedded analyst who reported both to the service line leader and the central analytics function. RACI matrices made clear that the central team owned definitions and quality, while embedded analysts owned local translation and adoption.

Over the next year, data quality scores improved, but so did usage. Clinicians reported that reports finally reflected their reality, and adoption of predictive tools for readmission risk and staffing decisions increased significantly. The balance between central control and local relevance was sustained through clear roles, not just better tools.

## Case Study #3: SaaS Company Reinvents Junior Roles in the Age of AI[14]

A mid-sized SaaS firm introduced AI-assisted coding and reporting tools that could draft SQL queries and generate standard dashboards in minutes. Senior leaders were excited, but junior analysts quietly worried that the work they had been hired to do would no longer be needed. Turnover began to tick up, and morale wavered.

Rather than allowing fear to fester, the analytics leader redesigned junior roles as "AI collaboration specialists." These analysts were trained in prompt engineering, intervention points for AI-generated code, and the basics of bias detection in models. Role charters were updated to emphasize reviewing AI outputs, exploring edge cases, and working directly with product managers to frame better questions.

Within six months, the team had doubled its throughput of analysis without increasing headcount. Innovation rates—measured by the number of new ideas tested per quarter—increased significantly. Most importantly, junior staff reported feeling more valuable, not less, because they were now closer to decision-making rather than buried in repetitive tasks.

# Success Metrics

Role clarity is not an abstract virtue; it has tangible performance signatures. Leaders can track a small set of metrics to see whether roles are "healthy" and functioning as intended.

## Measuring the Health of Roles and Responsibilities[15]

| Metric | What It Indicates | Healthy Range | Warning Sign |
|---|---|---|---|
| **Project On-Time Delivery** | Handoff clarity and decision speed | ≥ 80-85% of projects | Repeated delays without clear cause |
| **Stakeholder Satisfaction** | Perceived usefulness of analytics | ≥ 4.2 / 5 on surveys | Complaints about relevance or clarity |
| **Rework Rate** | Degree of duplication and misaligned expectations | ≤ 15% of effort | High percentage of redo work |
| **Cross-Functional NPS** | Quality of collaboration across roles | ≥ 70 (promoter-heavy) | Fragmented relationships, finger-pointing |
| **Role Clarity Survey Score** | How well people understand their own and others' roles | ≥ 85-90% positive responses | Frequent "I'm not sure who owns this." |

Tracking these metrics quarterly provides an early warning system. If on-time delivery drops or rework rises, for example, leaders can revisit RACIs and charters rather than blaming "the culture" in the abstract.

For organizations that want to track progress over time, it can be helpful to think about role clarity in stages. The table that follows offers a compact maturity model that leaders can use to self-assess and set targets. Leaders can use this model as a simple diagnostic in executive offsites or quarterly business reviews, asking, "Where are we now, and what would it take to move one stage up over the next year?"

### Role Clarity Maturity Model[16]

| Maturity Stage | Characteristics | Typical Symptoms | Priority Actions |
|---|---|---|---|
| **Ad Hoc** | Roles defined informally, vary by project | Frequent surprises, firefighting, rework | Run role clarity survey; pilot RACI on 1-2 projects |
| **Defined** | Core roles and high-level responsibilities documented | Less chaos, but many exceptions | Create role charters; standardize RACIs for major initiatives |
| **Integrated** | Roles, RACIs, and charters used consistently across teams | Faster decisions, fewer ownership disputes | Link role clarity to metrics and performance reviews |
| **Optimized** | Roles regularly revisited as AI and strategy evolve | Organization adapts quickly to change | Annual role evolution workshops; integrate with talent and AI governance roadmaps |

## Practical Advice for Leaders[17]

Leaders who want to move from theory to practice can focus on a short list of concrete moves over the next few months. Each of the actions below can be adapted to the size and maturity of the organization.

- **Run a brief role clarity survey.** Ask people whether they understand their own responsibilities, who they depend on, and where they see overlaps or gaps in analytics and AI work.
- **Map current roles against the core role table.** Identify where you have strong coverage, where roles are thin or

duplicated, and where important responsibilities (such as stewardship or ethics) have no clear owner.

- **Build a RACI for 2-3 flagship projects.** Use one or two important analytics or AI initiatives to pilot RACIs that clarify who is Responsible, Accountable, Consulted, and Informed for each major task.
- **Draft role charters for key roles.** Start with the roles most involved in high-value projects, writing concise charters that spell out purpose, scope, decision rights, interfaces, and success measures.
- **Host a cross-functional town hall.** Present the updated role model, explain how it will improve delivery and reduce friction, and invite questions so people can see themselves in the new structure.
- **Train managers on using RACIs and charters.** Equip frontline leaders to treat these artifacts as everyday tools in project planning, performance conversations, and onboarding.
- **Make RACI creation a standard kickoff task.** Require every significant analytics or AI project to document a RACI at the start and review it whenever scope changes.
- **Review and refresh role charters annually.** Revisit charters at least once a year, paying particular attention to how AI tools are changing day-to-day work and shifting responsibilities.
- **Add role clarity metrics to business reviews.** Track on-time delivery, rework, collaboration scores, and role clarity survey results alongside financial and operational metrics, and use changes as signals to adjust roles and interfaces.

By treating these steps as an ongoing leadership discipline rather than a one-off redesign, organizations stay ahead of both technological change and internal complexity.

## Special Consideration: Cross-Border and Multi-Region Teams[18]

Role clarity becomes even more important—and more delicate—when analytics and AI teams are distributed across countries or regions. Time zones, cultural norms, and local regulations can all influence how roles are interpreted and how decisions are made.

Three practical adjustments help:

- **Local co-owners, global standards:** Keep global definitions for core roles and governance (for example, what a data steward or AI ethicist is responsible for), but explicitly name local co-owners for region-specific execution. This balances consistency with responsiveness to local realities.
- **Time-zone-aware RACIs:** When building RACIs for cross-border projects, factor in who is realistically available to make decisions at different hours. In some cases, this means designating a "follow-the-sun" pattern of responsibility and clearly documenting escalation paths.
- **Cultural translation of charters:** Ensure role charters are not only translated linguistically but also contextualized culturally. In some regions, for instance, people may be reluctant to challenge decisions without explicit permission written into their role expectations.

By explicitly addressing these cross-border dynamics, organizations reduce the risk that carefully designed roles will be interpreted differently—or ignored entirely—once they cross borders.

## Conclusion[19]

Analytics and AI are, at their very core, human systems supported by technology. When roles are vague, even the best tools cannot deliver sustained value. When roles are clear, work flows more smoothly, risks are caught earlier, and teams move with greater confidence.

Defining roles and responsibilities isn't glamorous work. It requires careful listening, tough trade-offs, and a willingness to make implicit expectations explicit. Yet, it is precisely this work that separates organizations that "dabble" in analytics from those that turn data and AI into a durable competitive advantage.

## Notes

[1] Organization design, role clarity, and cross-functional AI roles—the themes running through this chapter's Abstract—are developed in Davenport's *The AI Advantage*; Brynjolfsson and McAfee's *The Second Machine Age*; and McKinsey's AI state-of-practice surveys.

[2] Definitions of Accountability, AI Ethicist, AI Governance, and Organizational Alignment used here synthesize common language from AI-governance and responsible-AI guidance on clear accountability, ethical oversight, and alignment with values/strategy, as found in relevant AI governance glossaries and practitioner guides (e.g., McKinsey responsible AI frameworks).

[3] Analytics Governance and Data Stewardship—framing stewardship as day-to-day data care (quality, lineage, policy enforcement) within broader governance—are defined in data-governance glossaries and practitioner guides.

[4] RACI Matrix, Role Charter, and Role Evolution—integrating responsibility-assignment guidance and operating-model practices for ownership clarity, actionable charters, and planned evolution—are defined in standard project-management and role-design resources.

[5] The Introduction's focus on failures in "the messy space between people" and explicit accountability for AI-assisted decisions aligns with McKinsey's AI surveys and Davenport's emphasis on governance and human oversight in *The AI Advantage.*

[6] Role ambiguity symptoms and "human in the loop" risks in AI deployment are illustrated through case discussions of deployment challenges and risk-management gaps in The State of AI in 2023: Generative AI's Breakout Year, *McKinsey.*

[7] The four principles of scope, accountability, interfaces, and evolution echo operating-model and role-design frameworks, consistent with Davenport's prescriptions for durable AI organizations, as developed in *The AI Advantage.*

[8] McKinsey's guidance on data/analytics leadership roles and Davenport's taxonomy of AI responsibilities together shape the core role map—CDO, data engineer, data scientist, data steward, AI ethicist, and related positions—reflecting patterns in AI organization and governance literature.

[9] RACI matrices for analytics and AI initiatives—formalizing Responsible, Accountable, Consulted, and Informed roles—follow standard project-management practice as set out in responsibility-assignment guidance.

[10] Concise, outcome-focused role charters as living documents reflect talent and organizational design practices in agile and AI-enabled organizations, as described in agile role-design resources.

[11] Role evolution and the shift of junior work toward higher-judgment tasks are grounded in Brynjolfsson and McAfee's argument to "race with machines" in *The Second Machine Age*; and in Davenport's view of AI augmenting knowledge workers in *The AI Advantage.*

[12] Case Study #1's pattern—resolving analytics bottlenecks by clarifying ownership using RACIs and charters rather than adding tools—draws on McKinsey AI case studies.

[13] A centralized-plus-embedded hybrid structure to support better predictive tool uptake in healthcare is the pattern in Case Study #2; see clinical analytics literature.

[14] Redesigning junior roles into "AI collaboration specialists"—as in Case Study #3—reflects recommendations to center new human roles on supervising, steering, and partnering with AI systems, as argued in Brynjolfsson and McAfee's *The Second Machine Age.*

[15] Role health metrics—project delivery, satisfaction, rework, NPS, and clarity scores—align with KPIs in analytics program management and AI value-realization dashboards, as reflected in industry AI surveys.

[16] The role clarity maturity model (Ad Hoc to Optimized) parallels maturity frameworks in AI governance and operating-model assessments, including McKinsey's stages of AI adoption, as documented in *McKinsey* AI adoption frameworks.

[17] A phased implementation roadmap—diagnose/map, design/communicate, embed/evolve—synthesizes change-management steps drawn from AI transformation case studies. This sequencing aligns with standard practice in AI transformation work.

[18] Cross-border and multi-region teams, shaped by time zones, regulations, and culture, are discussed with reference to global operating models and distributed analytics functions in global operating-model resources.

[19] The Conclusion's framing of analytics and AI as "human systems supported by technology" draws on Davenport's *The AI Advantage*; and Brynjolfsson and McAfee's *The Second Machine Age*.

65% of employees worry they will be replaced by someone who knows AI better, and 61% worry AI might reduce how others perceive their value.

*Harvard Business Review*

"Why AI Adoption Stalls, According to Industry Data"

Eatough et al.

February 2026

## Key topics explored in this chapter:

- The Strategic Value of Diversity in Analytics and AI
- Integrating Inclusion Without Compromising Your Standards
- Building an Inclusive Culture of Belonging
- Addressing Challenges and Resistance
- Diversity and Inclusion Maturity in Analytics and AI

# WAY 7
# Champion Diversity


## Abstract[1]

In analytics and AI, diversity is not only a values issue. It is also a performance, innovation, and risk issue. This chapter explains how diverse and inclusive teams improve decision quality, reduce blind spots, and help organizations build fairer, more trustworthy systems. It also shows how inclusion turns representation into real contribution by strengthening psychological safety, widening access to opportunity, and embedding diverse perspectives into hiring, promotion, governance, and model review. When diversity is treated as a core capability instead of a side initiative, organizations make better decisions and build AI systems people trust.


## Objective

After completing this chapter, you will be able to:

- Articulate the business and ethical case for diversity in analytics and AI teams.
- Identify key forms of diversity (cognitive, demographic, experiential) and how they strengthen model quality and decision-making.
- Design inclusive hiring and promotion practices that expand the talent pool without diluting standards.
- Build team cultures of belonging and psychological safety that unlock the full contribution of diverse talent.
- Integrate diversity into AI governance and bias mitigation processes.
- Track diversity and inclusion with meaningful metrics linked to innovation, fairness, and business outcomes.

# Terms to Know

**Algorithmic Bias**[2] - Systematic and unfair errors in model predictions that disproportionately affect certain groups, often due to skewed data, unrepresentative features, or design choices that encode historical inequities.

**Cognitive Diversity**[3] - Differences in how people think, problem-solve, and approach decisions, shaped by their experiences, disciplines, and perspectives; associated with better performance in complex, non-routine tasks.

**Diversity**[4] - The presence of meaningful differences in identity, background, and perspective (for example, gender, ethnicity, age, socio-economic background, professional path) within a team or organization.

**Inclusion**[5] - The extent to which people feel respected, valued, and able to contribute fully, regardless of their background or identity, often measured through belonging, voice, and perceived fairness.

**Psychological Safety**[6] - A shared belief that it is safe to speak up with ideas, questions, or concerns without fear of embarrassment or punishment.

**Representation Bias**[2] - A form of algorithmic bias that arises when training data does not adequately represent all relevant groups, as seen in facial recognition systems with markedly higher error rates for darker-skinned women than for lighter-skinned men.

**Talent Pipeline**[7] - The pool of potential candidates for current and future roles, shaped by sourcing strategies, employer brand, and development programs, and a central focus of diversity strategies.

**Tokenism**[5] - Superficial efforts to appear diverse—such as hiring or promoting a small number of underrepresented individuals—without giving them real influence, support, or equitable access to opportunities.

# Introduction

In analytics and AI, diversity is often framed as either a moral commitment or a brand concern. Both matter. But for leaders accountable for performance and risk, diversity is also a hard-edged business and safety lever: companies with more diverse executive teams are significantly more likely to deliver above-average profitability and stronger value creation, and organizations with diverse leadership tend to generate a larger share of their revenue from innovation compared with peers that have less diverse teams.

Inside analytics teams, the mechanism is straightforward. Diverse teams see around corners that homogeneous teams miss, challenge assumptions others treat as obvious, and are more likely to anticipate how models will behave for different demographic groups. People who recognize themselves or their communities in the data are better positioned to ask, "Who does this fail for?," especially in areas like lending, hiring, pricing, and healthcare where AI systems have already shown disparate error rates across groups. In a world where AI systems shape consequential decisions, the ability to anticipate harm is not a "nice-to-have"; it is a core competency.

## The Strategic Value of Diversity in Analytics and AI[8]

The business value of diversity goes beyond representation. In analytics and AI, it shows up in better problem framing, stronger innovation, and earlier detection of risk. Cognitive diversity helps teams challenge default assumptions, test alternatives, and notice where data, models, or decisions skew results.

Research on facial recognition and other AI systems has shown how unbalanced data and narrow design assumptions produce much worse outcomes for some groups than for others. Those failures are not just technical. They reflect missing perspectives during design, testing, and review. Diverse teams pressure-test those blind spots early and often.

Diversity also creates context advantages. Teams with broader cultural, linguistic, and professional experience are more likely to catch nuances in customer language, local behavior, and stakeholder expectations. This improves product relevance, change management, and adoption.

## Integrating Inclusion Without Compromising Your Standards[9]

One of the most common executive concerns is the false choice between diversity and excellence. In practice, inclusive hiring and promotion do not lower standards. They make it more likely that standards apply fairly and consistently. But that means reducing noise in the process. Practical strategies include:

- **Auditing and revising job descriptions** to remove unnecessary degree requirements, narrow "culture fit" language, and vague references to "top schools," and instead focusing on demonstrable skills, outcomes, and learning capacity.
- **Using structured interviews** and, where feasible, anonymized resumes in early screening, supported by standardized scoring rubrics, to keep evaluation focused on skills and achievements rather than names, schools, or demographic cues.
- **Building diverse interview panels** that mix disciplines, seniority levels, and backgrounds so that no single perspective dominates candidate evaluation.
- **Expanding sourcing** to include historically Black colleges and universities, women-in-tech networks, veterans' organizations, disability communities, and regionally diverse institutions, which enlarges the qualified talent pool without relaxing performance expectations.
- **Publishing evaluation criteria and promotion frameworks** so that people understand what is required to advance and can self-assess against clear standards, reducing the influence of informal networks and "like me" bias.

AI tools help manage scale in recruiting, but they need scrutiny of their own. Automated hiring and screening systems reproduce historical biases baked into training data. Leaders who deploy these tools need clear governance to monitor fairness and act when patterns point to disparate impact. When done well, these practices increase the chances, not reduce them, that capable people from all backgrounds can compete on equal footing and succeed.

## Building an Inclusive Culture of Belonging[10]

Hiring more diverse talent is only the beginning. If people arrive in an environment where they are not heard, cannot raise concerns safely, or see no fair path to advancement, diversity gains will not last. Inclusion turns representation into sustained contribution.

Psychological safety matters here. Teams perform better when people believe they can speak openly about risks, mistakes, and uncomfortable patterns without being punished for it. In analytics and AI, that may mean a junior team member questioning a model's subgroup error rate, an engineer admitting a data issue, or an analyst challenging a long-standing business assumption.

To build an inclusive culture of belonging, consider:

- Visible executive sponsorship.
- Clear promotion criteria.
- Bias and allyship training.
- Employee resource groups that serve as early reviewers of analytics products.
- Regular listening mechanisms such as surveys and forums.

These are not soft extras. They are operational supports for better learning, better design, and better decisions.

### Addressing Challenges and Resistance[11]

Even serious diversity efforts run into resistance. Sometimes it is explicit skepticism. More often, it shows up in quieter forms: old networks keep controlling opportunities, "culture fit" gets used as a stand-in for sameness, or diversity is treated like separate work instead of part of how strong analytics gets done.

Leaders can respond by grounding the conversation in evidence. Diversity improves innovation, reduces blind spots, and strengthens risk management. Framing it that way helps move the discussion from slogans to outcomes.

It also helps to build diversity and inclusion directly into analytics and AI workflows. When hiring processes, model reviews, governance forums, and promotion systems all include clear diversity and fairness checkpoints, inclusion becomes part of quality control rather than a side campaign.

## Case Studies

### Case Study #1: Reducing Bias in a Credit Scoring Model[12]

A regional bank rolled out a machine learning model to support credit decisions for small-business customers. Initial results looked promising on aggregate accuracy, but customer advocates raised concerns that approval rates seemed lower for certain communities. The original model team was technically strong but relatively homogeneous in background and experience, which meant they had not systematically analyzed performance by segment or examined whether features acted as proxies for protected characteristics.

The bank formed a cross-functional review group that included risk officers, community representatives, and data scientists from more diverse backgrounds. Together, they analyzed approval patterns by geography, business owner demographics, and industry and discovered that proxy variables for neighborhood and business age were disproportionately disadvantaging minority-owned firms. By revising features, introducing fairness constraints, and expanding the training dataset to better represent different segments, the bank improved approval equity without materially increasing default risk. The organization also instituted a governance requirement that any high-impact model undergo diverse review and subgroup performance analysis before deployment.

A strong diversity practice shows its value most clearly when teams catch harms before they scale. In credit scoring and similar high-stakes use cases, broader review groups, feature audits, and more representative data can improve fairness without creating unacceptable risk.

## Case Study #2: Global Product Team Uses ERGs as Red Teams[13]

A global consumer technology company was preparing to launch a new AI-powered recommendation system in multiple regions. Early tests showed strong engagement in North America and Europe, but regional leaders in Asia and Latin America were uneasy about the cultural fit and inclusiveness of the recommendations, echoing findings that diverse customer bases require local nuance to realize full innovation benefits.

The company invited several of its ERGs, representing different cultures, languages, and communities, to act as "red teams" for the product. ERG members received access to test environments, used the recommender as real customers would, and documented content that felt inappropriate, biased, or out of touch. Their feedback drove concrete changes in training data selection, localized content rules, and user controls. Post-launch, customer satisfaction scores were higher in the regions that had been involved in the review, and return-visit behavior improved. The product team adopted ERG red teaming as a standard step in AI product development, confirming that diversity directly improves both customer experience and business results.

The larger lesson is that better team composition and better technical review often reinforce each other. When more perspectives are present in design and governance, fairness problems are more likely to surface early enough to fix.

### Case Study #3: Inclusive Sourcing Expands the Talent Pipeline

An analytics organization that had historically recruited from a narrow set of schools broadened its sourcing approach to include regional universities, nontraditional programs, veterans, and women-in-tech networks. Hiring managers also shifted toward structured interviews and clearer, less ambiguous role criteria.

Within several hiring cycles, the candidate pool became more varied, representation improved across multiple levels, and leaders reported stronger team problem-solving because the new hires brought a wider mix of perspectives and experience.

## Success Metrics[14]

Diversity and inclusion efforts gain credibility when they are measured with the same discipline as other strategic priorities. Leaders don't require dozens of indicators; all they need is a focused set of metrics that can provide strong signals. The table on the next page summarizes some common measures, what they tell you, and how leaders typically use them.

Leaders can even start with a small subset of these metrics, review them quarterly alongside performance indicators, and refine them over time as data quality improves and governance matures.

## Diversity and Inclusion Metrics for Analytics and AI Teams

| Metric Category | Example Metric | What It Indicates | How Leaders Use It |
|---|---|---|---|
| **Representation** | % of women/ URGs in analytics roles and leadership | Who is in the room and who is missing | Set hiring and promotion priorities |
| **Pipeline** | Diversity of applicant pools and interview slates | Whether sourcing is reaching varied candidate pools | Adjust sourcing channels and brand messaging |
| **Inclusion** | Belonging and psychological safety scores in surveys | Whether people feel valued and able to speak up | Target team-level culture interventions |
| **Progression and Retention** | Promotion rates, tenure, voluntary exits by demographic | Whether opportunities and outcomes are equitable | Review promotion processes and sponsorship |
| **AI Fairness** | Model error and satisfaction scores by demographic segment | How different groups experience AI-driven decisions | Prioritize fairness reviews and model changes |

A simple dashboard for an analytics function can turn abstract commitments on diversity and safety into visible, trackable commitments. For example, it might monitor:

- Percentage of analytics leadership roles held by women and underrepresented groups, showing whether decision-making power is actually diversifying over time.
- Percentage of major AI projects that include diverse review panels, indicating how often different perspectives are built into model design, testing, and approval.
- Number of models with documented bias testing across key segments, making it clear where fairness checks are routine versus ad hoc or missing.
- Psychological safety scores for analytics teams from regular surveys, signaling whether people feel safe raising concerns, challenging assumptions, and questioning model behavior.

Together, these measures let leaders see whether the organization has embedded diversity, fairness, and safety in day-to-day analytics work. Not just in policy. Reviewing them alongside standard performance metrics in regular governance forums signals that diversity, inclusion, and fairness are integral to business outcomes, not separate from them. Over time, this integrated approach helps organizations refine targets, direct investment, and sustain momentum as their analytics and AI capabilities evolve.

## Diversity and Inclusion Maturity in Analytics and AI[15]

Just as analytics capabilities mature over time, so does an organization's approach to diversity and inclusion in data and AI. A simple maturity lens helps leaders diagnose the current state and, at the same time, set realistic improvement goals:

## D&I Maturity Matrix

| Stage | Characteristics | Typical Risks | Priority Moves |
|---|---|---|---|
| **Reactive** | Isolated initiatives; diversity seen as HR-led | Low trust, inconsistent practices, tokenism | Establish basic metrics and leadership sponsorship |
| **Programmatic** | Programs in place (ERGs, training), limited link to analytics | Efforts feel "separate" from core work | Tie D&I explicitly to analytics and AI outcomes |
| **Integrated** | Hiring, promotion, and model reviews include D&I by design | Better representation, still uneven inclusion | Standardize diverse panels and fairness checks |
| **Strategic** | D&I embedded in analytics strategy and AI governance | D&I seen as a source of innovation and risk advantage | Refresh goals annually; share impact stories widely |

Each stage reflects its own set of characteristics:

- **Stage 1 - Reactive:** Diversity is largely a compliance concern; analytics and AI teams are homogeneous; fairness issues are addressed only after incidents.
- **Stage 2 - Programmatic:** Formal initiatives and training exist; some diversity gains appear in hiring; AI teams occasionally run bias checks but without consistent governance.
- **Stage 3 - Integrated:** Diversity and inclusion considerations are embedded into hiring, promotion, and AI lifecycle processes; metrics are reviewed alongside performance; ERGs and diverse panels are regularly consulted.
- **Stage 4 - Strategic:** Diversity and inclusion are treated as core capabilities; diverse perspectives are deliberately sought for high-stakes AI decisions; the organization iterates on practices as markets, regulations, and technologies evolve.

Leaders can use this maturity lens in offsites or governance forums by asking, "Which stage best describes our analytics and AI teams today, and what specific actions would move us one stage higher over the next 12-18 months?" This framing helps position diversity and inclusion as capabilities to mature, not checkboxes to complete.

## Practical Advice for Leaders[16]

Leaders ready to champion diversity in their analytics and AI functions can focus on a concise set of moves over the next year:

- **Run a brief role and inclusion survey** within analytics and AI teams to understand current experiences of belonging, psychological safety, and perceived fairness.
- **Map diversity** across roles, levels, and locations in analytics and AI, identifying where representation and pipeline are strong and where gaps exist.
- **Review high-stakes models** or AI-enabled products to see who is involved in design, testing, and approval, and whether diverse perspectives are present in each stage.
- **Update hiring and promotion processes** to include structured interviews, clear criteria, and expanded sourcing networks that broaden the qualified pipeline without relaxing standards.

- **Integrate ERG red teaming** and diverse review panels into AI product and model governance so that diversity is built into the technical lifecycle.
- **Add a small set of diversity, inclusion, and fairness metrics** to existing analytics performance dashboards and discuss them in regular governance forums.
- **Share stories** where diverse perspectives changed a model, a decision, or a product for the better, making the impact of diversity concrete and visible.

By treating these steps as ongoing leadership disciplines rather than one-off campaigns, organizations embed diversity into "how we do analytics here" and position their AI efforts for more sustainable performance and trust.

# Conclusion[17]

Championing diversity in analytics and AI is not about choosing values over value. It's about recognizing that the quality of insights and the safety of systems depend on who is in the room and whether they can speak freely. Diverse, inclusive teams design better questions, build fairer models, and anticipate more of the world their organizations actually face, reducing blind spots and strengthening innovation.

Leaders who take this seriously move beyond slogans to structure: they redesign hiring, promotion, and governance so that diversity and inclusion are built into the way analytics work gets done. They protect psychological safety, reward those who raise hard questions, and use metrics to steer progress, aligning with evidence that inclusive, diverse teams ultimately outperform and sustain higher engagement with lower turnover.

Over time, leaders who champion diversity build analytics and AI functions that not only perform well in the short term but also earn the trust of customers, regulators, and employees—and that trust is one of the most valuable assets any data-driven organization can possess.

# Notes

[1] The Abstract synthesizes findings from Hunt's "Delivering through Diversity," BCG's work on diverse leadership and innovation, *Impax Asset Management*'s business-case reports, and fairness case studies such as Buolamwini and Gebru's "Gender Shades," all linking diversity to financial outperformance, innovation revenue, and safer AI systems.

[2] Algorithmic Bias and Representation Bias—grounded in demographic error disparities found across commercial computer vision and classification systems—are examined in Buolamwini and Gebru's "Gender Shades."

[3] Cognitive Diversity draws on BCG's diverse leadership and innovation studies, which show that varied thinking styles and backgrounds improve creativity and problem-solving in complex tasks.

[4] Diversity as used here reflects definitions and quantitative framing from Hunt et al., "Delivering through Diversity."

[5] Inclusion and Tokenism here draw on business-case DEI sources emphasizing belonging, equitable opportunity, and the limitations of superficial representation; see *Impax Asset Management*'s business-case reports; and Aurora50's DEI business-case materials.

[6] Psychological Safety is grounded in insights from Google's Project Aristotle; and LeaderFactor's psychological safety framing, both identifying it as a primary driver of effective, innovative teams.

[7] Talent Pipeline reflects DEI pipeline analyses in Gulf Business DEI coverage, emphasizing sourcing strategies, partnerships, and development as levers for expanding access without lowering standards.

[8] BCG's innovation findings, "Gender Shades" evidence on representation bias, and practitioner work on cognitive diversity and global product design converge to show how diversity drives innovation, blind-spot reduction, and resilience; see BCG's diverse leadership and innovation studies; and Buolamwini and Gebru's "Gender Shades."

[9] Impax's diversity-and-inclusion business-case work and broader IO psychology evidence on structured hiring, anonymized screening, and skills-based evaluation underpin this section's approach to improving fairness and predictive validity; see *Impax Asset Management*'s business-case reports.

[10] Project Aristotle, LeaderFactor's psychological safety framing, and commentary linking psychological safety to innovation, learning, and surfacing risk and bias in AI systems together support this section; see Google's Project Aristotle; and LeaderFactor's psychological safety framing.

[11] Common forms of organizational resistance to diversity—and the case for reframing it as core to strategy and risk management—are synthesized from *Impax Asset Management*'s business-case reports; Hunt's "Delivering through Diversity"; and Aurora50's DEI business-case materials.

[12] Patterns in fairness, lending, and oversight literature—where diverse review groups, feature audits, and expanded training data improve equity without unacceptable risk increases—are reflected here from arXiv fairness and bias analyses.

[13] Practitioner descriptions of ERGs acting as red teams and product-innovation writing on how diverse teams and local insight improve customer satisfaction and product-market fit inform this section; see Mind the Product innovation resources.

[14] Metrics guidance linking representation, inclusion, and fairness indicators to business performance is adapted from Hunt's "Delivering through Diversity"; and Aurora50's DEI business-case materials.

[15] Maturity-model thinking from McKinsey's DEI and governance frameworks—describing successive stages from reactive compliance to strategic integration—is combined with recommendations from *Impax Asset Management*'s business-case reports; Hunt's "Delivering through Diversity"; and Aurora50's DEI business-case materials, emphasizing diagnosis, process redesign, integrated metrics, and storytelling.

[16] The link between diversity and model quality draws on fairness and bias evidence—especially analyses of performance disparities in AI systems—from Buolamwini and Gebru's "Gender Shades"; and Digital Government Hub fairness coverage.

[17] Hunt et al., "Delivering through Diversity"; and BCG's diverse leadership and innovation studies jointly anchor the business case for diversity—enhanced innovation, reduced blind spots, better decision quality, and stronger financial performance—while cognitive-diversity and innovation research from BCG's diverse leadership and innovation studies shows that varied perspectives improve problem framing and hypothesis generation in complex tasks.

## Key topics explored in this chapter:

- The Imperative of a Long Term Talent View
- Strategic Recruitment: Casting Wide and Deep Nets
- Local Talent Development: Growing from Within
- Succession Planning and Knowledge Capture in the Age of AI
- Partnering with Institutions: Extending the Talent Ecosystem
- Emphasizing Resilience, Adaptability, and Inclusivity

# WAY 8

# Create Sustainable Talent Pipelines

## Abstract[1]

Analytics and AI capabilities rise or fall on one asset more than any other: talent. Tools, platforms, and methodologies will continue to change, but organizations that can reliably attract, develop, and retain skilled people will adapt faster than their competitors. This is especially true in an environment where the capabilities needed for gen AI and advanced analytics continue to evolve rapidly. Companies that successfully build sustainable talent pipelines look beyond this quarter's hiring targets to cultivate a resilient, diverse, future-ready workforce that can grow alongside technology and market demands. They treat skills as a renewable asset rather than fixed inventory. This chapter examines what it takes to construct these pipelines for analytics and AI—and how to do so in a way that advances diversity, inclusion, and long-term organizational health by integrating external recruitment, internal development, succession planning, and partnerships into a coherent system.

## Objective

After completing this chapter, you will be able to:

- Explain why a long-term, pipeline-oriented view of talent is essential for analytics and AI strategy, given shrinking skills half-lives and shifting role requirements.
- Develop recruitment approaches that reach diverse, high-potential candidates without lowering standards, aligned with skills-based hiring principles.
- Design internal development pathways that reskill and upskill current employees into analytics and AI roles at scale.

- Implement succession planning and knowledge capture practices to reduce key-person risk in critical analytics and AI positions.
- Build external partnerships that extend the organization's talent ecosystem and support continuous skill development.
- Monitor talent pipelines with meaningful metrics that link directly to performance, resilience, and inclusion.

# Terms to Know

**Career Pathway**[2] **-** A structured sequence of roles and learning experiences that show how employees can progress over time, often linked to clearly defined skills and competencies.

**Knowledge Capture**[3] **-** Systematic methods for recording and preserving essential know-how, decisions, and rationale from experts before they leave a role, supporting continuity, faster onboarding, and reduced key-person risk.

**Skills Half Life**[4] **-** The period during which a given skill remains at peak relevance before newer methods or tools make it partially obsolete, a phenomenon accelerated by gen AI and rapid technological change.

**Skills Velocity**[5] **-** The speed at which individuals or teams acquire and effectively apply new skills to real work, increasingly used as a measure of how quickly organizations can adapt to emerging needs.

**Succession Planning**[3] **-** A structured process for identifying and preparing people to fill key roles when incumbents move or leave, including high-potential technical and analytics experts as well as executives.

**Sustainable Talent Pipeline**[6] **-** A balanced, long-term approach to attracting, developing, and retaining talent that can keep pace with evolving business and technology needs, emphasizing skills-based planning, internal mobility, and continuous learning.

**Talent Marketplace**[6] **-** An internal or external platform that matches projects and roles with people based on skills, interests, and development goals, enabling more dynamic deployment and development of talent.

**Workforce Resilience**[7] **-** The capacity of a workforce to absorb shocks—such as technology changes or market shifts—and still deliver, supported by broad skill bases, adaptable talent, and flexible deployment models.

# Introduction

Analytics and AI transformations often begin with technology—new platforms, cloud migrations, model libraries. Over time, leaders discover that their real bottleneck is people: not just having enough headcount, but having the right skills at the right time, in the right places. The pace of change in tools and methods has shortened the shelf life of technical skills; a technique or platform that was leading-edge three years ago may now be expected baseline knowledge, reinforcing the idea that organizations must continually reassess and refresh their skills portfolios.

In this environment, relying on reactive hiring is risky. When every competitor is searching for the same limited pool of data scientists or engineers, vacancies stay open longer, salaries escalate, and important initiatives are delayed, amplifying the cost of slow hiring cycles. Sustainable talent pipelines offer a different path: instead of scrambling to fill gaps as they appear, leaders intentionally design systems to attract new talent, grow internal capabilities, preserve institutional knowledge, and adapt to new demands over time, using skills-based workforce planning as a competitive backbone.

## The Imperative of a Long-Term Talent View[4]

Analytics work spans multiple disciplines: data engineering, statistics, machine learning, domain expertise, visualization, governance, and change management. Very few people arrive fully formed, and gen AI is reshaping which tasks are automated and which require deeper human judgment, making role definitions more fluid. At the same time, the "half-life" of many technical skills is shrinking as new approaches, languages, and tools emerge, pushing organizations toward continuous upskilling models rather than occasional training.

Leaders who treat talent as a series of one-off hires will find themselves in a constant race they cannot win. A long-term view changes the questions leaders ask; instead of "Who can we hire this quarter?" they ask:

- What skills will we need more of in 18-36 months, given our AI roadmap and evolving business strategy?
- Which current roles are likely to evolve or disappear as AI automates routine tasks and augments knowledge work?
- Where are we heavily dependent on a small number of experts whose departure would create disproportionate risk?

- How do we ensure we have successors and documentation for critical roles, and pathways for emerging talent to step into them?

By framing talent pipeline creation as a strategic investment—on par with capital projects or product development—leaders can align budgets, incentives, and governance accordingly, recognizing that skills development is a primary lever for future competitiveness.

## Strategic Recruitment: Casting Wide and Deep Nets[6]

A sustainable pipeline begins with thoughtful external recruitment: to create an ongoing flow of candidates aligned with future skills needs and cultural expectations. That requires a clear employer brand, targeted outreach, and a disciplined approach to candidate experience.

### Employer brand and narrative

Analytics and AI professionals increasingly look for roles where their work has visible impact, where ethics are taken seriously, and where learning is supported. Organizations can strengthen the pipeline by:

- Telling concrete stories about how analytics has improved outcomes—for customers, patients, or communities—through public case studies and internal narratives.
- Highlighting commitments to responsible AI, strong governance, and skills-based development, signaling seriousness about long-term careers.
- Showcasing visible career paths, including how current analytics leaders have grown inside the organization through rotations and development programs.

### Targeted sourcing and outreach

Generic job postings will not reach all the talent you need. More effective tactics include:

- Participating in specialized communities (for example, competitions, technical forums, open-source projects) and engaging where talent already spends time.
- Building relationships with university programs, bootcamps, and professional associations focused on analytics, AI, and adjacent disciplines to access emerging talent early.

- Using alumni networks, practitioner conferences, and technology councils to identify potential candidates long before roles open, creating "warm" pipelines for future needs.

**Diversity-conscious pipelines**
To avoid perpetuating narrow talent pools, recruitment should intentionally reach underrepresented groups through partnerships with minority-serving institutions, global campuses, and targeted professional groups. When combined with consistent standards and structured assessments, this broadens access without compromising quality and aligns with evidence that skills-based hiring can improve both diversity and performance.

**Candidate experience as an asset**
The recruitment process itself influences reputation. Responsive communication, clear timelines, practical interview tasks, and respectful feedback—even for rejected candidates—can turn applicants into advocates in specialized analytics communities. Over time, this strengthens the brand and keeps the pipeline warm, reducing future time-to-fill and improving offer acceptance rates.

## Local Talent Development: Growing from Within

External hiring alone cannot keep up with demand for analytics and AI skills. Internal development complements recruitment by turning existing employees into future analytics professionals and leaders, which research shows can help close skills gaps more sustainably than external hiring alone. It also reinforces a culture of learning and loyalty: people who can see a path to growth are more likely to stay and invest in the organization's success. Key elements of effective internal development include:

- **Skills gap analysis:** Leaders map current roles and skills against future needs using skills inventories, manager assessments, and employee self-assessments, often supported by skills taxonomies and analytics to prioritize investments.
- **Personalized learning paths:** Structured efforts for different personas (aspiring analysts, engineers moving into ML, business professionals becoming analytics "translators") that blend external courses, internal workshops, project-based assignments, and mentoring.

- **Career path mapping:** Publishing explicit career paths—such as "Business Analyst → Analytics Translator → Analytics Product Owner" or "Data Engineer → Senior Engineer → Data Architect"—so employees know which skills and experiences matter at each step.
- **Champions and peer learning:** Top performers serve as "skills champions," leading communities of practice or internal bootcamps and creating apprenticeship-style learning opportunities for their peers.
- **Recognition and incentives:** Recognizing learning achievements in performance discussions and promotion decisions so that building new skills is clearly valued.

Taken together, these practices turn the existing workforce into a dynamic source of new analytics and AI capability, reducing dependence on external hiring alone and improving workforce resilience.

## Succession Planning and Knowledge Capture in the Age of AI[3]

Some roles carry outsized risk if vacated—principal data scientists, lead data architects, long-tenured domain experts, or analytics leaders with unique relationship capital. Sustainable talent pipelines require both a plan for who may step into these roles and a way to preserve their knowledge.

### Identifying critical roles and successors

Succession planning starts by identifying roles whose sudden vacancy would seriously disrupt operations or strategy. For each, leaders can identify potential successors at different readiness levels ("ready now," "ready in 1-2 years," "emerging talent") and define developmental experiences those successors need to be effective, such as leading key projects, owning major models, or managing stakeholders.

### Capturing institutional knowledge

AI and collaborative tools offer new and helpful ways to document and share expertise, including:

- Recording walkthroughs of key models, data pipelines, and decision flows with explanations of "why," not just "what," to preserve design rationale.
- Using search and Q&A systems to make past decisions, designs, and documentation more discoverable to future teams.

- Standardizing templates for model documentation, experiment logs, and post-implementation reviews so that knowledge is consistently captured.

This helps to ensure that when people move on, they don't leave behind a gap. Over time, this reduces vulnerability to turnover and retirement and accelerates onboarding for new hires.

## Partnering with Institutions: Extending the Talent Ecosystem[6]

No single organization can build all required talent in isolation. Strategic partnerships with universities, technical schools, bootcamps, and professional bodies extend the talent ecosystem and keep teams connected to emerging ideas and tools. Common partnership models include:

- **Internships and co-ops:** Students rotate through analytics and AI teams, contributing to real projects while learning in context, and organizations gain early access to potential hires.
- **Capstone projects:** Student teams work on defined business problems under joint supervision, giving the organization fresh perspectives and the chance to observe talent over time.
- **Advisory roles:** Senior leaders sit on academic advisory boards, helping shape curricula so that graduates are better prepared for real-world work and emerging skills requirements.
- **Certification programs:** Jointly developed programs that certify employees on widely used tools and platforms, often with technology providers, support consistent skill standards at scale.

These partnerships create a virtuous cycle: they feed the external pipeline, support local skill development, and enhance the organization's brand as a destination for analytics and AI careers, which is increasingly important in competitive talent markets.

## Emphasizing Resilience, Adaptability, and Inclusivity[7]

A sustainable pipeline is not just about volume; it is about resilience and adaptability. As AI automates some tasks and creates new ones, organizations will need people who can flex across roles, combine technical and business skills, and work effectively in diverse teams.

Talent strategies that support resilience and inclusivity often:

- Encourage cross-functional rotations and hybrid roles (for example, analytics translators who understand both data and operations) to bridge silos and build adaptable skill sets.
- Invest in "power skills" such as communication, influence, and critical thinking alongside technical training, recognizing that transversal skills are essential in dynamic environments.
- Ensure that reskilling opportunities are accessible to employees from many backgrounds, not just those already close to technical roles, which supports equity and maximizes workforce potential.

When diversity and inclusion are built into pipeline design, the result is a workforce that is not only technically capable but also better equipped to see around corners and serve diverse customers, reinforcing both performance and fairness goals.

# Case Studies[8]

## Case Study #1: A Bank Reduces Time-to-Fill for Data Engineers

A large regional bank struggled to hire experienced data engineers fast enough to support its cloud migration and AI roadmap. Key projects slipped because roles stayed open for months, and competition from technology firms was intense.

Leadership responded with a dual-track strategy. Externally, the bank sharpened its value proposition for technologists, emphasizing modern tooling, flexible work, and the opportunity to have measurable impact on financial inclusion initiatives. It built closer relationships with regional universities and sponsored hackathons to meet potential candidates earlier, effectively building a pre-qualified talent pool.

Internally, the bank created a reskilling program to move experienced ETL and database professionals into data engineering roles. Participants received intensive training, mentorship from senior engineers, and guaranteed placement upon completion. Within two years, time-to-fill for mid-level data engineering roles decreased significantly, a meaningful share of new capacity came from reskilled insiders, and external hires increasingly saw the bank as a place to build serious data careers rather than a stopgap role.

## Case Study #2: Health System Builds an Analytics Academy

A multi-hospital health system wanted to expand its use of analytics and AI in clinical operations but found that frontline staff and managers often lacked the skills to interpret dashboards or engage meaningfully with data scientists. Recruiting enough external analysts to embed in every unit was unrealistic.

The organization created an "Analytics Academy" that offered tiered learning paths for nurses, physicians, administrators, and aspiring analysts. Courses combined online content with in-person workshops focused on internal data and tools. Graduation unlocked new responsibilities and access to more advanced analytics capabilities. Over time, the academy produced a network of "analytics champions" in each department—people who understood both their clinical context and data concepts. These champions became vital partners to the central analytics team, helping frame use cases, validate model outputs, and drive adoption of new tools.

## Case Study #3: Tech Company Preserves Knowledge During Rapid Growth

A fast-growing technology company relied on several senior data scientists and machine learning engineers who had been with the firm from its early days. These individuals held important knowledge about model architectures, decision trade-offs, and the history behind key analytics systems. As the company scaled, leaders worried about what would happen if these experts left.

Analytics leadership introduced a structured knowledge capture program. Senior experts were asked to record deep-dive sessions walking through major models and pipelines, explain past decisions, and annotate repositories with richer context. The team standardized model documentation templates and created an internal knowledge base searchable by use case and model type. At the same time, each expert mentored one or two successors, involving them in critical reviews and strategic discussions. Over the following years, some early employees moved on, but their knowledge remained accessible, new team members ramped up more quickly, and the organization felt more confident that its analytics capabilities were not tied to a handful of individuals.

# Success Metrics[9]

To understand whether talent pipeline investments are working, it helps to track a small set of outcome-focused metrics. The table that follows highlights core measures, what they reveal, and typical targets for mature analytics functions, consistent with skills-based and data-driven talent practices.

## Key Metrics for Talent Pipelines

| Metric | What It Reveals | Illustrative Target | Leadership Use Case |
|---|---|---|---|
| **Time-to-Fill (Critical Roles)** | How quickly you can staff high-impact analytics jobs | 20-30% reduction over 2-3 years | Adjust sourcing strategy and budget |
| **Internal Fill Rate** | Share of roles filled by internal candidates | 30-50% for mid-level roles | Gauge effectiveness of internal pathways |
| **Skills Velocity** | Speed from hire/reskilling to defined proficiency | Productivity in 6-9 months | Fine-tune onboarding and learning design |
| **Retention of Critical Talent** | Ability to keep key analytics and AI roles | Voluntary exits < 10-12% annually | Identify hotspots and refine development offerings |
| **Diversity Across Pipeline** | Breadth of representation at each stage (apply→lead) | Year-over-year improvements | Check if inclusive sourcing and development work |
| **Bench Strength for Key Roles** | No. of "ready now/soon" successors per critical role | At least 1-2 per key position | Validate succession planning maturity |

Many organizations start by baselining these metrics, then set modest, time-bound improvement goals aligned with business priorities. Reviewing them quarterly alongside business KPIs helps ensure talent pipeline health remains a visible, managed part of analytics strategy, and supports continuous adjustment as conditions change.

Just as analytics capabilities mature, so do talent pipelines. The following table offers a simple way to gauge where an organization stands and what "better" looks like, synthesizing themes from skills-based and succession planning research.

### Talent Pipeline Maturity Model for Analytics and AI[10]

| Maturity Stage | Characteristics | Typical Risks | Priority Actions |
|---|---|---|---|
| **Ad Hoc** | Hiring is reactive; no clear pathways or succession | Chronic vacancies, burnout, key-person risk | Baseline metrics; identify critical roles; pilot reskilling |
| **Emerging** | Some programs (academies, partnerships) but fragmented | Mixed results; uneven access to opportunities | Align recruitment, development, and succession goals |
| **Integrated** | External hiring, internal development, and succession coordinated | Improved coverage; pockets of weakness remain | Standardize career paths; formalize knowledge capture |
| **Strategic** | Pipelines tied to business and AI strategy; measured regularly | Talent seen as strategic differentiator | Refresh pipeline plans annually; continuously refine metrics |

# Practical Advice for Leaders[11]

Leaders who want to move from ad hoc hiring to sustainable pipelines can focus on a concrete set of actions over the next 12-24 months:

- **Map current analytics and AI roles,** skills, and positions using a basic skills inventory and stakeholder interviews.
- **Identify critical roles** and create simple succession and development plans for each, including at least one "ready later" candidate and a knowledge capture plan.
- **Baseline key pipeline metrics** such as time-to-fill, internal fill rate, and retention of critical roles, and add them to regular business reviews.

- **Design or refine** two or three internal learning paths and career pathways for priority personas (for example, aspiring analysts, analytics translators, data engineers).
- **Launch a targeted reskilling program** that moves people from adjacent roles into analytics positions, with clear selection criteria, learning paths, and guaranteed placement.
- **Formalize or deepen a handful of strategic partnerships** with educational institutions or training providers aligned to your skill needs.
- **Communicate stories** where pipeline investments enabled faster response to a new opportunity or mitigated a critical risk, reinforcing the business value of long-term talent strategy.

By treating these steps as part of core leadership work rather than optional extras, organizations position themselves to keep pace with change instead of reacting to it, converting talent from a constraint into a repeatable advantage.

# Conclusion

Creating sustainable analytics and AI talent pipelines is not about predicting the future with perfect accuracy. It's about building the capacity to respond—by having people who can learn, adapt, and lead through change, supported by skills-based workforce planning and dynamic development ecosystems. When organizations invest in both external recruitment and internal development, preserve important knowledge, and extend their reach through partnerships, they turn talent from a constraint into a strategic competitive advantage that compounds over time.

The organizations that thrive in the next decade won't be the ones with the most sophisticated tools, but those with the most resilient, adaptable, and inclusive talent pipelines—companies that treat continuous skill-building as core infrastructure for AI-enabled competitiveness in an analytics world that is ever-changing.

# Notes

[1] Gen-AI skill shifts, skills-based workforce planning, and integrated talent strategies—synthesized in the Abstract and Objective—draw on McKinsey's skills and workforce reports; and Josh Bersin Company/Guild's talent strategy analyses.

[2] Career Pathway and internal development sections—drawing on structured pathways, blended learning, and internal academies to close skills gaps and support mobility—are grounded in Josh Bersin Company/Guild's people-development research; and McKinsey's talent pipeline guidance.

[3] Knowledge Capture, Succession Planning, and related sections on critical roles, high-potential successors, and systematic knowledge retention draw on Josh Bersin Company succession-planning guidance.

[4] Skills Half-Life and long-term views on gen-AI-driven skill change and the need for continuous reskilling are informed by McKinsey's skills half-life analyses; and Josh Bersin Company's gen-AI workforce reports.

[5] The Skills Velocity concept—measuring the rate of skill acquisition and application as an adaptability indicator—is developed in Josh Bersin Company dynamic skilling frameworks; and *McKinsey* talent velocity resources.

[6] Sustainable Talent Pipeline, Talent Marketplace, strategic recruitment, partnerships, and system design—synthesizing skills-based hiring, internal marketplaces, and external partnerships for resilient pipelines—draw on McKinsey's skills-based talent ecosystem guidance; and Josh Bersin Company/Guild's talent marketplace analyses.

[7] Workforce Resilience and adaptability sections draw on McKinsey workforce resilience research; and Josh Bersin Company talent adaptability reports.

[8] Case studies reflecting patterns in reskilling, academy, and succession literature—external branding with internal development to reduce time-to-fill, internal academies and champions to expand reach, and knowledge capture with mentoring to mitigate key-person risk—appear in Josh Bersin Company/Guild case studies; and McKinsey talent transformation cases.

[9] Success metrics adapting talent-pipeline measures—time-to-fill, internal mobility, retention, diversity, and bench strength—from workforce analytics and succession-planning sources, reviewed alongside business KPIs, are drawn from McKinsey workforce analytics guidance; and Josh Bersin Company succession metrics.

[10] The talent pipeline maturity model—applying maturity-model thinking from talent and organizational-capability research to pipelines, moving from reactive to strategic integration tied to business and AI strategy—is built from McKinsey talent maturity frameworks; and Josh Bersin Company capability models.

[11] Practical steps for leaders—synthesizing phased recommendations from skills-based talent strategy and people-development studies stressing diagnosis, coordinated external and internal strategies, formalized succession and knowledge capture, and disciplined measurement—draw on McKinsey skills-based talent strategy guidance; and Josh Bersin Company/Guild phased talent development recommendations.

## Key topics explored in this chapter:

- Recognizing the Ethical Imperative
- Foundational Ethical Frameworks and Principles
- Managing Algorithmic Bias and Fairness
- Establishing Transparent Standards in Data Handling and AI Application
- Building an Ethical Analytics Culture
- Governance and Oversight Mechanisms
- Ethics Governance Maturity
- Driving Responsible Innovation
- Stakeholder Engagement and Public Responsibility
- Continuous Learning and Adaptability

# WAY 9

# Establish Ethical Leadership in Data and AI


## Abstract[1]

As AI moves from pilot projects to core operating systems, ethical leadership becomes a strategic requirement, not a side concern. Executives increasingly oversee models that influence lending, hiring, pricing, clinical recommendations, service prioritization, and public-facing decisions—often at speed and scale. In these settings, ethical failures do more than create bad headlines. They can trigger regulatory scrutiny, legal exposure, operational disruption, and long-term erosion of trust. This chapter offers a practical method for ethical leadership in data and AI by connecting principles such as privacy, transparency, fairness, and accountability to everyday governance, culture, and decision-making.


## Objective

After completing this chapter, you will be able to:

- Articulate why ethical leadership in data and AI is a strategic and risk-management imperative, not just a compliance concern.
- Apply core ethical principles—privacy, transparency, fairness, and accountability—to real analytics and AI decisions.
- Recognize common sources of algorithmic bias and use practical techniques and processes to mitigate them.
- Design governance mechanisms, including ethics boards and escalation pathways, with real authority and "veto power."
- Foster an ethical analytics culture built on psychological safety, open dialogue, and ongoing education.

- Monitor ethical performance through meaningful metrics and adapt practices as technologies and societal expectations evolve.

# Terms to Know

**Accountability**[2] - Clear assignment of responsibility for decisions and outcomes, including the authority to approve, escalate, and remediate ethical issues, often supported by explicit governance and liability frameworks.

**Algorithmic Bias**[3] - Systematic and unfair errors in model predictions or decisions that disproportionately affect certain groups, often arising from skewed data, features, or deployment context, as demonstrated in facial analysis, credit, and health applications.

**Data Governance**[4] - The policies, processes, and roles that govern how data is collected, stored, used, and protected across an organization, providing the foundation for responsible AI.

**Ethical Guardrails**[2] - Boundaries and criteria that define what the organization will and will not do with data and AI, even when practices are technically feasible or legal, reflecting a commitment to go beyond minimum compliance.

**Explainable AI (XAI)**[4] - Methods and tools that make model behavior and outputs understandable to humans, especially non-technical stakeholders, enabling oversight, contestability, and trust.

**Fairness**[3] - The property of treating individuals and groups equitably in model training, evaluation, and deployment, minimizing unjustified differences in outcomes and aligning with principles of non-discrimination.

**Model Drift**[2] - Changes in model performance or behavior over time due to shifts in data, environment, or underlying relationships, which can introduce new ethical risks if not monitored and addressed.

**Privacy by Design**[4] - An approach that integrates privacy considerations into system design from the outset rather than as an add-on, as recommended by health and data-protection AI guidance.

**Responsible AI**[4] - An overall approach to designing, building, and deploying AI systems that align with ethical, legal, and societal expectations, operationalized through principles, processes, and oversight.

# Introduction

When AI and advanced analytics were experimental, ethical questions were easier to postpone. That is no longer true. Today, models influence decisions about access, opportunity, cost, risk, treatment, and priority in ways that affect real people every day. They recommend who should receive a loan, which job applicants move forward, what treatments clinicians consider, and which citizens receive services or scrutiny. In many organizations these systems operate at scale with limited direct human review. That scale magnifies both value and harm. A small design flaw, a weak dataset, or a poorly governed deployment can quickly become a broad fairness issue, a privacy problem, or a reputation crisis. Ethical leadership is not a philosophical add-on. It is a practical leadership discipline that shapes trust, resilience, and long-term legitimacy.

This chapter offers practical guidance on translating broad principles into concrete practices that teams embed in projects, policies, and culture. Ethics becomes an integral part of how the organization does data and AI, not an afterthought.

## Recognizing the Ethical Imperative[5]

Ethical leadership begins with recognizing the real-world impact of data and AI decisions. Each new use case—automated underwriting, predictive maintenance, dynamic pricing—touches people's lives in ways that rarely show up in a dashboard, especially when effects concentrate among specific populations. A model that misclassifies a small percentage of cases looks acceptable in aggregate but remains unacceptable when the misclassified group is consistently the same marginalized community. Real-world AI deployments in facial recognition and credit scoring have shown this pattern. Leaders who appreciate this dynamic:

- Treat ethics as integral to strategy, not an afterthought, tying ethical performance to brand strength, regulatory relationships, and long-term value.
- Ask early, "Who might be harmed by this system?" and "Who is not in the room as we design it?," bringing affected perspectives into the design and review process.
- Recognize that trust, once lost, is far more expensive to regain than any short-term gain from cutting corners, as seen in multiple AI incident and governance case studies.

This orientation shifts ethics from a "brake pedal" to a steering wheel—something that guides where and how to innovate, not merely something that slows things down.

## Foundational Ethical Frameworks and Principles[4]

Good intentions are not enough. Organizations need structured frameworks that help teams consistently navigate complex trade-offs. Comparative reviews of AI ethics frameworks show convergence around core principles—privacy, transparency, fairness, and accountability—even as sector-specific details vary.

## Core Ethical Principles for Data and AI

| Principle | Focus Question | Typical Practices |
|---|---|---|
| **Privacy** | Are we respecting people's data rights? | Data minimization, consent, strong security, access limits |
| **Transparency** | Can stakeholders understand what we do? | Clear data notices, model documentation, XAI tools |
| **Fairness** | Are outcomes equitable across groups? | Bias audits, fairness metrics, representative data |
| **Accountability** | Who owns outcomes and remediation? | Defined roles, ethics boards, escalation paths |

One way to operationalize these principles is through an internal framework such as Responsible, Sustainable, Transparent, Auditable (RSTA), applied at each stage of the analytics lifecycle. Responsible asks whether the use case aligns with mission and values. Sustainable asks whether the system can be monitored and governed ethically over time. Transparent asks whether non-technical stakeholders can understand the system. Auditable tests whether internal or external parties can review design, data, and decisions.

Embedding these frameworks into project intake forms, model approval checklists, and review templates ensures teams consider ethics systematically rather than sporadically. Ethics guidelines work best when formally integrated into concrete processes and oversight.

## Managing Algorithmic Bias and Fairness[3]

Algorithmic bias has moved from academic debate to the boardroom. One landmark study found that commercial facial-analysis systems showed error rates above 30 percent for darker-skinned women compared to less than 1 percent for lighter-skinned men—proof that unbalanced datasets and careless design choices produce stark disparities. Civil liberties groups and regulators have documented similar patterns of unequal performance in facial recognition, risk assessment, and automated decision tools.

Ethical leadership does not assume bias can be fully eliminated; instead, it insists that bias be actively understood, monitored, and mitigated. Practical steps include:

- **Diverse, cross-functional teams:** Involving data scientists, domain experts, legal, ethics, and representatives of affected communities in model design and review introduces multiple vantage points on fairness risks.
- **Data review and feature scrutiny:** Examining training data for representativeness and asking whether certain features (for example, ZIP code or school attended) act as proxies for protected attributes helps surface structural sources of bias.
- **Fairness testing:** Evaluating model performance across relevant subgroups and tracking metrics such as false positive and false negative rates by gender, ethnicity, or region, where lawful and appropriate, in line with demographic analysis recommendations.
- **Red teaming and scenario analysis:** Intentionally stress-testing models under edge cases or adversarial scenarios reveals where performance or fairness may break down before deployment.

Leaders should set a firm expectation: no high-impact model goes live without a documented fairness review and a plan for ongoing monitoring. This standard echoes the broader call for systematic impact assessment and continuous evaluation in high-risk AI domains.

## Establishing Transparent Standards in Data Handling and AI Application[4]

Principles gain real force when translated into policies and standards. Ethical leaders work with legal, compliance, and technology teams to codify expectations for how data and AI are used, and they make those expectations visible internally and, where appropriate, externally. Key components of transparent standards include:

- **Data collection and use policies:** Clear rules about what data can be collected, for which purposes, and under which legal bases, including retention and deletion schedules, consistent with data-protection and health-AI guidance.

- **Model risk tiers:** Categorization of models by impact (internal efficiency vs. customer-facing decisions vs. safety-critical use cases) with corresponding levels of scrutiny, reflecting risk-proportionate governance.
- **Approval criteria and documentation:** Requirements for model documentation (purpose, data sources, limitations, fairness results, explainability approach) before deployment, enabling auditability and regulatory readiness.
- **Disclosure and communication:** Guidelines on when and how to inform customers or employees that AI is being used in decisions, and what recourse they have, aligning with calls for transparency and contestability.

Some organizations establish AI or data ethics boards with representation from business, technology, legal, ethics, and external advisors. These boards must have real authority, including the power to delay or veto deployments that cross agreed-upon ethical red lines, or they function as symbolic, powerless bodies rather than genuine safeguards.

## Building an Ethical Analytics Culture[2]

Policies and methods are necessary but not sufficient. Ethical leadership ultimately lives in day-to-day behavior: which issues people feel safe raising, how leaders respond to concerns, and whether ethics is seen as part of "how we do business" rather than as an external constraint.

Key cultural levers include:

- **Leader role-modeling:** Executives and managers share real dilemmas they have faced, how they balanced competing considerations, and what they learned when things went wrong, signaling that ethics is taken seriously and not just delegated.
- **Scenario-based training:** Teams walk through realistic analytics and AI scenarios—biased datasets, ambiguous consent, unintended uses—and practice making decisions, which research suggests is more effective than generic training.
- **Psychological safety for escalation:** Team members at any level must feel safe saying, "I think this model might be unfair," without fear of retaliation; evidence on team effectiveness makes clear that such climates are vital for surfacing concerns and enabling learning.

- **Recognition and rewards:** When employees slow or reshape a project to address ethical concerns, leadership should acknowledge and celebrate that behavior rather than quietly penalize it for affecting timelines.

In high-performing organizations, ethics is not the exclusive worry of "the ethics team." It is a distributed responsibility shared across every role and function.

## Governance and Oversight Mechanisms[2]

Effective ethical leadership requires structures that see across projects and act when needed. Governance must integrate with existing risk and compliance systems rather than bolt on as an afterthought—a point emphasized throughout health and cross-sector AI ethics guidance. A practical governance setup includes:

- **Defined roles and authorities:** Clear responsibility for AI and data ethics at the executive level (for example, Chief Data or AI Officer, Chief Ethics Officer) and within lines of business, with explicit mandates.
- **Ethics or model-risk committees:** Cross-functional bodies that review high-impact projects, monitor key indicators (for example, bias incidents or complaints), and escalate issues to senior leadership or the board.
- **Ongoing monitoring:** Processes to detect model drift, performance deterioration, or new fairness issues over time, not just at launch, reflecting the need for continuous oversight.
- **Incident-response playbooks:** Pre-agreed steps for investigating, communicating, and remediating ethical incidents, including how to engage affected parties and adjust systems.

Good governance balances rigor with agility. Overly burdensome processes push teams to work "under the radar"; overly light ones leave the organization exposed. Leaders must match control levels to risk levels—stricter safeguards on safety-critical or rights-impacting systems, lighter requirements on lower-risk internal analytics.

## Ethics Governance Maturity[5]

Ethics in data and AI matures over time, like any other organizational capability. The model below gives leaders a practical lens for assessing where they stand today and what "better" looks like, grounded in studies of AI ethics practices.

## Ethics Governance Maturity Model

| Stage | Characteristics | Typical Risks | Priority Moves |
|---|---|---|---|
| **Ad Hoc** | Ethical issues handled case by case; no clear owners | Inconsistent decisions, surprise incidents | Assign executive owner; document basic principles |
| **Policy-Led** | Policies and codes of conduct exist but are lightly used | "Check-the-box" behavior, policy-practice gap | Embed ethics into intake and approval processes |
| **Embedded** | Ethics boards, reviews, and metrics integrated into AI lifecycle | Uneven adoption, local workarounds | Standardize templates, monitoring, and escalation |
| **Strategic** | Ethics informs strategy and product design; viewed as differentiator | Complacency if early success breeds overconfidence | Refresh methods regularly; share impact outcomes |

Leaders can bring this maturity model into executive offsites or board discussions by asking: "Which stage best describes our current ethics governance, and what specific actions would move us one stage higher over the next 12-24 months?" Framing governance as a capability to develop shifts ethics from reactive fixes to proactive system design.

## Driving Responsible Innovation[6]

Ethics and innovation are sometimes framed as opposites; in practice, they reinforce each other. Ethical guardrails enable teams to explore boldly within clearly defined boundaries, reducing the risk of expensive rollbacks after public or regulatory backlash. Leaders promote responsible innovation by:

- Asking better questions, shifting from "Can we do this?" to "Should we do this?" and "What conditions must be in place to do this safely?"
- Piloting with guardrails, running limited pilots with diverse user groups, monitoring for unintended consequences, and using findings to refine or halt initiatives.

- Embedding impact assessments by incorporating ethical and societal questions into business cases and model proposals, not just technical feasibility and ROI.
- Encouraging "red team" thinking, giving teams explicit license to think like critics or adversaries to identify where systems could fail or be misused before launch, including use of ERGs as red teams.

Organizations that build these practices into their innovation process discover more robust, trusted solutions and avoid costly mid-course corrections driven by public backlash or regulatory intervention.

## Ethical Decision Checklist for Leaders[4]

Before green-lighting a significant analytics or AI initiative, leaders should apply a simple checklist to pressure-test ethical readiness. Using this checklist in approval meetings and project reviews keeps ethical considerations visible alongside financial, technical, and operational criteria—consistent with guidance that ethics questions belong inside standard governance processes.

## Ethical Decision Checklist

| | Item | Key Question |
|---|---|---|
| ☐ | **Purpose** | Are we clear on the problem we are solving and why AI or advanced analytics is the right tool? |
| ☐ | **People Impact** | Who could be helped and who could be harmed by this system, directly or indirectly, especially among vulnerable groups? |
| ☐ | **Data and Fairness** | Is our data representative enough, and have we checked for proxies that could unfairly disadvantage certain groups? |
| ☐ | **Transparency** | Can we explain, in plain language, how this system influences decisions and what its limitations are? |
| ☐ | **Accountability** | Who is accountable for outcomes, monitoring, and remediation if issues arise, and is that responsibility clearly documented? |
| ☐ | **Guardrails** | Under what conditions would we pause, modify, or roll back this system, and are those conditions clearly documented and communicated? |

## Stakeholder Engagement and Public Responsibility[2]

Ethical leadership extends beyond the organization's perimeter. Many data and AI use cases affect people who have no direct relationship with the company—individuals whose data appears in third-party datasets, for instance, or communities shaped by location-based analytics. Engaging external stakeholders surfaces perspectives invisible inside the building and builds legitimacy and trust. Meaningful engagement includes:

- **Customer and community advisory panels:** Regular dialogues with representatives of affected groups to discuss new AI initiatives and gather feedback.
- **Public reporting:** Voluntary transparency reports that describe how AI is used, what safeguards exist, and how many ethical incidents or complaints were handled.
- **Collaboration with civil society and academia:** Partnering with researchers and advocacy organizations to stress-test systems, share best practices, and contribute to evolving standards.

These activities make known that the organization sees itself as part of a broader ecosystem, with responsibilities not only to shareholders but also to society at large. Over time, this can strengthen the "license to operate" in sensitive domains and support more constructive relationships with regulators and communities.

## Continuous Learning and Adaptability[5]

The ethical landscape for data and AI is not static. New capabilities, including generative models, autonomous agents, and multimodal systems, raise fresh questions. Legal guidelines and societal expectations keep evolving. What passed as acceptable two years ago observers now view as insufficiently protective or transparent. Ethical leaders respond by:

- Staying informed about regulatory developments, major industry incidents, and emerging academic work on AI ethics and governance.
- Refreshing methods and policies regularly rather than treating them as one-off projects, reflecting the need for adaptive governance.
- Learning from incidents, treating internal and external missteps as opportunities to improve systems, not only to assign blame.

- Participating in cross-industry forums and multi-stakeholder initiatives to share experiences and learn from peers.

A culture of continuous learning keeps ethical leadership in step with technological innovation rather than trailing it, closing the gap between principles and practice.

# Case Studies[3]

## Case Study #1: Credit Model Redesign to Address Fairness Concerns

A financial institution deployed a machine learning model to support small-business credit decisions. Overall default rates remained stable, but internal auditors noticed significant differences in approval rates across neighborhoods with different demographic profiles—a pattern consistent with broader concerns about algorithmic discrimination in automated decision-making.

The bank convened a cross-functional task force, including risk, legal, analytics, and community representatives, to investigate. The team found that features such as geographic indicators and historical credit patterns were acting as proxies for race and amplifying existing inequalities, mirroring documented issues in other high-stakes AI contexts. The bank removed or transformed those proxy features, expanded training data to better represent underserved segments, and introduced fairness constraints into the optimization process.

The revised model delivered more equitable outcomes without materially increasing credit risk. The bank then required every high-impact model to pass a fairness audit before deployment and periodic reviews thereafter, institutionalizing the practice and aligning with recommendations for continuous monitoring of high-risk AI.

## Case Study #2: Health System Implements an AI Ethics Board

A large health system was piloting AI-assisted tools for imaging, triage, and readmission-risk prediction. Clinicians and patient advocates raised concerns about opacity of models and potential biases against certain patient groups, reflecting broader discussions about AI's impact on patient safety and equity.

Leadership responded by establishing an AI Ethics and Safety Board composed of clinicians, data scientists, ethicists, patient representatives, and legal counsel. The board classified AI use cases by clinical risk and patient impact, required documentation of intended use, evidence base, fairness testing, and explainability approach for high-risk tools, and held authority to delay or veto deployments if safety or fairness concerns were unresolved.

Early decisions led to adjustments in one triage tool before full rollout and paused another project pending further study. While some teams initially viewed the extra scrutiny as a hurdle, over time clinicians reported greater confidence in AI tools that had passed the board's review, and the health system strengthened its reputation for responsible innovation.

## Case Study #3: Tech Company Uses ERG Red Teams to Test Generative AI

A technology company developing a generative-AI content assistant needed to ensure the system did not produce biased or harmful outputs, particularly for users from marginalized communities. Recognizing that technical evaluations alone would miss some harms, leadership engaged its employee resource groups (ERGs) to act as "red teams."

ERG members tested the system with prompts reflecting their lived experiences, languages, and contexts, documenting instances of stereotyping, exclusionary language, or unsafe suggestions. The AI team used those findings to refine training data, adjust safety filters, and improve prompt-handling logic. The result was a more robust and inclusive product. The company adopted ERG red teaming as a standard step in every new generative-AI feature launch and highlighted the practice in its public communication about AI responsibility.

# Success Metrics

To manage ethics with the same rigor as other strategic priorities, leaders should track a concise set of indicators.

## Ethical AI and Analytics Metrics

| Metric | What It Reveals | Illustrative Target | Leadership Use Case |
|---|---|---|---|
| **Model Fairness Review Coverage** | % of high-impact models w/documented fairness reviews | 100% of Tier-1/Tier-2 models | Ensure critical systems undergo scrutiny |
| **Ethical Incident Rate** | No. and severity of ethics- related incidents per period | Downward trend over time | Assess effectiveness of governance |
| **Time to Resolve Ethics Incidents** | Speed and quality of response to identified issues | Resolution within a defined SLA | Test responsiveness and process maturity |
| **Transparency and Documentation** | % of models with complete documentation and XAI artifacts | 90-100% for customer-facing models | Gauge explainability readiness |
| **Staff Confidence in Raising Concerns** | Survey results on psychological safety around ethics | ≥ 80-85% positive responses | Measure cultural health and escalation safety |
| **External Trust Indicators** | Complaints, regulatory inquiries, public sentiment trends | Stable or improving vs. baseline | Monitor broader license to operate |

Leaders baseline these metrics, set realistic improvement goals, and review progress in the same forums where they examine financial, operational, and risk metrics. That placement signals to everyone that ethical performance is integral to overall performance.

# Practical Advice for Leaders[5]

Moving from principles to practice requires deliberate sequencing. These four steps give leaders a manageable way to help signal the seriousness of their ethical agenda.

### Step 1: Establish Foundations

- Confirm executive ownership for data and AI ethics (for example, assign clear responsibility at C-suite level).
- Agree on a concise set of principles (privacy, transparency, fairness, accountability) and communicate them widely.
- Identify three to five high-impact AI or analytics use cases and conduct structured ethical reviews as pilots.

### Step 2: Build Governance and Tools

- Create or refine an ethics board or model-risk committee with defined scope and authority, including veto rights for high-risk deployments.
- Standardize model documentation templates, including fields for intended use, data sources, limitations, and fairness results.
- Introduce fairness testing and XAI practices into the analytics development lifecycle, prioritizing high-impact models.

### Step 3: Shape Culture and Capability

- Integrate scenario-based ethics discussions into team meetings, training, and leadership-development programs.
- Establish clear escalation pathways and communicate that raising concerns is expected and valued.
- Recognize individuals and teams who exemplify ethical decision-making in analytics projects.

### Step 4: Engage and Evolve

- Engage external stakeholders—customers, communities, regulators, and experts—in periodic dialogues about AI use and expectations.
- Monitor ethical metrics alongside business metrics in regular reviews and adjust controls as needed.

- Refresh policies, training, and frameworks regularly as technologies and regulations evolve.

By taking these steps, leaders turn ethics from a slogan into a real system—shifting it from something they talk about to something they demonstrate and continuously improve.

# Conclusion

Ethical leadership in data and AI is ultimately about stewardship: using the power of new technologies in ways that respect people, align with societal expectations, and build lasting trust. Organizations that invest in strong frameworks, governance, and culture will be better positioned to innovate with confidence, avoid preventable harm, and attract talent and partners who care about how work is done, not just what is achieved.

As AI systems become more capable, the true differentiator will not be access to models but the quality of leadership directing their use. Leaders who embrace this responsibility today help ensure that as machines get smarter, their organizations become not only more efficient but also more just, transparent, and worthy of trust.

# Notes

[1] Ethical leadership as a strategic and risk-management imperative—including documented harms, regulatory scrutiny, and core principles such as privacy, transparency, fairness, and accountability—is examined in World Health Organization's *Ethics and Governance of Artificial Intelligence for Health*; *Frontiers in Artificial Intelligence*'s "Ethical and Legal Considerations in Healthcare AI"; and *Journal of Medical Ethics*'s "The Real-World Impact of Artificial Intelligence Ethics Frameworks: A Scoping Review."

[2] Culture, governance structures, stakeholder engagement, psychological safety, and continuous monitoring in ethical AI programs—including clear accountability and escalation pathways—are laid out in *Frontiers in Artificial Intelligence*'s "Ethical and Legal Considerations in Healthcare AI"; *Journal of Medical Ethics*'s "The Real-World Impact of Artificial Intelligence Ethics Frameworks: A Scoping Review"; and World Health Organization's *Ethics and Governance of Artificial Intelligence for Health.* 141

[3] Algorithmic bias, fairness concerns, and impacts on specific groups—including facial-analysis results and broader issues in automated decision systems—are documented in Buolamwini and Gebru's "Gender Shades: Intersectional Accuracy Disparities in Commercial Gender Classification," Proceedings of Machine Learning Research; and American Civil Liberties Union of Minnesota's "Biased Technology: The Automated Discrimination of Facial Recognition."

[4] Ethical principles and operational frameworks—including privacy-by-design, explainable AI, model documentation, risk tiers, metrics, and leadership checklists—are set out in World Health Organization's *Ethics and Governance of Artificial Intelligence for Health*; and *Frontiers in Artificial Intelligence*'s "Ethical and Legal Considerations in Healthcare AI."

[5] *Journal of Medical Ethics*'s "The Real-World Impact of Artificial Intelligence Ethics Frameworks: A Scoping Review" and *Frontiers in Artificial Intelligence*'s "Ethical and Legal Considerations in Healthcare AI" examine the implementation and maturity of AI ethics frameworks in practice—including embedding ethics into governance, iteration over time, and supporting frameworks with tools, metrics, and organizational capabilities.

[6] Practitioner perspectives on responsible innovation, the use of guardrails, and examples of employee-resource groups and diverse teams acting as red- or "challenge"-teams in AI development draw on C-Suite Strategy's "Harnessing the Power of Employee Resource Groups for Business Success"; and World Health Organization's *Ethics and Governance of Artificial Intelligence for Health.*

55% of leaders say Responsible AI enhances customer experience and drives innovation, showing that strong ethical practices correlate with business value.

*PwC*

"2025 Responsible AI survey: From policy to practice"

Sen et al.

October 2025

## Key topics explored in this chapter:

- Cultivating a Culture of Experimentation and Psychological Safety
- Designing Rigorous, Purposeful Experiments
- Generative AI as Idea Multiplier and Experiment Accelerator
- Scaling Innovation from Prototype to Production
- Fostering Continuous Creative Thinking
- Breaking the Chains of Legacy Mindsets

# WAY 10

# Encourage Innovation and Experimentation


## Abstract[1]

Innovation isn't a side activity in analytics and AI; it is the engine that propels organizations to discover new value, adapt to disruption, and learn what truly works. Low-code tools, cloud analytics, and generative AI have sharply reduced the marginal cost of experimentation, but without structure they also create noise, technical debt, and unmanaged risk. True differentiation comes not from having the most ideas, but from rigorously testing and rapidly scaling the right ones, safely and quickly. That is how experiments become durable advantages rather than one-off pilots. This chapter shows how to build an analytics and AI experimentation engine by cultivating psychological safety, designing rigorous experiments, using generative AI as an idea multiplier, and responsibly moving from prototype to production.


## Objective

After completing this chapter, you will be able to:

- Explain why experimentation is essential to analytics and AI strategy—not merely a "nice-to-have."
- Cultivate cultures of psychological safety, encouraging teams to test ideas and learn from failure.
- Design structured experiments, linking hypotheses directly to business outcomes and risk boundaries.
- Use generative AI and self-service tools to broaden innovation participation without sacrificing control.

- Construct pathways for scaling promising prototypes into safe, maintainable production solutions.
- Monitor innovation performance using clear metrics and adapt practices over time.

# Terms to Know

**AI Sandbox**[2] - A controlled environment where users can explore and test AI tools and models on designated data with managed risk and governance, often inspired by regulatory and digital sandbox models in finance and AI policy.

**Citizen Developer**[3] - A non-IT professional who creates applications, workflows, or automations using low-code/no-code tools or managed AI platforms, within defined governance and security guardrails.

**Experiment Design**[4] - The structured process of framing hypotheses, defining success metrics, identifying treatment and control groups, and specifying guardrails for a test, which underpins rigorous experimentation.

**Fail Fast**[4] - An approach that emphasizes running small, time-bound experiments to quickly determine whether an idea is worth scaling or should be abandoned, minimizing sunk costs and allowing learning to compound.

**Hypothesis-Driven Experimentation**[4] - Running tests based on explicit, testable statements about expected outcomes rather than open-ended tinkering, typically tied to concrete business metrics.

**Minimum Viable Product (MVP)**[4] - The smallest functional version of a solution that can be deployed to learn from real users while limiting risk and investment, often used as a bridge between experiment and production.

**Psychological Safety**[5] - A shared belief that it is safe to speak up with ideas, concerns, or mistakes without fear of punishment or humiliation, which research links to higher experimentation rates and AI adoption.

**Time-to-Prototype**[6] - The elapsed time from initial idea to a usable prototype or MVP that can be evaluated by stakeholders, frequently used as a proxy for innovation speed.

# Introduction[5]

Many organizations claim to value innovation, but few treat it as a system. In analytics and AI, innovation isn't just about "big ideas"; it's about establishing a repeatable process for formulating hypotheses, testing them quickly and safely, and scaling what works. This demands leadership attention on culture, tooling, governance, and incentives—not just technology investments—because innovation founders when experiments remain ad hoc, invisible, or disconnected from strategic goals.

Consider generative AI, which has dramatically lowered the barrier to creation. A single analyst can now develop prototypes, code snippets, and draft dashboards in hours, not weeks. The risk is that organizations launch more pilots than they can responsibly evaluate or scale, echoing the "pilot purgatory" pattern observed in AI programs that stall after proof-of-concept. The big opportunity lies in capitalizing on this newfound speed within a disciplined experimentation engine—one that transforms curiosity into learning and learning into business impact.

## Cultivating a Culture of Experimentation and Psychological Safety[5]

Analytics and AI work inherently involve experimentation, as teams formulate hypotheses about essential inputs, test algorithms, and iterate on features. Yet cultural norms often stifle this work; people often fear they'll be blamed for failed pilots or punished for "wasting" time on ideas that don't pan out, especially when AI is perceived as a threat to jobs or competence. Leaders can counter this by explicitly framing experimentation as "core work effort." To deliberately cultivate psychological safety:

- Normalize incomplete ideas by inviting staff to share early sketches or rough prompts.
- Decouple exploration from performance evaluation, valuing participation in structured experiments—even unsuccessful ones.
- Protect safe sandboxes, ensuring sanctioned AI exploration isn't mistaken for policy violations.
- Share honest stories of failure, where leaders openly discuss what went wrong and what they learned.

When people recognize that thoughtfully designed experiments are encouraged, they're much likelier to try new approaches, challenge assumptions, and discover better ways of working. Conversely, where psychological safety is low, evidence suggests experimentation and learning dramatically slow.

## Designing Rigorous, Purposeful Experiments[4]

Encouraging experimentation does not mean encouraging chaos. The most innovative analytics organizations run many tests, but they do so in disciplined ways, distinguishing between tinkering and hypothesis-driven experimentation and recognizing that only the latter reliably leads to learning that can be scaled.

## Tinkering vs. Hypothesis-Driven Experimentation

| Dimension | Tinkering | Hypothesis-Driven Experimentation |
|---|---|---|
| **Primary Question** | "What happens if we try this?" | "If we do X, we expect Y change in Z metric." |
| **Problem Definition** | Vague or implicit | Explicit business problem stated up front |
| **Hypothesis** | Unstated or very loose | Clear, testable hypothesis captured in writing |
| **Success Metrics** | Decided after the fact or loosely defined | Pre-defined, tied to business outcomes |
| **Scope and Guardrails** | Often ad hoc | Time, data, and risk boundaries agreed before starting |
| **Use of Control / Baseline** | Rare, intuitive comparison | Uses baseline or control where feasible |
| **Documentation** | Minimal or absent | Short experiment log (setup, results, interpretation) |
| **Decision Criteria** | Subjective "looks good" or "feels bad" | Pre-agreed rules to scale, iterate, pause, or stop |
| **Learning Reuse** | Hard to find or replicate | Captured and shared so others can build on or avoid repeating |
| **Organizational perception** | "Playing with tools" side activity | Core work and disciplined path to value and risk reduction |

Key elements of rigorous experiment design include a clear problem and hypothesis (for example, "Using generative AI to triage customer emails will reduce average response time by 20 percent without lowering satisfaction"), defined success metrics tied to business outcomes, agreed scope and guardrails on time, data, and user exposure (often starting with anonymized or synthetic data), use of baselines or control groups where feasible, and explicit decision rules that prevent endless pilots.

One simple mindset shift is to move from "Can we build this?"—a question AI increasingly answers with "yes"—to "Should we build this, and how will we know?", anchoring experimentation in value creation and ethics rather than novelty.

## Generative AI as Idea Multiplier and Experiment Accelerator[6]

Generative AI can support experimentation in several concrete ways, but it works best when it's wrapped in guardrails and associated with clear roles for human judgment.

Practical uses range from brainstorming to reframing work: teams can prompt AI tools for alternative strategies, stakeholder personas, or "devil's-advocate" critiques that surface blind spots. It can also accelerate prototyping through AI-assisted code, simple pipelines, mock dashboards, or conversational interfaces that bring concepts to life before you commit scarce engineering capacity. Generative tools can further support experiment design by drafting hypotheses, outlining experimental plans, or suggesting sample-size estimates for experts to refine.

To harness these benefits safely, teams need an environment of managed AI sandboxes with approved tools, defined data boundaries, and clear rules of use. Leaders should provide training in prompt literacy and evaluation so teams can question outputs rather than accept them at face value. Just as importantly, leaders must draw a bright line between exploratory use and production workflows so quick prototypes don't silently morph into necessary, unreviewed systems. In this way, generative AI can amplify human creativity and experimentation.

## Embracing Failure as a Learning Catalyst[4]

Within any experimentation system, most ideas won't evolve into production solutions. This isn't waste; it's the cost of discovery. In fact, high-performing organizations distinguish themselves by how they handle "failed" experiments, treating them as structured learning opportunities rather than sources of embarrassment.

Effective practices include documenting experiments in brief and creating "experiment logs" that record the hypothesis, setup, results, and interpretations. Leaders should then share these learnings widely so others can build on them or avoid repeating the same tests. It's important to separate "outcome" from "process," evaluating teams on the quality of experiment design and learning, not just on positive results. Organizations should also celebrate "smart stops": cases where teams end a pilot early because evidence shows it lacks value or creates undue risk. Taken together, this posture turns failure into a strategic asset—a wellspring of institutional knowledge that improves the quality and efficiency of future experiments and helps organizations escape pilot purgatory.

## Scaling Innovation from Prototype to Production[7]

Today it's common for organizations to push promising prototypes into production too quickly without properly strengthening them. In studies of AI adoption—especially in healthcare—this is often called "pilot purgatory," a situation where pilot projects accumulate costs and fail to deliver meaningful, enterprise-wide results.

To avoid this, leaders need a clear, intentional path from experimentation to full production. This starts with **defining readiness criteria,** including specific thresholds for business value, technical performance, reliability, and risk that a prototype must meet before implementation. Organizations also benefit from **cross-functional transition teams** that bring together product, engineering, operations, risk, and change management to guide rollout and support. A **phased rollout,** beginning with smaller segments or regions and supported by strong monitoring before wider deployment, is equally important. Finally, assigning clear **operational ownership** for ongoing monitoring, maintenance, and improvement—along with defined communication channels for frontline staff to report issues—helps ensure long-term success. Without a way to embed successful experiments into the organization, innovation becomes little more than a series of "what could've been." The right pathway can make experimentation a real competitive advantage.

## Fostering Continuous Creative Thinking[6]

Innovation is more sustainable when creative thinking becomes part of everyday work rather than something reserved for occasional workshops. Leaders can reinforce this by building routines and structures that keep experimentation visible, practical, and easy to engage in.

Examples include **hackathons and innovation sprints,** where cross-functional teams explore new ideas in focused, time-bound sessions, often using AI tools for rapid prototyping. **"Innovation hours,"** or "20 percent time," give employees space to pursue self-directed experiments that align with strategic priorities. Regular **innovation showcases** also play an important role, allowing teams to share both successes and failures with peers and leadership, reinforcing a culture of learning. In addition, organizations should encourage the use of **AI as a "thinking partner"** for brainstorming, critique, and identifying edge cases. Together, these practices make it clear that innovation is everyone's responsibility, not just the domain of a central team. Over time, they help create an environment where curiosity and disciplined experimentation become a normal part of the daily routine.

### Breaking the Chains of Legacy Mindsets[7]

Often, the greatest barrier to innovation isn't technology or budget; it's mindset. Legacy structures and beliefs—like "only central IT can build anything" or "mistakes are career-limiting"—stifle experimentation.

To address this, helpful actions include **flattening decision-making,** allowing low-risk experiments to proceed with lighter approvals but within clear guardrails. **Enabling citizen developers** with tools, training, and governance lets business users safely build automations, dashboards, or AI-assisted workflows. Leaders should also **align incentives** so performance goals don't reward risk avoidance at the expense of learning. Furthermore, valuing "risk-aware experimentation" means praising teams that identify and de-risk problematic pilots, not just those that launch successful ones

Changing mindsets takes time. Yet, consistent signals about what's celebrated, funded, and protected can gradually reshape what people believe and how they behave.

## Case Studies[8]

### Case Study #1: Global Bank Launches an AI Sandbox for Experimentation

A global bank sought to encourage AI-driven innovation while upholding strict regulatory and security requirements. Historically, experimentation with new tools had been slow and tightly controlled, prompting business units to seek unsanctioned solutions.

Technology and risk leaders collaborated to create an AI sandbox: a secure environment where employees could utilize approved generative-AI tools on curated, de-identified datasets. Access required brief training on responsible use and data boundaries. The sandbox also included templates for common experiments, such as summarizing customer interactions, drafting analytics code, or exploring new dashboards. Within a year, hundreds of employees had participated in sandbox experiments. Some concepts, like AI-assisted call summarization and automated report drafting, were refined and transitioned into formal projects. Others were documented as useful learning but not pursued further. The bank reduced shadow-IT risks while simultaneously producing grassroots innovation, echoing reports that AI sandboxes effectively balance innovation with oversight in financial services.

## Case Study #2: Retailer Uses Hackathons to Accelerate Store-Level Analytics

A large retailer struggled to generate store-level innovation within its analytics program. Most initiatives originated centrally, leaving frontline teams feeling disconnected from data projects and AI tools. The retailer introduced quarterly "Store Analytics Hackathons," pairing store staff with analysts and engineers. Participants gained access to store-specific data in a safe environment and were encouraged to use AI tools to explore ideas around demand-forecasting, staffing schedules, and localized promotions.

Winning ideas were selected based on potential impact and feasibility. Several prototypes—for example, a generative-AI assistant to help managers interpret daily performance reports—were refined into pilots and then scaled. More importantly, store leaders reported feeling greater ownership of analytics, and the central team gained a deeper understanding of on-the-ground challenges. This outcome reflects findings that hackathons can foster cross-functional collaboration and uncover practical, high-value use cases in retail.

## Case Study #3: Health Insurer Learns from a "Failed" AI Pilot

A health insurer piloted an AI system designed to route member inquiries to the correct support channel. Early results revealed modest speed improvements but mixed member satisfaction; some segments reported confusion or frustration with AI-driven prompts.

Instead of quietly abandoning the project, the insurer conducted a structured after-action review. The team documented assumptions, experiment design, results, and member feedback. They discovered that expectations hadn't been clearly communicated and that certain segments preferred human contact for specific inquiry types. The insurer chose not to scale the original solution. Instead, it utilized the learning to redesign a hybrid human-AI routing strategy. A subsequent experiment, featuring clearer communication and more targeted AI use, yielded superior results. The organization treated the initial pilot as a valuable source of insight rather than a failure to conceal.

# Success Metrics[4]

Innovation benefits from measurement just as other strategic priorities do. Leaders should use a focused set of metrics to understand whether experimentation is healthy and productive.

## Innovation and Experimentation Metrics

| Metric | What It Reveals | Illustrative Target | Leadership Use Case |
|---|---|---|---|
| **Number of Active Experiments** | Volume of structured tests in a period | Steady, sustainable growth over time | Gauge experimentation energy |
| **Time-to-Prototype** | Speed from idea to usable MVP | Reduction by 30-50% over 1-2 years | Assess impact of AI tools and processes |
| **Experiment-to-Scale Rate** | % of experiments that progress to scaled deployment | Around 10-20% | Balance exploration vs. selectivity |
| **Learning Reuse Rate** | % of new experiments referencing prior experiment logs | Increasing trend | Measure institutional learning |
| **Participation Breadth** | Distribution of contributors across functions/levels | Growing diversity over time | Ensure innovation is not siloed |
| **Psychological Safety Scores** | Survey responses on safety to propose/test ideas | ≥ 80-85% positive | Track cultural readiness for experimentation |

Leaders do not need perfect numbers; rather, they need directional insight. Reviewing these or other metrics alongside business performance helps ensure experimentation remains intentional, supported, and sustainable rather than sporadic or purely technology-driven.

## Practical Advice for Leaders

Leaders who want to turn experimentation into a durable capability can follow a manageable, phased approach that converts curiosity into repeatable value.

### Phase 1: Signal and Enable

- Explicitly state that experimentation is expected in analytics and AI and connect it to strategic priorities.
- Identify and approve a small set of AI tools and sandbox environments, with clear usage guidelines.[2]
- Run a one-time or recurring "innovation day" or hackathon to surface early ideas and demonstrate support.[8]

### Phase 2: Structure and Protect

- Introduce simple experiment templates capturing problem, hypothesis, metrics, guardrails, and timeline.[4]
- Create a lightweight approval path for low-risk experiments so teams can move quickly within defined boundaries.
- Clarify that lessons from well-designed experiments—successful or not—are viewed positively in performance conversations, reinforcing psychological safety.[5]

### Phase 3: Connect and Scale

- Establish criteria and a process for moving prototypes into formal projects and production, including shared success metrics.[7]
- Form cross-functional review groups to assess which experiments to scale and how.
- Create a central repository of experiment summaries and learnings so future teams can reuse insights.

**Phase 4: Measure and Evolve**

- Track a small set of innovation metrics and share them in leadership forums.
- Adjust policies, tools, and capacity based on bottlenecks or unintended consequences, such as pilot overload or shadow experimentation.
- Refresh training and communication as AI tools and business priorities evolve, keeping experimentation aligned with strategy and ethics.

# Conclusion

Encouraging innovation and experimentation in analytics and AI is less about heroic creativity and more about building systems that make exploration safe, disciplined, and scalable. When leaders cultivate psychological safety, provide appropriate tools and guardrails, and value learning as much as outcomes, experimentation becomes a valuable and exciting part of everyday work.

Just be aware that experimentation isn't a short burst of activity, but a continuous process of discovery, learning, and renewal supported by structures that make innovation sustainable. As AI accelerates what can be built, the organizations that thrive will be those that know how to choose the best ideas, how to test them responsibly, and how to scale them into lasting competitive advantage.

# Notes

[1] Experimentation as a strategic capability in analytics and AI—encompassing the impact of generative AI, low-code tools, and cloud platforms on the cost and volume of experimentation, and the risks of pilot overload and technical debt—is examined in Nisum's "Scaling AI in Healthcare: Escaping Pilot Purgatory"; Concord's "Why Most AI Pilots Fail—and How Healthcare Enterprises Can Break the Pattern"; and Salesforce's "Why 95% of AI Pilots Fail—and What the Other 5% Do Differently."

[2] AI sandboxes as controlled environments for safe experimentation in financial services and other regulated sectors are detailed in *Organisation for Economic Co-operation and Development*'s "Regulatory Sandboxes in Artificial Intelligence"; NayaOne's "Why an AI Sandbox for Banks Is Key to Safe Innovation"; NayaOne's "Sandbox Environments and the Use of Technology in Finance"; and NayaOne's "Regulatory vs Digital Sandbox for AI: You Need to Know."

[3] Citizen developers and the conditions under which low-code and no-code experimentation can be safely democratized are characterized in NayaOne's "Sandbox Environments and the Use of Technology in Finance."

[4] The distinction between tinkering and hypothesis-driven experimentation—including "fail fast" approaches, experiment-to-scale funnels, and staged pathways from prototype to production—is drawn from Nisum's "Scaling AI in Healthcare: Escaping Pilot Purgatory"; Concord's "Why Most AI Pilots Fail—and How Healthcare Enterprises Can Break the Pattern"; Salesforce's "Why 95% of AI Pilots Fail—and What the Other 5% Do Differently"; and *Organisation for Economic Co-operation and Development*'s "Regulatory Sandboxes in Artificial Intelligence."

[5] Psychological safety as an enabler of experimentation—including cultural practices supporting safe risk-taking and the treatment of learning from failed experiments as positive performance evidence—is analyzed in Lab for Applied Artificial Intelligence, *Loyola University Chicago*'s "How AI Is Reshaping Work and Human Psychology"; *Psychology Today*'s "Psychological Safety Drives AI Adoption"; Hive HR's "Why AI and Psychological Safety Belong Together—with Insights from Hive"; and *Training Journal*'s "Psychological Safety Is the Missing Piece in Your AI Strategy."

[6] Generative AI as an accelerator of experimentation—supporting brainstorming, rapid prototyping, and experiment-design assistance while requiring human oversight—is discussed in Lab for Applied Artificial Intelligence, *Loyola University Chicago*'s "How AI Is Reshaping Work and Human Psychology"; and NayaOne's "Sandbox Environments and the Use of Technology in Finance"; and NayaOne's "Regulatory vs Digital Sandbox for AI: You Need to Know."

[7] Pilot purgatory, pilot-to-production rates, and related scaling challenges are analyzed in Nisum's "Scaling AI in Healthcare: Escaping Pilot Purgatory"; Concord's "Why Most AI Pilots Fail—and How Healthcare Enterprises Can Break the Pattern"; and Salesforce's "Why 95% of AI Pilots Fail—and What the Other 5% Do Differently."

[8] Hackathons, innovation sprints, and similar creative rituals in retail and other industries—and their role in surfacing practical analytics ideas and increasing frontline ownership—are explored in *Galp Upcoming Energies*'s "Galp Hackathon Retail 4.0 Harnesses the Power of AI"; *Thoughtworks*'s "What Can Retailers Learn from Hackathons?"; PlacementPreparation's "10 Best Retail Hackathon Project Ideas"; and Zigpoll's "Overcoming Brick-and-Mortar Retail Challenges with Hackathon Sponsorship."

Today,34% of companies are using AI to deeply transform their businesses; 37% are applying it only at a surface level.

*Deloitte*

"The State of AI in the Enterprise"

Rowan et al.

January 2026

# Key topics explored in this chapter:

- The Strategic Value of Generational Diversity
- Understanding Generational Differences in Workstyles and Learning Preferences
- Cross-Generational Leadership: Do and Don't
- Leveraging Knowledge Transfer and Reverse Mentoring
- Designing Inclusive Development Plans for All Generations
- Using Technology to Bridge Generational Gaps
- Cultivating an Intergenerational Culture
- Overcoming Challenges and Conflict
- The Vital Role of Leadership

# WAY 11

# Develop Cross-Generational Analytics and AI Talent

## Abstract[1]

Analytics and AI teams now comprise four or more generations, ranging from seasoned professionals who recall pre-digital processes to "AI natives" who treat intelligent tools as natural collaborators. This generational diversity is a potent asset: experienced colleagues bring context, judgment, and stakeholder credibility, while younger ones contribute digital fluency, experimental energy, and comfort with emerging tools. Yet, unmanaged, this diversity can breed friction, foster shadow-AI usage, and lead to missed learning opportunities. This chapter examines the strategic value of generational diversity, highlights differences in work styles and learning preferences, and explains how to design reverse mentoring, knowledge transfer, and inclusive development programs. It also explores how to cultivate cross-generational analytics and AI talent, ensuring each cohort can contribute fully while continuing to grow professionally.

## Objective

After completing this chapter, you will be able to:

- Articulate the strategic value of cross-generational collaboration within analytics and AI teams.
- Recognize common generational differences in work styles and learning preferences, and adapt leadership strategies accordingly.
- Design reverse mentoring and knowledge-transfer programs that benefit all generations.
- Create inclusive development plans and learning pathways supporting multiple career stages.

- Use technology to bridge generational gaps rather than widen them, including AI-enabled mentoring and collaboration tools.
- Monitor cross-generational engagement and learning using targeted metrics, and adjust interventions over time.

# Terms to Know

**AI Native**[2] - Individuals, often from younger cohorts, who've grown up with AI and digital tools view them as natural collaborators in their daily work, much like how Gen Z often mentors older colleagues on AI.

**Cross-Generational Collaboration**[3] - Intentional cooperation among employees from diverse age cohorts to achieve shared goals, leveraging their varied perspectives and skills. And research links this collaboration to higher innovation and decision quality, especially when well-led.

**Knowledge Transfer**[3] - Structured processes for sharing experience, context, and skills between individuals and across generations. These include mentoring, documentation, and project-based learning.

**Multigenerational Workforce**[3] - A workforce comprising two or more generational cohorts (e.g., Baby Boomers, Generation X, Millennials, Generation Z) collaborating. This structure is now prevalent in analytics and AI functions.

**Reverse Mentoring**[4] - A mentoring arrangement where junior or younger employees guide more senior or older colleagues. They often focus on technology, culture, or emerging trends, while the junior mentors simultaneously gain insights into strategy and institutional knowledge.

**Shadow AI**[5] - Employees' use of unsanctioned or unmanaged AI tools, often bypassing perceived friction in official systems. Recent surveys suggest a majority of workers now engage in some form of shadow AI, carrying significant data-risk implications.

**Wisdom Gap**[5] - The perceived divide between technical fluency (often seen in younger workers) and accumulated judgment and institutional knowledge (typically found in older workers). Cross-generational programs aim to transform this gap into a reciprocal "wisdom exchange."

# Introduction

Analytics and AI transformations seldom launch from a blank slate. Most organizations employ long-tenured staff deeply familiar with legacy systems, historical business decisions, and nuanced stakeholder dynamics.

Simultaneously, they also onboard new talent accustomed to smartphones, cloud tools, and AI assistants. This creates a multigenerational analytics workforce, reflecting diverse eras of technology, education, and work-related expectations.

When leaders intentionally harness these strengths, cross-generational teams become potent engines of innovation, resilience, and superior decision-making. Fail to do so, and organizations invite avoidable tension between older workers who might feel displaced or undervalued and younger colleagues who could resort to shadow AI and external networks for support.

## The Strategic Value of Generational Diversity[3]

Generational diversity is more than a mere demographic fact; it's a strategic resource. That's because distinct age cohorts contribute important complementary capabilities to analytics and AI initiatives.

## Generational Strengths in Analytics and AI Teams

| Typical Cohort | Key Strengths in Analytics and AI Context |
|---|---|
| **Seasoned Professionals (Boomers / Gen X)** | Deep domain expertise, historical context, pattern recognition, stakeholder trust; strong "gut checks" on model outputs |
| **Mid-Career (Older Millennials / Gen X)** | Translators between legacy processes and modern tools; pragmatic problem-solvers; change agents |
| **Early-Career (Younger Millennials / Gen Z)** | Digital and AI fluency, rapid experimentation, comfort with new platforms, fresh perspectives |

Leaders who intentionally combine these strengths produce powerful benefits. They **accelerate learning:** younger colleagues help senior staff adopt AI tools, while senior peers provide vital context and nuance. They also **mitigate knowledge loss** by capturing institutional memory earlier and more systematically. And they **strengthen innovation:** diverse, mixed-age teams generate more creative solutions than homogeneous groups, particularly when conflict is well managed. The real challenge is transitioning from informal collaboration to structured practices that embed cross-generational learning into daily routine operations.

## Understanding Generational Differences in Workstyles and Learning Preferences[3]

Effective leadership depends on understanding how generations differ in communication styles, expectations, and approaches to learning. While it is important to avoid stereotypes, recognizing broad patterns can still provide valuable insight for shaping thoughtful organizational design.

## Generational Workstyle and Learning Tendencies

| Generation | Workstyle Tendencies | Learning Preferences |
|---|---|---|
| **Baby Boomers** (1946-1964) | Value face-to-face dialogue, clear roles, stability | In-person workshops, context-rich explanations |
| **Generation X** (1965-1980) | Prefer autonomy, efficiency, pragmatism | Self-directed learning, concise resources |
| **Generation Y (Millenials)** (1981-1996) | Seek collaboration, feedback, purposeful work | Blended digital/live learning, social formats |
| **Generation Z** (1997-2012) | Expect speed, authenticity, intuitive tech | Microlearning, mobile-first content, peer learning |

These patterns highlight important leadership adaptations. Leaders must offer multi-modal learning (live sessions plus digital modules); provide more context and rationale for older cohorts, and greater flexibility and autonomy for younger ones; and clarify how AI changes (not eliminates) the invaluable contributions of older workers. These types of tailored strategies truly boost engagement, ensuring every generation finds its vital place in the evolving analytics and AI landscape.

## Cross-Generational Leadership: Do and Don't[3]

Leaders play an important role in turning generational diversity into a source of collaboration rather than friction. Clear behavioral guidelines help translate this intent into consistent, everyday practice, shaping how teams communicate, learn from one another, and work together.

## Behavioral Guidelines for Leaders

| Do | Don't |
|---|---|
| Ask individuals about their preferences rather than assume based on age. | Assume all Boomers dislike tech or all Gen Z embrace every new tool. |
| Mix experience levels on analytics and AI projects by design. | Assign "modern" work only to younger staff and "legacy" work only to older staff. |
| Explain the "why" behind changes and how AI affects each role. | Announce AI initiatives as faits accomplis without context, especially to long-tenured staff. |
| Offer multiple learning formats (live, digital, microlearning, mentoring). | Mandate a single learning format and expect it to work for everyone. |
| Recognize and reward mentoring and knowledge sharing across ages. | Treat mentoring as invisible extra work with no bearing on evaluations. |
| Use younger "digital ambassadors" to help colleagues adopt tools safely. | Tolerate uncontrolled shadow AI because official tools are too hard to use or poorly supported. |

## Leveraging Knowledge Transfer and Reverse Mentoring[4]

Traditionally, knowledge flowed primarily from more experienced workers to younger employees. In today's AI-enabled environment, however, knowledge moves in multiple directions. Reverse mentoring reflects this shift by pairing younger, tech-savvy employees with senior leaders and other seasoned professionals in structured relationships that complement traditional models.

Well-designed reverse-mentoring programs formalize pairings and objectives, match participants based on skills and learning goals (like AI tools or new platforms), and emphasize mutual learning. Here, younger mentors provide technology and culture insight, while senior mentees share strategy, judgment, and organizational context. Effective programs also mandate regular check-ins, supported by collaboration tools, and recognize contributions in performance and development discussions for both mentors and mentees. Ultimately, these programs build bridges across generations, improve AI literacy in leadership, and give younger colleagues vital visibility and confidence.

## Designing Inclusive Development Plans for All Generations[3]

If development opportunities appear targeted to one generation—say, only younger employees receiving AI training or only older employees receiving leadership development—resentment can grow. But inclusive development plans ensure all cohorts see clear pathways for growth. Key elements include:

- Regular skills and interest assessments that surface aspirations across all generations.
- Diverse learning modalities blending online courses, internal academies, project-based assignments, mentoring, and coaching.
- Flexible career paths offering both technical and leadership tracks, alongside lateral moves into translator, product-owner, or governance roles.
- Microlearning and just-in-time content that supports fast, focused learning.
- Comprehensive legacy-knowledge capture, enabling experienced staff to document processes, decisions, and "what we learned" narratives, with full recognition for this vital contribution.

These practices foster continuous development, respecting diverse career stages and motivations.

## Using Technology to Bridge Generational Gaps[3]

Technology can either narrow or widen the generational divide. When thoughtfully deployed, it becomes a "shared space" where generations learn from one another. Useful levers include:

- Collaboration platforms supporting synchronous and asynchronous communication (video, chat, shared workspaces) to cater to diverse preferences.
- Personalized learning platforms recommending content tailored to role, skill level, and goals, including AI-enabled mentoring features.
- Analytics portals with configurable views, allowing power users to delve deep while offering simplified views for occasional users.
- Co-pilot-style AI tools that assist both experienced and newer employees with summarization, drafting, or analysis. Younger employees can serve as digital ambassadors, helping colleagues

adopt these tools. Meanwhile, older employees can guide how tools are applied to solving real business problems, transforming technology into a shared language rather than a dividing line.

## Cultivating an Intergenerational Culture[3]

Policies and tools matter, but daily culture determines whether generations collaborate or retreat into silos. Leaders need to foster norms and rituals that promote mutual respect and shared purpose. Practical ways include:

- Offering training on generational perspectives to help teams grasp how different cohorts interpret behaviors, feedback, and change.
- Intentionally staffing cross-generational project teams for complex analytics initiatives.
- Creating story-sharing forums where employees describe major project lessons, "first AI use" stories, or career journeys.
- Explicitly addressing age-based stereotypes by correcting assumptions like "Boomers aren't tech-savvy" or "Gen Z doesn't want to work hard."

A culture that normalizes curiosity, questioning, and help-seeking across all ages ultimately drives better analytics and AI outcomes.

## Overcoming Challenges and Conflict[5]

Generational differences can sometimes create friction, including disagreements about remote work, skepticism about new tools, or misunderstandings of tone. Leaders should treat these situations as opportunities to strengthen collaboration, not as proof that generations "can't work together." Helpful practices include:

- Providing conflict-resolution training with generational awareness, so managers recognize when tensions stem from differing expectations rather than bad intent.
- Facilitating structured dialogues where people from different age groups share their experiences with change, feedback, and technology.
- Establishing transparent feedback mechanisms for employees to raise concerns about generational dynamics and then receive responses.
- Implementing sentiment monitoring to identify generational patterns in engagement, belonging, and workload perceptions.

Addressing tensions early prevents small misunderstandings from becoming persistent divides. And studies suggest that when managed well, cognitive conflict in age-diverse teams significantly enhances innovation.

## The Vital Role of Leadership[1]

Leadership determines whether generational diversity becomes an asset or a liability. Leaders of analytics and AI teams must actively champion cross-generational collaboration and development. Key behaviors include:

- Modeling learning across generations—for instance, senior leaders openly ask younger colleagues for help with AI tools while younger leaders, in turn, seek mentorship on strategy and influence.
- Framing AI as a collaborative tool that augments human capabilities, not as a replacement for experienced staff, thereby reducing anxiety among older cohorts.
- Ensuring equitable access to development by auditing who receives training, stretch assignments, and mentoring—then correcting any imbalances.
- Designing diverse teams by default, making cross-generational composition standard for all major analytics programs.

These types of actions send a clear signal: everyone, regardless of generation, has a vital stake and a crucial role in making the analytics and AI effort a successful one.

# Case Studies[6]

## Case Study #1: Reverse Mentoring for AI Literacy in a Manufacturing Firm

A global manufacturing company recognized a disconnect: senior leaders were setting AI strategy without hands-on experience with the tools, while younger employees were experimenting with AI independently but without clear strategic direction. To close this gap, the company launched a reverse mentoring program focused on AI literacy. High-potential Millennial and Gen Z employees were paired with senior managers and executives based on shared learning goals. Younger mentors introduced leaders to practical use cases such as AI-assisted maintenance, demand forecasting, and co-pilot tools, while leaders provided important context on operational constraints, regulatory requirements, and long-term business priorities.

Within a year, senior leaders reported greater confidence in discussing AI opportunities and risks. Notably, several pilot initiatives emerged directly from ideas developed during these sessions. Younger mentors gained visibility while strengthening their communication and leadership skills, and the program ultimately became an ongoing component of the firm's leadership development effort.

## Case Study #2: Health System Builds a Cross-Generational Analytics Academy

A regional health system aimed to expand analytics across clinical and administrative functions but encountered uneven adoption. Long-tenured staff often viewed data tools warily, while newer employees, though eager, lacked familiarity with health-system operations. The organization responded by creating a "Cross-Generational Analytics Academy" to bridge these gaps.

The academy offered tracks tailored to diverse roles and experience levels: foundational analytics for clinicians, advanced data skills for analysts, and leadership modules for managers. Each cohort intentionally mixed generations. Learning encompassed hands-on work with AI-assisted tools, case discussions led jointly by senior clinicians and younger analysts, and projects where teams tackled real hospital challenges. Over time, participation surged. Cross-generational teams delivered improvements in areas like patient flow and resource allocation. Surveys revealed increased data confidence across all age groups and a stronger sense that analytics was "for us"—not just for specialists or younger staff.

## Case Study #3: Tech Company Reduces Shadow AI Through Digital Ambassadors

A technology company observed a surge in unsanctioned AI tool usage, particularly among younger employees frustrated by sluggish internal processes. Security and compliance leaders grew concerned, yet leadership didn't want to stifle the company's innovative energy. So, the company launched a "Digital Ambassador" program, redirecting this energy into safer, sanctioned channels.

It selected younger, AI-fluent employees as digital ambassadors, training them in security, governance, and responsible-AI guidelines. These ambassadors then partnered with more experienced team members to redesign workflows using approved AI platforms—like internal co-pilots for documentation, testing, and meeting summaries. The program significantly reduced shadow-AI usage while simultaneously increasing the number of sanctioned AI use cases in production. Older employees reported greater comfort experimenting with AI, and younger employees felt recognized for their expertise and contributions to change.

# Success Metrics[5]

To intentionally manage cross-generational development, leaders should track progress using a focused set of indicators.

## Cross-Generational Talent Metrics

| Metric | What It Reveals | Illustrative Target | Leadership Use Case |
|---|---|---|---|
| **Participation in Mentoring Programs** | Reach of traditional and reverse mentoring across generations | Representation from all major cohorts | Assess inclusivity of mentoring and knowledge sharing |
| **Cross-Generational Project Mix** | % of key analytics projects with multi-generation teams | Upward trend over 1-2 years | Check team-design practices |
| **AI Training Coverage by Age Cohort** | Access to AI/analytics learning across generations | Comparable rates across age groups | Detect and address training inequities |
| **Shadow-AI Indicators** | Use of unsanctioned tools by cohort | Downward trend, especially where sanctioned options exist | Evaluate effectiveness of safe alternatives |
| **Engagement and Belonging Scores** | Sentiment by generation about inclusion and opportunities | Narrow gaps between generations | Identify where specific cohorts need attention |
| **Knowledge-Capture Activity** | Volume and quality of documented legacy knowledge and lessons | Steady or growing contributions | Monitor progress on wisdom preservation |

Reviewing these metrics alongside standard people and performance indicators helps ensure generational considerations remain part of analytics talent strategy and that interventions can be targeted where gaps appear.

# Practical Advice for Leaders[5]

Leaders can develop cross-generational analytics and AI talent using a structured multi-step approach like this one.

### Step 1: Diagnose and Acknowledge

- Map generational distribution across analytics, data, and adjacent functions to grasp current composition.
- Conduct surveys or interviews to understand each cohort's views on AI, learning, and collaboration, assessing their comfort with tools and change.
- Share findings with teams, acknowledging strengths and tensions without assigning blame. This builds transparency and trust.

### Step 2: Launch Structured Cross-Generational Programs

- Pilot reverse-mentoring programs focused on AI literacy and digital tools. Use best-practice guidelines to foster mutual learning.
- Design at least one cross-generational project team for a visible analytics initiative, ensuring clear sponsorship and deep support.
- Launch a small digital-ambassador or AI-guide program. Younger staff can then support the adoption of sanctioned tools within established guardrails.

### Step 3: Align Development and Technology

- Audit training offerings to ensure all generations, not just early-career staff, access AI and analytics learning.
- Introduce learning pathways tailored to diverse roles and experience levels, incorporating multiple formats and mentorship opportunities.
- Ensure collaboration and analytics platforms support varied workstyles and accessibility needs, enabling all cohorts to participate fully.

### Step 4: Measure, Celebrate, and Adjust

- Track key cross-generational metrics and discuss them in leadership meetings to maintain focus on inclusion.
- Highlight stories where cross-generational collaboration improved outcomes or averted missteps, reinforcing desired behaviors.
- Refine programs and communication based on feedback from all age groups, adjusting structures that unintentionally favor specific cohorts.

Together, these steps make generational diversity a purposeful and integrated component of an analytics and AI talent strategy.

# Conclusion

A multigenerational workforce isn't a problem to solve; it's a powerful engine for analytics and AI advancement when managed effectively. Seasoned professionals bring crucial context and judgment, making AI systems safer and more relevant. Meanwhile, younger colleagues offer fluency with new tools and an appetite for experimentation. Under shared leadership, this diversity significantly enhances innovation and decision quality.

By investing in reverse mentoring, inclusive development, thoughtful use of technology, and metrics that reveal each generation's strengths, organizations can transform the "wisdom gap" into a dynamic wisdom exchange. This exchange strengthens analytics capabilities today and prepares the workforce to adapt together as AI continues its evolution. Moreover, it aligns with emerging views that innovation's future hinges on cross-generational collaboration, not any single cohort.

# Notes

[1] Multigenerational analytics and AI workforces—including AI natives, shadow AI, and cross-generational collaboration as a strategic capability—are examined in this chapter's Abstract and Objective through "Bridging the Generational Divide: Fostering Intergenerational Collaboration in the Workplace"; "Generational Diversity and Team Innovation: The Roles of Conflict and Shared Leadership"; "AI and Reverse Mentoring: How Cross-Generational Learning Drives Innovation"; "Gen Z as AI Mentors: Bridging the Generational Divide at Work"; "Lurking in the Shadows: The Costs of Unapproved AI Tools"; "Shadow AI Is Widespread—and Executives Use It the Most"; and "How to Empower Leaders with AI for Generational Collaboration."

[2] AI natives and younger cohorts as natural users and coaches of AI tools in the workplace are characterized in "Gen Z as AI Mentors: Bridging the Generational Divide at Work" and "How to Empower Leaders with AI for Generational Collaboration."

[3] Cross-generational collaboration, along with evidence linking age-diverse teams to improved innovation and decision-making when conflict is well managed, is examined in "Generational Diversity and Team Innovation: The Roles of Conflict and Shared Leadership" and "Mentoring and Innovation: How Cross-Generational Teams Affect Decision-Making and Overall Organizational Performance."

[4] Mentoring, documentation, and project-based work as mechanisms for knowledge transfer across generations are discussed in "Bridging the Generational Divide: Fostering Intergenerational Collaboration in the Workplace" and "Mentoring and Innovation: How Cross-Generational Teams Affect Decision-Making and Overall Organizational Performance." Reverse-mentoring programs—in which younger employees mentor senior colleagues on technology and culture while receiving strategic guidance—are defined, structured, and assessed in "AI and Reverse Mentoring: How Cross-Generational Learning Drives Innovation"; "The Definitive Guide to Implementing Reverse Mentoring (in 2026)"; and "Bridging Generational Gaps with Reverse Mentoring."

[5] The "wisdom gap" between technical fluency and accumulated judgment—and its reframing as a reciprocal wisdom exchange through intergenerational programs—is explored in "Gen Z as AI Mentors: Bridging the Generational Divide at Work" and "AI and Reverse Mentoring: How Cross-Generational Learning Drives Innovation." Multigenerational workforces and typical cohorts (Baby Boomers, Generation X, Millennials, Generation Z) in contemporary organizations are surveyed in "Generational Diversity and Team Innovation: The Roles of Conflict and Shared Leadership" and "Bridging the Generational Divide: Fostering Intergenerational Collaboration in the Workplace." Generational work- and learning-preferences, intergenerational conflict, inclusive development plans, cultural practices, measurement, and staged leadership actions draw on "Bridging the Generational Divide: Fostering Intergenerational Collaboration in the Workplace"; "Generational Diversity and Team Innovation: The Roles of Conflict and Shared Leadership"; "Mentoring and Innovation: How Cross-Generational Teams Affect Decision-Making and Overall Organizational Performance"; "Cross-Generational Mentor Matching: Build Stronger Connections"; and "How to Empower Leaders with AI for Generational Collaboration."

[6] *Patterns* and illustrative details underpinning the manufacturing reverse-mentoring program, the health-system cross-generational analytics academy, and the tech-company digital-ambassador initiative are drawn from "AI and Reverse Mentoring: How Cross-Generational Learning Drives Innovation"; "The Definitive Guide to Implementing Reverse Mentoring (in 2026)"; "Gen Z as AI Mentors: Bridging the Generational Divide at Work"; "Mentoring and Innovation: How Cross-Generational Teams Affect Decision-Making and Overall Organizational Performance"; "Lurking in the Shadows: The Costs of Unapproved AI Tools"; and "Shadow AI Is Widespread—and Executives Use It the Most."

## Key topics explored in this chapter:

- The Rise of Citizen Analytics and Data Advocacy
- The Business Case for Democratizing Analytics
- Building Data and AI Literacy Across the Organization
- Providing Accessible, Conversational Tools
- Cultivating a Culture of Data Advocacy
- Governing Citizen Analytics and Shadow AI
- Measuring the Impact of Empowerment Initiatives
- Leadership's Role in Driving Empowerment
- Overcoming Common Barriers

# WAY 12

# Empower Data Advocates and Citizen Analysts


## Abstract[1]

Analytics and AI aren't confined to specialist teams anymore. Instead, business leaders, frontline staff, and citizen analysts now directly leverage data and intelligent tools to drive decisions, streamline processes, and enhance customer service. Generative AI and conversational interfaces have dramatically lowered the barrier to entry; natural language is fast becoming the de facto query language. This empowers users to ask questions and gain insights without writing a single line of code. When guided effectively, this democratization accelerates insight, innovation, and responsiveness. But left unmanaged, it fuels shadow AI, inconsistent practices, and new risks that security and governance experts increasingly highlight. This chapter explains the business case for democratizing analytics, outlines how to build data and AI literacy at scale, and covers deploying conversational tools and safe sandboxes. It also provides guidance on cultivating advocacy networks, measuring impact, and balancing decentralization with governance.


## Objective[2]

After completing this chapter, you will be able to:

- Explain why data advocates and citizen analysts are essential for scaling analytics and AI beyond central teams.
- Distinguish the roles of data advocates, citizen analysts, and specialist analytics professionals.
- Build literacy programs that help non-specialists interpret data, question AI outputs, and recognize escalation triggers.

- Select accessible self-service and conversational tools that reduce friction while preserving governance.
- Design advocate networks and communities of practice that spread capability through peer leadership.
- Track empowerment through practical metrics tied to adoption, time to insight, governance health, and shadow-AI reduction.

## Terms to Know

**AI Literacy**[1] **-** The capacity to grasp AI's utility, its limitations and inherent risks, and how to engage with AI tools effectively and ethically.

**Citizen Analyst**[3] **-** A non-specialist employee who uses governed data and analytics tools to answer business questions and support decisions in their own domain.

**Citizen Developer**[3] **-** A non-IT professional who builds automations, workflows, or simple applications using low-code/no-code and AI-assisted tools, all within defined governance guardrails.

**Conversational BI**[1] **-** Business intelligence tools that let users explore data through natural-language prompts and guided question-and-answer interfaces.

**Data Advocate**[2] **-** A local champion who encourages better use of data and analytics, supports peers, and connects business teams with central analytics resources.

**Data Democratization**[2] **-** The strategic distribution of data access, tools, and literacy across an organization, enabling more individuals to make data-driven decisions.

**Data Literacy**[2] **-** The ability to read, interpret, question, and communicate with data in context.

**Shadow AI**[1] **-** The use of unsanctioned AI tools or workflows outside approved security, privacy, and governance controls.

## Introduction

Most organizations say they want to be data-driven, but many still rely too heavily on a small analytics team for routine questions. That model does not scale well. It slows decisions, overloads specialists, and teaches the broader workforce to wait for answers instead of learning how to explore evidence responsibly.

Empowering data advocates and citizen analysts provides a more durable approach. It spreads basic analytics and AI capability outward so business teams can answer simpler questions themselves, identify better opportunities for advanced analysis, and collaborate more effectively with expert teams when complexity rises.

## The Rise of Citizen Analytics and Data Advocacy[2]

Two forces are driving the rise of citizen analytics: the natural-language revolution and the spread of accessible tools. Conversational BI and natural-language query engines let business users ask questions like "Why did customer churn spike last quarter?" and get clear answers with supporting visuals—no SQL required. At the same time, low-code platforms and embedded AI make it practical for non-specialists to build and refine analytics assets on their own.

Within this environment, three roles tend to take shape:

- **Citizen analysts:** Marketers, HR partners, operations managers—use self-service tools to explore data, test ideas, and guide decisions.
- **Citizen developers:** Build lightweight automations or apps using low-code/no-code platforms and AI co-pilots.
- **Data advocates:** Act as local champions, helping peers use data and AI responsibly while staying connected to central analytics teams.

With the right support, these roles expand analytics capacity, ease the load on central teams for routine work, and bring data-driven thinking into everyday decisions.

## The Business Case for Democratizing Analytics[2]

Democratizing analytics is a direct response to rising demand and complexity. As more processes go digital, the number and variety of data-driven decisions grow faster than specialist teams can keep up. Self-service and citizen roles become necessary just to maintain pace.

Done well, citizen analytics speeds up decisions. Frontline staff and managers can answer many questions themselves instead of waiting in a report queue. It also opens the door to more experimentation, since the people closest to customers and operations can explore patterns and test ideas quickly. Central teams benefit too, shifting away from routine reporting toward higher-value work like advanced modeling and governance. The point is straightforward: analytics and AI don't scale if access to data and tools stays locked inside a specialist silo.

## Building Data and AI Literacy Across the Organization[2]

Empowerment without literacy carries inherent risks. Employees must possess sufficient understanding to interpret results, question outputs, and discern when to escalate—a point repeatedly emphasized in data literacy and AI governance guidance.

Effective literacy programs typically encompass baseline assessments to identify current capabilities across roles; role-specific curricula for executives, managers, and frontline staff; blended delivery combining microlearning, workshops, peer coaching, and project-based assignments; and ongoing support structures like office hours, internal forums, and "ask an analyst" channels. Ultimately, you want to transition from one-off training to a continuous learning ecosystem where employees regularly update their data and AI skills as tools and needs evolve.

## Providing Accessible, Conversational Tools[2]

Even the strongest literacy program will stall if the tools are too complex or hard to reach. Citizen analysts only really engage when platforms meet them where they are, which is exactly what newer conversational BI tools aim to do for non-technical users.

Key capabilities include:

- Natural-language, question-and-answer style interfaces.
- Guided workflows and templates that help users pose better questions and make sense of what they see.
- Built-in explainers for metrics and models.
- Alerting and lightweight automation that proactively surface insights.
- Mobile-friendly, accessible interfaces.

Together, these features lower friction so non-specialists can fold data into their everyday work, staying aligned with established best practices for self-service BI and conversational analytics.

## Cultivating a Culture of Data Advocacy[2]

Tools and training create potential. Advocacy turns that potential into daily behavior. Data advocates matter because people often learn best from trusted peers who understand their local business reality.

Leaders can cultivate advocacy by:

- Identifying early adopters within each function and inviting them into a formal data advocate or analytics champion network.
- Clarifying expectations so advocates function as connectors and coaches, not unpaid support staff.
- Providing enhanced enablement through deeper training, early access to new tools, and direct links to central analytics teams.
- Recognizing advocacy in performance and promotion discussions.
- Creating community forums where advocates share stories and solutions.

When empowered and supported, advocates across departments become the local faces of the analytics transformation, making change feel peer-led rather than centrally imposed.

## Governing Citizen Analytics and Shadow AI[2]

Democratization without governance creates inconsistency, security exposure, and decision risk. The answer is not to block citizen analytics. It is to channel it into safe, understandable, well-supported pathways:

- **Approved tools and environments:** Make sanctioned analytics and AI tools easy to access.
- **Tiered risk rules:** Distinguish low-risk exploration from high-risk decisions or customer-facing use.
- **Auditability:** Ensure queries, outputs, and key actions can be reviewed when needed.
- **Escalation pathways:** Give users a clear route to specialist support for ambiguous or high-stakes issues.
- **AI-use guidance:** Explain what can and cannot be entered into tools, shared externally, or used in decisions.

Shadow AI often grows when the official path feels impractical. Leaders reduce it not only through policy, but by making sanctioned options genuinely usable.

# Case Studies

## Case Study #1: Insurance Firm Builds a Network of Data Advocates[2]

A regional insurance firm wanted to reduce dependence on emailed reports and static spreadsheets. It launched a data-advocate network by identifying employees who were already the informal go-to people for data questions inside business units.

Those advocates received deeper training in the firm's BI platform and AI assistant, hosted short support sessions, and partnered with the analytics team on dashboard improvements. Over time, dashboard use increased, simple report requests dropped, and several advocates grew into formal analytics roles.

## Case Study #2: Retailer Introduces Conversational BI for Store Managers[2]

A large retailer saw that store managers needed faster answers about staffing, inventory, and local performance, but most were not comfortable with traditional BI tools. The company introduced conversational BI with guided prompts and practical support tailored to store operations.

Managers could ask natural-language questions, explore local trends more easily, and act without waiting for a custom report. Adoption improved because the tool fit the rhythm of operational work rather than forcing users into analyst-style workflows.

## Case Study #3: Manufacturing Company Reins in Shadow AI with Safe Sandboxes[1]

Engineers and planners at a manufacturing firm began using public AI tools to summarize reports, draft communications, and explore optimization ideas. Productivity went up, but security and compliance leaders quickly flagged the risk of sensitive information leaving corporate boundaries—a familiar pattern that mirrors the broader concerns around shadow AI.

In response, IT and analytics leaders rolled out an internal AI sandbox tied to corporate login and approved data sources, created simple "use recipes" for common tasks, and asked employees to move their shadow-AI use cases into this safer environment. Over time, use of unsanctioned tools dropped as the sandbox became the default; the activity logs then made it easier to spot strong citizen-built workflows, which teams could harden and scale, turning grassroots experimentation into governed innovation.

# Success Metrics

Citizen-analytics and advocacy efforts work best when they track real behavior and outcomes, not vanity counts like "licenses purchased." Metrics should give leaders clear visibility into how well the organization is actually enabling people to use data.

## Citizen Analytics and Data-Advocacy Metrics

| Metric | What It Reveals | Illustrative Target | Leadership Use Case |
|---|---|---|---|
| **Data Literacy Participation** | Reach of traditional and reverse mentoring across generations | Sustained participation from key functions | Gauge awareness and interest |
| **Active Citizen-Analyst Count** | % of key analytics projects with multi-generation teams | Upward trend with representation across units | Monitor decentralization of analytics |
| **Time to Insight** | Access to AI/analytics learning across generations | 30-50% reduction over 1-2 years | Assess impact on decision speed |
| **Advocate Network Coverage** | Use of unsanctioned tools by cohort | Presence in all major business units | Ensure advocacy is organization-wide |
| **Shadow-AI Incidents** | Sentiment by generation about inclusion and opportunities | Downward trend as sanctioned options improve | Test governance effectiveness |
| **Linked Business Outcomes** | Volume and quality of documented legacy knowledge and lessons | Growing portfolio of stories and examples | Demonstrate value to sustain investment |

Leaders can review these measures alongside broader analytics and people dashboards. Based on what the data shows, they can tune programs and investments in line with the organization's self-service and AI-governance maturity, rather than relying on guesswork or anecdotes.

Beyond tracking advocacy, you also need visibility into growth and maturity. Citizen-analytics capabilities develop over time, so the model below offers a straightforward way to assess your current maturity and decide what to prioritize next, similar to staged approaches often used for self-service BI.

Leaders can use this model in planning sessions to agree on which stage best describes citizen analytics today, then set specific actions to move at least one stage higher over the next 12-24 months.

## Citizen Analytics Maturity Model

| Maturity Stage | Characteristics | Typical Symptoms | Priority Actions |
|---|---|---|---|
| **Ad Hoc** | Isolated power users; tools used inconsistently; no shared standards | Shadow AI growth, inconsistent insights, low trust | Define basic policies; pilot literacy and safe sandbox |
| **Tool-Led** | Self-service tools rolled out with limited enablement and governance | Low adoption, misuse, central team still overloaded | Launch literacy programs; identify data advocates |
| **Programmatic** | Structured literacy, advocate networks, and guardrails in place | Uneven engagement across functions | Expand advocate coverage; refine metrics and governance |
| **Embedded** | Citizen analytics part of everyday work; leaders model behavior | Complacency, underinvestment in continued learning | Refresh curricula; update tools; sustain advocacy and recognition |

## Leadership's Role in Driving Empowerment[2]

Citizen analytics succeeds when leaders communicate that responsible use of data is part of everyone's job, not a niche specialty. That message becomes credible only when leaders model it themselves.

Executives and managers should use live data in meetings, ask good questions about evidence, recognize advocates publicly, and fund the infrastructure that makes empowerment possible. Without visible leadership support, citizen analytics is easily dismissed as an optional side initiative.

### Overcoming Common Barriers

But even strong empowerment programs hit predictable obstacles:

- Central teams fearing loss of control.
- Business users feeling overloaded or generally skeptical.
- Complaints that tools are "too clunky."
- Some people overtrusting AI outputs.

This mix of friction can stall momentum. A more effective path is to recast central analytics as enablers and coaches, embed analytics into existing workflows, and make self-service tools fast and intuitive. Paired with clear governance and safe, sanctioned alternatives to shadow AI, these moves make it far more likely that citizen analytics will take root instead of staying a side project.[2]

## Practical Advice for Leaders[2]

- **Inventory current behavior.** Find where self-service, spreadsheet workarounds, and shadow AI already exist.
- **Identify your informal champions.** They are often the best starting point for an advocate network.
- **Start with a few high-value use cases.** Focus first on recurring business questions that are important but low risk.
- **Invest in role-based literacy.** Train people for the decisions they actually make, not for abstract technical mastery.
- **Make sanctioned tools easier than unsanctioned ones.** Convenience is a governance strategy.
- **Clarify escalation triggers.** Users should know when to proceed, when to pause, and when to call in experts.
- **Recognize advocacy in a visible way.** If peer enablement matters, reward it accordingly.

# Conclusion

Empowering data advocates and citizen analysts does not eliminate the need for specialist analytics teams. It makes those teams more effective by spreading responsible capability outward across the organization.

When literacy, accessible tools, advocate networks, and governance work together, analytics and AI stop being confined to experts and become part of how the enterprise learns, decides, and improves every day. That is how organizations turn democratization into durable advantage instead of unmanaged sprawl.

# Notes

[1] Shadow AI, conversational BI, AI sandboxes, and the need for governed experimentation and AI literacy are analyzed in "AI Gone Wild: Why Shadow AI Is Your IT Team's Worst Nightmare," Cloud Security Alliance, and "AI Sandboxes Let State Government Employees Experiment Safely," StateTech Magazine.

[2] The business case for citizen analytics, data literacy, self-service BI, maturity models, and leadership recommendations is developed in "Self-Service BI: Definition, Tools, Best Practices, and Real-World Use Cases," Toucan Toco; "How To Enable Self- Service Analytics Using Data Literacy," *CDO Magazine*; "Resources for Data Analysts & Business Intelligence Professionals," TDWI; and "How Conversational BI Is Changing the Way We Explore Data," element61.

[3] Citizen analysts and citizen developers—their roles, benefits, and governance risks—are covered in "Resources for Data Analysts & Business Intelligence Professionals," TDWI, and "How Citizen-Built Apps Expose Data and 5 Moves to Close the Gap," Citizen Development.

The primary obstacles
to AI impact are
organizational,
not technological.

*Boston Consulting Group*

"Five Barriers CEOs Must Overcome for AI Impact"

Berthion

March 2026

# **Part Two:** Process

In the age of AI, process is the connective tissue that orchestrates human and machine capabilities through agile, ethical, and continuously evolving workflows, balancing rapid innovation with unwavering trust and accountability.

## Key topics explored in this chapter:

- From Waterfall to Agile Analytics
- Theoretical Foundations and Methods
- Designing the Agile Analytics Workflow
- Backlog Management and Dynamic Prioritization
- Integrating Automation and AI into Agile Workflows
- Scaling Agile Analytics in Large Organizations
- Continuous Improvement as a Core Habit

# WAY 13

# Design Agile Analytics Workflows

## Abstract

Analytics and AI projects today need agility to handle constant change—from shifting markets and evolving customer behavior to new regulatory demands. Agile workflow design directly addresses this by emphasizing iterative development, rapid prototyping, and flexible prioritization. Instead of massive, infrequent releases, agile teams deliver smaller, testable pieces of value, which makes it easier to gather quick feedback and make important course corrections. They adapt agile practices (such as sprint planning, backlog management, and continuous stakeholder engagement) to data and AI initiatives, and they use DevOps-style automation and monitoring to support reliable, repeatable delivery. At scale, organizations spread agile analytics across multiple teams through shared patterns and portfolio-level alignment, all without sacrificing governance, quality, or ethical oversight. This chapter prepares readers to design and run agile analytics workflows that are both fast and resilient.

## Objective[1]

After completing this chapter, you will be able to:

- Explain why traditional, waterfall-style analytics projects struggle in volatile business environments and how agile principles—such as short iterations and continuous feedback—address these shortcomings.
- Design sprint-based analytics workflows that deliver minimum viable analytics (MVA) in short cycles while still maintaining data quality and governance.

- Build and manage an analytics backlog that reflects business priorities, technical dependencies, and risk, and allows for reprioritization as conditions change.
- Integrate automation and AI into agile workflows to modernize data pipelines, testing, deployment, and feedback analysis without creating opaque "black-box" processes.
- Scale agile analytics across multiple teams and business units by using centers of excellence, standard guidelines, and portfolio-level prioritization.
- Track key workflow and business metrics—such as cycle time, adoption, and rework rates—to drive continuous improvement in both process and outcomes.

# Terms to Know

**Agile Analytics**[2] **-** Applying agile principles—short iterations, continuous feedback, and adaptive planning—to design, develop, and deploy analytics and AI solutions. This extends agile software concepts to BI and data products.

**AI-Assisted Orchestration**[3] **-** The use of AI tools to automate or optimize parts of analytics workflows—such as pipeline monitoring, anomaly detection, backlog recommendation, or summarizing sprint outcomes—while still retaining human oversight for high-impact decisions.

**Backlog**[1] **-** A dynamic, prioritized list of analytics work items (user stories, enhancements, models, and technical improvements) that guides sprint planning and resource allocation, replacing static, one-time project plans.

**DevOps for Analytics**[3] **-** Practices that integrate development, operations, and data engineering to enable rapid, reliable release of analytics products. It uses automation, monitoring, and continuous integration/continuous delivery (CI/CD), informed by DevOps research and DORA-style metrics.

**Minimum Viable Analytics (MVA)**[4] **-** The smallest, quickest analytics artifact (like a simple dashboard, scorecard, or prototype model) that delivers real, testable value to stakeholders. It's analogous to a minimum viable product in software, but focuses on decision support.

**Retrospective**[2] - A structured meeting at the end of a sprint where the team reflects on successes, challenges, and necessary changes for the next iteration. It's a core mechanism for continuous improvement in agile analytics.

**Sprint**[2] - A fixed, short timebox—typically 1-3 weeks—where a cross-functional team commits to delivering a specific set of analytics tasks and insights. This cadence is common in agile BI and data-product teams.

# Introduction[1]

Analytics and AI teams work in environments where business models, customer behavior, and regulatory expectations change quickly. Traditional, plan-driven approaches like "waterfall" assume stable requirements and long lead times. By the time teams deliver a "final" report or model, the underlying questions or data sources have often already changed. Agile analytics reframes these efforts as ongoing learning journeys, not one-off projects. It matches the view of analytics as an iterative "sense-making" process rather than a purely technical solution pipeline.

Instead of designing the "perfect" solution upfront, agile analytics teams build in short cycles, share work early, and treat stakeholder feedback as a primary design input. Frequent delivery of small pieces of value reduces risk by surfacing issues earlier and keeps outputs aligned with operational needs. Automation and AI support this agility by handling repetitive tasks such as data checks, pipeline monitoring, and deployment—so human experts focus on interpretation, collaboration, and higher-order decisions.

## From Waterfall to Agile Analytics[1]

Traditional waterfall-style analytics assumes stable requirements and clean, predictable data. In practice, requirements emerge only after stakeholders review early prototypes. Data-quality or integration issues surface midway through a project, making change requests expensive and disruptive when processes are rigid. Agile analytics anticipates these surprises, managing them through iteration rather than exception handling.

Agile analytics introduces several key shifts:

- It moves from big upfront design to incremental design, where teams begin with a directional vision and refine details as they learn from data and feedback.

- It shifts from large releases to frequent, small deliverables, where each sprint produces something usable—even just an MVA—so value realizes earlier.
- And it transforms distant stakeholders into active collaborators, with business partners attending reviews, providing feedback, and helping reprioritize work.

These shifts don't eliminate planning; they alter its cadence. Vision and strategy remain essential, but teams revisit priorities frequently instead of relying on inflexible upfront schedules. AI tools can reveal emerging patterns that prompt earlier reprioritization.

## Theoretical Foundations and Methods[4]

Agile analytics builds on well-established ideas from project management and software delivery. Classical project-management literature distinguishes plan-driven approaches, best suited to stable environments, from adaptive ones, which work best under uncertainty and frequent change. Methods such as Scrum and Kanban bring adaptiveness to life through short timeboxes, limits on work in progress, and clear feedback loops. Applied to analytics and AI, these elements let teams respond to changing data sources, newly discovered patterns, and evolving business questions rather than staying locked to rigid upfront specifications.

At enterprise scale, organizations adopt portfolio-level frameworks such as the Scaled Agile Framework (SAFe) to keep local, experimental efforts aligned with broader strategic goals. In that context, organizations manage dashboards, predictive models, and data products as continuously evolving services rather than fixed, one-time deliverables.

Insights from DevOps and continuous-delivery research reinforce this approach. High-performing technology organizations show that frequent, small releases, supported by strong automation, testing, and monitoring, both increase delivery speed and improve overall stability. That directly challenges the assumption that velocity and reliability must always be traded off against each other. Agile analytics adapts these proven ideas to data pipelines and machine-learning models, borrowing key workflow metrics from DevOps—deployment frequency, lead time for changes, and change-failure rate—to guide and measure progress in data and AI initiatives.

## Designing the Agile Analytics Workflow[2]

A typical **agile analytics workflow** follows a repeating loop: plan, build, validate, adapt—centered on a backlog and initiated by a sprint.

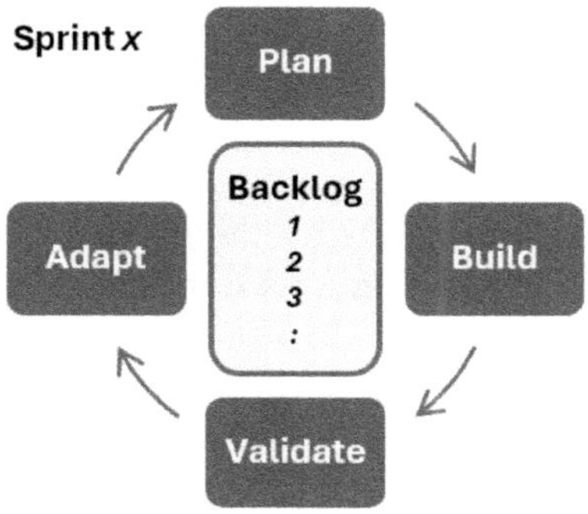


- **Plan:** At the start of a sprint, the team collaborates with stakeholders to select a small number of backlog items they can realistically deliver. They frame these as user stories, such as "As a regional sales leader, I need daily pipeline visibility so I can prioritize deals and coaching." The team then clarifies acceptance criteria, dependencies, and the definition of done.
- **Build:** Data engineers, data scientists, and analysts collaborate to prepare data, develop prototypes, and create visualizations or models. Automation, version control, and standard templates help maintain quality and address impediments, while daily standups keep work visible and support repeatable deployment.
- **Validate:** Near the sprint's end, the team demos outputs to stakeholders, explicitly seeking critique on what was answered, what's missing, and what would make artifacts more actionable. This feedback directly informs backlog refinement and future sprint planning.
- **Adapt:** In a retrospective, the team reviews successes, identifies areas of friction, and determines necessary changes. They add these improvement actions to the backlog alongside business features.

Over time, this cycle establishes a rhythm of delivery and learning: stakeholders expect regular, visible progress, and teams discover what truly drives business value, rather than guessing from a distance. AI can assist by flagging unusual data issues during the build phase, summarizing qualitative feedback across sprints, or surfacing similar user stories for reuse or adaptation.

## Backlog Management and Dynamic Prioritization[1]

The backlog is the beating heart of agile analytics. Unlike static project plans, it's designed to change as new ideas, regulatory requirements, technical-debt items, and improvement actions emerge. The challenge is avoiding chaos while ensuring the most valuable work rises to the top.

Effective backlog management involves clear prioritization criteria—business value, risk reduction, regulatory urgency, effort, and learning potential—regular refinement sessions where teams clarify, split, or merge items, and full transparency. Making the backlog visible to stakeholders keeps trade-offs explicit and reduces the influence of the "loudest voice." AI-enabled project tools assist by clustering similar requests, flagging stale items, and analyzing historical effort and impact patterns to propose more realistic priorities. Human judgment still balances strategic considerations and risk.

## Integrating Automation and AI into Agile Workflows[3]

Automation is essential for sustaining speed without eroding quality. When teams deliver meaningful increments every one or two weeks, manual testing, ad-hoc deployments, and fragile pipelines quickly become bottlenecks. That's why DevOps-inspired practices embed automation and monitoring throughout the analytics lifecycle.

Common patterns include:

- Automated data validation to check schema, completeness, and anomalies when pipelines refresh.
- CI/CD for analytics assets to keep dashboards, transformations, and models under version control and deploy them through automated pipelines.
- Monitoring and alerts for model-performance drift, pipeline failures, or unusual latency.
- AI itself can act as a collaborator by drafting documentation, summarizing model changes, proposing test cases, or recommending which models may need retraining.

At the same time, AI-assisted orchestration raises governance questions. Organizations need clear policies and human review points—especially for high-risk or regulated workflows—to ensure that AI-generated or AI-orchestrated code and decisions remain trustworthy.

## Scaling Agile Analytics in Large Organizations[4]

Enterprises that start with one or two agile analytics teams eventually face the question of how to spread these practices across many teams without recreating bureaucracy. Research on agile at scale highlights a few recurring patterns.

Organizations usually create standardization with flexibility by defining a minimal set of common practices (for example, sprint lengths, core ceremonies, and basic tooling) while allowing teams to adapt details to their own context. Centers of excellence or enablement often emerge as specialized groups that provide coaching, reusable patterns, and governance guidance for agile analytics, DevOps, and data engineering. Portfolio-level agility replaces rigid multi-year plans: analytics initiatives are treated as a portfolio of evolving products and experiments, and portfolio boards review evidence of value and learning to shift capacity based on impact and strategic fit. Coordination mechanisms—such as regular cross-team reviews, shared roadmaps, and clearly defined data domains—help prevent duplication and conflicting solutions while preserving team autonomy.

## Continuous Improvement as a Core Habit[2]

Agile analytics isn't just a set of ceremonies; it's a mindset of continuous improvement, with retrospectives serving as the key formal mechanism. In effective retrospectives, teams move beyond surface complaints to examine root causes, consider how process, architecture, or expectations contributed to issues, and generate specific improvement actions for future sprints.

Organizations often augment retrospectives with data-driven insights from workflow-analytics tools. These tools analyze sprint histories, ticket movements, and incident patterns to identify systemic bottlenecks. Mature teams track not only how fast they deliver but also whether outputs are used and generate measurable business value—like faster decisions, reduced waste, or higher revenue. They then use these insights to refine backlog priorities and design choices. Studies of agile and DevOps suggest that teams consistently transform retrospective insights into concrete changes. They outperform those that treat such practices as merely symbolic.

# Case Studies[5]

## Case Study #1: Agile Analytics for Retail Forecasting

A global retail chain historically produced quarterly demand forecasts via a lengthy, sequential process. Analysts gathered requirements, engineered features, and delivered models only after months of work. By the time results reached buyers and merchandisers, promotions and external shocks had often rendered the outputs less relevant, leading to skepticism and manual overrides.

To address this, the retailer introduced agile analytics squads responsible for specific product categories. Squads ran two-week sprints focused on minimum viable analytics—initially simple, near-real-time dashboards of store-level sales and inventory, later short-horizon predictive models updated weekly. Automation monitored data feeds and alerted teams when input distributions shifted, triggering faster recalibration and reducing performance drift. Over six months, forecast accuracy improved, and planning cycles shortened from quarterly to roughly biweekly. Buyers reported greater trust because they observed forecasts evolving in response to their feedback and current conditions, rather than arriving as static, opaque deliverables.

## Case Study #2: Agile Data Science in a Regulated Bank

A large financial institution faced pressure to accelerate model development for credit risk and fraud detection while meeting strict regulatory standards. Previously, model development followed a rigid governance path, featuring detailed upfront documentation, lengthy validation cycles, and a single, high-stakes approval gate. This delayed deployment and misaligned models with frontline needs.

The bank piloted cross-functional "risk analytics squads," combining risk officers, data scientists, validators, and IT engineers. Squads operated in three-week sprints, starting with transparent rule-based prototypes and simple scorecards to enable early engagement from risk and compliance stakeholders. Every sprint included a validation checkpoint where experts reviewed model changes, documentation, and performance metrics. DevOps practices automated testing and deployment into controlled environments, creating consistent audit trails. Over time, approval times dropped, frontline fit improved, and regulators gained confidence in the repeatable, auditable process built around iterative improvement, rather than last-minute negotiation.

### Evidence from Prior Studies[4]

Beyond individual case examples, multiple empirical and survey-based studies suggest that agile and DevOps-style practices can meaningfully improve analytics and software outcomes. Surveys of BI and analytics teams report that organizations using agile development practices see faster time-to-first-value and higher user satisfaction compared with those using traditional methods. These outcomes are often linked to incremental delivery, closer stakeholder collaboration, and iterative refinement.

Large-scale DevOps research, summarized through DORA-style metrics, connects continuous delivery, automated testing, and frequent releases to shorter lead times, lower change-failure rates, and improved reliability. This challenges the common myth that speed and stability must always be traded off against each other. Research on agile at scale and agile portfolio management also indicates that organizations which combine local team autonomy with portfolio-level alignment and standardized practices are better able to sustain performance gains, even though scaling remains challenging. While much of this literature focuses on software rather than analytics specifically, the underlying mechanisms—short feedback cycles, iterative delivery, and socio-technical coordination across roles—map directly to data and AI workflows.

## Success Metrics[3]

To move beyond anecdote, agile analytics teams benefit from tracking a small, consistent set of metrics, with a few examples shown in the table that follows. The aim is to see whether workflow changes improve both delivery performance and business outcomes, not to create extra reporting work.

Organizations usually adjust metric definitions, target ranges, and data sources to match their domain and regulatory context, combining workflow indicators with outcome-focused KPIs such as adoption rates, incident reduction, or revenue uplift.

## Key Metrics for Agile Analytics Workflows

| Metric | Definition | What It Tells You |
|---|---|---|
| **Cycle Time** | Time from a new idea entering the backlog to first usable output | Speed of learning and delivery |
| **Sprint Predictability** | % of sprint work completed vs. originally committed | Reliability of planning and execution |
| **Stakeholder Engagement** | Participation in reviews, feedback quality, follow-through | Strength of collaboration and trust |
| **Adoption and Usage** | Frequency of real decision use of dashboards/models | Real-world relevance and business uptake |
| **Quality and Stability** | Defects, incident counts, failure rates in pipelines and models | Robustness of analytics in production |
| **Improvement Follow-Through** | Share of retrospective actions completed in later sprints | Depth of continuous improvement culture |

# Practical Advice for Leaders[4]

Leaders who want agile analytics workflows to thrive must focus as much on culture and incentives as on process diagrams and tools. Practitioner reports and agile-at-scale guidance highlight several effective practices.

- **Model curiosity and humility.** Treat analytics outputs as hypotheses to explore together, rather than as infallible truths.
- **Protect focus.** Avoid overloaded sprints and frequent mid-sprint scope changes.
- **Invest in automation early.** Make sure multiple analytics squads do not reinvent the same technical plumbing.
- **Define value.** Align rewards with learning and measurable business impact, rather than the sheer volume of output.
- **Make agile visible.** Attend demos, ask about retrospective insights, and use sprint outputs in executive decision-making.

These behaviors signal that iterative, evidence-based work is both valued and expected.

## Anticipating and Managing Risks[5]

As agile analytics matures, a number of common risks emerge.

- **Process fragmentation** occurs when different teams reinvent agile practices and vocabulary, making collaboration and scaling difficult. Lightweight standards, shared playbooks, and coaching can harmonize practices without stifling autonomy.
- **Over-automation** introduces hidden defects or compliance gaps if automated pipelines or AI-generated code lack sufficient review. Clear human review checkpoints, periodic audits, and explicit ownership of workflows are essential.
- **Ethical blind spots** arise when rapid experimentation with AI overlooks fairness, transparency, or privacy considerations. Integrating ethics criteria and domain-expert input into "definitions of done" helps mitigate this risk.
- **Measurement fatigue** occurs if teams are overloaded with metrics. Focusing on a concise, balanced set of indicators helps keep attention on what matters most.

By identifying these risks and assigning ownership for monitoring them, organizations catch issues early on instead of waiting for visible, high-profile failures.

## Methodological Considerations and Limitations

The patterns presented in this chapter rest mainly on practitioner reports, case studies, and cross-sectional survey findings rather than controlled experiments. They are subject to survivorship and publication bias, likely over-represent successful agile-analytics initiatives, and cannot fully separate the impact of agile practices from other factors such as leadership quality or infrastructure investment.

Measurement itself shapes behavior: teams that know cycle time or adoption is being tracked optimize for those indicators at the expense of less visible dimensions, such as interpretability or long-term maintainability.

For these reasons, treat the practices and metrics discussed here as design patterns and hypotheses rather than strict formulas. Future studies, particularly long-term and mixed-methods work in analytics-heavy, regulated fields, could show which agile-analytics practices are suitable and most dependable.

# Conclusion

Designing agile analytics workflows is not just a matter of adding stand-ups and sprint boards to existing projects. It means rethinking how analytics and AI teams define value, work with stakeholders, and integrate automation into their daily work. When done well, agile analytics turns data initiatives into living systems that adapt alongside the organization's strategy and environment rather than static projects that quickly fall out of date. Leaders who combine iterative delivery, strong stakeholder engagement, thoughtful automation, and continuous learning put their organizations in a better position to respond faster, learn more deeply, and make better decisions. The same principles that guide agile software and DevOps now apply to analytics and AI — but with added responsibility: the insights these workflows produce shape how entire organizations see their world and decide what to do.

# Notes

[1] Agile versus waterfall project approaches, the role of short iterations and backlog-driven reprioritization in addressing changing requirements, and the use of backlogs in analytics planning are laid out in Tempo's "Waterfall vs Agile: Which Project Management Style for You?"; Saviom's "Agile versus Waterfall: Quick Comparison"; and Rigby, Sutherland, and Noble's "Agile at Scale," *Harvard Business Review.*

[2] Applying agile principles to BI and analytics—sprints, retrospectives, incremental delivery, and stakeholder engagement practices—is detailed in Sigma Computing's "Agile BI Reporting Workflows"; Mode's "Agile Analytics: Why You Should Embrace Incremental Shipments"; and *US-Analytics*'s "Does EPM/BI Project Methodology Really Matter? Waterfall vs. Agile vs. Blended."

[3] DevOps and DORA-style metrics, CI/CD, automated testing, change-failure rates, and their adaptation to analytics workflows are covered in Atlassian's "Atlassian DevOps: DORA Metrics"; *GitLab Docs*' "DevOps Research and Assessment (DORA) Metrics"; and Plandek's "Change Failure Rate—DORA Metrics."

[4] The theoretical grounding of agile analytics in agile software, agile BI, and agile-portfolio management—covering user stories, incremental delivery, portfolio alignment, and treating analytics as evolving products—is drawn from Mode's "Agile Analytics: Why You Should Embrace Incremental Shipments"; *Thoughtworks*'s "Introducing Agile Analytics"; and Laanti and Kangas's "Agile Portfolio Management: Benefits and Challenges," Journal of Modern Project Management.

[5] Examples of agile analytics in retail forecasting and regulated financial environments, along with risk and scaling considerations, appear in *MIT Sloan Management Review*'s "Pair People and AI for Better Product Demand Forecasting"; Rigby, Sutherland, and Noble's "Agile at Scale," *Harvard Business Review*; and *US-Analytics*'s "Does EPM/BI Project Methodology Really Matter? Waterfall vs. Agile vs. Blended."

High-performing organizations (top 6%) are nearly 3x more likely to fundamentally redesign workflows for AI, a key factor in achieving meaningful business impact.

*McKinsey & Company*

"The state of AI in 2025: Agents, innovation, and transformation"

Singla et al.

November 2025

## Key topics explored in this chapter:

- Foundations of AI Governance Structures
- Theoretical and Regulatory Foundations
- Nine Core Components of an Effective AI Governance Framework
- Scaling Governance in Large Organizations
- Governance as a Driver of Innovation and Control

# WAY 14

# Craft Effective Governance Structures


## Abstract

AI governance keeps analytics and AI work tied to the organization's goals while actively managing risks to people, operations, and compliance. As organizations embed AI into core processes—from credit decisions and hiring to healthcare and public services—weak governance significantly raises the stakes, inviting operational failures, legal penalties, and reputational damage. This chapter introduces practical AI governance methods that define decision rights, oversight bodies, and how policies are enforced across the AI lifecycle. It also shows how model inventories, standard controls, and continuous monitoring can live alongside experimentation and fast delivery, drawing on risk-based ideas from NIST's AI Risk Management Framework and established model-risk practices. The case examples show that effective governance can support innovation by channeling it safely, using clear guardrails, predictable approval paths, and audit-ready evidence that help with scale, trust, and long-term value.


## Objective[1]

After completing this chapter, you will be able to:

- Distinguish AI governance from traditional data governance and articulate why AI requires additional, model-centric controls.
- Design governance methods that cover model inventory, risk assessment, decision rights, and oversight bodies across the AI lifecycle.

- Define and operationalize decision rights for key roles including business owners, data science teams, risk, legal, and compliance.
- Implement policy- and compliance-enforcement mechanisms that scale through automation without becoming bureaucratic bottlenecks.
- Establish scalable monitoring, testing, and vendor-risk processes that keep pace with a growing AI portfolio.
- Use governance as an enabler of responsible innovation by creating freedom within a framework and clear, predictable pathways for experimentation and deployment.

# Terms to Know

**AI Governance**[2] - The formal set of policies, processes, roles, and tools that guide the responsible development, deployment, and oversight of AI systems, emphasizing lifecycle risk management, accountability, and trustworthiness.

**Decision Rights**[4] - Explicitly defined authority and accountability for decisions across the AI lifecycle—such as who can approve deployment, who owns risk, and who can override or retire a model—typically documented using RACI or similar governance tools.

**Model Inventory**[3] - A centralized, maintained catalog of AI models and other material analytics assets that records owners, purposes, risk levels, and lifecycle status, drawing on model-risk-management practice in banking and regulatory guidance.

**Oversight Body**[5] - A cross-functional group (for example, an AI governance committee or model-risk committee) that sets policies, reviews high-risk use cases, and arbitrates escalated issues, echoing structures in risk and compliance governance.

**Policy Enforcement**[6] - Procedural and automated mechanisms that ensure governance rules (for example, documentation, testing, and human-in-the-loop requirements) are consistently applied across tools and teams, often via workflow automation and control gates.

**Regulatory Compliance**[7] - Ongoing adherence to laws, standards, and supervisory expectations relevant to AI, data, and algorithms, including instruments such as the EU AI Act and frameworks like NIST's AI RMF.

**Vendor Risk Management**[8] - Structured processes for assessing, monitoring, and mitigating risks introduced by third-party or external AI solutions, including due diligence, contract controls, and continuous oversight.

# Introduction[9]

As AI systems move from pilots into everyday operations, gaps in governance can lead to serious failures in high-stakes areas. Models now influence creditworthiness, hiring, clinical decisions, pricing, and eligibility for services, making unmanaged risks more probable and more expensive. Traditional data governance focuses on controlling who can access which data and under what conditions. AI governance, however, extends this oversight to include what models do with data, how they were trained and validated, and who bears accountability for failures.

A solid AI governance structure answers these questions and gives leaders a way to move fast without losing control, so teams are less likely to run shadow AI outside the rules." Embedding AI governance into strategy, risk, and compliance processes helps organizations use AI in ways that reflect their mission and meet regulatory obligations, while building trust as AI becomes part of everyday operations.

## Foundations of AI Governance Structures[10]

AI governance spans the entire lifecycle of intelligent systems—from ideation and data selection through design, deployment, monitoring, and retirement. This approach treats AI as a managed asset, not a collection of disconnected experiments. Clearly defined and widely understood lifecycle elements enable organizations to align AI initiatives with business strategy, risk appetite, and ethical commitments.

Lifecycle-oriented governance clarifies responsibilities at each step, from model design to performance monitoring, ensuring every system has an identified owner and escalation path. It also enhances transparency and auditability, a condition regulators increasingly expect for deploying AI in high-risk contexts. And it formalizes AI's socio-organizational aspects: how humans and systems interact, who makes which calls, and how issues are escalated and resolved.

## Theoretical and Regulatory Foundations[11]

Modern AI governance builds on practices from risk management, corporate governance, and data protection. In financial services, for example, model-risk-management has, for a long time, required a list of important models, clear documentation of assumptions, and board-level oversight—providing a useful template for AI controls.

Frameworks like NIST's AI Risk Management Framework and the EU AI Act emphasize structured, risk-based governance across the AI lifecycle.

NIST's AI RMF defines core functions—Govern, Map, Measure, Manage—and encourages tailoring controls to context and risk. Meanwhile, the EU AI Act introduces high-risk categories, mandates documentation and monitoring, and requires human oversight, signaling how regulators expect organizations to manage AI risk in practice.

## Nine Core Components of an Effective AI Governance Framework[12]

Despite sector differences, effective AI governance methods share nine core components. Together, these components create a clear but flexible way to manage AI risk while still leaving room for innovation. This gives a clear view of each system, who owns it, what controls apply, and which groups actually oversee it—helping organizations avoid both uncontrolled experimentation and heavy, paralyzing bureaucracy.

### 1. AI Inventory Management[13]

An AI or model inventory is often the first practical step in setting up AI governance because it shows which systems exist, where they run, and who owns them. A comprehensive inventory should list in-scope AI and other material models, including their purpose, business and technical owners, risk ratings, deployment environment, and links to key documentation. Effective inventories reduce duplication, surface unmanaged models, and provide a foundation for risk assessments, internal audits, and regulatory inquiries. Supervisors and examiners increasingly expect organizations—especially in financial services and areas of essential infrastructure—to show that they have a complete model inventory and clear owners for each model. Inventory completeness thus becomes a visible indicator of governance maturity.

### 2. Risk Management and Assessment[14]

AI brings risks around fairness, privacy, security, operational resilience, and reputation, which is why risk-based approaches sit at the center of AI governance. Frameworks like NIST's AI RMF and sectoral model-risk guidance prompt organizations to classify AI systems by impact and likelihood, tailoring controls accordingly. Common practices involve structured impact assessments, bias and fairness testing across relevant subgroups, security and privacy reviews, and scenario or stress testing of models under unusual or adverse conditions. The resulting risk classifications decide who must review a system, how strict validation should be, and how often it needs to be checked in production, so governance effort matches the level of potential harm.

### 3. Decision Rights and Accountabilities[15]

Unclear decision rights can weaken even a well-designed governance framework, leaving teams unsure who can approve new AI use cases, deploy or retire models, accept remaining risk, or respond to incidents. Clear governance allocates authority for these decisions and employs tools like RACI matrices to specify Responsible, Accountable, Consulted, and Informed parties at each lifecycle step. In regulated contexts, regulators often expect boards and senior management to assume explicit oversight responsibilities, while operational ownership resides with designated business and technical roles. Clear decision rights speed up crisis response, cut down on duplicated effort and conflict, and make it easier to show supervisors that people understand their AI responsibilities and can act on them.

### 4. Oversight Bodies and Escalation Protocols[16]

Oversight bodies, such as AI governance committees or model-risk committees, provide a place for coordinated review and challenge and usually include people from business, data science, risk, compliance, legal, and sometimes audit. These groups establish policies and standards, review high-risk AI use cases, adjudicate escalated ethical or risk concerns, and track remediation of incidents and control gaps. Clearly documented escalation paths ensure issues identified at the technical or frontline level reach the appropriate decision-making tier quickly. This structure supports consistent handling of contentious or sensitive AI deployments, gives the board more confidence, and reduces the risk that concerns are handled informally or ignored.

### 5. Policy and Compliance Enforcement[17]

Policies spell out expectations—for example, that high-risk models must go through independent validation, fairness testing, and documentation review. But enforcement mechanisms translate these expectations into daily practice. Many organizations leverage workflow automation within MLOps or governance platforms to verify required documentation, test results, and approvals before a model progresses to the next stage. Automated policy gates ensure more consistent enforcement, ease manual burden on governance teams, and create audit trails for later review. Risk-sensitive settings allow lighter checks for low-risk models and stricter gates for high-risk systems, helping governance stay both thorough and workable as the AI portfolio grows.

## 6. Model Testing and Validation[18]

Model testing and validation are central to AI model-risk management. Testing typically evaluates performance (e.g., accuracy and stability), robustness (e.g., sensitivity to data shifts), and fairness (e.g., error rates across groups). Validation, conversely, independently assesses a model's fitness for purpose and documentation adequacy. In highly regulated sectors, independent model-validation units, separate from development teams, often must provide objective challenge and help prevent conflicts of interest. Periodic re-validation is recommended when data, usage, or regulatory expectations change materially. Strong testing and validation practices increase internal confidence in AI systems and make external reviews and audits easier.

## 7. Continuous Monitoring and Automated Alerts[19]

Because AI systems can drift or degrade over time, continuous monitoring becomes essential. Monitoring tracks shifts in input data, drops in key performance metrics, new biases in outputs, and security anomalies that might signal that data or models have been compromised. Automation typically detects and flags anomalies early. Governance must specify who reviews alerts, how to triage issues, and when to roll back, retrain, or augment models with human review. MLOps and model-monitoring guidance stresses that metrics and thresholds must reflect the level of risk and match documented tolerances, so alerts are meaningful and responses fit the size of the potential impact.

## 8. Vendor and Third-Party Risk Management[20]

Third-party AI tools and services create extra governance challenges because key functions and important details about training data or testing methods often sit outside the organization. Vendor-risk-management methods address this by mandating disclosures on training data, testing practices, security controls, and performance across relevant populations before procurement. Healthcare and financial-services guidance recommends embedding AI-specific clauses into vendor contracts—such as audit rights and notification obligations for significant model changes—and ensuring high-impact vendor models undergo testing on local data before broad rollout. Organizations are still responsible for the results, even when they use external tools. As a result, vendor AI should face scrutiny similar to in-house models.

## 9. Regulatory and Ethical Alignment[21]

Regulatory expectations for AI are changing quickly. The EU AI Act provides one of the most detailed AI-specific schemes, while NIST's AI

RMF offers a broadly applicable risk approach. Organizations must monitor developments in relevant jurisdictions and ensure their governance structures meet or exceed emerging requirements, particularly for high-risk systems subject to explicit legal obligations. Ethical alignment goes beyond simply meeting the law by asking whether each AI use fits the organization's values and broader norms about fairness, human rights, and transparency. Many responsible-AI frameworks recommend ethical review processes for novel or sensitive use cases, even where legal rules remain nascent. They also encourage multi-stakeholder dialogue to surface potential harms and trade-offs early.

## Scaling Governance in Large Organizations[22]

As AI portfolios grow, governance has to expand in a way that still works day to day, so teams aren't pushed into using informal workarounds. Large organizations often adopt a federated model: central teams define standards, maintain tools and inventories, and review high-risk systems, while local teams manage day-to-day implementation within those boundaries.

Centralized AI-governance platforms give the organization one place to manage model inventories, policies, documentation, testing evidence, and monitoring results. Automated workflows enforce standard steps while allowing for risk-based tailoring and local nuance. This helps keep practices consistent, lightens the load on individual teams, and gives leaders a clearer view of AI risk across the organization.

## Governance as a Driver of Innovation and Control[23]

Well-designed governance cultivates freedom within a framework. It clarifies which use cases qualify for simple, low-friction approval and which demand more intensive review. This allows low-risk experiments to move quickly while reserving deeper scrutiny for higher-risk initiatives. Clear rules, templates, and automated checks help teams understand requirements and avoid rework, while risk-proportionate expectations give innovators room to experiment responsibly.

Management literature on "freedom within a framework" similarly emphasizes how predictable guardrails can unlock creativity by reducing ambiguity and fear of arbitrary enforcement. When governance is seen as an enabler rather than a barrier, teams are more likely to engage early and openly on risk, improving both innovation and control.

# Case Studies[24]

## Case Study #1: Building a Central AI Governance Platform

A multinational financial-services firm discovered that AI models were being developed in multiple regions with inconsistent documentation and oversight, which made it hard to respond to supervisors' requests. To address this, the firm implemented a central model-governance platform connected to its model inventory, and the platform became the mandatory entry point for new AI initiatives.

The platform enforced standard steps: recording basic metadata, completing risk assessments, uploading validation results, and capturing approvals. Later, it was integrated with development pipelines so model changes automatically updated inventory records and triggered re-approval when required. Internal reviews reported sharp increases in documented model coverage and a reduction in the time needed to assemble evidence for regulatory examinations—from weeks to days—showing how governance can improve both control and efficiency.

## Case Study #2: Governance for Vendor-Provided AI in Healthcare

A regional healthcare provider adopted vendor AI tools for imaging, triage, and operational planning. At first, it allowed individual departments to buy solutions on their own, which led to uneven due diligence and unclear accountability for performance and safety issues. The organization then put an AI vendor-risk method in place that required vendors to disclose training data, testing on representative populations, security controls, and model-change processes before procurement.

Contracts for high-impact tools included audit rights and notification obligations. Clinical teams also tested vendor models on local data before wider rollout. According to internal audits, this structured approach reduced AI-related clinical incidents and improved consistency across vendor assessments, showing that AI-specific governance can be built into broader third-party-risk programs.

# Success Metrics[25]

To check if their governance is working at the right level, organizations usually track a short list of key metrics, including coverage, adherence, timeliness, incidents, remediation, and how well vendors are aligned.

## AI Governance Metrics

| Metric | Definition | What It Tells You |
|---|---|---|
| **Model Coverage** | Share of AI models recorded in central inventory | Visibility and control over the AI portfolio |
| **Policy Adherence Rate** | % of models meeting documentation/testing standards | Consistency of governance enforcement |
| **Approval Cycle Time** | Time from governance submission to decision | Efficiency and predictability of governance processes |
| **Incident Rate** | No. of material AI-related incidents over a defined period | Effectiveness of controls and monitoring |
| **Remediation Timeliness** | Time to resolve identified issues or violations | Responsiveness and organizational learning |
| **Vendor Compliance Alignment** | Proportion of critical vendors meeting governance requirements | Strength of third-party risk management |

Trend analysis helps leaders check whether systems still work well in practice. High incident rates can signal missing or weak controls, while long approval times can signal processes that are so complex they push teams toward workarounds and shadow AI.

# Practical Advice for Leaders[26]

Leadership commitment is the big enabler of effective AI governance.

- Senior leaders should present AI governance as a way to **protect people and support long-term innovation,** not just as extra paperwork for compliance.
- **Invest in a shared language** so terms like "high-risk model," "explainability," and "human-in-the-loop" mean the same thing across different functions.

- **Create visibility** by building a high-quality model inventory before adding more complex controls.
- **Co-design governance** processes with data scientists, engineers, and business owners to ensure workflows are realistic, not just theoretical.
- **Pilot new processes** with a small set of teams, refine them based on feedback and metrics, and then scale them step by step to improve adoption.
- **Keep governance from being seen as something to work around** by recognizing and rewarding teams that raise risks early, improve documentation, or create reusable governance templates.

## Anticipating and Managing Governance Risks[27]

Poorly designed governance systems can fail in several distinct ways. Over-centralization creates bottlenecks and delays, pushing teams toward shadow AI. Under-specified policies leave teams guessing, leading to inconsistent practices and potential non-compliance. A "check-the-box" culture focuses on filling out forms instead of having real discussions about risk. Static approaches can also develop blind spots around new risks and regulatory changes. Mitigation strategies include

- Delegating routine approvals and reserving central review for high-risk cases.
- Providing detailed procedures and concrete examples.
- Making sure board and committee reviews emphasize discussion and challenge, not just paperwork.
- Conducting regular framework reviews and pairing them with horizon scanning for new threats and obligations.

## Evidence and Limitations[28]

Most evidence on AI-governance effectiveness comes from case studies, industry surveys, and regulator feedback rather than controlled experiments, which makes it hard to prove cause and effect. Organizations with mature model-risk management, clear decision rights, and documented oversight processes tend to report fewer surprises in regulatory exams and higher internal confidence, but metrics such as low incident rates or fast approval times can be ambiguous.

For example, low incident counts may reflect either strong controls or under-reporting, and very short cycle times may indicate either efficient processes or superficial review. For these reasons, governance methods and metrics are best treated as design patterns to adapt and test in context, combining quantitative indicators with qualitative assessments and feedback to understand how governance is actually working.

## Conclusion

Crafting effective governance structures is essential to using AI's benefits in ways that stay safe and sustainable. Governance keeps AI work tied to the organization's purpose, clarifies who is accountable, helps ensure that models keep performing as intended over time, and provides the transparency that regulators, customers, employees, and the public increasingly expect.

When AI governance is thoughtfully designed, supported by the right automation, and anchored in clear roles and metrics, it can become a real source of competitive advantage. Organizations that invest in strong AI governance can keep innovating with confidence, adapt to new risks and rules, and maintain trust as AI becomes part of daily work.

## Notes

[1] NIST's risk-based lifecycle functions, including the emphasis on balancing agility with proportional controls that runs through this chapter's objective, are laid out in National Institute of Standards and Technology's *Artificial Intelligence Risk Management Framework* (*AI RMF* 1.0).

[2] AI governance, as used here, draws on *AuditBoard*'s "Safeguard the Future of AI: The Core Functions of the *NIST AI RMF*."

[3] Model inventories in AI governance: centralized registries covering ownership, risk ratings, and lifecycle tracking—are detailed in KPMG's "Model Risk Management."

[4] Decision rights across the model lifecycle, including RACI matrices and clearly articulated structures, are examined in *EY*'s "*Solutions* for Banks - EY Model Risk Management."

[5] Cross-functional oversight bodies—model-risk committees that set policies, review high-risk systems, and manage escalations—are treated in National Institute of Standards and Technology's *Artificial Intelligence Risk Management Framework* (*AI RMF* 1.0) and related supervisory guidance.

[6] Automated policy enforcement is addressed in *ModelOp*'s "*NIST AI RMF*" and similar governance-platform resources.

[7] Regulatory-compliance expectations for AI systems—documentation, monitoring, and human-oversight requirements—are detailed in National Institute of Standards and Technology's *Artificial Intelligence Risk Management Framework* (*AI RMF* 1.0) and EU AI Act commentary.

[8] Vendor-risk-management definitions and case studies—covering AI-specific vendor-risk processes such as disclosures, contract clauses, and monitoring—appear in Vanta's "Third Party Risk Management and Vendor Risk Management"; Censinet's "Healthcare TPRM Best Practices: Building a World-Class Vendor Risk Management Program"; and related third-party-risk guidance.

[9] High-impact domains, growing consequences of weak governance, and the extension from data governance to AI governance that frame the introduction are drawn from National Institute of Standards and Technology's *Artificial Intelligence Risk Management Framework* (*AI RMF* 1.0) and Wiz's "NIST *AI Risk Management Framework*: A tl;dr."

[10] Lifecycle-oriented AI governance aligned with strategy and ethics, including emphasis on ownership and auditability, is addressed in Wiz's "NIST *AI Risk Management Framework*: A tl;dr" and similar AI-security explainers; and KPMG's "Model Risk Management."

[11] Structured, risk-based governance: its theoretical and regulatory basis, core functions, and high-risk categories—is grounded in National Institute of Standards and Technology's *Artificial Intelligence Risk Management Framework* (*AI RMF* 1.0) and EU AI Act analyses.

[12] Recurring governance components—inventory, risk assessment, decision rights, oversight, enforcement, testing, monitoring, vendor risk, and ethics—are drawn from KPMG's "Model Risk Management"; *AuditBoard*'s "Safeguard the Future of AI: The Core Functions of the *NIST AI RMF*"; EY's "*Solutions* for Banks - EY Model Risk Management"; *ModelOp*'s "*NIST AI RMF*"; National Institute of Standards and Technology's *Artificial Intelligence Risk Management Framework* (*AI RMF* 1.0); Censinet's "Healthcare TPRM Best Practices"; and Wiz's "NIST *AI Risk Management Framework*: A tl;dr."

[13] Comprehensive model inventories, clear ownership, and regulator expectations in AI inventory management are addressed through model-risk-management practice, as summarized by KPMG's "Model Risk Management."

[14] Risk-based classification and assessments—covering impact and likelihood approaches, bias and security testing, and stress testing—are set out in *AuditBoard*'s "Safeguard the Future of AI: The Core Functions of the *NIST AI RMF*" and National Institute of Standards and Technology's *Artificial Intelligence Risk Management Framework* (*AI RMF* 1.0).

[15] Decision-rights allocation, board and senior-management oversight, operational ownership, and the use of RACI matrices are examined in EY's "*Solutions* for Banks - EY Model Risk Management" and KPMG's "Model Risk Management."

[16] Oversight-body composition, responsibilities, and escalation protocols are addressed in *AuditBoard*'s "Safeguard the Future of AI: The Core Functions of the *NIST AI RMF*"; National Institute of Standards and Technology's *Artificial Intelligence Risk Management Framework* (*AI RMF* 1.0); and Wiz's "NIST *AI Risk Management Framework*: A tl;dr."

[17] Policy enforcement, automated gates, and risk-sensitive workflows are illustrated in National Institute of Standards and Technology's *Artificial Intelligence Risk Management Framework* (*AI RMF* 1.0) and *ModelOp*'s "*NIST AI RMF*."

[18] Model testing and validation—covering performance, robustness, fairness, and independent validation—are addressed in EY's "*Solutions* for Banks - EY Model Risk Management" and KPMG's "Model Risk Management."

[19] Continuous-monitoring and alerting practices described here draw on National Institute of Standards and Technology's *Artificial Intelligence Risk Management Framework* (*AI RMF* 1.0) and model-monitoring/MLOps guidance from KPMG's "Model Risk Management" and similar sources.

[20] AI-specific vendor-risk management and the healthcare case study—covering vendor disclosures, contracting, and monitoring—draw on Vanta's "Third Party Risk Management and Vendor Risk Management" and Censinet's "Healthcare TPRM Best Practices: Building a World-Class Vendor Risk Management Program."

[21] Regulatory and ethical-alignment considerations, including ethical review practices, are addressed in National Institute of Standards and Technology's *Artificial Intelligence Risk Management Framework* (*AI RMF* 1.0); EU AI Act commentary; and responsible-AI guidance from global initiatives.

[22] Federated governance and platform-based scaling—covering risk management and governance in large organizations—are examined in EY's "*Solutions* for Banks - EY Model Risk Management"; *AuditBoard*'s "Safeguard the Future of AI: The Core Functions of the *NIST AI RMF*"; and Panorays's "How AI Is Transforming Third-Party Risk Management Workflows."

[23] Governance as an innovation enabler is explored in National Institute of Standards and Technology's *Artificial Intelligence Risk Management Framework* (*AI RMF* 1.0); *ModelOp*'s "*NIST AI RMF*"; and management literature on freedom within a framework.

[24] Financial-services model-risk case material and vendor-governance examples from Censinet's "Healthcare TPRM Best Practices" and Vanta's "Third Party Risk Management and Vendor Risk Management" underpin the financial-services and healthcare case studies in this chapter.

[25] The governance-metrics table is drawn from KPMG's "Model Risk Management"; National Institute of Standards and Technology's *Artificial Intelligence Risk Management Framework* (*AI RMF* 1.0); *AuditBoard*'s "Safeguard the Future of AI: The Core Functions of the *NIST AI RMF*"; and Censinet's "Healthcare TPRM Best Practices."

[26] Practical guidance for leaders on framing, shared language, co-design, piloting, and incentives draws on National Institute of Standards and Technology's *Artificial Intelligence Risk Management Framework* (*AI RMF* 1.0) implementation guides; EY governance-practice advice; and World Economic Forum's "Responsible AI: Design, Operationalize, and Govern."

[27] Over-centralization, under-specification, check-the-box culture, and blind-spot risks are addressed in governance-risk discussions in responsible-AI and risk-management literature, including World Economic Forum's "Responsible AI: Design, Operationalize, and Govern."

[28] Commentary on ambiguous metrics and the need for contextual adaptation—central to the evidence-and-limitations section—draws on KPMG's "Model Risk Management" and other governance surveys and regulator-feedback summaries.

## Key topics explored in this chapter:

- The Strategic Foundation of KPIs
- How AI Is Transforming KPI Design and Management
- Designing KPIs That Matter
- A KPI Design Blueprint
- KPI Governance in an AI Era
- Adapting KPIs as Business Needs Evolve
- Driving Accountability and Performance with KPIs
- Evidence from Practice and Research

# WAY 15

# Define Business-Driven KPIs

## Abstract

Key performance indicators (KPIs) measure the impact of analytics and AI by turning strategy into clear, trackable signals. This chapter explains how to define KPIs that stay tightly linked to strategic goals, focus attention on what matters most, and support accountability across teams. It introduces an end-to-end approach to KPI design that treats metrics as "living" rather than fixed. The chapter also shows how AI can uncover new performance drivers, enable predictive and real-time indicators, and help refine targets over time. Through case studies and practical tools, it illustrates how business-driven KPIs can turn analytics from a basic reporting function into a real engine for performance.

## Objective[1]

After completing this chapter, you will be able to:

- Directly link KPIs to strategic objectives, value drivers, and stakeholder needs.
- Distinguish between vanity metrics and actionable KPIs that truly influence decisions and behaviors.
- Balance leading and lagging indicators, understanding how AI can identify and strengthen crucial leading signals.
- Establish well-tested KPI governance practices that maintain consistency, quality, and relevance as conditions evolve.
- Build adaptive KPI systems that evolve with shifting business strategy, technology, and market dynamics.

- Use KPIs to drive accountability, foster learning, and enhance performance across all organizational levels.

# Terms to Know[2]

**Business-Driven KPI -** A KPI explicitly derived from strategic goals and value drivers, rather than from data availability or reporting tradition, ensuring tight linkage between metrics and strategy.

**Key Performance Indicator (KPI) -** A specific, measurable metric that indicates how successfully an organization, team, or process is progressing against defined objectives, often organized within frameworks like the Balanced Scorecard.

**KPI Catalog -** A centrally maintained repository describing each KPI's definition, formula, owner, data sources, and intended use, helping prevent confusion and duplication.

**KPI Governance -** The policies, roles, and processes used to define, approve, monitor, and retire KPIs, maintaining consistency, quality, and alignment over time.

**Lagging Indicator -** A metric that reflects outcomes after they occur (for example, quarterly revenue or customer churn) and is important for accountability and reporting.

**Leading Indicator -** A metric that provides early signals about future performance (for example, pipeline health as a predictor of revenue), enabling proactive adjustments.

**Predictive Metric -** A KPI generated or enhanced through statistical or machine-learning models to forecast future outcomes, often used as an AI-enabled leading indicator.

# Introduction[3]

Leaders often describe KPIs as the "language of performance": they turn strategy into numbers that can be tracked and managed. Yet many organizations struggle with metric overload—dozens, even hundreds, of loosely defined indicators. These metrics often lack a clear link to strategy and rarely shape real decisions. Research on balanced scorecards and strategy execution shows that too many poorly aligned metrics dilute focus and weaken accountability. The spread of AI and advanced analytics raises both the opportunities and the risks. Organizations can now track more signals, more often, and in greater detail. However, this also increases the risk of overload if metrics are not tied to clear objectives. The challenge is straightforward: is the organization measuring the right things, in the right ways, at the right times? Effective KPIs are business-driven, adaptive, and AI-enabled. They start from strategy, evolve with goals and objectives, and become part of everyday management routines.

## The Strategic Foundation of KPIs[4]

At their best, KPIs are a translation layer between strategy and execution. Rather than tracking everything that can be measured, organizations define a focused set of metrics that signal whether important business objectives are on track.

In a traditional model, senior executives select KPIs based on experience, industry norms, and historical practice. That approach has value, but static KPIs quickly become disconnected from shifting strategies, new product lines, and evolving customer expectations. Teams end up optimizing for metrics that no longer reflect what the organization actually needs to monitor for success.

A business-driven approach starts with a different premise: every KPI must trace directly to a strategic intent. For example:

- If the strategic goal is profitable growth, key KPIs might include customer lifetime value, unit margin, and cost-to-serve.
- If the point is risk reduction, metrics might focus on incident frequency, time-to-detect, and policy adherence.

Two principles underpin this foundation:

- **Business alignment:** KPIs must capture outcomes and drivers that leadership explicitly cares about. Counting "number of dashboards delivered" may say more about activity than impact. Measuring "percentage of key decisions informed by analytics" signals whether insights are truly being used.
- **Owned accountability:** KPIs drive behavior only when someone is responsible for monitoring them and acting on deviations. Clear ownership at the appropriate level—team, function, or executive—ensures that metrics are not just observed but managed.

When leaders explicitly map KPIs to strategic goals, they become a shared language for prioritization. Leaders then evaluate investments in analytics, AI, and process changes against their expected effect on the agreed metrics, reducing misalignment and conflict.

## How AI Is Transforming KPI Design and Management[5]

AI changes what, how, and when we measure KPIs.

### What We Measure

Traditional KPIs often focused on metrics that were easy to access and calculate. AI widens this range by analyzing large, complex datasets to find which factors most strongly predict desired outcomes. This can lead to new, more useful KPIs, such as:

- Behavioral engagement scores that better predict churn than simple login counts.
- Operational complexity indices that explain project overruns more accurately than budget variance alone.

AI can also map relationships among metrics, revealing that some commonly tracked KPIs are redundant or even misleading when viewed in isolation.

### How We Measure

Historically, many KPIs were compiled manually, which created delays and errors. AI-enabled analytics platforms now support:

- Automated ingestion and cleaning of data from multiple sources.
- Real-time or near-real-time calculation and visualization of KPIs.
- Automated anomaly detection that flags unusual patterns without requiring constant human monitoring.

These capabilities reduce reporting lag and free analysts to focus on interpretation, collaboration, and scenario exploration rather than data wrangling.

### When We Measure

In a stable environment, monthly or quarterly metrics might be enough. In fast-moving markets, slow measurement cycles mean slow reactions. AI-supported systems can update KPIs continuously, making it possible to:

- Adjust tactics in response to emerging trends.
- Run experiments and see early performance signals quickly.
- Re-evaluate whether thresholds and targets still make sense as conditions change.

Together, richer metrics, automated measurement, and higher frequency encourage a shift from reactive reporting to more proactive performance management.

## Designing KPIs That Matter[6]

A small number of well-chosen KPIs outperforms a long list of loosely relevant metrics. Designing KPIs that matter requires deliberate choices along several dimensions.

### Mapping KPIs to Strategic Objectives

The starting point is a strategy map or similar expression of how the organization creates value. For each strategic objective, teams ask:

- What outcome are we trying to achieve?
- What behaviors or processes most influence that outcome?
- Which metrics can reliably indicate whether those drivers are moving in the right direction?

Engaging cross-functional stakeholders in this process—strategy owners, finance, operational leaders, analytics teams—builds buy-in and reduces the risk that KPIs are seen as imposed from above.

### Focusing on Actionable Metrics

Actionable KPIs are ones that teams can directly influence and that point to a clear course of action when they move. For example:

- "Customer satisfaction score" indicates overall sentiment but may not point to a specific intervention.
- "Percentage of unresolved negative feedback after 48 hours" suggests a concrete action: improve response and resolution processes.

When designing KPIs, it helps to ask: if this metric changes, what decision or behavior should that trigger? If the answer is unclear, the metric may be better used as a contextual statistic rather than a core KPI.

### Balancing Leading and Lagging Indicators

Lagging indicators such as revenue, costs, and churn confirm what has already happened. They are essential for accountability but poor tools for early correction. Leading indicators—such as engagement levels, pipeline activity, or process adherence—offer early warning and opportunity for course correction.

AI can be especially helpful in identifying and refining leading indicators. By analyzing historical data, AI models can uncover which early behaviors or conditions most strongly predict later outcomes. Those insights can be translated into leading KPIs that teams can monitor and influence before results are locked in.

A healthy KPI set usually includes both lagging indicators to confirm results and leading indicators to anticipate them.

## A KPI Design Blueprint

To operationalize KPI design, organizations often employ a blueprint. This blueprint connects objectives, drivers, metrics, and actions into a single, clear line of sight.

## KPI Blueprint Model

| Element | Guiding Question | Example |
|---|---|---|
| **Strategic Goal** | What are we trying to achieve? | Increase profitable customer retention |
| **Value Driver** | What most influences this goal? | Quality of onboarding and early service |
| **KPI** | How will we measure that driver or outcome? | 90-day churn rate for new customers |
| **Target and Band** | What is acceptable, concerning, or excellent? | Target ≤ 5%; watch band 5-7%; critical > 7% |
| **Owner and Action** | Who owns this KPI and what happens when it moves? | CX director; triggers root-cause analysis and playbook actions |

## KPI Governance in an AI Era[7]

As metrics become more numerous, data-driven, and technically complex, governance becomes essential. Without it, organizations risk metric sprawl, conflicting definitions, and loss of trust in reported performance. Effective KPI governance typically includes:

### KPI Governance Committees

These cross-functional groups usually include analytics leaders, business owners, finance, risk, audit, and technology representatives. Their responsibilities often include:

- Approving new KPIs and ensuring they align with strategy.

- Reviewing and retiring metrics that are obsolete, redundant, or misleading.
- Resolving conflicts when different parts of the organization report similar metrics differently.

### Central KPI Catalog

A centralized repository is used to document important information associated with each KPI:

- Name and precise definition.
- Calculation formula and data sources.
- Frequency of calculation and reporting.
- Owner, stakeholders, and primary use cases.

This catalog helps prevent inconsistent interpretations and supports onboarding for new employees and teams.

### Automated Quality Control

AI-enabled monitoring tools can scan the KPI landscape for:

- Metrics that have not changed meaningfully for extended periods.
- KPIs that are rarely accessed or referenced in decisions.
- Inconsistencies between related metrics that suggest data or definition issues.

Identified KPIs can then be reviewed and either refined or retired, keeping the portfolio lean and relevant.

## Adapting KPIs as Business Needs Evolve[8]

No KPI portfolio should be considered permanent. That's because strategy evolves, markets shift, and AI can reveal new insights about what really drives business performance. Adaptive KPI systems incorporate regular review, adjustment, and change as a deliberate practice.

### Dynamic KPI Adjustment

Using historical and ongoing data, organizations can assess whether each KPI:

- Remains predictive of important outcomes.
- Still aligns to current strategic priorities.
- Is being used in high-stakes decisions.

### Scenario Analysis

AI-enabled scenario modeling can help test whether the existing KPI set would provide early warning under different conditions. For example:

- Would current indicators highlight a supply chain disruption in time to respond?
- Under a new pricing strategy, do existing revenue and margin KPIs provide sufficient visibility?

If the answer is no, then either new KPIs and/or supplemental indicators may be needed.

### Cadence of Review

Many organizations schedule formal KPI reviews annually or semi-annually, aligned with strategic planning cycles, while retaining the flexibility to update specific metrics more frequently as needed.

## Driving Accountability and Performance with KPIs[9]

KPIs only drive performance when they are built into day-to-day business management rather than being treated as a reporting afterthought. Strategy-execution research shows that organizations using metrics in regular management dialogue—forecast reviews, pipeline discussions, operations huddles—achieve better alignment and follow-through than those that review KPIs only in periodic scorecards.

Leaders can strengthen accountability by linking selected KPIs to incentives and recognition, ensuring transparency of definitions and formulas, tailoring dashboards to each level of the organization, and explicitly asking in reviews how KPI movements informed decisions and trade-offs. At the same time, leaders should encourage teams to revisit and retire KPIs that no longer influence behavior. This signals that metrics are tools for learning, not rigid constraints.

## Evidence from Practice and Research[10]

Field studies and industry surveys on performance management find that organizations tightly linking metrics to strategic objectives and decision processes tend to outperform those tracking large volumes of loosely connected indicators. Balanced-Scorecard research shows that a focused, well-aligned KPI set improves clarity and execution, whereas metric proliferation creates confusion and dilutes accountability.

Empirical work on AI-powered KPIs suggests that organizations using AI to create or refine their KPI portfolios see improvements in predictive accuracy, financial performance, and cross-functional collaboration when compared with peers relying solely on traditional metrics. These findings align with a business-driven, AI-enabled KPI approach but also emphasize that metrics must be interpreted contextually and complemented by qualitative judgment, especially in complex or uncertain environments.

# Case Study[11]

## Redesigning KPIs for a Subscription Business

A global SaaS company historically focused on new-sales KPIs: deals closed, total bookings, and quarterly revenue. As the business matured, leadership realized long-term value depended more on renewals and expansion than on acquisition. Yet, existing metrics continued to steer behavior toward short-term wins, often at the expense of fit and retention. A cross-functional redesign effort mapped the customer lifecycle, identified value drivers like product adoption and customer health, and introduced new KPIs. These included onboarding completion within 30 days, a product-adoption index, and net revenue retention by segment.

AI models analyzed historical data, identifying behaviors in the first 90 days that best predicted long-term retention. This converted those behaviors into leading indicators for customer-success teams to monitor and influence. Over the following year, compensation structures updated to incorporate retention and expansion KPIs. Quarterly reviews focused as much on customer health as on new bookings, shifting sales and success behaviors toward higher-fit deals and early-stage engagement that improved retention and sustainable growth.

# Success Metrics[12]

To understand whether KPI systems help or hinder performance, leaders can track a small set of health indicators focused on alignment, ownership, usage, adaptability, and portfolio size. Work on measurement and strategy execution stresses the importance of monitoring the KPI system itself as well. The indicators presented in the table that follows help leaders see whether their KPI environment is focused, aligned, and dynamic rather than static and cluttered, and whether they are actively pruning and evolving metrics as strategy, markets, and insights change.

### KPI System Health

| Metric | Definition | What It Tells You |
|---|---|---|
| **Strategic Alignment Rate** | % of KPIs mapped to explicit strategic objectives | Degree to which metrics support the current strategy |
| **Ownership Clarity** | Share of KPIs with named, active owners | Strength of accountability |
| **Usage in Key Decisions** | Proportion of major decisions documented as referencing KPIs | Extent to which KPIs influence real decisions |
| **Review and Refresh Cadence** | Frequency with which KPIs are reviewed and updated | Adaptability of the KPI portfolio |
| **KPI Portfolio Size** | No. of active KPIs at each level (enterprise, unit, team) | Risk of overload versus sufficiency |
| **Retirement Rate** | % of KPIs retired or replaced over a defined period | Willingness to remove obsolete or low-value metrics |

## Practical Advice for Leaders[13]

Leaders shape how KPIs are perceived and used when they start from business strategy rather than existing reports, ask which decisions and behaviors matter most, and then design or refining KPIs to support those choices. They should:

- **Demand clarity.** Insist on unambiguous definitions and transparent formulas.
- **Enforce limits.** Restrict the number of primary KPIs that are used at each level.
- **Focus.** Treat additional measures as "contextual" rather than "core," reinforcing the idea that focus beats volume.
- **Encourage experimentation.** Pilot new KPIs in selected areas, learn from outcomes, and then decide whether to scale. This helps keep the KPI portfolio adaptive.
- **Model healthy engagement.** In reviews, ask how KPIs informed decisions, what trade-offs were considered, and what changes followed decision-making.

- **Reinforce fundamentals.** Metrics are tools for learning, not just surveillance.

## Anticipating and Managing KPI Risks[14]

KPIs introduce risks when they are misapplied, including:

- **Metric myopia:** Over-focusing on a single KPI and neglecting broader impacts.
- **Vanity metrics:** Indicators that look impressive but rarely drive decisions.
- **Gaming and distortion:** Achieving targets through behavior that undermines true performance.
- **Overcomplexity:** Bloated KPI portfolios causing confusion and slow decision-making.

To mitigate these risks:

- Use balanced KPI sets that cover multiple performance dimensions.
- Regularly revisit incentive designs.
- Create channels for staff to raise concerns about unintended consequences.

Keep in mind that AI can both increase and reduce risk: opaque models can make gaming harder to detect, but AI can also spot unusual patterns that may signal manipulation or harmful side effects when monitoring is thoughtfully designed.

## Limitations and Contextual Factors[15]

The effects of KPIs are difficult to separate from broader organizational context because metrics both shape and are shaped by culture, incentives, and power dynamics. The same KPI design can have different impacts across industries, maturity levels, and regulatory environments, and aggressive incentive ties can sharpen focus while raising the risk of gaming or neglect of unmeasured dimensions.

For these reasons, the practices presented here should be treated as design patterns to test and adapt rather than universal prescriptions, and organizations can benefit from ongoing scrutiny, experimentation, and refinement of their KPI systems, informed by both quantitative results and qualitative feedback from the people who use them.

# Conclusion

In an AI-rich, rapidly changing business environment, KPIs can no longer function as static scorecards or after-the-fact reports; they must act as adaptive guides that evolve alongside strategy and technology. When supported by governance, automation, and a culture of learning, KPIs become a central way for organizations to sense change, respond thoughtfully, and sustain performance over time. The combination of strategic alignment, AI-enabled discovery of leading indicators, and disciplined KPI governance gives leaders a practical path to turn analytics and AI into a true performance engine rather than a reporting sideline.

# Notes

[1] The capabilities emphasized in this chapter's objective—linking KPIs to strategy, balancing leading and lagging indicators, and building adaptive, AI-enabled KPI systems—are grounded in Balanced-Scorecard and strategy-execution literature, including The Strategy Institute's "A Comprehensive Guide to Implementing the Balanced Scorecard Framework," Balanced Scorecard Institute's "Balanced Scorecard Basics," Lean Data Point's "Measuring Strategic Execution Success Using the Balanced Scorecard," and Kaplan and Norton's "The Balanced Scorecard—Measures That Drive Performance," *Harvard Business Review.*

[2] Definitions of KPIs, leading and lagging indicators, business-driven KPIs, predictive metrics, KPI governance, and KPI catalogs used here follow The Strategy Institute's "A Comprehensive Guide to Implementing the Balanced Scorecard Framework," Balanced Scorecard Institute's "Balanced Scorecard Basics," and Rhythm Systems Blog's "Balanced Scorecard KPI Examples Including a 2026 KPI Scorecard."

[3] The "language of performance," the problems of metric proliferation, and the need for business-driven, adaptive, AI-enabled KPIs are grounded in Boston Consulting Group's "How AI-Powered KPIs Measure Success Better," *Alteryx*'s "The Art of the AI KPI, Part 1," and *Metrology News*'s "Research Reveals That 90% of Organizations Using AI to Create KPIs Report Improvement."

[4] Kaplan and Norton's "The Balanced Scorecard—Measures That Drive Performance," *Harvard Business Review*, together with practical implementation guides in The Strategy Institute's "A Comprehensive Guide to Implementing the Balanced Scorecard Framework," Balanced Scorecard Institute's "Balanced Scorecard Basics," and Lean Data Point's "Measuring Strategic Execution Success Using the Balanced Scorecard," establish KPIs as a translation layer between strategy and execution and articulate the role of Balanced-Scorecard perspectives.

[5] Practitioner reports and industry research on AI-enabled KPI design and management are drawn from Boston Consulting Group's "How AI-Powered KPIs Measure Success Better," Google Cloud Blog's "KPIs for Gen AI: Measuring Your AI Success," Google Cloud's "KPIs for Gen AI: Measuring AI Success—Deep Dive," *Metrology News*'s "Research Reveals That 90% of Organizations Using AI to Create KPIs Report Improvement," and *Alteryx*'s "The Art of the AI KPI, Part 1."

[6] Designing "KPIs that matter" is addressed in Rhythm Systems Blog's "Balanced Scorecard KPI Examples Including a 2026 KPI Scorecard," The Strategy Institute's "A Comprehensive Guide to Implementing the Balanced Scorecard Framework," and Lean Data Point's "Measuring Strategic Execution Success Using the Balanced Scorecard."

[7] KPI governance practices are drawn from Balanced Scorecard Institute's "Balanced Scorecard Basics," The Strategy Institute's "A Comprehensive Guide to Implementing the Balanced Scorecard Framework," Boston Consulting Group's "How AI-Powered KPIs Measure Success Better," and *Alteryx*'s "The Art of the AI KPI, Part 1."

[8] Adaptive KPI systems, dynamic review and retirement of metrics, and AI-enabled scenario modeling to test KPI portfolios are explored in Boston Consulting Group's "How AI-Powered KPIs Measure Success Better," *Alteryx*'s "The Art of the AI KPI, Part 1," Google Cloud's "KPIs for Gen AI: Measuring AI Success—Deep Dive," and *Metrology News*'s "Research Reveals That 90% of Organizations Using AI to Create KPIs Report Improvement."

[9] For evidence that embedding KPIs into ongoing management routines improves alignment and performance, see The Strategy Institute's "A Comprehensive Guide to Implementing the Balanced Scorecard Framework," Lean Data Point's "Measuring Strategic Execution Success Using the Balanced Scorecard," and Rhythm Systems Blog's "Balanced Scorecard KPI Examples Including a 2026 KPI Scorecard."

[10] Performance-management research and AI-KPI case reports are summarized from Boston Consulting Group's "How AI-Powered KPIs Measure Success Better," *Metrology News*'s "Research Reveals That 90% of Organizations Using AI to Create KPIs Report Improvement," *Alteryx*'s "The Art of the AI KPI, Part 1," and Google Cloud's "KPIs for Gen AI: Measuring AI Success—Deep Dive."

[11] SaaS and retail case studies illustrating business-driven, AI-informed KPI redesign and its impact on retention and profitability draw on ScaleXP's "SaaS Benchmarks 2023 Part 4: Revenue Retention," LinkedIn's "Why Net Revenue Retention Could Be Your Most Important KPI," and Rhythm Systems Blog's "Balanced Scorecard KPI Examples Including a 2026 KPI Scorecard."

[12] Suggested KPI system-health indicators are examined in Balanced Scorecard Institute's "Balanced Scorecard Basics," Rhythm Systems Blog's "Balanced Scorecard KPI Examples Including a 2026 KPI Scorecard," and The Strategy Institute's "A Comprehensive Guide to Implementing the Balanced Scorecard Framework."

[13] Practical leadership behaviors for effective KPI are taken from Lean Data Point's "Measuring Strategic Execution Success Using the Balanced Scorecard," The Strategy Institute's "A Comprehensive Guide to Implementing the Balanced Scorecard Framework," and Rhythm Systems Blog's "Balanced Scorecard KPI Examples Including a 2026 KPI Scorecard."

[14] KPI-related risks are examined in The Strategy Institute's "A Comprehensive Guide to Implementing the Balanced Scorecard Framework," Rhythm Systems Blog's "Balanced Scorecard KPI Examples Including a 2026 KPI Scorecard," and *Alteryx*'s "The Art of the AI KPI, Part 1."

[15] Contextual factors and limitations of KPI-based management are analyzed in The Strategy Institute's "A Comprehensive Guide to Implementing the Balanced Scorecard Framework," Lean Data Point's "Measuring Strategic Execution Success Using the Balanced Scorecard," and Kaplan and Norton's "The Balanced Scorecard—Measures That Drive Performance," *Harvard Business Review*.

## Key topics explored in this chapter:

- Why Mapping Decision-Making Workflows Matters
- Documenting and Visualizing Decision Workflows
- Theoretical Foundations of Workflow Mapping
- Embedding AI in Decision Workflows
- Optimizing and Standardizing Workflows for Scale
- Clarifying Data Roles Throughout Decision Workflows

# WAY 16

# Map Decision-Making Workflows


## Abstract

Analytics and AI only create value when insights reliably flow into decisions and actions. This chapter explains how to map, optimize, and standardize decision-making workflows so data moves efficiently from dashboards, along clearly defined paths, to accountable decision-makers. It also shows how AI-enabled tools such as process mining, intelligent routing, and real-time decision support can help turn static procedures into adaptive, AI-integrated workflows.


## Objective

After completing this chapter, you will be able to:

- Explain why mapping decision workflows is vital for realizing the full value of analytics and AI.
- Identify high-value decisions within core business processes and document their end-to-end workflows.
- Use visual tools—like flowcharts and swim-lane diagrams—to clarify triggers, data inputs, roles, and handoffs.
- Integrate AI into decision workflows for real-time analytics, predictive automation, and dynamic task routing.
- Standardize and optimize workflows at scale, while still preserving flexibility for local context.
- Define data-related roles and responsibilities across workflows to ensure accountability and prevent dropped handoffs.

# Terms to Know

**AI-Integrated Workflow**[1] **-** A decision process in which AI systems provide recommendations, automate tasks, or route work dynamically alongside human decision-makers, following intelligent-automation patterns.

**Decision-Making Workflow**[2] **-** The series of steps, roles, data inputs, and actions through which a decision is initiated, analyzed, made, executed, and reviewed, consistent with business decision-management practices.

**Exception Handling**[3] **-** The subset of a workflow dealing with cases that deviate from standard patterns and require special attention or escalation, often highlighted in process-mining and BPM applications.

**Process Mining**[4] **-** The use of event logs and system data to reconstruct and analyze how work actually flows through an organization, revealing bottlenecks, delays, loops, and non-compliant variants.

**RACI Matrix**[5] **-** A framework that clarifies who is Responsible, Accountable, Consulted, and Informed for specific steps or decisions, widely used in process and decision-governance design.

**Task Routing**[6] **-** The assignment of work items to people or systems based on rules or AI models that consider skills, workload, and priorities, as described in intelligent task-routing and AI-routing guidance.

**Workflow Mapping**[7] **-** The practice of documenting and visualizing processes, typically using diagrams that show activities, decision points, and handoffs, as in BPMN-style process modeling.

# Introduction

Organizations invest heavily in analytics and AI—building data lakes, dashboards, and sophisticated models—yet leaders still question why insights do not translate into results. The problem often is not the analytics quality, but the lack of reliable pathways connecting analysis to decision and action. Decision-making workflows—how decisions start, who participates, which data informs them, and how outcomes are executed—are often undocumented or only partially understood. This forces teams to rely on informal practices and ad-hoc communication.

In an AI-rich environment, this gap becomes more visible and more costly. AI models continuously generate insights, but without well-mapped workflows, those insights may not reach the right person at the right time or may lack clear action paths. Process-mining and workflow-analytics studies consistently show that organizations discover major delays and rework not within the analytics itself, but in how insights move—or fail to move—through decision chains. This chapter argues that mapping, optimizing, and standardizing decision workflows is the missing link in many analytics transformations. It also shows how AI can help discover, orchestrate, and improve these workflows at scale.

## Why Mapping Decision-Making Workflows Matters[8]

Mapping decision workflows makes the invisible visible, exposing how work truly gets done and where data either supports or fails to support key choices. Documenting decision processes yields several key benefits.

- **Linking insights to action:** Without a mapped flow, no shared understanding exists regarding how analytical recommendations move from analysts to accountable decision-makers. Mapping clarifies where recommendations originate, who reviews them, and how they translate into concrete changes in pricing, staffing, risk posture, or customer experience.
- **Driving accountability:** Vague roles and decision rights can stall work at handoffs or lead to endless revisits. Clear workflow maps assign responsibility for each step—data preparation, analysis, interpretation, approval, and execution—enabling teams to trace and address delays and failures.
- **Standardizing best practices:** Once documented and refined, a workflow can serve as a template. Teams across different regions or business units can then adopt a proven decision pattern instead of inventing their own from scratch. This reduces variability, simplifies training, and improves control.

In short, mapping decision workflows transforms decision-making from an informal art into an inspectable, improvable process, aligning it with modern business decision-management approaches.

## Documenting and Visualizing Decision Workflows[9]

Mapping starts by understanding the most important decisions and their surrounding processes. A structured approach typically involves the following steps:

- **Identify key decisions:** Instead of documenting every decision, organizations focus on those significantly impacting revenue, risk, cost, or customer outcomes—for example, pricing approvals, credit decisions, fraud reviews, workforce planning, or major investments.

- **Define data entry and use points:** For each decision, teams identify data entry points and how it transforms, including source systems, quality checks, analytical models, and dashboards or reports used in decision meetings.
- **Clarify roles:** Stakeholders are listed with their contributions: data engineers prepare inputs, analysts produce or explain insights, subject-matter experts add context, and final decision-makers authorize actions.
- **Diagram flows:** Teams create flowcharts or swim-lane diagrams to show the sequence of activities and handoffs. Swim lanes can organize by role, system, or region and typically include triggers, activities, decision points, data touchpoints, and action checkpoints.
- **Highlight bottlenecks and pain points:** During mapping workshops, participants highlight areas where delays, errors, or rework occur. These often include unclear approval thresholds, duplicated reviews, or manual steps ripe for automation.

AI-supported process-mining tools complement human interviews by analyzing event logs from workflow, CRM, or ticketing systems. They generate process maps that reveal actual paths, wait times, rework loops, and deviations from intended flows. Combining human insight with data-driven process discovery yields a more accurate and actionable view of decision workflows.

## Theoretical Foundations of Workflow Mapping[10]

Workflow mapping and process mining build on established business process management (BPM) principles. BPM treats organizational processes as explicit, modeled objects that teams can analyze and improve. BPM practice emphasizes visually modeling processes and responsibilities. Meanwhile, decision-modeling approaches like Decision Model and Notation (DMN) explicitly model decision logic and dependencies within those processes.

Process mining extends traditional BPM, applying algorithms to event-log data to reconstruct actual process flows, identify bottlenecks, and uncover non-compliant variants. Decision-modeling guidance stresses that defining decision questions, inputs, and logic improves both automation and governance. It also notes that DMN models can link directly to process models in BPMN, enabling tighter integration between process and decision flows. In the context of decision-making, these tools help bridge the gap between official diagrams and how decisions truly get made, providing a more empirical basis for redesign.

## Embedding AI in Decision Workflows

Once documented, organizations can decide where AI should participate—as a recommender, an automation engine, or a task orchestrator. AI's role in decision flows unfolds across several dimensions.

- **Real-time analytics:** Instead of waiting for scheduled reports, AI-enabled decision-support systems deliver insights as new data appears—for example, an unusual transaction or a spike in demand. Organizations can design workflows so specific thresholds or patterns automatically trigger alerts or recommended actions, supporting near real-time responses.
- **Predictive automation:** AI models forecast likely outcomes and propose—or execute—predefined responses. For instance, a risk model might flag transactions exceeding a risk-score threshold, routing them to specialist queues while auto-approving low-risk items. This mirrors AI-assisted decisioning use cases.
- **Cognitive task routing:** Instead of static routing rules, AI assigns tasks based on workload, skills, and historical performance. It sends complex cases to experienced staff while routing simpler requests to newer staff or bots. This improves both speed and quality, mirroring best practices in AI-driven task routing for service and annotation workflows.
- **Bias mitigation and consistency:** Properly designed and monitored AI systems enforce standardized criteria for certain decisions. This reduces variability from personal preferences or inconsistent rule application, supporting fairness and compliance goals.

In all cases, AI should integrate through explicit workflow steps, not as a hidden layer. Diagrams should show where AI models invoke, what inputs they require, what outputs they generate, and who is accountable for reviewing or overriding them. This clarity is essential for trust, governance, and training.

## Optimizing and Standardizing Workflows for Scale[11]

Process-mining and workflow-analytics studies report that organizations with a formal approach to optimization routinely uncover hidden bottlenecks, unnecessary handoffs, and non-compliant variants, leading to measurable reductions in cycle time and rework when addressed. Leaders can use such insights to remove or consolidate redundant approvals, automate repetitive tasks, or adjust routing rules and AI logic to better balance workloads.

## Core Components of Effective Optimization

| Component | Primary Focus | Typical Outcomes |
|---|---|---|
| **Process Optimization** | Removing delays, redundancies, and rework | Faster cycle times, fewer errors |
| **Continuous Improvement** | Feeding outcomes back into designs and models | Better decisions and workflows over time |
| **Standardization at Scale** | Reusing proven workflows with local variations | Consistency with controlled flexibility |
| **AI-Enabled Process Discovery** | Using logs to reveal real, not assumed, flows | Data-driven identification of bottlenecks |
| **Template and Pattern Libraries** | Capturing and sharing best-practice workflows | Quicker onboarding and alignment across teams |

Continuous improvement involves tracking outcomes such as profitability, customer satisfaction, or risk incidents after key decisions and feeding this information back into models and process designs, creating closed loops where both decision quality and workflow design improve together. As workflows mature, they can be standardized across similar contexts; a "gold standard" process can be documented and adopted by multiple regions, with local variations clearly specified and governed.

## Clarifying Data Roles Throughout Decision Workflows[12]

Clear roles are crucial when decisions depend on complex data and AI systems. Without role clarity, analytics tasks may be duplicated, key checks skipped, and responsibility contested. Typical data-related roles in decision workflows include:

- Data stewards, who ensure data entering the workflow meets quality, completeness, and compliance standards and who own definitions and lineage.
- Data engineers, who build and maintain pipelines that supply data to decision points.
- Analysts and data scientists, who transform raw data into insights, design models, and explain results in decision forums.

- Citizen data users, who use self-service tools to perform local analyses.
- Business owners and decision authorities, who weigh insights alongside context and constraints and accept accountability for outcomes.
- AI systems and automation, which execute predefined steps such as preliminary reviews or routing as "digital team members" under human oversight.

RACI matrices help specify for each workflow step who is responsible, accountable, consulted, and informed, reducing confusion and clarifying expectations, especially when decisions span functions. Process and decision-modeling practice shows that such explicit role modeling is vital to making decision governance workable at scale.

# Case Studies

## Case Study #1: Transforming Exception Handling in Logistics[13]

A global logistics provider grappled with escalating delays resolving delivery exceptions—damaged goods, missed time windows, customs issues—despite robust analytics and tracking systems. Customers endured lengthy waits and inconsistent communication, and leaders suspected the root cause stemmed from decision-making processes, not merely data availability.

A cross-functional team mapped the exception-handling workflow for key markets via workshops. This revealed that frontline staff often escalated issues to multiple managers, each applying personal judgment and informal rules. Moreover, they inconsistently used shipment history and customer data. Process mining on ticketing and operational systems then revealed that some cases cycled through numerous handoffs and languished in queues far longer than actual handling time.

They designed a new workflow, clearly defining exception categories and paths. It embedded classification models to triage incoming exceptions by priority and customer value. This new system routed routine cases directly to empowered frontline staff using predefined rules, while sending complex cases to specialized teams. Automated notifications to customers and account managers cut down on back-and-forth communication. And, ongoing analysis of event logs provided crucial feedback to refine routing and rules. Within months, average resolution times plummeted, and customer satisfaction soared. This transformed exception handling into a continuously improving, data-driven workflow, moving beyond mere ad-hoc firefighting.

### Case Study #2: Mapping AI-Enabled Credit Decisions in Banking[14]

A regional bank deployed AI models to support small-business credit decisions, with early pilots showing strong predictive performance, but adoption was uneven and turnaround times varied widely across branches. Leadership also lacked clear visibility into how decisions were actually being made.

The bank launched a decision-workflow mapping initiative focused on small-business credit, combining interviews with process mining on loan-origination and document-management systems. The maps revealed inconsistent data collection and pre-screening steps, variation in when and how the AI model was invoked, and unclear escalation paths for borderline cases.

The redesigned workflow standardized data capture and verification steps before model use, specified when and how the AI model should be run and how recommendations should be presented to officers, and defined thresholds for auto-approval, manual review, and escalation. Roles and responsibilities for model monitoring, exception handling, and overrides were documented using RACI matrices, and training used workflow diagrams to explain the intended relationship between AI and human judgment. Over time, the bank observed faster, more consistent decisions, improved customer experience, and clearer evidence for audits and regulators about how AI was used in credit decisions.

## Success Metrics[15]

Process mining and bottleneck analysis suggest organizations monitor key metrics—such as cycle time, handoff counts, and rework. This delivers data-driven visibility into workflow health and enables targeted improvements. These metrics enable leaders to assess not just whether decisions are being made, but how effectively underlying workflows function. Tracking them over time, moreover, clearly highlights the impact of mapping and AI integration.

## Workflow Performance Metrics

| Metric | Definition | What It Tells You |
|---|---|---|
| **Decision Cycle Time** | Time from decision trigger to final decision and action | Speed and efficiency of the workflow |
| **Touchpoint Count** | No. of handoffs or approvals per decision | Complexity and risk of delays or errors |
| **Straight-Through Rate** | % of cases completed without manual intervention | Level of automation and process strength |
| **Exception Escalation Rate** | Share of cases requiring escalation beyond defined thresholds | Adequacy of rules and AI models; clarity of thresholds |
| **Rework Rate** | % of decisions reopened or revised after initial action | Quality of inputs, criteria, and execution |
| **Data Availability at Decision** | % of decisions where required data was available on time | Reliability of data pipelines supporting decisions |

# Practical Advice for Leaders[16]

- **Accelerate decision-workflow mapping and optimization** by starting with a small number of high-value decisions, rather than trying to map everything simultaneously.
- **Select high-impact processes** with clear performance problems and enough volume for effective analysis.
- **Combine interviews, workshops, and log reviews** to gain context and uncover paths and bottlenecks.
- **Reinforce trust and governance** by explicitly defining AI's role in diagrams and training to help staff grasp when and how to rely on models and where human oversight remains essential.
- **Use RACI matrices** to clarify data and decision roles, especially where responsibilities cross boundaries, to prevent dropped handoffs and contested accountability.
- **Treat workflow diagrams as living documents** that evolve with process changes and AI enhancements.

## Anticipating and Managing Workflow Risks[17]

As organizations formalize and automate decision workflows, they must manage new risks.

- **Over-reliance on automation** can foster excessive trust in AI or rules, diminishing important human judgment in novel or high-stakes situations. Mitigating this risk requires clear override paths, human-in-the-loop controls, and periodic human review of automated decisions.
- **Hidden complexity** presents another risk: as organizations add more AI components and process integrations, workflows can become more opaque. Maintaining clear, updated documentation and simplifying processes wherever possible helps reduce this.
- **Rigidity** can merge when standardization stifles essential local adaptations. Leaders should define which workflow elements are mandatory and where flexibility is allowed, and they should establish procedures for proposing and approving deviations.
- **Data blind spots** introduce further risks: when key data sources are missing or of low quality, workflows will yield suboptimal decisions. This highlights the need for strong data stewardship and continuous monitoring of data completeness and quality at every decision point.

Explicitly naming these risks empowers organizations to design workflows that are both powerful and resilient.

## Methodological and Practical Limitations[18]

Process maps and mining outputs are only as reliable as the underlying data and assumptions. Event logs can be incomplete, mistimed, or fail to capture informal workarounds. For these reasons, validate workflow designs with the individuals who actually perform the work. Decision-modeling and BPM literature also note that RACI matrices and DMN diagrams can oversimplify complex decision dynamics or leave gaps if they're not revisited as responsibilities and systems evolve.

The methods and patterns in this chapter should be treated as hypotheses to test and refine in context, not as fixed blueprints. Organizations benefit from iterative experimentation, monitoring how workflow changes affect performance metrics, and adjusting designs as strategies, technologies, and regulations evolve.

# Conclusion[19]

Mapping, optimizing, and standardizing decision-making workflows is important for unleashing the full value of analytics and AI. When workflows remain implicit, even the best models exert little influence on organizational actions. But when workflows are documented, clarified, and enhanced with AI, decisions move faster, become more consistent, and deliver the intended transparency.

From this perspective, decision workflows are not static procedures; they are living architectures that evolve with shifting strategies, advancing technologies, and accumulating insights. Organizations that invest in mastering these architectures—using workflow mapping, process mining, decision modeling, and AI-enabled orchestration—will convert data into appropriate action and turn it into lasting competitive advantage.

# Notes

[1] AI-integrated workflows place AI systems as explicit components in decision processes, providing recommendations, automation, or dynamic routing; see Marlabs's "10 Best Intelligent Automation Platforms You Can Use in 2025," INFORM Software's "Unlocking Business Efficiency with Process Mining," and IBM's "IBM Process Mining."

[2] Decision-making workflows are defined in decision-management literature as structured series of steps, roles, data inputs, and actions through which decisions move from trigger to execution and review; see Taylor and Debevoise's *The MicroGuide to Process and Decision Modeling in BPMN/DMN* and Blue Polaris's "New Book on BPMN and DMN."

[3] Exception handling—special cases that deviate from standard patterns and require escalation—receives focused attention in process-mining and intelligent-automation guidance; see Articsledge's "What Is Process Mining? Complete Guide," INFORM Software's "Unlocking Business Efficiency with Process Mining," and Nexright's "How IBM Process Mining Enables Workflow Optimization at Scale."

[4] Process mining uses event-log data to reconstruct actual process flows, revealing bottlenecks, delays, loops, and non-compliant variants; see Articsledge's "What Is Process Mining? Complete Guide," IBM's "IBM Process Mining," the Task Force on Process Mining's "Process Mining: A Database of Applications," and Nexright's "How IBM Process Mining Enables Workflow Optimization at Scale."

[5] RACI matrices are widely used in process and decision governance to clarify who is Responsible, Accountable, Consulted, and Informed for specific steps or decisions; see Taylor and Debevoise's *The MicroGuide to Process and Decision Modeling in BPMN/DMN* and Blue Polaris's "New Book on BPMN and DMN."

[6] Intelligent task-routing and AI-routing guidance describes assigning work items to people or systems based on skills, workload, and priority; see KeyLabs's "Intelligent Task Routing: Assigning the Right Labelers to the Right Jobs" and Marlabs's "10 Best Intelligent Automation Platforms You Can Use in 2025."

[7] Workflow mapping practices, including BPMN-style process diagrams showing activities, decision points, and handoffs, are described in resources on BPMN and DMN modeling; see Taylor and Debevoise's *The MicroGuide to Process and Decision Modeling in BPMN/DMN* and Blue Polaris's "New Book on BPMN and DMN."

[8] The benefits of mapping decision workflows—linking insights to action, driving accountability, and standardizing best practices—are highlighted in process-mining and BPM literature; see IBM's "IBM Process Mining," Articsledge's "What Is Process Mining? Complete Guide," the Task Force on Process Mining's "Process Mining: A Database of Applications," and Nexright's "How IBM Process Mining Enables Workflow Optimization at Scale."

[9] Structured approaches to documenting decision workflows—including identifying key decisions, defining data entry and use points, clarifying roles, diagramming flows, and highlighting bottlenecks—are discussed in BPMN/DMN and process-mining materials; see Taylor and Debevoise's *The MicroGuide to Process and Decision Modeling in BPMN/DMN*, Blue Polaris's "New Book on BPMN and DMN," Articsledge's "What Is Process Mining? Complete Guide," and IBM's "IBM Process Mining."

[10] Theoretical foundations for workflow mapping draw on business process management (BPM), Decision Model and Notation (DMN), and process mining; see Taylor and Debevoise's *The MicroGuide to Process and Decision Modeling in BPMN/DMN* and Blue Polaris's "New Book on BPMN and DMN" for BPMN/DMN integration. Real-time analytics, predictive automation, cognitive task routing, and bias mitigation are summarized in Articsledge's "What Is Process Mining? Complete Guide" and IBM's "IBM Process Mining," with KeyLabs's "Intelligent Task Routing" detailing AI-driven task routing.

[11] Core components of workflow optimization at scale—process optimization, continuous improvement, standardization with controlled flexibility, AI-enabled process discovery, and template libraries—are described in process-optimization materials; see Nexright's "How IBM Process Mining Enables Workflow Optimization at Scale," IBM's "IBM Process Mining," INFORM Software's "Unlocking Business Efficiency with Process Mining," and Marlabs's "10 Best Intelligent Automation Platforms You Can Use in 2025."

[12] Data and AI-related roles in decision workflows (data stewards, data engineers, analysts and data scientists, citizen users, business owners, and AI systems) and the use of RACI matrices for role clarity are addressed in discussions of decision governance and workforce design; see Taylor and Debevoise's *The MicroGuide to Process and Decision Modeling in BPMN/DMN*, Blue Polaris's "New Book on BPMN and DMN," KeyLabs's "Optimizing the Annotation Workforce: Building High-Performance Teams," and IBM's "IBM Process Mining."

[13] The logistics exception-handling case illustrates how mapping workflows, using process mining, and embedding AI-based triage and routing can reduce resolution times and improve customer satisfaction; see INFORM Software's "Unlocking Business Efficiency with Process Mining," Articsledge's "What Is Process Mining? Complete Guide," and KeyLabs's "Intelligent Task Routing: Assigning the Right Labelers to the Right Jobs."

[14] Workflow mapping, standardized data capture, clarified AI invocation, and RACI-documented roles improve consistency, adoption, and auditability in AI-enabled lending, as shown in Taylor and Debevoise's *The MicroGuide to Process and Decision Modeling in BPMN/DMN*, IBM's "IBM Process Mining," and Nexright's "How IBM Process Mining Enables Workflow Optimization at Scale."

[15] Success metrics for decision workflows—decision cycle time, touchpoint count, straight-through rate, exception escalation rate, rework rate, and data availability at decision—are recommended in workflow-analytics guidance; see IBM's "IBM Process Mining," Articsledge's "What Is Process Mining? Complete Guide," the Task Force on Process Mining's "Process Mining: A Database of Applications," and INFORM Software's "Unlocking Business Efficiency with Process Mining."

[16] Practical advice to make system data explicit, make AI's role explicit, use RACI matrices, and treat diagrams as living documents is drawn from process-mining guidance, BPMN/DMN resources, and intelligent-automation literature; see Taylor and Debevoise's *The MicroGuide to Process and Decision Modeling in BPMN/DMN*, IBM's "IBM Process Mining," Marlabs's "10 Best Intelligent Automation Platforms You Can Use in 2025," and Blue Polaris's "New Book on BPMN and DMN."

[17] Key workflow risks—over-reliance on automation, hidden complexity, rigidity, and data blind spots—and mitigations such as override paths, documentation, defined flex points, and strong data stewardship are discussed in process-mining and intelligent-automation guidance; see IBM's "IBM Process Mining," Articsledge's "What Is Process Mining? Complete Guide," Marlabs's "10 Best Intelligent Automation Platforms You Can Use in 2025," and INFORM Software's "Unlocking Business Efficiency with Process Mining."

[18] Methodological limitations of process maps and mining outputs—including incomplete or mis-timed logs and oversimplified RACI or DMN diagrams—and the need for iterative refinement are noted in process-mining and BPM literature; see Articsledge's "What Is Process Mining? Complete Guide," IBM's "IBM Process Mining," and Taylor and Debevoise's *The MicroGuide to Process and Decision Modeling in BPMN/DMN.*

[19] Decision workflows framed as living architectures that evolve with strategy, technology, and learning are supported by process-mining discussions and BPMN/DMN integration guidance; see Nexright's "How IBM Process Mining Enables Workflow Optimization at Scale," IBM's "IBM Process Mining," and Taylor and Debevoise's *The MicroGuide to Process and Decision Modeling in BPMN/DMN*. The claim that mapping decision workflows significantly impacts business performance beyond IT draws on Articsledge's "What Is Process Mining? Complete Guide" and INFORM Software's "Unlocking Business Efficiency with Process Mining" on process-mining-driven improvements in speed, consistency, and accountability.

## Key topics explored in this chapter:

- The Collaboration Stack for AI & Analytics
- Why Cross-Functional Collaboration Matters for AI and Analytics
- Best Practices for Fostering Collaboration
- How AI Improves Collaboration
- Overcoming Common Barriers

# WAY 17

# Streamline Cross-Functional Collaboration


## Abstract

To create sustained value from analytics and AI, organizations must break down silos. This chapter offers practical strategies for fostering cross-functional collaboration, including setting shared goals, building integrated workflows, and using collaborative technologies that connect data, people, and decisions. It also explains how AI can enhance collaboration by automating summaries, coordinating work, and detecting emerging communication gaps. Case examples and tools help leaders design collaboration environments where diverse teams move in step, improving innovation, decision quality, and business impact.


## Objective

After completing this chapter, you will be able to:

- Explain why cross-functional collaboration is essential for successful analytics and AI initiatives.
- Set shared, business-driven goals and KPIs that effectively align teams across departments.
- Design integrated workflows and role structures that reduce handoff friction and ambiguity.
- Use collaboration technologies and AI capabilities to coordinate work and share knowledge in real time.
- Identify and address common barriers to collaboration, including silos, fragmented tools, and language gaps.
- Embed collaborative behaviors into performance management and leadership practices so they endure over time.

# Terms to Know

**AI-Augmented Collaboration**[1] - The use of AI to assist with communication, summarization, task routing, translation, engagement monitoring, and data access within and across teams.

**Collaboration Glossary**[2] - A shared catalogue of key business and data terms that standardizes language across functions and reduces misinterpretation, commonly implemented as part of data-governance programs.

**Collaboration KPI**[3] - A metric that captures cross-team performance, such as shared goal achievement, time-to-decision across departments, or reuse of common assets, used to monitor collaboration health.

**Collaboration Technology**[4] - Digital tools—such as messaging platforms, shared workspaces, AI meeting assistants, and project-management systems—that support communication, coordination, and shared visibility across teams.

**Cross-Functional Collaboration**[5] - Coordinated work among people from different functions (such as marketing, operations, IT, finance, and analytics) who share responsibility for outcomes, a pattern emphasized in high-performing digital and AI organizations.

**Integrated Workflow**[6] - A process design where inputs, activities, and decisions cross functional boundaries smoothly, with clear handoffs, shared tools, and explicit decision rights.

**Knowledge Sharing**[7] - The exchange of expertise, insights, and lessons learned across individuals and teams, often via wikis, playbooks, and communities of practice, which research links to improved innovation and execution.

**Silo**[8] - A condition in which departments or teams work in isolation, with limited information sharing or joint accountability, widely cited as a barrier to data-driven transformation.

# Introduction[9]

Analytics and AI rarely sit within a single department. Their models draw on customer, operational, financial, and external data, while their outputs affect marketing, supply chain, risk management, and more. Without proven cross-functional collaboration, these interdependencies often lead to delays, misunderstandings, partial implementations, and "shadow" analytics projects that only duplicate and waste effort.

In modern organizations, collaboration functions as critical infrastructure. It shapes how quickly ideas advance, how well teams identify and mitigate risks, and how consistently customers experience the brand. AI raises the stakes further. The quality and trustworthiness of AI solutions depend on diverse expertise—ranging from technical fluency and domain knowledge to legal, privacy, and change-management insight. The goal is to ensure analytics and AI become catalysts for connection rather than sources of friction. Effective cross-functional collaboration can be visualized as a stack of reinforcing layers:

## The Collaboration Stack for AI & Analytics[10]

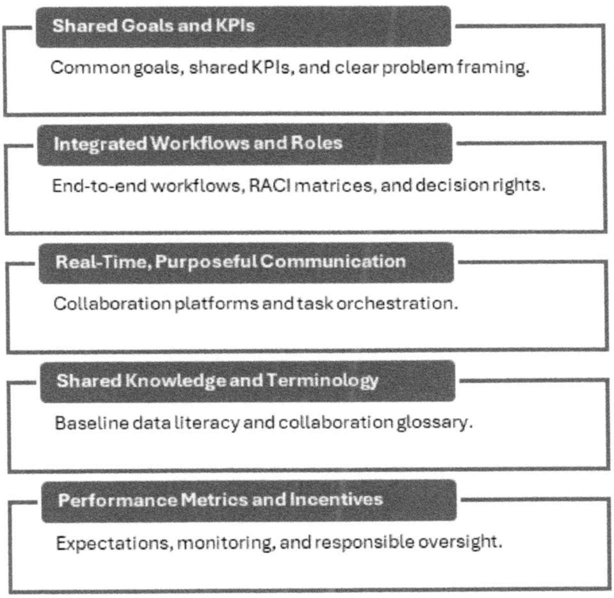


Research in strategy execution and collaboration metrics shows that gaps in any layer show up as rework, slow decisions, or technically sound AI that fails to achieve its full impact.

## Why Cross-Functional Collaboration Matters for AI and Analytics[11]

Cross-functional collaboration isn't merely a "nice-to-have"; it's a structural imperative for effective analytics and AI. Models demand rich, high-quality data that rarely resides in a single system. Collaboration across sales, operations, finance, legal, and risk builds a more comprehensive picture, reducing bias and enhancing relevance.

Complex use cases, such as fraud detection, personalization, or supply-chain resilience, demand diverse perspectives. These varied viewpoints ensure solutions are technically sound, operationally feasible, compliant, and aligned with stakeholder needs. Shared terminology, data, and goals help teams move from analysis to action faster, reducing duplicative analyses and conflicting narratives. Moreover, AI implementation and change management depend on collaboration. Projects that blend business, IT, analytics, risk, and legal expertise from the outset can better design guardrails, explainability artifacts, and communications that truly resonate across groups.

## Best Practices for Fostering Collaboration[12]

### Establish Shared Goals and KPIs

Collaboration falters when departments operate under conflicting metrics. Effective strategy and measurement guidance calls for clearly defined, cross-functional goals, such as improving end-to-end customer experience or reducing total cost-to-serve, then translates these into shared KPIs that multiple teams jointly own. For instance, a single "customer lifetime value" KPI might be co-owned by marketing, product, and service, or a "time-to-decision for AI approvals" KPI shared by risk, legal, and analytics.

When teams understand their success intertwines, conversations shift from "my metric versus yours" to "how do we move our shared indicators together?" Research on collaborative KPIs shows that organizations adopting shared measures achieve improved innovation, customer satisfaction, and time-to-market.

### Build Integrated Workflows and Decision Rights

Collaboration thrives when workflows cross boundaries by design rather than by exception. Mapping how work flows across functions, particularly for analytics- and AI-enabled decisions, surfaces critical handoffs, dependencies, and role gaps.

Swim-lane diagrams illustrate which function leads each step, which provides input, and when decisions require joint approval. RACI matrices clarify accountability for key decisions: model approvals, data access, or KPI changes, reducing "decision drift" where everyone is involved but no one is accountable. Clear decision rights accelerate joint decisions and cut rework from misaligned expectations.

### Enable Real-Time, Purposeful Communication

Timely collaboration depends on communication channels that match the pace of work. Modern platforms easily combine messaging, video, file-sharing, whiteboarding, and task tracking, often augmented by AI features like summarization and task extraction.

Teams benefit from establishing clear norms: where to post decisions, how to tag stakeholders, when to escalate from asynchronous chat to live working sessions, and which channels are reserved for urgent matters. AI meeting assistants that transcribe, summarize, and extract action items help keep stakeholders aligned. This means not everyone needs to attend every discussion, which is especially helpful for distributed teams.

### Encourage Knowledge Sharing and a Collaboration Glossary

Collaboration deepens when teams share not just outputs but also insights, terminology, and lessons learned. Regular cross-functional forums—such as "AI show-and-tell" sessions or data guilds—enable teams to present their successes, analyze failures, and highlight reusable assets.

A collaboration or business glossary, often housed in a data catalog, standardizes definitions for key metrics and AI terms (ex. churn, bias, model drift). This standardization reduces confusion and helps head off debates about semantics. Recognizing contributors who document playbooks, code snippets, and FAQs signals that knowledge sharing is both valued and career relevant.

### Integrate Collaboration into Performance and Incentives

Behavior follows measurement, so performance systems must explicitly reflect collaboration expectations. When performance reviews and promotion criteria include contributions to cross-functional initiatives, collaboration becomes an integral part of career progression.

For example, assess leaders on how effectively they staff and support cross-functional squads, and evaluate individual contributors on their tangible contributions to shared assets and joint projects. Publicly highlighting collaborative achievements reinforces that "collaboration wins" are just as valued as individual heroics.

## How AI Improves Collaboration[13]

AI is not only a consumer of cross-functional data; it can act as a collaboration engine. Several capabilities are already mainstream or rapidly emerging, as outlined in the table that follows:

## The Collaboration Value of AI

| AI Capability | Example in Practice | Collaboration Value | Watch-Outs / Risks |
|---|---|---|---|
| **Meeting Summarization** | Tools that transcribe meetings and auto-generate summaries, decisions, and tasks | Reduces note-taking burden; keeps absent stakeholders aligned | Requires consent, careful data handling, and accuracy checks |
| **Task Extraction and Routing** | NLP that identifies action items and syncs them into project boards | Increases follow-through; clarifies cross-team commitments | Risk of over-capturing sensitive content if scope is unclear |
| **Integrated AI Dashboards** | Role-aware views of shared metrics across functions | Grounds conversations in a single source of truth | Poor design can still encourage siloed interpretations |
| **Smart Workload Allocation** | Algorithms that match tasks to teams based on skills and capacity | Balances load; reduces bottlenecks in AI projects | Opaque logic can feel unfair if not explained |
| **Translation and Localization** | Real-time translation in global teams | Reduces language barriers; expands participation | Cultural nuance may be lost in automatic translation |
| **Engagement Pattern Analytics** | Aggregate views of participation, response times, and cross-team interactions | Helps spot disengaged or overloaded groups early | Can feel like surveillance if not governed responsibly |

Used thoughtfully, these capabilities make collaboration more reliable and less dependent on manual coordination, but they require clear guardrails on privacy, consent, and appropriate use to maintain trust.

## Overcoming Common Barriers[14]

Even with the best intentions and advanced tools, organizations still encounter recurring obstacles.

- One common barrier is **silo mentality:** departments often protect their information and priorities, viewing collaboration as a threat to their autonomy. Leaders can effectively counter this by communicating shared goals, forming cross-functional task forces for visible initiatives, and rotating high-potential talent across functions to build crucial empathy and networks.

- **Fragmented data and tools** often force manual reconciliation, hindering a shared understanding. Strategic investments in shared platforms, strong integration layers, and common glossaries can significantly reduce this friction.
- **Communication fatigue** presents another risk; too many messages, meetings, and channels can overwhelm staff. Here, AI can help filter notifications and summarize threads, while clear norms keep communication purposeful.
- **A lack of shared language and literacy** frequently causes misalignment. To counter this, cross-functional data- and AI-literacy programs, coupled with shared glossaries, help align understanding across the organization.
- **And equity and inclusion challenges** emerge when specific functions, regions, or demographics dominate discussions. Anonymous pulse surveys and participation analytics can reveal whose voices are present or missing, supporting more inclusive facilitation.

# Case Studies[15]

## Case Study #1: Cross-Functional AI Customer Analytics at a Global Retailer

A global retailer aimed to leverage AI for a deeper understanding of customer behavior across both online and offline channels. However, their initial analytics efforts were highly compartmentalized: e-commerce, in-store operations, and marketing each conducted their own analyses, resulting in conflicting definitions and overlapping pilot projects. To address this, leadership chartered a cross-functional "customer insights squad," bringing together experts from marketing, e-commerce, store operations, data science, and IT.

The squad quickly defined shared objectives—such as increasing multi-channel customer lifetime value—and established a common glossary for key metrics like "active customer" and "repeat visit." A unified, AI-enabled dashboard soon became the single source of truth for customer KPIs. Furthermore, an AI meeting assistant summarized weekly squad reviews, efficiently extracting action items into a shared project board.

Within the first year, the cycle time for joint campaign decisions fell substantially, and the reuse of experiment templates and code across channels significantly increased, a trend clearly tracked in their collaboration metrics.

## Case Study #2: Streamlining Collaboration in AI-Supported Clinical Workflows

A regional healthcare system introduced AI tools to augment clinical decision-making, offering features like risk scores for patient deterioration and readmission. While early pilots showed promise, they also revealed significant misalignment: clinicians questioned model outputs and workflows, IT focused solely on integration, and administrators primarily prioritized cost and compliance.

The organization responded by forming dedicated cross-functional working groups for each major AI use case. These groups convened clinicians from multiple specialties, data scientists, informatics experts, and compliance officers. These collaborative groups meticulously mapped current workflows using swim-lane diagrams and then co-designed precisely how AI outputs would appear within clinical systems and during team huddles. AI tools facilitated asynchronous review of design proposals and efficiently summarized feedback from numerous stakeholders into actionable themes. Crucially, training sessions co-led by clinicians and data scientists reinforced a shared vocabulary for important terms like "risk threshold," "false positive," and "alert fatigue." Ultimately, the adoption of AI decision-support tools significantly increased. Consequently, the organization recorded faster time-to-decision in critical cases and simultaneously improved performance on targeted quality metrics.

# Success Metrics[16]

## Collaboration Metrics

| Metric | Definition | What It Tells You | Linked Practices |
|---|---|---|---|
| **Cross-Functional Goal Coverage** | % of strategic initiatives with representation from key functions | Degree of cross-team involvement in critical work | Shared goals; cross-functional squads |
| **Shared KPI Adoption** | Proportion of teams measured against at least one common KPI | Alignment of incentives and performance focus | Shared KPIs; performance integration |
| **Cycle Time for Joint Decisions** | Time from proposal to decision for cross-functional initiatives | Efficiency of collaborative decision-making | Integrated workflows; clear decision rights |
| **Collaboration Participation Rate** | Share of invited functions that actively participate in joint forums | Breadth and depth of engagement | Protected time; inclusive facilitation |
| **Reuse of Shared Assets** | No. of times templates, code, or playbooks are used across functions | Effectiveness of knowledge-sharing mechanisms | Knowledge bases; recognition for sharers |
| **Perceived collaboration quality** | Survey-based rating of cross-functional collaboration effectiveness | Human experience and trust in collaborative processes | Leadership modeling; norms and culture |

A practical approach is to select one or two leading indicators (for example, shared KPI adoption or reuse of shared assets) and one or two lagging indicators (for example, joint decision cycle time or perceived collaboration quality) and review them in the same governance forums that oversee AI portfolios.

# Practical Advice for Leaders[17]

Leaders sculpt collaboration environments. They model cross-functional behavior by:

- **Participating in cross-functional reviews,** asking questions that bridge perspectives, and visibly crediting joint contributions over single-function wins.
- **Clearly defining decision rights** for major AI initiatives—who decides what, how to resolve disagreements, and where to escalate issues—through simple RACI charts allows teams to achieve clarity independently.
- **Investing in shared infrastructure**—like collaboration and data platforms used across functions—prevents tool sprawl that merely recreates digital silos.
- **Protecting collaborative time** reduces overload; give cross-functional teams dedicated bandwidth and use AI to automate low-value coordination tasks.
- **Telling collaboration stories** in town halls or internal communications. This reinforces that cross-functional work is a strategic capability, not just overhead.

## Anticipating and Managing Collaboration Risks[18]

As collaboration intensifies, organizations must remain vigilant against potential downsides.

- **Decision drift** occurs when too many voices slow or diffuse decisions. Mitigation strategies include clear agendas, effective facilitation, time-boxed discussions, and explicit decision owners.
- **Responsibility dilution** arises when "everyone" is involved, yet no one feels truly accountable; RACI matrices and unambiguous outcome owners effectively mitigate this risk.
- **Over-collaboration**—characterized by too many meetings and coordination tasks—saps productivity. Applying a "minimum necessary collaboration" principle and offloading routine follow-ups to AI tools can significantly help.
- **Tool proliferation** presents another concern: adopting numerous unintegrated tools can recreate digital silos. Periodic tool rationalization and integration are therefore essential.
- **Privacy and surveillance concerns** emerge when AI systems analyze communications or engagement patterns. Responsible

use demands explaining what's monitored and why, obtaining appropriate consent, aligning with privacy regulations, and limiting analysis to aggregated, purpose-bound data.

## Evidence and Limitations[19]

Much of the evidence supporting the practices in this chapter comes from practitioner case studies, industry surveys, and documented experiences within cross-functional AI programs rather than controlled experiments. These sources consistently link shared KPIs, integrated workflows, and structured collaboration forums to faster decision cycles and better alignment. However, they also make it difficult to separate the specific impact of any single practice from broader cultural and organizational factors. For this reason, the Collaboration Stack and related practices should be treated as design patterns and starting hypotheses, to be adapted, tested, and refined within each organization's unique context.

# Conclusion[20]

In AI-forward organizations, cross-functional collaboration isn't a mere side activity; it's a core capability woven into strategy, operations, and governance. Analytics and AI initiatives thrive when marketing, operations, finance, IT, risk, and other functions collaborate with shared goals, integrated workflows, common language, and mutual trust. AI technologies expand collaboration's potential—automating coordination tasks, boosting visibility, and revealing engagement patterns. But tools prove effective only when supported by the right culture and structures.

The most successful organizations combine a proven collaboration culture with thoughtful design of processes, roles, metrics, and responsible AI usage. This approach transforms cross-functional work into a durable advantage in the age of intelligent systems.

# Notes

[1] AI-augmented collaboration capabilities—summarization, routing, translation, and engagement analytics—are surveyed in Zapier's "The 9 Best AI Meeting Assistants in 2025."

[2] Business glossaries as a data-governance practice are examined in Select Star's "How to Build a Business Glossary for Data Governance."

[3] Collaboration KPIs and cross-team performance measures are developed in *MIT Sloan Management Review*'s "Build Better KPIs with Artificial Intelligence."

[4] Collaboration technologies and AI meeting assistants are surveyed in Kirenz's "25 Meeting Summarization - Gen AI & Prompting."

[5] Cross-functional collaboration patterns and the behavioral effects of collaboration tools and KPIs are explored in Averi AI's "Cross-Functional Knowledge Sharing: Best Practices."

[6] Shared KPIs that drive cross-functional alignment and outcome-based performance are addressed in Flevy's "How Can KPIs Be Designed to Drive Cross-Functional Collaboration?"

[7] Querio's "Top Collaboration KPIs for Data Governance Success" examines links between knowledge sharing, innovation, and execution.

[8] Silos, role clarity, and collaboration responsibilities across data and governance processes are addressed in Querio's "Top Collaboration KPIs for Data Governance Success."

[9] Collaboration as AI infrastructure and the need for diverse expertise are developed in Seth Mattison's "Ultimate Guide to Cross-Functional Collaboration Metrics" and *ScienceDirect* on cross-functional AI initiatives.

[10] The "Collaboration Stack" layers and their links to rework and adoption challenges are mapped in Flevy; Averi AI's "Cross-Functional Knowledge Sharing"; OvalEdge's "Data Governance Business Glossary for Trusted Terms"; Vertu's "Top AI Meeting Summarizer Tools for Streamlined Collaboration"; and Seth Mattison's "Ultimate Guide to Cross-Functional Collaboration Metrics."

[11] Structural drivers of cross-functional collaboration in AI projects—data sharing, bias reduction, feasibility, and compliance—are analyzed in Querio's "Top Collaboration KPIs" and *ScienceDirect* on cross-functional AI initiatives.

[12] Best practices on shared goals, integrated workflows, communication norms, glossaries, and performance incentives are drawn from Flevy's KPI guidance; Averi AI; Decision Management *Solutions*; Cube Software's "How Cube's AI-Powered Collaboration Transforms Cross-Functional Planning"; Kirenz; Querio; Alation's "Business Glossary vs. Data Dictionary"; and Seth Mattison.

[13] AI collaboration tools—meeting summarization, task extraction, dashboards, workload allocation, translation, and engagement analytics—and associated risks are covered in Vertu's "Top AI Meeting Summarizer Tools"; Kirenz; *MIT Sloan Management Review*; KeyLabs; FlowHunt's "The Ultimate Guide to AI Meeting Notes"; and Querio.

[14] Common collaboration barriers and mitigations—silo mentality, fragmented tools, communication fatigue, literacy gaps, and inclusion issues—are examined in Averi AI; FlowHunt; and Zapier's "The 9 Best AI Meeting Assistants."

[15] Case descriptions of global retail AI squads and healthcare AI collaboration appear in Cube Software's "How Cube's AI-Powered Collaboration Transforms Cross-Functional Planning"; Select Star; Zapier; Decision Management *Solutions*; and *ScienceDirect*.

[16] Collaboration metrics and the leading/lagging indicator distinction are developed in Seth Mattison's "Ultimate Guide to Cross-Functional Collaboration Metrics"; Averi AI; Flevy; and *MIT Sloan Management Review*'s "Build Better KPIs with Artificial Intelligence."

[17] Leadership behaviors, shared infrastructure investments, protected collaboration time, and storytelling draw on Cube Software and FlowHunt's "The Ultimate Guide to AI Meeting Notes."

[18] Collaboration risks—decision drift, responsibility dilution, over-collaboration, tool proliferation, and surveillance concerns—and governance responses are addressed in *Decision Management Solutions* and FlowHunt.

[19] On teaming and cross-boundary collaboration—especially in knowledge-intensive work—and the impact of cross-functional integration on innovation outcomes, see Edmondson, Amy C., and Jean-François Harvey. *Extreme Teaming: Lessons in Complex, Cross-Sector Leadership.*

[20] Collaboration as a strategic capability—and AI's role in expanding but complicating it—are examined in *MIT Sloan Management Review*'s "Build Better KPIs with Artificial Intelligence" and Vertu's "Top AI Meeting Summarizer Tools."

## Key topics explored in this chapter:

- The New Change-Management Landscape
- A Method for AI-Driven Change
- Mitigating Disruption During AI Transformation
- Governance and Policy in Managing Change
- Achieving Buy-In and Sustained Engagement
- How AI Is Changing Change Management

# WAY 18

# Manage Analytics Change

## Abstract

Change management is a core analytics discipline, especially in the age of AI. This chapter presents practical approaches for stewarding analytics and AI transformation, mitigating disruption, and securing stakeholder buy-in through structured change frameworks and transparent governance. It adapts classical change models—such as Lewin's phases and Prosci's ADKAR—to the unique pace, complexity, and cultural impact of AI initiatives, emphasizing people-centered leadership, communication, and workforce upskilling. It also illustrates how organizations can use both human and AI capabilities to guide employees through uncertainty, reduce resistance, and build durable readiness for continuous digital evolution.

## Objective

After completing this chapter, you will be able to:

- Describe how AI-enabled analytics alters the change-management landscape and why it demands specialized attention.
- Apply structured change methods tailored to AI initiatives, from vision setting through scaling and sustainment, in ways that complement models like ADKAR and Lewin.
- Anticipate nd mitigate disruption by assessing readiness, addressing fears, and supporting digital adoption in the flow of work.
- Design governance structures, roles, and policies that support responsible, transparent, and ethical AI transformation.
- Build stakeholder buy-in and engagement using communication strategies, ambassador networks, and recognition.

- Use AI tools—such as digital adoption platforms, predictive analytics, and sentiment analysis—to enhance change management itself.

## Terms to Know

**AI Transformation**[1] - Organizational change driven by the introduction and scaling of AI and advanced analytics, affecting processes, roles, and culture, typically unfolding in structured stages from assessment through sustainment.

**Ambassador (Change Champion) Network**[2] - A group of employees who advocate for change, provide peer support, and relay feedback between frontline teams and project leaders, often used to operationalize ADKAR at scale.

**Change Governance**[3] - The policies, roles, committees, and processes that oversee how change initiatives are prioritized, executed, and monitored, including AI-specific risk and ethics oversight.

**Change Management**[4] - A structured approach to preparing, equipping, and supporting people through change, with models like Prosci's ADKAR focusing on individual transitions across Awareness, Desire, Knowledge, Ability, and Reinforcement.

**Digital Adoption Platform (DAP)**[5] - Software that overlays applications to guide users in real time with in-app walkthroughs, tooltips, and analytics on usage and friction, helping drive behavioral adoption and reveal where users struggle.

**Predictive Change Analytics**[6] - The use of data and models to forecast adoption patterns, resistance hot spots, and likely outcomes of change strategies, often combining usage data, survey inputs, and sentiment.

**Readiness Assessment**[7] - A diagnostic process that evaluates how prepared people, processes, and systems are for a specific change, frequently using surveys and interviews to inform planning and tailoring interventions.

## Introduction[8]

In previous waves of digital transformation, organizations often treated change management as an "add-on": extra communications near go-live or training just before a launch. Yet, in an era where AI-driven analytics can reshape operating models and decision rights, this approach is no longer sufficient. AI affects not only tools but also how people make decisions, perceive their expertise, and trust systems.

The rapid pace of AI innovation, the opacity of some models, and the high stakes of automated decisions create a uniquely challenging change environment. Employees may worry about job security, fairness, and a loss of control. Meanwhile, leaders must balance ambition with caution amid evolving regulation and scrutiny. Managing this complexity requires integrating change management into analytics strategy from the outset, rather than treating it as a final implementation step.

## The New Change-Management Landscape[9]

AI-driven analytics transformation differs from many past changes in several key ways:

- First, **pace is higher:** AI projects can quickly move from pilot to scale, especially in software environments, bringing workflow and role shifts in weeks instead of years. This can amplify fatigue if support isn't adequate.
- Second, **complexity and uncertainty are greater:** some AI models prove difficult to explain, regulations and norms are still evolving, and unclear data usage can easily trigger mistrust in sensitive domains like HR, underwriting, or customer targeting.
- AI also carries **a deep cultural and identity impact:** it touches core aspects of professional identity for underwriters, clinicians, analysts, and frontline staff. This raises questions about expertise, autonomy, and surveillance that are often emotional, not just rational.

Recognizing these features helps leaders design change approaches that address not only process and skill gaps but also perceptions, fears, values, and opportunity.

## A Method for AI Change[10]

Classic change models—such as Lewin's unfreeze-change-refreeze and Prosci's ADKAR (Awareness, Desire, Knowledge, Ability, Reinforcement)—remain useful. However, AI's speed and ambiguity call for additional narrative emphasis. This chapter uses a three-part framing that complements these models. This framework, presented in the table that follows, keeps the human story of AI-driven analytics change visible while remaining compatible with established theory and practice.

## Three-Part Framework for AI-Driven Change[11]

| Path Element | Key Questions | Typical Actions (Linked to ADKAR & Lewin) | AI Enablers |
|---|---|---|---|
| **Path Framing** | Why AI? For whom? With what guardrails and outcomes? | Clarify vision, principles, success metrics; build Awareness; unfreeze | Scenario modeling; impact analysis |
| **Path Narrating** | How will change unfold over time? What experiments first? | Sequence pilots, communicate roadmap, co-create story; build Desire and Knowledge | Tailored comms; FAQ chatbots; translation |
| **Path Stretching** | How do we scale, govern, and sustain responsibly? | Redesign roles, embed governance; build Ability and Reinforcement; refreeze | Predictive analytics; DAPs; monitoring |

### Path Framing: Defining the AI Vision

Change begins with a compelling and concrete why. For AI-driven analytics, this means explaining which business problems or opportunities AI will address, how value will be measured (for example, cycle time, error rates, or new revenue), which principles will guide the work (fairness, transparency, augmentation over replacement, privacy by design), and what will and will not change for key groups in the near term.

People-centric AI guidance stresses that executive sponsors must connect the AI vision to strategy. They also need to frame AI explicitly as decision support rather than unchecked automation to reduce anxiety and build early Awareness and Desire. Clear framing also supports regulatory and ethical expectations around explainability and human oversight.

### Path Narrating: Timing and Execution

Path Narrating translates vision into a believable story about how change will unfold. This involves sequencing pilots and learning phases before broader rollout, setting expectations about experimentation rather than promising a linear path, and using AI-assisted communication—such as tailored message drafts, FAQ chatbots, and translation—to keep audiences informed in language they understand.

When employees see that feedback influences the roadmap and that missteps are acknowledged rather than hidden, Desire and Knowledge grow instead of eroding. Analytics on engagement (for example, open rates, DAP usage, and the number of FAQ queries) can further refine messaging and pacing.

### Path Stretching: Scaling for Sustainability

Path Stretching focuses on what happens after initial solutions deliver results. Organizations plan for ongoing skill development instead of one-time training, using adaptive learning platforms and DAPs that provide just-in-time guidance and analytics to build Ability in the flow of work. They design new or evolved roles—such as AI product owners, model-risk managers, data stewards, and human-in-the-loop reviewers—and clarify how performance expectations will shift.

Governance mechanisms for model risk, ethics, lifecycle management, and workforce impact are institutionalized and linked to Reinforcement mechanisms such as audits, KPIs, and continuous-improvement loops. These mechanisms help "refreeze" more adaptive, AI-infused ways of working while keeping them open to responsible evolution.

## Mitigating Disruption During AI Transformation[12]

Every significant change causes some disruption; effective change management reduces unnecessary friction and supports people through necessary adjustments. Up-front readiness assessments—using surveys, interviews, or focus groups—can surface data-literacy levels, AI familiarity, concerns, and prior change fatigue. This allows for differentiated communication and learning plans.

Digital adoption platforms provide embedded tutorials, checklists, and contextual help directly within AI tools, reducing time to proficiency and support tickets while offering analytics on where users struggle or abandon flows. Human-centered training addresses technical, emotional, and ethical dimensions. It explains what AI will and will not do to roles, how fairness and bias are handled, and how to interpret and challenge AI outputs via realistic scenarios. Transparent communication about what is known, what is being piloted, and how feedback is used builds credibility even when not all answers are available.

## Governance and Policy in Managing Change[13]

Governance structures guide both the technical aspects of AI and the human transition. Some organizations create an AI transformation or AI change-management office. This office coordinates initiatives, aligns change plans, and tracks adoption, value, and risk across programs. Oversight committees that include HR, legal, compliance, IT, analytics, and business leaders review high-impact deployments and monitor ethical, legal, and workforce implications, providing an escalation path for addressing tensions.

Formal AI and change policies clarify permissible and prohibited uses, responsibilities for bias monitoring and human oversight, expectations for training, and mechanisms for employees to report concerns or challenge AI-assisted decisions. Clear governance and policy help preserve trust and anchor Reinforcement, satisfying both internal expectations and emerging external standards.

## Achieving Buy-In and Sustained Engagement[14]

Lasting change is more likely when people feel involved and respected. Stakeholder involvement—engaging respected managers, informal leaders, and frontline experts early—improves solution design, surfaces risks, and seeds local advocates.

Ambassador or champion networks demonstrate new tools, collect feedback, and model constructive attitudes toward AI, bridging central teams and local realities. Recognition and incentives that celebrate teams integrating AI into workflows, individuals mentoring others, or those who raise critical concerns signal that thoughtful adoption—not blind enthusiasm—is valued, strengthening Desire and Reinforcement.

## How AI Is Changing Change Management[15]

AI doesn't just drive change; it also augments change-management practice itself. Generative tools can draft tailored messages for different audiences, maintain FAQ bots, and translate technical content into accessible language, allowing change teams to scale outreach and consistency.

Predictive change analytics can combine usage logs, DAP metrics, and survey or sentiment data to identify adoption hot spots and gaps, estimate where resistance is likely, and flag which interventions are working. AI-powered learning systems can assess baseline knowledge and recommend individualized training paths, micro-content, and refreshers. Sentiment analysis on employee feedback (with appropriate consent) can highlight emerging concerns and disengagement trends earlier than traditional surveys, while scenario-planning tools can simulate different rollout strategies and training mixes to compare likely impacts on adoption and risk.

# Case Study

## AI-Driven Underwriting Transformation in Financial Services[16]

A multinational financial-services firm launched a multi-year initiative to modernize underwriting using AI-powered risk models and workflow automation. Early prototypes showed strong predictive performance, but pilots revealed significant resistance among underwriters. They worried about reduced judgment and job security, and questioned the models' fairness.

The firm established a dedicated AI transformation office that partnered with HR, risk, and regional leaders to integrate change management into program design. Readiness assessments revealed wide variation in analytics comfort and deep concern about opaque decisions. This prompted vision workshops where leaders and underwriters co-created a Path Framing narrative that positioned AI as an augmentation tool and codified principles on explainability and human override.

A network of underwriting champions in each region acted as ambassadors, testing new tools, advising on workflow integration, and mentoring peers. The firm deployed a DAP overlay to guide users through new decision screens and capture friction points, while predictive change analytics tracked adoption, feature usage, and time to proficiency by branch. Locations where usage lagged despite training received targeted coaching and additional workshops. Over 18 months, underwriting turnaround time fell, exception rates dropped, and surveys showed rising confidence that AI-supported decisions were fair and efficient.

# Success Metrics[17]

Guidance on AI adoption recommends tracking a mix of **leading indicators** (adoption rate, champion coverage, readiness scores) and **outcome indicators** (time to proficiency, incident volume, sentiment) and reviewing them regularly in AI governance forums.

## Change Management Metrics

| Metric | Definition | What It Tells You | Linked Levers |
|---|---|---|---|
| **Adoption Rate** | % of target users actively using new analytics/AI tools | Uptake and integration into daily work | Communication; DAP design; manager support |
| **Time to Proficiency** | Avg. time for users to reach defined competency | Effectiveness of training and in-flow guidance | Training design; DAP; local coaching |
| **Change Readiness Score** | Pre/post survey index on understanding and confidence | Preparedness and perception of change | Path Framing; storytelling; manager briefings |
| **Incident and Exception Volume** | No. of significant issues or escalations post-go-live | Quality of planning, risk mitigation, and governance | Testing; phased rollout; support playbooks |
| **Champion Network Coverage** | Proportion of teams with active, trained ambassadors | Depth of local support and peer influence | Ambassador program design; recognition |
| **Sentiment Trend** | Direction of employee sentiment on AI and analytics over time | Cultural trajectory and emerging concerns | Listening channels; ethics; pacing |

# Practical Advice for Leaders[18]

Leaders who treat analytics change as both a technical and human challenge significantly increase their odds of success. They should start framing change early by emphasizing purpose, guiding principles, and how AI fits into their long-term strategy, aligning with the Awareness and Desire stages in ADKAR.

- **Listening** should be as systematic as communication: structured feedback loops such as surveys, office hours, and open forums provide insight and build trust when leaders show how input influences decisions.
- **Investing in managers** is important because they translate strategy into reality. Equipping them with context, FAQs, and coaching helps them support local Desire and Ability.
- **Coordinating across portfolios** to align pacing prevents multiple high-impact AI changes from landing on the same teams simultaneously.
- **Openly sharing learning and insight** also reinforces a culture of experimentation rather than blame.

## Anticipating and Managing Change Risks[19]

AI-driven change introduces predictable risks that leaders can manage proactively. **Change fatigue** arises when too many initiatives run at once; mitigation includes portfolio-level prioritization, realistic timelines, and occasional pauses or staging. **Shadow resistance** occurs when employees agree publicly but revert to old practices. Monitoring real behavior (for example, usage data), offering safe channels for dissent, and addressing root concerns can surface and resolve these issues. **Trust erosion** is a risk when AI deployments seem unfair, opaque, or rushed. Inclusive design processes, explainability, and visible governance structures support trust, especially in HR or workforce analytics. **Inequitable impact** may occur if some roles, regions, or demographics experience disproportionate disruption. Impact assessments and targeted support help balance burden and benefit. Privacy and surveillance concerns can arise when AI tools analyze behavior, usage, or sentiment. Best practice calls for purpose limitation, explicit consent, data minimization, and transparency to maintain trust.

# Conclusion[20]

Managing analytics and AI change is ultimately about creating conditions where people can experiment, learn, and grow alongside new technologies. Frameworks, governance, and tools are important, but they serve a deeper goal: helping individuals and teams reimagine how they contribute value in an AI-enabled organization.

When change management is woven into analytics strategy—from Path Framing through Path Stretching—organizations are better positioned to turn disruption into opportunity. In this view, AI becomes not just a technical asset but a catalyst for building more adaptive, transparent, and human-centered ways of working, making change capability itself a strategic differentiator in the era of intelligent systems.

# Notes

[1] Staged AI transformation impacting processes, roles, and culture is examined in Prosci's "AI Transformation: A People-Centric Guide to Leading Change."

[2] On ambassador networks as ADKAR-scale mechanisms, see Prosci's material on navigating AI adoption with champions (in "AI Change Management").

[3] On AI change governance structures and ethics oversight, see Prosci on AI transformation governance (in "AI in Change Management: Early Findings").

[4] ADKAR's focus on individual transitions and its use in AI contexts is laid out in 6sigma.us's "ADKAR Model: The Guide to Successful Change Management."

[5] DAP functions—overlays, walkthroughs, friction analytics—are surveyed in *Axero Solutions*'s "Top Digital Adoption Platforms" and *Futurum Group*'s "WalkMe's Digital Adoption Platform Helps Remove EX Friction Points."

[6] Predictive change analytics and sentiment analysis applied to adoption are developed in *Qandle*'s "AI-Powered Sentiment Analysis to Measure Employee Satisfaction" and *AllHR Software*'s "AI-Powered Sentiment Analysis for Employee Surveys: 5-Step Guide."

[7] For readiness assessments informing tailored interventions, see ADKAR/change-management guidance from 6sigma.us's "ADKAR Model" and Prosci's "AI Change Management."

[8] AI's new change landscape and the need to integrate change early are characterized in *MargOnline*'s "Leveraging ADKAR for Successful AI Adoption" and Prosci's "AI Transformation."

[9] AI's unique pace, opacity, and identity impact as change challenges are explored in Prosci's "AI in Change Management: Early Findings" and *MargOnline*'s AI adoption work.

[10] The Path Framing/Narrating/Stretching framework, aligned with ADKAR and Lewin, is set out in Prosci's "AI Transformation" and *Futurum Group* materials.

[11] People-centric framing, experimentation-focused narration, and scaling via roles, governance, and DAPs are developed in Prosci's "AI Transformation"; *MargOnline*'s "Leveraging ADKAR"; *Axero Solutions*'s "Top Digital Adoption Platforms"; and 6sigma.us's "ADKAR Model."

[12] Disruption mitigation through readiness assessments, DAPs, and human-centered training is addressed in Prosci's "AI Change Management"; *SAP Learning*'s "Exploring Digital Transformation and Digital Adoption"; and *Futurum Group*'s WalkMe guidance.

[13] AI transformation offices, oversight committees, and policy patterns are surveyed in Prosci's "AI in Change Management: Early Findings" and "AI Change Management."

[14] Stakeholder involvement, ambassador networks, and recognition for thoughtful AI use are discussed in *MargOnline*'s "Leveraging ADKAR" and Prosci webinars ("Live and On-Demand Webinars").

[15] AI augmenting change practice—gen-AI comms, predictive analytics, adaptive learning, sentiment analysis, and scenarios—is explored in Prosci's "AI Transformation"; *Qandle*'s sentiment analysis guide; and *AllHR Software*'s "AI-Powered Sentiment Analysis for Employee Surveys."

[16] The underwriting transformation case—combining champions, DAPs, predictive change analytics, and measurable outcomes—draws on Prosci's "AI Change Management" and *Futurum Group* materials.

[17] Change metrics—adoption, proficiency, readiness, incidents, champions, and sentiment—and their linkage to levers are mapped in Prosci's "AI Transformation" and *Axero Solutions*'s DAP resources.

[18] Leader practices—early framing, listening, manager enablement, pacing, and learning transparency—are set out in 6sigma.us's "ADKAR Model" and *AllHR Software*'s sentiment/employee experience guidance.

[19] Risks including change fatigue, shadow resistance, trust erosion, inequitable impact, and surveillance concerns are examined in *Futurum Group* materials and Brandon Hall Group's "Leverage AI for Sentiment Analysis for the Employee Experience."

[20] Change capability as a core AI competency—with AI as a catalyst for adaptive, human-centered work—is argued in Prosci's "AI Transformation" and *MargOnline*'s "Leveraging ADKAR."

# Key topics explored in this chapter:

- Why Continuous Improvement Matters in Analytics
- Implementing Feedback Loops for Analytics Excellence
- Benchmarking and Performance Tracking
- Choosing Improvement Methods
- Refining Processes, Technologies, and Models
- Drift, Retraining, and Champion-Challenger Models
- Building a Culture and Infrastructure of Ongoing Improvement
- AI and Automation for Faster Improvement

# WAY 19

# Build Continuous Improvement in AI and Analytics


## Abstract

Analytics capabilities must evolve as data, technologies, and business priorities change. This chapter describes how to design continuous-improvement systems for AI and analytics, including feedback loops, benchmarking, and structured refinement of processes, tools, and models. It shows how organizations can move from one-off projects to ongoing optimization cycles using methodologies such as PDCA, DMAIC, and agile sprints, and explains where each is best suited in an analytics lifecycle. Special attention is given to the role of AI and automation in accelerating learning, detecting performance drift, and enabling self-tuning systems under human oversight.


## Objective

After completing this chapter, you will be able to:

- Explain why analytics and AI require ongoing refinement rather than static implementation, especially in fast-changing environments where data and behavior drift.
- Design feedback loops that connect model and dashboard performance to business outcomes and user experience.
- Use benchmarking to evaluate analytics capabilities internally and against external standards.
- Apply structured improvement cycles (for example, PDCA, DMAIC, agile) to analytics processes, technologies, and models, choosing the right method for the problem.

- Build cultural and infrastructural support—such as leadership sponsorship, training, and knowledge sharing—that sustain improvement.
- Use tools to monitor performance, surface improvement opportunities, and reduce manual effort in the improvement cycle while maintaining appropriate guardrails.

# Terms to Know

**AutoML (Automated Machine Learning)**[1] - Tools that automate parts of the model-development and tuning process—such as feature selection, algorithm choice, and hyperparameter optimization—often embedded in MLOps workflows.

**Benchmarking**[2] - Comparing performance metrics to internal or external standards to identify strengths, gaps, and improvement opportunities, widely used in quality and analytics programs.

**Continuous Improvement**[3] - An ongoing effort to enhance products, services, or processes through incremental changes, often guided by structured methodologies like PDCA or DMAIC.

**DMAIC**[4] - A Six Sigma improvement framework—Define, Measure, Analyze, Improve, Control—used for structured, data-driven improvement of existing processes, particularly when causes are not well understood.

**Drift**[5] - A change in data distributions or relationships over time (data, concept, or performance drift) that can degrade model performance if not monitored and addressed.

**Feedback Loop**[6] - A system in which outputs or outcomes are measured and fed back into decision-making, enabling adjustments to inputs or processes and forming the basis of learning cycles.

**PDCA (Plan-Do-Check-Act)**[7] - A four-step, iterative method for continuous improvement—plan a change, implement it, evaluate results, and standardize successful changes—widely used in Lean and Kaizen contexts and adaptable to analytics work.

**Process Mining**[8] - The analysis of event logs to discover, monitor, and improve real processes by revealing actual workflows, bottlenecks, and deviations from standards.

# Introduction[9]

Analytics and AI systems are often launched with great fanfare, but without deliberate continuous improvement many stagnate as dashboards go unused, models degrade, and processes revert to old habits. Continuous-quality-improvement work in healthcare and industry shows that impact plateaus when teams treat solutions as "done" instead of as evolving capabilities.

In reality, analytics should be treated as a living system rather than a finished product. Data sources evolve, competitive dynamics shift, regulations tighten, and user needs change; models that were once state-of-the-art can become misaligned, and performance indicators that once mattered may lose relevance. Continuous-improvement methods such as PDCA and DMAIC, adapted for data and AI, keep analytics aligned with reality and ensure that insights remain accurate, actionable, and valuable.

## Why Continuous Improvement Matters in Analytics[10]

Analytics capabilities represent a portfolio of assets—models, dashboards, pipelines, and workflows—that must adapt with the organization and its environment. Market and customer behaviors shift over time, especially in digital channels, requiring updates to forecasts, segmentations, and recommendation logic to stay relevant.

Regulatory and risk dynamics, particularly in sectors such as finance and healthcare, introduce new constraints and expectations that force updates to models, thresholds, and KPIs. Technological progress in algorithms, platforms, and infrastructure creates opportunities to re-platform or retune existing solutions, improving accuracy, robustness, and cost-efficiency. Each analytics project also generates insights about data, processes, and behaviors; continuous-improvement practices ensure this learning is harvested and reused rather than trapped in one-off efforts.

## Implementing Feedback Loops for Analytics Excellence[11]

Feedback loops are the core mechanism through which analytics systems learn from experience. Internal stakeholder feedback from business users reveals whether outputs are understandable, timely, and actionable, and which metrics matter most in real decisions; structured review sessions and surveys are central to continuous-improvement programs.

Usage analytics—such as dashboard views, filters used, time on page, and frequency of overrides of model recommendations—show whether tools are embedded in daily work or being bypassed. External market and customer data, including churn, satisfaction, complaint themes, and industry benchmarks, indicate whether analytics-supported decisions deliver desired outcomes and where recalibration is needed. A feedback loop becomes closed only when owners interpret signals, implement changes, and then re-measure results to confirm impact. AI and automation can accelerate these loops by continuously monitoring performance and raising alerts when key indicators fall below baselines.

## Benchmarking and Performance Tracking[12]

Feedback shows how systems perform; benchmarking sets the bar for what "good" looks like. Internal benchmarking compares similar analytics use cases across regions or units (for example, forecast error, time from request to insight, adoption rates) to reveal internal best practices and outliers and to spread effective practices.

External benchmarking uses industry benchmarks or published case studies—such as typical error ranges, service-level targets, or quality indicators—to position performance against peers. Automated monitoring in modern analytics and MLOps platforms tracks key metrics in near real time and alerts when model performance drifts, delivery cycle times exceed service-level targets, or adoption declines in particular groups, supporting proactive improvement rather than ad hoc crisis response.

## Choosing Improvement Methods[13]

PDCA is ideal for iterative refinement and everyday issues, while DMAIC offers a more data-intensive approach for complex problems with unknown causes; agile provides structure for continuous, cross-functional product evolution. Organizations often use DMAIC to tackle significant analytics problems, then embed PDCA to sustain and refine improved processes, while analytics squads operate with agile sprints for ongoing AI-product development.

## Improvement Method Overview

| Method | Best Used For | Analytics/AI Example | Typical AI Assist |
|---|---|---|---|
| **PDCA** | Small, iterative refinements; broad, everyday use | Tuning dashboard layouts or alert thresholds based on feedback | Usage analytics to Check; automation to Act |
| **DMAIC** | Larger, complex issues needing rigor | Reducing model-driven error in a key underwriting or forecast | Statistical analysis; drift/root-cause tools |
| **Agile Sprints** | Ongoing product evolution; cross-functional product teams | Incrementally enhancing an AI product over 2-4-week sprints | Backlog prioritization; A/B-test design |

## Refining Processes, Technologies, and Models[14]

Continuous improvement is operationalized through iterative cycles and disciplined analysis. Teams apply PDCA, DMAIC, or agile cycles to plan small changes, implement them, check results, and act, repeating this across dashboards, pipelines, and models instead of relying on infrequent overhauls.

Root-cause analysis tools such as 5 Whys or fishbone diagrams help distinguish symptoms (for example, low usage) from underlying causes such as missing metrics, poor training, or conflicting incentives. Automation and AI enhance these efforts by spotting anomalies, suggesting retraining windows, and proposing A/B tests, while orchestration tools schedule reports, trigger retraining workflows, or roll out configuration changes after approvals, making improvements faster and more durable.

## Drift, Retraining, and Champion-Challenger Models[15]

Drift is one of the most important reasons AI systems need continuous improvement. Teams monitor input data distributions, model scores, and downstream KPIs to detect data or concept drift and performance drift when predictions diverge from actual outcomes. Drift-management practices use statistical tests and continuous tracking of metrics such as accuracy, AUC, and error rates to identify degradation.

Simple trigger rules—such as accuracy dropping beyond a threshold over a time window or key features drifting outside control limits—can generate retraining candidates or investigation alerts. Champion-challenger strategies train challenger models on recent data and evaluate them against the current champion via shadow deployment or online A/B tests; if a challenger consistently outperforms, it can be promoted. Some platforms support automated drift alerts, candidate retraining, and champion-challenger evaluation, with human oversight to validate changes and ensure alignment with business and risk objectives.

## Building a Culture and Infrastructure of Ongoing Improvement[16]

Continuous improvement depends as much on culture and structure as it does on tools and methods. Leaders who routinely ask "What did we learn and change?" alongside "What did we deliver?" show that refining systems is part of the work, not an optional extra. When leaders reserve time and resources for experimentation and data-driven review, improvement routines start to show up in everyday decisions rather than in occasional initiatives.

Training and cross-functional collaboration around data literacy, improvement methods, and problem-solving skills help domain experts and data professionals jointly interpret metrics, run cycles, and co-design solutions. Iteration and knowledge sharing through communities of practice, repositories of reusable assets, and structured lessons-learned sessions boost reuse and reduce duplicated effort. Dedicated "improvement sprints" or protected exploration time encourage curiosity and innovation, seeding new analytics capabilities.

## AI and Automation for Faster Improvement[17]

Teams can significantly accelerate continuous-improvement cycles by using AI and automation. For example:

- Predictive analytics can forecast where issues are likely to arise—such as when model performance will drop or processes will miss service-level agreements—enabling preventive action.
- Process mining reconstructs actual workflows from event logs, highlighting bottlenecks, wait times, and variants associated with poorer performance; integrated with PDCA or Kaizen, it supports a loop of analysis, intervention, and re-monitoring.

- RPA and workflow tools automate repetitive tasks, freeing humans for diagnostic and design work.
- Adaptive models and AutoML systems can periodically search for better algorithms or hyperparameters and schedule retraining on fresh data when drift or accuracy thresholds are exceeded, managing champion-challenger evaluation and versioning as part of an MLOps stack.
- Model-monitoring platforms integrate drift detection, alerting, and optional remediation triggers, shortening time from signal to response while supporting oversight.

# Case Study

## Continuous Improvement in Healthcare Analytics[18]

A leading healthcare provider invested in analytics for patient flow, resource allocation, and quality monitoring. Initial deployments produced gains in length-of-stay management and throughput, but over time performance plateaued and staff engagement waned. Leaders sought a more systematic continuous-improvement approach.

The organization formed a cross-functional analytics-improvement council including clinicians, operations leaders, data scientists, and quality specialists. For each major initiative, they designed feedback loops combining patient-satisfaction surveys, complaint themes, clinical outcome metrics such as readmission rates and average length of stay, and staff feedback on dashboard and alert usability. The council adopted PDCA cycles for high-impact workflows like discharge planning and used internal benchmarking to compare metrics across hospitals in the system.

Process-mining tools analyzed admission and discharge event logs, revealing process variants and bottlenecks correlated with longer waits and inconsistent protocol adherence. AI systems monitored input data and model performance continuously; when patterns suggested rising readmissions for specific segments, alerts triggered joint reviews of care processes and risk-scoring models. Improvement actions ranged from updating model features and thresholds to redesigning discharge checklists and patient-education steps. Over three years, the provider documented reductions in avoidable delays and 30-day readmissions for targeted cohorts, along with improved clinician satisfaction with analytics tools.

# Success Metrics[19]

Guidance on AI-adoption and quality-improvement metrics recommends tracking both throughput and outcome uplift so teams don't mistake activity for impact. These metrics are typically reviewed alongside business KPIs in governance forums to keep improvement tightly tied to value.

## Continuous Improvement Metrics

| Metric | Definition | What It Tells You | Key Levers |
|---|---|---|---|
| **Improvement Cycle Throughput** | No. of completed improvement cycles per period | Pace of learning and refinement | PDCA/DMAIC cadence; squad capacity |
| **Time to Implement Improvements** | Avg. time from identifying an issue to deploying a change | Responsiveness of the improvement system | Automation; governance; decision rights |
| **Performance Drift Detection Lag** | Time between onset of performance degradation and its detection | Effectiveness of monitoring and alerts | Monitoring stack; thresholds; alert routing |
| **Adoption of Improved Assets** | % of users transitioning to updated models/tools | Success of deployment and change management | Communication; DAP; training; manager advocacy |
| **Reuse of Lessons Learned** | No. of initiatives applying documented best practices | Strength of knowledge sharing | Repositories; communities of practice |
| **Outcome Uplift from Improvements** | Aggregate impact of improvement cycles on key business or quality metrics | Realized value of continuous improvement | Portfolio prioritization; experiment design |

# Practical Advice for Leaders[20]

Leaders play a decisive role in whether continuous improvement in analytics becomes reality. They can:

- **Make improvement part of initiative charters.** Require every major analytics effort to define monitoring and improvement plans, not just launch criteria.
- **Reinforce learning as a core expectation.** In reviews, ask "What did we learn and improve?" alongside "What did we deliver?"
- **Fund and protect time for improvement work on existing assets.** Don't dedicate all of your capacity to new builds.
- **Align incentives.** Make sure teams are recognized and rewarded for sustaining and improving existing assets, not only for launching new ones.
- **Encourage cross-functional investigation of performance issues.** Bring together data, process, and domain expertise that supports system-level thinking and avoids narrow, local fixes.

## Anticipating and Managing Improvement Risks[21]

Continuous improvement itself carries risks if not designed thoughtfully. **Over-tinkering**—making constant changes without proper evaluation—can create instability; disciplined experimentation with clear hypotheses and evaluation windows mitigates this. **Local optimization** occurs when improvements in one area degrade performance elsewhere; systems-thinking and benchmarking guidance highlight using cross-functional impact reviews and system-level metrics to detect and manage such trade-offs. **Measurement overload** can arise when teams track too many metrics, obscuring signal with noise; focusing on a concise, balanced set of process and outcome indicators keeps attention on what matters. **Automation overreach** is another risk: relying heavily on self-tuning systems without oversight can introduce hidden vulnerabilities, so periodic human review, clear guardrails, and explainability are needed.

Recognizing and planning for these risks allows continuous-improvement systems to enhance, rather than undermine, overall performance.

# Conclusion[22]

Continuous improvement in AI and analytics is both a philosophy and a disciplined practice, recognizing that models, dashboards, and processes are snapshots in time rather than permanent solutions. Organizations that embrace this mindset design feedback loops, benchmarking systems, and structured refinement cycles that keep analytics aligned with a changing world.

AI and automation strengthen these efforts by enabling faster detection of issues, more precise diagnosis, and more efficient execution of improvements, while governance and culture help ensure changes are safe and strategic. When leaders treat improvement as a core responsibility rather than an afterthought, analytics becomes a dynamic capability that helps the organization learn faster, adapt more intelligently, and sustain higher performance in a shifting environment.

# Notes

1 AutoML capabilities and their role in MLOps workflows are covered in *Databricks*'s "MLOps Workflows on *Databricks*."

2 Benchmarking definitions and types (internal and external) are drawn from *Crewhu*'s "6 Types of Benchmarking Your Business Should Use" and *CH Consulting Group*'s "Mastering Internal and External Benchmarking."

3 Continuous-improvement concepts and PDCA in quality/analytics contexts are examined in *Heliyon*'s "A Structured Model for Continuous Improvement Methodology" and *BuzzClan*'s "PDCA Cycle: The Ultimate Guide to Continuous Quality Improvement."

4 DMAIC as a structured, data-driven method applicable to digital processes is illustrated in the *University of Minho*'s "DMAIC for Process Digitalization: A Hospital Case Study."

5 Model drift types and the need for monitoring and retraining are detailed in *Aerospike*'s "Mitigating Model Drift in Machine Learning."

6 Feedback loops, model-monitoring best practices, and closed-loop optimization are addressed in *Dysnix*'s "Machine Learning Model Monitoring: Best Practices."

7 PDCA's four steps and their application in continuous quality improvement are laid out in *BuzzClan*'s "PDCA Cycle: The Ultimate Guide to Continuous Quality Improvement."

8 Process mining as an enabler of continuous improvement is situated within *Heliyon*'s "A Structured Model for Continuous Improvement Methodology."

9 Analytics as a living system and CQI lessons from healthcare are explored in 6sigma.us's "Continuous Quality Improvement (CQI): Driving Organizational Performance" and *CH Consulting Group*'s "Mastering Internal and External Benchmarking."

[10] The case for continuous improvement as essential to analytics portfolios and competitive positioning is made in *ThinkAI Corp*'s "Data-Driven Decision-Making in Healthcare Supply Chains" and *Solomon Insight*'s "The Advantages of External Benchmarking vs Internal Benchmarking."

[11] Feedback-loop design combining stakeholder feedback, usage analytics, and outcomes draws on *ThinkAI Corp*'s "Data-Driven Decision-Making" and *Crewhu*'s "6 Types of Benchmarking Your Business Should Use."

[12] Internal and external benchmarking patterns and automated monitoring are addressed in *CH Consulting Group*'s "Mastering Internal and External Benchmarking"; *PMC*'s "A Scoping Review of Continuous Quality Improvement in Healthcare"; and *Databricks*'s "MLOps Workflows on *Databricks*."

[13] Choosing among PDCA, DMAIC, and agile—along with typical AI assists—is addressed in *OrcaLean*'s "Integrating AI into DMAIC and PDCA: A Practical Framework"; 6sigma.us's "Continuous Quality Improvement (CQI)"; and the University of Minho's DMAIC case study.

[14] On applying improvement cycles and root-cause analysis tools (5 Whys, fishbone) in analytics, see *Adonis Partners*'s "Restoring CX with Continuous Improvement and Lean Six Sigma."

[15] Drift-monitoring metrics, triggers, and champion-challenger workflows are covered in *Aerospike*'s "Mitigating Model Drift in Machine Learning" and *DataRobot*'s "Challengers Tab - Submit Challenger Models."

[16] Culture and infrastructure enablers—leadership behavior, training, and communities of practice—are covered in 6sigma.us's "Continuous Quality Improvement (CQI)" and *BuzzClan*'s "PDCA Cycle."

[17] AI and automation enablers—process mining, RPA, AutoML, and model-monitoring platforms—are surveyed in *OrcaLean*'s "Integrating AI into DMAIC and PDCA" and *Dysnix*'s "Machine Learning Model Monitoring: Best Practices."

[18] The healthcare analytics continuous-improvement case—covering council structure, PDCA, process mining, and outcomes—is drawn from PMC's "A Scoping Review of Continuous Quality Improvement in Healthcare" and *ThinkAI Corp*'s "Data-Driven Decision-Making in Healthcare Supply Chains."

[19] Continuous-improvement metric definitions—throughput, time to implement, drift lag, adoption, reuse, and uplift—are drawn from *Heliyon*'s "A Structured Model for Continuous Improvement Methodology"; *Dysnix*'s "Machine Learning Model Monitoring"; *Aerospike*'s "Mitigating Model Drift"; PMC's "A Scoping Review"; and *OrcaLean*'s "Integrating AI into DMAIC and PDCA."

[20] Leadership behaviors that normalize improvement and system-level investigation are examined in the University of Minho's "DMAIC for Process Digitalization" and *Adonis Partners*'s "Restoring CX with Continuous Improvement and Lean Six Sigma."

[21] Risks of over-tinkering, local optimization, measurement overload, and automation overreach are surfaced in *Crewhu*'s "6 Types of Benchmarking" and *Databricks*'s "MLOps Workflows on *Databricks*."

[22] *Heliyon*'s "A Structured Model for Continuous Improvement Methodology" and *OrcaLean*'s "Integrating AI into DMAIC and PDCA" together support the conclusion that continuous improvement combined with AI and governance creates a dynamic analytics capability.

## Key topics explored in this chapter:

- Why Standardization Is Important for AI Effectiveness
- What to Standardize and Where to Flex
- What to Standardize: The Foundation
- The Case for Flexibility
- How to Harmonize Consistency and Adaptability
- Federated Governance in Practice
- Continuous Monitoring and Improvement of Standards

# WAY 20

# Standardize Practices with Flexibility


## Abstract

Consistency and adaptability must coexist in modern analytics and AI. This chapter presents strategies for standardizing core analytics and AI practices—such as common data models, quality controls, model-governance workflows, and semantic layers—while preserving room for innovation and business-specific customization. It explains what to standardize, where to remain flexible, and how to design modular frameworks and federated governance structures that support both reliability and experimentation.


## Objective

After completing this chapter, you will be able to:

- Articulate why standardization is important for AI effectiveness, scale, and trust, including data quality, explainability, and compliance.
- Identify which elements of analytics should be standardized.
- Distinguish between foundational standards and areas where business-specific customization is necessary.
- Design "guardrail" methods, modular architectures, and semantic layers that support both consistency and local adaptation.
- Implement federated governance mechanisms that review exceptions, capture learning, and evolve standards over time.
- Recognize common pitfalls of both excessive rigidity and unmanaged variation—and apply best practices to avoid them in AI and analytics initiatives.

# Terms to Know

**Common Data Model (CDM)**[1] **-** A shared representation of key entities, attributes, and relationships that standardizes how data is structured and interpreted across systems and teams, widely used as a foundation for large-scale analytics and AI.

**Exception Process**[2] **-** A formal mechanism for requesting, reviewing, and approving deviations from established standards, often run through a data or AI governance council.

**Federated Governance**[3] **-** A hybrid governance model in which a central group defines common policies and standards while domain teams have autonomy to implement them locally within defined guardrails; commonly used in data-mesh architectures.

**Guardrail**[4] **-** A constraint or rule—such as required access controls, quality checks, or content filters—designed to prevent harmful or risky variation while still allowing controlled flexibility, including safety policies for generative AI.

**Metadata**[5] **-** Information that describes data—such as definitions, formats, lineage, ownership, and calculation logic—used to improve understanding, quality, and governance, typically managed via catalog and governance tools.

**Modular Framework**[6] **-** An architecture composed of standardized core components (for example, ingestion, quality, semantic layer, model registry) with clearly defined interfaces for customizable or optional modules.

**Standardization**[7] **-** The process of defining and enforcing common practices, formats, and rules to ensure consistency, quality, interoperability, and compliance across teams and systems.

# Introduction[8]

As AI and analytics expand across an organization, the variety of data sources, tools, and use cases grows rapidly. Without shared standards, that variety turns into chaos: conflicting metrics, incompatible datasets, brittle integrations, and opaque models that erode trust. At the same time, overly rigid standardization stifles innovation, drives teams toward unsanctioned workarounds, and blocks adoption of new techniques.

The challenge is building a foundation stable enough to support scale and compliance, yet flexible enough to accommodate new technologies, business models, and local requirements. In AI terms, that means combining global "rules of the road" for data and models with local freedom to adapt and experiment within safe boundaries. This chapter examines how to make that balance explicit: deciding what must be common, what teams can customize, and how to evolve standards as the organization learns.

## Why Standardization Is Important for AI Effectiveness[9]

AI and analytics depend on consistent, reliable inputs, semantics, and processes. When foundational elements differ across systems and teams, complexity undermines value.

**Data Integrity and Semantics.**
Models trained or scored on inconsistent definitions—such as multiple meanings of "active customer," "churn," or "revenue"—produce outputs that cannot be reliably compared or governed. Common data models and shared metric definitions help prevent this.

**Reliability, Scale, and Interoperability.**
Reusing proven pipelines, feature stores, approval workflows, and monitoring patterns allows organizations to deploy AI across domains without reinventing basics; standardized components support "paved paths" in data-mesh and platform architectures that make compliant behavior the path of least resistance.

**Compliance, Ethics, and Auditability.**
Traceable, repeatable processes and transparent definitions make it easier to demonstrate how data and models are used, monitored, and retired. Consistent documentation, model-approval templates, and logging underpin Responsible-AI methods and regulatory expectations.

Automation and AI governance—such as policy-as-code, automated access controls, and AI guardrails—require predictable formats and controls, which become fragile and risky when standards are absent.

## What to Standardize and Where to Flex[10]

Different elements of the AI and analytics stack require different levels of standardization. Data-mesh and federated-governance patterns emphasize distinguishing global invariants from local degrees of freedom.

## Standardization vs. Flexibility Matrix

| Layer/Element | Standardized Globally | Flexible Locally |
|---|---|---|
| **Core Entities and Keys** | CDM for customers, products, assets, locations | Extension fields for local attributes |
| **Metrics and KPIs** | Enterprise KPI definitions and calculation logic | Supplemental metrics tailored to domain goals |
| **Data Quality and Access** | Baseline quality checks, PII rules, access policies | Additional checks or filters for local risk contexts |
| **Model Governance** | Approval templates, risk tiers, documentation, logging | Domain-specific evaluation criteria and thresholds |
| **Platform and Pipelines** | Shared ingestion, storage, monitoring, semantic layer | Domain-specific transforms, features, and models |
| **Tools and Experimentation** | Approved platforms and sandbox patterns | Choice of methods and prototypes within guardrails |

This matrix makes explicit where consistency is non-negotiable and where teams can differentiate responsibly.

## What to Standardize: The Foundation[11]

### Data Models and Definitions

A common data model defines how core entities—such as customers, products, transactions, and assets—are represented across systems. It specifies field names and meanings, units and formats, and key relationships such as customer-to-account mappings. Aligning sources to a shared model simplifies integration, model deployment, lineage tracking, and cross-domain analytics; AI-assisted mapping tools can suggest alignments, but human stewards own final definitions and governance.

### Metadata and Centralized Dictionaries

Centralized metadata repositories or catalogs describe business definitions of fields and metrics (including AI-specific concepts such as risk scores or fairness metrics), calculation logic for KPIs and derived variables, and data and model lineage. Living metadata and glossaries reduce misunderstandings, speed onboarding, and support explainability and auditability for analytics and AI systems.

### Validation, Quality, and Access Rules

Standard data-quality checks and access policies provide a baseline for trust and safety. Reusable checks—completeness thresholds, allowed ranges, referential integrity—should be defined centrally and applied automatically across pipelines and domains. Standard access controls, masking rules, and PII-handling practices help ensure AI systems do not inadvertently leak sensitive data, especially in generative-AI applications.

### Process Templates, Workflow Patterns, and Model Governance

Common analytics and AI use cases follow similar patterns. Process templates can define steps for model development (ingest, explore, model, validate, approve, deploy, monitor, retire) along with required checkpoints like ethics review, bias assessment, security review, and documentation. Standard model-governance workflows—risk tiering, approval matrices, registration in a central model registry—ensure consistent oversight while allowing evaluation criteria for performance and business fit.

## The Case for Flexibility[12]

Strict uniformity everywhere is neither practical nor desirable. Evolving technologies—such as new data types, cloud platforms, or domain-specific foundation models—often require tailored experimentation before they are candidates for standardization. Business-specific needs also vary: logistics may require fine-grained geospatial rules; risk teams may need specialized stress-testing that differs from marketing's needs.

Innovation and experimentation benefit from governed sandboxes where early-stage proofs of concept operate under lighter constraints (for example, using de-identified or synthetic data in non-production environments). Successful approaches can later be evaluated for promotion into the standard stack. Flexibility, when governed, allows the organization to explore new ideas and meet local needs without fracturing the shared foundation.

## How to Harmonize Consistency and Adaptability[13]

### Purpose-Driven Standards

Standards should be grounded in clear objectives. Compliance standards exist to meet regulatory and risk obligations; interoperability standards ensure that data and models can be reused across domains; innovation standards may focus on minimum documentation and safety for experiments rather than prescribing specific tools. By stating purpose, organizations clarify where strict adherence is mandatory versus where optionality is acceptable.

### Guardrails, Not Straightjackets

Effective standards define valuable constraints while leaving space around them. For example, non-negotiable fields, identifiers, and privacy rules in core datasets can coexist with flexible extension fields for local context; required quality and monitoring thresholds can be supplemented by domain-specific controls; fixed requirements for production models (registration, logging, risk tiering, approval) can be paired with looser rules in registered sandbox environments where risk is low. This "freedom within a framework" approach allows teams to innovate inside clear boundaries.

### Modular and Layered Frameworks

Modular designs separate standardized core components from customizable modules. A shared ingestion, storage, and quality layer feeds a universal semantic layer; domains then attach their own transformation logic, feature pipelines, and models on top. A common monitoring and alerting approach tracks drift, performance, and incidents, while thresholds and remediation playbooks can differ by use case and risk level.

Clear interfaces mean teams can evolve local modules without destabilizing upstream or downstream components, a pattern reflected in both data-mesh implementations and enterprise GenAI platform designs.

## Federated Governance in Practice[14]

Federated governance blends central standards with local autonomy. A central data/AI governance function defines global policies—such as CDM scope, baseline quality metrics, access criteria, and model-risk tiers—while domain teams implement them in their own pipelines and products.

Governance-as-code embeds policies into data pipelines and platforms so standards (quality checks, access rules, logging) are enforced automatically in design, build, and run stages rather than solely via manual review. Federated councils review exception requests, adjudicate cross-domain issues, and periodically revise standards based on field experience, aligning with data-mesh guidance on federated computational governance. This model helps avoid both centralized bottlenecks and unmanaged local divergence.

### Continuous Monitoring and Improvement of Standards[15]

Standards themselves require monitoring and evolution. Analytics on catalog usage, exception volume, and policy bypasses reveal where standards may be unclear, misaligned, or outdated. Periodic standards reviews examine which exceptions were approved, which local innovations succeeded, and where friction is highest, then update standards accordingly.

In this way, the standardization framework becomes a living system, not a static rulebook, echoing broader trends in adaptive AI governance. Organizations that revisit standards regularly can respond faster to technology shifts and regulatory change while keeping a coherent foundation.

# Case Study

## Harmonizing in Practice[16]

A multinational manufacturer set out to deploy predictive-maintenance analytics across dozens of plants, each with different equipment, local practices, and regulatory environments. Leadership recognized the need for a shared foundation to compare performance and scale AI solutions while respecting legitimate local differences.

The central analytics team, working with plant engineers, defined a CDM for equipment, failure events, and maintenance activities, along with global KPIs such as mean time between failures, unplanned downtime, and preventive-maintenance adherence. A shared ingestion and quality layer validated and standardized sensor and maintenance data before loading it into a common semantic layer. Each plant could extend the CDM with local attributes—as long as they documented them centrally—and implement specialized rules for sensor thresholds and alerts while using the global monitoring framework.

A federated data and AI governance council, with representatives from central and plant teams, managed the exception process. When multiple plants adopted similar custom attributes or rule sets that improved prediction accuracy or lowered downtime, those patterns were evaluated and, where appropriate, promoted into the global standard set. Within two years, the manufacturer achieved comparable, high-quality data and KPIs across plants while preserving flexibility for local optimization and experimentation, and time to onboard a new plant onto the predictive-maintenance stack dropped significantly.

# Success Metrics[17]

## Standardization and Flexibility Metrics

| Metric | Definition | What It Tells You | Key Levers |
|---|---|---|---|
| **CDM Coverage Rate** | % of critical entities using the common data model | Breadth of foundational standardization | CDM governance; data stewardship |
| **KPI Definition Consistency** | % of key KPIs with a single, approved definition across domains | Semantic alignment and comparability | Metadata catalog; glossary governance |
| **Exception Volume and Disposition** | No. of exception requests; % approved; % later standardized | Health of governance and learning from flexibility | Federated council; exception-process design |
| **Time to Onboard New Use Cases** | Avg. time to build a new use case on the standard stack | Speed and leverage provided by standards | Paved paths; modular architecture maturity |
| **Policy / Guardrail Incident Rate** | No. of significant incidents due to non-compliance or unmanaged variation | Effectiveness of guardrails and enforcement | Policy-as-code; automated controls |
| **Innovation Adoption Rate** | % of local innovations promoted into global standards | Ability to learn from the edge and evolve standards | Standards review cadence; federated council |

Data-governance and AI-governance guidance suggests regularly reviewing these metrics in data/AI governance forums to keep standardization tightly tied to value and learning.

## Potential Pitfalls of Rigidity and Chaos[18]

Finding the right balance means recognizing risks at both extremes.

- **Too little standardization:** Analytics outputs become inconsistent and hard to reconcile; integrations across products, regions, or vendors require extensive custom work; and compliance, security, and ethical risks increase due to ad-hoc data usage and undocumented models.

- **Too much rigidity:** Business units may resort to shadow IT and unsanctioned AI tools; innovation slows as teams feel blocked from experimenting; and standards grow stale, failing to keep pace with technology and regulatory change.

Leaders must routinely ask whether standards are serving their intended purpose and whether flexibility is used productively rather than as an escape from discipline.

## Best Practices Checklist[19]

Organizations seeking to standardize with flexibility can use the following checklist as a guide:

- Define non-negotiables for production, including core entities, keys, KPI definitions, quality and access rules, and model-governance steps.
- Maintain living documentation so data dictionaries, process templates, and governance policies are accessible and current.
- Automate enforcement where possible through schema checks, policy-as-code, and CI/CD gates for model and data changes.
- Create clear exception pathways with transparent criteria, turnaround times, and documentation of outcomes.
- Capture and reuse lessons: when exceptions or local innovations succeed, evaluate whether to integrate them into enterprise standards.
- Promote "freedom within a framework": communicate that guardrails exist to enable safe speed, not to police creativity.

## Practical Advice for Leaders[20]

Leaders can make or break the organization's effort to harmonize standards and flexibility. To help, they should:

- **Frame standards as enablers of speed, safety, and reuse.** Emphasize how shared foundations accelerate AI and analytics delivery.
- **Increase legitimacy and practicality.** Involve both business and technical stakeholders in designing and revising standards, especially those affecting AI and generative-AI use cases.

- **Drive relevance.** Make certain local teams see real pathways for their innovations to influence enterprise-level practices, so standards feel reciprocal rather than imposed.
- **Surface friction and improvement opportunities.** Ask regularly in reviews, "Where are standards helping you? and Where are they getting in the way?"
- **Think about incentives.** Make leaders accountable for both compliance with guardrails and the constructive use of flexibility to drive innovation.

# Conclusion[21]

Standardizing practices with flexibility is not a one-time design decision; it is an ongoing balancing act. Strong foundations in data models, metadata, quality rules, and governance workflows provide the reliability AI and analytics need to scale. Thoughtful flexibility, through guardrails, modular architectures, and federated governance, ensures those foundations never become a ceiling on innovation.

# Notes

[1] CDM structure and its benefits are set out in *OHDSI*'s "Standardized Data: The OMOP Common Data Model" and TDWI's "Speeding Time to Value: How a Common Data Model Allows You to Do More with Less."

[2] Exception-process design within data-mesh and governance programs is treated in *Branch Boston*'s "What Data Mesh Governance Really Means—and How to Implement It."

[3] Federated-governance concepts and hybrid central/local models are developed in Lifebit's "Federated Data Governance Explained Simply"; Promethium's "Data Mesh Principles & Implementation"; and *Decube*'s "Best Practices for Data Governance."

[4] Guardrails, policy-as-code, and governance of data fabrics and mesh are examined in *Sogeti Labs*'s "Emerging Trends: Policy as Code for Governance Enforcement" and *ServiceNow*'s "Responsible AI."

[5] Metadata, catalogs, and their role in governance and explainability are addressed in *Sogeti Labs*'s "Emerging Trends: Data Governance in Data Fabrics and Mesh" and Lifebit's "Federated Governance: The Blueprint for Data Democracy."

[6] Modular "freedom within a framework" architectures are examined in *CDAO Magazine*'s "An Enterprise Approach to GenAI Platforms: Freedom Within a Framework" and *Lean Construction Institute*'s "Leveraging AI in a Common Data Environment (CDE)."

[7] Standardization benefits and the risks of schema proliferation are addressed in *Patterns*/PMC on common data models and TDWI's "Speeding Time to Value."

[8] *Branch Boston*'s "What Data Mesh Really Is (and Isn't)" explores the balance between centralized and federated AI governance.

[9] Standardization's role in enabling scale, interoperability, and compliance is set out in TDWI's "Speeding Time to Value"; *OHDSI*'s "Standardized Data"; *Decube*'s "Data Mesh Architecture"; and *ServiceNow*'s "Responsible AI."

[10] The standardization-versus-flexibility matrix and data-mesh framing of invariants versus local autonomy are drawn from Promethium's "Data Mesh 101"; *Mesh-AI*'s "Data Mesh 101: Why Federated Data Governance Is the Secret Sauce"; and PMC articles on common data models.

[11] Foundations—CDM, metadata, quality, governance patterns—are covered in PMC articles; *ServiceNow*'s "Responsible AI"; Sogeti Labs; and *Mesh-AI*'s data mesh guidance.

[12] Purpose-driven standards, guardrails, and modular frameworks are treated across *Mesh-AI*; Lifebit's federated governance guides; TDWI; Promethium; *CDAO Magazine*'s "Freedom Within a Framework"; and Lean Construction's CDE patterns.

[13] Harmonizing consistency and adaptability through purpose-driven standards, guardrails, and modular layered frameworks is addressed across *Mesh-AI*; Lifebit; TDWI; Promethium; *CDAO Magazine*; and Lean Construction.

[14] Federated governance and exception handling in practice are covered in *Decube*'s "Best Practices for Data Governance" and Promethium's "Data Mesh Principles & Implementation."

[15] Continuous improvement of standards, catalog analytics, and adaptive AI governance are addressed in PMC articles and *ServiceNow*'s "Continual Improvement Management."

[16] The manufacturing/predictive-maintenance case pattern—CDM, shared layers, and federated council—is drawn from *Decube*; *Lean Construction Institute*'s "Leveraging AI in a Common Data Environment"; and *Branch Boston*'s data mesh governance discussions.

[17] Standardization-and-flexibility metrics—CDM coverage, KPI consistency, exceptions, onboarding time, incidents, innovation rate—are sourced from TDWI; *Branch Boston*; *Mesh-AI*; and Sogeti Labs.

[18] Pitfalls of too little or too much standardization—"data anarchy" versus rigidity—are flagged in TDWI, Sogeti Labs, and related governance sources.

[19] Best-practice checklist items—non-negotiables, living docs, automation, exception paths, reuse, freedom within framework—are compiled from TDWI; Sogeti Labs; *Branch Boston*; *Mesh-AI*; and *Decube*.

[20] Leader behaviors and incentives in federated data-governance models are examined in *CDAO Magazine*'s "An Enterprise Approach to GenAI Platforms" and Domo's "Federated Data Governance: A 2025 Guide."

[21] *OHDSI*'s "Standardized Data" and *CDAO Magazine*'s "Freedom Within a Framework" both affirm that flexible standardization is a core AI-governance pillar.

# Key topics explored in this chapter:

- Why AI Alignment Is Different–and More Complex–Than Analytics
- Building a Foundation for AI Strategy Alignment
- Adaptive Architectures to Support Business Strategy
- Leadership's Role in AI Strategy Alignment
- Measuring Direct AI Impact, Not Just Technical Output

# WAY 21

# Align AI and Analytics with Enterprise Strategy


## Abstract

Analytics and AI deliver lasting value only when tightly aligned with enterprise strategy. This chapter explains how to connect AI and analytics initiatives to business objectives, embed them in planning and portfolio processes, and measure their direct impact on outcomes. It introduces practical tools for value-based prioritization, strategic roadmapping, and governance that ensure AI investments serve business goals rather than technology curiosity.


## Objective

After completing this chapter, you will be able to:

- Explain how AI alignment differs from traditional analytics alignment and why stakes are higher.
- Build AI roadmaps that connect capabilities, initiatives, and resources directly to strategic objectives.
- Use value-based prioritization methods to select and sequence AI projects.
- Design governance structures and cross-functional forums that keep AI portfolios synchronized with enterprise strategy.
- Shape adaptive data and technology architectures that can pivot as strategy evolves.
- Measure AI's business impact using strategic KPIs and feedback loops, then retire or redirect misaligned initiatives.

# Terms to Know

**Adaptive Architecture**[1] - A data and technology environment designed to evolve with changing business and regulatory needs, supporting multiple AI use cases and rapid reprioritization.

**AI Portfolio**[2] - The set of AI and analytics initiatives, products, and capabilities an organization is pursuing at any given time, managed as a portfolio rather than isolated projects.

**AI Strategy Alignment**[3] - The deliberate linking of AI and analytics initiatives to clearly defined enterprise goals, priorities, and value drivers, often using strategy maps, OKRs, or scorecards.

**Strategic KPI**[4] - A metric that captures progress toward core strategic objectives such as growth, profitability, risk reduction, or customer experience, often enhanced by AI-powered measurement.

**Strategic Roadmap**[5] - A time-phased plan that connects AI capabilities and projects to business outcomes and milestones, typically refreshed in line with enterprise planning cycles.

**Value-Based Prioritization**[6] - A method of ranking initiatives based on expected impact, risk, and effort rather than technical novelty, widely recommended in AI and strategic-portfolio-management guidance.

# Introduction[7]

Organizations have long recognized the need to align analytics with business priorities, because reports and dashboards that do not serve strategic goals quickly lose attention. In the past, misalignment mostly led to wasted effort and underused deliverables. AI makes alignment even more important because models can influence individual customer experiences, automate entire workflows, and shape decisions with regulatory or ethical implications.

In fact, AI has the potential to entirely reshape products, processes, and business models. But this upside is realized only when AI efforts are rooted in enterprise strategy: where the organization aims to compete, how it plans to differentiate, what risks it is willing to take, and which stakeholders it intends to serve. This chapter explores how to build that alignment deliberately, so AI becomes a strategic instrument rather than a series of disconnected experiments.

## Why AI Alignment Is Different—and More Complex—Than Analytics[8]

Traditional analytics has focused on improving existing processes: better reports, more accurate forecasts, localized optimizations. When analytics misaligned with strategy, organizations produced underused reports or duplicated effort. AI changes this calculus in several important ways.

- **Capability outpaces alignment mechanisms:** It is increasingly possible to build powerful models and automations across many processes, making "Should we?" and "Where does this help us win?" more important than "Can we?". Without clear strategic intent, organizations risk deploying AI in areas that do not materially support competitive advantage or mission outcomes while neglecting domains where AI could be transformative.
- **Higher stakes and broader impact:** AI systems can directly interact with customers and partners, influence credit decisions, hiring choices, pricing, and safety outcomes, and create new regulatory exposures around fairness, transparency, and accountability. This breadth demands alignment with enterprise risk appetite, brand positioning, and stakeholder expectations.
- **Portfolio complexity:** As AI initiatives multiply, duplication, overlap, and conflict become more likely; systems built in one part of the organization can affect data, processes, or metrics in another. Alignment therefore requires viewing AI through a portfolio lens and managing dependencies and trade-offs across the enterprise.

## Building a Foundation for AI Strategy Alignment[9]

### Strategic AI Roadmap Development

Alignment starts with a clear, shared understanding of how AI will contribute to enterprise goals, captured in a strategic AI roadmap. A roadmap connects vision to execution by:

- Identifying priority domains where AI can meaningfully advance strategic objectives (for example, customer experience, risk management, operational efficiency, or product innovation).
- Outlining a sequence of initiatives and capability builds, along with enabling investments in data, platforms, and skills.

- Defining milestones and "value drops" that deliver tangible benefits along the way, improving stakeholder buy-in and funding continuity.

Practitioners recommend updating AI roadmaps in lockstep with enterprise planning cycles so AI initiatives reflect changing priorities, market conditions, and lessons from past projects.

### Governance: Moving Beyond Ad-Hoc Approvals

Given AI's complexity and risk profile, informal or siloed approval processes fall shortt. Effective alignment requires cross-functional governance that:

- Reviews proposed AI initiatives against strategic objectives and risk criteria.
- Prioritizes and sequences initiatives based on value, feasibility, and dependencies.
- Monitors portfolio progress, adjusting or retiring initiatives based on impact and strategic fit.

When creating an AI governance council, it is important to include leaders from key business lines, IT, risk, legal, and compliance—not just analytics and data science. Standardized project-intake templates, risk reviews, and ethics checks ensure that each proposal addresses business value, alignment, and organizational values—not just technical design.

### AI's Unique Demand for Cross-Functional Collaboration

Because AI touches multiple processes and stakeholder groups, cross-functional collaboration is a precondition for strategic alignment. Integrated problem selection, where business leaders, technologists, and analytics teams jointly identify which problems to tackle, ensures that use cases are strategically relevant, teams understand data and technical requirements upfront, and teams consider change implications early.

Portfolio and governance sources recommend regular alignment meetings, joint design sessions, and shared workspaces to keep solutions grounded in both business reality and technical constraints. Cross-functional communities of practice allow teams to share experiences across domains, spreading alignment practices and preventing fragmentation of AI strategy.

## Adaptive Architectures to Support Business Strategy[10]

Strategic alignment is not only about which AI initiatives are pursued. It is also about how the underlying architecture supports adaptation. Flexibility as a design principle means teams build data platforms, integration layers, and model-deployment pipelines to:

- Add new data sources without major rework.
- Support multiple model types and deployment patterns (batch, real time, in-app).
- Accommodate evolving regulations or security requirements.

Modular architectures, with reusable components for ingestion, feature engineering, model management, and monitoring, let business units plug in their own logic and context while drawing on shared capabilities. Domain-oriented data platforms mirror strategic domains (customer, product, risk), making it straightforward to see where AI capabilities support each objective. An adaptive architecture makes pivoting technically feasible when strategy shifts.

## Leadership's Role in AI Strategy Alignment[11]

Leadership is central to aligning AI with enterprise strategy. Executives must clarify the "why" by articulating how AI supports the organization's mission and competitive strategy: which strategic problems AI should help solve, which outcomes will be used to judge success, and which boundaries (such as certain data uses or automation levels) will not be crossed.

Resource allocation is equally important. Leaders must direct funding, talent, and time toward high-value AI initiatives, even when that means deprioritizing attractive but misaligned ideas. Champions of responsible use set the expectation that the organization will deploy AI thoughtfully, with attention to ethics, fairness, and transparency, so that AI serves brand and societal goals alongside financial ones. When leaders use AI-supported insights in their own decisions and challenge model outputs in meetings, they reinforce alignment through everyday practice.

## Measuring Direct AI Impact, Not Just Technical Output[12]

Alignment means nothing without measurement. Technical metrics: accuracy, AUC, latency, uptime, are necessary but not sufficient to judge strategic fit. Organizations must evaluate each AI initiative against business outcomes. For each one, organizations should define:

- Primary strategic KPIs (for example, revenue uplift, cost savings, risk losses avoided, customer-experience improvements).
- Secondary indicators (for example, time-to-decision, interaction quality, error rates).

These KPIs belong in existing performance dashboards and reviewed alongside other strategic metrics, not buried in separate technical reports. Transparent impact reporting: before-and-after comparisons, qualitative user and customer feedback, and unintended consequences discovered and addressed, builds trust and informs portfolio decisions. Continuous feedback loops between measurement and portfolio management retire or re-scope initiatives that no longer advance strategic goals and scale the ones that do.

# Case Studies[13]

## Case Study #1: Strategic AI Roadmapping in a Global Bank

A global bank had multiple AI pilots—fraud detection, credit-scoring enhancements, next-best-offer models—but local enthusiasm drove most of them. Executives grew worried about fragmented investments, inconsistent risk controls, and overlapping efforts.

The bank launched an AI strategy-alignment initiative, starting with cross-business workshops across retail, corporate, risk, and operations. Those workshops identified a small set of strategic objectives where AI could make the biggest difference: reducing fraud losses, improving customer engagement, and streamlining credit decisioning. A multi-year AI roadmap grouped initiatives under these themes and sequenced them by value potential, data readiness, and dependencies.

A cross-functional governance council reviewed new proposals against the roadmap and required each initiative to specify clear business KPIs and risk considerations. Over three years, AI investment shifted from scattered pilots to a focused portfolio: measurable reductions in fraud loss rates, faster credit-approval times, higher cross-sell success, all tracked by strategic KPIs. Leaders updated the roadmap annually as strategy evolved and as the bank learned from successes and failures.

## Case Study #2: Aligning AI for Customer Experience in Telecom

A telecommunications provider set out to improve customer experience and retention using AI, but early initiatives: chatbots, churn models, and personalization engines, launched across different units with little coordination. Customer feedback was mixed, and some AI interactions frustrated users.

Leadership reframed the entire AI effort around a single strategic objective: becoming the most trusted provider in priority markets. A cross-functional team spanning customer service, marketing, network operations, and analytics built a shared customer-experience framework with strategic KPIs—net promoter score, first-contact resolution, complaint volume. Teams then prioritized AI initiatives by expected impact on those KPIs.

The provider invested in AI-assisted agent tools that suggested next-best actions and responses, backed by integrated customer data, measuring both customer outcomes and operational metrics. Features that did not move strategic KPIs were redesigned or retired; teams scaled the successful ones. Retention and satisfaction improved measurably over time. Proof that AI aligned with a clear experience strategy creates value that technical innovation alone does not.

## Case Study #3: Product Innovation Alignment at a Consumer Goods Company

A consumer goods company experimented with AI to support product development, from demand forecasting to concept testing, but individual brand teams adopted tools independently, resulting in inconsistent methodologies and limited comparability across categories.

Senior leadership defined a strategic goal to accelerate innovation while improving hit rates for new products and established a central innovation and analytics hub to standardize core methods—such as conjoint analysis, social listening, and scenario modeling—while allowing brand teams flexibility to explore category-specific questions. AI-enabled platforms provided portfolio-level views of innovation performance, and brand-level AI initiatives were required to specify their contribution to enterprise KPIs such as innovation revenue, time from idea to launch, and post-launch performance.

As alignment matured, leadership could compare innovation outcomes across brands and prioritize investment in approaches that consistently delivered strategic results rather than those that merely showcased cutting-edge techniques.

# Success Metrics[14]

## Strategic Alignment Metrics

| Metric | Definition | What It Tells You |
|---|---|---|
| **Strategic Coverage of AI Portfolio** | % of AI initiatives mapped to explicit strategic objectives | Degree to which AI work supports enterprise goals |
| **Value-Based Approval Rate** | Share of approved AI projects that meet predefined value thresholds | Strength of prioritization discipline |
| **Roadmap Adherence and Agility** | % of roadmap milestones achieved, adjusted, or retired with justification | Balance of discipline and adaptability |
| **Strategic KPI Impact** | Aggregate change in key strategic KPIs attributable to AI initiatives | Real business impact of the AI portfolio |
| **Cross-Functional Sponsorship** | Proportion of AI initiatives with multiple business and technical sponsors | Depth of shared ownership and alignment |
| **Retirement/Redirect Rate** | % of AI initiatives retired based on impact review | Willingness to stop or pivot misaligned efforts |

Strategic-portfolio-management sources recommend tracking the series of metrics in this table to assess whether AI is genuinely aligned with strategy or drifting toward technical experimentation.

# Practical Advice for Leaders[15]

Leaders who want strong AI alignment should follow these practical steps.

- **Use strategy-first framing.** Start with "What are our most important strategic questions or problems?" before asking "Where can we use AI?"
- **Require explicit alignment in proposals.** Ask each AI initiative to state which strategic objectives and KPIs it supports. Reject or defer those that don't align.

- **Integrate AI into core planning.** Include AI capabilities and opportunities in annual and multi-year planning cycles, not as a separate technical track.
- **Make trade-offs visible.** Transparently shift investment from low-impact AI work to higher-impact initiatives, reinforcing that strategic value, not novelty, drives decisions.
- **Tell alignment stories.** Highlight examples where AI clearly contributed to strategic wins—growth, risk mitigation, customer trust—to build momentum and reinforce desired behaviors.

These practices move AI from tactical experimentation to a disciplined, strategy-driven capability.

## Risks and Pitfalls in AI Strategy Alignment[16]

Even with good intentions, organizations can fall into traps.

- **Unclear goals or shifting priorities:** AI projects launched without stable, well-communicated objectives struggle to define success and maintain support.
- **Resource fragmentation:** Multiple teams may pursue similar AI problems independently, diluting resources and creating conflicting solutions.
- **Overemphasis on technology:** Pursuing cutting-edge models for their own sake can divert attention from simpler solutions that better serve strategy.
- **Ignoring change readiness:** Even well-aligned AI initiatives can fail if stakeholders are not prepared or supported to use them, underscoring the need for integrated change management.

Mitigating these risks requires clear communication, disciplined portfolio management, and close collaboration between strategy, business, and technical leaders.

# Conclusion[17]

AI's potential is fully realized only when it is woven into the fabric of enterprise strategy. Alignment is not a single decision but a continuous practice of setting direction, choosing the right problems, building enabling capabilities, and systematically measuring impact.

Organizations that invest in roadmapping, governance, cross-functional collaboration, adaptive architectures, and business-centric measurement turn AI into a genuine strategic asset—one that consistently advances their goals, adapts as those goals evolve, and earns trust from stakeholders inside and outside the organization.

# Notes

[1] Adaptive architectures and compliance-first AI roadmaps are detailed in *SmartDev*'s "AI Transformation Roadmap for Finance and Compliance" and *Decube*'s "Data Mesh Architecture: Guide for Data Engineers."

[2] The case for treating AI initiatives as a managed portfolio is made in *FinOps Foundation*'s "Unlocking AI Business Value With FinOps."

[3] Strategic AI measurement and alignment—definitions and practices—are developed in *MIT Sloan Management Review*'s "Build Better KPIs With Artificial Intelligence."

[4] Strategic KPIs and AI-enhanced measurement are examined in *MIT Sloan Management Review*'s "Build Better KPIs With Artificial Intelligence" and *SwissCognitive*'s "Build Better KPIs With Artificial Intelligence (AI)."

[5] AI strategic roadmaps and banking/finance roadmapping patterns are laid out in *WhiteBlue Consulting*'s "Roadmap to an AI-First Enterprise for Banking and Finance" and Persistent's enterprise readiness guidance.

[6] Value-based prioritization and outcome-based AI selection are addressed in *Breakthrough Growth*'s "How to Identify and Prioritize High-Value AI Opportunities" and LinkedIn's value-first guidance.

[7] *McKinsey*'s "Extracting Value from AI in Banking: Rewiring the Enterprise" and *Breakthrough Growth* advance the argument that AI raises alignment stakes well beyond traditional analytics.

[8] Distinctions between analytics and AI alignment—capability, stakes, and portfolio complexity—are drawn in *MIT Sloan Management Review*'s "Strategic Alignment With AI and Smart KPIs"; *WhiteBlue Consulting*; *McKinsey*'s "Extracting Value from AI in Banking"; and *Breakthrough Growth.*

[9] Foundation building via roadmaps, governance, and cross-functional collaboration is addressed in Persistent's enterprise readiness guidance; *SmartDev*'s leadership strategies; *WhiteBlue Consulting*; *FinOps Foundation*; and *MIT Sloan Management Review.*

[10] Adaptive architecture principles—flexibility, modularity, and domain-oriented platforms—are treated in *SmartDev*; *WhiteBlue Consulting*; *McKinsey*'s enterprise AI insights; and *Decube*'s "Data Mesh Architecture."

[11] Leadership roles in AI alignment—vision, resource allocation, and responsible use—are examined in *SmartDev*'s "Mastering AI Adoption: Leadership Strategies" and *SwissCognitive.*

[12] Measuring direct AI impact with strategic KPIs and smart-KPI practices is developed in *SwissCognitive's* "Build Better KPIs With Artificial Intelligence."

[13] Banking, telecom, and consumer-goods alignment case patterns are drawn from *WhiteBlue Consulting*; Persistent; *McKinsey*'s "Extracting Value from AI in Banking"; *SmartDev*; *FinOps Foundation*; and *Breakthrough Growth.*

[14] Alignment metrics—portfolio coverage, value-based approvals, roadmap adherence, KPI impact, sponsorship, and retirement rate—are drawn from *Breakthrough Growth*; *WhiteBlue Consulting*; *MIT Sloan Management Review*; and *FinOps Foundation.*

[15] Leader practices—strategy-first framing, explicit alignment, integrated planning, visible trade-offs, storytelling—are surveyed across LinkedIn articles; *MIT Sloan Management Review*'s big ideas on AI strategy; *Breakthrough Growth*; and Persistent.

[16] Risks and pitfalls in AI alignment—unclear goals, fragmentation, tech-centrism, change readiness—are identified in LinkedIn's "AI Fragmentation Risk"; *FinOps Foundation*; *McKinsey*'s "The State of AI"; and *WhiteBlue Consulting.*

[17] Persistent's "Enterprise Readiness for AI" and *MIT Sloan Management Review*'s big ideas on AI business strategy argue that AI becomes a strategic asset when embedded in roadmapping, governance, and measurement.

## Key topics explored in this chapter:

- Why Ethics Must Be Operationalized
- Components of an Ethical AI Framework
- Risk-Tiered Ethics in Practice

# WAY 22

# Embed Ethical Guidelines


## Abstract

Ethics in AI and analytics cannot depend on ad-hoc reviews or informal norms; they must be built into everyday processes and decisions. This chapter explains how to operationalize ethical principles across the analytics lifecycle by creating clear internal guidelines, establishing oversight structures, and embedding decision checkpoints from design through retirement. It introduces practical mechanisms—such as risk-tiered impact assessments, model and system cards, and continuous monitoring—that make ethical risk management repeatable, proportional, and auditable.


## Objective

After completing this chapter, you will be able to:

- Explain why ethics must be operationalized rather than handled solely through periodic committee reviews.
- Describe the core components of an ethical AI framework, including guidelines, oversight, lifecycle checkpoints, transparency, and training.
- Design lightweight but effective ethical checkpoints throughout the model lifecycle, calibrated to risk tiers.
- Integrate documentation and monitoring practices that support audits, regulatory expectations, and internal learning.
- Build training and communication approaches that foster a culture where ethical concerns are surfaced early and acted upon.
- Balance the need for ethical rigor with the need for speed, experimentation, and innovation in AI initiatives.

# Terms to Know

**AI Ethics Board / Responsible AI Council**[1] - A cross-functional group that oversees high-risk AI initiatives, reviews exceptions, and steers the evolution of ethical guidelines and controls, increasingly recommended by regulators and governance approaches.

**Bias Mitigation**[2] - Techniques used to detect, reduce, or manage unfair differential treatment or outcomes produced by AI systems, through data balancing, algorithm choice, or post-processing corrections, and recognized as a trustworthiness characteristic in AI risk frameworks.

**Ethical AI**[3] - The design, development, deployment, and monitoring of AI systems in ways that align with principles of fairness, transparency, privacy, accountability, safety, and human well-being, as articulated in frameworks such as NIST AI RMF and UNESCO guidance.

**Impact Assessment (AI Impact Assessment)**[4] - A structured evaluation of potential risks and benefits associated with an AI system, focusing on affected populations, fairness, privacy, security, and compliance obligations; promoted as a core governance tool.

**Lifecycle Checkpoints**[5] - Defined moments in the AI development and deployment process where ethical and risk concerns are assessed and documented, and where go/no-go or mitigation decisions are made, spanning ex-ante and ex-post phases.

**Model Card / System Card**[2] - A concise document describing an AI system's intended use, data, evaluation methods, limitations, and known ethical considerations, updated over time to support transparency and governance, referenced in auditing and privacy guidance.

**Operationalization (of ethics)**[6] - Converting high-level values and principles into concrete processes, controls, tools, and metrics that shape day-to-day AI work at scale, often through policy-to-control mappings and integrated risk-management workflows.

**Risk Tiering**[7] - The classification of AI systems into categories (for example, low, medium, high, critical) based on potential impact, sensitivity, and harm, with controls and checkpoints proportional to each tier, mirroring risk-based regulatory approaches.

# Introduction[8]

As AI and advanced analytics move deeper into critical operations—credit decisions, hiring, medical triage, customer targeting—the potential for unintended harm grows. Regulatory scrutiny and public expectations are rising, making "trusty AI" a strategic requirement rather than a branding slogan. Many organizations have drafted responsible-AI principles, but principles alone do not guarantee responsible behavior. Without practical mechanisms embedded in workflows, teams inadvertently deploy models that conflict with stated values or regulatory obligations.

Ethics deserves the same treatment as security or quality: a design constraint and operational discipline built into processes, tools, and governance—not an after-the-fact review. This chapter describes how to embed ethical guidelines and controls directly into the AI lifecycle so every significant model or analytics product passes through consistent, risk-proportional, and documented checks.

## Why Ethics Must Be Operationalized[9]

Ethics becomes operational when it reliably shapes how systems are designed, built, and used—not just how they are discussed. Modern AI systems, often trained on large, heterogeneous datasets, influence high-impact decisions, and even well-intentioned teams can produce biased or privacy-compromising outcomes without structured safeguards.

Accountability is growing: regulations and standards now require evidence of risk assessments, documentation, and incident handling—not just value statements. As organizations run dozens or hundreds of AI projects, relying on informal ethical conversations or a single central review body is impractical. Operationalization does not replace human judgment; it channels and augments it through processes that are repeatable, transparent, risk-tiered, and auditable.

## Components of an Ethical AI Framework[10]

A framework for operationalizing ethics includes five components:

This framework aligns with core functions in NIST's AI Risk Management Framework (Govern, Map, Measure, Manage) and with lifecycle-based guidance from UNESCO's Recommendation on the Ethics of AI.

## Ethical AI Framework

| Component | Key Question | Example Practice |
|---|---|---|
| **Internal Guidelines** | What do our principles mean in practice? | Policy statements mapped to concrete requirements |
| **Oversight Structures** | Who decides on hard trade-offs / exceptions? | Ethics board; risk-tier review process |
| **Lifecycle Checkpoints** | When and how do we assess ethical risk? | Design impact assessments; pre-deploy reviews |
| **Transparency Mechanisms** | How do we explain and audit our systems? | Model cards; logs; versioned decisions |
| **Continuous Training** | How do people learn and feel accountable? | Role-specific training; speak-up channels |

### Internal Guidelines[11]

Ethical work begins with clarity about what responsible AI means for the organization. Guidelines define high-level principles—fairness, transparency, privacy, robustness, safety, human oversight—and map each to specific expectations, such as requiring high-risk models to undergo impact assessments and bias testing across agreed attributes.

Guidelines should cover both internally developed and third-party AI systems, including generative-AI services, ensuring procurement and vendor management follow the same standards. They typically reference external methods (NIST AI RMF, UNESCO, OECD, or sector rules) while tailoring details to the organization's mission, risk appetite, and stakeholder commitments. Clear guidelines provide the policy backbone that tools and processes operationalize.

### Oversight Structures[12]

Oversight bodies ensure ethical guidelines are applied proportionally and consistently. An AI Ethics Board or Responsible AI Council provides governance for high-risk uses, reviews exceptions, and approves or halts deployments in sensitive areas, in line with risk-based regimes such as the EU AI Act.

Membership typically spans data science, business lines, legal, compliance, security, HR, and sometimes external experts or user representatives to bring multiple perspectives to trade-offs. Risk tiering helps scale oversight by categorizing systems (for example, low/medium/high/critical) based on potential impact on individuals, data sensitivity, safety risks, regulatory exposure, and systemic implications, with controls calibrated accordingly.

### Lifecycle Checkpoints[13]

Ethical considerations must appear at multiple lifecycle stages, not just at the end.

- **Concept and design:** Teams conduct proportionate impact assessments to clarify system purpose, stakeholders, potential harms and benefits, and high-level mitigations; high-risk concepts may require explicit go/no-go approval before development.
- **Data readiness:** Data sources are assessed for suitability, consent, representativeness, and potential for bias; documentation captures lineage and constraints.
- **Development and testing:** Bias tests, robustness checks, and privacy/security reviews are integrated into pipelines; results and mitigations are logged.
- **Pre-deployment review:** For higher-risk systems, oversight bodies review model/system cards, test evidence, human-oversight design, and monitoring plans; approvals and conditions are recorded.
- **Deployment and monitoring:** Monitoring plans define metrics, thresholds, and escalation paths for issues such as drift, bias signals, and safety or security incidents; logs and dashboards support ongoing oversight.
- **Operational review and retirement:** Periodic reviews evaluate real-world impact, incidents, and evolving regulations; systems may be recalibrated, restricted, or retired when they no longer meet standards.

Documented checkpoints ensure ethics is baked into workflows rather than bolted on as a late review.

### Transparency Mechanisms[14]

Documentation is the connective tissue that enables understanding, accountability, and auditability. Model or system cards compile information about training and testing data, features, intended uses, limitations, and ethical considerations such as privacy and fairness, enabling both internal decision-making and external explanation.

Decision logs and version control record key design choices, trade-offs, approvals, and model updates with timestamps and owners, supporting audits and incident reconstruction. AI-auditing and data-protection resources highlight model cards, impact assessments, and incident logs as essential artifacts for demonstrating compliant, trustworthy AI and for supporting knowledge transfer.

### Continuous Training[15]

Even the best approach fails if practitioners do not understand it or feel responsible for applying it. Continuous training introduces responsible-AI principles, explains policies and workflows, and uses realistic case studies to illustrate both good and poor practices. Role-specific modules emphasize what product managers, engineers, data scientists, risk officers, and business owners must do differently at each lifecycle stage.

Clear, safe channels for raising concerns—such as confidential reporting lines, ethics champions in teams, or designated contacts in governance bodies—encourage staff to speak up early when they see potential issues. This helps embed ethics into culture rather than treating it as a compliance checkbox.

## Risk-Tiered Ethics in Practice[16]

A simple risk tier matrix can guide which controls apply where, mirroring risk-based regulation.

## Risk Tier Matrix

| Risk Tier | Example Use Case | Controls (Illustrative) |
|---|---|---|
| **Low** | Internal productivity aids, non-sensitive analytics | Basic checklist; brief impact note; model card; light monitoring |
| **Medium** | Marketing targeting, operations optimization | Standard impact assessment; bias checks; model card; periodic review |
| **High** | Credit, hiring, healthcare, safety systems | Detailed impact assessment; ethics-board review; strong monitoring/audits |

This proportionality allows speed to occur at the low end while applying rigor where stakes are highest.

# Case Studies[17]

## Case Study #1: Operationalizing Ethics in Consumer Lending

A large retail bank sought to deploy machine-learning models to refine credit decisions and pricing but recognized that errors or biases could harm vulnerable customers and attract regulatory scrutiny. The bank instituted a responsible-AI framework requiring formal impact assessments and risk-tier classification for any model influencing lending decisions.

Project teams documented model purpose, affected populations, risk tier, and potential fairness issues; the AI Ethics Board reviewed all high-risk applications. During development, teams used fairness-testing tools to compare approval and error rates across demographic segments and iterated on features and sampling strategies to reduce disparities. Before deployment, the board reviewed model cards summarizing data, evaluation results, limitations, monitoring plans, and human-in-the-loop controls, and in production, dashboards tracked fairness and performance metrics with alerts triggering investigations and retraining when patterns shifted.

## Case Study #2: Embedding Ethics in Healthcare Decision Support

A regional healthcare network implemented AI tools to support clinical decisions, such as predicting patient deterioration and recommending care pathways. Clinicians were concerned about over-reliance on opaque algorithms and potential inequities in care.

The organization established a clinical-AI review committee including clinicians, data scientists, ethics officers, and patient representatives. All decision-support tools were required to pass defined checkpoints: clinical-relevance assessment, bias and safety analysis, usability testing, and governance approval. Model cards described intended uses, contraindications, and limitations and were accessible from clinician interfaces, while continuous monitoring tracked both technical performance and patient outcomes across demographic groups, with periodic reviews to adjust models or workflows.

## Case Study #3: Responsible Personalization in Digital Media

A global digital-media platform expanded its use of recommendation algorithms to personalize content feeds but faced concerns about filter bubbles, addictive patterns, and exposure of sensitive groups to harmful content. The company created a responsible-personalization program with three pillars: principles (user agency, safety, diversity of exposure), processes (ethics checkpoints in recommendation development), and tooling (safety and fairness evaluation suites).

Teams were required to run impact assessments considering effects on different cohorts, including minors, and to define guardrails such as content filters, frequency caps, and opt-out mechanisms. Experiments and online tests included diversity and safety metrics, not just engagement, and monitoring systems flagged patterns of excessive exposure to potentially harmful content for certain groups, triggering human review and algorithm adjustments.

# Success Metrics[18]

Use ethical AI metrics to help demonstrate trustworthy AI, improve user trust, and reduce legal or regulatory challenges.

## Ethical AI Metrics

| Metric | Definition | What It Tells You |
|---|---|---|
| **Coverage of Impact Assessments** | % of medium/high-risk AI systems with completed AI impact assessments | Adherence to risk-based ethics processes |
| **Model Card / Documentation Coverage** | % of significant models with current model/system cards | Transparency and audit readiness |
| **Incident and Near-Miss Rate** | No. of recorded ethical incidents / near misses per period and time-to-resolution | Effectiveness of monitoring and response |
| **Fairness / Bias Indicators** | Disparity metrics across key groups (for example, false-positive gaps, precision equality) | Quality of bias detection and mitigation |
| **Training and Awareness Coverage** | % of relevant staff completing responsible-AI training | Cultural uptake of ethical practices |

## Benefits and Organizational Impact[19]

When ethical guidelines are embedded into processes, trust and reputation increase because organizations can demonstrate transparent, responsible AI practices to customers, employees, regulators, and investors. Risk mitigation and resilience improve as issues are detected and addressed early, reducing the likelihood of fines, reputational damage, or disruptive system rollbacks.

Clarity for innovation grows because teams understand boundaries and expectations, enabling faster experimentation within defined ethical and regulatory constraints. Ethics thus becomes a strategic capability that supports sustainable innovation rather than constraining it.

# Practical Advice for Leaders

Operationalizing ethics presents challenges that leaders must actively manage.

- **Balancing speed and oversight:** Overly heavy processes can slow innovation, while controls that are too light miss important risks; risk tiering and proportional controls help strike the right balance.
- **Keeping guidelines current:** As AI techniques, regulations, and social expectations evolve; policies, templates, and tools must be reviewed and updated regularly.
- **Ensuring broad engagement:** Ethics cannot be siloed in legal or compliance; business, technical, and operations teams must share ownership, with governance that spans functions.

Leaders should respond in specific ways:

- **Mandate risk-tiered impact assessments** for higher-risk systems.
- **Establish an AI Ethics Board** with clear authority and cross-functional membership.
- **Invest in documentation** and monitoring tools integrated with existing MLOps/DevOps pipelines.
- **Recognize and reward teams** that proactively surface and address ethical issues.

# Conclusion[20]

Embedding ethical guidelines into analytics and AI processes is now a core competence for organizations deploying AI at scale. By combining clear principles, structured oversight, risk-tiered lifecycle checkpoints, transparent documentation, and continuous training, organizations can translate values into daily practice.

This operational approach allows them to innovate confidently, manage risk proactively, and maintain the trust of the stakeholders whose lives and livelihoods their AI systems increasingly affect.

# Notes

[1] AI Ethics Boards and Responsible-AI Councils as cross-functional oversight structures are addressed in *NIST AI RMF* and related AI governance resources.

[2] Bias-mitigation techniques and the role of model cards in documenting risk are detailed in *Lumenova AI*'s "AI Risk Assessment Best Practices: *NIST AI RMF* Alignment."

[3] Ethical-AI principles and the NIST *AI Risk Management Framework* are set out in *NIST*'s "*AI Risk Management Framework* (*AI RMF*)" overviews and playbook.

[4] Ethical impact assessments across the lifecycle are addressed in *UNESCO*'s "Ethical Impact Assessment Tool" and related summaries.

[5] Lifecycle checkpoints are drawn from UNESCO's Recommendation on the Ethics of AI and *NIST AI RMF* Playbook.

[6] Operationalizing ethics through policy-to-control mappings, workflows, and metrics is addressed in Diligent and *NIST AI RMF* plain-English guides—including *Dawgen Global*'s "*NIST AI RMF* in Plain English."

[7] Risk-tiering regimes—spanning minimal to high risk—and proportional controls are laid out in the EU AI Act high-level summary (European Commission) and Intellias explainers.

[8] The shift from principles to practice and the imperative to embed ethics in workflows are addressed in *UNESCO Recommendation* commentary and evaluation-community guidance.

[9] Operationalizing ethics is shown to be necessary—driven by complexity, scale, and regulation—in *NIST AI RMF* commentaries and EU AI Act overviews.

[10] Framework components aligned to NIST's Govern/Map/Measure/Manage structure are set out in ISPartners LLC, *NIST AI RMF*, and UNESCO.

[11] Clear internal guidelines covering principles, expectations, and third-party systems are detailed in *LogicGate*'s "Understanding the *NIST AI RMF* Framework" and *NIST AI RMF* materials.

[12] Oversight structures, risk tiering, and cross-functional membership requirements are covered in EU AI Act explainers, Intellias, and NIST AI Resource Center.

[13] Lifecycle-embedded checkpoints spanning design, data, development, deployment, monitoring, and retirement are drawn from *NIST AI RMF* Playbook and UNESCO's Ethical Impact Assessment.

[14] Transparency and documentation practices—model cards, logs, and incident records—are addressed in *Lumenova AI* and UNESCO's AI-ethics materials.

[15] Continuous training, culture, and speak-up channels are discussed in *UNESCO Recommendation* commentary and *LogicGate.*

[16] On risk-tiered controls for low, medium, and high use cases, see Intellias and EU AI Act explainers.

[17] Case patterns in lending, healthcare, and digital media personalization are examined in AI-ethics case material summarized in UNESCO and AI-ethics commentary sources.

[18] Ethical-AI metrics—impact-assessment coverage, documentation, incidents, fairness, and training—are catalogued in *Lumenova AI, NIST AI RMF,* and ISPartners LLC.

[19] Benefits, organizational impact, and challenges—balancing speed against oversight, navigating evolving guidance, and establishing shared ownership—are discussed in EU AI Act implementation and *NIST AI RMF* practice guides.

[20] The conclusion that embedding ethics is a core competence for scaled AI draws on *NIST AI RMF, UNESCO Recommendation,* and governance best-practice summaries.

## Key topics explored in this chapter:

- The Data Value Chain and Where Agents Fit
- Understanding AI Agents in the Data Value Chain
- Orchestration Patterns and Where to Use Them
- Governance, Risk, and Human-in-the-Loop Control
- Core Benefits of AI-Driven Orchestration

# WAY 23

# Orchestrate Data Value Chains


## Abstract

Maximizing the value of enterprise data requires orchestrating every stage of the data value chain as a coherent whole—from sourcing and preparation through modeling, decision integration, and impact measurement. Fragmented tooling, manual handoffs, and siloed ownership have historically created latency, quality issues, and underused insights across analytics programs. Agentic AI and multi-agent systems now enable a new level of autonomous, adaptive coordination, where specialized agents manage data quality, harmonization, model lifecycle, and operational execution across integrated workflows. This chapter presents conceptual and architectural methods for orchestrating end-to-end data value chains with AI agents, explains orchestration patterns, and details implementation practices that balance automation with human oversight, security, and governance.


## Objective

After completing this chapter, you will be able to:

- Describe the concept of a data value chain and why end-to-end orchestration matters for AI and decisioning.
- Explain what AI agents and multi-agent systems are and how specialized agents can be deployed across the value chain.
- Understand common orchestration patterns—such as pipeline, parallel, supervisor, goal-driven, and market-based—and when to use them.
- Identify benefits and risks of AI-driven orchestration, including throughput, resilience, observability, and compliance.

- Outline practical steps for implementing agentic orchestration with appropriate governance, risk-tiered autonomy, and human-in-the-loop control.
- Use example metrics and case patterns to design, monitor, and continuously improve orchestrated data ecosystems.

# Terms to Know

**Agent Orchestration**[1] - The coordination of multiple AI agents—defining roles, interactions, control patterns, and guardrails—so they collectively deliver a coherent outcome, often using orchestration methods and patterns.

**AI Agent**[2] - An autonomous software entity that uses AI techniques to perceive context, reason about options, and act toward goals within defined constraints, typically through tools, APIs, and policies.

**Data Quality Agent**[3] - An AI agent dedicated to monitoring, validating, cleaning, and enriching data—often continuously—using rules and learned patterns to prevent or remediate issues across pipelines and BI layers.

**Data Value Chain**[4] - The end-to-end sequence of activities through which raw data is acquired, transformed, analyzed, and translated into decisions and measurable business impact.

**End-to-End Orchestration**[5] - Coordinated management of all stages of the data value chain, rather than local optimization of individual components or pipelines in isolation; often implemented via unified workflow and observability platforms.

**Multi-Agent System (MAS)**[2] - A collection of interacting AI agents that coordinate or compete to achieve individual or shared objectives within a shared environment, using orchestration patterns such as pipeline, parallel, and hierarchical/supervisor.

**Orchestration Pattern**[1] - A reusable design for how agents interact and are coordinated—for example, sequential (pipeline), parallel, supervisor/hierarchical, event-driven, or market-based negotiation.

# Introduction

Most organizations can point to dozens of analytics pipelines—some feeding dashboards, others training models, still others powering reports—often with different standards, schedules, and owners. Without orchestration, these networks generate duplicated effort, inconsistent metrics, manual reconciliation, and slow reactions to change, mirroring challenges documented in end-to-end supply-chain research.

The concept of a data value chain reframes analytics as an integrated system rather than a collection of tasks: sourcing, ingestion, quality control, harmonization, feature engineering, model development, deployment, decision integration, and impact measurement. When these stages are orchestrated end-to-end, organizations can move from sporadic insight delivery to continuous, adaptive decision support. Recent advances in agentic AI make it possible to coordinate this chain more autonomously.

## The Data Value Chain and Where Agents Fit[1,4]

End-to-end orchestration starts with understanding the stages of the data value chain and mapping where agents can add value.

## Data Value Chain with Agent Roles

| Stage | Purpose | Typical Agent Roles |
|---|---|---|
| **Sourcing and Ingestion** | Acquire and load raw data | Ingestion agents; schema-detection agents |
| **Quality and Validation** | Ensure data is complete, consistent, timely | Data-quality agents; anomaly-detection agents |
| **Harmonization and Modeling View** | Align schemas and entities; build shared views | Data-harmonization and entity-resolution agents |
| **Feature Engineering and Training** | Create features; train and evaluate models | Feature-engineering agents; model-lifecycle agents |
| **Deployment and Decisioning** | Serve models; embed outputs into workflows | Serving agents; decision-support and routing agents |
| **Monitoring and Impact Measurement** | Track technical and business performance | Monitoring agents; KPI-tracking agents |

Process-mining tools and architecture diagrams can help reveal how these stages currently operate, where manual handoffs and failure points exist, and where agents can be introduced incrementally. Multi-agent orchestrators, integrated with existing data platforms, can then coordinate these roles using patterns suited to each stage.

## Understanding AI Agents in the Data Value Chain[2,3]

AI agents differ from traditional scripts or workflow rules in autonomy, adaptability, and collaboration. They perceive state (for example, data profiles, model metrics, queue lengths), select actions under constraints, and coordinate with other agents through orchestration frameworks.

Within the data value chain, common roles include:

- **Data-quality agents** that continuously profile data streams, detect anomalies, validate constraints, and apply corrections or escalate issues; they can detect schema changes, unexpected nulls, or freshness violations and trigger remediation or alerts.
- **Data-harmonization agents** that map heterogeneous schemas into a common model, reconcile entity identities, and keep master records aligned, reducing downstream reconciliation work.
- **Model-lifecycle agents** that automate training, retraining, evaluation, and deployment, scheduling jobs based on data freshness, performance drift, or policy changes and routing evaluation results to humans when needed.
- **Insight and reporting agents** that use natural-language and visualization capabilities to assemble reports, answer ad-hoc questions, and tailor outputs to stakeholder needs.
- **Operational-orchestration agents** that tie analytics outcomes to operational systems by triggering tasks in ERP, CRM, or workflow platforms, monitoring KPIs, and escalating exceptions.

In a multi-agent ecosystem, agents share context via unified data layers, active metadata, or event buses and coordinate actions through orchestration patterns rather than operating as isolated bots.

## Orchestration Patterns and Where to Use Them[1]

Different orchestration patterns suit different parts of the value chain and different risk profiles as illustrated in the table that follows.

## Orchestration Pattern Matrix

| Pattern | Description | Best Fit Use Cases |
|---|---|---|
| **Pipeline (Sequential)** | Agents chained in sequence; each agent's output feeds the next | Batch ETL, nightly reporting, model-training flows |
| **Parallel** | Agents work concurrently and merge results | Cross-table validations; multiple model candidates in parallel |
| **Supervisor / Hierarchical** | Central orchestrator routes tasks, evaluates outputs, handles exceptions | Complex multi-step workflows; compliance-critical flows |
| **Goal-Driven** | Agents optimize toward explicit objectives and constraints | Personalization, dynamic pricing, multi-objective planning |
| **Market / Negotiation** | Agents bid for tasks or resources | Capacity allocation, compute scheduling, logistics routing |
| **Event-Driven (Choreography)** | Agents react to published events without a single coordinator | Asynchronous enrichment, telemetry, side-car tasks |

Combining patterns is common. A common example is a supervisor-controlled pipeline for high-risk decisions with parallel validation agents to speed checks and event-driven enrichment for non-essential metadata updates.

## Governance, Risk, and Human-in-the-Loop Control[4]

AI-driven orchestration changes how work is done, so governance and human oversight must be explicit. Risk-tiered autonomy enables low-risk tasks (such as schema tagging or non-sensitive quality checks) to be handled autonomously, while higher-risk decisions (for example, large inventory shifts, pricing changes, or regulatory reports) are proposed by agents for human approval.

Human-in-the-loop patterns—such as approval gates, interruptible flows, and fallback escalation—allow people to intervene at critical junctures, aligning with governance guidance that emphasizes human oversight for higher-risk AI decisions. Policy-as-code and access controls help ensure agents operate within defined data and system boundaries, with role-based controls and logging aligned to data-governance and security policies.

Designs must anticipate failure modes, including loops, deadlocks, silent failures, and conflicting actions; clear incident routes, rollback strategies, and audit-first logging—often supported by data-observability tools—are essential. Agent orchestration should plug into the broader AI-governance stack, including model-risk management, responsible-AI oversight, and security and compliance processes.

### Core Benefits of AI-Driven Orchestration[5]

When well governed, agentic orchestration delivers tangible benefits.

- **Higher speed:** Agent-driven monitoring and remediation can significantly reduce end-to-end latency from data arrival to decision and cut data downtime.
- **Better reliability and quality:** Continuous, autonomous checks increase data reliability, improving time-to-detection and time-to-resolution for issues and raising trust in downstream analytics and AI.
- **Resilience and scalability:** Distributed agents can reroute tasks or degrade gracefully when components fail, and new agents or checks can be introduced without redesigning entire flows.
- **Improved observability and compliance:** Orchestration layers with rich logging create detailed audit trails for compliance and internal assurance.

Analyst and vendor reports describe agentic data-quality and orchestration platforms that reduce critical incidents and improve SLA adherence when embedded into data operations.

## Success Metrics[3]

Orchestration metrics, like those presented in the following table, work best when they're visible on shared dashboards and reviewed in data and AI-governance forums. Reductions in incidents, time-to-detection, time-to-resolution, and improvements in SLA adherence are commonly highlighted as primary indicators of success.

## Orchestration Metrics

| Metric | Definition | What It Tells You |
|---|---|---|
| **End-to-End Latency** | Time from data creation to decision or action | Speed of the value chain |
| **Data Incident Rate** | No. of significant data-pipeline/quality incidents per period | Overall reliability |
| **Time-to-Detection (TTD)** | Avg. time to detect data or orchestration issues | Monitoring effectiveness |
| **Time-to-Resolution (TTR)** | Avg. time from detection to resolution | Operational responsiveness |
| **Automated vs Manual Interventions** | % of issues or decisions handled fully by agents vs by humans | Maturity of agentic orchestration |
| **SLA Adherence** | % of pipelines/decisions meeting freshness and uptime SLAs | Reliability for stakeholders |

## Practical Implementation Considerations

Moving to agent-orchestrated value chains is as much about the organization's operating model as it is technology.

- **Map one critical value chain:** Use workshops and, where helpful, process-mining tools to document current flows, bottlenecks, and manual handoffs for a domain such as supply chain, customer data, or regulatory reporting.
- **Pilot narrow, high-impact scenarios:** Examples include 24/7 agentic data-quality monitoring for regulatory data or end-to-end orchestration for a single product line.
- **Integrate with existing platforms:** Use standardized APIs and connectors to connect agents to data lakes, warehouses, workflow tools, and BI platforms rather than rebuilding everything.
- **Instrument for observability from the start:** Ensure agents and orchestrators emit logs, traces, and metrics so teams can debug and optimize end-to-end flows.
- **Invest in skills and change management:** Data engineers, analysts, and business users need training on agentic patterns, supervision responsibilities, and new workflows.

These steps reduce risk and build confidence as organizations transition from fragmented pipelines to orchestrated ecosystems.

# Case Studies[5]

## Case Study #1: Multi-Agent Orchestration in Global Supply Chain Planning

A global consumer-goods manufacturer faced chronic volatility in its supply chain due to demand shocks, transport delays, and supplier disruptions. Traditional planning systems reconciled data from sales, production, logistics, and external feeds only every few days, leaving planners reactive and reliant on manual interventions.

The company implemented a multi-agent orchestration layer on top of existing planning and execution systems. Specialized ingestion and quality agents pulled real-time signals from POS data, distributor inventories, IoT sensors, weather services, and transport networks; harmonization agents aligned these to a global data model. Planning agents continuously generated demand and supply scenarios, logistics agents evaluated routing options, and risk agents scored disruption likelihood based on external news and event feeds.

A supervisor agent coordinated these roles against global objectives such as service-level targets, cost constraints, and sustainability metrics, surfacing recommended actions to human planners through dashboards. Planners retained authority over major decisions like large inventory reallocations or supplier switches, while agents autonomously adjusted low-risk parameters such as shipment sequencing or safety-stock levels within approved bands. Over roughly 18 months, the manufacturer reported faster responses to disruptions, fewer stockouts and expedited shipments, lower overall inventory, and improved traceability of planning decisions via orchestrator logs.

## Case Study #2: Agentic Data-Quality Orchestration in Financial Services

A large financial-services firm struggled with inconsistent data quality across customer, product, and transaction systems, undermining analytics, regulatory reporting, and customer-facing AI services. Data stewards spent much of their time reacting to issues, and many incidents were discovered late by business users rather than by monitoring.

The firm adopted an agentic data-quality platform integrated with its data lake and core systems. Data-quality agents continuously profiled data, tracking signals such as schema changes, rule violations, and data downtime; when anomalies occurred, agents either auto-remediated known issues or raised prioritized alerts to data stewards. Harmonization agents resolved duplicate entities across systems, and governance agents enforced masking and access rules in non-production environments.

A supervisor agent orchestrated onboarding for new data sources by triggering schema inference, rule assignment, test runs, and registration in the catalog before enabling production use. Human stewards shifted focus to configuring rules, reviewing exceptions, and improving policies, with agents providing 24/7 monitoring and first-line correction. Over the first year, the firm saw fewer critical data incidents affecting regulatory reports and customer journeys, better TTD and TTR for quality issues, and shorter onboarding times for new sources.

## Practical Advice for Leaders[4,5]

Leaders play a decisive role in moving from fragmented pipelines to orchestrated data value chains. They can:

- **Frame orchestration as a business capability** that improves decision speed, reliability, and resilience rather than as a purely technical initiative.
- **Start with one strategically important value chain** and sponsor cross-functional mapping and orchestration pilots with clear metrics.
- **Insist on risk-tiered autonomy and human oversight,** defining where agents can act autonomously, where they only recommend, and where humans must approve.
- **Integrate orchestration metrics** like latency, incident rates, and automation share into regular data and AI-governance reviews.
- **Invest in skills and communication** so teams understand new patterns, their roles in supervising agents, and how early successes connect to strategic goals.

This leadership stance helps ensure that agentic orchestration strengthens, rather than destabilizes, enterprise decision infrastructures.

# Conclusion

Orchestrating end-to-end data value chains with AI agents represents a shift from brittle, static pipelines to dynamic, self-managing ecosystems. Instead of a tangle of point solutions and manual fixes, organizations can design multi-agent architectures where specialized agents coordinate to maintain data quality, adapt models, and drive operational decisions in near real time.

Achieving this requires clear mapping of the data value chain, thoughtful choice of orchestration patterns, well-tested governance and human-in-the-loop controls, and disciplined measurement. When done well, agentic orchestration turns the data value chain into an adaptive infrastructure that enhances resilience, accelerates insight-to-action, and amplifies the strategic impact of AI across the enterprise.

# Notes

[1] Agent orchestration and multi-agent patterns—including sequential/pipeline, parallel/concurrent, supervisor/hierarchical, goal-driven/adaptive, market/negotiation, and event-driven/choreography—are developed in *Azure Architecture Center*'s "AI Agent Orchestration *Patterns*"; *Dynamiq Blog*'s "Agent Orchestration *Patterns* in Multi-Agent Systems: Linear and Adaptive Approaches with Dynamiq"; *Google Developers Blog*'s "Developer's Guide to Multi-Agent *Patterns* in ADK"; *Kore.ai Blog*'s "Choosing the Right Orchestration Pattern for Multi-Agent Systems"; and Datagrid Blog's "How to Orchestrate AI Agents for Unified Data Access."

[2] AI agent and multi-agent system (MAS) concepts—autonomous entities perceiving environment, reasoning under constraints, selecting actions via tools/APIs, and collaborating in shared settings—are covered in *Microsoft Azure* Architecture Center guidance on agent design; *Google Developers Blog*'s "Developer's Guide to Multi-Agent *Patterns* in ADK" (coordinator, hierarchical, human-in-the-loop); and related architecture resources emphasizing perception, reasoning, action, and interaction.

[3] Data quality agent capabilities and data-reliability metrics—including continuous profiling, anomaly detection, constraint validation, auto-remediation, escalation, schema-change handling, freshness monitoring, end-to-end latency, data downtime/incident rate, time-to-detection (TTD), time-to-resolution (TTR), SLA adherence, and automated vs. manual intervention ratios—are detailed in *Acceldata*'s "Data Quality Agent | *Acceldata* ADM" and *Telmai Blog*'s "Telmai Brings Autonomous-Ready Data Observability for the Agentic AI Era."

[4] Data value chain, end-to-end orchestration, and governance—spanning sourcing/ingestion through quality control, harmonization, feature engineering, modeling, deployment, decision integration, monitoring, and impact measurement, with holistic alignment, digital enablement, capability roadmaps, agile program management, full-process integration, visibility, real-time responsiveness, risk-tiered autonomy, human-in-the-loop oversight, policy-as-code, and alignment with AI governance stacks—are drawn from *BCG*'s "A Unified Approach to End-to-End Supply Chain Transformation" and *Inbound Logistics*' "End-to-End Supply Chain: Meaning, Benefits, and How to Implement" (applied to data contexts).

[5] Agentic orchestration benefits and case experience—reductions in critical incidents, improved SLA adherence, faster time-to-detection/resolution, enhanced resilience, lower latency, better reliability, autonomous monitoring/remediation, continuous real-time data trust, and minimal human intervention in quality/harmonization/alerting—are reported in vendor outcomes from *Acceldata*'s data quality agent, Telmai's autonomous-ready observability, and related agentic data platforms.

## Key topics explored in this chapter:

- Comparing Traditional Analytics and AI at Scale
- Nuances of Scaling AI
- Best Practices for Scaling Analytics and AI Initiatives
- Operational Challenges in Practice

# WAY 24

# Scale Analytics and AI Initiatives Sustainably


## Abstract

Growth in analytics and AI introduces new layers of technical, organizational, and ethical complexity. Scaling traditional analytics typically means more reports, more data, and more users; scaling AI means managing evolving models, real-time decision workflows, and amplified risk. This chapter contrasts traditional analytics scale-up with AI scale-up, highlighting differences in lifecycle management, governance, and culture. It then presents best practices for prioritizing initiatives, allocating resources, building adaptive architectures, and embedding governance and monitoring. Consider this chapter a structured playbook for scaling analytics and AI programs responsibly. Its emphasis is on "scaling right, not just scaling fast," so that AI growth enhances value without overwhelming systems, people, or risk controls.


## Objective

After completing this chapter, you will be able to:

- Distinguish between scaling traditional analytics and scaling AI in terms of lifecycle, risk, and integration.
- Identify key nuances that make AI scale-up uniquely challenging.
- Apply best-practice principles for prioritization, resource allocation, governance, and agile processes at scale.
- Recognize common operational challenges—data diversity, technical debt, talent constraints—and plan mitigation strategies.
- Draw lessons from real-world patterns to design sustainable, enterprise-wide AI scaling initiatives.

# Terms to Know

**Model Lifecycle Management**[1] - The end-to-end process of designing, training, validating, deploying, monitoring, and retraining AI models, typically supported by MLOps or ModelOps practices.

**Scaling Analytics**[2] - Expanding the reach and sophistication of data analysis and reporting, usually through more users, data sources, and use cases, often with a primarily descriptive or diagnostic focus.

**Scaling AI**[2] - Growing the number, scope, and impact of AI/ML systems embedded in operations, including more models, domains, and automated decisions, under continuous monitoring and governance.

**Sustainable Scale**[3] - Growth in AI and analytics that maintains quality, governance, and organizational capacity, avoiding collapse under complexity, risk, or cost—often framed as "scaling right, not just scaling fast."

**Technical Debt (AI/ML)**[4] - The accumulated cost of quick, suboptimal design choices in models, data pipelines, and infrastructure that make future change and maintenance difficult, increasingly recognized as a major constraint on AI ROI.

**Value-Based Prioritization**[5] - A structured method of choosing initiatives based on expected business impact, feasibility, risk, and time-to-value rather than technical novelty alone, recommended in AI-strategy and portfolio-management guidance.

# Introduction

Many organizations begin their data journeys with a small analytics team building dashboards, descriptive reports, and ad-hoc analyses. Scaling that world often means adding more users, more data sources, and better self-service tools, which extends visibility but largely keeps humans in control of decisions.

AI changes the nature of scale. When models are embedded into front-line processes—from pricing and recommendations to credit decisions and fraud detection—systems can make or influence thousands or millions of decisions per day. Scaling AI therefore amplifies both benefit and risk: small flaws can propagate widely, and governance gaps can quickly become enterprise-level problems. This chapter examines what makes AI scale-up distinct, explores important nuances, and outlines how to grow capabilities without sacrificing agility, safety, or trust.

## Comparing Traditional Analytics and AI at Scale[2]

Traditional analytics and AI share foundations—data, infrastructure, and skills—but diverge sharply in how scale behaves.

## How Scale Behaves: Analytics vs AI

| Dimension | Traditional Analytics at Scale | AI at Scale |
|---|---|---|
| **Primary Output** | Human-interpreted reports and dashboards | Embedded, often automated, decisions in workflows |
| **Change Frequency** | Periodic updates to reports and metrics | Continuous model updates and data-driven adaptation |
| **Failure Impact** | Misleading insight for a limited set of users | Widespread incorrect or unfair decisions at speed |
| **Operational Integration** | Mostly "side-by-side" with processes | Deeply integrated into ERP, CRM, and operational systems |
| **Monitoring Focus** | Data loads and report refresh | Model performance, drift, bias, and system health |
| **Governance Scope** | Data quality, access, and definitions | Data plus model behavior, explainability, impact, and ethics |
| **Typical Talent Mix** | BI developers and analysts | Data scientists, ML/MLOps engineers, product owners, and risk specialists |

Traditional analytics scale-up historically involves standardizing data pipelines for reporting, expanding BI platforms and self-service tools, and training users to explore dashboards and run queries. These efforts extend visibility and literacy but depend on manual interpretation and action; reports may be updated regularly, but decisions occur at human cadence.

Scaling AI introduces dynamic data ingestion from diverse, often real-time sources; automated decisioning that triggers actions in operational systems; continuous monitoring of models for performance, drift, and bias; and deep integration with ERP, CRM, and customer-facing systems. The combination of automation, adaptivity, and embeddedness means AI scale-up inherently involves managing systemic risk, not just throughput.

## Nuances of Scaling AI

### 1. Continuous Learning and Model Lifecycle

AI models are not static assets; they degrade over time as data, behavior, and environments change. Sustaining performance at scale requires automated pipelines for retraining on new data, versioning and rollback mechanisms, and structured impact evaluation (such as A/B testing) to ensure new versions improve outcomes. As portfolios grow, model-by-model manual management becomes untenable. Standardized lifecycle automation—covering data preparation, training, validation, deployment, monitoring, and retirement—becomes essential for scalable, reliable AI.

### 2. Operational Integration and Automation

AI systems increasingly sit inside processes rather than beside them. Models may score transactions in real time for fraud risk, recommend next-best actions in contact centers, or adjust prices and inventory dynamically. Scaling this integration requires robust architecture—APIs, microservices, and event streams—and careful design of failover modes and human overrides. As enterprises embed AI deeper into operational systems, latency, uptime, and resilience become as important as accuracy.

### 3. Governance and Compliance Complexity

As AI use widens, organizations must govern not just data but also model behavior and its human impact. This includes ethical and fairness standards, regulatory compliance (for example, explainability, audit trails, non-discrimination), and internal policies on acceptable uses and escalation paths. Scaling AI without scaling governance exposes organizations to legal, reputational, and societal risk. Risk-management practice calls for integrating AI into enterprise risk and compliance models rather than managing it as an isolated technical concern.

### 4. Talent and Cultural Challenges

Scaling AI requires a broader mix of roles than traditional BI: data scientists and ML engineers to design and operationalize models, platform engineers to maintain infrastructure, product owners and domain experts to translate business needs into AI products, and risk/legal/ethics specialists to guide responsible deployment. Culturally, organizations must shift from project-based mindsets to product-like thinking, with ongoing ownership, iteration, and learning. Without such shifts, organizations often accumulate "pilot sprawl" rather than durable capabilities; embedding AI into "how we work" is as much a social and organizational project as a technical one.

**5. Risk and Impact Amplification**

When a report is wrong, a small group of decision-makers may be misled. When a scaled AI system is wrong, thousands of automated decisions can be affected quickly. Errors or biases can propagate across customer segments, markets, or processes; fixing issues requires not only model adjustments but also analysis of prior decisions and potential remediation. This amplification demands more stringent validation, testing, and monitoring before and after deployment. Practices such as stress-testing, red-teaming, and continuous monitoring become essential safeguards at scale.

## Best Practices for Scaling Analytics and AI Initiatives[5,6,7]

### Prioritization Aligned with Business Value

Clear approaches are needed to decide which analytics and AI initiatives to scale. Value-based prioritization methods recommend scoring use cases on strategic alignment, impact potential, feasibility, risk, and time-to-value. Balanced portfolios mix quick wins that build credibility with longer-horizon bets that can change trajectories, avoiding dilution of resources across too many pilots. Priorities should be revisited as the business environment and capabilities evolve so the scaled portfolio remains aligned with strategy rather than legacy choices.

### Adaptive Resource Allocation

Static staffing models rarely work as AI portfolios grow. Sustainable approaches form flexible, cross-functional squads around high-priority initiatives and use a mix of internal teams, partners, and vendors with clear ownership and knowledge-transfer plans. Investment in upskilling—data literacy for business staff and MLOps/architecture skills for technical teams—is consistently cited as essential for sustainable AI scale. Because talent is scarce, organizations must design for leverage via reusable platforms and shared assets, not just hiring more specialists.

### Governance Evolution

Governance has to broaden as AI scales. Data governance should extend to AI governance, specifically model documentation, approval processes, risk classification, monitoring requirements, and clear ownership. Multi-layered bodies (for example, steering committees and AI risk or ethics boards) that integrate business, technical, and risk perspectives are increasingly recommended. Risk-based approaches define tiered governance: lighter-touch for low-risk internal optimizations, heavier for customer- or citizen-facing models with material impact. Think "proportionate governance"—auditable where stakes are high, simplified where risk is low.

### Agile Processes and Pipelines

Agility is both more important and more challenging at scale. Effective practices include:

- Agile delivery with short iterations, frequent stakeholder feedback, and clear acceptance criteria.
- Automation of data pipelines and model training/testing/deployment (CI/CD for ML) to reduce manual handoffs and errors.
- Standardized templates for experiments, evaluations, and rollouts to make good practices repeatable.

Designing for repeatability rather than heroics—standardized pipelines, shared templates, and automated checks—helps teams adapt to new data, regulations, and strategic shifts without losing control.

### Enterprise Architecture and Infrastructure

Scaling AI and analytics without scalable infrastructure quickly hits a wall. Architectural principles include:

- Cloud-native platforms that elastically scale compute and storage.
- Modular, API-driven services to integrate models with existing systems.
- Centralized yet flexible data platforms that support batch, streaming, and real-time use cases.
- Monitoring and observability for data pipelines, models, and downstream services.

Investing early in shared platforms reduces duplication, accelerates future initiatives, and improves governance by centralizing model visibility and controls.

### Monitoring, Metrics, and Feedback

At scale, metrics and feedback loops become the nervous system of AI operations. Organizations should track:

- Model performance (accuracy, stability, drift), fairness metrics, and system health.
- Business outcomes tied to AI interventions—such as fraud-loss reduction, conversion uplift, or complaint rates.
- Portfolio-level metrics that help assess the health of scaling efforts.

# Success Metrics

## Scaling Analytics and AI Health Metrics

Tracking these signals supports proactive refactoring and portfolio decisions rather than reactive fixes.

| Metric | Definition | What It Tells You |
|---|---|---|
| **Portfolio Strategic Coverage** | % of AI/analytics initiatives mapped to strategic objectives | Alignment with enterprise strategy |
| **Time-to-Production** | Avg. time from idea to first production deployment | Delivery efficiency and pipeline maturity |
| **Model Fleet Health** | % of production models with active monitoring, retraining, and owners | Lifecycle robustness and governance |
| **Incident and Rollback Rate** | No. of significant AI incidents or rollbacks per period | Stability and governance effectiveness |
| **Technical Debt Burden** | Share of models/pipelines flagged for refactor or consolidation | Sustainability of the stack over time |
| **Talent Sustainability** | Signals such as attrition in key AI roles or % of staff trained | Capacity to sustain scale |
| **Strategic KPI Uplift from AI** | Changes in core KPIs attributable to AI | Real business value vs added complexity |

## Operational Challenges in Practice

Even with good design, organizations encounter recurring operational challenges.

- **Data diversity and volume:** New geographies, products, and channels introduce additional data sources and formats, making quality, lineage, and integration ongoing tasks rather than one-off projects.
- **Balancing flexibility and standardization:** Over-standardization can smother innovation, while excessive flexibility leads to incompatible systems and governance gaps, echoing concerns in data-mesh and AI-governance discussions.
- **Technical debt:** Unmanaged technical debt can consume a large share of development time and materially constrain AI ROI; proactive tracking and refactoring can significantly boost returns.
- **Talent retention and burnout:** High demand for AI expertise can lead to overextended teams; recommended responses include pacing initiatives, rotating staff between high-pressure and foundational work, and providing clear career paths in data and AI.

Recognizing these challenges early makes them easier to manage before they become systemic.

# Case Studies[6]

## Case Study #1: Enterprise-Wide AI Scaling at a Global Retailer

A global retail group began its AI initiative with a handful of pilots—demand-forecasting models in one region, a personalization engine in e-commerce, and fraud detection for online payments. These pilots delivered promising results but were isolated, each with its own pipelines and deployment methods.

Leadership decided to scale AI across markets and business lines to support growth and efficiency. The retailer created an AI roadmap aligned with strategic goals such as improving margin via better inventory, lifting customer-lifetime value, and reducing fraud losses. Use cases were prioritized based on impact, feasibility, and dependencies, allowing the company to identify "platform" capabilities—like forecasting and personalization—that could be reused across brands and geographies.

A central data and AI platform was established on cloud infrastructure, providing shared data services, model registries, experiment tracking, and monitoring. An AI governance board defined approval thresholds, documentation requirements, and risk classifications for models, focusing more stringent review on customer-facing and high-impact decisions. Agile, cross-functional squads formed around major initiatives, blending data scientists, engineers, merchandisers, supply-chain experts, and risk managers.

Over three years, the retailer refactored pilots into modular services: the forecasting engine was adapted to multiple regions via configuration rather than custom code, and the personalization engine supported multiple channels and brands from a common core. Dashboards gave executives visibility into performance and risk across the AI portfolio. The retailer reported improved inventory turns, higher conversion rates, and lower fraud losses, supported by a stable governance and platform foundation.

## Case Study #2: Scaling AI Risk Management in Financial Services

A large financial-services firm initially used AI models in pockets—for example, fraud detection in cards, churn prediction in retail banking, and marketing-campaign optimization—each managed by separate teams with different tools and processes. As regulators and boards increased scrutiny of AI risk, the firm realized it needed a more coherent, scalable approach.

The firm launched an AI scaling and governance program focused on risk-sensitive domains. It mapped existing and planned AI use cases and classified them by impact on customers, financial exposure, and regulatory relevance, prioritizing high-risk models (credit decisioning, fraud blocking, anti-money-laundering systems) for standardized lifecycle management. An enterprise MLOps platform was deployed to centralize model development, testing, deployment, and monitoring.

Policies were updated to require documentation, explainability assessments, fairness checks, and back-testing for high-risk models before production. An AI risk committee—including compliance, legal, risk, and business leaders—reviewed high-impact use cases and monitored incidents. Model owners were assigned for each AI system, with clear responsibilities for performance, monitoring, and remediation.

Regular reviews examined both technical metrics and business outcomes, such as false-positive rates in fraud detection and approval disparities in credit decisioning. Over time, the firm reduced duplicated models, simplified pipelines, and improved its ability to demonstrate control and accountability to regulators, turning AI scaling into a managed, transparent process.

# Practical Advice for Leaders

Leaders determine whether AI scaling becomes a sustainable capability or a sprawl of pilots. They can:

- **Anchor scale in strategy, not tools.** For every major initiative, require a clear link to strategic objectives and how success will be measured; proposals should specify value-based prioritization scores and strategic KPIs, not just accuracy gains.[5]
- **Fund platforms and governance, not just pilots.** Earmark budget for shared data/AI platforms, MLOps capabilities, and AI-governance functions (policies, risk reviews, monitoring) and treat them as enterprise infrastructure.[7]
- **Insist on model ownership and lifecycle plans.** Every production model should have named business and technical owners, defined monitoring and retraining approaches, and escalation paths.[1]
- **Run regular portfolio reviews.** Make trade-offs visible, pausing or retiring low-value or fragile solutions to free capacity for stronger bets.[3]
- **Invest in people and culture.** Launch data/AI literacy programs, reward responsible adoption, and set expectations for sustainable—rather than purely rapid—scaling.[3]

These practices help transform AI from a set of experiments into a durable, enterprise-wide capability.[3]

# Conclusion

Scaling analytics and AI sustainably is not simply a matter of "more data and more models." It requires acknowledging how AI changes the nature of scale: models that learn, systems that act autonomously, and decisions that propagate across the enterprise in real time. Organizations that succeed combine clear strategic prioritization, adaptive resource allocation, strong governance, agile processes, a comprehensive architecture, and intentional culture change.

They invest not only in building new capabilities but also in maintaining and improving them, managing risk, and learning from experience. In doing so, they transform AI from a cluster of pilots into a durable engine of competitive advantage.

# Notes

[1] Model lifecycle management and MLOps—end-to-end processes and tooling for training, deploying, monitoring, and retraining AI models—are laid out in *Databricks*'s "AI Governance Best Practices: Frameworks & Principles."

[2] The contrast between scaling analytics and scaling AI—traditional scale-up versus embedded decisioning, continuous learning, and heightened risk—is drawn in *AuditBoard*'s "Scaling AI and Analytics in Audit Programs: A Playbook" and *AWS*'s "Enabling AI Adoption at Scale Through Enterprise Risk Management."

[3] Sustainable scale, governance, and architecture—aligning AI growth with strategy, culture, and shared platforms to avoid pilot sprawl—are addressed in *Databricks*'s "AI Governance Best Practices" and AWS's enterprise risk management guidance.

[4] Technical debt in models and pipelines—and its constraining effect on AI ROI—is examined in IBM Institute for Business Value AI insights and *SentinelOne*'s "AI Risk Management: A Comprehensive Guide 101."

[5] Structured scoring for AI initiatives—impact, feasibility, risk, and time-to-value—is developed in *Breakthrough Growth*'s value-first guidance and *FinOps Foundation*'s "Unlocking AI Business Value With FinOps."

[6] Scaling case patterns in retail and financial services—via shared platforms, governance, and cross-functional teams—are detailed in Deloitte's "Scaling AI for Sustainable Value in Insurance" and *AuditBoard*'s scaling playbook.

[7] AI governance and risk management—model behavior, explainability, fairness, and regulatory alignment—are examined in *Databricks*'s "AI Governance Best Practices," *SentinelOne*'s AI risk guide, and AWS's enterprise risk management framework.

# **Part Three:** Technology

In the age of AI, technology is the great enabler that propels productivity and unlocks groundbreaking potential to serve people in innovative ways.

## Key topics explored in this chapter:

- Key Considerations in Technology Selection
- The Business-Technical-Governance (BTG) Selection Model
- Piloting and Proof-of-Concept Strategies
- Integrating Automation and AI into Agile Workflows
- Integration Planning and Change Management
- Emerging Trends and Future-Proofing

# WAY 25

# Choose Strategic AI and Analytics Technology


## Abstract

Strategic technology selection lays the groundwork for successful AI and analytics initiatives. This chapter offers a practical guide to evaluating, piloting, and integrating AI and analytics platforms so they align with business strategy, manage risk effectively, and adapt to emerging capabilities like generative and agentic AI.


## Objective[1]

After completing this chapter, you will be able to:

- Identify and articulate business-driven requirements for AI and analytics platforms across descriptive, diagnostic, predictive, prescriptive, and generative use cases.
- Evaluate AI/ML and analytics technologies with a repeatable framework that balances performance, scalability, security, governance, and user experience.
- Compare cloud, hybrid, and on-premises deployment options using total cost of ownership (TCO) and business value, not just license price.
- Design and run focused pilots and proofs of concept (POCs) that test business value, technical fit, and adoption risk before large-scale commitments.
- Plan for integration, change management, and governance so chosen platforms become part of a sustainable enterprise analytics operating model.

# Terms to Know

**Agentic AI**[2] - AI systems that can autonomously plan, execute, and adapt sequences of actions (often across tools or services) to achieve goals within defined constraints and governance controls.

**Analytics Platform**[1] - An integrated environment that supports data ingestion, storage, processing, analysis, visualization, and often AI/ML model development and deployment.

**AutoML**[3] - Automated machine learning capabilities that streamline data preparation, feature engineering, model selection, training, and tuning, lowering the expertise threshold to build useful models.

**Business Value Framework**[4] - A structured way of linking platform features and use cases to measurable outcomes such as revenue growth, cost reduction, risk mitigation, and experience improvement.

**Cloud-Native Analytics**[5] - Platforms architected specifically for cloud environments, typically separating compute and storage and offering elastic scaling and managed services.

**Data Governance**[6] - Policies, processes, roles, and tools that ensure data is accurate, secure, compliant, and used responsibly across its lifecycle, especially in AI/ML contexts.

**Federated Analytics**[7] - An approach that enables analysis across decentralized data sources without centralizing all data, often important for regulatory or operational reasons.

**Total Cost of Ownership (TCO)**[8] - The full cost of acquiring, operating, and evolving a platform over time, including licenses, infrastructure, support, and talent.

**Unified Analytics Platform**[1] - A technology environment that brings together data engineering, BI, and data science/ML capabilities in a single, integrated architecture.

# Introduction

Choosing the right analytics and AI/ML technologies lays the foundation for successful programs that deliver sustained business value. The rapid evolution of tools, exploding data volumes, and rising use case complexity make technology choice a strategic—not tactical—decision. It locks in both capability and constraint. The platforms you choose not only influence today's dashboards and models but also shape your ability to experiment, scale, comply with regulations, and govern emerging AI risks over the next decade.

## Key Considerations in Technology Selection[9]

A practical approach to platform selection treats it as a portfolio decision, driven by a consistent set of criteria applied across vendors and architectures. This mindset keeps the focus on business outcomes and risk management. Vendor feature checklists come last.

## The Business-Technical-Governance (BTG) Selection Model

The Business-Technical-Governance Selection Model offers a simple, reusable method for organizing these criteria. Imagine a triangle diagram with three labeled sides: Business, Technical, and Governance. Your candidate platform is represented as a point inside this triangle.

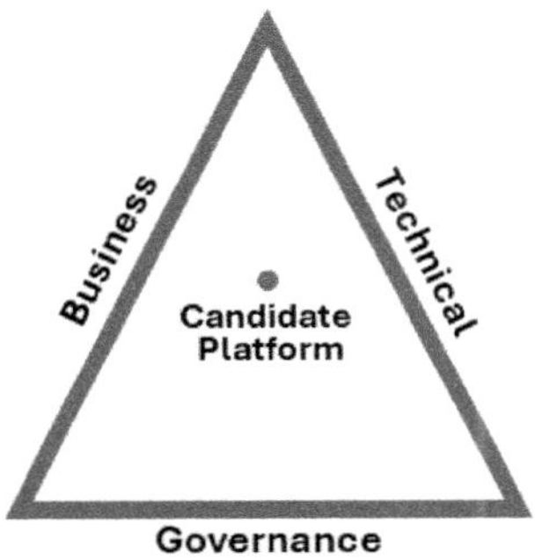


Apply the model like this:

- **Step 1 - Business:** Define the business goals and use cases.
- **Step 2 - Technical:** Identify architectural and integration requirements.
- **Step 3 - Governance:** Document the governance, risk, and compliance constraints.
- **Step 4 - Score** the candidate platform along each axis using common decision criteria and metrics.
- **Step 5 - Visually compare** platforms within the BTG triangle, then decide, pilot, or reject.

Throughout this chapter, when we discuss "core selection dimensions" or portfolio decisions, we use the BTG Selection Model as the organizing framework.

### Alignment with Business Needs[10]

Always begin with your highest-value use cases, not tool features. Clarify whether your priorities involve real-time personalization, operational reporting, regulatory risk models, or AI-assisted decision support, because each stresses the platform differently. Some tools optimize for governed dashboarding, others for data science experimentation, still others for natural language interaction or embedded AI capabilities. In BTG terms, this work defines the Business corner of the selection triangle.

### Performance and Scalability[11]

Modern platforms must support elastic growth in data volume, query complexity, and concurrent users without degrading the user experience. Cloud-native architectures, which separate storage and compute and support workload isolation, allow you to run batch ETL, streaming ingestion, BI, and ML on the same platform without resource contention. When evaluating options, look beyond peak benchmark numbers. Instead, test sustained performance under realistic mixes of queries, data refreshes, and model scoring. These considerations primarily shape the Technical corner of the BTG Selection Model.

### Integration and Ecosystem Compatibility[12]

An analytics platform rarely stands alone; it exists within an ecosystem of ERP, CRM, marketing, clinical, and operational systems. Favor platforms offering well-tested connectors, open APIs, and support for common formats and protocols to reduce integration friction and vendor lock-in. For many enterprises, a "best-of-breed within a coherent architecture" approach often outperforms a single monolithic tool, provided data and identity integration are designed deliberately. This makes integration and ecosystem fit important components of the Technical corner of the BTG model.

### Security, Compliance, and Governance

As AI and analytics move closer to core processes, security and governance become first-order selection criteria, not afterthoughts. Evaluate role-based access control, encryption at rest and in transit, audit logging, data lineage, and support for relevant industry standards (for example, HIPAA, GDPR, PCI-DSS, and sector-specific regulations). Increasingly, you must also scrutinize AI-specific controls like model cataloging, explainability, bias testing, and agent governance to ensure responsible use of generative and agentic AI capabilities. These elements define the Governance corner of the BTG Selection Model.

### User Enablement and Experience

Sustainable value emerges when business users, analysts, and data scientists all find the platform usable. Look for intuitive interfaces, self-service capabilities, collaborative features, thorough documentation, and training resources that reduce the learning curve. At the same time, confirm that advanced users can extend the platform through code, custom models, and APIs rather than remaining constrained by low-code boundaries. User experience links Business (adoption, value realization) and Governance (safe self-service) within the BTG model.

### Cost Structure and TCO

License or subscription price often represents less than half of a platform's true economic impact. Consider infrastructure, storage, data egress, upgrade overhead, and the specialized skills needed to operate and govern the platform. Cloud-native analytics may appear more expensive for steady, predictable workloads, but they can dramatically reduce TCO for variable workloads, faster innovation cycles, and managed services that shift operational burden to the provider. In BTG terms, we evaluate TCO relative to the benefits and risks at each corner of the model, not in isolation.

### Visual Synthesis: Core Selection Dimensions

A simple way to synthesize these criteria involves visualizing platform choices along three intersecting axes: business alignment, technical fit, and governance maturity. A platform that ranks high on technical performance but low on governance and user enablement often underperforms in real organizations. Conversely, a moderately capable platform with strong governance and adoption support can deliver outsized returns precisely because it gets used. This three-axis view is precisely the BTG Selection Model, rendered as a conceptual diagram and scorecard.

## Evaluating Emerging AI and ML Technologies

Integrating AI and machine learning into analytics platforms adds new dimensions to technology selection. Beyond core analytics functions, leaders must assess how AI capabilities impact risk, trust, and long-term maintainability.

### AutoML and Model Management

Platforms with AutoML simplify model creation for non-experts, enabling rapid experimentation across many use cases, from churn to anomaly detection. However, ease of use must pair with comprehensive model management—versioning, approval workflows, performance monitoring, and rollback—to avoid "shadow models" operating outside governance. In BTG terms, AutoML primarily affects Technical fit, while model management proves essential for Governance maturity.

### Explainability and Fairness Tools

Regulators and stakeholders increasingly expect explanations for model behavior and evidence that organizations have assessed and mitigated bias. Prioritize platforms that offer built-in tools for feature importance, scenario sensitivity, bias diagnostics across protected classes, and transparent documentation of training data sources. These capabilities not only support compliance but also build trust with frontline users whose decisions models influence, strengthening both Business adoption and Governance within the BTG model.

### Embedded AI Services

Many leading platforms now embed AI capabilities—like natural language querying, automated insights, anomaly detection, and forecasting—directly into the user experience. These features can accelerate adoption by lowering the barrier from "ask IT for a report" to "ask a conversational interface a question." But they must be configured against curated, governed data to avoid confidently wrong outputs. Embedded AI, therefore, touches all three corners of the BTG model.

### AI Orchestration Support

As organizations deploy more models and AI agents, orchestration—coordinating data prep, model execution, monitoring, and policy enforcement—becomes necessary. Evaluate whether platforms provide pipelines, workflow engines, or integration with MLOps tools that simplify operationalizing models and agents at scale while preserving observability and control. Strong orchestration is a hallmark of Technical fit and Governance maturity within the BTG Selection Model.

### Positioning the BTG Selection Model Among Established Governance Frameworks[13]

Several widely referenced AI governance frameworks guide how organizations manage risk and accountability. The OECD AI Principles emphasize inclusive growth, human-centered values, transparency, robustness, and accountability as core norms for responsible AI. Meanwhile, the NIST AI Risk Management Framework organizes AI risk practices into four functions—Govern, Map, Measure, and Manage. And the EU AI Act introduces a risk-based categorization of AI systems with strict obligations for high-risk uses. The BTG Selection Model aligns with these approachess but operates as a decision lens for comparing platforms. It helps you ask whether a candidate platform will make implementing those principles and risk practices across Business, Technical, and Governance dimensions easier or harder. Essentially, it acts as a pragmatic bridge between high-level governance frameworks and concrete technology selection.

## Piloting and Proof-of-Concept Strategies[14]

Conducting structured pilots minimizes risk and validates platform fit before committing budgets and organizational attention. A strong pilot approach includes clear success criteria, representative scope, side-by-side comparisons (where feasible), iterative feedback loops, and a willingness to walk away if no candidate meets minimum thresholds.

### Clear Success Criteria

Define specific business outcomes (e.g., reduced cycle time, increased conversion, or lower manual effort) and technical metrics (e.g., query latency, model training time, or user satisfaction) before the pilot begins. Align these criteria with BTG dimensions so you can coherently score pilot results.

### Representative Scope

Use real data, realistic data volumes, and actual user groups, even on a limited scale, to test the platform under conditions that mirror production. This reveals Business, Technical, and Governance strengths and gaps before full rollout.

### Side-by-Side Comparison

When feasible, run two candidate platforms against the same use case and data to compare usability, performance, and cost using a common scorecard. A BTG-aligned scorecard makes trade-offs explicit. For example, one platform might excel in Technical fit but lag on Governance.

### Iterative Feedback Loops

Incorporate feedback from business users, data engineers, data scientists, and risk/compliance stakeholders throughout the pilot, not just at its conclusion. This ensures the BTG model incorporates perspectives from all three corners.

### Decision and De-Risking

Use pilot results to refine your requirements and negotiate with vendors. Be willing to declare a "no decision" if no platform meets minimum thresholds. Documenting BTG-based trade-offs supports transparent, defensible decisions.

## Integration Planning and Change Management

Technology selection only creates value when the platform integrates into business processes and people's daily work. Effective integration and change management translate platform potential into realized outcomes.

### Architecture Alignment

Position the platform within your broader data and analytics architecture—data lake, warehouse, operational systems, and identity providers—ensuring data flows, metadata, and security controls remain consistent. This ensures Technical assumptions made during BTG evaluation hold true in production.

### User Readiness and Training

Tailor training to distinct personas, such as executives, operational managers, citizen analysts, and data scientists. Combine small-group workshops, self-paced learning, and office hours so early adopters become internal champions rather than isolated experts. Strong enablement is vital to realizing the Business potential identified in BTG scoring.

### Governance and Operating Model

Update data and AI governance processes to incorporate the new platform. This includes data quality responsibilities, model approval workflows, and AI risk assessments where relevant. Clarify who owns which parts of the lifecycle—from data onboarding to decommissioning models and dashboards—to avoid confusion and conflicts. These operating model decisions operationalize the Governance corner of the BTG model.

### Adoption Monitoring

Track metrics like active users, number of certified dashboards, models in production, and time from idea to deployment to ensure the platform genuinely moves the needle. Use these insights to refine training, adjust governance friction points, and prioritize platform enhancements. BTG-aligned scorecards help you see whether gaps in Business, Technical, or Governance dimensions are limiting adoption.

## Emerging Trends and Future-Proofing

Technology choices must anticipate—not merely react to—shifts in the analytics landscape. Emerging trends like cloud-first architectures, unified platforms, contextual AI assistants, and privacy-preserving analytics should inform selection criteria. This ensures today's decisions remain viable as capabilities evolve.

### Cloud-First and Serverless

Organizations increasingly adopt cloud-first and serverless analytics platforms to balance cost, flexibility, and time to value. These platforms reduce infrastructure management burden and offer rapid access to new features. But they also require conscious strategies for cost optimization, data residency, and vendor diversification. BTG evaluations should consider how cloud-first models affect each dimension.

### Unified Platforms and Data Products

Vendors converge data engineering, BI, and data science capabilities into unified analytics platforms, aiming to reduce fragmentation and integration overhead. At the same time, enterprises organize around "data products" and data mesh architectures. Here, domain teams own data and analytics capabilities while conforming to shared standards, which changes the balance among Business value, Technical complexity, and Governance maturity.

### Contextual AI Assistants

AI assistants integrated into analytics platforms change how users discover data, interpret metrics, and simulate scenarios. Selecting platforms that can host or integrate such assistants—with guardrails and lineage back to trusted data—positions your organization to benefit from these interaction shifts. This is a clear example where Business benefits and Governance risks must be weighed jointly within the BTG model.

### Federated and Privacy-Preserving Analytics

As data sovereignty and privacy regulations tighten, federated analytics and privacy-enhancing technologies (such as differential privacy and secure enclaves) gain importance in platform roadmaps. Assess how candidate platforms support analyses across regions, business units, and partners without centralized data movement that could introduce risk. These capabilities primarily influence Governance but also unlock Business use cases that would otherwise be infeasible.

# Case Studies

## Case Study #1: Retailer Choosing a Unified Cloud Analytics Platform[1]

A global specialty retailer faced fragmented reporting across regions and brands, grappling with multiple BI tools, departmental data marts, and inconsistent KPIs. Leadership sought near real-time visibility into store and e-commerce performance, predictive demand forecasting, and AI-driven personalization to support growth. After a requirements assessment, the team shortlisted two cloud-native analytics platforms combining data warehousing, streaming ingestion, and BI capabilities. They then designed a pilot around three high-value use cases: a consolidated executive performance dashboard, a demand forecast for a volatile product category, and a marketing attribution model. Using production-like data and involving planners, marketers, and store managers, they evaluated data refresh performance, dashboard responsiveness, forecast accuracy, and user satisfaction.

One platform delivered slightly faster queries, but the other offered stronger integrated ML, superior governance, and more intuitive self-service tools. The retailer chose the latter and, within 18 months, reduced manual reporting effort, improved forecast accuracy, and standardized KPIs globally. This illustrated a BTG-driven decision where Business and Governance outweighed a small Technical performance gap.

## Case Study #2: Financial Institution Balancing AI Innovation and Governance[3]

A regional bank aimed to deploy machine learning models for credit risk and fraud detection while experimenting with conversational AI for customer service. This occurred under regulatory expectations for transparent models, auditable decisions, and strong data privacy and model-risk controls. The bank evaluated several AI/ML platforms, focusing on explainability, bias detection, model registry capabilities, and integration with existing risk governance processes. They ran pilots using historical loan and transaction data to compare model performance and operational workflows.

One platform provided cutting-edge AutoML and a slick UX but offered limited support for formal model approval workflows and regulatory reporting. Another, however, featured complete governance capabilities—model lineage, challenger/champion management, detailed audit trails—even though its AutoML interface was less polished. The bank selected the latter and layered custom UI components for analysts on top of its APIs, preserving strong governance while keeping analysts productive. Over time, they expanded into agentic AI use cases, leveraging the platform's governance capabilities to manage risk as AI systems took on more autonomous actions across channels. This was a BTG decision where Governance outranked marginal Technical convenience.

### Case Study #3: Public Health Agency Selecting a Privacy-Preserving Analytics Platform[2]

A national public health agency required an analytics and AI platform to support disease surveillance, vaccine campaign planning, and near real-time hospital capacity monitoring. This needed to operate under strict health data privacy regulations and public-trust expectations. The team evaluated platforms offering strong support for federated analytics, pseudonymization, and fine-grained access controls. They also sought capabilities for explainable risk scores that clinicians could interpret and assessed alignment with global AI governance methods emphasizing transparency and accountability in high-impact public sector use cases.

One candidate platform offered powerful centralized data-lake capabilities but required extensive data movement and provided limited tooling for consent management and differential privacy. Another supported federated model training, audit-ready access logs, built-in explainability dashboards, and integration patterns aligned with NIST-style AI risk-management practices and EU-style risk-based regimes. The agency selected the latter, prioritizing Governance and ethical considerations alongside sufficient Technical performance. Viewed through BTG, the choice emphasized Governance and Business legitimacy (trust, compliance) over maximal Technical centralization.

## Success Metrics

Evaluate technology choices through metrics that connect platform capabilities to business outcomes, not just technical performance.

## Table of Illustrative Metrics

| Dimension | Example Metric | Why It Matters |
|---|---|---|
| **Business Value** | Incremental revenue, cost savings, or risk reduction directly attributable to analytics and AI use cases over 12-24 months | Shows whether the platform enables use cases that move financial and strategic needles |
| **Time to Insight** | Avg. time from question or idea to first useful dashboard or model in production | Reflects agility and friction across data, tooling, and governance |
| **Adoption and Engagement** | Active users by persona, certified dashboards used monthly, models used in key workflows | Indicates that the platform is embedded in daily decision-making |
| **Performance and Reliability** | Query latency, job failure rates, SLA adherence for critical workloads | Ensures user trust and suitability for operational or real-time use |
| **Governance and Risk** | % of models with documented lineage, explainability, and bias tests; no. of policy violations caught by governance tools | Demonstrates responsible AI and analytics practices |
| **Economic Efficiency** | TCO per active user, cost per query or per model scoring event, capacity utilization | Helps optimize spend and justify investments relative to alternatives |

Track these metrics on an "Analytics Platform Scorecard" and review them quarterly with a cross-functional steering group that includes business, technology, and risk leaders. Organize this group around BTG so no single perspective dominates.

# Practical Advice for Leaders[15]

Leaders don't need to become platform engineers, but they must ask the right questions and create the conditions for wise technology choices.

- **Anchor selection in strategy, not hype.** Ensure every major platform decision traces back to your top strategic priorities and a small set of signature analytics and AI use cases. Resist the urge to chase features that don't materially advance those goals, using the Business corner of the BTG model as the first filter.

- **Build a cross-functional selection team.** Include business owners, data and analytics leaders, enterprise architects, security and risk representatives, and end users to avoid blind spots. This diversity of perspectives helps reconcile performance ambitions with governance and change-management realities. And a BTG-aligned team ensures each corner of the model has a clear voice.
- **Think portfolio, not single tool.** Accept that different domains and maturity levels may require different tools. But insist on a coherent architecture and governance model that makes them work together. Applying BTG at a portfolio level can highlight where you're over-invested in Technical capabilities and under-invested in Governance, or vice versa.
- **Negotiate for value, not just discounts.** Beyond price, negotiate commitments around roadmap alignment, training, support, co-innovation, and metrics that matter to you. The BTG model provides language for specifying what "value" means in contracts and joint plans.
- **Invest early in governance and skills.** Allocate funding for training, enablement, and AI/analytics governance tooling as part of the initial business case, rather than as afterthoughts. This upfront investment reduces rework and risk as adoption scales and ensures you can meet expectations from external AI governance models while honoring internal BTG criteria.

# Conclusion

Choosing strategic analytics and AI/ML technologies requires a comprehensive approach—one that balances business alignment, performance, integration, governance, user experience, and cost over time. Emerging AI capabilities, especially generative and agentic AI, raise the stakes by amplifying both potential value and potential risk. That makes platform governance and explainability central to selection decisions. Organizations that use structured pilots, clear success metrics, cross-functional decision processes, and the disciplined Business-Technical-Governance Selection Model are the ones that get this right.

# Notes

[1] Platform selection criteria for enterprise analytics—requirement definition, evaluation criteria, pilots, and operating-model fit—are laid out in *CEI America*'s "Choosing an Enterprise Analytics Platform," Info-Tech Research Group's Business Intelligence and Analytics Platform Selection Guide, and *IBsolution*'s "Data and Analytics Platform Framework for Data-Driven Enterprises," which collectively emphasize requirement definition, evaluation criteria, pilots, and operating-model fit as core to platform success.

[2] Definitions of agentic AI, governance, federated analytics, and related concepts are drawn from *Dataiku*'s "Agentic AI Governance: Four Criteria to Evaluate Tools," IBsolution's platform framework, LinkedIn's article on scalable data governance, and the arXiv work on governance-ready AI infrastructure.

[3] AutoML and model-management practices—particularly the imperative to pair easy model creation with rigorous lifecycle control—are developed in *Datalere*'s "The AI/ML Tool Evaluation Template," LinkedIn's governance guidance for AI/ML, and *Dataiku*'s criteria for responsible agentic AI tools.

[4] The Business Value Framework, BTG scorecard, and success-metric examples are grounded in the *International Institute for Analytics*' "Returned Business Value Framework" and Confluent's "The Business Value of a Data Streaming Platform, Part 2," both of which link platform choices to measurable impact.

[5] Cloud-native analytics platform architectures—including separation of compute and storage, elastic scaling, and managed services—are documented in AWS, Google Cloud, and *Microsoft Azure* analytics platform guidance, and in Snowflake's cloud data platform whitepaper.

[6] Security, governance, and AI-risk considerations—explainability, bias testing, lineage, and policy enforcement among them—are addressed in *BigID*'s "AI Governance Principles," *Mimecast*'s "AI Governance," *Palo Alto Networks*' "AI Governance: What It Is and Why It Matters," and arXiv papers on governance-ready AI infrastructure.

[7] Architecture-alignment and integration guidance—emphasizing coherent data flows and consistent controls—is found in IBsolution's platform framework, *McKinsey*'s "From Raw Data to Real Profits," and the National Institute of Standards and Technology's *AI Risk Management Framework*.

[8] TCO and economic-efficiency perspectives—including warnings against evaluating price in isolation from utilization and value—are developed in Terrazone's cloud-cost analysis, Teradata's platform comparisons, and Info-Tech's BI and analytics selection guide. Total cost of ownership models covering licenses, infrastructure, support, and talent costs are also addressed in IDC's TCO analysis frameworks and Forrester's Total Economic Impact (TEI) methodology.

[9] User-experience and adoption themes—particularly time-to-insight and persona-based enablement—are stressed in Info-Tech's platform selection guide and *CEI America*'s "Choosing an Enterprise Analytics Platform," both of which treat these factors as practical success drivers.

[10] Trends such as unified analytics platforms, data products, contextual AI assistants, and cloud-first/serverless models are explored in *McKinsey*'s "From Raw Data to Real Profits" and *Improvado*'s "Contextual AI Assistants and the Data Analytics Framework."

[11] Structured pilots, side-by-side comparison, and evidence-based decisions are advocated in Confluent's business value series, Teradata's comparison work, and *McKinsey*'s recommendations on testing data platforms under real workloads before major commitments.

[12] Federated and privacy-preserving analytics, along with public-sector use cases, are covered in arXiv discussions of governance-ready AI infrastructure, IBsolution's federated analytics coverage, *Mimecast*'s "AI Governance," the National Institute of Standards and Technology's *AI Risk Management Framework*, and the EU AI Act summary on *ArtificialIntelligenceAct*.eu.

[13] The link between BTG and formal governance frameworks is established in *BigID*'s "AI Governance Principles," the National Institute of Standards and Technology's *AI Risk Management Framework*, and *ArtificialIntelligenceAct.eu*'s "High-Level Summary of the EU Artificial Intelligence Act," which position BTG as a practical selection lens within those norms.

[14] Portfolio-oriented negotiation and vendor-management advice are drawn from Confluent's guidance on co-innovation and value-oriented metrics, IIA-driven value frameworks, and Info-Tech's focus on strategic fit over feature counts in BI/analytics selection.

[15] Leadership-focused recommendations center on *McKinsey*'s "From Raw Data to Real Profits," the *International Institute for Analytics*' value framework, LinkedIn's governance guidance, IBsolution's operating-model discussions, and *Dataiku*'s AI-governance criteria, all of which highlight leaders' role in strategy-aligned platform choices.

## Key topics explored in this chapter:

- Architectural Principles for Scalability
- A Scalable AI Architecture Model
- Ingestion and Streaming for Scalable AI Workflows
- Storage and Next-Generation Databases
- Stream Processing and Real-Time Analytics
- Security, Governance and Observability
- Monitoring and Automation
- Integrating New Technologies Seamlessly
- Talent and Culture Considerations

# WAY 26

# Build a Scalable Analytics and AI Architecture


## Abstract

Strategic Scalable analytics and AI architectures are the infrastructure backbone that separates organizations that can continuously deliver data-driven value from those perpetually blocked by technical debt, fragile pipelines, and misaligned systems. This chapter provides a comprehensive, practitioner-oriented introduction to designing, building, and evolving that backbone. It covers the core architectural principles of elasticity, modularity, and cloud-native design; a practical five-layer reference model for AI architectures; ingestion and streaming workflows; modern storage and database options including vector and time-series databases; real-time stream processing; security, governance, and observability practices; and strategies for integrating emerging technologies seamlessly. The chapter also addresses talent and culture considerations, illustrates concepts through two detailed case studies, and offers practical leadership guidance. Readers will gain actionable knowledge and decision-making tools to build architectures that grow with business ambition rather than constrain it.


## Objective

After completing this chapter, you will be able to:

- Articulate the core principles of scalable, cloud-native AI and analytics architecture and explain why they matter for sustained business value.
- Apply a five-layer reference model to assess and design enterprise AI architectures.

- Select appropriate storage, streaming, and processing technologies for specific analytical and AI workload patterns.
- Design governance, observability, and security controls that scale alongside the architecture.
- Evaluate and integrate emerging technologies—including vector databases, feature stores, event-driven architectures, and data mesh approaches—into existing platforms.
- Lead talent and culture changes that enable cross-functional teams to build and sustain scalable AI architecture over time.

## Terms to Know

**Data Mesh**[1] **-** A decentralized data architecture paradigm in which domain teams own and serve their data as products, governed by shared standards, rather than centralizing all data in a single platform.

**Elasticity**[2] **-** The ability of a computing system to automatically scale resources up or down in response to workload demand, minimizing cost during idle periods and preventing bottlenecks during peak loads.

**Event-Driven Architecture (EDA)**[3] **-** A software design pattern in which system components communicate by producing and consuming discrete events, enabling loose coupling, real-time responsiveness, and independent scaling of producers and consumers.

**Feature Store**[4] **-** A centralized repository for storing, versioning, and serving pre-computed ML features to both training pipelines and real-time inference endpoints, ensuring consistency and reuse across models.

**Kappa Architecture**[5] **-** A stream-first data processing architecture that eliminates the separate batch layer found in Lambda Architecture by treating all data—historical and real-time—as a continuous stream, simplifying operations at the cost of higher reprocessing demands.

**Lambda Architecture**[5] **-** A data processing architecture that combines a batch layer (for high-throughput, accurate historical processing) and a speed layer (for low-latency real-time processing), merging their results in a serving layer.

**Microservices**[2] **-** An architectural style in which an application is structured as a collection of small, independently deployable services, each responsible for a specific business capability and communicating via lightweight APIs.

**MLOps**[6] - A set of practices, tools, and cultural norms that apply DevOps principles to the machine learning lifecycle—covering data versioning, model training, testing, deployment, monitoring, and retraining—to accelerate and reliably govern ML systems in production.

**Vector Database**[4] - A specialized database optimized for storing and querying high-dimensional vector embeddings—numerical representations of text, images, or other data—using approximate nearest-neighbor search to power semantic search, recommendation, and retrieval-augmented generation (RAG) use cases.

# Introduction

Architecture is the invisible infrastructure that either accelerates or constrains every analytics and AI initiative. Organizations that invest in scalable, well-governed architecture continuously compound their analytical capabilities. Those that neglect it repeatedly rediscover the same bottlenecks: slow pipelines, brittle integrations, inconsistent data, and models that perform in the lab but fail in production. The difference is rarely a shortage of talent or ambition—it is structural. This chapter builds a practical guide for leaders and practitioners who want to move from ad hoc data infrastructure to an architecture intentionally designed for scale, speed, and reliability. It addresses both the technical decisions and the organizational conditions that make those decisions stick.

## Architectural Principles for Scalability[7]

Scalable architecture is not simply "bigger" architecture—it is architecture designed from the outset to grow gracefully without requiring wholesale replacement. Several foundational principles distinguish scalable from brittle designs.

### Elasticity and Cloud-Native Design

Cloud-native architectures treat compute, storage, and networking as elastic resources that can expand or contract within minutes rather than months. Separating compute from storage—as platforms like Snowflake, Databricks, and BigQuery do—allows independent scaling of each dimension, matching cost to actual workload rather than provisioning for theoretical peaks. Serverless functions and managed containers extend this principle to individual pipeline steps and model inference endpoints. Elasticity is not free: it requires careful design of stateless services, idempotent operations, and cost-monitoring guardrails to prevent unbounded spending.

### Modular and Microservices Architectures

Monolithic data platforms are difficult to evolve because a change in one area risks breaking others. Modular architectures decompose the platform into independently deployable components—ingestion services, transformation engines, feature computation, model serving, and reporting layers—that communicate through well-defined APIs. This approach enables teams to upgrade or replace individual components without system-wide disruption, accelerates independent team delivery, and makes failures more contained and diagnosable. The trade-off is that distributed systems require thoughtful orchestration, service discovery, and observability to avoid coordination overhead.

## A Scalable AI Architecture Model[7]

A practical five-layer reference model organizes the key components of a scalable AI architecture into a coherent stack, from raw data sources at the bottom to business consumers at the top. The five layers are:

- **Data Ingestion and Integration:** Collects data from structured sources (databases, APIs, SaaS platforms) and unstructured sources (logs, documents, media) using batch, micro-batch, and streaming patterns. Key concerns are reliability, schema evolution, and lineage from the point of origin.
- **Storage and Data Management:** Organizes data into logical zones (raw, curated, enriched, feature-ready) across data lakes, lakehouses, warehouses, and specialized stores. Governance here means catalog registration, access control, and quality certification.
- **Processing and Transformation:** Applies business logic, joins, aggregations, and feature engineering using batch engines (Spark, dbt), stream processors (Flink, Kafka Streams), and SQL transformation layers. Automated testing and data quality gates belong at this layer.
- **AI/ML and Analytics:** Hosts model training, experimentation, feature stores, model registries, and inference endpoints alongside BI, reporting, and advanced analytics tools. MLOps practices govern the lifecycle from experiment to production.
- **Consumption and Activation:** Delivers insights and model outputs to decision-makers, operational systems, APIs, and embedded applications. Serving patterns range from dashboards and self-service analytics to real-time decisioning APIs and AI-augmented workflows.

## Five Layer Reference Model

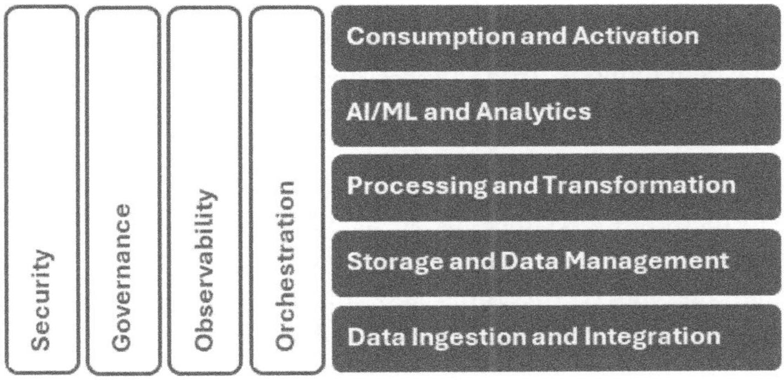


Cross-cutting concerns—security, governance, observability, and orchestration—span all five layers rather than residing in any single one. This layered view helps architecture teams identify gaps, prioritize investments, and communicate the platform's structure to non-technical stakeholders without overwhelming detail.

### Comparing the 5-Layer Model to Established Reference Architectures[8]

The five-layer model presented here synthesizes patterns from several widely cited reference architectures. The Databricks Data Ingestion Reference Architecture emphasizes reliable pipeline design, schema registry, and streaming-first ingestion—aligning closely with layer one. The Informatica Data Lakehouse Architecture Guide focuses on the storage and governance layer (layer two), particularly the lakehouse pattern that unifies warehouse-grade query performance with data lake flexibility. The Snowflake Data Lakes and Architecture Fundamentals documentation enriches the storage layer with cloud-native separation of compute and storage, and multi-cluster warehouse patterns. Microsoft's Azure Databricks Modern Analytics Architecture and the Azure Big Data Architectures documentation provide end-to-end reference designs spanning layers one through four, with particular depth on streaming, transformation, and ML workloads. AWS's Serverless Data Analytics Pipeline Reference Architecture introduces the consumption layer's serving patterns for event-driven and serverless scenarios. The five-layer model synthesizes these vendor-specific patterns into a platform-agnostic framework that teams can apply regardless of their cloud provider or tooling choices.

## Ingestion and Streaming for Scalable AI Workflows

Reliable, well-governed data ingestion is the foundation on which every downstream AI and analytics capability rests. Weak ingestion creates data debt that compounds over time—late-arriving records, inconsistent schemas, and lineage gaps that undermine trust in models and reports.

### Automated Pipelines

Modern ingestion pipelines must handle schema evolution without breaking downstream consumers, manage late-arriving data through watermarking and reprocessing, and enforce data quality checks at the point of entry. Tools like Apache Kafka, AWS Kinesis, and Azure Event Hubs provide durable, scalable streaming backbones. Orchestrators such as Apache Airflow, Prefect, and Dagster manage batch dependencies, retries, and alerting. The key design principle is that pipelines should be self-healing where possible—automatically retrying transient failures, dead-lettering unprocessable records, and alerting on anomalies rather than silently dropping data.

### CI/CD for Models

Applying continuous integration and continuous delivery (CI/CD) principles to ML model development dramatically reduces the time from experiment to production—and the risk associated with each deployment. A model CI/CD pipeline typically triggers on code or data changes, runs automated unit and integration tests, validates model performance against a holdout dataset, registers a new model version, and promotes it to staging and then production after approval gates. Infrastructure-as-code tools such as Terraform and Pulumi ensure deployment environments are reproducible. Container registries and Kubernetes clusters provide consistent model serving infrastructure across environments.

### Monitoring and Governance

Pipeline monitoring should track data freshness, volume anomalies, schema drift, and SLA compliance in real time. Governance at the ingestion layer means capturing origin metadata, transformation history, and access logs from the moment data enters the platform—not as a retroactive exercise. This lineage foundation is essential for regulatory compliance, audit readiness, and downstream model explainability.

### Collaboration Tools[9]

Scalable ingestion is a team sport. Shared data catalogs (Apache Atlas, Alation, Collibra) help engineers and analysts discover available datasets and understand their lineage. Version-controlled pipeline code in Git—reviewed through pull requests by data engineers and domain experts—applies software engineering discipline to data infrastructure. Notebook environments with built-in collaboration features (Databricks, JupyterHub, Google Colab Enterprise) reduce friction between exploration and operationalization of new data sources.

## Storage and Next-Generation Databases[10]

The storage landscape for AI and analytics has expanded far beyond the traditional relational database and data warehouse. Different workload patterns—high-throughput batch processing, low-latency serving, semantic search, time-series analysis, and graph traversal—call for different storage engines. Organizations with mature architectures typically maintain a portfolio of storage technologies unified by a governance and catalog layer.

### Vector Databases

Vector databases have emerged as an important component in AI architectures driven by large language models and multimodal AI. They store high-dimensional embeddings—numerical representations of text, images, audio, or code generated by embedding models—and support fast approximate nearest-neighbor (ANN) search. This enables semantic search ("find documents similar in meaning to this query"), recommendation systems, and retrieval-augmented generation (RAG) pipelines where a language model retrieves relevant context before generating a response. Leading options include Pinecone, Weaviate, Chroma, Milvus, and vector search extensions to existing databases (pgvector for PostgreSQL, Azure Cognitive Search, Elasticsearch). Choosing between standalone vector databases and vector-enabled general databases depends on query volume, latency requirements, and the team's existing operational expertise.

### Time-Series and Streaming Databases

Time-series workloads—IoT sensor data, financial tick data, application performance metrics, and operational telemetry—have access and write patterns that relational databases handle poorly at scale. Purpose-built time-series databases such as InfluxDB, TimescaleDB (a PostgreSQL extension), and Apache Druid optimize for high-frequency writes, time-range queries, and downsampling aggregations. For industrial and real-time monitoring use cases, these databases feed anomaly detection models and operational dashboards that require sub-second query latency across months of sensor history.

### Graph and Multi-Model Databases

Graph databases (Neo4j, Amazon Neptune, Azure Cosmos DB for Gremlin) excel at relationship-intensive queries—fraud detection networks, knowledge graphs, supply chain traceability, and recommendation engines based on connection patterns. Multi-model databases that support document, graph, and key-value workloads in a single engine (Azure Cosmos DB, ArangoDB) reduce operational complexity when a use case spans multiple data models. When combined with vector search, graph databases provide a powerful foundation for knowledge-graph-augmented RAG systems that retrieve structured facts alongside semantic passages.

## Stream Processing and Real-Time Analytics[11]

Real-time analytics capabilities have become a competitive differentiator across industries. Detecting fraud within milliseconds, personalizing digital experiences in the moment, and monitoring industrial equipment before failures occur all require stream processing architectures that go far beyond traditional batch data warehouses.

### Foundational Tools and Patterns

Apache Kafka remains the dominant event streaming backbone for high-throughput, durable message queuing and replay. Apache Flink provides stateful stream processing with exactly-once semantics, windowing operations, and complex event processing. Apache Spark Structured Streaming integrates stream processing within the broader Spark ecosystem. Managed cloud services—AWS Kinesis, Google Dataflow, Azure Stream Analytics—reduce operational burden for teams without deep distributed systems expertise. The choice among these tools depends on throughput requirements, latency targets, exactly-once semantics needs, and the existing skills of the engineering team.

### Lambda Architecture

Lambda Architecture addresses the challenge of building systems that are both highly accurate (from complete historical data) and highly responsive (from real-time streams) by maintaining parallel batch and speed layers whose outputs are merged at query time. The batch layer reprocesses all historical data periodically to produce accurate, comprehensive views. The speed layer processes only the most recent data with low latency to fill the gap until the batch layer catches up. While conceptually clean, Lambda Architecture introduces operational complexity because teams must maintain two separate processing codebases producing logically equivalent outputs—a burden that has led many organizations to evaluate Kappa Architecture as a simpler alternative.

### Kappa Architecture

Kappa Architecture eliminates the separate batch layer by treating all data as a stream and reprocessing historical data by replaying the event log from the beginning. This simplifies the codebase to a single processing paradigm but places higher demands on the stream processing engine's ability to handle large-scale reprocessing without falling behind real-time ingestion. Kafka's durable log retention and Flink's parallel backfill capabilities make Kappa Architecture increasingly practical. The right choice between Lambda and Kappa depends on the maturity of streaming tooling available, tolerance for reprocessing latency, and the operational burden teams can absorb.

## Security, Governance and Observability

Security, governance, and observability are not optional overlays to be added after an architecture is built—they are structural requirements that shape every architectural decision. Organizations that treat them as afterthoughts accumulate compliance debt, erode stakeholder trust, and face costly retroactive remediation.

### Security Controls

A defense-in-depth approach applies security controls at multiple layers: network segmentation and private endpoints for data stores, encryption at rest and in transit, identity-based access through centralized identity providers (Azure AD, AWS IAM, Okta), column-level and row-level security in data platforms, and secrets management through vaults (HashiCorp Vault, AWS Secrets Manager). Zero-trust principles—verifying every access request regardless of network location—are increasingly standard for cloud-native AI systems that span multiple environments and organizational boundaries.

### Lineage and Auditability

Data lineage tracking records the full provenance of every dataset and model—that is, where data originated, how it was transformed, which models were trained on it, and what decisions it influenced. This capability is essential for regulatory compliance (GDPR, CCPA, financial risk models), for investigating data quality incidents, and for meeting emerging AI governance requirements that demand traceability from model outputs back to training data. Catalog tools with automated lineage (Apache Atlas,

Alation, Microsoft Purview, dbt's column-level lineage) significantly reduce the manual effort of building and maintaining these records.

### Policy Enforcement

Governance policies—data classification rules, retention schedules, access approval workflows, and model deployment gates—should be enforced programmatically rather than through manual review alone. Policy-as-code tools (Open Policy Agent, AWS Lake Formation, Unity Catalog on Databricks) embed governance rules directly into the data platform so that access decisions, anonymization requirements, and data movement restrictions are applied consistently without depending on human vigilance at every step.

## Monitoring and Automation

The scale and complexity of modern AI architectures make manual monitoring untenable. Automated monitoring covers infrastructure health, pipeline reliability, data quality, model performance, and security events. Automation extends to remediation: self-healing systems detect and resolve known failure modes without human intervention, reserving engineer attention for novel problems.

### Full-Stack Observability[9]

Full-stack observability integrates three telemetry types—metrics (quantitative measurements), logs (event records), and traces (request-path timing across services)—into a unified view. Platforms such as Datadog, Grafana Stack (Prometheus + Loki + Tempo), and Elastic Observability correlate signals across the data pipeline, model serving layer, and application tier to enable rapid root-cause analysis. In AI architectures, observability must extend to model performance: tracking prediction distributions, feature drift, and business outcome metrics alongside traditional infrastructure KPIs.

### AI-Assisted Anomaly Detection

Traditional threshold-based alerting struggles with the complexity and seasonality of modern AI system telemetry. ML-powered anomaly detection—embedded in tools like Datadog, Dynatrace, and Monte Carlo (for data quality)—learns normal behavior patterns and surfaces deviations that static rules would miss. These systems reduce alert fatigue by distinguishing genuine anomalies from expected variation, and they surface correlations across data quality, model performance, and infrastructure metrics that human operators would not connect manually.

### Automation and Self-Healing

Self-healing architecture responds to detected anomalies with automated remediation: restarting failed pipeline tasks, triggering model retraining when drift exceeds thresholds, scaling compute resources in response to queue depth, or rolling back a problematic model deployment. Runbooks-as-code and automated playbooks (using tools like PagerDuty, AWS Systems Manager, or custom Kubernetes operators) codify institutional knowledge about failure modes so resolution is consistent, auditable, and fast. You are looking to automate the response to known, low-stakes failures so engineers can focus on novel problems that genuinely require expertise.

## Integrating New Technologies Seamlessly[11]

The pace of innovation in AI and analytics means that architecture must accommodate new technologies without requiring wholesale replacement of existing investments. Organizations that design for integration from the outset—rather than treating each new tool as a standalone deployment—dramatically reduce the cost and risk of adopting emerging capabilities.

### API-First Design

API-first design treats every platform capability—data access, model inference, feature serving, governance queries—as a service exposed through a well-documented, versioned API rather than a direct database connection or proprietary integration. This abstraction layer allows the underlying implementation to evolve independently of the consumers, and it enables new tools to plug into the platform without requiring architectural surgery. REST APIs, GraphQL endpoints, and gRPC services serve different latency and payload profiles; the key is that every capability is accessible programmatically from day one.

### Event-Driven Architectures

Event-driven architectures decouple producers and consumers of data through an event bus or message broker, making it straightforward to add new consumers (a new model, a new reporting pipeline, a new operational trigger) without modifying the producing system. This pattern is particularly valuable for integrating AI capabilities into operational workflows: a model inference service subscribes to transaction events and publishes risk scores without requiring changes to the transaction processing system. CloudEvents, a CNCF standard for event metadata, improves interoperability across heterogeneous event systems.

### Feature Stores as Shared Infrastructure

Feature stores resolve a persistent problem in ML platform integration: the same feature—for example, a customer's 30-day purchase frequency—is computed differently by different model teams, creating training-serving skew and duplicated work. A shared feature store centralizes feature computation, versioning, and serving, ensuring that the feature value seen during model training matches exactly what the model sees at inference time. Platforms such as Feast (open source), Tecton, and Vertex AI Feature Store provide both offline feature retrieval for training and low-latency online serving for production inference.

### Data Mesh Approaches

Data mesh shifts the integration challenge from a central platform team to domain teams that own and publish their data as products conforming to shared standards. Each domain team is responsible for the quality, freshness, SLAs, and discoverability of its data products, reducing the central bottleneck while maintaining interoperability through a federated governance layer. Integrating a new technology in a data mesh environment means certifying it as a compatible data product consumer or producer under the shared standards—a fundamentally different and often faster path than integrating through a central platform team.

### Hybrid Cloud and Edge

Not all AI workloads belong in the central cloud. Data sovereignty requirements, network latency constraints, and intermittent connectivity drive deployment of model inference to edge devices and on-premises infrastructure. Hybrid architectures use consistent APIs and governance standards across cloud and edge deployments, allowing a model trained centrally to be deployed to edge nodes with automated update management and monitoring. Platforms such as AWS IoT Greengrass, Azure IoT Edge, and NVIDIA Jetson provide managed edge inference capabilities that integrate with central AI platforms through standardized connectivity patterns.

## Talent and Culture Considerations

Architecture is ultimately built and operated by people. The most sophisticated technical design fails if the talent model and organizational culture do not support it. Scalable AI architecture requires not just individual technical skills but shared practices, cross-functional collaboration, and a learning culture that continuously adapts to new technologies and changing business requirements.

### Cross-Functional Teams

Scalable AI architecture is built by teams that combine data engineering, ML engineering, platform engineering, domain expertise, and product management skills—not by siloed teams that hand work over fences. The platform-product team model, popularized by Spotify's squad structure and adopted widely in data organizations, organizes teams around platform capabilities (data platform, ML platform, governance platform) that serve internal customers. Domain teams consume platform services to build AI and analytics products, maintaining ownership of their data and models while benefiting from shared infrastructure.

### DevOps and MLOps Culture

DevOps culture—characterized by shared ownership of reliability, automated testing, continuous delivery, and blameless post-mortems—is the organizational foundation that makes scalable architecture operational rather than aspirational. Extending these practices to ML through MLOps means data scientists and ML engineers adopt version control, automated testing, and deployment pipelines as standard practice rather than optional discipline. Organizations that achieve this cultural shift deploy models significantly faster, with fewer production incidents, than those where data science and engineering remain organizationally separate.

### Continuous Learning and Upskilling

The technology landscape for AI architecture evolves faster than traditional enterprise software. Teams need structured time and resources for learning: technology radar reviews that evaluate emerging tools against current needs, dedicated innovation sprints, internal conference days where teams share what they have learned, and partnerships with vendors and cloud providers to get early access to new capabilities. Upskilling programs should address not just technical skills but architectural thinking—helping engineers understand not only how a technology works but when and why to apply it, and how it fits into the broader architecture.

# Case Studies

## Case Study #1: Streaming Architecture for Industrial Monitoring[3]

A global industrial manufacturer operated more than 400 production lines across 18 facilities, each generating continuous telemetry from thousands of sensors monitoring temperature, vibration, pressure, and throughput.

Unplanned downtime cost an average of $150,000 per hour, and the maintenance team operated on fixed schedules that frequently resulted in either premature part replacements or missed early warning signs. The existing data architecture relied on batch exports to a central data warehouse updated nightly—far too slow to support predictive maintenance or real-time operational decisions.

The architecture team designed a Kappa Architecture-based streaming platform using Apache Kafka for event ingestion, Apache Flink for stateful stream processing, and InfluxDB for time-series storage. Edge gateways at each facility performed initial data validation and compression before forwarding to the central Kafka cluster over encrypted connections. Flink jobs computed rolling aggregations, applied rule-based anomaly filters, and invoked a pre-trained gradient-boosting model for predictive maintenance scoring in under 200 milliseconds per sensor event. Anomaly scores above threshold triggered automated work orders in the CMMS system through an event-driven integration, and real-time dashboards gave operations managers facility-level visibility with drill-down to individual equipment.

Within 12 months, unplanned downtime fell by 34%, maintenance cost per unit declined, and the architecture team published a set of reusable pipeline templates that three other business units adopted for their own monitoring use cases—demonstrating the value of building shared, scalable infrastructure rather than one-off solutions.

## Case Study #2: Vector Search and RAG for Customer Support[4]

A large telecommunications provider managed a customer support operation handling 2.5 million contacts per month across phone, chat, and digital channels. Support agents spent significant time searching across a fragmented knowledge base of 80,000 articles spread across three legacy systems, leading to inconsistent answers, long handle times, and high agent frustration. The company had experimented with keyword-based search improvements but found that customers phrased questions in ways that did not match article terminology—a classic semantic gap problem.

The architecture team implemented a retrieval-augmented generation (RAG) system built on a vector database (Weaviate) and a large language model served through an internal API gateway. All 80,000 knowledge articles were embedded using a sentence transformer model and indexed in Weaviate. An automated pipeline synchronized new and updated articles nightly, regenerating embeddings for changed content and retiring stale ones. At inference time, agent queries were embedded and used to retrieve the top-five semantically relevant articles, which were then passed as context to the LLM to generate a concise, grounded answer with citations. A feature store maintained agent-specific context in the form of customer service history, current issues, and previous interaction summaries to enrich the retrieval query for personalization. Governance controls ensured the LLM could only draw from the curated knowledge base and that all generated answers were logged with their source citations for audit purposes.

Average handle time fell by 22%, first-contact resolution improved, and agent satisfaction scores increased significantly—with the architecture team reporting that the feature store and vector database components were subsequently reused for three additional AI use cases within 18 months.

## Success Metrics

Architecture investments are difficult to justify with business cases alone—they require a set of technical and operational metrics that connect infrastructure quality to business outcomes. These types of metrics provide a balanced scorecard for assessing the health and scalability of an AI and analytics architecture.

Review them quarterly with a cross-functional architecture steering group that includes technology, business, and risk leadership. Use them not as performance scores but as diagnostic signals: a declining SLA adherence rate may indicate growing technical debt; a long time-to-production may point to governance friction that needs streamlining rather than elimination.

## Table of Illustrative Metrics

| Dimension | Example Metric | Why It Matters |
|---|---|---|
| **Elastic Scalability** | Time to scale a workload from baseline to 10× load; cost delta per additional unit of work at scale | Confirms the architecture can handle growth without manual re-engineering or excessive cost |
| **Reliability and SLAs** | Pipeline SLA adherence rate; data freshness vs. target; mean time to recovery (MTTR) for incidents | Measures whether the architecture reliably delivers data and models when the business needs them |
| **Time to Production** | Median elapsed time from approved model to live production serving; number of manual handoff steps in the ML pipeline | Indicates MLOps maturity and the architecture's ability to accelerate AI value delivery |
| **Real-Time Capability** | End-to-end latency from event ingestion to model output delivery; % of use cases served in real time vs. batch | Demonstrates whether the architecture can support latency-sensitive AI applications |
| **Architectural Flexibility** | Time to integrate a new technology component; number of API-breaking changes per quarter in platform services | Shows how well the architecture absorbs new capabilities without destabilizing existing systems |
| **Governance Coverage** | % of production datasets with complete lineage; % of models with documented bias tests and performance baselines | Reflects the organization's readiness for audits, regulatory inquiries, and responsible AI commitments |

# Practical Advice for Leaders[12]

Architecture decisions are fundamentally leadership decisions. They involve trade-offs between speed and stability, cost and capability, and centralization and autonomy that cannot be resolved purely by technical judgment. Leaders who understand these trade-offs can sponsor the right investments and create the conditions for architectural success.

- **Set architectural guardrails, not rigid blueprints.** Prescriptive architecture mandates that specify exact technologies breed resentment and slow delivery. Instead, define a small set of non-negotiable architectural principles—API-first design, lineage from day one, security controls at every layer, automated testing for pipelines—and give teams autonomy to choose how they implement those principles within approved technology patterns. This approach enables innovation without fragmentation.
- **Invest early in MLOps and observability.** Organizations consistently underestimate the operational cost of running models in production without MLOps infrastructure. Every hour spent deploying a model manually, debugging a pipeline failure without observability tooling, or rolling back a bad deployment without version control is an hour not spent on new AI capabilities. Investing in MLOps and observability platforms early pays compound returns as the model portfolio grows.
- **Favor incremental modernization over big-bang rewrites.** Large-scale architecture overhauls routinely run over budget, over time, and under expectations. A strangler-fig pattern—progressively replacing legacy components with modern equivalents while keeping the overall system running—delivers value incrementally and keeps risk manageable. Identify the highest-use components to modernize first, typically ingestion pipelines and model serving infrastructure, and build the business case from demonstrated wins rather than projected future value.
- **Tie architecture decisions to business scenarios.** Every significant architectural investment should be justified by one or more specific business scenarios it enables. "We need a vector database to support semantic search on our product catalog, which will improve recommendation relevance and increase attach rate by an estimated X%" is a defensible business case. "We need a vector database because vector search is the future" is not. Anchoring architecture in business scenarios also helps teams prioritize when they face capacity constraints.
- **Cultivate platform and product thinking.** Architecture teams that think like platform product managers—with internal customers, documented capabilities, SLAs, and roadmaps—build infrastructure that teams actually adopt. Architecture teams that think like pure engineers build systems that are technically impressive but poorly adopted because they optimize for elegance over usability. Invest in developer experience: documentation, self-service portals, starter templates, and

responsive support. The architecture's business value is realized only when it is widely used.

## Conclusion

Building a scalable analytics and AI architecture is not a one-time project—it's an ongoing practice of deliberate design, disciplined engineering, and organizational investment. The principles of elasticity, modularity, API-first design, and governance-as-code provide a stable foundation that can accommodate the rapid evolution of AI capabilities without constant architectural reinvention. The five-layer reference model gives teams a shared vocabulary for describing and evaluating their architecture against best practices. And the case studies illustrate that these principles translate into measurable business outcomes when applied with rigor and organizational commitment.

Leaders who understand these architectural imperatives—and who create the talent, culture, and investment conditions that support them—position their organizations to continuously compound AI and analytics value rather than starting from scratch with each new generation of technology.

## Notes

[1] Definitions of data mesh, governance coverage, and the architecture health-scorecard concept are drawn from *Bix-Tech*'s "AI-First Data Architecture: A Practical Blueprint for the Future of Enterprise Intelligence" along with vendor-neutral analytics-architecture guidance that treats data as a product and emphasizes domain ownership.

[2] *ChaosSearch*'s "Cloud Data Platform Architecture Guide," highlights autoscaling, microservices, and zero-trust controls as the foundations of elasticity and cloud-native security in scalable data platforms.

[3] Real-time analytics patterns, hybrid-cloud and edge integration, and Lambda/Kappa decisions are illustrated in *Microsoft Azure*'s big-data and modern analytics architecture guidance and MSSQLTips' coverage of lakehouse ingestion and processing options, both of which show how streaming engines and multi-layer designs support low-latency analytics.

[4] *Informatica*'s "Data Lakehouse Architecture: AI Guide," describes feature stores, vector databases, and governance coverage—specifically feature management, vector search, and end-to-end lineage—as central elements of AI-ready architectures.

[5] Lambda and Kappa architecture descriptions—contrasting batch-plus-speed designs with single-pipeline streaming approaches—are found in Azure and community presentations such as "Big Data Architecture on Azure Data Analytics Platform," which illustrate both approaches in a cloud-native context.

[6] MLOps practices, time-to-production metrics, reliability SLAs, and platform-product thinking are illustrated in *Databricks*' reference architectures for data ingestion and ML pipelines, which emphasize CI/CD, monitoring, governance, and internal platform stewardship.

[7] BePivotl's cloud-native data-platform reference architecture and *Bix-Tech*'s "AI-First Data Architecture: A Practical Blueprint for the Future of Enterprise Intelligence" set out the 5-Layer Scalable AI Architecture Model, elasticity patterns, and CI/CD for models, both emphasizing layered, modular designs and automated ML workflows.

[8] RE-CINQ's "AI Platform Reference Architecture" examines AI-assisted observability and continuous-learning culture, stressing AI-driven anomaly detection and ongoing upskilling as prerequisites for operating complex AI platforms.

[9] LinkedIn's "Enterprise AI Technology Stack: Layered Architecture" maps domain-aligned microservices, data mesh adoption, and cross-functional platform teams to organizational ownership and DevOps/MLOps practices.

[10] Polyglot persistence, data-lake and lakehouse roles, and the treatment of vector and graph databases in scalable architectures are explained in Snowflake's explanations of data-lake and data-lakehouse architecture for AI workloads.

[11] API-first, serverless, and architectural-flexibility patterns are demonstrated in AWS's "Serverless Data Analytics Pipeline Reference Architecture," which shows how loosely coupled components and managed services enable gradual upgrades and technology swaps.

[12] Leadership-level guidance on guardrails, modernization, and scenario-driven architecture positions leaders as stewards of principles and portfolios rather than specific tools; see *ChaosSearch, Bix-Tech, Databricks, Microsoft Azure* architectural solution ideas, and LinkedIn's "Enterprise AI Technology Stack: Layered Architecture."

## Key topics explored in this chapter:

- The AI Imperative in Legacy Integration
- Key Integration Challenges and AI-Driven Solutions
- Legacy-Modern Integration Layers
- Integration Strategies: An AI Enablement Perspective
- Comparing Major Modernization Strategies
- The Legacy-Modern AI Integration Matrix
- Best Practices for Successful AI-Informed Integration

# WAY 27

# Integrate Legacy and Modern Systems


## Abstract

Legacy systems often hold the core transaction, product, and customer records that AI and analytics need most. Yet they were not designed to feed modern data platforms or AI workloads. Modernizing only at the edges leaves these systems isolated and causes AI models to operate on partial, delayed, or inconsistent data. This, in turn, weakens insight quality and automation potential. This chapter explores AI-aware integration strategies, middleware patterns, and migration approaches that harmonize legacy and modern ecosystems, preserving operational stability while unlocking data for advanced analytics and automation.


## Objective

After completing this chapter, you will be able to:

- Explain why integrating legacy systems is central to effective AI/analytics initiatives and identify common technical, data, and organizational obstacles.
- Compare major integration patterns—APIs, data virtualization, messaging, and hybrid architectures—from an AI enablement perspective.
- Describe how middleware, AI-enabled connectors, and data harmonization tools help bridge technological disparities and data quality issues in legacy environments.
- Design incremental migration and modernization plans that wrap, refactor, or rehost legacy capabilities without unacceptable disruption.

- Outline governance, risk, and compliance practices that ensure integrated legacy-modern ecosystems remain secure, auditable, and regulator-ready.
- Define success metrics and operating practices for sustaining hybrid architectures where legacy cores and modern AI platforms coexist over time.

# Terms to Know

**AI-Enabled Connector**[1] - An integration component that uses AI techniques (for example, schema inference, protocol detection, or intelligent mapping) to accelerate and automate connectivity between legacy and modern systems.

**Data Harmonization**[2] - The process of aligning data from disparate systems into consistent formats, structures, and business definitions so it can be used jointly in analytics and AI models.

**Data Virtualization**[3] - A technology that provides a unified, queryable view of data across multiple sources—including legacy systems—without physically moving or duplicating all of it.

**Hybrid Architecture**[4] - An environment where legacy on-premises systems coexist and interoperate with cloud platforms and modern services, often connected through APIs, messaging, and integration platforms.

**Legacy System**[5] - An older application or platform that remains essential to operations but may use outdated technologies, architectures, and interfaces that complicate integration.

**Legacy-Modern AI Integration Matrix**[2] - A simple model that maps integration patterns (for example, APIs, messaging, virtualization, replication) against AI requirements (latency, data breadth, write-back) to guide pattern selection for specific AI use cases.

**Middleware**[6] - Software that sits between systems, handling communication, transformation, routing, and orchestration to connect legacy and modern components.

**Migration Strategy**[7] - A structured approach to evolving or replacing legacy systems—such as rehosting, replatforming, refactoring, or rewriting—often executed incrementally to reduce risk.

# Introduction[8]

Legacy platforms remain the backbone of many enterprises, encompassing core banking systems, policy administration, inventory control, hospital information systems, and mainframe billing applications. They often house the most valuable longitudinal and transactional data, yet present major integration hurdles for modern analytics platforms, cloud data lakes, and AI services. This difficulty stems from their proprietary protocols, batch-oriented processes, and limited APIs. From an AI perspective, the question isn't whether to keep or replace legacy systems, but rather how to connect them so models access timely, high-quality data and can drive decisions back into operational workflows without destabilizing the core.

## The AI Imperative in Legacy Integration[9]

AI's effectiveness hinges on data that is complete, timely, and context-rich. Legacy systems typically capture mission-critical transactions and master records that define customers, products, policies, or accounts. They also embed tacit business rules and validations within their data structures and processes, operating continuously to produce change logs and events that can feed streaming and real-time analytics. If these systems remain isolated, AI models will operate on partial views, potentially leading to biased risk scores, inaccurate forecasts, or misaligned personalization. Effective integration improves data completeness, enables real-time insights, and synchronizes operations, allowing recommendations to flow back into legacy transaction systems via APIs, messages, or automation.

## Key Integration Challenges and AI-Driven Solutions[10]

Legacy integration is hard precisely because technology, data, and process assumptions have changed dramatically since many of these systems were built.

### Technological Disparities

Monolithic architectures, proprietary protocols, green-screen interfaces, and tightly coupled codebases resist straightforward API integration. Fortunately, AI-enabled connectors and integration platforms can infer message structures, simulate APIs around screens or files, and translate between old and new protocols, significantly reducing the effort that results from manual engineering.

### Data Quality and Silos

Legacy schemas often reflect historical business logic, featuring overloaded fields, cryptic codes, and incomplete documentation. AI-driven profiling and metadata tools scan these landscapes to identify issues, automate cleansing, normalize reference data, and support entity resolution across systems.

### Latency and Throughput Requirements

Many legacy platforms were designed for overnight batches, not continuous access by AI models and cloud platforms. Event-driven middleware and streaming pipelines can offload logs or change-data-capture (CDC) feeds in near real time, ensuring AI workloads see fresh data without overloading the core systems.

### Risk Management and Compliance

Replatforming core systems risks business continuity and regulatory compliance. AI-powered observability, anomaly detection, and predictive maintenance tools help detect emerging issues in integrated environments, reducing downtime and safeguarding data integrity during and after migration.

## Legacy-Modern Integration Layers[3]

We can visualize AI-centric integration as distinct layers: legacy systems form the base, followed by an integration/middleware layer (APIs, messaging, data virtualization), a harmonized data/AI layer (lakehouse, feature stores, AI services), and finally, consumer layers (dashboards, applications, agents). Each layer abstracts complexity from the one below while exposing standardized interfaces upward. This design allows new AI capabilities to be added without directly coupling every consumer to fragile legacy cores.

## Integration Strategies: An AI Enablement Perspective[11]

There is no single approach to legacy integration. Most enterprises blend several strategies over time.

### Incremental Modernization

Wholesale replacement projects frequently exceed budget and timeline expectations while increasing operational risk. Instead, incremental modernization wraps legacy systems with APIs, messaging, and AI-aware middleware. This gradually shifts functionality and data workloads to modern platforms while enabling early AI use cases, such as analytics on replicated cloud data.

### Hybrid Architecture Design

Hybrid architectures connect on-premises legacy cores with cloud-based analytics and AI platforms via secure links, gateways, and integration hubs. Batch extracts populate historical tables while CDC and streaming feeds provide real-time views for time-sensitive AI models in a "dual-speed" setup.

### Middleware Harnessing AI

Modern integration platforms (iPaaS, API management, ESBs) increasingly embed AI to automate mapping, error handling, protocol conversion, and process orchestration. They can propose schema mappings, flag anomalies, and optimize routes based on observed usage.

### Data Virtualization and APIs

Data virtualization layers provide unified, queryable views over legacy and modern stores for analytics and AI prototypes. Meanwhile, API gateways mediate access, enforce security policies, and manage traffic, shielding fragile legacy endpoints from direct external load.

### Cloud-Based Data Lakes and Warehouses

Cloud data platforms often serve as hubs where legacy data is ingested, cleansed, harmonized, and combined with modern sources for AI consumption. This typically starts with rehosted workloads and evolves toward cloud-native patterns as pipelines and logic are refactored.

## Comparing Major Modernization Strategies[12]

Legacy modernization efforts increasingly draw on methods like the "5 Rs" and "7 Rs" for cloud migration, which classify options such as rehost, replatform, refactor, and rebuild or replace.

### Rehosting (Lift-and-Shift)

Rehosting moves applications to new infrastructure, often the cloud, with minimal code changes. This reduces hardware costs and offers some integration benefits while preserving many legacy constraints around data models and interfaces.

### Replatforming

Replatforming applies targeted optimizations such as containerization or managed databases to improve scalability and automation without fully redesigning the application. It represents a middle ground between speed and modernization depth.

### Refactoring (Re-Architecting)

Refactoring restructures the system—frequently into services or microservices—while preserving core behavior. This increases flexibility for AI-ready integration patterns and event streams but requires more investment.

### Rebuilding or Replacing

Rebuilding or replacing provides the cleanest slate for AI-optimized data and integration but carries high change-management and implementation risk.

From an AI-enablement perspective, rehosting and replatforming often rely more heavily on external integration patterns—APIs, messaging, and data replication—to connect legacy data to AI platforms. Refactoring and rebuilding, however, enable deeper embedding of streaming, event-driven, and service-oriented patterns within the core. Therefore, choose your strategy in tandem with AI integration plans and the Legacy-Modern AI Integration Matrix. This ensures modernization paths are evaluated not only on cost and risk but also on their ability to meet latency, data breadth, and write-back requirements.

## The Legacy-Modern AI Integration Matrix[2]

To make integration decisions more systematic, the Legacy-Modern AI Integration Matrix maps integration patterns against AI requirements. It focuses on four common patterns—APIs, messaging and streaming, data virtualization, and data replication—and three core AI requirements: latency, data breadth, and write-back or actuation.

## Simplified Legacy-Modern AI Integration Matrix

| Integration Pattern | Latency Suitability | Data Breadth Capability | Write-back / Actuation Support |
|---|---|---|---|
| **Direct or Mediated APIs** | Good for low-latency, synchronous requests | Typically narrow to moderate (specific entities and operations) | Strong: supports transactional updates and decisions |
| **Messaging / Streaming (CDC, events)** | Excellent for near real-time feeds and high throughput | Moderate to broad, especially for event-rich domains | Moderate: supports asynchronous commands and alerts back to systems |
| **Data Virtualization** | Moderate latency; best for read-heavy queries and prototyping | Broad logical views across multiple sources | Limited: typically read-oriented; write-back routed via APIs or other channels |
| **Data Replication (ETL/ELT)** | Variable latency–strong for analytics, weaker for strict real-time needs | Very broad, especially for historical and feature-rich datasets | Indirect: write-back usually handled via separate operational interfaces |

Practically, teams can locate each AI use case on this matrix—for example, "fraud scoring with millisecond latency and automatic transaction holds" versus "monthly churn modeling with no immediate write-back"—and choose integration patterns and modernization strategies accordingly. This allows them to shift from batch-heavy approaches toward event- and API-centric patterns as architectures mature.

## Best Practices for Successful AI-Informed Integration[14]

Disciplined practices ultimately determine whether integrations are adequate and sustainable.

### Executive Sponsorship and Cross-Functional Teams

Legacy integration projects touch core revenue and risk processes, so they require clear sponsorship, funding, and decision paths. Cross-functional teams that combine business, IT, data science, and compliance ensure AI use cases are grounded in real needs and constraints.

### Comprehensive Data Mapping and Documentation

Documenting legacy schemas, data flows, and embedded business rules is essential for safe integration. AI-driven metadata extraction and code analysis tools can accelerate this work by inferring lineage and constraints.

### Testing with Realistic AI Use Cases

Validate integration against representative AI workloads, including data volumes, latency targets, and failure scenarios. Testing with real or production-like data uncovers edge cases in quality, throughput, and concurrency that synthetic tests might miss.

### Monitoring and Continuous Improvement

Integrated observability—covering integration flows, middleware, data quality, and model behavior—supports continuous tuning and issue detection. AI-powered anomaly detection flags unusual patterns such as drops in data volume or shifts in distributions.

# Thought Experiment

## AI-Powered Legacy Integration in Financial Services[15]

Imagine a global bank with a mainframe core banking system and multiple regional loan-servicing platforms. Historically, its cloud-based AI models for credit risk and fraud detection relied on nightly batch files. The bank now designs a hybrid architecture where middleware and API gateways expose selected legacy functions and data through secure, standardized interfaces. A CDC pipeline streams transaction updates into a cloud data lake and event bus in near real time. AI-enabled connectors map legacy codes to harmonized schemas, and cloud-hosted models score transactions as they arrive, sending decisions and alerts back via APIs or messages to legacy systems and modern channels.

Integration progresses in phases—from read-only streams for analytics, to write-back of risk scores and alerts, to decomposing selected legacy functions into microservices. Throughout, observability and compliance tooling track data lineage, model usage, and control effectiveness to satisfy regulators and internal risk teams.

# Success Metrics[16]

Evaluating legacy-modern integration requires metrics that capture both operational stability and AI enablement.

Track these metrics in an "Integration and Modernization Scorecard" that is regularly reviewed with technology, risk, and business sponsors to guide priorities and funding.

## Table of Illustrative Metrics

| Dimension | Example Metric | Why It Matters |
|---|---|---|
| **Data Availability for AI** | % of priority legacy data elements accessible to AI/analytics platforms in near real time | Shows how fully legacy data is unlocked for modeling and insight |
| **Latency and Throughput** | End-to-end delay from legacy transaction to AI model input; sustained events per second supported without degradation | Indicates whether integration can support real-time or high-volume AI use cases |
| **Integration Reliability** | No. of integration incidents per quarter, MTTR, and data-delivery success rates | Reflects stability and robustness of middleware, APIs, and pipelines |
| **Modernization Progress** | Proportion of legacy interfaces exposed via APIs, messaging, or virtualization; No. of high-risk batch jobs retired | Measures structural progress from brittle point-to-point links to more flexible patterns |
| **Governance and Compliance** | % of integrated data flows with documented lineage, access controls, and monitoring for policy violations | Demonstrates that integration supports regulatory and internal governance expectations |
| **Business / AI Impact** | Uplift in model performance, reduction in manual reconciliation, or faster decision cycles attributable to legacy integration | Connects integration investments to tangible outcomes and AI value |

# Practical Advice for Leaders[17]

Leaders are accountable for balancing modernization ambition with operational safety.

- **Treat legacy integration as a strategic AI enabler, not just IT plumbing.** Frame integration investments in terms of AI use cases and business outcomes—such as real-time risk, personalization, or operational automation—rather than solely cost or technical-debt reduction.
- **Start with value-anchored, incremental steps.** Identify a handful of high-impact scenarios and the minimum legacy integration needed to support them. Then, expand once you've demonstrated benefits to build momentum and de-risk larger modernization efforts.
- **Invest in integration platforms and skills.** Prioritize robust middleware, API management, and data integration platforms—ideally with AI-enabled mapping and monitoring—alongside upskilling architects and engineers in hybrid patterns.
- **Align governance early.** Involve security, risk, and compliance teams from the outset to define access patterns, logging requirements, and control points in integrated flows, reducing approval friction and rework later.
- **Plan for coexistence, not instant replacement.** Assume legacy systems will coexist with modern platforms for years. Therefore, design integration patterns and operating models that can sustain that hybrid reality.

# Conclusion

From an AI standpoint, integrating legacy and modern systems represents a strategic capability that dictates how fully and quickly enterprises can exploit their historical and operational data. By leveraging AI-aware middleware, hybrid architectures, data virtualization, and incremental migration strategies, organizations can create legacy value while maintaining the reliability and compliance that core systems provide. When combined with clear success metrics, cross-functional governance, disciplined execution, and structured approaches—such as modernization-strategy comparisons and the Legacy-Modern AI Integration Matrix—legacy integration transforms from a barrier into a source of competitive advantage for AI maturity.

# Notes

[1] AI-Enabled Connector and related integration concepts are defined in "Expert Advice on Integrating APIs with Legacy Systems in 2025" from the *Moesif Blog.*

[2] Data Harmonization, the Legacy-Modern AI Integration Matrix, and associated metrics are mapped in "AI Integration with Legacy Systems: A Practical Modernization Guide" from the Tredence Blog and "Legacy Data Integration: Challenges and Strategies" from the *WaferWire* Blog.

[3] Legacy-Modern Integration Layers and Data Virtualization are explained in "Modernizing Legacy Systems: A Guide to Strategies" from the *WaferWire* Blog and "Strategies for AWS Migration: The New 7th R Explained" from the *NetApp Blog.*

[4] Hybrid Architecture examples, including financial services applications, are drawn from "Hybrid Cloud Internet Banking Architecture" from Teamvoy and "Navigating Hybrid and Multi-Cloud Maturity in Financial Services" from LinkedIn.

[5] Legacy System is defined, in its standard sense, in "Legacy System Modernization" from *Deloitte Insights* and "How Modernizing Legacy Systems Drives Success in 2025" from the Cygnis Blog.

[6] For Middleware and API patterns, including latency considerations in the matrix, see "Expert Advice on Integrating APIs with Legacy Systems in 2025" from the *Moesif Blog* and supporting IBM resources.

[7] Migration Strategy comparisons, including the 5 Rs and 7 Rs frameworks, are drawn from "Strategies for AWS Migration: The New 7th R Explained" from the *NetApp Blog*, "Cloud Modernization Approaches: Rehost, Replatform, or Refactor?" from the vFunction Blog, "Top Legacy Application Modernization Strategies" from the Nix United Blog, and *WaferWire* sources on migration options and trade-offs.

[8] Contextual background in the Introduction on legacy systems comes from "Legacy Application Modernization: Challenges and Strategies" from the Softura Blog and "Legacy Application Modernization with AI Integration" from *Varseno Solutions.*

[9] The AI Imperative is examined in "AI Integration with Legacy Systems: A Practical Modernization Guide" from the Tredence Blog and "Agentic AI in Legacy Transformation: Modernizing Through Intelligent Overlays" from Architecture & Governance Magazine.

[10] Key Integration Challenges and AI-Driven *Solutions* are surveyed in "Expert Advice on Integrating APIs with Legacy Systems in 2025" from the *Moesif Blog*, "Best Legacy Code Management Platforms: Top 5 Options in 2025" from Swimm Learn, and supporting WWT and AgileSoftLabs insights.

[11] Integration Strategies from an AI Enablement Perspective are laid out in "AI Integration with Legacy Systems: A Practical Modernization Guide" from the Tredence Blog and *WaferWire* resources.

[12] Major Modernization Strategies are compared across "Strategies for AWS Migration: The New 7th R Explained" from the *NetApp Blog*, "Cloud Modernization Approaches: Rehost, Replatform, or Refactor?" from the vFunction Blog, "Top Legacy Application Modernization Strategies" from the Nix United Blog, and *WaferWire* sources on migration options and trade-offs.

[13] Messaging and streaming patterns in the matrix draw on event-driven guidance in "AI Integration with Legacy Systems: A Practical Modernization Guide" from the Tredence Blog and IBM materials.

[14] Best Practices for Successful AI-Informed Integration are drawn from "Legacy System Modernization" from *Deloitte Insights*, "How Modernizing Legacy Systems Drives Success in 2025" from the Cygnis Blog, "Legacy Application Modernization with AI Integration" from *Varseno Solutions*, and "Legacy Application Modernization: Challenges and Strategies" from the Softura Blog.

[15] The Thought Experiment on AI-Powered Legacy Integration in Financial Services draws on "Hybrid Cloud Internet Banking Architecture" from Teamvoy, "WWT Helps Financial Institution Build Hybrid Cloud Integration for Analytics and AI" from World Wide Technology, "Navigating Hybrid and Multi-Cloud Maturity in Financial Services" from LinkedIn, "Expert Advice on Integrating APIs with Legacy Systems in 2025" from the *Moesif Blog*, "AI Integration with Legacy Systems: A Practical Modernization Guide" from the Tredence Blog, "Agentic AI in Legacy Transformation: Modernizing Through Intelligent Overlays" from Architecture & Governance Magazine, and AgileSoftLabs modernization insights.

[16] Success Metrics for AI-legacy integration are drawn from "AI Integration with Legacy Systems: A Practical Modernization Guide" from the Tredence Blog, *WaferWire* resources, and IBM modernization discussions.

[17] Practical Advice for Leaders on AI-legacy integration is offered in "Legacy System Modernization" from *Deloitte Insights*, "Using Gen AI-Driven Modernization on Premises" from IBM Think Insights, and incremental approaches discussed in AgileSoftLabs and *WaferWire* resources.

Spending on AI governance platforms is expected to surpass $1 billion by 2030, fueled by fragmented global regulations extending to 75% of economies.

*Gartner*

"Global AI Regulations Fuel Billion-Dollar Market for AI Governance Platforms"

Kornutick

February 2026

# Key topics explored in this chapter:

- The Distributed AI Collaboration Framework (DACF)
- AI Models as Services
- Frameworks for Evaluating and Procuring AI Model Vendors
- Comparing AI Risk and Procurement Methods
- AI Vendor Governance Lifecycle
- Governing AI Model Vendors Post-Procurement

# WAY 28

# Manage Vendor Relationships


## Abstract

External AI and analytics vendors deliver capabilities that aren't just tools, but embedded decision engines, continuously evolving services rather than static products. While these model- and SaaS-based offerings accelerate innovation and reduce time to value, they also introduce new dependencies, opaque behavior, and complex risk profiles that traditional vendor management processes weren't designed to handle. This chapter presents approaches for evaluating, procuring, and governing analytics and AI vendors. It also outlines strategies for co-innovation, contractual protection, and ongoing oversight that preserve agility without sacrificing control, ethics, or compliance.


## Objective

After completing this chapter, you will be able to:

- Describe how AI "models as a service" and analytics SaaS offerings transform traditional vendor-management dynamics and risk profiles.
- Apply structured frameworks to evaluate and select AI and analytics vendors, considering capability fit, transparency, ethics, and integration readiness.
- Design governance mechanisms—monitoring, reviews, and escalation paths—for ongoing oversight of AI vendors post-contract signing.

- Define risk-management and contractual controls (e.g., SLAs, audit rights, data protection, exit strategies, and IP clauses) tailored to AI and model-driven services.
- Structure co-innovation relationships with key AI vendors that align roadmaps, responsibly share insights, and maintain comprehensive governance.
- Establish success metrics and review cadences that link vendor performance to business value, ethical standards, and regulatory expectations.

# Terms to Know

**AI as a Service (AIaaS)**[1] - Cloud-hosted AI capabilities—such as models, APIs, or agent platforms—consumed on demand, rather than deployed and managed entirely in-house.

**AI Vendor Assessment Framework (VAF)**[2] - A structured framework guiding organizations to evaluate AI vendors across dimensions like risk, benefit, transparency, and return on investment.

**Distributed AI Collaboration Framework (DACF)**[3] - A layered model for coordinating AI decision-making across external vendors, internal systems, and humans. Its four layers—cloud intelligence, edge inference, human interface, and feedback/governance—together enable safe, adaptive, and auditable collaboration.

**Ethical AI Criteria**[4] - Principles and requirements—such as fairness, transparency, accountability, and privacy—that vendors must meet to ensure responsible AI use.

**Model Governance**[5] - Policies, processes, and controls for managing models across their lifecycle, including validation, monitoring, documentation, and vendor oversight for externally provided models.

**Service-Level Agreement (SLA)**[6] - A contractual commitment defining performance targets (e.g., uptime, latency, accuracy) and consequences if a vendor fails to meet them.

**Third-Party Risk Management (TPRM)**[7] - The discipline of identifying, assessing, and mitigating risks introduced by external vendors and service providers, including AI providers.

# Introduction

In the era of AI and analytics, vendor relationships increasingly center on hosted models, managed platforms, and embedded AI features, moving beyond traditional on-premises software and one-off consulting engagements. While these AI-as-a-service offerings can be powerful accelerators, they also blur the line between internal and external decision-making. Key predictions and recommendations now flow from opaque systems controlled by third parties. To manage this effectively, organizations must evolve vendor-management practices. They need to emphasize transparency, model governance, ethical alignment, and co-innovation, moving beyond just price and technical fit.

At the same time, AI decision-making is increasingly distributed across cloud platforms, local applications, and human reviewers, rather than concentrated in a single monolithic system. Many organizations run vendor-hosted models in the cloud, while internal services perform edge-level checks or enrichment. Human experts then approve or override decisions for high-stakes cases. This chapter therefore introduces a Distributed AI Collaboration Framework (DACF). You can use it alongside procurement and risk tools to understand how vendors, internal systems, and humans share decision-making responsibility over time.

## The Distributed AI Collaboration Framework (DACF)[3]

The Distributed AI Collaboration Framework offers a simple yet robust way to map how AI vendors integrate into your broader decision ecosystem and where governance must act. The approach features four interlocking layers: cloud intelligence, edge inference, human interface, and feedback/governance.

### Cloud Intelligence Layer

The cloud-intelligence layer comprises external and internal AI services that generate core predictions, scores, or recommendations. In an AI-vendor context, this layer includes hosted models, SaaS analytics platforms, and agent services invoked via APIs.

Key considerations include:

- Vendor models' capability and fit for your use cases.
- Transparency into model design, limitations, and update practices.
- Cloud-level SLAs for uptime, latency, and quality.

### Edge Inference Layer

The edge-inference layer includes systems closer to your operations—decision engines, rules engines, or local models—that contextualize, filter, or combine cloud outputs before impacting users or processes.

Examples of edge-inference controls include:

- Business rules that constrain vendor scores, such as capping credit-limit changes for certain segments.
- Local anomaly detection that flags suspicious vendor outputs for review.
- Data-quality checks before sending inputs to the vendor.

### Human Interface Layer

The human-interface layer covers how human decision-makers and reviewers interact with vendor-supplied AI, including dashboards, case-management tools, and human-in-the-loop workflows.

Design priorities include:

- Presenting explanations, confidence indicators, and key features that drive predictions.
- Ensuring override, escalation, and appeal paths are clear and usable.
- Providing training and guidance so humans grasp both the capabilities and limitations of vendor systems.

### Feedback and Governance Layer

The feedback-and-governance layer spans monitoring, risk assessment, incident response, and continuous improvement across the other three layers. It connects vendor models to enterprise-risk models like the NIST AI Risk Management Framework and sector-specific regulations.

Core activities include:

- Aggregating metrics on performance, fairness, reliability, and user impact across vendors.
- Conducting periodic audits and red-team exercises on vendor AI systems.
- Integrating incident learnings and user feedback into vendor discussions, internal controls, and future procurement.

Throughout this chapter, consider the DACF a mental model: when evaluating vendors, ask how they'll perform at the cloud-intelligence layer.

When designing controls, decide what should reside in edge inference or the human interface. And when structuring governance, ensure the feedback-and-governance layer has sufficient authority and data.

## AI Models as Services[8]

Traditional vendor engagements focused on software licenses, professional services, or hardware, featuring clear deliverables, version cycles, and acceptance criteria. In contrast, AI-model vendors often deliver distinct characteristics that demand a fundamentally different approach to evaluation and governance.

### Dynamic and Opaque Deliverables

Models are hosted and continuously retrained, meaning their behavior may change as vendors update training data or algorithms. This complicates reproducibility and raises questions about who controls when and how models evolve. Unlike traditional software updates arriving at predictable version milestones, model behavior can shift silently between API calls, making it essential to track version identifiers and establish contractual notice obligations for material changes.

### Intense Data-Privacy and Security Demands

Using external AI services often requires sending sensitive or regulated data to vendors' infrastructure. This makes strong data protection, jurisdictional awareness, and clear boundaries around retention and secondary use essential. Organizations must understand precisely where data travels, how long it is retained, and whether it could be used to train generic models that benefit other customers—a concern that has prompted many regulated industries to demand contractual prohibitions on secondary training use.

### Dependence on Third-Party Expertise

Internal teams may have limited visibility into architectures, limitations, and training data, heavily relying on vendor documentation and dashboards to understand performance and risk. This asymmetry of information creates a governance challenge: organizations are accountable for outcomes produced by systems they did not build and cannot fully inspect. Contractual transparency requirements, audit rights, and independent testing help close this gap, but they must be negotiated before contracts are signed rather than demanded after problems emerge.

### Service-Level Complexity

Performance is governed by SLAs for uptime, latency, throughput, and sometimes accuracy or response quality, rather than fixed deliverables. This new landscape compels buyers to interrogate not only what a vendor's product does, but also how it changes over time, its transparency, and how it will be governed. The DACF emphasizes that these questions demand answers at every layer of your decision stack—from cloud intelligence through edge inference and human interaction to feedback and governance—not just in the contract.

## Frameworks for Evaluating and Procuring AI Model Vendors[9]

A structured evaluation framework helps teams compare AI vendors consistently and defensibly. Emerging guidance—including AI-specific vendor-assessment tools and risk-management models—can significantly improve procurement decisions.

### Capability and Fit Assessment

Assessment begins with the use case: What decision will the model influence, under which constraints, and at what scale? Key questions include whether the vendor's model demonstrably solves the targeted problem with acceptable accuracy and coverage. Can it scale to expected volumes and geographies without prohibitive cost? And how configurable is it for thresholds, rules, and outputs? Pilot evaluations and benchmark tests against internal baselines provide evidence that goes beyond marketing claims.

### Transparency and Explainability

Since many AI vendors offer black-box models, transparency is essential for trust and regulatory compliance. Buyers should seek access to model documentation and intended-use statements, explainability tools like feature-importance and local-explanation APIs, and audit logs capturing inputs, outputs, and version identifiers for investigations and audits.

### Compliance and Ethics

Responsible AI requires aligning vendor practices with your organization's values and regulatory obligations. Evaluation should consider evidence of bias testing and remediation, alignment with AI-governance frameworks and standards, and data-protection certifications and controls for cross-border transfers.

### Integration and Support

Even strong models can fail if they're difficult to integrate or poorly supported. Buyers should assess API quality, SDKs, documentation, and reference architectures. They also need to evaluate support responsiveness and access to experts, along with compatibility with existing monitoring, identity, and security tooling.

### Pilot and Proof of Concept

Before large-scale commitments, controlled pilots validate performance, integration complexity, and operational fit. Pilots should use representative data and workflows, measure accuracy, latency, throughput, and user experience, and include clear exit criteria for advancing or disqualifying vendors. A useful mental model is to visualize AI-vendor evaluation as a multi-axis rubric—capability fit, transparency and ethics, integration and operability, and commercial risk. Here, high capability but weak governance or integration can disqualify vendors for high-risk or regulated applications.

## Comparing AI Risk and Procurement Methods[10]

Different AI-risk and procurement methods offer complementary lenses for evaluating third-party AI vendors. Two influential examples are the NIST AI Risk Management Framework (AI RMF) and the AI Vendor Assessment Framework (VAF) developed by the Data & Trusted AI Alliance.

### AI Risk Management Framework (AI RMF)

NIST AI-RMF-inspired approaches start from an overarching view of AI risk across design, development, deployment, and use, emphasizing functions like Govern, Map, Measure, and Manage. Applied to procurement, this prompts organizations to map AI use cases and risk profiles before engaging vendors, measure potential impacts and controls, and embed continuous management of vendor-related risk into enterprise processes.

### AI Vendor Assessment Framework (VAF)

The VAF, by contrast, focuses tightly on evaluating external AI vendors and systems. It uses structured criteria covering risk, benefit, transparency, security, and governance readiness, with scoring rubrics and artifacts tailored to due diligence and oversight. It operationalizes high-level principles into concrete questions, documentation requests, and evidence requirements that procurement and risk teams can apply consistently across a vendor portfolio.

The evaluation model in this chapter is compatible with both approaches: it borrows the risk-first lifecycle view from NIST AI RMF and the practical, criteria-driven structure of the VAF. The DACF and the AI Vendor Governance Lifecycle situate these evaluations within your technical and organizational architecture, clarifying where vendor services reside and how they interact with edge-inference, human-interface, and feedback-and-governance layers over time.

## AI Vendor Governance Lifecycle[11]

Beyond evaluation approaches, it's helpful to view AI-vendor relationships through a lifecycle lens that spans from initial need identification through decommissioning or replacement. An AI Vendor Governance Lifecycle provides that unifying conceptual model and aligns with generalized AI-lifecycle guidance used in governance and compliance.

A simple lifecycle has six stages:

1. **Need identification and problem framing:** Business and technology teams define the decision problem, risk appetite, and whether external AI is appropriate.
2. **Market scan and pre-screening:** Procurement and risk functions identify candidate vendors and filter them using high-level criteria such as sector fit, certifications, and ethical commitments.
3. **Deep evaluation and pilot:** Teams apply structured assessment methods, run pilots, and test how vendor solutions will integrate into the DACF layers.
4. **Contracting and onboarding:** Legal, procurement, and risk functions negotiate SLAs, data and IP terms, audit rights, and incident obligations. They then onboard the vendor into inventories, monitoring, and governance forums.
5. **Operational monitoring and co-governance:** Teams monitor performance, fairness, and compliance, review metrics via scorecards, and engage in joint governance and co-innovation aligned to the feedback-and-governance layer.
6. **Review, renewal, and decommissioning:** Periodic reviews assess ongoing value and risk, leading to renewal, renegotiation, or decommissioning with structured exit and data-portability steps.

References to ongoing governance and post-procurement oversight map primarily to stages 5 and 6, while evaluation and piloting align with stages 2 and 3. The DACF helps distribute responsibilities and controls at each stage across technical layers and human roles.

## Governing AI Model Vendors Post-Procurement[12]

Signing a contract marks the beginning, not the end, of vendor governance. Ongoing oversight ensures models remain performant, fair, and aligned as conditions change.

### Continuous Performance Monitoring

Organizations should instrument vendor models with dashboards that track indicators like accuracy, coverage, latency, uptime, and error types where feasible. Because access to ground truth often lags, monitoring can include proxy metrics, user feedback, and outlier detection on inputs and outputs. AI-assisted monitoring and agent-driven SLA systems increasingly support this by detecting breaches and anomalies in real time and escalating issues automatically. In DACF terms, this spans cloud-intelligence performance, edge-inference guards, and human-interface feedback, all feeding into the feedback-and-governance layer.

### Version Control and Update Management

Dynamic models require explicit agreements and processes for updates. Governance practices include requiring version identifiers in APIs and logs; establishing test environments and protocols to evaluate new versions against your data before rollout; and defining rollback options and notice periods for material changes, especially in regulated contexts. Within the lifecycle, these practices reside in operational monitoring and co-governance, ensuring model changes in the cloud-intelligence layer are tested against edge-inference logic and human workflows before impacting real decisions.

### Data Privacy and Security Controls[13]

Vendor governance must enforce strong controls around data shared externally. This includes data minimization, anonymization or pseudonymization where possible; encryption in transit and at rest; clear statements about retention, secondary data uses, and deletion processes; and periodic reassessment of security posture and regulatory alignment. These controls should be embedded from contracting and onboarding onward and reflected in how data flows between your systems and the vendor across all DACF layers.

### Ethical Oversight and Incident Management[14]

Organizations should define incident categories—such as discriminatory outcomes, harmful content, or privacy violations—and establish playbooks for investigation, reporting, and remediation when vendor models misbehave. Governance forums should regularly review vendor performance against ethical-AI principles and decide on mitigations or vendor changes when necessary, using evidence aggregated across DACF layers and lifecycle stages.

### Collaborative Co-Innovation[15]

Strategic AI vendors can be innovation partners, not just providers. Co-innovation practices include regular roadmap sessions to align on features, regulations, and use cases; joint experiments or pilots using de-identified data in controlled environments; and shared learning loops where both parties contribute domain knowledge, feedback, and risk insights to improve models over time. Co-innovation should be staged within the lifecycle—early pilots in evaluation, broader experiments in operational monitoring. And the DACF helps determine where to safely integrate new capabilities, while governance retains authority to pause or redirect work if risks emerge.

### Risk Management and Contractual Considerations[16]

Contracts are key instruments for embedding AI-governance and risk controls into vendor relationships. Important elements include:

- **SLAs:** Define uptime, response-time, support-response and resolution-time targets, and where appropriate, quality metrics such as accuracy or false-positive limits. Also include remedies such as service credits, termination rights, and escalation triggers.
- **Risk appetite and classification:** Use AI-procurement risk models to classify use cases by risk level and align contractual controls with the risk your organization is willing to accept.
- **Audit rights and transparency reporting:** Reserve rights to review relevant controls, receive transparency reports, and request evidence of testing, certifications, or independent audits.
- **Data usage, retention, and IP:** Specify ownership of input data, derived outputs, and model improvements; clarify whether your data can train generic models; and define retention and deletion obligations, especially after termination.

- **Exit strategies:** Plan for vendor failure or strategic changes by including rights to export data, obtain transitional support, and ensure continuity of critical services during migration.

These elements focus on contracting and onboarding but demand a revisit during vendor reviews. They also influence how you instrument DACF layers—for example, ensuring logs support audit and exit rights.

# Thought Experiment

## Managing an AI-Based Credit-Scoring Vendor[17]

Consider a financial institution contracting with an AI vendor that provides credit-risk scores via a hosted service in a highly regulated environment where explainability, fairness, and data protection are paramount.

- **Evaluation and procurement:** The bank uses an AI-vendor assessment method, classifies credit scoring as high-risk, and sets a conservative risk appetite. Vendors, therefore, must demonstrate bias testing, regulatory adherence, and strong security certifications.
- **Explainability and monitoring:** The contract requires access to explainability dashboards, segment-level performance metrics, and tools for generating case-specific rationales. It also demands real-time alerts for shifts in approval rates or model performance across protected groups.
- **Governance forums:** A joint governance committee meets quarterly to review performance, data drift, regulatory guidance, and incident reports, deciding on retraining, configuration changes, or safeguards.
- **Contractual safeguards:** SLAs cover uptime and latency. Clauses define data residency, retention, audit rights, and incident obligations, and model updates must be sandbox-tested with rollback options.

In DACF terms, the vendor's scoring model resides at the cloud-intelligence layer. The bank's decision engine and policy rules form the edge-inference layer, loan officers and committees occupy the human-interface layer, and the governance committee, dashboards, and regulators make up the feedback-and-governance layer. Over time, the relationship can be evaluated against the lifecycle by tracking reductions in manual review time, changes in default rates, and incident frequency and severity from onboarding through renewal or replacement.

# Success Metrics[18]

Evaluate vendor relationships with metrics that connect operational performance, risk, and business value.[19] Organizations can track these metrics in a "Third-Party AI and Analytics Vendor Scorecard," which procurement, risk, IT, and business sponsors periodically review. The scorecard acts as a key artifact for the feedback-and-governance layer and for operational-monitoring and review stages.

## Table of Illustrative Metrics

| Dimension | Example Metric | Why It Matters |
|---|---|---|
| **Service Reliability** | Uptime % for critical APIs; average and response times | Shows how fully legacy data is unlocked for modeling and insight |
| **Model Performance** | Changes in accuracy, precision/recall, or business KPIs attributable to vendor models | Indicates whether integration can support real-time or high-volume AI use cases |
| **Governance and Ethics** | % of high-risk vendor models with completed assessments, bias tests, and documented explanations | Reflects stability and robustness of middleware, APIs, and pipelines |
| **Compliance Posture** | No. of issues raised in audits, regulator interactions, or cyber-insurance reviews related to third-party AI | Measures structural progress from brittle point-to-point links to more flexible patterns |
| **Commercial Efficiency** | Total vendor cost versus realized or projected value; No. of redundant vendors consolidated | Demonstrates that integration supports regulatory and internal governance expectations |
| **Co-Innovation Impact** | Count and impact of jointly delivered enhancements, new use cases, or process improvements with strategic AI vendors | Connects integration investments to tangible outcomes and AI value |

# Practical Advice for Leaders[20]

Leaders set the tone for how aggressively to pursue external AI capabilities and how firmly to manage associated risks.

- **Anchor vendor decisions in risk appetite and use cases.** Clarify which AI decisions you're willing to outsource and under what risk conditions. Use that clarity to guide vendor selection and contractual safeguards, especially for high-risk use cases.
- **Elevate vendor oversight into AI governance.** Treat key AI vendors as extensions of your AI ecosystem. Subject them to the same governance forums, model inventories, and monitoring standards as internal models, ensuring governance understands how vendor systems operate across DACF layers.
- **Design for reversibility and competition.** Avoid single-vendor lock-in by negotiating data portability, maintaining the ability to stand up alternatives, and periodically benchmarking competitors. Make reversibility a design objective from early lifecycle stages.
- **Invest in procurement and legal literacy on AI.** Equip procurement, legal, and risk teams with AI-specific frameworks, training, and checklists. This allows them to challenge vendors and structure agreements that map onto DACF and lifecycle approaches.
- **Lean into co-innovation with guardrails.** With strategic vendors, create joint innovation programs tied to clear value hypotheses and shared guardrails around data use, ethics, and IP. Stage these carefully from pilots to scaled rollouts under governance oversight.

# Conclusion

Vendor management in AI and analytics demands an evolved mindset: organizations aren't just buying tools anymore; they're embedding external decision systems into their operations. To harness these capabilities responsibly, they must adopt structured evaluation approaches, risk-aware procurement practices, and robust post-procurement governance that monitors performance, ethics, and compliance in real time. By combining clear SLAs, strong contractual protections, lifecycle-based oversight, and co-innovation practices grounded in the DACF, leaders can transform AI-vendor relationships into engines of innovation while preserving control, trust, and regulatory readiness.

# Notes

[1] AI as a Service—cloud-hosted AI capabilities consumed on demand rather than fully managed in-house—is described through *Cloudelligent*'s case-study materials.

[2] The AI Vendor Assessment Framework is set out in the Data & Trusted AI Alliance's guidance on evaluating AI vendors across risk, benefit, transparency, and governance dimensions.

[3] The Distributed AI Collaboration Framework draws on Cranium, *BigID*, Alation, and NIST AI-RMF commentary about multi-layered AI governance across cloud intelligence, edge inference, human interfaces, and feedback/governance.

[4] Ethical-AI criteria and procurement-oriented governance—emphasizing fairness, transparency, accountability, and privacy in vendor selection—are addressed in *Art of Procurement*'s AI-governance framework for procurement.

[5] Model-governance practices and AI-procurement risk controls—including lifecycle controls for externally provided models—are outlined in *HubSpot*-hosted "Risk Management Framework for AI Procurement" materials.

[6] SLA definitions and AI-specific service-level management concepts are drawn from *Newgen*'s discussion of AI-agent-driven SLA management alongside EaglePoint Technologies' best practices for IT-vendor SLAs.

[7] Third-party risk management and AI-vendor monitoring—including AI-specific considerations within TPRM programs—are addressed in *Venminder*'s vendor-management news and guidance.

[8] The new AI-vendor landscape and the need for contractually embedded protections are examined in EaglePoint Technologies' vendor-management best practices, *BetterCloud*'s SaaS-vendor guidance, and *Internet Lawyer Blog*'s clauses for AI-vendor contracts.

[9] Evaluation-framework elements for capability, transparency, ethics, integration, and pilots are developed in the DTA Alliance's VAF, *Art of Procurement*'s governance framework, *Cloudelligent*'s and GEP's SaaS-vendor management guidance, and EaglePoint's IT-vendor practices.

[10] *NIST AI RMF* and the VAF are compared in NIST's AI-risk-management framework documentation, Vanta's interpretive resources, the DTA Alliance's VAF material, and UKAI's commentary on responsible-AI procurement.

[11] AI Vendor Governance Lifecycle stages are drawn from governance and lifecycle materials presented by Scrut, Saidot, and Nemko's AI-lifecycle guidance, as well as *HubSpot*-hosted AI-procurement risk frameworks and DTA Alliance materials.

[12] Post-procurement monitoring, version-control, and SLA-governance practices are covered in *Venminder*'s and *FlowGenius*'s best-practice guidance for vendor monitoring, *Internet Lawyer Blog*'s update-management clauses, *Newgen*'s SLA-monitoring advice, and *Atlas Systems*' vendor-governance framework.

[13] Data-privacy and security-control recommendations—covering retention, secondary use, and deletion—draw on *Venminder*'s and *Atlas Systems*' discussions of third-party controls with *Internet Lawyer Blog*'s contractual clauses.

[14] Ethical-incident oversight and escalation playbooks are addressed in the Ethical AI Institute's RFX guidance on responsible-AI procurement and oversight of third-party systems.

[15] Co-innovation practices—joint pilots, roadmap alignment, and shared learning loops with vendors—are illustrated in RTS Labs' AI-in-financial-services case studies and Lucid's AI-driven financial-planning case studies.

[16] Contractual-risk-management elements—SLAs, risk classification, audit rights, data usage, and exit strategies—are covered in *Atlas Systems*' vendor-governance framework, *FlowGenius*'s vendor-management best practices, *Art of Procurement*'s AI-governance framework, *HubSpot*-hosted risk-management guidance, and GEP's SaaS-vendor-management guide.

[17] The credit-scoring thought experiment draws on RTS Labs' financial-services case studies, DTA Alliance's VAF, *Newgen*'s AI-SLA examples, *Art of Procurement*'s governance principles, *Atlas Systems*' governance framework, and *Cloudelligent*'s fintech AI case study.

[18] Vendor performance metrics and scorecard design draw on EaglePoint's vendor-performance metrics, *HubSpot*-hosted AI-procurement KPIs, *Venminder*'s compliance indicators, *BetterCloud*'s SaaS-portfolio metrics, and *FlowGenius*'s vendor-scorecard practices.

[19] Portfolio-optimization, commercial-efficiency, and co-innovation metrics are developed in *BetterCloud*'s SaaS-vendor-management guidance and GEP's SaaS-vendor-management recommendations for measuring value and innovation.

[20] Leadership-level advice on risk appetite, governance elevation, reversibility, literacy, and co-innovation guardrails draws on the Ethical AI Institute's RFX, DTA Alliance's VAF, *BetterCloud*'s SaaS-management guide, *Cloudelligent*'s case study, Lucid's co-innovation case studies, and related governance sources.

## Key topics explored in this chapter:

- The Journey from Piloting to Full Adoption
- Comparing the Journey to MLOps Maturity Models
- Model Management at Scale
- Embedding Predictive and ML into Decision Processes
- Technology and Infrastructure Enablers
- Overcoming Challenges

# WAY 29

# Advance Predictive and ML Capability

## Abstract

Predictive analytics and machine learning enable organizations to move beyond merely reacting to past events. Instead, they anticipate future occurrences and act proactively before issues or opportunities fully materialize. Yet, many enterprises remain trapped in "pilot purgatory," where technically promising proofs of concept never scale. This often happens because model lifecycle management, governance, and operational integration are either missing or underdeveloped. This chapter offers a clear roadmap for advancing predictive and ML capabilities from initial pilots to enterprise-scale adoption. We emphasize strong model management, risk-aware governance, and seamlessly embedding models into everyday decision processes.

## Objective

After completing this chapter, you will be able to:

- Describe the stages of the ML journey from pilots to full-scale operational adoption and recognize common pitfalls like "pilot purgatory."
- Apply MLOps concepts and practices to standardize model development, deployment, monitoring, and retraining across various use cases.
- Design end-to-end model lifecycle management processes, including validation, drift detection, and orderly retirement.
- Establish governance structures that clarify accountability, manage risk, and weave ethical and regulatory considerations

into ML initiatives using a Model Lifecycle Governance Framework that combines preventive, detective, and response controls.

- Integrate predictive and ML outputs into operational workflows, change-management efforts, and data-driven culture building.
- Define success metrics for ML capability maturity and prioritize investments in technology, talent, and processes that support sustainable scaling.

## Terms to Know

**Concept Drift**[1] - A change over time in the relationship between input features and the target variable, causing model performance to degrade even if data quality remains acceptable.

**Data Drift**[2] - A shift in the statistical distribution of input data compared to what the model encountered during training, often serving as an early warning signal for declining performance.

**MLOps**[3] - A discipline that combines machine learning, software engineering, and operations to automate and standardize the ML lifecycle from development to deployment and monitoring.

**Model Lifecycle Governance Framework**[4] - A structured approach to governing ML models across their lifecycle that organizes controls into preventive (up-front design and validation), detective (continuous monitoring and audits), and response (rollback, retraining, and escalation) layers.

**Model Registry**[5] - A centralized system that tracks models, versions, metadata, ownership, status, and deployment history to support traceability and governance.

**Pilot Purgatory**[6] - A state where organizations repeatedly run ML pilots that demonstrate technical promise but never progress to robust, scaled production use.

## Introduction[7]

Predictive analytics and ML promise better forecasts, smarter resource allocation, and automated decisions that can reshape costs, risks, and customer experiences. In practice, though, many AI projects stall before reaching production or fail to deliver lasting value. They're often treated as one-off experiments rather than components of a managed capability. Advancing ML requires treating models as living systems that demand continuous improvement, monitoring, and strong links to human decision-makers and operational processes. A Model Lifecycle Governance Framework clarifies who is responsible for preventing, detecting, and responding to model-related risks at each stage, transforming scattered projects into a coherent capability.

## The Journey from Piloting to Full Adoption[8]

Organizations that successfully scale ML typically progress through a series of stages, with deliberate hand-offs between them.

### 1. Pilot Phase: Proof of Concept and Validation

Pilots should address concrete, high-value problems with measurable outcomes rather than open-ended curiosity projects. Effective pilots:

- Focus on well-scoped use cases with clear hypotheses and Key Performance Indicators (KPIs).
- Utilize realistic, production-like data and cross-functional teams comprising business, data, and technology stakeholders.
- Capture not only model metrics but also important operational insights regarding data readiness, workflow integration, and user trust.

A pilot truly succeeds only when it yields both a credible business case and a practical blueprint for operating the model at scale. Preventive controls in this phase include disciplined problem framing, thorough data quality checks, comprehensive validation protocols, and thorough documentation before exposing any results in production environments.

### 2. Scaling Beyond Pilots

The transition from pilot to production marks where MLOps practices become essential. Key activities include:

- Standardizing pipelines for data ingestion, feature engineering, training, validation, and deployment.
- Automating deployment and monitoring through Continuous Integration/Continuous Delivery (CI/CD), comprehensive tests, and interactive dashboards, rather than relying on manual handoffs.
- Formalizing governance by clearly defining approvers, required documentation, risk assessments, and review cadences.

At this point, the Model Lifecycle Governance Framework evolves from primarily preventive controls to a more balanced set that integrates preventive release gates, detective monitoring, and response runbooks for rollback and remediation when issues surface.

### 3. Enterprise Adoption and Continuous Improvement

At higher maturity levels, organizations treat ML as a product portfolio embedded across various functions. Hallmarks include:

- Centralized model registries and ML platforms that offer self-service capabilities to data teams.
- Continuous feedback loops where monitoring results and user feedback inform retraining and enhancement backlogs.
- Explicit alignment of each production model with business KPIs, risk classifications, and named owners.

In this phase, governance focuses heavily on detective controls—such as portfolio-level monitoring, periodic audits, and fairness reviews—alongside mature response mechanisms for planned retraining, controlled replacement, and decommissioning to maintain a healthy overall model estate.

## Comparing the Journey to MLOps Maturity Models[3]

Published MLOps maturity models typically outline a path from manual, experiment-driven workflows to automated, standardized, and governed ML operations, often using levels like ad hoc, repeatable, managed, and optimized.

- The **pilot phase** in this chapter roughly aligns with ad-hoc or initial maturity, where experiments often reside in notebooks and scripts. By adding structure—clear hypotheses, realistic data, and early governance artifacts—organizations begin to move beyond purely exploratory work.
- The **scaling phase** corresponds to repeatable or managed maturity, where standardized pipelines, CI/CD, and model registries enable consistent engineering and monitoring across projects.
- **Enterprise-wide adoption and continuous improvement** reflect optimized maturity, where ML functions as a strategic platform closely tied to business KPIs, risk management, and comprehensive governance.

Viewing the journey this way helps teams benchmark their current standing and plan the necessary investments to advance to the next level.

## Model Management at Scale[9]

As the number of models grows, informal practices quickly become fragile, making disciplined lifecycle management indispensable.

### Model Development

Model development should occur in collaborative environments that support experiment tracking, reproducibility, and shared components. Recommended practices include:

- Versioning training data, code, and configurations to ensure experiments can be reproduced reliably.
- Employing feature stores to centralize engineered features and maintain a single source of truth for feature definitions.
- Tracking experiments with rich metadata such as model type, hyperparameters, dataset slices, and performance metrics.

Within the Model Lifecycle Governance Framework, these practices serve as preventive controls, making downstream monitoring, auditing, and comparison much more feasible.

### Model Validation

Validation must extend beyond a single train-test split. Strong validation approaches include:

- Cross-validation and holdout datasets to rigorously test robustness across different segments and time periods.
- A/B tests and shadow deployments that compare new models against existing ones under real-world operating conditions.
- Stress testing across edge cases, rare events, and fairness-sensitive segments, with all results captured as essential governance artifacts.

In governance terms, validation acts as the final preventive checkpoint before models begin influencing real-world decisions.

### Model Deployment

Deployment patterns—whether batch scoring, real-time APIs, or edge deployments—must adhere to consistent engineering standards. These typically involve:

- Packaging models using containerization or similar techniques for reliable, repeatable releases.

- Running integration tests to ensure models function correctly with upstream data sources and downstream applications before a broad rollout.

### Monitoring and Drift Detection

Once a model goes live, the governance focus shifts from "should this model go live?" to "should this model continue to operate as-is?" Monitoring should:

- Track performance metrics such as accuracy, precision, recall, and calibration over time and across key segments.
- Monitor data distributions on features and outcomes to detect data drift and potential concept drift.
- Utilize alerting systems and runbooks to define acceptable thresholds and specify the actions to take when metrics deteriorate.

These monitoring activities form the core detective controls within the governance framework.

### Retirement and Replacement

No model should run indefinitely. Clear retirement criteria—such as persistent underperformance, material business-process changes, or regulatory shifts—prevent outdated models from silently undermining decisions. Retirement processes typically involve:

- Decommissioning or disabling endpoints and jobs.
- Archiving model artifacts, datasets, and documentation for audit and learning purposes.
- Updating or removing dependent workflows, dashboards, and training materials.

Retirement decisions and documented rollbacks are crucial response controls that effectively close the loop in the model lifecycle.

### Governance and Risk Management[10]

Scaling ML without strong governance significantly increases the likelihood of biased, brittle, or non-compliant systems. The Model Lifecycle Governance Framework categorizes controls into three broad areas:

- **Preventive:** design standards, risk assessments, validation protocols, documentation templates, and approval gates.

- **Detective:** performance and drift dashboards, fairness and bias reports, periodic reviews, and formal audits.
- **Response:** rollback and failover procedures, retraining and re-validation workflows, human override mechanisms, and escalation and communication plans.

Key governance elements include:

- **Defined accountability:** Assign specific roles—model owners, data stewards, platform owners, and a governance committee—with clear responsibilities for approvals, monitoring, and escalation.
- **Risk-based oversight:** Classify models by risk (for example, financial impact, regulatory exposure, impact on individuals) and calibrate requirements for documentation, explainability, and human oversight accordingly.
- **Ethics and bias management:** Incorporate fairness tests, disparate-impact analysis, and bias reviews into the lifecycle, especially for models affecting opportunities, access, or safety.
- **Transparency and explainability:** Favor interpretable models where feasible, and employ explanation tools when more complex models are necessary, ensuring key stakeholders can understand and challenge predictions.
- **Integrated controls:** Link up-front validation, ongoing monitoring and drift detection, and defined remediation actions into a single coherent control system rather than isolated checks.

Referencing the framework when designing governance charters, model-risk policies, runbooks, and dashboards helps ensure consistent control implementation, avoiding an ad hoc approach.

## Embedding Predictive and ML into Decision Processes[11]

Models only generate value when their outputs consistently inform real decisions in ways that users trust and find practical.

### Integration into Workflows

Effective integration approaches include:

- Surfacing predictions directly within systems people already use, such as CRM platforms, logistics tools, clinical applications, or decision support dashboards.

- Exposing model outputs through APIs and event streams that can trigger actions, notifications, or downstream workflows automatically.
- Providing contextual information alongside predictions, such as confidence scores, key drivers or features, and alternative scenarios, enabling users to interpret and, if necessary, challenge recommendations.

### Building a Data-Driven Culture

Human factors often dictate whether ML capabilities take root or simply fade away. Important practices include:

- Leaders demonstrating reliance on data and model outputs when making decisions, and consistently requesting evidence rather than intuition alone.
- Offering data literacy and ML literacy programs for both managers and frontline staff, ensuring they feel confident using, questioning, and improving models.
- Creating feedback channels where users can flag confusing or implausible predictions and observe how that feedback informs model updates or process changes.

These feedback loops also function as informal detective and response mechanisms, especially for high-impact models where user experience and trust prove invaluable.

## Technology and Infrastructure Enablers[12]

Technology choices can either bolster or hinder ML scaling. Key enablers include:

- **Scalable compute and storage:** Cloud and hybrid platforms offer elastic resources for experimentation, training, and production inference without lengthy procurement cycles.
- **Feature stores:** Shared feature stores ensure consistent feature definitions and align training and serving data, thereby reducing errors and duplicated effort.
- **Orchestration platforms:** Workflow orchestration coordinates complex ML processes—data ingestion, feature engineering, training, validation, deployment, and retraining—significantly improving reliability, observability, and recoverability.

When aligned with the Model Lifecycle Governance Framework, these platforms can enforce preventive checks in CI pipelines, support detective monitoring at scale, and automatically trigger response runbooks when alerts fire.

## Overcoming Challenges[13]

Several recurring challenges can stall progress if left unaddressed:

- **Data quality and availability issues:** Incomplete, inconsistent, or siloed data can severely undermine model performance and user trust. Therefore, robust DataOps practices and strong data governance foundations are often prerequisites for ML success.
- **User skepticism and explainability gaps:** If users perceive models as opaque or misaligned with their expertise, they may disregard outputs. Clear explanations, comprehensive training, and user involvement in design help build trust.
- **Change management hurdles:** New models frequently alter roles, workflows, and performance expectations. Without deliberate change management, even technically sound solutions can encounter significant resistance.
- **Tension between speed and control:** Teams may feel compelled to choose between rapid experimentation and strong governance. However, a risk-tiered governance approach allows for faster iteration with lower-risk models while reserving stringent controls for higher-impact use cases.

Explicitly addressing these challenges—and embedding responses into the Model Lifecycle Governance Framework—helps organizations overcome early roadblocks.

# Thought Experiment

## Advancing ML in Healthcare Operations[14]

Consider a hospital system piloting a predictive readmission model that flags patients at high risk of returning within 30 days of discharge. The pilot at a single hospital demonstrates that targeted follow-up calls and care-management interventions successfully reduce readmissions. To scale responsibly, the system:

- Builds automated pipelines with comprehensive data quality and completeness checks before scoring.

- Deploys the model as an API integrated into the electronic health record (EHR) system, ensuring clinicians see risk scores at the point of discharge planning.
- Implements monitoring dashboards that track performance, calibration, and fairness across hospitals, units, and key demographic groups.
- Establishes a governance committee that includes clinicians, data scientists, ethicists, compliance officers, and patient representatives to review performance, biases, and complaints.
- Provides training and quick-reference guides to clinicians on interpreting risk scores, discussing them with patients, and offering feedback on surprising or problematic predictions.

Using the Model Lifecycle Governance Framework, the hospital system combines:

- Preventive controls during design and validation (including fairness checks).
- Detective controls via dashboards, drift monitoring, and clinician feedback.
- Response controls such as adjusting thresholds, retraining with new data, temporarily rolling back to simpler rules, or updating workflows when necessary.

Over time, the model integrates into standard discharge planning, with governance ensuring it continues to improve rather than degrade or cause unintended harm.

## Success Metrics[15]

Evaluate ML capability advancement using metrics that reflect both technical maturity and business impact. Many organizations also track governance-focused indicators—such as the percentage of models with completed risk assessments, assigned owners, or up-to-date runbooks—as part of evaluating the Model Lifecycle Governance Framework's effectiveness.

### Table of Illustrative Metrics

| Dimension | Example Metric | Why It Matters |
|---|---|---|
| **Pilot-to-Production Rate** | % of ML pilots that reach production within 12-18 months | Shows the organization's ability to move from experimentation into stable operational use |
| **Time to Production** | Average time from model sign-off to production deployment | Reflects MLOps efficiency, engineering discipline, and bottlenecks |
| **Model Portfolio Health** | No. of models in production, share registered and actively monitored, and proportion meeting performance thresholds | Indicates maturity of lifecycle management and governance across the model estate |
| **Business-Outcome Impact** | Changes in revenue, cost, risk, or quality metrics that can be linked to key ML models | Connects ML capability to tangible enterprise value rather than technical metrics alone |
| **Drift and Incident Rates** | Frequency of significant drift events or model-related incidents and time to detection and remediation | Measures robustness of monitoring and effectiveness of response controls |
| **Cultural Adoption** | % of key decisions that reference ML outputs or analytics, plus survey-based measures of data-driven behaviors | Reflects the extent to which ML is embedded into organizational culture and daily decision-making |

# Practical Advice for Leaders[16]

Leaders play a pivotal role in transforming ML from isolated experiments into a core organizational capability.

- **Define a clear ML ambition and portfolio.** Identify a focused set of priority use cases with explicit KPIs, and manage them as a cohesive portfolio rather than scattered projects.
- **Invest early in MLOps and DataOps foundations.** Fund shared platforms, pipelines, and governance capabilities that make each successive model easier and safer to deploy.

- **Make accountability explicit.** Assign both business owners and model owners to each production model, ensuring clear responsibility for outcomes, monitoring, and compliance.
- **Champion culture and change.** Demonstrate data-driven decision-making, support training and literacy programs, and recognize teams that effectively use ML in real decisions.
- **Balance innovation with guardrails.** Encourage experimentation in low-risk domains while insisting on rigorous governance for higher-impact models, using the Model Lifecycle Governance Framework as a reference point.

# Conclusion

Advancing predictive and machine learning capability isn't a mere technology rollout; it's a managed initiative from initial pilots to broad, trusted adoption across the enterprise. Organizations that invest in strong MLOps foundations, disciplined lifecycle management, risk-aware governance, and intentional cultural integration can transform ML from isolated success stories into a scalable engine of operational change. By treating models as living systems, aligning stages with recognized MLOps maturity models, and applying a Model Lifecycle Governance Framework that combines preventive, detective, and response controls, they can harness the benefits of AI-driven operations while effectively managing risks.

# Notes

1 Concept drift—the changing of feature-target relationships as a key risk—is defined in Fiddler AI's articles on machine-learning model-lifecycle management.

2 Data drift, emphasizing shifts in input distributions as early indicators of performance issues, is detailed in Encord's model-drift best-practices guidance.

3 MLOps and its role in standardizing and automating ML workflows are characterized in Assist Software's overview of MLOps as a "game changer" and *MLOps Community* resources on AI in production.

4 The Model Lifecycle Governance Framework's preventive, detective, and response structure is organized in governance.aicareer's AI-model-lifecycle governance materials.

5 The model-registry concept—centralized tracking for models, versions, and metadata—is explained in *Clarifai*'s ML-lifecycle-management materials.

6 Pilot purgatory, pilot-to-production rates, and related scaling challenges are examined in *Business2OChannel*'s content on moving from pilot to production with MLOps.

[7] Stalled AI projects, the importance of treating models as living systems, and the need to link ML to measurable business outcomes are the subjects of *Nirvana Lab*'s writing on scaling ML-driven products across global operations.

[8] The staged journey from pilots through scaling to enterprise adoption, with its emphasis on explicit transitions, is mapped in guidance from Agility-at-Scale, *Business20Channel*, *MLOps Community*, *Saventech*, and governance.aicareer on scaling AI projects.

[9] Practices for model development, validation, deployment, monitoring, and retirement are recommended in *Databuzz*, Fiddler AI, Assist Software, *Clarifai*, Encord, and governance.aicareer on ML-lifecycle management.

[10] Governance elements—accountability, risk-based oversight, ethics and bias management, explainability, and tiered controls—are addressed in *Culture Partners*' AI-and-culture guidance, LinkedIn articles on data-driven culture and change management, Agility-at-Scale's risk-tiering, Fiddler AI's transparency practices, and Encord's drift-monitoring guidance.

[11] Embedding models into workflows, building data-driven culture, and using feedback loops are explored in *Burtch Works*' strategies for embedding analytics, *Saventech*'s MLOps content, *Culture Partners*' cultural-change guidance, LinkedIn articles on data-driven culture, *Nirvana Lab*'s scaling case studies, and governance.aicareer's governance framework.

[12] Technology enablers—scalable environments, feature stores, orchestration platforms, and their alignment with governance—are discussed in Assist Software, *Databuzz*, *Saventech*, *Business20Channel*, and *MLOps Community* resources on infrastructure for ML at scale.

[13] Common obstacles and approaches to overcoming them—DataOps investment, explainability, change-management programs, and risk-tiered governance—are catalogued in *MLOps Community* analyses, *Culture Partners*' change-management work, *Burtch Works*' culture insights, Agility-at-Scale's guidance, and governance.aicareer's framework.

[14] The healthcare readmission thought experiment and its application of preventive, detective, and response controls draw on *Nirvana Lab*'s scaling examples, Assist Software's MLOps practices, LinkedIn discussions on data-driven culture, *Clarifai*'s monitoring guidance, and *Culture Partners*' governance and culture perspectives.

[15] Success-metrics and governance-specific indicators for scaled AI programs are drawn from *Business20Channel*'s metrics for scaling AI, *Nirvana Lab*'s focus on outcome measures, governance.aicareer's governance-effectiveness indicators, and *Burtch Works*' measures of cultural adoption.

[16] Leadership-focused advice—on ambition and portfolio definition, early investment in MLOps and DataOps, explicit accountability, culture change, and balancing innovation with guardrails—is drawn from Agility-at-Scale, *Databuzz*, LinkedIn culture articles, *Burtch Works*, Assist Software, and governance.aicareer.

# Key topics explored in this chapter:

- AI-Specific Security and Privacy Challenges
- Best Practices for Securing AI-Powered Analytics
- Taxonomy of AI Attacks and Defense Patterns
- Governance and Culture

# WAY 30

# Prioritize Security and Privacy

## Abstract

Security and privacy in analytics and AI now dictate organizations' ability to trust their systems and meet escalating regulatory and societal expectations. As AI models ingest sensitive data and operate within complex, distributed pipelines, new threat classes—like prompt injection, model poisoning, and model extraction—significantly expand the attack surface beyond traditional IT risks. This chapter outlines end-to-end practices for securing AI-powered analytics environments, integrating technical controls, privacy-by-design pipelines, AI-specific defenses, and governance structures to collectively safeguard confidentiality, integrity, and trust.

## Objective

After completing this chapter, you will be able to:

- Identify AI-specific security and privacy risks and distinguish them from traditional IT threats.
- Design security controls for analytics pipelines that protect data at rest, in transit, and in use, while upholding privacy-by-design principles and regulatory compliance.
- Implement practical defenses against prompt injection and other LLM-centric threats, such as input filtering, architectural isolation, and adversarial testing.
- Apply privacy-enhancing techniques—including anonymization, tokenization, differential privacy, and federated learning—to minimize the exposure of personal and sensitive data.

- Establish governance structures, incident-response processes, and cultural practices that embed AI risk management into daily operations.
- Define success metrics that track the effectiveness of security and privacy controls across AI and analytics ecosystems.

# Terms to Know

**Adversarial Attack**[1] - A technique in which inputs are intentionally crafted to cause a model to produce incorrect or harmful outputs, often with minimal, hard-to-detect perturbations.

**Data Minimization**[2] - A privacy principle and regulatory expectation that organizations collect, use, and retain only the data necessary for specific, declared purposes.

**Differential Privacy**[3] - A set of techniques that inject controlled noise into outputs or computations so that insights can be derived from datasets without revealing information about any specific individual.

**Federated Learning**[4] - A machine-learning approach where models are trained across decentralized data sources, with only model updates—not raw data—aggregated centrally, reducing the need to move or centralize sensitive data.

**Model Poisoning**[5] - An attack where adversaries manipulate training data or update processes to embed malicious behavior or degrade model performance.

**Prompt Injection**[6] - An attack on LLMs and generative AI in which malicious instructions are embedded in user prompts or external content to override system instructions, exfiltrate data, or bypass safeguards.

**Security by Design / Privacy by Design**[7] - Engineering principles that embed security and privacy controls from the earliest stages of system and pipeline design instead of layering them on as afterthoughts.

# Introduction

As organizations deploy AI models across customer interactions, operations, and decision workflows, security and privacy failures carry increasingly severe and visible consequences. Generative AI and LLM-driven agents introduce dynamic behaviors adversaries can manipulate through carefully crafted prompts or poisoned data. Meanwhile, analytics pipelines swiftly move sensitive information across clouds, tools, and partners. Regulators are responding with stricter enforcement of data-protection rules and AI-specific governance expectations, making security and privacy a strategic imperative for any serious analytics and AI program.

## AI-Specific Security and Privacy Challenges[8]

### AI Model Vulnerabilities

AI models, especially large language models and other generative systems, face attack vectors not typically found in conventional applications.

- **Prompt-injection attacks** attempt to override or divert an AI system's instructions by embedding malicious directives within user input or referenced content. This includes hidden instructions in documents or web pages the model processes, creating risks of data leakage, policy bypasses, or unauthorized AI agent actions.
- **Evasion attacks** craft adversarial inputs that models misclassify. Meanwhile, model poisoning injects malicious data into training or fine-tuning to degrade performance or implant backdoors. Both actions undermine trust and can compromise downstream systems.
- **Reverse-engineering and model-extraction attacks** approximate or clone proprietary models by repeatedly querying exposed APIs. This risks intellectual-property loss and reveals embedded business logic or sensitive patterns.

### Complex and Distributed Data Flows

Modern analytics pipelines encompass ingestion, transformation, model training and inference, and consumption by dashboards, APIs, and AI agents across multiple clouds and regions. Each node—be it a streaming engine, feature store, model server, LLM gateway, or connector—can introduce vulnerabilities if access control, encryption, and privacy enforcement are inconsistently applied.

### Regulatory Landscape and Ethical Obligations

Data-protection laws such as GDPR, HIPAA, and CCPA, alongside emerging AI regulations, impose stringent requirements for consent, minimization, purpose limitation, data-subject rights, and breach notification. AI-governance guidance further emphasizes fairness, transparency, and accountability, framing biased or unsafe models as both ethical and compliance risks that demand active management.

## Best Practices for Securing AI-Powered Analytics[9]

### Comprehensive Data Encryption

Encryption remains a foundational protection.

- Encrypt data in transit using modern TLS configurations as information traverses endpoints, services, and clouds.
- Encrypt data at rest in databases, object stores, model repositories, and log stores with strong algorithms and key management.
- Extend encryption to intermediate artifacts such as feature stores, model snapshots, vector indexes, and prompt logs, which can contain sensitive attributes or business secrets.

### Fine-Grained Access Control and Zero-Trust Security

Zero-trust architectures assume no implicit trust based on network location; therefore, every request must be authenticated and authorized.

- Implement centralized identity and access management with role-based or attribute-based controls across data platforms, ML services, and LLM gateways.
- Apply least-privilege principles to both human users and AI agents, restricting access to only the data and functions essential for each role.
- Segment and isolate sensitive environments, such as production model-serving clusters or datasets containing regulated information, with stricter controls and enhanced monitoring.

### Input Filtering and Sanitization

Strong input handling proves crucial, as prompt injection and adversarial inputs target models directly through their inputs.

- Utilize input-validation and content-filtering proxies to inspect prompts or payloads for known injection patterns, malicious instructions, or anomalous structures.
- Separate system instructions from user content using strict schemas and delimiters. Additionally, design prompts with clear instruction hierarchies to limit user override.
- Log prompts and responses for red-teaming and forensic analysis; and protect these logs as sensitive data.

### Robust Adversarial Testing and Model Hardening

Security testing must extend to model behavior, not merely infrastructure.

- Conduct regular adversarial testing and red-teaming of models using crafted prompts or inputs to probe for jailbreaks, data exfiltration, and safety bypasses.
- Incorporate adversarial training and robustness techniques—exposing models to adversarial examples and edge cases during training—to enhance resilience.
- Evaluate and document trade-offs among robustness, performance, and latency, including any limitations and residual risks within model-governance artifacts.

### Complete Audit Trails and Real-Time Monitoring

Visibility proves essential for detecting and responding to incidents.

- Maintain immutable, centrally collected logs for data access, pipeline execution, model queries, parameter changes, and administrative actions.
- Utilize SIEM and observability platforms to aggregate logs and metrics, applying anomaly detection to flag unusual query volumes, access patterns, or output behaviors.
- Monitor model telemetry—confidence scores, output distributions, error rates, and drift—for sudden changes that could signal data poisoning, exploitation, or configuration errors.

### Privacy-Enhancing Techniques

To minimize the exposure of personal data while preserving analytic value, organizations can:

- Utilize anonymization and tokenization for direct identifiers and highly sensitive attributes.
- Apply differential privacy for statistical analyses and training on sensitive datasets.
- Adopt federated learning or on-device inference to keep data local where possible, transferring model updates instead of raw data.

### Regulatory Automation and Policy Enforcement

Manual compliance checks don't scale with modern pipelines.

- Embed data-classification, consent-checking, and geographic-routing rules into ingestion and transformation flows, automatically quarantining or blocking non-compliant records.

- Automate retention, masking, and minimization policies to ensure data lifecycles align with legal and internal requirements.
- Integrate compliance tests into CI/CD for data and AI pipelines, preventing deployments that violate policy baselines.

## Taxonomy of AI Attacks and Defense Patterns[10]

This table summarizes major AI-specific attack types and associated defense patterns, serving as a reusable reference for analytics and AI teams.

## Major AI Attack Types and Defenses

| Attack Type | Brief Description | Primary Targets | Example Defense Patterns |
|---|---|---|---|
| **Prompt Injection** | Malicious instructions embedded in user prompts or external content to override system behavior | LLM prompts, context windows, retrieval sources | Input-filtering proxies, strict prompt-schema separation, output validation, least-privilege connectors, red-teaming |
| **Data / Model Poisoning** | Malicious data injected into training or fine-tuning to corrupt behavior or implant backdoors | Training sets, feature stores, update pipelines | Data-quality gates, trusted sources, in-depth training, drift monitoring, supply-chain security |
| **Model Inversion** | Reconstruction of sensitive training data from model outputs or embeddings | Deployed models, embedding APIs | Limiting confidence-score exposure, rate-limiting, differential privacy, careful prompt/output design |
| **Model Extraction** | Replicating model functionality by systematically querying APIs and training a clone | Public model APIs, SaaS endpoints | API authentication and throttling, watermarking outputs, limiting returned information, monitoring for scraping-like behavior |

### Positioning This Guidance Relative to AI Risk Frameworks[11]

Prominent AI-risk and governance models, such as the NIST AI Risk Management Framework (AI RMF) and the OWASP Top 10 for LLMs, offer high-level structures for understanding and mitigating AI risks. The guidance in this chapter serves as a pipeline-focused implementation of these approaches.

- The NIST AI RMF's Govern function manifests here in the recommendations on cross-functional committees, risk appetite, and training, while the Map function aligns with AI-specific risk identification and the attack taxonomy.
- Suggestions around success metrics and monitoring support the Measure function. Incident-response practices correspond to the Manage function, especially when responding to and recovering from AI incidents.
- For OWASP's LLM Top 10, the chapter's advice on input filtering, logging, red-teaming, and access control maps directly to mitigations for prompt injection, sensitive-information disclosure, and poisoning categories.

Viewing the chapter through this lens helps readers perceive it as a concrete playbook that fits under NIST's functions and complements OWASP's LLM-specific risk catalog.

## Governance and Culture[12]

Technical controls are necessary but insufficient; governance and culture stabilize security and privacy over time.

### Cross-Functional Security and Privacy Committees

AI-governance best practices emphasize cross-functional oversight, encompassing IT, data, legal, compliance, and business leadership. Effective committees:

- Define AI risk appetite and approve high-risk use cases.
- Align security and privacy controls with enterprise-risk methods.
- Oversee policies for AI systems, including third-party services and agent platforms.
- Ensure findings from monitoring and incidents feed back into design, training, and procurement.

### Promoting a Culture of Responsible AI Use

Ultimately, security and privacy depend on everyday behaviors.

- Training should cover both technical and socio-technical aspects of AI risk, including secure prompt practices, appropriate data handling, and how to recognize AI misuse.
- Leadership should foster a safety-first mindset and encourage "effective challenge," making it acceptable to question AI-generated outputs and decisions.
- Clear channels for employees and affected individuals to report concerns about AI decisions, data exposure, or unfair outcomes help surface issues early.

### Incident-Response Protocols Aligned to AI Threats

Incident-response plans must account for AI-specific scenarios.

- Organizations should maintain dedicated AI incident playbooks for prompt injection, model poisoning, data leakage via models, and compromised agents. These playbooks must specify roles for detection, triage, containment, communication, and recovery.
- Tabletop exercises and simulated attacks help teams practice these playbooks, expose gaps, and enhance coordination.

# Thought Experiment

## Securing an AI Chatbot Service[13]

Imagine a healthcare provider launching an AI chatbot designed to answer patient questions and guide them through services. This chatbot would inevitably process sensitive health information.

- An input-validation proxy filters prompts before they reach the model, identifying prompt-injection attempts, disallowed requests, and suspicious instruction patterns.
- Conversation data is encrypted in transit and at rest. Logs are minimized, de-identified, and protected with strict access controls.
- Security and data-science teams regularly red-team the chatbot with adversarial prompts and edge cases, feeding findings into model hardening and prompt adjustments.

- SIEM and AI-based detectors monitor for unusual query patterns or response behaviors, triggering automated containment and human review when anomalies appear.
- A cross-functional AI-governance group periodically reviews fairness, consent handling, logging practices, and incident reports to maintain regulatory alignment and policy adherence.

This configuration enables the provider to benefit from conversational AI while preserving patient trust and ensuring compliance.

# Success Metrics[14]

Security and privacy programs should use metrics that help leaders demonstrate progress and target investments strategically.

## Table of Illustrative Metrics

| Dimension | Example Metric | Why It Matters |
|---|---|---|
| **Encryption and Access** | % of sensitive datasets and model artifacts encrypted and protected by fine-grained IAM | Shows coverage of core technical safeguards for confidentiality |
| **Pipeline Policy Coverage** | Share of critical pipelines enforcing policy-as-code for classification, consent, minimization, and retention | Indicates maturity of privacy-by-design and regulatory automation |
| **AI Incident Frequency** | No. of AI-related security/privacy incidents per quarter and mean time to detect | Reflects both resilience and monitoring effectiveness |
| **Adversarial Testing Depth** | Frequency of red-team exercises and number of identified issues remediated per cycle | Measures proactive effort to discover and fix vulnerabilities |
| **Training and Culture** | % of relevant staff completing AI security/privacy training and improved secure-usage behaviors | Links cultural readiness to technical controls |
| **Compliance Posture** | Audit findings related to data protection and AI governance, and avoidance of fines or enforcement actions | Gauges how well controls stand up to external scrutiny |

## Practical Advice for Leaders[15]

Leaders must ensure security and privacy evolve in step with AI ambition.

- **Declare a clear AI risk appetite and principles.** Articulate risk tolerance for various AI use cases and establish non-negotiable security and privacy principles, such as default encryption and human-in-the-loop oversight for high-risk decisions.
- **Integrate security and privacy into the pipeline.** Invest in pipeline-level controls and policy-as-code so every new model and data product automatically inherits consistent protections.
- **Treat AI security as an integral part of AI governance.** Integrate security and privacy experts into AI steering committees and risk reviews from the outset, not merely during compliance checks.
- **Fund red-teaming and resilience, not just prevention. Allocate** resources for adversarial testing, prompt-injection exercises, and response drills so the organization learns and adapts before real attacks occur.
- **Model ethical vigilance.** Set expectations that AI success encompasses safety and fairness, and recognize teams that identify and mitigate risks early, not solely those that deliver features fastest.

## Conclusion

Prioritizing security and privacy in analytics and AI means moving beyond traditional perimeter defenses to address model-level vulnerabilities, pipeline-level controls, and AI-specific regulatory and ethical demands. Organizations that embed encryption, zero-trust access, adversarial testing, and privacy-by-design into their analytics pipelines—supported by cross-functional governance and an informed culture—will build more trustworthy AI ecosystems, experience fewer incidents, and better withstand regulatory scrutiny. Connecting these practices to frameworks such as the NIST AI RMF and OWASP LLM Top 10 further strengthens their legitimacy and bridges high-level guidance with day-to-day engineering decisions.

# Notes

[1] Adversarial attacks are defined in "Navigating the Liminal Edge of AI Security: Deconstructing Prompt Injection, Model Poisoning, and Adversarial Perturbations in the Cognitive Cyber Domain" from the Cloud Security Alliance Blog.

[2] Data minimization is explained in "Privacy by Design in the Pipeline: Embedding Data Protection at Scale" from the Databahn *Blog*.

[3] Differential privacy is detailed in "Data Security in Analytics Pipelines: Safeguarding Sensitive Information in the Age of Big Data" from the Daydreamsoft Blog.

[4] Federated learning is examined in "Privacy by Design in the Pipeline: Embedding Data Protection at Scale" from the Databahn *Blog*.

[5] Model poisoning is detailed in "The Double-Edged Sword of Generative AI Security: 2025 Guide" from the Oligo Security Academy.

[6] Prompt injection—its risks and mechanisms—is addressed in "Prompt Injection in LLMs" from the *Obsidian Security* Blog and "Prompt Injection Attacks on LLMs" from the *Wiz Academy*.

[7] Security by design and privacy by design are examined in "Data Pipeline Security: Best Practices" from the Techment Blog.

[8] AI-specific security challenges—including complex data flows and regulatory obligations—are analyzed in "Navigating the Liminal Edge of AI Security" from the Cloud Security Alliance Blog, "AI Security Challenges: Best Practices for 2025" from the Invicti Web Security Blog, "AI Governance Best Practices" from the *Databricks Blog*, and "The Rise of the Security Data Pipeline" from the Software Analyst Substack.

[9] Best-practice guidance on encryption, zero-trust access, input filtering, adversarial testing, logging, monitoring, and privacy-enhancing techniques is drawn from the Daydreamsoft Blog, Techment Blog, Databahn *Blog*, Practical DevSecOps, *Wiz Academy*, NHIMG Community, *Databricks Blog*, Software Analyst Substack, and related sources.

[10] A taxonomy of AI attack types and defenses is assembled from "AI-Specific Attack Vectors" from Auxin, "Securing AI/ML Models" from the Yash Technologies Blog, "Prompt Injection Attacks on LLMs" from the *Wiz Academy*, "Navigating the Liminal Edge of AI Security" from the Cloud Security Alliance Blog, "Data Security in Analytics Pipelines" from the Daydreamsoft Blog, "AI Security Challenges" from the Invicti Web Security Blog, and "The Rise of the Security Data Pipeline" from the Software Analyst Substack.

[11] The mapping to *NIST AI RMF* and OWASP LLM Top 10 draws on "NIST *AI Risk Management Framework*" from NIST, "Web Security and AI: OWASP and *NIST AI RMF*" from the *AuditBoard* Blog, "OWASP Top 10 for Large Language Model Applications" from the OWASP Foundation, "The OWASP Top 10 for LLM: Updated 2025" from the Oligo Security Academy, "AI Governance" from *Palo Alto Networks Cyberpedia*, and "AIRMF Playbook: Govern" from NIST AIRC Resources.

[12] Governance and culture recommendations—covering cross-functional committees, training, safety-first mindset, reporting channels, and AI-incident playbooks—are drawn from "AIRMF Playbook: Govern" from NIST AIRC Resources, "AI Governance" from *Palo Alto Networks Cyberpedia*, "AI Governance Best Practices" from the *Databricks Blog*, "Navigating the Liminal Edge of AI Security" from the Cloud Security Alliance Blog, and "AI Security Challenges" from the Invicti Web Security Blog.

[13] The healthcare chatbot thought experiment draws on "AI Security Challenges" from the Invicti Web Security Blog, "A Guide to Prompt Injection Attacks" from the Lakera Blog, "Data Security in Analytics Pipelines" from the Daydreamsoft Blog, "LLM Security Best Practices 2025" from the NHIMG Community, "The Rise of the Security Data Pipeline" from the Software Analyst Substack, and "AIRMF Playbook: Govern" from NIST AIRC Resources.

[14] Success-metric examples and their rationales are assembled from "Data Security in Analytics Pipelines" from the Daydreamsoft Blog, "Privacy by Design in the Pipeline" from the Databahn *Blog*, "AI Security Challenges" from the Invicti Web Security Blog, "Navigating the Liminal Edge of AI Security" from the Cloud Security Alliance Blog, "AI Governance" from *Palo Alto Networks Cyberpedia*, and compliance discussions from the Databahn *Blog* and *Databricks Blog*.

[15] Leadership advice on risk appetite, pipeline-level controls, integrating security into AI governance, funding red-teaming, and modeling ethical vigilance is drawn from "AI Governance Best Practices" from the *Databricks Blog*, "The Rise of the Security Data Pipeline" from the Software Analyst Substack, "AI Governance" from *Palo Alto Networks Cyberpedia*, "Prompt Injection 101" from Practical DevSecOps, and "AIRMF Playbook: Govern" from NIST AIRC Resources.

Privacy teams are shrinking with the median staff size down from 8 to 5, even as AI heightens demands for data governance, quality tagging, and ethical compliance.

*ISACA Now*

"Five Key Findings from ISACA State of Privacy Report"

Kanouse

January 2026

# Key topics explored in this chapter:

- The Automation Imperative in Analytics
- Automation Opportunities Across the Analytics Lifecycle
- Comparing the Automation Lifecycle to Maturity Models
- Balancing Automation with Human Oversight
- Technology Enablers of Effective Automation
- Organizational and Cultural Considerations

# WAY 31

# Automate to Free Human Capacity


## Abstract

Automation in analytics reorients human effort, shifting it from manual data handling and routine reporting toward higher-order work such as interpretation, strategic framing, and influencing decisions. By deliberately automating repetitive activities across the analytics lifecycle—data ingestion and preparation, feature engineering, model deployment, reporting, and ongoing monitoring—organizations can accelerate operations and enhance consistency. This also creates more space for analysts to tackle complex, ambiguous problems where human judgment remains essential. This chapter examines concrete automation opportunities, crucial human-in-the-loop guardrails, enabling technologies, cultural considerations, and measurement practices that ensure automation amplifies, rather than displaces human capacity.


## Objective

After completing this chapter, you will be able to:

- Explain why automation serves as a cornerstone for scaling analytics and estimate how it shifts analyst time from low-value preparation work toward more valuable activities.
- Identify high-impact automation opportunities across the analytics lifecycle, from data ingestion and preparation through modeling, deployment, and reporting.
- Design automation patterns that integrate human-in-the-loop (HITL) oversight, explainability, and ethical safeguards to prevent blind trust in automated outputs.

- Choose and combine enabling technologies—RPA, AI/ML, workflow-orchestration platforms, and interactive tools—to build resilient, human-centered analytics automation.
- Address organizational and cultural dimensions of automation, including reskilling, change management, collaboration, and governance expectations.
- Define and monitor metrics that demonstrate how automation impacts efficiency, quality, analyst experience, and business outcomes.

# Terms to Know

**AI Augmentation**[1] **-** The use of AI and automation to enhance human capabilities and decision-making rather than to fully replace human involvement.

**Automation ROI**[2]**-** The net financial benefit derived from automation relative to its total cost, often measured through labor savings, error reduction, and business-outcome improvements.

**Human-Centered Automation Framework**[3] **-** A design approach that explicitly balances automated steps, human-in-the-loop checkpoints, and ethical guardrails, ensuring that automation augments human judgment rather than displacing it and that higher-risk decisions retain meaningful human oversight.

**Human-in-the-Loop (HITL)**[4] **-** A design pattern where humans supervise, validate, or override automated steps at defined decision points, especially in higher-risk or ambiguous situations.

**Workflow Orchestration**[5] **-** Coordination of tasks across systems and teams using tools that manage dependencies, scheduling, error handling, and monitoring for end-to-end processes.

# Introduction[6]

Analysts frequently report spending a significant share of their time locating, cleaning, and preparing data, leaving only a small slice for actual analysis, storytelling, and stakeholder engagement. As data volumes, sources, and expectations continue to rise, manual workflows simply can't keep pace without exhausting teams and slowing insight delivery. Automation offers a clear path forward, but only when we design it to complement human strengths—pattern recognition, judgment, and contextual understanding—instead of relegating people to passively watching opaque pipelines run. The Human-Centered Automation Framework, introduced in this chapter, provides a structure for deliberately designing these balanced workflows from the start.

## The Automation Imperative in Analytics[7]

Evidence across industries reveals that analysts and data scientists still dedicate a significant majority of their time to low-level data-preparation tasks, often termed the "80/20 problem." Without automation, we face several challenges:

- Teams can spend 60-80% of project time discovering, cleaning, structuring, and validating data.
- Manual handoffs, spreadsheet logic, and one-off scripts introduce inconsistencies and hard-to-detect errors.
- Scaling from a small set of reports or models to a large portfolio becomes impractical and fragile.

Well-designed automation counters these issues by:

- Reducing time spent on repetitive preparation tasks through automated ingestion, transformation, and quality checks.
- Standardizing processes so pipelines and reports behave consistently and become easier to reuse.
- Supporting self-service and on-demand reporting, enabling business users to obtain answers without overwhelming central analytics teams.

When positioned as AI augmentation within an appropriate framework, automation also tends to boost job satisfaction by allowing analysts to spend more time interpreting results, exploring scenarios, and engaging directly with business stakeholders.

## Automation Opportunities Across the Analytics Lifecycle[8]

Automation delivers its greatest value when it significantly reduces toil without sacrificing essential human oversight. The Human-Centered Automation Framework encourages teams at each lifecycle stage to ask:

- What can we automate?
- What must remain human?
- And where do we need explicit HITL checkpoints and guardrails?

## The Human-Centered Automation Framework

| Lifecycle Stage | Automated Work Segment | HITL Segment | Guardrail Segment |
|---|---|---|---|
| **Data Preparation and Ingestion** | Ingestion, profiling, transformations | Approve schema changes, review anomalies | Data-quality thresholds, lineage rules |
| **Feature Engineering and Modeling** | AutoML training, feature search | Problem framing, model selection, fairness review | Model-risk policy, documentation standards |
| **Deployment and Monitoring** | CI/CD, drift alerts, auto-rollback | Approve major releases, investigate alerts | Risk thresholds, audit logging |
| **Reporting and Visualization** | Refresh pipelines, NLG summaries, alerts | Curate insights, stakeholder narration | Access controls, usage monitoring |

### Data Preparation and Ingestion

Data preparation often provides the most fertile ground for automation gains. Modern tools can:

- Automatically discover and profile new data sources.
- Propose cleansing and transformation steps based on patterns, rules, or learned behaviors.
- Infer schemas and automatically map new sources into existing models.
- Capture metadata, lineage, and quality metrics as pipelines execute.

Within the framework, these automations run by default, while humans review exceptions, approve changes impacting key metrics or regulated fields, and adjust rules when context shifts.

### Feature Engineering and Model Development

Automation can significantly accelerate, but never fully replace, modeling work. AutoML and related platforms can:

- Automate feature selection, model training, and basic hyperparameter tuning.

- Use optimization methods to explore large parameter spaces.
- Standardize development workflows through template pipelines and experiment-tracking systems that capture configuration and results.

Human judgment remains central to correctly framing the problem, choosing appropriate loss functions, and balancing accuracy against fairness, interpretability, and operational resilience. Activities such as model selection, fairness assessments, and sign-off on production candidates function as explicit HITL checkpoints.

### Model Deployment and Monitoring

Deployment and monitoring lend themselves effectively to automation through MLOps practices:

- CI/CD pipelines can package models, run unit and integration tests, and push to staging or production with automated rollbacks if tests fail.
- Monitoring systems track performance, latency, drift, and error rates, triggering alerts and, where appropriate, automated retraining or rollback jobs.
- Canary and shadow deployments can expose new models to limited traffic, collecting evidence before a full rollout.

Human approvals at defined risk thresholds and clear escalation paths when monitoring alerts trigger keep humans in control of high-impact changes.

### Reporting and Visualization

Reporting is often where business stakeholders most visibly experience the benefits of automation:

- Automated data pipelines keep dashboards refreshed with minimal manual intervention.
- Natural-language-generation tools draft narrative explanations of key trends and anomalies.
- Conversational interfaces allow users to query curated datasets using everyday language.
- Event-driven alerts notify stakeholders when thresholds are crossed or anomalies arise.

Under the Human-Centered Automation Framework, these outputs serve as starting points for human analysis and communication rather than unquestioned recommendations.

## Comparing the Automation Lifecycle to Maturity Models[9]

Many analytics and automation maturity models outline a trajectory from manual, descriptive reporting toward increasingly predictive and prescriptive analytics, all underpinned by higher levels of automation.

- At **early maturity**, organizations rely heavily on ad hoc reports and manual data preparation. The data-preparation and reporting practices in this chapter demonstrate how to move beyond this stage by automating ingestion, cleaning, and refresh cycles.
- **Intermediate maturity** introduces standardized pipelines, some AutoML, scripted deployment routines, and rules that automate recurring analytics tasks. When combined with HITL checkpoints and workflow orchestration, these elements align closely with the automation lifecycle described here.
- At **advanced maturity**, organizations deploy real-time data, embedded machine learning, and self-optimizing decision engines operating within policy and risk constraints.

In this context, the Human-Centered Automation Framework becomes especially vital to ensure that, even when low-risk decisions are fully automated, humans remain accountable for policy choices, ethical considerations, and continuous evaluation.

## Balancing Automation with Human Oversight[10]

Automation without meaningful oversight can amplify mistakes, biases, and misinterpretations at scale. The Human-Centered Automation Framework formalizes a mode of calibrated collaboration between humans and machines, moving beyond a push for full autonomy. It achieves this by combining several strategic design approaches.

- **Human-in-the-loop designs** introduce explicit checkpoints where humans review, adjust, or approve automated outputs, particularly around high-impact decisions such as fraud flags, credit decisions, or major model releases.
- **Explainability and transparency** demand that automated outputs include rationales, key drivers, or feature-importance

views. This lets users interrogate and challenge results rather than simply accepting them.

- **Continuous feedback loops** provide users with clear mechanisms to report incorrect, low-quality, or harmful outputs. This feedback then informs model retraining, rule refinement, or interface changes.
- **Ethical guardrails** embed bias checks, protections for sensitive attributes, consent enforcement, and escalation workflows directly into automated processes.
- **Adaptive automation** modulates the degree of automation based on risk level, confidence, or context—for example, auto-approving low-risk decisions while routing medium- and high-risk cases to human reviewers.

Together, these patterns position automation as a powerful assistant whose work remains visible, contestable, and adjustable, rather than a black box.

## Technology Enablers of Effective Automation[11]

Several categories of technology typically collaborate to deliver end-to-end automation in analytics.

- **Robotic process automation (RPA)** handles highly repetitive, rule-based tasks—such as copying data between legacy systems, running standard reports, or reformatting flat files—especially where modern APIs are missing or incomplete.
- **Machine learning and AI** underpin "intelligent" automation by classifying documents, extracting entities, detecting anomalies, recommending transformations, and generating code, SQL, or documentation that accelerates analytics work.
- **Workflow-orchestration platforms** coordinate dependencies, retries, scheduling, and observability across data and analytics pipelines, providing a central control plane for complex, multi-system workflows.
- **Interactive analytics tools** combine automated insights with rich exploration capabilities. This enables analysts to drill into anomalies, change parameters, override defaults, and add contextual commentary while automation handles the heavy lifting underneath.

Within our approach, we intentionally assemble these components so automation handles more repetitive work, but humans still set context, retain override authority, and actively shape how tools are utilized.

## Organizational and Cultural Considerations[12]

Technology alone won't deliver on automation's promise; organizational structures, skills, and culture often dictate success or failure. As routine tasks become automated, analysts increasingly need capabilities in problem framing, experiment design, stakeholder communication, and ethical reasoning, along with training on how to collaborate effectively with AI tools.

Change-management efforts are essential because fears about job loss, loss of control, or fairness can easily derail automation programs. Transparent communication, visible commitments to reskilling, and involving teams in design and tool selection help build trust.

Cross-functional collaboration among analytics, IT, operations, security, and compliance ensures automated workflows are resilient, secure, and policy-aligned. Governance should clarify:

- Which activities are suitable for automation.
- Which decisions require HITL review and under what conditions.
- How exceptions and failures are handled.
- Who owns automated processes and is accountable for their outcomes.

Mechanisms like automation review boards, change-control processes, and formal documentation reduce the risk of "shadow automation" evolving outside oversight. Embedding the Human-Centered Automation Framework into governance charters, training, and role descriptions reinforces that automation and human judgment are a shared responsibility.

# Thought Experiment

## Automating Fraud-Detection Analytics[13]

Imagine a global insurance company modernizing its fraud-analytics capabilities. Previously, these capabilities relied on manually extracted claims data, batch-run models, and long queues of undifferentiated alerts.

In the updated design:

- Data pipelines automatically ingest and standardize claims data from multiple systems, applying quality checks and enrichment rules along the way.
- Machine-learning models score claims in near real time, highlighting suspicious patterns and assigning risk scores.
- Automated alerting routes high-risk claims to investigators via dashboards that display key contributing features, relevant history, and similar past cases.
- Investigators and analysts provide feedback on false positives and missed fraud, which then feeds into model retraining and rule refinements. Governance policies require human approval for any automated claim denials, and periodic audits review bias, performance, and impact across different customer segments.

The result is quicker detection, less manual triage, fewer unnecessary escalations, and more investigator time focused on genuinely complex cases—a practical illustration of Human-Centered Automation in action.

## Success Metrics[14]

Evaluating automation requires examining efficiency, quality, and the extent to which human work shifts toward higher-value activities. Pre- and post-automation baselines—comparing cycle time, error rates, and manual effort—are especially useful for quantifying ROI. Within the Human-Centered Automation Framework, additional measures can track the share of decisions with human-in-the-loop escalation and how often automated decisions are reversed or adjusted after human review.

## Table of Illustrative Metrics

| Dimension | Example Metric | Why It Matters |
|---|---|---|
| **Time Efficiency** | Reduction in cycle time from data arrival to insight or decision; % decrease in manual preparation time | Shows how automation accelerates insight delivery and frees analyst capacity |
| **Error and Quality** | Change in error rates, rework, and data-quality incidents before and after automation | Indicates whether automation improves reliability rather than just speed |
| **Analyst Capacity Shift** | % of analyst time spent on higher-value tasks versus preparation | Demonstrates whether automation truly frees human capacity |
| **Adoption and Satisfaction** | User adoption of automated tools, satisfaction scores, and qualitative feedback on workflows | Reflects cultural acceptance and practical usability |
| **Governance and Risk** | No. of policy violations, escalation rates for high-risk cases, and audit findings related to automated workflows | Shows whether automation operates within defined risk and compliance boundaries |
| **Explainability and Trust** | % of automated decisions with available explanations; trust scores from key user groups | Indicates whether stakeholders understand and trust automated outputs rather than treating them as black boxes |
| **Continuity and Resilience** | System uptime for automated pipelines, mean time to recovery (MTTR), and frequency of manual fallback activation | Demonstrates that automation is reliable under real-world conditions and does not create new failure points |
| **Business Outcomes** | Financial impact such as cost savings, revenue uplift, risk reduction, or customer experience improvements attributable to automation | Connects automation to tangible enterprise value |

## Practical Advice for Leaders[15]

Leaders play a pivotal role in positioning automation as a tool to unleash human potential rather than merely a cost-cutting lever.

- **Start with bottlenecks.** First, pinpoint the steps where analysts lose the most time or where errors prove especially costly, then prioritize automation in those areas.
- **Design with people in mind.** Involve analysts and business users in mapping workflows so tools support natural ways of working and preserve meaningful control points.
- **Institutionalize HITL and guardrails.** Define where human review is mandatory, how escalations function, and how automated decisions are logged and audited; codify the Human-Centered Automation Framework in policies and standards.
- **Invest in skills and storytelling.** Ensure that the time gained through automation intentionally redirects toward deeper analysis, experimentation, and narrative development, not simply filling new low-value tasks.
- **Track and communicate impact.** Utilize clear metrics to demonstrate improvements in speed, quality, and business results, and share these stories widely to reinforce trust and sustain investment.

## Conclusion

Thoughtfully implemented automation expands human capacity by relieving analysts of repetitive work and giving them more time to tackle complex, strategic questions. Organizations that gain the most from automation deploy it aggressively where appropriate but pair it with strong human-in-the-loop oversight, explainability, ethical safeguards, and cultural support. This keeps people as the ultimate stewards of analytic insight and action. By measuring results and continuously refining workflows under a Human-Centered Automation Framework, they build analytics programs that are both highly efficient and genuinely human-centered.

# Notes

[1] AI augmentation—using automation to enhance rather than replace human analytic work—is addressed in *Livelytics*' discussion of this approach.

[2] The Automation-ROI definition follows *Intalio*'s process-mining strategy, which focuses on using analytics to quantify automation value in workflows.

[3] The Human-Centered Automation Framework draws on *Fast Company*'s "human-in-the-loop safety net" and HCL Software's AI-guardrails guidance on protecting brands in the age of agentic AI.

[4] Human-in-the-loop patterns are explained through HCL Software's guardrails content and Sogolytics' overview of HITL AI.

[5] For workflow orchestration in data analytics, see Infomineo's analysis of AI and data-analytics trends that emphasize orchestration across processes.

[6] The introduction's statistics on analysts spending 60–80 percent of their time on data preparation draw on Aristotle Metadata's analysis of wasted data-team time and *McKinsey*'s talent-strategy insights for automated machine learning.

[7] The "80/20 problem," its impacts, and automation's benefits are examined in research from ProjectPro, *McKinsey*, Integrate.io, *Streamkap*, OptimusAI, *Intalio*, Infomineo, Sogolytics, and related sources.

[8] The automation-opportunity breakdown across data preparation, modeling, deployment, monitoring, and reporting is drawn from OptimusAI, Integrate.io, *Livelytics*, Infomineo, *McKinsey*, *Databuzz*, Fiddler AI, Governance.AICareer, *Clarifai*, Encord, *Streamkap*, and Sogolytics.

[9] The mapping from automation lifecycle stages to analytics-maturity levels is developed across AltexSoft's analytics-maturity model, DAS42's data-analytics-maturity framework, *McKinsey*'s AutoML commentary, Infomineo's 2026 trends, and *Fast Company* and HCL Software's work on human-in-the-loop guardrails.

[10] Balancing automation and human oversight—including adaptive automation and feedback loops—is taken up by Statsig on automation limits, *Fast Company* on HITL safety nets, HCL Software on guardrails, *Nirvana Lab* on production feedback loops, and *Culture Partners* on ethical and cultural considerations.

[11] The technology-enablers section draws on *Intalio*'s RPA and process-mining viewpoint, OptimusAI's data-engineering automation, Infomineo's orchestration emphasis, *Livelytics*' interactive analytics framing, and Sogolytics' human-in-the-loop automation commentary.

[12] Organizational and cultural guidance on reskilling, change management, collaboration, and governance comes from *Hypestudio*'s automation-ROI guide, Integrate.io's data-preparation-efficiency insights, HCL Software's guardrails recommendations, *Palo Alto Networks*' AI-governance content, *Fast Company*'s HITL article, and related sources.

[13] The fraud-detection thought experiment draws on patterns from OptimusAI's data-pipeline automation, *Saventech*'s MLOps pipelines, Fiddler AI's model-management guidance, Governance.AICareer's lifecycle-governance framework, Encord's drift-monitoring practices, *Hypestudio*'s ROI analysis, and *Fast Company*'s HITL design.

[14] The success-metrics table and baseline recommendations draw on OptimusAI's time-savings discussion, Integrate.io's data-quality statistics, *McKinsey*'s talent-strategy analysis, *Livelytics*' automation-value framing, *Intalio*'s ROI measurement strategy, *Streamkap*'s real-time analytics guidance, and Statsig's evaluations of automation limits.

[15] Leadership-focused advice on starting with bottlenecks, designing with people in mind, institutionalizing HITL, investing in skills, and tracking impact draws on Integrate.io's bottleneck data, Sogolytics' HITL design, *Fast Company*'s human-loop article, *Palo Alto Networks*' AI-governance principles, *McKinsey*'s talent-strategy guidance, and *Hypestudio*'s automation-ROI recommendations.

.

## Key topics explored in this chapter:

- The Strategic Imperative of AI-Centric Emerging Tech Vigilance
- Methods for Continuous Technology Assessment
- Practical Piloting of Experimental AI Tools
- Building Rigorous Business Cases for AI Adoption
- Scaling AI Innovation with Agility
- Managing Innovation Risks and Avoiding Pitfalls

# WAY 32

# Stay Agile with Emerging Technology

## Abstract

New technologies—especially fast-moving AI capabilities—tend to shift quickly from novelty to basic competitive requirements. Organizations that keep pace build a repeatable discipline around horizon scanning, focused experimentation, and evidence-based business-case development. This helps them selectively adopt what matters, set aside what does not, and adjust course as conditions evolve. This chapter presents AI-focused approaches for tracking trends, testing emerging tools, and scaling only those innovations that meet risk-adjusted value thresholds. It helps enterprises remain nimble and future-oriented without being tossed around by hype cycles.

## Objective

After completing this chapter, you will be able to:

- Explain why AI-centered vigilance around emerging technologies is strategically important and how it differs from conventional technology-upgrade schedules.
- Apply a structured approach to continuous technology assessment, including horizon scanning, capability inventories, opportunity and risk mapping, and cross-functional advisory mechanisms.
- Design pragmatic AI pilot initiatives using clear goals, realistic datasets, agile delivery practices, and "fail-fast, learn-fast" decision gates to prevent indefinite delays.

- Develop well-formed, risk-adjusted business cases for AI adoption that quantify benefits, model multiple scenarios, and involve stakeholders from across the enterprise.
- Describe methods for scaling AI innovation using adaptable architectures, governance structures, and cultural enablers that maintain long-term agility.
- Recognize common innovation traps—such as hype chasing, unchecked technical debt, and ethical or regulatory blind spots—and outline ways to mitigate them.

# Terms to Know

**AI Emerging-Tech Agility Cycle**[1] - A repeatable loop for managing AI innovation from Scan → Select → Pilot → Scale → Retire, emphasizing disciplined decision gates, risk-adjusted learning, and continuous portfolio refresh.

**AI Investment Lifecycle**[2] - A structured view of AI initiatives, from idea and pilot through scaling, optimization, and retirement, with continuous revisiting of ROI and risk hypotheses.

**Horizon Scanning**[3] - Systematic exploration of emerging trends, signals, and weak indicators to anticipate future technological developments and their implications.

**Risk-Adjusted ROI**[4] - An assessment of an AI investment's expected return that explicitly incorporates probabilities, scenarios, and downside risks, moving beyond just best-case benefits.

**Signal**[5] - A specific observation (e.g., a new paper, startup, tool, or regulation) that may indicate an emerging technological shift or trend.

**Technology (or Foresight) Radar**[6] - A visual mapping of technologies and trends across stages such as explore, experiment, adopt, and retire, often used to communicate priorities and track emerging tech.

# Introduction[7]

Emerging technologies have long-shaped competitive dynamics. But the speed and breadth of AI change have dramatically shortened the cycles for experimentation and adoption. Foundation models, generative systems, agents, and new toolchains can reshape how an organization operates within months, not years. Yet, studies indicate that most AI pilots stall or fail to deliver observable value. Staying agile in this environment means cultivating a repeatable organizational capability that can scan, test, and decide with rigor, treating AI innovation as a managed portfolio rather than a series of isolated bets. This chapter frames that important discipline as the **AI Emerging-Tech Agility Cycle** that looks like this:

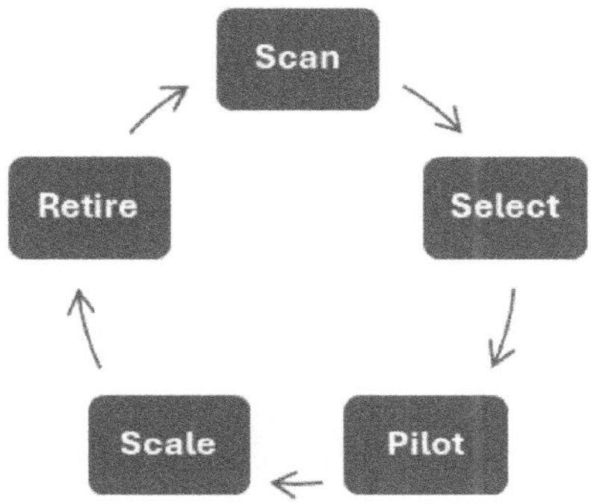


## The Strategic Imperative of AI-Centric Emerging-Tech Vigilance[8]

AI advances—from generative models and autonomous agents to AutoML tools and evolving governance models—often emerge through fast, open, and community-driven innovation cycles. Unlike more predictable technology shifts, organizations can roll out AI improvements almost immediately via APIs. This gives competitors the option to quickly match capabilities or even leap ahead.

At the same time, numerous studies indicate that a large share of enterprise AI initiatives never progress beyond pilot or fail to produce meaningful ROI. Some estimates even suggest that roughly 90-95 percent of generative-AI pilots stall out. The underlying problem often stems less from model performance and more from fuzzy business value, weak integration into real workflows, and inadequate risk and control structures. An AI-focused vigilance capability enables organizations to:

- **Detect** meaningful trends early enough to experiment ahead of the pack, while filtering out distracting noise.
- **Judge** how well new capabilities fit existing strategy and organizational strengths, instead of chasing novelty for its own sake.
- **Anticipate and manage** the ethical, regulatory, security, and operational risks that arise as AI capabilities mature.

In day-to-day practice, this vigilance means repeatedly moving through the AI Emerging-Tech Agility Cycle: scanning for signals, selecting promising candidates, running disciplined pilots, scaling what proves valuable, and retiring tools or approaches that no longer fit.

### Methods for Continuous Technology Assessment[9]

A sound assessment approach blends outward-looking scanning with inward-focused reflection and structured decision processes. These activities primarily occur in the scan and select phases of the AI Emerging-Tech Agility Cycle, ensuring that only the most relevant, strategically aligned ideas advance to pilots.

### Trend Intelligence and Horizon Scanning

Horizon-scanning practices utilize structured techniques—such as foresight radars, signal tracking, and clustering—to convert scattered signals into actionable patterns for leaders. For AI, this may involve:

- Reviewing research papers, preprint repositories, benchmark results, and major conferences to spot new architectures and capabilities.
- Watching patent activity, startup funding, and vendor roadmaps to gauge how quickly innovations move toward commercial use.
- Applying AI-driven tools for trend detection and market scanning that identify emerging themes and players in near real time.

Well-constructed radars then classify AI trends by time horizon and maturity, offering leaders clearer guidance on where to explore, experiment, and commit to adoption.

### Internal Capability Inventories

Organizations must interpret external developments alongside their actual preparedness to absorb them. Capability inventories document:

- Current AI assets (e.g., models, platforms, data pipelines), integration patterns, and known technical debt.
- Available skills and roles—spanning data science, MLOps, governance, and domain expertise—and existing gaps.
- Ongoing initiatives and pilots, including their goals, progress, and dependencies.

This visibility helps prevent "shiny object" pursuits that overlook constraints in data readiness, architecture, or talent.

### Opportunity and Risk Mapping

Emerging AI capabilities prove most useful when tied to concrete business needs rather than explored in isolation. Useful tools include:

- Grids that cross AI techniques (e.g., summarization, agents, or forecasting) with specific, high-value business problems to reveal promising opportunity areas.
- Risk maps that highlight where AI adoption might heighten ethical, security, or regulatory exposure, signaling a need for stronger governance.

### Cross-Functional Advisory Panels

Cross-functional groups—bringing together business owners, data leaders, architects, risk, and legal—offer a venue for collective evaluation of AI innovations. Such panels:

- Review trend radars and determine which topics warrant pilots or deeper investigation.
- Assess fit with strategic priorities, data and infrastructure readiness, and the organization's risk appetite.
- Ensure that governance considerations integrate into early experiments rather than being bolted on later.

Taken together, these assessment activities act as the "front end" of the AI Emerging-Tech Agility Cycle, significantly increasing the odds that ideas moving into pilot are both technically credible and genuinely business-relevant.

## Comparing This Approach to Established Foresight Frameworks[10]

Many organizations already rely on established foresight instruments—such as technology radars and formal horizon-scanning methods to track emerging trends. The AI Emerging-Tech Agility Cycle is designed to work alongside, rather than replace, these tools.

- **Technology or foresight radars** typically emphasize a technology's position in its maturity path (e.g., explore, experiment, adopt, retire) and when it might affect the organization. They excel at visual storytelling and portfolio-level prioritization, but often say less about the detailed operational work required to progress from exploration to scaled deployment.

- **Horizon-scanning approaches** focus on systematically identifying and clustering signals into trends, often using STEEP (social, technological, economic, environmental, political) lenses and scenario analysis. They broaden the organization's field of view and challenge assumptions, but may not spell out concrete steps for piloting, business-case development, and scaling.

The AI Emerging-Tech Agility Cycle aligns with these approaches in its early phases—utilizing horizon scanning and radars for scan and select—but extends further by explicitly modeling the pilot → scale → retire phases that often determine whether AI experimentation leads to lasting value.

In short, traditional foresight tools help you notice and classify what's on the horizon, while the agility cycle focuses on how you test, invest in, and eventually sunset AI capabilities in a structured way.

## Practical Piloting of Experimental AI Tools[11]

Pilots serve as the important link between theoretical potential and operational reality. Yet, evidence suggests most AI pilots never successfully cross that bridge. Therefore, careful pilot design becomes central. Within the AI Emerging Tech Agility Cycle, the pilot stage is where organizations evaluate hypotheses and build the evidence base for decisions to scale or retire.

Key design elements include:

- **Clear pilot objectives:** Pilots should anchor in specific business questions or processes, with explicit success criteria, rather than operating as open-ended "let's try this AI tool" experiments.
- **Representative data and users:** Using realistic datasets and involving real end-users helps uncover integration challenges, edge cases, and change-management needs early in the process.
- **Iterative, fail-fast methods:** Agile sprints and hypothesis-driven experiments allow teams to adapt or stop pilots quickly when signals are weak, limiting sunk costs and freeing capacity.
- **Flexible, safe sandboxes:** Cloud or hybrid environments with strong security and governance controls provide space for rapid testing while protecting sensitive data and limiting the blast radius.
- **Decision-gate reviews:** Planned gates (e.g., go/kill/pivot) evaluate pilots on impact, feasibility, risk profile, and

organizational readiness, preventing never-ending proofs of concept with no route to production.

Pilot evaluations should consider fairness, explainability, robustness, and operational fit—not only accuracy or novelty. These decision points are where the AI Emerging-Tech Agility Cycle explicitly determines whether an initiative advances into scale or loops back to scan/select, armed with new insights.

## Building Rigorous Business Cases for AI Adoption[12]

Because failure rates are high and the temptation to overspend is real, AI investments must rest on solid business cases. Within the AI Emerging-Tech Agility Cycle, this rigor becomes most visible at the pivot from pilot to scale, where funding and commitment decisions occur.

Core components include:

- **Quantitative impact assessment:** Estimate potential gains in efficiency, cost savings, revenue growth, error reduction, or risk mitigation across different adoption scenarios, grounded in pilot outcomes whenever feasible.
- **Qualitative and strategic benefits:** Account for non-financial advantages such as strategic differentiation, enhanced employee or customer experiences, or preparedness for emerging regulations.
- **Risk-adjusted ROI and scenarios:** Construct best-, base-, and worst-case projections, including risks around adoption pace, user uptake, or under-realized savings. Sensitivity analyses that show how ROI shifts under varying assumptions add credibility and support more nuanced decisions.
- **Stakeholder co-creation:** Engaging finance, operations, IT, legal, and risk teams in building the business case encourages more realistic assumptions and smoother approvals.
- **Phased investment roadmaps:** Link funding tranches to evidence milestones—initial pilot results, bounded deployments, then broader rollouts—allowing investment levels to recalibrate as new data emerges.

## Scaling AI Innovation with Agility[13]

Once pilots demonstrate promise, the focus shifts from experimentation to expansion—all without losing the ability to adapt. In the AI Emerging-Tech Agility Cycle, this corresponds to the scale phase, followed by intentional decisions about when to retire or refresh solutions as technologies and needs change.

Key enablers include:

- **Flexible architectures and platforms:** Modular, API-driven, and container-based designs simplify replacing models or services as capabilities improve, without re-engineering entire systems. Technology radars can signal when older components should be phased out and when newer options merit consideration.
- **Embedded governance:** AI-governance practices—such as model registries, risk classification schemes, explainability requirements, and human-in-the-loop policies—should integrate into deployment pipelines and operating procedures, not appended at the end.
- **Talent and cultural readiness:** Scaling innovation demands that AI knowledge reside within business units as well as technical teams. Training programs, communities of practice, and internal champions help weave new tools into everyday work.
- **Collaborative innovation ecosystems:** Relationships with universities, startups, and technology vendors can open access to leading-edge AI capabilities and shared learning, while also spreading innovation risk across partners.

As newer AI capabilities emerge, the retire step in the AI Emerging-Tech Agility Cycle becomes essential. Organizations must willingly decommission outdated tools and models to keep complexity manageable and free up resources for the next wave of experimentation.

## Managing Innovation Risks and Avoiding Pitfalls[14]

Being agile with emerging technology doesn't mean pursuing every new development; it implies disciplined responsiveness.

Common pitfalls and corresponding mitigations include:

- **Hype chasing:** Reacting to every AI headline can thinly spread resources and create a backlog of abandoned proofs of concept. Using technology radars and business-aligned prioritization criteria helps direct attention toward trends that truly matter.
- **Technical debt accumulation:** Rapid experimentation can leave behind prototypes, scripts, and unmanaged models that add complexity and risk. Establishing expectations for

documentation, ownership, and refactoring as projects mature keeps technical debt from spiraling.

- **Ethical and societal blind spots:** Emerging AI systems may inadvertently amplify bias, invade privacy, or propagate misinformation. Ongoing ethical review and engagement with affected stakeholders help bring these concerns to light early.
- **Regulatory shocks:** AI-related regulations and sector-specific guidance evolve quickly, so organizations need adaptable processes and architectures that can accommodate new rules with minimal disruption.

By explicitly including "retire" as a distinct stage in the AI Emerging-Tech Agility Cycle, organizations create a formal mechanism to tackle technical debt, ethical issues, and regulatory shifts instead of allowing legacy experiments to linger indefinitely.

# Thought Experiment

## Institution Supporting Research Through AI Innovation[15]

Consider a research university aiming to remain at the forefront of scholarship and grant funding. Seeing a surge of AI tools for literature review, grant support, and collaboration discovery, the institution decides to integrate AI innovation into its core operating model.

- A horizon-scanning team maintains an AI technology radar that tracks tools for grant summarization, reviewer recommendations, collaboration suggestions, and publication-trend mapping—all corresponding to the AI Emerging-Tech Agility Cycle's scan phase.
- Selected departments then run pilots—for instance, using generative AI to summarize calls for proposals and match them with researcher profiles—measured against indicators such as time saved, accuracy, and researcher satisfaction. These activities occupy the pilot stage.
- Business cases highlight reduced administrative load and faster grant processing, along with strategic benefits like higher funding success rates and better research visibility. Strong cases underpin the decision to scale.

- Ethics and data-protection committees set policies for using publication and grant content, ensuring confidentiality and academic integrity.
- AI-literacy programs help faculty and staff learn to use the tools effectively and responsibly, spreading adoption beyond early advocates.

In effect, the institution becomes more nimble in winning funding and nurturing collaboration while still honoring core academic values—operating within the AI Emerging-Tech Agility Cycle rather than treating AI initiatives as isolated, one-off projects.

## Success Metrics[16]

Evaluating agility with emerging technologies requires metrics that reflect both experimentation throughput and disciplined value capture. These measures can map directly to stages in the AI Emerging-Tech Agility Cycle—for example, scanning metrics to the scan stage, pilot throughput to the pilot stage, and ROI and governance indicators to the scale and retire stages.

## Table of Illustrative Metrics

| Dimension | Example Metric | Why It Matters |
|---|---|---|
| **Scanning and Insight** | Frequency of horizon scanning updates and count of AI trends reviewed each year | Signals a deliberate, repeatable scanning process instead of sporadic trend watching |
| **Experimentation** | No. of AI pilots launched and, more importantly, the % reaching a clear go/kill/pivot decision within a defined period | Demonstrates the ability to move beyond "permanent pilot" status |
| **Pilot-to-Production** | Proportion of successful pilots that transition into production deployments with measurable outcomes | Indicates how well the innovation pipeline converts experiments into operational solutions |
| **Value Realization** | Realized ROI compared with initial AI business-case estimates, including variation across best/base/worst assumptions | Connects innovation work to both financial and strategic impact |
| **Governance Coverage** | Share of AI efforts evaluated under formal governance processes and aligned to risk-adjusted policies | Shows that scaling is happening responsibly rather than through uncontrolled experimentation |
| **Cultural Readiness** | AI-literacy levels, training-completion rates, and survey results on willingness to work with AI-enabled change | Reflects how well the organization can absorb new capabilities |

# Practical Advice for Leaders[17]

Leaders largely determine whether emerging technologies become a durable advantage or a persistent distraction.

- **Anchor scanning in strategy, not curiosity.** Ensure that trend radars and horizon-scanning outputs explicitly tie back to strategic themes, focusing attention on AI developments that truly matter for the mission.
- **Treat AI innovation as a portfolio.** Manage AI work across explore, pilot, scale, and retire stages with clear criteria, funding

gates, and risk tolerances. The AI Emerging-Tech Agility Cycle offers a shared language for this portfolio view.

- **Insist on rigorous pilots and business cases.** Require well-articulated hypotheses, metrics, and risk-adjusted ROI scenarios before moving from pilot to scale, thereby limiting open-ended experimentation.
- **Integrate governance early.** Include risk, legal, and ethics partners from the outset of the innovation process rather than involving them only after pilots conclude.
- **Invest in literacy and narrative.** Develop AI fluency broadly and tell a coherent story about how emerging technologies support the organization's purpose and values, helping people understand why the work matters.

# Conclusion

AI-driven emerging technologies are reshaping how organizations create value, but their speed and unpredictability demand more than opportunistic adoption. By investing in disciplined practices for horizon scanning, focused experimentation, and risk-aware business-case development—backed by adaptable architectures, governance, and culture—organizations can remain nimble, avoid the "95 percent pilot failure" pattern, and responsibly harness AI innovation over time. The AI Emerging-Tech Agility Cycle connects these practices into a repeatable loop. Placing it alongside established foresight tools such as technology radars and horizon-scanning methods helps leaders weave strategy, experimentation, and scaling into a single coherent approach.

# Notes

[1] The term "AI Emerging-Tech Agility Cycle" and the Scan - Select - Pilot - Scale - Retire loop come from *RapidCanvas*'s analysis of why many AI projects fail and how to structure AI programs as a continuous cycle.

[2] The AI Investment Lifecycle is developed in *Augmented Capital*'s guidance on building strong AI investment cases and *Productboard*'s framing of AI initiatives from idea through retirement.

[3] Horizon scanning is detailed in Purpose & Means' guidance on building future radars and *Futures Platform*'s horizon-scanning guidelines.

[4] Risk-adjusted ROI and scenario-based planning are treated in *Innovation Partners*' "ROI of Intelligence" guide and *Augmented Capital*'s approach to AI investment cases.

[5] "Signals" and their role in trend identification are examined in the *ScienceDirect* article on signals, foresight, and technological change.

[6] For technology and foresight radars, see LTIMindtree's Tech Radar 2025 and LinkedIn examples of AI horizon-scanning activities.

[7] Mario Thomas's "The Year AI Grew Up," *RapidCanvas*'s generative-AI failure analysis, and *Fortune*'s report on MIT's generative-AI pilot findings supply the introduction's emphasis on compressed AI adoption cycles and high pilot-failure rates.

[8] Strategic imperative materials draw on NIHR's generative-AI report, *RapidCanvas*'s statistics on stalled pilots, *Futures Platform*'s scanning guidance, LTIMindtree's radar content, and National Academies materials on AI risks and governance.

[9] *Futures Platform* and LTIMindtree foresight methods, Purpose & Means' radar work, NIHR's generative-AI considerations, DCipher Analytics' scanning tools, *Productboard*'s lifecycle guidance, *Augmented Capital*'s capability and ROI lens, *Fortune*'s pilot-failure analysis, *Innovation Partners*' value-mapping guidance, *Process Excellence Network*'s agentic-AI risk mapping, National Academies' cross-functional advice, and *Palo Alto Networks*' AI-governance principles together underpin the continuous-assessment framework.

[10] Foresight frameworks are compared across *Futures Platform*, LTIMindtree, LinkedIn, Purpose & Means, and *ScienceDirect* foresight content, alongside *RapidCanvas*'s agility-cycle model and *Productboard*'s AI-investment-lifecycle stages.

[11] Practical piloting guidance is assembled from Mario Thomas's commentary on AI pilots, *Process Excellence Network*'s analysis of agentic-AI pilots, *Fortune*'s report on pilot failure, NIHR's experimentation advice, *RapidCanvas*'s gate design, and *Productboard*'s pilot-to-scale criteria.

[12] Business-case construction draws on *Augmented Capital*'s AI-investment guidance, *Innovation Partners*' ROI framework, *Productboard*'s lifecycle planning, and *RapidCanvas*'s risk-adjusted decision-making emphasis.

[13] Scaling and agility guidance is drawn from *Futures Platform*'s retirement patterns, *Productboard*'s lifecycle stages, NIST AIRC's governance playbook, *ScienceDirect*'s ecosystem and risk analysis, and *RapidCanvas*'s advocacy for formal retirement stages.

[14] Pitfall-management recommendations emerge from insights by Mario Thomas, *RapidCanvas, ScienceDirect, Innovation Partners,* National Academies, and NIHR's generative-AI report.

[15] Research-university thought experiment materials draw on Purpose & Means' radar methods, *Augmented Capital* and *Innovation Partners*' investment-case ideas, *Databricks*' AI-governance best practices, *Productboard*'s lifecycle approach, LTIMindtree's tech-radar content, and *RapidCanvas*'s agility-cycle framing.

[16] Success-metrics examples and their linkages to agility-cycle stages draw on *Futures Platform*'s scanning metrics, *Process Excellence Network*'s pilot-throughput focus, *Augmented Capital*'s ROI tracking, *Palo Alto Networks*' governance-coverage expectations, and *Productboard*'s lifecycle-stage monitoring.

[17] Leadership advice synthesizes *Futures Platform*'s strategy-aligned scanning guidance, LTIMindtree's radar use, *Process Excellence Network*'s portfolio recommendations, *Augmented Capital*'s investment discipline, *Palo Alto Networks*' AI-governance principles, and *Productboard*'s emphasis on literacy and storytelling.

# Key topics explored in this chapter:

- Enabling Self-Service Analytics at Scale
- Embedding Analytics into Daily Workflows
- Building Supportive Analytics Communities via Technology
- Governance and Security Embedded by Design
- AI and Automation to Support Democratization
- Technology Integration and Implementation Best Practices
- Democratized Analytics Technology Stack
- Architectural Patterns for Democratized Analytics

# WAY 33

# Democratize Analytics and AI Access


## Abstract

Democratizing analytics and AI access means enabling many more people—not just specialists—to work with data directly in their daily workflows. Technology plays a central role: scalable self-service platforms, embedded analytics, intelligent assistance, and governance-by-design all reduce friction. This lets non-technical users ask questions, explore data, and act on insights without creating chaos or risk. This chapter focuses on these technology levers, leaving broader culture and operating-model topics to other parts of the book.


## Objective

After completing this chapter, you will be able to:

- Describe the key technology capabilities that enable self-service analytics and AI for non-specialist users at scale.
- Design self-service and embedded analytics architectures that bring governed insights into the applications where people already work.
- Implement collaboration and community features—such as shared workspaces, templates, and usage analytics—that support thriving analytics user communities.
- Embed governance, security, and auditability into democratized environments so broader access doesn't compromise control.
- Use AI and automation (for example, augmented analytics, chatbots, adaptive learning) to lower barriers and guide users through analytics tasks.

- Draw lessons from real-world case studies to inform practical implementation roadmaps for data and analytics democratization.

# Terms to Know

**Augmented Analytics**[1] - Analytics platforms that embed AI and machine learning to automate insight discovery, suggest visualizations, and assist users in exploring data, especially non-experts.

**Embedded Analytics**[2] - The integration of analytics capabilities—such as charts, KPIs, and self-service exploration—directly inside business applications and portals used in daily work.

**Power User**[3] - A technically inclined business user who creates and curates analytics content (for example, datasets, dashboards) that others consume, often acting as a bridge between central data teams and general users.

**Self-Service Analytics**[4] - Tools and architectures that let business users access, explore, and analyze data with minimal IT involvement, within guardrails that ensure security and quality.

# Introduction

Expanding analytics access beyond data teams is one of the most powerful levers for improving day-to-day decision-making. While culture and literacy matter, many democratization efforts fail because the technology stack remains too technical, too fragmented, or too risky for broad use. This chapter therefore focuses on technology-specific foundations: self-service platforms, embedded analytics, collaboration features, and governance tooling that together enable a wide array of users to work with data safely. To make these foundations more actionable, we introduce a Democratized Analytics Technology Stack and compare common architectural patterns such as centralized self-service portals and embedded-first strategies.

## Enabling Self-Service Analytics at Scale[5]

Self-service doesn't mean "anything goes." It means providing intuitive, governed tools that let users answer many of their own questions.

### Modern Self-Service Platforms

Recent generations of BI and analytics platforms emphasize ease of use, guided exploration, and AI-assisted workflows. Core capabilities include:

- Drag-and-drop and low-code interfaces that let users to build dashboards and simple models without writing SQL or code.
- Augmented analytics features—such as auto-insight detection, recommended charts, and anomaly detection—that uncover patterns users might otherwise miss.
- Natural language querying (NLQ/NLP), which enables users to ask questions in everyday language and see visual answers, lowering the learning curve and extending access to front-line staff.
- Smart data preparation as the platform profiles data, suggests joins, cleans formats, and exposes curated semantic models so users interact with business concepts rather than raw tables.

Industry sources highlight how AI-powered self-service tools enable store managers, marketers, and operators to ask questions in natural language and receive auto-generated visual answers without submitting requests to data teams.

### Cloud-Native Scalability

Cloud-native analytics services underpin democratization, offering elastic compute and storage that handles many concurrent self-service users. Guides for platforms such as Power BI show how users build real-time self-service reports on DirectQuery models with automatic refresh and change-detection mechanisms, while administrators use capacity metrics and activity logs to track usage and resource impact. This combination delivers broad access with managed performance and oversight.

## Embedding Analytics into Daily Workflows[6]

Self-service portals get you partway there. Analytics must also appear where people already work.

### Embedded and Operational Analytics

Embedded analytics brings visualizations, KPIs, and exploration capabilities directly into operational applications, intranets, and customer-facing products. Examples include:

- Analytics within CRM, ERP, and line-of-business applications, where interactive reports, KPI cards, and drill-downs integrate seamlessly with transactional views.
- Micro-frontends and widget SDKs that developers use to embed self-service components in web apps and portals, employing shared authentication and governance.
- Event-driven alerts and in-app nudges that flag anomalies or opportunities directly inside tools such as POS systems or collaboration apps.

Embedded analytics vendors and case examples confirm that adoption rises when users access analytics through a single sign-on inside familiar applications, rather than switching to a separate BI portal.

## Building Supportive Analytics Communities via Technology[7]

Democratization becomes self-sustaining when users learn from each other, not just from documentation.

### Collaboration Platforms and Social Features

Modern analytics platforms build in collaboration features that drive peer learning:

- Commenting and discussions on dashboards and reports, enabling users to ask questions, annotate findings, and share interpretations.
- Tagging, favorites, and sharing mechanisms that highlight commonly used metrics and trusted content.
- Template galleries and content repositories with curated dashboards, semantic models, and how-to resources that reduce barriers for new users.

AI-driven content curation recommends relevant reports or datasets based on a user's role and prior activity, so new users find useful artifacts quickly instead of wandering.

### Usage Analytics and Power-User Identification

Usage telemetry within analytics tools is a powerful democratization asset. Most organizations underuse it.

- Platform activity logs and adoption reports reveal which dashboards see the most use, which features are under-utilized, and where performance bottlenecks occur.

- By analyzing activity patterns, organizations identify power users—those who create and maintain content for others—and support them with training and recognition.

Case guidance on self-service BI underscores the importance of power users working directly with data, building more complex integrations, and serving as local experts for their teams.

## Governance and Security Embedded by Design[8]

Broader access requires stronger, not weaker, governance. Technology must provide guardrails that are largely invisible to end users.

### Role-Based Access and Data Masking

Best-practice guides on data democratization make one thing clear: self-service and robust governance must be built together. Key capabilities include:

- Role-based access controls (RBAC) and, where needed, attribute-based access controls (ABAC) restrict who can see which tables, rows, or columns.
- Dynamic data masking for sensitive fields such as personal or financial data, enabling broader use of shared datasets without exposing raw values.

### Data Lineage, Audit Trails, and Policy Enforcement

Governance-by-design rests on visibility and automated enforcement:

- Lineage and catalog tools reveal how datasets and dashboards are constructed, which sources they depend on, and who uses them, fostering user trust and enabling impact analysis.
- Audit logs capture data access, sharing, and export events, providing evidence for compliance and supporting anomaly detection.
- Policy-driven automation can warn or block users when queries exceed defined thresholds, attempt to combine restricted datasets, or export sensitive information.

Data-governance providers show that embedding governance policies directly into analytics and catalog tools is what makes democratization possible "without compromising integrity."

## AI and Automation to Support Democratization[9]

AI isn't only an analytics subject. It is also what makes broader access practical. It provides:

- **Automated insight generation:** Augmented-analytics engines proactively surface anomalies, correlations, and trend changes, providing non-experts with a starting point for exploration.
- **Chatbots and virtual assistants:** Conversational agents integrated into analytics platforms guide users in building queries, choosing charts, or interpreting results.
- **Personalized learning experiences:** AI-driven learning modules recommend tutorials or micro-lessons based on each user's activity—tracking features they haven't tried or errors they encounter—embedding data-literacy support inside the tools themselves.

Across retail and other sectors, the evidence is consistent: combining natural language interfaces, embedded bots, and auto-visualizations cuts friction and makes data "part of everyday decision-making—for everyone."

## Technology Integration and Implementation Best Practices[10]

Integration patterns determine whether democratization holds together or fractures under load. Key practices include:

- Tight integration with core data platforms so that self-service tools use curated semantic models and governed data, not ad hoc extracts.
- Cloud or hybrid deployment for elastic scalability, with gateways where needed to connect on-premises sources while maintaining consistent governance.
- Open SDKs and APIs that allow product and IT teams extend analytics into custom applications and workflows.
- Containerization and microservices for analytics services where independent scaling, updates, and experimentation are valuable—especially for embedded and AI-assisted components.

Vendors and reference architectures agree: successful democratization treats analytics as a platform capability—wired into identity, governance, and observability—not as a standalone reporting tool.

## Democratized Analytics Technology Stack[11]

The "Democratized Analytics Technology Stack" organizes these elements into four reinforcing layers:

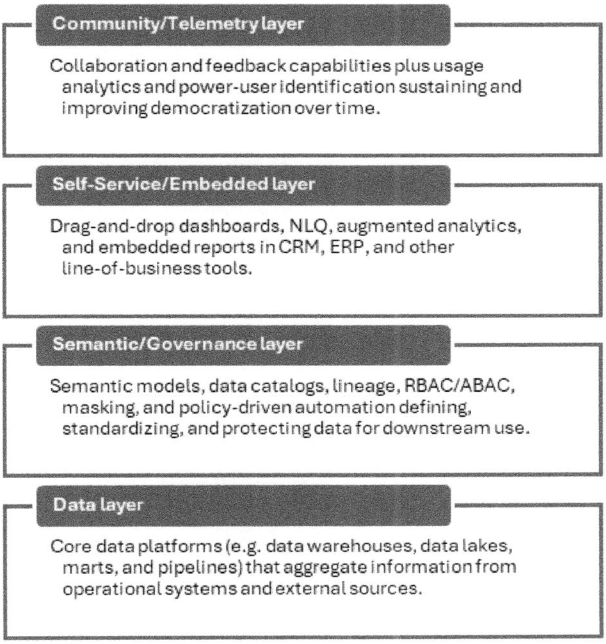


Mapping current investments onto these four layers shows leaders exactly where gaps live: strong tools but weak governance, for instance, or solid data infrastructure with no community or telemetry to sustain adoption.

## Architectural Patterns for Democratized Analytics[12]

Within this stack, organizations face a design choice: how do users primarily reach analytics? Two patterns dominate—a centralized self-service portal and an embedded-first strategy—and organizations can combine them in a hybrid approach.

## Centralized Self-Service Portal

In a portal-centric pattern, users go to one enterprise BI hub to access dashboards, reports, and self-service exploration.

| Pros | Cons |
|---|---|
| Provides a clear "front door" for analytics, simplifying discovery and centralizing governance of content and models | Requires users to leave their operational tools and log into a separate portal, which often reduces usage among busy front-line roles |
| Facilitates standardization of user experience, security, and semantic definitions across domains | Risks concentrating adoption among analysts and managers rather than truly democratizing access across the broader workforce |
| Works well for power users and analysts who need richer capabilities and cross-domain views | |

## Embedded-First Strategy

In an embedded-first pattern, analytics lives inside existing business applications, delivered through SDKs, widgets, and APIs.

| Pros | Cons |
|---|---|
| Meets users where they already work, increasing the likelihood that insights inform decisions in the flow of day-to-day operations | Demands closer coordination between application and analytics-platform teams, and more integration work to embed components consistently |
| Single sign-on and contextual views reduce friction and significantly boost adoption among non-technical and front-line users | Can fragment user experience if different applications embed analytics differently or rely on inconsistent semantic models |
| Aligns with event-driven alerts and in-app nudges that prompt timely action instead of passive report consumption | Demands careful design so embedded analytics retain central governance, lineage, and telemetry, rather than becoming isolated widgets |

In practice, most organizations land on a hybrid: a centralized portal for deeper self-service and cross-domain exploration, with embedded analytics in high-frequency workflows where speed and convenience matter most.

# Case Studies

## Case Study #1: Retail Data Platform Enabling Self-Service for Mid-Sized Retailers[13]

A European data-warehouse provider, incuda, collaborated with an analytics vendor to serve mid-sized multichannel retailers (stores, e-commerce, call centers, catalogs) through a full-stack data platform with embedded self-service BI. By integrating a white-labeled BI solution directly into their data platform, incuda allowed retail clients to connect multiple data sources, calculate their own metrics, and build customized dashboards without heavy IT involvement.

Over more than a decade, this embedded self-service approach led to at least a 50-percent increase in data adoption among end users at client organizations, with many more employees regularly working with data. Retailers used the platform to standardize reporting while still tailoring analytics to local merchandising and marketing needs, illustrating how embedded self-service underpinned a practical form of analytics democratization at scale.

## Case Study #2: Financial Services Firm Democratizing Access with a Data Catalog and Governance[14]

Financial-services company Oportun used a data catalog and governance-centric tooling to unify datasets and broaden access to trusted data across teams. By improving visibility into data assets and integrating policy controls (for example, role-based access, stewardship workflows) directly into the catalog, Oportun enabled hundreds of employees—from data scientists to business stakeholders—to access and analyze data independently.

This approach reduced reporting bottlenecks and improved compliance, allowing more self-service analysis without sacrificing regulatory obligations. Governance-by-design features, such as automated policy enforcement and integrated auditing, made democratization sustainable by ensuring that increased access didn't come at the cost of data quality or security.

# Success Metrics[16]

Measuring democratization requires metrics that capture both breadth of access and quality of use.

## Table of Illustrative Metrics

| Dimension | Example Metric | Why It Matters |
|---|---|---|
| **Adoption Breadth** | No. and % of employees using analytics tools monthly; growth in "data consumers" | Indicates how widely analytics access has expanded beyond specialist teams |
| **Self-Service Utilization** | Share of analytics interactions performed via self-service (for example, ad-hoc queries, user-built reports) versus centrally built content | Shows whether users can answer their own questions without heavy IT reliance |
| **Embedded Usage** | Proportion of analytics usage happening inside operational apps or portals versus standalone BI portals | Reflects how well insights are integrated into daily workflows |
| **Governance and Trust** | No. of governance violations, data-quality incidents, or unauthorized-access attempts; user-trust scores in survey feedback | Demonstrates whether democratization is occurring within safe guardrails |
| **Community Health** | No. of active power users, shared assets (templates, dashboards), and collaborative interactions (comments, shares) | Indicates whether a self-sustaining analytics community is forming |

# Practical Advice for Leaders[17]

From a technology perspective, leaders should:

- **Invest in platforms that combine ease of use with governance** so that self-service and embedded analytics can grow without fragmenting data or creating security gaps.
- **Start with high-value, high-frequency workflows** (for example, store operations, marketing campaigns, front-line service) when deploying embedded and self-service analytics, demonstrating clear value to everyday users.

- **Deliberately cultivate power users** by providing advanced tools, training, and recognition to serve as local analytics champions and content producers.
- **Leverage usage telemetry** to guide enablement and identify under-used features, friction points, and successful content; then tailor education and platform improvements accordingly.
- **Integrate governance tooling early** so that democratization is built on trusted data, clear policies, and auditable access, avoiding disruptive retrofits.

## Conclusion[18]

Democratizing analytics access is a technology-design challenge. The right platforms, embedded touchpoints, collaboration capabilities, and governance mechanisms let more people work with data safely and effectively. When organizations pair AI-augmented self-service tools and embedded analytics with governance-by-design and supportive communities, they build an enterprise-wide analytics ecosystem where informed decision-making is the norm, not the exception. The Democratized Analytics Technology Stack and the contrast between portal-centric and embedded-first architectural patterns give leaders concrete reference points for aligning technology choices with that goal.

## Notes

[1] Augmented analytics is defined in Toucan Toco's "Self-Service BI."

[2] For embedded analytics, see *Qrvey*'s "Embedded Analytics Examples."

[3] Power users are characterized in 3*Cloud Solutions*' "The Role of Power Users in a Self-Service BI Initiative."

[4] For self-service analytics, see *SailPoint*'s "Data Democratization."

[5] Enabling self-service analytics at scale draws on ThoughtSpot's "WEX Self-Service Analytics Journey," *ApplyData*'s "Data Democratization: Empowering All with Self-Service Analytics," Strategy Software's "What's Next for Retail in 2025? AI-Powered Analytics Trends and BI Innovation," Alation's "What Is Data Democratization?," Toucan Toco's "Self-Service BI," *Yellowfin*'s "Incuda Drives 50% Increase in Self-Service Analytics Adoption with *Yellowfin* BI," and Microsoft's "Power BI Implementation Planning: Usage Scenario—Self-Service and Real-Time Analytics."

[6] Embedding analytics into daily workflows is addressed in Microsoft's "Power BI Implementation Planning: Usage Scenario—Self-Service and Real-Time Analytics," *Elegant MicroWeb*'s "Enable User Adoption of BI Tools with Embedded BI," *Qrvey*'s "Embedded Analytics Examples," and Strategy Software's "What's Next for Retail in 2025? AI-Powered Analytics Trends and BI Innovation."

[7] The community and collaboration cluster draws on *Reveal BI*'s "Analytics Adoption: Turning Data into Everyday Decisions," *Yellowfin*'s "Incuda Drives 50% Increase in Self-Service Analytics Adoption with *Yellowfin* BI," *ApplyData*'s "Data Democratization: Empowering All with Self-Service Analytics," Alation's "What Is Data Democratization?," and 3*Cloud Solutions*' "The Role of Power Users in a Self-Service BI Initiative."

[8] Combining self-service with robust data-governance frameworks is shown to matter in *RecordPoint*'s "Data Democratization" and *SailPoint*'s "Data Democratization."

[9] This AI and automation section draws on Toucan Toco's "Self-Service BI," ThoughtSpot's "WEX Self-Service Analytics Journey," *Reveal BI*'s "Analytics Adoption: Turning Data into Everyday Decisions," and Strategy Software's "What's Next for Retail in 2025? AI-Powered Analytics Trends and BI Innovation."

[10] The technology-integration best-practices cluster draws on *Yellowfin*'s "Incuda Drives 50% Increase in Self-Service Analytics Adoption with *Yellowfin* BI," *Qrvey*'s "Embedded Analytics Examples," *Elegant MicroWeb*'s "Enable User Adoption of BI Tools with Embedded BI," and Microsoft's "Power BI Implementation Planning: Usage Scenario—Self-Service and Real-Time Analytics."

[11] Synthesized from ten sources, the Democratized Analytics Technology Stack concept and its four layers draw on Toucan Toco's "Self-Service BI," *Yellowfin*'s "Incuda Drives 50% Increase in Self-Service Analytics Adoption with *Yellowfin* BI," *SailPoint*'s "Data Democratization," *RecordPoint*'s "Data Democratization," Alation's "What Is Data Democratization?," ThoughtSpot's "WEX Self-Service Analytics Journey," *Elegant MicroWeb*'s "Enable User Adoption of BI Tools with Embedded BI," *Reveal BI*'s "Analytics Adoption: Turning Data into Everyday Decisions," *ApplyData*'s "Data Democratization: Empowering All with Self-Service Analytics," and 3*Cloud Solutions*' "The Role of Power Users in a Self-Service BI Initiative."

[12] This architectural-patterns section draws on *Elegant MicroWeb*'s "Enable User Adoption of BI Tools with Embedded BI," Microsoft's "Power BI Implementation Planning: Usage Scenario—Self-Service and Real-Time Analytics," *Qrvey*'s "Embedded Analytics Examples," *SailPoint*'s "Data Democratization," *Reveal BI*'s "Analytics Adoption: Turning Data into Everyday Decisions," Strategy Software's "What's Next for Retail in 2025? AI-Powered Analytics Trends and BI Innovation," *ApplyData*'s "Data Democratization: Empowering All with Self-Service Analytics," and 3*Cloud Solutions*' "The Role of Power Users in a Self-Service BI Initiative."

[13] The Incuda case study appears in *Yellowfin*'s "Incuda Drives 50% Increase in Self-Service Analytics Adoption with *Yellowfin* BI."

[14] Alation's "What Is Data Democratization?" and *RecordPoint*'s "Data Democratization" provide the Oportun case study.

[15] Power users' critical role in self-service BI initiatives is examined in 3*Cloud Solutions*' "The Role of Power Users in a Self-Service BI Initiative" and Toucan Toco's "Self-Service BI."

[16] Success metrics for this cluster draw on *Yellowfin*'s "Incuda Drives 50% Increase in Self-Service Analytics Adoption with *Yellowfin* BI," ThoughtSpot's "WEX Self-Service Analytics Journey," *Qrvey*'s "Embedded Analytics Examples," and Microsoft's "Power BI Implementation Planning: Usage Scenario—Self-Service and Real-Time Analytics."

[17] This practical-advice cluster draws on *SailPoint*'s "Data Democratization," Strategy Software's "What's Next for Retail in 2025? AI-Powered Analytics Trends and BI Innovation," ThoughtSpot's "WEX Self-Service Analytics Journey," *Reveal BI*'s "Analytics Adoption: Turning Data into Everyday Decisions," and Microsoft's "Power BI Implementation Planning: Usage Scenario—Self-Service and Real-Time Analytics."

[18] The conclusion's claim that democratizing analytics access is fundamentally a technology-design challenge is supported by Toucan Toco's "Self-Service BI" and *Elegant MicroWeb*'s "Enable User Adoption of BI Tools with Embedded BI."

## Key topics explored in this chapter:

- Cloud Analytics: The Central AI Brain Empowering Human Insight
- Edge Analytics: Bringing AI-Enhanced Context and Speed to Human Decision Points
- Hybrid Architectures: Orchestrating Human-AI Collaboration Across Cloud and Edge
- Migration and Implementation Strategies Focused on Human-AI Integration
- Challenges and Considerations in Aligning Technology with Human-AI Integration

# WAY 34

# Amplify Human Intelligence Through Distributed AI


## Abstract

Distributed AI analytics, spanning cloud and edge, builds the infrastructure that keeps human decisions continuously supplied with timely, context-rich, and computationally powerful insights. Cloud platforms serve as the centralized hub for heavy analytics and global learning, while edge computing delivers lightweight, real-time intelligence directly to the locations where people work, observe, and act. This chapter examines the technology strategies, architectures, and operating models that synchronize cloud-edge capabilities with human roles, so AI augments rather than displaces human judgment across distributed environments.


## Objective

After completing this chapter, you will be able to:

- Explain how hybrid cloud-edge architectures enable human-AI collaboration by separating training and global analytics from real-time, local inference.
- Design distributed AI architectures that use the cloud as a central model hub and the edge as a context-aware, low-latency decision layer for frontline staff.
- Outline model synchronization, feedback, and governance mechanisms that align edge models with centrally managed versions while incorporating local human insights.
- Evaluate migration and implementation strategies that prioritize human-AI touchpoints, modularity, and change management in hybrid deployments.

- Identify key challenges—latency, reliability, privacy, and interface diversity—and describe technical patterns that mitigate these without compromising human usability.
- Extract lessons from real-world cases in manufacturing, healthcare, and retail to inform practical distributed AI roadmaps.

## Terms to Know

**Edge AI**[1] **-** AI models deployed on or near data-generating devices—such as gateways, cameras, or medical monitors—to perform inference locally with low latency and reduced data transfer.

**Hybrid Cloud-Edge Architecture**[2] **-** An arrangement where cloud resources handle centralized, compute-heavy analytics and model management, while edge nodes handle real-time processing and human-facing decision support.

**Latency Optimization**[3] **-** Techniques for reducing response time between data capture, AI inference, and human feedback, often through local processing, efficient communication, and model compression.

**Model Synchronization**[4] **-** Processes and tooling that distribute centrally trained models to edge devices, collect telemetry and feedback, and coordinate updates across distributed deployments.

## Introduction[5]

Human expertise and AI capabilities reinforce each other best when insights arrive at the right time, in the right format, and with the right context for action. Centralized cloud platforms excel at training deep models, integrating data across organizational silos, and building comprehensive situational awareness. They struggle, though, with millisecond-level responsiveness and intermittent connectivity at operational frontlines. Edge AI reverses this: it works close to the action and draws on local context, but hits limits on compute and storage. Leading organizations therefore pursue hybrid cloud-edge architectures that treat the cloud as a central analytics hub and the edge as a network of context-aware nodes that work alongside humans in real time.

## Cloud Analytics: The Central AI Brain Empowering Human Insight[6]

Cloud platforms aggregate data across plants, stores, patients, or fleets and provide the deep computational power necessary for advanced analytics.

Key cloud-side roles include:

- Training sophisticated models on large historical datasets, such as predictive maintenance models built on multi-site equipment data or clinical risk models developed from broad patient cohorts.
- Running deep simulations and scenario analysis that inform strategic decisions—for example, modeling cost and risk trade-offs across entire manufacturing networks.
- Orchestrating model lifecycle management, including version control, A/B testing, performance monitoring, and coordinated deployment schedules for edge devices.
- Hosting collaborative data and analytics platforms, where cross-functional teams analyze patterns, review alerts from the field, and refine models based on human feedback.

Manufacturing case investigations demonstrate how cloud-based predictive maintenance systems use aggregated sensor data and machine learning to shift from reactive to proactive maintenance, substantially reducing downtime and advancing Industry 4.0 transformations.

## Edge Analytics: Bringing AI-Enhanced Context and Speed to Human Decision Points[7]

Edge computing extends centrally trained models to the locations where human operators, clinicians, or associates act.

Examples of edge AI roles include:

- Real-time anomaly detection and predictive maintenance on factory equipment, where edge sensors and local models monitor vibrations, temperatures, and operational states to flag issues before failure.
- In-store computer vision systems that perform live inference on multiple camera feeds to track queues, detect suspicious behavior, recognize products, or guide store layout decisions—often under challenging lighting and network conditions.

- Healthcare monitoring devices that analyze vital signs or behavior in real time at the patient's bedside or home, providing early warnings while preserving privacy by minimizing raw data transfers.

One retail implementation shows how an edge-based computer vision system let a chain run object recognition and queue monitoring in real time, route results to back-end systems via messaging, and give data scientists a fast path to deploying models for security, product recognition, and customer experience—all while maintaining GDPR compliance. Sam's Club took a similar path: an edge-enabled "seamless exit" system used real-time computer vision to eliminate manual receipt checks, improving customer experience and generating computing cost savings.

## Hybrid Architectures: Orchestrating Human-AI Collaboration Across Cloud and Edge[8]

Hybrid cloud-edge architectures deliberately partition responsibilities between centralized and local resources.

Here are the key architectural patterns:

- **Distributed processing:** Cloud systems perform batch analytics and model training, while edge nodes handle latency-sensitive inference and event handling. In predictive maintenance scenarios, for example, edge devices provide instant anomaly alerts while cloud models forecast degradation weeks in advance.
- **Model synchronization and feedback loops:** Edge devices regularly receive updated model versions from the cloud, while sending back telemetry on predictions, outcomes, and user interactions. This allows centralized teams to refine models based on field performance and operator feedback.
- **Unified data governance:** Security and privacy policies must consistently apply as data moves between edge and cloud. Healthcare architectures, for example, combine edge inference with encrypted, federated learning and blockchain-based audit trails to ensure confidentiality and trust.
- **Contextual enrichment:** Edge systems can augment local sensor data with cloud-derived insights—such as fleet-wide failure patterns or broader demand signals—allowing frontline staff to see both local context and global trends when making decisions.

Real manufacturing deployments confirm the payoff: combining edge's instant response with cloud's analytical depth produces faster anomaly detection and fewer false alerts compared with cloud-only or edge-only approaches. Humans decide faster and with greater confidence.

## Migration and Implementation Strategies Focused on Human-AI Integration[9]

Transitioning to a distributed AI architecture is as much a human interaction design challenge as a compute placement decision.

Practical strategies include:

- **Assessing human-AI touchpoints:** Map where people currently make time-critical decisions (for example, line operators, nurses, store associates) and prioritize edge deployments at those points, while retaining analysis, planning, and learning loops in the cloud.
- **Modularizing AI components:** Containerize models and analytics services so they can be deployed on edge gateways, industrial PCs, or clinical devices with consistent packaging and observability.
- **Piloting collaborative interfaces:** Initiate pilots where human users interact with AI recommendations via dashboards, mobile apps, or AR interfaces at the edge, and refine UI/UX based on real-world usage.
- **Investing in training and change management:** Train frontline staff on how to interpret local AI alerts, understand limitations, and feedback corrections, to ensure AI is viewed as a teammate rather than an opaque controller.
- **Establishing feedback loops:** Design explicit mechanisms for edge-side annotations (for example, "false alarm," "good catch") that feed back into cloud models, making the overall system a joint human-machine learning loop over time.

## Challenges and Considerations in Aligning Technology with Human-AI Integration[10]

Hybrid architectures introduce both technical and human-facing challenges that teams must actively manage:

- **Latency vs. model complexity:** Edge devices may require simplified or quantized models to meet latency and resource constraints, which can affect accuracy. Organizations must balance responsiveness with predictive quality for each use case.
- **Reliability and connectivity:** Edge systems must operate under intermittent connectivity, requiring local failover logic, buffering, and graceful degradation when cloud services are unavailable.
- **Security and privacy:** Sensitive operational or health data processed at the edge requires protection through encryption, secure communication, and, in some cases, federated learning and privacy-preserving techniques.
- **User interface diversity:** Different roles and contexts (for example, shop floor vs. ICU vs. retail floor) require tailored interfaces and alerting strategies to avoid overload and ensure clarity at the moment of decision.
- **Operational complexity:** Managing fleets of edge devices, model versions, and monitoring across sites requires DevOps/MLOps practices adapted to distributed environments.

# Case Studies

## Case Study #1: Hybrid Cloud-Edge Predictive Maintenance in Manufacturing[11]

Manufacturing is one of the clearest proving grounds for hybrid cloud-edge architectures. Facilities using optimized cloud-edge hybrids achieve as much as 80% faster anomaly detection and 55% fewer false alerts compared with other pure configurations.

In cloud-edge deployments:

- Edge devices attached to machines continuously monitor vibration, temperature, and operational parameters, running local models to detect anomalies and trigger immediate alerts to operators or control systems.
- Cloud platforms aggregate data across lines and plants, training more sophisticated models that predict degradation weeks in advance and identify process patterns not visible locally.
- Operators receive real-time edge alerts on HMIs or mobile devices while maintenance planners use cloud dashboards to

schedule interventions, balancing short-term safety and long-term asset optimization.

This hybrid configuration amplifies human intelligence by providing frontline staff with instant, localized warnings and giving planners a broad analytical view for strategic decisions.

## Case Study #2: Edge-AI Enabled Patient Monitoring in Healthcare[12]

Healthcare is embracing edge AI for patient-centric monitoring. A recent Edge-AI integrated IoT framework for real-time patient monitoring combined federated learning, homomorphic encryption, and blockchain logging to deliver secure anomaly detection at the edge.

In this case:

- Edge devices (for example, on-premises gateways or bedside units) run quantized models that analyze vital signs streams—such as heart rate and oxygen saturation—in real time, triggering local alerts for clinicians when anomalies occur.
- Cloud components collect encrypted model updates (not raw data) under federated learning schemes, improving global models without centralizing sensitive patient data.
- Clinicians use dashboards and mobile devices to view risk scores and trend summaries, with the ability to override or annotate alerts, feeding clinical feedback into model improvement.

This approach pairs the immediacy and privacy advantages of edge processing with the continuous learning and coordination strengths of the cloud. Human clinical judgment stays at the center.

## Case Study #3: Edge Computer Vision for In-Store Experience and Security[13]

Retailers are deploying edge AI and computer vision to sharpen staff decision-making and improve the customer experience. One retailer stood up an edge-based, in-store object recognition system that runs live inference on multiple video feeds. They integrated it with existing systems via messaging.

Significant benefits included:

- Continuous monitoring of checkout and parking queues, enabling staff to adjust staffing or open lanes before bottlenecks form.
- Support for deploying new models targeting security, fraud detection, and visual product recognition, enhancing both loss prevention and merchandising decisions.
- Integration with back-end systems while maintaining GDPR compliance for data security and retention.

Separately, Sam's Club piloted "Seamless Exit," using edge-based computer vision to analyze video feeds at store exits and eliminate the need for manual receipt checks, improving customer experience and generating 10-18% annual computing cost savings. In both cases, human associates stayed in control, using AI-generated signals to guide interventions rather than waiting on central reports.

## Success Metrics[14]

Distributed AI initiatives require evaluation across both technical and human-centric dimensions.

## Table of Illustrative Metrics

| Dimension | Example Metric | Why It Matters |
|---|---|---|
| **Detection Latency** | Reduction in time from event occurrence to AI alert at the edge for key use cases | Captures how well the architecture supports timely human responses |
| **Alert Quality** | Change in false positive and false negative rates for edge alerts compared with cloud-only or legacy systems | Indicates whether hybrid deployments improve signal-to-noise for users |
| **Availability and Resilience** | % of time edge AI services remain operational during network disruptions; success of local failover behaviors | Reflects robustness of AI support in real-world conditions |
| **Feedback Loop Utilization** | Volume of human feedback events from edge applications (for example, alert confirmations, overrides) and their incorporation into model updates | Shows whether human insights are systematically improving models |
| **Governance Compliance** | Incidents related to data privacy or security across cloud-edge workflows; adherence to sector-specific regulations | Confirms that distributed AI remains trustworthy and compliant |

# Practical Advice for Leaders[15]

Treat distributed AI as a way to amplify, not sideline, human judgment.

- **Start from frontline decisions, not from infrastructure diagrams.** Identify important edge decisions (for example, line shutdowns, triage, store interventions) and design cloud-edge patterns that support those humans first.
- **Adopt hybrid by design.** Use the cloud for deep learning and coordination, but commit to running the most time-sensitive inferences at the edge, with clear criteria for where each belongs.
- **Make feedback a feature.** Ensure every edge interface offers simple mechanisms for users to confirm, correct, or comment on AI outputs and route this data back into your model refinement pipelines.

- **Plan for observability and governance across tiers.** Invest in monitoring and policy enforcement that span both cloud and edge, so issues are visible and controllable regardless of where they arise.

# Conclusion

Amplifying human intelligence with distributed AI is an architectural and design challenge. The cloud must provide a reliable, ever-learning analytics backbone; edge systems must deliver fast, context-aware insights exactly where people act. Organizations that build hybrid cloud-edge architectures with explicit human-AI touchpoints, robust synchronization, and shared governance transform static data processing into a living intelligence layer woven through operations. The result is sharper, faster, more contextually aware decision-making: the central theme of this book.

# Notes

[1] Edge AI, as used here, comes from *IEB Media*'s "Edge Architectures and Cloud Computing Impact Manufacturing."

[2] Hybrid cloud-edge architecture, as used here, follows *JUIT*'s "Cloud-based Predictive Maintenance for Industrial Equipment."

[3] On latency optimization, see *IJCEM*'s "AI-Driven Predictive Maintenance in Automotive Manufacturing Using Edge Analytics."

[4] Model synchronization is drawn from *Travancore Analytics*' "Real-Time Decision-Making Using Cloud-Edge Collaboration."

[5] Hybrid cloud-edge architectures as a central "AI brain" with context-aware edge nodes are illustrated in *Korcomptenz*'s "Cloud IoT Analytics Manufacturing Case Study."

[6] This cloud analytics cluster draws on *Nature*'s "Edge-AI Integrated IoT Framework for Real-Time Patient Monitoring," *OxMaint*'s "Cloud vs. Edge Computing Predictive Maintenance," *SERENA Project*'s "A Cloud-to-Edge Architecture for Predictive Analytics," *IEB Media*'s "Edge Architectures and Cloud Computing Impact Manufacturing," and *JUIT*'s "Cloud-based Predictive Maintenance for Industrial Equipment."

[7] This edge analytics cluster draws on *IJCEM*'s "AI-Driven Predictive Maintenance in Automotive Manufacturing Using Edge Analytics," *Clarkston Consulting*'s "Edge Computing in Retail," *DelveInsight*'s "Artificial Intelligence in Remote Patient Monitoring," *VirtuLab*'s "Object Recognition ML Computer Vision Success Story," and vSoft *Consulting*'s "Retail Store AI Computer Vision Analytics Case Study."

[8] This hybrid architectures cluster draws on *Travancore Analytics*' "Real-Time Decision-Making Using Cloud-Edge Collaboration," *OxMaint*'s "Cloud vs. Edge Computing Predictive Maintenance," *Telit*'s "Edge AI in Connected Health Care Patient-Centric Approach," *Korcomptenz*'s "Cloud IoT Analytics Manufacturing Case Study," and *IEB Media*'s "Edge Architectures and Cloud Computing Impact Manufacturing."

[9] Migration and implementation draw on WWEMD's "Edge Analytics for Predictive Maintenance in Manufacturing Implementation Guide for 2025," *Advantech*'s "Success Stories Edge AI in Medical," *DelveInsight*'s "Artificial Intelligence in Remote Patient Monitoring," and *Nature*'s "Edge-AI Integrated IoT Framework for Real-Time Patient Monitoring."

[10] This challenges cluster draws on *VirtuLab*'s "Object Recognition ML Computer Vision Success Story," *Telit*'s "Edge AI in Connected Health Care Patient-Centric Approach," *Clarkston Consulting*'s "Edge Computing in Retail," and *SERENA Project*'s "A Cloud-to-Edge Architecture for Predictive Analytics."

[11] This case study draws on *OxMaint*'s "Cloud vs. Edge Computing Predictive Maintenance," *IJCEM*'s "AI-Driven Predictive Maintenance in Automotive Manufacturing Using Edge Analytics," *JUIT*'s "Cloud-based Predictive Maintenance for Industrial Equipment," and *Travancore Analytics*' "Real-Time Decision-Making Using Cloud-Edge Collaboration."

[12] For this case study, see *Nature*'s "Edge-AI Integrated IoT Framework for Real-Time Patient Monitoring," *Advantech*'s "Success Stories Edge AI in Medical," and *DelveInsight*'s "Artificial Intelligence in Remote Patient Monitoring."

[13] This case study draws on *VirtuLab*'s "Object Recognition ML Computer Vision Success Story," vSoft *Consulting*'s "Retail Store AI Computer Vision Analytics Case Study," and *Clarkston Consulting*'s "Edge Computing in Retail."

[14] The success metrics cluster is drawn from *Travancore Analytics*' "Real-Time Decision-Making Using Cloud-Edge Collaboration," *IJCEM*'s "AI-Driven Predictive Maintenance in Automotive Manufacturing Using Edge Analytics," *OxMaint*'s "Cloud vs. Edge Computing Predictive Maintenance," and *Nature*'s "Edge-AI Integrated IoT Framework for Real-Time Patient Monitoring."

[15] This practical advice cluster draws on *Korcomptenz*'s "Cloud IoT Analytics Manufacturing Case Study," *SERENA Project*'s "A Cloud-to-Edge Architecture for Predictive Analytics," *DelveInsight*'s "Artificial Intelligence in Remote Patient Monitoring," and *Telit*'s "Edge AI in Connected Health Care Patient-Centric Approach."

## Key topics explored in this chapter:

- Streaming Data Pipelines: The Backbone of Real-Time Intelligence
- Real-Time Decision Intelligence Reference Model
- Real-Time Dashboards and Visualization
- AI-Augmented Triggers and Alerts for Rapid Action
- Batch, Near Real-Time, and True Streaming Decision Patterns
- Human-AI Collaboration in Real-Time Decision Environments

# WAY 35

# Enable Real-Time Decision Intelligence


## Abstract

Real-time decision intelligence unites streaming data, analytics, and human judgment so organizations can respond to events within seconds instead of hours or days. Streaming platforms, low-latency dashboards, and AI-driven alerts build a continuously refreshed operational picture. That picture, in turn, enables proactive interventions across supply chains, manufacturing, banking, and other sectors. This chapter examines the technical infrastructure and human-AI collaboration patterns needed to turn data velocity into a durable decision-making advantage.


## Objective

After completing this chapter, you will be able to:

- Describe the core components of streaming data pipelines that underpin real-time decision intelligence.
- Design real-time dashboards and visualizations that present live metrics, anomalies, and AI insights in actionable formats for different roles.
- Explain how rule-based and AI-driven alerts can trigger rapid, context-aware responses while minimizing alert fatigue.
- Integrate human judgment into real-time environments through feedback loops, escalation paths, and training.
- Recognize key implementation considerations such as scalability, latency optimization, governance, and security for streaming systems.

- Draw lessons from real-world case studies in logistics, manufacturing, and fraud detection to shape practical roadmaps.

# Terms to Know

**Event-Driven Architecture (EDA)**[1] **-** A design style where events (for example, sensor readings, transactions) trigger downstream processing, alerts, or workflows as they occur.

**Real-Time Dashboard**[2] **-** A visualization system that auto-updates metrics, trends, and alerts as new data arrives, supporting rapid situational awareness.

**Real-Time Decision Intelligence**[3] **-** The coordinated use of streaming data pipelines, analytics (including AI), dashboards, and human workflows to continuously sense, decide, and act within operational timeframes.

**Streaming Data Pipeline**[4] **-** An architecture that continuously ingests, processes, and routes data events in near real time rather than in periodic batches.

# Introduction

As business cycles accelerate and operating environments grow more volatile, waiting for tomorrow's reports often proves inadequate. Streaming analytics lets organizations to continuously monitor operations, identify issues early, and orchestrate rapid responses. Yet, this only works when paired with interfaces and workflows that keep humans central. Therefore, real-time decision intelligence equally encompasses integrating AI and dashboards into frontline operations and deploying Kafka clusters or stream processors.

## Streaming Data Pipelines: The Backbone of Real-Time Intelligence[5]

Streaming pipelines deliver the continuous event flow that fuels real-time decisions.

Key components include:

- **Data ingestion technologies** such as Apache Kafka and cloud equivalents (for example, Confluent Cloud, Amazon Kinesis) capture events from transactional systems, devices, and external feeds with durability and horizontal scalability.

- **Stream processing approaches** (for example, Apache Flink, Kafka Streams, Spark Streaming, or cloud-native services): perform transformations, filtering, joins, windowed aggregations, and enrichment on the fly.
- **Integration with analytical stores:** Processed streams often flow into real-time databases or analytical warehouses, supporting both live dashboards and historical analysis.

Supply chain and logistics applications show how streaming platforms unify data from inventory systems, telematics, and external signals. This unification allows managers to base decisions on accurate, current views rather than outdated batch reports.

## Real-Time Decision Intelligence Reference Model[6]

Across logistics, manufacturing, and fraud detection, a recurring pattern emerges: events are ingested, processed in motion, evaluated by AI, persisted, and surfaced to humans through dashboards and workflows. A reference model makes these layers explicit, enabling teams to design and govern them deliberately.

This model captures the shift from "store-analyze-act" to "ingest-analyze-act-store," where logic operates on live data and where storage primarily supports learning, compliance, and long-term analysis.

## Real-Time Decision Intelligence Reference Model

| Layer | Description | Purpose |
|---|---|---|
| **Ingestion** | Connects to operational sources such as WMS, TMS, ERP, core banking, e-commerce, and IoT devices, as well as external feeds like carrier status, traffic, and weather | Uses CDC, APIs, and streaming platforms to capture events with minimal delay and normalized schemas |
| **Processing** | Performs real-time joins, enrichment (for example, customer, product, or route attributes), filtering, and windowed aggregations on streaming data | Computes streaming KPIs and features, such as delay-risk scores, machine-state summaries, or transaction-velocity indicators |
| **Storage** | Maintains hot operational stores plus warehouses or lakes for history, training data, and audit trails | Persists event logs, model inputs, and outcomes to support root-cause analysis and regulatory evidence |
| **AI and Analytics** | Hosts models for ETA prediction, route optimization, anomaly detection, and fraud scoring that operate on streams or micro-batches | Uses continuous feedback (for example, confirmed fraud, realized ETAs, machine failures) to retrain and recalibrate models |
| **Visualization and Decision-Support** | Provides real-time dashboards and alert panels for dispatchers, plant supervisors, fraud analysts, and executives | Surfaces role-appropriate metrics, anomalies, and AI insights, aligning with existing BI practices rather than replacing them wholesale |
| **Human-Workflow and Automation** | Connects alerts to workflows and playbooks such as rerouting shipments, launching maintenance tickets, expediting orders, or opening fraud cases | Encodes decision logic such as "re-allocate stock," "slow or stop the line," or "block and escalate," combining straight-through automation with human-in-the-loop review for ambiguous or high-risk events |

## Real-Time Dashboards and Visualization[7]

Dashboards translate streaming data into human-readable situational awareness.

Effective real-time dashboards typically provide:

- **Live metrics and KPIs** that update continuously to show production rates, inventory levels, or fraud indicators without manual refresh.
- **Visual alerts and anomaly cues** (for example, color changes, icons) that highlight when thresholds are breached or patterns deviate from normal.
- **Role-specific views** for operators, supervisors, and executives, ensuring each group sees the detail needed for their decisions.

In manufacturing settings, real-time dashboards integrating machine, ERP, and operator data allow teams to monitor dozens of parameters on always-visible displays. This eliminates cycling through multiple control screens and enables swifter responses to deviations.

## AI-Augmented Triggers and Alerts for Rapid Action[8]

Alerts translate streaming insights into timely prompts and actions.

Common patterns include:

- **Rule-based alerts** where thresholds on metrics—such as vibration levels, defect rates, or transit delays—trigger notifications to dashboards, mobile devices, or control systems.
- **AI-driven anomaly detection**, where models learn normal behavior and flag unusual patterns without requiring hard-coded rules.
- **Context-aware notifications**, which tailor alerts by user role, severity, and context to reduce noise and focus attention on the most critical issues.
- **Integration with automated workflows**, where high-confidence alerts can automatically trigger actions (for example, blocking a transaction, re-routing a shipment), with escalation paths to human experts for review of borderline cases.

In banking and payments, streaming systems built on Kafka and Flink enable real-time fraud detection. They analyze each transaction against behavioral profiles and execute immediate actions, such as freezing accounts or sending step-up authentication prompts. This substantially reduces fraud windows.

## Batch, Near Real-Time, and True Streaming Decision Patterns[9]

Comparing streaming and processing modes reveals that "real time" spans a continuum, from batch through micro-batch near-real-time to sub-second streaming. Choosing the appropriate pattern for each decision prevents over-engineering some use cases while under-serving others.

## Decision Latency Patterns

| Pattern | Typical Latency Window | Characteristics and Trade-Offs | Example Use Cases |
|---|---|---|---|
| **Batch** | Tens of minutes to 24 hours or more | High throughput and simpler operations; decisions delayed until scheduled runs complete. | Daily inventory and logistics reports, financial close, historical dashboards, offline model training. |
| **Near Real-Time** | Roughly 5-300 seconds (micro-batch) | Small windows processed frequently; balances freshness with cost and infrastructure complexity. | Control-tower shipment views, plant-floor status boards, warehouse dashboards where seconds-level delays are acceptable. |
| **True Streaming** | Sub-second to a few seconds end-to-end | Event-by-event processing; maximizes responsiveness but requires always-on, carefully tuned streaming infrastructure. | Card and payments fraud detection, real-time routing decisions, critical equipment protection where every second counts. |

Fraud detection research demonstrates that transitioning from batch to micro-batch and streaming architectures significantly shrinks the window during which attackers can exploit stolen credentials. This also enhances detection performance and resource efficiency. In supply chain and manufacturing contexts, near-real-time patterns often suffice, while true streaming is reserved for the most time-sensitive flows.

### Human-AI Collaboration in Real-Time Decision Environments[10]

Real-time systems work best when humans and AI complement each other. AI excels at volume and speed, continuously scanning streams to surface anomalies, correlations, and risks that humans would struggle to detect promptly. Humans contribute context and judgment, interpreting alerts against domain knowledge, local conditions, and ethical considerations, and determining when to override automated suggestions. Feedback loops—for example, marking alerts as true or false positives—enable teams to refine models and rules, strengthening performance and trust over time. Training and playbooks equip users to interpret dashboard signals, triage alerts, and escalate appropriately, balancing speed with caution.

## Case Studies

### Case Study #1: Streaming Logistics for Supply Chain Visibility[11]

FourKites, a supply chain visibility platform, uses cloud-hosted Kafka-based streaming to integrate transportation, inventory, and yard operations into a unified real-time logistics system. With over 3 million shipments tracked daily, streaming data feeds AI models that power estimated times of arrival, risk scores, and exception alerts. This allows customers to respond within seconds rather than hours.

Separately, Walmart leverages Confluent's streaming platform to process billions of events daily across more than 100 million SKUs. This enables real-time replenishment decisions throughout a vast store and distribution network. By continuously monitoring stock levels, local demand, and other parameters, the system triggers automatic replenishment and highlights emerging issues for planners, transforming replenishment into a near real-time decision process.

Within the reference model, these solutions continuously ingest order, inventory, and telematics events; process them into delay-risk metrics; store both live states and history; apply AI to forecast ETAs and demand; surface control-tower views to planners; and drive rerouting and exception-management workflows when issues arise.

## Case Study #2: Real-Time Manufacturing Dashboards Driving Operational Action[12]

Manufacturing plants increasingly deploy real-time dashboards that combine machine data, ERP information, and operator inputs into unified views. These are visible on the shop floor and in management offices. Specifically, these dashboards:

- Present live KPIs such as throughput, downtime, and quality metrics, often on "always-up" displays.
- Provide configurable alarms for deviations (for example, vibration exceeding thresholds, defect rates over set limits), enabling operators to act before small issues escalate.
- Offer role-specific perspectives: operators see machine status and job progress, supervisors see bottlenecks and staffing needs, and executives see plant-wide performance.

Such deployments correlate with increased operational efficiency, reduced downtime, and better alignment across plant roles. This is because decisions stem from a shared, live picture rather than lagging reports.

Mapped to the reference model, sensor and PLC data ingest into streaming platforms. Processing layers then compute real-time KPIs and anomaly scores, while historical traces store for root-cause analysis and predictive-maintenance training. Dashboards support different roles, and workflows trigger maintenance tickets and escalation protocols when alerts fire.

## Case Study #3: Real-Time Streaming Fraud Detection in Banking[13]

Banks and payment providers increasingly adopt real-time streaming architectures to detect and prevent fraud as transactions occur. One approach combining stream analytics with adaptive AI models reduced false negatives by 12.4%, maintained a false positive rate around 3.2%, and outperformed existing commercial systems by 22-35% across key metrics, all with 40% less compute usage.

In real-world deployments with banks like Citizens and Evo Banco, streaming architectures built on Kafka and Flink analyze every incoming transaction against behavioral baselines, device information, and historical patterns. When anomalies surface, the system can immediately block transactions, send alerts to customers, or route events to fraud investigators for manual review, reducing loss exposure and protecting customer trust.

Within the reference model, these architectures ingest transaction and context events. Processing layers then enrich and aggregate behavior over windows. Storage retains events and labels for investigations and training. AI models score risk in milliseconds. Dashboards and queues support analysts, and workflows automate blocks, step-up authentication, and escalations.

# Success Metrics[14]

Organizations should measure real-time decision intelligence on both speed and quality.

## Table of Illustrative Metrics

| Dimension | Example Metric | Why It Matters |
|---|---|---|
| **Decision Latency** | Time from event occurrence to action taken (for example, alert triggered, order re-routed, transaction blocked) | Lower latency demonstrates the system's ability to support time-sensitive interventions |
| **Accuracy and Precision** | For AI-driven alerts: false-positive and false-negative rates, precision, recall, and F1 score | Balances responsiveness with trust and reduces alert fatigue |
| **Operational Impact** | Downstream outcomes such as reduced downtime, fraud losses avoided, on-time delivery improvements, or inventory-optimization gains | Ties real-time capabilities to tangible business results |
| **System Performance** | Throughput (events processed per second), processing lag, and infrastructure cost per event | Ensures the streaming architecture scales sustainably |
| **User Engagement** | Dashboard usage, alert-response time, and user-satisfaction scores | Indicates whether humans are effectively collaborating with real-time systems |

## Practical Advice for Leaders[15]

Leaders implementing real-time decision intelligence should:

- **Start with high-impact, well-scoped use cases** (for example, fraud detection, shipment tracking, critical equipment monitoring) where latency reductions materially improve outcomes and prove value before scaling broadly.
- **Design for human-AI collaboration from day one** by building feedback loops, escalation workflows, and role-appropriate dashboards so that streaming systems augment rather than replace human judgment.
- **Invest in streaming infrastructure and governance together,** ensuring data quality, lineage, security, and audit trails are maintained at streaming speed, not bolted on afterward.
- **Match latency patterns to decision needs:** use batch for historical analysis, near-real-time for operational dashboards, and true streaming only where sub-second responsiveness is mandatory, avoiding needless complexity.
- **Monitor and optimize continuously** through metrics on decision latency, accuracy, operational impact, system performance, and user engagement. This supports ongoing refinement of models, alerts, and workflows based on real-world feedback.

## Conclusion

Real-time decision intelligence changes how organizations sense, decide, and act. It replaces delayed batch processing with continuous streaming pipelines, AI-augmented alerts, and live dashboards. When streaming architectures pair with thoughtful human-AI collaboration patterns and governance-by-design, they enable proactive, timely interventions across supply chains, manufacturing, fraud prevention, and other domains. The Real-Time Decision Intelligence Reference Model and the continuum of latency patterns offer leaders concrete frameworks for aligning technology investments with operational needs so that speed serves strategy rather than adding complexity.

# Notes

[1] Event-driven architecture (EDA) is defined in Confluent's "Real-Time Streaming Prevents Fraud."

[2] Real-time dashboards are defined and contextualized in *DataParc*'s "Real-Time Manufacturing Dashboard: Setup, Importance, and Benefits."

[3] Real-time decision intelligence is defined in Instaclustr's "Real-Time Streaming: Streaming Analytics Top 5 Use Cases, Challenges, and Best Practices" and *CrateDB*'s "Real-Time Analytics: Case Studies and Real-World Applications."

[4] Streaming data pipelines are defined and illustrated in Striim's "Use Cases: Real-Time Analytics in the Supply Chain."

[5] This section on streaming data pipelines is addressed in Instaclustr's "Real-Time Streaming," *CrateDB*'s "Real-Time Analytics," Kai Waehner's "Inside FourKites Logistics Platform," Confluent's "Real-Time Streaming Prevents Fraud," Propulsion Tech Journal's "A Framework for Real-Time Fraud Detection," IJFMR's "Investigating the Applications of AI Fraud Detection," Striim's "Use Cases: Real-Time Analytics in the Supply Chain," and SmartWarehousing's "Real-Time Supply Chain Analytics."

[6] This section on the Real-Time Decision Intelligence Reference Model draws on Instaclustr's "Real-Time Streaming," Striim's "Use Cases," Confluent's "Supply Chain Optimization," *CrateDB*'s "Real-Time Analytics," Propulsion Tech Journal's "A Framework," IJFMR's "Investigating the Applications," *NewMathData*'s "Senpex," and SmartWarehousing's "Real-Time Supply Chain Analytics."

[7] This section on real-time dashboards and visualization draws on HiveMQ's "The Business Impact of Real-Time Dashboards," *DataParc*'s "Real-Time Manufacturing Dashboard," *Starburst*'s "Lockheed Martin Case Study," and *Harmoni*'s "Manufacturing Dashboards."

[8] This section on AI-augmented triggers and alerts draws on Instaclustr's "Real-Time Streaming," IJFMR's "Investigating the Applications," Propulsion Tech Journal's "A Framework," Confluent's "Real-Time Streaming Prevents Fraud," and SmartWarehousing's "Real-Time Supply Chain Analytics."

[9] This section on batch, near-real-time, and true streaming decision patterns draws on Instaclustr's "Real-Time Streaming," Propulsion Tech Journal's "A Framework," IJFMR's "Investigating the Applications," Striim's "Use Cases," *DataParc*'s "Real-Time Manufacturing Dashboard," *Harmoni*'s "Manufacturing Dashboards," and HiveMQ's "The Business Impact of Real-Time Dashboards."

[10] For more on human-AI collaboration in real-time decision environments, see Striim's "Use Cases," Instaclustr's "Real-Time Streaming," *CrateDB*'s "Real-Time Analytics," *Michigan State University Online*'s "Improve Real-Time Decision Making," Confluent's "Real-Time Streaming Prevents Fraud," and IJFMR's "Investigating the Applications."

[11] This case study draws on Kai Waehner's "Inside FourKites Logistics Platform," Confluent's "Supply Chain Optimization," and Striim's "Use Cases: Real-Time Analytics in the Supply Chain."

[12] This case study draws on *Starburst*'s "Lockheed Martin Case Study," *Harmoni*'s "Manufacturing Dashboards," *DataParc*'s "Real-Time Manufacturing Dashboard," and HiveMQ's "The Business Impact of Real-Time Dashboards."

[13] This case study is examined in Propulsion Tech Journal's "A Framework for Real-Time Fraud Detection," Confluent's "Real-Time Streaming Prevents Fraud," and IJFMR's "Investigating the Applications of AI Fraud Detection."

[14] Success metrics draw on Instaclustr's "Real-Time Streaming," Propulsion Tech Journal's "A Framework," IJFMR's "Investigating the Applications," Confluent's "Real-Time Streaming Prevents Fraud," Striim's "Use Cases," HiveMQ's "The Business Impact," and SmartWarehousing's "Real-Time Supply Chain Analytics."

[15] This practical-advice cluster draws on Confluent's "Supply Chain Optimization," Confluent's "Real-Time Streaming Prevents Fraud," IJFMR's "Investigating the Applications," Striim's "Use Cases," *Michigan State University Online*'s "Improve Real-Time Decision Making," HiveMQ's "The Business Impact," SmartWarehousing's "Real-Time Supply Chain Analytics," and Propulsion Tech Journal's "A Framework."

Leading companies are building "AI factories"–integrated platforms of data, methods, and algorithms–to accelerate development across analytical, generative, and agentic AI.

*MIT Sloan Management Review*

"Five Trends in AI and Data Science for 2026"

Davenport and Bean

January 2026

## Key topics explored in this chapter:

- The AI Transparency and Explainability Model
- XAI Techniques
- Governance and Lifecycle Integration
- Human-AI Collaboration and Communication

# WAY 36

# Foster AI Transparency and Explainability

## Abstract

Transparency and explainability make AI systems open to scrutiny, questioning, and effective oversight. This chapter introduces a layered AI Transparency and Explainability Model, along with a focused set of explainable AI (XAI) techniques, to help organizations align governance, models, data, and user interfaces so that AI-driven decisions are understandable in practice—even in high-stakes contexts such as medical imaging.

## Objective

After completing this chapter, you will be able to:

- Define transparency and explainability within AI governance and regulatory contexts.
- Utilize a layered AI Transparency and Explainability Model (governance, model, data, interface) to assign responsibilities for documentation, controls, and user-facing explanations.
- Select appropriate XAI techniques (for example, SHAP, LIME, saliency maps, counterfactuals) by evaluating their strengths, weaknesses, and use cases.
- Integrate explainability into AI lifecycle governance, encompassing model approval, monitoring, and human-in-the-loop review.
- Communicate explanations effectively to diverse audiences (for example, executives, regulators, clinicians, and customers).

# Terms to Know

**Counterfactual Explanation**[1] - An explanation showing how small changes in input features could alter a model's prediction (for example, "If income were 10% higher, the loan would be approved").

**Explainable Artificial Intelligence (XAI)**[2] - Methods and practices that render AI model behavior and predictions understandable to humans, often through feature attributions, visualizations, or examples.

**LIME (Local Interpretable Model-agnostic Explanations)**[3] - A model-agnostic XAI method that approximates a complex model locally around a prediction using a simpler surrogate model.

**Saliency Map**[4] - A visual explanation, commonly used in medical imaging, that highlights image regions most influencing a model's prediction.

**SHAP (SHapley Additive exPlanations)**[5] - An XAI framework based on Shapley values from game theory, distributing a prediction among input features and offering consistent feature attributions.

**Transparency**[6] - The extent to which an AI system's information—its purpose, data, model, and limitations—is accessible and understandable to stakeholders and regulators.

# Introduction[7]

AI governance frameworks consistently emphasize transparency and explainability as essential for responsible use. Regulators stress that people affected by AI systems—as well as auditors and oversight bodies—need clear insight into how these systems work, what data they use, and where their limitations lie. In high-stakes areas like healthcare, finance, and public services, explainability plays a key role in building trust, supporting accountability, and meeting regulatory requirements. Research in medical imaging shows that clinicians are more likely to trust AI recommendations when they can see and understand how the system reached its conclusions—for example, through visual highlights or simple, rule-based explanations.

## The AI Transparency and Explainability Model[8]

To operationalize transparency, use an architecture that assigns accountability across four layers: governance, models, data, and interfaces.

### Layer 1: Governance

**Scope:** Policies, standards, and oversight structures defining what transparency and explainability mean for the organization.

**Responsibilities:**

- Set explainability requirements by risk level (for example, more stringent for medical or credit decisions).
- Define documentation standards (model cards, data sheets, audit logs).
- Mandate human oversight and establish processes for review and appeal.

### Layer 2: Model

**Scope:** Model design, training, validation, and monitoring practices that render behavior interpretable.

**Responsibilities:**

- Choose model families that balance performance and interpretability where necessary (for example, simpler models for some high-risk tasks).
- Integrate XAI methods (for example, SHAP, LIME, rule-based surrogates) into training and validation workflows.
- Track performance and explanation stability over time, especially under drift.

### Layer 3: Data

**Scope:** Data quality, labeling, and documentation underpinning meaningful explanations.

**Responsibilities:**

- Document data sources, representativeness, and known biases.
- Ensure labels are well-defined and audited, particularly in domains like medical imaging where ground truth can be ambiguous.
- Maintain lineage so explanations can link predictions back to underlying data.

### Layer 4: Interface and Communication

**Scope:** User-facing explanations, visualizations, and narratives tailored to diverse audiences.

**Responsibilities:**

- Present explanations at the right level of detail (for example, simple reasons for customers, richer detail for auditors or clinicians).
- Combine multiple explanation types (for example, saliency maps plus textual rationales) to support complete interpretation.
- Provide channels for feedback and challenge, making explainability interactive rather than static.

This layered architecture clarifies that transparency isn't solely delegated to a single XAI method; rather, it's important that accountability stretch across governance, model engineering, data management, and user experience design.

## XAI Techniques[9]

Different XAI techniques serve distinct needs and audiences. Research comparing SHAP, LIME, saliency maps, and counterfactual explanations reveals fundamental trade-offs in reliability, computational expense, and interpretability clarity.

Reviews of medical-imaging applications stress that saliency-based approaches let clinicians observe model attention regions. However, they require integration with additional explanation methods and clinical reasoning to prevent misinterpretation. Comparative studies of SHAP and LIME urge cautious interpretation of feature attributions, particularly when features exhibit collinearity or when models display strong nonlinearity.

## Summary of XAI Techniques

| Technique | Strengths | Weaknesses | Suitable Use Cases |
|---|---|---|---|
| **SHAP** | Theoretically grounded in game theory; provides consistent feature attributions; supports global and local explanations | Computationally expensive, especially with many features; sensitive to feature correlations; can be complex to explain to non-experts | High-stakes tabular models (for example, credit, clinical risk scores) where consistent explanations and feature importance matter |
| **LIME** | Model-agnostic, relatively fast; provides local explanations around specific predictions; easy to prototype | Approximations can be unstable; assumes local linearity; less reliable when features interact strongly | Interactive debugging, user-specific explanations, initial exploration of black-box models in lower-risk contexts |
| **Saliency Maps (for Images)** | Intuitive visual overlays showing where a model "looked" in an image; widely used in medical imaging; integrates well into clinician workflows | Often show "where" but not "what"; can be noisy or inconsistent; lack standard evaluation metrics; risk of over-trust if clinicians overinterpret heatmaps | Medical imaging (for example, highlighting lesions), radiology QA, visual model debugging and clinician-AI collaboration |
| **Counterfactual Explanations** | Provide actionable, human-friendly "what-if" scenarios; align closely with legal and ethical expectations for justification | Can be hard to generate realistically; may ignore feasibility or fairness constraints if not carefully designed | Individual-level decisions (for example, loans, hiring), policy-sensitive settings where users need to understand how to change outcomes |

## Governance and Lifecycle Integration[10]

AI governance methods advocate embedding transparency and explainability throughout the AI lifecycle, rather than treating them as retrospective attachments.

- **Design:** Define transparency objectives and XAI requirements based on risk and stakeholder needs.
- **Development:** Select model families and XAI techniques that can meet those requirements; document assumptions and limitations.
- **Deployment:** Integrate explanation services into applications and workflows, including logging and audit capabilities.
- **Monitoring:** Track not only model accuracy but also the stability of explanations (for example, whether feature importance patterns or saliency maps change unexpectedly under drift).

Legal and policy analyses warn against an "explainability illusion," where surface-level explanations mask unresolved issues with model risk or bias. The layered architecture combats this pitfall by making transparency explicit at every level: governance, data, model, and interface.

## Human-AI Collaboration and Communication[11]

Research examining clinician perspectives on XAI in medical imaging highlights that explanations gain value when integrated with human expertise and domain knowledge. Clinicians prefer explanations consistent with their mental models, enabling them to challenge AI outputs that conflict with clinical evidence.

More broadly, AI governance frameworks suggest tailoring explanations to audiences: concise justifications and rights information for consumers, deeper technical content for auditors, and interactive diagnostic tools for internal specialists. Effectively communicating explanations—including explicit acknowledgment of uncertainties and limitations—is just as vital as the underlying XAI technique itself.

# Case Studies

## Case Study #1: Explainability Requirements in Enterprise AI Governance[12]

Enterprise AI governance resources profile organizations that establish transparency and explainability as distinct policy categories, enforced through tangible controls such as model documentation, explanation APIs, and user-facing rationales. Requirements typically scale with risk tier; high-impact models must offer human-interpretable explanations and comprehensive audit logs, whereas low-risk models might only need foundational documentation.

## Case Study #2: Saliency Maps in Medical Imaging[13]

Medical imaging literature shows saliency maps are the predominant explanation method for deep learning models interpreting radiological images. Radiologists use heatmaps to visualize where models focus attention when flagging tumors or lesions, building confidence when patterns align with clinical expectations. However, studies also reveal inconsistent or misleading heatmaps when models react to image artifacts, prompting calls for standardized evaluation protocols and integrating saliency with complementary explanation forms.

## Case Study #3: SHAP and LIME in Clinical and Security Contexts[14]

Comparative investigations of SHAP and LIME across biomedical and security applications show SHAP delivers more stable feature attributions, making it suitable for high-stakes decision contexts. LIME, however, offers faster, localized explanations, valuable for debugging and user-specific insights. Yet, both methods remain vulnerable to feature interactions and collinearity, leading to recommendations for careful interpretation combined with domain expertise.

# Success Metrics[15]

## Table of Illustrative Metrics

| Dimension | Example Metric | Why It Matters |
|---|---|---|
| **Governance Coverage** | % of AI systems with defined transparency and explainability requirements by risk tier | Shows whether explainability is being managed systematically, not ad hoc |
| **Documentation Completeness** | Share of production models with current model cards, data sheets, and explanation method documentation | Indicates readiness to audit and communicate model behavior |
| **XAI Implementation** | % of high-impact models with integrated XAI methods (for example, SHAP, saliency maps) available to end-users or reviewers | Reflects actual use of explainability, not just policy statements |
| **Explanation Stability** | Frequency or severity of unexplained changes in explanation patterns (for example, feature importance or saliency) under stable conditions | Helps detect drift, model brittleness, or XAI method instability |

# Practical Advice for Leaders[16]

Leaders can strengthen AI transparency and explainability by starting with these recommendations:

- **Adopt a layered transparency model,** clarifying responsibilities at governance, model, data, and interface layers.
- **Define explainability requirements by risk,** tying XAI methods and documentation depth to the impact of each AI system.
- **Select XAI methods pragmatically,** using SHAP in high-stakes tabular settings, saliency maps for imaging, and LIME or counterfactuals for local, user-facing explanations.
- **Measure and communicate explanation quality,** including stability, interpretability for target users, and alignment with domain expectations.

# Conclusion

Transparency and explainability involve distributed responsibilities across governance, model design, data management, and user interfaces. A formal AI Transparency and Explainability Model, paired with XAI techniques suited to their strengths, weaknesses, and contexts, makes AI behavior comprehensible in high-stakes domains such as healthcare and finance. This layered approach supports trust, oversight, and human-AI collaboration beyond basic regulatory compliance.

# Notes

[1] A counterfactual explanation, as used here, follows *PMC*'s "Comparative Analysis of Explainable AI Techniques for Intrusion Detection Systems in Healthcare."

[2] On explainable artificial intelligence (XAI), this book follows Witness.ai's "AI Transparency."

[3] The working sense of LIME comes from *arXiv*'s "Explainability Techniques Applied to Road Traffic Forecasting Using Graph Neural Networks."

[4] A saliency map, as used here, is described in *Nature*'s "Enhancing Trust in AI-Assisted Medical Imaging."

[5] SHAP is understood here per *IJIRT*'s "Unlocking the Black Box: A Survey on Explainable AI and Privacy-Preserving AI."

[6] For transparency as used in this book, see *EWSolutions*' "AI and Data Governance."

[7] The case for transparency and explainability as organizational imperatives is made in Bradley's "Global AI Governance: Five Key Frameworks Explained" and Jones Walker's "The Explainability Illusion."

[8] The AI Transparency & Explainability Model is developed across *Tangibly*'s "A Layered Model for AI Governance," *AI21*'s "AI Governance Frameworks," *EWSolutions*' "AI and Data Governance," Liminal's "Enterprise AI Governance Guide," *arXiv*'s "Explainability Techniques Applied to Road Traffic Forecasting," *PMC*'s "Comparative Analysis of Explainable AI Techniques," *DiVA Portal*'s "Comparing XAI Methods LIME and SHAP," and Witness.ai's "Model Monitoring."

[9] XAI techniques are surveyed across *IJIRT*'s "Unlocking the Black Box," *arXiv*'s "Explainability Techniques Applied to Road Traffic Forecasting," *Nature*'s "Enhancing Trust in AI-Assisted Medical Imaging," *PMC*'s "Comparative Analysis of Explainable AI Techniques," *DiVA Portal*'s "Comparing XAI Methods LIME and SHAP," and *ScienceDirect*'s "Comprehensive Review of XAI Methods in Medical Imaging."

[10] Governance and lifecycle integration are addressed in Bradley's "Global AI Governance," *EWSolutions*' "AI and Data Governance," Liminal's "Enterprise AI Governance Guide," *PMC*'s "Enhancing Trust in AI-Assisted Medical Imaging," Witness.ai's "Model Monitoring," and Jones Walker's "The Explainability Illusion."

[11] Human-AI collaboration and communication are examined in *Nature*'s "Enhancing Trust in AI-Assisted Medical Imaging" and *arXiv*'s "Explainability Techniques Applied to Road Traffic Forecasting."

[12] The enterprise governance case study draws on Bradley's "Global AI Governance: Five Key Frameworks Explained" and Liminal's "Enterprise AI Governance Guide."

[13] The medical imaging case study is drawn from *Nature*'s "Enhancing Trust in AI-Assisted Medical Imaging" and *ScienceDirect*'s "Comprehensive Review of XAI Methods in Medical Imaging."

[14] *PMC*'s "Comparative Analysis of Explainable AI Techniques for Intrusion Detection Systems in Healthcare" and *DiVA Portal*'s "Comparing XAI Methods LIME and SHAP" supply the intrusion detection case study.

[15] For success metrics around AI transparency and governance, see *EWSolutions*' "AI and Data Governance," Liminal's "Enterprise AI Governance Guide," Witness.ai's "AI Transparency," and Witness.ai's "Model Monitoring."

[16] This practical-advice cluster draws on *Tangibly*'s "A Layered Model for AI Governance," *AI21*'s "AI Governance Frameworks," *arXiv*'s "Explainability Techniques Applied to Road Traffic Forecasting," and *PMC*'s "Enhancing Trust in AI-Assisted Medical Imaging."

Only 12% of organizations describe their AI governance committees as mature and proactive, while 23% still lack a dedicated AI governance body altogether.

*Cisco*

2026 Data and Privacy Benchmark Study:
"A Shifting Paradigm: Governance in the Age of AI"
January 2026

# **Part Four:** Data

In the age of AI, data forms the foundation of innovation and insight in the digital enterprise.

## Key topics explored in this chapter:

- The AI Data Stewardship Stack
- Comparison of Stewardship Models for AI
- Stewardship Across the AI Lifecycle
- Roles: CDOs, Stewards, and AI Teams

# WAY 37

# Redefine Data Stewardship for AI

## Abstract

Data stewardship can no longer live as a narrow, back-office governance function. It now sits close to model performance, ethical risk, and operational accountability, which means stewards need to understand not just what data means, but how it will be used, transformed, monitored, and challenged over time. This chapter argues for a shift from static control to active enablement: the objective is not simply to lock data down, but to help organizations use it well enough that AI systems stay reliable, explainable, and aligned with business intent. To make the shift practical, this chapter introduces an AI Data Stewardship Stack and explores centralized, domain-oriented, and federated stewardship models to help organizations align their operation with the most appropriate approach.

## Objective

After completing this chapter, you will be able to:

- Explain how AI alters the scope and impact of data stewardship responsibilities.
- Utilize the AI Data Stewardship Stack to assign clear owners, stewards, and risk controls across domains, data products, features/labels, and models.
- Differentiate between centralized, domain-oriented, and federated stewardship models for AI, understanding their pros, cons, and example contexts.

- Integrate stewardship into AI governance and data governance models, treating it as an essential strategic function rather than purely operational.
- Align AI stewardship roles with Chief Data Officer (CDO) responsibilities and broader data strategy.

# Terms to Know

**AI Data Stewardship**[1] - Stewardship extended to AI contexts, covering not just datasets but also features, labels, and models, with responsibility for quality, ethics, and regulatory alignment.

**Centralized Stewardship Model**[2] - A governance pattern where a central team owns most stewardship decisions, standards, and approvals across the enterprise.

**Data Products**[3] - Curated, documented, reusable datasets that are managed as products with clear contracts, quality expectations, and owners.

**Data Steward**[4] - A person or team responsible for the quality, definitions, and appropriate use of a specific data domain, dataset, or asset, often acting as the "owner in practice."

**Data Stewardship**[5] - The day-to-day execution of data governance—applying standards, managing quality, metadata, and access to ensure data is trustworthy, compliant, and usable.

**Domain-Oriented Stewardship**[6] - A model where stewardship responsibilities are embedded in domain teams (for example, marketing, risk, operations) that own their data and AI assets.

**Feature Stewardship**[7] - Stewardship applied to engineered features, including logic, lineage, access policies, and fitness for specific AI use cases.

**Federated Stewardship Model**[8] - A hybrid approach combining central policy-setting and oversight with distributed domain stewards who manage local data, features, and models under shared standards.

**Label Stewardship**[9] - Stewardship focused on labeling guidelines, annotation processes, and audits to ensure reliable and fair labels for supervised learning.

# Introduction[10]

AI systems are highly sensitive to the quality and context of their inputs. If source data is incomplete, mislabeled, stale, or unrepresentative, models can fail in ways that are hard to detect until damage is already visible. Problems that might once have stayed local now spread across automated workflows, recommendations, and downstream decisions.

In many organizations, stewardship was once treated as a custodial role focused on standards, access, and glossary work. Those remain important, but AI demands stronger accountability. Stewards increasingly need to work with engineers, modelers, legal teams, domain experts, and risk leaders to ensure data is fit for both analytical and operational use. This broader and more complex role includes documenting lineage, validating feature definitions, clarifying ownership, checking quality at crucial points, and helping teams understand where data should not be used.

Stewardship becomes most valuable when it helps people move faster with trusted data rather than simply enforcing rules after problems appear.

## The AI Data Stewardship Stack[11]

One effective way to bring order to this complexity is to frame it as an AI Data Stewardship Stack—a layered view that clarifies what exactly needs stewardship at each level and who is responsible for it. This section lays out the scope, responsibilities, and risk controls associated with each element of the stack.

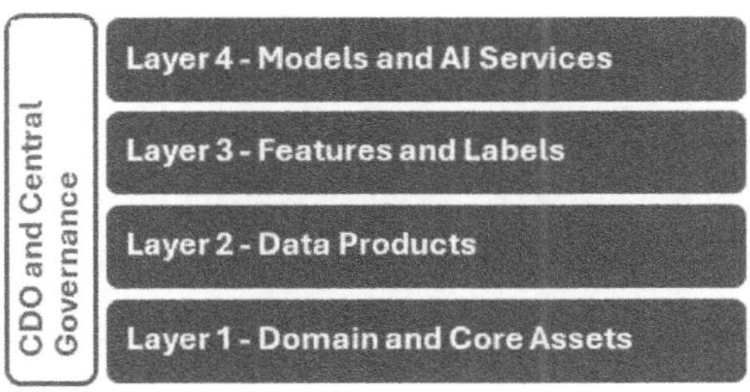


### Layer 1: Domains and Core Data Assets

**Scope:** Business domains (e.g., customer, claims, manufacturing, HR) and their foundational operational systems.

**Responsibilities:**

- Document business definitions and data standards comprehensively.

- Manage metadata, lineage, and classification (e.g., sensitivity levels, jurisdictional constraints).
- Ensure baseline data quality (correctness, completeness) and lawful collection practices.

**Risk Controls:** Data quality rules, privacy classification schemes, access control mechanisms, and retention policies enforced at both system and domain levels.

### Layer 2: Data Products

**Scope:** Curated, reusable datasets (e.g. "Customer 360," etc.) architected as data products.

**Steward Roles:** Data product owners/stewards who maintain contracts, service-level agreements (SLAs), and comprehensive documentation.

**Responsibilities:**

- Define schemas, semantics, and quality expectations explicitly.
- Publish documentation addressing purpose, lineage, and known limitations.
- Coordinate with central governance on standards alignment and compliance requirements.

**Risk Controls:** Product-level quality checks, de-identification where mandated, and documented allowed use cases (e.g., "analytics-only, no individual decisioning").

### Layer 3: Features and Labels

**Scope:** Engineered features and labels consumed by AI models (e.g., "90-day churn score," "on-time shipments ratio," "fraud label").

**Steward Roles:** Feature stewards (typically senior data scientists or MLOps engineers) and label stewards (typically domain experts overseeing annotation workflows).

**Responsibilities:**

- Document feature and label logic comprehensively, including temporal awareness and leakage prevention considerations.
- Maintain feature/label quality metrics and drift monitoring infrastructure.

- Ensure labels reflect fair, consistent criteria and undergo periodic auditing.

**Risk Controls:** Feature and label approval workflows, bias assessments, labeling guidelines, and human-in-the-loop (HITL) review for applicable population segments.

### Layer 4: Models and AI Services

**Scope:** Deployed models, model ensembles, and AI services (e.g., recommendation APIs, risk scoring engines, conversational agents).

**Steward Roles:** Model stewards (e.g., model owners, ML product managers) and AI risk stewards (e.g., risk/compliance representatives aligned to AI portfolios).

**Responsibilities:**

- Maintain model cards, comprehensive documentation, and performance metrics.
- Oversee monitoring protocols, retraining schedules, and incident management processes.
- Ensure models operate within approved use cases and respect data product contracts.

**Risk Controls:** Model risk classifications, approval gates, periodic review cycles, and model-level access control enforcement.

### Cross-Cutting: CDO and Central Governance

**Scope:** Enterprise-wide stewardship strategy, policies, and oversight architecture.

**Roles:** CDO, data governance council, and stewardship council establishing standards and RACI (Responsible, Accountable, Consulted, Informed) across the stack.

**Responsibilities:**

- Define trust and stewardship methods tailored to AI.
- Coordinate federated stewardship across organizational domains.
- Align AI data stewardship with regulatory imperatives and strategic priorities.

This AI Data Stewardship Stack clarifies that stewardship isn't confined to data tables; it extends through products, features/labels, and models, with tailored roles and risk controls at each layer.

## Comparison of Stewardship Models for AI[12]

| Aspect | Centralized Stewardship | Domain-Oriented Stewardship | Federated Stewardship (Hybrid) |
|---|---|---|---|
| **Who Owns Stewardship** | Central team (e.g., CDO office, enterprise data stewardship team) | Each domain team owns stewardship for its data and AI assets | Central governance sets standards; domain stewards apply them locally |
| **Strengths** | High consistency, strong compliance, clear single point of accountability | High agility, strong domain context, faster decisions for local AI projects | Balances consistency with autonomy; good fit for diverse, scaled AI portfolios |
| **Weaknesses** | Can become a bottleneck; may lack detailed domain context; risk of "ivory tower" governance | Risk of inconsistent definitions and uneven quality; harder to enforce compliance across domains | Requires strong coordination and clear RACI; failure in communication can re-create silos |
| **Best-Fit Contexts** | Highly regulated sectors needing tight control (e.g., financial reporting, small organizations) | Smaller or less regulated organizations; domains with unique data and fast-changing needs | Large, multi-domain enterprises, especially with both global and local regulatory requirements and many AI use cases |
| **AI Implications** | Establishes a strong baseline for AI risk, but may slow model development and local experimentation | Enables rapid AI innovation but can create fragmented AI risk controls and inconsistent feature/label practices | Supports scalable AI stewardship across the AI Data Stewardship Stack, with central guidance and domain-level ownership |

Recent studies recommend a federated approach for AI: a central CDO-led function that defines standards and trust methods, while domain stewards manage local data, features, and models within clearly-defined and communicated guardrails.

## Stewardship Across the AI Lifecycle[13]

Effective AI stewardship operates across the complete data and model lifecycle, not just during design.

- **Design and scoping:** Stewards assess whether adequate data exists to support a proposed AI use case, evaluating its quality, lineage, and consent.
- **Data preparation and feature engineering:** Feature and domain stewards verify engineered signals are valid, comprehensively documented, and policy-aligned.
- **Training and validation:** Stewards support dataset documentation, enforce labeling guidelines, and review fairness and bias assessments.
- **Deployment:** Model stewards ensure models deploy only into approved contexts, respecting data contracts and stewardship decisions.
- **Monitoring and evolution:** Stewards oversee performance tracking and data drift detection, coordinate remediation efforts, and update documentation and approvals when models or data products evolve.

## Roles: CDOs, Stewards, and AI Teams

Recent guidance on the Chief Data Officer role emphasizes that CDOs are central to establishing AI stewardship. They:

- Set stewardship strategy and oversee the organizational readiness of data for AI initiatives.
- Define enterprise standards for data, features, labels, and models.
- Convene stewardship councils, bringing together central and domain stewards for coordinated oversight.

Data stewards, in turn, function as the "enforcement arm" of governance, translating policy abstractions into concrete decisions about metadata management, access permissions, and usage appropriateness. For AI, this requires partnering with data scientists, MLOps teams, risk functions, and legal counsel to ensure data and models satisfy both technical and ethical standards.

# Case Studies

## Case Study #1: Centralized Stewardship in a Regulated Environment[14]

A stewardship guide profiles financial and public-sector organizations where a central governance team manages most stewardship decisions, particularly for highly regulated data domains. This model simplifies compliance auditing and ensures uniform standards but can constrain agility. Some organizations mitigate this by appointing domain data custodians who provide contextual expertise, while the central team retains final authority on policy interpretation and exception approval.

## Case Study #2: Domain Stewards for AI Data Products[15]

Data product and stewardship frameworks highlight organizations appointing stewards within functional domains (e.g., marketing or risk management) to own critical data products and associated AI features. These stewards manage quality, semantics, and access governance, while partnering with central governance on cross-domain standards and initiatives. This structure yields more relevant, timely data for domain-specific AI models while maintaining consistency through federated coordination.

## Case Study #3: Federated Stewardship for Multi-Domain AI[16]

Federated governance models illustrate large enterprises combining a central council with domain-level stewards to balance control and autonomy. The central body establishes AI stewardship standards and risk thresholds, while domain stewards manage local data, features, and models within those boundaries. This architecture enables AI initiatives to scale across geographies and business units without losing visibility into enterprise-wide risk and compliance obligations.

# Success Metrics[17]

## Table of Illustrative Metrics

| Dimension | Example Metric | Why It Matters |
|---|---|---|
| **Stewardship Coverage** | % of critical domains, data products, feature sets, and models with assigned stewards and documented responsibilities | Shows whether AI-relevant assets have clear owners accountable for their quality and appropriate use |
| **Policy Adherence** | No. or % of AI projects that pass stewardship/governance review before deployment | Indicates how effectively stewardship is embedded in the AI lifecycle rather than treated as optional |
| **Issue Response** | Time from detection of a data or model incident to steward acknowledgment and remediation plan | Measures operational effectiveness of stewardship in practice, not just on paper |
| **Federated Alignment** | Frequency of stewardship council meetings and % of domains represented, plus No. of cross-domain policies adopted | Reflects maturity of federated stewardship coordination and cross-domain collaboration |

# Practical Advice for Leaders[18]

Leaders can strengthen AI data stewardship with these recommendations:

- **Define the AI Data Stewardship Stack explicitly.** Assign roles at each layer (domain, data product, feature/label, model), ensuring no gaps in accountability.
- **Select an appropriate stewardship model.** Choose centralized, domain-oriented, or federated based on regulatory profile, organizational scale, and diversity of AI use cases. Document the rationale for the choice.
- **Equip stewards with tools and authority.** Give them access to metadata catalogs, lineage visualization, monitoring dashboards, and clear escalation paths for resolving cross-domain conflicts that arise.

- **Embed stewardship into AI governance.** Ensure stewards actively participate in risk assessments, model approval committees, and post-incident reviews rather than being consulted as an afterthought.

# Conclusion

AI amplifies the importance of data stewardship, extending accountability from raw data to data products, features, labels, and models. The AI Data Stewardship Stack, together with the comparison of centralized, domain-oriented, and federated models, provides a practical framework for assigning ownership and risk controls where they matter most. Organizations that invest in clear stewardship roles—especially federated models anchored by a strong CDO function—are better positioned to scale AI while preserving quality, compliance, and trust. When stewardship spans the full AI lifecycle and covers every artifact, AI becomes not just a technical capability, but a governed, trustworthy organizational asset.

# Notes

[1] AI data stewardship is defined in Deloitte's "Chief Data Officer: AI Governance."

[2] The centralized stewardship model is defined in LinkedIn's "Federated vs. Centralized Data Governance."

[3] Data products are defined in Liminal's "Enterprise AI Governance Guide."

[4] The role of the data steward is defined in Alation's "Role of Data Stewards."

[5] Data stewardship is defined in *Dataversity*'s "How to Become a Data Steward."

[6] Domain-oriented stewardship is defined in *Atlan*'s "Data Stewardship 101."

[7] Feature stewardship is defined in *getdbt*'s "AI Data Pipelines."

[8] The federated stewardship model is defined in Lifebit's "Federated Governance Complete Guide."

[9] Label stewardship is defined in Humans in the Loop's "How Humans in the Loop Powers Responsible AI Through Data Annotation."

[10] The case that stewardship must evolve for AI is made in *EWSolutions*' "Data Quality Framework" and *EWSolutions*' "Data Stewardship and Artificial Intelligence."

[11] The AI Data Stewardship Stack is assembled from *Ovaledge*'s "Data Stewardship Guide," *Dataversity*'s "How to Become a Data Steward," Alation's "Role of Data Stewards," *EWSolutions*' "Data Quality Framework," Gable's "Federated vs. Centralized Data Governance," *getdbt*'s "Data Governance Ownership," *Atlan*'s "Data Stewardship 101," *InTime Tec*'s "Data Quality in AI," Quinnox's "Data Governance for AI," Orq's "Managing the AI Lifecycle," Deloitte's "Chief Data Officer: AI Governance," Witness.ai's "Model Monitoring," and Lifebit's "Federated Governance Complete Guide."

[12] Stewardship models for AI are surveyed in Liqueo's "Centralised vs. Federated vs. Hybrid," Gable's "Federated vs. Centralized Data Governance," *Atlan*'s "Data Stewardship 101," LinkedIn's "Federated vs. Centralized Data Governance," Lifebit's "Federated Governance Complete Guide," Deloitte's "Chief Data Officer: AI Governance," Quinnox's "Data Governance for AI," and Domo's "Centralized or Decentralized Data."

[13] Stewardship across the AI lifecycle is treated in Orq's "Managing the AI Lifecycle," Quinnox's "Data Governance for AI," *InTime Tec*'s "Data Quality in AI," Humans in the Loop's "How Humans in the Loop Powers Responsible AI," Witness.ai's "Model Monitoring," *EWSolutions*' "Data Quality Framework," Deloitte's "Chief Data Officer: AI Governance," *Atlan*'s "Know Data Governance," and *Ovaledge*'s "Data Stewardship Guide."

[14] The centralized stewardship case study is drawn from LinkedIn's "Federated vs. Centralized Data Governance."

[15] The domain-oriented stewardship case is examined in Domo's "Centralized or Decentralized Data."

[16] The federated stewardship case is drawn from Liqueo's "Centralised vs. Federated vs. Hybrid."

[17] The success-metrics cluster is derived from *Atlan*'s "Data Stewardship 101," Quinnox's "Data Governance for AI," and Lifebit's "Federated Governance Complete Guide."

[18] Practical advice draws on *Atlan*'s "Data Stewardship 101," Gable's "Federated vs. Centralized Data Governance," *Dataversity*'s "How to Become a Data Steward," and Alation's "Understand Data Governance Models."

## Key topics explored in this chapter:

- AI Demands a New View of Data Quality
- Traditional vs AI-Focused Data Quality Programs
- Lifecycle-Aware Data Quality Practices
- Governance, Roles, and Shared Responsibility

# WAY 38

# Elevate Data Quality for AI Workloads


## Abstract

Data quality matters in every analytics program, but AI workloads raise the stakes because models learn from patterns, gaps, and distortions in the data they consume. A dashboard built on weak data may mislead a few decisions. An AI model trained on weak data can scale those errors across thousands or millions of outcomes. This chapter explains how organizations need to rethink data quality when data is being used not just to describe the past, but to shape predictions, classifications, recommendations, and automated actions. It introduces an AI Data Quality Stack that links AI-specific quality dimensions to each stage of the lifecycle. And it contrasts traditional data quality programs with AI-focused ones, which emphasize continuous monitoring, feature and label quality, and fit-for-purpose metrics rather than one-time cleansing efforts.


## Objective

After completing this chapter, you will be able to:

- Explain why traditional data quality methods fall short for AI and ML workloads.
- Use the AI Data Quality Stack to connect key dimensions such as relevance, drift, labeling, and feature quality to specific stages of the AI lifecycle.
- Distinguish traditional data quality programs from AI-focused ones based on monitoring cadence, scope (record-level vs. feature/label-level), and the metrics they track.

- Implement continuous data and model monitoring, including drift detection, as a core pillar of AI reliability.
- Embed governance, documentation, and feedback loops so that data quality becomes a shared responsibility across data, ML, and business teams.

# Terms to Know

**AI Data Quality**[1] **-** The degree to which data is accurate, complete, consistent, timely, relevant, and suitable for training, validating, and operating AI systems.

**Data Drift**[2] **-** Changes in data patterns over time that can reduce model reliability if not detected and addressed.

**Data Relevance**[3] **-** The degree to which data is directly related to the problem an AI model is trying to solve, avoiding unnecessary or misleading inputs.

**Feature Quality**[4] **-** The predictive usefulness, stability, and correctness of engineered features used by AI models, including absence of leakage and consistent definitions.

**Labeling Quality**[5] **-** Accuracy, consistency, and representativeness of labels used in supervised learning, often impacted by annotation processes and subjectivity.

**Model Monitoring**[6] **-** Continuous tracking of model performance, data drift, and other indicators in production to detect issues early and trigger retraining or rollback.

**Traditional Data Quality**[7] **-** Rule-based and largely batch processes focused on record-level correctness, completeness, and consistency in operational and reporting systems.

# Introduction

In the era of AI, quality management needs a broader lens. Traditional checks such as missing values, invalid formats, and duplicate records still matter, but they are no longer enough. Teams also need to ask whether the data is representative, whether labels are reliable, whether definitions are stable, and whether the data still reflects the environment in which the model is operating. In short, quality for AI is not just about clean data. It is about trustworthy input conditions for systems that can amplify both strengths and flaws.

## AI Demands a New View of Data Quality[8]

Poor data quality is one of the main reasons AI projects fail, and the problems rarely surface until models are running in production. AI systems amplify data quality issues. They don't hide them. Organizations must treat data quality as a continuous, end-to-end discipline built for AI, not a one-off cleansing task before model training.

To operationalize AI data quality, picture it as a layered stack that aligns quality dimensions (as rows) with lifecycle stages (as columns).[9]

## The AI Data Quality Stack

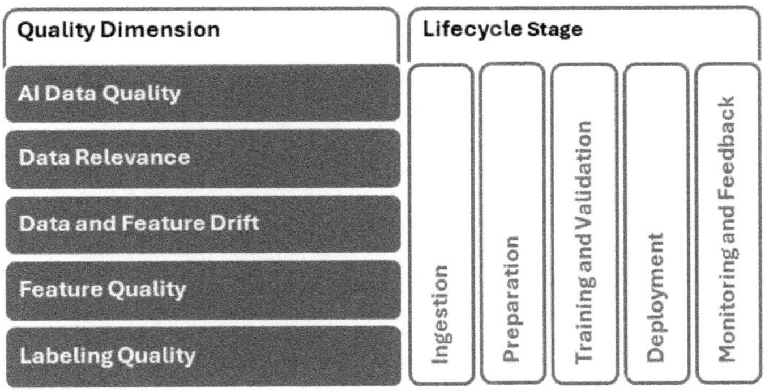


### Quality Dimension: AI Data Quality

- **Ingestion:** Apply automated validation rules, schema checks, and anomaly detection to ensure incoming data is structurally sound and falls within expected ranges.
- **Preparation:** Standardize formats, address missing values, eliminate duplicates, and comprehensively document transformations.
- **Training and Validation:** Profile datasets and features; quantify missingness, outliers, and class balance; exclude unreliable records from training corpora.
- **Deployment:** Verify serving data conforms to assumptions embedded in training pipelines (for example, identical encodings and units).
- **Monitoring and Feedback:** Track quality metrics over time; deploy AI-driven anomaly detection to intercept issues before they contaminate models.

### Quality Dimension: Data Relevance

- **Ingestion:** Prioritize sources directly reflecting the target problem; resist the temptation to hoard tangentially related data.
- **Preparation:** Use profiling and feature engineering to isolate genuine signals; discard features contributing noise or spurious correlations.
- **Training and Validation:** Evaluate feature importance and conduct ablation studies, confirming inputs materially contribute to performance and are conceptually justified.
- **Deployment:** Ensure only validated, relevant features are served to models; prevent unvetted inputs from infiltrating production inference.
- **Monitoring and Feedback:** Periodically reassess relevance as business context evolves; retire features that have lost meaningful connection to outcomes.

### Quality Dimension: Data and Feature Drift

- **Ingestion:** Track changes in source systems and schemas; systematically log version updates and upstream events.
- **Preparation:** Monitor distribution shifts in important columns and features, comparing historical baselines to current data.
- **Training and Validation:** Simulate future drift scenarios or employ time-based splits to evaluate model robustness under evolving conditions.
- **Deployment:** Continuously compare live feature distributions against training baselines; detect covariate drift and concept drift in real-time.
- **Monitoring and Feedback:** Use specialized tools and dashboards (for example, Evidently AI, NannyML) to detect drift and trigger retraining, rollback, or investigation protocols.

### Quality Dimension: Feature Quality

- **Ingestion:** Collect sufficient raw granularity to support strong feature engineering (for example, granular events with precise timestamps).
- **Preparation:** Engineer features with explicitly documented logic, scrupulously avoiding leakage by using only information available at actual prediction time.

- **Training and Validation:** Evaluate feature stability, predictive power, and correlation structure; monitor for redundant or unstable features that degrade model interpretability.
- **Deployment:** Ensure online and offline feature calculations remain consistent; validate feature freshness and latency against service-level agreements.
- **Monitoring and Feedback:** Track feature-level metrics (missingness rates, distribution shifts, latency spikes) and adjust pipelines as requirements change.

### Quality Dimension: Labeling Quality

- **Ingestion:** Define clear, comprehensive labeling guidelines; employ expert annotators or high-quality label sources wherever feasible.
- **Preparation:** Validate label distributions, check for systematic annotation errors or class imbalance, and correct mislabeled samples where practical.
- **Training and Validation:** Assess model sensitivity to label noise; experiment with comprehensive loss functions or noise-handling techniques to mitigate annotation imperfections.
- **Deployment:** Where online labels or user feedback are generated (for example, user ratings), validate and moderate them before treating them as ground truth.
- **Monitoring and Feedback:** Periodically audit labels; deploy human-in-the-loop (HITL) review to correct relevant cases and refine labeling policies based on observed patterns.

The AI Data Quality Stack gives teams a structured framework to ask, at each lifecycle stage, "Which dimension of quality are we managing, and with which controls?" It replaces the habit of treating data quality as a single, monolithic concept.

## Traditional vs AI-Focused Data Quality Programs[10]

Organizations that modernize typically run traditional data quality and AI-focused programs in parallel. The following table outlines the key distinctions.

## Comparison of Data Quality Programs

| Dimension | Traditional Data Quality Program | AI-Focused Data Quality Program |
|---|---|---|
| **Monitoring Cadence** | Batch checks (daily/weekly), periodic scorecards | Continuous or near-real-time monitoring of data and model metrics |
| **Focus Level** | Record-level validity, completeness, and consistency | Feature- and label-level quality, drift, relevance, and bias |
| **Rule Design** | Static, hand-crafted rules per column or system | Hybrid rules + ML-based anomaly detection and drift detection |
| **Metrics** | Generic metrics (for example, % nulls, duplicates, errors) | Fit-for-purpose metrics (for example, feature stability, label noise rates, data drift scores, model KPIs) |
| **Scope of Responsibility** | Primarily data engineering or governance teams | Shared across data engineering, ML, and domain teams; integrated with AI lifecycle management |

The comparison shows why AI demands its own dedicated approach rather than an extension of traditional data quality tooling.

## Lifecycle-Aware Data Quality Practices[11]

Best-practice guides align quality controls with the AI lifecycle at every stage.

- **Ingestion:** Implement automated validation and profiling to intercept anomalies and schema changes early in the pipeline.
- **Preparation:** Utilize reproducible transformations, version control, and automated tests for data and feature pipelines.
- **Training and Validation:** Combine cross-validation with dataset quality checks, drift simulations, and fairness/bias assessments to ensure model readiness.
- **Deployment:** Enforce contractual assumptions (for example, feature value ranges, data availability guarantees) within serving systems.

- **Monitoring and Feedback:** Continuously monitor model performance, data drift, and data quality metrics; feed detected incidents back into upstream pipelines and governance processes.

### Governance, Roles, and Shared Responsibility[12]

Data governance for AI affirms that data quality isn't merely a technical concern—it represents an organizational responsibility intrinsically tied to risk and compliance. Recommended practices include:

- Defining explicit owners for datasets, features, and labels, with clear accountability mechanisms for quality outcomes.
- Utilizing metadata catalogs and lineage tracking to make quality rules and issues visible to both data and ML teams, fostering transparency.
- Establishing cross-functional review forums where domain experts, data engineers, and data scientists jointly determine what "fit-for-purpose" data looks like for specific AI use cases, aligning technical and business perspectives.

## Case Studies

### Case Study #1: Continuous Data Quality Monitoring for AI Pipelines[13]

A data quality framework guide profiles organizations that moved from batch checks to continuous monitoring, detecting drift, schema changes, and upstream anomalies in real time. Teams integrated anomaly detection with alerting systems and lineage tracking, intercepting and resolving issues before they reached downstream AI models. Production incidents dropped significantly, and so did the business disruption that followed.

### Case Study #2: Managing Model Drift in the AI Lifecycle[14]

Deployment marks the beginning of ongoing maintenance, not the end of AI work. Organizations that monitored data and model drift, regularly refreshed training data, and maintained versioning and rollback strategies sustained model performance and trustworthiness even as their operational environments shifted in unpredictable ways.

## Case Study #3: AI-Powered Data Quality vs Traditional Methods[15]

Comparisons of traditional and AI-powered data quality approaches show that manual, rule-only methods buckle under modern data volume and variety. AI-driven quality frameworks automate profiling, anomaly detection, and rule generation on the fly. That shift enables predictive data quality—catching issues before they reach decisions—which matters most for AI workloads that depend on fresh, reliable signals for continuous learning.

# Success Metrics[16]

## Table of Illustrative Metrics

| Dimension | Example Metric | Why It Matters |
|---|---|---|
| **Drift Detection Coverage** | % of production models and key features with active drift monitors and alerts | Indicates how effectively the organization can detect changing data patterns before performance collapses |
| **Label Quality Oversight** | Share of labeled datasets that have documented labeling guidelines, inter-annotator agreement scores, or audit samples | Shows whether label noise and bias are being actively managed and controlled |
| **Feature Quality Metrics** | No. of critical features with tracked stability and leakage checks (for example, stability index, time-based leakage tests) | Reflects organizational attention to the "shape" and reliability of features driving AI models |
| **Issue Resolution Speed** | Time from detection of a critical data quality issue to mitigation (fix, rollback, or retrain) | Measures whether data quality management is keeping pace with AI's operational impact and risk velocity |

## Practical Advice for Leaders[17]

Leaders who want to elevate data quality short start here:

- **Adopt an AI-specific quality process.** Utilize the AI Data Quality Stack as a comprehensive checklist across ingestion, preparation, training, deployment, and monitoring phases.
- **Shift from static to continuous monitoring.** Deploy drift detection, anomaly detection, and real-time quality dashboards for mission-critical AI pipelines.
- **Embed quality into roles and incentives.** Ensure that feature owners, label owners, and model owners share collective responsibility for AI outcomes, with accountability mechanisms built into performance evaluation.
- **Treat data relevance and labeling quality as first-class concerns.** Ensure they are top-of-mind, not afterthoughts or secondary considerations, especially when it comes to high-impact AI applications affecting customer experience or regulatory compliance.

## Conclusion

Traditional data quality practices are necessary but not sufficient for AI. They must expand to address relevance, drift, feature integrity, and labeling across every stage of the AI lifecycle. The AI Data Quality Stack, and the sharp contrast between traditional and AI-focused programs, shows organizations how to move from static, record-centric checks to continuous, feature- and label-aware quality management. Organizations that make this investment will build AI systems that are more robust, explainable, and trustworthy, because their foundations, the data and features themselves, receive the same rigor and attention as the models built on top of them.

## Notes

[1] AI data quality draws its working sense from *InTime Tec*'s "Data Quality in AI: Challenges, Importance & Best Practices."

[2] Data drift, as used here, follows Witness.ai's "Model Monitoring."

[3] On data relevance, this book follows *ScienceDirect*'s "Data quality challenges in AI-driven decision making."

[4] The working sense of feature quality comes from *getdbt*'s "AI Data Pipelines."

[5] Labeling quality, as used in this chapter, is defined in *Dataversity*'s "12 Key AI *Patterns* for Improving Data Quality."

[6] Model monitoring is defined and contextualized in *Clarifai*'s "ML Lifecycle Management."

[7] Traditional data quality, as distinguished from AI-era approaches, is characterized in Digna's "AI-Powered Data Quality vs Traditional Methods."

[8] Why AI demands a new view of data quality is addressed in *EWSolutions*' "Data Quality Framework" and *DataShift*'s "4 Top Trends Transforming Data Quality in 2025."

[9] The AI Data Quality Stack is drawn from Orq's "Managing the AI Lifecycle," getElyxai's "Data Quality Best Practices," *InTime Tec*'s "Data Quality in AI," *Witness*.ai's "Model Monitoring," *ScienceDirect*'s "Data quality challenges," *Dataversity*'s "12 Key AI *Patterns*," getdbt's "AI Data Pipelines," and Humans in the Loop's "How Humans in the Loop Powers Responsible AI."

[10] Traditional vs AI-focused data quality programs are compared in *Acceldata*'s "How AI is Transforming Data Quality Management," *EWSolutions*' "Data Quality Framework," getdbt's "AI Data Pipelines," getElyxai's "Data Quality Best Practices," Orq's "Managing the AI Lifecycle," and BARC's "Redefining Data Quality for AI."

[11] Lifecycle-aware data quality practices are surveyed in *Clarifai*'s "ML Lifecycle Management," *DataShift*'s "4 Top Trends," *Dataversity*'s "12 Key AI *Patterns*," Orq's "Managing the AI Lifecycle," getdbt's "AI Data Pipelines," and Quinnox's "Data Governance for AI."

[12] Governance, roles, and shared responsibility in data quality are addressed in *Qualytics*' "Data Quality Trends," Quinnox's "Data Governance for AI," and getdbt's "Data Governance Ownership."

[13] The continuous monitoring case study draws on getElyxai's "Data Quality Best Practices."

[14] *Witness*.ai's "Model Monitoring" underpins the ongoing maintenance case study in this section.

[15] The AI-powered data quality case study is drawn from *Acceldata*'s "How AI is Transforming Data Quality Management."

[16] The success-metrics cluster draws on *Clarifai*'s "ML Lifecycle Management," Humans in the Loop's "How Humans in the Loop Powers Responsible AI," getdbt's "AI Data Pipelines," and *EWSolutions*' "Data Quality Framework."

[17] Practical advice in this section draws on *EWSolutions*' "Data Quality Framework," *DataShift*'s "4 Top Trends," *Qualytics*' "Data Quality Trends," and *InTime Tec*'s "Data Quality in AI."

70-85% of AI and ML project failures stem from data-related issues, primarily poor data quality, rather than flawed algorithms.

*AIMultiple*

"AI Data Quality in 2026: Challenges & Best Practices"

Dilmegani

March 2026

# Key topics explored in this chapter:

- How Silos Undermine AI and Human-AI Collaboration
- AI-Centric Integration Architectures for Breaking Silos
- Warehouse vs Lake vs Fabric vs Mesh for AI and Explainability
- Enterprise AI Data Fabric + Mesh Framework
- Semantic Layers and Shared Definitions
- Governance for Unified AI Data Access
- Change Management: Moving People, Not Just Data

# WAY 39

# Break Down Data Silos


## Abstract

To unlock AI and dismantle data silos, organizations need to move from isolated systems to an integrated data fabric plus data mesh architecture. In this model, domains own high-quality data products, while a shared fabric, semantic layer, and feature layer make cross-domain AI both safer and more explainable. This chapter introduces an Enterprise AI Data Fabric + Mesh framework and compares core data architectures—warehouse, lake, fabric, and mesh—specifically through the lens of AI workloads and explainability.


## Objective

After completing this chapter, you will be able to:

- Explain how data silos distort AI models, undermine explainability, and weaken human-AI collaboration.
- Differentiate AI-centric integration architectures—data warehouse, data lake, data fabric, and data mesh—and understand how each impacts AI scalability and explainability.
- Utilize the Enterprise AI Data Fabric + Mesh framework to clarify roles for domains, data products, semantic layers, and feature layers, including governance responsibilities at each level.
- Design feature sharing and unified data access approaches that combine cross-domain data while enforcing policy and consent.
- Embed cross-domain governance and change management practices, ensuring that breaking silos strengthens—rather than weakens—AI governance and trust.

# Terms to Know

**AI Data Integration**[1] - Architectures and pipelines that connect distributed, heterogeneous data sources, transforming them into AI-ready datasets and features while preserving governance and performance.

**Cross-Domain Governance**[2] - Federated or unified governance structures coordinate policies, access, and quality standards across multiple domains (e.g., sales, operations, risk) to support shared AI use.

**Data Fabric**[3] - A metadata-driven integration layer virtually connects data across systems, providing unified, policy-aware access and an enterprise data fabric for analytics and AI without centralizing all storage.

**Data Lake**[4] - A centralized, low-cost repository storing large volumes of raw, often unstructured data, typically for exploratory analytics and machine learning.

**Data Mesh**[5] - An organizational and architectural approach where domain teams own and publish data products under federated standards, supporting decentralized feature sharing and unified data access for AI.

**Data Warehouse**[6] - A centralized, structured repository optimized for reporting and BI, featuring curated schemas and strong performance guarantees.

**Enterprise Data Fabric**[7] - The enterprise-wide manifestation of data fabric, spanning hybrid and multi-cloud environments to unify access, security, and observability for AI and analytics workloads.

**Feature Sharing**[8] - The practice of making engineered features available across teams and models through governed repositories, enabling reuse and consistent semantics.

**Semantic Layer**[9] - A business-friendly abstraction over technical data structures, providing consistent definitions and metrics (e.g., "customer," "order," "active account") to BI tools and AI pipelines.

**Unified Data Access**[10] - The ability for humans and AI to query distributed data as if it were a single, coherent resource, with common semantics and governance.

# Introduction

Data silos—isolated departmental systems, local databases with no enterprise visibility, and unintegrated SaaS tools—have always slowed down analytics. For AI, the damage is much greater. When models train inside a single silo, they only see part of the story, learning narrow patterns that break as soon as they are used across the wider business. A churn model that never sees service tickets, or a risk model blind to supply-chain signals, are classic symptoms of silo-bound AI.

Silos also make explainability harder. When data from different domains cannot be traced or connected, it becomes nearly impossible to show how each source shapes a model's decisions, which erodes trust and weakens cross-domain governance. Breaking silos in an AI context does not mean forcing everything into one giant database. It means building safe, governed, interoperable AI data integration so humans and AI can use cross-domain data as a single, coherent, and understandable whole.

## How Silos Undermine AI and Human-AI Collaboration[11]

### Fragmented Views of Entities

Across many enterprises, representations of customers, patients, products, or assets are scattered across CRM, billing, support, marketing, and operational systems, each holding a partial—and often conflicting—view. Models trained inside any one of these silos misread signals because they lack cross-channel context; patterns that only emerge in the full customer or asset journey stay hidden. Human experts, who naturally stitch together this broader picture, then see AI outputs that conflict with their lived experience. Over time, trust erodes and human-AI collaboration weakens as domain expertise and algorithmic judgments drift further apart.

### Inconsistent Semantics and Metrics

What counts as an "active customer"? When is a shipment "on time"? How do you define "high risk"? In many organizations, different teams answer these questions in conflicting ways. Features engineered in one domain then become hard or impossible to reuse elsewhere because definitions are undocumented, or they clash with parallel work in other systems. When the underlying semantics are misaligned, cross-domain model comparisons stop being meaningful—they look precise on the surface but are measuring different things underneath.

### Governance and Compliance Gaps

Silos often develop their own access rules and risk practices, which leads to uneven enforcement of privacy, consent, and usage policies. Some domains overshare sensitive data and expose the organization to regulatory and reputational risk, while others lock data down so tightly that AI teams cannot access the signals they need. The result is a patchwork of underpowered AI in some areas and under-governed experimentation in others. Without cross-domain governance, enterprises cannot credibly show that AI respects the same policies across all contributing data sources.

## AI-Centric Integration Architectures for Breaking Silos[12]

Contemporary architectures offer several complementary patterns to reduce data silos and support AI at scale.

### Enterprise Data Fabric and Logical Integration

A data fabric connects distributed data sources via metadata-driven integration, comprehensive cataloging, standardized access interfaces, and policy-aware data virtualization. Rather than physically consolidating everything into a single storage layer, the enterprise data fabric constructs unified views and access paths. This allows AI models and feature pipelines to query consistent representations of entities regardless of where data physically resides. This approach reduces duplication, accelerates AI data integration, and enables central enforcement of governance and security policies across heterogeneous systems.

### Data Mesh with AI-Aware Domains

Data mesh emphasizes decentralized ownership, positioning domain teams as accountable stewards who treat data as a product with clear quality and usability commitments. For AI, this translates into:

- Domains (e.g., Sales, Operations, Risk) publishing curated data products and feature products that are discoverable, comprehensively documented, and governed according to shared standards.
- ML platforms and AI teams consuming these standardized products rather than creating custom extractions from siloed systems, reducing fragmentation and improving consistency.
- Combining data mesh (clarifying who owns what and why) with data fabric (automating integration and governance), delivering

domain autonomy while maintaining enterprise-level interoperability.

### Unified Feature Layer

A unified feature layer represents an important anti-silo mechanism for AI. Features are typically:

- Engineered once from multiple domains, combining behavioral, transactional, and service data into cohesive representations.
- Registered with explicit logic, lineage, and ownership metadata, rendering their construction transparent and auditable.
- Shared across teams and models with consistent semantics and fine-grained access controls.

Policies can be enforced at the feature level—e.g., "allowed for marketing models, disallowed for pricing"—enabling feature sharing that respects risk boundaries and consent constraints while maximizing reuse.

## Warehouse vs Lake vs Fabric vs Mesh for AI and Explainability[13]

As AI workloads grow, most organizations end up running on several architectures at once rather than a single "standard" platform. Each option—warehouse, lake, fabric, and mesh—supports AI and explainability in different ways, with its own strengths and blind spots. The table on the next page provides you with an overview.

In practice, large enterprises rarely choose just one. They assemble a portfolio: warehouses for well-structured, governed reporting and simpler models; lakes for large-scale, multi-modal training data; fabrics for unified access, metadata, and security; and meshes for domain-owned data products and scalable feature sharing. Over time, most organizations will operate with elements of all four, combining them to meet different AI and explainability requirements across use cases and business units.

## Comparison of Data Architectures for AI and Explainability

| Dimension | Data Warehouse | Data Lake | Data Fabric | Data Mesh |
|---|---|---|---|---|
| **Primary Role** | Curated, structured reporting and BI | Low-cost storage and exploration of raw, diverse data | Unified access layer across distributed sources | Domain-based ownership and data products |
| **Fit for AI Training** | Good for features derived from well-defined metrics; limited visibility into raw context | Strong for large-scale ML on raw logs, events, and semi-structured data | Supports AI by virtualizing data across systems without heavy copying | Provides high-quality, domain-specific datasets and features for AI |
| **Cross-Domain Context** | Often limited; cross-domain joins need heavy modeling | Possible but manual; depends on data science and ETL skills | Strong; semantic and metadata layers can represent entities across systems | Strong; domains publish interoperable products under shared standards |
| **Explainability Support** | Clear lineage and definitions for curated metrics; good for BI explainability | Raw provenance exists but can be messy; explainability requires extra curation | Centralized policy, lineage, and observability help trace AI inputs across sources | Data-as-product contracts document meaning and quality; explainability depends on consistent product standards |
| **Governance Model** | Centralized governance via warehouse team | Often centralized but lighter governance; risk of "data swamp" | Centralized policy with distributed enforcement; strong for regulated AI workloads | Federated computational governance; domains apply shared policies locally |
| **Typical AI Pattern** | Analytics and ML on curated aggregates | Exploratory ML and feature generation from logs, clickstreams, IoT, etc. | Cross-domain AI that needs near-real-time data and uniform policies | Many domain models plus cross-domain AI via shared data products and feature stores |

## Enterprise AI Data Fabric + Mesh Framework[14]

To operationalize hybrid architectures, the Enterprise AI Data Fabric + Mesh Framework shows how domains, data products, semantic layers, and feature layers work together under shared governance.

It clarifies the distinction between the two approaches: the mesh defines who owns and curates data and features, while the fabric determines how data is integrated, secured, and made usable across the enterprise.

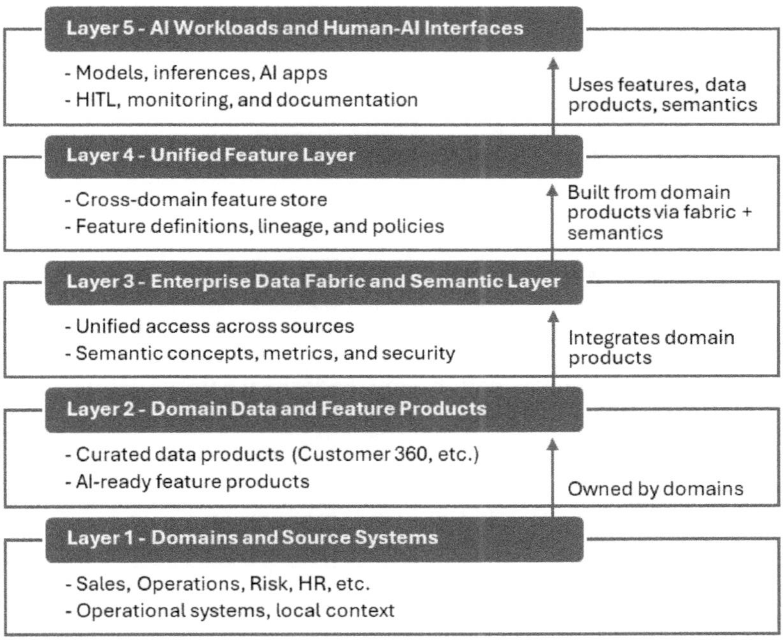


### Layer 1: Domains and Source Systems

**What It Is:** Business-aligned domains (for example, Sales, Operations, Risk, HR) own the source systems and have deep knowledge of their local context.

**Responsibilities:** They maintain high-quality operational data, identify AI-relevant signals, and participate in data classification and access policy decisions.

**Governance:** Domain data owners and stewards are accountable for data quality and regulatory compliance within their area.

### Layer 2: Domain Data and Feature Products

**What It Is:** Domains publish curated data products (e.g., "Customer 360," "Shipment events") and AI-ready feature products (e.g., "churn propensity features," "supplier reliability scores").

**Responsibilities:** Define schemas, semantics, service-level agreements (SLAs), and comprehensive documentation; ensure products are discoverable and reusable via catalogs.

**Governance:** Federated computational governance—shared policies (privacy, retention, masking) codified once and applied to each product via policy-as-code.

### Layer 3: Enterprise Data Fabric and Semantic Layer

**What It Is:** A fabric layer unifying access across data products and legacy sources, plus a semantic layer exposing consistent business concepts (e.g., customer, order, risk exposure).

**Responsibilities:** Virtualize and federate queries; manage metadata, lineage, and security; and provide standardized entity models and metrics to BI and AI pipelines.

**Governance:** Central platform and governance teams define global policies, semantic standards, and approval workflows for cross-domain AI uses.

### Layer 4: Unified Feature Layer

**What It Is:** A cross-domain feature store consuming domain data products via the fabric and semantic layer to create shareable features for models.

**Responsibilities:** Register features with logic, lineage, and owners; manage online/offline consistency; and implement access policies at the feature level (e.g., marketing vs. pricing).

**Governance:** Feature owners account for correctness and compliance; governance teams ensure features are tagged with purpose, sensitivity, and allowed use cases.

### Layer 5: AI Workloads and Human-AI Interfaces

**What It Is:** Model training, inference services, and AI-augmented applications consuming features, data products, and semantic views.

**Responsibilities:** Implement model documentation, explainability, and monitoring; ensure human-in-the-loop oversight where impact is high.

**Governance:** Model risk, AI ethics, and oversight committees approve high-impact use cases and monitor performance and drift.

## Semantic Layers and Shared Definitions[15]

Technology alone can't align meaning; semantics have to be explicitly shared and governed.

### Enterprise Semantic Layer

A semantic layer constructs business-friendly definitions of core concepts—customer, order, claim, policy, asset—and their attributes, along with standardized calculations and filters. It sits above physical storage, presenting a consistent abstraction to BI tools and AI pipelines. This ensures features and metrics derive from shared definitions rather than raw tables with ambiguous column names.

For AI, this means:

- Feature engineering starts from the semantic layer, dramatically improving interoperability across models and domains.
- Explanations, model cards, and documentation can reference these shared concepts, rendering AI behavior more interpretable to business users lacking technical data expertise.

### Ontologies and Knowledge Graphs

In complex domains, ontologies and knowledge graphs capture rich relationships across entities—e.g., patient-medication-diagnosis-provider chains, product-supplier-shipment-incident networks. Graph-based architectures stitch together siloed systems into navigable representations. Here, both AI and humans can traverse multi-hop relationships, revealing insights invisible in isolated tables.

For AI, this supports:

- Contextual recommendations and reasoning over cross-domain data, leveraging relationship patterns that simple feature vectors miss.

- More transparent human-AI collaboration, enabling humans to follow reasoning paths across domains within a unified conceptual graph rather than stitching together disjointed reports.

## Governance for Unified AI Data Access[16]

Breaking silos without evolving governance amplifies risk rather than mitigating it. The objective is controlled unification—integration bounded by policy and oversight.

### Policy-as-Code for AI Data

Policy-driven fabrics and governance platforms demonstrate how access and usage rules can be encoded as machine-readable policies and automatically enforced at scale. Policies specify:

- Who (or which workloads) can access specific data or features.
- Which purposes are permitted (e.g., analytics-only vs. individualized decisioning).
- How consent, retention, data locality, and masking rules apply across domains.

Policies are enforced at ingestion (filtering or flagging non-compliant data), transformation (applying masking, tokenization, or aggregation), and consumption (restricting which models and applications can access specific unified data access paths).

### Harmonized Access Controls and Cross-Domain Governance

Instead of allowing each silo to manage identity and access in isolation:

- Enterprises adopt a unified identity and access model spanning domains, integrated with the fabric's policy engine.
- Data, models, and features use role- and attribute-based controls aligned with governance standards, ensuring consistency.

For AI, model training jobs and inference services are treated as "users" whose access is governed with the same rigor as human analysts. Cross-domain models undergo approval processes, ensuring each data contribution is authorized, documented, and compliant.

## Change Management: Moving People, Not Just Data[17]

Silos and the barriers they create are as much about people and structure as they are technology.

### Aligning Incentives Around Shared AI Value

Success depends on aligning domain incentives with cross-domain AI outcomes. Organizations can achieve this by:

- Demonstrating to domains how cross-domain AI improves their own metrics—e.g., better risk signals, higher conversion rates, fewer operational surprises.
- Recognizing and rewarding teams that publish high-quality data products and features others reuse, embedding collaboration into performance evaluation.

### Addressing Fears of Loss of Control

Preserving domain ownership is essential: breaking silos doesn't mean centralizing all decisions into a data dictatorship. Clear messaging should emphasize:

- Domains retain ownership and stewardship of their data and data products.
- Enterprise integration and AI teams provide infrastructure, fabric, and shared standards—not control.
- Joint committees decide high-impact cross-domain AI uses, respecting domain expertise while serving enterprise goals.

### Training and Collaboration Mechanisms

Cross-functional working groups—comprising data stewards, data scientists, architects, compliance officers, and domain subject-matter experts—ensure AI data integration respects business realities and regulatory constraints. Shared documentation, playbooks, and communities of practice propagate lessons across domains, preventing new silos of expertise from forming as old technical silos dissolve.

# Case Studies

## Case Study #1: Enterprise Data Fabric for Cross-Domain AI[18]

Data fabric blueprints showcase organizations that use metadata-driven integration layers to virtualize access across on-premises databases, cloud warehouses, and SaaS platforms. By unifying lineage, cataloging, and policy enforcement, they let cross-domain AI models consume consistent entity views without massive data replication. This cuts deployment time and strengthens explainability by centralizing metadata and making data flows easier to trace and govern.

### Case Study #2: Data Mesh Adoption in Multi-Domain Organizations[19]

Data mesh case studies highlight large enterprises where domain teams—retail, supply chain, finance—assume ownership of publishing high-quality data products with explicit contracts and SLAs. AI teams consume these products through a shared feature store, resulting in accelerated model development, richer domain context, and stronger accountability for data quality at the source rather than downstream cleanup.

### Case Study #3: Hybrid Fabric + Mesh for Regulated Industries[20]

Guides on combining fabric and mesh describe financial services and healthcare organizations using mesh principles for domain ownership while leveraging fabric technologies for centralized policy enforcement, lineage tracking, and semantic consistency. This hybrid approach allows them to scale AI across heavily regulated domains while maintaining strict governance and auditability, satisfying both operational agility and compliance imperatives.

## Success Metrics[21]

To make the Enterprise AI Data Fabric + Mesh more than an architecture diagram, teams need concrete ways to measure whether it's actually reducing silos and improving trust. The metrics that follow offer a starting set of "health signals" across feature reuse, scalability, transparency, and governance. They are intentionally simple, so leaders can track progress over time and quickly spot where the framework is working and where it needs reinforcement.

## Table of Illustrative Metrics

| Dimension | Example Metric | Why It Matters |
|---|---|---|
| **Cross-Domain Feature Reuse** | % of production models using shared features from the enterprise feature store rather than custom features | Indicates whether the feature layer and mesh products are genuinely reducing silos |
| **Time to Onboard a New Domain** | Time from identifying a new domain (for example, ESG, cyber) to publishing its first governed data product and features | Measures how efficiently the fabric + mesh framework scales across the enterprise |
| **Lineage and Explainability Coverage** | Share of AI models that can trace inputs back through fabric lineage and domain data products to original sources | Shows whether integrated architectures are improving AI transparency and auditability |
| **Governance Policy Enforcement** | % of data products and features with policy-as-code rules attached and monitored (for example, PII masking, purpose limits) | Reflects maturity of federated computational governance |

# Practical Advice for Leaders[22]

Leaders can more effectively break silos for AI by taking these steps:

- **Adopt a hybrid fabric + mesh strategy.** Utilize mesh principles for domain ownership and data-as-product accountability, and fabric technologies for unified access, semantics, and governance automation.
- **Invest in semantic and feature layers.** Ensuring AI teams build on shared concepts and reusable features instead of re-creating logic within each silo. This reduces waste and improves consistency.
- **Make policy-as-code and lineage non-negotiable.** Require every data product and feature to carry governance metadata and traceability. This embeds compliance into architecture rather than treating it as an afterthought.
- **Treat domains as partners.** Align incentives and establish clear RACI (who owns quality, who owns access, who approves cross-domain models) across the Enterprise AI Data Fabric + Mesh stack. This fosters collaboration rather than control.

# Conclusion

Breaking down data silos for AI isn't about dumping everything into one giant database. It's about creating governed, semantically consistent, interoperable access so AI systems and human decision-makers can safely use the full richness of enterprise data. Within an Enterprise AI Data Fabric + Mesh framework, integration patterns like data fabric, data mesh, and unified feature stores work together—under strong governance and change management—to give AI a whole-of-enterprise view instead of fragmented snapshots. When this is done well, silos give way to a shared data and feature ecosystem where domain experts, data stewards, AI teams, and business leaders can actually collaborate. AI becomes a synthesizer of cross-domain insight, while humans stay in charge of how that integrated data is defined, governed, and applied.

# Notes

[1] AI data integration, as used here, draws on Impressico's "Data Fabric Blueprint."

[2] On cross-domain governance, see Promethium's "Data Mesh vs Data Fabric Comparison Guide."

[3] Data fabric follows IBM's "Data Management vs Data Fabric vs Data Mesh."

[4] Data lake is drawn from *ConnectWise*'s "Data Warehouse vs Data Lake vs Data Lakehouse vs Data Mesh."

[5] Data mesh follows USDSI's "Understanding Data Fabric and Data Mesh."

[6] Data warehouse comes from *Ocient*'s "Unraveling the Web: Data Mesh vs Data Fabric and the Role of Data Warehouses."

[7] On enterprise data fabric, see SAP's "What is Data Fabric."

[8] Feature sharing, as used here, draws on IBM's "Semantic Layer."

[9] The semantic layer is discussed in *Booz Allen*'s "Data Mesh or Data Fabric: Do Better with Both."

[10] Unified data access, as used here, follows Promethium's "Data Fabric vs Data Mesh vs Data Lake vs Data Warehouse."

[11] How silos undermine AI and human-AI collaboration is examined in *Atlan*'s "What is Data Fabric?," *Splunk*'s "Cisco Data Fabric Transforms Machine Data into AI-Ready Intelligence," *Ovaledge*'s "Data Mesh vs Data Fabric," and Databahn's "Policy-Driven Security Data Fabric."

[12] AI-centric integration architectures for breaking silos are drawn from IBM's "Data Lakehouse vs Data Fabric vs Data Mesh," *SR Analytics*' "Data Mesh vs Data Fabric," DataGalaxy's "Data Mesh vs Data Fabric," *Petronellatech*'s "Data Mesh or Data Fabric," Promethium's "Data Mesh vs Data Fabric Comparison Guide," and IBM's "Semantic Layer."

[13] Comparisons of warehouse vs lake vs fabric vs mesh for AI and explainability are drawn from *Atlan*'s "Data Mesh vs Data Lake," Promethium's "Data Fabric vs Data Mesh vs Data Lake vs Data Warehouse," IBM's "Data Management vs Data Fabric vs Data Mesh," DataGalaxy's "Data Mesh vs Data Fabric," and USDSI's "Understanding Data Fabric and Data Mesh."

[14] The Enterprise AI Data Fabric + Mesh framework is assembled from Alation's "Data Mesh vs Data Fabric," *Progress*' "Data Fabric vs Data Mesh," *Petronellatech*'s "Data Mesh or Data Fabric," *Ovaledge*'s "Data Mesh vs Data Fabric," Promethium's "Data Mesh vs Data Fabric Comparison Guide," *AtScale*'s "Semantic Layer 2025 in Review," IBM's "Data Management vs Data Fabric vs Data Mesh," USDSI's "Understanding Data Fabric and Data Mesh," DataGalaxy's "Data Mesh vs Data Fabric," and Bismart's "Data Fabric Data Integration 2025."

[15] Semantic layers and shared definitions are addressed in SAP's "What is Data Fabric," *Booz Allen*'s "Data Mesh or Data Fabric," and IBM's "Semantic Layer."

[16] Governance for unified AI data access is addressed in Databahn's "Policy-Driven Security Data Fabric," Promethium's "Data Fabric vs Data Mesh vs Data Lake vs Data Warehouse," *Progress*' "Data Fabric vs Data Mesh," DataGalaxy's "Data Mesh vs Data Fabric," and Promethium's "Data Mesh vs Data Fabric Comparison Guide."

[17] Change management in this context draws on *SR Analytics*' "Data Mesh vs Data Fabric," *Petronellatech*'s "Data Mesh or Data Fabric," *Progress*' "Data Fabric vs Data Mesh," and *Ovaledge*'s "Data Mesh vs Data Fabric."

[18] The data fabric case is taken from Impressico's "Data Fabric Blueprint."

[19] *Ovaledge*'s "Data Mesh vs Data Fabric" provides the data mesh case study.

[20] *Petronellatech*'s "Data Mesh or Data Fabric" provides the hybrid fabric + mesh case study.

[21] Success metrics for this cluster draw on Promethium's "Data Mesh vs Data Fabric Comparison Guide," DataGalaxy's "Data Mesh vs Data Fabric," SAP's "What is Data Fabric," and Databahn's "Policy-Driven Security Data Fabric."

[22] This practical-advice cluster draws on Alation's "Data Mesh vs Data Fabric," *AtScale*'s "Semantic Layer 2025 in Review," Databahn's "Policy-Driven Security Data Fabric," and USDSI's "Understanding Data Fabric and Data Mesh."

## Key topics explored in this chapter:

- Trust as a Deliberate Outcome, Not a Default
- The 5-Layer Trust Stack for Data and Analytics
- Data Lineage, Observability, and Integrity
- Transparency, Explainability, and Communication
- Accuracy, Quality, and the Risks of Rapid Automation
- Culture, Leadership, and Human-in-the-Loop
- External Trust: Security, Transparency Reports, and Public Confidence
- Traditional BI vs AI-Era Trust Practices

# WAY 40

# Build Trust in Data and Analytics


## Abstract

Building trust in data and analytics for AI requires a shift—from assuming outputs are correct to intentionally earning trust through layered practices. Transparency, explainability, governance, culture, and communication need to work together, not sit as separate initiatives. This chapter introduces a Trust Stack for Data and Analytics. It contrasts traditional BI approaches with AI-era practices such as continuous monitoring and human-in-the-loop (HITL) oversight. And it shows how organizations build and sustain confidence in their data and models while enabling responsible collaboration between people and AI.


## Objective

After completing this chapter, you will be able to:

- Define organizational trust in analytics and explain its importance in AI-driven decision-making.
- Implement data transparency practices, including data lineage and documentation, to make analytical processes inspectable and auditable.
- Apply model explainability and communicate uncertainty effectively, rendering AI-driven decisions understandable and contestable for non-technical stakeholders.
- Embed AI ethics, accountability, and human-in-the-loop (HITL) structures into analytics workflows, ensuring humans retain ultimate responsibility for outcomes.

- Utilize the Trust Stack for Data and Analytics to integrate transparency, explainability, governance, culture, and external communication into a coherent trust-building program.

## Terms to Know

**Accountability**[1] - Clearly assigning responsibility for data and AI-driven decisions, encompassing data use approvals, model risk ownership, and incident review and remediation.

**AI Ethics**[2] - Principles and practices that ensure AI and analytics respect human rights and align with organizational values such as fairness, privacy, and transparency, backed by clear governance, ongoing oversight, and well-defined review processes.

**Data Accuracy**[3] - The extent to which data accurately reflects the real-world objects or events it represents; a core component of data integrity and trust.

**Data Lineage**[4] - Documented tracing of data's origin, movement, and transformation, which enables explainability, compliance, and rapid issue investigation.

**Data Transparency**[5] - Openness regarding data collection, usage, transformation, and sharing, including clear communication to both internal and external stakeholders.

**Human-in-the-Loop (HITL)**[6] - A design pattern where people stay involved at critical moments in an AI workflow to provide oversight, real-world context, and ethical judgment.

**Model Explainability**[7] - Techniques and practices that render model behavior and individual predictions understandable to humans.

**Organizational Culture (for data and AI)**[8] - Shared norms and behaviors governing how data and analytics are used, questioned, and governed, including openness to scrutiny and learning from mistakes.

**Responsible AI**[9] - Operationalizing AI ethics through governance methods, risk controls, and lifecycle practices to ensure AI systems are safe, fair, and trustworthy in practice.

**Trust in Analytics**[10] - Stakeholders' confidence that data and AI-driven outputs are accurate, explainable, ethically produced, and align with institutional commitments.

# Introduction

Trust in data and analytics used to rest on a quiet assumption: if a report cleared basic accuracy checks, people treated it as reliable. That default no longer holds. AI systems trained on huge, messy datasets now make judgments in unfamiliar situations and directly shape decisions that carry real consequences—who gets credit, who is hired, which medical cases are prioritized, even how law enforcement deploys its attention and resources.

In this setting, models can pick up and amplify historical bias, drift as the world changes, fabricate patterns that sound reasonable but aren't real, or make decisions so opaque that even their creators struggle to explain them. Trust is no longer something we can assume; it has to be engineered. That means building interlocking systems for transparency, explainability, governance, culture, and communication. Done well, these systems let employees, customers, regulators, and the public work confidently with AI while still being able to challenge, audit, and correct it when it fails.

## Trust as a Deliberate Outcome, Not a Default[11]

Contemporary governance and ethics models redefine trust. It's no longer an assumed byproduct of technical competence; instead, it's a strategic asset demanding intentional design from inception, not post-hoc patching.

### From Assumption to Architecture

In many enterprises, data science has outpaced governance infrastructure, creating significant gaps. Models often reach production before their training data, inherent limitations, and risk profiles are properly documented. Dashboards shape pivotal decisions, yet often lack transparent definitions for metric calculation or underlying assumptions. Analytics teams often operate in organizational silos, lacking clear accountability structures for oversight or incident response. This misalignment creates operational and reputational risk. When stakeholders eventually discover that analytical conclusions lack confident explanations, challenge capabilities, or traceable origins, trust collapses—often publicly and irreversibly.

### Trust Begins with Transparency

Making data lineage, transformation logic, model development choices, and interpretive boundaries visible and comprehensible transforms analytics from an inscrutable black box into a disciplined, inspectable practice. Transparency invites scrutiny, which in turn drives improvement and accountability. When stakeholders understand not just a system's conclusions, but also how and why it reached them, uncertainty and suspicion recede. Collaboration between humans and AI becomes more effective; trust builds on knowledge, not blind faith.

## The 5-Layer Trust Stack for Data and Analytics[12]

Viewing trust as a layered architecture gives organizations a clear way to organize the many factors that shape stakeholder confidence. The Trust Stack frames trust-building as a set of mutually reinforcing layers, starting with data foundations and running all the way up to external communication and accountability. Each layer delivers a distinct capability, and together they form a practical approach for designing and evaluating trust across the organization.

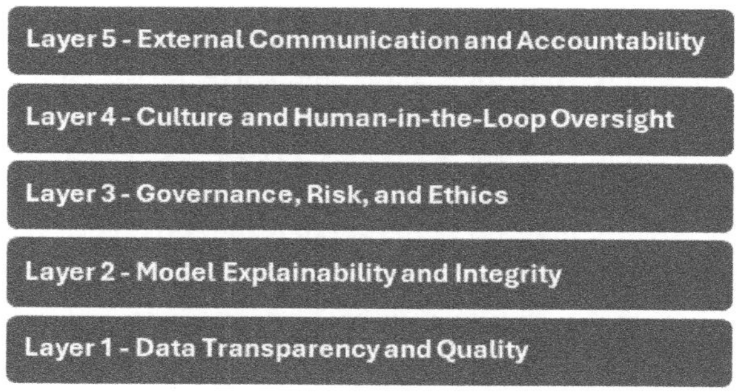


### Layer 1: Data Transparency and Quality

**What It Is:** Clear, well-documented data assets that show lineage, ownership, and definitions; automated quality checks; and explicit flags for missing, uncertain, or low-confidence data.

**Trust Contribution:** Stakeholders can see where numbers come from and how reliable they are, reducing the sense that figures are arbitrary, manipulated, or cherry-picked.

**Key Controls:** Automated lineage capture across pipelines, actively maintained data dictionaries, quality dashboards that track freshness and completeness, and observability tools that surface anomalies in real time.

### Layer 2: Model Explainability and Integrity

**What It Is:** Standardized model cards, clear feature documentation, explainability reports (for example, SHAP-based summaries), and validation logs that track performance over time.

**Trust Contribution:** Decision-makers understand why models behave the way they do, which makes it easier to spot errors, bias, or fragile correlations and to compare models on more than just top-line accuracy.

**Key Controls:** Explainable tools embedded in MLOps workflows, model registries that capture metadata and version history, and peer review of modeling choices before models go live.

### Layer 3: Governance, Risk, and Ethics

**What It Is:** AI governance councils with cross-functional membership, documented risk assessments for each system, bias audits, ethics charters that spell out acceptable uses, and clear policies for model deployment.

**Trust Contribution:** Stakeholders see that models are reviewed, approved, and monitored against explicit standards, rather than quietly released from isolated engineering teams.

**Key Controls:** Formal ethics frameworks, risk registers that link systems to potential harms, defined approval workflows with clear decision rights, and regular internal or third-party audits.

### Layer 4: Culture and Human-in-the-Loop Oversight

**What It Is:** HITL workflows that require human approval for high-impact decisions, open "analytics town halls" where results are challenged and debated, training on data literacy and responsible AI, and blameless post-mortems that examine analytical errors without focusing on punishment.

**Trust Contribution:** Analytics becomes something people can question and shape, not a black box they are expected to obey. Humans understand they have the authority to intervene, override, and improve systems, which builds ownership instead of alienation.

**Key Controls:** Clear escalation paths, structured training curricula, and regular forums that invite constructive critique and support organizational learning.

### Layer 5: External Communication and Accountability

**What It Is:** Published transparency reports, clear customer-facing explanations of automated decisions, easy-to-use channels for appeals or disputes, and regular public or stakeholder briefings on how AI is used and what outcomes it drives.

**Trust Contribution:** External audiences—customers, regulators, and civil society—see visible, repeatable commitments to responsible analytics instead of vague promises or marketing language.

**Key Controls:** Published ethics reviews, public explanations that meet accessibility standards, formal dispute and appeal pathways with documented resolution steps, and regulatory disclosures that align with legal and industry requirements.

## Data Lineage, Observability, and Integrity[13]

Trust requires understanding not merely a model's conclusions, but also where its input data originated and how that data transformed en route to the final output.

### Data Lineage As a Cornerstone of Trust

Data lineage serves as a foundational pillar of trustworthy analytics and AI. It demonstrates traceability from source systems through successive transformations into reports and predictive models. This traceability enables stakeholders to understand provenance, verify regulatory compliance, and rapidly investigate issues when anomalies surface. Effective lineage systems achieve three key goals:

- **Multi-level mapping:** Lineage should span technical pipelines (tables, scripts, APIs), business concepts (customer, order, risk exposure), and organizational accountability (domain stewards, data engineers).
- **Integration with quality checks:** Connecting lineage to data quality monitors and anomaly detection accelerates root-cause analysis when errors occur, allowing teams to pinpoint precisely where corrupted data entered the flow.
- **Governance integration:** Feeding lineage into governance models clarifies responsibilities, approval workflows, and escalation paths for data-related incidents, thus closing accountability gaps.

### Data Observability and Continuous Monitoring

Data observability platforms extend lineage by actively monitoring freshness, completeness, schema stability, and drift. They track how problems propagate into downstream analytics before corrupting decisions. Observability and lineage, working in tandem, signal to stakeholders that data remains under continuous vigilance, reinforcing perceptions of integrity and control. Observability dashboards alert teams to anomalies—sudden drops in record counts, unexpected null values, schema mismatches—enabling proactive intervention before corrupted data poisons AI outputs.

## Transparency, Explainability, and Communication[14]

Transparency and trust models converge on a core principle: sharing what data is collected, how it's used, and how AI-driven decisions are ultimately produced.

### Transparency in Analytics Parallels Transparency in Human Relationships

When people understand how something works and why specific decisions were made, uncertainty and suspicion diminish. Transparent analytics involves documenting not only final outputs but also underlying assumptions, data sources, transformation steps, model selection rationale, and acknowledged limitations. This openness signals respect for stakeholders' intelligence, treating them as partners rather than mere passive consumers.

### Model Explainability is Central

Explainable AI guidance highlights techniques such as feature attributions (for example, SHAP and LIME), local explanations for individual predictions, counterfactuals ("What if this feature changed?"), and natural-language rationales as core tools for building trust as models grow more complex. These capabilities need to be built into governance practices—like model documentation standards, review and approval forums, and customer-facing explanations—not treated as optional extras. They aren't. Explainability ultimately serves many groups at once:

- **Technical teams** leverage explainability to debug models, identify spurious correlations masquerading as insights, and refine feature engineering.
- **Business stakeholders** use explainability to validate that model logic aligns with domain knowledge and ethical standards, catching problems pure performance metrics might miss.

- **End-users**—customers, employees, and citizens—rely on explainability to understand decisions affecting them and to contest outputs they deem incorrect or unfair, exercising agency rather than passive acceptance.

### Communicating Limitations and Uncertainty

Transparent communication extends to candidly acknowledging limitations and uncertainty: clearly stating assumptions, articulating error margins, and identifying contexts where models perform less reliably. Counterintuitively, this honesty tends to increase, rather than decrease, perceived trustworthiness. It demonstrates intellectual rigor and respect for truth over overselling AI capabilities, calibrating stakeholder expectations and guarding against over-reliance.

## Accuracy, Quality, and the Risks of Rapid Automation[15]

Governance commentaries emphasize that as generative AI and automation scale rapidly, subtle errors can compound exponentially if validation and review mechanisms lag behind deployment velocity. AI systems can hallucinate—inferring plausible yet fundamentally false patterns—catastrophically threatening trust if unchecked.

### Maintaining Data Accuracy and Integrity

Sustaining data accuracy and overall integrity demands:

- **Upstream quality management:** Implementing disciplined data quality practices at the point of collection, not merely downstream in warehouses. Quality checks should embed across ingestion, transformation, and consumption layers.
- **Continuous validation loops:** Establishing ongoing tests, back-testing against historical outcomes, and monitoring model outputs for anomalies and drift. Automated alerts flag when performance degrades or predictions diverge from expected ranges, triggering human investigation.
- **Explicit uncertainty communication:** Presenting confidence intervals, risk ranges, and probabilistic language rather than falsely precise point estimates. Communicating uncertainty helps decision-makers calibrate their reliance on AI, avoiding overconfidence traps.

### Database and Pipeline Governance

Reports analyzing AI and database governance underscore that ungoverned changes to schemas, validation rules, or naming conventions can silently undermine model reliability. For instance, if a field is renamed or its semantic definition shifts without documentation, downstream models may fail silently or produce systematically incorrect outputs. Database and data pipeline governance—including rigorous change control, versioning, and impact analysis—is integral to AI trust, not an afterthought.

## Culture, Leadership, and Human-in-the-Loop[16]

Literature on human-in-the-loop and responsible AI consistently identifies human oversight as among the strongest predictors of successful, trusted AI adoption.

### HITL Design Embeds Human Judgment at Critical Points

Human-in-the-loop (HITL) design integrates human judgment strategically—during label review in training data curation, approval of high-impact decisions (e.g., loan denials, employee terminations), and escalation of uncertain or ethically ambiguous cases—preserving organizational accountability for fairness and context. HITL isn't a brake slowing AI adoption; it's a steering mechanism ensuring AI augments rather than displaces human expertise.

Effective HITL workflows incorporate:

- **Clear escalation criteria:** Defining when decisions route to humans, balancing efficiency with risk mitigation.
- **Documented overrides and rationales:** Creating audit trails of human interventions, capturing why humans disagreed with model recommendations.
- **Feedback loops:** Channeling human corrections back into model training, enabling continuous improvement grounded in real-world judgment.

### Building Organizational Culture Around Trust

To cultivate an organizational culture that sustains trust, you should:

- **Encourage critical inquiry:** Promote norms where teams question and interrogate data and models rather than accepting outputs uncritically. A culture of healthy skepticism supports iterative improvement and guards against complacency.
- **Demystify analytics:** Use internal workshops, "analytics town halls," and open forums to reveal how data becomes insight, helping employees perceive analytics as a collaborative craft rather than arcane wizardry.

- **Align leadership messaging:** Ensure executives and analytics leaders set realistic expectations, candidly discuss limitations and ethics, and visibly commit to continuous improvement. When leaders model transparency and accountability, organizational norms follow.

### AI Ethics and Responsibility

Ethics and responsibility underpin these cultural choices. Governance models recommend establishing formal ethics charters, trust frameworks, and bias audits that explicitly tie AI development to organizational values and stakeholder expectations. Transparent documentation of sources, transformations, and model usage becomes a visible signal of accountability, not mere compliance theater.

## External Trust: Security, Transparency Reports, and Public Confidence[17]

Trust extends beyond internal operations to how analytics affects customers, citizens, and the broader public. Governance analyses stress that external stakeholders expect clarity regarding how their data is used and how AI decisions affecting them are made.

### Practices That Bolster External Trust

External trust-building practices include:

- **Strong security and privacy controls:** Implementing access logging, encryption, data minimization, and incident response protocols. Security breaches destroy trust in a rapid and comprehensive fashion, so strong controls are a non-negotiable foundation.
- **Transparency reports or ethics reviews:** Publishing summaries of major AI deployments, monitoring results, and mitigation actions. Making these reports public demonstrates accountability and invites external scrutiny, signaling confidence rather than defensiveness.
- **Mechanisms for explanation, appeal, and opt-out:** Providing customer-facing explainability and formal dispute pathways where AI decisions significantly affect individuals in areas like credit and employment. These mechanisms demonstrate that AI is accountable to people, not the reverse.

**Building Public Confidence**

Organizations that provide clear, accessible explanations of automated decisions, publish regular transparency reports, and respond promptly and substantively to concerns cultivate public confidence that AI will be deployed responsibly. This external trust complements internal governance and can become a competitive differentiator in industries where consumer trust drives market position.

## Traditional BI vs AI-Era Trust Practices[18]

As enterprises move from traditional business intelligence to AI-driven decision systems, their trust practices have to change with them. Instead of relying mainly on periodic, human-only checks, organizations need continuous, system-level controls embedded across the full AI lifecycle. The table below highlights how these trust practices are evolving.

## Comparison of Traditional BI and AI-Era Trust Practices

| Dimension | Traditional BI Trust Practices | AI-Driven System Trust Practices |
|---|---|---|
| **Monitoring Cadence** | Periodic report validation and scheduled audits | Continuous model and data monitoring for drift, anomalies, and security events |
| **Review Pattern** | Human review of static dashboards and ad hoc investigations | HITL review for high-impact AI decisions, with documented overrides and audit trails |
| **Transparency Focus** | Metric definitions and report logic documentation | End-to-end transparency: data lineage, model logic, and explanation of individual predictions |
| **Error Handling** | Fix report logic, re-issue corrected dashboards | AI incident management (e.g., bias or drift events), with root-cause analysis, model updates, and communication plans |
| **Stakeholder Engagement** | Mainly consumers of reports, with limited feedback loops | Cross-functional engagement across design, review, and improvement cycles |

This comparison shows why trust in the AI era requires capabilities—continuous monitoring, explainability, HITL workflows, and structured incident response—that go far beyond traditional reporting disciplines.

# Case Studies

## Case Study #1: Data and AI Ethics Framework in the Public Sector[19]

A government Data and AI Ethics Framework illustrates how public bodies self-assess AI projects against principles including fairness, transparency, and accountability. The model provides structured prompts about data sources, consent mechanisms, explainability approaches, and human oversight roles, helping project teams identify risks early and systematically document mitigations. Publishing the approach and associated tools publicly signals commitment to responsible AI, building citizen trust that governmental AI deployment will align with democratic values and legal norms, not technocratic opacity.

## Case Study #2: Governance Structures for Trustworthy Analytics in Industry[20]

A governance guide profiling trust-building in AI and analytics describes how a large financial institution established a cross-functional data governance council. This council codified ethical principles and defined explicit roles for overseeing AI models. This council set enforceable standards for data quality, privacy protections, and model validation. It also mandated transparency and explainability requirements for customer-facing use cases. Over time, this governance structure evolved from a perceived compliance burden into a strategic asset—improving stakeholder confidence, reducing operational incidents, and accelerating responsible innovation.

## Case Study #3: Human-in-the-Loop as "Architecture of Trust"[21]

Analyses of human-in-the-loop (HITL) implementations describe HITL not as a brake impeding AI velocity but as a steering mechanism preserving organizational accountability for fairness and contextual judgment. By embedding expert review directly into operational workflows and documenting decisions and overrides, organizations generated comprehensive audit trails. These trails demonstrated that humans remained ultimately responsible for outcomes. Studies cited in these analyses argue that HITL design correlates with higher adoption rates and stronger trust among both workers and customers, validating the investment in oversight infrastructure.

# Success Metrics[22]

## Table of Illustrative Metrics

| Dimension | Example Metric | Why It Matters |
|---|---|---|
| **Transparency and Lineage** | % of critical reports and AI models with documented, searchable data lineage and transformation logic | Shows whether stakeholders can trace how data translates into decisions |
| **Explainability and Oversight** | Share of high-impact models with documented explainability methods, user-facing rationales, and HITL checkpoints | Indicates whether decisions are understandable and controllable |
| **Ethics and Governance** | No. of AI projects reviewed against an ethics framework or trust checklist before deployment | Reflects how systematically ethics and responsible AI are applied |
| **Incident Learning** | Time from detection of an analytics incident (e.g., erroneous output, bias, outage) to internal or public communication of root cause and remediation | Measures whether the organization responds to errors with transparency and accountability |

# Practical Advice for Leaders[23]

- **Treat trust as a core design objective.** Integrate transparency, explainability, HITL, and ethics into AI and data strategies from inception, rather than retrofitting them post-deployment.
- **Institutionalize data lineage, observability, and quality checks.** Ensure all critical analytics can be traced, validated, and monitored continuously over time, not just at project launch.

- **Embed human-in-the-loop workflows and clear accountability.** Ensure AI augments rather than replaces human judgment and that responsibility is never ambiguous or diffused across siloed teams.
- **Communicate openly about limitations, uncertainty, and ethics.** Use accessible storytelling and transparency reports to align technical practices with company values and stakeholder expectations and to build credibility through honesty.

# Conclusion

Trust in data and analytics forms the bedrock for responsible AI and data-driven decision-making. It emerges when transparency reveals how systems work, accuracy and quality assure their reliability, and ethics, governance, and human oversight ensure they operate in ways people can accept. In an era of rapid automation and generative AI proliferation, organizations investing in the full Trust Stack—data transparency, explainability, governance, culture, and external communication—will be better positioned to innovate sustainably while maintaining the confidence of employees, customers, regulators, and the public. When executed well, trust transforms from a fragile assumption into a durable organizational capability, enabling humans and AI to collaborate responsibly and effectively toward shared goals.

# Notes

[1] Accountability, as applied to data governance, is defined in TrustCloud's "Data Governance in 2025."

[2] For AI ethics and responsible AI, see ThoughtSpot's "Responsible AI."

[3] For data accuracy as a trust dimension, see Smart Data Institute's "Building Trust in AI and Data Analytics."

[4] Data lineage is defined in *Data Crossroads*' "Part 1: Technological Challenges—Data Lineage."

[5] On data transparency, see ISACA's "Building Trust Through Transparency."

[6] Human-in-the-loop (HITL) is defined in LinkedIn's "Human in the Loop: The Key to Ethical and Effective AI in 2025."

[7] Model explainability is defined in Bismart's "Explainable AI: Business Trust."

[8] Organizational culture, as applied to data and AI, is defined in Strategy Software's "Building Trust and Governance into Your Data and AI Organization."

[9] On responsible AI, see Data in Government Blog's "Building Trust in Data and AI."

[10] Trust in analytics is defined in DataGalaxy's "The Increasing Need for Data Trust."

[11] Trust as a deliberate outcome is addressed in Liminal's "Enterprise AI Governance Guide" and DataGalaxy's "Top Data Observability Tools."

[12] The Trust Stack for Data and Analytics is assembled from DataGalaxy's "Governance Hype Trust Models," TrustCloud's article, Alation's "What is Explainable AI Governance," *Athena Solutions*' "AI Governance 2025," *Parseur*'s "Human in the Loop AI," and *Forbes*' "Building Trust in Motion."

[13] Data lineage, observability, and integrity are addressed in *Data Crossroads*' "Part 1: Technological Challenges—Data Lineage," Journal WJAETS' "Transparency and Explainability in AI-Driven Decision Making," DataGalaxy's "Top Data Observability Tools," and *RiseUpLabs*' "AI Security."

[14] Transparency, explainability, and communication are examined in Journal WJAETS' article, *McKinsey*'s "Building AI Trust," and Liquibase's "2025 DORA Report."

[15] Accuracy, quality, and the risks of rapid automation are treated in *MyData Trust*'s "Data Governance 2025-2026," Smart Data Institute's article, Liquibase's article, ISACA's article, and TrustCloud's article.

[16] Culture, leadership, and human-in-the-loop practices are covered in *Xcelerator Siemens Community*'s article, *Solutions Review*'s "Keeping Humans in the Loop," Strategy Software's article, Data in Government Blog's article, and ThoughtSpot's article.

[17] External trust is addressed in *Forbes*' article, *RiseUpLabs*' article, Data in Government Blog's article, and Humans in the Loop's "How Humans in the Loop Powers Responsible AI."

[18] Traditional BI versus AI-era trust practices are contrasted across *RiseUpLabs*' "AI Security," TrustCloud's article, DataGalaxy's "Top Data Observability Tools," Strategy Software's article, *Xcelerator Siemens Community*'s article, ISACA's article, Alation's article, Smart Data Institute's article, and SuperAGI's "AI vs Traditional Methods."

[19] The government ethics framework case study is drawn from Data in Government Blog's "Building Trust in Data and AI."

[20] The financial institution governance case study is drawn from DataGalaxy's "Governance Hype Trust Models."

[21] The human-in-the-loop case study draws on Ping Identity's "Human in the Loop AI" and *Xcelerator Siemens Community*'s article.

[22] The success-metrics cluster is drawn from *Data Crossroads*' article, Alation's article, Data in Government Blog's article, and Smart Data Institute's article.

[23] This practical-advice cluster draws on *Athena Solutions*' article, *Data Crossroads*' article, LinkedIn's article, and ISACA's article.

## Key topics explored in this chapter:

- Understanding the Frameworks
- Data Classification, Lineage, and Lifecycle Controls
- AI Risk Assessment and Model Governance
- Policy Frameworks and Policies-as-Code
- RegTech and Automated Compliance Auditing
- Data Retention, Erasure, and Machine Unlearning
- Coordination Between Technical and Legal Teams
- International Data Transfers and Jurisdictional Complexity

# WAY 41

# Govern Data for Compliance and Regulation

## Abstract

As data regulation intensifies globally—from GDPR and CCPA to industry-specific rules in healthcare, finance, and AI—organizations face mounting pressure to demonstrate documented, auditable compliance. Data governance is no longer a back-office obligation. In the AI-enabled organization, it's a necessary operating discipline that shapes how data is collected, used, protected, retained, shared, and audited. As regulatory expectations expand and data moves across more systems, models, vendors, and jurisdictions, leaders need governance that is both rigorous and practical. This chapter explains how to build methods that meet regulatory requirements while supporting business value through clear policies, privacy-by-design practices, consent management, cross-border controls, and continuous monitoring that catches compliance gaps before they become violations.

## Objective

After completing this chapter, you will be able to:

- Describe how major frameworks shape AI governance and regulatory compliance expectations.
- Design governance controls that align AI data pipelines with privacy and security obligations.
- Apply responsible AI, ethics and accountability principles to risk assessments, policy frameworks, and model governance.

- Use regulatory technology (RegTech) and automation to monitor compliance, manage evidence, and support AI-specific risk management.
- Address complex topics such as data retention, deletion, and machine unlearning under rights like GDPR's Right to Be Forgotten.

## Terms to Know

**AI Auditability**[1] - The ability to reconstruct and demonstrate how AI systems were designed, trained, and operated, using documentation, logs, and lineage to support internal and external audits.

**AI Governance**[2] - Structures, policies, and tools that guide the design, deployment, and oversight of AI systems, integrating risk management and regulatory requirements.

**Data Lineage**[3] - A documented, often automated record of where data originates, how it moves, and how it transforms from source systems into AI models and reports.

**Data Privacy**[4] - Legal and ethical protection of personal data, including principles like lawfulness, transparency, minimization, and rights of access, rectification, and erasure under laws such as GDPR.

**Data Retention**[5] - Policies and technical controls defining how long data and related artifacts—logs, models, documentation—are kept, and how they are securely deleted or anonymized when no longer needed.

**Model Governance**[6] - Processes and controls that manage model lifecycles—development, validation, approval, deployment, monitoring, and retirement—under regulatory and risk guidance.

**Policy Frameworks**[7] - Structured sets of internal policies and standards (for example, data handling, model use, documentation) mapped to external regulations.

**Regulatory Compliance**[8] - Ongoing adherence to applicable laws, regulations, and standards, demonstrated through controls, evidence, and readiness for inspection or audit.

**Regulatory Technology (RegTech)**[9] - Software and AI-driven tools that automate aspects of compliance, such as obligation extraction, control mapping, monitoring, and regulatory reporting.

**Responsible AI**[10] - Practices that ensure AI systems are fair, transparent, safe, and aligned with societal values, with clear accountability for impacts.

# Introduction[11]

AI introduces complexities that have no precedent in traditional IT. Data flows shift dynamically, models infer new attributes from raw inputs, and automated decisions propagate at scale, affecting individuals, institutions, and entire markets. Systems once considered mere software now occupy a gray zone between product, service, and decision agent. Governance must match that reach and risk.

Frameworks like GDPR, the EU AI Act, NIST's AI RMF, and ISO/IEC 42001 converge on the same theme: transparency, documentation, and accountability are regulatory mandates, not optional virtues. Organizations deploying AI must explain how data moves through their systems—tracing origins, documenting transformations, controlling access, and stating purposes, especially when systems shape high-risk decisions affecting employment, credit, healthcare, or public safety. What began as industry best practice has become a compliance baseline. Risk-based governance, structured documentation, and continuous monitoring have moved from aspirational goals to essential requirements.

## Understanding the Frameworks[12]

Frameworks don't exist in isolation; they overlap, complement, and sometimes complicate one another. Comparative analyses stress that GDPR, the EU AI Act, NIST AI RMF, and ISO/IEC 42001 serve distinct but interlocking purposes. Treating them as "interchangeable" risks missing obligations or unnecessarily duplicating effort.

- **GDPR** functions as a binding data-protection law governing personal data across the European Economic Area. Its requirements—lawful processing bases, transparency notices, data minimization, security safeguards, Data Protection Impact Assessments (DPIAs), and individual rights such as access and erasure—apply to any processing of personal data, whether by AI or traditional systems.

- The **EU AI Act** takes a different approach: it applies a risk-based regulatory model specifically to AI systems. High-risk systems—those affecting fundamental rights, safety, or critical infrastructure—face obligations including formal risk management, comprehensive technical documentation, human oversight provisions, data governance standards, and post-market monitoring. While GDPR governs data, the AI Act governs the system built on that data.

- **NIST's AI RMF** offers a voluntary framework designed to help organizations identify, assess, and manage AI-related risks like fairness, transparency, robustness, security, and interpretability. It doesn't impose legal obligations, but many entities adopt it to structure internal practices and demonstrate due diligence to stakeholders and regulators.
- **ISO/IEC 42001** establishes an AI management system standard, defining governance structures, risk-management processes, documentation protocols, and continual-improvement practices. Organizations can seek certification against this standard, signaling to customers, auditors, and regulators that they operate under a recognized responsible-AI model.

Rather than viewing these frameworks as competing mandates, governance professionals increasingly build compliance requirements matrices—tools that map each AI system to applicable regulations and approaches. Then they link those requirements to concrete controls, responsible owners, and sources of evidence, creating a traceable path from obligation to implementation.

## Data Classification, Lineage, and Lifecycle Controls[13]

Effective governance begins with knowing what data you hold and how it moves throughout the organization.

Data classification serves as the entry point: tagging datasets by sensitivity (personally identifiable information, special-category data under GDPR), jurisdiction, usage rights, and lifecycle stage. Metadata-driven platforms propagate these classifications downstream, ensuring that when a dataset enters a model-training pipeline or feeds a production dashboard, its constraints travel with it—triggering anonymization, encryption, access controls, or outright exclusion where policy dictates.

Data lineage transforms classification from static labeling into dynamic oversight. Automated lineage tools capture data's path across ingestion, transformation, training, and inference, building visualizations that link business metrics and model outputs back to their original sources. When a regulator or auditor asks, "How did this prediction arise?" lineage provides the answer, mapping intermediate transformations, applied policies, and upstream controls. More practically, lineage enables impact analysis: when a schema changes or a policy tightens, organizations can quickly identify which models, reports, and dashboards are affected, avoiding surprises during regulatory inspections.

Lifecycle controls extend this logic to time: retention policies define how long data persists in training sets, logs, and model validation archives, and specify how data is deleted or anonymized when its retention period expires or its legal basis lapses. For models themselves, governance must track versioning, approvals, monitoring baselines, and retirement decisions, creating an auditable model governance trail that shows not only what a model does but when, why, and under whose authority it was deployed, updated, or decommissioned.

## AI Risk Assessment and Model Governance[14]

Both the NIST AI RMF and the EU AI Act promote risk-based governance, urging organizations to classify their AI systems by use case, potential impact, and affected populations. Leading governance platforms now embed risk-classification workflows that guide cross-functional teams through structured questions—Does this system influence hiring decisions? Could it affect access to credit or healthcare? What populations are most exposed?—and maintain decision logic documenting how each system received its risk tier.

AI-specific risks differ from traditional operational failures. Beyond performance degradation or system outages, organizations must contend with algorithmic bias and discrimination, where skewed training data or proxy variables systematically disadvantage protected groups; lack of explainability, where opaque models produce decisions without meaningful human understanding of their reasoning; data poisoning and adversarial attacks, where malicious actors manipulate inputs to corrupt outcomes; and misuse or out-of-scope deployment, where a model built for one purpose is repurposed without appropriate revalidation.

Effective model governance addresses these risks through layered controls: an AI risk register mapping each model to potential failure modes and mitigation strategies; comprehensive evaluations that extend beyond accuracy to measure fairness, robustness, and interpretability; and version-controlled documentation—often called model cards or datasheets—that captures training data, assumptions, performance benchmarks, and known limitations, updated whenever models are retrained or regulations change.

## Policy Frameworks and Policies-as-Code[15]

Internal policy methods serve as the operational bridge between abstract regulatory text and daily practice. Governance experts emphasize that policies must define who may access, modify, or deploy data, features, and models; specify acceptable uses of synthetic data and derived attributes; and establish requirements for human oversight, documentation, and approval workflows, especially for high-risk systems subject to DPIAs or AI Act conformity assessments.

Modern platforms go further, implementing policies as code: machine-readable rules that automatically enforce compliance. Examples include preventing personally identifiable information from landing in unclassified storage, blocking high-risk model deployments until documented human oversight and DPIA completion are verified, and flagging data-retention violations before they escalate into regulatory breaches. By embedding compliance logic directly into the pipeline, organizations shift from reactive auditing to preventive control, generating machine-readable evidence of enforcement—audit logs, approval records, policy-check results—ready for regulators without manual collection.

## RegTech and Automated Compliance Auditing[9]

RegTech platforms automate compliance tasks that once required armies of lawyers and auditors. Case studies describe systems using natural language processing to scan regulatory documents—EU AI Act articles, GDPR recitals, sector-specific guidance—extracting "shall" obligations, grouping them into control themes (data governance, transparency, risk management, human oversight), and mapping them to organizational controls.

Evidence-management platforms track existing controls, their owners, last test dates, results, and supporting documentation. These systems generate near-real-time compliance dashboards, surfacing gaps before audits and enabling rapid response when regulations change. Monitoring tools continuously track model versions, data sources, and control coverage, raising alerts when new models lack required documentation or when external feeds introduce unvalidated data.

Regulatory reporting automation tools emphasize that data governance and lineage form the non-negotiable foundation: without clean, traceable data, no amount of intelligent automation can produce defensible reports. But where that foundation exists, RegTech dramatically reduces manual effort, accelerates audit readiness, and frees human judgment for the complex, interpretive work—assessing fairness, systemic risk, and ethical trade-offs—that machines can't yet handle.

## Data Retention, Erasure, and Machine Unlearning[16]

GDPR's Right to Be Forgotten (Article 17) now reaches into AI contexts, raising questions that database-centric compliance programs never confronted: How do you delete personal data from a trained neural network? Analyses of machine unlearning highlight the challenge—residual influence of training data can persist in model parameters even after source datasets are purged, complicating simple erasure.

Organizations experimenting with GDPR-compliant unlearning adopt multi-level approaches: removing individual records from training sets and retraining models from filtered data; applying incremental unlearning algorithms that selectively adjust parameters to reduce or eliminate specific data points' influence without full retraining; and documenting every action taken—what data was removed, which models were affected, what validation confirmed reduced influence—in auditable workflows that demonstrate good-faith compliance even where perfect deletion remains technically elusive.

Compliance-by-design therefore demands explicit retention schedules for both data and models, technical mechanisms enabling model refresh or unlearning on demand, and governance artifacts—policy documents, test results, audit trails—that record erasure decisions and the evidence supporting them. Controllers who can show regulators a structured, documented unlearning process signal that they take data rights seriously, even when technology imposes limits.

## Coordination Between Technical and Legal Teams[17]

Enterprise AI governance guides consistently identify siloed teams as a root cause of compliance failure. Data scientists build systems optimized for performance, lawyers review contractual terms months later, and neither understands the other's constraints until production deployment surfaces a regulatory gap. Better practice embeds compliance-by-design—integrating legal and compliance expertise into architecture and model design from the start, treating regulatory requirements as first-class constraints alongside latency and accuracy.

Training programs now teach AI practitioners the legal basics—consent, intellectual property, export controls, explainability obligations—so compliance becomes part of professional competence, not an external imposition. Cross-functional AI governance committees bring together technical leads, legal counsel, ethicists, privacy officers, and business stakeholders to oversee high-risk systems, ensuring that human-oversight mechanisms are not afterthoughts but integral design features. This coordinated ecosystem transforms compliance from a deployment checkpoint into a design standard and quality criterion.

## International Data Transfers and Jurisdictional Complexity[18]

AI systems rarely respect borders. Training data may originate in Europe, models train in US cloud regions, and inference serves users globally, creating overlapping jurisdictional claims and conflicting legal obligations. Governance frameworks must map data and workloads to jurisdictions, documenting where personal data is stored and processed, which laws apply, and what cross-border transfer mechanisms (standard contractual clauses, adequacy decisions) authorize those flows.

Privacy-enhancing technologies—federated learning, which trains models locally and aggregates only updates, not raw data; secure multiparty computation, which enables joint analysis without data pooling; and homomorphic encryption, which allows computation on encrypted data—offer pathways for cross-border AI collaboration without centralizing sensitive information. Organizations that master these techniques, integrating them into governance models that document their use and validate their protections, gain a competitive edge: the ability to scale AI globally while respecting local law signals regulatory maturity and earns stakeholder trust.

## A Concise AI Compliance Control Matrix[19]

To translate abstract frameworks into operational practice, many organizations adopt a compliance control matrix that maps regulatory sources to key control areas. The following tables offer a working artifact you can adapt to your own portfolio:

## AI Compliance Control Matrix, Part 1

| Framework / Control Area | Data Lineage and Training | Model Documentation and Transparency | Risk Assessment and Monitoring |
|---|---|---|---|
| **GDPR** | Maintain processing records and lineage for personal data flows; document sources, lawful basis, and transformations in RoPA and DPIAs | Document processing purposes, categories of data, recipients, and logic of automated decisions where applicable (e.g., Articles 13-15 notices) | Conduct DPIAs for high-risk processing; monitor impacts on rights and freedoms; maintain risk registers tied to processing activities |
| **EU AI Act (High-Risk Systems)** | Maintain datasets' provenance and lineage; document data quality, representativeness, and bias mitigation in technical documentation | Provide technical documentation, model cards, and logs sufficient for conformity assessment and post-market monitoring | Implement a formal risk management system, including identification, analysis, mitigation, and continuous monitoring of AI risks |
| **NIST AI RMF (Voluntary)** | Encourage traceability and data governance practices, including lineage, quality, and documentation across training and evaluation datasets | Promote documentation of system goals, context, assumptions, performance, and limitations in model cards or equivalent artifacts | Structure risk identification, measurement, and management across categories like validity, robustness, fairness, security, and explainability; support continuous monitoring |
| **ISO/IEC 42001** | Require an AI management system with documented data governance processes, including lineage, ownership, and quality controls | Mandate systematic documentation for AI assets within the management system, with audit-ready records | Embed AI risk management into the management system, including periodic assessments, control selection, and performance reviews |

## AI Compliance Control Matrix, Part 2

| Framework / Control Area | Retention and Unlearning | Human Oversight and Accountability |
|---|---|---|
| **GDPR** | Enforce purpose-based retention limits and deletion/anonymization, including plans for removing personal data from training sets and logs | Ensure meaningful human review for decisions with legal or similarly significant effects (e.g., safeguards under Article 22), with clear roles and escalation paths |
| **EU AI Act (High-Risk Systems)** | Define policies for data and model updates; maintain logs to support corrective actions and potential recall; align with data governance and quality requirements | Implement "appropriate human oversight" so operators can understand, supervise, and override AI decisions; document oversight design and training |
| **NIST AI RMF (Voluntary)** | Recommend policies for data and model lifecycle management as part of risk treatment, including archival and decommissioning practices | Emphasize governance functions that define roles, assign accountability, and ensure human involvement commensurate with risk, including oversight of high-impact uses |
| **ISO/IEC 42001** | Define organization-wide retention and disposal rules for AI-related data and artifacts, documented and periodically reviewed | Require role definitions, "four eyes" review, and governance processes to ensure adequate human oversight, peer review, and incident response for AI decisions |

You can extend these matrices with additional rows (ex. sector-specific regulations, internal policies) or columns (ex. security controls, third-party model documentation), but even this concise version clarifies where controls exist—and where gaps threaten compliance.

# Case Studies

## Case Study #1: Implementing an AI Compliance Requirements Matrix[20]

Organizations profiled in enterprise AI governance guides have operationalized compliance by building compliance requirements matrices that map each AI system to its applicable regulations—EU AI Act classifications, GDPR processing categories, sector-specific mandates, NIST AI RMF risk tiers. They then drill down to concrete controls (risk assessments, documentation templates, human-oversight mechanisms), assign responsible owners, and link to evidence repositories. This structured mapping accelerates audit readiness, aligns cross-functional teams, and surfaces gaps before external inspections, turning abstract regulatory language into actionable work.

## Case Study #2: RegTech for AI-Enabled Compliance[9]

Case studies of RegTech deployments show platforms scanning legal texts—using natural language processing to extract "shall" clauses, clustering them into control themes (transparency, risk management, data governance, human oversight), and continuously monitoring whether organizational evidence exists for each requirement. These systems generate real-time compliance dashboards, perform horizon scanning for regulatory updates, and flag missing documentation or control coverage automatically. Experts stress that while RegTech automates monitoring and evidence aggregation, human judgment remains indispensable for interpreting ambiguous legal language, assessing fairness, and evaluating systemic risk—tasks that require contextual understanding machines can't yet replicate.

## Case Study #3: Right to Be Forgotten and Machine Unlearning[16]

Analyses of GDPR's Right to Be Forgotten in AI contexts document organizations piloting machine unlearning protocols—workflows designed to remove or minimize the influence of specific personal data from trained models. Approaches range from retraining from scratch with filtered datasets to incremental unlearning algorithms that selectively adjust parameters, and cryptographically verifiable deletion workflows that produce audit trails proving data removal. These efforts demonstrate to regulators and data subjects that controllers take erasure obligations seriously, even when achieving perfect deletion from complex AI systems remains a frontier research challenge.

# Success Metrics[21]

## Table of Illustrative Metrics

| Dimension | Example Metric | Why It Matters |
|---|---|---|
| **Regulatory Coverage** | % of AI systems mapped to applicable regulations/ frameworks with documented controls and owners | Indicates how systematically compliance is addressed across the AI portfolio |
| **Lineage and Auditability** | Share of regulatory reports and high-risk models with automated end-to-end data lineage and model documentation | Shows readiness to explain and justify outcomes to regulators and auditors |
| **Risk Assessment Maturity** | % of high-risk AI systems with documented risk assessments covering bias, explainability, robustness, and monitoring plans | Reflects whether AI risk is being managed beyond accuracy alone |
| **Erasure and Retention Compliance** | Time to process valid erasure requests across data stores and models; % of systems covered by documented retention and unlearning processes | Measures ability to honor data rights and retention obligations in AI contexts |

# Practical Advice for Leaders[22]

- **Treat compliance as a risk-management discipline.** Integrate GDPR, the EU AI Act, NIST AI RMF, and ISO standards into a coherent program with clear control mappings rather than fragmenting efforts across siloed initiatives.
- **Invest in classification, lineage, and policies-as-code.** Ensure regulatory constraints are enforced automatically and remain auditable across data and model lifecycles, reducing manual burden and compliance drift.
- **Deploy RegTech capabilities judiciously.** Use automation for obligation tracking, evidence management, and horizon scanning while reserving human judgment for ethics, fairness, and systemic-risk decisions—balancing efficiency with accountability.
- **Embed legal and ethical expertise early in AI design.** Training technical teams on compliance basics and aligning governance with

organizational values and public expectations transforms compliance from a barrier into a strategic advantage. This signals to regulators, customers, and society that your AI development work proceeds with both conscience and capability.

## Conclusion

Governing data for compliance in the AI era isn't about paperwork. It's about building systems that are lawful, auditable, and accountable by design. As GDPR and the EU AI Act mature and NIST AI RMF and ISO 42001 gain traction, organizations that embed regulatory intelligence into classification, lineage, model governance, retention policies, and risk-management processes will outpace those still treating compliance as a deployment checklist. At that level, compliance becomes a visible commitment. It signals to regulators, customers, and the public that AI development proceeds with conscience as well as capability.

## Notes

[1] AI auditability is understood here per LinkedIn's "Regulatory Reporting and AI Data Governance."

[2] For AI governance as used in this book, see RSI Security's "ISO 42001 and *NIST AI RMF* Alignment" and Liminal's "Enterprise AI Governance Guide."

[3] Data lineage draws its working sense from *Data Crossroads*' "Part 1: Technological Challenges—Data Lineage" and LinkedIn's "Regulatory Reporting and AI Data Governance."

[4] GDPR principles and distinctions with the EU AI Act are explained in *ModelOp*'s "NIST vs GDPR: AI Regulations and Standards."

[5] Data retention policies and the Right to Be Forgotten are examined in Emergent Mind's "Right to Be Forgotten GDPR Art. 17."

[6] Model governance and lifecycle management are addressed in ISMS.online's "ISO 42001 and the EU AI Act."

[7] Policy frameworks mapped to regulations are surveyed in Anecdotes AI's "AI Regulations in 2025."

[8] Regulatory compliance, as used here, follows *Wiz Academy*'s "AI Compliance Guide."

[9] RegTech capabilities and case studies are developed in *Centraleyes*' "Top AI Compliance Tools," Nemko's "RegTech for AI-Enabled Systems," Inventive AI's "AI Compliance Questionnaire Guide," *FinTech Global*'s "Is RegTech Ready for the Age of AI Model Risk Management," and *Atlan*'s "Regulatory Reporting Automation."

[10] On responsible AI, this book follows *NIST*'s "NIST *AI Risk Management Framework*."

[11] The regulatory frontier and compliance frameworks are surveyed in Liminal's "Enterprise AI Governance Guide," *Obsidian Security*'s "Understanding AI Regulations," and SecurePrivacy's "AI Governance Framework Tools."

[12] Mapping GDPR, EU AI Act, *NIST AI RMF*, and ISO 42001 draws on *Obsidian Security*'s "Understanding AI Regulations," Software Seni's "EU AI Act, *NIST AI RMF*, and ISO 42001 Compared," *Wiz Academy*'s "AI Compliance Guide," ISMS.online's "ISO 42001 and the EU AI Act," and Vanta's "Choosing an AI Compliance Standard."

[13] Classification, lineage, and lifecycle controls are covered in Regulativ.ai's "AI Regulations Overview," *Atlan*'s "Regulatory Reporting Automation," LinkedIn's "Regulatory Reporting and AI Data Governance," and *FinTech Global*'s "Is RegTech Ready for the Age of AI Model Risk Management."

[14] AI risk assessment and model governance are examined in Cloud Security Alliance's "Strategic Implementation of the CSA AI Controls Matrix," Nemko's "RegTech for AI-Enabled Systems," Centraleyes' "Top AI Compliance Tools," RSI Security's "ISO 42001 and *NIST AI RMF* Alignment," and Liminal's "Enterprise AI Governance Guide."

[15] Policy frameworks and policies-as-code draw on Anecdotes AI's "AI Regulations in 2025," Future of Privacy Forum's "GPA 2025," Cloud Security Alliance's "Strategic Implementation," and Nemko's "RegTech for AI-Enabled Systems."

[16] GDPR's Right to Be Forgotten and machine unlearning are examined in EMIL-DAI's "What Happens to the Right to Be Forgotten When AI Never Forgets?," Emergent Mind's "Right to Be Forgotten GDPR Art. 17," Tech Policy Press's "Addressing GDPR's Shortcomings," and Leiden Law Blog's "Erasing Personal Data in an AI Era."

[17] Coordination between technical and legal teams is addressed in Vanta's "Choosing an AI Compliance Standard," SecurePrivacy's "AI Governance Framework Tools," *Vodworks*' "AI Compliance Blog," and Future of Privacy Forum's "GPA 2025."

[18] International data transfers and privacy-enhancing technologies are covered in *Vodworks*' "AI Compliance Blog," *ModelOp*'s "NIST vs GDPR," *Obsidian Security*'s "Understanding AI Regulations," and NIST's "NIST *AI Risk Management Framework*."

[19] The AI compliance control matrix draws on ISMS.online's "ISO 42001 and the EU AI Act," *Obsidian Security*'s "Understanding AI Regulations," NIST's "NIST *AI Risk Management Framework*," SecurePrivacy's "AI Governance Framework Tools," and ISACA's "The Control Matrix Rebooted."

[20] This case study on implementing an AI compliance requirements matrix draws on *Atlan*'s "Regulatory Reporting Automation" and Liminal's "Enterprise AI Governance Guide."

[21] Success metrics—including regulatory coverage, lineage, risk assessment, and erasure compliance—are drawn from Liminal's "Enterprise AI Governance Guide," *Data Crossroads*' "Part 1: Technological Challenges—Data Lineage," NIST's "NIST *AI Risk Management Framework*," and Emergent Mind's "Right to Be Forgotten GDPR Art. 17."

[22] Treating AI compliance as risk management is the practical stance advocated in Software Seni's "EU AI Act, *NIST AI RMF*, and ISO 42001 Compared," LinkedIn's "Regulatory Reporting and AI Data Governance," Centraleyes' "Top AI Compliance Tools," and *Wiz Academy*'s "AI Compliance Guide."

44% of leaders cite regulatory, ethical, or legal concerns as the second-top barrier to AI adoption.

*McKinsey & Company*

"The State of Organizations 2026"

Krivkovich et al.

February 2026

## Key topics explored in this chapter:

- AI Techniques for Unstructured Data
- Architectures for Semantic Search and Contextual Analytics
- Unstructured and External Data Value Stack
- Governance, Security, and Ethics for Unstructured and External Data
- Integrating External Data and Data Enrichment
- Challenges: Volume, Ambiguity, and Integration into Decisions

# WAY 42

# Drive Value from Unstructured and External Data


## Abstract

Most organizational data remains trapped in unstructured formats—emails, documents, images, audio, video—that traditional analytics cannot easily process. Meanwhile, valuable external data from social media, public records, third-party providers, and IoT sensors often goes unused. This chapter explains how to create value from both unstructured and external data through modern techniques including natural language processing, computer vision, data partnerships, and integration architectures that combine internal and external sources for richer insights. And we'll cover how to put into place the governance framework and ethical safeguards essential for transforming unstructured and external data into trusted strategic assets.


## Objective

After completing this chapter, you will be able to:

- Identify high-value use cases for unstructured and external data in your organization.
- Select appropriate technologies for processing text, images, audio, and video at scale.
- Design data partnerships and acquisition strategies that expand analytical capability while managing quality and compliance risks.

- Build integration architectures that combine structured, unstructured, and external data sources.
- Measure value creation from alternative data sources through business impact metrics.

# Terms to Know

**Contextual Analytics**[1] - Analytics that uses context from unstructured and external data—text, images, events—to interpret and explain patterns that raw numbers alone cannot reveal.

**Data Enrichment**[1] - Adding external or unstructured information—sentiment, topics, entities, macroeconomic variables—to internal records to enhance analysis and models.

**External Data Integration**[1] - The process of acquiring, validating, and incorporating data from outside the organization—open data, third-party feeds, web content—into AI pipelines.

**Generative AI**[2] - Models such as large language models and multimodal transformers that generate text, images, or other content, increasingly used to summarize and analyze unstructured and external data.

**Knowledge Graphs**[3] - Graph-structured representations of entities and relationships that integrate structured, unstructured, and external data into a semantically rich, machine-readable form.

**Multimodal AI**[4] - Models and systems that jointly process multiple data types—text, images, audio, video—to infer richer patterns and provide more holistic insights.

**Retrieval-Augmented Generation (RAG)** - An AI technique where a language model first retrieves relevant information from external data sources and then uses that information, along with its own training, to generate an answer.

**Semantic Search**[5] - Search that uses vector embeddings and similarity rather than keywords, allowing users to retrieve content by meaning across text and multimedia.

**Unstructured Data**[6] - Data that does not fit neatly into tables—free text, documents, images, audio, video, and logs—often requiring AI methods for processing.

# Introduction[7]

Roughly 80 percent of enterprise information sits outside traditional row-and-column structures. Emails, contracts, call recordings, sensor logs, images, and videos accumulate at extraordinary rates, but most never enter an analytics workflow. For decades, technical and economic constraints pushed organizations toward the data they could most easily store and query—transactional records, invoices, CRM entries—leaving messier but richer sources unused.

Not anymore. Natural language processing now parses legal contracts at scale, computer vision inspects manufacturing defects in real time, and speech analytics detects customer frustration before complaints are filed. Organizations are also discovering the strategic value of external data. Open government databases, satellite imagery, economic indicators, social media streams, and scientific literature all offer perspectives internal systems cannot replicate. When internal transaction histories combine with external sentiment, weather patterns, or competitive intelligence, the resulting models detect opportunities and risks far earlier than either source could reveal alone.

## AI Techniques for Unstructured Data

### Natural Language Processing and Textual Analytics[8]

Large language models and advanced NLP systems excel at converting enormous volumes of text into structured insights. They identify entities, extract relationships, gauge sentiment, and infer intent across documents that would demand thousands of human hours to review manually. Contract review teams now deploy models that flag critical obligations, financial risks, and renewal clauses buried in thousands of pages of legal language. Customer experience groups mine support tickets, chat transcripts, and product reviews to spot dissatisfaction patterns long before customers churn. Research divisions transform technical manuals, patent filings, and scientific articles into searchable knowledge repositories that surface connections no single analyst would notice.

Knowledge graphs built from these collections of text take the process further. They represent concepts and entities as nodes, with edges capturing how those entities relate. This graph structure enables semantic queries. Users can ask not just "Which papers mention protein folding?" but "What are the upstream and downstream relationships between protein folding and disease pathways discussed in recent literature?" These capabilities accelerate discovery and make implicit connections explicit.

### Computer Vision and Audio Analysis[9]

Computer vision systems, trained on labeled image datasets, now recognize defects on manufacturing lines, classify objects in satellite and drone footage, and assist radiologists in interpreting medical scans. Meanwhile, speech and audio models extract tone, emotion, and conversational intent from recorded calls, adding layers of meaning previously unidentifiable in transcripts alone. When a customer's voice reveals frustration even as their words remain polite, audio analysis flags the interaction for follow-up.

The convergence of these techniques—something called multimodal AI—delivers even greater value. Retailers align product images with customer reviews and social media posts to detect emerging style trends before those trends appear in sales figures. Supply chain managers cross-reference shipping photos with sensor data and logistics records to identify packaging damage patterns. In each case, combining visual, textual, and numerical signals produces a fuller understanding than any single data type could provide.

### Knowledge Graphs as Contextual Scaffolding[3]

Both academic research and enterprise practice demonstrate that knowledge graphs serve as connective tissue between diverse AI systems and heterogeneous data sources. Unlike flat tables or document stores, knowledge graphs organize information as networks of entities and relationships, making it easy to traverse connections that span structured databases, unstructured text, and external feeds.

This graph-based representation improves how NLP and multimodal models interpret ambiguous references. When a document mentions "Apple," context from the graph clarifies whether the text refers to the technology company, the fruit, or a record label. Knowledge graphs also support explainable AI by letting users trace how a model arrived at a conclusion—following edges from input entities through intermediate relationships to final predictions.

In domains such as life sciences and healthcare, multimodal knowledge graphs link clinical notes, lab images, genomic data, and published research into unified frameworks. Clinicians can query these graphs to discover diagnostic patterns, identify candidate therapies, and generate personalized treatment recommendations grounded in the latest evidence.

## Architectures for Semantic Search and Contextual Analytics

### Data Lakes, Vector Databases, and Semantic Layers[10]

Storing and querying unstructured and external data at enterprise scale demands architectural foundations that differ sharply from traditional data warehouses. Data lakes and lakehouses provide the raw storage capacity, but retrieving relevant information from millions of documents, images, or audio files requires more than keyword indexes. Vector databases address this challenge by converting content into mathematical embeddings—high-dimensional vectors that capture semantic meaning. Two documents about supply chain disruptions will possess similar embeddings even if they use entirely different vocabulary, enabling retrieval systems to find conceptually related material rather than just exact phrase matches.

These architectures enable several powerful capabilities. Semantic retrieval answers natural-language questions by pulling relevant passages from vast document libraries. Cross-modal search lets users find images that match a text description or discover text that explains a visual pattern. Retrieval-augmented generation (RAG) pipelines ground generative AI responses in curated enterprise and external content, reducing the risk that models fabricate information.

A semantic or knowledge layer sits atop the raw storage, connecting embeddings, graph entities, and business concepts. When an executive asks, "What supply risks do we face in Q3?" the semantic layer translates that intent into queries across transaction logs, supplier contracts, news feeds, and weather forecasts, then assembles a coherent, contextual answer.

### How Traditional Search Differs from Semantic Search and RAG[11]

The evolution from keyword-based search and static business intelligence to semantic search and RAG-driven analytics represents a shift from literal pattern matching to meaning-aware information retrieval. Traditional systems excel when users know exactly what record or phrase they need, but they struggle with exploratory questions, ambiguous language, or conceptual queries that span multiple sources.

## Comparison: Traditional Search vs Semantic Search

| Aspect | Traditional Search | Semantic Search |
|---|---|---|
| **Query Method** | Exact word or phrase matching against indexes and column names | Uses embeddings and semantic context to interpret intent and retrieve related content, even without exact terms |
| **Data Types** | Primarily structured data and well-labeled text fields | Structured plus unstructured data and external sources (documents, media, open data) |
| **Result Relevance** | High for precise, known-item lookups; can return many irrelevant hits for ambiguous queries | Higher relevance for conceptual and ambiguous queries; one enterprise study reports 25-35% precision gains and up to ~40% fewer irrelevant results for complex queries |
| **Typical Use Cases** | Finding a specific record (for example, invoice ID), simple log searches, fixed-schema BI dashboards | Exploratory research, question-answering over knowledge bases, cross-document analysis, conversational analytics |
| **Explainability and Context** | Limited context; users often must inspect many results and know schema details | Can surface explanations, related concepts, and source snippets; in RAG, answers link back to underlying documents |
| **Integration with Generative AI** | Not designed to feed LLMs directly; mainly supports manual review | Designed to power generative AI via RAG/GraphRAG, providing grounded, context-aware responses from enterprise and external content |

This shift from keywords to semantic context underpins the transition from conventional business intelligence to contextual analytics powered by intelligent assistants that operate across unstructured and external data.

## Unstructured and External Data Value Stack[12]

Translating unstructured and external data into business value requires a layered architecture. Each layer builds upon the one below, transforming raw content into increasingly refined and actionable insights.

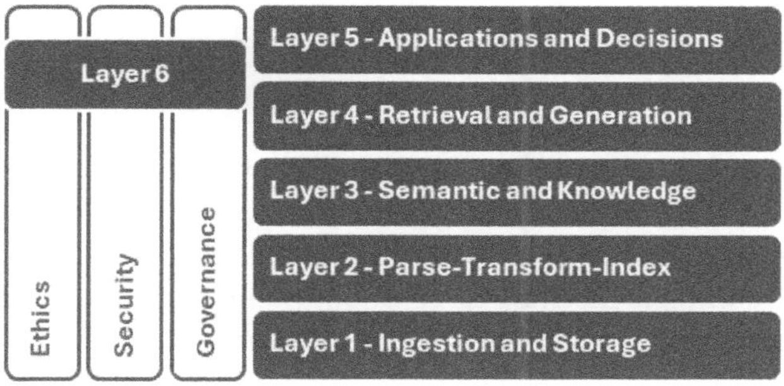


**Layer 1: Ingestion and Storage**

At this foundational layer, raw unstructured data and external feeds from APIs, open data portals, and web content flow into data lakes or lakehouses. Systems capture basic metadata and apply preliminary quality checks: format validation, de-duplication, and high-level compliance screening. The key is to preserve fidelity while filtering out obvious noise.

**Layer 2: Parse-Transform-Index**

Content moves through parsing pipelines that extract text from images, transcribe audio, and pull structured elements from PDFs. NLP and other AI services then extract entities, topics, and categorical labels, enriching each item with descriptive metadata. Vector embeddings—in other words, mathematical representations of semantic meaning—are generated for text, images, and other data types that are then stored in vector databases optimized for similarity search and multimodal AI workloads.

**Layer 3: Semantic and Knowledge**

This is where knowledge graphs and semantic models connect entities, relationships, and business concepts across structured tables, unstructured documents, and external sources. This layer exposes an abstraction that maps user intent to underlying data. So, when someone asks about "supply risk in Q3," the semantic layer can translate that question into relevant metrics, entity relationships, and document collections, enabling a truly contextual analytics experience.

**Layer 4: Retrieval and Generation**

This layer uses retrieval-augmented generation and semantic search services to fetch relevant context for user queries and AI agents. Natural-language interfaces allow generative models to compose summaries, comparisons, and scenario analyses grounded in retrieved evidence. APIs expose these capabilities to downstream applications, ensuring generated insights remain traceable to their source material.

### Layer 5: Applications and Decisions

Here, user-facing applications like intelligent assistants, investigative search tools, risk monitors, and recommendation engines blend structured dashboards with unstructured data and external insights. Rather than replacing traditional metrics, these applications augment them, giving decision-makers richer context without overwhelming them. Integration into existing business intelligence and operational workflows ensures unstructured signals enhance rather than disrupt established processes.

### Layer 6: Governance, Security, and Ethics

Governance, security, and ethics cut across all layers. This is where provenance tracking tags content with its source information and other important data like acquisition timestamp, license terms, and processing history. Source quality ratings are used to distinguish trusted providers from questionable ones. Access controls protect sensitive content. Policy checks ensure compliance with licensing, privacy, and regulatory requirements. Continuous monitoring assesses RAG quality, hallucination rates, and drift in external feeds. And human-in-the-loop review safeguards all of the-important, high-stakes decisions.

## Governance, Security, and Ethics for Unstructured and External Data[14]

Unstructured and external data introduces governance challenges rarely posed by structured internal data. Misinformation, manipulation, bias, copyright disputes, privacy violations, and security breaches all become more likely when organizations ingest content from sources they don't control. Best-practice governance methods address these risks through several mechanisms.

Provenance tracking records where each piece of content originated, when it was acquired, under what license, and through which processing steps it passed. This metadata accompanies embeddings and knowledge graph nodes, ensuring every insight traces back to its source. Source quality management curates which domains and providers the organization trusts, filtering out manipulated content such as deepfakes or synthetic reviews designed to distort models.

Role- and attribute-based access controls determine who can retrieve sensitive documents and use derived embeddings. It's important to remember that ethical use requires careful attention to intellectual property, fair use, and privacy law. That's because public availability doesn't imply lawful processing. Scraping a website may violate terms of service or infringe copyright, and seemingly open content may still be subject to privacy protections.

Governance frameworks emphasize that unstructured content must meet the same quality, lineage, access, and compliance standards applied to structured data. Organizations treating unstructured sources as second-class data assets expose themselves to unacceptable legal, reputational, and operational risk.

## Integrating External Data and Data Enrichment[13]

External data enriches internal records by adding context that organizational systems can't generate themselves. Open government databases, commercial datasets, and web-sourced content all offer signals that improve forecasting, risk assessment, and customer understanding. Effective enrichment begins with selecting sources aligned to specific analytical questions. Credit risk models benefit from macroeconomic indicators; retail forecasts improve with mobility and foot-traffic data; supply chain planning draws on climate and weather feeds.

Harmonizing identifiers and geographies is essential. External signals must link cleanly to internal entities in CRM, ERP, and risk management systems. A dataset providing unemployment rates by county does the organization no good if customer records lack geocoded addresses. Once linked, external features require periodic revalidation. Economic conditions shift, data providers update methodologies, and what was accurate six months ago may no longer represent current reality.

When done well, external enrichment produces hybrid models that fuse transactional data with broader context. Customer purchase histories combined with sentiment from online reviews and local economic indicators yield churn predictions far more accurate than purchase data alone. These models detect early warning signs and surface opportunities that competitors, relying solely on internal data, will miss.

## Challenges: Volume, Ambiguity, and Integration into Decisions[15]

Projects that create value from unstructured data confront three persistent challenges:

- The first is scale. Enterprises accumulate documents, media files, and logs at rates that quickly overwhelm traditional indexing and search systems. Without scalable infrastructure for storage, semantic search, and embedding generation, content libraries become unsearchable "data graveyards."

- The second challenge is ambiguity. Unstructured content resists neat categorization. Language is context-dependent, images can be interpreted multiple ways, and audio recordings carry subtleties that transcripts miss. Automating metadata extraction and entity recognition is essential, but these systems make mistakes. Over-reliance on automated tagging without human review can lead to misclassified content and possible missed insights.
- The third challenge involves integrating insights into decision workflows. AI-derived insights from unstructured sources often arrive with uncertainty. A sentiment analysis model may be 85 percent confident that customer feedback is negative, but what should a manager do with that 15 percent doubt? Clear communication of confidence intervals and model limitations is critical. High-impact decisions—those affecting reputation, regulatory compliance, or financial risk—demand important human-in-the-loop review.

Generative AI raises the stakes. Without a grounding in curated data and clear provenance, these systems can produce outputs that sound convincing but lack evidence. Left unchecked, these fabrications erode trust and weaken the credibility of analytics.

# Case Studies

## Case Study #1: Knowledge Graphs for Research and Enterprise Intelligence[16]

A large-scale knowledge graph, constructed from millions of computer science research papers, illustrates how unstructured external text transforms into structured, queryable knowledge. Researchers used natural language processing to extract entities—authors, institutions, concepts, methodologies—and relationships among them. The resulting graph enables discovery queries impossible with keyword search alone: identifying emerging research clusters, tracing the intellectual lineage of ideas, and predicting collaboration opportunities.

Industry practitioners have adopted similar approaches to connect fragmented enterprise data. One technology vendor described knowledge graphs as "missing links" that integrate siloed systems, external feeds, and unstructured documents into unified semantic layers. These graphs improve question-answering systems, enhance semantic search relevance, and provide the contextual scaffolding that makes AI-driven decision support both powerful and interpretable. What begins as scattered, incompatible content becomes networked understanding accessible to both humans and machines.

## Case Study #2: Semantic Search and Vector Databases for Multimodal AI[17]

Several organizations have deployed vector databases to power semantic search across text, images, and audio, enabling use cases that traditional keyword indexes can't support. Recommendation engines use image embeddings to suggest visually similar products even when metadata is sparse or inconsistent. Visual search applications let users upload a photo and retrieve related images from vast archives based on semantic similarity rather than tags. Conversational agents answer questions by retrieving relevant passages from internal documentation and external content, then using retrieval-augmented generation to synthesize coherent, contextually grounded responses.

These architectures demonstrate that semantic search delivers faster, more relevant discovery than keyword-based methods. Users spend less time sifting through irrelevant results and more time analyzing the insights they need. The shift from literal matching to meaning-aware retrieval fundamentally changes how knowledge workers interact with organizational information.

## Case Study #3: Governance for RAG and Enterprise GenAI[18]

Organizations deploying retrieval-augmented generation at scale have learned that governance can't be an afterthought. Without well-tested data quality controls, metadata management, and provenance tracking, RAG systems propagate outdated, inconsistent, or sensitive content into generated answers. Best-practice implementations profile all ingested content, maintain comprehensive metadata catalogs, enforce role-based access controls, encrypt embeddings at rest and in transit, and align embeddings with source lineage so that every generated insight can be audited back to its origin.

One financial services firm described how inadequate governance led to a RAG system citing deprecated risk policies in client-facing reports. The error was caught before external distribution, but the incident prompted a full governance overhaul. The revised system tags every document with version history, approval status, and access restrictions. Generated responses now include source citations and confidence scores, and high-stakes outputs route through human review before release. These measures increased stakeholder trust and reduced compliance risk, demonstrating that governance and provenance aren't obstacles to innovation—they're enablers of responsible, scalable generative AI.

# Success Metrics[19]

## Table of Illustrative Metrics

| Dimension | Example Metric | Why It Matters |
|---|---|---|
| **Unstructured Data Coverage** | % of high-value use cases that incorporate unstructured or external features alongside structured data | Indicates how broadly unstructured and external data are being used |
| **Semantic Search Effectiveness** | Click-through or satisfaction scores for semantic search/RAG applications vs. baseline keyword search | Measures whether semantic and contextual retrieval improves user outcomes |
| **Knowledge Graph Adoption** | No. of AI applications and reports powered by knowledge graphs or semantic layers, rather than isolated sources | Reflects progress toward contextual, inter-connected analytics |
| **Provenance and Governance** | Share of retrieved/generated insights that expose source citations and provenance metadata to users | Shows whether traceability and governance are integral to GenAI and RAG |

# Practical Advice for Leaders[20]

- **Invest in foundational infrastructure.** Data lakes, vector databases, knowledge graphs, and semantic layers support today's multimodal AI and semantic search use cases, and they also enable emerging techniques like GraphRAG by creating the underlying conditions for diverse data types to be stored, indexed, and queried at scale.

- **Make governance and provenance first-class requirements from day one.** Every unstructured and external source—especially those feeding generative AI systems—should carry metadata about origin, quality, license, and processing history. Provenance tracking and access controls protect the organization from legal, ethical, and reputational risk while building stakeholder trust in AI-driven insights.
- **Prioritize enrichment opportunities where external or unstructured signals demonstrably improve outcomes.** Focus on domains where context matters most: forecasting that improves when internal sales data is combined with economic indicators and sentiment signals, risk detection that sharpens when transaction patterns are enriched with news and social media data, and customer understanding that deepens when purchase histories are linked with support interactions and product reviews.
- **Maintain human-in-the-loop review for ambiguous or high-stakes insights.** When reputational, regulatory, or ethical consequences are significant, generative AI outputs should surface sources, confidence scores, and uncertainty ranges. Systems that expose their reasoning and acknowledge their limitations earn trust; those that present conclusions as unchallengeable facts erode it.

# Conclusion

Driving value from unstructured and external data is about expanding the organization's analytical capability beyond traditional structured sources. When text, images, video, and external signals are integrated with operational data, organizations see patterns and opportunities that were previously invisible.

The technical challenges are real—quality, integration, privacy, and bias all require careful management. But organizations that build the capability to work with alternative data sources create analytical advantages that are difficult for competitors to replicate.

# Notes

[1] Contextual analytics, data enrichment, and external data integration are defined in *DataHub Analytics*' "Unstructured Data: Unlocking Insights with AI" and IBM's "Enable AI Unstructured Data Integration Governance."

[2] Generative AI's role in analyzing unstructured and external data is examined in RAGflow's "RAG Review 2025: From RAG to Context" and *All Things Open*'s "Vector Databases & Semantic Search AI."

[3] Knowledge graphs and their role in connecting structured and unstructured data are surveyed in PingCAP's "Machine Learning Knowledge Graphs 2025," PingCAP's "Knowledge Graph Tools AI Development 2025," *YouTube*'s "Knowledge Graphs in AI: Applications and Future Trends," Beam AI's "5 Ways Knowledge Graphs Are Quietly Reshaping AI Workflows," and Ontoforce's "Knowledge Graphs: Multi-Modal Data and the Next Era of AI in Life Sciences."

[4] On multimodal AI—its definition and applications—see *UnitX Labs*' "Unstructured Data Machine Vision System 2025 Trends & Impact."

[5] Semantic search and its comparison with keyword search are explained in Capsula AI's "Search Engines," *All Things Open*'s "Vector Databases & Semantic Search AI," Whisper IT's "Semantic Search vs Keyword Search," Couchbase's "Semantic Search vs Keyword Search," and Celerdata's "Semantic Search vs Keyword Search."

[6] Unstructured data as an underused enterprise asset is examined in Collibra's "Making Unstructured Data AI-Ready" and TechNative's "What to Expect in AI Data Governance: 2025 Predictions."

[7] Why unstructured and external data matter is addressed in TechNative's "What to Expect in AI Data Governance," Collibra's "Making Unstructured Data AI-Ready," and *CIO*'s "Knowledge Graphs: The Missing Link in Enterprise AI."

[8] NLP techniques, contract analytics, customer-feedback mining, and knowledge graphs from text are covered in Elsherief et al.'s "Navigating the Landscape of Multimodal AI in Medicine," Collibra's "Making Unstructured Data AI-Ready," *CIO*'s "Knowledge Graphs: The Missing Link," Chu et al.'s "Scientific Knowledge Graphs," and *YouTube*'s "Knowledge Graphs in AI."

[9] For computer vision, audio analysis, and multimodal AI applications, see Aperture Data's "Multimodal Data Introduction Part 2" and PingCAP's "Knowledge Graph Tools AI Development 2025."

[10] Data lakes, vector databases, semantic layers, and RAG architectures are covered in Kitemetric's "Top 11 Vector Databases for AI Workloads in 2025," *All Things Open*'s "Vector Databases & Semantic Search AI," Enterprise Knowledge's "Data Governance for Retrieval Augmented Generation (RAG)," and Querio's "Why Semantic Context Is Key to Better AI Analytics."

[11] Traditional keyword search versus semantic search and RAG-driven analytics are compared in Whisper IT's "Semantic Search vs Keyword Search," *All Things Open*'s "Vector Databases & Semantic Search AI," Couchbase's "Semantic Search vs Keyword Search," RAGflow's "RAG Review 2025," *DATAVERSITY*'s "Semantic Search and AI," and Celerdata's "Semantic Search vs Keyword Search."

[12] The six-layer unstructured and external data value stack draws on *UnitX Labs*' "Unstructured Data Machine Vision System," PingCAP's "Machine Learning Knowledge Graphs 2025," Capsula AI's "Search Engines," Wang et al.'s "Data Governance in the Age of Large-Scale Data-Driven Language Technology," Wu et al.'s "Improving Retrieval Augmented Generation Systems," *AtScale*'s "Semantic Layer 2025 in Review," Querio's "Why Semantic Context Is Key," *SAS*'s "The Strategic Imperative," and *Meibel AI*'s "Structure Augmented Generation."

[13] Integrating external data and data enrichment strategies are addressed in Chu et al.'s "Scientific Knowledge Graphs," IBM's "Enable AI Unstructured Data Integration Governance," *CIO*'s "Knowledge Graphs: The Missing Link," Enterprise Knowledge's "Data Governance for Retrieval Augmented Generation (RAG)," and *Meibel AI*'s "Structure Augmented Generation."

[14] Governance, ethics, provenance tracking, and compliance for unstructured and external data are examined in Wang et al.'s "Data Governance in the Age of Large-Scale Data-Driven Language Technology," *SAS*'s "The Strategic Imperative," Enterprise Knowledge's "Data Governance for Retrieval Augmented Generation (RAG)," and IBM's "Enable AI Unstructured Data Integration Governance."

[15] Challenges in unstructured data projects are documented in Aperture Data's "Multimodal Data Introduction Part 2," Whisper IT's "Semantic Search vs Keyword Search," *DataHub Analytics*' "Unstructured Data," *CAS eForum*'s "Bridging Data Divides," and RAGflow's "RAG Review 2025."

[16] Case Study 1 on knowledge graphs for research and enterprise intelligence draws on Beam AI's "5 Ways Knowledge Graphs," Chu et al.'s "Scientific Knowledge Graphs," *CIO*'s "Knowledge Graphs: The Missing Link," and *YouTube*'s "Knowledge Graphs in AI."

[17] Semantic search and vector databases for multimodal AI—Case Study 2—draw on Couchbase's "Semantic Search vs Keyword Search," *All Things Open*'s "Vector Databases & Semantic Search AI," and Kitemetric's "Top 11 Vector Databases."

[18] Governance for RAG and enterprise GenAI—Case Study 3—is grounded in Wu et al.'s "Improving Retrieval Augmented Generation Systems," Enterprise Knowledge's "Data Governance for Retrieval Augmented Generation (RAG)," and *SAS*'s "The Strategic Imperative."

[19] Success metrics—unstructured data coverage, semantic search effectiveness, knowledge graph adoption, and provenance and governance—are drawn from *UnitX Labs*' "Unstructured Data Machine Vision System," *All Things Open*'s "Vector Databases & Semantic Search AI," PingCAP's "Machine Learning Knowledge Graphs 2025," *YouTube*'s "Knowledge Graphs in AI," and Enterprise Knowledge's "Data Governance for Retrieval Augmented Generation (RAG)."

[20] GoodData's "From RAG to GraphRAG," *CAS eForum*'s "Bridging Data Divides," Ontoforce's "Knowledge Graphs: Multi-Modal Data," and RAGflow's "RAG Review 2025" collectively supply the practical leadership advice in this section.

# Tables and Charts Index

## Tables and Charts Index

### WAY 6: Define Roles and Responsibilities



### WAY 7: Champion Diversity



### WAY 8: Create Sustainable Talent Pipelines



### WAY 9: Establish Ethical Leadership in Data and AI



### WAY 10: Encourage Innovation and Experimentation



### WAY 11: Develop Cross-Generational Analytics and AI Talent



### WAY 12: Empower Data Advocates and Citizen Analysts



### WAY 13: Design Agile Analytics Workflows



### WAY 14: Craft Effective Governance Structures

## WAY 36: Foster AI Transparency and Explainability



## WAY 37: Redefine Data Stewardship for AI



## WAY 38: Elevate Data Quality for AI Workloads



## WAY 39: Break Down Data Silos



## WAY 40: Build Trust in Data and Analytics



## WAY 41: Govern Data for Compliance and Regulation



## WAY 42: Drive Value from Unstructured and External Data

# Terms to Know Index

*A term may appear in multiple Ways, with its definition varying slightly depending on the source and context in which it is used.*

## Terms to Know Index

## Terms to Know Index

## Terms to Know Index

# Bibliography

"10 Best Intelligent Automation Platforms You Can Use in 2025." *Marlabs,* 31 Dec. 2024, marlabs.com/post/10-best-intelligent-automation-platforms-you-can-use-in-2025. Accessed 8 Jan. 2026.

"10 Best Retail Hackathon Project Ideas." *PlacementPreparation,* 25 Dec. 2025, placementpreparation.io/blog/hackathon-project-ideas-for-retail. Accessed 19 Jan. 2026.

"2025 DORA Report: AI Trust, Database Governance." *Liquibase Blog,* liquibase.com/blog/2025-dora-report-ai-trust-database-governance. Accessed 1 Feb. 2026.

"2026 AI and Data Analytics Trends in Business Research." *Infomineo,* infomineo.com/services/data-analytics/2026-ai-and-data-analytics-trends-in-business-research/. Accessed 8 Jan. 2026.

"2026: File Data Preparation Efficiency Stats." *Integrate.io Blog,* Integrate.io, integrate.io/blog/file-data-preparation-efficiency-stats/. Accessed 8 Jan. 2026.

"2026 Real-Time Analytics Use Cases." *Streamkap,* streamkap.com/resources-and-guides/real-time-analytics-use-cases. Accessed 8 Jan. 2026.

"5 Steps for Task-Specific Generative AI Model Routing." *Prompts.ai,* 18 Jan. 2026, prompts.ai/blog/5-steps-for-task-specific-generative-ai-model-routing. Accessed 21 Jan. 2026.

"6 Types of Benchmarking Your Business Should Use." *Crewhu,* 2020, crewhu.com/blog/6-types-of-benchmarking-your-business-should-use. Accessed 21 Jan. 2026.

"80% of Your Data Team's Time Is Wasted. It's Time to Fix That." *Aristotle Metadata,* aristotlemetadata.com/80-of-your-data-teams-time-is-wasted-its-time-to-fix-that/. Accessed 8 Jan. 2026.

Acceldata. "Data Quality Agent | Acceldata ADM." *Acceldata,* 23 May 2025, acceldata.io/agentic-data-management/use-cases/data-quality-agent. Accessed 21 Jan. 2026.

Acceldata. "How AI is Transforming Data Quality Management." *Acceldata Blog,* acceldata.io/blog/how-ai-is-transforming-data-quality-management. Accessed 1 Feb. 2026.

"Addressing GDPR's Shortcomings in AI Training Data Transparency with the AI Act." *Tech Policy Press,* techpolicy.press/addressing-gdprs-shortcomings-in-ai-training-data-transparency-with-the-ai-act/>. Accessed 1 Feb. 2026.

"ADKAR Model: The Guide to Successful Change Management." *6sigma.us,* 2025, 6sigma.us/six-sigma-in-focus/adkar-model-change-management/. Accessed 21 Jan. 2026.

Adonis Partners. "Restoring CX with Continuous Improvement and Lean Six Sigma." *Adonis Partners,* 2025, adonispartners.com/restoring-cx-continuous-improvement-lean-six-sigma/. Accessed 21 Jan. 2026.

## Bibliography

Advantech. "Success Stories Edge AI in Medical." *Advantech*, advantech.com/en-us/resources/case-study/success-stories-edge-ai-in-medical. Accessed 8 Jan. 2026.

Aerospike. "Mitigating Model Drift in Machine Learning." *Aerospike Blog*, 2026, aerospike.com/blog/model-drift-machine-learning/. Accessed 21 Jan. 2026.

"Agentic AI Governance: Four Criteria to Evaluate Tools." *Dataiku Stories*, dataiku.com/stories/blog/agentic-ai-governance-4-criteria-to-evaluate-tools. Accessed 8 Jan. 2026.

"Agentic AI in Legacy Transformation: Modernizing Through Intelligent Overlays." *Architecture & Governance*, architectureandgovernance.com/applications-technology/agentic-ai-in-legacy-transformation-modernizing-through-intelligent-overlays/. Accessed 8 Jan. 2026.

"Agile BI Reporting Workflows." *Sigma Computing*, 31 Dec. 2024, sigmacomputing.com/blog/agile-bi-reporting-workflows. Accessed 21 Jan. 2026.

"Agile versus Waterfall: Quick Comparison." *Saviom*, 23 Mar. 2025, saviom.com/blog/agile-versus-waterfall-quick-comparison. Accessed 21 Jan. 2026.

"AI Agents: Human-in-the-Loop Isn't Going Away; It's Getting Smarter." *Squirro Blog*, squirro.com/squirro-blog/ai-agents-human-oversight. Accessed 16 Dec. 2025.

"AI and Data Analytics Maturity Model." *AltexSoft Blog*, altexsoft.com/blog/analytics-maturity-model/. Accessed 8 Jan. 2026.

"AI and Reverse Mentoring: How Cross-Generational Learning Drives Innovation." *LinkedIn Articles*, 21 Aug. 2024, linkedin.com/pulse/ai-reverse-mentoring-how-cross-generational-learning-drives-padin-0pf6f. Accessed 19 Jan. 2026.

"AI Automation ROI and Business Impact: The Complete Guide (2025)." *Hype Studio*, hypestudio.org/ai-automation-roi-business-impact-the-complete-guide-2025/. Accessed 8 Jan. 2026.

"AI Compliance Blog." *Vodworks*, vodworks.com/blogs/ai-compliance/. Accessed 1 Feb. 2026.

"AI Compliance Guide." *Wiz Academy*, wiz.io/academy/ai-security/ai-compliance. Accessed 1 Feb. 2026.

"AI Compliance Questionnaire Guide." *Inventive AI*, inventive.ai/blog-posts/ai-compliance-questionnaire-guide. Accessed 1 Feb. 2026.

"AI-Driven Business Transformation: Strategies and Frameworks." *The Art of Service Academy*, theartofservice.com/course/view.php?id=1503. Accessed 8 Jan. 2026.

"AI-Driven Financial Planning Case Studies." *Lucid*, lucid.now/blog/ai-driven-financial-planning-case-studies. Accessed 8 Jan. 2026.

"AI-Driven Predictive Maintenance in Automotive Manufacturing Using Edge Analytics." *International Journal of Creative Engineering and Management*, ijcem.in/wp-content/uploads/AI-DRIVEN-PREDICTIVE-MAINTENANCE-IN-AUTOMOTIVE-MANUFACTURING-USING-EDGE-ANALYTICS.pdf. Accessed 8 Jan. 2026.

"AI Financial Services Case Studies." *RTS Labs*, rtslabs.com/ai-financial-services-case-studies/. Accessed 8 Jan. 2026.

"AI-First Data Architecture: A Practical Blueprint for the Future of Enterprise Intelligence." *Bix-Tech,* bix-tech.com/aifirst-data-architecture-a-practical-blueprint-for-the-future-of-enterprise-intelligence/. Accessed 8 Jan. 2026.

"AI Gone Wild: Why Shadow AI Is Your IT Team's Worst Nightmare." *Cloud Security Alliance,* cloudsecurityalliance.org/blog/2025/03/04/ai-gone-wild-why-shadow-ai-is-your-it-team-s-worst-nightmare. Accessed 19 Jan. 2026.

"AI Governance 2025: Guide to Responsible Ethical AI Success." *Athena Solutions,* athena-solutions.com/ai-governance-2025-guide-to-responsible-ethical-ai-success/. Accessed 1 Feb. 2026.

"AI Governance and Transparency." *UC AI Council,* universityofcalifornia.edu/governance-transparency. Accessed 16 Dec. 2025.

"AI Governance Best Practices: A Framework for Data Leaders." *Alation Blog,* alation.com/blog/ai-governance-best-practices-framework-data-leaders/. Accessed 8 Jan. 2026.

"AI Governance Best Practices: Frameworks & Principles." *Databricks Blog,* 19 Jan. 2026, databricks.com/blog/ai-governance-best-practices-how-build-responsible-and-effective-ai-programs. Accessed 21 Jan. 2026.

"AI Governance Best Practices: How to Build Responsible and Effective AI Programs." *Databricks Blog,* databricks.com/blog/ai-governance-best-practices-how-build-responsible-and-effective-ai-programs. Accessed 8 Jan. 2026.

"AI Governance Framework Tools." *SecurePrivacy AI Blog,* secureprivacy.ai/blog/ai-governance-framework-tools. Accessed 1 Feb. 2026.

"AI Governance Frameworks." *AI21 Knowledge,* ai21.com/knowledge/ai-governance-frameworks/. Accessed 28 Jan. 2026.

"AI Governance." *Mimecast,* mimecast.com/content/ai-governance/. Accessed 8 Jan. 2026.

"AI Governance Principles." *BigID,* bigid.com/blog/ai-governance-principles/. Accessed 8 Jan. 2026.

"AI Governance: What It Is and Why It Matters." *Palo Alto Networks,* paloaltonetworks.com/cyberpedia/ai-governance. Accessed 8 Jan. 2026.

"AI Guardrails: Protecting Your Brand in the Agentic AI Age." *HCL Software Blog,* hcl-software.com/blog/unica/ai-guardrails-protecting-your-brand-in-the-agentic-ai-age. Accessed 8 Jan. 2026.

"AI Implementation Is a Classical Change Management." *Data Invision,* datainvision.com/blog/ai-implementation-is-a-classical-change-management. Accessed 8 Jan. 2026.

"AI in Production 2025 Collection." *MLOps Community,* mlops.com. Accessed 8 Jan. 2026.

"AI Integration with Legacy Systems." *Tredence Blog,* tredence.com/blog/ai-integration-with-legacy-systems. Accessed 8 Jan. 2026.

"AI Investment Lifecycle." *Productboard Blog,* productboard.com/blog/ai-investment-lifecycle/. Accessed 8 Jan. 2026.

"AI Lifecycle." *Digital Nemko Insights,* nemko.com/insights/ai-lifecycle. Accessed 8 Jan. 2026.

"AI Lifecycle." *Scrut Glossary,* scrut.io/glossary/ai-lifecycle. Accessed 8 Jan. 2026.

## Bibliography


"The AI/ML Tool Evaluation Template: A Guide to Smarter Selection." *Datalere,* datalere.com/articles/the-ai-ml-tool-evaluation-template-a-guide-to-smarter-selection. Accessed 8 Jan. 2026.

"AI Model Lifecycle Governance." *AI Career Governance Blog,* governance.ai. Accessed 8 Jan. 2026.

"AI Model Lifecycle Governance." *Governance.AICareer,* Governance.AI. Accessed 8 Jan. 2026.

"AI Platform Reference Architecture." *RE-CINQ,* re-cinq.com/blog/ai-platform-reference-arch. Accessed 8 Jan. 2026.

"AI Regulations Overview." *Regulativ.ai,* Regulativ.ai. Accessed 1 Feb. 2026.

"AI Sandboxes Let State Government Employees Experiment Safely." *StateTech Magazine,* statetechmagazine.com/article/2025/10/ai-sandboxes-let-state-government-employees-experiment-safely-perfcon. Accessed 19 Jan. 2026.

"AI Security Challenges: Best Practices for 2025." *Invicti Web Security Blog,* invicti.com/blog/web-security/ai-security-challenges-best-practices-for-2025. Accessed 8 Jan. 2026.

"AI Security." *RiseUpLabs,* riseuplabs.com/ai-security/. Accessed 1 Feb. 2026.

"AI-Specific Attack Vectors: Prompt Injection, Data Poisoning, and Model Extraction." *Auxin,* auxin.io/ai-specific-attack-vectors-prompt-injection-data-poisoning-and-model/. Accessed 8 Jan. 2026.

"AI Transparency." *Witness.ai Blog,* Witness.ai. Accessed 28 Jan. 2026.

"AI Vendor Assessment Framework." *Data & Trusted AI Alliance,* dtaalliance.org/work/ai_vendor_assessment_framework. Accessed 8 Jan. 2026.

"AI vs Traditional Methods: A Comparative Analysis of Customer Data Risk Management Approaches in 2025." *SuperAGI,* superagi.com/ai-vs-traditional-methods-a-comparative-analysis-of-customer-data-risk-management-approaches-in-2025/. Accessed 1 Feb. 2026.

"AIRMF Playbook: Govern." *NIST AIRC Resources,* nist.gov/airmf-resources/playbook/govern/. Accessed 8 Jan. 2026.

Al-Hawari, Mohammad A., et al. "Consequence of Resistance to Change on AI Readiness: Mediating-Moderating Role of Task-oriented Leadership and High-Performance Work System in the Hospitality Sector." *SAGE Open,* 5 Dec. 2023, doi:10.1177/21582440231217731. Accessed 8 Jan. 2026.

Alation. "Business Glossary vs. Data Dictionary: What Your Team Needs." *Alation,* 25 Sept. 2025, alation.com/blog/data-dictionary-vs-business-glossary/. Accessed 21 Jan. 2026.

Alation. "Data Mesh vs Data Fabric." *Alation Blog,* alation.com/blog/data-mesh-vs-data-fabric/. Accessed 1 Feb. 2026.

Alation. "Role of Data Stewards." *Alation Blog,* alation.com/blog/role-of-data-stewards/. Accessed 28 Jan. 2026.

Alation. "Understand Data Governance Models: Centralized, Decentralized, Federated." *Alation Blog,* alation.com/blog/understand-data-governance-models-centralized-decentralized-federated/. Accessed 28 Jan. 2026.

Alation. "What Is Data Democratization?" *Alation*, alation.com/blog/what-is-data-democratization/. Accessed 8 Jan. 2026.

Alation. "What is Explainable AI Governance." *Alation Blog*, alation.com/blog/what-is-explainable-ai-governance/. Accessed 1 Feb. 2026.

All Things Open. "Vector Databases & Semantic Search AI." *All Things Open*, allthingsopen.org/articles/vector-databases-semantic-search-ai. Accessed 1 Feb. 2026.

AllHR Software. "AI-Powered Sentiment Analysis for Employee Surveys: 5-Step Guide." *AllHR Software*, 2024, allhrsoftware.com/blog/ai-powered-sentiment-analysis-for-employee-surveys-5-step-guide/. Accessed 21 Jan. 2026.

"Allied OneSource. From Training to Transformation: How Continuous Learning Cultivates a Future-Ready Workforce." *Allied OneSource*, 2024, alliedonesource.com/from-training-to-transformation-how-continuous-learning-cultivates-a-future-ready-workforce. Accessed 8 Jan. 2026.

"Analytics Adoption: Turning Data into Everyday Decisions." *Reveal BI Blog*, revealbi.io/blog/analytics-adoption. Accessed 8 Jan. 2026.

Anecdotes AI. "AI Regulations in 2025: US, EU, UK, Japan, China, and More." *Anecdotes AI*, anecdotes.ai/learn/ai-regulations-in-2025-us-eu-uk-japan-china-and-more. Accessed 1 Feb. 2026.

Aperture Data. "Multimodal Data Introduction Part 2." *Aperture Data Blog*, aperturedata.io/blog/multimodal-data-intro-part2. Accessed 1 Feb. 2026.

ApplyData. "Data Democratization: Empowering All with Self-Service Analytics." *ApplyData*, applydata.io/data-democratization-empowering-all-with-self-service-analytics/. Accessed 8 Jan. 2026.

"Applying NIST's AI RMF to Third-Party AI: Why Your Vendors Are Your Risk Surface." *Cranium*, cranium.ai/resources/blog/applying-nists-ai-rmf-to-third-party-ai-why-your-vendors-are-your-risk-surface/. Accessed 8 Jan. 2026.

"The Art of the AI KPI, Part 1." *Alteryx*, 9 Mar. 2025, alteryx.com/blog/the-art-of-the-ai-kpi-part-1. Accessed 26 Jan. 2026.

"Artificial Intelligence Use in Collaborative Network Processes." *ScienceDirect*, sciencedirect.com/science/article/pii/S2452414X25001062. Accessed 8 Jan. 2026.

arXiv. "Explainability Techniques Applied to Road Traffic Forecasting Using Graph Neural Networks." *arXiv*, arxiv.org/abs/2305.02012. Accessed 28 Jan. 2026.

Atlan. "Data Mesh vs Data Lake." *Atlan*, atlan.com/data-mesh-vs-data-lake/. Accessed 1 Feb. 2026.

Atlan. "Data Stewardship 101." *Atlan*, atlan.com/data-stewardship-101/. Accessed 28 Jan. 2026.

Atlan. "Know Data Governance: Data Governance Models." *Atlan*, atlan.com/know/data-governance/data-governance-models/. Accessed 28 Jan. 2026.

Atlan. "Regulatory Reporting Automation." *Atlan*, atlan.com/know/data-governance/regulatory-reporting-automation/. Accessed 1 Feb. 2026.

Atlan. "What is Data Fabric?" Atlan, atlan.com/what-is-data-fabric/. Accessed 1 Feb. 2026.

## Bibliography


"Atlassian DevOps: DORA Metrics." *Atlassian*, atlassian.com/devops/frameworks/dora-metrics. Accessed 21 Jan. 2026.

AtScale. "Semantic Layer 2025 in Review." *AtScale Blog*, atscale.com/blog/semantic-layer-2025-in-review/. Accessed 1 Feb. 2026.

Attupurathu, Thomas. "Organizational Resistance to AI: A Strategic Approach." *LinkedIn*, 4 Jan. 2025, linkedin.com/pulse/organizational-resistance-ai-strategic-approach-attupurathu-pcwgc. Accessed 8 Jan. 2026.

AuditBoard. "Safeguard the Future of AI: The Core Functions of the NIST AI RMF." *AuditBoard Blog*, 13 Jan. 2025, auditboard.com/blog/nist-ai-rmf. Accessed 21 Jan. 2026.

AuditBoard. "Scaling AI and Analytics in Audit Programs: A Playbook." *AuditBoard Blog*, 13 Jan. 2025, auditboard.com/blog/playbook-how-ai-and-analytics-can-scale-your-audit-program. Accessed 21 Jan. 2026.

Averi AI. "Cross-Functional Knowledge Sharing: Best Practices." *Averi AI*, 10 Oct. 2025, averi.ai/guides/cross-functional-knowledge-sharing-best-practices. Accessed 21 Jan. 2026.

AWS Security Blog. "Enabling AI Adoption at Scale Through Enterprise Risk Management Framework." *Amazon Web Services*, 24 Sept. 2025, aws.amazon.com/blogs/security/enabling-ai-adoption-at-scale-through-enterprise-risk-management-framework-part-2/. Accessed 21 Jan. 2026.

Axero Solutions. "Top Digital Adoption Platforms." *Axero Solutions*, 2025, axerosolutions.com/insights/top-digital-adoption-platforms. Accessed 21 Jan. 2026.

Azure Architecture Center. "AI Agent Orchestration Patterns." *Microsoft*, last updated 12 Feb. 2026, learn.microsoft.com/en-us/azure/architecture/ai-ml/guide/ai-agent-design-patterns. Accessed 21 Jan. 2026.

"Azure Big Data Architectures and Patterns." *Microsoft Learn*, microsoft.com/en-us/azure/architecture/databases/guide/big-data-architectures. Accessed 8 Jan. 2026.

"Azure Databricks: Modern Analytics Architecture." *Microsoft Learn*, microsoft.com/en-us/azure/architecture/solution-ideas/articles/azure-databricks-modern-analytics-architecture. Accessed 8 Jan. 2026.

Babych, Oleksii. "Agent Orchestration Patterns in Multi-Agent Systems: Linear and Adaptive Approaches with Dynamiq." *Dynamiq Blog*, getdynamiq.ai/post/agent-orchestration-patterns-in-multi-agent-systems-linear-and-adaptive-approaches-with-dynamiq. Accessed 21 Jan. 2026.

"Balanced Scorecard Basics." *Balanced Scorecard Institute*, 5 Nov. 2025, balancedscorecard.org/bsc-basics-overview. Accessed 26 Jan. 2026.

"Balanced Scorecard KPI Examples Including a 2026 KPI Scorecard." *Rhythm Systems Blog*, 7 Jan. 2026, rhythmsystems.com/blog/kpi-examples-list. Accessed 26 Jan. 2026.

BARC. "Redefining Data Quality for AI." *BARC Research*, barc.com/redefining-data-quality-for-ai/. Accessed 1 Feb. 2026.

Baum, Kevin, et al. "On the Quest for Effectiveness in Human Oversight: Interdisciplinary Perspectives." *arXiv*, 5 Apr. 2024, arxiv:2404.04059. Accessed 16 Dec. 2025.

Beam AI. "5 Ways Knowledge Graphs Are Quietly Reshaping AI Workflows in 2025-2026." *Beam AI*, beam.ai/agentic-insights/5-ways-knowledge-graphs-are-quietly-reshaping-ai-workflows-in-2025-2026. Accessed 1 Feb. 2026.

"Best Legacy Code Management Platforms: Top 5 Options in 2025." *Swimm Learn,* swimm.io/learn/legacy-code/best-legacy-code-management-platforms-top-5-options-in-2025. Accessed 8 Jan. 2026.

"BI and Analytics Tool Selection Framework: Core Components Required for Success." *Analytics8,* analytics8.com/blog/bi-and-analytics-tool-selection-framework-core-components-required-for-success/. Accessed 8 Jan. 2026.

"Bias Busters: The Cognitive Brakes on the Gen AI Accelerator." *McKinsey & Company,* 15 Oct. 2025, mckinsey.com/capabilities/strategy-and-corporate-finance/our-insights/bias-busters-the-cognitive-brakes-on-the-gen-ai-accelerator. Accessed 8 Jan. 2026.

"Biased Technology: The Automated Discrimination of Facial Recognition." *American Civil Liberties Union of Minnesota,* 28 Feb. 2024, aclu-mn.org/news/biased-technology-automated-discrimination-facial-recognition. Accessed 19 Jan. 2026.

"Big Data Architecture on Azure Data Analytics Platform." *SlideShare,* slideshare.net/slideshow/big-data-architecture-on-azure-data-analytics-platform-229767637/229767637. Accessed 8 Jan. 2026.

Bismart. "Data Fabric Data Integration 2025." *Bismart Blog,* blog.bismart.com/en/data-fabric-data-integration-2025. Accessed 1 Feb. 2026.

Bismart. "Explainable AI: Business Trust." *Bismart Blog,* blog.bismart.com/en/explainable-ai-business-trust. Accessed 1 Feb. 2026.

Boadi, Emmanuel. "Data-Driven Culture - Key Strategies and Case Studies." *LinkedIn,* 11 Mar. 2025, linkedin.com/pulse/building-data-driven-culture-your-organisation-key-strategies-boadi-wkfee. Accessed 8 Jan. 2026.

Booz Allen. "Data Mesh or Data Fabric: Do Better with Both." *Booz Allen Insights,* boozallen.com/insights/data-optimization/data-mesh-or-data-fabric-do-better-with-both.html. Accessed 1 Feb. 2026.

Boston Consulting Group. "A Unified Approach to End-to-End Supply Chain Transformation." *BCG,* 2024, bcg.com/publications/2024/transformative-end-to-end-supply-chain-approach. Accessed 21 Jan. 2026.

Bradley. "Global AI Governance: Five Key Frameworks Explained." *Bradley Insights & Publications,* bradley.com/insights/publications/2025/08/global-ai-governance-five-key-frameworks-explained. Accessed 28 Jan. 2026.

Brandon Hall Group. "Leverage AI for Sentiment Analysis for the Employee Experience." *Brandon Hall Group,* 2024, brandonhall.com/leverage-ai-for-sentiment-analysis-for-the-employee-experience/. Accessed 21 Jan. 2026.

"Brazil's Nubank Is Leveraging OpenAI to Transform Customer Support." *Weekly Fintech Pulse,* substack.com/p/weeklyfintechpulse341. Accessed 8 Jan. 2026.

Breakthrough Growth. "How to Identify and Prioritize High-Value AI Opportunities." *Breakthrough Growth,* 25 Nov. 2024, breakthroughgrow.com/insights/how-to-identify-and-prioritize-high-value-ai-opportunities. Accessed 21 Jan. 2026.

"Bridging Data Divides: AI as a New Paradigm for Unstructured Data." *CAS eForum,* casact.org/article/142716-bridging-data-divides-ai-as-a-new-paradigm-for-unstructured-data. Accessed 1 Feb. 2026.

"Bridging Generational Gaps with Reverse Mentoring." *Chronus,* 28 May 2024, chronus.com/blog/reverse-mentoring. Accessed 19 Jan. 2026.

## Bibliography

"Bridging the Generational Divide: Fostering Intergenerational Collaboration in the Workplace." *PUIIJ*, 24 June 2024, puiij.com/index.php/research/article/view/136. Accessed 19 Jan. 2026.

Brynjolfsson, Erik, and Andrew McAfee. *The Second Machine Age: Work, Progress, and Prosperity in a Time of Brilliant Technologies.* W. W. Norton, 2014.

"Building a Data-Driven Culture: Four Key Elements." *MIT Sloan Management Review*, 23 Jan. 2025, sloanreview.mit.edu/article/building-a-data-driven-culture-four-key-elements. Accessed 8 Jan. 2026.

"Building a Data-Driven Culture: Strategies for Embedding Analytics across the Organization." *Burtch Works Industry Insights*, burtchworks.com/industry-insights/building-a-data-driven-culture-strategies-for-embedding-analytics-across-the-organization/. Accessed 8 Jan. 2026.

"Building a Strong AI Investment Case for Maximum ROI." *Augmented Capital Blog*, augmentedcapital.co/blog/building-a-strong-ai-investment-case-for-maximum-roi. Accessed 8 Jan. 2026.

"Building AI Trust: The Key Role of Explainability." *McKinsey QuantumBlack*, mckinsey.com/capabilities/quantumblack/our-insights/building-ai-trust-the-key-role-of-explainability. Accessed 1 Feb. 2026.

"Building Trust and Governance into Your Data and AI Organization." *Strategy Software Blog*, strategysoftware.com/blog/building-trust-and-governance-into-your-data-and-ai-organization. Accessed 1 Feb. 2026.

"Building Trust in AI and Data Analytics: Implementing Effective Governance Frameworks." *Smart Data Institute*, smartdatainstitute.com/building-trust-in-ai-and-data-analytics-implementing-effective-governance-frameworks/. Accessed 1 Feb. 2026.

"Building Trust in Data and AI: The New Data and AI Ethics Framework and Self-Assessment Tool." *Data in Government Blog*, dataingovernment.blog.go. Accessed 1 Feb. 2026.

"Building Trust Through Transparency." *ISACA Journal*, isaca.org/resources/isaca-journal/issues/2025/volume-3/building-trust-through-transparency. Accessed 1 Feb. 2026.

Buolamwini, Joy, and Timnit Gebru. "Gender Shades: Intersectional Accuracy Disparities in Commercial Gender Classification." *Proceedings of Machine Learning Research*, vol. 81, 2018, pp. 77-91, proceedings.mlr.press/v81/buolamwini18a.html. Accessed 8 Jan. 2026.

"The Business Case for Diversity and Inclusion." *Impax Asset Management*, impaxam.com/assets/pdfs/reports/the-business-case-for-diversity-and-inclusion-us.pdf. Accessed 8 Jan. 2026.

"The Business Case for Diversity and Inclusion -- in Numbers." *Aurora50*, aurora50.com/the-business-case-for-diversity-and-inclusion-in-numbers. Accessed 8 Jan. 2026.

"The Business Impact of Real-Time Dashboards for Industrial IoT Data Streaming Analytics." *HiveMQ Blog*, hivemq.com/blog/the-business-impact-real-time-dashboards-industrial-iot-data-streaming-analytics/. Accessed 28 Jan. 2026.

"Business Intelligence and Analytics Platform Selection Guide." *Info-Tech Research Group*, infotech.com/research/ss/business-intelligence-and-analytics-platform-selection-guide. Accessed 8 Jan. 2026.

"The Business Value of a Data Streaming Platform, Part 2." *Confluent Blog*, confluent.io/blog/business-value-of-data-streaming-platform-part-2/. Accessed 8 Jan. 2026.

BuzzClan. "PDCA Cycle: The Ultimate Guide to Continuous Quality Improvement." *BuzzClan*, 2026, buzzclan.com/quality-assurance/pdca-cycle/. Accessed 21 Jan. 2026.

Bérubé, Vincent, et al. "Redefine AI Upskilling as a Change Imperative." *McKinsey & Company*, 1 Dec. 2025, mckinsey.com/capabilities/people-and-organizational-performance/our-insights/the-organization-blog/redefine-ai-upskilling-as-a-change-imperative. Accessed 8 Jan. 2026.

Calvino, Manuel. "Many Workers Are Using Unapproved AI Tools at Work." *LinkedIn*, 3 Oct. 2025, linkedin.com/posts/manuel-calvino_many-workers-are-using-unapproved-ai-tools-activity-7380208450359726080-Eccb. Accessed 19 Jan. 2026.

"Can Data Analytics Be Automated." *Livelytics*, livelytics.ai/can-data-analytics-be-automated/. Accessed 8 Jan. 2026.

"Case Study: Retail Store AI Computer Vision Analytics." *vSoft Consulting Blog*, vsoftconsulting.com/blog/case-study-retail-store-ai-computer-vision-analytics. Accessed 8 Jan. 2026.

CDAO Magazine. "An Enterprise Approach to GenAI Platforms: Freedom Within a Framework." *CDAO Magazine*, 22 Dec. 2024, cdomagazine.tech/opinion-analysis/an-enterprise-approach-to-genai-platforms-freedom-within-a-framework. Accessed 21 Jan. 2026.

Celerdata. "Semantic Search vs Keyword Search." *Celerdata Glossary*, celerdata.com/glossary/semantic-search-vs-keyword-search. Accessed 1 Feb. 2026.

Censinet. "Healthcare TPRM Best Practices: Building a World-Class Vendor Risk Management Program." *Censinet Perspectives*, 23 Dec. 2025, censinet.com/perspectives/healthcare-tprm-best-practices-building-a-world-class-vendor-risk-management-program. Accessed 21 Jan. 2026.

Centraleyes. "Top AI Compliance Tools." *Centraleyes*, centraleyes.com/top-ai-compliance-tools/. Accessed 1 Feb. 2026.

CH Consulting Group. "Mastering Internal and External Benchmarking." *CH Consulting Group*, 2025, chconsultinggroup.com/masteringinternalandexternal-benchmarking/. Accessed 21 Jan. 2026.

"Challengers Tab -- Submit Challenger Models." *DataRobot Documentation*, datarobot.com/en/docs/mlops/monitor/challengers.html. Accessed 21 Jan. 2026.

"Change Failure Rate—DORA Metrics." *Plandek*, plandek.com/blog/change-failure-rate. Accessed 21 Jan. 2026.

"Choosing an AI Compliance Standard." *Vanta Resources*, vanta.com/resources/choosing-an-ai-compliance-standard. Accessed 1 Feb. 2026.

"Choosing an Enterprise Analytics Platform." *CEI America*, ceiamerica.com/choosing-enterprise-analytics-platform/. Accessed 8 Jan. 2026.

## Bibliography

"Choosing the Right Orchestration Pattern for Multi-Agent Systems." *Kore.ai Blog,* kore.ai/blog/choosing-the-right-orchestration-pattern-for-multi-agent-systems. Accessed 21 Jan. 2026.

Chu, Runhui, et al. "Scientific Knowledge Graphs and Discovery Enhanced by Large Language Models." *Nature Scientific Data,* vol. 12, 2025, nature.com/articles/s41597-025-05200-8. Accessed 1 Feb. 2026.

CIO. "Knowledge Graphs: The Missing Link in Enterprise AI." *CIO,* cio.com/article/3808569/knowledge-graphs-the-missing-link-in-enterprise-ai.html. Accessed 1 Feb. 2026.

"Cisco Data Fabric Transforms Machine Data into AI-Ready Intelligence." *Press Release,* q4cdn.com/812015656/files/doc_news/Cisco-Data-Fabric-Transforms-Machine-Data-into-AI-Ready-Intelligence-2025.pdf>. Accessed 13 April 2026.

Clarifai. "ML Lifecycle Management." *Clarifai Blog,* clarifai.com/blog/ml-lifecycle-management/. Accessed 1 Feb. 2026.

Clarkston Consulting. "Edge Computing in Retail." *Clarkston Consulting Insights,* clarkstonconsulting.com/insights/edge-computing-in-retail/. Accessed 8 Jan. 2026.

"Cloud-Based Analytics Platforms Comparison." *Teradata,* kr.teradata.com/getattachment/70ce540f-027f-4670-844d-74d0dd3bc457/cloud-based-analytics-platforms-comparison-v5.pdf. Accessed 8 Jan. 2026.

"Cloud-based Predictive Maintenance for Industrial Equipment." *JUIT Institutional Repository,* ir.juit.ac.in:8080/jspui/bitstream/123456789/11450/1/Cloud-based%20Predictive%20Maintenance%20for%20Industrial%20Equipment.pdf. Accessed 8 Jan. 2026.

"Cloud Data Platform Architecture Guide." *ChaosSearch Blog,* chaossearch.io/blog/cloud-data-platform-architecture-guide. Accessed 8 Jan. 2026.

"Cloud IoT Analytics Manufacturing Case Study." *Korcomptenz Case Studies,* korcomptenz.com/case-studies/cloud-iot-analytics-manufacturing-case-study/. Accessed 8 Jan. 2026.

"Cloud Modernization Approaches: Rehost, Replatform, or Refactor?" *vFunction Blog,* vfunction.com/blog/cloud-modernization-approaches-rehost-replatform-or-refactor/. Accessed 8 Jan. 2026.

"A Cloud-to-Edge Architecture for Predictive Analytics." *SERENA Project,* serena-project.eu/wp-content/uploads/2019/02/A-cloud-to-edge-architecture-for-predictive-analytics.pdf. Accessed 8 Jan. 2026.

"Cloud vs. Edge Computing Predictive Maintenance." *OxMaint Blog,* oxmaint.com/blog/post/cloud-vs-edge-computing-predictive-maintenance. Accessed 8 Jan. 2026.

"Co-Lab AI Horizon Scanning Activity." *LinkedIn Posts,* linkedin.com/posts/co-lab-engineering_co-lab-ai-horizon-scanning-activity-7366024132234276864-PZEf. Accessed 8 Jan. 2026.

Collibra. "Making Unstructured Data AI-Ready: Unlocking Value for GenAI and Agents." *Collibra Blog,* collibra.com/blog/making-unstructured-data-ai-ready-unlocking-value-for-genai-and-agents. Accessed 1 Feb. 2026.

"Comparative Analysis of Explainable AI Techniques for Intrusion Detection Systems in Healthcare." *PMC,* nih.gov/articles/PMC12252469/. Accessed 28 Jan. 2026.

"A Comprehensive Guide to Implementing the Balanced Scorecard Framework." *The Strategy Institute*, 21 Mar. 2024, thestrategyinstitute.org/insights/a-comprehensive-guide-to-implementing-the-balanced-scorecard-framework. Accessed 21 Jan. 2026.

A Comprehensive Guide to Implementing the Balanced Scorecard Framework." *The Strategy Institute*, 21 Mar. 2024, thestrategyinstitute.org/insights/a-comprehensive-guide-to-implementing-the-balanced-scorecard-framework. Accessed 27 Jan. 2026.

"Comprehensive Review of XAI Methods in Medical Imaging." *Medical Image Analysis*, 2025, sciencedirect.com/science/article/pii/S1361841525002129. Accessed 28 Jan. 2026.

Confluent. "Real-Time Streaming Prevents Fraud." *Confluent Blog*, confluent.io/blog/real-time-streaming-prevents-fraud/. Accessed 28 Jan. 2026.

Confluent. "Supply Chain Optimization with Real-Time Data Streaming." *Confluent Blog*, confluent.io/blog/supply-chain-optimization/. Accessed 28 Jan. 2026.

ConnectWise. "Data Warehouse vs Data Lake vs Data Lakehouse vs Data Mesh: A Comprehensive Comparison." *ConnectWise Blog*, connectwise.com/blog/data-warehouse-vs-data-lake-vs-data-lakehouse-vs-data-mesh-a-comprehensive-comparison. Accessed 1 Feb. 2026.

"Consequence of Resistance to Change on AI Readiness: Mediating." *SAGE Open*, sagepub.com/doi/10.1177/21582440231217731. Accessed 8 Jan. 2026.

"Contextual AI Assistants and the Data Analytics Framework." *Improvado Blog*, improvado.io/blog/data-analytics-framework. Accessed 8 Jan. 2026.

"Continuous Quality Improvement (CQI): Driving Organizational Performance." *6sigma.us*, 2025, 6sigma.us/six-sigma-in-focus/continuous-quality-improvement-cqi/. Accessed 21 Jan. 2026.

"Continuous Quality Improvement (CQI): Driving Organizational Performance." *6sigma.us*, 6sigma.us. Accessed 21 Jan. 2026.

"The Control Matrix Rebooted." *ISACA Now Blog*, isaca.org/resources/news-and-trends/isaca-now-blog/2025/the-control-matrix-rebooted. Accessed 1 Feb. 2026.

"Cross-Generational Mentor Matching: Build Stronger Connections." *Qooper*, 2 July 2025, qooper.io/blog/cross-generational-mentor-mentee-matching. Accessed 19 Jan. 2026.

Cube Software. "How Cube's AI-Powered Collaboration Transforms Cross-Functional Planning." *Cube Software*, 2 June 2025, cubesoftware.com/blog/how-cubes-ai-powered-collaboration-transforms-cross-functional-planning. Accessed 21 Jan. 2026.

"Cultivating a Data-Driven Culture: Leadership Strategies for Success." *Newmath Data Blog*, 22 May 2024, blog.newmathdata.com/cultivating-a-data-driven-culture-leadership-strategies-for-success-594a0a25fe75. Accessed 8 Jan. 2026.

"Cultural Levers Driving Digital Transformation in Banking." *DOOR Training & Consulting*, 27 Oct. 2025, doortraining.com/insights/blog/the-three-cultural-levers-that-drivesuccessful-digital-transformation-in-banking. Accessed 8 Jan. 2026.

Dastin, Jeffrey. "Amazon Scraps Secret AI Recruiting Tool That Showed Bias against Women." *Reuters*, 10 Oct. 2018, reuters.com/article/us-amazon-com-jobs-automation-insight-idUSKCN1MK08G. Accessed 16 Dec. 2025.

"Data & Trusted AI Alliance Launches New Framework to Streamline Responsible AI Procurement." *UKAI*, ukai.co/resource/data-trusted-ai-alliance-launches-new-framework-to-streamline-responsible-ai-procurement.html. Accessed 8 Jan. 2026.

## Bibliography


"Data Analytics Maturity Framework." *DAS42 Newsroom*, das42.com/newsroom/data-analytics-maturity-framework/. Accessed 8 Jan. 2026.

"A Data and AI Driven Culture." *Pointury*, pointury.com/publications/data-culture. Accessed 8 Jan. 2026.

"Data and Analytics Platform Framework for Data-Driven Enterprises." *IBsolution*, ibsolution.com/academy/blog_en/data-and-analytics/business-analytics-platform-framework-for-data-driven-enterprises. Accessed 8 Jan. 2026.

Data Crossroads. "Part 1: Technological Challenges—Data Lineage." *Data Crossroads*, 1 Oct. 2025, datacrossroads.nl/2025/10/01/part-1-technological-challenges-data-lineage/. Accessed 1 Feb. 2026.

"Data Democratization." *RecordPoint Blog*, recordpoint.com/blog/data-democratization. Accessed 8 Jan. 2026.

"Data-Driven Culture - Key Strategies and Case Studies." *LinkedIn*, 11 Mar. 2025, linkedin.com/pulse/building-data-driven-culture-your-organisation-key-strategies-boadi-wkfee. Accessed 8 Jan. 2026.

"Data-Driven Culture Measurement Framework: Foundation of Data Literacy." *CDO Magazine*, 9 July 2023, cdomagazine.tech/opinion-analysis/data-driven-culture-measurement-framework-foundation-of-data-literacy. Accessed 8 Jan. 2026.

"A Data-Driven Culture Will Differentiate the Winners from the Losers." *KPMG*, kpmg.com/us/en/media/news/data-driven-culture-kpmg-insight-2024.html. Accessed 8 Jan. 2026.

"Data-Driven Decision-Making: How to Foster a Culture of Analytics." *LinkedIn*, 28 Dec. 2024, linkedin.com/pulse/data-driven-decision-making-how-foster-culture-analytics-sidd-tumkur-cukpe. Accessed 8 Jan. 2026.

"Data-Driven Decision-Making in Healthcare Supply Chains." *ThinkAI Corp*, 2025, thinkaicorp.com/data-driven-decision-making-a-case-study-in-healthcare-supply-chain-analytics/. Accessed 21 Jan. 2026.

"Data Governance 2025--2026." *MyData Trust*, mydata-trust.com/2026/01/07/data-governance-2025-2026/. Accessed 1 Feb. 2026.

"Data Governance Business Glossary for Trusted Terms." *OvalEdge*, 16 June 2021, ovaledge.com/blog/data-governance-business-glossary. Accessed 21 Jan. 2026.

"Data Governance for AI." *Quinnox Blogs*, quinnox.com/blogs/data-governance-for-ai. Accessed 28 Jan. 2026.

"Data Governance in 2025: What Enterprises Need to Know Today." *TrustCloud Community*, trustcloud.ai/article/data-governance-in-2025-what-enterprises-need-to-know-today/. Accessed 1 Feb. 2026.

"Data Governance in 2025: What Enterprises Need to Know Today." *TrustCloud*, trustcloud.ai/article/data-governance-in-2025-what-enterprises-need-to-know-today/>. Accessed 13 April. 2026.

"Data Governance in the Age of Large-Scale Data-Driven Language Technology." *SIGMOD Record*, sigmodrecord.org/?smd_process_download=1&download_id=14333. Accessed 1 Feb. 2026.

"Data Governance Ownership." *getdbt Blog*, getdbt.com/blog/data-governance-ownership. Accessed 28 Jan. 2026.

"Data Ingestion Reference Architecture." *Databricks Resources*, databricks.com/resources/architectures/data-ingestion-reference-architecture. Accessed 8 Jan. 2026.

"Data Lakehouse Architecture: AI Guide." *Informatica Resources*, informatica.com/resources/articles/data-lakehouse-architecture-ai-guide.html. Accessed 8 Jan. 2026.

"Data Lakes and Data Lake Architecture Fundamentals." *Snowflake*, snowflake.com/en/fundamentals/data-lakes-and-data-lake-architecture/. Accessed 8 Jan. 2026.

"Data Mesh 101: Why Federated Data Governance Is the Secret Sauce of Data Innovation." *Mesh-AI*, 31 Dec. 2024, mesh-ai.com/case-studies/data-mesh-101-why-federated-data-governance-is-the-secret-sauce-of-data-innovation. Accessed 21 Jan. 2026.

"Data Mesh Architecture: Guide for Data Engineers." *Decube Blog*, 1 Oct. 2024, decube.io/post/data-mesh-explained. Accessed 21 Jan. 2026.

"Data Mesh Principles & Implementation: Your Complete Roadmap." *Promethium*, 27 Oct. 2025, promethium.ai/guides/data-mesh-principles-implementation-guide/. Accessed 21 Jan. 2026.

"Data Mesh vs Data Fabric." *Alation Blog*, alation.com/blog/data-mesh-vs-data-fabric/. Accessed 1 Feb. 2026.

"Data Pipeline Security: Best Practices." *Techment Blog*, techment.com/blogs/data-pipeline-security/. Accessed 8 Jan. 2026.

"Data quality challenges in AI-driven decision making." *ScienceDirect*, sciencedirect.com/science/article/pii/S0306437925000341. Accessed 1 Feb. 2026.

"Data Quality Framework." *EWSolutions*, ewsolutions.com/data-quality-framework/. Accessed 28 Jan. 2026.

"Data Security in Analytics Pipelines: Safeguarding Sensitive Information in the Age of Big Data." *Daydreamsoft Blog*, daydreamsoft.com/blog/data-security-in-analytics-pipelines-safeguarding-sensitive-information-in-the-age-of-big-data. Accessed 8 Jan. 2026.

"Data Steward -- Responsibilities, Types & Tips for Success." *Collate*, 31 Dec. 2024, getcollate.io/learning-center/data-steward. Accessed 16 Dec. 2025.

"Data Stewardship 101." *Atlan*, atlan.com/data-stewardship-101/. Accessed 28 Jan. 2026.

"Data Stewardship: Definition, Importance, and Best Practices." *Denodo*, 31 Oct. 2025, denodo.com/en/glossary/data-stewardship-definition-importance-best-practices. Accessed 16 Dec. 2025.

"Data Stewardship: Definition, Responsibilities, and Governance." *Alteryx Blog*, 18 Mar. 2025, alteryx.com/blog/data-steward. Accessed 16 Dec. 2025.

Databahn. "Policy-Driven Security Data Fabric: Automating Compliance at Network Scale." *Databahn Blog*, databahn.ai/blog/policy-driven-security-data-fabric-automating-compliance-at-network-scale. Accessed 1 Feb. 2026.

Databricks. "MLOps Workflows on Databricks." *Databricks Documentation*, 2024, docs.databricks.com/aws/en/machine-learning/mlops/mlops-workflow. Accessed 21 Jan. 2026.

## Bibliography


DataGalaxy. "Data Mesh vs Data Fabric." *DataGalaxy Blog*, datagalaxy.com/en/blog/data-mesh-vs-data-fabric/. Accessed 1 Feb. 2026.

DataGalaxy. "Governance Hype Trust Models." *DataGalaxy Blog*, datagalaxy.com/en/blog/governance-hype-trust-models/. Accessed 1 Feb. 2026.

DataGalaxy. "The Increasing Need for Data Trust." *DataGalaxy Blog*, datagalaxy.com/en/blog/the-increasing-need-for-data-trust/. Accessed 1 Feb. 2026.

DataGalaxy. "Top Data Observability Tools." *DataGalaxy Blog*, datagalaxy.com/en/blog/top-data-observability-tools/. Accessed 1 Feb. 2026.

Datagrid. "How to Orchestrate AI Agents for Unified Data Access." *Datagrid Blog*, 10 Oct. 2025, datagrid.ai/blog/ai-agent-orchestration-guide. Accessed 21 Jan. 2026.

DataHub Analytics. "Unstructured Data: Unlocking Insights with AI." *DataHub Analytics*, datahubanalytics.com/unstructured-data-unlocking-insights-with-ai/. Accessed 1 Feb. 2026.

"DataOps and MLOps in 2025: Building Smarter, Scalable Data Pipelines." *Saventech*, saventech.com/dataops-mlops-in-2025-building-smarter-scalable-data-pipelines/. Accessed 8 Jan. 2026.

DataShift. "4 Top Trends Transforming Data Quality in 2025." *DataShift Blog*, datashift.eu/blog/4-top-trends-transforming-data-quality-in-2025. Accessed 1 Feb. 2026.

Dataversity. "12 Key AI Patterns for Improving Data Quality." *Dataversity Articles*, dataversity.net/articles/12-key-ai-patterns-for-improving-data-quality-dq/. Accessed 1 Feb. 2026.

Davenport, Thomas H., and Randy Bean. "Why Companies That Wait to Adopt AI May Never Catch Up." *Harvard Business Review*, 6 Dec. 2018, hbr.org/2018/12/why-companies-that-wait-to-adopt-ai-may-never-catch-up. Accessed 8 Jan. 2026.

Davenport, Thomas H. *The AI Advantage: How to Put the Artificial Intelligence Revolution to Work*. MIT Press, 2018.

Dawgen Global. "NIST AI RMF in Plain English: Govern, Map, Measure, Manage—Done Right." *Dawgen Global*, 14 Oct. 2025, dawgen.global/nist-ai-rmf-in-plain-english-govern-map-measure-manage-done-right/. Accessed 21 Jan. 2026.

DBS Bank. *Digital Transformation Annual Report 2022*. DBS, 2022, dbs.com/investor-relations. Accessed 16 Dec. 2025.

Decision Management Solutions. "Collaboration Governance and Decision-Making Risks." *Decision Management Solutions*, 2024, decisionmanagementsolutions.com/resources/decision-management-references-briefs/. Accessed 21 Jan. 2026.

Decube. "Best Practices for Data Governance." *Decube Blog*, 14 Nov. 2024, decube.io/post/best-practices-data-governance. Accessed 21 Jan. 2026.

"The Definitive Guide to Implementing Reverse Mentoring (in 2026)." *Academy to Innovate HR*, 23 Nov. 2025, aihr.com/blog/reverse-mentoring. Accessed 19 Jan. 2026.

Deloitte. "Chief Data Officer: AI Governance." *Deloitte Insights*, deloitte.com/us/en/insights/industry/government-public-sector-services/chief-data-officer-government-playbook/2026/chief-data-officer-ai-governance.html. Accessed 28 Jan. 2026.

Deloitte. "Scaling AI for Sustainable Value in Insurance." *Deloitte Insights,* 24 Mar. 2025, deloitte.com/us/en/industries/financial-services/articles/scaling-ai-in-insurance.html. Accessed 21 Jan. 2026.

DelveInsight. "Artificial Intelligence in Remote Patient Monitoring." *DelveInsight Blog,* delveinsight.com/blog/artificial-intelligence-in-remote-patient-monitoring. Accessed 8 Jan. 2026.

"Design with AI -- Learn from Google Experts." *Google Design,* design.google/library/people-ai-research. Accessed 8 Jan. 2026.

"DevOps Research and Assessment (DORA) Metrics." *GitLab Docs,* gitlab.com/user/analytics/dora_metrics. Accessed 21 Jan. 2026.

Digna. "AI-Powered Data Quality vs Traditional Methods: A Game-Changer for Modern Enterprises." *Digna Blog,* digna.ai/ai-powered-data-quality-vs-traditional-methods-a-game-changer-for-modern-enterprises. Accessed 1 Feb. 2026.

DiVA Portal. "Comparing XAI Methods LIME and SHAP on Binary Classification." *DiVA Portal,* diva-portal.org/smash/get/diva2:1874387/FULLTEXT01.pdf. Accessed 28 Jan. 2026.

"Diversity by the Numbers: The Business Case for DEI." *The Diversity Movement,* thediversitymovement.com/content/files/2023/03/By-The-Numbers_Update_2022_Final.pdf.[tdmlibrary.thediversitymovement]. Accessed 8 Jan. 2026.

"Does EPM/BI Project Methodology Really Matter? Waterfall vs. Agile vs. Blended." *US-Analytics,* 31 Dec. 2024, us-analytics.com/hyperionblog/does-epm-and-bi-project-methodology-really-matter. Accessed 21 Jan. 2026.

Domo. "Centralized or Decentralized Data: The Answer Might Be Both." *Domo Blog,* domo.com/blog/centralized-or-decentralized-data-the-answer-might-be-both. Accessed 28 Jan. 2026.

Domo. "Federated Data Governance: A 2025 Guide." *Domo Glossary,* 2025, domo.com/glossary/federated-data-governance. Accessed 21 Jan. 2026.

"The Double-Edged Sword of Generative AI Security: 2025 Guide." *Oligo Security Academy,* oligo.security/academy/the-double-edged-sword-of-generative-ai-security-2025-guide. Accessed 8 Jan. 2026.

"Drafting AI Vendor Contracts: The 10 Clauses That Protect Your Business." *Internet Lawyer Blog,* internetlawyer-blog.com/drafting-ai-vendor-contracts-the-10-clauses-that-protect-your-business/. Accessed 8 Jan. 2026.

Dysnix. "Machine Learning Model Monitoring: Best Practices." *Dysnix,* 2025, dysnix.com/blog/ml-model-monitoring-in-production. Accessed 21 Jan. 2026.

"Edge-AI Integrated IoT Framework for Real-Time Patient Monitoring with Federated Learning and Blockchain-Based Security." *Scientific Reports,* 2025, nature.com/articles/s41598-025-30150-x. Accessed 8 Jan. 2026.

"Edge Architectures and Cloud Computing Impact Manufacturing." *IEB Media,* iebmedia.com/technology/edge-cloud/edge-architectures-and-cloud-computing-impact-manufacturing/. Accessed 8 Jan. 2026.

Edmondson, Amy C., and Jean-François Harvey. *Extreme Teaming: Lessons in Complex, Cross-Sector Leadership.* Emerald, 2017.

## Bibliography

Elsherief, Mai, et al. "Navigating the Landscape of Multimodal AI in Medicine." *Science Direct,* 2025, sciencedirect.com/science/article/abs/pii/S0957417425032580. Accessed 1 Feb. 2026.

"Embedded Analytics Examples." *Qrvey Blog,* qrvey.com/blog/embedded-analytics-examples/. Accessed 8 Jan. 2026.

Emergent Mind. "Right to Be Forgotten GDPR Art. 17." *Emergent Mind,* emergentmind.com/topics/right-to-be-forgotten-gdpr-art-17. Accessed 1 Feb. 2026.

EMIL-DAI. "What Happens to the Right to Be Forgotten When AI Never Forgets?" *EMIL-DAI,* emildai.eu/what-happens-to-the-right-to-be-forgotten-when-ai-never-forgets-is-data-erasure-an-illusion/. Accessed 1 Feb. 2026.

"Empowering Customer Support Agents with Generative AI." *Building Nubank,* nubank.com/empowering-customer-support-agents-with-generative-ai. Accessed 8 Jan. 2026.

"Enable User Adoption of BI Tools with Embedded BI." *Elegant MicroWeb,* elegantmicroweb.com/uncategorized/enable-user-adoption-of-bi-tools-with-embedded-bi.htm. Accessed 8 Jan. 2026.

"End-to-End Supply Chain: Meaning, Benefits, and How to Implement." *13 Feb. 2025,* inboundlogistics.com/articles/end-to-end-supply-chain/. Accessed 21 Jan. 2026.

"Enhancing Trust in AI-Assisted Medical Imaging: A Structured Review of Explainability Techniques." *Nature Digital Medicine,* 2025, nature.com/articles/s41746-025-02023-0. Accessed 28 Jan. 2026.

"Enhancing Trust in AI-Assisted Medical Imaging: A Structured Review of Explainability Techniques." *PMC,* nih.gov/articles/PMC12809972/. Accessed 28 Jan. 2026.

"Enterprise AI Governance Guide." *Liminal Blog,* liminal.ai/blog/enterprise-ai-governance-guide. Accessed 28 Jan. 2026.

"Enterprise AI Technology Stack: Layered Architecture." *LinkedIn Articles,* linkedin.com/pulse/enterprise-ai-technology-stack-layered-architecture-mahmoud-abufadda-qw76f. Accessed 8 Jan. 2026.

Enterprise Knowledge. "Data Governance for Retrieval Augmented Generation (RAG)." *Enterprise Knowledge,* enterprise-knowledge.com/data-governance-for-retrieval-augmented-generation-rag/. Accessed 1 Feb. 2026.

"Enterprise Strategy Group Evaluates BigQuery TCO." *Google Cloud Blog,* google.com/blog/products/data-analytics/enterprise-strategy-group-evaluates-bigquery-tco/. Accessed 8 Jan. 2026.

"Equity, Diversity & Inclusion Report 2024." *Impax Asset Management Group plc,* impaxam.com/assets/pdfs/reports/Impax-Equity-Diversity-and-Inclusion-Report.pdf.[impaxam]. Accessed 8 Jan. 2026.

"Erasing Personal Data in an AI Era." *Leiden Law Blog,* leidenlawblog.nl/articles/erasing-personal-data-in-an-ai-era. Accessed 1 Feb. 2026.

"Ethical and Legal Considerations in Healthcare AI." *Frontiers in Artificial Intelligence,* nih.gov/articles/PMC12076083/>. Accessed 19 Jan. 2026.

"Ethics and Governance of Artificial Intelligence for Health: WHO Guidance." *World Health Organization,* 2021, who.int/publications/i/item/9789240029200. Accessed 19 Jan. 2026.

"EU AI Act, NIST AI RMF, and ISO 42001 Compared: Which Framework to Implement First." *Software Seni,* softwareseni.com/eu-ai-act-nist-ai-rmf-and-iso-42001-compared-which-framework-to-implement-first/. Accessed 1 Feb. 2026.

European Commission. "High-Level Summary of the AI Act." *Artificial Intelligence Act,* 26 Feb. 2024, digital-strategy.ec.europa.eu/en/policies/regulatory-framework-ai. Accessed 21 Jan. 2026.

EWSolutions. "AI and Data Governance." *EWSolutions,* ewsolutions.com/ai-and-data-governance/. Accessed 28 Jan. 2026.

EWSolutions. "Data Stewardship and Artificial Intelligence." *EWSolutions,* ewsolutions.com/data-stewardship-and-artificial-intelligence/. Accessed 28 Jan. 2026.

"Expert Advice on Integrating APIs with Legacy Systems in 2025." *Moesif Blog,* moesif.com/blog/monitoring/Expert-Advice-on-Integrating-APIs-with-Legacy-Systems-in-2025/. Accessed 8 Jan. 2026.

"Exploring Digital Transformation and Digital Adoption -- WalkMe Fundamentals." *SAP Learning,* sap.com/courses/starting-your-digital-adoption-journey-walkme-fundamentals/exploring-digital-transformation-and-digital-adoption. Accessed 8 Jan. 2026.

"Extracting Value from AI in Banking: Rewiring the Enterprise." *McKinsey & Company,* 2023, mckinsey.com/industries/financial-services/our-insights/extracting-value-from-ai-in-banking-rewiring-the-enterprise. Accessed 21 Jan. 2026.

EY. "Solutions for Banks - EY Model Risk Management." *EY,* 28 Nov. 2024, ey.com/en_sk/solutions-for-banks-ey-model-risk-management. Accessed 21 Jan. 2026.

Family Medicine and Community Health. "A Scoping Review of Continuous Quality Improvement in Healthcare." 2024, pmc.ncbi.nlm.nih.gov/articles/PMC11031995/. Accessed 21 Jan. 2026.

"Federated Governance Complete Guide." *Lifebit Blog,* lifebit.ai/blog/federated-governance-complete-guide/. Accessed 28 Jan. 2026.

"Federated vs. Centralized Data Governance: Which Model is Right for Your Business." *LinkedIn Pulse,* linkedin.com/pulse/federated-vs-centralized-data-governance-which-model-vijay-6tfdc. Accessed 28 Jan. 2026.

"Finding the Right Balance Between Centralised & Federated AI Governance." *LinkedIn Articles,* 22 July 2025, linkedin.com/pulse/finding-right-balance-between-centralised-federated-ai-gonzalez-u9i2e/. Accessed 21 Jan. 2026.

FinOps Foundation. "Unlocking AI Business Value With FinOps." *FinOps Foundation Working Group,* 12 May 2025, finops.org/wg/unlocking-ai-business-value-with-finops/. Accessed 21 Jan. 2026.

"Fintech Company Uses Gen AI to Improve Customer Experience." *Cloudelligent Case Studies,* cloudelligent.com/case-study/fintech-company-gen-ai/. Accessed 8 Jan. 2026.

Flevy / Accenture Insight. "How Can KPIs Be Designed to Drive Cross-Functional Collaboration?" *Flevy,* 31 Dec. 2024, flevy.com/topic/key-performance-indicators/question/optimizing-kpis-enhanced-cross-functional-collaboration-innovation. Accessed 21 Jan. 2026.

## Bibliography


FlowHunt. "The Ultimate Guide to AI Meeting Notes in 2024." *FlowHunt*, 21 July 2025, flowhunt.io/blog/the-ultimate-guide-to-ai-meeting-notes-in-2024/. Accessed 21 Jan. 2026.

Forbes. "Building Trust in Motion: Ethical Data and Responsible AI." *Forbes Technology Council*, forbes.com/councils/forbestechcouncil/2025/03/24/building-trust-in-motion-ethical-data-and-responsible-ai/. Accessed 1 Feb. 2026.

"Foster a Culture of Data Literacy." *IBM*, 18 Sept. 2024, ibm.com/think/insights/data-differentiator/data-literacy-culture. Accessed 8 Jan. 2026.

Fountaine, Tim, et al. "Building the AI-Powered Organization." *Harvard Business Review*, July-Aug. 2019, hbr.org/2019/07/building-the-ai-powered-organization. Accessed 8 Jan. 2026.

"A Framework for Real-Time Fraud Detection Using Stream Analytics and Adaptive Machine Learning." *Propulsion Technology Journal*, propulsiontechjournal.com/index.php/journal/article/download/9543/5822/16152. Accessed 28 Jan. 2026.

"From Pilot to Production: How Enterprises Are Successfully Scaling AI with MLOps (10 December 2025)." *Business20Channel*, business20channel.tv/from-pilot-to-production-how-enterprises-are-successfully-scaling-ai-with-mlops-10-december-2025. Accessed 8 Jan. 2026.

"From Pilot to Production: Scaling ML-Driven Products across Global Operations." *The Nirvana Lab Blog*, thenirvanalab.com/blog/from-pilot-to-production-scaling-ml-driven-products-across-global-operations/. Accessed 8 Jan. 2026.

"From Raw Data to Real Profits: A Primer for Building a Thriving Data Business." *McKinsey & Company*, mckinsey.com/capabilities/tech-and-ai/our-insights/from-raw-data-to-real-profits-a-primer-for-building-a-thriving-data-business. Accessed 8 Jan. 2026.

"The Future of Jobs Report 2025." *World Economic Forum*, 24 Aug. 2025, weforum.org/publications/the-future-of-jobs-report-2025. Accessed 8 Jan. 2026.

*The Future of Jobs Report 2025*. World Economic Forum, 7 Jan. 2025, weforum.org/publications/the-future-of-jobs-report-2025. Accessed 8 Jan. 2026.

Futurum Group. "WalkMe's Digital Adoption Platform Helps Remove EX Friction Points." *Futurum Group*, 2023, futurumgroup.com/insights/walkmes-digital-adoption-platform-helps-remove-ex-friction-points/. Accessed 21 Jan. 2026.

Gable. "Federated vs. Centralized Data Governance." *Gable Blog*, gable.ai/blog/federated-vs-centralized-data-governance. Accessed 28 Jan. 2026.

"Galp Hackathon Retail 4.0 Harnesses the Power of AI." *Galp Upcoming Energies*, 31 May 2025, galp.com/pt/upcomingenergies/en/node/180. Accessed 19 Jan. 2026.

"The Gen-AI Divide: Why 95% of AI Projects Fail." *RapidCanvas Blog*, rapidcanvas.ai/blogs/the-gen-ai-divide-why-95-of-ai-projects-fail. Accessed 8 Jan. 2026.

"The gen AI skills revolution: A new talent strategy." *McKinsey & Company*, 28 Aug. 2024, mckinsey.com/capabilities/tech-and-ai/our-insights/the-gen-ai-skills-revolution-rethinking-your-talent-strategy. Accessed 19 Jan. 2026.

"Gen Z as AI Mentors: Bridging the Generational Divide at Work." *LLSSA*. Accessed 19 Jan. 2026.

"Gen Z Is Teaching the Workplace: The Rise of Reverse Mentoring." *Davron,* 20 Oct. 2025, davron.net/genz-reverse-mentoring-workplace. Accessed 19 Jan. 2026.

"Gender Diversity on the Rise across UAE Boards, Reveals Aurora50 Report." *Gulf Business,* gulfbusiness.com/gender-diversity-on-the-rise-across-uae-boards-reveals-aurora50-report.[gulfbusiness]. Accessed 8 Jan. 2026.

"Generational Diversity and Team Innovation: The Roles of Conflict and Shared Leadership." *Frontiers in Psychology,* 6 Jan. 2025, pmc.ncbi.nlm.nih.gov/articles/PMC11753251. Accessed 19 Jan. 2026.

"Generative AI: Report, May 2025." *NIHR,* io.nihr.ac.uk/wp-content/uploads/2025/05/Generative-AI-Report_May-2025_.pdf. Accessed 8 Jan. 2026.

getdbt. "AI Data Pipelines." *getdbt Blog,* getdbt.com/blog/ai-data-pipelines. Accessed 1 Feb. 2026.

getElyxai. "Data Quality Best Practices." *getElyxai Blog,* getelyxai.com/en/blog/data-quality-best-practices. Accessed 1 Feb. 2026.

GoodData. "From RAG to GraphRAG: Knowledge Graphs, Ontologies, and Smarter AI." *GoodData Blog,* gooddata.com/blog/from-rag-to-graphrag-knowledge-graphs-ontologies-and-smarter-ai/. Accessed 1 Feb. 2026.

Google Developers Blog. "Developer's Guide to Multi-Agent Patterns in ADK." *Google,* 16 Dec. 2025, developers.googleblog.com/developers-guide-to-multi-agent-patterns-in-adk/. Accessed 21 Jan. 2026.

"Governance Playbook: Govern." *NIST AIRC Resources,* nist.gov/airmf-resources/playbook/govern/. Accessed 8 Jan. 2026.

"GPA 2025: AI Development and Human Oversight." *Future of Privacy Forum,* fpf.org/blog/gpa-2025-ai-development-and-human-oversight-of-decisions-involving-ai-systems-were-this-years-focus-for-global-privacy-regulators/. Accessed 1 Feb. 2026.

Green, Aaron. "How Growth-Focused Organizations Can Meet the Needs of a Shifting Workforce." *Harvard Business Review,* 21 Sept. 2023, hbr.org/sponsored/2023/09/how-growth-focused-organizations-can-meet-the-needs-of-a-shifting-workforce. Accessed 20 Jan. 2026.

"A Guide to Prompt Injection Attacks." *Lakera Blog,* lakera.ai/blog/guide-to-prompt-injection. Accessed 8 Jan. 2026.

"Harnessing the Power of Employee Resource Groups for Business Success." *C-Suite Strategy,* 11 June 2025, c-suite-strategy.com/blog/harnessing-the-power-of-employee-resource-groups-for-business-success. Accessed 19 Jan. 2026.

Hazan, Eric, et al. "A New Future of Work: The Race to Deploy AI and Raise Skills in Europe and Beyond." *McKinsey Global Institute,* May 2024, mckinsey.com/mgi/our-research/a-new-future-of-work-the-race-to-deploy-ai-and-raise-skills-in-europe-and-beyond. Accessed 9 Jan. 2026.

"High-Level Summary of the EU Artificial Intelligence Act." *ArtificialIntelligenceAct.eu,* artificialintelligenceact.eu/high-level-summary/. Accessed 8 Jan. 2026.

## Bibliography

"How AI Is Reshaping Work and Human Psychology." *Lab for Applied Artificial Intelligence,* 31 Mar. 2025, luc.edu/quinlan/whyquinlan/centersandlabs/labforappliedartificialintelligence/research/2025/3rdquarter2025/howaiisreshapingworkandhumanpsychology. Accessed 19 Jan. 2026.

"How AI-Powered KPIs Measure Success Better." *Boston Consulting Group,* 11 Feb. 2024, bcg.com/publications/2024/how-ai-powered-kpis-measure-success-better. Accessed 27 Jan. 2026.

"How Citizen-Built Apps Expose Data and 5 Moves to Close the Gap." *Citizen Development,* 22 July 2025, linkedin.com/posts/citizendevelopment_cimulate-activity-7353755847128170498-rBsZ. Accessed 19 Jan. 2026.

"How Cultural Change Drives Successful Data Transformation." *Meritshot Blogs,* meritshot.com/blogs/how-cultural-change-drives-successful-data-transformation. Accessed 12 Dec. 2025.

"How Diverse Teams Unlock Product Innovation." *Mind the Product,* 31 Jan. 2024, mindtheproduct.com/how-diverse-teams-unlock-product-innovation.[9]. Accessed 8 Jan. 2026.

"How Humans in the Loop Powers Responsible AI Through Data Annotation." *Humans in the Loop,* humansintheloop.org/how-humans-in-the-loop-powers-responsible-ai-through-data-annotation/. Accessed 28 Jan. 2026.

"How IBM Process Mining Enables Workflow Optimization at Scale." *Nexright,* nexright.com/enterprise-process-mining-workflow-optimization/. Accessed 8 Jan. 2026.

"How Modernizing Legacy Systems Drives Success in 2025." *Cygnis Blog,* 9 Dec. 2024, cygnis.co/blog/legacy-system-modernization-2025/. Accessed 8 Jan. 2026.

"How to Avoid Talent Gaps with Data-Driven Succession Planning." *Visier,* 22 Nov. 2022, visier.com/blog/how-to-avoid-talent-gaps-with-data-driven-succession-planning. Accessed 19 Jan. 2026.

"How to Become a Data Steward." *Dataversity Articles,* dataversity.net/articles/how-to-become-a-data-steward/. Accessed 28 Jan. 2026.

"How to Build a Business Glossary for Data Governance." *Select Star,* 19 Feb. 2025, selectstar.com/resources/business-glossary-data-governance. Accessed 21 Jan. 2026.

"How to Build a Data-Driven Culture with AI." *AZTech Training,* aztechtraining.com/articles/how-to-build-a-data-driven-culture-with-ai. Accessed 8 Jan. 2026.

"How to Build a Future Radar That Actually Works." *Purpose & Means,* purposeandmeans.io/how-to-build-a-future-radar-that-actually-works. Accessed 8 Jan. 2026.

"How to Build Your Talent Pipeline: Succession Planning Starts with High-Potential Employees." *Page Executive,* 13 Dec. 2023, pageexecutive.com/advice/insights/how-build-your-talent-pipeline-succession-planning-starts-high-potential-employees. Accessed 19 Jan. 2026.

"How to Empower Leaders with AI for Generational Collaboration." *Aquent,* 4 Dec. 2025, aquent.com/blog/how-to-empower-leaders-with-ai-for-generational-collaboration. Accessed 19 Jan. 2026.

"How to Horizon Scan: A Guideline." *Futures Platform,* futuresplatform.com/blog/how-to-horizon-scanning-guideline. Accessed 8 Jan. 2026.

"How Value-First Thinking Transforms Organizational AI Success." *LinkedIn Articles,* 17 Aug. 2025, linkedin.com/pulse/outcome-based-ai-management-how-value-first-thinking-andre-d8cqe/. Accessed 21 Jan. 2026.

"Human-Centred Mechanism Design with Democratic AI." *DeepMind Blog,* deepmind.google/blog/human-centred-mechanism-design-with-democratic-ai. Accessed 8 Jan. 2026.

"Human in the Loop AI." *Parseur Blog,* parseur.com/blog/human-in-the-loop-ai. Accessed 1 Feb. 2026.

"Human in the Loop AI: Why People Still Matter in an Automated World." *Sogolytics Blog,* sogolytics.com/blog/human-in-the-loop-ai/. Accessed 8 Jan. 2026.

"Human-in-the-Loop for AI: A Collaborative Future in Research Workflows." *metaphacts Blog,* blog.me. Accessed 16 Dec. 2025.

"The Human-in-the-Loop Safety Net." *Fast Company,* fastcompany.com/91475665/the-human-in-the-loop-safety-net. Accessed 8 Jan. 2026.

"Human in the Loop: The Key to Ethical and Effective AI in 2025." *LinkedIn,* linkedin.com/pulse/human-in-the-loop-key-ethical-effective-ai-2025-radu-sargu-naoxf. Accessed 1 Feb. 2026.

"Human in the Loop: Why Trust and Responsibility Are the True Accelerators of AI." *Xcelerator Community,* siemens.com/public/blogs/human-in-the-loop-why-trust-and-responsibility-are-the-true-accelerators-of-ai-2025-10-14. Accessed 1 Feb. 2026.

"Human-Loop Evals and Automation Limits." *Statsig Perspectives,* statsig.com/perspectives/humanloopevals-automationlimits. Accessed 8 Jan. 2026.

Hunt, Vivian, et al. "Delivering through Diversity." *McKinsey & Company,* Jan. 2018, mckinsey.com/capabilities/people-and-organizational-performance/our-insights/delivering-through-diversity. Accessed 8 Jan. 2026.

"Hybrid Cloud Internet Banking Architecture." *Teamvoy,* teamvoy.com/portfolio/hybrid-cloud-internet-banking-architecture/. Accessed 8 Jan. 2026.

IBM. "Data Lakehouse vs Data Fabric vs Data Mesh." *IBM Think Topics,* ibm.com/think/topics/data-lakehouse-vs-data-fabric-vs-data-mesh. Accessed 1 Feb. 2026.

IBM. "Data Management vs Data Fabric vs Data Mesh." *IBM Think Topics,* ibm.com/think/topics/data-management-vs-data-fabric-vs-data-mesh. Accessed 1 Feb. 2026.

IBM. "Enable AI Unstructured Data Integration Governance." *IBM Think Insights,* ibm.com/think/insights/enable-ai-unstructured-data-integration-governance. Accessed 1 Feb. 2026.

IBM Institute for Business Value. "AI - Research, Reports, and Insights." *IBM,* 11 Dec. 2025, ibm.com/thought-leadership/institute-business-value/en-us/technology/ai-cognitive. Accessed 21 Jan. 2026.

"IBM Process Mining." *IBM,* 2024, ibm.com/products/process-mining. Accessed 8 Jan. 2026.

## Bibliography

IBM. "Semantic Layer." *IBM Think Topics*, ibm.com/think/topics/semantic-layer. Accessed 1 Feb. 2026.

"Implementing and Scaling AI Projects." *Agility-at-Scale*, agility-at-scale.com/ai/ai-strategy/scaling-ai-from-pilots-to-enterprise-wide-deployment/. Accessed 8 Jan. 2026.

Impressico. "Data Fabric Blueprint." *Impressico*, impressico.com/blog/data-fabric-blueprint/. Accessed 1 Feb. 2026.

"Improve Real-Time Decision Making with Real-Time Supply Chain Data and Visibility." *Michigan State University Online Resources*, michiganstateuniversityonline.com/resources/supply-chain/improve-real-time-decision-making-with-real-time-supply-chain-data/. Accessed 28 Jan. 2026.

"Improving Retrieval Augmented Generation Systems via Answer Selection and Reflection." *Science Direct*, sciencedirect.com/science/article/pii/S2666792425000551. Accessed 1 Feb. 2026.

"Innovative Human Capital: Applied Agentic AI for Organizational Transformation." *Innovative Human Capital*, 27 Dec. 2025, innovativehumancapital.com/article/applied-agentic-ai-for-organizational-transformation. Accessed 8 Jan. 2026.

"Inside FourKites Logistics Platform: Data Streaming for AI and End-to-End Visibility in the Supply Chain." *Kai Waehner Blog*, kai-waehner.de/blog/2025/07/14/inside-fourkites-logistics-platform-data-streaming-for-ai-and-end-to-end-visibility-in-the-supply-chain/. Accessed 28 Jan. 2026.

"Intalio's Process Mining Strategy: Using Analytics to Identify and Quantify Automation ROI in Workflow." *Intalio Blogs*, intalio.com/blogs/intalio-s-process-mining-strategy-using-analytics-to-identify-and-quantify-automation-roi-in-workflow. Accessed 8 Jan. 2026.

"Integrating AI in Cultural Change Management: A Strategic Guide to Data-Driven Transformation." *Culture Partners Insights*, culturepartners.com/insights/integrating-ai-in-cultural-change-management-a-strategic-guide-to-data-driven-transformation/. Accessed 8 Jan. 2026.

"Intelligent Task Routing: Assigning the Right Labelers to the Right Jobs." *KeyLabs Blog*, keylabs.ai/blog/intelligent-task-routing-assigning-the-right-labelers-to-the-right-jobs/. Accessed 8 Jan. 2026.

InTime Tec. "Data Quality in AI: Challenges, Importance & Best Practices." *InTime Tec Blog*, blog.intimetec.com/data-quality-in-ai-challenges-importance-best-practices. Accessed 28 Jan. 2026.

"Introducing Agile Analytics." *Thoughtworks*, 19 July 2023, thoughtworks.com/en-us/insights/blog/introducing-agile-analytics. Accessed 21 Jan. 2026.

"Investigating the Applications of AI Fraud Detection in Real-Time Transaction Monitoring." *International Journal For Multidisciplinary Research*, ijfmr.com/papers/2025/6/61545.pdf. Accessed 28 Jan. 2026.

"Is Human Oversight to AI Systems Still Possible." *Technology in Society*, sciencedirect.com/science/article/pii/S1871678424005636.[21]. Accessed 8 Jan. 2026.

"Is Human Oversight to AI Systems Still Possible." *Technology in Society*, sciencedirect.com/science/article/pii/S1871678424005636. Accessed 16 Dec. 2025.

"Is RegTech Ready for the Age of AI Model Risk Management." *FinTech Global*, fintech.global/2025/10/30/is-regtech-ready-for-the-age-of-ai-model-risk-management. Accessed 1 Feb. 2026.

"ISO 42001 and NIST AI RMF Alignment." *RSI Security Blog*, rsisecurity.com/iso-42001-nist-ai-rmf-alignment/. Accessed 1 Feb. 2026.

"ISO 42001 and the EU AI Act." *ISMS.online*, isms.online/iso-42001/eu-ai-act/. Accessed 1 Feb. 2026.

"IT Vendor Management Best Practices." *EaglePoint Technologies*, eaglepointtech.com/it-vendor-management-best-practices/. Accessed 8 Jan. 2026.

Jones Walker. "The Explainability Illusion: Why AI Transparency Requirements Miss the Point." *Jones Walker AI Law Blog*, joneswalker.com/en/insights/blogs/ai-law-blog/the-explainability-illusion-why-ai-transparency-requirements-miss-the-point.html?id=102kzle. Accessed 28 Jan. 2026.

The Josh Bersin Company and Guild. "Dynamic Skilling: Anticipating and Mitigating Current and Future Skills Gaps," *Guild*, Mar. 2025. guild.com/report/dynamic-learning-ecosystem-bersin. Accessed 9 Jan. 2026.

Kaplan, Robert S., and David P. Norton. "The Balanced Scorecard—Measures That Drive Performance." *Harvard Business Review*, Jan.–Feb. 1992, hbr.org/1992/01/the-balanced-scorecard-measures-that-drive-performance-2.

"Keeping Humans in the Loop While Building the Future of AI." *Solutions Review*, solutionsreview.com/keeping-humans-in-the-loop-while-building-the-future-of-ai/. Accessed 1 Feb. 2026.

Kesari, Ganes. "Building a Data-Driven Culture: Four Key Elements." *MIT Sloan Management Review*, 23 Jan. 2025, sloanreview.mit.edu/article/building-a-data-driven-culture-four-key-elements. Accessed 8 Jan. 2026.

Keylabs. "Navigating AI Model Deployment: Challenges and Solutions." *Keylabs*, 8 Feb. 2024, keylabs.ai/blog/navigating-ai-model-deployment-challenges-and-solutions/. Accessed 21 Jan. 2026.

Kirenz. "25 Meeting Summarization - Gen AI & Prompting." *Kirenz*, 14 Apr. 2024, kirenz.github.io/generative-ai/tasks/task-meeting-summarization.html. Accessed 21 Jan. 2026.

Kitemetric. "Top 11 Vector Databases for AI Workloads in 2025." *Kitemetric Blogs*, kitemetric.com/blogs/11-top-vector-databases-for-ai-workloads-in-2025. Accessed 1 Feb. 2026.

"Knowledge Graphs in AI: Applications and Future Trends." *YouTube*, youtube.com/watch?v=k1gwZQgCBhc. Accessed 1 Feb. 2026.

Kore.ai. "Choosing the Right Orchestration Pattern for Multi-Agent Systems." *Kore.ai Blog*, kore.ai/blog/choosing-the-right-orchestration-pattern-for-multi-agent-systems. Accessed 21 Jan. 2026.

Koster, Raphael, et al. "Human-Centred Mechanism Design with Democratic AI." *DeepMind Blog*, 3 July 2022, deepmind.google/blog/human-centred-mechanism-design-with-democratic-ai. Accessed 8 Jan. 2026.

"KPIs for gen AI: Measuring AI Success—Deep Dive." *Google Cloud*, 2024, cloud.google.com/transform/gen-ai-kpis-measuring-ai-success-deep-dive. Accessed 28 Jan. 2026.

## Bibliography

"KPIs for Gen AI: Measuring Your AI Success." *Google Cloud Blog,* 25 Nov. 2024, cloud.google.com/transform/gen-ai-kpis-measuring-ai-success-deep-dive. Accessed 28 Jan. 2026.

KPMG. "A Data-Driven Culture Will Differentiate the Winners from the Losers: What Businesses Should Do To Stay Ahead." *KPMG,* 20 Feb. 2024, kpmg.com/us/en/media/news/data-driven-culture-kpmg-insight-2024.html. Accessed 8 Jan. 2026.

KPMG. "Model Risk Management." *KPMG International,* 19 Jan. 2025, kpmg.com/us/en/articles/2025/model-risk-management.html. Accessed 21 Jan. 2026.

KPMG. *Model Risk Management.* KPMG International, 2021, assets.kpmg.com/content/dam/kpmg/ie/pdf/2020/11/ie-model-risk-management.pdf. Accessed 21 Jan. 2026.

Laanti, Maarit, and Petri Kangas. "Agile Portfolio Management: Benefits and Challenges." *Journal of Modern Project Management,* vol. 11, no. 2, 2024, journalmodernpm.com/manuscript/index.php/jmpm/article/view/JMPM02501. Accessed 21 Jan. 2026.

Lamarre, Eric, et al. *Rewired: The McKinsey Guide to Outcompeting in the Age of Digital and AI.* McKinsey & Company, 2023, mckinsey.com/capabilities/mckinsey-digital/our-insights/rewired-to-outcompete. Accessed 16 Dec. 2025.

"Law & Compliance in AI Security & Data Protection." *European Data Protection Board,* June 2025, edpb.europa.eu/system/files/2025-06/spe-training-on-ai-and-data-protection-legal_en.pdf. Accessed 19 Jan. 2026.

"A Layered Model for AI Governance: Practical Ties to Trade Secrets." *Tangibly,* tangibly.com/a-layered-model-for-ai-governance-practical-ties-to-trade-secrets/. Accessed 28 Jan. 2026.

"Leading Data-Driven Culture and Change Management in Banks and Firms." *LinkedIn Articles,* linkedin.com/pulse/building-data-driven-culture-change-management-banks-firms-zarikar-h0vxf. Accessed 8 Jan. 2026.

"Legacy Application Modernization: Challenges and Strategies." *Softura Blog,* softura.com/blog/legacy-application-modernization-challenges/. Accessed 8 Jan. 2026.

"Legacy Application Modernization with AI Integration." *Varseno Solutions,* varseno.com/legacy-application-modernization-ai-integration/. Accessed 8 Jan. 2026.

"Legacy Data Integration: Challenges and Strategies." *WaferWire Blog,* waferwire.com/blog/legacy-data-integration-challenges-strategies. Accessed 8 Jan. 2026.

"Legacy Software Modernization Strategies---Complete Guide." *SKMGp Blog,* skmgp.com/blog/legacy-software-modernization-strategies---complete-guide. Accessed 8 Jan. 2026.

"Legacy System Modernization." *Deloitte Insights,* deloitte.com/us/en/insights/topics/digital-transformation/legacy-system-modernization.html. Accessed 8 Jan. 2026.

"Leveraging ADKAR for Successful AI Adoption." *MargOnline,* 2024, margonline.com/blog/leveraging-adkar-for-successful-ai-adoption/. Accessed 21 Jan. 2026.

"Leveraging AI in a Common Data Environment (CDE)." *Lean Construction Institute Blog,* 24 Mar. 2025, leanconstruction.org/blog/leveraging-ai-in-a-common-data-environment-cde/. Accessed 21 Jan. 2026.

"Leveraging AI to Support Value-Based Decision-Making." *LinkedIn Articles,* 28 July 2025, linkedin.com/pulse/leveraging-ai-support-value-based-decision-making-matthew-khoury-ou3pe/. Accessed 21 Jan. 2026.

Lifebit. "Federated Data Governance Explained Simply (Yes, Really!)." *Lifebit Blog,* 11 July 2025, lifebit.ai/blog/federated-data-governance/. Accessed 21 Jan. 2026.

Lifebit. "Federated Governance: The Blueprint for Data Democracy." *Lifebit Blog,* 16 Sept. 2025, lifebit.ai/blog/federated-governance-complete-guide/. Accessed 21 Jan. 2026.

Liqueo. "Centralised vs. Federated vs. Hybrid: Choosing the Right Data Governance Model." *Liqueo,* liqueo.com/centralised-vs-federated-vs-hybrid-choosing-the-right-data-governance-model/. Accessed 28 Jan. 2026.

"LLM Security Best Practices 2025." *NHIMG Community,* nhimg.org/community/nhi-best-practices/llm-security-best-practices-2025/. Accessed 8 Jan. 2026.

"Lockheed Martin Case Study." *Starburst Resources,* starburst.io/resources/lockheed-martin-case-study/. Accessed 28 Jan. 2026.

LogicGate. "Understanding the NIST AI RMF Framework." *LogicGate Blog,* 2024, logicgate.com/blog/understanding-the-nist-ai-rmf-framework/. Accessed 21 Jan. 2026.

Lohr, Steve. "Your A.I. Radiologist Will Not Be With You Soon." *The New York Times,* 14 May 2025, nytimes.com/2025/05/14/technology/ai-jobs-radiologists-mayo-clinic.html. Accessed 8 Jan. 2026.

Lorenzo, Rocío, et al. "How Diverse Leadership Teams Boost Innovation." *Boston Consulting Group,* 23 Jan. 2018, bcg.com/publications/2018/how-diverse-leadership-teams-boost-innovation. Accessed 8 Jan. 2026.

Lumenova AI. "AI Risk Assessment Best Practices: NIST AI RMF Alignment." *Lumenova AI Blog,* 2024, lumenova.ai/blog/ai-risk-assessment-best-practices-nist-ai-rmf/. Accessed 21 Jan. 2026.

"Lurking in the Shadows: The Costs of Unapproved AI Tools." *Journal of Accountancy,* 11 Nov. 2025, journalofaccountancy.com/news/2025/nov/lurking-in-the-shadows-the-costs-of-unapproved-ai-tools. Accessed 19 Jan. 2026.

"Machine Learning in Medicine." *New England Journal of Medicine,* vol. 380, no. 14, 4 Apr. 2019, pp. 1347-58, doi:10.1056/NEJMra1814259. Accessed 8 Jan. 2026.

"Machine Learning Model Drift: Best Practices." *Encord Blog,* encord.com/blog/model-drift-best-practices/. Accessed 8 Jan. 2026.

"Machine Learning Model Lifecycle Management." *Fiddler AI Articles,* fiddler.ai/articles/machine-learning-model-lifecycle-management. Accessed 8 Jan. 2026.

"Machine Learning Model Monitoring: Best Practices." *Dysnix,* 2025, dysnix.com/blog/ml-model-monitoring-in-production. Accessed 21 Jan. 2026.

"Manufacturing Dashboards." *Harmoni,* harmoni.io/manufacturing-dashboards/. Accessed 28 Jan. 2026.

## Bibliography


"Mastering AI Adoption: Leadership Strategies and SmartDev Solutions." *SmartDev*, smartdev.com/mastering-ai-adoption-leadership-strategies-and-smartdev-solutions/. Accessed 21 Jan. 2026.

"Mastering Internal and External Benchmarking." *CH Consulting Group*, 2025, chconsultinggroup.com/masteringinternalandexternal-benchmarking/. Accessed 21 Jan. 2026.

McKinsey & Company. "Developing a Resilient, Adaptable Workforce for an Uncertain Future." *McKinsey & Company*, 6 Dec. 2024, mckinsey.com/capabilities/people-and-organizational-performance/our-insights/developing-a-resilient-adaptable-workforce-for-an-uncertain-future. Accessed 8 Jan. 2026.

McKinsey & Company. "Taking a Skills-Based Approach to Building the Future Workforce." *McKinsey & Company*, 15 Nov. 2022, mckinsey.com/capabilities/people-and-organizational-performance/our-insights/taking-a-skills-based-approach-to-building-the-future-workforce. Accessed 8 Jan. 2026.

McKinsey & Company. "The Upskilling Imperative: Required at Scale for the Future of Work." *McKinsey & Company*, 13 May 2025, mckinsey.com/industries/public-sector/our-insights/the-upskilling-imperative-required-at-scale-for-the-future-of-work. Accessed 8 Jan. 2026.

"Measuring Strategic Execution Success Using the Balanced Scorecard." *Lean Data Point*, 2 July 2024, leandatapoint.com/blog/strategic-execution. Accessed 28 Jan. 2026.

"Mentoring and Innovation: How Cross-Generational Teams Affect Decision-Making and Overall Organizational Performance." *Psico-Smart Blog*, 28 Nov. 2024, blogs.psico-smart.com/blog-how-crossgenerational-teams-affect-decisionmaking-and-overall-organizational-performance-182689. Accessed 19 Jan. 2026.

"Mentoring and Reverse Mentoring: Two Sides of a Valuable Coin." *Workspan Daily*, worldatwork.org/publications/workspan-daily/mentoring-and-reverse-mentoring-two-sides-of-a-valuable-coin. Accessed 19 Jan. 2026.

"MIT Report: 95% of Generative AI Pilots at Companies Are Failing, CFOs Warn." *Fortune*, fortune.com/2025/08/18/mit-report-95-percent-generative-ai-pilots-at-companies-failing-cfo/. Accessed 8 Jan. 2026.

MIT Sloan Management Review. "Build Better KPIs With Artificial Intelligence." 2023, sloanreview.mit.edu/projects/the-future-of-strategic-measurement-enhancing-kpis-with-ai/. Accessed 21 Jan. 2026.

MIT Sloan Management Review. "Strategic Alignment With AI and Smart KPIs." 2024, sloanreview.mit.edu/article/strategic-alignment-with-ai-and-smart-kpis/. Accessed 21 Jan. 2026.

Moats, David, and Chandrima Ganguly. "Bringing AI Participation Down to Scale." *Patterns*, 9 May 2025, doi:10.1016/j.patter.2025.101241. Accessed 8 Jan. 2026.

Mode. "Agile Analytics: Why You Should Embrace Incremental Shipments." *Mode Blog*, 12 Mar. 2023, mode.com/blog/what-is-agile-analytics. Accessed 21 Jan. 2026.

ModelOp. "NIST AI RMF." *ModelOp*, 29 Apr. 2024, modelop.com/ai-governance/ai-regulations-standards/nist-ai-rmf. Accessed 21 Jan. 2026.

"Modernizing Legacy Systems: A Guide to Strategies." *WaferWire Blog*, waferwire.com/blog/modernizing-legacy-systems-guide-strategies. Accessed 8 Jan. 2026.

"The Most Important On-Time Delivery (OTD) Metrics." *SourceDay Blog,* sourceday.com/blog/on-time-delivery-metrics. Accessed 16 Dec. 2025.

"My AI Governance Framework for Procurement." *Art of Procurement Blog,* artofprocurement.com/blog/my-ai-governance-framework-for-procurement. Accessed 8 Jan. 2026.

Nair, Devadrita, and Maria Jesus Saenz. "Pair People and AI for Better Product Demand Forecasting." *MIT Sloan Management Review,* 29 Jan. 2024, sloanreview.mit.edu/article/pair-people-and-ai-for-better-product-demand-forecasting. Accessed 21 Jan. 2026.

National Academies. "National Academies AI Risk and Governance Materials." *nationalacademies.org,* nationalacademies.org/units/DEPS-NMMB-25-01. Accessed 8 Jan. 2026.

National Institute of Standards and Technology. "NIST AI Risk Management Framework (AI RMF)." *NIST Information Technology Laboratory,* nist.gov/itl/ai-risk-management-framework. Accessed 21 Jan. 2026.

National Institute of Standards and Technology. "NIST AI RMF Core." *NIST AI Resource Center,* 4 Mar. 2025, airc.nist.gov/airmf-resources/airmf/5-sec-core/. Accessed 21 Jan. 2026.

National Institute of Standards and Technology. "NIST AI RMF Playbook." *NIST AI Resource Center,* 5 Feb. 2025, nist.gov/itl/ai-risk-management-framework/nist-ai-rmf-playbook. Accessed 21 Jan. 2026.

"Navigating AI Model Deployment: Challenges and Solutions." *Keylabs,* 8 Feb. 2024, keylabs.ai/blog/navigating-ai-model-deployment-challenges-and-solutions/. Accessed 21 Jan. 2026.

"Navigating Hybrid and Multi-Cloud Maturity in Financial Services." *LinkedIn,* by Enrique Peláez, 14 Jul. 2025, linkedin.com/pulse/navigating-hybrid-multi-cloud-maturity-financial-services-pel%C3%A1ez-ng3oc. Accessed 8 Jan. 2026.

"Navigating the Liminal Edge of AI Security: Deconstructing Prompt Injection, Model Poisoning, and Adversarial Perturbations in the Cognitive Cyber Domain." *Cloud Security Alliance Blog,* cloudsecurityalliance.org/blog/2025/12/01/navigating-the-liminal-edge-of-ai-security-deconstructing-prompt-injection-model-poisoning-and-adversarial-perturbations-in-the-cognitive-cyber-domain. Accessed 8 Jan. 2026.

"New Book on BPMN and DMN -- Building More Effective Processes by Integrating Process Modeling with Decision Modeling." *Blue Polaris,* bluepolaris.com/new-book-on-bpmn-and-dmn-building-more-effective-processes-by-integrating-process-modeling-with-decision-modeling/. Accessed 8 Jan. 2026.

"New Economy Skills: Unlocking the Human Advantage." *World Economic Forum,* weforum.org/docs/WEF_New_Economy_Skills_Unlocking_the_Human_Advantage_2025.pdf. Accessed 8 Jan. 2026.

"New Radar Modes: Smarter Horizon Scanning and Trendspotting." *DCipher Analytics Blog,* dcipheranalytics.com/blog/new-radar-modes-smarter-horizon-scanning-trendspotting. Accessed 8 Jan. 2026.

Newgen. "AI Agent-Driven Service-Level Agreement (SLA) Management." *Newgen,* newgensoft.com/resources/article/ai-agent-driven-service-level-agreement-sla-management/. Accessed 8 Jan. 2026.

## Bibliography


"NIST vs GDPR: AI Regulations and Standards." *ModelOp*, modelop.com/ai-governance/ai-regulations-standards/nist-vs-gdpr. Accessed 1 Feb. 2026.

"Nubank Elevates Customer Experiences with OpenAI." *OpenAI*, openai.com/index/nubank. Accessed 8 Jan. 2026.

Nussbaumer Knaflic, Cole, et al. *Storytelling with Data: Before & After: Practical Makeovers for Powerful Data Stories.* Wiley, 2025.

Nussbaumer Knaflic, Cole. *Storytelling with Data: A Data Visualization Guide for Business Professionals.* 10th anniversary ed., Wiley, 2025.

"Object Recognition ML Computer Vision Success Story." *VirtuLab Success Stories*, virtuslab.com/success-stories/object-recognition-ml-computer-vision/. Accessed 8 Jan. 2026.

Ocient. "Unraveling the Web: Data Mesh vs Data Fabric and the Role of Data Warehouses." *Ocient*, ocient.com/blog/unraveling-the-web-data-mesh-vs-data-fabric-and-the-role-of-data-warehouses/. Accessed 1 Feb. 2026.

OHDSI. "Standardized Data: The OMOP Common Data Model." *OHDSI*, 31 Aug. 2021, ohdsi.org/data-standardization/. Accessed 21 Jan. 2026.

"On the Quest for Effectiveness in Human Oversight." *arXiv*, arxiv.org/html/2404.04059v1. Accessed 16 Dec. 2025.

"On the Quest for Effectiveness in Human Oversight." *arXiv*, arxiv.org/html/2404.04059v1.[arxiv]. Accessed 8 Jan. 2026.

Ontoforce. "Knowledge Graphs: Multi-Modal Data and the Next Era of AI in Life Sciences." *Ontoforce Blog*, ontoforce.com/blog/knowledge-graphs-multi-modal-data-and-the-next-era-of-ai-in-life-sciences. Accessed 1 Feb. 2026.

"Optimizing the Annotation Workforce: Building High-Performance Teams." *KeyLabs Blog*, keylabs.ai/blog/optimizing-the-annotation-workforce-building-high-performance-teams. Accessed 8 Jan. 2026.

OrcaLean. "Integrating AI into DMAIC and PDCA: A Practical Framework." *OrcaLean*, 2025, orcalean.com/article/integrating-ai-into-dmaic-and-pdca:-a-practical-framework. Accessed 21 Jan. 2026.

Orq. "Managing the AI Lifecycle." *Orq Blog*, orq.ai/blog/managing-the-ai-lifecycle. Accessed 28 Jan. 2026.

OvalEdge. "Data Stewardship Guide." *Ovaledge Blog*, ovaledge.com/blog/data-stewardship-guide. Accessed 28 Jan. 2026.

"Overcoming Brick-and-Mortar Retail Challenges with Hackathon Sponsorship." *Zigpoll*, . Accessed 8 Jan. 2026.

"Overcoming the 80/20 Rule in Data Science." *Pragmatic Institute*, pragmaticinstitute.com/resources/articles/data/overcoming-the-80-20-rule-in-data-science/. Accessed 8 Jan. 2026.

OWASP Foundation. "OWASP Top 10 for Large Language Model Applications." *OWASP*, owasp.org/www-project-top-10-for-large-language-model-applications/. Accessed 8 Jan. 2026.

"The OWASP Top 10 for LLM: Updated 2025 Examples and Mitigation Strategies." *Oligo Security Academy*, oligo.security/academy/owasp-top-10-llm-updated-2025-examples-and-mitigation-strategies. Accessed 8 Jan. 2026.

Panorays. "How AI Is Transforming Third-Party Risk Management Workflows." *Panorays Blog,* 4 Nov. 2025, panorays.com/blog/ai-in-third-party-risk-management. Accessed 21 Jan. 2026.

"People + AI Guidebook." *Google PAIR,* withgoogle.com/guidebook. Accessed 15 Dec. 2025.

"People + AI Research (PAIR)." *Google Research,* withgoogle.com. Accessed 8 Jan. 2026.

Persistent. "Enterprise Readiness for AI: More Than Just Data." *Persistent Blog,* persistent.com/blogs/enterprise-readiness-for-ai-more-than-just-data/. Accessed 21 Jan. 2026.

"Perspective Review: Will Generative AI Make Common Data Models Obsolete?" *Patterns,* vol. 6, 20 Apr. 2025, pmc.ncbi.nlm.nih.gov/articles/PMC12033412/. Accessed 21 Jan. 2026.

Petronellatech. "Data Mesh or Data Fabric: Charting Your Enterprise's Future." *Petronellatech,* petronellatech.com/data-mesh-or-data-fabric-charting-your-enterprises-future/. Accessed 1 Feb. 2026.

PingCAP. "Knowledge Graph Tools AI Development 2025." *PingCAP,* pingcap.com/article/knowledge-graph-tools-ai-development-2025/. Accessed 1 Feb. 2026.

PingCAP. "Machine Learning Knowledge Graphs 2025." *PingCAP,* pingcap.com/article/machine-learning-knowledge-graphs-2025/. Accessed 1 Feb. 2026.

"Power BI Implementation Planning: Usage Scenario—Self-Service and Real-Time Analytics." *Microsoft Learn,* learn.microsoft.com/en-us/power-bi/guidance/powerbi-implementation-planning-usage-scenario-self-service-real-time-analytics. Accessed 8 Jan. 2026.

"Privacy by Design in the Pipeline: Embedding Data Protection at Scale." *Databahn Blog,* databahn.ai/blog/privacy-by-design-in-the-pipeline-embedding-data-protection-at-scale. Accessed 8 Jan. 2026.

"Process Mining: A Database of Applications." *Task Force on Process Mining,* 2021, tf-pm.org/upload/1612166268135.pdf. Accessed 8 Jan. 2026.

Progress. "Data Fabric vs Data Mesh." *Progress,* progress.com/data-fabric-vs-data-mesh. Accessed 1 Feb. 2026.

"Project Aristotle: Google's Data-Driven Insights on High-Performing Teams." *Aristotle Performance,* 2024, aristotleperformance.com/post/project-aristotle-google-s-data-driven-insights-on-high-performing-teams.[13]. Accessed 8 Jan. 2026.

"Project Aristotle Psychological Safety." *LeaderFactor,* leaderfactor.com/learn/project-aristotle-psychological-safety.[leaderfactor]. Accessed 8 Jan. 2026.

"Project Aristotle Reveals the Value of a Human Workplace." *Inc.,* 11 May 2025, inc.com/peter-economy/how-googles-project-aristotle-made-teams-better-by-reminding-us-work-is-human/91185766.[15]. Accessed 8 Jan. 2026.

Promethium. "Data Fabric vs Data Mesh vs Data Lake vs Data Warehouse." *Promethium,* promethium.ai/guides/data-fabric-vs-data-mesh-vs-data-lake-vs-data-warehouse/. Accessed 1 Feb. 2026.

## Bibliography

Promethium. "Data Mesh vs Data Fabric Comparison Guide." *Promethium*, promethium.ai/guides/data-mesh-vs-data-fabric-comparison-guide/. Accessed 1 Feb. 2026.

"Prompt Injection 101." *Practical DevSecOps*, practical-devsecops.com/wp-content/uploads/2025/12/Prompt-Injection-101-guide.pdf. Accessed 8 Jan. 2026.

"Prompt Injection Attacks on LLMs." *Wiz Academy*, wiz.io/academy/ai-security/prompt-injection-attack. Accessed 8 Jan. 2026.

"Prompt Injection in LLMs." *Obsidian Security Blog*, obsidiansecurity.com/blog/prompt-injection. Accessed 8 Jan. 2026.

Prosci. "AI Change Management." *Prosci*, 2023, prosci.com/ai-change-management. Accessed 21 Jan. 2026.

Prosci. "AI in Change Management: Early Findings." *Prosci Research Note*, 2026, prosci.com/blog/ai-in-change-management-early-findings. Accessed 21 Jan. 2026.

Prosci. "AI Transformation: A People-Centric Guide to Leading Change." *Prosci Change Management Blog*, 2026, prosci.com/blog/ai-transformation. Accessed 21 Jan. 2026.

Prosci. "Live and On-Demand Webinars." *Prosci*, 2024, prosci.com/resources/webinars. Accessed 21 Jan. 2026.

"Psychological Safety Drives AI Adoption." *Psychology Today*, 22 Sept. 2025, psychologytoday.com/us/blog/decisions-decisions/202509/psychological-safety-drives-ai-adoption. Accessed 19 Jan. 2026.

"Psychological Safety Is the Missing Piece in Your AI Strategy." *Training Journal*, 16 Nov. 2025, trainingjournal.com/2025/content-type/features/psychological-safety-is-the-missing-piece-in-your-ai-strategy. Accessed 19 Jan. 2026.

Qandle. "AI-Powered Sentiment Analysis to Measure Employee Satisfaction." *Qandle*, 2025, qandle.com/blog/ai-powered-sentiment-analysis/. Accessed 21 Jan. 2026.

Qualytics. "Data Quality Trends." *Qualytics Resources*, qualytics.ai/resources/in/data-quality-trends. Accessed 1 Feb. 2026.

Querio. "Top Collaboration KPIs for Data Governance Success." *Querio*, 18 Jan. 2026, querio.ai/articles/top-collaboration-kpis-for-data-governance-success. Accessed 21 Jan. 2026.

Querio. "Why Semantic Context Is Key to Better AI Analytics." *Querio AI Articles*, querio.ai/articles/why-semantic-context-is-key-to-better-ai-analytics. Accessed 1 Feb. 2026.

"RACI Chart Guide: Roles, Examples, and Best Practices." *TeamGantt Blog*, 23 Aug. 2025, teamgantt.com/blog/raci-chart-definition-tips-and-example. Accessed 16 Dec. 2025.

"RACI Matrix." *HPT by DTS Blog*, hptbydts.com/raci-matrix. Accessed 16 Dec. 2025.

"RACI Matrix: Responsibility Assignment Matrix Guide." *Project-Management.com*, Project-Management.com. Accessed 16 Dec. 2025.

"RACI Matrix: The Management Tool for Effective Role Assignment." *Furious Squad*, 27 Apr. 2025, furious-squad.com/en/factsheets/raci-matrix. Accessed 16 Dec. 2025.

"RACI Template [FREE Download] & RACI Matrix Guide." *AIHR*, 11 Jan. 2026, aihr.com/blog/raci-template. Accessed 16 Dec. 2025.

RAGflow. "RAG Review 2025: From RAG to Context." *RAGflow Blog*, ragflow.io/blog/rag-review-2025-from-rag-to-context. Accessed 1 Feb. 2026.

"Real-Time Analytics: Case Studies and Real-World Applications." *CrateDB*, cratedb.com/real-time-analytics/case-studies-and-real-world-applications. Accessed 28 Jan. 2026.

"Real-Time Decision-Making Using Cloud-Edge Collaboration." *Travancore Analytics*, travancoreanalytics.com/en-us/real-time-decision-making-using-cloud-edge-collaboration/. Accessed 8 Jan. 2026.

"Real-Time Manufacturing Dashboard: Setup, Importance, and Benefits." *DataParc Blog*, dataparc.com/blog/real-time-manufacturing-dashboard-setup-importance-benefits/. Accessed 28 Jan. 2026.

"Real-Time Streaming: Streaming Analytics Top 5 Use Cases, Challenges, and Best Practices." *Instaclustr Education*, instaclustr.com/education/real-time-streaming/streaming-analytics-top-5-use-cases-challenges-and-best-practices/. Accessed 28 Jan. 2026.

"Real-Time Supply Chain Analytics: Key Features, Technologies, and Trends." *SmartWarehousing Blog*, smartwarehousing.com/blog/real-time-supply-chain-analytics. Accessed 28 Jan. 2026.

"Real-Time Upskilling: How HR Keeps Pace with AI." *SHRM News and HR Trends*, 2025, shrm.org/topics-tools/news/hr-trends/real-time-upskilling. Accessed 8 Jan. 2026.

"The Real-World Impact of Artificial Intelligence Ethics Frameworks: A Scoping Review." *Journal of Medical Ethics*, nih.gov/articles/PMC12626214>. Accessed 19 Jan. 2026.

"RegTech for AI-Enabled Systems." *Nemko Digital Insights*, nemko.com/insights/regtech-for-ai-enabled-systems. Accessed 1 Feb. 2026.

"Regulatory Reporting and AI Data Governance: The Future of Financial Compliance." *LinkedIn*, linkedin.com/pulse/regulatory-reporting-ai-data-governance-future-financial-i5tnc. Accessed 1 Feb. 2026.

"Regulatory Sandboxes in Artificial Intelligence." *Organisation for Economic Co-operation and Development*, 12 July 2023, oecd.org/en/publications/regulatory-sandboxes-in-artificial-intelligence_8f80a0e6-en.html. Accessed 19 Jan. 2026.

"Regulatory vs Digital Sandbox for AI: You Need to Know." *NayaOne*, nayaone.com/knowledgebase/regulatory-vs-digital-sandbox-for-ai-you-need-to-know. Accessed 19 Jan. 2026.

"Reimagining people development to overcome talent challenges." *McKinsey & Company*, 2 Mar. 2023, mckinsey.com/capabilities/people-and-organizational-performance/our-insights/reimagining-people-development-to-overcome-talent-challenges. Accessed 19 Jan. 2026.

"Research Reveals That 90% of Organizations Using AI to Create KPIs Report Improvement." *Metrology News*, 18 Mar. 2024, metrology.news/research-reveals-that-90-of-organizations-using-ai-to-create-kpis-report-improvement/. Accessed 28 Jan. 2026.

"Reskilling: Key Insights to Get Started." *SHIFT eLearning*, 2024, shiftelearning.com/blog/reskilling-key-insights-get-started. Accessed 8 Jan. 2026.

## Bibliography


"Resources for Data Analysts & Business Intelligence Professionals." *TDWI*, tdwi.org/pages/persona/data-analysts-bi-pros.aspx. Accessed 19 Jan. 2026.

"Responsibility Assignment Matrix." *Wikipedia*, wikipedia.org/wiki/Responsibility_assignment_matrix. Accessed 16 Dec. 2025.

"Responsible AI at Google Research: PAIR." *Google Research Blog*, research.google/blog/responsible-ai-at-google-research-pair. Accessed 8 Jan. 2026.

"Responsible AI: Design, Operationalize, and Govern." *Global Responsible AI Initiative*, 2023, weforum.org/stories/2019/04/business-case-for-diversity-in-the-workplace. Accessed 21 Jan. 2026.

"Responsible AI Governance." *BigID Blog*, bigid.com/blog/responsible-ai-governance/. Accessed 8 Jan. 2026.

"Rethinking AI Talent Strategy as Automated Machine Learning Comes of Age." *McKinsey & Company*, mckinsey.com/capabilities/quantumblack/our-insights/rethinking-ai-talent-strategy-as-automated-machine-learning-comes-of-age. Accessed 8 Jan. 2026.

"Returned Business Value Framework: Assessing Strategic Alignment in Analytics and AI." *International Institute for Analytics*, iianalytics.com/community/blog/returned-business-value-framework-assessing-strategic-alignment-in-analytics-and-ai. Accessed 8 Jan. 2026.

Rigby, Darrell K., et al. "Agile at Scale." *Harvard Business Review*, vol. 96, no. 3, May-June 2018, hbr.org/2018/05/agile-at-scale. Accessed 21 Jan. 2026.

"The Rise of the Security Data Pipeline." *Software Analyst Substack*, substack.com/p/the-rise-of-security-data-pipeline. Accessed 8 Jan. 2026.

"Risk Management Framework for AI Procurement." *HubSpot File Library*, hubspotusercontent-na1.net/hubfs/20596328/Risk%20Management%20Framework%20for%20AI%20Procurement-4.pdf. Accessed 8 Jan. 2026.

"Roadmap to an AI-First Enterprise for Banking and Finance." *WhiteBlue Consulting*, 2024, whiteblue.com/post/roadmap-to-an-ai-first-enterprise-for-banking-finance. Accessed 21 Jan. 2026.

"The ROI of Intelligence: A Definitive Guide to Measuring AI Value in Professional Services Marketing and Business Development." *Innovation Partners*, innovaitionpartners.com/blog/the-roi-of-intelligence-a-definitive-guide-to-measuring-ai-value-in-professional-services-marketing-and-business-development. Accessed 8 Jan. 2026.

"The Role of Data Literacy in Building a Data-Driven Culture." *Visium*, 8 Sept. 2024, visium.com/articles/the-role-of-data-literacy-in-building-a-data-driven-culture. Accessed 8 Jan. 2026.

"The Role of Power Users in a Self-Service BI Initiative." *3Cloud Solutions*, 3cloudsolutions.com/resources/the-role-of-power-users-in-a-self-service-bi-initiative/. Accessed 8 Jan. 2026.

Rojas, Silvia. "The Urgent Case for Reskilling: Key Insights to Get Started." *SHIFT eLearning*, 2024, www.shiftelearning.com/blog/reskilling-key-insights-get-started. Accessed 8 Jan. 2026.

"SaaS Benchmarks 2023 Part 4: Revenue Retention." *ScaleXP*, 10 June 2024, scalexp.com/saas-benchmarks-revenue-retention. Accessed 28 Jan. 2026.

"SaaS Vendor Management Guide." *GEP Blog*, gep.com/blog/technology/saas-vendor-management-guide. Accessed 8 Jan. 2026.

"SaaS Vendor Management: The Definitive Guide for 2025." *BetterCloud Monitor*, bettercloud.com/monitor/saas-vendor-management-the-definitive-guide-for-2025/. Accessed 8 Jan. 2026.

"Sandbox Environments and the Use of Technology in Finance." *NayaOne*, nayaone.com/knowledgebase/sandbox-environments-and-the-use-of-technology-in-finance. Accessed 19 Jan. 2026.

"SandboxAQ Launches AQtive Guard AI-SPM to Stop the Rapid Spread of Shadow AI Across the Enterprise." *PR Newswire*, 3 Dec. 2025, prnewswire.com/news-releases/sandboxaq-launches-aqtive-guard-ai-spm-to-stop-the-rapid-spread-of-shadow-ai-across-the-enterprise-302631705.html. Accessed 19 Jan. 2026.

"Scaling AI and Analytics in Audit Programs: A Playbook." *AuditBoard Blog*, 13 Jan. 2025, auditboard.com/blog/playbook-how-ai-and-analytics-can-scale-your-audit-program. Accessed 21 Jan. 2026.

"Scaling AI for Sustainable Value in Insurance." *Deloitte Insights*, 24 Mar. 2025, deloitte.com/us/en/industries/financial-services/articles/scaling-ai-in-insurance.html. Accessed 21 Jan. 2026.

"Scaling AI in Healthcare: Escaping Pilot Purgatory." *Nisum*, 8 Dec. 2025, nisum.com/nisum-knows/scaling-ai-in-healthcare-escaping-pilot-purgatory. Accessed 19 Jan. 2026.

"Scaling AI Projects with MLOps: The Secret to Moving ML Models from Prototype to Production." *Databuzz Ltd. Blog*, databuzzltd.com/blog-posts/mlops-the-secret-to-moving-ml-models-from-prototype-to-production. Accessed 8 Jan. 2026.

"Scaling Data Governance for AI and ML: A Practical Guide." *LinkedIn*, linkedin.com/pulse/building-scalable-data-governance-framework-ai-ml-guide-sunil-zarikar-o0xyf. Accessed 8 Jan. 2026.

"SCALING Self-Service Analytics Using Data Literacy." *CDO Magazine*, 9 July 2023, cdomagazine.tech/opinion-analysis/how-to-enable-self-service-analytics-using-data-literacy. Accessed 19 Jan. 2026.

"SCIKIQ Natural Language Query: AI-Powered Conversational Analytics." *SCIKIQ*, scikiq.com/SCIKIQ-natural-language-query-conversational-analytics. Accessed 19 Jan. 2026.

"Search Engines." *Capsula AI Topics*, capsula.ai/topics/search-engines. Accessed 1 Feb. 2026.

Secureframe. "Understanding the NIST AI RMF: What It Is and How to Put It into Practice." *Secureframe Blog*, 20 May 2024, secureframe.com/blog/nist-ai-rmf. Accessed 21 Jan. 2026.

"Securing AI/ML Models: Adversarial Attacks and Defenses." *Yash Technologies Blog*, yash.com/blog/securing-ai-ml-models-adversarial-attacks-and-defenses/. Accessed 8 Jan. 2026.

## Bibliography

Select Star. "How to Build a Business Glossary for Data Governance." *Select Star,* 19 Feb. 2025, selectstar.com/resources/business-glossary-data-governance. Accessed 21 Jan. 2026.

"Self-Service BI: Definition, Tools, Best Practices, and Real-World Use Cases." *Toucan Toco,* 1 Oct. 2025, toucantoco.com/en/blog/self-service-bi. Accessed 19 Jan. 2026.

"Self-Service BI." *Toucan Toco Blog,* toucantoco.com/en/blog/self-service-bi. Accessed 8 Jan. 2026.

"Semantic Search and AI: From Days of Discovery to Seconds of Answers." *DATAVERSITY,* dataversity.net/articles/semantic-search-and-ai-from-days-of-discovery-to-seconds-of-answers/. Accessed 1 Feb. 2026.

"Semantic Search vs Keyword Search: What's the Difference." *Couchbase Blog,* couchbase.com/blog/semantic-search-vs-keyword-search-whats-the-difference/. Accessed 1 Feb. 2026.

"Senpex: Real-Time Generative AI Logistics Case Study." *NewMathData Case Studies,* newmathdata.com/case-studies/senpex-real-time-generative-ai-logistics/. Accessed 28 Jan. 2026.

SentinelOne. "AI Risk Management: A Comprehensive Guide 101." *SentinelOne Cybersecurity 101,* 22 Mar. 2025, sentinelone.com/cybersecurity-101/cybersecurity/ai-risk-management/. Accessed 21 Jan. 2026.

"September 2025 Vendor Management News." *Venminder Blog,* venminder.com/blog/september-2025-vendor-management-news. Accessed 8 Jan. 2026.

"Serverless Data Analytics Pipeline Reference Architecture." *AWS Big Data Blog,* amazon.com/blogs/big-data/aws-serverless-data-analytics-pipeline-reference-architecture/. Accessed 8 Jan. 2026.

ServiceNow. "Continual Improvement Management." *ServiceNow,* servicenow.com/products/continual-improvement.html. Accessed 21 Jan. 2026.

ServiceNow. "Responsible AI." *ServiceNow,* servicenow.com/platform/responsible-ai.html. Accessed 21 Jan. 2026.

ServiceNow. "The Four Essential Elements to Responsible AI Governance." *ServiceNow Resource Center,* 19 Aug. 2025, servicenow.com/standard/resource-center/white-paper/wp-now-on-now-ai-governance.html. Accessed 21 Jan. 2026.

Seth Mattison. "Ultimate Guide to Cross-Functional Collaboration Metrics." *Seth Mattison,* 19 May 2025, sethmattison.com/thoughts-blog-posts/ultimate-guide-to-cross-functional-collaboration-metrics. Accessed 21 Jan. 2026.

"Shadow AI: A Guide from Security Risk to Competitive Advantage." *The AI Hat,* theaihat.com/the-executive-guide-to-shadow-ai-from-security-risk-to-competitive-advantage. Accessed 19 Jan. 2026.

"Shadow AI: A Wake-Up Call for AI Security and Governance." *Zenity,* zenity.io/blog/current-events/shadow-ai-a-wake-up-call. Accessed 19 Jan. 2026.

"Shadow AI Is Widespread—and Executives Use It the Most." *Cybersecurity Dive,* 11 Nov. 2025, cybersecuritydive.com/news/shadow-ai-employee-trust-upguard/805280. Accessed 19 Jan. 2026.

"Shadow AI on the Rise: 50% of Employees Using Unapproved AI Tools." *ISC² Community,* 14 May 2025, community.isc2.org/t5/Industry-News/Shadow-AI-on-the-Rise-50-of-Employees-Using-Unapproved-AI-Tools/td-p/79019. Accessed 19 Jan. 2026.

"Signals, Foresight, and Technological Change." *ScienceDirect,* sciencedirect.com/science/article/pii/S0169534724002866. Accessed 8 Jan. 2026.

"Singapore's Biggest Bank DBS to Cut 4,000 Roles as It Embraces AI." *BBC News,* 24 Feb. 2025, bbc.com/news/articles/c4g7xn9y64po. Accessed 8 Jan. 2026.

"Singapore's DBS Girds for AI as Tellers Morph Into Bankers." *Bloomberg,* 7 Nov. 2025, bloomberg.com/news/articles/2025-11-07/singapore-s-dbs-girds-for-ai-as-tellers-morph-into-bankers. Accessed 8 Jan. 2026.

"Skills 2025: The Half-Life of Capabilities in a Tech-Driven World." *TD Magazine,* 2025, td.org/content/td-magazine/skills-2025. Accessed 8 Jan. 2026.

"Skills Development Is Becoming More Dynamic, Complex, but also Essential, The Josh Bersin Company Finds." *Guild,* guild.com/news-press/skills-development-dynamic-complex-essential-bersin-company-guild-find. Accessed 19 Jan. 2026.

SmartDev. "AI Transformation Roadmap for Finance and Compliance." *SmartDev Blog,* 2024, smartdev.com/ai-transformation-roadmap-finance-compliance/. Accessed 21 Jan. 2026.

Sogeti Labs. "Emerging Trends: Data Governance in Data Fabrics and Mesh." *SogetiLabs Blog,* 2 July 2025, labs.sogeti.com/emerging-trends-data-governance-in-data-fabrics-and-mesh/. Accessed 21 Jan. 2026.

Sogeti Labs. "Emerging Trends: Policy as Code for Governance Enforcement." *SogetiLabs Blog,* 27 Nov. 2025, labs.sogeti.com/emerging-trends-policy-as-code-for-governance-enforcement/. Accessed 21 Jan. 2026.

Sogeti Labs. "Why Data Governance Is Crucial in Getting Data Ready for AI." *SogetiLabs Blog,* 13 June 2025, labs.sogeti.com/why-data-governance-is-crucial-in-getting-data-ready-for-ai/. Accessed 21 Jan. 2026.

Solomon Insight. "The Advantages of External Benchmarking vs Internal Benchmarking." *Solomon Insight,* 2024, solomoninsight.com/blog/the-advantages-of-external-benchmarking-vs-internal-benchmarking-in-the-oil-gas-and-energy-industry-blog. Accessed 21 Jan. 2026.

"Speeding Time to Value: How a Common Data Model Allows You to Do More with Less." *TDWI,* tdwi.org/articles/2020/08/03/ba-all-data-model-do-more-with-less.aspx. Accessed 21 Jan. 2026.

"SQL Server and Azure Data Lakehouse Ingestion and Processing Options." *MSSQLTips,* mssqltips.com/sqlservertip/7037/azure-data-lakehouse-ingestion-processing-options/. Accessed 8 Jan. 2026.

"The State of AI in 2023: Generative AI's Breakout Year." *McKinsey & Company,* 31 July 2023, mckinsey.com/capabilities/quantumblack/our-insights/the-state-of-ai-in-2023-generative-ais-breakout-year. Accessed 16 Dec. 2025.

Steffine, Gregory P. *Hyper: Changing the Way You Think About, Plan, and Execute Business Intelligence for Real Results, Real Fast!* Sanderson Press, 2015.

Steffine, Gregory P. *Think Fast!: The Insight You Need to Compete and Win with Self-Service Analytics.* Sanderson Press, 2018.

## Bibliography


Stiepan, DeeDee. "Using AI in Radiology Clinical Practice." *Mayo Clinic News Network*, 13 Sept. 2022, newsnetwork.mayoclinic.org/discussion/using-ai-in-radiology-clinical-practice. Accessed 8 Jan. 2026.

"The Strategic Imperative: Governance for Retrieval Augmented Generation." *SAS Blogs*, sas.com/content/sascom/2025/11/25/the-strategic-imperative-governance-for-retrieval-augmented-generation/. Accessed 1 Feb. 2026.

"Strategic Implementation of the CSA AI Controls Matrix." *Cloud Security Alliance Blog*, cloudsecurityalliance.org/blog/2025/08/08/strategic-implementation-of-the-csa-ai-controls-matrix-a-ciso-s-guide-to-trustworthy-ai-governance. Accessed 1 Feb. 2026.

"Strategies for AWS Migration: The New 7th R Explained." *NetApp Blog*, netapp.com/blog/aws-cvo-blg-strategies-for-aws-migration-the-new-7th-r-explained/. Accessed 8 Jan. 2026.

"Structure Augmented Generation: Bridging Structured and Unstructured Data for Enhanced RAG Systems." *Meibel AI*, meibel.ai/post/structure-augmented-generation-bridging-structured-and-unstructured-data-for-enhanced-rag-systems. Accessed 1 Feb. 2026.

"A Structured Model for Continuous Improvement Methodology." *2024*, sciencedirect.com/science/article/pii/S2405844024160653. Accessed 21 Jan. 2026.

SwissCognitive. "Build Better KPIs With Artificial Intelligence (AI)." 17 Nov. 2023, swisscognitive.ch/2023/11/18/build-better-kpis-with-artificial-intelligence-ai/. Accessed 21 Jan. 2026.

"Talk to Your Data: How Conversational BI Is Changing the Way We Explore Data." *element61*, 22 Dec. 2025, element61.be/en/event/talk-your-data-how-conversational-bi-changing-way-we-explore-data. Accessed 19 Jan. 2026.

Taylor, James, and Tom Debevoise. *The MicroGuide to Process and Decision Modeling in BPMN/DMN*. 3rd ed., Decision Management Solutions, 2014, decisionmanagementsolutions.com/wp-content/uploads/2014/11/MicroGuide-to-BPMN-and-DMN-Sampler.pdf. Accessed 8 Jan. 2026.

"Team Productivity: Top Metrics for Project Success." *Orangescrum Blog*, orangescrum.com/top-metrics-to-measure-team-productivity-in-projects. Accessed 16 Dec. 2025.

"Technology Radar 2025." *LTIMindtree*, ltimindtree.com/tech-radar-2025/. Accessed 8 Jan. 2026.

Telit. "Edge AI in Connected Health Care Patient-Centric Approach." *Telit Blog*, telit.com/blog/edge-ai-in-connected-health-care-patient-centric-approach/. Accessed 8 Jan. 2026.

Telmai. "Telmai Brings Autonomous-Ready Data Observability for the Agentic AI Era." *Telmai Blog*, 27 Oct. 2025, telm.ai/blog/telmai-brings-autonomous-ready-data-observability-for-the-agentic-ai-era/. Accessed 21 Jan. 2026.

Tessler, Michael Henry, et al. "AI can help humans find common ground in democratic deliberation." *Science*, 18 Oct. 2024, doi:10.1126/science.adq2852. Accessed 8 Jan. 2026.

Thoropass. "Key Insights from the NIST AI Risk Management Framework." *Thoropass Blog*, 27 July 2025, thoropass.com/blog/nist-ai-rmf. Accessed 21 Jan. 2026.

"Top AI Meeting Summarizer Tools for Streamlined Collaboration." *Vertu,* 22 July 2025, vertu.com/ai-tools/top-ai-meeting-summarizer-tools-for-collaboration-2025/. Accessed 21 Jan. 2026.

"Top Collaboration KPIs for Data Governance Success." *Querio,* 18 Jan. 2026, querio.ai/articles/top-collaboration-kpis-for-data-governance-success. Accessed 21 Jan. 2026.

"Top Digital Adoption Platforms." *Axero Solutions,* 2025, axerosolutions.com/insights/top-digital-adoption-platforms. Accessed 21 Jan. 2026.

"Top Legacy Application Modernization Strategies." *Nix United Blog,* nix-united.com/blog/legacy-application-modernization-strategies/. Accessed 8 Jan. 2026.

"Towards a Governance-Ready AI Infrastructure." *arXiv,* 2026, arxiv.org/html/2601.11702v1. Accessed 8 Jan. 2026.

"Transparency and Accountability in AI: Building Trust in Automated Decisions." *Dialzara Blog,* dialzara.com/blog/ai-transparency-and-accountability-principles-differences. Accessed 16 Dec. 2025.

"Transparency and Explainability in AI-Driven Decision Making." *World Journal of Advanced Engineering Technology and Sciences,* journalwjaets.com/sites/default/files/fulltext_pdf/WJAETS-2025-0720.pdf. Accessed 1 Feb. 2026.

"The Ultimate Guide to AI Meeting Notes in 2024." *FlowHunt,* 21 July 2025, flowhunt.io/blog/the-ultimate-guide-to-ai-meeting-notes-in-2024/. Accessed 21 Jan. 2026.

"Uncontrolled AI: Navigating Ethical Dilemmas and Shadow AI Risks." *CentralEyes,* 28 Apr. 2025, centraleyes.com/shadow-ai-risks. Accessed 19 Jan. 2026.

"Understanding AI Regulations." *Obsidian Security Blog,* obsidiansecurity.com/blog/understanding-ai-regulations. Accessed 1 Feb. 2026.

"Understanding Data Fabric and Data Mesh: Modern Data Management Approaches." *USDSI,* usdsi.org/data-science-insights/understanding-data-fabric-and-data-mesh-modern-data-management-approaches>. Accessed 13 April 2026.

"Understanding On-Prem vs. Cloud TCO." *Terrazone,* terrazone.io/on-prem-vs-cloud-tco/. Accessed 8 Jan. 2026.

"Understanding the 7 Rs of Cloud Migration." *IBM Think Insights,* ibm.com/think/insights/7-rs-cloud-migration. Accessed 8 Jan. 2026.

UNESCO. "UNESCO Recommendation on the Ethics of Artificial Intelligence." *AEPia Edition of UNESCO Impact Assessment,* 2024, aepia.org/wp-content/uploads/2024/04/UNESCO_impacto_etico.pdf. Accessed 21 Jan. 2026.

UNESCO. "UNESCO Recommendation on the Ethics of Artificial Intelligence: Ethical Impact Assessment Tool." 2023, unesco.org/en/articles/ethical-impact-assessment-tool-recommendation-ethics-artificial-intelligence. Accessed 21 Jan. 2026.

University of Minho. "DMAIC for Process Digitalization: A Hospital Case Study." *Repositorium,* 2021, repositorium.sdum.uminho.pt/bitstream/1822/70726/1/Ramires_Sampaio.pdf. Accessed 21 Jan. 2026.

## Bibliography

"Unlocking AI Business Value With FinOps." *FinOps Foundation Working Group,* 12 May 2025, finops.org/wg/unlocking-ai-business-value-with-finops/. Accessed 21 Jan. 2026.

"Unlocking Business Efficiency with Process Mining." *INFORM Software,* 3 Sept. 2025, inform-software.com/en/blog/artificial-intelligence/what-is-process-mining. Accessed 21 Jan. 2026.

"Unlocking the Black Box: A Survey on Explainable AI and Privacy-Preserving AI." *International Journal of Innovative Research in Technology,* ijirt.org/publishedpaper/IJIRT169215_PAPER.pdf. Accessed 28 Jan. 2026.

"Upskilling for AI: Workforce Training Strategies." *Paylocity,* 25 June 2025, paylocity.com/resources/learn/articles/ai-upskilling. Accessed 8 Jan. 2026.

"Use Cases: Real-Time Analytics in the Supply Chain." *Striim Blog,* striim.com/blog/use-cases-real-time-analytics-in-the-supply-chain/. Accessed 28 Jan. 2026.

"Use Conversational Analytics API for Natural Language AI." *Google Cloud,* google.com/blog/products/business-intelligence/use-conversational-analytics-api-for-natural-language-ai. Accessed 19 Jan. 2026.

"Using AI in Radiology Clinical Practice." *Mayo Clinic News Network,* 13 Sept. 2022, newsnetwork.mayoclinic.org/discussion/using-ai-in-radiology-clinical-practice. Accessed 8 Jan. 2026.

"Using Gen AI-Driven Modernization on Premises." *IBM Think Insights,* ibm.com/think/insights/gen-ai-driven-modernization-on-premises. Accessed 8 Jan. 2026.

"Using the NIST AI RMF Core Functions." *IS Partners,* ispartnersllc.com/hubs/nist-ai-rmf/core-functions/. Accessed 8 Jan. 2026.

"Using Unified Analytics Platforms for Data Products and Mesh." *McKinsey & Company,* mckinsey.com/capabilities/tech-and-ai/our-insights/from-raw-data-to-real-profits-a-thriving-data-business. Accessed 8 Jan. 2026.

Vanta. "Third Party Risk Management and Vendor Risk Management." *Vanta,* 2024, vanta.com/products/third-party-risk-management. Accessed 21 Jan. 2026.

"Vendor Governance Framework for AI and IT Services." *Atlas Systems Blog,* atlassystems.com/blog/vendor-governance-framework. Accessed 8 Jan. 2026.

"Vendor Management Best Practices for 2025." *FlowGenius Blog,* flowgenius.ai/post/9-vendor-management-best-practices-for-2025. Accessed 8 Jan. 2026.

"Waterfall vs Agile: Which Project Management Style for You." *Tempo,* 6 July 2025, tempo.io/blog/waterfall-vs-agile. Accessed 21 Jan. 2026.

"Web Security and AI: OWASP and NIST AI RMF." *AuditBoard Blog,* auditboard.com/blog/nist-ai-rmf. Accessed 8 Jan. 2026.

Welch, Neville. Overcoming Leadership Barriers in AI Adoption: A Socio-Technical Ambidextrous Approach. Zenodo, 2025, doi.org/10.5281/zenodo.16218385.

"WEX Self-Service Analytics Journey." *ThoughtSpot Data Trends & Best Practices,* thoughtspot.com/data-trends/best-practices/wex-self-service-analytics-journey. Accessed 8 Jan. 2026.

"What Can Retailers Learn from Hackathons." *Thoughtworks,* 19 July 2023, thoughtworks.com/insights/blog/what-can-retailers-learn-hackathons. Accessed 19 Jan. 2026.

"What Data Mesh Governance Really Means---and How to Implement It." *Branch Strategic Advisory,* branchboston.com/what-data-mesh-governance-really-means-and-how-to-implement-it/. Accessed 21 Jan. 2026.

"What Data Mesh Really Is (and Isn't)." *Branch Strategic Advisory,* branchboston.com/what-data-mesh-really-is-and-isnt/. Accessed 21 Jan. 2026.

"What Is AI Governance? How to Use AI Responsibly." *BigID Blog,* bigid.com/blog/what-is-ai-governance. Accessed 16 Dec. 2025.

"What Is AI Governance? -- IBM Think." *IBM,* 9 Oct. 2024, ibm.com/think/topics/ai-governance. Accessed 16 Dec. 2025.

"What Is AI Governance." *Palo Alto Networks Cyberpedia,* 12 Mar. 2024, paloaltonetworks.com/cyberpedia/ai-governance. Accessed 16 Dec. 2025.

"What Is Data Stewardship." *Reltio,* 29 Apr. 2025, reltio.com/glossary/data-governance/what-is-data-stewardship. Accessed 16 Dec. 2025.

"What Is Process Mining? Complete Guide." *Articsledge,* 3 Nov. 2025, articsledge.com/post/process-mining. Accessed 8 Jan. 2026.

"What It Really Takes to Scale Artificial Intelligence." *McKinsey & Company,* 17 Jun. 2019, mckinsey.com/capabilities/tech-and-ai/our-insights/digital-blog/what-it-really-takes-to-scale-artificial-intelligence. Accessed 21 Jan, 2026.

"What's Next for Retail in 2025? AI-Powered Analytics Trends and BI Innovation." *Strategy Software Blog,* strategysoftware.com/blog/whats-next-for-retail-in-2025-ai-powered-analytics-trends-and-bi-innovation. Accessed 8 Jan. 2026.

"What's Next in Talent." *McKinsey & Company,* 3 Feb. 2024, mckinsey.com/featured-insights/themes/whats-next-in-talent. Accessed 19 Jan. 2026.

"What to Expect in AI Data Governance: 2025 Predictions." *TechNative,* technative.io/what-to-expect-in-ai-data-governance-2025-predictions/. Accessed 1 Feb. 2026.

"Why 95% of AI Pilots Fail --- and What the Other 5% Do Differently." *Salesforce,* 12 Nov. 2025, salesforce.com/news/stories/why-ai-pilots-fail. Accessed 19 Jan. 2026.

"Why AI and Psychological Safety Belong Together---with Insights from Hive." *Hive HR,* 8 Oct. 2025, hive.hr/blog/ai-and-psychological-safety. Accessed 19 Jan. 2026.

"Why an AI Sandbox for Banks Is Key to Safe Innovation." *NayaOne,* nayaone.com/knowledgebase/why-an-ai-sandbox-for-banks-is-key-to-safe-innovation. Accessed 19 Jan. 2026.

"Why Companies That Wait to Upskill Their Workforce Will Struggle." *Harvard Business Review,* hbr.org/article/why-companies-that-wait-upskill-will-struggle. Accessed 16 Dec. 2025.

"Why Data Preparation Is an Important Part of Data Science." *ProjectPro,* projectpro.io/article/why-data-preparation-is-an-important-part-of-data-science/242. Accessed 8 Jan. 2026.

## Bibliography

"Why Data Scientists Spend 80% of Their Time Cleaning Data (and How to Fix It)." *OptimusAI*, optimusai.ai/data-scientists-spend-80-time-cleaning-data/. Accessed 8 Jan. 2026.

"Why Ethical AI Requests for Proposals (RFX) Matter." *Ethical AI Institute*, ethical.institute/rfx.html. Accessed 8 Jan. 2026.

"Why MLOps Is the Real Game Changer for AI." *ASSIST Software Business Insights*, assist-software.net/business-insights/why-mlops-real-game-changer-ai. Accessed 8 Jan. 2026.

"Why Most Agentic AI Pilots Fail—and How to Fix Them." *Process Excellence Network*, processexcellencenetwork.com/ai/articles/why-most-agentic-ai-pilots-fail-and-how-to-fix-them. Accessed 8 Jan. 2026.

"Why Most AI Pilots Fail --- and How Healthcare Enterprises Can Break the Pattern." *Concord*, concord.net/why-most-ai-pilots-fail-and-how-healthcare-enterprises-can-break-the-pattern. Accessed 19 Jan. 2026.

"Why Net Revenue Retention Could Be Your Most Important KPI." *LinkedIn*, 28 Aug. 2023, linkedin.com/pulse/why-net-revenue-retention-could-your-most-important-kpi-adam-turinas. Accessed 28 Jan. 2026.

"Why Your AI Vendors Are Your Risk Surface." *Vanta Resources*, vanta.com/resources/nist-ai-risk-management-framework. Accessed 8 Jan. 2026.

Witness.ai. "Model Monitoring." *Witness.ai Blog*, witness.ai/blog/model-monitoring/. Accessed 1 Feb. 2026.

Wiz. "NIST AI Risk Management Framework: A tl;dr." *Wiz Academy*, 30 Jan. 2025, wiz.io/academy/ai-security/nist-ai-risk-management-framework. Accessed 21 Jan. 2026.

WWEMD. "Edge Analytics for Predictive Maintenance in Manufacturing Implementation Guide for 2025." *WWEMD*, wwemd.io/edge-analytics-for-predictive-maintenance-in-manufacturing-implementation-guide-for-2025/. Accessed 8 Jan. 2026.

"WWT Helps Financial Institution Build Hybrid Cloud Integration for Analytics and AI." *World Wide Technology*, wwt.com/case-study/financial-institution-hybrid-cloud. Accessed 8 Jan. 2026.

"The Year AI Grew Up." *Mario Thomas Blog*, mariothomas.com/blog/the-year-ai-grew-up/. Accessed 8 Jan. 2026.

Yellowfin. "Incuda Drives 50% Increase in Self-Service Analytics Adoption with Yellowfin BI." *Yellowfin BI Blog*, yellowfinbi.com/blog/incuda-drives-50%-increase-in-self-service-analytics-adoption-with-yellowfin-bi. Accessed 8 Jan. 2026.

Zapier. "The 9 Best AI Meeting Assistants in 2025." *Zapier*, 30 July 2025, zapier.com/blog/best-ai-meeting-assistant/. Accessed 21 Jan. 2026.

www.ingramcontent.com/pod-product-compliance
Ingram Content Group UK Ltd.
Pitfield, Milton Keynes, MK11 3LW, UK
UKHW020202290926
15471UKWH00005B/1017